Masterplots

Revised Second Edition

Masterplots

1,801 Plot Stories and Critical Evaluations
of the World's Finest Literature

Revised Second Edition

Volume 4
Dum – Gen
1869 – 2490

Edited by
FRANK N. MAGILL

Story Editor, Revised Edition
DAYTON KOHLER

Consulting Editor, Revised Second Edition
LAURENCE W. MAZZENO

SALEM PRESS
Pasadena, California   Englewood Cliffs, New Jersey

Editor in Chief: Dawn P. Dawson

Consulting Editor: Laurence W. Mazzeno *Managing Editor:* Christina J. Moose
Project Editors: Eric Howard *Research Supervisor:* Jeffry Jensen
Juliane Brand *Research:* Irene McDermott
Acquisitions Editor: Mark Rehn *Proofreading Supervisor:* Yasmine A. Cordoba
Production Editor: Cynthia Breslin Beres *Layout:* William Zimmerman

Library of Congress Cataloging-in-Publication Data
Masterplots / edited by Frank N. Magill; consulting editor, Laurence W. Mazzeno. — Rev. 2nd ed.
   p.   cm.
Expanded and updated version of the 1976 rev. ed.
Includes bibliographical references and indexes.
1. Literature—Stories, plots, etc. 2. Literature—History and criticism. I. Magill, Frank Northen, 1907-1997. II. Mazzeno, Laurence W.
PN44.M33   1996
809—dc20   96-23382
ISBN 0-89356-084-7 (set)   CIP
ISBN 0-89356-088-x (volume 4)

Revised Second Edition
Third Printing

PRINTED IN THE UNITED STATES OF AMERICA

LIST OF TITLES IN VOLUME 4

Revised Second Edition

THE DUMB WAITER

Type of work: Drama
Author: Harold Pinter (1930-   )
Type of plot: Absurdist
Time of plot: Mid-twentieth century
Locale: England
First performed: 1959, in German translation; first performed and published in English, 1960

> *Principal characters:*
> BEN, a hit man
> GUS, his fellow hit man

The Story:

Ben and Gus were in a basement room with two beds and a closed serving hatch between the beds. Ben read aloud two different stories from the newspaper. Gus complained about the room's not having a window, about coming in the dark to a strange place, sleeping all day, doing the job, and going away again in the dark. Ben said that Gus needed hobbies, like his own woodwork. Gus wanted Ben to tell him why Ben had stopped the car in the middle of the road, when it was still dark, that morning. Ben said that he thought Gus was asleep, that he was not waiting for anything, and that they were too early. When Gus objected that they had done as they were told, Ben replied that he, not Gus, took the call. Ben repeated that they were too early, but refused to say more.

Gus wanted to know what town they were in (Ben said Birmingham) and, since it was Friday, wanted to go to watch the football team the next day (Ben said there was no time). Gus reminisced about the Birmingham Villa team losing a game in a disputed penalty to the White Shirts. Gus remembered that the other team was from Tottenham, so that the game had to have been in Birmingham. Ben said he was not there, yet he disagreed emphatically about the penalty, but denied that the game was in Birmingham. An envelope slid under the door. Gus saw it, unsealed it, and found twelve matches but no writing.

When Ben told him to "light the kettle," Gus responded that Ben meant "light the gas" and "put on the kettle." Ben refused to back down. When Gus persisted, Ben asserted that he was the senior partner and then lost his temper, grabbing Gus by the throat. Gus tried to make tea, but there was a meter on the stove, and neither of them had any money. Gus lamented that Wilson did not do well by them, such as leave enough gas available for a cup of tea. He had questions for Wilson, but found Wilson difficult to talk to. Gus wanted to know if anyone cleaned up after they were gone, and who that would be if so. Another question occurred to him: How many jobs had the two of them done? What if no one had ever cleaned up? Ben pointed out that their employer had departments for everything. The noise of the dumbwaiter descending made them grab their revolvers. Gus opened the dumbwaiter and removed a piece of paper that read, "Two braised steak and chips. Two sago puddings. Two teas without sugar."

Ben said the place was probably under new management. Gus wanted to know who had it now. A second piece of paper read, "Soup of the day. Liver and onions. Jam tart." Ben looked in the serving hatch but not up it. When Gus put his finger to his mouth and looked up it, Ben was alarmed. The meager contents of Gus's bag were brought out and put on a plate, but the dumbwaiter had already gone up. Gus questioned how could a gas stove with three rings service a busy place? What happened when no one was there? Had those menus been coming down and going up for years? The third piece of paper read, "Macaroni Pastitsio. Ormitha Maca-rounada." Gus put the plate in the box and called the contents up the hatch. Ben corrected Gus for shouting.

Gus wanted to know if there was another kitchen, other gas stoves. Why, he wondered, did Wilson not get in touch? Did Ben not believe that the two of them were reliable? (Ben said nothing.) The box came down. The fourth note read, "One Bamboo Shoots, Water Chestnuts, and Chicken. One Char Siu and beansprouts." Their packet of tea had been sent back.

A speaking tube was suddenly discovered, which Gus did not understand why he had not seen before. Gus followed Ben's directions—blowing into it, then speaking—but he could not hear anything. Ben took the tube and listened and talked into it. The voice on the other end, Ben told Gus, said everything they had sent up was defective. Ben gave Gus his instructions, but he forgot to tell Gus to take out his gun—which Ben had never omitted before.

Gus wanted to know what they would do if it was a girl—the mess made by the girl on their last job bothered Gus—but Ben replied they would do just the same.

Gus pointed out that they had passed their tests years ago. They had taken the tests together; they had proved themselves. What was he playing these games for? The fifth note read, "Scampi." Gus yelled up that they had nothing left. Ben seized the tube from Gus, hung it up, went back to his bed and picked up the paper. Gus exited left. The whistle on the speaking tube went off. Ben answered, noted that the usual procedure would be followed, and said they were ready. Ben went to the left, the door to the right opened. Ben turned, leveled his revolver at the door. Gus stumbled in, stripped of jacket, waistcoat, tie, holster, revolver. Gus and Ben stared at each other in silence.

Critical Evaluation:

In all likelihood the most original British playwright of the last half of the twentieth century, Harold Pinter has written not only for the theater but also for radio, television, and film. Pinter focuses on the individual in relation to others and on the threatening nature of late twentieth century society. In Pinter's world, what one is responsible for is not at all clear. Written at the beginning of Pinter's career, *The Dumb Waiter* presents Ben and Gus, professional hit men, with many hits on their record. It seems, as the play unfolds, that Gus is going to be killed by Ben because Gus asks too many questions. Pinter describes a world in which everything is unreliable, including consciousness, memory, personal relationships, and any kind of social contract. The nature of human beings is at issue in Pinter's plays; he presents them without nostalgia and with no sentimentality.

The extent to which Ben and Gus are responsible for their own lives remains unknown. Is Gus, for instance, acting in good faith to question the life he has lived? Or was he acting in good faith when he simply followed orders? What, as a soldier, is he expected to do? Pinter's characters may be simultaneously victors, victimizers, and victims. What is most menacing to the individual occurs by surprise and remains unexplained. However murky the world may appear to the individual and the individual to the world, Pinter's recurrent themes are clear enough: the alienation of the individual from him- or herself, from others, and from the environment; the uncertainty of truth, on any level; the impossibility of interpersonal relation-ships; the ironies and frequent contradictions of life.

The language of Pinter's plays is often contradictory and uses opposition such as the repeated references to black and white in *The Dumb Waiter*. While Ben reads and rereads the newspaper at any free moment, focusing on what is "down in black and white," Gus, in a stunning non sequitur, finds the black and white crockery thoroughly satisfying. It is the only thing he admires in their present location. Ben accepts what he reads. Gus bets that the newspaper story that Ben read that said that an eight-year-old girl killed a cat is a lie. More likely, the eleven-year-old boy killed the cat and blamed it on his eight-year-old sister. Ben agrees, but that is the last time he agrees with Gus.

For Pinter, words typically conceal more than they reveal. Silence indicates an inner life, the nature of which may well mystify both the self and others. Ben's silence is opaque, possibly without a self: He reads the newspaper or pursues his hobbies. Since he is not idle, who can criticize him? By carefully describing the outer lives of Ben and Gus, in a seemingly naturalistic manner, Pinter leaves readers and audience members to speculate about the two characters' inner lives.

For Ben, everything is a matter of black and white. The importance to him of the past he shares with Gus remains unknown. Gus continues to be plagued by unanswered questions. These include: Why did Ben stop the car in the middle of the road that morning? Why was an envelope with twelve matches slid under the door when they had no money for the gas meter? Why is there no different method for a hit on a woman? Why does Wilson not treat them better? Why is the suddenly active dumbwaiter making requests of them? Who is upstairs?

The significance of what is not said is as important as what is. What is not said may amount to more emphatic communication than what is stated. Ben, for example, does not like Gus's questions, which is apparent by his silence and by the fact that if he answers, he tends to contradict himself or lose his temper. Pinter's characters are frequently called lower class, and, it is argued, therefore predictably easily frustrated and violent. They defy, in truth, such easy categorization. If Ben is less aware or less intelligent, is that the problem? Is it not rather Ben's lack of courage that threatens Gus, Ben's willingness to victimize anyone and his unwillingness to question, much less to criticize, anyone more powerful? Ben is a "company man" with, it seems, no convictions or restraints to keep him from doing whatever his supervisors want him to do.

With the dumbwaiter becoming active in the middle of the play, Ben accepts as fact—without any questioning—that they must meet the demands that come from above, down in black and white, no matter how unreasonable or increasingly bizarre those demands may be. Gus wants to know why. For example, when he and Ben are both in need of their tea, why should they send up their few supplies? Even though Gus sends everything up, he later asks Ben, and then himself, why did they send everything up? Who is upstairs? Why is he playing all these games? Why does not whoever is upstairs understand that they have nothing left? These simple questions, in Pinter's play, become the riddles of existence.

Unlike Gus, Ben does not question. He lives in a black-or-white world in which he seems neither happy nor unhappy but secure. The tube next to the dumbwaiter, through which one alternately listens and talks, does not work for Gus, just as the toilet does not flush for him—until the very end. The tube does work for Ben, who is ready, when his supervisors say so, to do his job. He is even ready to kill his partner when his supervisors instruct him to do so.

Carol Bishop

Bibliography:
Burkman, Katherine H. *The Dramatic World of Harold Pinter: Its Basis in Ritual*. Columbus: Ohio State University Press, 1971. A provocative study, with notes, bibliography, and index.
Esslin, Martin. *Pinter: A Study of His Plays*. Expanded ed. New York: W. W. Norton, 1976. Originally published in 1970 under the title *The Peopled Wound: The Work of Harold Pinter*, a good book to use as a starting point. Bibliography, index.

Hynes, Joseph. "Pinter and Morality." *The Virginia Quarterly Review* 68 (Autumn, 1992): 740-752. Examines Pinter's comedy and compares his work to that of Henrik Ibsen and George Bernard Shaw.

Kennedy, Andrew. *Six Dramatists in Search of a Language: Shaw, Eliot, Beckett, Pinter, Osborne, Arden.* New York: Cambridge University Press, 1975. Focuses on Pinter's linguistic modes. Bibliography, index.

Schroll, Herman T. *Harold Pinter: A Study of His Reputation (1958-1969) and a Checklist.* Metuchen, N.J.: Scarecrow Press, 1971. Argues that Pinter's works have lasting significance. Bibliography, index.

THE DUNCIAD

Type of work: Poetry
Author: Alexander Pope (1688-1744)
Type of plot: Mock-heroic
Time of plot: Eighteenth century
Locale: England and the underworld
First published: 1728-1743

> *Principal characters:*
> DULNESS, a goddess
> TIBBALD, hero of the first edition, a Shakespearian scholar
> COLLEY CIBBER, hero of the second edition, playwright, producer,
>   and poet laureate

When Alexander Pope set out to criticize the general literary climate of his time and to avenge the slights given his own work by other writers, he took the theme of John Dryden's *Mac Flecknoe* (1682), in which the poetaster Thomas Shadwell is crowned ruler of the Kingdom of Nonsense, and expanded it to make a true mock epic of three books. He added a fourth book when he rewrote the poem in 1742. *The Dunciad* acclaims the goddess Dulness, daughter of Chaos and Night, and her chosen prince. In the first edition the prince of dullness is the scholar Lewis Theobald (Tibbald); in the second edition he is Colley Cibber, playwright and poet laureate.

This poem lacks the close-knit quality of Pope's other fine mock epic, *The Rape of the Lock* (1712). *The Dunciad* is longer, and the fact that the hero appears only at intervals explains a certain disunity. Tibbald-Cibber appears at the middle of book 1, is present only as a spectator at the epic games described in book 2, and merely dreams the trip to the underworld, modeled on that of Aeneas in book 4 of Vergil's *Aeneid* (c. 29-19 B.C.E.). The important points in the poem are made in the descriptive passages in these episodes and in conversations that contain criticism of individuals and trends.

Pope relied, for satirical effect, on the classical epic as his model. *The Dunciad*, like *The Rape of the Lock*, begins with a parody of the *Aeneid*:

> The mighty Mother, and her Son, who brings
> The Smithfield Muses to the ear of Kings,
> I sing.

The invocation is appropriately directed not at a muse but at the Patricians, the patrons whose purses inspire dull writing. The dedication to the author's friend Jonathan Swift which follows is an eighteenth century, rather than a classic, convention.

Pope describes in detail the abode of Dulness and the allegorical figures gathered around her throne: Fortitude, Temperance, Prudence, and Poetic Justice, who is weighing truth with gold and "solid pudding against empty praise." The gods are notoriously interested in the affairs of mortals; Dulness looks out upon the ingredients of dull writing and the numerous creators of it. Her eye lights upon the hero, who is raising to her an altar of tremendous tomes of his writing. She anoints him as king of her realm, and the nation croaks Aesop's line, "God save King Log."

In the second book Pope designs appropriate contests for his various groups of enemies. The booksellers race to win a phantom poet. A patron is designated for the poet who tickles best, but he is carried off by an unknown sycophantic secretary. Journalists swim through the muck of the Thames River:

> Who flings most filth, and wide pollutes around
> The stream, be his the Weekly Journals bound;
> A pig of lead to him who drives the best;
> A peck of coals a-piece shall glad the rest.

As a final test the goddess promises her "amplest powers" to anyone who can remain awake as he listens to the verses of "Three College Sophs, and three pert Templars." The book ends with the whole company lying asleep.

Grandiose heroic couplets and numerous parallels with classical visits to the underworld fill the third book. John Taylor, the Water Poet, replaces the ferryman Charon; Elkanah Settle, a Restoration poet, takes Anchises' part in showing the hero the future of Dulness and her offspring. The high point of this book is the crowning of Tibbald-Cibber with a poppy wreath by Bavius, prototype of the worst of poets from ancient times.

The 1742 *Dunciad*, centering on the triumph of Dulness over England, reveals a slightly more mature outlook in the poet than does the earlier version. Tibbald was the object of a vindictive attack, occasioned by his criticism of Pope's edition of Shakespeare. Cibber is representative of the dull poet; as laureate he was well known for his poor occasional verse. The fourth book is far more concerned with the institutions promoting the rise of dullness than with individuals. The more frequent use of classical names, rather than contemporary ones, indicates the poet's movement toward universality.

The last book is almost an entity in itself. It opens with a new invocation, to Chaos and Night. The pseudo-learned notes, effective satire written by Pope, point out the precedents for a second invocation when important new matter is introduced. Evil omens presage the coming destruction as Dulness ascends her throne and Cibber reclines in her lap, making his only appearance in this book.

Around the goddess are Science, Wit, Logic, Rhetoric, and other abstractions in chains, reminiscent of several scenes in Edmund Spenser's *The Faerie Queene* (1590). Various personages appear to tell of Dulness' victory over the many arts and institutions. First to come is a harlot representing the Italian opera; she rejoices in the banishment of Handel to Ireland and the supremacy of chaos in music.

Pope uses an epic simile to describe the nations clustering around the goddess: ". . . orb in orb, congloved are seen/ The buzzing Bees about their dusky Queen." Present are the passive followers of Dulness and those who lead the advance: pompous editors who make mincemeat of good poets with notes and commentary, patrons who set up a bust of a poet after he has died neglected.

A specter, the head of Westminster School, modeled on Milton's Moloch, speaks on the state of education:

> As Fancy opens the quick springs of Sense,
> We ply the Memory, we load the brain,
> Bind rebel Wit, and double chain on chain,
> Confine the thought, to exercise the breath;
> And keep them in the pale of Words till death.

Pope criticizes the hair-splitting grammarians in Aristarchus' boasts that he has turned good verse into prose again. Science is also satirized as the study which loses itself in detail; but Dulness still fears science, for an object of nature is capable of awakening a mind. Religion does not escape; the poet says that it has degenerated into a belief in a mechanistic God, made in man's image.

Knowing the state of her kingdom, the goddess celebrates her mysteries, reflecting Pope's interest in ceremony. As the rites are concluded a state of dullness encompasses the country, schools, government, army. Truth, philosophy, and religion perish as "Universal Darkness buries All."

The Dunciad contains more of the heroic spirit than most other mock epics. Most mock epics are directed toward the amusement of the reader, and do not age well past the time in which their jokes are caught without footnotes. *The Dunciad*, however, reveals Pope's passionate conviction that the triumph of dullness was a real danger to art, science, and learning. He chose to deliver his warning to England in a humorous form, but his seriousness about his subject raises the latter part of the fourth book to the level of real heroic poetry.

There are many fine lines of poetry in *The Dunciad*, but it is more diffuse and less brilliant satire than either *Mac Flecknoe* or Pope's own *Epistle to Dr. Arbuthnot*. Missing are the biting, succinct couplets such as Dryden's "The rest to some faint meaning make pretense,/ But Sh—— never deviates into sense" or Pope's lines on Addison, "Damn with faint praise, assent with civil leer,/ And without sneering, teach the rest to sneer."

The greatest deterrent to the modern reader's easy enjoyment of *The Dunciad* is probably the fact that so much of the poet's criticism of contemporary people and issues is almost unintelligible; few names die faster than those of the fifth-rate writers of an era. Yet the satirical comments on universal conditions remain fresh and pointed. *The Dunciad* is worthy of a high place among mock-heroic poems.

Bibliography:

Clark, Donald B. *Alexander Pope*. New York: Twayne, 1967. Provides a thorough examination of all of Pope's major works. Interpretations and criticisms of several individual poems comprise the bulk of this study. Historical and biographical information are also provided.

Regan, J. V. "The Mock-Epic Structure of the *Dunciad*." *Studies in English Literature 1500-1900* 19, no. 3 (Summer, 1979): 459-473. Focuses on the structure of *The Dunciad*. To illustrate how Pope's poem follows epic conventions, as well as how it departs from them, Regan draws parallels between *The Dunciad* and Vergil's *Aeneid*.

Rogers, Robert. *The Major Satires of Alexander Pope*. Champaign: University of Illinois Press, 1955. Convincingly argues that each of Pope's satires reflects his own moral concerns on the ethical dilemmas he faced himself. This comprehensive overview of Pope's satiric poems is essential for any discussion pertaining to the poet's use of irony and wit.

Sitter, John E. *The Poetry of Pope's "Dunciad."* Minneapolis: University of Minnesota Press, 1971. This full-length study devoted to *The Dunciad* concentrates on the poem's imagery, structure, and origins. Use of textual evidence makes the work an excellent starting place for critical analysis.

Williams, Aubrey L. *Pope's "Dunciad": A Study of Its Meaning*. Baton Rouge: Louisiana State University Press, 1955. In order to interpret Pope's meaning and to comment on his imaginative powers, Williams examines the poem from every possible angle. Provides one of the most thorough treatments of *The Dunciad*.

DUTCHMAN

Type of work: Drama
Author: Amiri Baraka (Everett LeRoi Jones, 1934-   )
Type of plot: Political
Time of plot: 1960's
Locale: New York City
First performed: 1964; first published, 1964

Principal characters:
CLAY, a twenty-year-old black man
LULA, a thirty-year-old white woman

The Story:
   Scene i. Clay and Lula exchanged glances as Clay sat inside a subway car pulling into a station and Lula stood outside waiting to board. At first, Clay smiled at Lula "without a trace of self-consciousness," but then he felt a growing sense of embarrassment. The smile that crossed Lula's face was "premeditated." After eating an apple, Lula offered one to Clay. She attempted to engage him in sexual banter, and she ridiculed him for adopting the posture and dress of the white middle class, telling him, "You look like death eating a soda cracker." At the same time that Lula made explicit sexual overtures to Clay, she harassed him about his middle-class identity and his resulting status as a dislocated African American man in America: "Everything you say is wrong. . . . Boy, those narrow-shoulder clothes come from a tradition you ought to feel oppressed by. . . . Your grandfather was a slave, he didn't go to Harvard."
   Scene ii. Clay and Lula decided to go to a party together. Lula verbally created the scenario of a sexual encounter between them. As the conversation continued, Lula became more derogatory, her language more racial and aggressive, and she jumped up into a wild dance, shouting slurs at Clay and demanding that he get up to dance and have sex with her.
   Clay tried to calm her down. At first nervously bemused, he became more agitated and forceful. When Lula continued to holler epithets and slurs at him, he slapped her hard across the mouth and threw her into a seat. Telling Lula to "shut up and let me talk," Clay then verbally (and figuratively) abused Lula, stripping her of her delusions of power, insight, and security. He declared that a potentially revolutionary violence underlay African American experience, though it was "for now" present only in the subterranean and indirect modes of jazz and poetry: "If Bessie Smith had killed some white people she wouldn't have needed that music. She could have talked very straight and plain about the world. No metaphors. . . . Just let me bleed you, you loud whore, and one poem vanished."
   Lula's response to Clay's furious challenge was cold and detached: "I've heard enough." Clay, too, was suddenly tired, and abruptly he was ready to end the conversation. He turned to leave the subway car saying, "Looks like we won't be acting out that little pageant you outlined before." As he bent over her to grab his things from the seat, Lula stabbed him twice in the chest with a knife. He was dead immediately. Lula turned to the other passengers on the train, both black and white, who had been sitting passively during the entire exchange, and commanded them to dump Clay's body from the train and to disembark at the next station. The passengers did as they had been told.
   Another young African American man boarded the subway, carrying his books. "An old Negro conductor," walking through the car, acknowledgd the young man with a quick "Hey,

1876

brother," then passed Lula "doing sort of a restrained soft shoe." He tipped his hat to her and left the car. Lula and the young man were left alone.

Critical Evaluation:

Dutchman, an early play by the poet, dramatist, and political writer Amiri Baraka, was written when his name was still LeRoi Jones and at a transitional time for both the playwright and the Black Arts (or Black Aesthetics) movement. *Dutchman* reflects that transition in its aesthetic structure, its political content, and its implied audience.

This transition in African American drama can be characterized as a shift from aesthetics as they had been traditionally defined by a primarily white, European-oriented theater community to an explicitly politicized and black nationalist art directed toward and arising from the African American community. Baraka's work throughout the 1960's marks a critical existential shift in stark terms: After winning an Obie Award for *Dutchman* in 1964 ("Best Off-Broadway Play"), he then in 1968 changed his name to emphasize his African and Kawaida identity and became Imamu Amiri Baraka. At the same time, his shift from artist-activist to black nationalist and Marxist-Leninist socialist critic marked his abandonment of the New York arts scene (including the avant-garde) to focus instead on literary forms deeply tied to African American revolutionary politics. Readers of *Dutchman* who pursue its critical reception will find revealing contrasts in interpretation depending on the political and aesthetic stance of the critic, especially in relation to historical changes and debates within African American liberation politics.

The play itself opens on a subway, "in the flying underbelly of the city," a subterranean metaphor for both the rattling dissonance of American culture and the psychological interior terrain of American racial politics. Baraka sets up the association: "Steaming hot, and summer on top, outside. Underground. The subway heaped in modern myth."

The play consists of two short scenes between the two characters as they ride the subway together. A metaphoric and ironic Eden is suggested when Lula first eats an apple and offers one to Clay. Their first exchange, in which Lulu ridicules the image Clay seems to be trying to project, establishes the pivotal issue of power (that is, who controls the conversation) and unveils both Clay's aspirations to the middle class and Lula's moral instability. As the scene proceeds, the tension between them builds. Lula pushes hard, making sexual overtures that are seductive one moment and arrogant and derogatory the next. Clay stays almost entirely reactive to Lula's definition of his identity; he lets her control the conversation while joking to defuse the confrontation, and he refuses to counterattack her verbally. Baraka closes the scene with an explicitly historical and political frame. As Lula declares,

> And we'll pretend the people cannot see you. That is, the citizens. And that you are free of your own history. And I am free of my history. We'll pretend that we are both anonymous beauties smashing through the city's entrails.

The mythic elements of the play deepen in the course of the first scene, even while the dramatic style itself stays naturalistic. Several critics see class and racial struggle as the central themes, with turbulent intensity building in Clay as a symbol of the African American middle class, who must repress black-defined identity in order to assimilate into white-dominated society. In this view, Lula represents the failed moral order of white supremacy, which although obviously unstable and erratic, remains at least apparently in control. The explicit sexual dynamics and underlying sexual tension represent, in this context, a playing out (and reversal) of racial stereotypes, and Lula's behavior reveals the complex blend of desire and psychosis characteristic of white racism. Other interpretations focus on Clay as representing repressed African American art and artists. Claiming at one point to be "Baudelaire," Clay becomes the Black Aesthetic movement struggling to fit into the constraints of European clothing.

The second scene continues to develop the themes of the first. Clay's revelatory outburst is defined, in the context of a dialogue that had been controlled by Lula's fantasies and delusions of power, as a response. Although his self-expression is genuine, deeply realized, and powerful (he speaks both as an artist and as a representative of the African American middle class now alert to its historical dilemma), it leads to his destruction precisely because he chose to remain in conversation with Lula, whose murderous intolerance of Clay's self-assertion reveals white supremacy in brutal terms. Although Lula is willing to conduct a white liberal charade with Clay, she responds with predictable violence to Clay's potentially revolutionary insight. The second young man and the old conductor present the same dangerous stance toward Lula, who calmly prepares for the next encounter, and as the curtain falls, the audience senses that the cycle is about to begin again. The play's conclusion suggests Baraka's increasingly emphatic call for African Americans to break off conversation both artistically and politically with the failed (and violent) white American culture. In *Dutchman*, Clay's self-defined expression of power and identity leads to his own death. The mythic, symbolic, and historical/political depth in the play makes it clear that Baraka's subterranean travelers are moving beneath, and through, the landscape of American history.

Several issues are important in *Dutchman*. During the 1960's, Baraka increasingly rejected the imperatives of protest literature. Critics have pointed to the class politics of the play as indicative of Baraka's emerging socialist critique, and some have compared *Dutchman* with the broader sociological analysis of E. Franklin Frazier's *Black Bourgeoisie* (1957). Another key issue concerns the tension in African American cultural politics between claims of racial essentialism (that is, the Black Aesthetics movement as being rooted in racial essence) and pressures toward assimilation into the American middle class. *Dutchman* suggests that the road toward assimilation is the road to individual and collective destruction. A comparative reading of *Dutchman* with other works can reveal the complexity and urgency of questions related to African American identity and power. Related to this is the relationship between political ideology and artistic form, the relationship between community identity and the role of drama as political ritual, and the role of art in revolutionary change. The play's title has been called a metaphoric reference to the first slave ships. Amiri Baraka's work profoundly engages the implications of history for African American political critique.

Sharon Carson

Bibliography:

Baraka, Imamu Amiri. *Selected Plays and Prose of Amiri Baraka/LeRoi Jones*. New York: William Morrow, 1979. An important source for reading *Dutchman* in the context of several of Baraka's political essays from the 1960's and 1970's.

Benston, Kimberly W. *Baraka: The Renegade and the Mask*. New Haven, Conn.: Yale University Press, 1976. A challenging study of Baraka's literary and political writings in the context of cultural politics. Notable for its endorsement by Larry Neal, a leading Black Aesthetics movement critic, and for its perceptive interpretation of *Dutchman*.

Brown, Lloyd. *Amiri Baraka*. Boston: Twayne, 1980. Includes a useful chapter on drama, with reference to *Dutchman*. Good annotated bibliography.

Hudson, Theodore R. *From LeRoi Jones to Amiri Baraka: The Literary Works*. Durham, N.C.:

Duke University Press, 1973. Puts *Dutchman* and other Baraka writings within the framework of his shift from avant-garde literary artist to practicing black cultural nationalist. Provides political and historical context for Baraka's transition, and notes and bibliography point readers to useful articles and interviews from the 1960's and early 1970's.

Lacy, Henry C. *To Raise, Destroy, and Create: The Poetry, Drama, and Fiction of Imamu Amiri Baraka (LeRoi Jones)*. Troy, N.Y.: Whitston, 1981. Includes an excellent and extensive interpretive reading of *Dutchman*. Also provides substantial biographical and political/cultural context, as well as insightful analysis of Baraka's role as inspiration to later African American writers.

THE DYNASTS

Type of work: Drama
Author: Thomas Hardy (1840-1928)
Type of plot: Historical
Time of plot: 1806-1815
Locale: Europe
First published: 1903-1908; 1910 (complete); first performed, 1914 (abridged version)

Principal characters:
NAPOLEON I
JOSEPHINE, his first wife
MARIE LOUISE, his second wife
KING GEORGE III OF ENGLAND
TSAR ALEXANDER OF RUSSIA
EMPEROR FRANCIS OF AUSTRIA
SIR WILLIAM PITT, prime minister of England
SPIRIT OF YEARS,
SHADE OF EARTH,
SPIRIT OF PITIES,
SPIRIT SINISTER, and
SPIRIT IRONIC, allegorical figures

The Story:
The Spirit of Years, Shade of Earth, Spirit Sinister, Spirit Ironic, Spirit of Pities, and their accompanying choruses, forgathered somewhere above the earth to watch the larger movements of humans in western Europe in 1805. The design of the Immanent Will manifested itself at the time in Napoleon's preparations for the invasion of England.

In England, Sir William Pitt contended with isolationist members of Parliament to secure proper defense against the invasion, while Napoleon went to Milan to be crowned King of Italy. The spirits made light of the chicanery and pomp that attended the coronation. The Spirit of Pities descended to earth and disturbed Napoleon by reminding him of his original intention to champion liberty.

At sea, a Pyrrhic victory of the French and Spanish over the English prevented the support required for the planned invasion. On the south coast of England, the Phantoms of Rumor caused great disturbance. A fleet of fishing craft was mistaken for the invasion fleet, and civilians fled from the coastal towns as signal fires flared upon the cliffs and hills.

When Napoleon learned that his admiral, Villeneuve, had returned to Cadiz, he discarded his invasion plan and moved eastward against Austria and Russia, countries that Pitt had enlisted in the English cause. The Spirit of Years remarked that the ensuing campaign would be a model in tactics for all time. At Ulm, Napoleon defeated the Austrians, who had hoped that the English fleet would hold the French forces in northern France. In London, Pitt, unsuccessful in gaining permission from the king to form a coalition government, visibly declined in health under his terrible burden.

Villeneuve was ordered out of Cadiz. The British under Nelson met the French and Spanish off Trafalgar and defeated them. Nelson was killed in the engagement; Villeneuve subsequently ended his own life in an inn at Rennes. Napoleon defeated the Austrians and Russians at Austerlitz. Then, hearing of the English victory at Trafalgar, he declared his intention of closing all continental ports to English ships. He dictated peace terms to Emperor Francis of Austria while attendant Austrian officers stood by in disgust at the sight of a nobody dictating to true royalty. In Paris, the Spirit of Rumor commented on the way Napoleon was uprooting old dynasties and founding new ones.

Pitt having died and King George III being mentally ill, Charles James Fox negotiated for England with Napoleon for peace, but Napoleon used the negotiations as a screen for his real plans. He marched on Prussia and defeated the Germans at the Battle of Jena. In Berlin, he decreed that all British ships were barred from continental ports. Napoleon and Tsar Alexander of Russia met at the River Niemen, where the two drew up a Franco-Russian alliance. During this meeting, Napoleon expressed the desire to cement his various alliances with blood ties. The Spirit of Years remarked ironically that Napoleon was one of the few men who could see the working of the Immanent Will.

Napoleon invaded Spain as a friend to help the Spanish gain Portugal. The Spanish Bourbons abdicated and Napoleon's brother, Joseph, was proclaimed king. Bourbon partisans enlisted English aid, and an English invasion fleet sailed for Portugal.

Back in Paris, Napoleon told his wife, Josephine, that he wished a divorce. Josephine had borne him no children, and he was anxious to perpetuate the dynasty he had founded. The British invasion of the Iberian Peninsula drew him to Spain to direct the campaign there. Austrian preparations for war induced Napoleon next to invade that country, and he defeated its forces at Wagram. The British, under the Duke of Wellington, held their own against the French in Spain. At that point, the Spirit Sinister reminded the Spirit Ironic not to sneer for fear Immanent Will would cut short the comedy that was taking place.

A British force was sent to the Scheldt, but the expedition ended disastrously when the army was decimated by miasmal fever. Napoleon, fearful of assassination and still anxious to perpetuate his line, negotiated with the Russians for the hand of a Russian princess, and with the Austrians for the hand of Princess Marie Louise. The tsar accepted the offer, but Napoleon had already arranged, through Metternich, for a marriage with the Austrian princess, Marie Louise. The marriage was performed with the conspicuous absence of many high clergy; the Russians, feeling insulted, prepared for war. In the meantime, the British in Spain under the Duke of Wellington gained a decisive victory at Albuera.

In due time, Marie Louise gave birth to Napoleon's heir. The insane king of England died after hearing of British successes in Spain. On the continent, war became imminent between France and Russia. On the banks of the Niemen, Napoleon received an evil portent when he was thrown from his horse. The Spirit of Pities foresaw misery for the French Grand Army in the Russian campaign. Wellington in Spain defeated the French at Salamanca. Napoleon gained a costly victory over the Russians at Borodino, and the French entered Moscow to find the city deserted and in flames. The French thereupon retreated across snow-covered Russian steppes to Lithuania. Thousands perished from the cold or were killed by harassing Russian cavalry. Napoleon deserted his army and raced back to Paris so as to anticipate the news of his failure in Russia. His chief task now was to hold his empire together.

As the British continued their successes in Spain, Austria joined the allies. Napoleon met defeat at the hands of the Austrians and Prussians at Leipzig. The allies invaded France. Napoleon, forced to abdicate, was exiled to Elba, an island in the Mediterranean. Marie Louise and the infant king of Rome went to Austria. The Bourbons reassumed the throne of France, and a congress to deliberate on general peace in Europe met in Vienna.

Napoleon escaped from Elba and returned to Paris at the head of an army he had picked up on his way. The allies outlawed Napoleon and prepared to overthrow him again.

A private ball in Brussels was broken up by the news that the French army was nearing the Belgian frontier. Almost overnight, Napoleon had organized and put into the field a large army, but he failed to separate the British and Prussians in Belgium, and he was brought to utter defeat on the fields south of Waterloo. The Hundred Days had ended.

The Spirit of Years pointed out to the assembled spirits that the human beings below them behaved as though they were in a dream, as though they were puppets being drawn by strings manipulated by Immanent Will. The Spirit of Years pointed to Napoleon in defeat and compared him to a tiny insect on an obscure leaf in the chart of the Ages. When the Spirit of Pities asked for what purpose the events below had taken place, the Spirit of Irony answered that there was no purpose, for only a dumb thing turned the crank that motivated and directed human behavior.

Critical Evaluation:

In *The Dynasts,* Thomas Hardy realized his lifelong ambition to dramatize the events of the Napoleonic period. He had already touched on the subject in his novel *The Trumpet-Major* (1880), and he had noted in his journal plans to execute a "Homeric ballad, in which Napoleon is a kind of Achilles." Hardy was an anxious witness to the cultural changes brought about by so-called progress. Yet while he regretted such changes as the dissolution of traditions and folk beliefs, he was at the same time suspicious of conventional religious and social institutions. In *The Dynasts*, he tries, in effect, to "rescue" history by giving comparatively recent human events epic stature.

Much of *The Dynasts* is written in blank verse (unrhymed iambic pentameter), but the work also includes prose passages, lyrics, rhymed couplets, and various other stanza forms. Some critics have suggested that Hardy may have chosen verse because a great novel on the subject already existed in Leo Tolstoy's *War and Peace* (1865-1869). More probably, Hardy chose an "antique" form to achieve the all-inclusiveness of epic and to claim association with classical epics, such as Homer's *Iliad* (c. 800 B.C.E.), which contain all verse forms and represent all levels of human society. Hardy too designs his epic to chronicle "the dull peoples and the Dynasts both," seeking to recover the heroic dimension of the human experience.

The greatest obstacle to this goal is what Hardy calls the Immanent Will. In Hardy's cosmology, worldly destiny and ambition are driven by an unconscious, motiveless force rather than by personal initiative or by a watchful, just God. Even the great powers appearing in the drama—Napoleon, Nelson, Wellington—are subject to this force, which works "like a knitter drowsed." Although he denied that it represented a systematic philosophy, *The Dynasts* seems to reinforce the determinism or fatalism prevailing in such earlier novels as *Tess of the D'Urbervilles* (1891). All the characters of the verse drama, whether high-born or humble, are caught in what Hardy calls "satires of circumstance"; whether king, commander, or whore, none seems capable of expressing individual purpose or intention.

To illustrate these satires, Hardy uses a chorus of Spirits or Intelligences. From various perspectives, they comment on the role of the Immanent Will in worldly experience. Themselves subject to the Will, they are free to meddle only superficially in human affairs. They may spread unreliable gossip, as does the Spirit of Rumour, or speak a word or two to an individual in a crisis (for example, to Villeneuve as he considers suicide, or to the defeated Napoleon after Waterloo). Only the Spirit of the Pities has any compassion for human misery; the others stand as indifferent, sometimes amused, witnesses to history.

A multitude of human actors crowd the drama. In addition to the key historical figures, Hardy includes many nonspeaking characters whose presence in these events the reader is merely intended to register. (This may be one of the reasons why Hardy stipulated that *The Dynasts* is intended "for mental performance alone.") Some of the more eminent characters serve principally to advance the action. Even Napoleon seems opaque when he makes rhetorical pronouncements; he is most sharply characterized as a victim of the Will: "a solitary figure on a jaded horse." As to the anonymous figures with whom Hardy peoples history, they, too, are caught in the Will's "knitting," as when a group of English deserters cheerfully drink themselves insensible in the ruins of a Spanish farmhouse, waking only when they are overtaken by Napoleon himself.

Hardy's epic vision is panoramic, and his sweeping aerial views of countryside and battlefield are, as the critic John Wain observed, cinematic achievements. Hardy also captures grotesque, anecdotal moments. For example, after Nelson's death at Trafalgar, his body is transported back to England preserved in a keg of rum, which his loyal, but thirsty sailors drain before arriving in port. For chronicling such extremes, Hardy develops a curious, even stilted vocabulary that is native neither to poetry nor prose. At times, he uses the speech of Wessex rustics that is familiar to readers of his novels; panicked at the rumor of Napoleon's approach, English country folk assert that he "lives upon human flesh, and has rashers o' baby every morning for breakfast." The poet invoked a completely different language when his Intelligences speak of the Immanent Will: "These are the Prime Volitions," they explain, "Their sum is like the lobule of a Brain/ Evolving always that it wots not of." In this twentieth century epic, Hardy proved himself to be a virtuoso of metrical form, and a keen, if eccentric, observer of historical detail.

"Critical Evaluation" by Sarah A. Boris

Bibliography:
Bailey, James Osler. *Thomas Hardy and the Cosmic Mind: A New Reading of "The Dynasts."* Chapel Hill: University of North Carolina Press, 1956. Presents a strong analysis of Hardy's philosophical views as expressed in *The Dynasts.*
Dean, Susan. *Hardy's Poetic Vision in "The Dynasts."* Princeton, N.J.: Princeton University Press, 1977. A thorough and accessible discussion of Hardy's epic vision and of his concept of the Immanent Will.
Maynard, Katherine Kearney. *Thomas Hardy's Tragic Poetry: The Lyrics and "The Dynasts."* Iowa City: University of Iowa Press, 1991. Examines *The Dynasts* in the context of Hardy's shorter poems and helps to define his sense of tragedy in a secular age.
White, R. J. *Thomas Hardy and History.* New York: Barnes & Noble Books, 1974. An invaluable study of Hardy's treatment of history in *The Dynasts* and elsewhere.
Wright, Walter F. *The Shaping of "The Dynasts": A Study in Thomas Hardy.* Lincoln: University of Nebraska Press, 1967. Especially useful in assessing Hardy's verse forms, as well as his indebtedness to the German philosopher Arthur Schopenhauer.

EARTH

Type of work: Novel
Author: Émile Zola (1840-1902)
Type of plot: Naturalism
Time of plot: 1860's
Locale: La Beauce, France
First published: La Terre, 1887 (English translation, 1888)

> *Principal characters:*
> FOUAN, an old peasant farmer
> ROSE, his wife
> HYACINTHE, called Jésus-Christ, his older son
> FANNY, his daughter
> BUTEAU, his younger son
> DELHOMME, Fanny's husband
> LISE, Fouan's niece and the daughter of Old Mouche
> FRANÇOISE, Lise's sister
> JEAN MACQUART, a soldier and artisan and later a farm laborer in
> La Beauce

The Story:

As Jean Macquart finished sowing each furrow with grain, he paused and gazed over the wide, rich plain. As far as he could see, farmers were scattering their wheat, anxious to finish sowing before the frosts came. He met and talked with Françoise about the coming division of old Fouan's property among his sons and son-in-law. In the notary's office, plans for the division were being discussed with anger. Fouan could not bear to lose the land that had taken all of his strength to work and that he had loved more passionately than his wife. The rent and food he asked in return for his property seemed excessive to his children, who, now that the land was within their grasp, intended to keep as much of its yield as possible. Buteau declared that the old man had money saved in bonds. This claim so enraged Fouan that he exhibited some of his old ferocity and authority. Finally, the notary completed the transaction and arranged that the surveyor divide the land.

Buteau drew the third lot of land. He declared that it was the worst and refused to take that part of the property. His refusal distressed Lise, Françoise's sister, for Buteau was her lover and she was pregnant. She had hoped that when he obtained the land he would marry her.

Old Mouche, the father of Lise and Françoise, had a stroke and died in his home. As the village women watched by his deathbed, a violent hailstorm laid waste the village crops. The peasants examined the damage by lamplight, their animosities forgotten in their common anguish at this devastation. Lise and Françoise stayed in the house after their father's death. Lise's son had been born and still Buteau had not married her. Jean became a constant visitor in the household. Believing that he was attracted by Lise, he proposed to her. Before accepting him, she decided to consult Buteau because of the child. At the autumn haymaking, Jean and Françoise worked together. While the girl stood atop the growing rick, Jean forked up bales of hay to her. She was flushed and laughing, and Jean found himself violently attracted to her. Because he was years older than Françoise, he was greatly upset when he suddenly realized that it was she who had drawn him to the house and not Lise.

Jean and the sisters met Buteau at the market in Cloyes. Because Lise now had property of her own and because he had at last accepted his share of land, Buteau decided to marry Lise. Buteau was now delighted by the land, and he plowed and sowed with vigor and passion, determined never to relinquish one inch of the earth. As the wheat grew, its rolling greenness covered La Beauce like an ocean. Buteau watched the weather as anxiously as a sailor at sea. Although Françoise wished to have her share of the land decided, Buteau managed to avoid a final settlement.

When Fouan's older son, nicknamed Jésus-Christ, took to buying brandy with the money that Buteau had grudgingly given his parents as their allowance, Buteau was so infuriated that he struck his mother to the floor. Rose did not recover, and she died three days later. That left Fouan completely alone. Finally, much against his will, he decided to make his home with Delhomme, his son-in-law.

By harvest time, the green sea of wheat had turned to a fiery gold, and the whole village worked at the harvest. Meanwhile, Jean was tormented by his desire for Françoise. Finally, exhausted by her struggle to resist his attentions, she yielded to him. Buteau, fearing he might lose both the girl and her land, asserted that they could never be married while Françoise was under age.

Fouan was bullied and restricted in Delhomme's home; he had no money for tobacco, and he was allowed little wine. Completely miserable, he went to live with Buteau and Lise. There he was appalled by Buteau's pursuit of Françoise, whose resistance made Buteau so angry that even Lise expressed the wish that her sister would surrender in order to have peace once more in the household. Françoise, however, continued proudly to refuse Buteau, and she was gradually transformed into a domestic drudge.

In desperation, Françoise agreed to marry Jean when she was of age. Fouan, drawn into these household quarrels, was no happier than he had been with Delhomme. At last, because Buteau and his wife begrudged every mouthful of food that he ate, he accepted Jésus-Christ's offer of a home. Jésus-Christ was the only one of Fouan's children without a passion for land. Although it distressed Fouan to see his hard-won acres go to buy brandy for Jésus-Christ, he enjoyed the jokes and the occasional excellent meals cooked in the nearly ruined house by Jésus-Christ's illegitimate daughter.

Before the time of the vintage, Jésus-Christ discovered that his father was spending his bonds on an annuity by which he hoped to acquire some land of his own once more. Amazed, first Fanny and then Buteau tried to bribe the old man to return to them. Fouan's relationship with Jésus-Christ was never close again after the discovery.

After a final explosion with Lise, Françoise left the house and went to live with her aunt. It was arranged that she should soon marry Jean and claim her full share of the property. The ill will between the sisters was intensified when the land was divided and Françoise secured the house at auction. Buteau and Lise moved to an adjacent house, where Fouan joined them, fearing that Jésus-Christ would steal his bonds.

Jean and Buteau were forced to work side by side in the fields. One day, while Jean was manuring the earth, Lise told Buteau that Fouan had suffered a stroke and that she would bring the doctor. To everyone's surprise, the old man recovered. During his illness, however, Lise had discovered his bonds. When they refused to return them, he left.

Homeless and desperate, Fouan wandered to Delhomme's farm, where he stayed wearily looking into the house. Next, he went to Jésus-Christ's hovel, but fear and pride again prevented him from entering. That night, during a terrible storm, Fouan, wretched and exhausted, dragged himself around to look once more at the land he had owned. Finally his hunger became so great that he returned to Buteau, who jeeringly fed him.

Françoise was pregnant. Enraged by the fear that the property might not revert to him and by the fact that Jean's plow had cut into their land, Buteau, aided by Lise, raped Françoise. With revulsion, the young woman realized that she had always loved him. In her jealousy, Lise knocked Françoise against a scythe in the field, and the blade pierced her abdomen. As she lay dying, Françoise refused to will her share of the farm to Jean; although he was her husband, she still regarded him as an outsider. After her death, Jean was evicted from the land.

Greedy for more money and terrified that the old man would betray the manner of Françoise's death, Lise and Buteau murdered Fouan by smothering him with a pillow and then setting fire to his bed. Jean Macquart, having no further ties with La Beauce, decided to become a soldier again. After a final tour of the land, he left the region forever. He reasoned that if he could not cultivate the land, he would at least be able to defend the earth of France.

Critical Evaluation:

Émile Zola began as a literary romantic and an idealist. In his youth, he wrote fairy tales and dreamed of perfect beauty and perfect love. The poverty he experienced early in life and the general European literary climate, however, brought him to try to picture an imperfect but real "corner of nature."

Earth, the fifteenth volume of the Rougon-Macquart series, is Zola's horrifying vision of the French peasantry before the Franco-Prussian War. In the relationships between Fouan and his family, Zola consciously adopted the theme of William Shakespeare's *King Lear* (1605-1606), although the realistic detail with which Fouan is drawn includes none of the nobility of Shakespeare's king. Zola's introduction of Rabelaisian humor in the character Jésus-Christ was an innovation in literary realism. The earth itself dominates the novel, and its beauty and indifference contrast vividly with the peasants' passionate absorption in possessing the land and with the crimes they commit in order to do so.

A magnificent example of Zola's groping for the authentic details in life, *Earth* can be best understood when placed in the literary context of realism and naturalism. Literary realism developed in the nineteenth century partly as a response to the conditions of modern society. It stressed fidelity to the facts of everyday existence. Scenes, characters, motives, and conflicts were presumably drawn from experiences in life rather than from dreams of other worlds or of the supernatural. Within the realist tradition are distinct and coherent groupings—naturalism is one of them—but it is easier to place a work such as *Earth* in the naturalist tradition than it is to define literary naturalism. In general, however, for the purposes of examining *Earth*, two basic points can be established: Naturalism attempts to portray the actual and significant details of life and especially (though not exclusively) the life of poor and working people, and naturalism most often attempts to uncover those forces in the environment and in the genetic makeup of the individual that determine the course of life.

Earth tries to give an accurate picture of French rural life in the 1860's. This picture is not merely a general account, but a brilliantly detailed canvas that conveys the humanity and density of rural life. The basis of the action of the novel is the division of an old man's land. Much of the novel, therefore, describes the unending, vicious, implacable hatreds and the unyielding tensions that emerge within the farmer's family. Domestic life is described through the conversations, the cooking and cleaning utensils, the jealous glances, and the dirt, cobwebs, and small, damp rooms of the peasant households. The smells of the fields, the manure, the sweat, and the musky odors of water and age saturate every scene.

The life of the countryside is also explored in relation to the fields, skies, and weather. The division of these fields, the run-down cottages, and the seeding and fertilization of the fields are depicted in meticulous detail. Pages are devoted to storms of various kinds, including a hailstorm, but unlike the romantics, for whom the excesses of the weather are often merely spectacular, these storms are viewed as destructive and, toward the end of *Earth*, as brutalizing and humbling.

Main events in the harvest are not omitted. Zola sketches a grape harvest, for example, in which the workers pick grapes, stuff themselves, and get sick. In fact, sickness, drunkenness, perversity, and violence are presented as being ever-present in the life of these times. Zola leaves out nothing, including all aspects of the sexual side of life. From the beginning of the novel, where Zola describes a young man and woman working together without embarrassment to help a bull and a cow to mate, the sexual theme is established as a central part of life.

Zola's accumulation of detail from real experience becomes increasingly powerful as the novel advances. These details, linked through action, character, and theme, become the tightly woven, actual fabric of life. Reading *Earth* is, in fact, to be submerged in this life; and this feeling of submersion no doubt accounts for the powerful influence the novel continues to exert. At the same time, Zola's selection of details led to his being accused of presenting only the sordid side of life, and of unnecessarily emphasizing the nasty aspects of life. *Earth* was sharply attacked precisely for these reasons when it was first published. Some even thought the novel to be deliberately pornographic. A good argument can be made that these scenes are included not for their shock value but for more serious reasons that are connected to Zola's understanding of science.

The second important feature of literary naturalism, its attempt to portray the underlying forces that shape human destiny, is especially evident in Zola's work, who understood these forces in a scientific context. They were describable, measurable, and inevitable. In his view, in fact, by understanding the genetic and environmental forces working on his characters, and by altering these forces, he could explain his characters scientifically and, at the same time, actually experiment on them and test them in his fiction. Zola did not, however, carry out this experimental procedure vigorously in his novels.

In *Earth*, the forces that are most evident are those associated with the land. The greed for the land, which is manifest in the character Buteau, overcomes all obstacles. Buteau will have the land or destroy it, himself, and his competitors and family. The power of sex is likewise connected with the earth. The opening scene of the novel deals with the fertilization of the land, and it describes a sexual life "close to the earth." Sexual activity takes place in the fields as well as in the home.

Finally, there is the genetic composition of the characters. Their strengths and weaknesses, determined by the strengths and weaknesses of their ancestors, provide a spectrum of responses to the conditions of rural France. The family thus helps place *Earth* in its proper position in the massive architecture of Zola's Rougon-Macquart series. Although Zola may have seen his characters as more or less determined by forces outside their control, *Earth* leaves the impression that men and women can, within limits, choose their course in life. It should be said that some other practitioners of naturalist fiction—such as Frank Norris in the United States—took a much more mechanical approach to the so-called scientific forces that shape human life. In Norris' work, the reader is left with the impression that human freedom is simply low farce. In *Earth*, however, Zola does not communicate this sense of a claustrophobic fate. No matter how awful Fouan's end may be, Zola never shifts the responsibility away from Fouan himself. *Earth* certainly demonstrates the limits and the narrowness of the life of the peasant in nineteenth century France, but within those limits, Zola shows that freedom survives, and with freedom the refreshing possibilities of birth.

"Critical Evaluation" by Howard Lee Hertz

Bibliography:

Grant, Elliott M. *Émile Zola*. New York: Twayne, 1966. Includes an extensive discussion of *Earth* and concludes that the central concept of the novel concerns the cycle of birth, growth, decay, death, and rebirth. Also includes poetic descriptions of La Beauce and informative discussions of dramatic action, subthemes, comedy, character, religion, and politics in the novel.

Hemmings, F. W. J. *Émile Zola*. Oxford, England: Clarendon Press, 1966. Intelligent discussion and criticism of Zola's life and works. Sees *Earth* as Zola's novel of Nature, with its emphasis on French peasants' passionate and erotic love for the earth. Concludes that the character Buteau is transported to madness by this lust for the soil.

Knapp, Bettina L. *Émile Zola*. New York: Frederick Ungar, 1980. Handbook-style summaries and analysis of the Rougon-Macquart cycle. Describes the purpose of *Earth* as a depiction of the reality of the life of French peasantry. Zola contrasts love of the soil with avarice, possessiveness, immorality, and cruelty. Knapp also discusses the outraged public and critical reaction to the novel.

Turnell, Martin. *The Art of French Fiction*. New York: New Directions, 1960. Contains a long, informative chapter on Zola. Discusses naturalism and themes of the Rougon-Macquart cycle. Also includes an analysis of *Earth's* fertility imagery.

Wilson, Angus. *Émile Zola: An Introductory Study of His Novels*. New York: William Morrow, 1952. A comprehensive examination of Zola's life, principles, influences, and themes. Wilson finds Earth the most complete of Zola's novels, bringing together strands of emotions and methods of expression from individual novels in the Rougon-Macquart series.

THE EARTHLY PARADISE

Type of work: Poetry
Author: William Morris (1834-1896)
First published: 1868-1870

Of all the poems of William Morris, the most successful, in terms of popularity, is *The Earthly Paradise*, published originally in five thick volumes. Following closely the plan of Geoffrey Chaucer's *The Canterbury Tales* (1387-1400), this composition reveals Morris' attraction to Chaucer's method as well as his sense of beauty. Like Chaucer, Morris found in medieval legends and ancient myths material for his poetic narrative art; and he also found a general plan according to which these unrelated stories could be brought together harmoniously by a technique in which Eastern cultures had long anticipated Chaucer and other Europeans. Unlike Chaucer, whose plan was so large that he could not complete it, Morris, upon an almost equal scale, brought his work to a happy conclusion.

The prologue introduces a company of Norsemen who have fled the pestilence and set sail to seek the fabled Earthly Paradise "across the western sea where none grow old." Not having succeeded in their quest, they have returned "shrivelled, bent, and grey," after lengthy wanderings abroad, to a "nameless city in a distant sea" where the worship of the ancient Greek gods has not died out. In this hospitable city they spend the rest of their lives. Twice each month they participate in a feast at which a tale is told, alternately, by one of the city elders and one of the wanderers. The former tell tales on classical subjects, and the latter draw their tales from Norse and other medieval sources. Thus, of the twenty-four stories, twelve are Greek and classical and twelve are medieval or romantic. Each pair of stories corresponds with one of the twelve months, the first two being told in January, the second two in February, and so on. Thus the long poem is neatly partitioned into twelve books with interpolated prologues and epilogues in the form of lyrics about the progressive changes in nature. *The Earthly Paradise* actually revived in England an enthusiasm for long romances. Despite their high cost, many thousands of Morris' books were sold, and the effect was a favorable one for the new revival of romantic feeling which Morris was fostering in art and decoration as well as in literature. Instead of exhausting Morris, this poetic effort inspired him to embark on other vast projects such as the translation of Homer and Vergil and a modern version of a Scandinavian epic, *Sigurd the Volsung*.

Among the tales told by the wanderers in *The Earthly Paradise*, the most striking is "The Lovers of Gudrun," a version of the Icelandic Laxdaela Saga. It tells of Gudrun, daughter of a great lord in Iceland, who was loved by many men but especially by Kiartan, a youth of manly deeds and kindly disposition. Although Gudrun passionately returns his love, Kiartan, before he will marry her, goes with his bosom friend and cousin Bodli to seek fame in Norway, where he remains some years at the court of Olaf Trygvesson. When Bodli returns alone to Iceland, he yields to his passion for Gudrun and tells her that Kiartan has fallen in love with King Olaf's sister Ingibiarg and will marry her. Convinced of Kiartan's unfaithfulness, Gudrun brokenheartedly marries Bodli. When Kiartan returns to claim his bride, Gudrun curses Bodli, and the desolate Kiartan, half in contempt, spares his life. Despairing and taunted by those about him, Bodli participates in an ambush set up by Kiartan's enemies, treacherously slays his friend, and is in turn killed by Kiartan's brothers. Although Gudrun marries again, what remains indelibly with the reader is Morris' picture of her agonized realization of what, in her faithlessness, she has done:

She cried, with tremulous voice, and eyes grown wet
For the last time, what e'er should happen yet,
With hands stretched out for all that she had lost:
"I did the worst to him I loved the most."

Morris was a natural creator; that his hand could not outspeed his brain is evidenced by his composing seven hundred lines of poetry in a day. Years after the composition of *The Earthly Paradise* he explained the nonchalant attitude toward the writing of poetry which enabled him to race undaunted through that enormous project: "Waiting for inspiration, rushing things in reliance on inspiration, and all the rest of it, are a lazy man's habits. Get the bones of the work well into your head, and the tools well into your hand, and get on with the job, and the inspiration will come to you."

In spite of its quantity, his poetry has a remarkably high quality. Although somewhat lacking in humor, pathos, and rich humanity, it shows none of the crabbed complaints of many poets. His range of subject matter is as broad as his composition was fluent. The very spacious cycle of stories in *The Earthly Paradise* includes these titles: "The Story of Theseus," "The Son of Croesus," "Cupid and Psyche," "The King's Treasure-House," "Orpheus and Eurydice," "Pygmalion," "Atalanta's Race," "The Doom of King Acrisius," "Rhodope," "The Dolphin and the Lovers," "The Fortunes of Gygis," "Bellerophon," "The Watching of the Falcon," "The Lady of the Land," "The Hill of Venus," "The Seven Sleepers," "The Man Who Never Laughed Again," "The Palace East of the Sun," "The Queen of the North," "The Story of Dorothea," "The Writing on the Image," "The Proud King," "The Ring Given to Venus," and "The Man Born to Be King."

These stories are so arranged that, with the revolving calendar, their temper becomes darker and stronger, developing into a sinister tone at the end. The full effect thus depends upon a continuous and consecutive reading. Conversely, the problem which arises as the reader progresses through this lengthy work is that the embroidery becomes too profuse to be sustained by the fabric. The result is the taint of decoration inherent in the Pre-Raphaelites—too much of beauty, love, languor, everything—so that the reader longs for a little substantial simplicity and cheerfulness. One might, therefore, argue for an occasional and selective reading of the stories, so long as their total scope is kept in mind.

The interludes give readers glimpses into the poet's mind, and these glimpses give evidence that despite his disapproval of introspective poetry, Morris did not always avoid it. While the stories of *The Earthly Paradise* come from all parts of the medieval world, these poems of the months are unequivocally English; they give an admiring description of the land of Morris' birth and life. With variations, they repeat the keynote of the prologue in which he characterizes himself as "the idle singer of an empty day" who has no power to sing of hell or heaven or to make death bearable. By "idle" Morris does not mean "useless" but, rather, one who can, by the scenes he presents, distract from "empty," daily cares. In this manner he acknowledged spiritual emptiness in his time.

Throughout this poetic work there runs a strain of despondency, doubt, and mild skepticism which records the poet's genuine pity for humanity. Although there is in the work an elemental vigor, glorying in youth, power, love, and possessions, these aspects of life are presented primarily through old men's memories. Despite the swift-moving action, the narrative generally seems grandly slow. Neither the tale-tellers nor the actors in the tales are particularly individualized as characters. Finally readers see a vast, intricate tapestry with its panorama of interwoven figures.

Bibliography:

Boos, Florence Saunders. *The Design of William Morris' "The Earthly Paradise."* Lewiston, N.Y.: Edwin Mellen Press, 1990. An analysis of the literary design of *The Earthly Paradise*. Discusses the literary structure of the work, the influences and sources for the poems, and their critical reception.

Calhoun, Blue. *The Pastoral Vision of William Morris: "The Earthly Paradise."* Athens: The University of Georgia Press, 1975. Places *The Earthly Paradise* within the genre of the pastoral. This perspective reveals motifs that can be connected to Morris' socialism and artistic endeavors.

Hodgson, Amanda. *The Romances of William Morris*. Cambridge, England: Cambridge University Press, 1987. A study that examines why William Morris utilized the genre of romance as a vehicle to express his views. A chapter analyzes The Earthly Paradise as a romance within the context of Morris' development of this literary form.

Skoblow, Jeffrey. *Paradise Dislocated: Morris, Politics, Art*. Charlottesville: University Press of Virginia, 1993. Sets *The Earthly Paradise* within the context of modernism and Marxism. Argues that *The Earthly Paradise* expresses a sense of estrangement or dislocation that is a part of modern culture.

Tompkins, J. M. S. *William Morris: An Approach to the Poetry*. London: Cecil Woolf, 1988. A complete study of the poetic works, including prose romances, written by William Morris. Two chapters are devoted to analysis of *The Earthly Paradise*, examining the tales particularly for what they reveal about Morris' feelings about society and his life.

EAST OF EDEN

Type of work: Novel
Author: John Steinbeck (1902-1968)
Type of plot: Regional
Time of plot: 1865-1918
Locale: California
First published: 1952

> *Principal characters:*
> ADAM TRASK, a settler in the Salinas Valley
> CATHY AMES, later Adam's wife
> CALEB and
> ARON TRASK, their twin sons
> CHARLES TRASK, Adam's half brother
> SAMUEL HAMILTON, a neighbor of the Trasks
> LEE, Adam's Chinese servant
> ABRA BACON, Aron's fiancée

The Story:

The soil of the Salinas Valley in California was rich, although the surrounding foothills were poor and life shriveled during the long dry spells. The Irish-born Hamiltons, arriving after American settlers had displaced the Mexicans, settled on the barren hillside. Sam Hamilton, full of talk, glory, and improvident inventions, and Liza, his dourly religious wife, brought up their nine children there.

In Connecticut, Adam Trask and his half brother Charles grew up in harmony despite the differences in their natures. Adam was gentle and good; Charles was roughly handsome and had a streak of wild violence. After Adam's mother committed suicide, his father had married the docile woman who became Charles's mother. Adam loved his stepmother but hated his father, a rigid disciplinarian whose fanatic militarism had begun with a fictitious account of his own war career and whose dream was to have a son in the army. He hoped to fulfill his dream through Adam. Charles, whose passionate love for his father went continually unnoticed, could not understand this rejection of himself. In despair, he beat Adam almost to death.

Adam served in the cavalry for five years. Then, although he hated regimentation and violence, he reenlisted, for he could neither accept help from his father, who had become an important figure in Washington, nor return to the farm Charles now ran alone. Afterward, Adam wandered through the West and the South, served time for vagrancy, and finally came home to find that his father had died, making him and Charles rich. In the years that followed, the two brothers lived together on the farm. Their bickering and inbred solitude drove Adam to periodic wanderings. Feeling that their life was one of pointless industry, he talked of moving west but he did not do anything about it.

Meanwhile, Cathy Ames was growing up in Massachusetts. She was born unable to comprehend goodness, but she had a sublimely innocent face and a consummate knowledge of how to manipulate and deceive others to serve her own ends. After a thwarted attempt to leave home, she burned down her parents' house, killing them, and left evidence to indicate that she had been murdered. She became the mistress of a man who ran a string of brothels and used his love for her against him. When he realized her true nature, he took her to a deserted spot and beat her savagely. Near death, she crawled to the nearest house—the Trasks'—where Adam and

Charles cared for her. Adam thought her innocent and beautiful; Charles, who had an empathetic knowledge of evil, wanted her to leave. Cathy, who knew she temporarily needed protection, enticed Adam into marrying her. On their wedding night, she gave him a sleeping draught and went to Charles.

Aware that Charles disapproved of Cathy, Adam decided to carry out his dream of going west. He was so transfigured by his happiness that he ignored Cathy's protests seriously; since she was his ideal of love and purity, he thought that she could not disagree with him. Adam bought a ranch in the richest part of the Salinas Valley and worked hard to prepare it for his wife and the child she expected. Cathy hated her pregnancy and tried unsuccessfully to abort the child. After giving birth to twin boys, she recuperated for a week; she then shot Adam, wounding him, and left, abandoning her sons.

Changing her name to Kate, Cathy went to work in a Salinas brothel. Her beauty and seeming goodness endeared her to the proprietress, Faye, and Kate gradually assumed control of the establishment. After Faye made a will leaving Kate her money and property, Kate engineered Faye's death. Making her establishment one that aroused and catered to sadistic tastes, she became legendary and rich.

Adam was like a dead man for a year after his wife left him, unable to work his land or even to name his sons. Finally, Sam Hamilton woke him by deliberately angering him. Sam, Adam, and Lee, the Chinese servant and a wise and good man, named the boys Caleb and Aron. The men talked of the story of Cain and Abel, and Lee declared that rejection terrifies a child most and leads to guilt and revenge. Later, after much study, Lee discovered the true meaning of the Hebrew word *timshel* (thou mayest) and understood that the story meant in part that man can always choose to conquer evil.

Sam had grown old and he knew he would soon die. Before he left his ranch, he told Adam about Kate and her cruel, destructive business. Adam visited her and suddenly knew her as she really was. Though she taunted him, telling him that Charles was the true father of his sons, and tried to seduce him, he left her a free and curiously exultant man. Yet he was unable to bring himself to tell his sons that their mother was not dead.

Caleb and Aron were growing up very differently. Golden-haired Aron inspired love without trying, but he was single-minded and unyielding; Caleb was dark and clever, a feared and respected leader whom others left much alone. When Adam moved to town, where the schools were better, Aron fell in love with Abra Bacon, who told him that his mother was still alive. Aron could not believe her because to do so would have destroyed his faith in his father and in everything.

About this time, Adam had the idea of shipping lettuce packed in ice to New York. When the venture failed, Aron was ashamed of his father for failing publicly. Caleb vowed to return the lost money to his father. As they faced the problems of growing into men, Aron became smugly religious, which was disturbing to Abra because she felt unable to live up to his idealistic image of her. Caleb alternated between wild impulses and guilt. Learning that Kate was his mother, he began following her until she, noticing him, invited him to her house. As he talked to her, he knew with relief that he was not like her; she felt his knowledge and hated him. Kate herself, obsessed by the fear that one of the old girls had discovered Faye's murder, plotted ways to destroy this menace. Although Caleb could accept Kate's existence, he knew that Aron could not. To get the boy away from Salinas, Caleb talked him into finishing high school in three years and beginning college. Adam, knowing nothing of Caleb's true character, was extravagantly proud of Aron.

When World War I broke out, Caleb went into the bean business with Will Hamilton and made a fortune because of food shortages. With growing excitement, he planned an elaborate presentation to his father of the money once lost in the lettuce enterprise. First he tried to persuade Aron, who seemed indifferent to his father's love, not to leave college. Caleb presented his money to Adam, only to have it rejected in anger because Adam's idealistic nature could not accept money made as profit from the war. He wanted Caleb's achievements to be like his brother's. In a black mood of revenge, Caleb took Aron to meet his mother. After her sons' visit, Kate, who was not as disturbed by those she could hurt as she was by someone like Caleb, made a will leaving everything to Aron. Then, burdened by age, illness, and suspiciousness, she committed suicide.

Aron was unable to face the new knowledge of his parents' past, so he joined the army and went to France. Adam did not recover from the shock of his leaving. Abra turned to Caleb, admitting that she loved him rather than Aron, whose romantic stubbornness kept him from facing reality. When the news of Aron's death arrived, Adam had another stroke. As he lay dying, Caleb, unable to bear his guilt any longer, told his father of his responsibility for Aron's enlisting and thus his death. Lee begged Adam to forgive his son. Adam weakly raised his hand in benediction and, whispering the Hebrew word *timshel*, died.

Critical Evaluation:

When John Steinbeck received the Nobel Prize in Literature in 1962, critics considered *The Grapes of Wrath* (1939) his best work, but Steinbeck himself always believed *East of Eden* to be his greatest achievement. The novel disappointed critics upon its first appearance because they were expecting something resembling his previous works. However, in *East of Eden* Steinbeck departed from his usual concise narration to explore complex philosophical and psychological themes about which he had been preparing to write since the late 1930's. As a fictional epic of the area around Salinas, California, where Steinbeck had grown up, the subject is much more personal than that of previous books. In fact, Steinbeck names himself as the grandson of the model for Sam Hamilton. The epic traces the history of two families—one a deteriorating New England family and the other a large family of recent Irish immigrants.

The novel's central theme is the struggle of good against evil, most obviously symbolized by the recurring discussion of the story of Cain and Abel. Steinbeck presents characters in pairs—Adam and Charles, Aron and Caleb, Abra and Cathy—using first initials to identify clearly which characters are inherently good and which must struggle to overcome the seeds of evil within them. Also associated with this theme is the Hebrew word *timshel* (thou mayest). In the Old Testament, God tells Cain that he may overcome evil and gain salvation. *Timshel* does not command that he must overcome evil or guarantee that he will; rather, it provides the opportunity to overcome evil if he chooses to do so. Ironically, it is Lee, the Chinese Presbyterian, who appeals to a group of Confucian scholars to solve the meaning of *timshel*. After learning Hebrew and spending months reading and discussing the Talmud, they give Lee the answer: "Thou mayest." *Timshel* appears again at the end of the novel when Adam, paralyzed by a stroke, whispers the word to Caleb, who had just confessed the evil he had done by taking Aron to meet Kate. The father tells the son, "thou mayest." Hence, the answer to Steinbeck's urgent question—can human beings overcome evil?—is left undetermined.

The philosophical discussion of *timshel* also influences the psychological portions of the novel. Through Steinbeck's explorations of how trying to overcome evil affects the human mind, we wee unsettling glimpses of the darkness of the human soul. Customers at Kate's house of prostitution illustrate the varieties of torture and perversion of which the human mind is capable.

"Eden" as symbol for both the biblical garden and the Salinas Valley in Northern California also has ambiguous meaning. Parts of the valley are lush and fertile, but others, like the Hamilton farm, are virtual wastelands—dry and barren. Even the lush Trask ranch is a deceptive ambiguous Eden: Although it is one of the most fertile properties in the county, the fields, orchards, and gardens have been allowed to go wild and the deteriorating old house crumbles to ruins.

In addition to its literary merits, *East of Eden* offers a wealth of social and historical information. In tracing the history of two families, Steinbeck depicts the waves of settlers passing through California, first the Mexicans, then the white Americans, and finally the Irish immigrants. A community cringes at the arrival of its first automobile and gets a lesson on how to crank-start a Ford. New inventions either work (Sam's new windmill) or dreadfully fail (Adam's attempt to exploit icebox railroad freight cars). Through Caleb and Will Hamilton, Steinbeck shows how profitable speculating in food was during wartime, and through Cathy Trask/Kate Ames he shows a great deal about organized prostitution across the country.

Since the late 1970's, some significant trends developed in the criticism of *East of Eden*. No longer content to say merely that the novel is not like the rest of Steinbeck's work, critics began looking for value in the differences. Whereas earlier novels are more naturalistic, objective, and detached, *East of Eden* is more subjective and personal. Steinbeck remained satisfied with that work's indeterminacy rather than striving to make order where none exists. After a period in which studies focused primarily on the Trask men and Sam Hamilton, criticism turned to some of the peripheral characters, mainly women, and their contribution to the complex fabric of Salinas society. These included perseverent Eliza, Dessie, in whose relaxed dress shop women could laugh and break wind, and Lee, the Trasks' Chinese servant, who is really the voice of wisdom and reason—the mouthpiece for Steinbeck's own views on philosophy and religion. In 1952, readers were not ready for a book like *East of Eden* from an author like John Steinbeck, but the novel seems to age like the fine fermented apple wine in Lee's jug—it gets better with each critical discussion, and its content never diminishes.

East of Eden's psychological explorations of good and evil find predecessors in nineteenth century American novels such as Nathaniel Hawthorne's *The Scarlet Letter* (1850) or Herman Melville's *Moby Dick* (1851). At the same time, in its thorough, almost encyclopedic chronicling of Salinas places, people, and events, Steinbeck's techniques foreshadow those used by William Kennedy in his Albany novels such as *Ironweed* (1983) and *Quinn's Book* (1988), for example. Steinbeck's comfort with indeterminacy also suggests a connection to other postmodern fiction.

"Critical Evaluation" by Geralyn Strecker

Bibliography:
Etheridge, Charles L., Jr. "Changing Attitudes Toward Steinbeck's Naturalism and the Changing Reputation of *East of Eden*: A Survey of Criticism Since 1974." In *The Steinbeck Question: New Essays in Criticism*, edited by Donald R. Noble. Troy, N.Y.: Whitston, 1993. Discusses the novel's disastrous reception in 1952 and its improving critical reputation since.
Gladstein, Mimi R. "The Strong Female Principle of Good—or Evil: The Women of *East of Eden*." *Steinbeck Quarterly* 24, nos. 1/2 (Winter/Spring, 1991): 30-40. This significant discussion of women in the novel divides the female characters into the Trask women and the Hamilton women. Calls Abra the principle of good, the second Eve, and the mother of future generations.

Hayashi, Tetsumaro. "The 'Chinese Servant' in *East of Eden.*" *San Jose Studies* 18, no. 1 (Winter, 1992): 52-60. On one level, Lee, an ignored, often invisible character, is a stereotypical servant, but he also provides a bridge between the spiritual and material worlds and offers an objective, transcendent view of life. Praises Lee's multifaceted role as servant, manager, surrogate parent, preacher, and scholar.

Steinbeck, John. *Journal of a Novel: The "East of Eden" Letters.* New York: Viking, 1969. Steinbeck used this journal, in the form of a letter to his friend and editor Pascal Covici, to work out problems with plot and subject matter. It is an indispensable companion to the novel.

Timmerman, John H. *John Steinbeck's Fiction: The Aesthetics of the Road Taken.* Norman: University of Oklahoma Press, 1986. The chapter on *East of Eden* argues that Cathy is the thematic and structural center of the novel, a Satan figure against whom all others are measured.

EASTWARD HO!

Type of work: Drama
Authors: George Chapman (c. 1559-1634) with Ben Jonson (1573-1637) and John Marston (1576-1634)
Type of plot: Comedy
Time of plot: c. 1605
Locale: London
First performed: 1605; first published, 1605

> *Principal characters:*
> TOUCHSTONE, a goldsmith
> MISTRESS TOUCHSTONE, his wife
> GERTRUDE, his haughty daughter
> MILDRED, his dutiful daughter
> FRANCIS QUICKSILVER, his idle and prodigal apprentice
> GOLDING, his diligent apprentice
> SIR PETRONEL FLASH, a new-made knight
> SECURITY, an old usurer
> WINIFRED, his young wife
> SINDEFY, Quicksilver's mistress

The Story:

Touchstone, a goldsmith, had two daughters, Gertrude, a flutter-brained social climber, and Mildred, a modest, gentle girl. He also had two apprentices, Francis Quicksilver, a fellow as unstable as his name, and Golding, who was steady and conscientious. Caught while trying to slip away from the shop, Quicksilver made a spirited defense of his way of life, especially of his prodigality among the town gallants. Touchstone answered with a severe moral lecture and pointed out the exemplary behavior of his fellow apprentice. The lecture was interrupted by a messenger from Sir Petronel Flash, who wished to make arrangements to marry Gertrude. As soon as Touchstone was out of hearing, Quicksilver abused the old citizen; Golding defended his master and warned and rebuked Quicksilver.

Mildred, with the help of a tailor and a maid, attired Gertrude elegantly to receive her knight, while Gertrude rattled away, full of herself and contemptuous of her bourgeois family. Touchstone brought in Sir Petronel and concluded the arrangements for the wedding, warning both Gertrude and the knight that they need not expect any gifts beyond the agreed dowry. Gertrude treated him impudently and left with the knight, with Mistress Touchstone fluttering in attendance on her soon-to-be-married daughter. After their departure, Touchstone proposed a match between Mildred and Golding.

From the wedding feast Quicksilver returned to the shop drunk, hiccuping and quoting lines from popular plays. Touchstone, losing patience with the fellow, released him from his indenture and discharged him. After Quicksilver's defiant and staggering exit, Touchstone told Golding that he too would no longer be an apprentice, but a full-fledged member of the guild and his master's son-in-law. At the home of old Security, where Quicksilver and his mistress Sindefy lived, the old usurer plotted with them to trap Sir Petronel and to gain possession of Gertrude's property. Quicksilver was to encourage the knight to borrow money for a proposed voyage to Virginia, and both Quicksilver and Sindefy, who was to become Gertrude's maid, were to encourage the bride to put up her land to cover the debt. Before leaving to set his plans in motion, Security delayed to bid farewell to his pretty young wife, Winifred.

Sir Petronel confessed to Quicksilver that he had no castle, but that he intended to send his bride on a wild goose chase to an imaginary castle in the country in order to get her out of the way while he carried off old Security's young wife on the Virginia voyage. Security brought in Sindefy and placed her with Gertrude as a maid, then took Sir Petronel to his home for breakfast. Captain Seagull, Scapethrift, and Spendall joined Sir Petronel there to make the final plans for the voyage.

As Gertrude prepared for her ride into the country to see her husband's nonexistent castle, Touchstone entered with his other daughter and his new son-in-law, Golding. Gertrude heaped contempt on all three, and Sir Petronel made disparaging remarks about the groom's lack of nobility. Touchstone distributed a few ironical barbs and led away the newlyweds. After their departure, Security presented Gertrude with papers, supposedly to cover a loan for new furnishings for the country castle. At Sir Petronel's request she signed the papers without even reading them and set out in her coach after urging the knight to follow as soon as possible. Sir Petronel and Quicksilver convinced Security that the knight was planning to elope with a lawyer's wife; and Security, maliciously delighted at the chance to injure another man, promised to lend them his wife's gown as a disguise. He also felt that lending the gown would be a good way to make certain that his wife did not leave home.

Sir Petronel, the disguised Winifred, Quicksilver, and the other adventurers ignored storm warnings and set out in their boats for the ship. Security discovered his wife's absence and tried to follow them. Slitgut, a butcher coming to Cuckold's Haven to set up a pair of horns, saw from his elevated vantage point a boat overturned in the waves. A few minutes later old Security crawled ashore bemoaning the appropriateness of his place of shipwreck. As soon as he had crept away, the butcher saw a woman struggling in the waves and a boy plunging in to save her. The boy rescued a very repentant Winifred, brought her ashore, and offered her shelter and dry clothes. A third victim of the storm was washed ashore at the foot of the gallows—a bad omen, Slitgut thought. The man was Francis Quicksilver, who passed by cursing his fate. Finally, Sir Petronel and Captain Seagull reached shore and met Quicksilver. Sir Petronel, having lost his money in the water, had no hope of saving his ship, which he expected to be confiscated. Winifred, now dry and freshly dressed, convinced Security that she had not left home until she began to worry about him. Slitgut made a few wry remarks about marriage and went home, unobserved by any of the adventurers.

Touchstone, thoroughly angered by the knight's desertion and by his wife's and daughter's foolishness, turned out Gertrude and Sindefy to shift for themselves, but having borne his wife as a cross for thirty years, he felt he should continue to do so. Golding, made an alderman's deputy on his first day in the guild, reported that Sir Petronel and Quicksilver had been arrested and the ship attached. Mistress Touchstone had learned her lesson; but Gertrude, in spite of her mother's entreaties that she beg forgiveness, treated her father with her customary contempt. Sir Petronel and Quicksilver were brought in by a constable, and Quicksilver was charged with the theft of five hundred pounds, a capital offense. A warrant was also sent out for old Security for his share in the business. Sir Petronel and Quicksilver reached a peak of repentance that made them the talk of the prison. Golding and the jailer joined Mistress Touchstone and her daughters in pleading with Touchstone to show mercy to the offenders; Touchstone was adamant. Finally Golding had himself arrested, sent for Touchstone to come to release him, and arranged for the latter to overhear Quicksilver's ballad of repentance, sung for the edification of other prisoners to the tune of "I Wail in Woe, I Plunge in Pain." Touchstone's heart was moved, and he offered forgiveness to his prodigal son-in-law and prodigal apprentice. Old Security, hearing that a song of repentance had worked such wonders, rushed up howling a lamentable song in a most lamentable voice; he too received mercy. At Golding's urging, Quicksilver agreed to marry Sindefy. Security returned to Winifred. Even Gertrude forgave her erring husband and asked forgiveness from her father. Thus all differences were reconciled.

Critical Evaluation:

Eastward Ho! first performed in 1605, is one of the most remarkably successful collaborative efforts in English literature. The talents of three considerably different playwrights—Ben Jonson, Thomas Marston, and George Chapman—went into its creation. Although Jonson and Marston had cooperated before (as well as having periods of intense, often bitter, competition), *Eastward Ho!* is Chapman's only known collaboration with other dramatists. The almost seamless blend of the three writers' different styles and concerns into a single, coherent play is an outstanding achievement.

The immediate impulse for the collaboration was to compete with the immense popular success of *Westward Ho!* (1604), a comedy of contemporary London life by Thomas Dekker and John Webster that was playing at a rival theater. Several commentators have suggested that a primary reason for the triple collaboration of Chapman, Jonson, and Marston was the need to produce a rival script as quickly as possible. It is likely that the three writers worked on different sections of the drama simultaneously, in order to expedite production.

Although it is impossible to assign definitively acts or scenes to any single one, or even a combination, of the three authors, linguistic and stylistic evidence strongly suggests that Jonson and Marston were largely responsible for the opening and closing sections of the play, where the language is sharper and more satirical, and that Chapman was the author of the middle section, including the major subplot involving Sir Petronel Flash's relationship with Security, the old usurer, and his wife, Winifred. Despite its highly satirical vein, this middle section, critics have noted, has a more genial and accessible humor, characteristic of Chapman's other dramas.

The play as a whole displays a remarkable unity and cohesion that is rarely found in a work by multiple authors. It has been conjectured that much of this unity is the result of an original plan, or outline, and a final revision, probably done either by Jonson himself or with his close supervision. Whatever the case, the play as finally written combines most of the strengths and few of the weaknesses of its three authors.

Eastward Ho! seeks to be a realistic comedy, with characters involved in entertaining but not totally implausible situations. The play's setting was intended to be familiar to its contemporary audience. In a sense, it is a combination of the city comedy play, based on London life, and the comedy of humors, based on individuals who represent types of human personality. In a comedy of humors, the major characters are motivated by their particular ruling passion, or humor (greed, lust, phobias of one kind or another, and so on). The work also has a strong moralistic vein, which was characteristic of the period and which no doubt reflects Marston's and Jonson's satirical viewpoints.

One such expression of views in *Eastward Ho!* was construed as an insult to the Scots in general and by extension to King James I himself, who had recently come to the English throne. The offending passage was reason for Chapman's and Jonson's being arrested and imprisoned for a time—although, ironically, it seems likely that Marston was the actual author of the particular lines. He escaped punishment by prompt flight.

A conventional moral framework guides the characters in the play. Touchstone, the London goldsmith, has two apprentices, Quicksilver and Golding. As their names suggest, the two young men have vastly different personalities. Quicksilver is an aimless wastrel who ends the play as a prison inmate. Golding is an ambitious, hardworking lad. Touchstone's two daughters, Gertrude and Mildred, duplicate this pattern: Gertrude, the older, is vain and pretentious, and allows herself to be gulled by Sir Petronel Flash. Mildred, engaged to Golding, is chaste and responsible. While some may see Golding and Mildred as too virtuous to be true, and unsympathetic in their relentless goodness and self-conscious morality, they do represent conventional ideas of proper action appropriate to their stations in life, just as Quicksilver and Gertrude are examples from the opposite end of the moral spectrum. By the end of the play, the various characters have received the rewards or punishments due to them and harmony is restored.

The play is also in the tradition of the journey narrative, in which a group of characters come together for a trip and share stories and experiences. In this case, the group is heading east, going down the Thames River for a variety of reasons. For example, Sir Petronel and the two adventurers Scapethrift and Spendall are bound for the new colony of Virginia. Hence the title, *Eastward Ho!*, which parodies the title of the earlier play, whose characters were headed in the opposite direction. Ironically, the trip is even shorter than the one in *Westward Ho!*, in which the travelers are shipwrecked and washed up on the shores of the Thames before they leave London.

Another notable feature about the play is its numerous references and parodies of other theatrical pieces, including a number of William Shakespeare's plays. At one point, the old usurer Security, desperately seeking a way to get down river, cries out, "A boat, a boat, a boat. A full hundred marks for a boat!" In addition to the literary touches, *Eastward Ho!* is remarkable for the number and range of its proverbial allusions, most of them delivered by Touchstone, and many of them heavily moralistic or didactic in tone. The use of these helps identify Touchstone as an individual character, while the everyday, colloquial flow of the language makes the play more immediate and accessible.

The combination of the two devices of literary allusion and proverbial wisdom draws attention to the play as a self-conscious artifact that is teaching a lesson. In a sense, *Eastward Ho!* comments on its own purpose as a play—to bring the lives of contemporary Londoners to the stage and to draw entertainment and edification from those lives.

"Critical Evaluation" by Michael Witkoski

Bibliography:
Adams, J. Q. "*Eastward Hoe* and Its Satire Against the Scots." *Studies in Philology* 28 (1931): 157-169. Treats an isolated, but interesting, facet of the play, helping to fit it into the larger political and legal circumstances of the period.
Brettle, R. E. "*Eastward Ho*, 1605, by Chapman, Jonson and Marston: Bibliography and Circumstances of Production." *The Library* 4th series, no. 9 (1928-1929): 287-302. A close examination of the origins and initial presentation of the drama. More for the advanced than the general student.
Petter, C. G. Introduction to *Eastward Ho!* London: Ernest Benn, 1973. A brief but highly informative survey of the drama that provides a wealth of information for the serious student and the casual reader. Additional material offers background on contemporary social issues, as well as Jonson's and Chapman's imprisonment for their supposed slur on the Scots.

Spivack, Charlotte. *George Chapman*. New York: Twayne, 1967. A general overview of Chapman's life and career, including his role as a collaborator on *Eastward Ho!* Does an excellent job in placing Chapman's dramatic work within the context of his life.

Van Fossen, R. W. Introduction to *Eastward Ho!* Manchester, England: Manchester University Press, 1979. Examines various aspects of the play, including authorship, contents, stage history, staging, and other issues. Includes background material on the plot and a selection of letters by Chapman and Jonson relating to the drama.

EAT A BOWL OF TEA

Type of work: Novel
Author: Louis Chu (1915-1970)
Type of plot: Domestic realism
Time of plot: 1941-1949
Locale: Chinatown, New York, and Chinatown, San Francisco
First published: 1961

> *Principal characters:*
> WANG BEN LOY, a young Chinese American waiter
> WANG WAH GAY, his father
> LEE MEI OI, his bride
> LEE GONG, her father
> AH SONG, her lover

The Story:

Early one morning in New York's Chinatown, two newlyweds were awakened by the sound of their doorbell. Wang Ben Loy, the young husband, opened their door to find an undesirable figure, a prostitute, from his past. The woman did not believe he was married and only became convinced when shown a pair of his wife's underwear on a clothesline. Ben Loy returned to bed with his beautiful wife, Mei Oi, but not to rest. Instead, thoughts of his recent impotence tormented him.

Ben Loy had been a young, hardworking Chinese American waiter in "Stanton," Connecticut. Dominated by a stern Confucian father, Ben Loy had found his only freedom from patriarchal strictures in surreptitiously meeting prostitutes in nearby New York City during his days off work. He and a fellow waiter had even expressly rented a hideout in New York, the apartment now tenanted by Ben Loy and his bride.

Ben Loy's father, Wah Gay, had migrated from China several decades before to make his fortune in America but eventually ended up running a Chinatown gaming establishment. During his thirty years in America, Wah Gay had returned to China once to marry and father a son, returning to New York to work. At age seventeen, Ben Loy had joined his father. After Ben Loy had reached his twenties and served in the U.S. Army in World War II, his mother wrote his father suggesting that their son marry.

Lee Gong, an old friend and mah-jongg partner of Wah Gay, who had led a life similar to Wah Gay's, also wanted to marry off his daughter, Mei Oi, who still lived in China. These two elders had tacitly arranged a marriage between their children. Ben Loy was then sent to their ancestral village, where he met Mei Oi; fortunately, the intended couple were attracted to each other. After a happy wedding, followed by a blissful few weeks, the couple had left for Hong Kong, then New York. Much to the newlyweds' dismay, Ben Loy had lost his potency once he left China. Blaming his previous licentiousness, Ben Loy felt guilty and incompetent; Mei Oi felt undesirable and neglected.

On the couple's arrival in New York, their fathers threw a huge wedding banquet. Many guests hinted that the couple was expected to have a child in the next year. Mei Oi became depressed and frustrated as time passed and her hopes of conceiving a child dimmed. It was then that Ah Song, a regular at Wah Gay's establishment, seized his opportunity. Ah Song was a notorious philanderer who preyed on credulous women with tales of exaggerated wealth and protestations of love. He quickly seduced the vulnerable Mei Oi, who soon became pregnant. Ben Loy, pleased to save face by his wife's pregnancy, avoided thinking about how their child had been conceived.

The secret was exposed, however, when Ah Song was spied leaving Mei Oi's apartment. Gossip spread rapidly and reached Lee Gong, who chided his daughter. Then Wang Chuck Ting, the Wang Family Association's president, informed Wah Gay of the situation and advised that the couple move to Stanton to minimize the family scandal. Wah Gay berated Ben Loy, who had received intimations of his cuckoldry from the barbershop gossips, and he slapped Mei Oi in anger. Although the couple moved to Connecticut, hostile relatives there forced them back to New York, where Ah Song and Mei Oi resumed their trysts.

On one such rendezvous, the furious Wah Gay ambushed Ah Song and cut off his left ear. Ah Song pressed charges, and Wah Gay hid from the police in an old friend's laundry in New Jersey. Wang Chuck Ting, joined by the Ping On Tong (the association that informally governed Chinatown), then intervened. With their political clout, this informal judiciary persuaded Wah Gay to emerge from hiding and coerced Ah Song to drop charges. Ah Song was then banished for five years. However, the loss of face Lee Gong and Wah Gay suffered because of the scandal forced them to seek anonymity in other states. Ben Loy and Mei Oi also decided to move westward to San Francisco to start a new life. All was forgiven between the couple, and the birth of the baby, whom Ben Loy accepted as his, added joy to their lives. Free from the oppressive presence of his father, Ben Loy flourished and sought remedies for his impotency. He found a Chinese herbalist who prescribed that he eat a bowl of bitter, medicinal tea regularly. This cure worked, Ben Loy regained his virility, and the couple reunited with thoughts of a new baby and renewed life together.

Critical Evaluation:

Eat a Bowl of Tea was neglected for almost two decades until a post-1960's generation of Asian American readers and scholars rediscovered and acclaimed it as the first authentic Chinese American novel. Since then, it has often been reprinted, has been made into a sensitive and entertaining film, and has become an Asian American classic. It is most often praised for its honest realism, classic comic structure, and deeply American themes. Louis Chu's novel is the first by a Chinese American insider depicting Chinatown life in a realistic mode. Certainly, more popular works about Chinatown life had preceded it, including Lin Yutang's novel *Chinatown Family* (1948) and Chin Yang Lee's *Flower Drum Song* (1957); however, these works depicted Chinatown life in a stereotypical manner. Chu's observation and recording of his Chinatown is, by comparison, more authentic and knowledgeable of life and work in Chinatown.

Unlike Lin and Lee, who neither lived nor worked there, Chinatown is integral to Chu's life and career. Born in Toishan, China, Chu immigrated to America when he was only nine. After graduating from college, he became director of a New York social center, host of the radio program *Chinese Festival*, and executive secretary of Chinatown's Soo Yuen Benevolent Society.

Chu's realism is especially original in his dialogue. Chu renders the language of his Chinatown characters with such a fine ear that one can hear the cadences of Cantonese underlying the broken English and savor the authenticity of the speakers' banter. Early book reviewers who expected Chu's ghetto characters to speak in polite standard English or Hollywood's stereotype of Chinese American speech patterns were bewildered by Chu's raw, unadulterated language.

Chu's novel also faithfully mirrors the "bachelor society" of America's Chinatowns. This society of men without women had been created by racist American immigration statutes of the early 1900's forbidding working-class Chinese from bringing wives into the United States, while equally racist miscegenation laws prevented Chinese from marrying Americans and establishing families in America. (Only wealthier Chinese merchants were allowed to bring wives into the United States.) Thus men such as Wah Gay and Lee Gong had to leave their wives in China, while working in America, enjoying a conjugal visit perhaps only once a decade. In the Chinatowns of that period, then, the population was overwhelmingly male, mostly "married bachelors." Hence, a woman like Mei Oi, a war bride of a Chinese American soldier, would have been a precious rarity in the Chinatown community.

In addition to its realist qualities, *Eat a Bowl of Tea* is a comic novel of archetypally classic construction. Classic comedy usually depicts a change from one kind of society to another. Initially, the negative characters who obstruct this change control the society; eventually, the incidents of plot that unite the hero and heroine cause a new society to crystallize around the hero. Indeed, the conflict in Chu's novel is one between a society of elders and a society of youth, between the tradition-bound Chinese sojourners (in America to make money) and the new Chinese Americans (in America to stay). Ideologically, the Confucian Chinese ethic of family hierarchy clashes with the American Dream of the individual's right to pursue happiness and identity. Wah Gay and Lee Gong represent the older Confucian sojourner generation, while Ben Loy and Mei Oi represent the younger Chinese American settler generation. Typical of the Confucian father, Wah Gay initially allows Ben Loy no opportunity to develop his individuality, making decisions for Ben Loy's travel, job, and even marriage. Chu shows that this oppressive familial structure breeds hypocrisy. For instance, Wah Gay's playing the role of the moral father is ironic because his means of livelihood, a gambling joint, is more suitable for a gangster than for a model Confucian father. Similarly, Ben Loy keeps up appearances as an obedient, hardworking son, but he secretly resorts to prostitutes as a release.

After Wah Gay's wounding of Ah Song, the Confucian family hierarchy begins to disintegrate as the representatives of the older generation, Lee Gong and Wah Gay, go into exile. The action then focuses on the younger generation, Ben Loy and Mei Oi, as they attempt to rebuild their marriage unencumbered by repressive expectations. The young couple's new sense of family is a loving partnership, not an authoritarian hierarchy. Here, Chu's novel becomes attuned to a profoundly American theme as its young couple moves from the old American East (New York) to the new American West (San Francisco). In so doing, they are following the archetypal journey of the American explorer who voyages westward to seek a second chance at life on new frontiers. Thus, rooting his novel in Chinese America, Louis Chu brings to fruition a work that consorts with themes deep in the American grain: the dream of the individual to pursue happiness and self-actualization, the desire that America be another Eden. *Eat a Bowl of Tea* is Louis Chu's only published novel, but, with it, he has deservedly been designated Chinese America's first novelist, the worthy forerunner of Frank Chin, Maxine Hong Kingston, and Amy Tan.

Jarrell Chua
C. L. Chua

Bibliography:
Chan, Jeffrey. Introduction to *Eat a Bowl of Tea*. Seattle: University of Washington Press, 1979. Excellent introduction by a distinguished Chinese American scholar and writer. Praises Chu

for his transcription of Cantonese idiom and satirical analysis of Chinatown society. Includes brief biography of Chu.

Chua, Cheng Lok. "Golden Mountain: Chinese Versions of the American Dream in Lin Yutang, Louis Chu, and Maxine Hong Kingston." *Ethnic Groups* 4 (1982): 33-57. A comparison of Chu with Lin and Kingston. Analyzes the conflict between the Chinese ideal of family and the American Dream of success, happiness, and individual identity. The critical approach is historical and archetypal.

Gong, Ted. "Approaching Cultural Change Through Literature." *Amerasia Journal* 7, no. 1 (1980): 73-86. Traces cultural development from Chinese to Chinese American in Monfoon Leong, Louis Chu, and Frank Chin. Examines common themes of the father-son relationship and generational conflict.

Hsiao, Ruth Y. "Facing the Incurable: Patriarchy in *Eat a Bowl of Tea*." In *Reading the Literatures of Asian America*, edited by Shirley Geok-lin Lim and Amy Ling. Philadelphia: Temple University Press, 1992. Places Chu in the tradition of literary debunking of patriarchy. Theorizes that while patriarchy is portrayed as the real villain in the novel, Chu fails to free his own creative imagination from male images of women; patriarchy remains an incurable malady of Chinese society.

Kim, Elaine H. *Asian American Literature: An Introduction to the Writings and Their Social Context*. Philadelphia: Temple University Press, 1982. A groundbreaking book on Asian American literature. Chapter 4, "Portraits of Chinatown," contains an illuminating discussion of the literary and sociological qualities of Chu's novel.

ECLOGUES

Type of work: Poetry
Author: Vergil (Publius Vergilius Maro, 70-19 B.C.E.)
First published: c. 43-37 B.C.E. (English translation, 1575)

> *Principal characters:*
> TITYRUS, an aging shepherd, sometimes thought to represent Vergil
> MALIBOEUS, an exile
> CORYDON, a lovelorn shepherd boy
> DAPHNIS, in the fifth eclogue, a shepherd hero who had recently died
> GALLUS, a poet and military leader, a friend of Vergil

Vergil's ten eclogues made their young author a nationally renowned figure when they were first made public approximately 39 B.C.E. Although these poems do not reach the heights of the *Georgics* (36-29 B.C.E.) or the *Aeneid* (30-19 B.C.E.), they are the work of a master, not the hesitant stumblings of an apprentice writer. Vergil made the pastoral form, first popularized by Theocritus, his own and paved the way for many English poets who imitated him, among them Edmund Spenser, Philip Sidney, John Milton, Percy Bysshe Shelley, and Matthew Arnold.

Vergil's pastoral world is not populated by Dresden-china shepherdesses in a never-never landscape; while his shepherds have their light-hearted moments, they inhabit real Italian hills and farms from which they can be evicted by unjust landlords. Exile, loneliness, and poverty threaten many of the characters in the poems. Even the traditional lovelorn shepherds are tied to Vergil's world by the naturalness of the landscape in which they lament; the heat of the Italian summer, the shade of the willow tree, the rocky hillsides where sheep pasture—all are part of the total effect of the eclogues.

Much scholarly effort has been directed toward proving that these poems are allegories that deal with contemporary events. It seems more fruitful and more realistic to accept the fact that Vergil is commenting on conditions of his age. One need not search for disguised poets and government officials. There is no certainty that any shepherd represents the poet's own view, although he has often been identified with Tityrus in the first eclogue.

This poem is one of the most realistic of the group; it reflects the days after Julius Caesar's assassination when residents of northern Italy were dispossessed to provide land for discharged soldiers. Maliboeus, one of the speakers, is among the exiles. He has left his newborn goats on the rocky road as he makes his way toward a new home in Africa, Scythia, or Britain. He laments the fact that the land he has labored to cultivate must fall into the hands of some barbarous veteran, and he inquires how his friend Tityrus has managed to escape the general desolation. Tityrus explains that he went to Rome to plead for his land and that a youth, whom some have identified with Augustus, granted his request, leaving him free to enjoy the humming of the bees on his neighbor's land. He offers his sympathy and his simple hospitality to the unfortunate Maliboeus.

The second eclogue is the disjointed lament of the Sicilian shepherd, Corydon, for his disdainful beloved, Alexis. Vergil conveys the character of Corydon brilliantly in his passionate, illogical outbursts, uttered as the boy wanders in the hot midday sun, when even lizards have sought shelter, recognizing the futility of his love, yet unable to forget the scornful youth and settle down to care properly for his vines.

Among the most vividly conceived personages of the eclogues are the two brash young shepherds who amicably insult each other in the third poem. Damoetas and Menalcas taunt each other with misdeeds they have witnessed; Damoetas has seen his friend slashing at a farmer's grapevines, while Menalcas suspects Damoetas of trying to steal a goat from Damon's flock. Damoetas spiritedly defends himself; he had won the goat legitimately in a singing match, but Damon refused to pay the prize. Menalcas scoffs at the notion of Damoetas' possessing such skill, and he is immediately challenged to a contest. The ensuing song follows the traditional pattern; the challenger sings one verse, then his opponent adds a second in keeping with the first, and the song moves from invocations to Jove and Apollo to tributes to the sweethearts of each singer to realistic comments on the scene. Each singer concludes with a riddle, and Palaemon, who has been brought in as judge, decides that both deserve prizes, as do all who know the joy or bitterness of love.

The most famous of these poems is the fourth, or Messianic, eclogue, in which Vergil prophesies the birth of a child who will usher in a new golden age when peace will prevail, humanity and nature will become self-sufficient, commerce will cease, and the land will need no further plowing and pruning. The poet laments that he will not survive to see this new age come to fruition, but he rejoices at being able to bid the infant smile at his mother.

The identity of the expected child has been cause for extensive speculation; both Antony and Augustus became fathers about this time, and Vergil may have refused out of political expediency to single out one or the other. Throughout the Middle Ages, however, Vergil was thought to have foreseen the birth of Christ; for this reason, he became for later ages a kind of pagan saint.

The pastoral elegy, the form of the fifth eclogue, has been imitated more often than any of the other types of poetry in this collection. Readers of English poetry may find many echoes of Mopsus' lament for Daphnis, who is mourned by nymphs, lions, and by the men whom he taught to celebrate Bacchic rites. Since his death, crops have failed, as if the flowers also lamented; only thorns and thistles grow where the violet and narcissus were planted. Mopsus' elegy concludes with a request for shepherds to build a mound for Daphnis and to carve an epitaph commending his fame and loveliness.

Menalcas rhapsodizes over his friend's verse, then begins his own elegy, in which he places Daphnis, now deified, at the gate of heaven, bringing peace to all the countryside. The mountains and rocks rejoice and the shepherds worship their new god in joyous rites. The contrasting moods of grief and exaltation remained a part of the pastoral tradition throughout succeeding ages, in poems like Milton's *Lycidas* (1637; published 1638) and Shelley's *Adonais* (1821).

The prologue to the sixth eclogue gives interesting insight into Vergil's poetic ambitions. The speaker, Tityrus, comments that his earliest poetry was in the Sicilian vein, pastoral, but that he had turned to kings and battles for a time, until Apollo cautioned him that a shepherd poet should sing of the countryside. Therefore, he depends on others to celebrate the great deeds of his friend Varus, while he must be content to dedicate to him his rustic song about the old satyr, Silenus, who tells young satyrs and naiads old tales about the creation, the Golden Age, the fate of Prometheus, and many other mythological legends. The reference within the poem to a scene in which the Muses bestowed a reed pipe upon Gallus, one of the best-known writers of Vergil's time, has led to the suggestion that, in this eclogue, allusions are made to Gallus' own work. The range of subject matter is wide, and there seems to be little connection between the various episodes in Silenus' narrative.

In the seventh eclogue, another singing match is described. The song of Corydon and Thyrsis reflects Vergil's deep love for the countryside and for the simplicity of the life of the shepherds. The reader can almost see the mossy springs, the budding vines of the early spring, and the chestnuts.

The eighth poem is addressed to a Roman hero, variously identified as the consul, Pollio, who is mentioned within the body of the poem, or as Augustus. Vergil will attempt to please this nobleman with the pastoral song he requested, while he waits for a chance to record his heroic exploits. In the lyric itself, Damon and Alphesiboeus recite songs for each other. The first is a lament for the infidelity of Nysa, Damon's beloved, who has married Mopsus. The deserted shepherd is both scornful and sentimental—at one moment, recalling his first childhood meeting with the girl, at another, bitterly berating the bridegroom or mourning the cold cruelty of the god of love. All nature should be upturned, with the wolf fleeing from the lamb and apples growing on oak trees, when such a love does not take its natural course. The singer sees no final recourse but death; he will plunge from the mountain top into the waves below.

Alphesiboeus' song is a curious one. He speaks as a young girl who is trying to lure her lover home from town by witchcraft, and the song begins with a number of spells. The ashes on the girl's altar flame spontaneously in the last stanza, and she expresses her hope that the absent shepherd is, indeed, coming.

The mood of the first poem is re-created in the ninth as Moeris tells his friend Lycidas that he has been evicted from his property by a new owner. Lycidas expresses surprise; he had heard that Menalcas' poetry had preserved that land. Moeris, made wise in the world's ways by misfortune, replies that there was such a rumor, but that poetry has no force against the soldiers who are taking over the land. He and Menalcas barely escaped with their lives. The thought that they might have lost the best of their shepherd poets recalls some of his lines to Lycidas and Moeris, and they quote them as they talk. One passage, referring to the new, beneficent star of "Olympian Caesar," has aroused special interest, since it obviously refers to the recently deceased Julius Caesar. This eclogue ends with an appealing scene, as Lycidas urges Moeris to stop and rest beside the calm lake they are passing and to sing as they watch countrymen pruning their vines.

The final poem is another tribute to Gallus, who was a highly competent military leader, as well as a fine poet; he was viceroy of Egypt after the defeat of Marc Antony at the battle of Actium. Unfortunately, his pride led to his political downfall and probably also to the loss of his poetry; we must rely on Vergil's praise for an estimate of his talents.

Gallus' mistress, Lycoris, to whom most of his love poetry had been addressed, had run away to the north of Italy with another soldier. In Vergil's poem, her betrayed lover laments her loss, followed by sympathetic shepherds. He resolves to seek what comfort he can in writing pastoral verse and hunting the wild boar, yet he cannot restrain a poignant hope that the sharp glaciers of the Alps will not cut the feet of his lost lady. He realizes, finally, that even poetry and hunting are powerless to mollify the god of love; he can only yield and accept his misery. The *Eclogues* present a theme constant throughout Vergil's writings: a longing for a return to a Golden Age. In these verses, he hints at what will become apparent in his magnum opus, the *Aeneid*: the establishment of the Roman Empire as it was to exist under Augustus after the Pax Romana was declared and Roman rule preserved peace throughout the Mediterranean region for more than a century. As early as 39 B.C.E., Vergil saw in the rise of his friend Octavian (the future Augustus) the fulfillment of a form of manifest destiny for the Roman people. The coming age, celebrated in the fourth eclogue, was to be one much like that Arcadian era celebrated in the poems of the Greek writer Theocritus, Vergil's model for his first sustained poetic endeavor.

Vergil borrows heavily from Greek predecessors, especially the poet Theocritus, whose short poems celebrating the pastoral life were models for a number of Roman writers. Like Theocritus, Vergil speaks wistfully of the simple country life where political cares rarely intrude and where love, not war, serves as the primary agent of both discord and harmony. Even in these early compositions, Vergil expresses the sentiment for which he has become famous for two millennia: The *lachrymae rerum*, the "tears in things," a sensitive, melancholy realization that even the most idyllic scenes and experiences possess within themselves the power to move one to sadness when one realizes the transitory nature of existence.

After reading these highly ornate poems, it is easy to find oneself agreeing with critics who complain about the artificiality of their composition, and about the forced union of mythology and philosophy. Readers caught up in the beauty and sentiment of individual eclogues may miss an important element that gives further significance to Vergil's composition. The arrangement of the ten poems exhibits a careful pattern, deliberately chosen by the author to provide an implicit contrast between the pastoral world of his shepherds and the political situation in his own country. The references to contemporary events highlight the contrasts between the world of political and military strife of the decades immediately preceding the composition of the *Eclogues*, and the Arcadian world of perpetual peace that Vergil celebrates in these ten poems.

The *Eclogues* are carefully divided into two sets of five poems each: The first five are forward-looking, peaceful, and patriotic; the second five are ambiguous, concerned with the past, and dominated by discussions of unworthy love. Individual eclogues from the first group seem to be paired with complementary (or contrasting) ones in the second. The neat structure gives the work a unity of purpose that transcends the focus of any single eclogue; this pattern is one repeated infrequently in literature until the nineteenth and twentieth centuries, when the assemblage of fragments to create a unified impression becomes an acceptable method for reflecting the concerns of the modern world; Alfred, Lord Tennyson's *Idylls of the King* (1859-1885) and T. S. Eliot's *The Waste Land* (1922) are inheritors of this Vergilian method of composition.

Vergil's *Eclogues* brought a new note of personal feeling and a fresh appreciation of nature into the highly artificial and rhetorical poetic tradition of his time. It is in large part this element of humanity that has sustained the appeal of his pastorals.

Updated by Laurence W. Mazzeno

Bibliography:
Griffin, Jasper. *Virgil*. Oxford, England: Oxford University Press, 1986. Basic introduction to Vergil's poetry. The second chapter exclusively addresses the *Eclogues* and provides a rewarding discussion of the themes of Arcadia and the tension between nature and the urban life in Rome. Index and bibliography.
Leach, Eleanor Winsor. *Vergil's Eclogues: Landscapes of Experience*. Ithaca, N.Y.: Cornell University Press, 1974. Detailed introduction and analysis of the work. Includes a sophisticated reading of poetic symbolism of the *Eclogues* and Vergil's poetry in general, as well as interpretation of Roman views on nature and the world. Copious illustrations and photographs enhance the text. Index.
Lee, Guy, trans. *Virgil: The Eclogues*, by Vergil. Harmondsworth, Middlesex, England: Penguin Books, 1984. Introduction provides a general but thorough discussion of pastoral poetry, Vergil's contribution to the tradition, and a historical overview of the poet's life and the poems' composition. Useful bibliography of primary and secondary sources.
Putnam, Michael C. J. *Virgil's Pastoral Art: Studies in the Eclogues*. Princeton, N.J.: Princeton

University Press, 1970. Detailed, scholarly analysis of all important aspects of the *Eclogues*, including themes and their historical context.

Slavitt, David R. *Virgil*. New Haven, Conn.: Yale University Press, 1991. Chapter 1 focuses on the *Eclogues* and provides a straightforward explanation of its relation to ancient poetry and its influence on subsequent and modern literature. A solid source. Bibliography of primary and secondary sources; index.

THE EDGE OF THE STORM

Type of work: Novel
Author: Agustín Yáñez (1904-1980)
Type of plot: Social realism
Time of plot: Spring, 1909, to spring, 1910
Locale: Near Guadalajara, Mexico
First published: Al filo del agua, 1947 (English translation, 1963)

Principal characters:
DON DIONISIO, the parish priest
MARÍA and
MARTA, his nieces
PADRE ISLAS and
PADRE REYES, assistant priests
DAMIÁN LIMÓN, a young man
MICAELA RODRÍGUEZ, a spoiled young woman
VICTORIA, a young widow, visiting from Guadalajara
GABRIEL, a young man reared by Don Dionisio
LUIS GONZAGA PÉREZ, a seminary student
MERCEDES TOLEDO, another young woman
LUCAS MACÍAS, a soothsayer

The Story:

Don Timoteo Limón was finishing his personal devotions when he became aware that a dog had been continuously howling and that he had forgotten to pray to several saints. Terrorized by the plaintive sound of the dog, which recalled to him the tragedy of his young daughter Rosalía, Don Timoteo had visions of past events. One such event that made him feel guilty was his killing a man in self-defense. The officials had exonerated him, but the image of the dead man's face still haunted him. He then linked the dog's howling to the fate of his son Damián who had gone to the United States to seek his fortune. Soon after going to bed, Don Timoteo Limón was disturbed by his visualizations of desirable women and finally got up to sprinkle holy water over his pillow, sheets, and windows. He concluded that his evil thoughts resulted from superstitions concerning the dog's howling and decided to attend a religious retreat.

The same night Mercedes Toledo was unable to sleep after having received Julián's letter. As did Don Timoteo Limón, Mercedes wrestled with horrifying thoughts and contemplated taking refuge in a religious institution. Later that night upon her return from Mexico City, Micaela Rodríguez was restless because of visions of a happy, modern life away from her small hometown. She resolved to scandalize the Daughters of Mary, an organization for unmarried maidens with strict rules, in the following manner: first, arousing envy with her pretty clothes, second, conversing about the interesting life outside the village, and third, stealing the attractive men away from the maidens. Her plan involved scandalous conduct, and Micaela thought she would be hated and therefore would have to leave the stagnant, hypocritical people of the village. She was pleased.

At the men's retreat, the principal parish priest, Dionisio Martínez, met with Father Reyes and five other priests; they heard confessions and meditated on sin, death, judgment, hell, the

Lord's Passion, and the parable of the prodigal son. Although Don Timoteo Limón and other villagers felt uneasy because they found themselves standing next to their enemies, Father Reyes used tact to quell the bitter feelings. The priests frightened the men by talking about the terrible assaults of the devil and ended the retreat by depicting the impending days of sadness.

Don Dionisio was caring for his orphaned nieces, María and Marta, as well as the bell ringer, Gabriel. The priest quit his subscription to a magazine because it stimulated María's interest in travel; he forbade her to read geography books or to visit Micaela Rodríguez since she dressed indecently and conversed inappropriately after her trip to Mexico City. Marta loved children and wanted to adopt Leonardo's child Martinita after the death of her mother. Marta showed her devotion to her religious beliefs and demonstrated her ability to give helpful advice, but she expressed thoughts and feelings that she could not understand. Gabriel became infatuated with the widow Victoria. As a result of his confused emotions, he rang the church bells excessively and later left the village.

Luis Gonzaga Pérez returned from the seminary with strict moral standards and projects that must be implemented on a timetable. Holy Week brought him great joy. His change from a fearful to a happy personality was shown by his desire to create great harmonies, paint impressive murals, or compose a poem that would become recognized in world literature. He became angered when Father Martínez would not allow him to carry the canopy in the procession. Pérez fled to the mountains as he felt mystical rapture increasing on Good Friday. The hot sun beating down upon his head, he contorted his face to drive away evil thoughts but, overwhelmed with despair, lost consciousness. Shortly thereafter, Pérez's mind became permanently impaired.

Father Islas was the Chaplain of the Daughters of Mary Immaculate. He advocated the traditional beliefs of the Catholic Church, using the idea of the purity of the maidens in order to discourage the young women from marrying. In spite of his unhealthy appearance, Islas commanded the maidens' loyalty, gaining authority through various superstitious devices: amazing examples of prophecy and healing, levitation, trances, and the multiplication of food. The maidens esteemed Father Islas as a saint beyond reproach; but, after having collapsed from an attack of epilepsy, he had to leave the priesthood, disillusioning his parishioners. The highly qualified Don Dionisio was then appointed head priest.

Damián Limón returned home and was castigated for having gone to such a sinful place where Mexicans were mistreated. After having precipitated his father's heart attack over a dispute about his inheritance, Damián murdered Micaela after an illicit love affair. The light sentence given to him by a corrupt political boss enabled him to join the revolutionaries at the end. After learning that Gabriel had declared his love for her because of Victoria, who had also encouraged him to study music, María chose to seek love. Condemned by the villagers for protecting the killer Damián, she decided to join the revolutionary army. Lucas Macías, the chronicler, linked the appearance of Halley's Comet with the coming of Francisco Madero, the man who was to provide leadership against the tyranny of Porfirio Díaz.

"The Story" by Linda Prewett Davis

Critical Evaluation:

Al filo del agua (literally, on the edge of the water) is a Spanish phrase with two meanings. It signifies the moment that the rain begins. The phrase is also used in reference to something imminent. The imminent in Agustín Yáñez's novel, the Mexican Revolution, was brought on by dissatisfaction with the political situation and by social unrest. The Roman Catholic church was one of Mexico's institutions on which the unrest was focused; hence the emphasis on religion in the novel. Reform of the political system and land distribution were other causes for the revolution.

In 1910, Porfirio Díaz had been dictator of Mexico for more than thirty years. He had ruled with an iron hand and only recently had the dream of political freedom and social improvement begun to filter through to the many semi-isolated towns of Mexico. The same few families had always been the social leaders and political bosses in the towns, and Díaz's thirty-odd years of rule had done nothing to lessen this inequity or to improve the lot of the common people. Education was nonexistent except for the privileged few, and superstition was rampant.

Another force that held the people in its grip was the church, a circumstance especially true in rural areas where Juarez's 1859 Reform Laws seldom reached. These laws had greatly reduced the political power of the church, and such things as processions and public religious festivities were forbidden. In the small towns, however, the priests often continued such clerical activities in spite of the law.

Yáñez has painted against this historical background a series of character studies portraying the effects of a narrow, rigid, dull, and conventional life on people of different ages, with varying degrees of education and exposure to outside influences. These influences, being, in the eyes of the village, outside ones and therefore bad, include such things as freemasonry, bright clothing, strangers, uncensored writings, fun, spiritualists, and people who had been to the United States. The list could go on and on. Yáñez creates a sense of monotonous gloom with the sure hand of an artist who has experienced this kind of life himself. The fictitious but typical town in which the action takes place is set in the state of Jalisco, of which the author was a native.

Each morning the church bells in this town call the people out of their beds as early as four o'clock to begin another dreary, quiet, prayerful day. Life is taken very seriously. The women wear dark somber colors and do not leave the house except to go to church or to do necessary errands. There is no visiting except in the case of extreme illness or a death in the house of a neighbor. There is little laughter, dancing, or singing. Strangers and strangeness are condemned. Nonconformity, even in small things, starts tongues wagging. At the end of each unvarying day, the church bells send the people to bed, an act that for many means the onset of sleepless hours of anxiety or of wrestling with guilty consciences and of wondering when and in what form God's wrath will be brought down upon their heads.

With this daily pattern providing the atmosphere, broken only by funerals, special fiesta days, and an occasional scandal, the action in the story begins as the people are preparing for their Lenten and Easter activities. The panorama of people and events proceeds on through the year, displaying the special religious days of June, the expected deaths, illnesses, bad luck in August, the celebration of patriotic holidays in September, the scandalous prank of the students home for vacation in November, the Christmas season with its festivities, which continues on into the New Year, at which time the people are awaiting the appearance of Halley's Comet. This event is being anticipated so intently by Lucas Macías, the soothsayer, that the rest of the people prepare for trouble, for Lucas has from the start associated the appearance of the comet with the stepping onto the scene of Francisco Madero, the man who is to lead the revolution against the tyranny of Díaz.

The person who can most nearly be described as the main character is Don Dionisio, the stern and upright but just and compassionate parish priest. He alone touches in some way upon the lives of all the other characters in the book. His help comes from two assistant priests, who present a vivid contrast to each other. One, Padre Reyes, is liberal and forward-looking; the other, Padre Islas, is narrow and conservative beyond belief. Although Padre Reyes is much more likable, it is Padre Islas, scurrying along the street from church to home so as to avoid meeting his parishioners on a personal basis, who wields more influence on the lives of the townspeople, for it is he who directs the organization to which all the unmarried girls belong. Into their minds he instills the urgent need to stay pure by remaining single, and he imbues them with a sense of guilt for thinking even wholesome thoughts connected with the opposite sex. This narrow man never uses the chapel of the Holy Family but always the chapel of the Virgin Mary, and Padre Reyes, the other assistant, is not above teasing him by asking if he thinks María and Juan will make a nice couple, or if he is aware that Mercedes is about ready to make someone a good wife. These questions are calculated to enrage Padre Islas. Padre Reyes, with his modern ideas about such things as life insurance—too far removed from the imaginations of the people to be noticed—is largely ignored, while Padre Islas is revered as a saint beyond the temptations and afflictions of ordinary man. Great is the disillusionment when the good Father Islas is found collapsed on the floor of the church in a fit of epilepsy, which results in his having to be removed permanently from the priesthood. The archbishop chose wisely when Don Dionisio was made head priest, for he approaches the problems of his parishioners with the best elements of the philosophies of his two assistants—an urgent sense of responsibility for their souls accompanied by a forgiving and understanding heart.

Two other personalities who present a study in contrasts are María and Marta, the orphaned nieces of Don Dionisio, who has reared them since they were very small. At the time the story begins, they are in their twenties, unmarried, and on the verge of taking opposite paths in life. Marta is contented with her love for children, her work in the hospital, and other gentle occupations. She is the ideal end product of the social and religious forces at work in her environment. María is rebellious. She has read forbidden literature—for example, *The Three Musketeers* (1844), and newspapers from the capital—behind her uncle's back. María runs away with a woman of very questionable reputation to follow the revolutionary army. She is a creature of reaction against her unnatural environment.

What happened to María happens, with variations, to nearly all the young people who have had contact in any way with the outside world. Luis Gonzaga Pérez, a young and talented seminary student, is unable to reconcile his inhibitions concerning the opposite sex with his natural desires, and at the end of the novel, he is drawing lewd pictures on the walls of his room in an insane asylum.

Damián Limón, the young son of a fairly prosperous landowner, leaves home, like the prodigal son, and goes to the United States to work. Upon his return home, when criticized for going to such a sinful place, where Mexicans are treated like dogs, he counters by stating that at least there Mexicans are paid in money instead of in promises as in Mexico. Damián becomes scandalously involved in a flagrant love affair and kills the woman, Micaela, after having just caused his father to have a fatal heart attack over an argument about his father's will. A corrupt political boss has a disgracefully light sentence placed upon him, and at the end of the story, he rides away to join the ranks of the revolutionaries.

The parents of Micaela Rodríguez, a spoiled only child, make the mistake of taking her to Mexico City for a few months. There she sees the parties, pretty clothes, and merriment of the capital's young people. Never again is she satisfied to stay in her dreary hometown and, failing to force her parents to move away to a livelier place, she threatens vengeance on the environment that binds her and shocks the town to its roots with her shameless flirting and indecent dress. She is finally stabbed by a jealous lover but dies forgiving him and putting the blame for her death on her own actions.

Doubt seems to be the villain that causes the downfall of these unfortunate young people. They have tasted of the world, compared it with their narrow surroundings, and found the surroundings wanting. Being few in number, these unlucky ones have fallen under the weight of a relentless social system that will tolerate no questioning. They turn their doubt of the system inward and begin to doubt themselves.

In the novel, the time is near at hand, however, when many doubters will join together with enough force to make a crack in the wall of hypocrisy that characterized Mexican society at the time. That crack would become ever wider as education seeped through. This is the meaning of the title of the novel. Yáñez gives the reader an unprejudiced and intricately detailed view of life in a Mexican town shortly after the beginning of the twentieth century. The book is not a call to arms to reform; rather, it presents an understanding, scathingly honest, and touching portrait.

Bibliography:

Brushwood, John S. *The Spanish American Novel: A Twentieth-Century Survey.* Austin: University of Texas Press, 1975. Situates Yáñez's novel in the nineteenth century by discussing the major characteristics and innovations of fiction. Analyzes the contribution of *The Edge of the Storm* to Spanish American literature.

Langford, Walter M. *The Mexican Novel Comes of Age.* Notre Dame, Ind.: University of Notre Dame Press, 1971. Explains why the publication of *The Edge of the Storm* marks a significant accomplishment in the development of the Mexican novel. Discusses the structure of Yáñez's work.

Lindstrom, Naomi. *Twentieth-Century Spanish American Fiction.* Austin: University of Texas Press, 1994. Defines the continuities that link the different periods in modern Spanish American literature. Discusses significant elements in *The Edge of the Storm.*

O'Neill, Samuel J. "Interior Monologue in '*Al filo del agua.*'" *Hispania* 51 (1968): 447-455. Presents the psychological technique involving the stream of consciousness. Gives a fascinating interpretation of Yáñez's portrayal of the inhabitants living in a small isolated town.

Sommers, Joseph. *After the Storm: Landmarks of the Modern Mexican Novel.* Albuquerque: University of New Mexico Press, 1968. Evaluates the significance of Yáñez's work in the history of the novel. Furnishes an informative commentary on the novelist's epoch.

THE EDUCATION OF HENRY ADAMS

Type of work: Autobiography
Author: Henry Adams (1838-1918)
Locale: United States, England, and France
First published: 1907

> *Principal personages:*
> HENRY ADAMS, an American
> CHARLES FRANCIS ADAMS, his father
> JOHN HAY, his friend
> CLARENCE KING, whom he admired

The Story:

Henry Brooks Adams was born of the union of two illustrious Massachusetts families, the Brookses and the Adamses, and he was, in addition, the grandson and the great-grandson of presidents. His wealth and social position should have put him among the leaders of his generation. Although the period of mechanical invention had begun in 1838, Henry Adams was raised in a colonial atmosphere. He remembered that his first serious encounter with his grandfather, John Quincy Adams, occurred when he refused to go to school and that gentleman led him there by the hand. For Henry Adams, the death of the former president marked the end of his eighteenth century environment.

Charles Francis Adams, Henry's father, was instrumental in forming the Free-Soil Party in 1848, and he ran on its ticket with Martin Van Buren. Henry considered that his own education was chiefly an inheritance from his father. Henry's education centered around Puritan morality and interest in politics and literary matters. In later life, looking back on his formal education, he concluded that it had been a failure. Mathematics, French, German, and Spanish were needed in the world in which he found himself an adult, not Latin and Greek. He had opportunity to observe the use of force in the violence with which the people of Boston treated the antislavery activist Wendell Phillips, and he had seen slaves returned to the South.

Prompted by his teacher, James Russell Lowell, he spent nearly two years abroad after his graduation from college. He enrolled to study civil law in Germany, but finding the lecture system atrocious, he devoted most of his stay to enjoying the paintings, the opera, and the theater in Dresden. When he returned to Boston in 1860, Henry Adams settled down briefly to read Blackstone. In the elections that year, however, his father became a congressman, and Henry accompanied him to the capital as his secretary. There he met John Hay, who was to become his best friend.

In 1861, President Lincoln named Charles Francis Adams minister to England. Henry went with his father to Europe. The Adams party had barely disembarked when they were met by bad news. England had recognized the belligerency of the Confederacy. The North was her undeclared enemy. The battle of Bull Run proved so crushing a blow to American prestige that Charles Francis Adams felt he was in England on a day-to-day sufferance. The Trent Affair and the second battle of Bull Run were equally disastrous abroad. Finally, in 1863, the tide began to turn. Secretary Seward sent Thurlow Weed and William Evarts to woo the English, and they were followed by announcements of victories at Vicksburg and Gettysburg. Charles Francis Adams remained in England until 1868, for Andrew Johnson had too many troubles at home to make many diplomatic changes abroad.

At the end of the war, Henry Adams had no means of earning a livelihood. He had, however, developed some taste as a dilettante in art, and several of his articles had been published in the *North American Review*. On his return to America, Henry Adams was impressed by the fact that his fellow countrymen, because of the mechanical energy they had harnessed, were all traveling in the same direction. Europeans, he had felt, were trying to go in several directions at one time. Handicapped by his education and by his long absence from home, he had difficulty in adapting himself to the new industrial America. He achieved some recognition with his articles on legal tender and his essays in the *Edinburgh Review*, and he hoped that he might be offered a government position if Grant were elected president. However, Grant, a man of action, was not interested in reformers or intellectuals like Henry Adams.

In 1869, Adams went back to Quincy to begin his investigation of the scandals of the Grant administration, among them Jay Gould's attempts to obtain a corner on gold, Senator Charles Sumner's efforts to provoke war with England by compelling her cession of Canada to the United States, and the rivalries of congressmen and cabinet members. He decided it would be best to have his article on Gould published in England, to avoid censorship by the powerful financier. Gould's influence was not confined to the United States, however, and Adams was refused by two publications. His essay on Gould was finally published by *The Westminster Review*.

Adams became assistant professor of medieval history at Harvard and taught at Cambridge for seven years. During that time he tried to abandon the lecture system by replacing it with individual research. He found his students apt and quick to respond, but he felt that he needed a stone against which to sharpen his wits. He gave up his position in 1871 and went west to Estes Park with a government geological survey. There he met Clarence King, a member of the party, with whom he could not help contrasting himself. King had a systematic, scientific education and could have his choice of scientific, political, or literary prizes. Adams felt his own limitations.

After his flight from Harvard he made his permanent home in Washington, D.C., where he wrote a series of books on American history. In 1893, he visited the Chicago Exhibition. From his observations of the steamship, the locomotive, and the newly invented dynamo, he concluded that force was the one unifying factor in American thought. Back in Washington, he saw the gold standard adopted, and concluded that the capitalistic system and American intervention in Cuba offered some signs of the direction in which the country was heading. During another visit to the exhibition in 1900, Adams formulated an important theory. In observing the dynamo, he decided that history is not merely a series of causes and effects, of people acting upon people, but the record of forces acting upon people. For him, the dynamo became the symbol of force acting upon his own time as the Virgin had been the symbol of force in the twelfth century.

During the next five years, Henry Adams saw his friends drop away. Clarence King was the first to go. He lost his fortune in the panic of 1893 and died of tuberculosis in 1901. John Hay, under McKinley, became American minister to England, and then secretary of state. He was not well when he accepted the president's appointments, and the enormous task of bringing England, France, and Germany into accord with the United States, and of attempting to keep peace, unsuccessfully, between Russia and Japan, caused his death in 1905.

Adams considered that his education was continuous during his lifetime. He had found the tools which he had been given as a youth utterly useless, and he had to spend all of his days forging new ones. As he grew older, he found the moral standards of his father's and grandfather's times disintegrating; corruption and greed existed on the highest political levels.

According to his calculations, the rate of change, due to mechanical force, was accelerating, and the generation of 1900 could rely only on impersonal forces to teach the generation of 2000. He himself could see no end to the multiplicity of forces which were so rapidly dwarfing humanity into insignificance.

Critical Evaluation:

The theme of *The Education of Henry Adams* is the process of multiplication and acceleration of mechanical forces that, during Henry Adams' lifetime, led to the breakdown of moral relationships between people and the degeneration of their pursuits into money-seeking or complete lassitude. The book is, too, an excellent autobiography, tracing Adams' thought processes intimately, and on an intellectual plane not generally achieved by most writers. For style and for content this book ranks with the finest of American autobiographies.

As a work of literature, *The Education of Henry Adams* may be read in at least three ways: first, as a conventional autobiography; second, as a work in the mainstream of the European *Bildungsroman* tradition, a personal narrative of one person's intellectual and emotional coming-of-age; and third, as a critical treatise on Western civilization and culture. In this latter sense, Adams anticipated the twentieth century's preoccupation with the relationship between technological science and humanistic cultural assumptions.

No matter how Adams' work is read, however, the key chapter is "The Dynamo and the Virgin." Here he uses the two symbols of the "Dynamo" and the "Virgin" to spell out his analysis of the shaping forces of civilization, a synthesis of ideas reflecting his entire education. This excursion into historiography places Adams in the front rank of nineteenth century historical philosophers, for it is at this point that he posits the thesis that belief is the guiding force of sociopolitical and cultural phenomena.

Just as religious beliefs—the Virgin—created the great works of the Middle Ages, he says, so also the modern belief in science and technology—the Dynamo—will shape the major creations of the modern age. At last, though, he views that latter age with trepidation and anxiety, for he realizes that in some ways the humanistic education he received from his forefathers did not suit him for the Age of the Dynamo. Indeed, he sees that moral values of great worth, values that underlie the significant achievements of his grandfather, John Quincy Adams, and his father, are being destroyed by the machine. At last, then, Henry Adams defines for us the major conflict of twentieth century American civilizations, a drama whose denouement still remains undecided.

Bibliography:

Dusinberre, William. *Henry Adams: The Myth of Failure.* Charlottesville: University Press of Virginia, 1980. Argues that Adams' literary career should not be judged from *The Education of Henry Adams* alone, and relates the book to Adams' other historical writings to show that his negative assessment of them is misleading.

Jordy, William H. *Henry Adams: Scientific Historian.* New Haven, Conn.: Yale University Press, 1952. Evaluates Adams' claims that he was writing a "scientific" history. Demonstrates the weaknesses of the scientific arguments that Adams advanced.

Levenson, J. C. *The Mind and Art of Henry Adams.* Boston: Houghton Mifflin, 1957. One of the first important studies to consider Adams' thought in its entirety. Contains an analysis of how *The Education of Henry Adams* fits in the writing life of its author.

O'Toole, Patricia. *The Five of Hearts: An Intimate Portrait of Henry Adams and His Friends, 1880-1918.* New York: Clarkson N. Potter, 1990. An engaging narrative about Adams and

his closest associates. Provides good insights into the events and emotions that lay behind the writing of *The Education of Henry Adams.* The most accessible of the books on Adams.
Samuels, Ernest. *Henry Adams.* Cambridge: The Belknap Press of Harvard University Press, 1989. The best one-volume biography of Adams, with an excellent discussion of the writing of *The Education of Henry Adams* that links the book well to the events of Adams' life.

EDWARD II

Type of work: Drama
Author: Christopher Marlowe (1564-1593)
Type of plot: Historical
Time of plot: Fourteenth century
Locale: England and France
First performed: The Troublesome Reign and Lamentable Death of Edward the Second, c.
   1592; first published, 1594

Principal characters:
>   EDWARD II, king of England
>   PRINCE EDWARD, his son
>   EDMUND, Earl of Kent, half brother to the king
>   PIERCE DE GAVESTON, earl of Cornwall
>   GUY, earl of Warwick
>   THOMAS, earl of Lancaster
>   LORD MORTIMER, the elder
>   LORD ROGER MORTIMER, the younger
>   HUGH SPENCER, earl of Gloucester
>   QUEEN ISABELLA, wife of King Edward

The Story:

King Edward II recalled his favorite, Pierce de Gaveston, from exile; Gaveston joyfully returned to England. While hurrying to Westminster to rejoin his monarch, he came upon the king talking to his courtiers. Secretively, he hid from the royal assemblage and overheard the noblemen discussing his repatriation.

They discussed how Edward, an immature and weak-minded yet stubborn man, nourished for Gaveston an unwholesome and unyielding love, in spite of the fact that Edward's father had originally banished the man. The noblemen of England, sworn to uphold the decree of exile, hated the royal favorite. Most passionate in his fury was young Mortimer. Others were not far behind Mortimer in their antipathy, and they threatened the king with revolt if Gaveston remained in England. None but the king's brother Edmund would harbor Gaveston. The fiery discussion ended, the nobles stalked off in haughty displeasure.

Gaveston, still in hiding, rejoiced in his knowledge of the king's love, for Edward revealed his pettiness by his unconcern for the welfare of his kingdom as weighed against his desire to clasp Gaveston to his bosom once more. When Gaveston revealed his presence, Edward ecstatically rewarded him with a series of titles and honors, the scope of which caused even Edmund to comment wryly that Edward had outdone himself. Gaveston smirkingly claimed that all he desired was to be near his monarch. To add salt to the kingdom's wounds, Edward sentenced the Bishop of Coventry, the instigator of Gaveston's exile, to die in the Tower of London.

This action, coupled with the titles and estates lavishly bestowed upon Gaveston, so incensed the rebellious nobility that under the leadership of the two Mortimers, Warwick, and Lancaster, they plotted to kill Gaveston. The Archbishop of Canterbury, protesting the damage inflicted upon the Church by the king's folly, allied himself with the plot. Queen Isabella, who professed to love her lord dearly, complained to the noblemen that since Gaveston's return Edward had snubbed her beyond endurance. She agreed that Gaveston must be done away with, but she cautioned the angry noblemen not to injure Edward.

When the rebellious nobility seized Gaveston, Edward, yielding to the archbishop's threat to enforce his papal powers against the king, could do nothing but stand by and allow his beloved friend to be carried off. A bitter exchange of words between the king and his lords was tempered by the gentle sentiments of Gaveston as he bade Edward farewell. Driven by childish anger, perhaps incensed by an intuitive knowledge, Gaveston attacked the queen and accused her of a clandestine association with the younger Mortimer, a charge which she denied. Sensing his advantage, Edward seized upon the accusation as a wedge to undermine his enemies, and he compelled the queen to use her influence to save Gaveston. The queen, because of her love for Edward and her hopes for a reconciliation, resolved to mend the rift by abetting her husband.

At first the nobles disdainfully refused to hear her entreaties. Then, having prevailed upon young Mortimer's sympathy, she disclosed to him a plot whereby Gaveston could be overthrown and the king obeyed at the same time. Mortimer then convinced the other nobles that if Gaveston were allowed to remain in England, he would become so unpopular that the common people would rise in protest and kill him. There was peace in England once more. Edward affected renewed love for his queen and the lords humbly repledged their fealty to Edward. An undercurrent of meanness prevailed, however, in the bosom of young Mortimer, whose sense of justice was outraged at the fact that Edward had chosen such a baseborn villain as his minion. He still believed that it would be a service to his country to unseat Gaveston, and thus he plotted secretly.

At the ceremonial in honor of Gaveston's return the lords could not stomach the presence of the king's minion. Bitter sarcasm was showered upon Gaveston, and young Mortimer tried to stab him. So outraged was Edward at this show of independence by his peers that he vowed vengeance for his dear Gaveston's sake. Even the loyal Edmund could not brook this display of pettiness on the part of his brother; he deserted Edward to join the nobles.

Edward renewed the smoldering accusation against Isabella that she was Mortimer's lover. Defeated in battle, the king's forces, with Gaveston in flight, were split up to confuse the enemy. Warwick, Lancaster, and others succeeded in capturing the king's minion and ordered his death, but Arundel, a messenger from Edward, pleaded that Gaveston be allowed to say farewell to the king. One of the nobles, unable to scorn the king's wishes, arranged to escort Gaveston to Edward. With a servant in charge, Gaveston was conducted to a hiding place to spend the night. Warwick, driven by blind hatred and an irrational patriotism, kidnapped the prisoner.

Meanwhile Valois, king of France and Isabella's brother, had taken advantage of the revolt in England and had seized Normandy. Edward, displaying the corruption of his statesmanship, dispatched his son, Prince Edward, and Isabella to negotiate a parley with Valois. Arundel, meanwhile, reported to Edward that Warwick had beheaded Gaveston. Edward, in a wild rage against his lords, swore to sack their lands and destroy their families. Characteristically, having lost his beloved friend, he also declared that henceforth young Spencer would be his favorite. He continued to resist the rebels, and before long Warwick, Lancaster, and Edmund were captured and sentenced to death.

In France, the earl of Gloucester suspected that Isabella was gathering forces to place her son upon the throne. Isabella, in the meantime, had been rejected by Valois. Sir John of Hainault rescued the queen and prince by offering to keep the pair at his estate in Flanders until Edward had matured sufficiently to rule England. The young prince was already showing signs of royal character and a depth and magnitude of personality which promised to make him a suitable monarch.

The condemned Mortimer and Edmund escaped to France, where Sir John agreed to help them in levying forces to aid Isabella and the prince. Landing at Harwich, the forces of Mortimer and Edmund routed the king, who fled toward Ireland. Stalwart, sincere, and intellectually honest, Edmund, who had broken with his brother only after the king had driven him too far, relented in his feelings against Edward; he was further disturbed by a suspicion that Isabella was in love with Mortimer. Mortimer became a despot in his triumph. Edward was captured and sent to Kenilworth Castle, a prisoner. There he was prevailed upon to surrender his crown to the prince.

With the queen's consent, Mortimer outlined a crafty scheme to kill Edward. He drew up an ambiguous note which ordered the king's death in one sense and abjured it in another. When Prince Edward, Isabella, Edmund, and Mortimer argued fiercely to decide upon the prince's protector, the prince revealed his distrust for Mortimer. Edmund, fearing greater disunion, resolved to rescue the imprisoned king. His attempt failed.

Prince Edward was crowned by the Archbishop of Canterbury. Shortly after the coronation the deposed Edward, tortured cruelly in a dungeon, was murdered by Mortimer's hireling, and Edmund was beheaded. Thereupon Edward III, now monarch, ordered Mortimer to be hanged and Isabella, who was suspected of being the nobleman's accomplice in plotting her husband's death, to be taken to the Tower of London.

Critical Evaluation:

The Troublesome Reign and Lamentable Death of Edward the Second, the last play written by Christopher Marlowe before his untimely death, is a chronicle in its highest form. In fact, the drama has in the past been assigned to William Shakespeare. Unlike Marlowe's earlier work, this play is polished in form, sustained in theme, and consistent in characterization. Marlowe's first real success in the field of historical drama, *Edward II* sacrifices for a highly dramatic and tragic ending the lyrical beauty of language and metaphor present in his other plays. A further accomplishment to be noted here is Marlowe's use of a large group of dominant characters; in his earlier plays he had employed only two central figures.

Edward II, Marlowe's last drama—the dating of Marlowe's dramas is conjectural—is regarded by many as his finest work, showing tighter structure and greater clarity and unity than his earlier works. Since it was published almost immediately after his death, the text escaped the corruption that his other works suffered, and there are relatively few problems with establishing an accurate text. Scholars also possess the source material for the work, Holinshed's *Chronicles of England*, in the edition of 1577 or 1587. By comparing this play with others of its genre and with its source, it is possible to arrive at an appreciation of Marlowe's achievement.

Holinshed's account of the reign of Edward II (1307-1327) is relatively unstructured and, though providing much material, does not establish clear relationships or a connected series of events. Marlowe, who worked closely enough with Holinshed's text to incorporate actual phrases from the chronicle, nevertheless set about to structure the story and bring out salient features, developing relationships and characterizations, and compressing the events of over twenty years—from Gaveston's return in 1307 to the execution of Mortimer in 1330—into what seems on stage to be a relatively short span. While this creates some problems in terms of improbably swift shifting of loyalties and changes of policy, it gives the drama a tightness of structure and a forward movement that underscores the alienation of all Edward's associates—his wife, the loyal Edmund, and the outraged barons.

It is this surging wave of hostility that is the central event of the play, which begins with the return of the king's beloved Gaveston from exile. Marlowe makes it quite clear that the two men are lovers, but it is not the homosexual relationship that disturbs the barons—in fact, at one point the elder Mortimer explains "the mightiest kings have had their minions," and lists famous pairs of male lovers in history. Rather it is the fact that Edward ignores his role as king for the sake of Gaveston that enrages the nobles. Gaveston is lowborn, but Edward elevates him to share the throne, and in his infatuation, he forgets his duties to his realm. He is following his personal will, and shows this weakness in his inability to give up his personal pleasure for the good of his kingdom. He is childish both in his willfulness and in his stubbornness, and he remains blind to the facts of his own misrule and of the justice of the nobles' grievances.

Yet the Tudor world saw rebellion against an anointed king as the most grievous breach of natural law, and the play documents the slow evolution of rebellion. At first it is solely against Gaveston that the hostility is directed. Only gradually does this hostility spread to the king, first after the death of Gaveston, and then when Edward fastens his affections upon new flatterers, primarily Spencer. Whereas the loyalty of Gaveston and Edward, for all its folly, had a touch of nobility about it, Spencer is merely a sycophant, and the king, in listening to him, reveals his fatal weakness of character. His early frivolousness turns to vengeance when the barons move to open revolt, and even his loving queen and the loyal Edmund slowly turn against him. It is perhaps a weakness of the play that neither party in the conflict can arouse the audience's admiration; there is no moral framework to the play, no good side and evil side, or even wisdom to oppose the folly. The misrule of the king is overthrown by a Machiavellian villain, the hypocritical Mortimer. Whereas Shakespeare tended to glorify those who put an end to misrule, as does Bolingbroke in *Richard II* (c. 1595-1596, which bears many similarities to *Edward II*), Marlowe paints a picture of unrelieved gloom, as the rebels, led by the unfaithful queen and the power-grabbing Mortimer, depose the king. It is only at the very end, as Edward III comes to the throne, executing Mortimer and imprisoning the queen, that rightful rule is restored. Edward III specifically seeks the counsel of his nobles before he acts and in so doing restores the reciprocity upon which the well-being of the realm rests.

Beyond the concept of divine right, there remains the concept that the king must rule not by whim, but with concern for the welfare of his land, and in concert with his nobles, who, like him, are born to their station. Though the play has strong political overtones, the absence of any developed conflict between right and wrong robs it of the sort of symbolic value that is possessed by Shakespeare's finest history plays. Indeed, the absence of a figure with whom the audience can identify may be in part responsible for the unpopularity of the play, which perhaps because of its historicity lacks the fascination of the powerfully imaginative Tamburlaine the Great, Part I (1587) or *Doctor Faustus* (1588).

Marlowe's genius was at its best when expressing powerful emotions and characters with extravagant poetic imaginations. In *Edward II* there is less opportunity for such luxuriant language, and for many, the play does not really come alive until the downfall of the king, when in spite of his unsympathetic character, the pathos of his situation commands the involvement of the audience. To be sure, Gaveston is also very much a Marlowe character, perhaps much like Marlowe himself—impulsive, poetic, a lover of pleasure and beauty, both irresponsible and passionate. It is Edward, however, who sticks in the mind. Aside from his touching and loyal love for Gaveston, he has no redeeming qualities, the extremity of his suffering gives him a nobility that is not destroyed even by his anguish. Even at the end he can exclaim "I am still king!" Marlowe has constructed one of the most harrowing death scenes to be found in Elizabethan drama—though he actually softened the even more horrible historical fact—and the pathos of Edward's intense emotional suffering elevates the play beyond the level of historical chronicle and assures its place among the world's great dramas.

"Critical Evaluation" by Steven C. Schaber

Bibliography:

Levin, Harry. *The Overachiever: A Study of Christopher Marlowe*. Cambridge, Mass.: Harvard University Press, 1952. Discusses how in Marlowe's plays men's passions ultimately betray them. Asserts that whereas Shakespeare deals with the well-being of the state, Marlowe focuses upon individual tragedies.

Marlowe, Christopher. *Edward the Second*. Edited by Charles R. Forker. Manchester, England: Manchester University Press, 1994. Contains an excellent 136-page introduction. Considers the relationship between *Edward II* and Shakespeare's histories.

Ribner, Irving. *The English History Play in the Age of Shakespeare*. Princeton, N.J.: Princeton University Press, 1957. Describes *Edward II* as the first fully developed Elizabethan history play and tragedy of character. Discusses the personalities of Edward and Mortimer and the theoretical underpinning of political issues.

Sales, Roger. *Christopher Marlowe*. New York: St. Martin's Press, 1991. Considers the Elizabethan mentality as revealed in Marlowe's life. In the analysis of *Edward II*, the emphasis is on Mortimer and the difficulties posed by deposing and executing a monarch.

Weil, Judith. *Christopher Marlowe: Merlin's Prophet*. Cambridge, England: Cambridge University Press, 1977. A study of Marlowe's satiric and tragic irony, examining the playwright's relationship to his public. Argues that Edward becomes sympathetic, one in whom reason is reborn between his defeat and his death.

EFFI BRIEST

Type of work: Novel
Author: Theodor Fontane (1819-1898)
Type of plot: Domestic realism
Time of plot: Second half of the nineteenth century
Locale: Germany
First published: 1895 (English translation, 1914)

> *Principal characters:*
> EFFI VON BRIEST, the only child of the Briest family
> FRAU VON BRIEST, her mother
> RITTERSCHAFTSRAT VON BRIEST, her father
> BARON VON INNSTETTEN, Effi's husband and a government official
> in Kessin
> ANNIE, Effi's daughter
> MAJOR VON CRAMPAS, the district commander in Kessin
> ROSWITHA, Effi's maid

The Story:

Effi Briest was sixteen years old when her mother cheerfully announced that Baron von Innstetten had asked for her hand in marriage. Effi had seen Innstetten only once, but she knew he had wanted to marry her mother years before. During a time when Baron von Innstetten had been absent for a long period, her mother had married Effi's father, Ritterschaftsrat von Briest, for he seemed too good a match to give up. Since then Innstetten had become a government official with a promising future.

Half an hour earlier, Effi had been sitting on a swing enjoying her happy childhood. Now she was to be a bride and in a few weeks, she would be the wife of an important government official. After the excitement of preparations, the wedding, and a honeymoon trip to Italy, the couple arrived in Kessin, a small town on the Baltic Sea. At first, Effie found her new surroundings interesting, but soon she began to feel uncomfortable in the strange house, which had formerly been owned by a seafaring captain; his relics and souvenirs gave the place a bizarre character. A stuffed shark, stories about the captain's mysterious Chinese servant, and a mentally ill maidservant, who sat in the kitchen with a black chicken on her lap, gave Effi nightmares, and she claimed that she heard noises in an unoccupied upstairs room. Innstetten was considerate toward his young wife and never failed to show his devotion. A practical man, however, he paid no attention to Effi's tales of supernatural happenings in the house. He was convinced that his wife's childish imagination would soon calm down.

After having paid the obligatory social visits to the local aristocracy, Effi realized that she would not find friends in that circle. The first friend she made was the town apothecary. Her second friend was Roswitha, her maid, whom she met in the graveyard where the girl had been grieving for the loss of her former mistress. Effi was pregnant and needed a maid. Once she learned that Roswitha was Catholic, she was convinced that Roswitha's faith would conquer the unexplained noises in the house. Roswitha never heard ghosts, and her straightforward manner was a relief from the formal stiffness of Effi's social world. The birth of her daughter, Annie, gave Effi new activities, but she continued to be bored in Kessin.

The new military commander in Kessin, Major von Crampas, was another addition to Effi's social world. The major's carefree behavior and witty conversation were quite a contrast to the well-disciplined and formal Innstetten, but the two men respected each other and became friends. Crampas often visited the Innstetten home, and he and Effie rode horses along the seashore and participated in community plays. Effi soon realized the danger of this situation and tried to avoid him. During a sleigh ride, Crampas overstepped the boundaries of friendship.

One day, Innstetten informed Effi that he had been promoted to a new post in a Berlin Ministry, a position that would take them to Berlin. Effi was happy to leave the strange house, the boring people, and above all Crampas, for their relationship, although they had kept it secret, increasingly burdened her conscience. Innstetten noticed Effi's great joy when he told her about the transfer to Berlin, and he felt guilty for not having considered leaving sooner.

In Berlin, Innstetten made a special effort to provide her with a cheerful house and an enjoyable social life. Though Innstetten's duties at the ministry kept them from spending much time together, the years in Berlin were happy ones until Effie was sent to a spa at Ems to recuperate after an illness. Innstetten and Annie remained in Berlin. One day, when Annie fell and cut her forehead, Roswitha searched through Effi's belongings to find a bandage. When Innstetten thereupon tried to restore order in Effi's room, he found a bundle of love letters from Crampas, written six years earlier. Innstetten did what he considered his duty regardless of his personal feelings: He called a friend to make the necessary arrangements for a duel with Crampas. Although his friend pointed out that the letters were more than six years old, Innstetten, who would have preferred to pardon Effi, decided to go through with the duel because he felt the insult to his honor had not been diminished by time. The two men fought near Kessin, and Crampas was fatally shot.

While these events took place, Effi was still in the Rhine country, wondering why Innstetten's daily letters had ceased. Finally, a letter from her mother informed her of the duel and of the pending divorce. Innstetten was given custody of Annie. The Briest family was willing to assist Effi financially, but they refused to allow her to return home. Heartbroken, she went back to Berlin, where she lived in a small apartment, a social outcast. Only Roswitha remained faithful to her.

Effi's health declined. Once she accidentally saw Annie leaving school, but she avoided meeting the child. Finally, moved by a desire to see her daughter again, Effi requested legal permission to have Annie visit her. When Annie arrived at the apartment, however, she gave only evasive and well-rehearsed answers. Discouraged, Effi sent the child home without the hope of seeing her again. Soon after this, Effi's health declined severely. Her doctor reported her condition to her parents, hinting that their continued rejection could mean her death. When she was finally permitted to return home, her health did improve again. Aside from her parents and the local minister, however, Effi had no friends or social intercourse. Roswitha, concerned for her mistress' loneliness, wrote to Innstetten asking him to give Effi the family dog. Innstetten was glad to fulfill her desire. He had been extremely successful in the ministry, but none of his promotions had lessened the pain in his heart, for he still loved Effie.

After a beautiful summer at her parents' home, Effi died. In her last conversation with her mother, she asked Frau von Briest to tell Innstetten that he had done the only correct thing possible for him. She wanted to die as Effi Briest, for she had not honored her married name.

Critical Evaluation:

Effi Briest is Theodor Fontane's masterpiece. Surprised at how easily it came to him, he compared it to a psychogram. Based loosely on an actual case, the novel treats sensational topics, including adultery and a duel, but in his tolerant, nonjudgmental stance, Fontane keeps a discreet narrative distance from intimate scenes.

The main theme of the novel, death, is pervasive and eclipses individual incidents. By the end of the novel Effi's death seems inevitable. It is her fate, the accumulation of myriad factors beyond her control. Her inclinations, circumstances, and surroundings combine so that the reader, with Fontane, can only say "Poor Effi."

Effi is a remarkably passive and detached heroine. The plot is advanced not so much by what she does as by what is done to her. The opening scene of Effi playing in the garden with her friends shows her as a carefree child, quite unprepared for the arranged marriage her mother springs on her. As she stands trembling before Innstetten, her friend Hertha calls to her from outside, "Effi, come." Even Innstetten finds the call fraught with meaning, as if Effi is being called away from him to finish her childhood. In the original German edition, these words are given even more weight when near the end of the book Effi's father says exactly the same thing when he calls her to come home. Effi feels at home only in her parents' manor house in Hohen-Cremmen and thinks of herself to the end as Effi Briest, her parents' child, and not as Innstetten's wife.

If violence was done to Effi, figuratively speaking, by interrupting her childhood, then violence was also done to her by moving her as a bride into the very house in Kessin where the previous bride had met with a mysterious end, leaving the house haunted by the ghost of a Chinese man who had presumably been her secret lover. The ghost bodes ill for Effi. It links the house with adultery and death, and it is the point of contention that widens the gap in communication between Effi and Innstetten. Effi wants to move out, but Innstetten is insensitive and insists they stay.

Fontane was a master at writing dialogue and often manages to convey as much through what is not said as through what is said. One such dialogue, at the beginning of chapter 20, reveals that the rift between Effi and Innstetten is beyond repair. After arranging to have Effi ride home from a party with Crampas, who is known to have had illicit affairs, Innstetten expresses suspicion of Effi in their conversation the following morning. Crampas had, in fact, availed himself of the opportunity to make advances, but Effi discloses none of this to her husband and finds herself defending Crampas as the perfect gentleman. The dialogue shows that Effi's loyalty has shifted from Innstetten to Crampas.

It is also through dialogue that Fontane illustrates the rift between Effi and her only child, Annie. Showing rare initiative, Effi arranges for the child to visit her and promises herself much from the meeting. Effi loves nothing more than a good chat, but she despairs when she is confronted with a rigid, uncommunicative little girl who answers like a parrot, repeating the phrase: "Oh yes, if I may." This one effort convinces her of the futility of establishing any sort of meaningful relationship with her daughter. It is another nail in Effi's coffin.

A close reading of the novel reveals that Effi was doomed from the start. Apparently incidental details reinforce one another, forming an artistic web of references to the forces that contribute to her demise. Hertha is not just the girl who calls out to Effi from the garden. In chapter 24, Effi and Innstetten visit Lake Hertha, the site of ancient rites of Hertha worship, which involved sacrificial victims. Seen in this light, the call from Hertha can be interpreted as the call to death, not a good omen at the moment of betrothal. Fontane introduces the topic of adultery as early as the opening scene with Effi and Hertha in which the girls ceremoniously drown discarded gooseberry skins, commenting that in days gone by unfaithful wives were given the same treatment. How ingenious of Fontane to have Effi visit Lake Hertha as an alternative to visiting a town called Crampas. She turns aside from adultery only to face death.

Indeed, it becomes increasingly apparent that Hertha's seemingly harmless call was the more sinister of Effi's two options on that opening day. The choice was between Innstetten, who is indoors, and Hertha, who is outdoors in the fresh air. Effi's mother has already remarked that Effi should always be in the air. Initially, it seems that by going with Innstetten Effi has made the wrong choice, a choice that leads to adultery and ignominy. When her father finally sends his two-word telegram: "Effi, come," the reader would like to think that this would take her life back to the point where she heard those words from Hertha, thus undoing the unhappy marriage and letting Effi take the other option back into her parents' garden where she belongs. Ironically, this is just where she does belong. When she spends the autumn nights sitting at her window, the night air kills her and she is buried in the garden.

The associations built up around Hertha exemplify the exceptionally rich texture of *Effi Briest*. Written when Fontane was over seventy, the novel reflects the wise realization that there is seldom a simple explanation. Life is extraordinarily complex. For those who would seek a single cause for Effi's decline and death, Fontane speaks through her father in the closing words of the novel: "That is *too* big a subject."

"Critical Evaluation" by Jean M. Snook

Bibliography:
Greenberg, Valerie D. "The Resistance of Effi Briest: An (Un)told Tale." *PMLA* 103, no. 5 (October, 1988): 770-782. A revisionist interpretation of the novel as Effi's struggle for liberation. A close reading of Effi's last remarks to her mother reveals that each point can be read in opposition to its surface meaning.
Riechel, Donald C. "*Effi Briest* and the Calendar of Fate." *Germanic Review* 48, no. 3 (May, 1973): 189-211. Points out that the narrative structure and content of *Effi Briest* are informed by Fontane's autumnal sense of the existence and influence of an order inaccessible to reason.
Subiotto, Frances M. "The Ghost in *Effi Briest*." *Forum for Modern Language Studies* 21 (1985): 137-150. Analyzes the ghost as a metaphor for all that is absent: suitable living quarters, action, love, and opportunities for women in Prussian society. Sees *Effi Briest* as a paradigm of the solitary state of the individual.
Turner, David. "Theodor Fontane: *Effi Briest*." In *The Monster in the Mirror*, edited by D. A. Williams. Oxford, England: Oxford University Press, 1978. Examines *Effi Briest* in the context of contemporary European literature. Discusses what makes Fontane's treatment of the subject matter realistic, as well as his accurate detail and skillful use of leitmotivs and symbols.
Zwiebel, William L. *Theodor Fontane*. New York: Twayne, 1992. Contains a concise summary of important critical observations on the genesis of *Effi Briest*, the four narrative sections, the role of predestination, Fontane's criticism of Prussian society, and the function of the ghost.

EGMONT

Type of work: Drama
Author: Johann Wolfgang von Goethe (1749-1832)
Type of plot: Tragedy
Time of plot: Sixteenth century
Locale: Brussels
First published: 1788 (English translation, 1837); first performed, 1789

> *Principal characters:*
> COUNT EGMONT, the lord of Gaure
> CLÄRCHEN, his beloved
> BRACKENBURG, a citizen in love with Clärchen
> THE DUKE OF ALVA, an emissary of Philip II
> MARGARET OF PARMA, the regent of The Netherlands
> WILLIAM, Prince of Orange

The Story:
 The people of The Netherlands were unhappy in the state of their homeland. Philip II of Spain was tightening his absolute control of the Lowlands, particularly in religious matters, for Philip was the main instrument of the Inquisition. A new regent had been appointed to administer his rule. The populace had hoped the office would go to Count Egmont, who, after his defeat of the French at Gravelines, had become a national hero. Besides, although Egmont was a Catholic, he treated Protestants with kindness, and he had even gone to Madrid to plead with Philip to lessen the strictures of Catholic repression.

 The king, however, had given the office to Margaret, his half sister. She, like Philip, tolerated no dissent from the established church, yet by firmness and tact she had pacified the burghers who stubbornly resisted any laws but their own. She had even managed to conciliate Egmont and William of Orange, so that outwardly at least there was harmony among the nobility.

 Margaret summoned Machiavel, her secretary, to hear his account of new uprisings. He told her how throughout Flanders mobs were breaking into cathedrals and despoiling the monuments of the hated foreign religion. He counseled Margaret to be firm but not cruel toward the Protestants. Margaret told him that her efforts toward conciliation would mean little, for it was rumored that the cruel Duke of Alva was on his way to assume control of the provinces. Machiavel reminded her that as regent she would hold the final power, but Margaret was wise in the ways of kings. Officially or not, Alva would rule The Netherlands, and she would be able to circumvent him only by appealing directly to her brother. She was especially fearful of what might happen to Egmont and William of Orange and of the effects of Alva's harsh rule on the people.

 In her humble house, Clärchen was happily singing, for she expected Egmont that night. Brackenburg watched her anxiously. He loved her and was certain that no good would come of the love between a count and a commoner. When Clärchen, looking out of her windows, saw a mob in the street, she asked Brackenburg to learn the cause of the disturbance. While he was gone, her mother reproached Clärchen bitterly for having rejected Brackenburg's suit. Even now, the mother declared, the burgher would be glad to marry Clärchen. Brackenburg returned to tell them the people had heard of the outbreaks in Flanders and were heartened by that uprising against their oppressors.

A group of commoners argued about their rights as citizens. One, who could read, told them of their rights under the constitution and of their forefathers' vigilance in protecting their privileges. Egmont, arriving on the scene, advised them to be moderate in their talk but to preserve their ancient liberties. After he left, a keen observer remarked that Egmont's head would make a dainty morsel for the headsman.

In his residence, Egmont attended to duties of state. One of his letters came from Count Oliva, his old preceptor, who counseled him to be more circumspect in his behavior and less free in his talk. Egmont threw the letter aside, remarking that everyone was different; he himself believed in doing what was right without fear or favor. Let others play the part of fawning courtier.

William of Orange arrived to talk over Alva's coming. William was in favor of caution; they would do nothing until they knew what Alva had been sent to accomplish. Egmont reminded him that they were both Knights of the Golden Fleece. As members of that order, they could not be punished except by a trial by their peers. Prince William was inclined to place little trust in their rights, however, for Philip was a determined and ruthless ruler. William declared that he himself would remain on his own estate and refuse to meet the Duke of Alva. Egmont decided to speak his mind freely. If he had to be a rebel, he would openly do his best to advance the welfare of The Netherlands.

Margaret, in the meantime, had received a dispatch from Philip. The letter was gentle and considerate in tone, a fact ominous in itself. The king informed her officially of Alva's mission and gave details of the formidable army the duke was bringing to garrison the recalcitrant towns. Margaret knew that her authority as regent had been superseded.

In the evening, Clärchen joyfully received Egmont. For a time, Egmont was remote, even keeping on his mantle. Then he showed her that he was wearing his full uniform, decorated with the emblem of the Golden Fleece, and said that he had come thus attired because she had asked him to do so as a favor. Clärchen, particularly impressed by the decoration of the Golden Fleece, was touched by that evidence of his regard.

The inhabitants of the town grew fearful. Alva's soldiers had been stationed at every strategic point and his spies were everywhere, so that the citizens dared not congregate to discuss their new woes. The ordinary people were afraid for Egmont; it was rumored that he would be killed.

In his palace, Alva had made his plans, with his trusted guards forming so tight a cordon around the residence that no one could get in or out. To his natural son Ferdinand he announced that he was expecting Egmont and William of Orange. At the end of the audience, Alva would detain Egmont on a pretext. Prince William would be arrested outside. As soon as he was safely in custody, Ferdinand, acting as the duke's messenger, was to return to the reception chamber. His arrival would be the signal to arrest Egmont. Ferdinand, uneasy over the success of the plot, was nevertheless flattered by the part he was to play.

William of Orange was too cautious to fall into the duke's trap, however, and he stayed away from the audience. Egmont, who knew no fear, went without hesitation and discussed at great length the troubled situation in The Netherlands. He was a skillful debater. At every point he upheld the dignity of the burghers and wisely counseled patience and tact in dealing with them. At last, Alva became impatient and abruptly ordered his arrest. He read a document in which Philip decreed that Egmont had been tried and found guilty of treason. Because the king of Spain did not acknowledge the authority of the Knight of the Golden Fleece, Egmont failed in his demand for immunity.

Clärchen was distraught when she heard of Egmont's arrest. Accompanied by the faithful Brackenburg, she wandered about the town in an attempt to incite the citizens to rescue Egmont.

Alva had done his work well, however; the burghers were afraid even to discuss the matter. Returning to the house, Clärchen thought of the vial of poison that Brackenburg had once shown her when he was disconsolate. Thinking to quiet her temporarily, he gave her the vial. Clärchen immediately drank the poison.

In the palace prison, Egmont had been wakeful. When he finally dozed off he was wakened by Ferdinand and Silva, who read him his sentence: He was to be executed publicly in the marketplace as a warning to the people. Silva left, but Ferdinand remained behind to condole with the count. Although he had had a part in the plot, he actually sympathized with Egmont.

When Egmont slept again, a vision appeared. Freedom was reclining on a cloud. Her features were those of Clärchen. She held above his head a wreath of victory. Egmont awoke at dawn to strains of martial music. The guards were at his door.

Critical Evaluation:

Partly a historical drama and partly a character drama, Johann Wolfgang von Goethe's *Egmont* links public and private realms in a way that was somewhat unusual for eighteenth century literature. In his crowd scenes, Goethe provided historical breadth through the comments of ordinary folk, and he made deft and accurate use of the biographies of the important public figures around Count Egmont: the regent, Margaret of Parma, the Duke of Alva, and Prince William of Orange. Yet it is useful to view the work as at heart a character drama. Count Egmont represents a way of living and a philosophy of life that has continued to fuel controversy about the play. Because most characters in the drama and fiction of Goethe's era were devoted either to public duty or to private desires, Count Egmont, who integrates the two realms effortlessly, dazzles as an exception. This aspect of Egmont affects the way Goethe treats the essential underlying theme of freedom, and it requires that the plot concerning his political career be complemented by the largely separate (and fictive) story of his love for the commoner Clärchen.

In literary tradition, love between a nobleman and a woman from a lower class usually illustrates class conflict and ends tragically; Goethe's drama *Faust* (1808) is one of many examples of this. It is an innovation that for Clärchen and Count Egmont, class and morality are never at issue. Clärchen resists her mother's suggestion that she will be scorned for engaging in an affair that could not lead to marriage. Indeed, it was offensive to many of Goethe's contemporaries that the play depicts Clärchen as being virtuous and the bourgeois morality of her mother and the pitifully weak Brackenburg as being deplorable. Clärchen and Egmont illustrate the continuity of the personal and the political. Because she loves Egmont both as the human being and as the hero of her people, her attempt to launch a movement to rescue him is privately as well as publicly justified. When he embraces his sweetheart in full Spanish dress uniform, Count Egmont shows symbolically the fusion of public and private life. What he wants for himself and what he fights for on behalf of his people is unified: freedom to enjoy life, not just the freedom of speech or assembly. As a further token of the possible union of private and public, the goddess Freedom, who promises national liberation in the Count's dream, physically resembles Clärchen.

Written between the time of the American and French revolutions, the play *Egmont*, in the spirit of its era, joins liberty to nationalism without being nationalistic. The religious conflict that motivates the rioters to destroy churches and smash images is presented as an aspect of the political struggle for self-rule. Egmont tells Alba that the people consider imposed Catholicism just a façade to hide tyrannous governmental policies. The riots in Flanders are thus less a matter of conscience than a political protest fanned by oppression. Nationalism becomes a forced product of the tyranny of foreign rulers rather than a natural, healthy assertion of common identity, as it was for later German nationalists. Count Egmont is perfectly content to serve a Spanish king; Margaret is presented as a capable and lenient ruler, praised by Clärchen and the townspeople, despite the fact that she is a Spaniard. Although Goethe's contemporaries were shocked by the political radicalism of the play, Egmont subdues the burgher who advocates revolutionary violence by telling the people that rights cannot be secured by rioting. It is only on the eve of his execution that Egmont can accept the inevitability of a national war for independence from Spain. His desire to prevent the devastations of war was one reason he had refused to flee with the Prince of Orange when Alba entered Brussels with Spanish troops.

Structurally, this play is organized to display Egmont's temperament and attitude toward life. The count speaks of his ability to enjoy parties, hunting, and food and drink without letting anxiety for the future hamper him. The burghers of Brussels approve, for it makes them feel that he understands them and is one of them. Several characters speak of Egmont's prowess in past battles, his generous, open nature, and his relative tolerance for Protestant preachers. Those who criticize the count's way of life attack his lavish entertainments, irresponsibility, and lack of circumspection. By walking into the trap set for him by Alba, Count Egmont demonstrates imprudence and overconfidence; but if this is a flaw, it is also inseparable from his strength and charm. The nobles Margaret, Alba, and Orange function as foils for Egmont in their caution, practicality, and ability to maneuver better politically. Although Egmont is not like them, he is far happier as a human being for entrusting himself to fate; and his political idealism does him credit. Egmont is neither calculating nor sober, but rather playful and free; because he does not worry about the future, he can enjoy the present moment. It is this freedom to live life to the fullest, as well as political freedoms for his people, for which Egmont claims he is dying.

Some critics take a dim view of Egmont's happy-go-lucky temperament, and others have faulted Goethe's play for the lack of action on stage and for the dream sequence near the end. It is true that the characters tend to talk about their attitudes and values rather than to show these through their actions. Like all Goethe's plays, this one is more reflective and poetic than outright dramatic. Besides the fascination with Egmont's character, the strength of the play lies in its artful exploration of the philosophy and psychology of all the characters, in its absorbing analysis of the historical forces at work, and in its treatment of the issues of nationalism, freedom, and power politics. Although it is true that the count's death sparked the great uprising of The Netherlands, the ironic fact is that Brussels and Egmont's province Flanders, both part of Belgium today, never succeeded in throwing off the foreign yoke as the northern Dutch provinces did several decades after the historical Egmont was executed. That Egmont is consoled in prison by a dream that predicts the future Dutch victory, inspired by his own martyrlike death, perhaps detracts from the realism and tragedy of the play, but poetically it is compelling.

"Critical Evaluation" by Julie D. Prandi

Bibliography:
Goethe, Johann Wolfgang von. *Egmont: A Tragedy in Five Acts.* Translated by Charles E. Passage. New York: Ungar, 1985. Included in this careful translation of Goethe's play is a very useful ten-page introduction to the work. Provides a good overview of theme, character, style, and structure. Also places the work in its historical and literary context.
Gray, Ronald. *Goethe: A Critical Introduction.* London: Cambridge University Press, 1967. Provides a concise account of Goethe's works, including not only information about sources,

influences, and relationship to the author's life and position in German literature but also insightful critical assessment. Chapter 4 discusses Goethe's major dramatic works, including *Egmont*. Includes bibliography and chronology of Goethe's life and works.

Hatfield, Henry C. *Goethe: A Critical Introduction*. Cambridge, Mass.: Harvard University Press, 1964. Provides interpretations of Goethe's works with a minimum of biographical and background material. In chapter 3, "Resolution and Maturity," the author discusses Goethe's turn toward "objective" verse in *Egmont* and several other works. Includes a bibliography.

Peacock, Ronald. *Goethe's Major Plays*. Manchester, England: Manchester University Press, 1959. Excellent though dated introduction to and interpretation and assessment of Goethe's major plays. Discusses *Egmont* as a historical tragedy, personal portrait, and hymn to freedom. Also places the play in the context of Goethe's development as a dramatist.

Wells, G. A. "Criticism and the Quest for Analogies: Some Recent Discussions of Goethe's *Egmont*." *New German Studies* 15, no. 1 (1988-1989): 1-15. Summarizes critical viewpoints on Goethe's play. Among other perspectives, the work is viewed as a drama of innocence versus experience and a conflict between romanticism and social/moral realities.

THE EGOIST
A Comedy in Narrative

Type of work: Novel
Author: George Meredith (1828-1909)
Type of plot: Psychological realism
Time of plot: Nineteenth century
Locale: England
First published: 1879

> *Principal characters:*
>   SIR WILLOUGHBY PATTERNE, the egoist
>   VERNON WHITFORD, his cousin
>   COLONEL DE CRAYE, his relative
>   LAETITIA DALE, a neighbor
>   CLARA MIDDLETON, Sir Willoughby's betrothed
>   DR. MIDDLETON, her father
>   CROSSJAY PATTERNE, Sir Willoughby's distant kinsman

The Story:

On the day of his majority, Sir Willoughby Patterne announced his engagement to Miss Constantia Durham. Laetitia Dale, who lived with her old father in a cottage on Willoughby's estate, loved him—she thought—secretly, but everyone, including Willoughby himself, was aware of it. Ten days before the wedding day, Constantia astonished everyone by eloping with Harry Oxford, a military man. For a few weeks after the elopement, Willoughby courted Laetitia, and the neighborhood gossiped about her chances to become his wife. There was great disappointment when he suddenly decided to go abroad for three years. On his return, he brought with him his cousin, Vernon Whitford, to advise him in the management of his properties, and a young distant kinsman named Crossjay Patterne.

Laetitia was at first overjoyed at Willoughby's return, but she soon saw that she was to lose him again, for he became engaged to Clara Middleton, the daughter of a learned doctor. Middleton and his daughter came to Willoughby's estate to visit for a few weeks. Over Willoughby's objections, Vernon encouraged Crossjay to enter the Marines, and the young man was sent to Laetitia to be tutored for his examination. Vernon, a literary man, wanted to go to London, but Willoughby overruled him. Noting Willoughby's self-centered attitude toward Crossjay, his complete and selfish concern with matters affecting himself, and his attempt to dominate her own mind, Clara began to feel trapped by her betrothal. She reflected that Constantia had escaped by finding a gallant Harry Oxford to take her away, but she sadly realized that she had no one to rescue her.

When Clara attempted to break her engagement, she found Willoughby intractable and her father too engrossed in his studies to be concerned. Willoughby had decided that Laetitia Dale should become Vernon's wife, so that he would have near him both his cousin and the woman who fed his ego with her devotion. According to Willoughby's plan, Vernon could retire to one of the cottages on the estate and write and study. When Willoughby asked Clara to help him in his plan, Clara took the opportunity to ask Vernon's advice on her own problem. He assured her that she must move subtly and slowly.

In desperation, she persuaded Dr. Middleton to agree to take a trip to France with her for a few weeks. She hoped never to return to Willoughby, but the wary lover introduced Dr. Middleton to his favorite brand of claret, and after two bottles of the wine, the doctor was putty in Willoughby's hands. When Clara asked him if he were ready to go to London with her, he told her that the thought was preposterous.

Colonel De Craye, who arrived to serve as best man at the wedding, gradually sensed that Clara was not happy at the prospect of her approaching marriage. In desperation, Clara wrote to her friend, Lucy Darleton, and received an invitation to visit her in London.

Clara gave Crossjay the privilege of accompanying her to the train station. A hue and cry was raised at her absence from the estate, and Vernon, accidentally discovering her destination, followed her to the station and urged her to come back. She did so only because she believed that her behavior might injure Crossjay's future. Vernon was soon to go to London to follow his writing career, and if she were to leave, too, Willoughby would have full control of the young boy.

Complications resulted from Clara's attempted escape. At the station, Vernon had persuaded her to drink some brandy to overcome the effects of the rainy weather. The neighborhood began to gossip. Willoughby confronted Crossjay, who told him the truth about Clara's escape. Clara hoped that Willoughby would release her from her engagement, but he again refused. Dr. Middleton, determined that his daughter should fulfill her pledge to marry Sir Willoughby, ignored what was happening. In any case, he liked Willoughby's vintage wines and the estate.

Gradually, though, the egoist realized that his marriage to Clara would not take place. To soothe his wounded vanity, he asked Laetitia to become his wife. She refused, declaring she no longer loved him. Colonel De Craye shrewdly surmised what had happened. He told Clara the hopeful news. Clara felt that her only remaining obstacle was her father's insistence that she must not break her promise to Willoughby. Now, however, she could show that Willoughby had broken his promise first by proposing to Laetitia while still pledged to her.

Dr. Middleton announced firmly that Clara need not marry Willoughby. He had decided that he admired Vernon's scholarship more than he liked Willoughby's wines. The twice-jilted lover tried to even the score by manipulating Clara to consent to marry Vernon, which he felt would have the ironic touch that would be some measure of recompense to him. He was denied even this satisfaction when Clara told him it was already her intention to wed Vernon as soon as her engagement to Willoughby was officially broken. The egoist's selfishness and arrogance had brought them together.

Defeated, the egoist went to Laetitia, offering her his hand even if she were only willing to marry him for his money. Laetitia accepted on the condition that Crossjay be permitted to enter the Marines. Clara and the doctor planned to leave for Europe. Vernon arranged to meet them in the Swiss Alps, where he and Clara would marry.

Critical Evaluation:

The Egoist by George Meredith is a remarkable depiction of a sensitive and intelligent woman's mental, moral, and emotional agonies as she attempts to free herself from her engagement to an egotistical man. With an unusual degree of self-awareness, honesty, and perceptivity, Meredith identifies with Sir Willoughby Patterne's egotism and convinces his readers that egotism is characteristic of all humans.

Several parallels to Meredith's life are significant. In 1849, when Meredith was twenty-one years old, he married Mary Ellen Nicolls, who was twenty-seven, the widow of a marine officer, and the daughter of Thomas Love Peacock. The marriage lasted seven years and was full of tension and quarrels. Meredith believed that his egotism drove her away. The breakup of this relationship underlies the deep psychological probing in the fifty poems of Meredith's *Modern*

Love (1861). There, Meredith indicates that he, like Willoughby, had sought control, expected others to submit to him, entertained an artificial but quite conventionally sentimental conception of femininity, and thought of himself as the center of the universe. In the poems and in the novel, he emphasizes suffering of the woman and concludes that both men and women are trapped in tragic circumstances by insincerity and lack of mutual understanding.

In *The Egoist*, Clara Middleton, like Mary Ellen Meredith, is caught in a nexus of relationships because of her virtues: purity, docility, and usefulness to men. Meredith allows the reader to share her thought processes as she works her way through a labyrinth of dilemmas. Willoughby is in everyone's eyes the perfect husband; she faces social disgrace. Fortunately Clara escapes before the wedding instead of after and manages to gain her freedom without sacrificing her reputation or hurting anyone.

Meredith not only shared with Willoughby a self-esteem based on thoughtless self-importance but he also shared the scholarly interests of Dr. Middleton, Clara's father, who values the opportunity to use the library and to drink the aged wine at Patterne Hall above his responsibility toward his daughter. Dr. Middleton, who is thought to be a fictional portrayal of Thomas Love Peacock, is also an egoist; his confidence in his own judgment blinds him to Clara's needs.

Vernon Whitford is thought to be modeled on two of Meredith's friends, Sir Leslie Stephen, the father of Virginia Woolf—which is particularly interesting in view of the fact that Vernon is portrayed as being fully worthy of Clara—and Meredith's close companion Henry Wallis, with whom Mary Ellen ran away from her marriage. As a writer, Vernon also has several characteristics in common with Meredith, who had written eight novels and several volumes of poetry before *The Egoist*. After writing this novel, he, like Vernon, turned to periodical journalism and became a literary adviser.

In form, the novel is a comedy that follows the principles Meredith had laid out two years earlier in an essay entitled "The Idea of Comedy and the Uses of the Comic Spirit" (1877). Here, he advocated the therapeutic value of laughter in correcting vanity and promoting common sense. In the prelude to the novel Meredith alludes to the feminine comic spirit who "proposes the correction of pretentiousness." Meredith's women conspire with the comic imps who love to "uncover ridiculousness in imposing figures": and gather wherever egoism is found. In the last sentences of the novel, the "grave and sisterly": comic muse accompanies the lovers in their escape to the Alps, which represent all that is natural and freeing.

In many ways, the novel is like a comic drama. "The curtain falls" in the last chapter, and the action follows the unities of place (Patterne Hall), action (Clara's attempts to free herself), and even of time, as it takes place over a few days. The women are impishly clever, witty, and wise as well as well bred and well educated, thus resembling Mary Peacock Nicolls, who learned classical languages and attended plays as a child. The women are also superior in unselfishness, intuition, and innate common sense. Their dialogues approach those of a brilliant drawing-room comedy. Laetitia Dale is a writer and a woman of deep thoughts and emotions, who moves from idealistic worship of Willoughby to a more mature and objective view of him. By the end of the novel, she has seen his faults, forgiven him, and accepted him on her own terms. Constantia Durham, who "had money and health and beauty, the triune of perfect starriness which makes all men astronomers," was intelligent enough to leave Willoughby. The delightful comments of Mrs. Mountstuart Jenkinson and Lady Busshe include clever predictions and sparkling dinner-table conversation. Even Willoughby's devoted aunts wield the corrective comic spirit. Significantly, it is the women who comment on the artificiality of the conventional codes of drawing-room conduct and the false values that have shaped their society.

Meredith's richly poetic narrative is noteworthy for its use of recurrent symbols, including that of the most cherished dinnerware of the nineteenth century, the "willow pattern." The idea of ancient artificial china is echoed in Willoughby's name, in Mrs. Montstuart Jenkinson's references to Clara as a "dainty rogue in porcelain," and in the breaking of a porcelain vase, one of Clara's wedding gifts.

Many of the patterns of imagery suggest the prevalence of Darwin's ideas in contemporary thinking. Willoughby feels that since he is "the fittest" he has a responsibility to help breed the noblest race of men to come. The young Crossjay embodies the animal innocence and natural exuberance of the primitive instinct that still exists in human beings. Meredith implies that culture has not yet totally cut off the primal passions that are restricted by rules of a society in which the supernatural has been replaced by the principles of evolution with no regard for the individual. Even Vernon's "holy tree," the double-blossomed cherry, is threatened by scientific breeders, but his appreciation of its beauty indicates that blood, brain, and spirit join in him in joyful wholeness. Crossjay instinctively knows that Vernon is right for Clara, who runs and plays with him as if her "real vitality had been in suspense."

"Critical Evaluation" by Constance M. Fulmer

Bibliography:
Handwerk, Gary J. "Linguistic Blindness and Ironic Vision in *The Egoist.*" *Nineteenth Century Literature* 39, no. 2 (September, 1984): 163-185. Handwerk discusses the irony of the relationship between self-knowledge and language.
Hill, Charles J. "Theme and Image in *The Egoist.*" *University of Kansas City Review* 20, no. 4 (Summer, 1954): 281-285. Reprinted in *The Egoist*, edited by Robert M. Adams, pp. 518-524. New York: W. W. Norton, 1979. Hill reads the novel as a document in Meredith's campaign to encourage men to support women's emancipation.
Mayo, Robert D. "*The Egoist* and the Willow Pattern." *English Literary History* 9 (1942): 71-78. Reprinted in *The Egoist*, edited by Robert M. Adams, pp. 453-460. New York: W. W. Norton, 1979. This significant article explains how Sir Willoughby Patterne is identified with the unrealistic conventionalism of the willow design as it is so charmingly described by Charles Lamb in his essay "Old China."
Sundell, Michael C. "The Functions of Flitch in *The Egoist.*" *Nineteenth-Century Fiction* 24, no. 2 (September, 1969): 227-235. Reprinted in *The Egoist*, edited by Robert M. Adams, pp. 524-531. New York: W. W. Norton, 1979. Sundell discusses how Adam Flitch, the coachman at Patterne Hall who was dismissed as a result of Willoughby's brutal egoism, symbolizes the perennial servitor.
Williams, Carolyn. "Natural Selection and Narrative Form in *The Egoist.*" *Victorian Studies* 27, no. 1 (Autumn, 1983): 53-79. An enlightening study of the impact of Darwinism on the novel.

THE ELDER STATESMAN

Type of work: Drama
Author: T. S. Eliot (1888-1965)
Type of plot: Allegory
Time of plot: Mid-twentieth century
Locale: London and Badgley Court, a nursing home
First performed: 1958; first published, 1959

Principal characters:
> LORD CLAVERTON, the elder statesman
> MICHAEL CLAVERTON-FERRY, his son
> MONICA CLAVERTON-FERRY, his daughter
> CHARLES HEMINGTON, her fiancé
> FEDERICO GOMEZ, formerly Fred Culverwell
> MRS. CARGHILL, Maisie Batterson, alias MAISIE MONTJOY, a woman out
> of Lord Claverton's past

The Story:

Lord Claverton's daughter's fiancé, Charles, was protesting that, should he stay for tea in the Claverton town house, he would not be able to have any private conversation with Monica because of her father's presence. Monica worshiped her father, who had been a famous man in the political and financial worlds of England but who was currently, on his doctor's orders, retired from public life. Lord Claverton was preparing for a rest cure at Badgley Court, a nursing home in the country. Lord Claverton entered. He had become querulous over the emptiness of his future. Like most men of affairs who have been compelled to give up their former activities, he realized the hollowness of his past eminence, yet could not endure the prospect of a life devoid of his former important activities. Life had become a mere waiting for death for him. He recognized himself as a ghost and, with dramatic irony, remarked that he smiled when he thought people were frightened of ghosts.

Hardly had this remark been uttered when the first ghost from his own past arrived in the form of one Señor Gomez, from the Latin American Republic of San Marco. Almost immediately Gomez was revealed as Fred Culverwell, a friend of Lord Claverton's Oxford days. The unbearably suave expatriate was in possession of a damaging secret. Years before, the two university students were driving at night with two young women, when Claverton—then plain Dick Ferry—ran over a man and did not stop because he feared the possible scandal. Culverwell also accused Claverton of having been the cause of Culverwell's ruin in England. By taking Culverwell up at Oxford and teaching him expensive tastes that he, a poor boy, lacked the means to gratify, Claverton had forced him to resort to theft and finally to forgery, which had led to a prison sentence and flight from England. In San Marco, with its peculiar political situation, he had done well. Culverwell was no crude blackmailer and wanted only Claverton's friendship, something to give him reality after thirty-five years of homesick exile under an assumed name. He was a realist; he knew that, although a worldly success, he had failed, although not so badly as had Claverton, who had had to keep on pretending to himself that he had succeeded. To his credit, Claverton stood the attack well, maintained his dignity, and showed no fear of the moral blackmail that Culverwell was so subtly exercising.

Lord Claverton's doctor had ordered him to Badgley Court, a nursing home run in a grimly cheerful fashion, for a complete rest. Hardly had he arrived when another ghost from his past appeared, this time in the form of Mrs. Carghill. A generation before she had been Maisie Montjoy, a star of the music halls. She was currently a prosperous widow. The Dick Ferry of those far-off days had been in love with her and she with him—or so she claimed. She had settled her breach-of-promise suit out of court, and now she retained only sentimental memories and all of his letters. Again Lord Claverton, in spite of her sarcastic comments, maintained his unruffled dignity, even when she pointed out that there was only a negligible difference between being an elder statesman and posing as one. Twice the ghosts brought home to him his essential emptiness.

The ultimate trial came in the form of his son Michael, a spendthrift and ne'er-do-well who, even in his effort to see his father, had become involved in a motor accident, although not a serious one. In a sense, Michael was also a ghost, the ghost of the boy Claverton might have been had he not been possessed by a devil who was prudent as well as wayward. The son, although obviously a weakling, had his side of the story. He was desperately eager to get out of England into some country where he could have a life of his own, free from the oppressive shadow of his father's great name. It was clear that the father had dominated the son too much. The situation between the two seemed to have reached an impasse, but a solution was provided by the two ghosts. Mrs. Carghill suggested to Gomez that he take Michael back with him to the mysterious business in San Marco. The price that has to be paid for this solution is that Claverton must have all his past errors laid bare before his daughter and her fiancé. This is his act of contrition, after which he receives absolution in the form of Monica's forgiveness and understanding. The ghosts from his past are at last exorcised, to return into the darkness whence they came. Claverton went out into the grounds of the nursing home to await death, much as Oedipus left the grove at Colonus to find his appointed end. The mask of the "elder statesman" was dropped forever. Claverton was himself, the real man under the mask.

Critical Evaluation:

Although often treated as a minor work, *The Elder Statesman* embodies some of T. S. Eliot's finest achievements in verse drama. As Eliot's final play, this work represents a culmination of many of Eliot's themes and techniques. His ability to make each character on stage an aspect of the central character, his technique of forming characters into competing triangles, and his facility for depicting spiritual conflicts through visible, human struggles all reach a zenith in this play.

Many of the characters in *The Elder Statesman* fit into the recognizable roles of pilgrim, witness, watcher, and tempter, roles used in Eliot's earlier plays, and do so more naturally than in any of Eliot's previous dramas. Lord Claverton is the pilgrim who gains his redemption through facing his past failures. Monica Claverton-Ferry and Charles Hemington serve as witnesses whose love and forgiveness enable Lord Claverton to discover his real self and make peace with his past. These three form a triangle of compassion and forgiveness. Michael Claverton-Ferry is a watcher who sees much but learns little, and like most of Eliot's watchers is destined to failure. Mrs. Carghill and Federico Gomez are the tempters who haunt Lord Claverton and complete their merciless revenge by tutoring Michael in their diabolical habits. Mrs. Carghill and Señor Gomez entice Michael into a triangle of hate and unforgiveness. The only other prominent character not fitting into one of these triangles is Mrs. Piggott. As the meddlesome manager of Badgley Court, she prods and prompts characters into action or self-expression. Her treatment in the play is too scant to allow the audience to observe her full character, but Mrs. Piggott seems to function as a watcher, an observer who gains little from the events of the play.

Lord Claverton's escape from the triangle of hate involves more than overcoming guilt, a potentially healthy emotion. He struggles against the hate that would use guilt as a weapon for revenge. His cure takes place in two stages. First, Lord Claverton must accept his true self and his past. He must likewise recognize the potential for good his friends once had. Lord Claverton accomplishes this first step when he confesses to Charles and Monica how he has failed his friends Fred and Maisie. Second, Lord Claverton must accept only his part of the guilt and refuse the rest. In both of these processes, his daughter's all-accepting love is vital to his final redemption from a deadening past. Through this love he finds the courage to die and, ironically, experience a new life. Lord Claverton's struggle ends in self-acceptance, peace, and completion. His recognition that "in becoming no one, I begin to live" shows that he has grasped the essence of childlike humility. With the yielding of vanity and pride the ghosts of fear over humiliation also dissipate.

As a completion of Eliot's treatment of Christian community, *The Elder Statesman* illustrates how witnesses can function as agents of redemption for the pilgrim. This pattern of action is the opposite of that in *Murder in the Cathedral* (1935), in which the pilgrim-martyr pours out his life as a blessing upon his contrite parishioners. While Lord Claverton, the pilgrim, remains the focal point of the play throughout, he is dependent upon the love of the two witnesses, Monica and Charles, to make possible his spiritual pilgrimage from ghostly hollowness to wholeness. In this play divine love is portrayed through human love, as reflected in Monica's self-sacrificing love for her father. For the first time in Eliot's works, human love functions as an agent of divine love. Thus the opening and closing love scenes create a fitting frame for the play, and mark a high achievement in Eliot's career.

Eliot's treatment of tempters nearly comes full circle in *The Elder Statesman* for in this final play he used the morality play as a model. Eliot uses characters surrounding Thomas Becket to portray his inner qualities and struggles, and so Eliot uses various characters around Lord Claverton in *The Elder Statesman* to represent his strengths and deficiencies. In Eliot's last play he discovers how to depict spiritual struggles as the visible trials of human beings. Consequently, the tempters are far more natural and believable than in Eliot's earlier plays. As Eliot learned to appreciate the value of the natural world, he also discovered how to use it as the basis for his drama on spiritual themes. In this sense, his plays demonstrate a definite improvement in characterization.

Eliot made use of Sophocles' *Oedipus at Colonus* (401 B.C.E.) as a foundation for *The Elder Statesman*. In *The Elder Statesman* Lord Claverton functions as the aged and dying Oedipus who is aided by his daughter as he seeks a happy death, or translation into a new life. Although some critics find Eliot's use of Greek models too subtle for comparison, these models nevertheless form an important reference point for interpreting the patterns of Eliot's plays. Another element often overlooked in Eliot's dramas is his use of poetry of the common person. In fact the first viewers of *The Cocktail Party* (1949) and subsequent plays did not perceive that the plays were written in verse at all. Certainly *The Elder Statesman* reads smoothly and only skillful actors can capture the written music without overplaying it. In this matter, too, Eliot was an experimenter, one who finally achieved his stated objective of writing such natural verse that listeners would declare "I could speak in verse, too."

The Elder Statesman is an excellent example of Eliot's ideals for verse drama. Although this drama is not considered by many to be his best work, it nevertheless points toward a new mode of writing verse drama in which few have excelled as Eliot did.

"Critical Evaluation" by Daven M. Kari

Bibliography:

Chiari, Joseph. *T. S. Eliot: Poet and Dramatist*. New York: Barnes & Noble Books, 1972. Sees *The Elder Statesman* as a fitting culmination of Eliot's verse dramas and offers a positive interpretation of its accomplishments.

Hinchliffe, Arnold P., ed. *T. S. Eliot, Plays: "Sweeney Agonistes," "The Rock," "Murder in the Cathedral," "The Family Reunion," "The Cocktail Party," "The Confidential Clerk," "The Elder Statesman": A Casebook*. New York: Macmillan, 1985. A concise selection of critical reviews by prominent critics. Many insights.

Jones, David E. *The Plays of T. S. Eliot*. London: Routledge & Kegan Paul, 1960. Chapter 7 concludes that in this play Eliot has complemented the motifs in *The Family Reunion* (1939) and resolved his dramas into a naturalistic surface. Discusses the Greek model for this play.

Kari, Daven Michael. *T. S. Eliot's Dramatic Pilgrimage: A Progress in Craft as an Expression of Christian Perspective*. Studies in Art and Religious Interpretation 13. Lewiston, N.Y.: Edwin Mellen Press, 1990. Finds the play a fitting completion of Eliot's Christian and artistic ideals. Addresses the criticism that Eliot's poetic skills waned in this work, and instead finds the play a model for future religious verse dramas.

Smith, Carol H. *T. S. Eliot's Dramatic Theory and Practice: From "Sweeney Agonistes" to "The Elder Statesman."* Princeton, N.J.: Princeton University Press, 1963. Chapter 7 provides a useful summary of the play's main characteristics and concludes that the play succeeds as a theatrical fable designed to project religious insights.

ELECTIVE AFFINITIES

Type of work: Novel
Author: Johann Wolfgang von Goethe (1749-1832)
Type of plot: Love
Time of plot: Eighteenth century
Locale: Germany
First published: Die Wahlverwandtschaften, 1809 (English translation, 1872)

> *Principal characters:*
> EDWARD, a wealthy nobleman
> CHARLOTTE, his wife
> OTTILIE, Charlotte's protégée
> THE CAPTAIN, Edward's friend
> LUCIANA, Charlotte's daughter by a previous marriage
> NANNY, a youngster and Ottilie's protégée
> HERR MITTLER, a self-appointed marriage counselor

The Story:

Edward, a wealthy nobleman, had long been in love with Charlotte, but each had been forced to wed someone else. Their first spouses died, however, before many years had elapsed, and soon afterward Edward and Charlotte were married. With Charlotte's daughter Luciana placed in a good school, the pair, happily married at last, settled down to an idyllic existence at Edward's rural castle. They spent their time working at pleasant tasks about the castle and its park, leading together the kind of life for which they had long hoped and dreamed.

One day, a letter came to the happy couple. The Captain, long a friend of Edward, was out of a position. Edward immediately suggested that his friend be invited to the castle, where the Captain could help in improving the grounds and buildings. At first Charlotte withheld her consent, but finally she agreed to her husband's earnest desire. She revealed that she, too, had thought of inviting someone to the castle, the daughter of a dead friend. Charlotte had taken the young woman, Ottilie, as her protégée because of her friendship with the girl's mother. Ottilie, who was at school with Luciana, was not immediately invited for the visit Charlotte planned.

The Captain arrived shortly, and his presence soon made marked differences in the household. In order that he and Edward might work together undisturbed and with greater convenience, Edward moved from the wing in which Charlotte's rooms were located to the wing in which the Captain had been placed. Charlotte saw less and less of her husband. One evening, the three read about the elective affinities of chemical elements and speculated on how people were also attracted to one another in different combinations and in varying degrees. The invitation to Ottilie was again discussed. Since Ottilie was not doing well in school, and because Charlotte clearly needed additional companionship, Ottilie was immediately sent for.

When Edward had seen Ottilie and been in her company on previous occasions, Ottilie had made no impression on him. Seeing her in the same household, however, he soon became aware of her attractiveness. It became obvious, too, that Ottilie found Edward attractive. The two fitted together strangely well. When they played duets, Ottilie's mistakes coincided with Edward's. Gradually, as the two spent more and more time together, Charlotte and the Captain often found themselves together, much to their delight. After some weeks had passed, Edward realized the extent of his passion and his influence on Ottilie, all of which made him rejoice. Recognizing the force of his passion, he made efforts to cause it to grow, as it did steadily and swiftly. Although Charlotte noticed the attentions he paid Ottilie, she refused to become upset by them; since she had discovered her own regard for the Captain, she could more easily overlook her husband's behavior.

One day, while Charlotte and the Captain were out boating, their passion for each other could no longer be concealed. Considering themselves mature people, however, they immediately controlled their emotions and resolved, after a few kisses, to adhere strictly to the moral path in their conduct. Also, during one of their periods together, Ottilie and Edward discovered their love for each other. More easily swayed and emotionally immature, they welcomed the passion and did not try to curb their emotions.

While the relationships among the four were developing, more guests came to the castle. They were a countess and a baron who were spending a vacation as lover and mistress while away from their respective spouses. On the night of their arrival, Edward showed the baron the way to the countess' rooms, that the lovers might be together. While wishing he could enter Ottilie's room with the same freedom as the baron had entered that of his mistress, Edward found himself at his wife's door. He knocked and was admitted. He remained the night with Charlotte, but when he and his wife embraced they did not think of each other, but of Ottilie and the Captain.

The four people had all been working on plans for improving the grounds of the castle, with the hope, especially on Edward's part, that everything might be finished in time for Ottilie's birthday. On the day of the birthday celebration, Edward made a public spectacle of himself, proving almost a fool in his ardor for Ottilie. Finally, Charlotte suggested that Ottilie be returned to school or sent to live with other friends. Edward, angry and frustrated in his love, left the castle. When he left, he vowed he would have nothing more to do with Ottilie, as Charlotte wished, so long as Ottilie remained. On the same day, the Captain, who had received a position which promoted him to the rank of major, also left the castle.

Shortly after Edward's departure, Charlotte, discovering that she was pregnant as the result of the night her husband had spent in her apartments, called on the services of Herr Mittler, a volunteer marriage counselor. Herr Mittler, however, was unable even to begin a reconciliation with Edward, whose passion for Ottilie had conquered him completely. Edward had been accustomed all of his life to doing as he pleased and could not see why he should not have his way in this matter. When war broke out, he entered the king's service. He served gallantly and won many honors. He believed that if he lived through the war he was fated to have Ottilie.

Meanwhile, Charlotte endured her pregnancy, but she and Ottilie were no longer so close to each other, for the younger woman had become suspicious of Charlotte. For a time life at the castle was enlivened when Luciana arrived for a visit with a large party of her friends. During the entertainment of the visit, Luciana pointedly left Ottilie out of the activities arranged for the guests.

Ottilie's friend during the trying weeks after Edward had gone was a young architect hired to supervise the building of a summerhouse. Although his work was completed, Charlotte had kept him on to redecorate the local church. The young man admired Ottilie very much. A young schoolmaster who had taught Ottilie also expressed interest in marrying her, but Ottilie could think only of Edward.

At last a son was born to Charlotte. At the christening Ottilie and Herr Mittler, who stood as sponsors for the baby, were surprised to note how much the infant resembled both Ottilie and the Captain, a resemblance soon noted by others. Charlotte, remembering how she had dreamed of the Captain while embracing her husband, guessed that Edward had been dreaming at the same time of Ottilie. In a sense the child, named Otto, was a symbol of the parents' double adultery.

Edward returned to a nearby farm when the war ended. He met the Captain and made a proposal to solve everyone's problems. He suggested that he and Charlotte divorce, so that he could marry Ottilie and Charlotte could marry the Captain. Although the ethics of the plan did not appeal to him, the Captain agreed to take the suggestion to Charlotte. When the Captain set out for the castle, Edward also visited the grounds in the hope of seeing Ottilie. They met, and Ottilie was extremely upset, so much so that while returning to the castle alone in a small boat she dropped Charlotte's baby overboard. The child was drowned. When the Captain arrived at the castle, Charlotte showed him the little corpse that was a miniature of himself.

Ottilie decided to go away. Edward met her at an inn and persuaded her to return to the castle with him. There the four—Edward, Charlotte, Ottilie, and the Captain—tried to resume the happy life they had known before. Ottilie, however, seldom spoke and ate her meals in her rooms. One day she died suddenly, having starved herself to death. It came out that Nanny, her little protégée, had been persuaded to eat the food intended for Ottilie. Edward also began a fast. When he died a short time later, although not as the result of his fasting, he was laid in a tomb beside the woman he had loved. In death for one, in life for the other, the two couples were finally united.

Critical Evaluation:

Johann Wolfgang von Goethe's middle years as a classicist were bracketed by early and late years dominated by Romantic characteristics. *Elective Affinities* is a product of that late Romanticism. As he aged, however, Goethe was less adamant than he was in his younger days about his own adherence to any set of aesthetic principles. As a consequence, *Elective Affinities* contains elements of both classicism—primarily in form—and Romanticism—mainly in content. The novel has a classic symmetry of form which complements the symmetrical arrangement of the four protagonists, dividing the married couple, Edward and Charlotte, between their two guests, Ottilie and the Captain. The classic harmonious structure of *Elective Affinities* is created by its cool, formal, generally unemotional style—particularly evident in the distancing between narrator and action evoked by Goethe's use of a third-person narrator. These classical qualities lead to the expectation that the issues with which the novel deals will be rigorously pursued to the necessary logical conclusion.

Such, however, is not the case, because Goethe treats content from a predominantly Romantic perspective. In *Elective Affinities*, the absolute moral imperative of classicism collides with the irresistible force of Romantic natural law. The classical view would mandate that society emerge the victor. Indeed, classic orthodoxy would reject the simultaneous existence of two immutable but antithetical laws in the universe. Romanticism, on the other hand, would argue for the victory of the individual and allows for paradox and contradiction. Rather than affirm a clear-cut endorsement of either law, however, Goethe concludes the novel ambiguously: Although death is the fate of the lovers who defied the moral code of society, those disciples of natural law ironically carry off a moral victory of sorts by wringing sympathetic comments from the narrator, who thinks about the existence of some higher plane where there is no conflict between social order and natural law. The implication—a thoroughly Romantic one—is that the two lovers, buried side by side, may yet reach that plane.

In addition to the fusion of classic and Romantic elements typical of Goethe's works, *Elective Affinities* also illustrates another of the author's lifelong preoccupations: the nature of the learning process. From *The Sorrows of Young Werther* (1774) to *Faust* (1833), Goethe was concerned with epistemology and its relation to education, although that concern is most pronounced in the two Wilhelm Meister novels. The *Bildungsroman*, as these novels were called, is a tale of character development and the shaping of one's innate endowments. As such, the term also applies to *Elective Affinities*, since this novel subtly delineates the evolving mental and emotional qualities of the four protagonists as each one's elective affinity—in chemistry, the irresistible mutual attraction between two elements—changes over the course of the story. To be sure, *Elective Affinities* is much more than a novel about the philosophy of learning or a study in classic versus Romantic, but a delicately woven, intense psychological drama.

Bibliography:
Dieckmann, Liselotte. "Novels: The Elective Affinities." In *Johann Wolfgang von Goethe*. Boston: Twayne, 1974. Discusses the way irony, symbolism, and other narrative elements shape the novel. Contains an annotated list of Goethe criticism.
Lange, Victor. Introduction to *Elective Affinities*, by Johann Wolfgang von Goethe. Translated by Elizabeth Mayer and Louise Bogan. Chicago: Regnery, 1963. Written by a well-known Goethe scholar, this is an excellent introduction to the philosophical and moral issues raised in the novel. Emphasizes the ambivalence of love and marriage in the story.
Peacock, Ronald. "The Ethics of Goethe's *Die Wahlverwandtschaften*." *Modern Language Review* 71, no. 2 (April, 1976): 330-343. Examines the novel's ethical sensibility regarding marriage as an institution. Places Ottilie at the center of the story as an affirmative ethical statement, despite her tragic life.
Tanner, Tony. "Goethe's *Die Wahlverwandtschaften*." In *Adultery in the Novel: Contract and Transgression*. Baltimore: The Johns Hopkins University Press, 1979. A study of the four main characters. Highly critical of Ottilie, who is usually idolized. Analyzes the symbolic value of particular objects, activities, and landscape descriptions so prominent in the novel.
Vietor, Karl. "Elective Affinites." In *Goethe the Poet*, translated by Moses Hadas. Cambridge, Mass.: Harvard University Press, 1949. Represents the classical view of the novel in German scholarship, which points to the inevitable conflict between nature and civilization. Argues that the solution lies in restraint, balance, and resignation. Emphasizes the tragic necessity of the plot.

ELECTRA

Type of work: Drama
Author: Euripides (c. 485-406 B.C.E.)
Type of plot: Tragedy
Time of plot: After the fall of Troy
Locale: Argos
First performed: Ēlektra, 413 B.C.E. (English translation, 1782)

> *Principal characters:*
> ELECTRA, the daughter of Agamemnon
> ORESTES, her brother
> CLYTEMNESTRA, her mother
> AEGISTHUS, the lover of Clytemnestra

The Story:

When Agamemnon, the king of Argos, returned home from the Trojan War, he was murdered in cold blood by his wife, Clytemnestra, and her lover, Aegisthus. Afterward, Aegisthus and Clytemnestra were married, and Aegisthus became king. Orestes, the young son of Agamemnon, was sent by a relative to Phocis before Aegisthus could destroy him. Electra, the daughter, remained, but was given in marriage to an old peasant, lest she marry a warrior powerful enough to avenge her father's death.

One day, after Electra and the peasant had gone out to do the day's work, Orestes came in disguise with his best friend, Pylades, to the farm to seek Electra. They heard her singing a lament for her fate and for the death of her father. A messenger interrupted her lament with word that a festival was to be held in honor of the goddess Hera and that all Argive maidens were to attend. Electra said she preferred to remain on the farm away from the pitying eyes of the people of Argos. The messenger advised her to honor the gods and to ask their help. Electra mistook Orestes and Pylades for friends of her brother. She told them her story and spoke of her wish that Orestes avenge the death of Agamemnon and the ill treatment of his children. Aegisthus, meanwhile, had offered a reward for the death of Orestes.

The peasant returned from his work and asked Orestes and Pylades to remain as his guests. Electra sent her husband to bring the relative who had taken Orestes away from Argos. On his way to the peasant's cottage, the old foster father noticed that a sacrifice had been made at the tomb of Agamemnon and that there were red hairs on the grave. He suggested to Electra that Orestes might be in the vicinity, but Electra answered that there was no chance of his being in Argos. When Orestes came out of the cottage, the old man recognized a scar on his forehead; thus brother and sister were made known to each other.

At the advice of the old peasant, Orestes planned to attend a sacrificial feast over which Aegisthus would preside. Electra sent her husband to tell Clytemnestra that she had given birth to a baby. Electra and Orestes invoked the aid of the gods in their venture to avenge the death of their father.

Orestes and Pylades were hailed by Aegisthus as they passed him in his garden. The pair told Aegisthus that they were from Thessaly and were on their way to sacrifice to Zeus. Aegisthus informed them that he was preparing to sacrifice to the nymphs and invited them to tarry. At the sacrifice of a calf, Orestes plunged a cleaver into Aegisthus' back while Aegisthus was examining the beast's entrails. Orestes then revealed his identity to the servants, who cheered the son of their former master. Orestes carried the corpse of Aegisthus back to the cottage, where it was hidden after Electra had reviled it.

At the sight of Clytemnestra approaching the peasant's hut, Orestes had misgivings about the plan to murder her. He feared that matricide might bring the wrath of the gods upon him. Electra was, however, determined to complete the revenge. She reminded Orestes that an oracle had told him to destroy Aegisthus and Clytemnestra.

Clytemnestra defended herself before Electra with the argument that Agamemnon had sacrificed Iphegenia, their child, as an offering before the Trojan venture and that he had returned to Argos with Cassandra, princess of Troy, as his concubine. Electra indicted her mother on several counts and claimed that it was only just that she and Orestes murder her. The queen entered the hut to prepare a sacrifice for Electra's supposed first-born; within, Orestes killed her, though he moaned in distress at the violence and bloodshed and matricide in which the gods had involved him.

The Dioscuri, twin sons of Zeus and brothers of the half-divine Clytemnestra, appeared to the brother and sister, who were overcome with mixed feelings of hate, love, pride, and shame at what they had done. The twin gods questioned Apollo's wisdom, whose oracle had advised this violent action; they decreed that Orestes should give Electra to Pylades in marriage and that Orestes himself should be pursued by the Furies until such a time as he would face a trial in Athens, from which he would emerge a free man.

Critical Evaluation:

Electra is a compelling example of Euripides' dramaturgy. At the same time, it affords a means of comparing his purpose and techniques with those of Aeschylus and Sophocles, for all of them used the same legend and presented roughly the same action. Aeschylus in *The Libation Bearers*, part of *The Oresteia* trilogy (458 B.C.E.), Sophocles in *Electra* (418-410 B.C.E.), and Euripides in his *Electra* all treat Orestes' return to Argos, his presenting himself to his sister Electra, their planning of the revenge against Aegisthus and Clytemnestra, and the execution of that revenge. The different treatments are, however, quite individual and show the distinctions between these three tragedians.

With Aeschylus, the twin murders of Aegisthus and Clytemnestra are the culminating crimes in a family polluted by generations of kin slayings. Regicide and matricide are evils instigated by Apollo to punish and purge the earlier murder of Agamemnon. Orestes alone takes on the burden of these crimes. Electra, a minor character, offers him encouragement to the deeds, but her nature shrinks from being an actual accomplice. Aeschylus shows Orestes' revenge as an act of divine justice, a crime that will in time earn an acquittal. Sophocles takes a different view of the matter. The regicide and matricide are justifiable for him in human terms as the proper retribution for Agamemnon's killing. Electra is portrayed as a hard, bitter, determined young woman who aids her brother as a rightful duty. This perspective is similar to that in Homer's *Odyssey* (c. ninth century B.C.E.).

Euripides calls both points of view into question. He sees the murders of Aegisthus and Clytemnestra as wholly unmitigated evils that are neither humanly nor divinely justifiable. Euripides says in effect that no killing is permissible for any reason. He carries this logic to its logical conclusion—that killers have as much right to live as anyone else no matter how twisted their psyche or how questionable their motives. This is a radical stand, but it is based on Euripides' firm conviction of the value of every human life, a belief that shines through the whole of *Electra* and makes the idea of just retribution a mockery. Euripides gives the impression that he would have liked to abolish all courts and prisons, turning justice into a matter of individual conscience. What is interesting is the way he worked out these ideas dramatically.

Whereas Aeschylus and Sophocles concentrate on royalty and heroes, Euripides does not hesitate to depict an honorable peasant or to show ignoble blue bloods. In fact, the entire action of *Electra* takes place in front of a peasant's hut. To Euripides, each life has worth, and the index to that worth is strength of character. Position, wealth, power, beauty, and physique were nothing to him. Rather, he was chiefly interested in accurate, realistic psychology.

Each of the main characters is shown as a clearly defined personality in relation to a specific environment. Euripides tends to concentrate on the sordid aspects in *Electra* as the legend would seem to demand, yet it is here that his faith in human dignity reveals its power. It is easy to love good people, but to love people as warped by circumstances as Electra, Orestes, or Clytemnestra requires moral courage. Euripides possessed that courage, and he portrayed their pain as though it were his own.

Electra has fallen from lavish prosperity to squalor and a forced, loveless marriage to a peasant, although that peasant is a compassionate man. She is slovenly and full of self-pity and spite. She envies her mother, Clytemnestra, who lives in luxury and power, and she hates Aegisthus. Her single passion is to kill them both, and when she discovers Orestes, she uses him to obtain revenge. Orestes himself is a neurotic vagabond of no status but with authorization from Apollo to kill his mother and her lover, and he declaims pompously about nobility of character. Clytemnestra seems like a housewife in queen's clothing, operating by a retaliatory logic. She takes a lover because her husband had a mistress, and she kills Agamemnon because he killed their daughter Iphigenia. Yet none of this has made her happy, and when she visits Electra out of motherly concern, she is hacked to death by her two children. Even Aegisthus appears to have decent aspects to him. It is precisely the ordinariness of Clytemnestra and Aegisthus that makes the realistic descriptions of their murders so sickening. Euripides convinces his readers and audiences that they deserved to live.

Once their passion for revenge is spent, Orestes and Electra are filled with self-revulsion and feel utterly degraded. Euripides brings two gods on stage, Castor and Polydeuces, to settle the matter, a *deus ex machina* ending that places the action in a new light. Apollo is directly responsible for the murders, just as Zeus is responsible for the Trojan War. These are not wise or just gods by human standards, and Euripedes shows those human standards to have infinitely more worth than the abominable edicts of the gods. Euripides is supremely confident in his position, and he does not shrink from judging gods by it.

Consistent with his faith in humanity's value, he allows Orestes and Electra a good measure of compassion in the end. They are both exiled, and Orestes will be driven mad by the Furies, which only he can see. Nevertheless, they too deserve to live, Euripides declares, and in time they too will win forgiveness. Rarely has the belief in human dignity had such a steadfast champion as Euripides.

"Critical Evaluation" by James Weigel, Jr.

Bibliography:

Grube, G. M. A. *The Drama of Euripides*. London: Methuen, 1941. Offers a detailed interpretation of *Electra*, which Grube admires for its psychological insights into all the characters.

Kitto, Humphrey Davy Findley. *Greek Tragedy: A Literary Study*. London: Methuen, 1939. Labeling *Electra* a melodrama, Kitto argues that the play succeeds because of its characterization but lacks a universal theme. Compares Euripides' version with what Kitto regards as the more tragic treatment of the story by Sophocles.

McDonald, Marianne. *Terms for Happiness in Euripides*. Göttingen, Germany: Vandenhoeck & Ruprecht, 1978. Analyzes *Electra* as a work that stresses the theme of friendship and shows that the traditional view of happiness is mistaken. Wealth, power, and victory do not produce the happiness enjoyed by the peasant who is married to Electra.

Michelini, Ann Norris. *Euripides and the Tragic Tradition*. Madison: University of Wisconsin Press, 1987. The first four chapters offer an overview of Euripidean criticism and discuss the literary conventions he inherited, his audience, and his style. Chapter 7 focuses on *Electra*, which Michelini regards as balancing comedy and tragedy.

Norwood, Gilbert. *Greek Tragedy*. Boston: John W. Luce, 1920. A good survey. Norwood admires Euripides' handling of Electra and argues that Euripides refuses to take sides. Concludes that the play demonstrates the inscrutability of life.

ELECTRA

Type of work: Drama
Author: Hugo von Hofmannsthal (1874-1929)
Type of plot: Tragedy
Time of plot: Antiquity
Locale: The inner courtyard of the palace at Mycenae, Greece
First performed: 1903; first published, 1904 as *Elektra* (English translation, 1908)

> *Principal characters:*
> ELECTRA, a daughter of the murdered king Agamemnon
> CHRYSOTHEMIS, her younger sister
> ORESTES, their brother
> CLYTEMNESTRA, the widow of Agamemnon and mother of Electra,
>   Chrysothemis, and Orestes
> AEGISTHUS, Clytemnestra's consort

The Story:

As the reddish glow of the setting sun flooded the inner courtyard of the palace, five women servants came to fill their pitchers at the well. While they were speaking, Electra, Agamemnon's eldest daughter, appeared, dressed in ragged clothing. Startled by their presence, she quickly disappeared like a frightened animal. Four of the women exchanged contemptuous observations about the mourning rites that Electra practiced each evening for her father, and they ridiculed both her and the wretched conditions of life that her mother and Aegisthus had imposed upon her. Disdainfully, they mentioned that she preferred eating on the ground with the dogs to sharing the servants' table, and that she insulted all the servants of the house and stared at them fiercely like a wild cat. When the young fifth servant expressed her admiration for the abused princess, she was ordered inside, where she was promptly beaten for her insolence. Their pitchers filled, the servant women reentered the palace.

Electra returned and, speaking alone, revealed her secret thoughts and feelings. She recalled in vivid detail the murder of her father who, upon his return from the Trojan War, was at this very twilight hour slaughtered in his bath with an ax by his wife and her lover. She prayed for her father's spirit to appear to her again, promising that his blood would one day be avenged. She vowed to sacrifice at his grave when that day came and swore that she, along with her sister Chrysothemis and her brother Orestes, would dance around his tomb in royal pageantry to commemorate his greatness.

Chrysothemis appeared in the doorway, interrupting Electra's fantasy, to alert her that she had overheard Clytemnestra and Aegisthus plotting to imprison her in a dungeon. Electra replied contemptuously, which led Chrysothemis to plead with her to understand her personal unhappiness. She explained that if they were to relinquish the hope of Orestes' return and his subsequent revenge, they would both be able to lead relatively normal lives, to love and marry, to bear children, and to experience the joys of family life. She would quite willingly tolerate the injustice of their father's murder in exchange for an ordinary happy life. Not so Electra, who reproached her sister severely and reassured her that their brother would indeed return one day, and that together they would punish the criminals. Sounds from within alerted them of Clytemnestra's approach. Chrysothemis fled, but Electra resolutely awaited a confrontation.

1950

Clytemnestra, covered with jewels and charms that she believed to possess magical powers, appeared in the window with her attendants and spoke insultingly to Electra, who answered deceptively, inducing her mother to descend into the courtyard to seek her council. Clytemnestra complained that her sleep was often troubled by bad dreams and that a terrible "nothing" tormented her soul, causing her to feel horror of sinking alive into chaos; whatever demon was responsible could be appeased by an appropriate sacrifice, and she solicited assistance in discovering it. Electra offered elusive and evasive responses: To dispel the dreams, a man of their house, but yet a stranger, must slay some unidentified impure woman in any place, at any hour. Receiving indifferent answers to her questions about Orestes' return, Electra, overcome by hysterical rage, screamed that Clytemnestra herself must be the sacrificial victim and that Orestes would slay her with the same ax she had used to kill his father. Taken aback, Clytemnestra shook with voiceless fear.

A servant entered and whispered something in Clytemnestra's ear, at which the expression on her face changed to one of evil triumph; calling for lights, she swept inside. Chrysothemis returned to tell Electra of the arrival of two strangers who had announced the death of Orestes. A young manservant came looking for a horse, so that he might carry such important news immediately to Aegisthus. Electra now determined to kill the guilty rulers herself, and when her frightened sister refused to participate in such a deed and ran away, Electra resolved to accomplish it alone. She was digging in the earth for the ax that she had buried years before when she noticed a stranger enter the courtyard.

She spoke with him cautiously, since he claimed to have information about Orestes' death, but when she revealed her name, he disclosed that he was indeed Orestes. Brother and sister embraced. Rejoicing at their reunion, Electra explained that the expectation of his return had sustained her through terrible times. A servant led Orestes into the palace to meet the queen, and soon after her screams could be heard. The servants became frightened and bewildered. When Aegisthus returned home, Electra met him with a torch and conducted him to the palace door. Within minutes, he appeared at a window crying for help, but he was quickly dragged out of sight.

Chrysothemis entered the courtyard with other women and told her sister that the wicked had all been slaughtered by Orestes and his followers. Electra seemed to be able to hear only the triumphant music in her own head, to which she danced like a maenad, arms stretched wide, knees flung high, in a mad dance of triumph. She suddenly fell to the ground, while Chrysothemis pounded on the palace door, calling helplessly for her brother.

Critical Evaluation:

Hugo von Hofmannsthal's poetic tragedy *Electra* is an adaptation of Sophocles' drama *Electra* (418-410 B.C.E.). The work adheres closely to the structure and dramatic organization of the original but omits the chorus of women of Mycenae and develops and interprets the poetic materials in an entirely original fashion. In some instances, Hofmannsthal also drew on Aeschylus' *Oresteia* (458 B.C.E.) and Euripides' *Electra* (413 B.C.E.) for promptings pertaining to diction and poetic imagery.

Hofmannsthal added no new twists to the plot of his Greek sources, but his conception of the characters differs radically from theirs. In Sophocles' play, Electra is overwhelmed by grief and sorrow, Clytemnestra seeks to justify her crimes with rational explanations, and Orestes returns wielding a sword of justice with which to reestablish order within the corrupted kingdom; there he was not tormented by the Furies, as in Aeschylus and Euripides. Hofmannsthal created an Electra possessed by an insane, all-consuming hatred and sustained by the expectation of eventual revenge; his superstitious Clytemnestra is tormented by insomnia produced by a guilty conscience; his Orestes (Hofmannsthal had at one time considered omitting him entirely from the play) is merely an agent of revenge, a character who lacks any strong personal definition. The secondary characters of Aegisthus and Chrysothemis are retained relatively unchanged, though the latter appears somewhat less sympathetic and more willing to serve as a partner in evil in the modern work.

Hofmannsthal's decision to omit the chorus found in all the Greek versions resulted in substantial shifts in the meaning and emotional tone of the drama. In Sophocles, the chorus functioned as sensible representatives of a traditional moral order. There, Electra found the chorus sympathetic to her sorrowful laments, and their commiseration and approval of her grief legitimized her sufferings; the women of Mycenae represented uninvolved persons who could judge morally from a position emotionally outside the framework of the tragic situation. Lacking an anchor in any such continuing moral order, Hofmannsthal's characters struggle in a fundamental moral chaos that remains unredeemed at the play's conclusion by either choral statements affirming the restoration of traditional values, as in Sophocles, or a strong-minded Orestes who promises to establish a new moral order for his new society. Hofmannsthal thereby enunciates his theme that at the dawn of the twentieth century human beings stood alone in the ruins of their old values yet powerless to create significant new ones to replace them.

The world of Hofmannsthal's *Electra* is one in which hatred and oppression are the ruling forces in society and political legitimacy is shown to reside in the effective use of force to gain and maintain power and authority. Other ideas that shape Hofmannsthal's world derive from such sources as Sigmund Freud and Josef Breuer's 1895 study on hysteria and Freud's 1900 *The Interpretation of Dreams*. Like most intellectuals at the time, Hofmannsthal owned both books and was thoroughly familiar with them. His depictions of neurotic obsession in the character of Electra and those of guilt-induced dreams in the character of Clytemnestra rank among the finest early examples of the impact Freud had on literature.

Hofmannsthal employs ordinary, mundane language, similar to that of Sophocles and Aeschylus, which he arranges into simple, clear, and direct lines of free verse that convey the characters' thoughts forcefully and vividly. His frequent use of violent images relating to blood, murder, slaughter, and butchery, which impart this work's gruesome tone, has a precedent in the Greek sources: Where Hofmannsthal has Electra urge her brother on by saying, "Once more, strike!" Sophocles wrote, "Strike her again, strike!" Eschewing any display of feats of poetic virtuosity, Hofmannsthal avoided a stilted and convoluted rhetorical style and shunned any images reminiscent of "lofty and sublime" imitations of classical Greek harmony and serenity. His clear, simple style was easily understood by a theater audience, and it proved to be ideal for being set to music in an opera.

When the German composer Richard Strauss saw Max Reinhardt's production of *Electra* in Berlin, he immediately recognized its operatic potential. He had met Hofmannsthal in Paris in 1900, and the two had enthusiastically considered the mutual benefits to be derived from working together. The stage play *Electra*, appropriately modified to meet the musical require-ments of an opera libretto, offered an ideal opportunity for collaboration and proved to be the first of several of the greatest musical-dramatic collaborations in operatic history. Serious work on the opera began in 1906. Hofmannsthal's drama of approximately 1,500 lines was too long and was reduced to about 825 lines, including two new short passages Strauss requested from the poet. Hofmannsthal's conception remained intact; cuts merely eliminated elaborations from speeches, insignificant scenes of comic relief, and reduced the importance of minor charac-ters. The opera was first produced in Dresden in 1909, and though received coolly at first, was soon recognized as a masterpiece. It is the operatic version, rather than Hofmannsthal's spoken drama, which has most consistently held the international stage and become known to a world-wide audience.

Raymond M. Archer

Bibliography:

Del Mar, Norman. *Richard Strauss: A Critical Commentary on His Life and Works.* 3 vols. London: Barrie & Rockliff, 1962. Includes a highly readable account of Hofmannsthal's play and its transformation into an opera.

Hamburger, Michael. *Hofmannsthal: Three Essays.* Princeton, N.J.: Princeton University Press, 1972. An excellent introduction to Hofmannsthal's poems, plays, and libretti for English-speaking readers.

_____. *A Proliferation of Prophets: Essays on German Writers from Nietzsche to Brecht.* Manchester: Carcanet Press, 1983. Contains a highly readable essay tracing Hofmannsthal's poetic and artistic development, with advice for readers new to his work on how to approach his poetry. An excellent section on *Electra.*

Hammelmann, Hanns, and Ewald Osers, trans. *A Working Friendship: The Correspondence Between Richard Strauss and Hugo von Hofmannsthal.* New York: Random House, 1961. Contains the twenty-one letters exchanged between Hofmannsthal and Strauss concerning the preparation of the libretto of *Electra.* Essential.

Puffett, Derrick, ed. *Richard Strauss: "Elektra."* New York: Cambridge University Press, 1989. A collection of eight essays from renowned scholars to examine in depth all aspects of the opera based on Hofmannsthal's drama.

ELECTRA

Type of work: Drama
Author: Sophocles (c. 496-406 B.C.E.)
Type of plot: Tragedy
Time of plot: c. 1250-1200 B.C.E.
Locale: Outside the royal palace at Mycenae, Greece
First published: 418-410 B.C.E. (English translation, 1649)

> *Principal characters:*
> PAEDAGOGUS, a servant of Orestes
> ORESTES, the son of the murdered King Agamemnon
> ELECTRA, the daughter of Agamemnon
> CHRYSOTHEMIS, sister of Electra and Orestes
> CLYTEMNESTRA, Agamemnon's widow
> AEGISTHUS, Agamemnon's cousin and Clytemnestra's lover
> CHORUS, women of Mycenae

The Story:

When Clytemnestra and Aegisthus murdered King Agamemnon, Electra had her brother, Orestes, spirited away by the Paedagogus, a loyal servant charged with caring for the boy. When Orestes became a man, he, the Paedagogus, and Orestes' friend Pylades returned to avenge the murder. Urged on by Electra, Orestes had been counseled by Apollo to gain vengeance stealthily. Wishing to take the culprits off guard, Orestes pretended that he and his companions were strangers, that Orestes had been killed in a chariot accident, and that they had come to return the princely ashes to his mother.

Even as Orestes explained his plan to the Paedagogus, intending also to lay an offering at Agamemnon's grave, Electra, wailing, emerged from the palace. The three men left, and Electra bemoaned her lost youth, spent in mourning for her slain father. Oppressed with sorrow, she had remained unbedded (A-lectra), a virgin obsessed with vengeance against her adulterous mother and Aegisthus. The Chorus' advice about reasonable limits to mourning and expressions of rage did not sway her from her course. She had seen Aegisthus kill her father at his hearth, and she was anguished to see the murderer ruling her father's kingdom, wearing her father's clothes, and sleeping with her father's wife. Electra was now beyond childbearing, beyond marrying, and her life seemed incapable of gaining meaning except through avenging the murder.

Electra's sister, Chrysothemis, arrived bearing burial offerings that Clytemnestra, troubled by dreams, had ordered her to take to Agamemnon's grave. Chrysothemis, though outraged, hoped to live comfortably, and she advised Electra to control herself; otherwise, Electra would be imprisoned, and she would have to live out her life alone. The prospect did not frighten Electra, who relished the thought that Clytemnestra had dreamed that Agamemnon returned, planted his scepter at his hearth, and produced foliage that covered all Mycenae. With the Chorus' approval, she urged Chrysothemis to offer locks of her own hair and Electra's hair and belt, rather than what their corrupt mother had sent.

Clytemnestra, emerging from the palace, accused Electra of bringing sorrow upon herself by her insolence. Although the Chorus and Electra believed that Clytemnestra had assassinated Agamemnon out of lust for Aegisthus, Clytemnestra claimed that she had slain him because, on his way to Troy, he had sacrificed their daughter Iphigenia. Electra retorted that Iphigenia had been sacrificed because Agamemnon, having mistakenly killed a stag of Artemis', was doomed with all his crew to be stranded, unable to proceed or retreat, unless he sacrificed the girl. Even if Agamemnon had had a wrong motive for the sacrifice, she argued, Clytemnestra's act remained unacceptable.

After Clytemnestra prayed to Apollo for a peaceful life with loving children, the Paedagogus entered to report Orestes' death. Clytemnestra claimed that she did not know whether to respond with joy at the end of a potential threat, or with sorrow at the loss of her child. Actually, however, she was relieved. Electra, on the other hand, was crushed by the report. She resolved to bring on her own death by wasting away at the gate.

Chrysothemis returned with news that Orestes was back. She had found a lock of his hair at Agamemnon's grave, along with other offerings. Believing their brother to be dead, however, Electra guessed that someone had left the offerings as a tribute to the deceased Orestes. Chrysothemis accepted the explanation.

Electra, devoid of hope of getting help from the outside, resolved to kill Aegisthus herself. She invited Chrysothemis to lend a hand, the rewards being twofold: admiration from the dead, who would honor their piety, and freedom for Chrysothemis to marry someone worthy. Chrysothemis was fearful, however, and argued that justice is sometimes harmful to the just. Electra was undeterred, and the Chorus praised her.

When Orestes arrived, pretending that he was a Phocian, he handed Electra what he claimed to be her brother's ashes; she lamented the death of the child she had saved from being murdered. Orestes, moved to reveal himself, was loath to do so in front of the Chorus, which advised Electra to moderate her mourning. Assured that the Chorus was on Electra's side, however, he identified himself, cautioning the joyous Electra to restrain herself and focus on what they had to know and do in order to succeed.

The Paedagogus reappeared with the news that Clytemnestra and Aegisthus were relieved by the thought that Orestes was dead. Orestes and Pylades entered the palace, and, after hearing vain cries for mercy from Clytemnestra, the Chorus and Electra heard the queen die. Orestes returned in a sober mood, hoping that Apollo's prophecy and his fulfillment of it would have positive results.

Aegisthus arrived almost immediately, happily expecting more news about Orestes' death. Electra led him to believe that Orestes' body was in the palace, and he ordered the doors to be thrown open, so that any who still hoped for Orestes' return could see the proof of his demise. Confronted by Clytemnestra's corpse, Aegisthus thought that it was Orestes' but he soon recognized his plight. Orestes forced him to enter the palace where, like Clytemnestra, he met his end.

Critical Evaluation:

Sophocles, the most successful of the ancient Greek playwrights, garnered between eighteen and twenty-four victories in yearly competitions at the Festival of Dionysus. He wrote about 123 tragedies, of which seven are preserved. Three concern the family of Oedipus; one relates the story of Deianira and her husband, Heracles; and three are devoted to the Trojan War and its consequences. *Electra*, Sophocles' only surviving play about the family of Agamemnon, preserves the basic story as Aeschylus had revised it from Homer's *Odyssey* (c. 800 B.C.E.) but alters the details yet again. The changes help us to understand Sophocles' interpretation of the myth and the yield for humanity that he saw in it.

Homer carefully avoids the horror of matricide in his account of Orestes' vengeance, recalling that Orestes murdered Aegisthus and properly buried both him and Clytemnestra. Though a number of alternative explanations for Clytemnestra's death could be advanced, Aeschylus sees matricide implicit in the situation, and in the last two plays of the *Oresteia*, his trilogy about the family of Agamemnon, Orestes is plagued by Furies in the vernacular of later ages, "driven mad by guilt") for slaying his mother. He is acquitted when the goddess Athena's utterly unjustified vote of not guilty breaks the deadlock of an evenly divided jury. Aeschylus is concerned with exploring matters of state: how personal anguish relates to one's obligations to a slain king and father; how humanity progresses; and what is involved in moving from one system of justice to another, here from blood vengeance to trial by jury.

Sophocles is more interested in the ways in which experience, working with innate qualities, determines a human being's character. The gods hardly figure in his play, and guilt is not the issue. Given their innate proclivities and experiences, his characters do what they think or feel they must do; the worst of them, Clytemnestra, sees and regrets in some measure the horrors she has perpetrated, and the best, Electra, is goaded into encouraging and supporting horrors of equal magnitude.

Noble and idealistic Electra, obsessed by the loss of the father she loved and feeling repugnance for her mother that is tainted with jealousy, abandons all hope of marrying, loving a husband, and bearing children. Instead, she commits herself to the past, to avenging her father's murder. She hates the usurper Aegisthus and her mother because they mistreat her, and, to a degree, that hatred compromises her desire for moral vengeance. She not only wants revenge but she also wants to cause her enemies pain. Her great fear is that she may herself possess traits inherited from her mother, and the fear is justified. Clytemnestra, if her account of her motive for killing Agamemnon carries any weight, was, like Electra, fiercely committed to justice by blood vengeance. Her hatred and lust too were implacable. She waited ten years for revenge, and, having gained it, mutilated the corpse of her victim, husband though he had been. She celebrated the anniversaries of his death with festivals. Electra's transcendent hatred and the lust for vengeance that she nurtures for years mirror Clytemnestra's; Electra, too, is determined to dishonor the corpse of a culprit, intending to toss the slain Aegisthus as carrion to birds and dogs. Warped by her experiences, the expression of her noble intent is unavoidably impious.

Chrysothemis, Clytemnestra's middle child, who is less proud and determined than her sister, accepts the condition of servitude in the household of her father's murderers. She subordinates her unhappiness and hopes for a better life in the future. Unwilling to risk her life to avenge Agamemnon (presumably she did not know him as well as Electra did), she is not made of the fierce, unyielding stuff that characterizes her sister and mother. She can be swayed to deliver her mother's offerings to the tomb of her father, she can then be swayed not to do so. Aware of Aegisthus and Clytemnestra's power, however, she will not openly oppose them.

Orestes, on the other hand, knows his father and mother only theoretically. He was taught that his father was treacherously slain, and he is dedicated to vengeance against the murderers, one of whom happens to be a person he does not recall, his mother. The anguish he causes Electra does not deter him from deceiving her when he sees an advantage in doing so. Neither rash nor timid and without the memory of family relationships to impede him, he is calculating and efficient, the perfect killer; he happens to be attached to the side of what passes for justice.

Guilt and pollution are endemic to the House of Atreus. As Sophocles sees the conflicts, the issue is how people deal with the problems, what in their characters, compounded of inherited traits and experiences, determines their actions. Clytemnestra, proud, bold, sexual, and vengeful, is the wrong kind of woman to outrage by murdering her child, the wrong kind, too, to leave unserviced for ten years. Her lover, now husband, Aegisthus, has motives of his own for hating the family of his cousin Agamemnon, whose father, Atreus, had killed Aegisthus' brothers and fed them to their father. The untrustworthy scion of an untrustworthy family with a history of savagery and pain, Aegisthus in a minor way reinforces the vision of character that Sophocles presents. Chrysothemis, yielding by nature, is a survivor, a follower who, like her uncle Aegisthus, can swell a scene or two but cannot create or dominate one. Orestes, deprived of the emotional complications engendered by family life, is an instrument of whatever purpose he embraces. Electra, by contrast, is indeed her mother's daughter—and, like her, proud, bold, sexual in her obsession, and vengeful. Tragically twisted into a woman for whom destruction is the only positive prospect, magnificent in both her love and her hatred, Electra stretches beyond the deaths of her enemies in a vain search for peace. Hers is a tragedy about the fruits of the past, the ways in which violence and perversity warp people, and the consequences for their lives.

Albert Wachtel

Bibliography:

Reinhardt, Karl. *Sophocles*. Translated by Hazel Harvey and David Harvey. New York: Barnes & Noble Books, 1979. A structural appreciation of *Electra* as the first of Sophocles' uniquely related last plays.

Sophocles. *Electra*. Translated by William Sale. Englewood Cliffs, N.J.: Prentice-Hall, 1973. Sensitive, detailed analyses of theme, meaning, and structure. Introduced by Eric A. Havelock's excellent general survey and Adam Parry's sketch on metrics.

Webster, T. B. L. *An Introduction to Sophocles*. 2d ed. New York: Methuen, 1969. A challenging portrait of a pious Sophocles, for whom god-inspired matricide is good.

Whitman, Cedric H. *Sophocles: A Study of Heroic Humanism*. Cambridge, Mass.: Harvard University Press, 1966. Sees *Electra* as a play that embraces the Homeric values of the *Odyssey*. Celebrates Electra's suffering, endurance, and wise triumph.

Winnington-Ingram, R. P. "The *Electra* of Sophocles: Prolegomena to an Interpretation." In *Oxford Readings in Greek Tragedy*, edited by Erich Segal. New York: Oxford University Press, 1983. Presents an interpretation in which the Furies were operative on Electra and Clytemnestra before her murder, allowing for both Homeric and Aeschylean interpretations.

THE ELEGY OF LADY FIAMMETTA

Type of work: Novel
Author: Giovanni Boccaccio (1313-1375)
Type of plot: Love
Time of plot: Fourteenth century
Locale: An Italian city, possibly Naples
First published: Elegia di Madonna Fiammetta, 1343-1344 (English translation, 1587)

> *Principal characters:*
> FIAMMETTA, a noble lady
> PANFILO, a young man

The Story:

Fiammetta had a dream that a serpent bit her while she was lying in a meadow and that, as darkness came, the wound festered and brought her close to death. When she woke she discovered that she had no injury and, failing to realize that the dream was a warning and a prophecy, she dismissed it from her thoughts.

Fiammetta was admired by the ladies and gentlemen who surrounded her when she went to church on a certain festival day, but of all her admirers none struck her fancy until she saw a young gentleman leaning against a marble pillar of the church. The glances that she and the young man exchanged proved that the attraction was mutual.

Realizing that she had been overtaken by love, Fiammetta spent hours in her chamber picturing the young man and hoping to see him again. As other chance meetings increased her interest in him, she became so disturbed and changed by love that her nurse commented on it and warned her of the dangers of passion and of betraying her husband. Fiammetta, however, was too much enamored of the young man to heed such warnings; she dreamed that Venus came to her and told her of the delight and power of love, urging her to ignore her nurse's warnings and to submit to love's promptings.

Encouraged by her fond glances, the young man became familiar with Fiammetta's friends and with her husband, so that he and Fiammetta might converse together, hiding their love. The young man taught her by his example how to converse in the company of others so as to reveal their love only to each other; he pretended to be telling of two lovers, Fiammetta and Panfilo, in order to show how deeply his own passion moved him. Although Fiammetta grew adept at this word game, she knew that their love could not forever be kept within the bounds of propriety.

Despite Fiammetta's refusals, which Panfilo took as coy signs of encouragement, he finally gained what all lovers desire. He and Fiammetta spent innumerable nights together, learning new delights of love. Nothing else mattered to Fiammetta. She thanked Venus for encouraging her in love, and she laughed at other gentlewomen who imagined that they knew what passion was.

Fiammetta's happiness, however, was fated to come to an end. One night, while she and Panfilo were together in her chamber, Fiammetta awoke to find Panfilo weeping. She hesitated to inquire into the cause of his distress for fear that he would reveal some other love for whom he was secretly longing. Pretending that she had not seen him weeping, she suddenly cried out as if in her sleep. When he wiped his tears and turned to her, she told him that she had suddenly feared that she had lost him. He answered that neither fortune nor death could change his love for her; he then began to sob and sigh again. Answering her question concerning his sorrow, Panfilo told her that he had to leave the city for four months because of his father's illness.

Fiammetta argued that if he loved her he would not leave her. She was sure of his love and could not bear to part with it; as one so desperately in love, she deserved his presence more than his father did. She feared for his health and safety if he were to leave her. Finally, she concluded, a storm was coming; no man of sense would go out in such weather.

In spite of her protests, Panfilo insisted that it was his duty to see his dying father, but he assured her that he would return at the end of four months. After a long and loving farewell, she accompanied him to the gate. Then, overcome with sorrow, she fainted and had to be revived by her maid.

During the first four months of Panfilo's absence, Fiammetta spent her days remembering the delights she had shared with him, wondering whether he was falling in love with someone else, counting the days and scolding the moon for being slow in its course, and imagining and dreaming that he had returned to her.

Even the satisfaction of daydreaming was denied to Fiammetta when she learned from the conversation of a merchant that Panfilo was married. She was plunged into jealousy and grief, but as time went on, she began to hope that Panfilo might not find happiness with his wife. She offered prayers to Venus asking that he be striken again with love for her so that he would return.

Fiammetta's husband noticed that she had lost her appetite and was having difficulty sleeping. Ignorant of the cause, he at first had medicines prescribed for her and then took her on a vacation to some beautiful islands. The medicines, however, had no effect on her passion, and the islands only reminded her of the delightful times she had spent with Panfilo. Feasts and shows failed to please her, and she spent her days sighing and praying to the gods of love and fortune.

Fiammetta learned from one of her servants that Panfilo was not married, as she had supposed from the merchant's tale, but rather that he was in love with a beautiful gentlewoman who loved him. Her misery intensified more than ever by this news. She found no comfort in her husband's loving and compassionate words, and her nurse could not bring her to her senses. She considered many ways of suicide, all of which seemed too painful or too difficult to be considered. She then reasoned that if she killed herself she would never see Panfilo again. Finally, fearing that worse torments were to come, she attempted to leap from the house, but she was stopped by the nurse and other servants.

After her nurse told her that Panfilo was returning, Fiammetta, for a time, hoped to see him again. The rumor, however, had confused Fiammetta's Panfilo with another man having the same name, and Fiammetta was forced to realize that she had lost him forever. She compared her condition to that of other betrayed lovers, supposing herself to be more unfortunate than they. She told her story in order that others might take it as an example of what misery may befall an amorous gentlewoman.

Critical Evaluation:

Giovanni Boccaccio's elegy has often been touted by scholars as the first psychological work of literature written in a modern language. It is an account of specific emotions occurring in an individual's mind, whereas most medieval literature relates physical actions, such as the exploits of knights or pilgrims, or expresses idealized emotions, such as in courtly love poetry. Boccaccio's work is composed as a letter written by the principal character, Fiammetta, to be sent as advice to other women who may find themselves in a similar situation, that is, seemingly duped by a man.

The elegy relates her emotional history from when she first saw and fell in love with her lover, Panfilo, through his leaving her, temporarily as she believed at first, up to her ultimate realization that he must have chosen never to return, thus rejecting her as his lover. Fiammetta seeks to express her feelings; the actions she leaves to readers to imagine. For example, she describes their trysts in only the vaguest of terms, but she expresses fully the emotions she felt during their affair.

Although, by her own account, happily married, she is impressed by the handsomeness of a young man. Becoming acquainted, they fall in love and carry on an affair secret to almost everyone. Even their pretend names for each other reveal the emotional nature of their relationship: Fiammetta ("endearing flame") and Panfilo ("all-loving," or "lover of all"). In a stream-of-consciousness literary style, she expresses the agonies of facing separation from her lover and then of wondering why he has stayed away far longer than he said he would, without communicating. Finally, she describes the despair that paralyzes her life. She blames herself, him, and the misfortune of the circumstances that divided them initially. Her emotions revolve between intense anguish in missing Panfilo and extreme anger because of his presumed rejection of her. She contemplates and even acts on thoughts of suicide. Her letter is meant to warn other women of the dangers of loving a man so deeply as to be as vulnerable to his abandonment as she proved to be.

The Elegy of Lady Fiammetta, although one of Boccaccio's minor works, has become better known as literary critics and historians have paid greater attention to gender-related issues in their research. It is one of only a few works of its time that have a woman as a principal character and of even fewer whose story is actually told through a female voice. Judged by modern social criteria, this work does not stand as a source of enhancing woman's status. Fiammetta's language describes her not only as victimized by a particular man but also more generally as a woman who is by nature vulnerable, culpable, and weak. The impression is one of a woman treated by her lover merely as a sexual object to be discarded after use. As Fiammetta relates so vividly, her beauty, her dignity, and her being dissipate in Panfilo's absence. The reader can choose, however, to evaluate this work in its own historical context. Accordingly, *The Elegy of Lady Fiammetta* stands as a departure from traditional literature. It portrays a woman in a social role beyond mere subservience, someone who desired a man who was not her husband and sought to gain him. It does not condemn Fiammetta as a mere adulteress or seductress but presents her as an individual with full awareness of her own life and wishes. The account is sympathetic. She schemes to betray her husband and she may be naïve, but Boccaccio depicts her above all as a victim of fortune.

A particular feature of Boccaccio's writing unrelated to either its psychological style or its content deserves mention. Reflecting a familiarity with classical literature, Boccaccio frequently refers to stories and characters from ancient history and mythology. Fiammetta and other speakers in the work often draw parallels between her trials and the relationships of other lovers of the past. In some cases, Boccaccio cites long series of classical references. These would have been readily recognized by his contemporary readers; what a modern reader may take as tedious, esoteric references would have reinforced the story and increased its impact for earlier readers.

Scholarly consensus has turned away from an earlier autobiographical interpretation of this work, by which Boccaccio seemed to be describing an affair of his own with a noblewoman in Naples in the late 1330's. Instead, Fiammetta appears to have been mostly a literary creation. She appears in other of his works, and the evidence linking her to a specific woman is not wholly persuasive. If one were to prefer a historical approach to the work, considering it as an autobiographical revelation, another interpretation offers itself. Boccaccio had lived most of his early life in Naples before leaving for Florence, where he composed this elegy, and one could view it as an emotional parallel to his travels, because he preferred Naples. He perhaps saw himself as Panfilo, the one who loved his southern city but was constrained by circumstances to leave for the north. Accordingly, he also envisaged Fiammetta (Naples) mourning his absence and torn emotionally over why he was no longer in her presence.

The beauty of *The Elegy of Lady Fiammetta* is in how much Boccaccio leaves to the reader to imagine. Fiammetta's psyche is revealed, but the women recipients of her letter (and all readers of the work) are left to imagine the specifics of the circumstances of the affair. The affair thus is general; it adapts to individual situations. The reader is left not knowing even if Panfilo eventually returns. *The Elegy of Lady Fiammetta* is a work that draws the reader into the mind of its principal character and elicits an emotional response. Whether Fiammetta is indicting men or fortune, whether she is medieval in her behavior or modern, and whether Boccaccio was expressing a male perception of society though through a female character or was antedating feminism—these issues remain open to interpretation.

"Critical Evaluation" by Alan Cottrell

Bibliography:
Boccaccio, Giovanni. *The Elegy of Lady Fiammetta*. Edited and translated by Mariangela Causa-Steindler and Thomas Mauch. Chicago: University of Chicago Press, 1990. The most elegant modern translation into American English. Introduction presents an overview of the author's life, the elegy, and the various sources of its inspiration.

_____. *The Elegy of Madonna Fiammetta Sent by Her to Women in Love*. Translated by Roberta L. Payne and Alexandra Hennessey Olsen. New York: Peter Lang, 1992. Contains a fine, brief introduction to the work's literary features. The translation is of a slightly different original text than Causa-Steindler and Mauch's, and thus can serve for comparison.

Griffin, Robert. "Boccaccio's *Fiammetta*: Pictures at an Exhibition." *Italian Quarterly* 18, no. 72 (Spring, 1975): 75-111. An appraisal of the techniques by which Boccaccio uses Fiammetta to present a series of emotions. Discusses the elegy's literary, linguistic, and classical features.

Iannucci, Amilcare A. "*L'Elegia di Madonna Fiammetta* and the First Book of the *Asolani:* The Eloquence of Unrequited Love." *Forum Italicum* 10, no. 4 (1976): 345-359. Compares *The Elegy of Lady Fiammetta* with a later Italian Renaissance work. Highlights Boccaccio's stylistic features.

Smarr, Janet Levarie. *Boccaccio and Fiammetta: The Narrator as Lover*. Champaign: University of Illinois Press, 1986. A chapter on *The Elegy of Lady Fiammetta* discusses the character of Fiammetta as she appears in other of Boccaccio's works. Discusses the variety of perspectives found in the voices of reasoned narrators and impassioned characters, who often were the same person playing differing roles.

ELEGY WRITTEN IN A COUNTRY CHURCHYARD

Type of work: Poetry
Author: Thomas Gray (1716-1771)
First published: 1751

Thomas Gray probably began "Elegy Written in a Country Churchyard" about 1746. It was originally a somewhat shorter poem than the version he published in 1751, and some have speculated that the poem may have been occasioned by an actual death, perhaps that of Gray's friend Richard West in 1742. When Gray designated his work as an elegy, he placed it in a long tradition of meditative poems that focus on human mortality and sometimes reflect specifically on the death of a single person. By setting his meditation in a typical English churchyard with mounds, gravestones, and yew trees, Gray was also following a tradition. Some of the most popular poems in the middle of Gray's century were set in graveyards and meditated on death.

"Elegy Written in a Country Churchyard" is cast in four-line stanzas, or quatrains, in which the first line rhymes with the third, the second with the fourth. This *abab* pattern, at this time associated with elegiac poetry, gives the poem an appropriately stately pace. The last three stanzas are printed in italic type and given the title "The Epitaph."

In the first three stanzas (lines 1 to 12), Gray sets the scene for his private and quiet meditations. He is far from the city and looking out from a country churchyard at a rural scene, but the sights and sounds of this rural world of men and beasts fade away. Although the scene is beautiful, life is not joyous, and Gray reflects that this day dies just like the one before it, as the plowman plods wearily home. The poet is alone, but he is not tired. The text gives a sense of the vitality of his solitude and of the stillness of the scene by describing the few things that remain to disturb it: the tinkling of the cattle who have returned home, the drone of the beetle, and the sound of an owl from the church tower. This owl—a "moping," secret, solitary ruler over the churchyard since ancient times—strikes an ominous note and protests that the poet is challenging its reign. With these descriptions, Gray creates the backdrop for his melancholy reflections about eternal truths.

In the next four stanzas (lines 13 to 28), Gray uses the churchyard scene to invoke important images: the strength of the elms, death as symbolized by the graves, and the comfort provided by the yews shading bodies that sleep. The poet begins by reflecting that death for the humble and lower class means a cessation of life's simple pleasures: waking up to the songs of birds, sharing life with a wife and children, and enjoying hard and productive work. Gray reflects not on the untimely death of young people but on the death that comes after a normal life span.

In the next four stanzas (lines 29 to 44), the poet addresses the upper classes—those with ambition, grandeur, power, nobility, and pride—and exhorts them not to mock the poor for their simplicity or for not having elaborate statues on their graveyard memorials. He tells the living upper classes (perhaps the people Gray envisions as his readers) that ultimately it does not matter what glory they achieve or how elaborate a tombstone they will have. They will die just like the poor.

The eight stanzas (lines 45 to 76) that follow provide the central message of the poem: The poor are born with the same natural abilities as members of the upper classes. Who can say what humble people might have accomplished in the great world had they not been constrained by their condition and their innate powers not been frozen by "Chill Penury." Gray implies that the innocence and beauty of these souls, wasted in their isolated rural environment, and resembling hidden deserts and ocean caves, could have flourished in better circumstances:

> Full many a gem of purest ray serene,
> The dark unfathomed caves of ocean bear:
> Full many a flower is born to blush unseen,
> And waste its sweetness on the desert air.

The churchyard graves may also contain the remains of a person who had the ability to become a great scholar, a generous national leader, or a man who could have been a great poet but is in the end no more than a "mute inglorious Milton." Gray goes on to speculate, however, that poverty may have prevented some dead men from doing not good but evil; now death has made them (unlike Oliver Cromwell) "guiltless" of shedding blood; they have not been able to slaughter, to refuse mercy, to lie, or to wallow in luxury and pride. Far from the "ignoble strife" of the great world, the village people have led "sober" and "noiseless" lives. Gray implies that, even though the village dead have accomplished nothing in the world, on balance they may be morally superior to their social betters.

Gray returns to the churchyard in the next section (lines 77 to 92), remarking on the graves' simple markers with their badly spelled inscriptions, names, and dates. Some bear unpolished verses or consoling biblical texts; some are decorated with "shapeless sculpture." Gray is touched that such grave markers show the humanity these dead people share with all men and women (including, by implication, the famous who took paths of glory). Those who remain can sense that the dead "cast one long lingering look" back on what they were leaving and were comforted by at least one loved one. Gray reflects that the voice of general human nature can be heard crying from these graves. In the last line of this section, Gray reflects that what he has learned will apply to himself and his readers: The "wonted fires" of his life and those of his readers will continue to burn in the ashes of all graves.

This more personal line provides a transition to the next six stanzas (lines 93-116), where it seems (the grammar is confusing) that Gray is addressing himself when he writes:

> For thee, who mindful of the unhonoured dead
> Dost in these lines their artless tale relate,
> If chance, by lonely contemplation led,
> Some kindred spirit shall inquire thy fate

Gray imagines an old farmer, who is described as a "hoary-headed swain," replying to this question in lines 98 to 116. The farmer's story describes Gray as a man who does not fit into either of the classes described earlier; he is neither a poor man nor a man of noble achievement. He is a wanderer, a man who vigorously meets the sun at dawn, yet later lies by a favorite tree and gazes listlessly at a brook. He mutters his fancies, resembling a madman or a hopeless lover. He is everything that Gray's contemporaries thought a poet should be—a man of exquisite sensibility, unfit for the world's work, meditative, and sad.

The farmer recounts that he saw the poet's funeral procession to a church, presumably the one where the poem is set. He does not seem to have helped arrange the funeral nor, unlike the reader, can he read the epitaph that concludes the poem (Gray may be indicating that the farmer's social class is not that of the poet and the reader). Perhaps Gray, in indicating that the poet chose to be buried where people of his class are not usually buried, intended to reinforce that the poem's theme applies to all humankind.

In the three stanzas of the epitaph (lines 117 to 128), Gray speaks of his grave being "upon the lap of Earth" and not inside the church. He accords himself modest praise and justifies his life as worthwhile. Despite his "humble birth," he was well educated. Although some may consider the poet's natural melancholý a disadvantage, he himself probably thought it the source of his poetic temperament. Gray describes himself as generous and sincere, for which his reward was not worldly fame or fortune (the "paths of glory") but Heaven "recompense," undoubtedly the "friend" mentioned in line 124. The epitaph concludes by telling the reader not to ask more about the poet's virtues and frailties but to leave him to God.

"Elegy Written in a Country Churchyard" moves from a meditation in a particular place upon the graves of the poor to a reflection on the mortality of all humankind and on some of the benefits of being constrained by poverty. The poem alludes to the wish of all people not to die and to the ways in which each is remembered after death. Gray concludes by imagining his own death and how he hopes to be remembered. If this progression of thought is not entirely logical, it is all the more understandable. One reason for the long popularity of Gray's elegy lies in the universal chord he managed to strike not only with the thoughts he expressed but, perhaps even more important, with the progression he gave those thoughts. Beyond that, the poem contains some of the most striking lines of English poetry.

George Soule

Bibliography:
Brady, Frank. "Structure and Meaning in Gray's *Elegy*." In *From Sensibility to Romanticism: Essays Presented to Frederick A. Pottle*, edited by Frederick W. Hilles and Harold Bloom. New York: Oxford University Press, 1965. In his lucid and careful reading of Gray's elegy, Brady stresses the appropriateness of the closing "epitaph." (The book contains two other essays on the "Elegy Written in a Country Churchyard.")

Brooks, Cleanth. "Gray's Storied Urn." In *The Well Wrought Urn: Studies in the Structure of Poetry*. New York: Reynal & Hitchcock, 1947. In a celebrated and important close reading of the poem, Brooks argues that the "Elegy Written in a Country Churchyard" is rich in irony and implication. Essential reading for any interpreter of the work.

Lonsdale, Roger, ed. *The Poems of Thomas Gray, William Collins, Oliver Goldsmith*. London: Longman, 1969. Lonsdale's introduction to Gray's elegy and his notes to the text are invaluable, especially on the difficulties of lines 93 to 96.

Sells, A. L. Lytton, assisted by Iris Lytton Sells. *Thomas Gray: His Life and Works*. London: George Allen & Unwin, 1980. This biography includes frequent references to Gray's elegy and includes a lengthy discussion of the work. Sells believes that the epitaph refers to Richard West.

Weinfield, Henry. *The Poet Without a Name: Gray's "Elegy" and the Problem of History*. Carbondale: Southern Illinois University Press, 1991. A scholarly book that employs a variety of critical methods to establish the poem's significance. Weinfield, who gives his own intricate reading of the work in chapter 3, considers the "thee" in line 93 to refer to all of humanity.

ELMER GANTRY

Type of work: Novel
Author: Sinclair Lewis (1885-1951)
Type of plot: Satire
Time of plot: 1915-1925
Locale: Midwestern United States
First published: 1927

> *Principal characters:*
> ELMER GANTRY, a minister
> MRS. GANTRY, his mother
> CLEO BENHAM GANTRY, his wife
> LULU BAINS, his mistress
> HETTIE DOWLER, another of his mistresses
> OSCAR DOWLER, Hettie's husband
> JIM LEFFERTS, Elmer's companion in rowdiness during his days at
> Terwillinger College
> JUDSON ROBERTS, a former football star and state secretary of the YMCA
> FRANK SHALLARD, a minister and Elmer's chief antagonist
> EDDIE FISLINGER, a minister and distant admirer of Gantry
> WALLACE UMSTEAD, the director of physical culture at Mizpah
> Theological Seminary
> HORACE CARP, one of the high churchmen in the seminary
> HARRY ZENZ, the seminary iconoclast
> JACOB TROSPER, the dean of Mizpah Theological Seminary
> AD LOCUST, a traveling salesman for the Pequot Farm Implement
> Company
> SHARON FALCONER, a woman evangelist
> CECIL AYLSTON, her assistant
> ART NICHOLS, the cornet and French horn player in Sharon Falconer's
> three-piece orchestra
> MRS. EVANS RIDDLE, an evangelist and a New Thought leader
> T. J. RIGGS, a rich associate of Elmer in Zenith

The Story:

Elmer Gantry, known as "Hell-cat" to his classmates at Terwillinger College in Kansas in 1902, was a large man, six feet one, with a loud booming voice. He led the team as football captain and was twice elected class president. Although he was assumed to be popular, Gantry was not really well liked by his classmates. Elmer's father, Logan Gantry, a feed dealer, had died at a young age, leaving his widow to support herself and her son with her sewing. She was a religious woman and made Gantry go to church, where he learned about religion but failed to learn decency or kindness.

When the evangelist Judson Roberts spoke at the college for the YMCA Week of Prayer, Gantry was moved to kneel in prayer and announce that he had been saved. The crowd cheered for the passionate speech Gantry delivered following his conversion, and the president of the college told him he was a born preacher. Gantry's mother, who had attended the meeting, said it was her happiest moment. College officials and his mother urged Elmer to become a minister.

Gantry attended Mizpah Seminary, where he was ordained as a Baptist minister. While he was preaching in a small town, Gantry met Lulu Bains, the daughter of a deacon at the church, and seduced her. He promised to marry her but quickly tired of her. When Floyd Naylor and Deacon Bains threatened to beat him if he did not marry Lulu, Gantry claimed he had always planned to marry her, and they announced the engagement. In a scheme to get out of his commitment, however, he staged a fight with Lulu, and then left her alone with Floyd. As Floyd innocently embraced Lulu to comfort her, Gantry led Deacon Bains to the spot and shined a flashlight on the couple. Outraged to see his daughter kissing Floyd, the deacon forced Lulu to marry Floyd. Gantry pretended to be devastated by Lulu's betrayal and asked the dean for a transfer.

On his way to the new church, Gantry got drunk with a stranger he met on the train, passed out, and missed the church service. He was fired from the seminary and had to find work as a salesman for a farm implement company. On his travels, he fell under the spell of a female evangelist named Sharon Falconer. Acting as her assistant, Gantry paid people to fake being saved or feigned his own conversion. Following her rise to eminence as a healer of the sick, Sharon bought a resort on the New Jersey coast that she named "Waters of Jordan Tabernacle." By holding meetings there, she did not have to share her profits with local churches. When a workman carelessly discarded a cigarette, the tabernacle went up in flames and killed 111 people, including Sharon and her crew. Gantry had tried to lead Sharon to safety, but she had stubbornly kept her station, holding a wooden cross in front of her. Only Gantry survived.

Unable to earn a living as an independent evangelist, Gantry worked for Mrs. Evans Riddle, another evangelist, until he was fired for stealing from the collection plate. In 1913, Gantry met the Methodist church leader Bishop Toomis, who was impressed with Gantry's style. Gantry became a Methodist, and Toomis arranged for Gantry to serve as a minister in the small town of Banjo Crossing. There he courted and married Cleo Benham because he thought she would help his career. Gantry never returned the love Cleo felt for him, and after the birth of their second child, they moved into separate bedrooms.

At the age of thirty-nine, Gantry was given a large church in Zenith, a city with a population of 400,000. He became friends with T. J. Riggs, a famous trial lawyer and a trustee of the church. Gantry was a popular preacher and soon built up attendance. Preferring to spend time on church work and organizations, Gantry was seldom home and, when he was, he was so surly and critical that his own children were afraid of him.

One Sunday, Lulu and Floyd showed up at Gantry's church. Lulu was still in love with Gantry, and he felt physical attraction for her. Soon Lulu and Gantry were meeting secretly in the church on Tuesday nights.

Gantry met with other ministers in town on a regular basis, and after he had been in Zenith for a year and a half, he organized a committee on public morals to conduct an attack on the red-light district. He won attention in the press through a few carefully staged raids on small-time bootleggers and prostitutes.

Gantry's hellfire and damnation sermons continued to attract attention from the public and the press. Gantry also used his pulpit to denounce the religious views of his former classmate, Frank Shallard, who preached in the same town. As a result of Gantry's smear attack, Shallard was fired from his church. Later, thugs calling him a heretic beat Shallard so brutally that he lost the sight in one eye. Gantry called to offer condolences and said he would find and punish the offenders, but Shallard never heard from Gantry again.

As Gantry's success continued, he joined the Rotary Club, played golf with the wealthy men of the community, and spent money on expensive clothes. He convinced the officials of

Abernathy College to award him a Doctor of Divinity Degree so that people could call him Dr. Gantry. When his sermons were broadcast on the radio, his audience increased from 2,000 to 10,000. He traveled to London, New York, Los Angeles, and Toronto to preach.

Gantry fired his longtime secretary and hired Hettie Dowler, a beautiful young woman who soon became his mistress. To get rid of Lulu, Gantry told her that Cleo had found out about the affair and that he had to end their relationship. That left Gantry free to concentrate on Hettie. When Hettie and her husband tried to blackmail Gantry with the letters that Gantry had written to her, the press got hold of the news and denounced Gantry. A detective, hired by Gantry's friend T. J. Riggs, investigated Hettie and discovered enough information on her past activities to force her to sign a confession that exonerated Gantry. The newspapers announced Gantry's innocence, and the congregation cheered him on Sunday. Gantry vowed to avoid temptation in the future, but even as he knelt in prayer with his congregation, he noticed a pretty woman in the choir whom he wanted to meet.

"The Story" updated by Judith Barton Williamson

Critical Evaluation:

Sinclair Lewis wrote *Elmer Gantry* at the height of his fame, in the middle of the 1920's. That decade began for Lewis with *Main Street: The Story of Carol Kennicott* (1920) and ended with *Dodsworth* (1929) and included not only *Babbitt* (1922) and *Arrowsmith* (1925) but also their author's refusal of a Pulitzer Prize. Curiously, *Elmer Gantry* gives the first hint of the waning of Lewis' powers. Before this novel, Lewis had served a long apprenticeship and achieved great success. Between 1915 and 1920, he wrote fifty short stories and five novels, experimenting with his themes and characterizations and sketching out his satiric portraits of various types, not the least of these being religious types. The climax of that kind of portraiture came with *Elmer Gantry*.

Lewis spent years perfecting his method of research to establish the realistic foundation on which his satires rest. *Main Street* was a sensational best-seller, and apparently it occurred to Lewis that he could repeat his success if he would, in a programmatic way, turn his satiric eye upon the various aspects of American life in sequence. After his exposure of the village, he next chose Zenith, a middle-sized city, and George F. Babbitt, a middle-class businessman. Thereafter he applied his attention (in collaboration with Dr. Paul de Kruif) to medicine, public health, and medical experimentation. Finally, he found a challenging topic in the ministry. Undertaking an exposure of hypocrisy in religion was a formidable and dangerous task, but Lewis felt confidently ready for it. In *Babbitt*, he had written of Mike Monday, the evangelist; Mrs. Opal Emerson Mudge, leader of the New Thought League; and the Reverend John Jennison Drew, author of *The Manly Man's Religion*.

Following his usual method of research, he sought expert advice to provide the background for his novel. He turned to a minister in Kansas City, with whom he was acquainted, and he hosted a weekly seminar of local pastors of many faiths and sects; after luncheon, there might be a session on "The Holy Spirit," with Lewis challenging, pressing, arguing, and thus absorbing material. Gradually, the characters and plot of his novel took shape. In Elmer Gantry, Lewis created his most extravagant faker, a salesman of religion with no real knowledge of theology and no scruples or morals, a stupid man who would exploit his parishioners as he climbed to success from village to town to city, a seducer of women, and a man of greed.

Lewis gave much of his attention to his portrait of Sharon Falconer, the beautiful and somewhat mad female evangelist who preaches in a majestic temple and then leads Gantry to her retreat in the hills where she allows herself to be seduced on an altar she has built to such pagan goddesses as Astarte. Sharon says she has visions and confesses that she hates little vices like smoking and swearing but loves big ones like lust and murder. Yet from some confused notions about God, Sharon derives sufficient strength to stand at the pulpit in her burning tabernacle and attempt to quell the panic of the mob of her parishioners. By contrast, Gantry knocks aside dozens of helpless people and is able to escape. Into such scenes as these, and into the final episode in which Gantry is narrowly saved from entrapment in the old badger game, Lewis poured all his vitality. What critics have missed, however, and what seems to suggest the first waning of Lewis' powers, is the lack of any real opposition. In Gantry himself there seems to be no decency, therefore there are no alternatives contending in his soul. In the "good" characters there is insufficient understanding and fortitude, and they neither supply important alternatives nor force Gantry to any choices. In this book, Lewis displayed his virtuosity as a satirist, but he also indulged it and failed to find for it any opposition in positive values.

Bibliography:
Dooley, D. J. "Aspiration and Enslavement." In *The Art of Sinclair Lewis*. Lincoln: University of Nebraska Press, 1967. Examines Elmer's picaresque journey through American religion in the early twentieth century. Charges that the novel fails as satire because it is neither realistic nor witty.
Geismar, Maxwell. "Sinclair Lewis: The Cosmic Bourjoyce." In *The Last of the Provincials: The American Novel, 1915-1925*. New York: Hill and Wang, 1949. Suggests that Lewis has little insight into religious motivation or the commercial exploitation of religion. Criticizes the character of Sharon Falconer as neoprimitive and that of Elmer as archetypal opportunist and false prophet.
Grebstein, Sheldon Norman. "The Great Decade." In *Sinclair Lewis*. New York: Twayne, 1962. Explores the novel's background and describes its having been written in "the most hotly charged religious atmosphere in America since the Salem witch burnings."
Hilfer, Anthony Channell. "Elmer Gantry and That Old Time Religion." In *The Revolt from the Village, 1915-1930*. Chapel Hill: University of North Carolina Press, 1969. Perceives the novel as an attack on small-town provincialism. Discusses contemporary social changes such as the Scopes Monkey Trial, Prohibition, and the hypocrisy and corruption of some religious extremists.
Schorer, Mark, ed. *Sinclair Lewis: A Collection of Critical Essays*. Englewood Cliffs, N.J.: Prentice-Hall, 1962. Contains earlier criticism of *Elmer Gantry*, including Rebecca West's famous attack on the novel as ineffective satire and Joseph Wood Krutch's praise of the book, as well as Schorer's classic study, "Sinclair Lewis and the Method of Half-Truths."

ÉLOGES AND OTHER POEMS

Type of work: Poetry
Author: Saint-John Perse (Alexis Saint-Léger Léger, 1887-1975)
First published: Éloges, 1911 (English translation, 1944)

Alexis Saint-Léger Léger, who wrote under the name of Saint-John Perse, was born in Guadeloupe and had a long and very distinguished career in both the prewar and postwar French diplomatic service. He thus represents that peculiarly French combination of the public servant and the man of letters. Though his *Anabasis* (1924) was translated by so famous a writer as T. S. Eliot, he remained little known outside Europe. It is improbable that his work will ever achieve any wide degree of popularity; nevertheless, because of his marked influence on twentieth century poetry, he remains an important figure.

"Pictures for Crusoe," the earliest of the poems included in the volume, should be read first; they are the clearest and, once understood, provide a sort of key to the other sections. In them, the reader is made immediately aware of the author's childhood spent in the tropics; there is a succession of luxuriant images from the island left behind by Robinson Crusoe and the expression of nostalgia for clean wind, sea, and sand, and for the brilliant colors of dawn and sunset. It is the theme of this series of short poems that Crusoe's real disaster occurs when he returns to the cities of men and leaves forever the lost tropic island. Everything that he brings with him, every symbol of the island—the goatskin parasol, the bow, the parrot—decays in the sour dirt of the city; the seed of the purple tropic flower that he plants will not grow; even Goodman Friday, as he steals from the larder, leers with eyes that have become sly and vicious. Crusoe weeps, remembering the surf, the moonlight, and other, distant shores.

The same theme of nostalgia, much less clearly stated, runs through the longer poems entitled "To Celebrate a Childhood" and "Praises." Here the poet tries to recapture, by the same device of a series of pictures, the lost world of a childhood against the background of violent contrasts of brilliant light and shining water and crowding vegetation. The lush images succeed one another with bewildering rapidity until the lost childhood is re-created. Indeed, the images are heaped with such profusion that the poems become almost cloying, like overripe fruit. There is a shift of emphasis here also, for no longer is there a contrast between two worlds, the island and the city, but rather an almost total recall of both the beauty and the squalor of the tropics.

The second section of the book, "The Glory of Kings," consists of four poems, two written in 1910 and two in 1924. These poems are much more obscure than those in the first section. In them, Perse seems to have moved from the background of his childhood in Guadeloupe to the world of some primitive people where nameless speakers address praises to their half-human, half-divine rulers—the queen, a mysterious sphinxlike creature, at once the queen and the mother; the prince, with his towering headdress, the healer and enchanter, keeping vigil. It may be that Perse is trying to express something of the spirit in which members of a primitive society identify themselves with their rulers, until the king becomes the symbol, indeed the very soul, of his people and is rejoiced in as such. By implication, this belief is set against the critical, questioning attitude of twentieth century human beings, shorn of reverence, cut off from "the sources of the spirit." "The Glory of Kings" seems to develop further a theme that was already implicit in "Pictures for Crusoe," the cult of the primitive that appeared in the work of so many twentieth century writers.

Under the first pen name of their author, these early poems by Perse are referred to by Marcel Proust, who, in *Cities of the Plain* (1922), gives an appreciation of them and an indication of the likely reaction of the average reader: Lying on the narrator's bed was a book of the admirable but ambiguous poems of Saint-Léger Léger; Madame Celeste Albaret picks up the book and asks if he is sure that they are poems and not riddles. It is natural that Proust, preoccupied as he was with the evocation of the past in all of its subtle ramifications in time and place, would have delighted in a poet bent on the same task of recapturing the totality of the experiences of childhood—including the sights, the sounds, the odors. Nor is it surprising that these pictures from the tropics, so different from the hothouse, artificial life that Proust knew, should, by their very contrast, have appealed to him.

Yet by including the remark of Madame Celeste, so distressing to the narrator, Proust succinctly indicates the probable response of most readers of poetry who approach Perse for the first time. It cannot be denied that these poems make very difficult reading. T. S. Eliot, in his preface to his translation of Perse's *Anabasis*, tries to defend the author against the charge of willful obscurity by claiming that their seeming obscurity results from the linkage of explanatory and connecting matter, not to incoherence. Eliot's advice to the reader was to allow the images of the poem to fall into the memory with unquestioning acceptance, each contributing to a total effect that will be apparent at the end of the poem. It is an indication of the contribution that Perse makes to poetic technique that this analysis could equally well be applied to much of Eliot's own work.

It is by means of sequences of images, abruptly shifting into one another, that Perse achieves his total effects. This aspect of his poetry elicited the special praise of Valéry Larbaud, who considers his descriptions far superior to those of François-Auguste-René Chateaubriand because they are concrete, exact, precise, and filled with meaning. The result is a blending of the ugly and the beautiful, the whole a passionate rendering of experience. In his descriptions Perse makes full use of a device so characteristic of contemporary poetry: the sudden juxtaposition of the so-called poetic and the deliberately ugly or grotesque. A coconut, tossed into the street, "diverts from the gutter/ the metallic splendor of the purple waters mottled with grease and urine, where soap weaves a spider's web." It is intriguing to consider that such lines were being written in France in 1910, at a time when English poetry was dominated by the Georgians.

Few modern poets so little known to the reading public have received from their fellow poets such high praise as has Perse. His work has been translated into English, German, Spanish, Italian, Russian, and Romanian. Hugo von Hofmannsthal considered that a direct road leads from Arthur Rimbaud to the early work of Stefan George and to that of Perse. Valéry Larbaud maintained that between 1895 and 1925 perhaps a hundred poets appeared in France, of whom at least thirty would continue to be worthy of attention; of these thirty, only a few would survive. To both of these critics, Perse is valuable because of his attempt, through the manipulation of language and his brilliant descriptions, to revivify French lyricism. It may well be, however, that Perse will remain essentially a poets' poet, important to other writers because of what they can learn from his method, rather than a poet for the general reader. It is no longer necessary for the poet to appeal to the community and the wider view. He may now appeal to himself and the urgencies of his private vision.

Bibliography:
Archambault, Paul J. "Westward the Human Spirit: Saint-John Perse's Vision of America." *Papers on Language and Literature* 23 (1987): 365-381. A good discussion of Perse's poetry. Concentrates primarily on the influence of Perse's exile in America, but also discusses the influence of the poet's life upon his poetry.

Galand, René. *Saint-John Perse*. New York: Twayne, 1972. Ideal for serious research. Discusses the themes, symbolism, and influences on Perse's poetry in a systematic and chronological order. Also includes a chronology of Perse's life and an extensive bibliography.

Little, Roger. *Saint-John Perse*. London: Athlone Press, 1973. Excellent discussion of the collected poems. Extremely helpful for beginning study on the poet. Includes chapters on Perse's other writings and ways in which to interpret his poetry. Bibliography.

Ostrovsky, Erika. *Under the Sign of Ambiguity: Saint-John Perse/Alexis Léger*. New York: New York University Press, 1984. A chronological discussion of Perse's life in relation to his poetry. Ostrovsky attempts to take away the ambiguities inherent in Perse's poetry. Also includes a bibliography.

Sterling, Richard L. *The Prose Works of Saint-John Perse: Towards an Understanding of His Poetry*. New York: P. Lang, 1994. A good source for twentieth century French aesthetics, especially in relation to Perse's poetry. Includes a good bibliography.

THE EMIGRANTS OF AHADARRA
A Tale of Irish Life

Type of work: Novel
Author: William Carleton (1794-1869)
Type of plot: Regional
Time of plot: 1840's
Locale: Ireland
First published: 1848

Principal characters:
    BRYAN M'MAHON, an honest young farmer
    KATHLEEN CAVANAGH, Bryan M'Mahon's beloved
    HYACINTH "HYCY" BURKE, a well-to-do libertine and rascal
    JEMMY BURKE, Hycy's father
    NANNY PEETY, a beggar girl
    KATE HOGAN, Nanny's aunt and a tinker's wife
    PATRICK O'FINIGAN, a drunken schoolmaster

The Story:

Hycy Burke was the son of a wealthy and respected peasant who had allowed his wife, a woman with social pretensions of her own, to spoil the young man. With his mother's approval, Hycy had become a dissolute young man. Because his father, Jemmy Burke, tried to curb him, Hycy entered into partnership with whiskey smugglers to supplement the diminished allowance from his father.

When one of the prettiest girls in the area, Kathleen Cavanagh, caught Hycy's eye, he determined to seduce her. Unfortunately for his plans, he misdirected two letters. One, intended for Kathleen, went to Bryan M'Mahon, who truly loved the girl; another, intended for young M'Mahon, went to Kathleen. Later, publicly snubbed on more than one occasion, Hycy resolved to have revenge on the girl and her true admirer. Any additional villainy could scarcely put him in greater danger; he had already been an accomplice to burglarizing his father's house, taking a large sum of money, as well as being an active accomplice of smugglers. It was through his fellow smugglers that he planned to get his revenge.

At the time, there was a law in Ireland that required the inhabitants of a township to pay fines for illegal distillation and smuggling of whiskey if the actual culprits were not known. Bryan M'Mahon's farm at Ahadarra covered an entire township; if he were required to pay such a fine by himself, he would be ruined. To carry out his plan, Hycy tried to get the help of the nephew of the local gauger. Hycy promised the exciseman's nephew the chance to lease a fine farm if the latter would press Hycy's suit for his sister's hand. The farm, of course, was Bryan M'Mahon's.

Bryan was not the only member of his family facing tragedy. Both his and his father's farm leases had run out, and death had prevented the absentee landlord from renewing them. The new landlord, a well-meaning but weak and inexperienced young man, was ruled by his agent, who wished to see the M'Mahons lose their farms, leased by the family for generations.

Hycy carefully made his plans. What he failed to realize, however, was that he had made enemies while Bryan had made friends; consequently, some persons who knew of his villainy were prepared to take measures to thwart him. In his father's house was Nanny Peety, a pretty, virtuous beggar girl who resented Hycy's attempts to seduce her. She knew something of his plans, and she had been a witness to the burglary that Hycy and his accomplice had committed. Nanny Peety's aunt, Kate Hogan, loved her niece and thought highly of Kathleen Cavanagh. She was willing and able to help them, because she was married to one of Hycy's smuggling associates. Patrick O'Finigan, a drunken schoolmaster, was also friendly to Kathleen and Bryan.

The plot against Bryan was put into operation when Hycy's anonymous letter sent the gauger to discover the illicit still at Ahadarra, on Bryan's farm. Faced with financial ruin and his family's loss of their leases, the young peasant did not know what to do. Because his own honesty kept him from believing that Hycy was working against him in such a manner, Bryan even took advice from the man who was bent on ruining him. Before long, he found himself worse off by taking the advice. A parliamentary election was about to take place in which the M'Mahons' landlord was standing for a seat. The voting turned out to be a tie until Bryan, angry with his landlord and following Hycy's advice, voted for his landlord's opponent. By doing so, he made himself appear false in everyone's eyes, for his landlord was a liberal who favored the Irish peasantry and religious freedom, while the opponent was a conservative who worked against the peasants and the Roman Catholic church.

When Hycy sent another letter enclosing a fifty-pound note, it looked as if Bryan had accepted a bribe for his vote. The evidence was so damning that even Kathleen, who loved Bryan sincerely, was forced to believe him guilty. Faced with calamity and disfavor in his community, Bryan and his family planned, like so many unfortunate Irish at the time, to emigrate to America in order to start a new and more successful life.

Bryan's friends, however, began to work for him. Displeased at Hycy's treatment of her niece and the troubles facing Kathleen when she lost her fiancé, Kate Hogan began investigating Hycy's activities. She, Patrick O'Finigan, Nanny Peety's father, and others gathered additional information and presented it to the magistrates with demands for a hearing. At the hearing, it was proved that Hycy had robbed his father, had been an accomplice of the whiskey smugglers, had placed the still at Ahadarra to incriminate Bryan, had plotted to make his victim appear to have taken a bribe, and had also become a counterfeiter. Confronted with these proofs, Jemmy Burke gave his son two hundred pounds to leave the country and stay away. Hycy's accomplices were arrested, convicted, and transported as criminals from Ireland, thus becoming the "emigrants" of Ahadarra. Cleared of all charges, Bryan resumed his rightful place in the community and in the affections of Kathleen.

Critical Evaluation:

By the time that he wrote *The Emigrants of Ahadarra* in 1848, William Carleton was considered the truest novelist of Ireland's "awfullest hours," and William Butler Yeats was to concede that the Irish novel began with him. *The Emigrants of Ahadarra* was avowedly written not to amuse but to reform and inform. Published while the Potato Famine was raging, it is informative and readable. Folkloric value is enhanced by Carleton's exuberance and hyperbole, which are similar to the imaginative flights that created the ancient Celtic wonder tales. The novel loftily defends virtue. Kathleen's simple dignity and virtue are not cloying but almost biblical and contrast with the paler virtues of other characters. Bridget M'Mahon is also convincingly admirable and uniquely graces the story, which expounds human ideals. Landlords are near-ogres, members of secret societies, and Orangemen (although to a less prominent degree than in other of Carleton's works), but many individuals are tenderly etched. The novel is realistic, and, in the Spain of the same era, it would have been classified as *costumbrista*, owing to its museum-like presentation of customs.

Modern critics sometimes flay *The Emigrants of Ahadarra* for allegedly sloppy construction, mushy sentiment, and—curiously enough—vagueness of purpose. Carleton is also accused of inserting excessive scenery and folklore for their own sake rather than to augment the novel's dramatic effect. Carleton did lack the benefit of proofreading by his publishers, but the novel accomplished its obvious objective of dramatizing the life of the Irish country people of the time. Even its supposedly overdone rhetoric does not bore the reader.

One may maintain that readers have an accurate picture of the famine-ravaged Irish peasants from Carleton alone. Carleton was an enigmatic novelist who hated landlordism and the Penal Laws and who was a convert to Protestantism in a very Catholic land, but he scarcely owed loyalty only to his own pen as has been accused. Furthermore, some critics concede that they did not really know Irish life until they read *The Emigrants of Ahadarra*.

Carleton's fiction is best known for its realistic pictures of Irish peasant life during the nineteenth century, and *The Emigrants of Ahadarra* is one of his best novels in this respect. The most noteworthy sections are the chapters describing such things as a "kemp" (a spinning contest among the peasant women), a country funeral, an election, and the illegal distillation of whiskey. While his treatment of these matters is outstanding, the entire novel is filled with specific and colorful details of peasant life. The speech and character of the people, their homes, the farm routine, landlord-peasant relations, and whiskey smuggling, all are related with a view to giving the reader a true picture of rural Irish life in the nineteenth century.

Bibliography:
Flanagan, Thomas. *The Irish Novelists 1800-1850*. New York: Columbia University Press, 1959. An influential overview which did much to reestablish Carleton in the context of nineteenth century Irish literature and culture. Three chapters of the study are devoted to Carleton's work, though treatment of the short fiction is more extensive than that of the novels. The author's historicist approach emphasizes content rather than form.
Kiely, Benedict. *Poor Scholar*. Dublin: Talbot Press, 1948. Drawing on Carleton's *Autobiography*, this study remains the most accessible and sympathetic introduction to the novelist's world. The approach is essentially biographical, emphasizing Carleton's peasant background, awareness with the nature of which is indispensable for an appreciation of his work. Kiely does not provide a systematic treatment of Carleton's oeuvre, but the study contains some relevant commentary on the major works, including *The Emigrants of Ahadarra*.
Sloan, Barry. *The Pioneers of Anglo-Irish Fiction 1800-1850*. Gerrards Cross: Colin Smythe, 1986. Ranging more widely than Flanagan's *The Irish Novelists*, this study includes coverage of various phases of Carleton's career as a novelist. The brief comments on *The Emigrants of Ahadarra* locate the novel in the appropriate phase, and enable the reader to see connections between the novel's preoccupations and those of contemporary nineteenth century Irish fiction. The study includes a bibliography and an elaborate chronology of the literary period in question.
Sullivan, Eileen. *William Carleton*. Boston: Twayne, 1983. A critical introduction to Carleton's life and works. Discussion of *The Emigrants of Ahadarra* links it to Oliver Goldsmith's *The Deserted Village*, and the significance of the novel's theme of reconciliation is briefly noted. The study contains a comprehensive bibliography of primary and secondary sources.
Wolff, Robert Lee. *William Carleton, Irish Peasant Novelist*. New York: Garland, 1980. A brief general overview of Carleton's fiction. Commentary on *The Emigrants of Ahadarra* concentrates on the way the novel treats the social aspects of emigration. The novel's political context is also outlined.

ÉMILE
Or, Education

Type of work: Novel
Author: Jean-Jacques Rousseau (1712-1778)
Type of plot: Novel of ideas
Time of plot: Eighteenth century
Locale: France
First published: Émile: Ou, De l'éducation, 1762 (English translation, 1762-1763)

Principal characters:
JEAN-JACQUES ROUSSEAU, in the role of tutor
ÉMILE, a healthy and intelligent French orphan
SOPHIE, a wellborn, warmhearted young woman

Jean-Jacques Rousseau's treatise on education—a novel in name only—is addressed to mothers in the hope that, as a result of learning Rousseau's ideas on education, they will permit their children to develop naturally without letting them be crushed by social conditions. Children cannot be left to themselves from birth, because the world as it is would turn them into beasts. The problem is to educate a child in the midst of society in such a manner that society does not spoil her or him.

In *Émile,* Rousseau argues that education comes from nature, from other people, and from things. The education from other people and from things must be controlled, so that habits conformable to nature will develop. Children have natural tendencies that should be encouraged, for nature intends children to be adults; the aim of education, according to Rousseau, is to make a child an adult. Yet by swaddling children, by turning them over to wet nurses, and by punishing them for not doing what is said to be their duty, parents turn children from natural ways of acting and spoil them for life.

Rousseau insists that the proper way to bring up a child is to begin by having the mother nurse the child and the father train the child. If substitutes must be found, however, a wet nurse of good disposition who was lately a mother should be selected, and a young tutor should be chosen, preferably one with the qualities of Rousseau.

In order to explain his theory of education, Rousseau refers to an imaginary pupil, Émile. The child should come from France, since inhabitants of temperate zones are more adaptable and more intelligent than those from other climates. The child should be from a wealthy family, since the poor are educated by life itself, and should be an orphan in order to allow Rousseau free range as tutor. Finally, the child should be healthy in body and mind.

Rousseau recommends a predominantly vegetable diet, particularly for the nurse, since the milk would be better if meat were not eaten. The tutor should see to it that the child is taken out to breathe the fresh air of the country, and, if possible, the family should live in the country: "Men are devoured by our towns."

The child should become accustomed to frequent baths, but should not be softened by warm water or by other pampering that destroys natural vigor. The child should also not be allowed to fall into habits other than that of having no habits. Neither regular mealtimes nor bedtimes should be imposed, and, as far as possible, the child should be free to act as he or she chooses. Injuries or illness may result, but it is better for a child to learn how to live naturally than to become a weak and artificial adult.

"The natural man is interested in all new things," wrote Rousseau, and he urged that the child be introduced to new things in such a way that things that were not naturally fearful would not be feared. He offers, as an example of the proper kind of education in this respect, an account of what he would do to keep Émile from becoming afraid of masks. He would begin with a pleasant mask, proceed to less pleasing, and, finally, hideous ones, all the while laughing at each mask and trying it on different persons. Similarly, to accustom Émile to the sound of a gun, Rousseau would start with a small charge, so that Émile would be fascinated by the sudden flash, then proceed to greater charges, until Émile could tolerate even large explosions.

Rousseau maintained that cries and tears are the child's natural expression of needs. The child should not be thwarted, because there is no other way to learn to live in the world, and education begins with birth. On the other hand, the child should not be allowed to control the house, demanding obedience from the parents.

It was Rousseau's conviction that children must be given more liberty to do things for themselves so that they will demand less of others. A natural advantage of the child's limited strength is that a child cannot do much damage, even when using his or her power freely. A child will learn to speak correctly, to read and write, when it is advantageous to do so; threats and coercion only hinder progress.

Speaking of a mode of education that burdens a child with restrictions and that is, at the same time, overprotective, Rousseau wrote, "Even if I considered that education was wise in its aims, how could I view without indignation those poor wretches subjected to an intolerable slavery and condemned like galley-slaves to endless toil. . . ? The age of harmless mirth is spent in tears, punishments, threats, and slavery. You torment the poor thing for his good; you fail to see that you are calling Death to snatch him from these gloomy surroundings." Instead of torturing children with excessive care, he argues, one should love them, laugh with them, send them out into the meadows, and play with them.

"When our natural tendencies have not been interfered with by human prejudice and human institutions, the happiness alike of children and men consists in the enjoyment of their liberty." Here, the principle behind Rousseau's theory of education becomes clear. The tutor or parent should educate the child in such a way that the child will learn through his or her own efforts to be as free as possible within society. A child who is educated by rules and threats becomes a slave and, once free, seeks to enslave others. The most satisfactory general rule of education, Rousseau argued, is to do exactly the opposite of what is usually done.

Since the child is supposed to learn through personal experience, misdeeds should be punished only by arranging matters so that the child comes to experience the natural consequences of what has been done. If there is any rule that can be used as a moral injunction, it would be, "Never hurt anybody"; only trouble comes from urging children or adults to do good to others.

Rousseau rejected the use of tales and fables for children. An amusing analysis illustrates his conviction that even the simplest fable, such as "The Fox and the Crow," strikes the child as ridiculous and puzzling, and encourages the careless use of language and foolish behavior.

After the child has reached adolescence, intellectual education should begin. Prior to this time, the concern of the tutor was to give Émile the freedom to learn the natural limits of his powers. Now he teaches Émile by showing him the natural advantages of the use of the intellect. The tutor answers questions, but only enough to make the child curious. His explanations are always in language the child can understand, and he encourages the child to solve problems independently and to make his or her own investigations. Interest should lead the child to increase his or her experience and knowledge; it is a mistake to demand that the child learn.

Jean-Jacques, as the tutor, shows Émile the value of astronomy by gently encouraging him to use the knowledge that he possesses in order to find his way out of the woods.

Rousseau's accounts of his efforts to teach Émile owe some of their charm to the author's willingness to show himself unsuccessful in some of his efforts. Nevertheless, the pupil never becomes a distinctive character: Émile is merely a child-symbol, just as Sophie, the author indicates, is a woman-symbol devised to enable Rousseau to discuss marriage problems.

By the time Émile is fifteen years of age, he has gained a considerable amount of practical and scientific knowledge; he can handle tools of all sorts, and he knows he will have to find some trade as his life's work. In book 4 of *Émile*, Rousseau discusses the most difficult kind of education: moral education, the study of the self in relation to others.

Rousseau presents three maxims that sum up his ideas concerning human sympathy, the foundation of moral virtue:

First Maxim.—It is not in human nature to put ourselves in the place of those who are happier than ourselves, but only in the place of those who can claim our pity.

Second Maxim.—We never pity another's woes unless we know we may suffer in like manner ourselves.

Third Maxim.—The pity we feel for others is proportionate, not to the amount of the evil, but to the feelings we attribute to the sufferers.

These maxims fortify the tutor, but they are not imparted to Émile. The youth is gradually made aware of the suffering of individuals; his experience is broadened; and he comes to know, through personal experience, the consequences of various kinds of acts. The important thing is to turn his affections to others.

Émile is given insight concerning religious matters by hearing a long discourse by "a Savoyard priest" who tells of the difficult passage from doubt to faith. He affirms humanity's natural goodness and the reliability of conscience when uncontaminated by philosophers or by mere convention.

Sophie, or "Woman," is introduced in book 5, since Émile must have a helpmate. Rousseau begins curiously by saying, "But for her sex, a woman is a man"; but when he considers her education, it is apparent that sex makes quite a difference. Woman need not be given as many reasons as man, and she can get along with less intellect; but she must have courage and virtue. Rousseau offers a great deal of advice, even concerning Sophie's refusal of Émile's first attempt to share her bed. After a charming digression on travel, the book closes with Émile's announcement that he is about to become a father and that he will undertake the education of his child, following the example of his beloved tutor.

As a literary work, *Émile* stands near the beginning of a tradition common in European fiction: the novel of ideas. Character and incident serve only as pretext for Rousseau's more important task: the explanation of his ideas about the kind of education proper for men and women if humankind is to free itself from the self-imposed chains of social and political custom that have stifled individual happiness. Although dated in its precepts (Rousseau makes it clear that boys should receive significantly more elaborate and extensive education than girls), *Émile* espouses an attitude toward education that links its author with the great European Romantics who held that expression and imagination should take precedence over reason and socialization in human development. The hallmark of his plan for education is the liberation of the self from conformity to artificial social norms. For Rousseau, education should be a process of individualization, not socialization. Émile's tutor (a veiled portrait of the author) is little more than a conduit through whom Nature works her magic on the youngster, leading, rather than cajoling, him to appreciate both himself and the world around him.

In *Émile* and elsewhere, Rousseau attacks the conventional wisdom that elevates refined civilization as the greatest good toward which human society can aspire. He is especially vitriolic in castigating the intellectuals of his day who denigrate the simple life of country folk; in Rousseau's eyes, these people are promoting false values, especially in their praise for commercial and financial success. In this way, Rousseau is predecessor to two of the great figures of nineteenth century letters: William Wordsworth and Karl Marx. From Rousseau, Wordsworth takes up the cause of the rustic communities whose lifestyles seem to make people happier. His poetry celebrates the same qualities of natural inquisitiveness and appreciation for natural beauties that Rousseau recommends as the hallmarks of education. Marx's railings against the upper classes and his insistence on economic equality also have their roots in Rousseau's writings. Unlike the father of Communism, however, Rousseau was not an advocate of revolution; instead, he stresses in *Émile* the necessity for gradual change as means for achieving desired social ends.

Updated by Laurence W. Mazzeno

Bibliography:
Blanchard, William H. *Rousseau and the Spirit of Revolt: A Psychological Study.* Ann Arbor: University of Michigan Press, 1967. Explores the psychological motivation for the educational reforms developed in *Émile.* Describes well the many contradictions in Rousseau's writings on education.
Cranston, Maurice. *The Noble Savage: Jean-Jacques Rousseau, 1754-1762.* London: Penguin Press, 1991. Explores Rousseau's aesthetic and literary evolution during this prolific period in his career as a writer. The chapter on *Émile* describes both practical and unreasonable recommendations by Rousseau on educational reform.
Crocker, Lester G. *The Prophetic Voice (1758-1778).* Vol. 2 in *Jean-Jacques Rousseau.* New York: Macmillan, 1968. Analyzes the last twenty years of Rousseau's career. The lengthy chapter on *Émile* examines the conflict between Rousseau's praise of freedom and his desire for the teacher to control his pupils' activities.
Havens, George R. *Jean-Jacques Rousseau.* Boston: Twayne, 1978. Contains an excellent general introduction to Rousseau's life and career and an annotated bibliography of important critical studies on his work. The analysis of *Émile* stresses the positive elements in Rousseau's desire to sensitize parents and teachers to the emotional needs of children.
Wokler, Robert. *Rousseau.* New York: Oxford University Press, 1995. A thoughtful study of Rousseau's belief that successful educational reform will eventually make citizens unwilling to tolerate despotic governments. Describes well the many connections between *Émile* and Rousseau's *Social Contract* (1762).

EMILIA GALOTTI

Type of work: Drama
Author: Gotthold Ephraim Lessing (1729-1781)
Type of plot: Tragedy
Time of plot: Early eighteenth century
Locale: Guastalla and Sabionetta, two mythical principalities in Italy
First performed: 1772; first published, 1772 (English translation, 1786)

Principal characters:

EMILIA GALOTTI, a beautiful, middle-class young woman
ODOARDO GALOTTI, her father
CLAUDIA GALOTTI, her mother
HETTORE GONZAGA, the prince of Sabionetta and Guastalla
COUNT APPIANI, betrothed to Emilia
THE MARQUIS MARINELLI, chamberlain to the prince
THE COUNTESS ORSINA, a mistress spurned by the prince

The Story:

Prince Hettore Gonzaga, once happily in love with and loved in return by Countess Orsina, had fallen in love with Emilia Galotti. She was the daughter of a soldier who resisted the conquest of Sabionetta by the prince, and she was betrothed to Count Appiani from the neighboring principality of Piedmont. This union of a nobleman and a beautiful, middle-class woman was the result of her mother's studied plan.

The treacherous Marquis Marinelli proposed that the prince retire to his palace at Dosalo after sending Count Appiani on a mission to the Princess of Massa, to whom the prince had affianced himself after leaving Countess Orsina. Once her betrothed was away, Emilia would be vulnerable to the prince's designs. The ruler eagerly agreed to this plan.

Odoardo Galotti readied his villa at Sabionetta in preparation for the wedding of his daughter and returned to his wife in Guastalla to accompany the bridal party. A young assassin gathered these facts from a family servant so that he could plan the abduction of Emilia. Count Appiani, disturbed by presentiments of evil, had rejected the prince's proposal to send him off on his wedding day. He was killed for his temerity when the bridal party was attacked. Closely guarded, Emilia was taken to the palace by the prince's people, under pretense that they were rescuing her from brigands. There the prince, playing the gallant, allayed Emilia's fears by apologizing for his former behavior and promising to escort her to her mother. Claudia, in the meantime, was frantic at having been separated from her daughter. Grieving over the death of Count Appiani, she accused Marinelli of plotting this deed of treachery and violence.

The prince, beset by a furious mother and a swooning young woman whom he desperately desired, had not reckoned with the wrath of a rejected mistress as well. The Countess Orsina, whose spies had uncovered the prince's guilty secrets, arrived at the palace in Dosalo and, failing in an attempt to blackmail him, revealed Prince Hettore's guilt to Odoardo Galotti when he came in haste and unarmed to the aid of his daughter and wife. The countess, determined to have revenge on her former lover, gave Galotti the dagger she had intended to use herself. Galotti insisted on his rights as a father to take his daughter to her home, but his petition was denied by the crafty Marinelli. Meanwhile, the prince, unaware of Galotti's knowledge and purpose, tried to appear as a benefactor who would see justice done in the courts. Until that time, however, he would keep Emilia apart for security's sake. To this arrangement Galotti pretended to agree, ironically commenting on each provision of treachery as it was proposed.

When the anxious father was finally allowed to see his daughter, she told him that she feared her virtue might yield where force could never prevail, for the arts of seduction were brilliantly practiced in Prince Hettore's court. To protect her virtue, Galotti stabbed Emilia, presented her body to the lustful prince, threw the dagger at his feet, and went off to give himself up to the authorities.

Critical Evaluation:

There has never been a simple interpretation of Gotthold Ephraim Lessing's *Emilia Galotti*. The tragedy portrays a father-daughter theme at the same time that it portrays the tensions between the bourgeoisie and the nobility in eighteenth century Germany. Setting the play in Italy at the court of Hettore Gonzaga, Lessing skillfully used the Italian prince's character to criticize the nobility that rules its subjects according to whim and fancy. The prince gives his consent to a woman's request merely because her name is Emilia; because he is in a hurry, he carelessly pronounces a death sentence. The prince represents the corrupt and lascivious court where rulers who possess the weapon of gallantry indulge their romantic desires to the fullest and destroy women's lives without remorse. The prince's flaws become even more pronounced when Lessing introduces the character of Odoardo Galotti, Emilia Galotti's proud, upright father, who belongs to the middle class and remains purposefully aloof from the court because he regards it as a place of decadence. His contempt for the court is so strong that he has only unwillingly allowed his wife and his daughter to stay in the city in its vicinity for the sake of Emilia's education. He himself spends his retirement years on his country estate.

Despite portraying the prince as a man with great shortcomings, Lessing is successful in also making him a likable character. He is a young man who finds it hard to exercise control over his amorous leanings, prevaricates when he should be firm, and trusts his aides too much. Because he is diffident about making decisions, he depends on his chamberlain, Marinelli, who sets the various plots in motion. To some extent, Lessing directs his audience's wrath away from the prince toward his chamberlain, which may be interpreted as a softening of his stance toward the ruling class. The prince is thus presented as a victim of his circumstances who is exploited through his vulnerability. At the conclusion of the play, the prince even bemoans the fact that to be a prince and a human being is tragic. A prince must be able to rule his emotions to rule effectively, but being a human being he finds it difficult to control his emotions. In the prince's exclamation: "Is it not enough, for the misery of the many, that princes are human? Must it also be that devils disguise themselves as their friends?" Lessing shifts the blame of Emilia Galotti's tragic death to Marinelli. The prince is reduced to a mere puppet in the hands of his corrupt court official.

Because Emilia knows that her father values chaste thoughts and conduct above everything else, she asks him to stab her so that her virtue may remain intact, crying out, "What we call brute force is nothing: seduction is the only true force.—I have blood pulsing in my veins, my father, blood that is as youthful, as warm as anyone's. And my senses are senses too. I vouch for nothing. I will be responsible for nothing." In his depiction of Odoardo Galotti's regard for virtue that exceeds his love for his daughter, Lessing draws attention to the emptiness of the concept of bourgeois morality. He forces the audience to ask whether this bourgeois concept of virtue must indeed be upheld at the cost of human life.

Lessing's characterization of the prince's previous mistress, Countess Orsina, provides yet another character type, a fiercely independent, active woman. The dagger she carries with her when she visits the prince in Dosalo shows that she is even ready to avenge her humiliation caused by the prince's rejection. In fact, she is indirectly responsible for Emilia Galotti's stabbing, because she provokes Odoardo by saying, "The bridegroom is dead: the bride—your daughter—worse than dead." Countess Orsina's characterization also reveals Lessing's concern about the strict imposition of gender roles during his time. Orsina correctly understands the limitations imposed on her sex. When the prince rejects her, she responds, "How can a man love a thing that wants to think in spite of him? A woman who thinks is as loathsome as a man who powders his nose." Lessing may have given these words to Orsina, who is on the verge of madness and an ambiguous character in the play, so as to disassociate himself from too obvious an endorsement of her views. Their mere expression, however, brings to the fore the subject of gender inequality and its tragic consequences.

"Critical Evaluation" by Vibha Bakshi Gokhale

Bibliography:

Allison, Henry E. *Lessing and the Enlightenment.* Ann Arbor: University of Michigan Press, 1966. Excellent source for information on Lessing's philosophy of religion.

Brown, F. Andrew. *Gotthold Ephraim Lessing.* New York: Twayne, 1971. Remains a good introduction to Lessing's life as a critic, dramatist, and theologian. Lessing's major works have been discussed against the backdrop of eighteenth century German literature and culture.

Graham, Ilse. *Goethe and Lessing: The Wellsprings of Creation.* New York: Barnes & Noble Books, 1973. Offers a new reading of *Emilia Galotti* by concentrating on the ideal image of the character and the failure of its realization. Discusses Lessing and Johann Wolfgang von Goethe's different sources of creativity.

Lessing, Gotthold Ephraim. *Emilia Galotti.* Translated by Edward Dvoretzky. New York: Felix Ungar, 1962. Introduction provides information about the source of this play and its reception in eighteenth century Germany. Translation has successfully retained the original flavor of the play by taking into account its rhetorical devices.

_____. *"Nathan the Wise," "Minna von Barnhelm," and Other Plays and Writings.* Edited by Peter Demetz. New York: Continuum, 1991. Includes a foreword by Hannah Arendt, which discusses Lessing's idea of friendship and fraternity and its political relevance in eighteenth century Germany. Also provides translations of selections from Lessing's philosophical and theological writings.

EMINENT VICTORIANS

Type of work: Biography
Author: Lytton Strachey (1880-1932)
First published: 1918

Principal personages:
HENRY EDWARD MANNING, a cardinal of the Roman Catholic church
FLORENCE NIGHTINGALE, a nineteenth century career woman
DR. THOMAS ARNOLD, an English educator
CHARLES GEORGE GORDON, a British general

Although they have been considered controversial, the biographical writings of Lytton Strachey are never dull. When he addresses himself to the Victorian period, those writings possess a special interest, for the biographer himself was a product of that period, and his feelings about it, while mixed, were far from being vague or uncertain. The age of Victoria at once fascinated and repelled him. Its pretentiousness exasperated the artist in Strachey, but he could not help acknowledging its solidity and force and its many outstanding scientists and individuals.

Four such individuals are his subjects in *Eminent Victorians*. Not the greatest of their time, these four, superficially diverse in their activities, yet belong among the most appropriate representatives of the age. Strachey picked an ecclesiastic, a woman of action, an educational authority, and a man of adventure to illustrate the multifaceted era in which they lived and worked. The quartet of portraits proved to be a critical and financial success, and it became the cornerstone of an increasingly solid career. After its publication, Strachey was no longer in need of assistance from family or friends. Yet his treatment of Cardinal Manning, Florence Nightingale, Arnold of Rugby, and General Gordon did not go unchallenged. He was accused of having been unduly severe with his subjects, of handling facts with carelessness, and of indulging in superficial judgments. Such indictments often came from partisans of one or more of the subjects of *Eminent Victorians*, but not infrequently they were joined by more objective critics as well.

Some of these critics overlooked the point that Strachey's biographical method aimed at verisimilitude, not photographic realism. His determination to rise above mere facts sometimes carried him too far—to outright and even outrageous caricature—but the writing remained brilliant and stimulating. The intelligent reader is more likely to be diverted than deceived by the author's prejudices and dislike, for they are hardly disguised. Whatever charges may be brought against Strachey today, it is generally admitted that he brought to biographical writing good proportion, good style, and colorful realism.

Cardinal Manning provided ideal biographical material and, despite his distinction as a churchman, he does not escape a touch of the Strachey lash. This representative of ancient tradition and uncompromising faith is revealed as a survivor from the Middle Ages who forced the nineteenth century to accept him as he was. Practical ability, rather than saintliness or learning, was the key to his career. In the Middle Ages, says Strachey, he would have been neither a Francis nor an Aquinas, but he might have been an Innocent.

Very early in his life, Manning had fixed his hopes on a position of power and influence in the world. Upon leaving college he aspired to a political career, but its doors were abruptly closed to him by his father's bankruptcy. He tried the Church of England as an alternative, perhaps less promising, avenue to fulfillment. By 1851, already over forty, he had become an archdeacon, but this was not enough for him. For some time his glance had been straying to other pastures; finally, he made the break and became a convert to Roman Catholicism. In the process he lost a friend—a rather important one—named William Gladstone.

Thereafter his ecclesiastical career was an almost unbroken series of triumphs and advances. One important asset was the ability to make friends in the right places, especially in the Vatican. Manning became the supreme commander of the Roman Church in England, then a cardinal. His magnetism and vigor spread his influence beyond church boundaries; and at his death crowds of working people thronged the route of his funeral procession. At the end of a long and twisted road, his egoism, fierce ambition, and gift for intrigue had brought him desired as well as some unexpected rewards, not least among them the regard of the poor.

The second of Strachey's eminent Victorians is Florence Nightingale. In his treatment of one of the most remarkable women of any age, the biographer is conspicuously successful in resisting any urge to be gallant. What her friends called calm persuasiveness, he characterized as demoniac fury; it is clear that to him the "Lady with a Lamp" might have been extremely capable but she was also tiresomely demanding and disagreeable. His account makes clear the almost miraculous energy and endurance that carried Nightingale past the many obstacles in her path.

For the sake of convenience, Strachey divides Florence Nightingale's accomplishments into two phases. The first is her dramatic contribution to the welfare of the British wounded during the course of the Crimean campaign; the second deals with her unflagging efforts after the war to transform the Army Medical Department, revolutionize hospital services, and work much-needed reform in the War Office itself. These aims dominated her completely, and in their execution she drove her friends ruthlessly but used herself with even less mercy. Enduring to the age of ninety, she became a legend, though, ironically and cruelly, her last years brought senility and softness upon her. They also brought, after consciousness had dulled almost into insensibility, the Order of Merit.

Dr. Thomas Arnold, the father of the poet and critic Matthew Arnold, is generally considered to have been the founder of the British public school system. Strachey's bias against the doctor is obvious in *Eminent Victorians*, based largely on the fact that Dr. Arnold was determined to make good Christians, as well as good Englishmen, out of his public school boys. (Strachey had little patience with either Christianity or Christian institutions, a point of view that colors his attitude toward all his subjects in *Eminent Victorians*.) Strachey also disapproved of the prefectorial system Arnold instituted at Rugby, which Strachey credits with two dubious, if unexpected, effects on later English education: the worship of athletics and the worship of good form. Although to some Victorians, Arnold was one of the most influential pedagogues, Strachey considered him the apostle of harmful and absurd ideas.

It is with apparent relief that the biographer turns to his fourth and final portrait, which provides a strong contrast between the single-mindedness of the educator and the maddening inconsistencies of General Charles George Gordon. The general's personality is unveiled as a mass of contradictions whom no biographer could ever hope completely to unravel. A mischievous, unpredictable boy, he developed into an undisciplined, unpredictable man, and a romantic legend wove itself about his early, swashbuckling exploits in China and Africa. His deeds were genuinely heroic—no one has ever questioned Gordon's bravery—but they combined oddly with his passion for religion. He was influenced strongly, and to an approximately equal degree, by brandy and the Bible. Inclined, on the whole, to be unsociable, he maintained an icy reserve, except for fits of ungovernable temper vented upon unlucky servants or trembling subordinates.

This is the man who, in his fifties, was chosen by the English government for a delicate African mission. The mission, a military one requiring the utmost of a negotiator's self-control, tact, and skill, was the arrangement for the inglorious evacuation of British forces from the Sudan, a project for which Gordon was disqualified by his opinions, his character, and everything in his life. What followed was the tragedy at Khartoum, an episode seldom matched in military annals for the mystery and horror with which it enveloped the fate of the principal actor.

Thus the biographer's searching glance at four eminent Victorians ends on a dramatic note. Widely differing in background, vocation, and personality, the four individuals illustrate different phases of the England of the later nineteenth century. They are related to one another, however, by the possession of a restless, questing vitality, by the fact that each left a mark upon the age.

Bibliography:

Altick, Richard. "Eminent Victorianism: What Lytton Strachey Hath Wrought." *American Scholar* 64, no. 1 (Winter, 1995): 81-89. Argues that Strachey's aim in *Eminent Victorians* was explicitly literary. Because he took such liberties with historical fact, it is Strachey's method that came to be discredited, rather than the Victorian ethos he attempted to subvert.

_____. "The Stracheyan Revolution." In *Lives and Letters: A History of Literary Biography in England and America*. New York: Alfred A. Knopf, 1966. An excellent summary of the pivotal role played by *Eminent Victorians* in the development of biography as a genre. Surveys Strachey's iconoclastic strategies.

Holroyd, Michael. *Lytton Strachey: The New Biography*. New York: Farrar, Straus, and Giroux, 1995. Provides a rich historical context for understanding the development of *Eminent Victorians*, including information regarding negotiations with Strachey's publisher. The first and fuller version of this biography (published in 1968) contains more literary criticism.

Powell, John. "Official Lives: Lytton Strachey and the Queen Victoria's Ministers." *Nineteenth Century Prose* 22, no. 2 (Fall, 1995): 129-152. An analysis of Strachey's introductory indictment of so-called official lives. Argues that a preoccupation with aesthetic form obscured his concern for accurate biographical representation.

Stratford, Jenny. "Eminent Victorians." *British Museum Quarterly* (Spring, 1968): 93-96. Provides a full description of Strachey's four exercise books of notes and drafts, which are now in the British Library. Discusses the various influences on Strachey's writing.

EMMA

Type of work: Novel
Author: Jane Austen (1775-1817)
Type of plot: Domestic realism
Time of plot: Early nineteenth century
Locale: Surrey, England
First published: 1816

Principal characters:
EMMA WOODHOUSE, the heiress of Hartfield
MR. WOODHOUSE, her father
HARRIET SMITH, Emma's protégée
MISS BATES, the village gossip
JANE FAIRFAX, Miss Bates's niece
MR. GEORGE KNIGHTLEY, a landowner of the neighborhood
MRS. WESTON, Emma's former governess
FRANK CHURCHILL, the stepson of Emma's former governess
MR. ELTON, a rector
ROBERT MARTIN, a yeoman

The Story:

A rich, clever, and beautiful young woman, Emma Woodhouse was no more spoiled and self-satisfied than one would expect under such circumstances. She had just seen her friend, companion, and former governess, Miss Taylor, married to a neighboring widower, Mr. Weston. While the match was suitable in every way, Emma could not help sighing over her loss, for now only she and her father were left at Hartfield, and Mr. Woodhouse was too old and too fond of worrying about trivialities to be a sufficient companion for his daughter.

The Woodhouses were the great family in the village of Highbury. In their small circle of friends, there were enough middle-aged ladies to make up card tables for Mr. Woodhouse, but there was no young lady to be a friend and confidante to Emma. Lonely for her beloved Miss Taylor, now Mrs. Weston, Emma took under her wing Harriet Smith, the parlor boarder at a nearby boarding school. Although not in the least brilliant, Harriet was a pretty seventeen-year-old girl with pleasing, unassuming manners and a gratifying habit of looking up to Emma as a paragon.

Harriet was the natural daughter of some mysterious person; Emma, believing that the girl might be of noble family, persuaded her that the society in which she had moved was not good enough for her. She encouraged her to give up her acquaintance with the Martin family, respectable farmers of some substance though of no fashion. Instead of thinking of Robert Martin as a husband for Harriet, Emma influenced the girl to aspire to Mr. Elton, the young rector.

Emma believed from Mr. Elton's manner that he was beginning to fall in love with Harriet, and she flattered herself on her matchmaking schemes. Mr. Knightley, the brother of a London lawyer married to Emma's older sister and one of the few people who could see Emma's faults, was concerned about her intimacy with Harriet. He warned her that no good could come of it for either Harriet or herself, and he was particularly upset when he learned that Emma had influenced Harriet to turn down Robert Martin's proposal of marriage. Emma herself suffered from no such qualms, for she was certain that Mr. Elton was as much in love with Harriet as Harriet—through Emma's instigation—was with him.

Emma suffered a rude awakening when Mr. Elton, finding her alone, asked her to marry him. She suddenly realized that what she had taken for gallantries to Harriet had been meant for herself; he had taken what Emma had intended as encouragement to his suit of her friend as encouragement to aspire for her hand. His presumption was bad enough, but the task of breaking the news to Harriet was much worse.

Another disappointment occurred in Emma's circle. Frank Churchill, who had promised for months to come to see his father and new stepmother, again put off his visit. Churchill, Mr. Weston's son by a first marriage, had taken the name of his mother's family. Mr. Knightley believed that the young man now felt superior to his father. Emma argued with Mr. Knightley, but she found herself secretly agreeing with him. Although the Hartfield circle was denied Churchill's company, it did acquire an addition in the person of Jane Fairfax, a niece of the garrulous Miss Bates. Jane rivaled Emma in beauty and accomplishment; this was one reason why, as Mr. Knightley hinted, Emma had never been friendly with her. Emma blamed Jane's reserve for their somewhat cool relationship.

Soon after Jane's arrival, the Westons received a letter from Churchill setting another date for his visit. This time he actually appeared, and Emma found him a handsome, well-bred young man. He frequently called on the Woodhouses and also on the Bates family, because of a prior acquaintance with Jane Fairfax. Emma rather than Jane was the recipient of his gallantries, however, and Emma could see that Mr. and Mrs. Weston were hoping that the romance would prosper.

About this time, Jane Fairfax received the handsome but anonymous gift of a pianoforte. It was presumed to have come from wealthy friends with whom Jane, who was an orphan, had lived, but Jane seemed embarrassed with the present and refused to discuss it. After Mrs. Weston pointed out to Emma that Mr. Knightley seemed to show great preference and concern for Jane, Emma began to wonder if the gift had come from him. Emma could not bear to think of Mr. Knightley's marrying Jane Fairfax; after observing them together, she concluded to her own satisfaction that he was motivated by friendship, not love.

It was now time for Frank Churchill to end his visit, and he departed with seeming reluctance. During his last call at Hartfield, he appeared desirous of telling Emma something of a serious nature; but she, believing him to be on the verge of a declaration of love, did not encourage him because in her daydreams she always saw herself refusing him and their love ending in quiet friendship.

Mr. Elton returned to the village with a hastily wooed and wedded bride, a lady of small fortune, extremely bad manners, and great pretensions to elegance. Harriet, who had been talked into love by Emma, could not be so easily talked out of it. What Emma had failed to accomplish, however, Mr. Elton's marriage did, and Harriet at last began to recover. Her recovery was aided by Mr. Elton's rudeness to her at a ball. When he refused to dance with her, Mr. Knightley, who rarely danced, offered himself as a partner, and Harriet, without Emma's knowledge, began to think of him instead of Mr. Elton. Emma had actually begun to think of Churchill as a husband for Harriet, but she resolved to do nothing to promote the match. Through a series of misinterpretations, Emma thought Harriet was praising Churchill when she was really referring to Mr. Knightley.

The prematrimonial entanglement was further complicated because Mrs. Weston continued to believe that Mr. Knightley was becoming attached to Jane Fairfax. In his turn, Mr. Knightley saw signs of some secret agreement between Jane Fairfax and Frank Churchill. His suspicions were finally justified when Churchill confessed to Mr. and Mrs. Weston that he and Jane had been secretly engaged since October. The Westons' first thought was for Emma, for they feared that Churchill's attentions to her might have had their effect. Emma assured Mrs. Weston that she had at one time felt some slight attachment to Churchill, but that time was now safely past. Her chief concerns now were that she had said things about Jane to Churchill which she would not have said had she known of their engagement, and also that she had, as she believed, encouraged Harriet in another fruitless attachment.

When she went to break the news gently to Harriet, however, Emma found her quite unperturbed by it; after a few minutes of talking at cross-purposes, Emma learned that it was not Churchill but Mr. Knightley upon whom Harriet had now bestowed her affections. When she told Emma that she had reasons to believe that Mr. Knightley returned her sentiments, Emma suddenly realized the state of her own heart; she herself loved Mr. Knightley. She now wished she had never seen Harriet Smith. Aside from the fact that she wanted to marry Mr. Knightley herself, she knew a match between him and Harriet would be an unequal one, hardly likely to bring happiness to either.

Emma's worry over this state of affairs was ended when Mr. Knightley asked her to marry him. Her complete happiness was marred only by the fact that she knew her marriage would upset her father, who disliked change of any kind; she was also aware that she had unknowingly prepared Harriet for another disappointment. The first problem was solved when Emma and Mr. Knightley decided to reside at Hartfield with Mr. Woodhouse as long as he lived. Harriet's situation remained problematic; when Mr. Knightley had been paying attention to her, he was really trying to determine the real state of her affections for his young farm tenant. Consequently, Mr. Knightley was able to announce one morning that Robert Martin had again offered himself to Harriet and had been accepted. Emma was overjoyed that Harriet's future was now assured. She could always reflect that all parties concerned had married according to their stations, a prerequisite for their true happiness.

Critical Evaluation:

Jane Austen had passed her fortieth year when her fourth published novel, *Emma*, appeared in 1816, the year before her death. Although *Pride and Prejudice* (1813) has always been her most popular novel, *Emma* is generally regarded as her greatest. In this work of her maturity, she deals once more with the milieu she preferred: "3 or 4 Families in a Country Village is the very thing to work on." The seventh of eight children of the learned village rector, she had grown to womanhood in her native Hampshire village of Steventon. She spent the remainder of her life, except for brief intervals in Bath and Southampton, in another Hampshire village, Chawton, and was thoroughly familiar with the world she depicted.

The action of *Emma* cannot be properly considered apart from the setting of Highbury, the populous village only sixteen miles from London. Its physical attributes are presented in such circumstantial detail that it becomes a real place. London seems far away, not because of the difficulty of travel but because of the community's limited views. It is a village where a light drizzle keeps its citizens at home, where Frank Churchill's trip to London for the alleged purpose of getting a haircut is foppery and foolishness, where the "inconsiderable Crown Inn" and Ford's "woollen-draper, linen-draper, and haberdasher's shop united" dominate the main street. Emma's view of the busiest part of town, surveyed from the doorway of Ford's, sums up the life of the village:

> Mr. Perry walking hastily by, Mr. William Cox letting himself in at the office door, Mr. Cole's carriage horses returning from exercise . . . a stray letter boy on an obstinate mule . . . the butcher with his tray, a tidy old woman . . . two curs quarrelling over a dirty bone, and a string of dawdling children round the baker's little bow-window.

The novel concerns the interrelationship between an inconsequential place of this sort and Emma Woodhouse, a pretty, clever young lady almost twenty-one years old, who is rich and has few problems to vex her. Ironically, her world is no bigger than the village of Highbury and a few surrounding estates, including her father's Hartfield; in that small world, the Woodhouse family is the most important. As the author states, the real dangers for Emma are "the power of having rather too much her own way, and a disposition to think a little too well of herself."

These dangers are unperceived by Emma. In the blind exercise of her power over Highbury, she involves herself in a series of ridiculous errors, mistakenly judging that Mr. Elton cares for Harriet rather than for herself; Frank Churchill for herself rather than for Jane Fairfax; Harriet for Frank rather than for Mr. Knightley; and Mr. Knightley for Harriet rather than for herself. It is the triumph of Austen's art that however absurd or obvious Emma's miscalculations, they are convincingly a part of Emma's charming egotism. The reader finally agrees with Mr. Knightley that there is always "an anxiety, a curiosity in what one feels for Emma."

Emma's vulnerability to error can in part be attributed to inexperience, since her life has been circumscribed by the boundaries of Highbury and its environs. Although Emma's only sister lives in London, no mention is made of visits there. She has never been to the seacoast, nor even to Box Hill, a famous scenic attraction nearby. She is further restricted by her valetudinarian father's gentle selfishness, which resists any kind of change and insists on a social life limited to his own small circle; he is exclusive to the degree of admitting only four people as his closest acquaintances and only three to the second group.

Emma's own snobbery binds her to the conclusion that she has no equals in Highbury. Mr. Knightley well understands the underlying assumption of superiority in Emma's friendship for Harriet Smith: "How can Emma imagine she has anything to learn herself, while Harriet is presenting such a delightful inferiority?" Emma fears superiority in others as a threat. Of the capable farmer Robert Martin, Harriet's wooer, she observes: "But a farmer can need none of my help, and is therefore in one sense as much above my notice as in every other way he is below it." Her resolution to like Jane Fairfax is repeatedly shattered by the praise everybody else gives Jane's superior attractions.

While Emma behaves in accordance with her theory that social rank is too important to be ignored, she fails to perceive that she is nearly alone in her exclusiveness. Indeed, the Eltons openly assume airs of superiority, and Jane Fairfax snubs Emma. Emma's increasing isolation from Highbury is epitomized in her resistance to the Cole family, good people of low rank who have come to be regarded socially as second only to the Woodhouse family. Sure that the Coles will not dare to invite the best families to an affair, she finds only herself uninvited. She imagines her power in Highbury to be flourishing even as it is already severely diminished.

Emma's task is to become undeceived and to break free of the limitations imposed by her pride, by her father's flattering tyranny, and by the limited views of Highbury. She must accomplish all this without abandoning her self-esteem and intelligence, her father, or society. The author prepares for the possibility of a resolution from the beginning, especially by establishing Mr. Knightley as the standard of maturity for which Emma must strive. Emma is always somewhat aware of his significance, and she often puts her folly to the test of his judgment. There are brief, important occasions when the two, united by instinctive understanding, work together to create or restore social harmony; however, it is not until Harriet presumes to think of herself as worthy of his love that Emma is shocked into recognizing that Mr. Knightley is superior to her as well as to Harriet.

Highbury itself, which seems so confined, also serves to enlarge Emma's views simply by proving to be less fixed than it appears. As Knightley observes: "Your neighbourhood is increasing, and you mix more with it." Without losing her desire for social success, Emma increasingly suffers from it. She is basically deficient in human sympathy, categorizing people as second or third rank in Highbury or analyzing them to display her own wit. She begins to develop in sensitivity, however, as she experiences her own humiliations. While still disliking Jane, she is capable of "entering into her feelings" and granting a moment of privacy. Her rudeness to Miss Bates is regretted, not only because Mr. Knightley is displeased but also because she perceives that she has been cruel.

Despite her love of schemes, Emma shares an important trait with Mr. Knightley, one which he considers requisite for his wife—an "open temper," the one quality lacking in the admirable Jane. Emma's disposition is open, her responsiveness to life counteracting the conditions in herself and her circumstances, which tend to be constricting. Her reaction to news of Harriet's engagement to Robert Martin is characteristic: She is "in dancing, singing, exclaiming spirits; and till she had moved about, and talked to herself, and laughed and reflected, she could be fit for nothing rational." Too ready to laugh at others, she can as readily laugh at herself. Impulsive in her follies, she is quick to make amends. She represents herself truthfully as she says, in farewell to Jane, "Oh! if you knew how much I love every thing that is decided and open!"

A fully realized character who develops during the course of the action, Emma is never forced by the author to be other than herself, despite her new awareness. Once Harriet is safely bestowed on Robert Martin, she complacently allows their friendship to diminish. The conniving to keep her father reasonably contented is a way of life. If he wishes to marry her, Mr. Knightley is required to move into Hartfield. Serious reflection upon her past follies is inevitably lightened by her ability to laugh at them—and herself. The novel is complete in every sense, yet Emma is so dynamic a characterization that one shares Mr. Knightley's pleasure in speculation: "I wonder what will become of her!"

"Critical Evaluation" by Catherine E. Moore

Bibliography:
Bloom, Harold, ed. *Jane Austen's "Emma."* New York: Chelsea, 1987. In this representative selection of criticism, Austen scholars focus on aspects such as Emma's imagination and Austen's power of understatement. Also includes consideration of *Emma* in terms of feminist literary criticism. Index and bibliography.
Dwyer, June. *Jane Austen.* New York: Continuum, 1989. A good basic reference for the general reader. The chapter on *Emma* gives a reading of the novel and discusses the novel's focus on the problems that life poses for someone like the title character. Includes a bibliography.
Kirkham, Margaret. *Jane Austen, Feminism and Fiction.* New York: Methuen, 1986. Kirkham asserts that Austen's viewpoint on such topics as the status of women, female education, marriage and authority, and women in literature is strikingly similar to that of eighteenth century English feminists. Includes a twenty-page chapter on *Emma*.
Lauber, John. *Jane Austen.* New York: Twayne, 1993. The chapter on *Emma* gives a reading of the novel with special attention to the title character. It also discusses the novel's place in Austen's canon. The novel is also considered in the chapter "Austen and Her Critics." Includes a chronology, annotated bibliography, and index.
Lodge, David, ed. *Jane Austen: "Emma."* 1968. Rev. ed. London: Macmillan, 1991. Part of a highly regarded series of critical studies on well-known authors and their works. Includes reviews and critical readings by Austen contemporaries and more recent writers that were collected from books and journals. For the seriously interested reader.

THE EMPEROR JONES

Type of work: Drama
Author: Eugene O'Neill (1888-1953)
Type of plot: Expressionism
Time of plot: Early twentieth century
Locale: West Indies
First performed: 1920; first published, 1921

> *Principal characters:*
> BRUTUS JONES, the emperor
> SMITHERS, a Cockney trader
> LEM, a native

The Story:

Henry Smithers, a Cockney adventurer, learned from a woman that the followers of Brutus Jones, the self-styled emperor of a West Indian island, were about to desert their ruler. With Smithers' help, Jones, a former Pullman porter and escaped convict, had duped the natives into believing that he was a magician. The superstitious natives made him emperor of the island. Smithers disclosed to the emperor the disaffection of his subjects, who had been taxed and cheated by the pair beyond human endurance. Jones had judged that he had six more months of power before the natives caught on to his skullduggery. He had had a silver bullet cast as a good luck charm; it would be a useful tool if he were ever caught by his subjects.

At Smithers' suggestion, Jones rang a bell for his attendants; no one appeared. Jones resigned his position as emperor on the spot and made immediate plans to escape through the jungle to the coast. Drums began to beat in the hills. The former emperor gave the palace to Smithers, took up his white Panama hat, and walked boldly out the front door.

At the edge of the jungle, Brutus Jones searched unsuccessfully for the canned food he had cached for such an emergency. The drums continued to beat, louder and more insistent. Night fell, and formless fears came out of the jungle to beset Jones. The moon rose. Jones came into a clearing and there in the moonlight saw Jeff, a Pullman porter he had killed in a razor duel. Jeff was throwing dice. When the kneeling figure refused to answer him, Jones shot at him. The phantom disappeared. Drums still thudded in the distance. Jones, now sick with fright, plunged into the inky jungle.

After a while, he came upon a road and paused to rest. A chain gang came out of the forest. The guard of the gang motioned to Jones to take his place in the gang and to get to work. When the guard whipped him, Jones lifted his shovel to strike him, but he discovered that he actually had no shovel. In his rage of fear and frustration, he fired his revolver at the guard. The road, the guard, and the chain gang disappeared; the jungle closed in. The louder beat of the tom-toms drove Jones on in frantic circles.

Now in tatters, the terrified Jones repented of the murders he had committed and of the way he had cheated the islanders. He came next upon a slave auction attended by white people dressed in the style of the 1850's. An auctioneer put Jones on the auction block. Frightened, Jones shattered this apparition by firing one shot at the auctioneer and another at a planter. He dashed into the forest, mad with fear. The drums continued to beat.

At three o'clock, Jones came to a part of the jungle that strangely resembled the hold of a slave ship. He found himself one of a cargo of slaves who were swaying slowly with the motion of the ship. Jones and the other slaves moaned with sorrow at being taken away from their homeland. Having only the silver bullet left in his revolver, Jones saved it and dashed on again into the dark of the night.

Next he came upon an altarlike arrangement of boulders near a great river. He sank to his knees as if to worship. A Congo witch doctor appeared from behind a large tree and began a primitive dance. Jones was hypnotized by the ritual. The witch doctor indicated to Jones in pantomime that the former emperor must offer himself as a sacrifice in order to overcome the forces of evil. A great green-eyed crocodile emerged from the river; Jones fired the silver bullet at the monster, and the witch doctor disappeared behind a tree, leaving Jones lying on the ground completely overcome by fear.

At dawn Lem, the leader of the rebels, came with Smithers and a group of natives to the edge of the jungle, where Jones had entered it on the previous night. Lem had been delayed in pursuing Jones because of the necessity of manufacturing silver bullets, which, Lem believed, were the only means of taking Jones's life. Several of Lem's men entered the jungle. They soon found the prostrate Jones, who had been running in circles throughout the night. One of them shot Jones through the chest with a silver bullet. Jones's body was brought back to Lem, who thought that the silver bullet was what had really killed Jones. Smithers, however, looking at Brutus Jones's fear-contorted face, knew differently.

Critical Evaluation:

The production of *The Emperor Jones* by the Provincetown Players was a turning point for Eugene O'Neill. The play, a huge success both in Provincetown and in New York, represented O'Neill's first foray into expressionism, the European movement influenced by the work of Sigmund Freud and Carl Jung that emphasized presenting psychological reality on stage. With this production, O'Neill earned a reputation as an important playwright both in the United States and in Europe.

The play is a long, tightly constructed, one-act play with eight scenes. The first and last scenes form a realistic frame, beginning with Smithers informing Jones that the natives are preparing to hunt him down to finish his two-year reign as emperor, and ending with the native leader, Lem, and Smithers discussing the death of Jones.

The middle scenes portray a journey into the jungle that is both physical and psychological, for when Jones fearfully plunges into the dark tangle of trees, he is also entering the troubled recesses of his mind. During this journey, he must face hunger and heat, repressed violent incidents from his own past, and his collective racial past—from slave auction to a face-to-face encounter with an African crocodile god. Jones's journey into racial memory demonstrates O'Neill's debt to Carl Jung's concept of the collective unconscious.

O'Neill portrays Jones's psychological quest in striking stage images. The first scene features Jones's throne room, blindingly white except for accents of red and a huge rough throne dominating the stage. Jones enters in a red uniform, an imposing figure who clearly inspires fear in the cowardly Smithers, to whom he displays his pistol with its six bullets, the last one being silver, for Jones has convinced the natives that only a silver bullet can kill him.

When Jones leaves his palace and enters the jungle, he finds himself in an area of shadows and increasing darkness, the fading of the light paralleling Jones's movement into his own blackness. Sounds are also important. Before Jones leaves his palace, Lem's men start beating their drums at the tempo of a normal heartbeat, increasing this as Jones progresses, feeding his nervousness and the audience's tension. The pistol shots, which Jones uses to dispel his hallucinations, punctuate several scenes. The audience counts the shots (as Lem is surely doing as well), realizing that when the sixth shot, the silver bullet, is fired, Jones is defenseless—ready to become the sacrifice demanded by the crocodile god.

Another significant stage image is Jones's gradual loss of pieces of his uniform, a costume parody of white power and grandeur that Jones "has a way of carrying . . . off." When he is finally stripped to a remnant of clothing resembling a breechcloth, Jones has lost the overlay of white civilization and seems ready for his journey on a slave ship and a confrontation with the African culture of his ancestors.

The figure of Brutus Jones himself is a significant stage image. In 1920, American audiences were accustomed to the "stage Negro" stereotype, but O'Neill shatters expectations in two ways. The stereotype is a comic one. (On the rare occasions when African Americans were serious characters, they were portrayed as light-skinned, sometimes even "passing" as white.) The usual theatrical practice was also to cast white actors, who played black roles in blackface. Instead, O'Neill presented a black actor, Charles Gilpin, as a character who could be viewed as a tragic hero.

Jones displays a number of attributes of the Aristotelian hero. His status is elevated, and he is intelligent. He has learned the native language and has skillfully used the opportunities that have presented themselves. When a shot from a would-be assassin misses Jones, he quickly invents the myth of the silver bullet, keeping the natives under his control for a longer period of time. Jones also demonstrates the typical pride, and his hamartia, or tragic error in judgment, is clear. He has adopted the "garments" of the white civilization that had oppressed him in the United States, cutting himself off from his own culture.

Chief among these overlays are his greed and his emphasis on material gain for himself without consideration of the effect his rapacity will have on the native people for whom he should feel kinship. Instead, he contemptuously refers to them as "bush niggers" and "bleeds 'em dry," sending money to European bank accounts while planning his own escape. He tells Smithers he has learned his methods by listening to the "white quality" on the Pullman cars where he served as a porter. Another overlay of white society is the Christian religion. Although Jones "lays [his] Jesus on the shelf" as he exploits the natives, he expects "Lawd Jesus" will rescue him from the ghosts of his past. This does not happen, and he becomes the sacrifice demanded by the African god, slain by the natives he has exploited. They use a silver bullet made from melted money, an appropriate symbol for the fallen would-be capitalist.

O'Neill's use of dialect and of some stereotypical attributes has been seen as problematic, as is the fact that Jones's dialect becomes "blacker" as he progresses in his psychological journey, moving away from the trappings of "civilization" that he has assumed. Both Jones and the white Smithers are outsiders, speaking what is considered by insiders to be debased forms of the language. O'Neill's interest in sympathetically portraying outsiders is a consistent thread running through his plays, often attributed to his own experience with prejudice as part of the Irish minority in New England.

In addition to the theme of the outsider, O'Neill was concerned with the emphasis that American society places on materialism, which he viewed as a dangerously destructive force. Brutus Jones's fall becomes more tragic when one considers that, if Jones had resisted the values of white American society, he might have provided positive leadership for the natives on "his" island, thus advancing his people. From a historical perspective, it may be significant that O'Neill was inspired to create Jones in part by his knowledge of two Haitian dictators: President Sam, who spread the rumor that he could only be killed by a silver bullet; and Henri Christophe, who proclaimed himself emperor of part of Haiti, then later committed suicide.

The Emperor Jones marked the beginning of O'Neill's experimentation with expressionism and related theatrical devices. The success of this experimentation was mixed, but this play, with its interesting blend of realism and expressionism, is clearly a theatrical success.

"Critical Evaluation" by Elsie Galbreath Haley

Bibliography:
Bogard, Travis. *Contour in Time: The Plays of Eugene O'Neill.* New York: Oxford University Press, 1972. Bogard's study of O'Neill's plays revolves around his assertion that O'Neill's experiments with theatrical devices were part of his attempt to create theater from his quest for identity. The section on *The Emperor Jones* compares the play to Henrik Ibsen's *Peer Gynt* (1867).

Falk, Doris V. *Eugene O'Neill and the Tragic Tension.* New Brunswick, N.J.: Rutgers University Press, 1958. A study of O'Neill's plays with emphasis on the psychoanalytic theories of depth psychology, noting the influence of Carl Jung's theory of the collective unconscious on *The Emperor Jones.*

Floyd, Virginia. *The Plays of Eugene O'Neill: A New Assessment.* New York: Frederick Ungar, 1985. This study for general readers features analyses of fifty plays, supplemented with information from O'Neill's notebooks. The section on *The Emperor Jones* discusses O'Neill's use of expressionism, noting similarities to August Strindberg's *A Dream Play* (1907). Floyd considers this a "landmark drama" for the American stage, with its first use of an African American actor in a leading role in New York theater.

Frenz, Horst. *Eugene O'Neill.* Translated by Helen Sebba. New York: Frederick Ungar, 1971. Provides an assessment of the man whose experiments transformed American drama. In his analysis of *The Emperor Jones* as one of O'Neill's expressionist experiments, Frenz compares the play to Georg Kaiser's *From Morn to Midnight* (1917).

Martine, James J., ed. *Critical Essays on Eugene O'Neill.* Boston: G. K. Hall, 1984. Two essays in this collection are of interest to students of *The Emperor Jones.* Frank R. Cunningham's "Romantic Elements in Early O'Neill" views Jones as one of O'Neill's failed romantics. Lisa M. Swerdt's "Blueprint for the Future" examines the play as a seminal work, introducing themes that O'Neill would develop more fully in later plays.

ENAMELS AND CAMEOS

Type of work: Poetry
Author: Théophile Gautier (1811-1872)
First published: Émaux et camées, 1852; enlarged edition, 1872 (English translation, 1903)

Théophile Gautier's poetry forms the transition between Romanticism and the Parnassus school in France. As a young man, Gautier was a prominent member of the group surrounding Victor Hugo in the battle of *Hernani* (1830). Later, however, though he did not formally renounce his support of Romanticism, his name was to become associated with the doctrine of Art for Art's sake, and it is especially in connection with his body of ideas that his name is remembered.

Gautier's earliest poetry was collected into a volume entitled, simply, *Poésies*, first published in 1830. A pronounced taste for the middle ages, a love of lonely places, an impression of alienation, all traditional sources of inspiration for the Romantic poets, find a place in this collection, which is remarkable mainly for its lack of originality.

"Albertus, or the Soul and Sin," a long narrative poem describing a young painter's fatal infatuation with a witch, appeared in 1833. This work is little read today and indeed has little to recommend it. Worthy of note, however, is Gautier's use of the stock-in-trade of the somewhat unwholesome lesser Romantic writers: Slugs and toads, phantoms and vampires all have their place in this work.

"La Comédie de la mort" (*The Comedy of Death*), a long poem that came out in 1838, is in two parts. In the first, titled "Life in Death" and involving a dialogue in a graveyard between a worm and a corpse, the poet's intention to shock his reader is obvious. In the second part, "Death in Life," Gautier again tends to reveal the grotesque if superficial side of his Romanticism. Yet here the intensity with which the poet insists that death overshadows all of life would seem to suggest in Gautier a deep-seated pessimism with which he has not always been credited. This impression is reinforced by several pieces in his *Poésies diverses*, a collection of poems that appeared in one volume with *La Comédie de la mort*. Especially worthy of mention is a short piece called "La Caravane." Gautier develops beautifully the symbol of a caravan crossing the Sahara as suggestive of humankind in the world. The only oasis, the only resting place, claims the poet, is the graveyard; this idea is evoked in the simplest of terms: ". . . a wood of cypresses strewn with white stones."

Not all of the poems in this collection are pessimistic, however. "Chinoiserie" ("Chinese Fantasy") illustrates Gautier's taste for distant lands and things exotic. The poet affirms that his love goes out not to Shakespeare's Juliet, Dante's Beatrice, or Petrarch's Laura. Rather, he loves a girl in China who lives in a tower of porcelain:

> The one I love, at present, is in China;
> She is living with her old parents,
> In a tower of fine porcelain,
> At the Yellow River, where the cormorants are.

In no way profound, "Chinoiserie" is a delightful piece, which was subsequently set to music. It is worth remarking that even at this relatively early stage in his development, Gautier could offer his dream vision in a precise, finely executed form.

In 1840, Gautier went to Spain and stayed there for six months. The first edition of *España* appeared in 1845; in it the reader has the impression that the starkness and acute relief of the Spanish landscape and the paintings in the art galleries of Spain appealed to, and even sharpened, Gautier's eye.

In "Ribera" and "À Zurburan," two poems in *España* written in *terza rima*, Gautier reveals a remarkable talent for giving a life in verse to the paintings of the two Spanish masters. Moreover, in trying to understand José Ribera's love of ugliness, and the cruelty and violence of Francisco de Zurburán's studies of early Christian martyrs, Gautier makes his art criticism into a powerful art form in its own right. Elsewhere in this edition, Gautier's approach to his art is perhaps more characteristic of the plastic arts than of poetry. In "Le Pin des Landes," for example, it is the scene viewed that calls to mind the symbol, whereas more commonly a poet will seek out a symbol to illustrate or clothe an idea.

Gautier describes how in the Landes, an area of southwest France, the only tree to be seen is the pine, with a gash in its side, to allow its resin to drip into a bowl. He develops the symbolic value of the tree beautifully; the poet, standing upright and alone, is like the tree. For the poet is cut off from others by his superiority and their jealousy. When he is unhurt, he keeps his treasure, Gautier claims; he needs a deep wound in his heart to make him release his works, his golden tears:

> Without regretting its blood that flows drop by drop,
> The pine pours out its balsam and its frothing sap,
> And still it stands upright by the side of the road,
> Like a wounded soldier, who wishes to die on his feet.

> The poet is thus in the wastes of the world;
> While he is unwounded, he keeps his treasure.
> He must have a deep gash upon his heart
> To release his verses, these divine, golden tears!

"Dans la Sierra," which is also in *España*, involves a landscape as a symbol, too. Here Gautier, inspired by the arid mountains of Spain, insists that he prefers them to the fertile plains. The cult of beauty for its own sake, suggested in this poem, was to be worked up into a whole new poetic doctrine by Gautier.

The collection *Enamels and Cameos*, to which additions were made in the five editions between 1852 and 1872, marks a major development in Gautier's poetry; it is the collection for which he is best remembered as a poet, that which illustrates his doctrine of Art for Art's sake.

In order to understand this doctrine, it is worth recalling that, about 1930, writers were being urged to participate in the general effort toward social progress. As early as 1832, in the preface to his *Poésies*, Gautier declared that the value of art lay in its beauty and not in its usefulness: It was not the artist's business to exercise an influence on the crowd. "In general," he wrote, "as soon as a thing becomes useful, it ceases to be beautiful." Art, he claimed, was a luxury, offered to a small, elite public capable of understanding it. In the preface to his novel *Mademoiselle de Maupin* (1835-1836), moreover, Gautier went on to say that only that which serves no purpose is beautiful. In an article in *L'Artiste* he insisted that the artist's sole aim was to capture beauty.

Although it is dangerous to seek an explanation of Gautier's poetic doctrine in his life, two possible influences might be considered. In the first place, it should not be forgotten that if the subordination of idea to form brings to mind the plastic arts, Gautier did in fact start his career as a painter. In addition, it is worth mentioning that he earned his living as a journalist, drama critic, and art critic at a time when the writer risked becoming a commodity, the prey of unscrupulous editors and publishers. He was only too aware of the difficulties a writer faced in trying to retain his integrity.

On the other hand, Gautier had lived too close to the Romantic movement and was too much of a critic not to see that in trying to follow all the movements of their soul, the Romantics had frequently sacrificed accuracy for effect; he was aware that his companions had on occasion been guilty of expressing more than they had to say. It is against this background that one must understand the doctrine of art for art's sake.

In *Enamels and Cameos* can be seen an attempt to return to precision and clarity, even at the expense of subject matter. The title of the collection is significant; the poems grouped under it are highly polished, exquisitely crafted pieces. The tone of the edition is set by the preface. Here Gautier states that just as Johann Wolfgang von Goethe at Weimar cut himself off from the world to write, so he, Gautier, has disregarded the storms lashing his windows and has written *Enamels and Cameos*.

If Gautier's aim in poetry was now beauty, he tells how the poet might achieve this effect in a poem written in 1857 and added as a conclusion to *Enamels and Cameos*. In "L'Art," Gautier claims that like painting or sculpture, poetry is both an art and a skill to be learned. The poet, a craftsman, must have a firm grip on all the resources of the language. If he succeeds in overcoming all the problems of rhyme and syntax and vocabulary, while creating no artificial obstacles, the work of art will resist the ravages of time as no other human creation can:

> All things pass on.—Robust art
> Alone possesses eternity;
>   The bust
> Survives the city.
> The very gods die,
> But verse, sovereign,
>   Remains
> Stronger than the sword

In this collection Gautier's extreme attachment to form results in carefully executed, sophisticated poetry, which is generally more impersonal than anything he had previously done. On the other hand, the subject matter is often very slight: "Study of Hands," "To a Red Gown," and "The Tea-Rose" are representative titles.

In *España*, especially, Gautier had already attempted artistic transpositions, trying to achieve or reproduce in verse the effect obtained by a work of art in another medium. In *Enamels and Cameos*, such attempts become more ambitious. In "Variations on the Carnival of Venice," for example, the poet offers a series of four pieces in which the point of departure is a musical phrase from a Venetian song. In rhythmic, colorful verse, Gautier creates a picture of Venice as he imagines it once was.

In "Symphony in White Major," Gautier again attempts an artistic transformation, showing all the nuances and associations of white. This is perhaps a fine display of virtuosity, but there is little development within the poem, and the question arises whether poetry is in fact a suitable medium for such an exercise.

The appeal of *Enamels and Cameos* is by its very nature limited. In trying to banish himself from his work, Gautier is on occasion guilty of creating "cold" poetry. By shutting himself off from the world, he severely restricts his choice of subjects. It might be argued, moreover, that Gautier's choice of art for its own sake is made at the expense of content—that beauty of form is not enough.

It must be recognized that the "impersonal" poetry of the Parnassians owed much to Gautier, and that his artistic transpositions were of great consequence for Charles Baudelaire and the Symbolists. Moreover, if Gautier's creative talents were limited, he did, nevertheless, by his respect for his calling and for the word, renew a tradition that began with François Malherbe. Baudelaire no doubt lavished excessive praise on Gautier, but in writing that Gautier was a poet for whom the inexpressible did not exist he was probably paying his compatriot a compliment he merited.

Bibliography:

Cutler, Maxine. *Evocations of the Eighteenth Century in French Poetry 1800-1869*. Geneva: Librarie Droz, 1970. Examines ten of Gautier's poems to reveal how he relies on both the poetic tradition and a sense of the immediate past as stimuli for his work.

Dillingham, Louise. *The Creative Imagination of Théophile Gautier: A Study in Literary Psychology*. Princeton, N.J.: Princeton University Press, 1927. Provides a psychological explanation for the production of Gautier's works, including the poems. Useful for understanding the unconscious sources of the poet's imagination.

Grant, Richard B. *Théophile Gautier*. Boston: Twayne, 1975. Introductory study aimed at providing an understanding of Gautier's work to general readers. A chapter on *Enamels and Cameos* discusses Gautier's vision of art as he expressed it in these poems; also comments on structure and theme.

Richardson, Joanna. *Théophile Gautier: His Life and Times*. London: Max Reinhardt, 1958. Comprehensive biography of the writer. Comments on the publication of *Enamels and Cameos* and discusses its place in Gautier's canon. Also explores the diversity of ideas expressed in the poems which make up the volume.

Tennant, P. E. *Théophile Gautier*. London: Athlone Press, 1975. General introduction to the writer's works. Devotes part of a chapter to a discussion of *Enamels and Cameos*. Praises the variety of the collection, calling it "the melting pot of so many literary and artistic trends."

ENCHEIRIDION

Type of work: Philosophy
Author: Epictetus (c. 55-135 C.E.)
First published: c. 138 C.E. (English translation, 1567)

The *Encheiridion*, or "manual," is a collection of short essays representing the principal teachings of the Greek philosopher Epictetus. Born as a slave in Phrygia (now Turkey), Epictetus was brought to Rome by his master, who was an influential freedman of the Roman Emperor Nero. Epictetus was permitted to study under the famous philosopher Musonius Rufus. After he obtained his freedom, he began to lecture informally on philosophy at Rome, where, however, he found few followers. Later, when Greek philosophers were exiled from Rome by Emperor Domitian, Epictetus traveled to Nicopolis in Greece and established a school that attracted large numbers of students. Like Socrates, Epictetus wrote nothing himself, but a devoted student, Flavius Arrian, transcribed his brilliant lectures and gave them the title *Discourses*; a considerable portion of this work survives. Arrian made a short selection of these lectures and published them separately as the *Encheiridion*. These two works, the only surviving examples of actual academic teaching by a Stoic philosopher, had enormous influence on the later development of this school of philosophy. Moreover, the *Encheiridion*, with its convenient distillation of the philosopher's powerful ethical message, left its mark on the thought of a wide range of later readers who include Marcus Aurelius, Michel Eyquem de Montaigne, Matthew Arnold, and Adam Smith.

Epictetus propounded the philosophy of Stoicism, which is named for the stoa or portico in ancient Athens where the earliest representatives of this school congregated. A chief objective of Stoicism is to secure happiness by overcoming the confusion caused by the emotions and to demonstrate the liberating powers of reason. The earlier Stoics also frequently engaged in academic disputes about physics, logic, and epistemology. By contrast, Epictetus cultivated a kind of popular philosophical sermon called the diatribe. His message was not directed primarily at specialists but at students of philosophy, though in fact most of these were, like Arrian, from aristocratic families. Accordingly, the *Encheiridion* in its fifty-three short chapters seeks to encourage, to exhort, even to convert readers to the philosopher's life. Some scholars have emphasized Epictetus' beginnings as a slave and the influence of that experience on his teaching. Indeed, while the *Encheiridion*'s emphasis on the liberating power of reason is consistent with the writings of other Stoics, the personal style of the diatribe frequently suggests that the author was familiar with the realities of enslavement. Another striking difference between Epictetus and earlier Stoics is the religious tone in his work. Because he viewed reason as an aspect of the universe and of the divine, Epictetus demands a virtual conversion to philosophy. He goes far beyond philosophical predecessors in expecting his readers not merely to study philosophy but to ensure that each step taken in life is in harmony with divine reason.

The *Encheiridion* opens with a discussion of this important theme of the liberating power of reason, which allows people to differentiate between those aspects of life that can and those that cannot be controlled. Human attitudes, choices, desires, and aversions can be controlled through the exercise of reason; possessions, bodies, and lives cannot. True happiness can be secured only by abandoning the frustrating pursuit of or flight from the uncontrollable things. Control of desire and aversion is key to the philosophy of Epictetus. Reason will tell people, for example, that if a piece of pottery they admire breaks, that pottery was merely something subject to breakage. Similarly, if a beloved child or spouse dies, reason will remind individuals that the loved ones were mortal and were subject to death. People seek to avoid what they think is harmful, but reason reveals that this perception actually resides in the human being, not in the thing itself. Epictetus applies the same analysis to the petty annoyances of life as to the fear of death: Whatever cannot be controlled should not be seen as dreadful. A famous dictum of Epictetus offers a summation of his teaching: "It is not things that disturb human beings, but their attitudes toward things."

The *Encheiridion* cites numerous everyday examples—repetition was a characteristic technique of the philosophical diatribe—to reinforce its message. Reason dictates that to take pride in a fine stallion one owns is, in fact, to take pride in what is not truly one's own and can be taken away. Disease or a handicap may be impediments to the body, but they need not be impediments to moral choice or to the exercise of reason. In a memorable comparison, Epictetus stresses that all the pleasures of life should be seen as merely given on loan. On a sea voyage, if people wander away from the ship at a port of call, captivated by the attractions of the unfamiliar place, they must be prepared to abandon everything and return to the ship when the captain calls. So also in life, where when the time comes, people must be prepared to leave behind spouse and child and all material things. Accordingly, Epictetus advises people to say of something not, "I have lost it," but rather, "I have returned it." Whatever takes away what was possessed should be seen as the instrument by which the Giver takes back what is given.

With his primarily aristocratic audience in mind, Epictetus addresses himself to the concerns of youthful ambition. By not striving for wealth or fame, people may indeed end up with fewer external things than could have been possible, but through the exercise of reason and moral choice, they will gain freedom and true happiness. The aspiring philosopher, attempting to maintain the proper attitude toward external things, may appear ridiculous and clumsy. (Epictetus' vivid depiction of the ridicule the aspirant can expect may reflect his own early experience of teaching at Rome.) Yet despite this opposition, the philosopher will know how to live properly. Just as when delicacies are passed around at a feast and polite guests wait patiently until the dish comes their way (or not, as the case may be), so the philosopher will accept with equanimity what is given (or not given) in life. Like Heracleitos or Diogenes, the true philosopher may even take less than is given, as he attaches less importance to externals than do others.

In some respects, the Stoic attitude toward strong human emotions may seem brutal or simplistic. Epictetus warns his readers not to be moved too much by the apparent misfortune of another who has lost property or a child, because this event is no more than that, an apparent misfortune. All the same, the philosopher does recommend the expression of sympathy in moderation. Superstitious fear caused by an evil omen will yield to reason, which says, "Every omen is favorable, if I wish it so." Envy and jealousy are similarly vanquished by a sense of proportion and an understanding of what is, and is not, under control. The philosopher will understand that anger and irritation arise not from events themselves but from the human attitude toward events. Epictetus subjects friendship and patriotism to the same analysis. To the objection that without power or wealth people must abandon their friends, Epictetus answers that friends who require others to have what they have risk losing their moral purpose and are not true friends. Stoicism found great favor among the Romans because it did not preach a withdrawal from politics as the Epicureans did. At the same time, Epictetus urges that such service should be undertaken only to the extent that it does not compromise an individual's moral purpose.

Another central idea that Epictetus weaves into his work is the Stoic command to "follow Nature," that is, to learn to accept whatever happens as part of the natural order and not as misfortune. When a slave breaks one of the host's drinking cups, remarks Epictetus, all the guests say, "It happens." So should everyone say when their own cup is broken, or even when their child dies. Nature is not evil, and the philosopher's moral purpose must be brought into harmony with it. Epictetus even analyzes social relationships in this way. A son who complains of a bad father was, after all, just "given" this father by nature; he should consider not what the father does, but what he himself should do to bring his own life in harmony with nature. Living according to nature will even bring an individual into a proper relationship with the gods, for by accepting whatever happens that individual acknowledges their just and proper governance of the universe.

In later chapters, the *Encheiridion* moves from these lofty thoughts to seemingly more trivial ones, such as how the philosopher should speak and behave in company; what kinds of entertainment to avoid; and how food, drink, and sex fit into the philosopher's lifestyle. These admonitions, which form a sizable proportion of this short work, are intended to cover the range of roles that the individual, like an actor, may be compelled to play in life. The metaphor of acting is conscious. As in learning a role for the theater, preparation for the philosophical life can be arduous, as difficult as becoming a master of rhetoric or competing at Olympia. Rather than specify each and every human situation, Epictetus offers what could be viewed as a simple rule of thumb: In a moment of perplexity, the philosopher might ask, "What would Socrates or Zeno do in this circumstance?" Epictetus clearly assigns great importance to showing others how to act by example, not merely by lecturing them. He notes that Socrates was eager to be a philosopher, but not at all eager to be recognized as one.

The *Encheiridion* exercised an enormous influence over later thinkers. Intended by Arrian as a useful epitome of his master's teaching, for some the manual came to represent pagan philosophy generally. Freethinkers such as Baruch Spinoza eagerly embraced a moral system that depends only vaguely on divine sanction, whereas Christian thinkers detected fascinating intimations of divine revelation in the writings of this Greek slave. In fact, the *Encheiridion* had the distinction of being the only pagan work adopted by early Christianity as a religious text. Paraphrases were prepared for use by monastic orders, with only slight alteration of the text. Later readers saw other merits and defects in the work. Blaise Pascal fulminated against the arrogance of Epictetus. Frederick the Great slept with a copy of the *Encheiridion* under his pillow. Matthew Arnold saw in Epictetus and his spiritual descendant, Marcus Aurelius, "the great masters of morals." It is arguable that no single book, excepting the New Testament, has provided so many with spiritual sustenance, solace, and sanity as the *Encheiridion* of Epictetus.

John M. Lawless

Bibliography:
Arnold, E. V. *Roman Stoicism.* Cambridge, England: Cambridge University Press, 1991. A valuable work on the development of Stoicism during the Roman Empire. Notable for careful choice of citations in recounting Epictetus' philosophy.
Epictetus. *The Discourses as Reported by Arrian, the Manual, and Fragments.* Edited and translated by W. S. Oldfather. 2 vols. Cambridge, Mass.: Harvard University Press, 1925-1928. Standard edition of the complete works with Greek text and facing translation. Translation is very literal and therefore useful to consult for difficult passages. Contains a somewhat dated but still important introduction, as well as extensive English indexes.
_____. *Handbook of Epictetus.* Edited and translated by Nicholas White. Indianapolis, Ind.: Hackett Publishing Company, 1983. An excellent, updated translation of the

Encheiridion for use by students of philosophy. The introduction suggests connections between Epictetus and earlier ancient philosophical systems. Provides excellent footnotes on key concepts and difficult passages.

Long, A. A. *Hellenistic Philosophy*. New York: Charles Scribner's Sons, 1974. Chapter 4 provides background absolutely essential to understanding the philosophy of Epictetus. Provides an accurate sketch of the main tenets of Greek Stoicism that were modified by Epictetus.

Stadter, Philip A. *Arrian of Nicomedia*. Chapel Hill: University of North Carolina Press, 1980. An interesting study of Arrian, who edited Epictetus' works but was also a biographer of Alexander the Great. Deals with problem of the transcription of Epictetus' lectures and provides insights into the period in which Epictetus lived.

THE END OF THE ROAD

Type of work: Novel
Author: John Barth (1930-   )
Type of plot: Existentialism
Time of plot: 1951-1955
Locale: Wicomico, Maryland
First published: 1958

Principal characters:
> JACOB HORNER, a teacher of English and the narrator
> JOE MORGAN, a teacher of history
> RENNIE MORGAN, his wife
> PEGGY RANKIN, a teacher of English
> THE DOCTOR, a doubtful M.D.

The Story:

The End of the Road begins with some doubt as to the narrator's, Jacob Horner's, existence. He tells readers that he became a teacher of English at Wicomico State Teachers College on the advice of the Doctor, never given a name, who operates a Remobilization Farm for the treatment of functional paralysis. Between this doubtful beginning and the nonending, John Barth examines the problems of existence and identity that began with his first novel, *The Floating Opera* (1956). Read on a literal level, the story is a rather banal love triangle involving Jacob, Joe Morgan, and Joe's wife. Read on a serious abstract-ethical level, it becomes the setting for a duel of opposing points of view, both concerned with the problems of nihilism.

Jacob meets the Doctor in a railroad station, where he has come after finishing his oral examination for his master's degree. In trying to decide where to go for a vacation, he has been overcome by paralysis. He is unable to make a choice. No one destination seems better than another; his will to do anything at all is paralyzed. The Doctor takes him to his Remobilization Farm near Wicomico and begins a series of therapy sessions designed to avoid situations involving complicated choices, the point being to make some choice, any choice, in order to keep moving, so that he would not fall into immobility again. Mythotherapy, based on the existentialist premises that existence precedes essence, and that people are free not only to choose their essence but also to change it at will, is the chief therapy prescribed for Jacob. It is a process of assigning a role to himself and carrying it out logically. It is essentially a mask to protect the ego.

At the college, Jacob becomes acquainted with Joe Morgan and his wife Rennie. The relationship quickly develops into a love triangle, but one in which the moral responsibility is shared equally by all three. Here, as elsewhere, Barth gives readers no chance to make any judgments, to fasten onto any solid ethical ground. *The End of the Road* is a short novel with the characters sketched and filled in quickly, with very little background or examination of motivational processes.

Jacob's modus operandi is mythotherapy. Joe's is one of ethical positivism; he has a set of consistent, relative values that he is trying to impress on Rennie. It is on Rennie that the action centers. While teaching Jacob to ride horseback, she tells him of her meeting with Joe and their subsequent relationship and marriage. Until she met Joe, she had no philosophy of her own, and she willingly erased her own personality to adopt that of her husband. She is still unsure of herself and not quite at ease with her adopted role. Later on, she comes to see Jacob as Satan, tempting her to abandon her assumed personality. She sees him as inconsistent, as having nothing but ever-changing masks, donning one after the other as the situation demands. Following logically, she sees Joe as a god: consistent, moral, and logically right. Over the battleground of Rennie, Jacob and Joe fight out their opposing points of view: Jacob with the shifting inconsistencies and limited goals of existentialism, Joe with his relative ethical values that deny any absolutes.

After Rennie and Jacob commit adultery, Barth abandons any consideration of Rennie and concentrates on the relationship between Jacob and Joe. The adultery had happened almost casually, while Joe was away. The seeds had been planted for it when Jacob and Rennie, peeking in on Joe after one of their rides, watched him making faces at himself in the mirror and engaging in a series of disgusting sex activities. Rennie is shattered; her god has his inconsistencies too.

Rennie tells Joe of her infidelity, and he confronts Jacob with it. Instead of behaving like an outraged husband, Joe tries to find the reasons behind the deed. All Jacob can say is that he does not know why it happened. Joe's search for causes goes so far beyond the point of believability that one is forced to view it in abstract terms. Here, as elsewhere, Barth carries action to an extreme and exaggerated point until it becomes parody.

Jacob's relationship with Peggy Rankin is a parody of Joe and Rennie's relationship. Both fail: Joe's because it is too intellectualized and Jacob's because it is too physical. Barth implies a middle way, one would assume, but he never says so directly. In fact, Barth provides no absolutes, but merely presents a set of actions. He seems to suggest that human involvement is the answer to the problems posed by nihilism.

Upon Joe's urging, Rennie visits Jacob several more times. She tells him that she does not know whether she hates or loves Jacob, but she wants to find out. When both Rennie and Joe visit Jacob one evening, it is to tell him that Rennie is pregnant and that they do not know whose child it is. All she knows is that she will commit suicide if she cannot have an abortion. This situation drives Jacob to decision and action. Through a series of lies, impersonations, and gall, he convinces one of the local doctors to give Rennie something to make her abort. When he tells Rennie what he has done and that she must give a false name and story, she refuses. She would rather shoot herself than lie. Jacob, by his imperfect realization of his role and his readiness to assume all the responsibility, has become fully involved, but his commitment is the very thing that the Doctor had told him he must avoid. Joe also has failed in his personal absolutism by turning to Jacob for an answer.

In desperation, Jacob goes to the Doctor and asks him to perform an abortion. The Doctor finally agrees on the condition that Jacob will give him all his money and go with him to a new location in Pennsylvania. Jacob agrees and brings Rennie to the Remobilization Farm. While on the operating table, Rennie dies.

Jacob is afraid that Joe will inform the police. Several days later, he receives a telephone call from Joe, who tells him that he has taken care of everything. Joe and his convictions have suffered a mortal blow. He is lost and desperate. He turns to Jacob for an explanation, but Jacob has nothing to offer. Both positions, moral nihilism and ethical positivism, have been wrecked in their encounter with reality. Joe is left to reconstruct his life. Jacob returns to the Doctor because he is not yet ready to assume the responsibilities of life.

The End of the Road is a bitter commentary on the plight of humanity. Barth, in his examination of nihilism, has given no answers. There are no moments of high good humor, as in *The Sot-Weed Factor* (1960), only an unrelieved pessimism. On the surface, the novel is akin to the Theater of the Absurd in its insistence on telling only the observable actions of a story. John Barth points no morals and draws no conclusions. The actions of his characters show that nihilism, in its several guises, is not an end in itself.

Critical Evaluation:

There is no real moral center for any of the major characters in John Barth's *The End of the Road*. Those who begin by believing that they are in secure possession of such a central, unshakable core of moral certitude—most notably, Joe Morgan and his wife, Rennie—are forced to accept the realization that they have deluded themselves, first in claiming that their philosophy offers a coherent view and response to the world, and second when it is made clear that they did not, in fact, even fully embrace their own supposed philosophy. In effect, they have been living a lie, and it turns out to be a lie that was not even a useful one. This realization destroys them. In the case of Rennie Morgan, she is literally destroyed.

For the Doctor and especially for his patient Jacob Horner, there is not even the pretense of an overriding moral philosophy to guide their actions and shape their perceptions of the world. Things simply are, and the Doctor quotes, without attribution, the philosopher Ludwig Wittgenstein: "The world is everything that is the case." The world, including human existence, must be accepted as it is, in all its conflicting confusion. There is no way to fashion it into an understandable unity. In this sense, both the Doctor and Horner are existentialists, accepting the essential absurdity of their situation and dealing with it by fashioning their own interpretations and even identities—interpretations and identities that are arbitrary and frequently changed. Yet, in the end, the tactics and response of existentialism prove as impractical as the moral absolutism espoused by Joe Morgan.

Ultimately, *The End of the Road* is concerned with two basic questions of identity and meaning: Who am I? and What am I to do? Neither question is answered, and Barth's unspoken but inescapable conclusion is that there are no answers. The novel introduces the theme of identity and meaning in its opening sentence: "In a sense, I am Jacob Horner," writes the narrator, and throughout *The End of the Road* the sense of Jacob Horner's reality—indeed, the reality of all of the characters—constantly shifts and changes. Horner is encouraged in his mutability by the Doctor's highly idiosyncratic cures, most notable of which is mythotherapy, which demands the creation of a series of outward personalities totally unrelated to any inner condition. The point is for Horner to continue acting in order to avoid the state of paralysis in which the Doctor initially found him. Choice is essential, even if it is meaningless. As the Doctor advises Horner, "If the alternatives are side by side, choose the one on the left; if they're consecutive in time, choose the earlier. If neither of these applies, choose the alternative whose name begins with the earlier letter of the alphabet."

Just as there is no morality to the Doctor's precepts for selection, there is no morality for Jacob Horner's actions. His emotionally brutal seduction of Peggy Rankin, the English teacher he picks up on the beach, and his adultery with Rennie Morgan are equally without emotion or purpose. Traditional human motives, such as passion or even simple lust, are not truly applicable. Horner is acting only to be acting, to assert his existence. That the results are terribly destructive in terms of human life and suffering is, in the end, to him a matter of indifference, perhaps of incomprehension.

As counterpoint to Horner's frightening flexibility, Barth presents Joe Morgan's mental and moral rigidity. In place of conventional morality he has erected his own system of rigorous intellectual honesty: Every action, every word, even every thought, must be capable of being explained and defended to the utmost. He is scornful and contemptuous of those who do not measure up to this standard, which he pursues to its logical, if absurd, conclusion. When he learns that his wife, Rennie, has committed adultery with Horner, Morgan reacts not as an outraged and deceived husband, but as a philosopher whose central tenets have been improperly and carelessly challenged. His response is to force Rennie to continue seeing Horner, perhaps even having sex with him, until she can logically explain her actions—and Horner's—to Morgans' satisfaction. Since Rennie's actions have an emotional, rather than logical basis, and since Horner's actions have no reason at all, this proves impossible. The contradiction not only destroys the Morgans' marriage, it ultimately proves the cause for Rennie's death on the operating table during a botched abortion performed by the Doctor. By refusing to accept the reality and power of irrationality, Joe Morgan reveals the emptiness of his own philosophy and his life based on it.

To present this bleak and arbitrary world, Barth creates a plot that is simple, even banal in its events, and presents it in a style of scrupulous meanness. Events and actions are described flatly, unemotionally, in language that tends to keep the reader uninvolved with the characters and their fates. The clarity of the language, which presents outward activities clearly and precisely, underscores the ambiguity and arbitrary nature of the human motives for those actions. With only one exception, a flashback that describes the initial meeting between Jacob Horner and the Doctor, the novel is recounted in strictly chronological terms that could be broadly paraphrased as: "This happened and then this happened and then nothing else happened." Since no action has any more meaning than any other action, nothing is emphasized, little is analyzed. The plot is presented but the meanings of actions are not revealed; characters are described but their personalities are not disclosed. The reason for this is quite simple. In the world Barth has fashioned for his novel, actions have no meaning, and there are no personalities. For those involved, it is indeed the end of the road.

"Critical Evaluation" by Michael Witkoski

Bibliography:
Bowen, Zack. *Readers Guide to John Barth*. Westport, Conn.: Greenwood Press, 1994. An accessible and helpful survey of Barth's writings, with valuable insights into the underlying philosophical themes which are at the core of *The End of the Road*.
Fogel, Stanley. *Understanding John Barth*. Columbia: University of South Carolina Press, 1990. An excellent introductory account of Barth's fictions, including his early "ethical" novels, *The Floating Opera* and *The End of the Road*.
Harris, Charles. *Passionate Virtuosity: The Fiction of John Barth*. Champaign: University of Illinois Press, 1983. A scholarly and in-depth discussion of Barth's fictions, ranging over philosophical and psychological sources.
Tharpe, Jac. *John Barth: The Comic Sublimity of Paradox*. Carbondale: Southern Illinois University Press, 1974. Through his concentration on the philosophical content of Barth's works, Tharpe sheds light on the ethical and existential situations in *The End of the Road*.
Walkiewicz, E. P. *John Barth*. Boston: Twayne, 1986. This brief but informative book is undoubtedly the best place to start in a study of John Barth.

ENDGAME
A Play in One Act

Type of work: Drama
Author: Samuel Beckett (1906-1989)
Type of plot: Absurdist
Time of plot: Indeterminate
Locale: Indeterminate
First performed: 1957; first published, 1957 as *Fin de partie* (English translation, 1958)

> *Principal characters:*
> HAMM, a blind, crippled mythomaniac
> CLOV, Hamm's attendant, possibly his son
> NAGG and
> NELL, Hamm's parents, confined to trash cans

The Story:

The world was nearing its end when Clov, the only character capable of movement, began another day. Carefully surveying the unfurnished living space, looking out the windows with and without the aid of a stepladder, he uncovered two trash cans one at a time, looking inside with a brief laugh before replacing the covers. He then removed the sheet covering Hamm in his makeshift wheelchair, in fact a wooden armchair on casters. Hamm, dressed in a housecoat, socks, a felt hat, and dark glasses over his sightless eyes, awakened slowly, pulling off the bloodstained handkerchief that had been covering his face. No sooner had Clov informed the audience that "it" was nearly finished and that he would retire to the kitchen and wait for Hamm to "whistle" him than Hamm came fully awake, talking stagily to himself and issuing orders to Clov. The extended dialogue that followed seemed to replicate the two men's daily routine, with only a few indications that the present day might be different, that something might, in fact, be coming to an end. As both men observed, there are always the same questions and the same answers.

Clov, although able to stand and walk, was also crippled, unable to sit down. Through habit, it seemed, he had learned to parry Hamm's orders and insults, "talking back" and taking his time about doing as he was told. More than once, Clov had threatened to leave for good, yet the dialogue would resume, interrupted only when Hamm's father, Nagg, lifted the lid on his trash can to beg for food: gruel or a cracker. There were no more bicycle wheels for Hamm's chair because there were no more bicycles, there was no more gruel for Nagg, and seeds that Clov had planted were not likely to sprout. Nagg again raised the lid on his can, pounding on the lid of the other can until his wife, Nell, poked her head out, grotesquely asking Nagg if he wanted to make love.

From their conversation, it soon became clear that Nagg and Nell lost their legs years earlier in an accident on a tandem bicycle and that the sawdust in their bins had long since been replaced by sand fetched from the beach, presumably by Clov. Hamm, supposedly trying to sleep, told his parents to be quiet, yet Nagg rambled on, regaling Nell with a long, involved joke about a tailor that presumably had made her laugh years earlier, when they were young, healthy, and in love at Lake Como. Hamm, furious, ordered Clov to close the lids on the cans and push him on a "ride" around the room, hugging the walls but leaving him precisely in the center at the end of the ride. Looking out the window at Hamm's request, Clov reported that the weather was the same, "light black from pole to pole," but that the lighthouse had sunk and that something was "taking its course." Both men were alarmed when Clov felt a flea on his body, fearing that "humanity" would start all over again. Haranguing Clov with reminders of his own generosity, Hamm then asked if his toy dog were ready. Like the wheelchair, the dog was a makeshift creature, having only three legs, yet Hamm insisted on putting it through its paces even as Clov lied about its looks and color.

Hamm, showing himself to be Nagg's son, then prepared to tell a long and involved story, inviting his father, as well as Clov, to listen. The story was even longer than Nagg's, recalling Hamm's lordship of a large estate, a beggar, and the beggar's son, who may or may not have been Clov himself. Nagg then recalled Hamm's own childhood, admitting without shame that both parents neglected his cries in the night in order to get their own sleep. Nagg then rapped on the lid of Nell's can, getting no answer. Clov would soon decide that she was dead.

Hamm continued his story, then lapsed into monologue as Clov continued to busy himself about the room, still threatening to leave. There seemed to be a rat in the kitchen and perhaps a small boy visible against the horizon in the distance. Clov packed his bags and prepared to leave, delivering a monologue of his own. Hamm then settled down to sleep, or to die, with a rambling speech incorporating lines of poetry and fragments of his "story." At the end, Nagg apparently remained alive, although closed up in his bin, and Clov remained poised for departure, yet with no real place to go.

Critical Evaluation:

Born in Dublin, Ireland, in 1906, Samuel Beckett lived in Paris during the 1920's and made his permanent residence there from 1937 until his death more than fifty years later. In the late 1940's, Beckett, who had published a few novels and some poetry in English, began writing in French, with almost immediately positive results. Beginning with *Molloy* (1951), Beckett achieved critical if not popular success, exploring the possibilities and limits of the novel. Ironically, however, it was as a playwright, composing originally in French, that Beckett achieved his full measure of fame and critical acclaim, initially with *En attendant Godot* (1952; *Waiting for Godot*, 1954). As with his novels, Beckett prepared his own English translations of the plays, achieving an originality of style that had eluded him when he wrote originally in English. *Endgame* was his second play to be performed and published, its fortunes closely rivaling those of the earlier, groundbreaking *Waiting for Godot*. Together with the early efforts of Eugène Ionesco and Jean Genet, Beckett's first two plays helped to define and illustrate the trend described, analyzed, and labeled by Martin Esslin in *The Theatre of the Absurd* (1961). Although the three playwrights were, as Esslin pointed out, more different than similar, their combined works served to redefine and reorient the "serious" Paris stage for two or three decades to come, with worldwide repercussions.

Interpreted by certain observers as a "psychodrama" portraying the fragmentation of the human personality, or perhaps the inside of the human skull, *Endgame* is nevertheless a powerful and entertaining play, with many memorable lines both in French and in English. Of particular interest is the "stage business," prescribed in the written text, that accounts for a fair share of the action: Clov folding sheets, moving or mounting the stepladder, wheeling Hamm around the room, or gathering his meager possessions as he prepares to leave. Hamm, although stationary, is far from immobile, with gestures and poses that constitute "stage business" as well. "Psychodrama" or not, *Endgame* presents four highly individuated and memorable characters, their interaction no less "dramatic" for the compression of dialogue and plot that often borders on the cryptic. The end of the world is at hand, and play, or playing, is all that is left to do. Taking its title from the end game in chess, the play manages to encompass, and to exemplify, most senses of the related terms of "play" and "game" as its characters, like those in Beckett's novels, express their humanity through ingenuity.

If the desolate landscape of *Waiting for Godot* can be likened to that of war-torn, occupied France, the ravaged interior of *Endgame* seems to suggest the threat of a world laid to waste by nuclear war. In neither case, however, is the equation expressly stated. Interpretation is left to the director, actors, and spectators. Arguably, *Endgame* is addressed even more to the actor than to the spectator, its greatest potential impact deriving from participation in the "play" portrayed.

Following the success of *Endgame*, Beckett went on to write *Krapp's Last Tape* (1958), an equally remarkable spectacle featuring a single actor and a tape recorder on which the character has attempted to keep track of time and of time's effects on his personality. Unlike most of Beckett's other mature work in any genre, *Krapp's Last Tape* was written first in English, then translated into French. Although Beckett would continue to write for the theater well into the 1970's, none of his later pieces achieved quite the success or impact of his first three efforts for the theater, of which *Endgame* remains perhaps the most remarkable, rivaled only by *Waiting for Godot*.

David B. Parsell

Bibliography:
Chevigny, Bell Gale, ed. *Twentieth Century Interpretations of "Endgame."* Englewood Cliffs, N.J.: Prentice-Hall, 1969. Contains illuminating contributions by director Alan Schneider, critics Ross Chambers and Hugh Kenner, and others. Also contains an excerpt from Martin Esslin's landmark book *The Theatre of the Absurd*.
Cohn, Ruby. *Just Play: Beckett's Theater*. Princeton, N.J.: Princeton University Press, 1980. This volume by a "lifelong" student and critic of Beckett contains a useful comparison/ contrast of French and English texts of *Endgame*.
Kalb, Jonathan. *Beckett in Performance*. New York: Cambridge University Press, 1989. An exhaustive and perceptive production study of Beckett's plays, primarily in Western Europe. Good on productions of *Endgame*.
Kennedy, Andrew K. *Samuel Beckett*. New York: Cambridge University Press, 1989. Published shortly before Beckett's death, Kennedy's study provides a balanced view of all of his work. Particularly stimulating analysis of Beckett's plays in general and *Endgame* in particular.
McMillan, Dougald, and Martha Fehsenfeld. *From "Waiting for Godot" to "Krapp's Last Tape."* Vol. 1 in *Beckett in the Theatre*. London: Calder, 1988. Complements Kalb's study of *Beckett in Performance*. Useful production notes and history on *Endgame*.

ENDYMION
A Poetic Romance

Type of work: Poetry
Author: John Keats (1795-1821)
Type of plot: Narrative
Time of plot: Ancient times
Locale: Mount Latmos, the Garden of Adonis, caverns, a place under the ocean, Neptune's palace, the sky, and the Cave of Quietude
First published: 1818

> *Principal characters:*
> ENDYMION, a shepherd
> PEONA, his sister
> CYNTHIA, the moon goddess
> GLAUCUS, an ancient man condemned by Circe
> INDIAN MAIDEN, an incarnation of Cynthia

The Story:

The narrator begins the poem with the famous line "A thing of beauty is a joy for ever" and the brief argument that "All lovely tales that we have heard or read" bring happiness because they "Haunt us until they become a cheering light/ Unto our souls." The narrator then traces the story of Endymion, a young shepherd. Endymion and his people gathered to worship the shepherd-god Pan at an altar on Mount Latmos. Endymion was not caught up in the mood of the festivities. Instead, he was depressed and dreamy. His sister, Peona, worried about him and pulled him aside to ask about the source of his sorrow. Endymion told her about the dream he had. In the dream, he saw his idealized version of womanly perfection. He told Peona that he fell in love with the woman in his dream, and when he awoke to find himself alone, the world seemed repulsive and he felt heartbroken. Peona urged her brother not to waste away his life on a dream woman whom he would never find.

Endymion digressed and told his sister that there are various degrees of happiness, from the simplest to the loftiest. Peona asked her brother why he would pursue love over fame and he replied that there were three sources of happiness. The first was sensual pleasure that comes from direct experience with nature, such as the music the wind makes with an aeolian harp. The second was pleasure that comes from art, especially of old heroic stories. The third was the best source of happiness: relationships. Endymion spoke of the happiness of human "entanglements" that allow people to get beyond the self and the limits of a single existence. Endymion determined that friendship is a "steady splendor," but love is loftier—a "radiance" where two souls "interknit." Endymion explained that men who might have achieved deeds of heroism have chosen love instead, finding in it contentment because love made the soul feel its immortality. Endymion suggested to Peona that love is worth more than fame. Endymion told Peona that since his dream, he saw the face of his dream lover in a well and heard her voice coming from a cave. Endymion resigned himself to a life of unrequited love and took Peona's hand and "stept into the boat, and launch'd from land."

Endymion began his search for his dream lover. He met a naiad who warned him that he must search in remote regions for the woman of his dreams if he wished to find consummation. When a voice urged him to descend, a despondent Endymion moved onward to the Garden of Adonis. He found Adonis, Venus' love, asleep. Venus arrived as Adonis awoke. Adonis beseeched Venus to have pity on Endymion. Venus and her minions vanished. Endymion wandered farther and found a giant eagle that flew him farther into caverns. With the "power to dream deliciously," Endymion found his dream lover. She told him that she loved him, but she could not bring him to Olympus. She did not reveal her name. (She was Cynthia, Moon goddess and the goddess of chastity.) After they made love, Endymion fell asleep and she left him. Endymion woke up in deeper despair. He came upon two streams, Alpheus and Arethusa—two streams who wanted to intermingle but could not because Cynthia would not allow it. Endymion pled his case to the "gentle Goddess of [his] pilgrimage" to "assuage" the lovers' pains of Alpheus and Arethusa. The vision of the rivers disappeared and Endymion saw "the giant sea above his head."

At the bottom of the sea, Endymion met Glaucus, an ancient man who was condemned to sit at the bottom of the sea for a thousand years because he had witnessed Circe deform some of her lovers and turn others into beasts. Glaucus welcomed Endymion as his savior who fulfilled the end of Circe's curse. Glaucus' curse had begun when he entered the sea. There, he had encountered his first love, Scylla, dead. Glaucus had placed Scylla's body in a crystal mausoleum. Many years passed before he encountered another being. A ship capsized and Glaucus found a dead man clenching a scroll. The scroll foretold that a youth would rescue Glaucus at the end of his thousand years of suffering. Until the rescue, it was Glaucus' responsibility to place all drowned lovers at each other's side in the crystal mausoleum. Endymion was moved by Glaucus' tale and helped the old man regain his youth by performing rituals that reanimated the dead lovers in the crystal mausoleum.

Rejoicing, the lovers went to Neptune's palace. During the festivities at Neptune's palace, Venus told Endymion that she had discovered the identity of his immortal lover. Endymion fainted and was carried upward by Nereids to a crystal bower. While passed out, Endymion heard in his "inward senses" the voice of his beloved, who promised him that they would soon be together and bade him to awake.

Endymion awoke near a placid lake in a green forest and met a beautiful Indian Maiden. She longed desperately for love because she had been deserted by Bacchus. Despite his love for his dream lover, Endymion fell in love with the Indian Maiden (who was actually Cynthia). Endymion was torn between the two lovers. Two flying horses appeared to Endymion and the Indian Maiden. The lovers mounted the winged pair and flew upward. During the journey, they fell asleep. While asleep, Endymion learned that his dream lover and Cynthia were the same entity. Endymion was still also drawn to the Indian Maiden. When the Indian Maiden disappeared, Endymion entered the Cave of Quietude.

Endymion returned to earth, still torn between his earthly love for the Indian Maiden and his divine love for Cynthia. Endymion encountered the Indian Maiden and told her their love was hopeless because of his love for Cynthia. Endymion decided to live out the rest of his life as a hermit. The Indian Maiden revealed that she was Cynthia. Peona watched as the two lovers disappeared together.

Critical Evaluation:

John Keats died at age twenty-five. He wrote at a feverish pace and left behind a body of work distinguished by its genius. His poetry ranks him among the greatest Romantic poets. Keats was deeply influenced by Edmund Spenser's *The Faerie Queene* (1590) and the works of Leigh Hunt. This influence is especially evident in *Endymion: A Poetic Romance*. Keats wanted to write a "long poem," that would be a "trial of invention." The poem was *Endymion: A Poetic Romance*, an effort of four thousand lines that he wrote in less than a year, the result of Keats's self-imposed poetic apprenticeship. In it, he appropriates (and often changes) Greek myth.

Keats was not satisfied with *Endymion: A Poetic Romance*, aware of the extent and nature of the poem's shortcomings. In a letter to John Taylor, his publisher, Keats wrote, "I am anxious to get *Endymion* printed so that I may forget it." Keats thought the poem a tool in his growth as a poet. Still, he put forth his negative thoughts on *Endymion: A Poetic Romance* in the "Preface" to the poem, where he spells out his regret that he made it public: "What manner I mean, will be quite clear to the reader, who must soon perceive great inexperience, immaturity, and every error denoting a feverish attempt, rather than a deed accomplished." Keats places himself somewhere between the healthy "imagination of a boy" and the "mature imagination of a man"—a place where the soul "ferments." From such fermentation derives what Keats called the "mawkishness" of *Endymion: A Poetic Romance*.

The structure of *Endymion: A Poetic Romance* follows what Jack Stillinger calls a "spatial conception of two realms in opposition and a mythlike set of actions involving characters shuttling back and forth between them." In book 1, Endymion and his sister occupy the actual world, although Endymion wants to move up to the realm of the ideal world—a place of higher reality. In books 2, 3, and 4, Endymion journeys on a quest for his dream lover, occupying realms of the fantastic. In book 4, Endymion briefly returns to the actual world, but disappears back into the ideal world. The pain-pleasure dichotomy of life is addressed in *Endymion: A Poetic Romance*—as in most of Keats's works—with the painful aspect existing in the actual world and the pleasure aspect existing in the idealized world. To make this dichotomy work, Keats, at his best, generally employs character pairings of mortals and immortals.

In *Endymion: A Poetic Romance*, Keats freely borrows from Greek mythology, using the character of Endymion, a chieftain king, and his passion for the moon goddess Cynthia (known in Greek mythology as Diana). Keats is very free in his interpretation of Cynthia, generally considered a goddess of chastity, the moon being out of reach. The "pleasure thermometer" passage, so named from a letter Keats sent to his publisher, Taylor, sets the tone of the poem and allows the introduction of eroticism and sexual imagery. Endymion's encounters with his dream lover Cynthia occur in dreams, but they are anything but chaste. Instead, they are very erotic; the lovers entwine, pant, sigh, faint, caress—the supposedly chaste Cynthia speaks of melting into Endymion. This eroticism is balanced by sexual imagery in the poem. The love between Adonis and Venus in the Garden of Adonis is presented as a sexual relationship that can never develop or mature. On the other hand, the relationship between Glaucus and Circe symbolizes the destructive nature of mature sexuality. The sexual relationship that Endymion seeks with Cynthia lies somewhere between that of Adonis and Venus and that of Glaucus and Circe—an idealized, mature sexual relationship that is emotionally fulfilling. By combining Endymion's dream lover into the earthly Indian Maiden and the spiritual Cynthia, Keats allows Endymion to attain the highest level of pleasure on the pleasure thermometer: an immortal love in which two souls "interknit."

Through the use of dream visions, Keats makes a statement about the growth of the human mind through the imagination—one of the principles of the Romantics. Although *Endymion: A Poetic Romance* is an immature work, it is interesting in its approach to the inner workings of the mind involved in a young man's experience of erotic love, which seems to be the poem's central idea. Fluent and facile, *Endymion's* power comes from Endymion's search for self-fulfillment through beauty and sex. Given the poem's abrupt ending, it may well be that Keats discovered the full meaning of a young man's experience of erotic love after he finished writing *Endymion: A Poetic Romance*.

Thomas D. Petitjean, Jr.

Bibliography:

Ende, Stuart A. "Keats's Music of Truth." *English Literary History* 40 (Spring, 1973): 90-104. Drawing on Yeats's theory that for each poet there is a single myth that underlies his or her deepest meditations, Ende considers Keats's poetic development in terms of the conflict between his desire for vision or imagination and his sense of separation from such redeeming states. Discusses *Endymion: A Poetic Romance*.

Mayhead, Robin. *John Keats*. Cambridge, England: Cambridge University Press, 1967. Discusses *Endymion: A Poetic Romance* in the context of Keats's entire body of works. This study serves as a basic introduction to Keats and his works.

Stillinger, Jack, ed. Introduction to *John Keats: Complete Poems*, by John Keats. Cambridge, Mass.: The Belknap Press of the Harvard University Press, 1982. Stillinger, the definitive Keats scholar, presents all of Keats's poems with a readable introduction that defines a basic critical approach.

Thurston, Norman. "Biography and Keats's Pleasure Thermometer." *Wordsworth Circle* 4 (Autumn, 1973): 267-270. Thurston discusses the "pleasure thermometer" in the letter to John Taylor as "a coherent and unified expression of Keats's attitude toward *Endymion*" at the time Keats wrote the letter.

Walsh, William. *Introduction to Keats*. New York: Methuen, 1981. Walsh uses the commentaries of a number of respected Keats scholars to place *Endymion: A Poetic Romance* in the appropriate critical context and rank among Keats's other works.

ENDYMION
The Man in the Moon

Type of work: Drama
Author: John Lyly (c. 1554-1606)
Type of plot: Comedy
Time of plot: Antiquity
Locale: Ancient Greece
First performed: 1588; first published, 1591

Principal characters:
ENDYMION, a courtier
CYNTHIA, the queen, loved by Endymion
TELLUS, in love with Endymion
EUMENIDES, Endymion's friend
SEMELE, loved by Eumenides
CORSITES, in love with Tellus
DIPSAS, an enchantress
GERON, her long-lost husband
SIR TOPHAS, a fop
FLOSCULA, Tellus' friend

The Story:

To his friend Eumenides, Endymion declared his love for Cynthia, goddess of the moon. Eumenides chided Endymion, reminding him of the moon's inconstancy, whereupon Endymion extolled inconstancy and change as virtues, attributes of everything beautiful. Convinced that Endymion was bewitched, Eumenides prescribed sleep and rest for the lovesick swain, but Endymion rejected the advice and berated his friend.

In hopes of misleading his friends, Endymion had also professed love for Tellus, a goddess of the earth. Enraged by his apparent perfidy, Tellus swore to take revenge. Since she still loved Endymion, Tellus was unwilling for him to die; therefore, she resolved to resort to magic and witchcraft in order to awaken his love for her. Her friend Floscula warned that love inspired by witchcraft would be bitter, but Tellus ignored the warning and left to consult Dipsas, an enchantress.

In contrast to Endymion and Tellus, Sir Tophas habitually scoffed at love and dedicated his life to war—against blackbirds, mallards, and wrens. When mocked by Endymion's and Eumenides' pages, Dares and Samias, Sir Tophas swore to kill them, but pardoned them when they explained that they had been speaking in Latin. Meanwhile, Tellus had found Dipsas, whom she consulted about the possibility of killing Endymion's love for Cynthia and supplanting it by magic with love for the earth goddess herself. Dipsas declared that since she was not a deity, she could only weaken love, never kill it. At Tellus' request, Dipsas agreed to enchant Endymion in such a way that his protestations of love for Cynthia would be doubted. Accompanied by Floscula and Dipsas, Tellus confronted Endymion in a garden and tried to make him confess his love for Cynthia. Although he admitted that he honored Cynthia above all other women, he insisted that he loved Tellus.

Later, the two pages, Dares and Samias, strolled in the gardens with their own lady loves, whom they had shown Endymion and Eumenides in the act of mooning over their loves. As a jest, Dares and Samias asked the two women to feign love for Sir Tophas, who, as usual, was playing at warfare in the gardens. The women complied, but Sir Tophas, ignoring them, reiterated his contempt for love and his passion for war.

Still later, Dipsas came upon Endymion asleep in a grove. Assisted by Bagoa, her servant, Dipsas spelled Endymion into a sleep from which he would not awaken until he was old and gray. In a dream, three women appeared to Endymion, and one of them started to stab him. When asked by the third woman to stop, the first woman peered into a looking glass and threw down her knife. At this moment, an old man appeared carrying a book that contained only three pages. Endymion refused to read the book until the man had torn up two of the pages.

When informed of Endymion's mysterious slumber, Cynthia agreed with Eumenides that the sages of the world should be consulted about a remedy. Angered by the impertinence of Tellus, Cynthia made her a prisoner in Corsites' palace, where she was to weave tapestries depicting stories of people who had been punished for their long tongues.

On the way to Thessaly, where Cynthia was sending him to seek a cure for Endymion, Eumenides met Geron, an old hermit. Geron said that if Eumenides were a faithful lover, he could learn the cure from a magic fountain nearby. Since Eumenides had always been true to Semele, the fountain promised to grant any single wish he might make. Although tempted to wish that his love for Semele might be requited, he dutifully asked for a cure for his friend. The fountain answered that the cure was a kiss from Cynthia.

Tellus, slowly pining away in prison, promised Corsites, her jailer and suitor, that she would marry if he could perform the impossible task of bringing Endymion to a cave, where she might see him once more. Corsites undertook this task, but was put to sleep by fairies guarding Endymion's body.

Thus Cynthia found two sleeping men when she came to the grove accompanied by wise men who she hoped would wake Endymion. The sages succeeded in waking only Corsites, who freely confessed his love for Tellus and what that love had inspired him to do. At last, Eumenides returned and persuaded Cynthia to attempt the cure. Upon her kiss, Endymion awoke, but his forty-year slumber had withered him: He was so senile that he could not stand. At Cynthia's request, however, he related his strange dream, explaining that, in the book that the old man had given him to read, he saw Cynthia being attacked by beasts of ingratitude, treachery, and envy. Cynthia promised to listen later to a fuller account of this vision.

A short time later, Bagoa disclosed that Tellus and Dipsas had been responsible for enchanting Endymion. For her pains, Bagoa was transformed into an aspen tree by Dipsas. Cynthia was more lenient than Dipsas. Learning that Tellus had been motivated by unrequited love, Cynthia forgave her and gave her to Corsites as his wife. Dipsas, too, was pardoned on condition that she would be reunited with Geron, her husband, whom she had sent away many years ago. This reunion displeased Sir Tophas, who had discarded his armor out of love for Dipsas; he was content, however, when Cynthia disenchanted Bagoa and gave her to Tophas as his wife. To Eumenides, she promised Semele, but Semele objected on the grounds that Eumenides had not asked for her at the magic fountain. She was placated, however, when Geron explained that Eumenides would not have learned the fountain's secret had he not been faithful. Most important, Cynthia restored the youth of Endymion and told him to persevere in his love.

Critical Evaluation:

Most famous for his novel *Euphues, The Anatomy of Wit* (1579), John Lyly was also a prolific playwright. He was the most fashionable English writer in the 1580's, praised as the creator of a "new English." Certainly *Endymion* made possible such later plays as William Shakespeare's *Midsummer Night's Dream* (1595-1596) and *As You Like It* (1599-1600). Lyly's comedies were a great advance over those of his predecessors. He possessed a unique skill in taking the Italian pastoral and Latin comedy of intrigue and adapting them to the English style, by combining them with fanciful plot and mythological characters as well as characters from the lower levels of English life. The grace and charm of his witty dialogue and his analysis of love were not surpassed until Shakespeare's later comedies.

Lyly was chief dramatist for the company of boy players attached to St. Paul's Cathedral, the favorite entertainers of Queen Elizabeth's court. The structure and style of *Endymion* would have been appreciated by their educated audience. The play is filled with references and allusions directed especially to this audience. The division of *Endymion* into acts and scenes is molded on Latin precedent, and the stage directions are of the classical pattern also employed by Ben Jonson: At the head of each scene are listed the characters who take part in it. The stage setting, however, is romantic; places separated by vast distances (the lunary bank, castle in the desert, and fountain) were represented by sections of the same platform stage, and the journey visualized by stepping across the stage. The treatment of time in the play was that of a fairy tale.

The story of Cynthia, the moon goddess, and Endymion was probably borrowed from the Roman poet Lucian. Sir Tophas is a blend of Latin parasite and braggart soldier. To the Elizabethan court, the main interest in the play lay in its reference to contemporary personalities. Cynthia was the Queen, and Tellus—in her jealousy, captivity in a desert castle, and her wiles—must have recalled Mary, Queen of Scots, who was beheaded in 1586. Endymion must have suggested the Earl of Leicester.

Endymion is undeniably an effete, even trivial play. The plot is inconsequential and artificial, the characters unreal, the dialogue pedantic. *Endymion* is important historically in that Lyly was trying to make the English theater a high art. Writing for the court rather than the populace, Lyly replaced the earthiness and crudity of earlier English plays with refinement and polish, thereby setting new standards that later dramatists, including Shakespeare, emulated. Although today's audiences will likely find the play precious, it nevertheless possesses great charm and wit, much beauty and humor, and probably has been unjustly neglected in the centuries since Lyly's death.

Bibliography:

Hunter, G. K. *John Lyly: The Humanist as Courtier.* London: Routledge & Kegan Paul, 1962. The work against which subsequent criticism of Lyly is compared. Suggests that Lyly was motivated primarily by a desire to establish himself at Elizabeth's court. Concentrates on *Endymion* more than any other play.

Knapp, Robert S. "The Monarchy of Love in Lyly's *Endimion*." *Modern Philology* 73 (May, 1976): 353-367. Argues that Lyly is intentionally enigmatic, mixing a wide range of possible interpretations under the general heading of love allegory.

Lenz, Carolyn Ruth Swift. "The Allegory of Wisdom in Lyly's *Endimion*." *Comparative Drama* 10, no. 3 (Fall, 1976): 235-257. Analyzes the play in terms of sixteenth century religious and philosophical thought, with special reference to Neoplatonic conceptions of love.

Saccio, Peter. *The Court Comedies of John Lyly: A Study in Allegorical Dramaturgy.* Princeton, N.J.: Princeton University Press, 1969. Suggests a complex dramaturgical structure involving both moral and political allegory. Includes an eighteen-page section on *Endymion* and many other references to the play.

Weltner, Peter. "The Antinomic Vision of Lyly's *Endymion*." *English Literary Renaissance* 3, no. 1 (Winter, 1973): 5-29. Self-consciously rejects historically based readings of the play, arguing instead for a symbolic reading based on Jungian archetypes. Idiosyncratic but interesting.

ENEMIES
A Love Story

Type of work: Novel
Author: Isaac Bashevis Singer (1904-1991)
Type of plot: Domestic realism
Time of plot: Mid-twentieth century
Locale: New York City and upstate New York
First published: Sonim, de Geshichte fun a Liebe, 1966 (English translation, 1972)

> *Principal characters:*
> HERMAN BRODER, a young Jewish immigrant from Poland
> TAMAR RACHEL BRODER (TAMARA), his first wife
> YADWIGA PRACZ, his present wife
> MASHA TORTSHINER, his mistress
> SHIFRAH PUAH BLOCH, her mother
> RABBI MILTON LAMPERT, Herman's wealthy employer

The Story:

On a summer morning, Herman Broder stirred from his troubled dreams, wondering if he could be in Nazi-occupied Poland, perhaps in the hayloft where his parents' servant girl, Yadwiga, had concealed him in order to save his life. Then, fully awake, he realized that he was in the apartment in Brooklyn which he shared with Yadwiga, whom he married after learning of the deaths of his wife and his children.

Herman told Yadwiga that he must make another of his overnight train trips to sell books. Actually, he remained in New York City, spending the day in the office of Rabbi Milton Lampert, for whom Herman worked as a ghostwriter, and the night at the apartment of his mistress, Masha Tortshiner, and her mother, Shifrah Puah Bloch, who were also Holocaust survivors. Although Masha knew that Herman was married, her mother did not. She was determined to have Masha get a divorce from her husband, Leon, so that she could marry Herman.

One day, Shifrah Puah called Herman's attention to a notice in the newspaper asking him to telephone a certain number. When he made the call, Herman found himself speaking to the uncle of his first wife, Tamara, who, it seemed, was alive and in New York. When Herman and Tamara were reunited, he was surprised to find her prettier than ever and considerably easier to get along with than she had been in the past. Although Herman knew that he must choose between his two wives, he had to admit that he would like to keep them both, and the volatile Masha as well.

Herman's trips to see Tamara aroused Masha's suspicions, even though she did not guess that Herman's first wife had come back from the dead. Herman thought he might be able to reassure Masha about his feelings for her during a vacation in the Adirondack Mountains that they had been planning. At first, they did relax and enjoy themselves, but then Masha told Herman that she was pregnant. Taken by surprise, Herman rashly promised to marry Masha.

Blithely ignoring the fact that Herman was already married, which, after all, involved only a mere Gentile, Masha worked on getting a divorce. Meanwhile, Herman's other two relationships with women were becoming even more complicated. On an outing in the Catskill

Mountains, he and Tamara, who had been merely friends, found themselves making love and enjoying it. Then, Yadwiga decided that she could become closer to her husband if she converted to Judaism and gave him a Jewish child. Though he did not want to bring a child into a world so full of cruelty and suffering, Herman could not refuse her.

Herman was still managing to keep the three women apart. However, he worried constantly about exposure, which he knew would cost him his job with the rabbi and might well lead to his being imprisoned or deported. He did have a little time to decide about which of his present wives to keep, because he had married Yadwiga in all innocence, believing Tamara to be dead. However, he would have no excuse, moral or legal, for acquiring a third wife.

Quite unexpectedly, Leon Tortshiner offered Herman a way out. He met with Herman in order to warn him that Masha was a promiscuous, deceitful woman. Leon told Herman not only that Masha had been consistently unfaithful during their marriage but also that she had already betrayed Herman by sleeping with Leon as the price of obtaining her divorce. Herman's immediate response was to end the relationship with Masha; however, she managed to convince him that it was Leon who was lying, and the two were married after all.

By the time winter arrived, Herman was in serious financial trouble. Not only was Yadwiga expecting a baby, which meant more bills in Brooklyn, but, after Masha's pregnancy had turned out to be purely psychological, she was too depressed to work, and so Herman had to provide all the support for the Bronx household as well. As a new convert to Judaism, Yadwiga was also driving Herman crazy with her questions about a faith he no longer observed.

Finally, the inevitable happened. First, Tamara dropped in at the Brooklyn apartment, and Yadwiga recognized her. Then some neighbors brought a gossipy man named Nathan Pesheles to meet Mrs. Broder, and, though Tamara pretended to be Herman's cousin, Pesheles took a good look at Yadwiga. When Rabbi Lampert found out that Herman had recently married, he visited Masha and invited the newlyweds to a party. One of the rabbi's guests was the observant Mr. Pesheles. He promptly informed Masha that he had met a Tamara Broder at Herman's apartment in Brooklyn, thus tipping her off to the fact that the dead wife was not dead, and then went on to tell everyone else, including the rabbi, that, in addition to Masha, Herman also had a pretty, pregnant wife named Yadwiga.

Before the evening ended, the kindly rabbi offered Masha a job and both Masha and her mother a place to live. Masha accepted, telling Herman that she never wanted to see him again. Tamara came to Herman's rescue, taking him in, giving him a job in her uncle's bookstore, and even helping Yadwiga in any way she could.

Then, just when things were going well, Masha came back into Herman's life. Now she wanted him again, and he agreed to run away with her. However, she was delayed, first by finding that her apartment had been burglarized, then by her mother's death. Herman and Masha considered a double suicide, but finally Herman decided to leave not only Masha, but everyone else.

Masha did kill herself. Yadwiga moved in with Tamara, who ran the bookstore while Yadwiga took care of their place and of her baby girl, little Masha. No one ever knew what happened to Herman.

Critical Evaluation:

Generally considered the most important Yiddish writer of the twentieth century, Isaac Bashevis Singer won a Nobel Prize in Literature in 1978, in large part because of his re-creation of a world which no longer exists. Singer often wrote about life in Polish-Jewish villages before they and their inhabitants were destroyed by the Nazis. *Enemies*, however, is set in the postwar, post-Holocaust period. Its subject is serious: the ways in which those who survived the Holocaust dealt with their memories and built new lives.

Appropriately, *Enemies* begins with Herman Broder's reliving the past. Even though he is now safe, Herman has been forever changed by his experiences. He has lost his faith in God and in human life. While he has married again, Herman hedges his bets by also keeping a mistress and remaining open to other possibilities. He is adamantly opposed to having more children, for it is clear that one cannot count on a beneficent God to preserve them. In fact, all that Herman now believes in is lust, which existed even in the death camps, and deceit, which he believes is the only way one can make it through the world.

Singer also shows how his four major women characters have responded to the Holocaust. Shifrah Puah wears black to keep alive the memories of those who died and feels guilty because she is alive. However, Shifrah still believes in God and observes the Jewish rituals.

Masha hates God as much as her mother loves him. Now, the central reality in her life is the Holocaust. Masha finds sexual stimulation in telling stories of those days while she and Herman are making love. Masha is enchanted with death, and, indeed, she does finally commit suicide.

In a sense, Tamara did die in the Holocaust, for she has become a new person: more unselfish, more considerate, and far wiser than she was before the war. After she and Herman are reunited, Tamara asks nothing for herself, not even that he return to her. Ironically, it is Tamara who now becomes Herman's only real friend and confidante. Even when he tells her that he is running off with Masha, Tamara accepts his decision with grace, and it is she who will fill Herman's place at the bookstore and care for his wife and his child.

It is also ironic that it is a Polish Catholic, Yadwiga, who replaces Herman within the Jewish community. What begins as her attempt to please her husband by observing his rituals ends with her wholeheartedly accepting the faith in which he no longer believes. Although Herman would blame his Holocaust experience for his actions, Singer points out that Herman's character was formed long before the Nazis came to power. It is appropriate that, at the end of the novel, the self-centered Herman, if not dead, is alone somewhere, while the generous Yadwiga is being cherished by her new community.

The tone of *Enemies* is not uniformly serious. Like the village storytellers from whom he drew his inspiration, Singer delights in the eccentricities of human behavior and in the capacity of human beings to make fools of themselves. Herman Broder's adventures in *Enemies* are essentially farcical, and Herman himself, though appealing, is devoid of common sense. After he has escaped from the Nazis by hiding from them and from God by denying him, Herman uses his new freedom to become the willing slave of lust, especially as it is embodied in the equally irrational Masha.

Of his three wives, Masha alone is as irrational and as self-destructive as Herman. While both Tamara and Yadwiga try to keep Herman out of trouble, Masha always encourages him to behave like a fool. She gets him to marry her at the risk of being imprisoned or deported, and eventually she causes him to lose his job. Then, after ending the relationship with him, she quits her job and persuades him to quit his so that they can run off together; she even agrees with him that, because of a slight hitch in their plans, they might as well commit suicide. Ironically, at that point Herman is saved by his own irrationality. When Masha confesses that she deceived him about sleeping with her husband, Herman fails to see the parallel with his lying about sleeping with his wife Tamara, and he decides not to kill himself after all. Like a thwarted child, he decides to quit the whole world.

As it is applied to Herman and Masha, Singer's subtitle, "A Love Story," points to the accuracy of the title "Enemies." Certainly these two lovers are each other's worst enemies.

However, the epilogue suggests that love can be redemptive rather than destructive. Thus, after Herman has rejected their aid and turned his back on life, Yadwiga and Tamara find gratification in helping each other, in loving the child Herman left them, and in being a part of the community which, through this new Jewish child, will itself be renewed.

Rosemary M. Canfield Reisman

Bibliography:
Alexander, Edward. *Isaac Bashevis Singer: A Study of the Short Fiction*. Boston: Twayne, 1980. A thorough and insightful work. The chapter devoted to *Enemies* emphasizes the importance of the Holocaust in the novel and in Jewish intellectual history.
Farrell, Grace, ed. *Isaac Bashevis Singer: Conversations*. Jackson: University Press of Mississippi, 1992. A collection of interviews in which *Enemies* is frequently mentioned. Singer points out that he understands Herman Broder's lack of belief in God but does not share his attitude.
Friedman, Lawrence S. *Understanding Isaac Bashevis Singer*. Columbia: University of South Carolina Press, 1988. Shows how the novel reflects its post-Holocaust setting. The Jews who survived and immigrated to America had to deal with religious doubt, along with their loss of a common language and of a sense of community.
Kresh, Paul. *Isaac Bashevis Singer: The Magician of West Eighty-sixth Street*. New York: Dial Press, 1979. An insightful critical biography. The brief but useful discussion of *Enemies* argues that Singer himself was the model for Herman Broder.
Lee, Grace Farrell. *From Exile to Redemption: The Fiction of Isaac Bashevis Singer*. Carbondale: Southern Illinois University Press, 1987. Systematically traces the development of Singer's thought, classifying the late work *Enemies* as a story of redemption. Although Herman exiles himself from God, Yadwiga and Tamara affirm their faith by nurturing a Jewish child.

AN ENEMY OF THE PEOPLE

Type of work: Drama
Author: Henrik Ibsen (1828-1906)
Type of plot: Social criticism
Time of plot: Late nineteenth century
Locale: Southern Norway
First published: En folkefiende, 1882 (English translation, 1890); first performed, 1883

> *Principal characters:*
> DR. THOMAS STOCKMANN, a medical officer
> MRS. STOCKMANN, his wife
> PETRA, his daughter
> EJLIF and
> MORTEN, his sons
> PETER STOCKMANN, his brother, the mayor
> MORTEN KIIL, Mrs. Stockmann's father
> HOVSTAD, an editor
> BILLING, a subeditor
> ASLAKSEN, a printer
> CAPTAIN HORSTER, Dr. Stockmann's friend

The Story:

All the citizens of the small Norwegian coastal town were very proud of the Baths, for the healing waters were making the town famous and prosperous. Dr. Stockmann, the medical officer of the Baths, and his brother Peter, the mayor and chairman of the Baths committee, did not agree on many things, but they did agree that the Baths were the source of the town's good fortune. Hovstad, the editor of the *People's Messenger*, and his subeditor, Billing, were also loud in praise of the Baths. Business was good and the people were beginning to enjoy prosperity.

Then Dr. Stockmann received from the University a report stating that the waters of the Baths were contaminated. Having become suspicious when several visitors became ill after taking the Baths, he had felt it his duty to investigate. Refuse from tanneries above the town was oozing into the pipes leading to the reservoir and infecting the waters. This meant that the big pipes would have to be relaid, at a tremendous cost to the owners or to the town. When Hovstad and Billing heard this news, they asked the doctor to write an article for their paper about the terrible conditions. They even spoke of having the town give Dr. Stockmann a testimonial to honor him for his great discovery.

Dr. Stockmann wrote up his findings and sent the manuscript to his brother so that his report could be acted upon officially. Hovstad called on the doctor again, urging him to write articles for the *People's Messenger*. It was Hovstad's opinion that the town had fallen into the hands of a few officials who did not care about the people's rights, and it was his intention to attack these men in his paper and urge the citizens to get rid of them in the next election.

Aslaksen, a printer who claimed to have the compact majority under his control, also wanted to join in the fight to get the Baths purified and the corrupt officials defeated. Dr. Stockmann could not believe that his brother would refuse to accept the report, but he soon learned that he was wrong. Peter went to the doctor and insisted that he keep his knowledge to himself because the income of the town would be lost if the report were made public. He said that the repairs would be too costly, that the owners of the Baths could not stand the cost, and that the townspeople would never allow an increase in taxes to clean up the waters. He even insisted that Dr. Stockmann write another report, stating that he had been mistaken in his earlier judgment. He felt this action necessary when he learned that Hovstad and Billing knew of the first report. When the doctor refused either to change his report or to withhold it, Peter threatened him with the loss of his position. Even his wife pleaded with him not to cross his powerful brother; he was sustained in his determination to do right only by his daughter Petra.

Hovstad, Billing, and Aslaksen were anxious to print the doctor's article so that the town could know of the falseness of the mayor and his officials. They thought his words so clear and intelligible that all responsible citizens would revolt against the corrupt regime. Aslaksen did plead for moderation, but promised to fight for what was right.

Peter Stockmann appeared at the office of the *People's Messenger* and cleverly told Aslaksen, Hovstad, and Billing that the tradespeople of the town would suffer if the doctor's report were made public. He said that they would have to stand the expense and that the Baths would be closed for two years while repairs were being made. The two editors and the printer then turned against Dr. Stockmann and supported Peter, believing that the majority would do so.

The doctor pleaded with them to stand by the promises they had given him, but they were the slaves of the very majority opinion they claimed to mold. When they refused to print his article, the doctor called a public meeting in the home of his friend, Captain Horster. Most of the citizens who attended already disliked him because the mayor and the newspaper editors had spread the news that he wanted to close the Baths and ruin the town. Aslaksen, nominated as chairman by the mayor, so controlled the meeting that a discussion of the Baths was ruled out of order.

Nevertheless, Dr. Stockmann took the floor and in ringing tones told the citizens that it was the unbelievable stupidity of the authorities and the great multitude of the compact majority that caused all the evil and corruption in the world. He said that the majority destroyed freedom and truth everywhere because the majority was ignorant and stupid. The majority was really in slavery to ideas which had long outlived their truth and usefulness. He contended that ideas become outdated in eighteen or twenty years at the most, but that the foolish majority continued to cling to them and deny new truths brought to them by the intelligent minority. He challenged the citizens to deny that all great ideas and truths were first raised by the persecuted minority, those few men who dared to stand out against the prevailing opinions of the many. He said that the real intellectuals could be distinguished as easily as could a thoroughbred animal from a cross breed. Economic and social position had no bearing on the distinction. It was a man's soul and mind that separated him from the ignorant masses.

His challenge fell on deaf ears. As he knew, the majority could not understand the meaning of his words. By vote they named him an enemy of the people. The next day they stoned his house and sent him threatening letters. His landlord ordered him to move. He lost his position as medical director of the Baths, and his daughter Petra was dismissed from her teaching position. In each case the person responsible for the action stated that it was public opinion that forced that action. No one had anything against him or his family, but no one would fight the opinion of the majority. Even Captain Horster, a friend who had promised to take the Stockmanns to America on his next voyage, lost his ship because the owner was afraid to give a ship to the only man who had stood by the radical Dr. Stockmann.

The doctor learned that his father-in-law had bought up most of the now undesirable Bath stock with the money that was to have gone to Mrs. Stockmann and the children. The townspeople accused the doctor of attacking the Baths so that his family could buy the stock and make a profit, and his father-in-law accused him of ruining his wife's inheritance if he persisted in his stories about the uncleanliness of the Baths. Reviled and ridiculed on all sides, Dr. Stockmann determined to fight back by opening a school. Starting only with any urchins he could find on the streets, he would teach the town and the world that he was stronger than the majority, that he was strong because he had the courage to stand alone.

Critical Evaluation:

The Norwegian playwright Henrik Ibsen, considered by many to be one of the greatest dramatists of all time, is also called the father of modern drama. In the mid-1870's, he created a new tradition of realistic prose drama that dealt boldly with contemporary social problems and individual psychology, offering an alternative to the melodrama that had dominated early nineteenth century theater. In the first twenty-five years of his career, Ibsen wrote romantic and historical dramas designed to glorify Norway and to wean Norwegian audiences from popular Danish plays. With his later, major works—twelve prose dramas of increasing complexity, beginning with *The Pillars of Society* (1877) and ending with *When We Dead Awaken* (1899)— Ibsen set a standard for realistic theater that would be emulated throughout the Western world. Ibsen's nineteenth century audiences were often shocked by the new and realistic subject matter of his plays. *Ghosts* (1881) openly referred to inherited venereal disease, and *A Doll's House* (1879) displayed an astonishingly liberal attitude toward the emancipation of women. Both plays were attacked as "immoral" and banned from several cities in Europe.

An Enemy of the People (1882), though somewhat less controversial, was revolutionary in its unflinching portrayal of the greed and self-interest in small-town politics. Ibsen spares almost no one as he examines the power of self-interest to shape human attitudes toward truth and civic responsibility. The townspeople are portrayed in Act IV as little more than an unthinking mob. In fact, Ibsen at times seems so critical of the power of the "compact majority" that some scholars interpret his play as an elitist attack on democracy. The extreme vacillation of the newspapermen, Hovstad and Billing, seems marked for special scorn. They enthusiastically support but then quickly abandon Dr. Stockmann as soon as they perceive their self-interest differently. Even Stockmann himself, heroic figure that he might be, is clearly motivated by self-interest. In the first act, his excitement over the discovery of pollution in the Baths is obviously motivated, at least in part, by extreme and petty competitiveness with his brother Peter. Stockmann is so absorbed in the singularity of his discovery that he naïvely ignores its obvious ramifications, hoping instead for rewards from the town. At the end of the play, Stockmann declares that "the strongest man in the world is he who stands alone," but he is ignoring his family, who will have to stand and suffer along with him. With nearly everyone in the play motivated and blinded by self-interest, Ibsen seems to imply that this distorting power dominates nearly all human minds and thus all aspects of human life.

Only the minor character, Captain Horster, seems free from the motivations of self-interest. Horster offers his house for Stockmann's speech in Act IV when no one else in the town dares support him, and at the end of the play Horster offers his house to the Stockmanns permanently, even though he has been dismissed from his ship's command as a result of his support of Stockmann. Captain Horster has nothing to gain from helping Stockmann and no particular interest in the political issues involved. He helps Stockmann simply because Stockmann is a friend in need.

Captain Horster functions in this play as a kind of *raisonneur*, a type of character who usually appears as a minor figure somewhat detached from the action and who represents a calm, levelheaded, rational standard against which the usually more irrational behavior of other characters is contrasted and measured. Ibsen's use of this traditional kind of dramatic character is unusually subtle. Horster is almost a shadowy figure in the play, appearing infrequently and saying little, though his presence can be very powerful in a sensitive reading or state production of the play. In his entrance with Stockmann in the first scene, Horster's reluctance to take advantage of Stockmann's somewhat extravagant largess is very subtly contrasted with the gluttony of Billing, who greedily gobbles up Stockmann's roast beef. Though he says little, Horster's words are powerfully indicative of the rational standard that underlies the play. When Billing loudly asserts that "a community is like a ship; every one ought to be prepared to take the helm," Captain Horster responds to this easy platitude with one line of hard, common sense: "Maybe that is all very well on shore; but on board ship it wouldn't work."

Ibsen's realistic style inaugurates a new style of drama because the settings, characters, and issues of his plays comment directly and forcefully on the life of his audiences. Ibsen is also called the father of modern drama because his plays possess a rich, thematic complexity typical of twentieth century literature. In his later plays, an increasing use of symbolism generates an even more complex, dense, and poetic drama. Ibsen's technical brilliance in the service of thematic complexity is already clear in *An Enemy of the People*. In Stockmann's discovery of the polluted Baths, Ibsen presents a very modern situation—the genuine dilemma with no satisfactory solution. The Baths are obviously dangerous and must be closed, but the closing of the Baths will also destroy the town, and it is the unresolvable nature of this dilemma between social responsibility and business interests that dominates the play. The accumulation of incidents in the play makes that dilemma clearer until the audience must accept a dramatic situation with no satisfactory resolution. In the play's first two acts, Peter Stockmann stands alone because all "right-thinking" people appear to agree that the Baths must be closed. In Act III, when Peter specifically outlines the economic devastation that will result from the closing of the Baths, nearly everyone in town shifts to Peter's point of view. Now Dr. Stockmann is the one who stands alone. In Act V, Ibsen adds a final twist to the situation. Stockmann's father-in-law, Morten Kiil, has used Mrs. Stockmann's inheritance to purchase the remaining stock in the Baths. Stockmann's persistence in closing the Baths now financially endangers his entire family and could destroy them as well as him. The price of idealism has been raised to an uncomfortable level. Thus, at the end of the play, Ibsen makes it impossible for the audience to choose sides comfortably. Stockmann can easily appear supercilious, even unbalanced, as he announces in the last scene that he will remain in town and start his own school, recruit "street urchins—regular ragamuffins," and "experiment with curs." Is Stockmann a hero, a fool, or both? The audience is unable to resolve their ambiguous attitudes toward Stockmann and the town that turned against him. They thus experience through Ibsen's play the radical uncertainty that typifies much of twentieth century literature and thought.

"Critical Evaluation" by Terry Nienhuis

Bibliography:
Gray, Ronald D. "*An Enemy of the People*." In *Ibsen: A Dissenting View*. Cambridge, England: Cambridge University Press, 1977. Gray develops in a very interesting way the widely held theory that *An Enemy of the People* is an allegory on the hostile reception generally given Ibsen's previous play, *Ghosts*.
Hornby, Richard. "The Validity of the Ironic Life: *An Enemy of the People*." In *Patterns in Ibsen's Middle Plays*. Lewisburg, Pa.: Bucknell University Press, 1981. An extremely

thorough and convincing interpretation of the play as an ironic portrait of Dr. Stockmann, a "multifaceted" character "mixing noble and base impulses."

Knutson, Harold C. *"An Enemy of the People*: Ibsen's Reluctant Comedy." *Comparative Drama* 27 (Summer, 1993): 159-176. Analyzes the comic tone of the play. In Stockmann's inflated ego Ibsen is, to some extent, consciously parodying himself.

Shaw, George Bernard. *"An Enemy of the People*: 1882." In *The Quintessence of Ibsenism.* 1891. Reprint. New York: Hill and Wang, 1958. Shaw's book introduced Ibsen to England and helped make Ibsen's works popular worldwide. It remains an indispensable guide to the plays.

Weigland, Hermann J. *"An Enemy of the People."* In *The Modern Ibsen: A Reconsideration.* New York: E. P. Dutton, 1960. Originally published in 1925, Weigland's essay is still one of the most thorough examinations of the play.

LES ENFANTS TERRIBLES

Type of work: Novel
Author: Jean Cocteau (1889-1963)
Type of plot: Psychological
Time of plot: Early twentieth century
Locale: Paris
First published: 1929 (English translation, 1930)

Principal characters:
    PAUL, a sensitive, imaginative boy
    ELISABETH, his sister
    GÉRARD, their friend
    AGATHA, Gérard's wife and a friend of Paul and Elisabeth
    MICHAEL, an American

The Story:

Paul and Elisabeth lived with their paralyzed mother in an old quarter of Paris. They lived in a private, instinctual world, dissociated from adults by passivity, imagination, and secret, mysterious rites. One night, when the quarter was transformed by snow, Paul was wandering among the snowballing groups in search of the school hero Dargelos, whom he worshiped. Dargelos, who possessed great charm, was both vicious and beautiful. As Paul moved toward him, Dargelos, perhaps accidentally, knocked him down with a stone-packed snowball. Although he injured Paul, he escaped immediate punishment but was later expelled from the school. Paul was taken home by Gérard, who loved Paul as much for his weakness as Paul loved Dargelos for his strength. Elisabeth was extremely angry with them when they reached Paul's home. She was then sixteen years old, two years older than Paul and utterly absorbed in him. She was frequently transported by fury when he appeared to be leaving her sphere of influence.

The three children went into the Room where Paul and Elisabeth ate, slept, read, fought, and played the Game. The Room was the central fixture in their lives; the Game was their inner world. The Room existed in an established chaos of boxes, clothes, papers, and books. Paul left it only for school and Elisabeth only to look after their mother or to buy magazines. Essentially the Game was daydreaming, a willed withdrawal to an imaginary world of submerged consciousness. After Elisabeth had sent Gérard away, she undressed Paul and put him to bed. Their doctor decided that Paul was unfit to return to school, a decision that plunged Paul into despair until he learned of Dargelos' expulsion. After that, school held no interest for him.

The Room held hidden treasures, the artifacts of their unconscious minds—keys, marbles, aspirin bottles—and when Gérard told Paul that Dargelos had disappeared, a photograph of him dressed as Athalie was added to the collection. The mother died suddenly. When Paul and Elisabeth saw her, rigid and transfixed in her chair, staring forward, the image haunted them; it was the one they retained. The mother's nurse, Mariette, remained in the household, content to care for and love Paul and Elisabeth without altering them.

Now an accepted visitor in the Room, Gérard was aware of the almost tangible tension, expressed in fights, recriminations, and reconciliations, between the two siblings. When Paul was well enough, Elisabeth, surprisingly, accepted an invitation from Gérard's uncle to take a holiday by the sea. On the journey she watched Paul while he was sleeping and was disgusted by the air of weakness that his illness had accentuated. She decided to remold him according to her own plans.

Once by the sea, they established a Room as much like their own as possible. Paul gained strength under Elisabeth's tutelage, in part through stealing useless objects from local shops while on raids that she had planned. Their booty formed a treasure imitating that in the Paris Room.

When they returned to Paris, Elisabeth was suddenly aware that Paul had outstripped her and that she had become the subordinate party in their relationship. Paul spent his evenings wandering around Montmartre, watching girls, drinking, and finally meeting Gérard and bringing him home for the night. On these occasions, Elisabeth would use him as a means of tormenting Paul. The first time she succeeded in rousing her brother came when she declared that she too would go into the world. Her position, she felt, had become untenable, and she subsequently obtained work as a mannequin. This act enraged Paul, who declared that she was prostituting herself; she thought the same about his nightly excursions.

At the dressmaker's establishment where she worked, Elisabeth met Agatha, an orphan whose drug-addicted parents had committed suicide. For Agatha she felt, for the first time, warm affection, but Agatha's introduction to the Room precipitated Paul's and Elisabeth's destruction when Agatha became devoted to Paul. The photograph revealed a startling likeness between Dargelos and Agatha, and Paul enthralled her as he had been in thrall to Dargelos. Agatha felt at home in the Room, but at the same time she recognized the strange, dreamlike existence her friends led.

As they matured, the Game failed to absorb Paul and Elisabeth completely. This situation so distressed Elisabeth that when she met Michael, an American friend of Gérard, she transferred her dream life to him. Paul was excluded from this friendship with Michael, but his anger at learning of it evaporated when he discovered that Michael wanted to marry Elisabeth and not, as he had subconsciously feared, Agatha. Elisabeth did marry Michael, but true to Gérard's vision of her, the marriage was never consummated: Michael was killed while driving alone in his sports car a few hours after the wedding.

Elisabeth inherited his fortune and his Paris house, into which the four moved. Lonely and disoriented in separate rooms, they gravitated to the Room that Paul finally established in the dining hall. Their lives moved slowly to a climax from the moment that Paul realized he was in love with Agatha. Afraid to tell each other of their love, they each told Elisabeth. Terrified that Paul might leave her, Elisabeth moved tirelessly between them all one night to dissuade them from marrying. Lying, she told Paul that it was Gérard whom Agatha loved, and she told Agatha that Paul was too selfish ever to love anyone. She also convinced Gérard that by friendship he had won Agatha's love and that it was his duty to marry her. Elisabeth was so dedicated to the idea of possessing Paul and so trusted by the others that she succeeded completely in her scheme.

A short time after his marriage to Agatha, Gérard met Dargelos. The former schoolmate sent Paul a gift, part of his collection of poisons. Paul and Elisabeth were delighted with the present which, to Agatha's horror, was added to the treasure.

Weeks later, when Paris was again covered in snow, Elisabeth dreamed that Paul was dead. She woke to find Agatha at the door. Agatha was convinced that Paul had killed himself; she had received a letter from him threatening suicide. They ran to the Room and found Paul choking on poison fumes which filled the screened-in corner where he lay. Although he could barely speak, with Agatha he reconstructed Elisabeth's scheme. When he cursed her, she felt that her heart had died. After admitting her guilt and jealousy, she snatched a revolver; by that violent act, she was able to regain their attention and thus to captivate Paul once more. Elisabeth worked to charm him back into their world of the Room and the Game, far from Agatha, who seemed less real to him than the snowstorm outside. The two women watched each other until Paul fell back exhausted. Thinking him dead, Elisabeth shot herself. Crashing against the screens, she destroyed the Room and let in the enemy world. Paul saw visions of people playing with snowballs crowding the windows, watching as he died. Theirs was the tragedy of outcasts who, unaware that they lived on borrowed time, died fighting for their private existence.

Critical Evaluation:

Les Enfants Terribles is the most claustrophobic of all Jean Cocteau's works, although its intense concentration on the vagaries of love is matched by its later companion piece *Les Parents terribles* (1938). In Cocteau's fantasies based on myth or folklore (in the case of *La Belle et la bête*, 1945), love can play a redemptive role, rescuing characters from distortions of their inner being imposed by other forces. In his domestic dramas, however, love is a distortive affliction that leads to disaster.

Cocteau's film version of *Les Enfants Terribles* (released in 1950) was given a restrictive X rating in Britain because the censors deemed the relationship between Paul and Elisabeth to be implicitly incestuous. This is a misleading simplification of a more complicated and more problematic network of feelings. Although Paul initially leaves the Room only to go to school, while Elisabeth clings even more closely to its sanctuary, they broaden their horizons conspicuously as they grow to sexual maturity. The Game, which absorbed them completely in their childish innocence, is dramatically transformed as they struggle to come to terms with the greater game of the social world. The possessiveness reflected in Elisabeth's attempt to keep Paul and Agatha apart is not only a simple desire to cling fast to what she and her brother have always had. It also arises out of the fact that they have both begun to yearn for something different, while fearing that what they want might be impossible to achieve. She is reacting against her own impulses as well. The siblings are inextricably bound together, but not by anything as straightforward as lust or sexual jealousy.

Paul's nemesis, Dargelos, is based on a real person of that name whom Cocteau encountered during his schooldays, and to whom the author refers in several other works. Although he can hardly be said to figure large in *Les Enfants Terribles* as a character, Dargelos moves the two most important levers of the plot. Dargelos injures Paul with the stone hidden in the snowball; through this incident Gérard is drawn into the lives of Paul and Elisabeth, disrupting their privacy. Dargelos also provides the poison that Paul takes after Elisabeth convinces him that Agatha does not love him. Dargelos is tacitly present at the novel's end as well as its beginning, still armed with his deadly snowball. His cold cruelty brackets the entire tragedy in such a fashion as to suggest that if only he had looked with favor upon his acolyte, all might have been well. If, in fact, the reader decides that Agatha was only a substitute for the charismatic Dargelos, then Elisabeth might be deemed to have had some reason to judge that it might be better, in the long run, to keep them apart.

Through the actions and reactions of Gérard, the fascinated voyeur, Cocteau testifies to the fact that there is something precious in the Game, but not in the sense that it is some kind of tiny utopia. The Game provides Paul's and Elisabeth's lives with a fundamental structure that Gérard's lacks, but it is essentially something to fall back on when other projects fail. Wherever they go they can always return to the Room, or some simulacrum of it, to provide safe haven for themselves—but that is all the Room is; it can never provide an answer to their inner needs.

There is a certain ironic paradox in the fact that the Game that Paul and Elisabeth play allows Paul to build up the strength he requires for his periodic ventures into the world beyond. He comes to appreciate this paradox when Elisabeth retaliates by moving outside herself, raising the possibility that when he next needs to recover from the personal disasters he constantly courts, she might not be there for him. The irony is, of course, redoubled when Elisabeth's expedition to the outer world brings back Agatha, a much more dangerous invader than Gérard.

It is not easy to weigh Elisabeth's decision to marry Michael. Perhaps it is an authentic attempt to begin a new Game and move into a new Room, whose tragic interruption seals the fate of Elisabeth and Paul in a relatively straightforward fashion. If Gérard's judgment of the matter is correct, however, her gesture is a feint that Michael's death merely serves to terminate in a relatively tidy fashion. If so, it is not entirely clear whether Elisabeth's halfhearted and doomed attempt to escape should be construed as a flight from Paul or as a flight from Agatha. To the extent that her subsequent determination to keep them apart is motivated by jealousy, it is not obvious which of them she is more jealous of—it was, after all, she who first became enamoured of Agatha. Given Gérard's inherent manipulability, marrying Agatha to him cannot seem such a definite loss as allowing her to marry Paul.

If this interpretation is accepted, Elisabeth's emotions and motives are more complicated than she realizes, and certainly far more complicated than Gérard realizes. Her final attempt to rebuild the Room and restart the Game is clearly a matter of desperation rather than constructive desire, and its failure is inevitable. The snow that conceals sharp stones ultimately blankets everything, banishing all the possible varieties of human warmth with evenhanded cruelty.

The Room is depicted throughout the novel as a prison, not so much because it embodies "the shadowy instincts of childhood" that are mentioned in the first few pages, but more because the world outside is full of sharp stones and subtle poisons. The apparent freedom of the world of adult relationships is spoiled by the lurking presence of Dargelos. He is the handsome and charming but ultimately treacherous object of desire. He is free, but the exercise of his freedom condemns others to their prisons, and ultimately to death row.

"Critical Evaluation" by Brian Stableford

Bibliography:
Brée, Germaine, and Margaret Guiton. *An Age of Fiction: The French Novel from Gide to Camus.* New Brunswick, N.J.: Rutgers University Press, 1957. Cocteau's novels are discussed form page 140 to page 148, which describe him as "a modern Daedalus."
Brown, Frederick. *An Impersonation of Angels: A Biography of Jean Cocteau.* New York: Viking, 1968. Like most studies of Cocteau this concentrates more on his work for the cinema than on his novels. Considers the relationship between the two versions of *Les Enfants Terribles.*
Crosland, Margaret. *Jean Cocteau.* London: Peter Nevill, 1955. A biography and critical analysis. Discusses the novel version of *Les Enfants Terribles* on pages 166-169.
Fowlie, Wallace. *Jean Cocteau: The History of a Poet's Age.* Bloomington: Indiana University Press, 1966. A sensitive study that includes a discussion of *Les Enfants Terribles.*
Steegmuller, Francis. *Cocteau: A Biography.* London: Constable, 1986. A biography that is fuller than Crosland's and less florid than Brown's.

THE ENORMOUS ROOM

Type of work: Novel
Author: e. e. cummings (1894-1962)
Type of plot: Autobiographical
Time of plot: 1917
Locale: France
First published: 1922

Principal characters:
> E. E. CUMMINGS, an American ambulance driver
> W. S. B., his American friend
> APOLLYON, the head of the French prison
> ROCKYFELLER,
> THE WANDERER,
> ZOO-LOO,
> SURPLICE, and
> JEAN LE NÈGRE, other prisoners

The Story:

The poet e. e. cummings and his friend B. were unhappy as members of the Norton-Harjes Ambulance Service, a unit sent by Americans to aid the French during World War I. One day they were arrested by French military police. From hints dropped during an investigation, cummings gathered that B. had written letters the censor found suspicious. Because they were good friends, both men were held for questioning. They never found out exactly what they were suspected of doing. On one occasion, cummings was asked whether he hated the Germans. He replied that he did not, that he simply loved the French very much. The investigating official could not understand how one could love the French and not hate Germans. Finally, cummings and B. were separated and sent to different prisons. Again and again cummings was questioned and moved from one spot to another, always under strict guard.

Late one night, he was taken to a prison in the little provincial town of Macé. There he was thrown into a huge darkened room, given a straw mattress, and told to go to sleep. In the darkness, he counted at least thirty voices speaking eleven different languages. Early the next morning he met B. in the room, who told him that all the prisoners there were suspected of being spies, some only because they spoke no French.

That morning, he learned the routine of the prison. The enormous room was lined with mattresses down each side, with a few windows to let in light at one end. It smelled of stale tobacco and sweat. Some of the men in the room were insane, and most of the others were afraid they might become so. The dull routine began at five-thirty in the morning, when someone was sent down to the kitchen under guard to bring back a bucket of sour, cold coffee. After coffee, the prisoners drew lots to see who would clear the room, sweep the floors, and collect the trash. At seven-thirty, they were allowed to walk for two hours in a small, walled-in courtyard. Then came the first meal of the day, followed by another walk in the garden. At four, they were given supper. At eight, they were locked in the enormous room for the night.

There was little entertainment except fighting and conversation. Some of the men spent their time trying to catch sight of women, who were kept in another part of the prison. The poet began to accustom himself to the enormous room and to make friends among the various inmates. One of the first of these was Count Bragard, a Belgian painter who specialized in portraits of horses. The count was a perfect gentleman, even in prison, and always looked neat and suave. He and cummings discussed painting and the arts as if they were at a polite party. Before cummings left, the count began to act strangely and withdraw from his friends. He was losing his mind.

One day, cummings was taken to see the head of the prison, a gross man he called Apollyon. Apollyon had no interest in the prisoners as long as they made no trouble for him. He questioned cummings for a considerable time in an effort to learn why the American was there, a circumstance over which the American himself often puzzled.

When new inmates arrived in the room, everyone looked them over with anticipation, some to find a man with money he could lend, some to find a fellow countryman, and some to find a friend. One day, a very fat, rosy-cheeked man arrived. He had been a successful manager of a disreputable house, and because he had a large sum of money with him, he was nicknamed Rockyfeller. He hired a strong man to act as his bodyguard. Nobody liked him, for he bought special privileges from the guards.

During his stay in the room, cummings met three men, very different from one another, whose personal qualities were such that they made life seem meaningful to him. He called them the Delectable Mountains, after the mountains Christian found in Paul Bunyan's *Pilgrim's Progress* (1678-1684). The first was the Wanderer, whose wife and three little children were in the women's ward of the prison. He was a strong man, and simple in his emotions and feelings; cummings liked to talk with him about his problems. One of the Wanderer's children, a little boy, sometimes came to the enormous room to visit his father. His pranks and games both bothered and amused the men. The Wanderer treated his son with love and the deepest kind of understanding. Until he was sent away, he remained cummings' best friend.

The second Delectable Mountain was Zoo-loo, a Polish farmer who could speak neither French nor English but who could communicate by signs. In a short time, he and cummings knew all about each other. Zoo-loo had a knack for hiding money, and despite the fact that the head of the prison repeatedly had him and his belongings thoroughly searched, he always seemed able to produce a twenty franc note from his left ear or the back of his neck. His kindnesses to cummings and B. were innumerable.

The third Delectable Mountain was a little man named Surplice. Everything astonished him. When cummings had some candy or cheese, Surplice was sure to come over to his cot and ask questions about it in a shy manner. His curiosity and friendly conversation made everything seem more important and interesting than it really was.

One morning, Jean Le Nègre was brought to the enormous room, a gigantic, simple-minded black man whom cummings was to remember as the finest of his fellow prisoners. Jean was given to practical jokes and tall tales; he had been arrested for impersonating an English officer and had been sent to the prison for psychopathic observation. The women prisoners called their approval and admiration of his powerful body when he walked in the courtyard. His favorite among the women was Lulu, who smuggled money and a lace handkerchief to him. When she was sent to another prison, Jean was disconsolate. When one of the prisoners pulled at Lulu's handkerchief, Jean fought back, and a scuffle followed. The guards came, and Jean was taken away for punishment. Calls from the women prisoners aroused him so that he attacked the guards and sent them flying until he was quieted and bound by a fellow prisoner whom he trusted. After that experience, Jean grew quiet and shy.

Just before cummings was released, B. was sent away. Jean Le Nègre tried to cheer cummings with his funny stories and exaggerated lies, but without much success. Although cummings was afraid that B. might never be freed from the prisons of France, he later learned that

B. was eventually released. Cummings himself left the enormous room knowing that in it he had learned the degradation, nobility, and endurance of human nature.

Critical Evaluation:

When *The Enormous Room* was first published in 1922, it was viewed as a war book, a "realistic" story exposing the horrors of World War I, as one representative critic put it. The book is indeed about war, but it is also about other things—society, language, and art—and about e. e. cummings himself. An examination and evaluation of the various aspects of *The Enormous Room* reveal its strength as an experimental autobiography and a portrait of modern culture.

Although it is a book about war, cummings' work is more a parody than a protest. The tone of the opening paragraph reveals this when the narrator pokes fun at the pompous rhetoric of "Our Great President" and contrasts it with the simple, honest language of a man like e. e. cummings, who was in a war started by the rhetoric of politicians. Cummings sustains this tone throughout the book as he contrasts those who are imprisoned with those who are their captors. The prisoners, particularly those whom cummings calls the Delectable Mountains, are simple, innocent, and naïve victims, whereas the victimizers are ruthless, uncaring bureaucrats. Using Paul Bunyan's book *Pilgrim's Progress* as his organizing principle, cummings shows how he, the pilgrim, progresses through the war. He experiences the brutality of such figures as the one he calls Apollyon (named after Bunyan's devil), and learns that in war innocent human beings battle against manipulative predators.

This context of war is actually a microcosm of society, another theme cummings develops. The qualities at which cummings the poet pokes fun and satirizes are the same ones he criticizes in *The Enormous Room*: the dehumanizing qualities of modern culture, its mechanization, and its substitution of thinking for feeling. Cummings rails against such institutions of culture as religion, education, and government and he uses the individual prisoners in the French jail as reminders of the power of the self against society.

Cummings uses experimental language in describing the prisoners, showing that a new use of language can be a tool for understanding, and that language and art are means of celebrating individuals who successfully rebel against the old order of living, speaking, and writing. Cummings uses antirhetoric to contrast with the pompous language of politicians, and he shows that language can help people see things in a new way. He describes the reason for his linguistic manipulation at the end of the autobiography when he points out that "to create is first of all to destroy." Indeed, cummings does destroy the predictable, ordinary, traditional ways of writing and speaking, and he creates his story through wrenched syntax, poetic descriptions, and shocking imagery.

In addition to war, society, language, and art, *The Enormous Room* is about e. e. cummings himself. He paints a portrait of a brash Bostonian who goes off to war, not because of any passionate commitment to a cause, but for the adventure of it. The young man is elitist and overly sensitive to the smells and sights of the prison into which he is thrown; above all, he is a detached observer who, as he views his surroundings and fellow prisoners, believes that he occupies a privileged position. As this pilgrim progresses, he learns about himself through the lives of those with whom he shares his small space. He learns from Surplice the importance of being amusing and amused, and that this quality of being mocked while mocking the world is integral to the suffering inherent in the human condition. He learns from Zoo-loo the power of unwritten and unspoken language and discovers that he, a person who luxuriates in the written and spoken word, must remain connected to language that transcends those human tools.

Finally, he learns the quiet strength of loyalty to others from the Wanderer, who is separated from his wife and children through the crass brutality of the "little, very little, *gouvernement français.*" These three Delectable Mountains, together with the other innocent prisoners, teach cummings about his relationship with humanity. Thus the detached, isolated cummings is transformed into an involved, connected one who emerges from his temporary confinement with a more mature sense of himself as a person and as an artist. When he writes a poem at the end of his narrative, it is with a maturity and serenity that he had not possessed at the beginning of his captivity when he had simply been playing with language and poking fun at bureaucrats. In the concluding chapter, entitled "I Say Good-Bye to La Misère," cummings bids farewell to his prison while greeting New York as a person whose liberation from his old self could only have occurred through his imprisonment.

It has been noted that *The Enormous Room* follows not only the pattern outlined in Bunyan's *Pilgrim's Progress* but also the classical pattern of the Dark Night of the Soul in which, as cummings once wrote in a letter, "a spirit descends to ascend." The spirit in this autobiography does indeed descend into himself and into a confining yet expansive prison before ascending to assume a new identity and a new role in the postwar America to which he returns. An enormous room is thus also an enormous journey.

"Critical Evaluation" by Marjorie Smelstor

Bibliography:

Cooperman, Stanley. *World War I and the American Novel.* Baltimore, Md.: Johns Hopkins University Press, 1967. Calls *The Enormous Room* "a carnival in a graveyard" and shows how cummings avoids conventional rebellion by manipulating language to depict the prison as adding foolishness to tragedy.

Dougherty, James P. "E. E. Cummings: *The Enormous Room.*" In *Landmarks of American Writing*, edited by Hennig Cohen. New York: Basic Books, 1969. In *The Enormous Room*, cummings' intent was to expose the stupidity and cruelty of wartime governments. Victims are implicitly advised to undergo a process of "unlearning" previously accepted values.

Gaull, Marilyn. "Language and Identity: A Study of E. E. Cummings' *The Enormous Room.*" *American Quarterly* 19 (Winter, 1967): 645-662. Demonstrates that since insincerely idealistic language had betrayed realists, cummings felt compelled to create new relationships between his use of language and its accurate expression of his experiences.

Kennedy, Richard S. *E. E. Cummings Revisited.* New York: Twayne, 1994. An introductory critical biography that identifies factual bases of *The Enormous Room*, notes its three-part structure, and details its allusions and correspondences to John Bunyan's *The Pilgrim's Progress.* Defines the work's antiwar and antiauthority themes and its comic-opera descriptions. Lauds cummings' preference for feeling, nature, children, and ignorance.

Lineham, Thomas M. "Style and Individuality in E. E. Cummings' *The Enormous Room.*" *Style* 13 (Winter, 1979): 45-59. Shows that, despite posturing, cummings in *The Enormous Room* uses a versatile style to attack dangerous gentility, conservatism, and complacency and thus to inspire readers to assert their own world-transforming individuality.

AN ENQUIRY CONCERNING HUMAN UNDERSTANDING

Type of work: Philosophy
Author: David Hume (1711-1776)
First published: 1748

"Philosophical decisions," says David Hume toward the end of his *An Enquiry Concerning Human Understanding*, "are nothing but the reflections of common life, methodised and corrected." This simple, homely epigram conceals a great deal. For one thing, *An Enquiry Concerning Human Understanding* is actually a sort of popularized revision of ideas that were systematically developed in book 1 of his precocious *Treatise of Human Nature* (1739-1740), which, although it was completed before the author was twenty-five, has been characterized as one of the most profound, thoroughly reasoned, and purely scientific works in the history of philosophy. Second, Hume's method for correcting the reflections of common life actually involves a thorough attack on the obscurities of metaphysical idealists.

Born in an age of reason, Hume at first shared the optimism of those who were certain that pure reason could unlock the secrets of nature, and as he read Francis Bacon, John Newton, Thomas Hobbes, and John Locke, he longed for fame equal to theirs. Yet as he reported in a letter to Sir Gilbert Elliot, although he "began with an anxious search after arguments, to confirm the common opinion; doubts stole in, dissipated, returned; were again dissipated, returned again; and it was a perpetual struggle of restless imagination against inclination, perhaps against reason." That last, "perhaps against reason," is the crucial phrase, for no philosopher before Hume used reason so brilliantly in an attack against the certainties of reason. The twelve essays of *An Enquiry Concerning Human Understanding* reflect Hume's three principal attacks against rationalism: against the doctrine of innate ideas and faith in ontological reasoning and an ordered universe; against empiricism, both the kind that led to Lockian dualism and the kind that led Berkeleyan idealism, on the ground that neither the physical nor the spiritual can be proved; and against deism, based on universal axioms and the law of causality. It is not surprising that religions since Hume have largely made their appeals to faith rather than to reason.

Considering what remains when such thoroughgoing skepticism rejects so much of the beliefs of rational human beings, Hume himself readily admitted (in the fourth essay, "Sceptical Doubts Concerning the Operations of the Understanding") that as a man he was quite satisfied with ordinary reasoning processes but that as a philosopher he had to be skeptical, for reasoning was not based on immediate sense experience. "The most lively thought is still inferior to the dullest sensation," he asserted in his second essay, "The Origin of Ideas." Unless the mind is "disordered by disease or madness," actual perceptions have the greatest "force and vivacity," and it is only on such matters of basic mental fact rather than on the abstract relations of ideas, as in mathematics, that human beings must depend for certainties about life. No amount of reasoning, for example, could have led Adam in the Garden of Eden to believe that fluid, transparent water would drown him or that bright, warm fire would burn him to ashes. "No object ever discovers, by the qualities which appear to the senses, either the causes which produced it, or the effects which arise from it." In dealing with this idea, Hume doggedly backs every argument into a corner, into some "dangerous dilemma." What is more, he enjoys himself immensely while doing it—"philosophers that gave themselves airs of superior wisdom and sufficiency, have a hard task when they encounter persons of inquisitive dispositions," he says. Concerning cause and effect, he argues that similar effects are expected from causes that appear similar, yet this relationship does not always exist and, even when observed, is not reasoned. Furthermore, it is merely an arbitrary assumption, an act of faith, that events that are remembered as having occurred sequentially in the past will continue to do so in the future. Causation thus was merely a belief, a belief he defined as a "lively idea related to or associated with a present impression."

This seemed to Hume not merely an impractical philosophical idea, but a momentous discovery of great consequence. Since causation was an a priori principle of both natural and moral philosophy, and since causation could not be reasonably demonstrated to be true, a tremendous revolution in human thought was in preparation. Only in the pure realm of ideas, logic, and mathematics, not contingent on the direct sense awareness of reality, could causation safely (because arbitrarily) be applied—all other sciences are reduced to probability. The concluding essay, "Of the Academical or Sceptical Philosophy," reaches grand heights of eloquence when Hume argues that a priori reasoning can make anything appear to produce anything: "the falling of a pebble may, for aught we know, extinguish the sun; or the wish of a man control the planets in their orbits."

> When we run over libraries, persuaded of these principles, what havoc must we make? If we take in hand any volume; of divinity or school metaphysics, for instance; let us ask, Does it contain any abstract reasoning concerning quantity or number? No. Does it contain any experimental reasoning concerning matter of fact and existence? No. Commit it then to the flames: for it can contain nothing but sophistry and illusion.

The polemic vigor of the essays stems in large part from the bitter experiences Hume had in the years immediately preceding the publication of *An Enquiry Concerning Human Understanding*. In 1744, he had sought to fill a vacancy in the chair of ethics and pneumatical philosophy at Edinburgh University, but to his astonishment his *Treatise of Human Nature* was invoked to prevent the appointment: "such a popular clamor has been raised against me in Edinburgh, on account of Scepticism, Heterodoxy, and other hard names . . . that my Friends find some Difficulty in working out the Point of my Professorship." Then he was dismissed without full salary as tutor to the mad son of the marquis of Annandale. These experiences played a part in sharpening the cutting edge of his thought and prose style.

After refining his conception of reason and its modes of function, Hume applies it to four crucial problems: "Liberty and Necessity," "Reason of Animals," "Miracles," and "Particular Providence and a Future State." Concerning the first, Hume argues that since the subject relates to common life and experience (unlike such topics as the origin of worlds or the region of spirits), only ambiguity of language keeps the dispute alive. For a clear definition, he suggests that it be consistent with plain matters of fact and with itself. Difficulty arises when philosophers approach the problem by examining the faculties of the soul rather than the operations of body and brute matter. In the latter, people assume that they perceive cause and effect, but in the functioning of their minds they feel no connection between motive and action. However, the doctrine of cause and effect cannot be invoked without, ultimately, tracing all actions— including evil ones—to the deity whom people refuse to accept as the author of guilt and moral turpitude in all creatures. As a matter of fact, freedom and necessity are matters of momentary emotional feeling "not to be controuled or altered by any philosophical theory or speculation whatsoever."

The reason of animals, according to Hume, consists—as it does in children, philosophers, and humankind in general—not so much in logical inferences as in experience of analogies and sequential actions. Observation and experience alone teach a horse the proper height that he can leap or a greyhound how to meet the hare in her tracks with the least expenditure of energy. Hume's learning theory here seems to be based on the pleasure-pain principle and forms the background for certain theories of twentieth century psychology. However, Hume ends this essay with a long qualification in which he cites the "Instincts," unlearned knowledge derived from the original hand of nature, and then adds this curious final comment: "The experimental reasoning itself, which we possess in common with beasts, and on which the whole conduct of life depends, is nothing but a species of instinct or mechanical power, that acts in us unknown to ourselves."

The essay on miracles is perhaps the most spirited of the entire collection, and it is the one which Hume expected, correctly, would stir the greatest opposition. Nevertheless, he was certain that his argument would be for the wise and the learned "an everlasting check to all kinds of superstitious delusion, and consequently . . . useful as long as the world endures." Events can be believed to happen only when they are observed, and all reports of events not directly observed must be believed only to the degree that they conform with probability, experimentally or experientially derived. A miracle is a violation of the laws of nature; therefore it violates all probability; therefore it is impossible. History gives no instance of any miracle observed by a sufficient number of unquestionably honest, educated, intelligent individuals. Despite the surprise, wonder, and other pleasant sensations attendant upon reports of novel experiences, all new discoveries that achieve credibility among people have always resembled in fundamentals those objects and events that have already been experienced. The most widespread belief in miracles exists among so-called primitive peoples. Finally, since there is no objective way of confirming miracles, believers have no just basis for rejecting those claimed by all religions. "So that, on the whole, we may conclude, that the Christian Religion not only was at first attended with miracles, but even at this day cannot be believed by any reasonable person without one. Mere reason is insufficient to convince us . . . to believe what is most contrary to custom and experience."

In the 1777 posthumous edition of *An Enquiry Concerning Human Understanding* appeared the announcement that these unsystematic essays should be regarded only as containing Hume's philosophical sentiments and principles. Although professional philosophers, especially the logical positivists, still prefer Hume's earlier *Treatise of Human Nature*, it is *An Enquiry Concerning Human Understanding*, with its livelier style and popular appeal, that stands as his personal testament. In it he said that he would be "happy if . . . we can undermine the foundations of an abstruse philosophy, which seems to have hitherto served only as a shelter to superstition, and a cover to absurdity and error." The irony is that he succeeded so well in undermining reason that he opened the door to the Romanticism of the late eighteenth and early nineteenth centuries. His voice has, however, outlasted that babel and his humanistic skepticism survives. "Be a philosopher," he cautioned himself, "but amidst all your philosophy, be still a man."

Bibliography:
Hume, David. *An Enquiry Concerning Human Understanding*. Edited by Charles W. Hendel. Indianapolis: Bobbs-Merrill Educational, 1955. Includes a thorough introduction to the essentials of Hume's philosophy and the place that *An Enquiry Concerning Human Understanding* played in the author's life. Also contains criticisms and explanations of the text.
Huxley, T. H. "Hume." In *English Men of Letters*. Vol. 7, edited by John Morley. London: Macmillan, 1895. An excellent source, in which Huxley provides an intriguing discussion of Hume's life and places his philosophical work in that context.

Noxon, James. *Hume's Philosophical Development*. Oxford, England: Clarendon Press, 1973. Compares *Treatise of Human Nature* and *An Enquiry Concerning Human Understanding*.

Olshewsky, Thomas M. "The Classical Roots of Hume's Skepticism." *Journal of the History of Ideas* 52, no. 2 (April-June, 1991): 269-288. Interprets Hume's work through an analysis of skepticism on the basis of the Stoic philosophy of Sextus Empiricus.

Stumpf, Samuel E. *Philosophy: History and Problems*. New York: McGraw-Hill, 1977. Stumpf's chapter on empiricism in Britain is one of the clearest explanations of the issues and responses that form the context of the philosophies of that trio of thinkers, Locke, George Berkeley, and Hume. An understanding of the first two is essential to grasping the importance of Hume's *An Enquiry Concerning Human Understanding*.

AN ENQUIRY CONCERNING POLITICAL JUSTICE

Type of work: Politics
Author: William Godwin (1756-1836)
*First published: An Enquiry Concerning Political Justice, and Its Influence on General
Virtue and Happiness*, 1793

In 1793, William Godwin, the first philosopher of anarchism, published *An Enquiry Concerning Political Justice*. This three-volume work gives evidence of being strongly influenced by the ideas of the French Revolution and argues that the rational being, the human, must be given complete freedom to exercise pure reason. All forms of government, being founded on irrational assumptions, are tyrannical and eventually must be eliminated. Laws have not been produced by wisdom but by greed and fear, so they should be replaced by the products of reasonable people's ability to make decisions. Accumulated property is a means of exploitation and, consequently, must be abolished. This last point was, however, modified in a later edition. With its varying degrees of indebtedness to Aristippus, Plato, Jean-Jacques Rousseau, and Claude-Adrien Helvétius, and despite its equivocating alterations in the final revision, Godwin's book gave evidence of original thinking and provided generations of revolutionary thinkers with stimulation and guidance.

Godwin asserts that the general human objective is happiness, that politics, the promotion of individual good, is humanity's most important pursuit, and that the two traditional articles of political liberty have been first, "security of our persons" and second, "security of our property." Godwin asks, however, would not a good government "take away all restraints upon the enquiring mind"? The early chapters of the book develop Godwin's view that throughout history government has had a corrupting influence, but only because people have not lived up to their potential truthfulness and to their ability to see what is evil and what is good. The assumption is that if people will define clearly to themselves the genuinely good principles of life, government will improve.

Godwin surveys historically the destructiveness and futility of war, and to emphasize its irrational causes, he quotes at some length from the satire on war in book 2 of Jonathan Swift's *Gulliver's Travels* (1726). In the present condition, Godwin continues, punishment is the only means of repressing the violent revolt of the deprived masses. If government is a subject for discussion, however, then people might reasonably agree about it some day and see the advantages of freedom and equality.

From these premises Godwin proceeds to demonstrate that, of the three principal causes of moral improvement, both literature and education, though beneficial, have limitations, and that the third cause, political justice, is strong where the first two are weak. Political justice is strong in the extent of its operation. When political justice is equally addressed to all, it will impart virtue to all. Since error and injustice tend to destroy themselves, it is doubtful whether they could be perpetuated without governmental support, for government "reverses the genuine propensities of mind, and instead of suffering us to look forward, teaches us to look backward for perfection." To exemplify how political institutions have in the past militated against moral improvement, Godwin points out the destructive passions engendered by the inequality of property, the magnificence accorded to enormous wealth, and the insolence and usurpation of rich persons. Traditionally, both legislation and administration of the law have favored the rich and have repressed the freedom of the poor to resist the rich.

Godwin asserts strongly that humanity's most distinguished and most important characteristic is its perfectibility, by which he means not the capacity to become perfect but, rather, the capability to improve. Evidences of humanity's progressive nature are the development of language and the invention of alphabetical writing. Having asserted that all science and all art are capable of being further perfected, Godwin asks why the same should not be true of morals and social institutions. On the usefulness of history in this regard, he comments: "Let us look back, that we may profit by the experience of mankind; but let us not look back as if the wisdom of our ancestors was such as to leave no room for future improvements."

The true instruments of moral influence, in Godwin's opinion, are not direct physical causes such as climate but, rather, such concepts as desire and aversion or punishment and reward. Definitely restrictive to moral progress are the institutions or professions that always operate to produce a certain character or stereotype and thus suppress frankness of mind. The example cited by Godwin is the priesthood, which requires that all priests must be alike in their subservience. Godwin is certain that free people in any country will be "firm, vigorous and spirited in proportion to their freedom," as, conversely, slaves will be "ignorant, servile and unprincipled."

When the magic of the indoctrinated idea is dissolved and the great majority of any society seek true benefits, the struggle need not involve tumult or violence. Indeed, "the effort would be to resist reason, not to obey it." Just views must be infused into the liberally educated, but this process must come about gradually. Humanity's basic error in politics is the supposition that a change is impracticable, with the result that humanity does not look forward incessantly to the accomplishment of change. People, Godwin asserts, do not choose evil when they see it to be evil. Therefore, once having shaken off an injurious evil, a society will not permit its revival unless its conviction of truth becomes obliterated.

An Enquiry Concerning Political Justice develops a theme that is in close agreement with Thomas Paine's belief that society, being produced by human wants, is a blessing, but that government, necessitated by human wickedness, is at its best a necessary evil. Godwin defines the term justice as meaning that the individual should contribute everything in his or her power to the benefit of the whole, the whole not being the state but other individuals. The importance to the general weal must be the only standard, and a benefit conferred upon an individual to the detriment of the society is wrong. Even one's self-preservation must be based on the premise of one's good to the society—to all. An important theme in Godwin's book is the propriety of applying more justice in order to ascertain political truth.

Society is bound to do for its members everything that can contribute to their welfare. In Godwin's view, what most enlarges the mind—virtue and consciousness of independence—contributes most to this welfare. Individuals, for their part, must follow the best knowledge obtainable. Regarding the possibility that a wrong action may result even from the individual's best intention, Godwin says: "If the disposition by which a man is governed have a systematical tendency to the benefit of his species, he cannot fail to obtain our esteem, however mistaken he may be in his conduct." Virtue is essentially the incessant search for accurate knowledge about utility and right, in which search the exercise of private judgment and the dictates of individual conscience must be accorded primary importance. Since pleasure is to be desired and pain to be avoided, individuals should contribute to the pleasure and benefit of one another and should oppose the despot's power, which is based on indoctrination and is productive of pain.

Moral equality consists in "the propriety of applying one unalterable rule of justice to every case that may arise." Two persons cannot have opposite rights. Moreover, people really have no rights. Since rights can apply only to totally indifferent issues (where to sit and the like), and since an intelligent person immediately becomes a moral person with duties, rights and duties are absolutely exclusive of each other. Although society, composed of individuals, also has no rights, people must, under the present inadequate government, assert some "rights."

Godwin argues further that judgment is founded on evidence, so compulsion cannot bring people to uniformity of opinion. Government needs to be perfected away from the concept of compulsion; the insignificant individual must be made free to criticize the august senate. Countries in which decrees instead of arguments are what rule contain "mere phantoms of men," who give no indication of what they might be if they were entirely free to follow the dictates of conscience and to speak and act as they think. Finally, individual justice—equality and freedom—must be the basis and goal of improvement in government.

Having set forth the underlying principles of his theory, Godwin proceeds to criticize existing society, develop his system of social ethics, and predict conditions of the future. His confidence in the power of reason gives the book an optimism which has frequently been criticized as unresponsive to the lessons of history. While it is true that his emphasis on necessity (cause and effect viewed as an invariable sequence) is inconsistent with his simultaneous assertion of the efficacy of education, Godwin has been unfairly criticized for maintaining that enlightened education could rectify the falsity and the ignorance of human judgment. Such a criticism cannot be fairly administered until after the society has made a concerted effort to educate itself as Godwin proposed.

Bibliography:
Clark, John P. *The Philosophical Anarchism of William Godwin.* Princeton, N.J.: Princeton University Press, 1977. A major study of Godwin's vision of a fundamentally reformed society.
Kelly, Gary. *The English Jacobin Novel, 1780-1805.* Oxford, England: Clarendon Press, 1976. Discusses Godwin's novels as reflections of his political philosophy.
Monro, D. H. *Godwin's Moral Philosophy: An Interpretation of William Godwin.* New York: Oxford University Press, 1953. Emphasizes the closely related connections between Godwin's political thinking and his ethics.
Philp, Mark. *Godwin's "Political Justice."* Ithaca, N.Y.: Cornell University Press, 1986. An excellent starting point. The most restricted and the most helpful commentary of Godwin's *An Enquiry Concerning Political Justice.*
St. Clair, William. *The Godwins and the Shelleys: The Biography of a Family.* New York: W. W. Norton, 1989. A biography with a unique point of view. William Godwin married Mary Wollstonecraft, the noted feminist, and their daughter, Mary, became the wife of Percy Bysshe Shelley. Contains some of the most up-to-date information on Godwin.

EPICŒNE
Or, The Silent Woman

Type of work: Drama
Author: Ben Jonson (1573-1637)
Type of plot: Comedy
Time of plot: Early seventeenth century
Locale: London
First performed: 1609; first published, 1616

Principal characters:
> MOROSE, a gentleman who loves no noise
> SIR DAUPHINE EUGENIE, his nephew
> NED CLERIMONT, one of Sir Dauphine's friends
> TRUEWIT, another friend
> SIR JOHN DAW, a ridiculous knight
> SIR AMOROUS LA-FOOLE, another silly knight
> CUTBEARD, a barber
> CAPTAIN OTTER, a heavy drinker
> MISTRESS OTTER, his wife
> MISTRESS EPICŒNE, the supposed Silent Woman

The Story:

Clerimont and Truewit, young men about town, met and discussed various matters, including the relative merits of natural beauty and the use of cosmetics. Shifting the topic to their friend Sir Dauphine Eugenie, they wondered how he was able to put up with his uncle Morose, an eccentric character who could abide no noise except the sound of his own voice. Clerimont's page amused them with accounts of various noisy pranks played on the ridiculous old man. Sir Dauphine joined them and complained that his uncle blamed all the pranks on him and his friends and threatened to marry and leave his fortune to his new wife instead of to his nephew. Morose had heard of a soft-voiced woman, extremely frugal of speech, and had negotiated with his silent barber, Cutbeard, to arrange a meeting, possibly even a marriage.

Truewit, amazed at hearing of a silent barber and a silent woman, was struck with a sudden inspiration and excused himself. After Truewit's departure on his undisclosed mission, Sir Amorous La-Foole arrived to invite the gentlemen to a feast at the home of his kinswoman, Mistress Otter. The guests were to include the silent Mistress Epicœne, Lady Haughty, Lady Centaur, Mistress Mavis, and Sir John Daw. Sir Dauphine and Clerimont bracketed Sir John and Sir Amorous as ridiculous targets for comedy.

Meanwhile, Morose was instructing his servant Mute to use only sign language, or in extreme emergencies to speak through a tube, when they were interrupted by a loud blast from a post-horn. Mute went to the door and returned, followed by Truewit, carrying a post-horn and a halter. Morose and Mute were overwhelmed by a volley of words and intimidated by a dagger when they attempted to leave the room. Truewit suggested that Morose choose some way of self-destruction other than marriage and offered him the halter to hang himself. After another voluble outpouring he left, but he added the final torture of another blast from his horn. When Cutbeard arrived, he found Morose in such a state that he had to be put to bed.

In the company of Mistress Epicœne, Sir Dauphine and Clerimont encouraged the fantastic knight Sir John Daw to quote and explain his own poetry, to show off his copious but confused mass of knowledge, and to boast of his romantic prowess. They were interrupted by Truewit, returning with his horn. Sir Dauphine was greatly disturbed at the account of the prank, which Truewit assured him would break off the intended marriage; he told Truewit that the marriage was his own plot abetted by his confederates, Cutbeard and Mistress Epicœne. Cutbeard hastened in to announce that Morose, furious with Truewit and certain that Sir Dauphine had sent him to break off the match, had determined to marry immediately. Cutbeard conducted Mistress Epicœne away, and the young gentlemen commented on her apparent desertion of her gallant, Sir John. They encouraged him to indulge his melancholy.

Morose welcomed Cutbeard and Mistress Epicœne, who spoke so softly that she could hardly be heard. Cutbeard did all his speaking by signs only. Carried away with Mistress Epicœne's noiseless charm, Morose promised large rewards to the barber, reminding him to deliver his thanks silently, and sent him to find a soft-voiced minister to perform the marriage ceremony. He gloated over his imminent marriage and his begetting of children to inherit his estate after he had cast out his impudent nephew.

When Cutbeard announced the results to Sir Dauphine and his friends, Truewit suggested that the whole of Sir Amorous' party be transported to Morose's house to celebrate the wedding with proper sound effects. The young men left and joined the crowd gathered at the Otters' house for the party. Clerimont and Sir Dauphine stirred up trouble between Sir Amorous and Sir John Daw by making each believe that the other was putting a slight on him. They made it seem that Sir Amorous knew that Morose was taking Sir John's sweetheart from him and that Sir John was taking Sir Amorous' guests to the wedding feast. They suggested to Sir Amorous that he have his provisions carried to Morose's home, in the hope that the smell of the venison would attract some fiddlers and trumpeters on the way.

Morose had the wedding ceremony performed by a person who could hardly be heard because of a bad cold; he rewarded him handsomely, but a crashing cough angered him, so he demanded that part of the reward be returned. Cutbeard suggested that making change would be difficult for the parson, but that he could cough out the rest. This suggestion silenced Morose, who dismissed the parson. Immediately following the ceremony, Mistress Epicœne exhibited her voice in an outburst of shrewish scolding. Reeling from this shock, Morose looked around to see Truewit entering with loud congratulations, shortly followed by the whole procession of noisy guests. The collegiate ladies invited Mistress Epicœne to join their circle. When they began to whisper confidentially, Morose had a gleam of hope which was immediately dashed by their loud criticisms of the lack of wedding festivities. Clerimont ushered in a host of musicians playing fortissimo, and Captain Otter followed with his drinking mugs and a group of drummers and trumpeters to sound for toasts. Morose fled, groaning, to lock himself in the attic with a nest of nightcaps pulled over his ears. The party continued noisily, enlivened by a quarrel between Captain Otter and his wife; she beat him until he howled repentance. Morose returned with his sword to drive away the party, but, overcome by the clamor, he fled again, followed by Sir Dauphine, who endeavored to console him, and Truewit, who reminded him of his warning about the dangers of marriage. Morose accepted Truewit's advice that he sue for a divorce.

Continuing their pranks on Sir John and Sir Amorous, the young men reduced them into such a state of terror that they hid from each other. At last each was persuaded to consent to be blindfolded and to accept indignities from his furious opponent. Sir John was to receive five kicks from Sir Amorous and to surrender his sword; Sir Amorous was to surrender his sword, receive a blow on the mouth, and have his nose tweaked. Sir Dauphine, impersonating each in turn, inflicted the indignities on the hoodwinked knights. On Morose's return, Truewit showed him the swords and said that the quarrel had arisen over the bride's amorous favors. Since Morose had not been able to face the noise in the law courts, Truewit promised to find legal help for the divorce proceedings. Prodded by the young men, both Sir John and Sir Amorous boasted of successful love affairs with Mistress Epicœne.

Truewit returned with Cutbeard disguised as a lawyer and Captain Otter disguised as a parson. These engaged in a noisy dispute on secular and canon law concerning divorce proceedings. During the dispute, which was exquisite torture to Morose, Mistress Epicœne and the ladies entered screeching about her wrongs. Every effort of Morose to free himself failed, even the accusation of adultery, for neither knight could claim intimacy after the marriage. Sir Dauphine proposed to his uncle that if he could free him from his tormenting bride Morose would restore him as heir. Morose eagerly accepted the terms and signed an agreement, at which Sir Dauphine pulled off Mistress Epicœne's wig to disclose that the supposed silent woman was a boy. Sir John and Sir Amorous were discredited and discomfited; the collegiate ladies were covered with embarrassment at having exposed feminine mysteries to a member of the opposite sex; and Morose retired to welcome silence.

Critical Evaluation:

A landmark in English theatrical history, *Epicœne* was written by Ben Jonson, whose abilities have long been ranked alongside those of William Shakespeare. One of Jonson's four greatest comedies, following *Volpone* (1605) by four years, *Epicœne* was followed by *The Alchemist* (1610) and *Bartholomew Fair* (1614), Jonson's last prose comedy. Of his seventeen plays, *Epicœne* occupies the midpoint in Jonson's career. Its contemporary and continued popularity through the Restoration—William Congreve probably patterned Mirabell in his play *The Way of the World* (1700) after Truewit and certainly patterned Heartwell in his play *The Old Batchelor* (1693) after Morose—was due in part to its superbly constructed prose. Lauded at length by John Dryden, in his *Essay of Dramatic Poesy* (1668), as the most nearly perfect example of English drama, *Epicœne* offers a number of obstacles—quite surmountable obstacles, but obstacles nevertheless—for a twentieth century reader.

Paradoxically, Jonson's expert use of the theatrical conventions of his time, such as boys playing women's parts and whole companies of boy actors, by whom *Epicœne* was first performed, now requires an agility of imagination to appreciate. Most crucially, no commentary or analysis can do justice to the force and vitality of Jonson's linguistic achievement, which can only be savored in Jonson's own words, whether read or heard, and its difference from Shakespeare's achievement is problematic to some audiences. Long witty speeches, which do not provide motivation or create suspense, are no longer valued for their own sake. Furthermore, Jonsonians, such as Jonas A. Barish and John J. Enck, emphasize that of all Tudor and Stuart playwrights, only Jonson is condemned because he is not Shakespeare.

Barish points out that, while Shakespeare deals in causality, Jonson does not. Consider, for example, Shakespeare's *Twelfth Night* (1599-1600), from which Jonson most probably derived the idea for contriving a duel between Sir John Daw and Sir Amorous La-Foole. While in *Twelfth Night*, the duel between Cesario, who is really Viola, and Sir Andrew Aguecheek ultimately redounds to no one's discredit because a woman and a clown are free not to enjoy physical combat, the fact that Sir John Daw and Sir Amorous La-Foole are so afraid of each other only reveals them as cowards. In Shakespeare, the audience learns how the characters are motivated and why they relate to one another as they do. Hence, Shakespeare's Malvolio, victim of a hoax as is Jonson's Morose, causes confusion in the audience, which Morose never does. It is much easier to laugh at those we do not have to understand. In Jonson's dramatic world, motivation is not at issue, and while not all of Jonson's characters are types or humors, their reactions are not caused by the actions of others.

In *Epicœne*, Dauphine wants his inheritance; Morose hopes to beget an heir and keep Dauphine from inheriting anything; Clerimont and Truewit amuse themselves with their prank pulling, while assisting their friend Dauphine; and each character pursues his own course, colliding now and then with others. The audience is not told why Dauphine needs his uncle's money—unlike Bassanio in Shakespeare's *The Merchant of Venice* (1596-1597) who needs money to win Portia as his wife—nor does the audience learn why Morose is pathologically unable to tolerate any sound around him. Possible reasons for Morose's intolerance of sound, such as childhood trauma, are irrelevant and would ruin the comedy.

The story plays with gender and gender expectations. The action, which consists of tricking Morose into making Dauphine his heir, involves "unmanly," cowardly men who are gossips and "unwomanly," promiscuous, deliberately barren women who fear the effects of aging. Different from the standard comedy that ends with everyone rightly married, *Epicœne* ends with the right couple divorced. Morose, who has been reduced to asserting that he is impotent, discovers that in marrying Epicœne he has wed a boy. Furthermore, silent Epicœne is neither male nor female, since speech is a virtue in a man, but a vice in a woman.

In *Epicœne*, silence is associated with cold, impotence, and the country; noise, with animals, procreation, and the town. The play maintains a precarious balance between extremes. At one moment, Truewit maintains that women want men to take them by force; the next moment, he is maintaining that a man must adapt to a woman; hence, if a man wants a woman who loves wit, he must give her verses. *Epicœne* continues to offer a magnificent play on the ways men relate to men, women to women, and men to women; it provides a series of brilliant variations without pretending to resolve what must remain irresoluble.

"Critical Evaluation" by Carol Bishop

Bibliography:

Barish, Jonas A. *Ben Jonson and the Language of Prose Comedy*. New York: Norton, 1960. An influential work, one that is essential to any study of Jonson's comedies.

Brock, D. Heyward. *A Ben Jonson Companion*. Bloomington: Indiana University Press, 1983. A valuable source of information on Jonson's work, life, and times. A bibliography is included.

Enck, John J. *Jonson and the Comic Truth*. Madison: University of Wisconsin Press, 1966. Essential to any study of Jonson's comedies. Barish and Enck's studies are in many ways complementary.

Mirabelli, Philip. "Silence, Wit and Wisdom in *The Silent Woman*." *Studies in English Literature, 1500-1900* 29 (Spring, 1989): 309-336. Argues that Truewit knows all, sees all, and knows that Epicœne is a boy. Purports that Jonson has a moral commentator, Truewit, who is motivated by the highest ideal of friendship.

Newman, Karen. "City Talk: Women and Commodification in Jonson's *Epicœne*." *English Literary History* 56 (Fall, 1989): 503-518. An insightful, feminist essay on history, but admittedly extra-literary.

Noyes, Robert Gale. *Ben Jonson on the English Stage: 1660-1776*. New York: Benjamin Blom, 1963. Provides valuable information on performers and productions, as provided in contemporary records by such diverse notables as John Dryden, John Dennis, Samuel Pepys, Jeremy Collier, Thomas Shadwell, and William Congreve.

EPIGRAMS

Type of work: Poetry
Author: Martial (Marcus Valerius Martialis, c. 40-c. 104 C.E.)
First transcribed: 86-98 C.E. (English translation, 1860)

The fourteen books of epigrams that were written at the rate of about one per year by Martial during a pivotal period in the history of Rome display a rare literary accomplishment: the complete mastery of a literary form by one man. From the time of his arrival in Rome at about the age of twenty-three until his return to his birthplace in Spain, Martial wrote verse epigrams on a wide variety of subjects and in many different styles.

Almost all that is known of Martial is known from his epigrams, and a great deal of the present knowledge of Rome from the death of Nero (68 C.E.) until the end of the first century comes from the same source. What Martial has preserved is the sort of information that could not, perhaps, be gained in any other way. One of the most common subject areas of Martial's verse is the everyday life of ancient Rome. He took an active part in that life, and it is realistically mirrored in his writings.

There are roughly five other kinds of epigrams that Martial produced. The first of these, probably the most important to him personally, is the epigram written in praise of the emperor or some other man of wealth and power. This type was written largely as a means of subsistence, patronage being the primary system by which poets lived. The contemplative epigrams, usually addressed to friends, show that Martial was realistic almost to the point of cynicism. He reached no great heights of philosophy, wishing only to be comfortable and peaceful. His desire for peace and solitude is expressed in another type of epigram in which he praises life in the country. In these Martial sees the country with the enthusiasm often found in the city dweller, but he did not write pastoral verse; he saw the Italian countryside as it really existed. The epigrammatic epitaphs, often written about children or animals, are among his best work, revealing sentiments that are rare in Martial, feeling often leavened by humor. In the epigrams on friendship he comes the closest to unironic emotion. Romantic love is usually treated satirically, and his discussions of that passion in himself seem devoid of sincere feeling.

Perhaps the chief fault that has been found with his work is found in Martial's personal situation, his toadying to men of position. When he begged the Emperor Domitian, whose name has become synonymous with cruel despotism and wicked licentiousness, for a special position, pleading as the father of three children, for example, his epigram has a self-abasement that may disgust the modern reader:

> Welfare and glory of the earth, while thee
> We safe behold, we gods believe to be;
> If my slight books did e'er thee entertain,
> And oft to read them thou didst not disdain,
> What nature does deny, do thou bestow:
> For father of three children make me go.
> When my verse takes not, this will be an ease;
> A high reward, in case it thee do please.

It is important, however, to understand the position poets held in Rome at that time. Only through patronage, from the emperor if possible, could a poet lead a comfortable life. Everyone who hoped to be looked upon as a gentleman wrote verses, and those who wrote for a living were compelled to praise and praise highly in order to be heard. Martial was certainly not alone in this respect. Completely a product of his time, he accepted the necessity to praise great men as a part of the literary milieu in which he lived.

Criticism that may carry more weight today is Martial's lack of poetic vision. He is never profound, seldom lyrically imaginative. His subjects are the people and things around him, and he depicts them as they are. It is this accuracy of portrayal that makes his verse so valuable in understanding his era. Counterbalancing his absence of elevated vision, however, is Martial's technical grasp of the form in which he wrote. Although he did not create the epigram, he is usually considered the first epigrammatist. He adopted the form, wrote exclusively in it, and did with it all that could be done.

The verse epigram customarily has two major parts, the exposition and the conclusion. The parts may vary in length—Martial's epigrams are from two to over thirty lines long—but usually the exposition takes up most of the poem, with the conclusion being short, often containing a sharp twist of meaning. Within this general framework Martial used direct address, questions, brief transition from exposition to conclusion, satire, irony, and sarcasm. Striking exaggerations and sudden surprises are common, as are plays on words and brief aphorisms. Rhetorical devices abound. His epigram "On a Pretender," for example, shows the quick turn of meaning at the close:

> He whom you see to walk in so much state,
> Waving and slow, with a majestic gait,
> In purple clad, passing the nobles' seat,
> My Publius not in garments more complete;—
> Whose new rich coach, with gilt and studded reins,
> Fair boys and grown-men follow in great trains,
> Lately his very ring in pawn did lay
> For four poor crowns, his supper to defray.

Along with his technical skill goes an animation and a lively perception that make his epigrams often sound like casual conversation. With all the conciseness so necessary for the successful epigram, Martial has an ease that removes from his verses the tenseness that very often causes epigrams to be painful reading.

Although he was poor, Martial was the associate of rich men, and so had full opportunity to see Roman life in all its aspects. Slaves as well as emperors are the subjects of his epigrams. Dinner parties are described along with great monuments. Everywhere he shows a sharp eye and a penetrating wit. Hating pretension, he pricks many a pompous bubble. Few elements of physical or human nature escape his attention.

Apart from Martial's clear pictures of Rome at the end of the first century, probably his greatest importance lies in his influence upon later writers of the epigram. Certainly it would be difficult to find any seventeenth or eighteenth century writer of this form in England who did not turn to Martial as his inspiration and guide. That there are at least seven French translations of the epigrams testifies to his popularity on the Continent.

Shortly after the accession of the Emperor Trajan, whom Martial flattered in verse with little success, the poet returned, in 94, to his birthplace, Bilbilis, a Roman colony in Spain, where he lived on a comfortable estate given to him by a woman whom he probably later married. Characteristically, he was given money for the trip by a friend because of some verses written to him. It is equally characteristic that Martial continued his writing in Spain, sending his epigrams to Rome promptly, with frequent expressions of longing for the excitements and pleasures of the city.

Bibliography:

Conte, Gian Biagio. *Latin Literature: A History*. Translated by Joseph B. Solodow, revised by Don Fowler and Glenn W. Most. Baltimore: The Johns Hopkins University Press, 1994. Brief but thorough examination of the poet's achievements and their place in the Roman literary tradition.

Hadas, Moses. *A History of Latin Literature*. New York: Columbia University Press, 1952. A standby in the study of classical literature; perceptive and persuasive in discussing Martial.

Howell, Peter. *A Commentary on Book One of the Epigrams of Martial*. London: Athlone Press, 1980. Examines nuances and hidden meanings; a place to start in a close reading of Martial.

Key, N. M. *Martial Book XI: A Commentary*. London: Duckworth, 1985. Concentrates on one portion of the poet's work in order to point out significant details.

Palmer, Robert. "Martial" in *Ancient Writers: Greece and Rome*. New York: Charles Scribner's Sons, 1982. Excellent introductory essay gives necessary basic information on Martial's career and achievements.

EPIGRAMS

Type of work: Poetry
Author: Meleager (c. 140-c. 70 B.C.E.)
First transcribed: First century B.C.E. (English translation, 1890)

Meleager is one of the few surviving voices in Greek literature from the early first century B.C.E. This century, so rich for Roman literature, was perhaps the scantiest of all the classical period for Greek literature. Our sense of dearth is intensified by the kind of literature which survived. Ancient Greek literature at no time produced seriously realistic writing, and when the mythical core vanished, the remains took the form of history, philosophy, or artificial styles such as New Comedy, Romance, and Epigram. Ironically, in this unsettled century, when the details of daily life would have been so fascinating, the chief creative writer transmitted some 130 epigrams consisting chiefly of picturesque variations on standard themes and topics of earlier epigrammatic love poets. The incongruity is made all the keener by the fact that Meleager's home until manhood was Gadara in Syria, the town in which Jesus was to cast devils into swine. The juxtaposition is startling.

Meleager's work might be taken for somewhat less the hothouse orchid it is if his earlier efforts had been preserved. His earliest writings were satirical dialogues in prose, modeled on the writings of Menippus, the famous Cynic philosopher and teacher at Gadara. Something of their character may be sensed from the later dialogues of Lucian. The subject of one is reported as a comparison of pease porridge with lentil soup. These were lost, however, and Meleager's literary heritage now consists of the epigrams found in the great collection known as *The Greek Anthology* (c. 90-80 B.C.E.). His epigrams and those of others he imitated may be found in this volume.

The last of Meleager's literary productions was one of the early entries of that anthology: His *Stephanos* (usually translated as *Garland*, also c. 90-80 B.C.E.) is a collection of epigrams of some fifty poets, himself included, with a famous verse preface that compares each poet to that flower that most suggests his poetic character. Later anthologists included *Garland* in larger gatherings; the final collection (apart from the additions derived from Planudes) was made in the tenth century. The poetically significant sections of that collection are the love poems, dedicatory inscriptions, epitaphs, and declamatory, moralizing, convivial, and satiric epigrams. Only about twenty of Meleager's epigrams, however, are to be found outside the love poems.

There is a tendency in the anthology, even within the major sections, to arrange poems on the same theme in a sequence. This tendency provides the most important clue for the appreciation of Meleager. The innocent reader on first encounter is likely to ascribe to Meleager both a hectic variety of erotic liaisons and a continuous intensity of emotion reflected in the extravagant language, both of which in fact distract the reader from the true poetic center of most of the epigrams. The poems are best approached as exercises in various types, attempts at overbidding previous treatments of a topic—overbidding in wit, imagery, and rhetoric. To illustrate, here is an epigram by the earlier poet Asclepiades:

> Let this that is left of my soul, whatever it be, let this at least, ye Loves, have rest for heaven's sake. Or else no longer shoot me with arrows but with thunderbolts, and make me utterly into ashes and cinders. Yea! yea! strike me, ye Loves; for withered away as I am by distress, I would have from you, If I may aught, this little gift.

Meleager takes up the notion of the incinerated lover and exploits it in various ways. For example:

> I am down; set thy foot on my neck, fierce demon. I know thee, yea by the gods, yea heavy art thou to bear: I know, too, thy fiery arrows. But if thou set thy torch to my heart, thou shalt no longer burn it; already it is all ash. If I perish, Cleobulus (for cast, nigh all of me, into the flame of lads' love, I lie, a burnt remnant, in the ashes), I pray thee make the urn drunk with wine ere thou lay it in earth, writing thereon, "Love's gift to Death."

The practice of poetry-as-one-upmanship comes all the more naturally to Meleager in that he was part of the wave of rhetorical fashion known as the Asianic. Meleager was a Syrian, but race or culture has nothing to do with Asianism, which is a name for a development within classical literature. The Asianic style sought for something like the Baroque: extravagance in diction and imagery, special tricks and effects in word arrangements. Most of this is hard to illustrate outside the original Greek, but the use of repetition and fancy compounds in the following may give some of the flavor: "Tears, the last gift of my love, even down through the earth I send to thee in Hades, Heliodora—tears ill to shed, and on thy much-wept tomb I pour them in memory of longing, in memory of affection." The witty side of Meleager's Asianism brings him close at times to the Metaphysicals' conceits: "Love-loving Asclepias, with her clear blue eyes, like summer seas, persuadeth all to make the love-voyage."

None of the foregoing is meant to deny the existence of genuine emotion in Meleager's poetry. The point is that, where emotion is found, it emerges from, launches, or sets on fire the already existing framework of artificial craft, and artifice is inseparable from the result. In various ways, of course, the same can be said of all poetry, but this pattern is so dominant in Meleager (and other epigrammatists) that it needs special emphasis as a defining characteristic.

There is a mystical, almost medieval strain in Meleager's love poetry. Meleager at times approaches a religious quality: More than the other epigrammatists, he expresses the total subjection, abasement, and humiliation of the lover, much as the courtly lover of the Middle Ages conceived himself as the abject servant of his lady. For example: "The goddess, queen of the Desires, gave me to thee, Theocles; Love, the soft-sandalled, laid me low for thee to tread on."

Along with the intermittent intensity of his passion, however, there is an element of coyness and sentimentality that pervades Meleager as well as most of the other love epigrammatists of the *Greek Anthology*. This element is absent from the love poetry of the great lyric age of Greece (c. 700-500 B.C.E.). Perhaps it is possible to account for the change by the fact that the great lyric age's love poetry was written when Eros was integrated within or demonically opposed to a genuine religious framework. For most educated people of Meleager's time there was no serious religion, rather only philosophy.

One other feature of Meleager's love poetry that needs simply to be noted, at least for contemporary readers, is the characteristic type of the beloved. Meleager's loved ones fall exclusively into two classes: *hetaerae* (professional female entertainers or courtesans) and boys in their early teens. Since these two classes account for practically all extant ancient Greek love poetry (Sappho is the exception), this phenomenon needs no special discussion in connection with Meleager.

One should not overemphasize Meleager as a love poet; nor should one be concerned with seeking out those poems that embody "genuine passion," as if these must necessarily be his best. Sheer flights of linguistic dexterity and brilliant variations of traditional themes can produce fine epigrams. Perhaps the most memorable characteristic of Meleager is an outgrowth of this side of his poetry; his bursts of wit often have an element of playfulness and tender humor. In one poem he sends forth a gnat on the dangerous Herculean mission of rousing Heliodora from the side of her current lover to bring her back: The reward will be Hercules' club and lion skin. In another he asks the dew-drunk cicada to strum in antiphon with Pan's piping at high noon and lull him to sleep. An epitaph he wrote for himself makes fun of his own garrulity. In all this one can see a survival of the Meleager who wrote on pease porridge and lentil soup.

Meleager's oeuvre is a curious mixture of the complex and the trivial, the passionate, and the sophisticated. Connoisseurs of the short lyric will be immensely rewarded by reading Meleager's epigrams.

Bibliography:

Cameron, Alan. *The Greek Anthology from Meleager to Planudes*. Oxford, England: Clarendon Press, 1993. Superb analysis of the texts, composition, and sources of Meleager's poetry. Traces the literary history of the work as it has been preserved through the centuries.

Gow, A. S. F., and D. L. Page. *The Greek Anthology: Hellenistic Epigrams*. 2 vols. Cambridge, England: Cambridge University Press, 1965. Comprehensive scholarly assessment of Meleager's work. An introduction provides information on dating, influences, and content, the arrangement of texts in *Garland*, and an analysis of several poems. The commentary section explicates individual works and includes extensive information on variants.

Jay, Peter. Introduction to *The Poems of Meleager*, by Meleager. Berkeley: University of California Press, 1975. Brief sketch of the poet's life; concentrates on efforts to assemble the collection of epigrams that are included in *Garland*. Notes the influence of the philosophical movement of Cynicism on Meleager's poetry.

Webster, T. B. L. *Hellenistic Poetry and Art*. New York: Barnes & Noble Books, 1964. Discusses the love epigrams that Meleager included in *Garland*. Cites numerous examples of the poet's techniques for presenting amorous themes.

Wright, F. A. *A History of Later Greek Literature*. London: Routledge & Kegan Paul, 1951. Brief summary of the poet's literary achievements. Discusses the various women who inspired Meleager's work, and the principles he employed in selecting works for inclusion in *Garland*.

EPISTLES

Type of work: Letters
Author: Horace (Quintus Horatius Falccus, 65-8 B.C.E.)
First transcribed: Epistulae, book 1, c. 20 B.C.E.; book 2, c. 15 B.C.E. (English translation, 1567)

The close and intimate life of the Greek city state gave rise to most of the literary forms of ancient literature, the greater number of which were adopted and adapted by the Romans. However, the epistle, the letter in verse, was a Roman literary invention brought to perfection by Horace during the first days of the Roman imperial period. With Rome administering most of the known world, friends would often be separated in different parts of the empire for years; even those who remained in Italy would often, as did Horace, retire to their country estates. Letter writing not only became a matter of occasional necessity but was often the only means of communication. It was natural that poets and men of letters should turn the epistle into a literary form so that even at a distance friends could share both poetry and, in some measure, epistolary conversation.

Horace's epistles were published in two books; the first, containing twenty letters, appeared about 20 or 19 B.C.E. The second, containing two long letters, probably appeared in 13 B.C.E. Some scholars argue that the second book of epistles should contain the famous *Epistle to the Pisos,* the *Ars Poetica.* However, this work has traditionally been published separately.

In his first book, Horace is a moralist, in the second, a literary critic. The shorter epistles in the first book, some less than fifteen lines long, are familiar and intimate; there is no doubt that they were written as letters first and poems second. In these shorter letters we see Horace, a man of forty-five who claims his days of writing lyric poetry are finished, expressing interest in the writing of the younger generation, inviting a friend to dinner, or the like. The longer epistles of the first book, however, are much more formal and tend to the didactic; they smack of the tour de force, and although they may well have been sent to the persons to whom they are addressed, they read more like open letters to the poet's entire audience. Typical of these longer letters, and setting the moral tone of the first book, is epistle 1, addressed to the poet's friend and patron, Maecenas. In it the poet bids farewell to poetry and states that in his declining years he will devote himself to philosophic inquiry. He will, however, be an eclectic, limiting his speculation to the precepts of no one school of philosophy, for his interest is to find what is ultimately and lastingly profitable for the achievement of virtue. The calm pursuit of wisdom, he states, is the highest good, not the frantic pursuit of things. Showing himself to be as much a Stoic as anything else, he claims that the secret of happiness is not to value anything too much. Other matters he speaks of in the first epistle are the need to control the passions so as not to ruin enjoyment, the need to train one's character, and the need to adapt oneself to both company and oneself alone. In conclusion, Horace's wish from life is enough books and enough food to keep him comfortable.

Having thus set the tone, Horace proceeds to write of the following matters in the successive epistles of the first book. Epistle 2, to Lollius, begins with the old doctrine that important moral lessons are to be learned from the study of Homer. Horace quickly turns to his real subject, however, which is the foolishness of putting off or not exerting the effort requisite for moral self-improvement. Epistle 3, to Julius Florus, was written to a friend who was abroad campaigning with Claudius; the poet inquires about other young friends on Claudius' staff. He is particularly interested in their literary activity. Epistle 4, to Tibullus, the poet, is a short note of warm friendship in which Horace gently recommends the Epicurean idea that one should live each day as if it were the last. Epistle 5, to Torquatus, is an invitation to a frugal but cheerful and friendly dinner party. Epistle 6, to Numicius, is a lay sermon on the famous Horatian phrase *Nil admirari* (wonder at nothing). The wise man should love nothing but virtue: Live, and be happy. Epistle 7, to Maecenas, is a note of appreciation for various favors. Horace apologizes for absenting himself from Rome for so long, and he uses the occasion to describe the ideal giver and, with some humor, the ideal receiver. Self-sufficiency, he claims, is preferable to all other blessings. Epistle 8, to Celsus Albinovanus, is a letter to a member of Tiberius' staff. The poet describes his own ill health and admonishes Celsus to bear up well under prosperity. Epistle 9, to Claudius Tiberius Nero, is a graceful letter of recommendation for Horace's friend Septimus. Epistle 10, to Aristius Fuscus, praises the superiority of country life as being more conducive to the contented mind and more favorable to liberty of spirit than the city life of Fuscus.

Epistle 11, to Bullatus, is an attempt to call this friend back to Rome from Asia, where he has retired because of his despair over the civil wars. Happiness, Horace says, is not in travel but in the mind and is to be achieved anywhere or nowhere. Epistle 12, to Iccius, ironically ridicules miserliness, introduces a friend, and gives news of recent events in the empire. Epistle 13, to Vinnius Asina, cautions Asina, Horace's emissary, to present certain of Horace's writings to Augustus at a propitious and proper moment and with due decorum. Epistle 14 chastises the caretaker of his farm, to whom the letter is written, for missing city life. Horace briefly reminisces about his wild younger years and then advises the wisdom of contentment. Epistle 15, to C. Numonius Vala, asks about the situation and conditions of the town of Velia, where Horace has been advised by his physician to take a cure. Again he comments on country life. Epistle 16, to Quinctius, describes the situation and advantages of Horace's Sabine farm. His description is detailed enough that its position can be determined. The poet goes on to philosophize on the nature of true virtue and the self-sufficiency and freedom of the virtuous man. Epistle 17, to Scaeva, is a letter of advice to one who would seek advantage by frequenting the company of the great. The friendship of the great, the poet says, is a good thing, but one must always solicit favors from them with modesty and caution. Epistle 18, to Lollius, in a more elaborate way treats the same topic as the seventeenth. Horace discusses the tact and discretion a client of the great must have; he concludes with remarks concerning peace of mind, a quality difficult to achieve when one depends on the favor of the great. Epistle 19, to Maecenas, is a review of the poet's literary career; he decries the folly of slavish imitation, and he attacks his detractors. Epistle 20, addressed to his book, is developed as an argument between the poet and his now completed first book of epistles. The book is addressed as if it were a young slave, a favorite of his master, who wants to be sold out of a quiet country household and into an exciting city house where he can seek advancement. Horace explains all the troubles and chances he must undergo. He ends the poem with remarks on what he expects from posterity. The tone of the nineteenth and twentieth epistles implies that the poet is finished now with his writing career.

The impression we receive from these twenty letters is that middle-aged Horace is feeling old and is in delicate health, and that he will write no more. Perhaps he really did believe he was through with poetry; however, he still had a few more poems to write, and among them were the two long discourses on literature (companion pieces, in effect, to the *Ars Poetica*) that make up the second volume of epistles.

The first of these two letters is to Augustus. After first paying the emperor the highest kind of compliments, Horace plunges into a consideration of the current state of literature. First he intervenes in the then raging Roman "battle of the ancients and the moderns." He acknowledges the greatness of the earlier Greek poets, but he wants to have the early Latin poets respected more than they usually are. Horace sketches out the history of Latin poetry from the beginnings up through the Greeks' "capture" of their captor, Rome, and then on to his own day. Looking at the present state of letters, Horace judges (and history shows him to have been quite correct) that the drama would not reach great heights in Rome: The taste of the people was for spectacle, mimes, and elaborate staging. Yet nondramatic poetry he thinks will do very well, for Augustus, whose taste is impeccable, will encourage poetry and will not be deceived by second-rate poets.

The second epistle of the last book is to Julius Florus, a friend of the poet who apparently wanted also to be a poet. This letter is much more personal in tone than the letter to Augustus and full of intimate detail. Horace begins by testifying that he is rather lazy and undependable now that he no longer must write poetry in order to stay alive, as he did when he was young. Moreover, poetry is one of the follies of the young and, now that he is growing old, he must give it up as he has his other youthful pastimes. How, he asks, can a man write real poetry amid the hustle and bustle and distractions of Rome? The real poet must live and write in the quiet countryside. The poets who stay in the city form worthless mutual admiration societies out of which comes no true criticism. A good poet is a good critic too, and he can take and use valid criticism of his own work. Bad poets hate criticism of any kind. Perhaps the happiest writer is the madman who writes very badly, but who thinks he writes divinely. At any rate, Horace concludes, at his age it is proper to think of gaining happiness, which is found in calm and content, not wealth.

Bibliography:

Armstrong, David. *Horace*. New Haven, Conn.: Yale University Press, 1989. A general introduction to Horace's works that covers the developing stages of his life and his relation to his changing society. Chapter 4 on the *Epistles*, which analyzes important themes in the poems, is especially good. An excellent source for beginners. Includes a useful index, notes, and a rewarding bibliography of primary and secondary sources.

Fraenkel, E. *Horace*. Oxford, England: Clarendon Press, 1957. An important analysis of the major aspects of Horace's life and the relationships between his works. Also provides an introduction to issues of classical scholarship in the study of Horace.

Kilpatrick, Ross. *The Poetry of Friendship*. Edmonton, Canada: University of Alberta Press, 1986. A detailed and scholarly discussion of Horace's first epistle and its thematic relation to other works in the ancient world.

Reckford, Kenneth J. *Horace*. New York: Twayne, 1969. An extremely accessible introduction to Horace. Includes a useful chronology of his life, an index, and a rewarding bibliography of primary and secondary sources. A solid overview of all important issues in Horace's poetry. The section on the *Epistles* is a good beginner's source.

Rudd, Niall. Introduction to *The Satires of Horace and Persius: A Verse Translation*. Harmondsworth, Middlesex, England: Penguin Books, 1973. A thoroughly enjoyable translation of Horace's *Epistles*. Also provides useful notes and commentary to the text and translation, and a sound introduction to the poems and life of Horace as well as his continuing influence. An excellent source for beginners who seek both a lively translation and a solid basic introduction.

EPITAPH OF A SMALL WINNER

Type of work: Novel
Author: Joaquim Maria Machado de Assis (1839-1908)
Type of plot: Philosophical realism
Time of plot: 1805-1869
Locale: Rio de Janeiro, Brazil
First published: Memórias póstumas de Bras Cubas, 1881 (*The Posthumous Memories of Brás Cubas*, 1951; *Epitaph of a Small Winner*, 1952)

> *Principal characters:*
> BRAZ CUBAS, a wealthy, cultured Brazilian
> MARCELLA, his first mistress
> VIRGILIA, his fiancée and later his mistress
> LOBO NEVES, Virgilia's husband
> QUINCAS BORBA, a philosopher and pickpocket

The Story:

Braz Cubas, a wealthy Brazilian, died of pneumonia in his sixty-fifth year. After his death, he decided to write his autobiography, to while away a part of eternity and to give humanity some record of his life. Braz was born in 1805. His childhood was an easy one, for his father was extremely wealthy and indulgent, only pretending to be severe with his child for the sake of appearances. One of the earliest experiences the boy remembered was the elation of the Brazilians over the defeat of Napoleon, an occasion marked in his memory by the gift of a small sword. The sword was the most important aspect of the occasion, and Braz remarked that each person has his own "sword" that makes occasions important.

As a child, Braz Cubas did not like school. In his seventeenth year, he had his first love affair with a courtesan named Marcella. Trying to please his mistress, Braz spent all the money he could borrow from his mother, and then gave promissory notes to fall due on the day he inherited his father's estate. His father, learning of the affair, paid off his son's debts and shipped him off to a university in Spain. At first, Braz hoped to take Marcella with him. She refused to go.

Graduated from the university and awarded a degree, Braz admitted that he knew very little. He then took advantage of his father's liberality and wealth and spent several years traveling about Europe. Called back to Rio de Janeiro by news that his mother was dying of cancer, he arrived home in time to see her before she died. After her death, he went into retirement, remaining in seclusion until his father came to him with plans for a marriage and a seat in the Brazilian legislative body. After some vacillation, Braz decided to obey his father's wishes. The reason for his hesitation was a love affair with a rather beautiful girl. His discovery that she was lame, however, turned him away from her. On his return to social life, he learned that the young woman his father had picked out for him, a girl named Virgilia, had position, wealth, and beauty. It was through her father's influence that the elder Cubas expected his son to get ahead politically. Unfortunately for the schemes of both father and son, Virgilia met Lobo Neves, a young man with more ambition and greater prospects. She decided to marry him, a decision that ended, at least temporarily, prospects of a political career for Braz.

Disappointed and disgruntled with life, he accidentally met Marcella, his former mistress. He found her greatly changed, for smallpox had destroyed her beauty. After losing her looks, she had left her earlier profession to become the keeper of a small jewelry shop.

Disappointment over his son's failure to win Virgilia was too much for his father, who died shortly afterward. There was a great to-do after the father's death, for Braz's brother-in-law turned out to be an avaricious man who wanted his wife, Braz's sister, to have as much of the estate as possible. Braz accepted calmly the selfish and unfortunate aspect of human nature thus revealed, and agreed, for his sister's sake, to be reconciled with his greedy brother-in-law.

Not very long after his father's death, Braz learned from Virgilia's brother that Virgilia and her husband were returning to Rio de Janeiro. Braz was pleased; he was still in love with her. A few days after the return of Virgilia and her husband, he met them at a ball. Virgilia and Braz danced several waltzes together and fell more deeply in love than they had ever been while Braz was courting her. They continued to meet, and before long, Virgilia became his mistress.

One day, Braz found a package in which were several bundles of banknotes. He kept the money and later used it to establish a trust fund for Dona Placida, a former servant of Virgilia's family, who maintained the house in which Virgilia and Braz kept their assignations. They managed for several years to keep their affair a secret, so that Braz could be a guest in Virgilia's home as well. In fact, he and Lobo Neves were good friends.

One day, Braz met Quincas Borba, an old schoolmate who had been reduced to begging. The man took some money from Braz and, as he discovered later, also stole his watch. That night, Braz suggested to Virgilia that they run away. She refused to do so. They had a lovers' quarrel, followed by a tender scene of repentance.

A short time later, Lobo Neves was offered the governorship of a province, and he suggested that Braz accompany him as his secretary. The situation was inviting to the two lovers, but they knew that in the smaller provincial capital their secret could not long be hidden. Their problems were unexpectedly solved when superstitious Neves refused the government post because the document appointing him was dated on the thirteenth of the month.

The love affair continued until Virgilia became pregnant. Neither of the lovers doubted that Braz was the father of the child, and he acted very much like a husband who expected to be presented with his firstborn. The child, not carried the full term, died at birth, much to the sorrow of Virgilia and Braz, and of the husband as well, who thought the child was his.

One day, Braz received a letter from Quincas Borba, the begging schoolmate who had stolen his watch. Having improved his finances, the beggar had become a philosopher, a self-styled humanist. Borba's ideas fascinated Braz, who had always fancied himself an intellectual and a literary man. He was also pleased when Borba sent him a watch as good as the one he had stolen. Braz spent a great deal of time with Borba, for Neves had become suspicious of the relationship between his wife and her lover, and the two were discreet enough to stay away from each other for a time.

At last, Virgilia and her husband left Rio de Janeiro after Neves received another political appointment. For a time, Braz felt like a widower. Lonely, he turned to public life. Defeated for office, he then became the publisher of an opposition newspaper, but his venture was not successful. He also fell in love and finally decided to get married. Once more, he was disappointed, for his fiancée died during an epidemic.

The years passed rather uneventfully. Braz grew older, and so did his friends. Not many weeks after the death of Quincas Borba, who had become a close companion, Braz fell ill of pneumonia. One visitor during his last illness was Virgilia, whose husband had died, but even her presence was not enough to keep Braz from slipping into delirium. In his dying moments, he cast up the accounts of his life and decided that in the game of life he was the winner by only a small margin, in that he had brought no one else into the world to suffer the misery of life.

Critical Evaluation:

Joaquim Maria Machado de Assis is one of the most remarkable figures of Brazilian literature. He is often regarded as its central figure and has been compared with such giants of world literature as Henry James, Gustave Flaubert, and Jorge Luis Borges. Machado was a mestizo (a person of mixed racial descent) and was reared in poor circumstances. Nevertheless, he taught himself English, German, and French and read widely in American and European literature. He lived almost his entire life in his home city of Rio de Janeiro, where he worked as a journalist, dramatist, translator, government official, and theater critic. A sociable man, Machado de Assis moved easily among the more intellectual circles of Brazilian society. An epileptic, he was often sick as a child, and his ill health continued into his adulthood. He began *Epitaph of a Small Winner*, which was a sharp departure from his earlier, more conventionally Romantic works, while taking a rest cure in Tijuca, outside Rio de Janeiro. Several chapters of this novel were dictated to his wife Carolina, as Machado de Assis' eyesight was too poor for him to be able to write them out himself.

Epitaph of a Small Winner is the first of what are sometimes called Machado de Assis' carioca novels, which refers to their focus on the society of Rio de Janeiro. These novels, including Machado de Assis' acknowledged masterpiece *Dom Casmurro* (1899), share many stylistic and thematic concerns. Some general themes include: problems of good and evil, the destructive nature of time, the dangers of the human ego, the unreliable nature of human judgment, the contrast between human longing for perfection and the frailty of human nature, the danger of totalizing scientific and philosophical systems, and the correlation between pleasure and disillusionment.

Many of these themes are readily apparent in *Epitaph of a Small Winner*. The humanism of Quincas Borba is the sort of explain-everything philosophy that Machado de Assis considers dangerous. Braz Cubas demonstrates the natural laziness of human nature; he is often all too willing to accept the easy answer. Braz Cubas accepts things as they happen to him; he reacts, rather than acts. He yearns for great things, yet accepts his mundane life.

One of the most obvious features of *Epitaph of a Small Winner* is the remarkable narrator. The novel is told in the first person by a narrator who is already dead. The narrator's memories of past events are highly subjective, and Braz Cubas demonstrates himself to be egotistical, self-interested, and not particularly bright; in short, the reader is presented with an untrustworthy narrator. This narrator often pauses to address the reader, even going to far as to say that, if there is a flaw in the book, the reader is that flaw. Not only is the narrator untrustworthy, he is arrogant.

This feature affects the reader's response to the novel. The reader's role in the storytelling process is emphasized, as it is impossible to relax and let the story happen. This calls into question the veracity of Cubas' entire narrative. There are times when Braz Cubas seems to be trying to justify himself; he may be telling his story in such a way as to make himself look good. If a reader cannot trust the narrator of a novel, who can be trusted? The novel thus proposes questions regarding the reliability of language, and with that, a doubting of the nature of reality itself, as reality seems to change according to the words used to describe it. If Braz Cubas describes his life in a particular way, then that is what that life becomes, regardless of what may have actually happened, or how another character might tell the story.

Thus, the stylistic innovations of the story emphasize some of the thematic concerns, as the reader is called on to interact directly with a flawed human being, in the form of the narrator. The reader must question not only Cubas' judgment but also the reader's own. This demonstrates Machado de Assis' primary concern in his novels—the inner life of his characters.

Machado attempts to get at problems of good and evil, not merely by describing human cruelty, violence, or injustice, but by demonstrating how easy it is for one individual to accept evil, not necessarily because evil is attractive, but because it is easy to accept evil.

Despite the novel's somewhat pessimistic view of life, it is often admired for its satirical and ironic humor. Braz Cubas' pessimism is often mistakenly applied to Machado de Assis. It is true that Braz Cubas certainly draws pessimistic conclusions about life, but attributing them to Machado de Assis may not be entirely appropriate, and not only because the author warned against biographical readings of his works. Braz' pessimism is not presented as an admirable thing; rather, it makes him appear ridiculous. It is clear that Machado was certainly aware of humanity's shortcomings; however, there would be no point in illustrating them so well if he did not at least hope, as every good satirist does, that they could be amended.

"Critical Evaluation" by Kelly C. Walter

Bibliography:
Caldwell, Helen. *Machado de Assis: The Brazilian Master and His Novels*. Berkeley: University of California Press, 1978. One of the primary translators of Machado de Assis' work into English focuses upon his novels, with special emphasis on *Epitaph of a Small Winner*.
Fitz, Earl E. *Machado de Assis*. Boston: Twayne, 1989. An excellent general introduction to Machado de Assis' life and work. Discusses all of Machado de Assis' novels, as well as his plays, short stories, poetry, and journalism.
Nunes, Maria Luisa. *The Craft of an Absolute Winner: Characterization and Narratology in the Novels of Machado de Assis*. Westport, Conn.: Greenwood Press, 1983. Focuses on Machado's novels, paying particular attention to the characters and to Machado de Assis' ideas about time.
_____. "Story Tellers and Character: Point of View in Machado de Assis' Last Five Novels." *Latin American Literary Review* 7, no. 13 (1978): 52-63. Discusses how these novels, including *Epitaph of a Small Winner*, use their unusual narrators to involve the reader in the text. Discusses Machado de Assis' ironic humor.

EQUUS

Type of work: Drama
Author: Peter Shaffer (1926-   )
Type of plot: Psychological realism
Time of plot: Late twentieth century
Locale: Great Britain
First performed: 1973; first published, 1973

> *Principal characters:*
> MARTIN DYSART, a child psychiatrist
> ALAN STRANG, a disturbed boy of seventeen
> FRANK STRANG, Alan's father
> DORA STRANG, Alan's mother
> HESTHER SALOMON, a magistrate
> JILL MASON, a worker at the stables
> HARRY DALTON, the owner of the stables

The Story:

Martin Dysart, a child psychiatrist, recognized that his life was filled with emptiness and pain. He was confronted by this recognition through his treatment of Alan Strang, an adolescent who has inexplicably blinded six horses with a horsepick. It was a crime which shocked and outraged the owner of the stables, who believed that Alan should be imprisoned. However, Hesther Salomon, the magistrate in charge of the case, recognized a deep need in the boy, and she brought him to Dysart hoping that he could make the boy "normal." Dysart came to recognize that he could, but at a terrible cost.

At first distrustful of Dysart, Alan sang jingles to block Dysart's overtures. Unperturbed, Dysart began seeing Alan and then began to make inquiries. He found the Strang household to be absolutely normal superficially, but, beneath this appearance of normality, strange tensions vibrated. Mr. Strang was dictatorial and repressed; Mrs. Strang was filled with religious mania. Neither was able to deal in any real way with what had happened.

Alan himself seemed unable to deal with his actions, and Dysart worked to find ways to allow Alan to tell him things that would help to explain the blinding of the horses. Using a small recorder, Alan told Dysart of his first encounter with a horse on a beach when he was six years old. A rider took him up and down through the surf, Alan glorying in the ride until his enraged father pulled him down from the horse, claiming that the horse and rider were menaces to safety. For Alan, it was a moment of great passion; it began his sense of a godlike spirit in horses, a god he named Equus.

From Mr. Dalton, Dysart learned that Alan was introduced to the stable by Jill Mason, and at first he believed that he had found a good worker, since Alan did much more than his share of grooming the horses and cleaning the stables. Oddly, however, Alan never rode the horses, though Mr. Dalton suspected that periodically they were ridden at night. Clearly, Alan was passionately fascinated by horses; in fact, he worshiped the god Equus in them, something Mr. Strang discovered disconcertingly when he saw Alan chanting before a picture of a horse, putting a bit in his own mouth, and beating himself.

Dysart was more and more taken with Alan; he saw in him someone who was filled with a passion, whose life was filled with worship, and he envied Alan. His own life seemed so safe and secure, so empty of energy and passion that he questioned whether his treatment of Alan was anything less than a monstrous sacrifice to the normal.

Under hypnosis, Dysart took Alan's mind back to one of the nights when he took a horse, Nugget, out riding. It was an evening of passionate devotion, of the worship of the god Equus. Alan led the horse gently out from the stables to a field, where he stripped and bowed to the god. He inserted a bit in his own mouth, and then, in complete worshipful ecstacy, he galloped around the field. Afterwards, he stood beside the horse, fully devoted, fully alive. It was a sense of passion that Dysart had never experienced.

Soon after, Mrs. Strang came to visit Alan, and, in a terrible fight, he silently accused her of some responsibility for his behavior. She refused to be accused, and, when Dysart intervened, she claimed that what Alan did was Alan's responsibility, not that of his parents. Nevertheless, she also blamed the Devil and left without any real understanding of what was troubling her son.

Alan suggested obliquely to Dysart that he was waiting to be given a truth pill; Dysart picked up on the suggestion and, giving Alan a placebo, had him tell about the night he blinded the horses. Before he began, Alan revealed that he knew that Dysart was in pain; Dysart was startled by Alan's perception but led him back hypnotically to that night. It began on a date with Jill to see a pornographic film, at which they discovered Mr. Strang. After the initial shock and embarrassment, Alan suddenly recognized that his father too had a secret inner life, that everyone did. It was a freeing recognition for him.

When they walked back to the stables and Jill proposed that they make love, Alan sensed the confining and overpowering presence of his god, Equus, who would always be watching. He found himself impotent in the face of his god, and, after chasing Jill away, he blinded the horses so that Equus could not see him.

The crisis having been reached, the episode having been lived through again, Alan fell asleep, dreamless for the first time in a long time. Dysart recognized that he was now beginning a recovery, but his recovery meant that he would no longer be passionate, that he would no longer gallop with a god. Dysart recognized that, in destroying this passion, he too had stabbed at faces with picks.

Critical Evaluation:

In many ways, *Equus* bears strong connections to classical drama, particularly Greek drama. Its solemn, stately, and ceremonial manner duplicates classical ceremonies. The strongest connection, however, is the presence of the chorus, which in Greek drama was meant to comment upon and explain the meaning of what was happening on the stage. Here, the chorus is played by a group of six actors who play the horses. The presence of the god is suggested by the Equus noise that they make in chorus, and it seems that they watch the action throughout; they see everything.

This "seeing" is an important part of Alan's perception of his god. In one way, Equus is a god-slave, in that Alan can lead Equus out and control him, making him gallop in the field. In this sense, Equus recalls Christ in his chains being led to Calvary. In fact, Alan keeps a gruesome picture of Christ in chains until his father tears it down; he replaces it with a picture of a horse with enormous eyes.

Yet, in another way, Equus is a beloved. After the gallop, Alan and the horse stand neck to neck, and there is a wonderful intimacy that fills Alan with life and passion. In yet another way, Equus is completely demanding and compelling, taking on the role of the avenging God that Mrs. Strang can envision so vividly. "God sees you Alan, he sees you," she insists, presenting

God as always hovering, waiting to avenge. Thus, in the stable scene, Alan, though he has come to recognize that he is not the only one with a secret inner life, also senses that the god will always demand him completely, that he will never find passion elsewhere, that he is always within in the sight of Equus. It is this consuming sight against which he strikes.

Perhaps the central crisis of the play, though, is within Dysart. In a dream, he imagines himself wearing a classical mask and being the chief priest at a sacrifice of five hundred children. He must go on with his task, but he cannot continue. This becomes for him a symbol of what he does to children through his psychiatry. He sacrifices essential parts of them that make them uniquely themselves. In fact, he sacrifices them to the god of the normal. When Hesther suggests that at the least he is able to take their pain away, Dysart realizes that even in doing this he has taken away something which is uniquely theirs, substituting only the bland and safe normal.

Equus is a play about passion and worship, and the strong suggestion of the dramatist is that modern society has lost its ability to worship anything, let alone worship it passionately. Dysart realizes that while he looks at books on classical Greece and travels there with all accommodations booked and all eventualities covered, out on a field a young boy is trying to become a centaur; he is galloping with a god. This worship is that for which Dysart longs, this awareness of gods springing out at every turn. Instead, he lives in a dry, sterile flat, in a dry, sterile marriage, taking away passion from children.

Dysart is not the only one in this situation. Dora and Frank lead proper, secure British lives; they will not let their son ride a horse on a beach. They have sublimated all passion in their own lives, Dora into a religious mania, Frank into prurient films which he goes to see secretly. Dora talks about her relatives indulging in "equitation": dressing in a stately manner and riding horses in a proper and sedate manner. Alan has a safe and secure job, working in an electrical shop and handling brands of merchandise. It is this proper and secure world that Alan fights when he rides, naked on a naked horse, filled with ecstacy. Only Dysart seems to recognize this and envy it. Only he seems to realize the consequences of taking this passion from Alan, consequences damaging to both Alan and himself.

The form of the play contributes to the focus upon Dysart and the dilemma of worship. The setting is minimal, with several benches and railings around a revolving set. All actors are present onstage throughout the performance, and the sense is that they are all witnesses, particularly Dysart, who is trying to discern the pattern in what he is seeing. The horses are noble and stately, but they are mimetic in that there is no attempt to reproduce them with any realism or to make them domestic and safe. They are the carriers of the god Equus, who, thus, is always on stage as well.

Though Alan is riveting, the central dilemma is Dysart's, and Peter Shaffer indicates this by beginning the play with a rambling statement of that dilemma, even before the audience is aware of the action that has led to it. The first act is in essence a long flashback, and it is composed of a series of vignettes, each of which contributes to Dysart's understanding. Many of these are reflections of Alan's sessions with Dysart, and they are played out simultaneously as Alan's spoken revelations to Dysart and as actions on the stage. Alan reacts with his parents as he is torn from the horse on the beach, but he also is answering—and sometimes not answering—Dysart's questions.

The result of this technique is to bridge the past and the present and to make them occur simultaneously. It is also to maintain a focus on Dysart, who is helping Alan relive these memories. This focus is particularly striking when Dysart slips away from the action and addresses the audience directly; this kind of address both opens and closes the play. In these addresses, Dysart struggles with his role and explicitly ponders the questions of worship, of passion, and of the normal. By the end of the play, he is unable to rescue the tensions between these or, to put it in his own words, to "account for Equus."

At the end of the play, the audience too is left to account for Equus, a complex and powerful symbol of all that seems to have been lost in a modern society driven to eradicate its own pain. In becoming normal, it has lost the sublime. In eradicating pain, it has lost the chance of utter delight. In creating a world superficially proper, it denies passions that must come to the surface. In all this, what is left to worship, to which to be utterly committed? Is it possible for modern humanity to gallop with gods? All these questions, which are spiritual questions at their center, are posed by *Equus*.

Gary D. Schmidt

Bibliography:
Beckerman, Bernard. "The Dynamics of Peter Shaffer's Drama." In *The Play and Its Critic: Essays for Eric Bentley*, edited by Michael Bertin. Lanham, Md.: University Presses of America, 1986. This article examines the stagecraft of Peter Shaffer by examining the dramatic structure of several of his plays.
Gianakaris, C. J. *Peter Shaffer*. New York: St. Martin's Press, 1992. This book-length study focuses on thematic issues in Shaffer's dramatic works, examining particularly the role of stagecraft in terms of the presentation of those themes.
Klein, Dennis A. "A Note on the Use of Dreams in Peter Shaffer's Major Plays." *Journal of Evolutionary Psychology* 9 (March, 1989): 25-32. This article is an examination of Dysart and the role that dreams play in *Equus*, focusing both on the dreams of Alan and those of Dysart in terms of progress of the play's meaning.
_____. *Peter Shaffer*. Boston: Twayne, 1979. One of three book-length studies of Shaffer's work, this one begins with a chapter of biography before it moves to a chronological handling of Shaffer's plays, providing basic background as well as major thematic concerns.
_____. "Peter Shaffer's *Equus* as Modern Aristotelian Tragedy." *Studies in Iconography* 9 (1983): 175-181. After detailing Aristotle's vision of the nature of tragedy and how it is encapsulated in drama, Klein examines the ways in which *Equus* fits the patterns of tragic drama that Aristotle outlines.
Mustazza, Leonard. "A Jealous God: Ritual and Judgement in Shaffer's *Equus*." *Papers on Language and Literature* 28 (1992): 174-184. Focusing on the treatment of Equus as the jealous, demanding god figure in Alan's life, this article examines the relationship of the play's meanings to the mythic figure of Dionysius.
Plunka, Gene A. *Peter Shaffer: Roles, Rites, and Rituals in the Theater*. Rutherford, N.J.: Fairleigh Dickinson University Press, 1988. This study of Shaffer's dramas examines the uses to which Shaffer puts ritual and rite—particularly religious ritual and rite—in his theatrical productions and notes the effects of these rites, both in terms of the meaning of the dramas and in terms of how the dramas are produced on stage.
Witham, Barry B. "The Anger of *Equus*." *Modern Drama* 22 (1979): 61-66. Focuses on Dysart's dilemma of whether he should "heal" Alan, thus depriving him of his ability to worship passionately, or allow Alan to keep the passion that Dysart is missing.

EREC AND ENIDE

Type of work: Poetry
Author: Chrétien de Troyes (c. 1150-c. 1190)
Type of plot: Arthurian romance
Time of plot: Sixth century
Locale: Arthurian England
First transcribed: Érec et Énide, c. 1164 (English translation, 1913)

Principal characters:
KING ARTHUR
QUEEN GUINEVERE
EREC, a knight of the Round Table and son of King Lac
ENIDE, his bride
GUIVRET THE LITTLE, Erec's friend and benefactor

The Story:

One Easter season, while King Arthur held his court in the royal town of Cardigan, he summoned all of his knights to a hunt for the white stag. Sir Gawain, hearing of the king's wish, was displeased and said that no good would come of that ancient custom, for the law of the hunt decreed that the successful hunter must also kiss the lady whom he considered the most beautiful damsel of the court. As Sir Gawain noted, there was likely to be dissension among the assembled knights and each, believing his own true love as the loveliest and gentlest lady in the land, would be angered by the slight if she were not so considered by the others.

At daybreak, the hunters set out. After them rode Queen Guinevere, attended by Erec, a fair and brave knight, and one of the queen's damsels. While they waited by the wayside to hear the baying of the hounds or the call of a bugle, they saw coming toward them a strange knight, his lady, and a dwarf who carried a knotted scourge. The queen sent her damsel to ask who the knight and his fair companion might be, but the dwarf, barring her way, struck the damsel across the hand with his whip. Then Erec rode forward and the dwarf lashed him across the face and neck. Being unarmed, Erec made no attempt to chastise the dwarf or his haughty master, but he vowed that he would follow the strange knight until he could find arms to hire or borrow that he might avenge the insult to the queen.

In the fair town to which the strange knight and his companions presently led him, Erec found lodgings with a vavasor, who told him the reason for all the stir and bustle that Erec had seen as he rode through the gates. On the next day, a fine sparrow hawk would be given to the knight who could defend against all comers the beauty and goodness of his lady. The haughty knight had won the bird in two successive years and would be allowed to keep it if his challenge went unanswered the next day. At the home of the vavasor, Erec met his host's daughter, Enide, who was despite her tattered garments the most radiantly beautiful damsel Erec had ever seen. With her as his lady and with arms borrowed from his host, Erec challenged and defeated in single combat the arrogant knight, whose name was Yder. Then Erec dispatched the vanquished knight, along with his lady and his dwarf, to Queen Guinevere to do with as she pleased. He also sent word that he would return with his beautiful bride, the damsel Enide.

Erec promised Enide's father great riches and two towns to rule in his own land, but he refused all offers to have Enide dressed in robes suitable to her new station: He wished all in King Arthur's court to see that even in her humble garments she was the most beautiful lady who ever lived. So great was her beauty that King Arthur, who had killed the White Stag, kissed her, and there was no demur from the assembled knights and ladies. The king also granted Eric the boon of a speedy marriage, so eager was the young knight for the love of his promised bride. The ceremony was performed by the archbishop of Canterbury at the time of the Pentecost before an assemblage of knights and ladies from every corner of the kingdom, and the celebration continued for a fortnight.

A month after Pentecost, a great tournament was held near Tenebroc, and in the lists there Erec showed himself the most valiant of all the knights assembled. On his return, he received from the king permission to visit his own land, and he and Enide set out with an escort of sixty knights. On the fifth day, they arrived in Carnant, where King Lac welcomed his son and Enide with much honor. Erec found so much pleasure in his wife's company that he had no thought for other pastimes. When tournaments were held in the region around, he sent his knights to the forays but himself remained behind in dalliance with the fair Enide. At last people began to gossip and say that he had turned a craven in arms. These reports so distressed Enide that one morning while they were still abed she began to lament the way in which the brave and hardy knight had changed because of his love for her. Overhearing her words, Erec was moved to anger, and he told her to rise and prepare herself at once to take the road with him on a journey of knight-errantry in search of whatever perils he might encounter by chance. At the beginning of the journey he gave orders that she was never to tell him of anything she might see, nor to speak to him unless he addressed her first.

As Enide rode ahead, forbidden to speak, she lamented her disclosure and the sudden loss of the life she had enjoyed with her loving husband. She disobeyed him, however, when they were about to be attacked by three robber knights, and again when they were assailed by five recreants. Erec, having overcome all who opposed him, felt no gratitude for her wifely warnings and fears for his safety and spoke harshly to her because she had disobeyed his command.

That night, since they knew of no town or shelter nearby, they slept in an open field. There, the squire of Count Galoin came upon them the next day and conducted them to lodgings in the town where the count was master. That nobleman, going to pay his respects to the strange knight and his lovely lady, was much smitten with Enide's beauty, so much so that, going to the place where she sat apart, he expressed his pity for her obvious distress and offered to make her mistress of all his lands. When Enide refused, he declared that he would take her by force. Fearing for her husband's life, Enide pretended to accede to his wishes. It was arranged that on the next day the count's knights were to overtake the travelers and seize Enide. Erec, coming to her rescue, would be killed, and she would be free to take the count as her lord. Once again, Enide disobeyed her husband and told him of Count Galoin's plan. Forewarned, Erec overcame his assailants and knocked the count senseless from his steed. When Galoin's followers would have pursued Erec and Enide, the count restrained them, praising Enide's prudence and virtue and the bravery of her knight.

Departing from Count Galoin's lands, the travelers came to a castle from which the lord came riding on a great steed to offer Erec combat at arms. Enide saw him coming but did not dare tell her husband for fear of his wrath. At last she did speak, however, and Erec realized that it was her love for him that made her disobedient to his commands. The knight who challenged Erec, Guivret the Little, was of small stature but stout heart and both he and Erec were wounded in the fight. Though the courageous little knight lost, he had put up such a good fight that he and Erec became friends. Guivret invited Erec to have his wounds dressed and to rest at his castle, but Erec thanked him courteously and rode on with Enide.

At length, they arrived at a wood where King Arthur had come with a large hunting party. By then, Erec was so begrimed and bloodied that Sir Kay the seneschal did not recognize him.

When he would have taken the wounded knight to the king's camp, Erec refused and they fought until Sir Kay was unhorsed. Sir Gawain then rode out to encounter the strange knight, and he was able to bring Erec to the place where the king had ordered tents set up in anticipation of their coming. There was great joy in that meeting for the king and Queen Guinevere, but distress at Erec's wounds. Although the king pleaded with Erec to rest there until his hurts were healed, the knight refused to be turned aside or delayed on his journey, and early the next morning he and Enide set out once more.

In a strange forest, they heard the cries of a lady in distress. Leaving Enide to await his return, Erec rode in the direction of the sound and found a damsel weeping because two giants had carried away her knight. Riding in pursuit, Erec killed the giants and rescued the knight, whose name was Cadoc of Tabriol. Later, he sent Cadoc and the damsel to King Arthur's camp, to tell the story of how he fared. Meanwhile, Erec's wounds had reopened, and he lost so much blood that he fell from his horse in a swoon.

While Enide was weeping over his prostrate body, a count with his suite came riding through the forest. The nobleman gave orders that the body was to be taken to Limors and prepared for burial. On their arrival at the palace, the count declared his intention of espousing Enide at once. Although she refused to give her consent, the ceremony was performed in great haste and guests were summoned to a wedding banquet that night.

Erec, recovering from his deep swoon, awoke in time to see the count strike Enide across the face because in her great grief she could neither eat nor drink at her new husband's bidding. Springing from the funeral bier, he drew his sword and struck the count on the head with such force that blood and brains gushed out. While the other guests retreated in fear of the ghostly presence that had so suddenly returned to life, Erec and Enide made their escape. Erec assured his wife that he was now convinced of her devotion and love.

Guivret the Little had received word that a mortally wounded knight had been found in the forest and that the lord of Limors had carried off the dead man's wife. Coming to see that the fallen knight received proper burial and to aid his lady if she were in distress, the doughty little knight came upon Erec, whom he failed to recognize in the murky moonlight, and struck a blow that knocked Erec unconscious. Enide and Guivret remained by the stricken man all that night, and in the morning they proceeded to Guivret's castle. There Erec was nursed back to health by Enide and Guivret's sisters. After his recovery, escorted by Guivret and burdened with gifts, the couple prepared to return to King Arthur's court.

Toward nightfall, the travelers saw in the distance the towers of a great fortress. Guivret said that the town was named Brandigant and that there was a perilous passage called the "Joy of the Court." King Evrain welcomed the travelers with great courtesy, but that night, while they feasted, he also warned Erec against attempting the mysterious feat that no knight had thus far survived. Despite the disapproval of his friend and his host Erec swore to attempt the passage.

The next morning he was conducted into a magic garden filled with all manner of fruits and flowers, past the heads and helmets of the unfortunate knights who had braved danger to blow the magic horn whose blast would signify joy to King Evrain's land. At the end of a path he found a beautiful damsel seated on a couch. While he stood looking at her, a knight appeared to engage him in combat. They fought until the hour of noon had passed; then the knight fell exhausted. He revealed that he had been held in thrall in the garden by an oath given to his mistress, whose one wish had been his eternal presence by her side. Erec then blew the horn and all the people rejoiced to find him safe. There was great joy also when the knight of the garden was released from his bondage and the beautiful damsel identified herself as the cousin of Enide.

Erec and Enide, accompanied by Guivret, continued their journey to the court of King Arthur, where they were received with gladness and honor. When his father died, Erec returned to reign in his own land. There he and Enide were crowned in a ceremony of royal splendor in the presence of King Arthur and all the nobles of his realm.

Critical Evaluation:

Erec and Enide is the first of a collection of metrical romances by Chrétien de Troyes, a master tale-teller of the medieval period about whom very little is otherwise known. The poem is the oldest romance on Arthurian materials extant in any language. It has sometimes been called the first novel because of its consistent plot. Written in eight-syllable rhyming couplets, the story provides the most idealized expression of the code of chivalry by a single writer of medieval times.

Like the author's *Yvain* (after 1164), *Erec and Enide* deals among other things with the conflict between and the attempt to reconcile knightly and marital responsibilities. Apparently Chrétien himself thought much of the work: In the romance's first paragraph he states that "now I shall begin the tale which will be remembered so long as Christendom endures. This is Chrétien's boast."

His scarcely modest claim was well founded, for this romance of Arthurian England in the sixth century has outlived myriad other medieval romances. The poem offers various and contrasting riches, including a mélange of real and unreal incidents, exact and exaggerated statistics, logical and implausible motivation, and wildly supernatural events in close juxtaposition with homely, concrete ones. From this often unlikely material, Chrétien devised a well-constructed plot. Moreover, the author, in welding his diverse and sometimes incongruous elements together, had a serious purpose, for he was interested in problems of individual conscience and in the choices individuals had to make in the face of conflicting loyalties and personal emotions. Chrétien was intrigued with how humans solve these problems as members of a social group. All the usual and contrived situations of medieval romance served Chrétien as a means of setting forth these problems and providing complicated webs to entrap the protagonists.

Although Erec, a king's son, married the daughter of a poor vavasor, or country squire, Chrétien takes care to make them equal in beauty and breeding. However, when because of excessive love of his wife, reports circulate that Erec has permitted himself to desert the tourneys and quests and fail to continue proofs of his knighthood, the story becomes the tale of married love subjected to the pressures of the man's other obligations and duties. It is also a story of a wife's patient endurance of her husband's eccentricities and abuse. In many respects, Chrétien intended *Erec and Enide*, for all its comic incidents and exaggerated postures, to be a straightforward narrative of love being testing. In this it is similar to Geoffrey Chaucer's late fourteenth century "Clerk's Tale" on the familiar theme of the patient Griselda.

It is characteristic of Chrétien that he focuses on the analysis of love, particularly as felt by his heroines. Such subtleties of thought are rare in medieval romance, but Chrétien's women in love verbalize their considerations in matters of the heart. Enide, for example, upbraids herself for false pride after she told Erec what others were saying about his valor, and in a soliloquy she tells herself it is right that she suffers: "One does not know what good fortune is until he has made trial of evil." Not until the fourteenth century, in Chaucer's Criseyde, is there a romance heroine engaged in such subtle love analysis.

Chrétien provides convincing characters, not merely stock figures. In *Erec and Enide*, he does not focus on battles or such farcical scenes as the one in which Enide must marry the Count against her will but rather on Erec's gradual realization of the great love his wife has for him. The plot development takes Erec to the point where at the end he says, "for I love you now more than ever I did before." He has learned the value of humility and faithfulness.

In a time when *fin amour*, or courtly love (in other words, adulterous love), was supposed to be the reigning material for poets and romance writers, Chrétien showed far more concern for love within the marriage bond. As a matter of fact, he stressed this kind of love as the ideal union. When he dealt with adulterous love as in his *Lancelot* (after 1164), he seems ill at ease and handles both plot and characterization with less finesse. Most critics as a result conclude that in this latter work he wrote on demand and not out of inclination. In both *Yvain* and *Erec and Enide*, however, he concentrates on the difficulties in marriage and on solutions of those difficulties.

Chrétien said at the beginning of his romance that "jongleurs were accustomed to garble and mutilate" the story, but that he himself had ordered his material into a unified, coherent whole. Chrétien not only successfully develops the plot but also shows progression in character development. He combines descriptions of lavishly ornamented watered silk, ivory, gold tapestries, and red armor; of the ragged garments of a peasant girl in a poor household; of the hardships of wayfaring on roads infested with evils of all sorts; and finally of a brilliant coronation ceremony and a happy ending for the reconciled Erec and Enide. With consummate artistry he makes his poem entertaining and at the same time poses comments on the problems of married love.

"Critical Evaluation" by Muriel B. Ingham

Bibliography:
Buckbee, Edward J. "*Erec et Enide.*" In *The Romances of Chrétien de Troyes: A Symposium*, edited by Douglas Kelly. Lexington, Ky.: French Forum, 1985. Buckbee argues that Erec and Enide are a perfect couple who fit the ideal of Arthur's elite society of knights and ladies, but he also notes that the characterization is ambiguous because Chrétien does not state their motives clearly.

Frappier, Jean. "Chrétien de Troyes." In *Arthurian Literature in the Middle Ages*, edited by R. S. Loomis. Oxford, England: Clarendon Press, 1959. Provides a good overview of Chrétien's work and deals primarily with his sources. An admirable starting point for new readers.

Loomis, Roger Sherman. *Arthurian Tradition and Chrétien de Troyes*. New York: Columbia University Press, 1949. Loomis shows how most episodes in Chrétien's romances have their parallels in other Irish, Welsh, and Breton stories. Some of Loomis' work has been questioned, but he remains an acknowledged authority in the field.

Luttrell, Claude. *The Creation of the First Arthurian Romance: A Quest*. Evanston, Ill.: Northwestern University Press, 1974. A study specifically of *Erec and Enide*, which focuses on Chrétien's sources and the meaning as revealed by the poem's structure. Also discusses romances that resemble *Erec and Enide*.

Noble, Peter S. *Love and Marriage in Chrétien de Troyes*. Cardiff: University of Wales Press, 1982. Examines the theme of love and marriage in all of Chrétien's romances. Concludes that *Erec and Enide* is a celebration of married rather than unmarried or pre-marital "courtly love."

EREWHON
Or, Over the Range

Type of work: Novel
Author: Samuel Butler (1835-1902)
Type of plot: Utopian
Time of plot: 1870's
Locale: Erewhon and England
First published: 1872

> *Principal characters:*
> HIGGS, a traveler in Erewhon
> CHOWBOK, a native
> NOSNIBOR, a citizen of Erewhon
> AROWHENA, his daughter

The Story:

Higgs, a young man of twenty-two years, worked on a sheep farm. From the plains, he looked often at the seemingly impassable mountain range that formed the edge of the sheep country and wondered about the land beyond those towering peaks. He learned from an old native named Chowbok that it was forbidden to visit that land. Chowbok assumed a strange pose when questioned further and uttered unearthly cries. Curious, Higgs persuaded Chowbok to go on a trip with him into the mountains.

They were unable to find a pass through the mountains. One day, Higgs came upon a small valley and went up it alone. He found that it led through the mountains. When he went back to get Chowbok, he saw the old native fleeing toward the plains. He went on alone. After climbing down treacherous cliffs and crossing a river on a reed raft, he finally came to beautiful rolling plains. He passed by some strange manlike statues, which made terrifying noises as the wind circled about them. He recognized in them the reason for Chowbok's performance.

Higgs awoke next morning to see two girls herding a flock of goats about him. When the girls saw him, they ran and brought some men to look at him. All of them were physically handsome. Convinced at last that Higgs was a human being, they took him to a small town close by. There his clothing was searched, and a watch he had with him was confiscated. The men seemed to be especially interested in his health, and he was allowed to leave only after a strict medical examination. He wondered why there had been such confusion over his watch until he was shown a museum in which was kept old pieces of machinery. Finally, he was put in jail.

In jail, he learned the language and some of the strange customs of the country, which was called Erewhon. The oddest custom was to consider disease a crime; anyone who was sick was tried and put in jail. On the other hand, people who committed robbery or murder were treated sympathetically and given hospital care. Shortly afterward, the jailor informed Higgs that he had been summoned to appear before the king and queen and that he was to be the guest of a man named Nosnibor. Nosnibor had embezzled a large sum of money from a poor widow, but he was now recovering from his illness. The widow, Higgs learned, would be tried and sentenced for allowing herself to be imposed upon.

In the capital, Higgs stayed with Nosnibor and his family and paid several visits to the court. He was well received because he had blond hair, a rarity among the Erewhonians. He learned a great deal about the past history of the country. Twenty-five hundred years before, a prophet had preached that it was unlawful to eat meat, since man should not kill his fellow creatures. For several hundred years, the Erewhonians were vegetarians. Then another sage showed that animals were no more the fellow creatures of man than plants were; if man could not kill and eat animals, he should not kill and eat plants. The logic of his arguments overthrew the old philosophy. Two hundred years before, a great scientist had presented the idea that machines had minds and feelings and that, if man were not careful, the machine would finally become the ruling creature on earth. Consequently, all machines had been scrapped.

The economy of the country was unusual. There were two monetary systems—one worthless except for spiritual meaning, one used in trade. The more respected system was the valueless one, and its work was carried on in Musical Banks where people exchanged coins for music. The state religion was a worship of various qualities of godhead, such as love, fear, and wisdom, and the main goddess, Ydgrun, was at the same time an abstract concept and a silly, cruel woman. Higgs learned much of the religion from Arowhena, one of Nosnibor's daughters. She was a beautiful girl, and the two fell in love.

Because Nosnibor insisted that his older daughter, Zulora, be married first, Higgs and his host had an argument, and Higgs found lodgings elsewhere. Arowhena met him often at the Musical Banks. Higgs visited the University of Unreason, where the young Erewhonian boys were taught to do anything except that which was practical. They studied obsolete languages and hypothetical sciences. He saw a relationship between these schools and the mass-mind, which the educational system in England was producing. Higgs also learned that money was considered a symbol of duty; the more money a man had, the better man he was.

Nosnibor learned that Higgs was meeting Arowhena secretly. Then the king began to worry over the fact that Higgs had entered the country with a watch, and he feared that Higgs might try to bring machinery back into use. Planning an escape, Higgs proposed to the queen that he make a balloon trip to talk with the god of the air. The queen was delighted with the idea. The king hoped that Higgs would fall and kill himself.

Higgs smuggled Arowhena aboard the balloon with him. The couple soon found themselves high in the air and moving over the mountain range. When the balloon settled on the sea, Higgs and Arowhena were picked up by a passing ship. They were married in England, and Higgs tried to get up an expedition to go back to Erewhon. Only the missionaries listened to his story. Then Chowbok, Higgs's faithless native friend, showed up in England teaching religion, and his appearance convinced people that Erewhon actually did exist. Higgs hoped to return to the country soon to teach it Christianity.

Critical Evaluation:

Samuel Butler's utopian satire *Erewhon* is a series of essays written between 1860 and 1870 that anticipates the works of Aldous Huxley and George Orwell. Like these later utopian writers, Butler attempts to expose and deflate the hypocrisies that flawed the England of his day rather than to prophesy or to propose corrective measures. As a result, his novel is really dystopian in vision. It savages a society full of easy self-congratulation and at the same time remains pitiless toward misfortune. Butler's artistic versatility—he was an accomplished, though unappreciated, painter, musician, and essayist—enabled him to offer social commentary from a variety of perspectives. *Erewhon* also helped Butler sharpen social critiques that he voiced even more effectively in his great autobiographical novel, *The Way of All Flesh* (1903), published only after his death.

In his preface to *Erewhon*, Butler concedes that the book contains "hardly any story, and little attempt to give life and individuality to the characters." He tries throughout the work to keep readers at a critical distance from the usual distractions of the novel genre. As a satirist, Butler asks the readers to examine every issue with detachment and to register every distortion and shift in perspective. Yet he makes his task treacherous with various techniques such as his use of anagrams—"Erewhon" is an anagram of "Nowhere." Just as the readers must untwist the title to assess its meaning, so they can never fully trust the novel's narration. In his unabashed desire both to exploit Erewhon and to convert its natives, the adventurer-narrator, Higgs, is clearly himself a target of Butler's satire. Yet, despite his own hypocritical bent, Higgs also records and loudly decries Erewhonian foibles. Himself insensitive to irony, he provides readers access to duplicities Butler wishes to reveal.

In general, Erewhonian society, like its English counterpart, confuses individual responsibility with bad luck, moral choice with mischance. By punishing disease as criminal, for example, Erewhon reflects Victorian England's desire to maintain appearances; visible blemishes—the hapless sick or poor—mar society's self-image and are eradicated. Because they are living reminders of the costs of progress and industry, they must be treated severely by being hidden away in poorhouses or prisons. In a sort of moral anagram, crime in Erewhon becomes a disease; it is attended by solicitous "straighteners" and wins the sympathy of the "patient's" friends. Here, Butler takes aim at English society's willingness to ignore all sorts of moral failures in the name of order and profit. He tacitly implies that people admire those who thrive by immoral means, blaming instead those who are so weak and gullible as to be victimized by them. Thus, Nosnibor, Higgs's host, is treated for having embezzled and is allowed to keep his ill-gotten profits, while the widow he cheated is prosecuted.

Similarly, children in Erewhon, rather than their parents, are made responsible for their birth and upbringing. The unborn commit a "felony" in inflicting themselves upon the living, for which they must make "obedient and abject" amends throughout their lives. In return, truly exemplary parents spend great sums educating their offspring at the Colleges of Unreason, "in order to render their children as nearly useless as possible." In this tortured relationship, Butler rehearses the account of his own childhood, which he later provides in *The Way of All Flesh*. In accord with family tradition, and against his own inclination, Butler was educated for the ministry, though he failed to enter the church. Through the Erewhonian "birth formulae," he exposes the coercion, guilt, and estrangement that troubled his typically Victorian family. Butler also mocks his expensive but irrelevant Cambridge education in the obsolete "hypothetical language" (that is, Latin) taught to Erewhonian students.

Butler also depicts Victorians as being confused about objects of worship. Erewhon's two systems of currency reflect a similar religious hypocrisy. Commercial interests supplant genuine religious feeling so that, finally, worship is expressed through commerce. Though publicly lauded, the "coin" of the Musical Banks is worthless, and the banks themselves are rarely visited. In the same way, Victorians went through the motions of religious observance, paying their tithes on Sunday, but their offerings remained worthless. They kneeled instead to the goddess Ydgrun, Butler's anagram for the Victorian "Mrs. Grundy," who enforces only a shallow social conformism.

Finally, in "The Book of the Machines," Butler ridicules the Victorians' misunderstanding and fear of Charles Darwin's theory of evolution, as well as their disproportionate faith in progress through industrialization. While the Erewhonians fear the "evolution" of machines (Higgs's watch is therefore regarded as dangerous), such an evolution was already at work in industrialized England. For the greedy Victorians, a factory possesses more life and potential than the workmen who operate it; machines—and the profit they sustain—threaten to become more real than the needs of colorless and expendable workers. At the same time, society fretted about the question of descent of man and resented being linked to the animal world as strongly as the Erewhonians mistrust the machine. Butler's twist neatly exposes the blindness of a society that neglects living, breathing individuals, all the while insisting upon humans' divine origin.

"Critical Evaluation" by Sarah A. Boris

Bibliography:

Cannan, Gilbert. *Samuel Butler: A Critical Study*. Folcroft, Pa.: Folcroft Press, 1969. A sound, general introduction to Butler's literary work, diverse talents, and interests.

Greenacre, Phillis. *The Quest for the Father: A Study of the Darwin-Butler Controversy*. New York: International Universities Press, 1963. A psychoanalytic account of Butler's connection with Darwin that sets "The Book of the Machines" into interpretative context.

Holt, Lee E. *Samuel Butler*. New York: Twayne, 1964. A fine overview of Butler's work.

Muggeridge, Malcolm. *The Earnest Atheist: A Study of Samuel Butler*. London: Eyre and Spottiswode, 1936. A lively and insightful account of Butler's attitudes. Helps to explain the ferocity of his attack on religion in *Erewhon*.

Stillman, Clara G. *Samuel Butler: A Mid-Victorian Modern*. Port Washington, N.Y.: Kennikat Press, 1972. Offers a helpful chapter on *Erewhon*, analyzing Butler's satirical methods.

AN ESSAY CONCERNING HUMAN UNDERSTANDING

Type of work: Philosophy
Author: John Locke (1632-1704)
First published: 1690

John Locke's purpose in *An Essay Concerning Human Understanding* is to inquire into the origin and extent of human knowledge. His conclusion—that all knowledge is derived from sense experience—became the principal tenet of empiricism, which has dominated Western philosophy ever since. Even George Berkeley, who rejected Locke's distinction between sense qualities independent of the mind and sense qualities dependent on the mind, produced his idealism in response to Locke's provocative philosophy and gave it an empirical cast that reflected Western culture's rejection of innate or transcendental knowledge.

An Essay Concerning Human Understanding is divided into four books: book 1, "Of Innate Notions"; book 2, "Of Ideas"; book 3, "Of Words"; and book 4, "Of Knowledge, Certain and Probable."

In preparation for his radical claim that all ideas are derived from experience, Locke begins his essay with a careful consideration of the thesis that there are innate ideas. Locke first examines the notion that there are ideas that are a necessary part of human understanding and are, therefore, common to all people. Locke's attack on this thesis is from two directions. He argues that many of the ideas that are supposed to be innate can be and have been derived naturally from sense experience, that not all people assent to those ideas that are supposed to be innate. Locke maintains that even if reason enables people to discover the truth of certain ideas, those ideas cannot be said to be innate; for reason is needed to discover their truth.

In book 2, "Of Ideas," Locke considers the origin of such ideas as those expressed by the words "whiteness," "hardness," "sweetness," "thinking," "motion," "man," and the like. The second section states his conclusion:

> Let us then suppose the mind to be, as we say, white paper void of all characters, without any ideas. How comes it to be furnished? . . . Whence has it all the materials of reason and knowledge? To this I answer, in one word, from experience. . . . Our observation, employed either about external sensible objects, or about the internal operations of our minds perceived and reflected on by ourselves, is that which supplies our understandings with all the materials of knowledge.

The two sources of ideas, according to Locke, are sensation and reflection. By the senses people come to have perceptions of things, thereby acquiring the ideas of yellow, white, or cold, for example. Then, by reflection, by consideration of the mind in operation, people acquire the ideas of thinking, doubting, believing, knowing, willing, and so on.

By sensation people acquire knowledge of external objects; by reflection people acquire knowledge of their own minds. Ideas that are derived from sensation are simple; that is, they present "one uniform appearance," even though a number of simple ideas may come together in the perception of an external object. The mind dwells on the simple ideas, comparing them to one another, combining them, but never inventing them. By a "simple idea" Locke means what some modern and contemporary philosophers have called a "sense-datum," a distinctive, entirely differentiated item of sense experience, such as the odor of some particular glue, or the taste of coffee in a cup. He calls attention to the fact that people use sense experience to imagine what they have never perceived, but no operation of the mind can yield novel simple ideas.

By the quality of something, Locke means its power to produce an idea in someone sensing the thing. The word "quality" is used in the essay in much the same way the word "characteristic" or "property" has been used by other, more recent, writers. Locke distinguishes between primary and secondary qualities. Primary qualities are those that matter has constantly, whatever its state. As primary qualities Locke names solidity, extension, figure, motion or rest, and number. By secondary qualities Locke means the power to produce various sensations that have nothing in common with the primary qualities of the external objects. Thus, the power to produce the taste experience of sweetness is a secondary quality of sugar, but there is no reason to suppose that the sugar itself possesses the distinctive quality of the sensation. Colors, tastes, sounds, and odors are secondary qualities of objects. Locke also refers to a third kind of quality or power, called simply "power," by which he means the capacity to affect or to be affected by other objects. Thus, fire can melt clay; the capacity to melt clay is one of fire's powers, and such a power is neither a primary nor a secondary quality.

Locke concluded that primary ideas resemble external objects, but secondary ideas do not. It is this particular claim that excited other professional philosophers, with Berkeley arguing that primary qualities can be understood only in terms of human sensations, so that whatever generalization can be made about secondary qualities would have to cover primary qualities as well, and other philosophers arguing that Locke had no ground for maintaining that primary ideas "resemble" primary qualities, even if the distinction between primary and secondary qualities is allowed.

Complex ideas result from acts of the mind, and they fall into three classes: ideas of modes, of substances, and of relations. Modes are ideas that are considered to be incapable of independent existence since they are affections of substance, such as the ideas of triangle, gratitude, and murder. To think of substances is to think of "particular things subsisting by themselves," and to think in that manner involves supposing that there is a support, which cannot be understood, and that there are various qualities in combination which give various substances their distinguishing traits. Ideas of relations are the result of comparing ideas with each other.

After a consideration of the complex ideas of space, duration, number, the infinite, pleasure and pain, substance, relation, cause and effect, and of the distinctions between clear and obscure ideas and between true and false ideas, Locke proceeds to a discussion, in book 3, of words and essences. Words are signs of ideas by "arbitrary imposition," depending upon observed similarities that are taken as the basis for considering things in classes. Words are related to "nominal essences," that is, to obvious similarities found through observation, and not to "real essences," the actual qualities of things. Locke then discusses the imperfections and abuses of words.

In book 4, Locke defines knowledge as "the perception of the connection of and agreement, or disagreement and repugnancy, of any of our ideas." An example cited is one's knowledge that white is not black, Locke arguing that to know that white is not black is simply to perceive that the idea of white is not the idea of black.

Locke insisted that knowledge cannot extend beyond the ideas one has, and that people determine whether ideas agree or disagree with each other either directly, by intuition, or indirectly, by reason or sensation. Truth is defined as "the joining or separating of signs, as the things signified by them do agree or disagree one with another." For example, the proposition "White is not black" involves the separation by "is not" of the signs "white" and "black," signifying the disagreement between the ideas of white and black; since the ideas are different, the proposition is true. Actually to have compared the ideas and to have noted their disagreement is to know the fact which the true proposition signifies.

Locke devoted the remaining chapters of book 4 to arguing that people have knowledge of their existence by intuition, of the existence of God by demonstration, and of other things by sensation. Here the influence of Descartes is clearly evident. It is the empiricism of the earlier parts of the book that won for Locke the admiration of philosophers.

Bibliography:
Aarsleff, Hans. *From Locke to Saussure: Essays on the Study of Language and Intellectual History*. Minneapolis: University of Minnesota Press, 1982. In the introduction, Aarsleff explains how book 3 of *An Essay Concerning Human Understanding* influenced thinking about language as a human creation. Early chapters trace Locke's influence in the eighteenth and nineteenth centuries. Not a general work about Locke.
Ayers, Michael. *Locke*. 2 vols. London: Routledge & Kegan Paul, 1991. Perhaps the most comprehensive account of Locke's thought. Devotes separate sections to Locke's doctrines of ideas, of knowledge and belief, of particulars and universals, of substance and mode, of God and nature, and of identity. Establishes Locke's position in the empiricist tradition.
Dunn, John. *Locke*. New York: Oxford University Press, 1984. Offers a sketch of Locke's life, followed by chapters on his political and philosophical thought. Includes a clear account of his theory of knowledge.
Squadrito, Kathleen M. *John Locke*. Boston: Twayne, 1979. A convenient survey of Locke's life and writings, with a full chapter on *An Essay Concerning Human Understanding*. Treats Locke more as a writer and less as an analytical thinker.
Wood, Neal. *The Politics of Locke's Philosophy: A Social Study of "An Essay Concerning Human Understanding."* Berkeley: University of California Press, 1983. Discusses Locke's place in the social and scientific thought of seventeenth century England, emphasizing the Baconian tradition.
Yolton, John W. *Locke and the Compass of Human Understanding: A Selective Commentary on the "Essay."* Cambridge, England: Cambridge University Press, 1970. A standard study by a well-known Lockean, concerned with the methodology and morality of science as Locke understood it.

AN ESSAY ON CRITICISM

Type of work: Poetry
Author: Alexander Pope (1688-1744)
First published: 1711

Published when Alexander Pope was twenty-two years of age, *An Essay on Criticism* remains one of the best known discussions of literary criticism, of its ends and means, in the English language. It is the source of numerous familiar epigrams known to the reading public. Pope was very young when he wrote the work; existing evidence points to 1708 or 1709 as the probable period of composition. Pope wrote of its composition: "The things that I have written fastest, have always pleased the most. I wrote the *Essay on Criticism* fast; for I had digested all the matter in prose, before I began upon it in verse."

Although Pope may seem to rely too heavily upon the authority of the ancient authors as literary masters, he recognizes, as many readers fail to note, the "grace beyond the reach of art" that no model can teach. True genius and judgment are innate gifts of heaven, as Pope says, but many people possess the seeds of taste and judgment that, with proper training, may flourish. The genius of the ancients cannot be imitated, but their principles may be.

The poem is structured in three parts: the general qualities of a critic; the particular laws by which a critic judges a work; and the ideal character of a critic. Part 1 opens with Pope's indictment of the false critic. He remarks that as poets may be prejudiced about their own merits, so critics can be partial to their own judgment. Judgment, or "true taste," derives from nature, as does the poet's genius; nature provides everyone with some taste, which, if not perverted by a poor education or other defects, may enable the critic to judge properly. To be a critic, one's first job is to know oneself, one's own judgment, tastes, abilities; in short, to know one's personal limitations.

The second task of the critic is to know nature, which is the critic's standard as it is the poet's. Nature is defined ambiguously as

> Unerring Nature, still divinely bright,
> One clear, unchanged, and universal light,
> Life, force, and beauty, must to all impart,
> At once the source, and end, the test of Art.

Nature thus becomes a universal or cosmic force, an ideal sought by poet and critic alike in the general scheme, things universally approved throughout history by all persons. This ideal must be apprehended through the critic's judicious balance of wit and judgment, of imaginative invention and deliberative reason.

The rules of literary criticism may best be located in those works that have stood the test of time and universal approbation, the works of antiquity. From the ancient authors, critics have derived rules of art that are not self-imposed at the whim of the critic, but are discovered justly operating in the writings of the best authors. Such rules are "Nature still, but Nature methodized."

Formerly, critics restricted themselves to discovering rules in classical literature; in Pope's time, however, critics had strayed from the principles of these earlier critics whose motive was solely to make art "more beloved," and prescribed their own rules, which are pedantic, unimaginative, and basely critical of literature. What was once a subordinate sister to creative

2073

art has replaced or turned against its superior, assuming a higher place in the order of things. Criticism, once destined to teach the "world . . . to admire" the poet's art, now presumes to be master.

The true critic must learn thoroughly the ancients, particularly Homer and Vergil, for "To copy nature is to copy them." There are beauties of art that cannot be taught by rules; these intangible beauties are the "nameless graces which no methods teach/ And which a master-hand alone can reach." Modern writers should avoid transcending, unless rarely, the rules of art first established by the great artists of the past.

Part 2 traces the causes hindering good judgment—that chief virtue of a true critic. Pope advises critics to avoid the dangers of blindness caused by pride, the greatest source of poor judgment, by learning their own defects and by profiting even from the strictures of their enemies. Inadequate learning is another reason a critic errs: "A little learning is a dangerous thing;/ Drink deep, or taste not the Pierian spring." A critic who looks too closely at the parts of a poem may come to prefer a poem dull as a whole yet perfect in parts to one imperfect in part but pleasing as a whole. It is the unity of the many small parts in one whole that affects readers: "'Tis not a lip, or eye, we beauty call,/ But the joint force and full result of all." Faultless art can never exist. Finally, a critic who condemns a work for failing to achieve that which its author never intended errs: One should "regard the writer's End,/ Since none can compass more than they intend."

As some critics deviate from nature in judging "by a love to parts," others confine their attention to conceits, images, or metaphors. Poets who dissimulate their want of art with a wild profusion of imagery have not learned to control their imagination; they overvalue mere decoration and paint, not "the naked nature and the living grace," but the external variables of nature. "True Wit," Pope says, "is Nature to advantage dressed,/ What oft was thought, but ne'er so well expressed."

Other critics too highly praise style and language without respect for content; true eloquence clarifies and improves the thought, revealing nature at her finest, but false eloquence imposes a veil upon the face of nature, obscuring with its finery the truths of nature. Proper expression, in addition, should fit with the content; the poet should never attempt to lend false dignity by archaic words. Proper diction is neither too old nor too modern.

Most false critics judge by meter, criticizing according to the roughness or smoothness of the verse. Overfondness for metrics results in the dull clichés of poetry, such as "the cooling western breeze," and the like. Pope avers that rough or smooth verse should not be the poet's ideal; the poet should aim rather to fit the sound to the sense:

> Soft is the strain when Zephyr gently blows,
> And the smooth stream in smoother numbers flows;
> But when loud surges lash the sounding shore,
> The hoarse, rough verse should like a torrent roar.

Lines 344-383 of the poem constitute a digression by Pope to illustrate "representative meter." The true critic generally abides by rules of tolerance and aloofness from extremes of fashion and personal taste. The critic who indulges in petty predilections for certain schools or kinds of poets sacrifices objectivity. Be a patron of no separate group, whether ancient or modern, foreign or native, Pope advises. The critic should be pledged to truth, not to passing cults. Nor should a critic fear to advance his or her own judgment merely because the public favors other poets and schools; no critic should echo fashion or be influenced by a writer's name. Especially reprehensible is that critic who derives opinions about literature from lords of quality.

The final pitfall of the false critic is subjectivity, measuring by personal preferences. Private or public envy may distort one's evaluation. The critic must put aside personal motives and praise according to less personal criteria. Nor should the critic be led astray by self-love: "Good-nature and good-sense must ever join." A critic may justly attack more worthy targets, of which many exist in "these flagitious times." Obscenity, dullness, immodesty—all should concern the critic and be exposed. The vices of an age, however, should not infect a critic's judgment on other matters.

Part 3 outlines the ideal character of a critic. It lists rules for a critic's manners and contrasts the ideal critic with the "incorrigible poet" and "impertinent Critic," concluding with a brief summary of literary criticism and the character of the best critics. It is not enough for the critic to know, Pope writes; a critic must also share the qualities of a good person, worthy of respect not only for intellect but also for character. Integrity stands at the head of a list of good qualities for a critic. Modesty that forbids both unseemly outspokenness and rigid adherence to errone-ous opinion, tact that supports truth without alienating by bluntness, and courage to pursue truth despite censure are important attributes for the true critic. As some dull and foolish poets are best not maligned for fear of provoking them to greater folly, so the critic full of pedantry and impertinence should be ignored. Nothing is too sacred for the learned fool, who rushes in "where Angels fear to tread." The true critic is one "Still pleased to teach, and yet not proud to know." Such a person has knowledge both "of books and human kind."

Having outlined the characteristics of true critics, Pope catalogs the most famous critics, "the happy few" of Greece and Rome: Aristotle, Horace, Dionysius, Quintilian, Longinus. Aristotle, "Who conquered Nature" respected by the poets as the lawgiver; Horace, who "still charms with graceful negligence"; Quintilian's "justest rules, and clearest method": such are the true critics who flourished along with the great empires of their nations.

With the fall of the empire came the fall of learning, enslavement of mind and body. Desiderius Erasmus stemmed the barbarian's reign of ignorance, and Nicolas Boileau of France signified the advancement of critical learning in Europe. England, however, almost entirely despises and remains untouched by the return to the "juster ancient cause."

Many twentieth century critics, following the lead of their nineteenth century predecessors, have dismissed *An Essay on Criticism* as a mere collection of well-worn epigrams and dated restatements of literary commonplaces. Ironically, Pope might agree in part with that assess-ment. *An Essay on Criticism* is not radical, in the way Percy Bysshe Shelley's *Defence of Poetry* (1840) is. It offers no clear statement of poetics that differs markedly from those of Pope's contemporaries; it is, in one sense, little more than an eighteenth century updating of the precepts espoused by the Latin poet Horace in *Ars poetica*, a kind of handbook for writers and critics who might want to create art that pleases while it teaches.

Such a glib assessment, however, masks the major achievement of the poem. In *An Essay on Criticism*, Pope manages to use art as a means of commenting on it. Most significant, he provides a convincing, eloquent statement of what was then a new form of literary evaluation, a method that has been dubbed "the criticism of judgment." Modeling his argument on the premises outlined by philosopher John Locke, Pope argues that judgment gives critics an objective, external standard that permits them to escape the hegemony of authority—slavish adherence to the rules derived from the writings of the ancients—while not succumbing to the anarchy inherent in accepting the vagaries of taste. Pope's criteria for assessing the value of a literary work provide ways for critics to accept as great the works of writers as diverse as the French playwright Pierre Corneille and William Shakespeare.

Underlying Pope's discussion of the nature of criticism is the belief that the function of the critic is essentially evaluative. Pope is concerned with establishing the overall value of a literary production, as were other seventeenth and eighteenth century critics. Not surprisingly, therefore, interpretation was, for him, a secondary activity; the chief role of the discerning reader was to determine if a work of art deserved the accolade of greatness, or if it should be relegated to the ranks of the merely amusing—or worse, to the literary trash heap. In this role, he stands with John Dryden and Samuel Johnson as one of the chief arbiters of his age.

Updated by Laurence W. Mazzeno

Bibliography:
Barnard, John, ed. *Pope: The Critical Heritage*. London: Routledge & Kegan Paul, 1973. Contemporaneous reaction to *An Essay on Criticism* is showcased here in six essays dating from 1711 to 1741. Later responses to the whole of Pope's writings are represented by essays dating to 1782. Brief bibliography with helpful annotations.

Hotch, Ripley. "Pope Surveys His Kingdom: *An Essay on Criticism*." In *Critical Essays on Alexander Pope*, edited by Wallace Jackson and R. Paul Yoder. New York: G. K. Hall, 1993. Reviews the structure and meaning of *An Essay on Criticism*. Argues that the work is less about criticism than about Pope himself; the poet offered the poem as a demonstration that he merits the throne of wit.

Isles, Duncan. "Pope and Criticism." In *Alexander Pope*, edited by Peter Dixon. Athens: Ohio University Press, 1972. Connects *An Essay on Criticism* to its predecessors and to Pope's later critical writings, following the development of Pope's critical ideas in his writings and conversations.

Mack, Maynard, ed. *Essential Articles for the Study of Alexander Pope*. Hamden, Conn.: Archon Books, 1964. Includes three important studies: "Pope on Wit: The *Essay on Criticism*," Edward Niles Hooker; "Wit in the *Essay on Criticism*," William Empson; and "The Unity of Pope's *Essay on Criticism*," Arthur Fenner, Jr.

Morris, David B. *Alexander Pope: The Genius of Sense*. Cambridge, Mass.: Harvard University Press, 1984. Chapter 2 discusses the originality of Pope's critical thinking and delineates the components of Pope's critical theory.

AN ESSAY ON MAN

Type of work: Poetry
Author: Alexander Pope (1688-1744)
First published: 1733-1734

Pope's *An Essay on Man* stands as an intellectual landmark of the eighteenth century because it embodies the cosmological, theological, and ethical thought of its age. Heavily influenced by Pope's friend Lord Bolingbroke, whose philosophy was congenial to Pope, *An Essay on Man* actually sums up the leading principles of the time. Arthur Lovejoy's *The Great Chain of Being* (1936) provides the essential background for a thorough understanding of the traditions upon which Pope drew.

The central conception of this poem rests, however, upon the ideas of plenitude, gradation, and continuity. Plenitude, for Pope, meant the overwhelming fullness of creation, of a universe inhabited by all possible essences created by God. The abundance and variety of creation is also marked by gradation, the notion that there exists a graduated chain or rank among creation, moving from the lowest created thing up to God. This chain implies, of course, subordination of lower creatures to higher because each step up the ladder marks a slight variation upon the preceding step. Thus man (given the poem's title, the use of this word, rather than "people" or "humanity" may be considered accurate) is superior by virtue of his reason to lower beings. The ordered harmony of the entire creation depends upon the proper ordering of parts. Continuity, this ordered continuum of creation, is for Pope the principle of social and divine love which ties together all forms of creation in measured rule.

Epistle 1 explains the relationship of man to the universe. Man's knowledge of the universe must be limited to this world only; however, because evil exists on earth, one should not question God's ways or his justice. It is enough to know that God, because of his infinite goodness, created a perfect system and that man is merely a small part of the gigantic whole. God created the universe in one vast chain; somewhere along this chain man's place may be found. The imperfections in his nature man pretends to find are not really imperfections, for God created man suited to his place and rank in creation. Our happiness here consists in two things: our ignorance of the future and our hope for better things in the future. "Hope springs eternal in the human breast:/ Man never Is, but always to be blest."

Man's chief error is his pride which causes him to aspire to be better than he is, to question Providence about the fitness of things. Such pride inverts the real order since people are the judged, not the judges. We must not presume to doubt the justice of God's dispensations. Another error is that man sees himself wrongly as the final cause of all creation, as though all nature exists to serve him alone.

Equally unjust is man's wish for the strength of wild beasts or the power of angels, because God made the earth and all its inhabitants in a graduated scale; at the bottom of this scale are the lowest of creatures, man stands in the middle, and above men are multitudes of angels and, finally, God:

> Vast chain of Being! which from God began,
> Natures ethereal, human, angel, man,
> Beast, bird, fish, insect, what no eye can see,
> No glass can reach; from Infinite to thee,
> From thee to Nothing.

Each animal is subordinated to the ranks above and superior to those below. Man, by virtue of his reason, rules all creation below, but he is not of ethereal substance, as an angel is, and does not possess angelic power. Therefore it is absurd to claim another's place since each is a part of the whole ordained by God. To break this vast chain at any point would destroy the whole and violate God's plan. Man should not view creation as imperfect because he can envision only a part of it. His middle place on the scale implies a limited perception of the complete plan, and what he sees as evil is actually from God's larger vision, partial evil contributing ultimately to his universal good.

> All partial Evil, universal Good:
> And, spite of Pride, in erring Reason's spite,
> One truth is clear, WHATEVER IS, IS RIGHT.

Epistle 2 discusses the nature and state of man as an individual whose tragic situation is that he is in this middle state, both god and beast, both spirit and body. In human nature two principles, self-love and reason, operate often at odds with each other. Neither is entirely good nor bad; when each does its function properly and works in conjunction with the other, good results occur. Pope compares these two principles to the mechanism of a watch; within men self-love is the spring, reason the balance wheel. Without one man could not act; without the other action would be aimless. Without self-love men would vegetate; without reason men would consume themselves in lawless passion. Self-love motivates, inspires, while reason checks, advises. Self-love judges by present good and reason by future consequences. Reason through time acquires power to control impulsive self-love.

The passions are modes of self-love good as long as they conform to reason's dictates. One, the Ruling Passion, often dominates all others and determines the character of a man. No virtue arising from any passion can be wholly without value if subdued, as lust may be turned to gentle love, anger to zeal.

Although man contains both vice and virtue, Heaven compensates by converting individual defects into the strength of all. Our weaknesses motivate mutual reliance. Since each man is given his due portion of happiness and misery no one should wish to exchange his state for another's. Each should rest content with his own lot.

Epistle 3 discusses the role of man in society. Pope sees the whole universe as one comprehensive society, a complex system of interrelations cementing all creation. Each part relates to others but rank in the chain of being confers power and control over inferior ranks. However, with rule comes responsibility, and man, the imperial race, must care for his underlings as God cares for him.

Whether ruled by animal instinct or human reason each enjoys that power best suited to his place. Although God set the necessary bounds to each species, allotting to each its particular share of happiness, he designed to ensure the happiness of the whole rather than of the part. The happiness of all depends entirely upon maintaining the proper relations among the individuals; each should love itself and others.

In the primitive state of society self-love and social love existed. Man's reason then learned useful rules from instinct. Reason observed principles of government from monarchical bees and republican ants. Man constructed his own cities and societies and soon common interest suggested the need for a ruler, who was chosen for his virtues in learning and arms. True religion and government were united in love. Superstition and tyranny arose to invert nature's order, but man's self-love taught him to protect his interests by erecting governments and laws, finding private good in public. Self-love directed to social love returned general social harmony. It is this charity that renders particular forms of government and religion unessential, for charity always seeks the happiness of all, linking self-love with social love, enlisting all ranks of creation into a harmonious order.

Epistle 4 views man in relation to happiness. Since God works by general laws, he intends all to be happy, not merely a few. Order is Heaven's first law, so there can be only one result: some beings will be greater than others. Yet, if Heaven intended all to be equally happy, to be greater is not to be happier. True happiness is not located in external condition or possessions. God compensates those who lack them with hope for the future; those who have them fear the future.

Individual bliss on earth rests on three possessions: health, peace, and competence. To good or bad men fortune may bestow its blessings, but gifts of fortune dispose the individual as he obtains them to enjoy them less. In achieving bliss the virtuous man has most advantages. One must not impute injustice to God because the virtuous man often finds calamities his reward for virtue. Calamity occurs through fortune or natural law; God does not dispense with his laws merely to favor a special person. Virtue, moreover, is not rewarded with material gifts.

Virtue's reward is not earthly and external. Its reward resides in the peace and joy of the heart. Earthly recompense would either be disdained as unworthy or would destroy the very virtue that prompted it. No shame or honor arises from one's station in life. True honor comes from faithful employment of one's responsibility. It is character that distinguishes a man, not his worldly fortune or fame. History teaches that those who attained worldly prizes frequently paid dearly for them. What deeds made the hero often corrupted the man.

Only true virtue is happiness. It is the sole thing a man may possess without loss to himself. Heaven's bliss is bestowed on him who avoids the extremism of sect and who observes in the creation the presence of God and the divine chain that links all to God. Such a man knows that true happiness belongs not to the individual but to the whole creation, that the source of all faith, law, morality, and happiness is love of God and of man. Self-love, transcending self in pursuing social love and divine, showers blessings upon all things. Self-love awakens the virtuous mind, and like a pebble dropped into water, stirring ripples on the surface, ever embraces wider and wider spheres, from friend, to parent, to neighbor, until it encompasses all living creation.

Bibliography:

Cutting-Gray, Joanne, and James E. Swearingen. "System, the Divided Mind, and the *Essay on Man*." *Studies in English Literature, 1500-1900* 32, no. 3 (Summer, 1992): 479-494. Considers the poem from philosophical and religious viewpoints, questioning whether Pope was merely compiling accepted truths or undermining the system that the poem claims to support.

Mack, Maynard. *Alexander Pope: A Life*. New Haven, Conn.: Yale University Press, 1985. Definitive biography of Pope, written by a great scholar. References to the poem appear throughout the book, but the major commentary is in chapter 21.

Nuttall, A. D. *Pope's Essay on Man*. Winchester, Mass.: Allen & Unwin, 1984. Addresses the poem as the major philosophical statement in eighteenth century English. Views the poem as including religious issues. Section on public and critical reaction to the poem.

Piper, William Bowman. "Pope's Vindication." *Philological Quarterly* 67, no. 3 (Summer, 1988): 303-321. Confronts questions related to the poem's religious issues by comparing it to John Milton's *Paradise Lost*. Although traditional readings have disregarded this comparison, Piper asserts that Pope is more persuasive concerning the reality of God than Milton is.

Pope, Alexander. *An Essay on Man*. Edited by Maynard Mack. London: Methuen, 1964. Contains a detailed introduction that analyzes the structure and artistry of the poem, its philosophical context, and Pope's Roman Catholic background. The scholarly notes are not intrusive.

ESSAYS

Type of work: Essays
Author: Sir Francis Bacon (1561-1626)
First published: 1597; revised, 1612, 1625

Sir Francis Bacon was a man of many accomplishments—scientist, philosopher, and politician; he was adept, too, at taking bribes, and for that was imprisoned. Yet it is as a literary man that he is perhaps best remembered, a writer so competent with the pen that for decades there have been persons willing to argue that Bacon wrote the plays attributed to William Shakespeare.

The essay form is rare in the modern age, although there are some faint signs of its revival. As Bacon used it, the essay is a carefully fashioned statement, both informative and expressive, by which a person comments on life and manners, on nature and its puzzles. The essay is not designed to win people to a particular cause or to communicate factual matter better put in scientific treatises. Perhaps that is one reason why it is not so popular in an age in which the truth of claims and their practical importance is always questioned.

The *Essays* first appeared, ten in number, in 1597. They were immediately popular because they were brief, lively, humane, and well-written. Perhaps they were effective in contrast to the rambling, florid prose written by most writers of the time. A considerable part of their charm lay in their civilized tone. In these essays, Bacon reveals himself as an inquisitive but also an appreciative man with wit enough to interest others. The first edition contained the following essays: "Of Studies," "Of Discourse," "Of Ceremonies and Respects," "Of Followers and Friends," "Of Suitors," "Of Expense," "Of Regiment of Health," "Of Honour and Reputation," "Of Faction," and "Of Negociating."

By 1612, the number of essays had been increased to thirty-eight, the earlier ones having been revised or rewritten. By the last edition, in 1625, the number was fifty-eight. Comparison of the earlier essays with those written later shows not only a critical mind at work but also a man made sadder and wiser, or at least different, by changes in fortune.

The essays concern themselves with such universal concepts as truth, death, love, goodness, friendship, fortune, and praise. They cover such controversial matters as religion, atheism, "the True Greatness of Kingdoms and Estates," custom and education, and usury, and they consider such intriguing matters as envy, cunning, innovations, suspicion, ambition, praise, vainglory, and the vicissitudes of things.

The *Essays or Counsels, Civil and Moral*, as they are called in the heading of the first essay, begins with an essay on truth entitled "Of Truth." The title formula is always the same, simply a naming of the matter to be discussed, as, for example, "Of Death," "Of Unity in Religion," "Of Adversity," "What is Truth? said jesting Pilate; and would not stay for an answer." One expects a sermon, and one is pleasantly surprised. Bacon uses his theme as a point of departure for a discussion of the charms of lying, trying to fathom the love of lying for its own sake. "A mixture of a lie doth ever add pleasure," he writes. This pleasure is ill-founded, however; it rests on error resulting from depraved judgment. Bacon reverses himself grandly: " . . . truth, which only doth judge itself, teacheth that the inquiry of truth, which is the love-making or wooing of it, the knowledge of truth, which is the presence of it, and the belief of truth, which is the enjoying of it, is the sovereign good of human nature."

When it comes to death, Bacon begins by admitting that tales of death increase humanity's natural fear of it, but he reminds the reader that death is not always painful. By references to

Augustus Caesar, Tiberius, Vespasian, and others, Bacon showed that, even in their last moments, great men maintained their characters and composure. Death is natural, he concludes, and it has certain advantages: It opens the gate to good fame and puts an end to envy. The good man is in no fear of death because he has better things to do and think about, and, when he dies, he knows he has obtained "worthy ends and expectations."

The essay "Of Adversity" is particularly interesting since it reflects Bacon's own experience after imprisonment, the loss of friends and position, and enforced retirement. He writes, "Prosperity is the blessing of the Old Testament; Adversity is the blessing of the New; which carrieth the greater benediction, and the clearer revelation of God's favour." Adversity puts life's brighter moments into effective contrast, and it allows a person the chance to show his or her virtues.

Bacon is no casual essayist. One does not need the report of history to know that the essays as they are found are the product of numerous revisions. Sentences do not achieve a careful balance and rhythm accidentally, nor does a moment's reflection provide apt allusions, pertinent Latin phrases, and witty turns of thought. The essay "Of Beauty" begins with a well-fashioned, complex statement: "Virtue is like a rich stone, best plain set; and surely virtue is best in a body that is comely, though not of delicate features; and that hath rather dignity of presence, than beauty of aspect." The essay continues by commenting on the sad fact that beauty and virtue are not always conjoined, but then Bacon remembers some noble spirits who were "the most beautiful men of their times"—Augustus Caesar, Titus Vespasianus, Philip le Bel of France, Edward the Fourth of England, Alcibiades of Athens, and Ismael the Sophy of Persia. Then he comes to a striking thought in a simple line: "There is no excellent beauty that hath not some strangeness in the proportion."

Although appreciative of beauty, Bacon was modern in his appreciation of use. "Houses are built to live in," he writes in the essay "Of Building," "therefore let use be preferred before uniformity, except where both may be had." He is aware of the importance of location; he warns the reader to be wary of an "ill seat" for his house and mentions in particular the discomfort that results from building a house in a hollow of ground surrounded by high hills. So aware is he of the mistakes that a builder can make that Bacon follows a catalog of dangers and difficulties with a charming and involved description of an ideal dwelling: a place for entertaining, a place for dwelling, and the whole a beautiful construction of rooms for various uses, courts, playing fountains—all of large, but proper dimensions, and built to take account of summer sun and winter cold.

Although there is a prevailing moral character to the essays so that, in retrospect, they seem to be a series of beautiful commands to erring spirits, there is enough of wisdom, education, humor, and common sense in them to save the author from the charge of moral arrogance. For example, Bacon does not begin his essay on anger by declaring how shameful anger is; he says instead, "To seek to extinguish Anger utterly is but a bravery of the Stoics." He then gives practical advice. To calm anger there is no other way but to consider the effects of anger, to remember what it has done in the past. To repress particular angry acts, Bacon advises the reader to let time pass in the belief that the opportunity for revenge will come later, and he particularly warns against the bitterness of words and the doing of any irrevocable act.

In writing of atheism, Bacon combined philosophical argument with moral persuasion and intensity of expression. If it seems strange that a scientist, the father of induction, should so easily accept the teachings of traditional Christianity, it is only because one tends to think of people as playing single roles and as living apart from their times. In any case, Bacon's philosophical skill was most at evidence in scientific matters, and there is no more reason to expect that he would be adept at philosophizing about religion than to expect that he should have anticipated Albert Einstein's reflections about science. The essay contains the famous line: "It is true, that a little philosophy inclineth man's mind to atheism; but depth in philosophy bringeth men's mind about to religion."

Although the essays naturally reflect a lifetime of experience, they do so in general, not in particular. One looks in vain for reports of adventures and misadventures at court—and Bacon had many of both. His ideas sound a bit like those of Niccolò Machiavelli in his essay on simulation and dissimulation, but there are no personal references to events in which he was involved and from which he acquired the knowledge imparted here. Nor would one suspect that Bacon was one of the leading scientific minds of his age; he discourses on friendship, parents and children, gardens, study, and the rest, as a gentle, humane scholar. One realizes that in the *Essays* Bacon gave up the roles which ambition made him play. In his contemplative moments, he sought to satisfy a twofold goal: to present the wisdom of his living, the wisdom that comes from experience and reflection on it, and to make this presentation by means of a style designed to be economical and ornamental at the same time.

Bibliography:

Bowen, Catherine D. *Francis Bacon: The Temper of a Man*. Boston: Little, Brown, 1963. Although this work is basically a biography of Bacon, Bowen includes some discussion of the publishing history of the essays and analysis of Bacon's style, concentrating particularly on his aphorisms and wit.

Bush, Douglas. *English Literature in the Earlier Seventeenth Century, 1600-1660*. 2d ed. rev. New York: Oxford University Press, 1962. Bush examines Bacon's essays in the light of his other prose writings, noting particularly the limitations of Bacon's understanding which led him to evaluate success in rather materialistic terms.

Patrick, John Max. *Francis Bacon*. London: Longmans, Green, 1966. This short work is a general introduction to Bacon's life and work. Patrick notes that the essays are not intended to be a personal expression and examines Bacon's fondness for balance, antithesis, three-item series, and aphorism.

Quinton, Anthony. *Francis Bacon*. Edited by Keith Thomas. New York: Hill and Wang, 1980. Quinton discusses the literary quality of the essays giving particular attention to their aphoristic style; he notes that their subjects range from public affairs to private life and frequently deal with abstractions such as truth or beauty. He also notes the cynical quality of Bacon's thought.

Williamson, George. *The Senecan Amble: A Study in Prose from Bacon to Collier*. Chicago: University of Chicago Press, 1951. Williamson uses the essays, as well as the other prose, to examine Bacon's style in detail, noting that Bacon considered the function of rhetoric to be the joining of imagination and reason. He considers the relationship between Bacon and the classics.

THE ESSAYS

Type of work: Essays
Author: Michel Eyquem de Montaigne (1533-1592)
First published: Essais, books 1-2, 1580; books 1-2, revised, 1582; books 1-3, 1588; books
1-3, revised, 1595 (English translation, 1603)

Michel Eyquem de Montaigne began his essays as a stoical humanist, continued them as a skeptic, and concluded them as someone concerned with the condition of human beings. This evolution, one substantially agreed upon by Montaigne scholars, is apparent in his *Essais*. The three volumes include writings such as "To Philosophize Is to Learn to Die," in which Montaigne considers how human beings should face pain and die; writings such as the famous "Apology for Raimond Sebond," in which the skeptical attack on dogmatism in philosophy and religion is most evident; and writings such as "The Education of Children," in which Montaigne makes a constructive effort to encourage humans to know themselves and act naturally for the good of all.

Montaigne retired to his property when he was thirty-eight. Public life had not satisfied him, and he was wealthy enough to live withdrawn from active life and give himself to contemplation and the writing of essays. He did spend some time in travel a few years later, and he was made mayor of Bordeaux, but most of his effort went into the writing and revision of his writings, the attempt to essay, or test, his ideas.

An important essay in the first volume, "That the Taste for Good and Evil Depends in Good Part upon the Opinion We Have of Them," begins with a paraphrase of a quotation from Epictetus to the effect that humans are bothered more by opinions than by things. The belief that all human judgment is, after all, more a function of the person than of the things judged suggested to Montaigne that by a change of attitude human beings could alter the values of things. Even death can be valued, provided those who are about to die are of the proper disposition. Poverty and pain can also be good, provided a person of courageous temperament develops a taste for that. Montaigne concludes that "things are not so painful and difficult of themselves, but our weakness or cowardice makes them so. To judge of great and high matters requires a suitable soul."

This stoical relativity is further endorsed in the essay "To Philosophize Is to Learn to Die." Montaigne's preoccupation with the problem of facing pain and death was caused by the death of his best friend, Étienne de La Boétie, who died in 1563 at the age of thirty-three, and by the deaths of his father, his brother, and several of his children. Montaigne was also deeply disturbed by the Saint Bartholomew Day massacres. As a humanist, he was well educated in the literature and philosophy of the ancients, and from them he drew support of the stoical philosophy suggested to him by the courageous death of his friend La Boétie.

The title of the essay is a paraphrase of Cicero's remark "that to study philosophy is nothing but to prepare one's self to die." For some reason, perhaps because it did not suit his philosophic temperament at the time, perhaps because he had forgotten it, Montaigne did not allude to a similar expression attributed by Plato to Socrates, the point there being that the philosopher is interested in the eternal, the unchanging, and that life is a preoccupation with the temporal and the variable. For Montaigne, however, the remark means either that the soul in contemplation removes itself from the body, or that philosophy is concerned to teach us how to face death. It is the second interpretation that interested him.

Asserting that all human beings strive for pleasure, even in virtue, Montaigne argued that the thought of death is naturally disturbing. He refers to the death of his brother, Captain St. Martin, who was killed when he was twenty-three by being struck behind the ear by a tennis ball. Other instances enforce his claim that death often comes unexpectedly to the young, for which reason the problem is urgent. With these examples, he writes, how can people "avoid fancying that death has us, every moment, by the throat?" The solution he recommends is to face death and fight it by becoming so familiar with the idea of death that we are no longer fearful. "The utility of living," he writes, "consists not in the length of days, but in the use of time." Death is natural, and what is important is not to waste life in the apprehension of death.

In the essay "Of Judging the Death of Another," Montaigne argues that people reveal their true character when they show how they face a death they know is coming. A "studied and digested" death may bring a kind of delight to a person of the proper spirit. Montaigne cites Socrates and Cato as examples of men who knew how to die.

Montaigne's most famous essay is his "Apology for Raimond Sebond," generally considered to be the most complete and effective of his skeptical essays. Yet what Montaigne is skeptical of is not religion, as many critics have asserted, but the pretensions of reason and dogmatic philosophers and theologians. When Montaigne asks "Que sais-je?" (What do I know?), the expression becomes the motto of his skepticism, not because he thinks that people should give up the use of the intellect and imagination but because he thinks it wise to recognize the limits of these powers.

The essay is ostensibly in defense of the book titled *Theologia naturalis: sive Liber creaturarum magistri Raimondi de Sebonde*, the work of a philosopher and theologian of Toulouse, who wrote the book about 1430. Montaigne considers two principal objections to the book: the first, that Sebond is mistaken in the effort to support Christian belief on human reason; the second, that Sebond's arguments in support of Christian belief are so weak that they are easily confuted. Montaigne agrees that the truth of God can be known only through faith and with God's assistance, but he argues that Sebond is to be commended for his noble effort to use reason in the service of God. If one considers Sebond's arguments as an aid to faith, they may be viewed as useful guides. Montaigne's response to the second objection takes up most of the essay, and since the work is, in some editions, more than two hundred pages long, the length alone may be considered to reflect the intensity of Montaigne's conviction. Montaigne argues against those philosophers who suppose that by reason alone human beings can find truth and happiness. The rationalists who attack Sebond do not so much damage the theologian as show their own false faith in the value of reason. Montaigne considers "a man alone, without foreign assistance, armed only with his own proper arms, and unfurnished of the divine grace and wisdom," and he sets out to show that such a man is not only miserable and ridiculous but grievously mistaken in his presumption. Philosophers who attempt to reason without divine assistance gain nothing from their efforts except knowledge of their own weakness. Yet that knowledge has some value, for ignorance is then not absolute ignorance. Nor is it any solution for the philosopher to adopt the stoical attitude and try to rise above humanity, as Seneca suggests; the only way to rise is by abandoning human means and by suffering and causing oneself to be elevated by Christian faith.

In the essay "Of the Education of Children," Montaigne writes that the only objective he had in writing the essays was to discover himself. In his opinions, Montaigne shows how studying himself led him from the idea of philosophy as a study of what is "grim and formidable" to the idea of philosophy as the path to the health and cheerfulness of mind and body. He claims that "The most manifest sign of wisdom is a continual cheerfulness," and that "the height and value of true virtue consists in the facility, utility, and pleasure of its exercise." Philosophy is "that which instructs us to live." The aim of education is to lead children so that they will come to love nothing but the good, and the way to this objective is an education that takes advantage of youth's appetites and affections. Though his love of books led Montaigne to live in such a manner that he was accused of slothfulness and "want of mettle," he justifies his education by pointing out that this is the worst men can say of him.

Not all of Montaigne's essays reflect the major stages of his transformation from stoic and skeptic to a man of good will. Like Ernest Bacon, he found satisfaction in working out his ideas about the basic experiences of life. Thus he wrote of sadness, constancy, fear, friendship (with particular reference to La Boétie), moderation, solitude, sleep, names, and books. These essays are lively, imaginative, and informed with the knowledge of a gentleman well trained in the classics. Yet he is most eloquent when he writes of pain and death, as when he refers to his own long struggle with kidney stones and to the deaths of those he loved, and when he writes of his need for faith and of the human need for self-knowledge. In such essays, the great stylist, educated thinker, and struggling human being are one. It was in the essaying of himself that Montaigne became a great essayist.

Bibliography:
Frame, Donald Murdoch. *Montaigne in France, 1812-1852*. New York: Octagon Books, 1976. A book that sets the tone for all further criticism of Montaigne by the foremost English-speaking critic of the author and best translator of his works. Examines nineteenth century criticism of Montaigne after his popularity had declined in previous centuries.
Regosin, Richard L. *The Matter of My Book: Montaigne's "Essais" as the Book of the Self*. Berkeley: University of California Press, 1977. A lucid work that examines the sense of self developed by Montaigne in *The Essays* by examining his reading, friendships, and other external influences.
Sayce, R. A. *The Essays of Montaigne: A Critical Exploration*. London: Weidenfeld & Nicolson, 1972. An examination of the text and form of Montaigne's *Essays*, with special attention to his views on the human condition, movement and change, religion and skepticism, and politics and government. Also considers his place in the history of Renaissance thought.
Starobinski, Jean. *Montaigne in Motion*, translated by Arthur Goldhammer. Chicago, Ill.: University of Chicago Press, 1985. Examines the impact on *The Essays* of Montaigne's travels, his friendships, and his interaction with the turbulent politics of his day. Shows the "honest dissimulation" that he practiced to protect and develop his true views.
Tetel, Marcel. *Montaigne*. New York: Twayne, 1974. The best book with which to begin a study of Montaigne. Examines briefly his life, sources, and influences, as well as the process by which he rendered those influences into *The Essays*. Also contains a useful bibliography for further reading.

ESSAYS OF ELIA and LAST ESSAYS OF ELIA

Type of work: Essays
Author: Charles Lamb (1775-1834)
First published: Essays of Elia, 1823; *Last Essays of Elia,* 1833

The essays Charles Lamb wrote for the *London Magazine* in the early 1820's, which were collected in the *Essays of Elia* and *Last Essays of Elia,* mark the acme of his literary achievement and are an enduring and loved contribution to English letters. Lamb had written familiar essays since 1802. After "The Londoner" appeared in the *Morning Post* (February 1, 1802), Thomas Manning wrote to him to express admiration for the piece, adding, "If you were to write a volume of essays in the same stile you might be sure of its succeeding." Although Lamb did not immediately take Manning's advice, he did over the next sixteen years produce other periodical essays, volumes of criticism, books for children, and a farce. In 1818, his collected works appeared in two volumes.

Then in 1820, John Scott, the editor of the newly established *London Magazine,* asked Lamb to contribute. Lamb's "Recollections of the South Sea House" appeared in the August issue, the first of the essays written under the pseudonym "Elia." Most of the fifty-three items collected in the two volumes of Elia essays were written for the *London Magazine* between 1820 and 1823, though the last piece in the second volume, "Popular Fallacies," appeared in the *New Monthly Magazine* in 1826 (January-June, September).

In the introduction to the *Last Essays of Elia,* ostensibly written by "a Friend of the Late Elia," Lamb accuses the essays of being "pranked in an affected array of antique models and phrases." The same accusation had been raised by Mary Lamb, the writer's sister and sometime coauthor of children's books, who criticized his fondness for outdated words. Lamb replied, "Damn the ages! I will write for antiquity!" This love for the past, which was, as Elia's "friend" conceded, natural to the author, surfaces in a variety of ways, particularly in literary debts, allusions, and subject matter. In "Oxford in the Vacation," the second essay, Lamb observes that the reader of his previous piece might have taken the author for a clerk. Lamb adds, "I do agnize something of the sort." The word agnize, acknowledge, probably came to Lamb from William Shakespeare's *Othello* (1604); by 1820, it was no longer a common word. Lamb claims that the libraries of Oxford "most arride and solace" him; arride, to please, is an Elizabethan word that Lamb probably took from Ben Jonson's *Every Man out of His Humour* (1599). Similarly, his use of "perigesis" for journey is likely a borrowing from Jonson's *Underwoods* (1627) and is the first recorded use of the word in the *Oxford English Dictionary* since Jonson's nearly two hundred years earlier. "Visnomy" for physiognomy (in "The Two Races of Men"), "pretermitted" instead of overlooked and "reluct" for rebel against (in "New Year's Eve"), and "keck" for reject (in "Imperfect Sympathies") all derive from seventeenth century authors. In at least two instances—"obolary" (having little money) in "The Two Races of Men" and "raucid" for raucous in "To the Shade of Elliston"—Lamb imitated these earlier writers by inventing words; the *Oxford English Dictionary* credits Lamb as the origin of both.

Lamb knew many of the leading authors of the age, including William Wordsworth, Samuel Taylor Coleridge, John Keats, William Hazlitt, Thomas De Quincey, and William Godwin. Yet his shelves and mind admitted almost no modern literature. His 1808 *Specimens of English Dramatic Poets, Who Lived About the Time of Shakespeare* called attention to Elizabethan and Jacobean authors whom Lamb admired and whose influence is evident in his Elia essays. Although Lamb's formal education ended at the age of fourteen, he read extensively, as is evident from the more than 130 authors he quotes in his work. For example, the epigraph for "A Quaker Meeting" comes from a 1653 poem by Richard Fleckno; that of "Imperfect Sympathies" is taken from Thomas Browne's *Religio Medici* (1642). "Christ's Hospital Five-and-Thirty Years Ago" presents the "wit-combats" between Coleridge and a fellow student in the same way that Thomas Fuller in his *History of the Worthies of England* (1662) describes the rivalry between Shakespeare and Ben Jonson. The very term "wit-combats" comes from Fuller, whom Lamb called "the dear, fine, silly, old angel." "Popular Fallacies" is modeled on Thomas Browne's seventeenth century exploration of "vulgar errors." In "Detached Thoughts on Reading," Lamb lists some of his favorite authors; among them Christopher Marlowe, Michael Drayton, William Drummond, and Abraham Cowley; the youngest of them, Cowley, died in 1667.

This love for the past is evident in the very titles of the essays: "Christ's Hospital Five-and-Thirty Years Ago," "The Old Benchers of the Inner Temple," "On Some of the Old Actors," "On the Artificial Comedy of the Last Century," "The Old Margate Hoy," and "Old China." "Oxford in the Vacation" includes a paragraph-long paean to antiquity, a quality that endears the university to Elia. In "The Old and the New Schoolmaster" Lamb praises the life of the old schoolmaster as idyllic and contrasts it with the hectic existence of the new one. "The Old Benchers of the Inner Temple" laments the passing of the old familiar faces as well as the fashion for fountains and objects to the remodeling of the entrance to the Inner Temple. Elsewhere Lamb observes that "the gardens of Gray's Inn . . . were then far finer than they are now" ("On Some of the Old Actors"). "Dream Children: A Reverie" again criticizes the modern. Lamb here relates that Blakesware, a country house in Hertfordshire, contained an old chimney piece bearing the carved story of the Children in the Wood. The new owner removed this mantlepiece in favor of a sterile "marble one of modern invention . . . , with no story upon it." The title of "Barrenness of the Imaginative Faculty in the Production of Modern Art" summarizes Lamb's conviction; he here compares the skills of the great Renaissance masters with what he regards as the diminished achievement of more recent painters. "There is a cowardice in modern art," he maintains. The same falling off strikes him in the theater, where no one could any longer perform Shakespeare's *Twelfth Night* (1601) or Richard Brinsley Sheridan's *The School for Scandal* (1777) as they could in Lamb's youth, and where the delightful escapism of Restoration comedy had yielded to the "all-devouring drama of common life" ("On the Artificial Comedy of the Last Century").

In this love for the past Lamb is one with the Romantic movement. Other Romantic traits that surface in the essays are the emphasis on the autobiographical and the dream state. Introspective, Lamb could have said with Michel Eyquem de Montaigne, "It is myself that I portray." The eighteenth century essays of Joseph Addison and Samuel Johnson adopted a familiar style and a persona—the Tatler, Mr. Spectator, the Rambler, the Idler—but they used this persona to separate writer and subject. The Elia pseudonym may be an anagram for "a lie" as well as for "Lamb." On August 16, 1820, just before the appearance of "Recollections of the South-Sea House," Lamb wrote to Barron Field, "You shall have soon a tissue of truth and fiction impossible to be extricated, the interlacing shall be so delicate, the partitions perfectly invisible, it shall puzzle you . . . , & I shall not explain it." Yet unlike his essayistic predecessors, Lamb used his persona to gain the freedom to get closer to, not further away from, the self. Though reality is thinly disguised, Lamb's life beats clearly just beneath the veiled surface of his work.

One method of camouflage is the change of names, beginning with Elia himself. Lamb's father appears as Lovel in "The Old Benchers of the Inner Temple." Lamb's brother John becomes his cousin James Elia, and his sister Mary appears as Cousin Bridget. Lamb's first love, Ann Simmons, is the Alice W—(n) of "Dream Children" and "New Year's Eve." Blakesware is translated to Blakesmoor. When Lamb describes his schooldays at Christ's Hospital, he writes as Elia writing as Samuel Taylor Coleridge; his own experiences are presented as those of a third person, L. Changing dates is another masking device. "The Superannuated Man" deals with Lamb's retirement but alters his last day at the East India House from March 29 to April 12, 1825. "Recollections of the South-Sea House" supposedly recounts events of 1780, when Lamb was only five years old.

The essential truth of Lamb's life, particularly his childhood, is, however, little altered. As he recounts in "Oxford in the Vacation," he was in fact "defrauded . . . of the sweet food of academic institution," and he enjoyed spending his limited free time at one or the other of the English universities. Coleridge's habit of borrowing, annotating, and sometimes returning Lamb's books is accurately depicted in "The Two Races of Men." Lamb enjoyed the quiet of a Quaker meeting; "My First Play" is a factual account of the beginning of his life-long love affair with the theater. Even the fictional "A Dissertation upon Roast Pig" includes a recollection of a schoolboy incident in which he gave a beggar an entire plum cake.

"A Dissertation upon Roast Pig" is rightly regarded as one of the finest examples of Lamb's wit, which relies on exaggeration, word play, and absurdity. Lamb here relates that Bo-bo accidentally burns down the family hut, and that in the conflagration nine suckling pigs perish. Horrified at first, Bo-bo and his father, Ho-ti, soon discover the excellent taste of roast pig (one of Lamb's favorite dishes). Ho-ti's cottages thereafter regularly burn down. Once others taste this delicacy, their houses also catch fire, until someone finds a way to cook a pig without consuming a house in the process. Yet his essay also contains the story of the plum cake and so demonstrates how Lamb used humor to distance the tragedies and disappointments of his life. The burnt house and the dead pigs transformed into a delicious food could serve as a metaphor for the transformation of Lamb's sorrows into the delightful essays of Elia.

The dream also allows Lamb to get closer to his experience through seeming distance. "The Child Angel: A Dream" purports to recount a vision concerning Ge-Urania, an infant angel. In its imaginative portrayal it seems a tale that Coleridge might have written, and its concerns with childhood and reverie place it squarely within the Romantic sensibility. Yet it is uniquely Lamb's in its nostalgic melancholy, just as the child angel itself is yet another avatar of Lamb, with his fear of hereditary madness and his limp: Ge-Urania "was to know weakness, and reliance, and the shadow of human imbecility, and it went with a lame gait." In the similarly titled and better-known "Dream Children: A Reverie," Lamb presents his youthful love for Ann Simmons and his sometimes troubled relationship with his brother John in the guise of a reverie. The piece contains humor and expresses no bitterness, but a gentle sadness suffuses the writing, a sense of loss and regret for what might have been. Like many other Lamb pieces, it plays variations on the *ubi sunt* theme: Where are all the great actors, the great artists of the past, one's former friends and acquaintances, where is one's first love, one's youth?

Though most of the Elia essays are personal as well as familiar, occasionally they demonstrate Lamb's skill as a critic. "On the Artificial Comedy of the Last Century" explains that because Restoration comedy is not meant to be taken seriously, it should not be regarded as immoral. "Stage Illusion" extends this argument to comedy in general. Whereas Coleridge argued that at a play the audience engages in a willing suspension of disbelief, Lamb more persuasively maintains that the spectator can enjoy the representation of a coward or a miser only when one recognizes that such a despicable character is being acted, not actually present on the stage. In his essay on the sonnets of Sir Philip Sidney, Lamb takes on another leading

Romantic critic, William Hazlitt, to defend the Elizabethan poet. Like Romantic criticism generally, Lamb's is subjective. Still, his assessments, whether of William Hogarth or Sidney or his favorite actors, are invariably fascinating and usually correct.

Joseph Rosenblum

Bibliography:
Aaron, Jane. *A Double Singleness: Gender and the Writings of Charles and Mary Lamb.* Oxford, England: Clarendon Press, 1991. A feminist reading. Aaron maintains that Charles Lamb's writings "encode his resistance to the cult of manliness prevalent during his period." The last chapter looks specifically at the Elia essays, but discussions of individual pieces are scattered throughout the book.
Barnett, George L. *Charles Lamb.* Boston: Twayne, 1976. A critical biography that devotes a long chapter to the Elia essays. Barnett argues that Lamb's essays resemble Romantic poetry in their emphasis on the dream state and the past. Also discusses Lamb's style and maintains that it is not an imitation of seventeenth century writing.
_____. *Charles Lamb: The Evolution of Elia.* Bloomington: Indiana University Press, 1964. Analyzes the development of Lamb's writing, especially that seen in his essays, and places him in the tradition of the familiar essay. Pays particular attention to the relationship between Lamb's private letters and his published work.
Lucas, E. V. *The Life of Charles Lamb.* London: Methuen, 1905. In this standard biography, Lucas identifies 1821 as Lamb's "golden year," in which he wrote most of his best Elia essays. Discusses Lamb's activities while he was writing these essays and provides essential biographical background.
Monsman, Gerald. *Confessions of a Prosaic Dreamer: Charles Lamb's Art of Autobiography.* Durham, N.C.: Duke University Press, 1980. Examines Lamb's use of a persona in his essays, arguing that such a mask was necessary for Lamb in dealing with the difficulties of his life. Monsman also considers the place of the Elia essays in the Romantic movement and concludes that Lamb "rejects the visionary and demonic poetry of the egotistical sublime and replaces it with a prose model of a safe and nourishing social reality."

ESTHER WATERS

Type of work: Novel
Author: George Moore (1852-1933)
Type of plot: Naturalism
Time of plot: Late nineteenth century
Locale: England
First published: 1894

> *Principal characters:*
> ESTHER WATERS, a servant girl
> WILLIAM LATCH, her betrayer
> MRS. BARFIELD, her mistress
> SARAH TUCKER, her enemy
> JACKIE, her son
> FRED PARSONS, her betrothed
> MISS RICE, her employer

The Story:

The first person Esther Waters met when she arrived at Woodview was William Latch, the son of the cook under whose direction Esther was to work. William was the worry of his mother's life, for, like his dead father, he was a gambler. Mrs. Latch had hoped that William would become a delivery boy and leave Woodview, but William was determined to go into service for Mr. and Mrs. Barfield, the owners of Woodview, so that he could observe their racing stable.

The position as kitchen maid at Woodview was a godsend to Esther, for her stepfather, claiming that he had too many mouths to feed, had forced her to leave home. The workhouse might have been her only refuge if she had not secured a position with the Barfields. In spite of her efforts to do her work well, however, it was hard for her to get along with the other servants. Mrs. Latch seemed to go out of her way to make life unpleasant for her, and the maids teased her because she was religious. William was at first her only champion among the servants, for which she was grateful to him. Then Esther found an unexpected friend in her mistress, Mrs. Barfield. She, too, was deeply religious, and she invited Esther to join the services she held in her room each Sunday morning. Learning that Esther could not read, Mrs. Barfield tried to teach her. Mrs. Barfield became Esther's friend as well as her employer, and this made Esther's life easier for a time. William continued to pay her special attention, to the anguish of Sarah Tucker, another of the maids. After a servants' ball in celebration of the victory of one of the Woodview horses, William took Esther out to some wheatstacks and seduced her, telling her they would be married as soon as he had enough money. By the following morning, Esther had convinced herself that she had been betrayed, and she refused to speak to William. He tried to reason with her and told her that he loved her and that they would be married soon, but she would not listen. Tiring at last of her sulking, he turned to Peggy Barfield, a cousin of his master, and after a few weeks eloped with her.

Three months later, Esther realized that she was pregnant. Strangely, the servant girls who had been her former tormentors became kind and sympathetic, which only made her feel more ashamed of her wickedness. Mrs. Barfield was sympathetic, too, but she had to send Esther away, for she had become a bad example for the other girls.

There was no place for her to go but to her home, where she found that her mother was also pregnant. Her stepfather was crueler than ever, but he tolerated her as long as she paid rent and gave him money to buy beer. At last, realizing that she had to leave before all of her savings disappeared and there was nothing left for her baby, Esther took lodgings close to the hospital where she was to be confined. After her son was born, she was filled with a happiness she had never known before, but her joy was lessened when she learned that her mother had died in childbirth, just a few days after Esther's Jackie was born. Soon afterward, Esther's stepfather and the other children went to Australia; Esther felt that she was now entirely alone in the world.

The next few years were terrible ones for Esther. She had to work as much as seventeen or eighteen hours a day. Once she had to go to the workhouse. Her greatest grief was the need to leave her child in the care of others while she worked, for Jackie was her whole life. When he was six years old, Esther found work with Miss Rice, a writer whose home was a haven to Esther. Miss Rice knew Esther's story and tried to make the girl's life easier for her.

One day, Esther met Fred Parsons, a colorless but honest, dependable, and religious man. When Esther told him her story, he readily forgave her. She took Fred to see Jackie, and the man and the boy became fast friends from the first meeting. Esther and Fred planned to be married as soon as Miss Rice could get another servant, for Esther refused to leave her mistress without someone to care for her. One evening, while on an errand for Miss Rice, Esther unexpectedly met William Latch, who told her that Peggy had left him. When he learned that Esther had borne his child, he pleaded to come back to her and hinted that it was her Christian duty to Jackie to give the boy his rightful father. Esther knew that she would be better off with Fred, as would Jackie, for William had become a tavernkeeper and a bookie. Jackie, however, met his father and loved him instantly. For his sake, Esther and William were married.

At first, William made money. Jackie was placed in a good school, and Esther had two servants to wait on her. Nevertheless, there were many days of anxious waiting to hear the results of a race. Often William had thousands of pounds to cover if the favorite won. After a time, he began to lose heavily. It was illegal to accept bets at the tavern, and William was in constant danger of being reported to the police. Fred Parsons came to warn Esther to leave William, to tell her that the tavern was to be raided, but she refused to desert her husband. Then Sarah Tucker came to her tavern to ask for help after she had stolen a silver plate from her employer. The police found her there. After the tavern was raided, William was heavily fined. Business began to dwindle, and Esther and William had lean times.

After William contracted tuberculosis, the dampness and fog of the racetracks only made him cough more, and at last he had to go to the hospital. There the doctors told him that he must go to Egypt for his health. He and Esther gambled all of their money on a single race and lost. Esther tried to be cheerful for William's sake, but when he died a few days later, she wished that she too had died. She had no money and no place to go. Her only blessing was that Jackie was old enough to take care of himself.

Esther went back to Woodview. Only Mrs. Barfield was left, and she was poor. Most of the land had gone to pay racing debts. Esther, however, was ready to stay with Mrs. Barfield without wages, for she had never forgotten her old friend's kindness. Jackie enlisted in the army and went to Woodview to tell his mother good-bye. With pride, she introduced him to Mrs. Barfield. She knew that her sin had been redeemed and that she would never have to be ashamed again. She had given her country a fine soldier. Few women could do more.

Critical Evaluation:

Nineteenth century fiction maintained a delicate balance between realism and Romanticism, often with a strong underlayer of sentimentality. In England at the end of the century, George Moore was leading the way toward the kind of literary realism represented in France by Gustave Flaubert and Émile Zola, but he believed that the most carefully observed facts are insufficient unless seen through the glass of imagination and humanity. Marked by unprecedented frankness, *Esther Waters* was the first English novel to reveal the pilgrimage through life of a human being as a physical creature. The novel caused a scandal almost as great as that caused by Thomas Hardy's *Jude the Obscure* (1895) and was for a time banned from circulating libraries; it had a tremendous influence on the works of younger writers, among them W. Somerset Maugham's first novel, *Liza of Lambeth* (1897).

Moore deliberately took a mundane subject and wrote about it in circumstantial, realistic detail and without melodrama; his simple prose style established place and setting with surprising poetic impact. From the first, the heroine is presented as a sensual young woman when it is explained that she is fond of touching living creatures. Her physical desires are, however, in conflict with her strict Christian background and later with her responsibilities as a mother. Moore creates a powerful scene when he describes Esther confronting Mrs. Spires in front of the cradles of sickly babies and refusing Mrs. Spires's offer to free her from responsibility and murder her baby for five pounds. The horror Esther feels is transmitted to the reader.

The novel presents a vivid picture of the life of a servant in the nineteenth century in large country houses and lower-middle-class homes. Often the only alternatives for a girl like Esther were prostitution or suicide. Moore shows these realities without exaggeration but with great feeling. Always, Esther is absorbed by one central thought: how to save her child, raise him, and make him into a decent man. Her struggle is told in human terms, and she emerges as a heroine of majestic proportions, all the more magnificent because in her own eyes she is only a miserable creature doing the best she can with little hope and few expectations. In the process, Moore also exposes the narrowness and hypocrisy of the middle-class households through which Esther passes, which by their very contrast illuminate the genuine goodness of Esther, Miss Rice, Mrs. Barfield, and a few others.

Bibliography:

Cave, Richard Allen. *A Study of the Novels of George Moore.* New York: Barnes & Noble Books, 1978. Discusses specific texts from George Moore's oeuvre and provides an overview of the texts and the stylistic subheadings under which they may be categorized. Also includes concise notes and references for further research.

Farrow, Anthony. *George Moore.* Boston: Twayne, 1978. Provides a chronology of the significant events of Moore's life and explores the influences and other factors to which he was exposed as a writer.

Federico, Annette. "Subjectivity and Story in George Moore's Esther Waters." In *English Literature in Transition, 1880-1920.* Greensboro: University of North Carolina, 1993. A study of the motivations that led Moore to write this socially provocative text. Also explores the cultural significance of the character of Esther.

Gerber, Helmut E., ed. *George Moore in Transition: Letters to T. Fisher Unwin and Lena Milman, 1894-1910.* Detroit, Mich.: Wayne State University Press, 1978. The letters contained in this text offer some indication of the reflective artfulness of Moore's craft. Also provides personal glimpses into his life, instincts, processes, and creative genius.

Owens, Graham, ed. *George Moore's Mind and Art.* New York: Barnes & Noble Books, 1970. A collection of nine critical essays that examine Moore's novels. Offers excellent insight into the author's themes and issues.

ETHAN FROME

Type of work: Novel
Author: Edith Wharton (1862-1937)
Type of plot: Psychological realism
Time of plot: Late nineteenth century
Locale: Starkfield, Massachusetts
First published: 1911

Principal characters:
ETHAN FROME, a New England farmer
ZENOBIA "ZEENA" FROME, his wife
MATTIE SILVER, Zeena's cousin

The Story:

Ethan Frome was twenty-one years old when he married Zenobia Pierce, a distant cousin who nursed his sick mother during her last illness. It was a wedding without love. Zenobia, called Zeena, had no home of her own, and Ethan was lonely. So they were married. Zeena's talkativeness, which had been pleasing to Ethan during his mother's illness, quickly subsided, and within a year of their marriage, Zeena developed the sickliness that was to plague her husband all her life. Ethan became increasingly dissatisfied with his life. He was an intelligent and ambitious young man who had hoped to become an engineer or a chemist. He soon, however, found himself stuck with a wife he detested and a farm he could not sell.

The arrival of Mattie Silver brightened the gloomy house considerably. Mattie, Zeena's cousin, had come to Starkfield partly because she had no other place to go and partly because Zeena felt in need of a companion around the house. Ethan saw in Mattie's goodness and beauty every fine quality that Zeena lacked.

When Zeena suggested that Ethan help Mattie find a husband, he began to realize how much he was attracted to the girl. When he went to a church social to bring Mattie home and saw her dancing with the son of a rich Irish grocer, he realized that he was jealous of this rival and in love with Mattie. On his way home with her, Ethan felt his love for Mattie more than ever, for on that occasion as on others, she flattered him by asking him questions on astronomy. His dreams of happiness were short-lived, however, for when he reached home, Zeena was her nagging, sour self. The contrast between Zeena and Mattie impressed him more and more.

One day, Ethan returned from his morning's work to find Zeena dressed in her traveling clothes. She was going to visit a new doctor in nearby Bettsbridge. Ordinarily, Ethan would have objected to the journey because of the expensive remedies that Zeena was in the habit of buying on her trips to town. On this occasion, however, he was overjoyed at the news of Zeena's proposed departure, for he realized that he and Mattie would have the house to themselves overnight.

With Zeena out of the way, Ethan again became a changed man. Later in the evening, before supper, Ethan and Mattie sat quietly before the fire, just as Ethan imagined happily married couples would do. During supper, the cat broke Zeena's favorite pickle dish, which Mattie had used to brighten up the table. In spite of the accident, they spent the rest of the evening happily. They talked about going sledding together, and Ethan told Mattie shyly—and perhaps wistfully—that he had seen Ruth Varnum and Ned Hale, a young engaged couple, stealing a kiss earlier in the evening.

In the morning Ethan was happy, but not because of anything out of the ordinary the night before. In fact, when he went to bed, he remembered sadly that he had not so much as touched Mattie's fingertips or looked into her eyes. He was happy because he could imagine what a wonderful life he could have if he were married to Mattie. He got glue to mend the pickle dish, but Zeena's unexpected return prevented him from repairing it. His spirits were further dampened when Zeena told him that the Bettsbridge doctor considered her quite sick. He had advised her to get a girl to relieve her of all household duties, a stronger girl than Mattie. She had already engaged the new girl. Ethan was dumbfounded by this development. In her insistence that Mattie be sent away, Zeena gave the first real hint that she may have been aware of gossip about her husband and Mattie.

When Ethan told Mattie of Zeena's decision, the girl was as crestfallen as Ethan. Zeena interrupted their lamentations, however, by coming downstairs for something to eat. After supper, she required stomach powders to relieve a case of heartburn. In getting the powders, which she had hidden in a spot supposedly unknown to Mattie, Zeena discovered the broken pickle dish, which had been carefully reassembled in order to give the appearance of being unbroken. Having detected the deception and learned that Mattie was responsible for the broken dish, Zeena called Mattie insulting names and showed plainly that the girl would be sent away at the earliest possible moment.

Faced with the certainty of Mattie's departure, Ethan thought of running away with her. His poverty, as well as his sense of responsibility to Zeena, offered no solution to his problem, only greater despair. On the morning Mattie was to leave Starkfield, Ethan, against the wishes of his wife, insisted on driving Mattie to the station. The thought of parting was unbearable to both. They decided to take the sleigh ride that Ethan had promised Mattie the night before. Down the hill they went, narrowly missing a large elm tree at the bottom. Mattie, who had told Ethan that she would rather die than leave him, begged until Ethan agreed to take her down the hill a second time and run the sled into the elm at the bottom of the slope; but they failed to hit the tree with force sufficient to kill them. The death they sought became a living death, for in the accident Mattie suffered a permanent spine injury and Ethan an incurable lameness. The person who received Mattie into her home, who waited on her, and who cooked for Ethan was Zeena.

Critical Evaluation:

Ethan Frome has enjoyed greater popularity than any other of Edith Wharton's twenty-two novels and novellas. It is also better known than any of her short stories, nonfiction, or poetry. Appearing first as a three-part serial in *Scribner's* magazine, the 1911 book got its start around 1907 when Wharton developed aspects of the narrative as an exercise in writing French. The story appeared as a play in 1936. Moving away from depicting the manners of high society, Wharton treats, in *Ethan Frome*, poor, inarticulate people living in the countryside. Early critics complained that a New York sophisticate such as Wharton knew nothing about the lives of the kind of people depicted in *Ethan Frome*. The book's popularity argues otherwise.

Wharton frames her story. Prior to chapter 1, an engineer observes Ethan coming to town and inquires about his history. Later, caught in a snow storm, the engineer spends a night at the Frome house, and the engineer intuits events of long ago. An omniscient narrator relates nine chapters that conclude with the accident. In the epilogue the engineer comments on Ethan, Zeena, and Mattie living in the lonely farm house for twenty-four years.

The novel employs few symbols. Beside the emblematic landscape, the cat implies the witchlike influence of Zeena on Mattie and Ethan, and the family graveyard suggests that Ethan will never escape Zeena or the farm. In her foreword to a 1922 edition, Wharton writes that

Ethan Frome intends to convey a sense of the harsh and beautiful New England countryside. Thus, Wharton adopts an austere realism, a tone in keeping with the hard landscape and with the shocking outcome.

This harsh tone informs the theme of Ethan's isolation. Wharton describes Ethan as like the landscape, mute and melancholic, as if he were one of the outcroppings of slate that push up through the snow. Ethan is "an incarnation of the land's frozen woe with all that was warm and sentient in him fast bound below the surface." The central narrative occurs in winter, but flashbacks contrast happy summer occasions. Ethan recalls to Mattie a picnic the previous summer at Shadow Pond when he found her locket; then he points to a tree trunk recalling that there they sat together in the summer evening. Yet at the time when he speaks the winter snow has nearly buried that tree trunk.

Isolation pervades the novel. When Ethan comes to town from his farm, he speaks to no one. Four or five years prior to the main action, Ethan had had one year of study at a technological college in Worcester, and he had been to Florida. The encounter with the greater world contrasts with Ethan's confinement to his rural farm. The isolation drives Ethan's mother crazy. The road past the house has lost its traffic and the mother can no longer see passersby. Once a talker, the mother grows silent and seldom speaks. Ethan, desperate in the long winter evenings for the sound of a voice, asks why she does not say something; his mother, insane, answers that she is listening to the people talking out in the storm. Then Zeena—a distant relative—comes to nurse the mother. After his mother's funeral, fearful of being left alone, Ethan too quickly proposes marriage.

Ethan is trapped on the farm. A villager notes early that most of the smart people got away from the area, but Ethan had to care first for his father, then his mother, then his wife, and then Mattie. Ethan made some attempts to get away. When his mother dies, Ethan hopes to move to a town, but Zeena prefers notoriety as a sickly person in Starkfield to anonymity in a city. Ethan considers running off with Mattie; he even writes a note to Zeena explaining his desertion. He recalls that a man in the area did run off to the West and that he found happiness.

Ethan, however, cannot bring himself to abandon Zeena. She cannot support herself on the farm. Then his eye fastens on a newspaper advertisement offering train trips to the West at reduced rates. He has no money with which to buy train fare for himself and Mattie. The facts of poverty and his marital obligation act like prison guards to chain him, "a prisoner for life." The toboggan accident leaves him lame so that his every step seems checked by the jerk of a chain. Circumstances and his own conscience prohibit Ethan from ever leaving Starkfield.

Zeena Frome counters her husband of seven years in all his desires. She speaks in a flat whine, keeps her hair tight with crimping pins, dresses always in dark calico, and complains constantly about imagined illness. She demands that the lovely Mattie Silver be banished from the house and that a new girl come to wait on her. Zeena, witchlike, dominates Ethan. After the crash, Zeena creates a living hell for Mattie and for Ethan.

"Critical Evaluation" by Emmett H. Carroll

Bibliography:
Lewis, R. W. B. *Edith Wharton: A Biography.* New York: Harper & Row, 1975. Excellent presentation of Wharton's life. Offers a relationship between the novel and Wharton's divorce from her husband Teddy.
McDowell, Margaret B. *Edith Wharton.* Boston: Twayne, 1976. In an overview of the novel, McDowell sees that the engineer-narrator emphasizes the terrible defeat of Ethan and Mattie.

Nevius, Blake. *Edith Wharton: A Study of Her Fiction*. Berkeley: University of California Press, 1953. Fixes the novel in the main tradition of Mrs. Wharton's fiction.

Trilling, Lionel. "The Morality of Inertia." *Edith Wharton: A Collection of Critical Essays*. Edited by Irving Howe. Englewood Cliffs, N.J.: Prentice-Hall, 1962. Trilling caused a major controversy in the study of *Ethan Frome*. Holds that Ethan is weak, and the novel only demonstrates the suffering he endures.

Wolff, Cynthia Griffin. *A Feast of Words: The Triumph of Edith Wharton*. New York: Oxford University Press, 1977. Wolff offers a psychological study of Wharton and the novel.

ETHICS

Type of work: Philosophy
Author: Baruch Spinoza (1632-1677)
First published: Ethica ordine geometrico demonstrata, 1677 (English translation, 1870)

A geometric demonstration of ethics is a novelty in the history of thought, but Baruch Spinoza's *Ethics* is famous not because of, but in spite of, its novelty of method. The principal advantage of the method is that it reveals Spinoza's thought as clearly as possible. Although the demonstrations may not satisfy critics who concern themselves only with definitions and logical form, they are strongly persuasive for those who, already committed to the love of the good and of God, need clarity and structure in their thoughts.

Spinoza begins with definitions, proceeds to axioms (unproved but acceptable), and then to propositions and demonstrations. If one wished to find fault with Spinoza's argument, any place is vulnerable: One can quarrel about the definitions, doubt the truth of the axioms, or question the validity of the demonstrations. To reject the book, however, one would need to question the integrity of Spinoza's spirit.

It has long been regarded an error in philosophy to attempt to deduce what people ought to do from a study of what people do, but what Spinoza attempts is a deduction of what people ought to do from a study of what must be, according to his definitions and axioms. The primary criticism of his method, then, is not that he errs—although most critics find errors in Spinoza— but that he tries to use logical means to derive ethical truths. The criticism depends on the assumption that ethical truths are either matters of fact, not of logic, or that they are not truths at all but, for example, emotive expressions.

Spinoza begins *Ethics* with definitions of "cause," "finite," "substance," "attribute," "mode," "free," "eternity," and "God," the latter term being defined to mean "Being absolutely infinite, that is to say, substance consisting of infinite attributes, each one of which expresses eternal and infinite essence." To understand this definition one must relate it to the definitions of the terms within it—such as "substance," "finite," and "attribute"—but one must also resist the temptation to identify the term, so defined, with any conventionally used term. Spinoza's God is quite different from others' God, at least in conception. The point of the definition is that what Spinoza means by "God" is whatever is "conceived through itself" (is substance), has no limit to its essential characteristics (has infinite attributes), and maintains its character eternally. As one might suspect, the definition of "God" is crucial.

The axioms contain such logical and semantical truths as "I. Everything which is, is either in itself or in another"; "II. That which cannot be conceived through another must be conceived through itself"; "VI. A true idea must agree with that of which it is the idea"; and "VII. The essence of that thing which can be conceived as not existing does not involve existence." At first, the axioms may be puzzling, but they are not as extraordinary as they seem. Axiom number seven, for example, means only that anything that can be thought of as not existing does not, by its nature, have to exist.

The propositions begin as directly implied by the definitions: "I. Substance is by its nature prior to its modifications" follows from the definitions of "substance" and "mode," and "II. Two substances having different attributes have nothing in common with one another" is another consequence of the definition of "substance." As the propositions increase, the proofs become longer, making reference not only to definitions but also to previous propositions and their corollaries. For those interested in technical philosophy, the proofs are intriguing even when they are unconvincing, but for others they are unnecessary; the important thing is to understand Spinoza's central idea.

Proposition 11 is important in preparing the way for Spinoza's main contention: "XI. God or substance consisting of infinite attributes, each one of which expresses eternal and infinite essence, necessarily exists." Although one may be tempted to seize upon this proposition as an instrument to use against atheists, it is necessary to remember that the term "God" is a technical term for Spinoza and has little, if anything, to do with the object of religious worship.

Proposition 14 makes the startling claim that "Besides God no substance can be nor can be conceived." A corollary of this proposition is the idea that God is one; that is, everything that exists, all of nature, is God. Individual things do not, by their natures, exist, but only through God's action, and God is not only the cause of their existence but also of their natures (24, 25). Readers might expect, consequently, that a great deal of the universe is contingent; that is, it depends upon something other than itself and need not be as it is. Spinoza argues in proposition 24 that "In Nature, there is nothing contingent, but all things are determined from the necessity of the divine nature to exist and act in a certain manner." Consequently, the human will is not free but necessary (32). This was one of the ideas that made Spinoza unpopular with both Jews and Christians.

Having used part 1 of *Ethics* to develop the conception of God, Spinoza goes on in part 2, after presenting further definitions and axioms, to explain the nature and origin of mind. He concludes that "In the mind there is no absolute or free will." (48). In part 2, he also develops the idea that God is a thinking and extended being.

In part 3, "On the Origin and Nature of the Emotions," Spinoza argues that emotions are confused ideas. "Our mind acts at times and at times suffers," he contends in proposition 1 of part 3; "in so far as it has adequate ideas, it necessarily acts; and in so far as it has inadequate ideas, it necessarily suffers." One should note that Spinoza defines "emotion" as any modification of the body "by which the power of acting of the body itself is increased, diminished, helped, or hindered, together with the ideas of these modifications."

By this time, Spinoza has created the idea that God, as both thinking and extended substance, is such that all nature is both thinking and extended (since everything that is, must be part of God). Another way of expressing this idea is that everything that exists does so both as body and as idea. Thus, the human being exists as both body and idea. If the human being, as idea, does not adequately comprehend the modifications of the human body, the mind suffers.

In part 4, "Of Human Bondage: Or, Of the Strength of the Emotions," Spinoza defines the good as "that which we certainly know is useful to us." In a series of propositions, he develops the ideas that each person necessarily desires what is considered to be good; that in striving to preserve his or her being, a person acquires virtue; and that the desire to be happy and to live well involves desiring to act, to live, "that is to say, actually to exist." In this attempt to relate freedom to one's will to act, and in the identification of the good with the striving toward existence, Spinoza anticipated much of the more significant work of the twentieth century existentialists.

In proposition 28 of part 4, Spinoza writes that "The highest good of the mind is the knowledge of God, and the highest virtue of the mind is to know God." This claim has been prepared for by previous propositions relating the good to what is desired, the desire to action, action to being, and being to God. Because of the intricacy of Spinoza's argument, it becomes possible for him to argue that to seek being, to seek the good, to use reason, and to seek God are one and the same. To use reason involves coming to have adequate ideas, having adequate ideas involves knowing the nature of things, knowing the nature of things involves knowing God.

It might appear that Spinoza's philosophy, for all its references to God, is egoistic, in that this crucial phase of his argument depends upon the claim that all people seek to preserve their own beings. A full examination of part 4, however, shows that Spinoza transcends the egoistic base of action by arguing that to serve the self best, one uses reason; but to use reason is to seek an adequate idea of God and, consequently, to seek what is good for all people. In fact, Spinoza specifically states that whatever causes people to live in harmony with one another is profitable and good, and that whatever brings discord is evil.

A person's highest happiness or blessedness, according to Spinoza, is "the peace of mind which springs from the intuitive knowledge of God." This conclusion is consistent with Spinoza's ideas that humanity's good consists in escaping from the human bondage of the passions, that to escape from the passions is to understand the causes that affect the self, that to understand the causes involves action, and that action leads to God.

When, through rational action, people come to determine themselves, they participate in the essence of all being; they become so at one with God that they possess an intellectual love of God, which is humanity's blessedness and virtue. The eternal is known only by the eternal; hence, in knowing God, one becomes eternal—not in a finite or individual way, but as part of God's being.

Spinoza is usually bracketed with René Descartes and Gottfried Wilhelm Leibniz as a rationalist philosopher. Eschewing the approach of the classic philosophers and the Scholastics alike, he relies almost exclusively on reason, devoid of any imaginative or theological super-structures, to develop his system of metaphysics. Like Descartes, he finds the method of the mathematician the best approach to philosophical inquiry: In identifying and developing the logical relationships between statements about the world, he is able to show how all things are related causally. Unlike Descartes, however, he does not hesitate to question traditional notions of God and construct a metaphysics that eliminates the need for a conventional deity.

The system Spinoza presents in all of his writings, but especially in *Ethics*, has been described alternatively as pantheistic and atheistic. Although he makes frequent references to God, Spinoza is not simply another in the line of Scholastic philosophers who, like St. Thomas Aquinas, devoted his life to proving the rationality of theological belief. Spinoza's God is not a personal, transcendent being on whom all creation depends; for Spinoza, "God" is equivalent to "Nature," an infinite substance in whom all finite substances reside. God and all that people generally consider "creation" are actually one. A similar monism characterizes Spinoza's view of "mind" and "body"; these two aspects of human nature, often described as dualistic components of humanity, are, for Spinoza, merely different modes of expressing the essential "oneness" of humanity—which, in turn, is simply an expression and extension of the infinite substance, which he calls God.

Within his highly structured mathematical approach, Spinoza devotes considerable attention to the notion of human desires and emotions. Reversing the traditional Aristotelian notion that people innately desire what is good, Spinoza argues that whatever one desires becomes viewed as a good. Much of the central sections of *Ethics* is devoted to explaining how people may overcome emotions and desires to reach a genuine understanding of what is truly good, and come to some appreciation of the infinite.

This complicated and highly theoretical system of metaphysics was castigated by Spinoza's contemporaries, and, for more than a century after his death, his works were little more than footnotes in the history of philosophy. His insistence that God is simply a part of nature and not a distinct being worthy of reverence led to charges of atheism; his complex analysis of philosophical questions, organized in the form of geometric propositions, caused many in the seventeenth century to dismiss him as too obscure. Not until the rise of Romanticism did his ideas—with their overtones of pantheism and insistence on the essential unity of all reality—become popular with thinkers and writers. Then they were embraced enthusiastically by Gotthold Ephraim Lessing and Johann Wolfgang von Goethe in Germany and Samuel Taylor Coleridge in England. Since the eighteenth century, Spinoza has risen in stature to become one of the most revered thinkers in European philosophy. He has been linked with the Stoics, who also found little real freedom in human activities and believed that much of human behavior was determined by forces that people simply could not identify. He also has been described as a kind of Socrates, working diligently to uncover the truth despite the hardships he experienced in his own life.

Updated by Laurence W. Mazzeno

Bibliography:
Bennett, Jonathan. *A Study of Spinoza's "Ethics."* Indianapolis: Hackett, 1984. In outline form, expounds *Ethics* in considerable detail. Raises hard questions of the text; judges the second half of part five to be worthless.
Curley, Edwin. *Behind the Geometrical Method: A Reading of Spinoza's "Ethics."* Princeton, N.J.: Princeton University Press, 1988. Relates *Ethics* to Cartesian philosophy, thereby hoping to make the work less esoteric to contemporary readers. Considers Spinoza a sophisticated materialist.
Kashap, S. Paul, ed. *Studies in Spinoza: Critical and Interpretive Essays.* Berkeley: University of California Press, 1972. Eighteen essays by British, U.S., and Norwegian scholars attempt to make Spinoza's thought more accessible by explaining it in terms of a modern philosophic vocabulary. Each essay is a self-contained discussion of a particular aspect of Spinoza's philosophy.
Lloyd, Genevieve. *Part of Nature: Self-Knowledge in Spinoza's "Ethics."* Ithaca, N.Y.: Cornell University Press, 1994. Illuminates the connection between Spinoza's metaphysics and ethics in relationship to the dilemma of alienation inherited with Descarte's notion of self. Argues that Spinoza, in his strangeness, exposes Western philosophy's assumptions of individuality while offering an alternative understanding.
Sullivan, Celestine J., Jr. *Critical and Historical Reflections on Spinoza's "Ethics."* University of California Publications in Philosophy 32. Berkeley: University of California Press, 1958. A brief review of certain difficulties in *Ethics.* Determines that the many paradoxes in Spinoza's thought—suppressed by his overpowering rationalism—reveal a division of mind characteristic of his age.

EUGENE ONEGIN

Type of work: Poetry
Author: Alexander Pushkin (1799-1837)
Type of plot: Impressionistic
Time of plot: Nineteenth century
Locale: Russia
First published: Evgeny Onegin, 1833 (English translation, 1881)

> *Principal characters:*
> EUGENE ONEGIN, a Russian dandy
> VLADIMIR LENSKY, his friend
> TATYANA LARIN, a woman in love with Eugene
> OLGA, her sister

The Story:

Eugene Onegin was brought up in the aristocratic tradition. Although he had little classical background, he had a flashing wit and he was well read in economics. He had become an accomplished man of the world by the time he reached young adulthood. In fact, he had been so successful in love and so accustomed to the social life of Moscow that he habitually felt a supreme boredom with life. Even the ballet had lately failed to hold his attention.

Eugene's father had led the usual life. He gave parties regularly and tried his best to keep up his social position by borrowing recklessly. Just as he declared bankruptcy, Eugene received word that his uncle was dying. Since he was the heir, he left in haste to attend the dying man. Grumbling meanwhile at the call of duty, he was thankful to be coming into an inheritance.

His uncle, however, died before he arrived. After the relatives had departed, Eugene settled down to enjoy his uncle's handsome country estate. The cool woods and the fertile fields charmed him at first, but after two days of country life his former boredom returned. He soon acquired a reputation as an eccentric. If neighbors called, Eugene found himself obliged to leave on an urgent errand. After a while, the neighbors left him to himself.

Vladimir Lensky, however, remained his friend. At eighteen, Vladimir was still romantic and filled with illusions of life and love. He had been in Germany, where he was much influenced by the philosopher Immanuel Kant and the poet-dramatist Friedrich von Schiller; this more German temperament set him apart. He and Eugene became more and more intimate.

The Larins had two daughters, Olga and Tatyana. Olga was pretty and popular, and although she was the younger, she was the leader in their group. Tatyana was reserved and withdrawn, but a discerning observer would have seen her real beauty. She made no effort to join in the country life. Olga had long been betrothed to Vladimir, but the family despaired of finding a husband for Tatyana.

On Vladimir's invitation, Eugene reluctantly agreed to pay a visit to the Larins. When the family heard that the two men were coming, they immediately thought of Eugene as a suitor for Tatyana. Eugene, however, was greatly bored with his visit. The refreshments were too ample and too rustic, and the talk was heavy and dull. He paid little attention to Tatyana. After he left, Tatyana was much disturbed. Having fallen deeply in love with Eugene, she had no arts with which to attract him. After confiding in her dull-witted nurse, she wrote Eugene a passionate, revealing love letter.

Eugene, stirred by her letter, paid another visit to the Larins and found Tatyana in a secluded garden. He told her the brutal truth. He was not a good man for a husband, for he had had too much experience with women and too many disillusionments. Life with him would not be at all worthy of Tatyana. The girl, making no protest, suffered in silence.

On his lonely estate Eugene lived the life of an anchorite. He bathed every morning in a stream, read, walked and rode in the countryside, and slept soundly. Only Vladimir called occasionally.

That winter the Larins celebrated Tatyana's name-day. When Vladimir represented the gathering as only a small family affair, Eugene consented to go. He felt betrayed when he found the guests numerous, the food heavy, and the ball obligatory. For revenge, he danced too much with Olga, preventing Vladimir from enjoying his fiancée's company. Vladimir became jealously angry and challenged Eugene to a duel. Eugene stubbornly accepted the challenge.

Before the duel, Vladimir went to see Olga. His purpose was to reproach her for her behavior, but Olga, as cheerful and affectionate as ever, acted as if nothing had happened. More lighthearted but somewhat puzzled, Vladimir prepared to meet Eugene on the dueling ground.

When the two friends met, Eugene shot Vladimir through the heart. Remorseful at last, Eugene left his estate to wander by himself. Olga soon married an army man and left home. In spite of the scandal, Tatyana still loved Eugene. She visited his house and made friends with his old housekeeper. She sat in his study reading his books and pondering his marginal notes. Eugene had been especially fond of cynical works, and his notes revealed much about his selfishness and disillusionment. Tatyana, who had hitherto read very little, learned much bitterness from his books and came to know more of Eugene.

At home, Tatyana's mother did not know what to do. The girl seemed to have no interest in suitors and had refused several proposals. On the advice of relatives, the lady decided to take Tatyana to Moscow, where there were more eligible men. They were to visit a cousin for a season in the hopes that Tatyana would become betrothed. From her younger cousins, Tatyana learned to do her hair stylishly and to act more urbanely in society. At a ball, a famous general, a prince, was attracted to Tatyana. In spite of the fact that he was unattractive, she accepted his proposal.

After more than two years of wandering, Eugene returned to Moscow. Still indifferent to life, he decided to attend a fashionable ball, simply to escape from boredom for a few hours. He was warmly greeted by his host, whom he had known well in former times. While the prince was reproaching him for his long absence, Eugene could not keep from staring at a queenly woman who dominated the gathering. She looked familiar. When he asked the prince about her, he was astounded to learn that she was Tatyana, his host's wife.

The changed Tatyana showed no traces of the shy rustic girl who had written so revealingly of her love. Eugene, much attracted to her, frequently went to her house, but he never received more than a cool reception and a distant hand to kiss. Finally, Eugene began to write her letters in which he expressed his hopeless longing. Still, Tatyana gave no sign. All that winter Eugene kept to his gloomy room, reading and musing. At last, in desperation, he called on Tatyana unannounced and surprised her as she was reading his letters.

Tatyana refused to give in to his importunate declarations. She did not understand why he had scorned her when she was a country girl but pursued her now that she was a married woman. She would rather listen to his brutal rejection than to new pleadings. She had once been in love with Eugene and would gladly have been his wife; perhaps she was still in love with him. Perhaps she had been wrong in listening to her mother, who had been insistent that she marry the prince. However, she was now married, and she would remain faithful to her husband until she died.

Critical Evaluation:

Eugene Onegin is generally considered Alexander Pushkin's most outstanding and characteristic work. Written between 1823 and 1831, the verse novel reflects Pushkin's development as a poet and marks a transition to prose fiction, which occupied his later years. The time of the fictional action of the novel spans the years 1820 to 1825, ending with the period of the Decembrist uprising in a fragmentary tenth chapter. The eight full cantos, or chapters as Pushkin called them, were published individually and as a complete edition in 1833.

The work is written in a highly ornate stanza form that is based on sonnet form and has rarely been attempted since. The plot is shaped by symmetrical refusals of love. First Onegin rejects Tatyana; then Tatyana dismisses Onegin. Although the form is highly polished, the plot is frequently overshadowed by the narrator's digressions, many of which explore the author's own biography and the process of writing the novel itself. Only about one-third of the novel concerns the plot, while the rest presents descriptions of life in St. Petersburg and the provinces and digressions on the theater, contemporary politics, amorous adventure, or literary craftsmanship. The work combines the pathos of a psychologically plausible affair with epigrammatic wit.

In spite of the strong French influence in his works, Pushkin expressed Russian life in lively Russian. The depth of his insight into Russian life led contemporary critics to call *Eugene Onegin* "an encyclopedia of Russian life," even though the novel ignores the concerns of the peasantry and the growing urban middle class. The novel depicts, however, a lively account of Russian customs and beliefs as well as a variety of contemporary portraits, interiors, and landscapes. *Eugene Onegin* brings together conflicting discourses and worldviews; including the hackneyed provincial taste of Tatyana's family, which lags several years behind that of fashionable society, the simple wisdom of peasant culture represented by the nanny, and the contemporary cosmopolitan lifestyle interpreted by the author-narrator, embodied in Eugene, and presented in Tatyana's salon at the end of the novel.

Eugene Onegin raises a series of problems concerning the relationship between literature and life. It also concerns the limits on social action and artistic expression imposed by the conventions and expectations of polite society. Life and literature repeatedly intersect. Pushkin inserts readers, both friends and foes, whom he addresses throughout the text. In this way, the audience also enters the fictional world of the novel. The author-narrator enters his created world to befriend Eugene. The narrator's muse merges with the novel's heroine, Tatyana. Tatyana, Lensky, and Eugene attempt to re-create the literature they have read while the author-narrator parodies these same works. Tatyana models herself on the sentimental heroines of Samuel Richardson and Madame de Staël. Lensky acts out patterns of romantic verse, like that written by Vasily Zhukovsky or André-Marie de Chénier. Eugene plays the role of the disillusioned hero, typically found in the works of George Gordon, Lord Byron, who abandons civilization. Both Eugene, a dandy, and Tatyana, hostess of a fashionable salon, ultimately play roles that unite social and aesthetic goals. At the same time, the author-narrator, as a published writer, counters the literary aspirations of the young poet, Lensky, and the Byronic hero, Eugene.

The main characters, including the author-narrator and the fictionalized readers, belong to the Westernized gentry of Russia and therefore acknowledge the same cultural conventions. During the course of the novel, the characters trace several stages of development, which occur at different rates but span youthful enchantment, a period of disenchantment, and then mature re-enchantment. The author-narrator develops from a child writing sentimental verse to the author of the novel itself. Tatyana, who begins as a young girl who sees people as literary stereotypes, learns that life's imitation of literature can be a parody and emerges as the hostess of a salon, which was the highest form of aesthetic creativity open to a woman at the time. Although Tatyana develops her ability to utilize cultural convention, Eugene finds himself trapped by a literary paradigm, while Lensky is never able to integrate life and art. All the characters live within a world from which there is no lasting retreat into the refuges of romantic imagination: nature, dream, and primitive society.

Although in the preface he refers to the novel as a satirical work, written "in the manner of Byron's *Don Juan*," Pushkin later diminished its satirical content. He did, however, admire the structure of Byronic poems. Like Byron, Pushkin shapes elliptical narratives with digressive asides and develops a stylistic link between the poet and his hero, who is also a product of contemporary society. Romantic irony, which presents the same ideas or events from conflicting points of view, colors the entire plot of Pushkin's narrative and is emphasized in a number of ways. Internal discrepancies are consciously inserted to allow for variations of meaning. Pushkin purposefully does not introduce a unifying scheme of images to enhance the impression of an open novel. In addition, the author-narrator frequently interrupts with comments on the text itself. He also parodies contemporary literary works and the sentimental moods of the characters. The tone alternates between frivolous and profound, derisive and sentimental.

Eugene Onegin does not, however, merely copy Byronic elements but evaluates and extends popular Byronic conventions. Although the narrator's point of view is frequently ironic, he, unlike Byron's narrators, mocks the romantic mood rather than poetry itself. Eugene's characters seems to exhibit the bitter rebelliousness, aristocratic arrogance, and passionate excess of one of Byron's heroes, yet the imitation is conscious on Eugene's part and parodic on the author-narrator's. By the end of the novel, the pose is considered outmoded in St. Petersburg society, unwittingly leaving Eugene in a state of truly Byronic alienation.

Pushkin's predilection for linguistic clarity, sparkling wit, and elegance was enhanced by a light touch, or the ability to make the complex configuration of plots, digressions, and intricate poetic arrangements appear easy. The loose structure of *Eugene Onegin* allows Pushkin to experiment with stylistic and generic convention while including a varied commentary on contemporary Russian life by way of the plot and the digressions from it. *Eugene Onegin* amply exemplifies Pushkin's powers of observation and insight into life and art.

"Critical Evaluation" by Pamela Pavliscak

Bibliography:
Driver, Sam. *Pushkin: Literature and Social Ideas*. New York: Columbia University Press, 1989. The book considers the poet as an engaged social thinker rather than as an alienated Romantic poet. Traces the development of Pushkin's social ideas and his involvement in contemporary politics. The chapter devoted to dandyism offers an insightful discussion of *Eugene Onegin* in light of European fashion.

Hoisington, Sona S., trans. *Russian Views of Pushkin's "Eugene Onegin."* Bloomington: Indiana University Press, 1988. A varied collection of Russian considerations of Pushkin's work. Contains several famous essays by nineteenth and twentieth century writers and critics, including Fyodor Dostoevski, Yuri Lotman, and Mikhail Bakhtin. Includes a discussion of the social significance of the novel, an elaboration of the novel as multiple-voice text, and an evaluation of the narrative structure.

Nabokov, Vladimir. *Eugene Onegin: A Novel in Verse by Aleksandr Pushkin*. 4 vols. Rev. ed. Princeton, N.J.: Princeton University Press, 1975. Nabokov's translation of *Eugene Onegin* includes an extensive and thorough commentary on the style and content of Pushkin's novel. Although his gloss on *Eugene Onegin* is eclectic and often digressive, Nabokov's discussion is always interesting.

Simmons, Ernest J. *Pushkin*. Cambridge, Mass.: Harvard University Press, 1937. A solid survey of Pushkin's life combined with discussion of his major works. Still considered the standard biography of the poet.

Vickery, Walter. *Alexander Pushkin*. New York: Twayne, 1970. Provides extensive plot commentary and a detailed consideration of Pushkin's versification. The chapter on *Eugene Onegin* offers a good, basic introduction to the work.

EUGÉNIE GRANDET

Type of work: Novel
Author: Honoré de Balzac (1799-1850)
Type of plot: Naturalism
Time of plot: Early nineteenth century
Locale: Saumur, France
First published: 1833 (English translation, 1859)

Principal characters:
MONSIEUR GRANDET, a miser
EUGÉNIE, his daughter
CHARLES GRANDET, his nephew
NANON, his servant
MONSIEUR DE GRASSINS, a banker
MONSIEUR CRUCHOT, a notary

The Story:

In the French town of Saumur, old Grandet was a prominent personality, and the story of his rise to fortune was known throughout the district. He was a master cooper who had married the daughter of a prosperous wood merchant. When the new French Republic offered for sale the church property in Saumur, Grandet used his savings and his wife's dowry to buy the old abbey, a fine vineyard, and several farms. Under the consulate, he became mayor and grew still more wealthy. In 1806, he inherited three additional fortunes from the deaths of his wife's mother, grandfather, and grandmother. By this time he owned the abbey, a hundred acres of vineyard, thirteen farms, and the house in which he lived. In 1811, he bought the nearby estate of an impoverished nobleman.

He was known for his miserliness, but he was respected for the same reason. His manners were simple and his table was meager, but his speech and gestures were the law of the countryside. His household consisted of his wife, his daughter, Eugénie, and a servant, Nanon. Old Grandet, who used his wife as a screen for his devious financial dealings, had reduced his wife almost to slavery. Nanon, who did all the housework, was gaunt and ugly but very strong. She was devoted to her master because he had taken her in after everyone else had refused to hire her because of her appearance. On each birthday, Eugénie received a gold piece from her father and a winter and a summer dress from her mother. Each New Year's Day, Grandet would ask to see the coins and would gloat over their yellow brightness.

He begrudged his family everything except the bare necessities of life. Every day, he would carefully measure and dole out the food for the household—a few lumps of sugar, several pieces of butter, and a loaf of bread. He forbade the lighting of fires in the rooms before the middle of November. His family, like his tenants, lived under the austere circumstances he imposed.

The townspeople wondered whom Eugénie would marry. There were two rivals for her hand. One of them, Monsieur Cruchot, was the son of the local notary. The other, Monsieur de Grassins, was the son of the local banker. On Eugénie's birthday, in the year 1819, both called at the Grandet home. During the evening, there was an unexpected knock at the door, and in came Charles Grandet, the miser's nephew. Charles' father had amassed a fortune in Paris, and Charles himself, dressed in the most fashionable Parisian manner, exemplified Parisian customs and habits and tried to impress these awkward, gawking provincials with his superior airs.

Eugénie outdid herself in an effort to make the visitor welcome, even defying her father in the matter of heat, candlelight, and other luxuries for Charles. Grandet was polite enough to his nephew that evening. Charles had brought a letter from his father, in which Grandet's brother announced that he had lost his fortune, was about to commit suicide, and entrusted Charles to Grandet's care. The young man was quite unaware of what his father had written, and when Grandet informed him next day that his father's business had failed and he had committed suicide, Charles burst into tears and remained in his room for several days. Finally, he wrote to a friend in Paris, asking him to dispose of his property and pay his debts. He gave little trinkets to Eugénie, her mother, and Nanon. Grandet looked at them greedily and said he would have them appraised. He informed his wife and daughter that he intended to turn the young man out as soon as his father's affairs were settled.

Charles felt that there was a stain on his honor. Grandet felt so too, especially since he and his late brother had the same family name. In consultation with the local banker, Monsieur de Grassins, he arranged a plan whereby he could save the family reputation without spending a penny. Monsieur de Grassins went to Paris to act for Grandet, but instead of returning he enjoyed a life of pleasure in the capital.

Eugénie fell in love with Charles. She sympathized with his penniless state and gave him her hoard of coins so that he would be able to go to the Indies and make his fortune. After the two young people had pledged everlasting love to each other, Charles left Saumur.

On the following New Year's Day, Grandet asked to see Eugénie's money. Her mother, who knew her daughter's secret, kept silent. In spite of Eugénie's denials, Grandet guessed what she had done with the gold. He ordered her to stay in her room and announced that he would have nothing to do with either her or her mother. Rumors began to circulate in town. The notary, Monsieur Cruchot, told Grandet that if his wife were to die, Eugénie could insist on a division of the property. The village whispered that Madame Grandet was dying of a broken heart caused by her husband's treatment of her. Realizing that he might lose a part of his fortune, Grandet relented and forgave his wife and daughter. When his wife died, he tricked Eugénie into signing over her share of the property to him.

Five years passed with no word from Charles to brighten Eugénie's drab existence. In 1827, when Grandet was eighty-two years old, he was stricken with paralysis. He died urging Eugénie to take care of his money.

Eugénie continued to live with old Nanon and to wait for Charles to return. One day, a letter came from Charles, in which he told her that he no longer wished to marry her. Instead, he hoped to marry the daughter of a titled nobleman and secure his father-in-law's title and coat of arms. Eugénie released Charles from his promise, but Monsieur de Grassins hurried to Charles and told him that his father's creditors had not been satisfied. Until they were, his fiancée's family would not allow a marriage. When she learned of his predicament, Eugénie paid the debt, which enabled Charles to marry.

Eugénie continued to live alone. Her routine was exactly what it had been while Grandet lived. Suitors came to the house again. Young de Grassins had been disgraced by his father's loose life in Paris, but Monsieur Cruchot, who had risen to a high post in the provincial government, continued to press his suit. At last, Eugénie agreed to marry him, providing he did not demand the prerogatives of marriage; she would be his wife in name only. They were married only a short time before Monsieur Cruchot died. To her own property, Eugénie thereupon added his. Nanon herself had married, and she and her husband stayed with Eugénie. Convinced that Nanon was her only friend, the young widow resigned herself to a lonely life. She lived as she had always lived in the bare old house. She had great wealth but, lacking everything else in life, was indifferent to it.

Critical Evaluation:

Eugénie Grandet is part of Honoré de Balzac's grandly designed *La Comédie humaine* (*The Human Comedy*). Rather late in his prolific writing career, Honoré de Balzac conceived the idea of arranging his novels, stories, and studies in a certain order. He first described his plan in *Avant-propos* (1842), claiming that the idea had originated as early as 1833, and named the project *The Human Comedy*. Balzac was influenced in his idea by the naturalists Georges Louis Leclerc de Buffon, Étienne Geoffroy Saint-Hilaire, and Jean Lamarck, whose scientific principles—especially the taxonomic system—Balzac sought to apply to literature, particularly for the purpose of organizing information. Balzac firmly believed that "social species" could be classified just as zoological species were, and he retroactively attempted to classify his fifty-odd previous works as well as all future writings to fit his scheme. To accommodate his plan, he adopted eight major topic headings: "Scenes from Private Life," "Scenes from Provincial Life," "Scenes from Parisian Life," "Scenes from Political Life," "Scenes from Military Life," "Scenes from Rural Life," "Philosophical Studies," and "Analytical Studies." The works were arranged, rearranged, and arranged again. *Eugénie Grandet* finally came to be categorized with the "Scenes of Provincial Life." In line with this ambitious organizational plan, Balzac tailored his earlier output to the new standards, with some predictably disastrous results. The literary qualities of the novels, however—notably of *Eugénie Grandet*—are irrefutable testimony to the triumph of art over science.

Balzac realized his goal of presenting typical human species in spite of, not because of, his "scientific" system of taxonomy. As the unsurpassed historian of the French middle class during the first half of the nineteenth century, he incarnated the stereotypes that were new then but so well known today, among them the snob, the provincial, the prude, the miser, and the lecher. He did so on the strength of his artistic skill and not by virtue of scientific analysis, for Balzac was not a systematic philosopher or a scientist but an artist. His novels, though they are often marred by his insensitivity to language and his proclivity for excessive details, outlined the essential characteristics of the nineteenth century French middle class more clearly than anyone else has ever done. Matching Juvenal and Martial, Balzac satirized avarice, ambition, lust, vanity, and hypocrisy. Greed, however, was his *bête noire*, and money is a pervasive theme in Balzac's novels. The figure of the greedy miser Monsieur Grandet epitomizes greed and furnishes Balzac with one of his best characters. Ironically, the novel reflects Balzac's own preoccupation with money and his desire to earn vast sums of it. Like many of his characters, he wanted wealth and social position. As a young man, he was poor and constantly in debt, but he never did learn how to manage money, even after his novels began earning him sizable sums. He was constantly in debt because he lived extravagantly and beyond his means. While writing, he lived like a monk, working furiously for long hours with virtually no time out even for eating. When the novel was completed, however, Balzac devoted that same energy to nonstop revelry. His feasts were legendary and his capacity for fine foods was gargantuan; he is said to have consumed one hundred oysters as an *hors d'oeuvre*, for example. His drinking and other debauches were no less excessive. He agreed with Monsieur Grandet that money is power and power is all that matters; therefore, money is the only important factor in life.

The difference between Balzac and his fictional characters, however, is that Balzac wanted money for what it would buy, whereas Grandet wanted money for its own sake. Balzac cultivated his Dionysian lifestyle with the same single-minded dedication with which Grandet cultivated abstemiousness. He enjoyed a grand style, in contrast to Grandet, who took pleasure from self-denial.

Though the novel is entitled *Eugénie Grandet*, it is Monsieur Grandet who dominates the novel just as he dominated his family. He is the force that determines his wife's destiny—who is ultimately killed by his penny-pinching vindictiveness—and that of his daughter—who is emotionally warped by his miserly indoctrination. Thus the novel is as much about Grandet as it is about Eugénie.

Monsieur Grandet is what literary critics call an undeveloped or a "flat" character. He undergoes no change in the course of the novel and experiences no enlightenment. From start to finish, he is venal and miserly. In fact, Eugénie is the only character who undergoes change, for she progresses from innocence to experience. The others remain as they were at the beginning.

Although Eugénie knows nothing of Grandet's machinations in accumulating his fortune, she is nevertheless shaped by her father's influence. Grandet thus exerts his wishes even beyond the grave, since his training of Eugénie—implicit and explicit—is reflected in her behavior long after he is dead. Although she is publicly charitable, she adopts his parsimonious living habits. Without effort, but presumably because she learned from her father, she increases her fortune. Eugénie would not be what she is without having grown up with such a father. The matrix of this relationship illustrates one of Balzac's major premises, which was to become a tenet of late nineteenth century literary naturalism: that the combined effects of genetics and environment cannot be surmounted. This phenomenon is labeled "determinism," more precisely, "mechanistic determinism," to distinguish it from its religious counterpart of predestination. Eugénie is born into a given social environment with a given genetic makeup. She is unable to change those factors, and they are the twin determinants of her fate. The novel traces her development up to the time when she accepts that fate that was foreordained at the outset: She is very, very rich and very, very unhappy. The inescapable forces of determinism work through to their inevitable conclusion.

Eugénie Grandet is an unusually moving work, for the reader can hardly fail to sympathize with Eugénie while despising her father. It comes as something of a shock, then, to realize that Eugénie bore her father no malice. Even her response to Charles's betrayal is so subtle that it is untainted; Charles is oblivious to subtlety, and the reader does not begrudge Eugénie her one, lone exercise of financial power. Balzac's incredible prestidigitation is at work here, manipulating the readers so that they accept the novel's point of view without imposing extraneous judgments. *Eugénie Grandet* is a tribute to Balzac's craft and art.

"Critical Evaluation" by Joanne G. Kashdan

Bibliography:
Bertault, Philippe. *Balzac and the Human Comedy.* Translated by Richard Monges. New York: New York University Press, 1963. A general survey of Balzac's novels, offering little in-depth analysis of individual works but usefully locating them in relation to Balzac's major themes and interests. Includes a brief biographical sketch.
Hemmings, F. W. J. *Balzac: An Interpretation of "La Comédie Humaine."* New York: Random House, 1967. Chapter 4, "The Cancer," presents a comparative analysis of *Eugénie Grandet*, *Cousin Bette*, and *Père Goriot* as a trilogy of works centering around a father whose private obsession jeopardizes his family.
Levin, Harry. *The Gates of Horn: A Study of Five French Realists.* New York: Oxford University Press, 1963. A study of literary realism in France. In chapter 4, Levin includes several specific references to *Eugénie Grandet*.
Maurois, André. *Prometheus: The Life of Balzac.* Translated by Norman Denny. Harmondsworth, Middlesex, England: Penguin Books, 1971. The definitive biography of Balzac,

which provides detailed context for and some commentary on all of the major works, including *Eugénie Grandet*.

Schor, Naomi. *Breaking the Chain: Women, Theory, and French Realist Fiction*. New York: Columbia University Press, 1985. In chapter 5, "*Eugénie Grandet:* Mirrors and Melancholia," Schor presents a closely detailed feminist reading of the novel, relying on the insights provided by psychoanalytic theory.

THE EUNUCH

Type of work: Drama
Author: Terence (Publius Terentius Afer, c. 190-159 B.C.E.)
Type of plot: Comedy
Time of plot: Fourth century B.C.E.
Locale: Athens
First performed: Eunuchus, 161 B.C.E. (English translation, 1598)

> *Principal characters:*
> PHAEDRIA, a young Athenian in love with Thais
> THAIS, a courtesan
> THRASO, a soldier and rival of Phaedria
> PARMENO, Phaedria's slave
> CHAEREA, Phaedria's younger brother, in love with Pamphila
> PAMPHILA, a slave
> CHREMES, Pamphila's brother

The Story:

Phaedria, a young Athenian of good family, was disturbed because he had been excluded from the house of Thais, a courtesan. He was also perturbed because of the love he felt for the woman. Phaedria's slave, anxious to help his master, advised that Phaedria retire to the country for a time and try to forget her. Parmeno, the slave, really believed the woman was wicked and that his master would be better off without her. As master and slave stood before Thais' house, which was next to Phaedria's father's residence, the courtesan herself came out to explain why she had refused to admit the young man. She explained that Thraso, a warrior, had purchased a slave who had formerly belonged to her mother. Thais believed that the slave, a young woman, was actually a free citizen of Athens. In order to get a good name in Athens, to which city she had recently come, Thais hoped to learn the woman's identity and restore her to her family. Thais had to humor the captain in order to get possession of the slave.

Phaedria believed Thais and promised to go away into the country for two days, so that she could work on the captain with her charms and get possession of the young slave woman. Before he left, Phaedria gave Parmeno orders to go into his father's house and get the two slaves whom he had purchased for Thais. One of the slaves was an Ethiopian woman, the other a eunuch. Thais wanted a eunuch because royalty preferred them.

On his way to get the slaves for Thais, Parmeno met Phaedria's younger brother, Chaerea, who had seen the slave woman Thais wanted and had fallen in love with her. Chaerea persuaded Parmeno to introduce him into Thais' household in place of the eunuch, and the exchange was made. In the meantime Thraso's parasite had brought the slave woman to Thais' house as a present to the courtesan from the warrior. He also bade Thais meet his master for dinner.

Thais and some of her maids went to Thraso's house as he had requested. While they were gone, Chaerea, in the person of the eunuch, was entrusted with the care of Pamphila, the slave woman. He sent her to be bathed by other slaves. When she was returned, he was so overcome by her charms, aided by a picture of Jupiter's rape of Danae, that he raped her. Ashamed at what he had done, he fled.

While Thais was gone, Pamphila's brother Chremes came to the house at the request of Thais. Told that she was not at home, he went in search of her at Thraso's residence. Thraso,

2112

thinking Chremes a rival for Thais' affections, behaved boorishly. Disgusted, Thais took her leave, after telling Chremes to meet her shortly thereafter at her own house.

Phaedria, in the meantime, had left for the country, but, overcome by his affection for Thais, he turned back. Arriving at his father's house, he was met by one of Thais' maids, who told him that the eunuch had raped Pamphila. Phaedria, swearing that such things could not happen, found the eunuch, who was dressed in Phaedria's brother's clothing. The maid, upon seeing the eunuch, realized that the guilty man was not the eunuch but Phaedria's brother. The brother, meanwhile, had gone off to a dinner with some friends. He was both sorry and glad for his deed; most of all, he wanted to marry the slave.

Thais returned, distressed and angry when she heard what had happened. Her anger was cut short by the arrival of Chremes, who thought that Pamphila was his sister, stolen in infancy. To make sure, he went off to get the nurse who had been in charge of his sister. Before he could leave, however, he had to chase off Thraso, who had arrived with a band of servants to reclaim the slave he had given to Thais.

Chaerea returned and confessed his actions to Thais. When she accused him of doing the deed to spite her, a courtesan, he demurred, swearing that he had raped the slave because he loved her overmuch. He still claimed that he wanted to marry her. Chremes returned with the nurse, who quickly identified Pamphila as Chremes' long-lost sister, a free citizen of the city, a member of a good family, and a fine wife for Chaerea, if the lad could get his father's consent.

While they were conferring, Thais' maid resolved to have her own revenge on Parmeno, Phaedria's slave. She told Parmeno that Chaerea had been seized and that he was about to be mutilated, as was the customary treatment of rapists in ancient Athens. Parmeno ran to Laches, the father of Phaedria and Chaerea, to get the older man's help.

When Laches learned the true facts, he was quite willing to permit a marriage between his younger son and the woman whom he had dishonored. More than that, the father became reconciled to his older son's love for the courtesan, since she had proved herself in her efforts to restore the slave to freedom and her proper position in life. He agreed to look after the courtesan's welfare and to permit his older son to live with her. This plan made Phaedria and Thais very happy, for they truly loved each other.

When Thraso returned for one last attempt to regain the favor of the courtesan, Phaedria threatened to kill him if he appeared in that street again. Thraso's parasite suggested to Phaedria and Thais that they keep the braggart for entertainment. The parasite pointed out that Thraso was very foolish, had a lot of money, and could be kept dangling a long time by the courtesan without ever receiving any of her favors. Phaedria, seeing the humor of the situation, agreed to the terms. The warrior, not realizing he was to be made a fool, was so happy with the arrangement that he promised to behave himself and to be more generous than ever with the parasite who had got him into the silly situation.

Critical Evaluation:

Of the two major Roman comic playwrights (the other was Plautus), Terence has always been considered the more thoughtful. Like Menander, the Greek writer whose works he imitated, Terence used the genre not simply to amuse his audience but also to explore human psychology and moral issues. Because some characters and scenes seem to have been introduced into *The Eunuch* merely for their farcical value, however, it has been suggested that Terence may have written this play primarily to please his audience. *The Eunuch* is often called Terence's most Plautine work; certainly it is his most lighthearted. Nevertheless, there is evidence that even in *The Eunuch*, Terence meant to touch on a serious theme.

As is typical of a play by Terence, *The Eunuch* has a double plot. The first story involves the love of Phaedria for Thais, and the second story involves Chaerea's desire for Pamphila. In *The Eunuch*, however, Terence also adds an underplot to his play. His source for the characters of Thraso and Gnatho has not been determined, but they could have been drawn from an ample supply of stereotypes available to Roman dramatists. The boastful soldier appears often in Roman comedy, as does the parasite, who makes his living by flattering wealthy dupes. The important question is why Terence introduced these characters into the play; some critics argue that their presence is gratuitous. Gnatho's description of his activities is, in itself, uproarious. Thraso is a variation of the stereotype he represents. As a soldier who, though stupid, is not brave, and though boastful, is proud not of his military exploits but of his wit, Thraso adds color and humor to the play. His siege of Thais' house is one of the most humorous scenes in *The Eunuch*. Nevertheless, neither that scene nor the characters of Thraso and Gnatho can be considered essential to the two primary plotlines. Thraso does not need to be as fully developed a character as he is, nor does he need to be as involved in the action as he is.

It may be that even in this atypical play, Terence wished to challenge the comfortable assumptions of his audience. This argument is supported by the fact that the frequent derogatory comments about courtesans are contradicted by the actions of the courtesan-protagonist. Thais wishes to return Pamphila to her family because she wants to win the respect of the Roman nobility; however, she is also motivated by unselfish love. In fact, except for Thais' conscientious maid, Pythias, Thais is the least motivated by self-interest. At the end of the play, when Laches takes Thais under his protection and permits Phaedria to retain her as his mistress, Laches is more than just a perceptive father or even a wise elder citizen; he is also acting as an agent of poetic justice and as a spokesperson for the playwright.

None of the male characters in *The Eunuch* can be compared to its courtesan protagonist in terms of generosity, integrity, and courage. Like Thais, Gnatho must be self-sufficient. Unlike her, however, he is willing to be dishonest and self-centered in order to survive. The slave Parmeno is drawn more sympathetically, since, unlike the scheming slave in most Roman comedies, Parmeno does try to draw a moral line. He is shocked when Chaerea acts upon his idle comment about masquerading as a eunuch. More important, however, he fears that he will be blamed for Chaerea's misconduct. Terence held Parmeno responsible, at least to some degree, for Chaerea's misconduct; Terence's feelings are evident in the punishment that he allows Pythias to mete out to Parmeno. It can also be argued that the fictional castration is meant to symbolize the punishment that Chaerea deserves.

In the first scene of *The Eunuch*, Parmeno defines love, which constitutes the subject of the play; its theme is self-interest. Love, Parmeno says, is a madness, subject to no rules, and once people are overtaken by love, their best hope is to pay as small a price as possible. Phaedria is willing to stay away from Thais for two days, not because he cares about her feelings, but because he hopes that by obeying her now, he will have her favors in the future.

The love Chaerea professes for Pamphila is another example of self-interest. Not only does he deceive an innocent, but he also rapes her. The reason that Terence never brings Pamphila onstage, even to show her reinstated with her family and betrothed to Chaerea, may be that he thinks it best not to dispel the comic mood.

Another example of self-interest is represented by Thraso and Chremes. During the siege, both are concerned about themselves. While Thais courageously defends her home, Chremes cowers beside her, and Thraso hides behind his small army of servants. The siege scene may have been added in order to expose two more male characters.

If Terence means *The Eunuch* to be taken seriously, however, it is difficult to explain why

Phaedria makes the accommodation he does at the end of the play. Though his love may be selfish, it seems to motivate everything he does. He wants to eliminate his rival and to have his mistress to himself. For financial reasons, however, he is willing to share her with Thraso. Either Terence has decided to end his play with a cynical comment on human nature, or he is primarily concerned with entertaining his audience. It is hardly surprising that critics continue to debate Terence's intentions in *The Eunuch*.

"Critical Evaluation" by Rosemary M. Canfield Reisman

Bibliography:

Forehand, Walter E. *Terence*. Boston: Twayne, 1985. Examines *The Eunuch* from the standpoint of plot, structure, and theme. Discusses the eight most important characters in the play. Includes extensive notes and an annotated bibliography.

Goldberg, Sander M. *Understanding Terence*. Princeton, N.J.: Princeton University Press, 1986. A study of the playwright. Includes an index to passages and an analysis of *The Eunuch* in the chapter titled *"Contaminatio."* The bibliography contains numerous citations to foreign-language publications.

Hunter, R. L. *The New Comedy of Greece and Rome*. Cambridge, England: Cambridge University Press, 1985. Sees the play as an exploration of male-female relationships. In a dramatic reversal, a woman protagonist attains power over men. The three primary male characters are also thematically important, however, since they represent various aspects of love.

Lowe, J. C. B. "The *Eunuchus:* Terence and Menander." *Classical Quarterly* 33, no. 2 (1983): 428-444. An attempt to resolve the question of Terence's intent by examining the ways in which he altered his source in Menander. Argues that an answer can be found in Terence's development of two key scenes.

Sandbach, F. H. *The Comic Theatre of Greece and Rome*. London: Chatto & Windus, 1977. Both the chapter on Menander and the chapter on Terence include observations about *The Eunuch*. Discusses Terence's alterations and additions to the works of Menander, his Greek source.

EUPHUES, THE ANATOMY OF WIT

Type of work: Novel
Author: John Lyly (c. 1554-1606)
Type of plot: Didactic
Time of plot: Sixteenth century
Locale: Naples and Athens
First published: 1578

Principal characters:
>EUPHUES, a young gentleman of Athens
>PHILAUTUS, a nobleman of Naples and his friend
>DON FERARDO, a governor of Naples
>LUCILLA, his daughter and Philautus' fiancée
>LIVIA, her friend
>EUBULUS, an old gentleman of Naples

The Story:

Euphues, a young gentleman of Athens, was graced by nature with great personal beauty and by fortune with a large patrimony, but he used his brilliant wit to enjoy the pleasures of wickedness rather than the honors of virtue. In his search for new experiences, the young man went to Naples, a city famed for loose living. There he found many people eager to encourage a waste of time and talent, but he was cautious, trusting no one and taking none for a friend. Thus, he escaped real harm from the company of idle youths with whom he associated.

One day, Eubulus, an elderly gentleman of Naples, approached Euphues and admonished the young man for his easy ways, warning him of the evil results that were sure to follow and urging him to be merry with modesty and reserve. In a witty reply, Euphues rebuffed the old man's counsel and told him that his pious urgings only resulted from his withered old age. In spite of the sage warning, Euphues remained in Naples, and after two months there he met a pleasing young man named Philautus, whom he determined to make his only and eternal friend. Impressed by the charm of Euphues, Philautus readily agreed to be his firm friend forever. Their friendship grew, and the two young men soon became inseparable.

Philautus had long before earned the affection and trust of Don Ferardo, a prominent official of Naples, and he had fallen in love with his beautiful daughter Lucilla. While Don Ferardo was on a trip to Naples, Philautus took his friend with him to visit Lucilla and a group of her friends. After dinner, Euphues was given the task of entertaining the company with an extemporaneous discourse on love. He declared that one should love another for his mind, not for his appearance. When the conversation turned to a discussion of constancy, Lucilla asserted that her sex was wholly fickle. Euphues began to dispute her, but, suddenly struck by Lucilla's beauty and confused by his feelings, he broke off his speech and quickly left.

Lucilla discovered that she was attracted to the young Athenian. After weighing the respective claims of Euphues and Philautus on her affections, she convinced herself that it would not be wrong to abandon Philautus for Euphues; however, she decided to pretend to each that he was her only love. Euphues, meanwhile, had persuaded himself that Lucilla must be his in spite of Philautus: Friendship must give way before love. In order to deceive his friend, Euphues pretended to be in love with Livia, Lucilla's friend. Philautus was overjoyed and promised to help him win Livia.

The two young men went immediately to the house of Don Ferardo. While Philautus was attending the governor, who had finally completed arrangements for his daughter's marriage to the young man, Euphues and Lucilla engaged in a subtle debate about love and finally declared their passion for each other. When Don Ferardo told his daughter of his plans for her marriage to Philautus, she told him of her love for Euphues.

Philautus, betrayed at once by his friend and his beloved, blamed first one and then the other. He wrote a scathing letter to Euphues, saying that they were friends no longer and that he hoped Euphues would soon be in his own unhappy situation; he warned that Lucilla, having proved untrue, might be faithless again. Euphues replied in a taunting letter that deception in love is natural. He expressed confidence that Lucilla would be faithful to him forever.

After what had happened, however, it was impossible for Euphues to visit Lucilla while her father was at home. During her lover's absence, she fell in love again, this time with Curio, a gentleman who possessed neither wealth nor wit. When Euphues at last went to apologize for being away so long, Lucilla replied curtly that she had hoped his absence would be longer. Admitting that her new lover was inferior to both Philautus and Euphues, she supposed God was punishing her for her fickleness. Although she realized that her life was likely to be unhappy, a fate she had earned, she did not hesitate to scorn Euphues. Don Ferardo argued that it was her filial duty to give up the worthless Curio. When she refused, her father died of grief shortly thereafter.

Having renewed his friendship with Philautus before departing from Naples, Euphues left with his friend a written discourse against the folly of love. It stated that love, although it started with pleasure, ended in destruction and grief, and he urged his friend to forget passion and to turn his attention toward more serious pursuits.

After returning to Athens where he engaged in long hours of study, Euphues wrote a treatise on the proper way to rear a child. His own upbringing had not steered him away from the shoals of sloth and wickedness. With this weakness of upbringing in mind, he urged that a young man should be legitimately born and reared under the influence of three major forces: nature, reason, and use. In this manner, the young man would be educated in the ways of virtue as well as in the customs of use. Euphues wrote many other letters and treatises: In one, he urged the gentlemen scholars of Athens to study with the laws of God in mind; in another, he debated with an atheist and converted him to godliness; a letter to Philautus encouraged him to abandon his dissolute life in Naples; in a letter to Eubulus, Euphues thanked the old man for his good advice and told him of his return to righteousness; another letter to Philautus expressed regret at the death of Lucilla and at the irreligious character of her life; two letters to a pair of young men told them to accept their destiny and to live virtuously; in response to a letter in which Livia told of her intention to be virtuous, Euphues praised her and told her of Philautus' possible visit to Athens.

Critical Evaluation:

John Lyly's *Euphues, the Anatomy of Wit*, is one of the most significant works in the development of English prose style. First published in 1578, the novel was one of the most popular fictions of the period, going through thirteen editions by 1613 and inspiring imitation among a number of contemporary writers, including Robert Greene, Thomas Lodge, and even, in a parodic tone, William Shakespeare. While the ornate, balanced, and highly artificial style that came to be known as euphuism did not originate with the novel, *Euphues* did make the style immensely popular and transformed the way in which English prose was written.

The essential hallmarks of euphuism are rhetorical; they undeniably emphasize sound over sense. Chief among these devices are balance, in the form of antithesis and in the form of parallelism, in which grammatical forms are kept carefully even. Alliteration and assonance, in which similarities in sound help tie phrases and sentences together, are also important to the style.

Antithesis, which comes form a Greek word meaning "opposition," combines and contrasts ideas in a balanced rhetorical form that gives equal weight to both. Euphues' advice to Lucilla, "If you will be cherished when you be old, be courteous when you be young" is an example of a balanced, antithetical statement. The second half of the sentence duplicates the grammatical structure of the first half, while the two parts of the sentence complement each other in form and meaning. "Cherished" is balanced against "courteous" and "old" against "young."

This balanced, antithetical pattern is the most characteristic feature of *Euphues*, and Lyly's obsessively regular use of it has caused some critics and scholars of the novel to remark on its metronomic rhythm, and to complain that the work is all sound and no sense. The perception that Lyly is obsessed with sound at the total expense of sense is mistaken; in *Euphues*, antithesis is used to express Lyly's view of human life as a conflict between appearance and reality. Lyly uses his specific rhetorical devices to examine the paradox of human perceptions and feelings.

"Do we not commonly see that in painted pots is hidden the deadliest poison, that in the greenest grass is the greatest serpent, in the clearest water the ugliest toad?" Under the moralizing tone of this exclamation from Euphues, and implicitly expressed in its rhetorical form, is the recognition that human life consists of a series of contradictions, all equally valid at their particular moment. Lyly's euphuistic prose is not merely a rhetorical performance; it is an analytic instrument for examining human feelings and emotions.

Parallelism, in which grammatical forms are kept carefully even, is another important part of Lyly's style. Carried to the extreme that Lyly achieves in *Euphues*, it attains a highly artificial level, but, as with balance and antithesis, with which parallelism is often associated in the novel, parallelism serves to reinforce the paradoxical nature of human existence.

A notable example, cited by Joseph Houppert in his study of Lyly, is the rebuke of the nominally good man Eubulus for his normal human distress over the loss of a loved one: "Thou weepest for the death of thy daughter, and I laugh at the folly of the father; greater vanity is there in the mind of the mourner, than bitterness in the death of the deceased." Here, the parallelism is obsessively exact, since "tears" and "laughter" contrast, while "death" and "daughter" alliteratively balance "folly" and "father," at the same time that the verb pattern is strictly maintained. Yet, as Houppert notes, the seeming paradox between death and life, and grief and joy, is resolved if one places this quotation in the context of the religious sentiment of Elizabethan England.

This quotation also illustrates a third major facet of Lyly's prose style, alliteration and assonance. Alliteration, the recurrence of initial consonant or vowel sounds, is clearly present in the passage: "Death" and "daughter," and "folly" and "father" are examples. Assonance, a similarity in sounds, is also present in this passage, as the sequence of vowels in "laugh," "folly" and "father" indicate. Lyly uses a sophisticated, even artificial rhetorical device to knit his narrative more closely together in terms of sense and content.

Euphues, the Anatomy of Wit is not an important landmark in English literature simply because of its style. The basic movement of the plot—Euphues' journey to ultimate wisdom after passing through the temptations and dangers of courtly society—is based to a large degree on the story of the prodigal son, as found in the New Testament. The novel's central theme, that life is a pilgrimage during which the truly wise person learns to disregard the appearance of the world, is a highly moral one. Lyly expresses this theme in a highly moralistic fashion. Quite consciously and deliberately, *Euphues* intends to teach its readers some important lessons.

Euphues contains a large number of dialogues, discourses, and letters in which the characters advise, admonish, and encourage one another in the pursuit of virtue and the avoidance of sin. Repeatedly, Lyly's highly structured prose style emphasizes the distance between what seems and what is. The Elizabethan Age was profoundly concerned with this topic and obsessively fearful of hypocrisy and dissimulation. Lyly's elaborate and ornate handling of it helps explain the considerable enthusiasm for the book.

In the end, however, it is the combination of theme, content, characters, and especially style that makes *Euphues* a singular element of English writing. The novel opened new and largely unparalleled avenues for English literature.

"Critical Evaluation" by Michael Witkoski

Bibliography:

Barish, Jonas A. "The Prose Style of John Lyly." *English Literary History* 22 (1956): 14-35. An early and unsurpassed study of Lyly's linguistic and rhetorical techniques, especially as they are employed in *Euphues, the Anatomy of Wit*. Essential for study of Lyly or of his most famous work.

Croll, Morris. Introduction to *Euphues, the Anatomy of Wit*, by John Lyly. New York: Russell & Russell, 1964. Discusses the novel's themes and style. Perceptive and instructive.

Houppert, Joseph W. *John Lyly*. Boston: Twayne, 1975. An excellent starting place for the student of Lyly who wishes to achieve a well-rounded sense of the political, cultural, and artistic setting in which Lyly lived and wrote.

Hunter, G. K. *John Lyly: The Humanist as Courtier*. Cambridge, Mass.: Harvard University Press, 1962. Places Lyly within the context of his times and the social status to which he aspired. Interesting in its study of how Elizabeth's court viewed—and used—language.

Wilson, John Dover. *John Lyly*. New York: Haskell House, 1970. A reprint of the 1905 edition, this volume remains one of the best studies of Lyly's life and works, and is especially sensitive to the use of language in *Euphues, the Anatomy of Wit*.

THE EUSTACE DIAMONDS

Type of work: Novel
Author: Anthony Trollope (1815-1882)
Type of plot: Social realism
Time of plot: Late nineteenth century
Locale: London and Scotland
First published: serial, 1871-1873; book, 1873

Principal characters:
  LIZZIE GREYSTOCK EUSTACE, a young, wealthy widow
  FRANK GREYSTOCK, Lizzie's cousin, a lawyer and politician
  LUCY MORRIS, a governess engaged to marry Frank Greystock

The Story:

Lizzie Greystock was the only child of old Admiral Greystock, a retired naval officer and widower who had devoted his declining years to wine, whist, and wickedness. Raised without the usual parental guidance, Lizzie entered womanhood headstrong, independent, strikingly beautiful, and, within the constraints of Victorian society, a little immoral. Her father died when she was nineteen; he left her penniless. She was taken in by her aunt, Lady Linlithgow, a truculent old dowager who was as rigid in her principles as she was poor. She and her niece, for the brief period they lived together in genteel poverty, despised each other.

Lizzie managed to attract the attention of a wealthy young nobleman, Sir Florian Eustace. After a brief courtship, they were married. The marriage was also brief, but it was long enough to produce a male heir and for Sir Florian to become disillusioned with his bride, who was a liar and a spendthrift. Sir Florian, not a well man, died within a year of his marriage. He left Lizzie a wealthy young widow, with four thousand pounds a year, a castle in Scotland, and a diamond necklace worth ten thousand pounds.

In the settling of the estate, Mr. Camperdown, the Eustace family lawyer, pressured Lizzie to place the necklace, which he declared a family heirloom, in a bank or some other place of security, but Lizzie claimed the necklace as personal property, given to her expressly as a gift from Sir Florian. She refused to comply with the lawyer's request. Determined to protect the family's interests, Mr. Camperdown began a prolonged legal campaign to have the diamonds returned. As the lawyer began his efforts, Lizzie was working her charms on Lord Fawn, a noble but impoverished member of Parliament for the Liberal Party. For the aspiring politician, marriage to the lovely and wealthy Lady Eustace seemed, at first, a definite asset, but as the diamond necklace controversy became increasingly public, Fawn, a timid and self-centered man, began to question the wisdom of his marriage proposal. Rather than face the formidable Lizzie Eustace, he simply neglected her. Lizzie turned for assistance to her cousin, Frank Greystock. Frank was a Conservative member of Parliament, and a political opponent of Fawn. As a matter of honor, Frank took up the cause of his widowed cousin, accepting her story that Sir Florian had given her the diamonds as an outright gift, to do with as she pleased. The story, however, was another of Lizzie's many fabrications.

Lord Fawn and Frank Greystock became personal, as well as political, enemies, and the issue was further complicated by the fact that Frank had fallen in love with Lucy Morris, a young woman with no fortune. She was the highly regarded governess for the Fawn family. Lucy was a great favorite of Lord Fawn's unmarried sisters, and a particular favorite of Lady Fawn, their mother. She enthusiastically returned Frank's affections, and she agreed to marry him at a time in the near future, when he would be able to provide for her. The match was opposed by everyone close to either of them. When Lord Fawn, on a visit to his mother and sisters, spoke disparagingly of Frank Greystock, Lucy vigorously defended him. To the profound regret of Lady Fawn and her daughters, Lucy then felt that she must leave the Fawn family home, in order not to divide a family she loved. She found a position as companion to Lady Linlithgow.

Lizzie then took a particular interest in her handsome cousin, and she considered the possibility of marrying him instead of Lord Fawn. To lure Frank away from Lucy, she began a course of seduction, initiating it by repeatedly stressing to Frank that she was alone and friendless, besieged by Mr. Camperdown, who was determined to make her relinquish what she continued to assert was her personal property. To escape the pressure, she left London for a prolonged visit to Portray, her castle in Scotland. She invited Frank for a visit. At the castle, Frank was introduced to some of Lizzie's new and rather peculiar friends. There were Mrs. Carbuncle and her niece, Lucinda Roanoke; Lord George de Bruce Carruthers, an adventurer and soldier of fortune whom Lizzie considered another candidate for a second husband; Sir Griffin Tewett, an unpleasant, ill-tempered young nobleman intermittently in pursuit of Lucinda Roanoke; and Mr. Emilius, a preacher with a popular following and a suspicious character. Frank found them all rather unsavory; he left at the earliest opportunity.

Fearful that Mr. Camperdown would use some legal means to seize the diamonds, Lizzie kept them in an iron box, and she took them with her on her travels. On the return trip to London, the entourage spent the night at a hotel in Carlisle. Lizzie's room was burglarized during the night, and the box was taken. During the investigation, she did not inform the police that the diamonds were not in the box at the time; instead, they were under her pillow. She was then, technically, guilty of perjury. In London, she became the guest of Mrs. Carbuncle, who tried to manipulate her titled guest to her best advantage. Mrs. Carbuncle's primary objective was to arrange a marriage between her niece, Lucinda Roanoke, and Sir Griffin. Sir Griffin had no real interest in Lucinda, but he was perversely determined to marry her because she so openly loathed him. In the meantime, there was a second burglary, and this time the diamond necklace was stolen. It was discovered that the burglary was a conspiracy between Lizzie's maid, Patience Crabstick, and Mr. Benjamin, a jeweler and money lender to whom Lizzie was in debt; she had consulted him about the possibility of disposing of the necklace. The police soon apprehended the culprits, and Lizzie was advised, under threat of severe penalty, to tell the truth, which she did. The diamonds, however, had been sold through foreign criminal channels; they were never recovered.

Pressured toward marriage with a man she despised, Lucinda had a nervous breakdown. Sir Griffin left the country; Lucinda and Mrs. Carbuncle also left the country, the latter without paying Lizzie the money she had borrowed from her. Lord George was not interested in marriage, and Frank, thoroughly disillusioned with Lizzie's lying and duplicity, followed his heart and married Lucy Morris. Lizzie returned to Portray Castle, where she charmed a Scottish doctor into giving her a medical certificate in order to prevent her from having to return to London for further legal proceedings. At that point, the fortune-hunting Mr. Emilius returned, and, seeing his main chance, he proposed marriage, and Lizzie accepted.

Critical Evaluation:

Anthony Trollope is noted for his penetrating analysis of Victorian society; he is particularly noted for the manner in which he treats the understated interaction between virtue and hypocrisy. The values that motivate this interaction are the primary themes of the novel:

marriage and money. In *The Eustace Diamonds*, marriage, the sanctioned union between man and woman in love, is an ill-considered venture for the bachelor without a personal fortune. Love, although ostensibly revered and idealized, is a secondary concern. Lizzie Eustace, the protagonist of the novel, is very beautiful and engagingly clever, but it is quite clearly the income inherited from her deceased husband that attracts her suitors. Her counterpart and diametric opposite, in both values and outward appearance, is Lucy Morris, plain, virtuous, highly principled, and penniless. Characteristic of Victorian novels, both women are orphans who enter adulthood without money; however, Lizzie, motivated by material ambition, seduces and charms a wealthy young nobleman in order to alter this condition. Lucy, however, is fundamentally incapable of seduction and duplicity. Once Frank Greystock has proposed marriage (to take place at some future undetermined time) her fidelity is constant and unwavering. Even when she is close to believing the popular view that Frank's proposal had been hasty and impractical, and that the pressures of his fledgling political career may make it necessary for him to rescind his offer, she is quite willing to release him if that is his choice. She remains resolute and unvindictive in her belief in his goodness and integrity. Conversely, Lord Fawn's second thoughts regarding his proposal to Lizzie inspire Lizzie to thoughts of vengeance and humiliation. The reader is fully aware of the fact that Lizzie would feel no ethical impediment in exacting her revenge. Lucy is incapable of telling a lie; Lizzie is almost incapable of telling the truth.

In *The Eustace Diamonds*, Trollope creates the same literary paradox that makes John Milton's Satan a more compelling character than Christ in *Paradise Lost* (1667). Although Lucy Morris is a paragon of Victorian womanhood, in her constancy she is relatively static. She lacks complexity, and she is eminently predictable. By contrast, Lizzie Eustace is by far the more interesting character, perhaps the most engaging bad woman in English literature since William Thackerary created Becky Sharpe in *Vanity Fair* (1847-1848). For readers removed by time from the social environment of Victorian England, Lizzie, compared to Lucy, is considered by some critics the more admirable of the two. Her pragmatism and ingenuity in a society dominated by men and masculine values reveal a commendable fortitude and, in an oblique way, a personal integrity. Pressured by the formidable legal establishment of conventional London to relinquish the diamond necklace to the Eustace estate as a protected heirloom, she has the temerity to resist. When Mr. Camperdown redoubles his efforts to intimidate her into compliance, she cleverly circumvents both coercion and persuasion, becoming in the process a *cause célèbre*, London's notorious woman.

The diamonds, however, and the burden of the money they represent, remain a symbol of discord. Throughout the novel, money brings disruption rather than stability, discontent instead of tranquillity. The diamond necklace, which Lizzie seeks to appropriate from the holdings of the Eustace family, affords her no personal pleasure. She has the constant anxiety that it will be seized by Mr. Camperdown, whom she stubbornly, and often inexplicably, resists. Paradoxically, even as she wishes to be free of the necklace, she guards it constantly, trusting no one.

Unlike Lucy Morris, Lizzie is a solitary figure. Other than her credulous and naïve cousin, Frank Greystock, Lizzie has no friends; she has only parasitic adherents like Mrs. Carbuncle and Lucinda Roanoke. Money remains central to Lizzie's eligible suitors, and it is continually conflicting in its roles of lure and impediment. Frank Greystock and Lord Fawn recognize that their careers require a marriage that brings with it a significant financial advantage. Marriage to Lizzie is for both men a very genuine and promising option. Frank's marriage to Lucy Morris, however, is Trollope's sentimental concession to his readers, in direct contradiction to the reality of the society in which Frank has made his way. As Lizzie's notoriety in the matter of the necklace threatens to be a full-blown scandal, Fawn realizes that his marriage for money may, conversely, prove to be prohibitively expensive to his career in other ways. Lord George de Bruce Carruthers, whom Lizzie realizes is a cynical fortune hunter—and, perversely, finds him more appealing because of it—concludes that the dangers outweigh the financial incentive. Mr. Emilius, the preacher (the confidence) man who is far more cunning and deceptive than the roguish but straightforward Lord George, waits in the figurative shadows, making his advances to Lizzie only after the scandal of the diamonds is resolved, and there is no danger that those close to her will be drawn into it.

Although Trollope concludes the Lucy Morris/Frank Greystock relationship with a conventional happy ending, *The Eustace Diamonds* reveals the degree to which Trollope sees nineteenth century British society as governed by what Thomas Carlyle termed the "cash nexus." It is a world in which the honored values of civilized society are inevitably subsumed by wealth and the social position that such wealth creates and sustains.

Richard Keenan

Bibliography:
Cecil, David. *Victorian Novelists: Essays in Revaluation.* Chicago: University of Chicago Press, 1961. A classic work in Victorian studies. Still the best basic introduction to Trollope, it establishes the quality of his work in comparison to his literary contemporaries.
Glendinning, Victoria. *Anthony Trollope.* New York: Alfred A. Knopf, 1993. A thorough biography particularly helpful in its treatment of the relationship between Trollope's attitude toward women in his personal life and the genesis of heroines such as Lizzie Eustace.
Harvey, Geoffrey. *The Art of Anthony Trollope.* New York: St. Martin's Press, 1980. Excellent analysis of character and psychological motivation, particularly in the commentary on the fox hunting chapters as a metaphor for social forms of maneuvering and entrapment.
McMaster, Juliet. *Trollope's Palliser Novels: Theme and Pattern.* New York: Oxford University Press, 1978. A thorough analysis of Lizzie Eustace's penchant for lying and her preoccupation with pseudoromanticism. Discusses the influence of other contemporary literary heroines, particularly Thackeray's Becky Sharp and Blanche Amory, in the development of Lizzie's amoral character.
Tracy, Robert. *Trollope's Later Novels.* Berkeley: University of California Press, 1978. Examines the role of the recurring character in later Palliser novels, particularly Lizzie Eustace's reappearance in *The Prime Minister.* Tracy draws an effective and helpful character analogy between Lizzie and Lady Glencora Palliser, whom Lizzie both admires and, to some degree, imitates.

EVANGELINE

Type of work: Poetry
Author: Henry Wadsworth Longfellow (1807-1882)
Type of plot: Pastoral
Time of plot: Mid-eighteenth century
Locale: French Canada and the United States
First published: 1847

> *Principal characters:*
> EVANGELINE BELLEFONTAINE, an exile
> GABRIEL LAJEUNESSE, her betrothed
> BASIL LAJEUNESSE, Gabriel's father
> BENEDICT BELLEFONTAINE, Evangeline's father

The Story:

In the Acadian province, in the village of Grand-Pré, lived a peaceful farming people who were undisturbed by the wars between the French and British. In a land where there was enough for all, there was no covetousness and no envy, and everyone lived at peace with his neighbor. Benedict Bellefontaine had his farm somewhat apart from the village. His daughter, Evangeline, directed her father's household. Although she had many suitors, she favored only one, Gabriel Lajeunesse, the son of Basil, the village blacksmith. Their fathers were friends, and the children had grown up together.

One fall day, while Benedict rested by the fire and Evangeline sat at her spinning wheel, Basil brought word that the men of the village were to meet at the church the next day. They were to be told the plans of the English, whose ships were riding at anchor in the harbor. That night Benedict and Basil signed the wedding contract that would unite their children. Then, while their fathers played draughts, Evangeline and Gabriel whispered in the darkening room until it was time to say goodnight.

The next morning everyone, including the folk from the outlying districts, came to the village to hear the announcement the English commander was to make. Everybody wore holiday dress, as if the occasion were one for celebration. At the Bellefontaine farm there was special joy, for with a feast and dancing the family and its guests were celebrating the betrothal of Gabriel and Evangeline. In the afternoon the church bell rang, summoning the men to the church. When they filed in, they were followed by the guard from the ship. Outside, the women stood waiting.

The news the English commander had for the little community rendered a crushing blow. By order of the king, their land, houses, and cattle were forfeited to the crown, and the entire population of Grand-Pré was to be transported. The men were to consider themselves his prisoners.

The tragic news spread quickly through the village, and to the farm where Evangeline was awaiting Benedict's return. At sunset she started toward the church, on her way comforting the downcast women she met. Outside she called Gabriel's name, but there was no answer from the church where the men were imprisoned.

The men were held prisoners for five days. On the fifth, the women brought their household goods to the shore to be loaded in boats, and late that afternoon the men were led out of the church by their guards. Evangeline, standing at the side of the road, watched them coming toward her. She was able to comfort Gabriel with the assurance that their love would keep them from harm, but for her father she could do nothing. In the five days he had aged greatly.

Basil and his son were put on separate ships. Evangeline remained on the beach with Benedict. That night the villagers of Grand-Pré watched their homes go up in flames, and listened to their animals bellowing as the barns burned. Turning from the sight, Evangeline saw that her father had fallen dead. She dropped in a swoon upon his breast and lay there until morning; then with the aid of Father Felician, the village priest, the Acadians buried Benedict Bellefontaine by the shore. That day Evangeline sailed with the other exiles.

The scattered exiles from Grand-Pré wandered far over the face of North America in search of their friends and families. Sometimes Evangeline lingered for a while in a town, but always she was driven on by her longing for Gabriel. Looking at unmarked graves, she imagined they might contain her lover. Sometimes she heard rumors of his whereabouts; sometimes she spoke with people who had actually seen and known him, but always long ago. The notary's son, Baptiste Leblanc, followed her faithfully and loyally through her years of searching, but she would have no one but Gabriel for a husband.

Finally a band of exiles rowed down the Mississippi River, bound for Louisiana, where they hoped to find some of their kinsmen. Evangeline and Father Felician were among them, Evangeline heartened because she felt she was nearing Gabriel at last. Then in the heat of the noonday, the voyagers pulled their craft to shore and lay down to sleep behind some bushes. While they slumbered, Gabriel, in the company of hunters and trappers, passed the spot on his way to the West. That evening, when the exiles went to explore the area, the prosperous herdsman who welcomed them proved to be Basil. Evangeline learned that Gabriel had left home that day, too troubled by thoughts of his love to endure the quiet life in his father's house.

For a time Basil helped Evangeline carry on her search. Leaving his peaceful home in the South, the herdsman traveled with the young woman to the base of the Ozark Mountains. They were guided by rumors of Gabriel's whereabouts, and sometimes, from the distance, they saw, or thought they saw, his campfire. When they reached the spot, he had already gone ahead.

One evening a Shawnee Indian woman came into the camp on her way back to her own people after her husband's murder by Comanches. In the night, after the others were asleep, she and Evangeline exchanged stories. When Evangeline had finished hers, the woman told the tale of Mowis, the bridegroom made of snow, and of the Indian woman who married and followed him, only to see him dissolve and fade with the sunshine. She told of Lilinau, who had followed her phantom lover into the woods until she disappeared forever. Evangeline felt that she, too, was following a phantom.

The next day the party traveled to the Jesuit Mission on the western side of the mountains, where they hoped to hear some word of Gabriel. A priest told them Gabriel had gone to the north to hunt six days before. It seemed certain he would pass that way on his journey home in the fall, so Evangeline decided to wait at the mission. Basil and his companions returned to their homes.

Autumn and winter passed and spring came, with no news of Gabriel. Finally Evangeline heard that he was camping in the forests of Michigan on the Saginaw River. When she reached his camp, it was deserted and in ruins.

For many years she wandered over the country in search of her lover, but always she met with disappointment. At last, grown gray, her beauty gone, she became a Sister of Mercy in Philadelphia, where she went because the soft-spoken Quakers reminded her of her own people. When pestilence struck the town, she visited the almshouse to nurse the destitute. One Sunday morning, she saw on the pallet before her a dying old man. It was Gabriel. In his last moments he dreamed of Evangeline and Grand-Pré. Trying to utter her name, he died. Evangeline murmured a prayer of thanks as she pressed her lover to her. The lovers lie side by side in nameless graves in Philadelphia, far from their old home in the north, but a few peasants who wandered back from exile still keep their story alive.

Critical Evaluation:

It is difficult in an unsentimental age to appreciate and understand the enormous appeal this poem had for readers in Henry Wadsworth Longfellow's time. It was hailed from the beginning as a truly "American" poem and its success was virtually unlimited. This pastoral romance relates an odyssey of sorts and dwells on the idea of search, wandering, and Evangeline's constancy. Longfellow sought to imbue the poem with a classical flavor within the framework of the American landscape. It is enriched with elaborate descriptions of the historic American drive toward the west and the south. The rivers, forests, and prairies about which Longfellow writes are the imaginative product of his reading and research, for most of the places mentioned he had never seen.

The basic story revolves around the cruel displacement of the Acadians by the British. Longfellow does not elaborate on the inequities of the British mandate to drive people from their homes; he is more interested in achieving a melancholy emotional tone by concentrating on the reality of exile and the frustration of search. The mood is a tranquil one. Longfellow looks at his two lovers from a distance, creating a hazy image of things far away; much of the poem's action takes place at night, or by moonlight. There is no doubt that the constancy and patience of Evangeline were appealing to Longfellow and his readers. Evangeline's loyalty and fidelity play a major role in the structuring of this romance. While Evangeline is the embodiment of feminine virtue, tenderness, and chastity, she does not have the dimension of a heroic figure. The poem suggests minor poetic form, certainly not of epic grandeur. Evangeline and Gabriel are not realistic lovers, but exponents of the romanticism of the times.

Longfellow felt that the English world was not sufficiently awakened to the beauty of the classical hexameter, so he decided from the beginning to employ this meter in *Evangeline*. There are difficulties with the use of this meter in English and Longfellow was aware of them; yet he painstakingly sought to adhere to this classical measure. The meter does add an intrinsic charm and appropriateness to the tale, despite the sometimes monotonous quality of the lines. Longfellow's use of hexameter triggered a new interest in the meter and inspired much critical evaluation of its use and value.

Bibliography:

Arvin, Newton. *Longfellow: His Life and Work.* Boston: Little, Brown, 1963. A benchmark study of Longfellow as a man and writer. Devotes a full chapter to an articulate and insightful exploration of *Evangeline*, including narrative structure, characters, settings, symbols, themes, and verse form. Places the poem squarely in the idyllic tradition.

Chevalier, Jacques M. *Semiotics, Romanticism and the Scriptures.* Berlin: Walter de Gruyter, 1990. The only book-length examination of the poem. Offers a sophisticated and very detailed line-by-line analysis of the prologue and first canto of book 1. Concentrates on scriptural and romantic elements in light of the poem's role as a variation on the myth of the lost paradise.

Hirsh, Edward L. *Henry Wadsworth Longfellow.* Minneapolis: University of Minnesota Press, 1964. Analyzes *Evangeline* in the context of Longfellow's other long narrative poems, especially *Hiawatha* and *The Courtship of Miles Standish.* Emphasis on Longfellow's tendency to mythologize his subjects and his preference for pastoral coloring.

Wagenknecht, Edward. *Henry Wadsworth Longfellow: His Poetry and Prose*. New York: Frederick Ungar, 1986. Offers focused analyses of Longfellow's major works, including a full chapter on *Evangeline*. Especially valuable in its treatment of Longfellow's original authorial intentions and his alterations to and expansion of the text. Good notes and suggestions for further reading.

Williams, Cecil B. *Henry Wadsworth Longfellow*. Boston: Twayne, 1964. Contains one chapter on Longfellow's verse narratives, including *Evangeline*. An adequate introductory treatment of the author's sources and influences, and the poem's meter, plot, and critical reception. Argues that *Evangeline* provides a sentimental journey that even a cynical modern reader may find attractive.

THE EVE OF ST. AGNES

Type of work: Poetry
Author: John Keats (1795-1821)
Type of plot: Romance
Time of plot: Middle Ages
Locale: A castle
First published: 1820

Principal characters:
  MADELINE, a young woman
  PORPHYRO, her lover
  ANGELA, an old nurse

The Story:

It was a cold St. Agnes' Eve—so cold that the owl with all its feathers shivered, so cold that the old Beadsman's fingers were numb as he told his rosary and said his prayers. Passing by the sculptured figures of the dead, he felt sorry for them in their icy graves. As he walked through the chapel door, he could hear the sound of music coming from the castle hall. He sadly turned again to his prayers. The great hall of the castle was a scene of feasting and revelry, but one among the merry throng was scarcely aware of her surroundings. The lovely Madeline's thoughts were on the legend of St. Agnes' Eve, which told that a maiden, if she followed the ceremonies carefully and went supperless to bed, might there meet her lover in a dream.

Meanwhile, across the moonlit moors came Porphyro. He entered the castle and hid behind a pillar, aware that his presence meant danger, because his family was an enemy of Madeline's house. Soon the aged crone, Angela, came by and offered to hide him, lest his enemies find him there and kill him. He followed her along dark arched passageways, out of sight of the revelers. When they stopped, Porphyro begged Angela to let him have one glimpse of Madeline. He promised on oath that if he so much as disturbed a lock of her hair, he would give himself up to the foes who waited below. He seemed in such sorrow that the poor woman gave in to him. She took Porphyro to the maiden's chamber and there hid him in a closet, where was stored a variety of sweetmeats and confections brought from the feast downstairs. Angela then hobbled away, and soon the breathless Madeline appeared.

She came in with her candle, which blew out, and kneeling before her high arched casement window, she began to pray. Watching her kneel there, her head a halo of moonlight, Porphyro grew faint at the sight of her beauty. Soon she disrobed and crept into bed, where she lay entranced until sleep came over her.

Porphyro stole from the closet and gazed at her in awe as she slept. For an instant a door opened far away, and the noises of another world, boisterous and festive, broke in; but soon the sounds faded away again. In the silence he brought dainty foods from the closet—quinces, plums, jellies, candies, syrups, and spices that perfumed the chilly room. Madeline slept on, and Porphyro began to play a soft melody on a lute. Madeline opened her eyes and thought her lover a vision of St. Agnes' Eve. Porphyro, not daring to speak, sank upon his knees until she spoke, begging him never to leave her or she would die.

St. Agnes' moon went down. Outside the casements, sleet and ice began to dash against the windowpanes. Porphyro told her that they must flee before the house awakened. Madeline, afraid and trembling, followed her lover down the cold, gloomy corridors, through the wide deserted hall, and past the porter, asleep on his watch. So they fled—into the wintry dawn.

Critical Evaluation:

John Keats wrote "The Eve of St. Agnes" in January and February of 1819, the first of an astonishing spate of masterpieces that came one after another, despite his failing health and emotional turmoil. "La Belle Dame Sans Merci," "Lamia," and six great odes were all written before October of that year. The circumstance of his death shortly afterward seems to throw into a kind of relief the luscious descriptions of physical beauty in this and other poems. More striking still is the poet's refusal to take comfort in the simplistic assurances of any religious or philosophical system that denied either the complexity of mind or the reality and importance of sense. "The Eve of St. Agnes" manifests Keats's characteristic concern with the opposition and subtle connection of the sensual world to the interior life. He shared this preoccupation with other Romantic poets, notably Samuel Taylor Coleridge and William Wordsworth, taking as his subject the web of an antithesis at the heart of human experience; like them, he cloaked his meditations in sensuous imagery.

In this and other ways, Keats and all the Romantics abandoned the poetic theory of the century before. Eighteenth century poetry was formal, didactic, and objective in stance. Its chief aim was to show to humanity a picture of itself for its own improvement and edification. Its chief ornament was wit: puns, wordplay, satiric description, and so forth. In short, what eighteenth century poets saw as virtue in poetry was logic and rigid metrics. Nineteenth century poets wrote from a radically different philosophical base, due in part to the cataclysmic political changes surrounding the American and French revolutions. Before these upheavals occurred, a belief in order and measure extended into all facets of life, from social relations to literature; extremes were shunned in all things as unnatural, dangerous, and perhaps blasphemous.

After 1789, when the social order in France turned upside down, an expectation of the millennium arose in England, especially in liberal intellectual circles; the old rules of poetry were thrown off with the outworn social strictures, and a new aesthetic bloomed in their place. Its ruling faculty was imagination. The world seemed made new, and poetry released from bondage. Romantic poets frequently stated that poems ought to be composed on the inspiration of the moment, thereby faithfully to record the purity of the emotion. In fact, Keats and his contemporaries labored hard over their creations; they exerted themselves not to smoothness of meter but to preserving the grace of spontaneity while achieving precision in observation of natural and psychological phenomena. Poets saw themselves as charting hitherto unexplored reaches of human experience, extremes of joy and dejection, guilt and redemption, pride and degradation. They wrote meditations, confessions, and conversations, in which natural things were seen to abet internal states, and they wrote ballads and narratives, such as "The Eve of St. Agnes," set in the past or in distant parts of the world and using archaic language and rhythms to make the events related seem even more strange and wonderful. Over and over they described epiphanous moments when the human consciousness becomes one with nature, when all is made new, when divinity animates the inanimate, and the lowest creature seems wondrous. This way of seeing was thought to be a return to an earlier consciousness lost in early childhood, and is the theme of Wordsworth's seminal "Ode: Intimations of Immortality."

In "The Eve of St. Agnes," Keats attempts, among other things, to maintain this elevated state of mind throughout the narrative. He sets the story in medieval times, so that the familiar fairy-tale characters take on charm from their quaint surroundings, and from the archaic language in which they speak and are described. Its verse form is the smooth, supremely-difficult-to-write Spenserian stanza, with its slightly asymmetric rhyme scheme that avoids the monotony of couplet or quatrain, and the piquant extension of the ninth line which gives to the whole an irregularity echoing ordinary speech. The first five stanzas contrast the Beadsman, coldly at his prayers, with the "argent revelry" of the great hall. This imagery of cold and warmth, silver and scarlet, chastity and sensuality continues throughout the poem, a comment on the plot.

That the poem is named for a virgin martyr yet tells the story of an elopement is likewise significant; for the point of the poem, on the one hand, is that piety and passion are opposing but inseparable drives. Each without the other has no point of reference. Porphyro without Madeline becomes the gross Lord Maurice, the savage Hildebrand; Madeline without Porphyro becomes the Beadsman with his deathlike abrogation of sense. Instead, Porphyro is made to faint at the celestial beauty of Madeline at her prayers, Madeline to be wooed by songs and colors and delicacies. The passage describing the array of food that Porphyro set out is understandably famous; these are not mere groceries but rather the glowing essence of fruitfulness, tribute to a love match of the meditative and emotional faculties that, when accomplished in one individual, fulfills the whole human potential.

The other theme, or perhaps the other face of the same theme, is the relentless press of quotidian misery on the poetic personality, another favorite arena of reflection among the Romantics, and one that was poignantly near Keats's heart, menaced by tuberculosis as he was, and his younger brother having died of the disease the previous winter. The lovers are shown, unearthly fair, escaping from a house where wrath and drunkenness hold sway, bound for a dream-vision of happiness. Significantly, the poet does not follow them to their southern sanctuary. Instead he relates the wretched end of Angela, who dies "palsy-twitched" in her sleep; the cold sleep of the Beadsman among the ashes; the drunken nightmares of the Baron and his guests. The ending, in short, is not unreservedly happy, but partakes of that bittersweet emotion which in the midst of joy acknowledges wretchedness, the mark of a mind that strives for aesthetic detachment while believing in its duty to the rest of humankind.

"Critical Evaluation" by Edward E. Foster

Bibliography:

Danzig, Allan, ed. *Twentieth Century Interpretations of "The Eve of St. Agnes."* Englewood Cliffs, N.J.: Prentice-Hall, 1971. Excellent source for beginning discussion of Keats's poem. Contains seven essays exploring such topics as narrative structure, contrary states of imagination, musical and pictorial settings, techniques of composition, literary influences and the darker side of seduction.

Gibson, Gail McMurray. "Ave Madeline: Ironic Annunciation in Keats's 'The Eve of St. Agnes.'" *Keats-Shelley Journal* 26 (1977): 39-50. Examines how the religious details of the poem function as a parody of the Christian Annunciation and thus a measure of the inadequacies of the lover's spiritualized romance.

Stillinger, Jack. Introduction to "The Eve of St. Agnes," by John Keats. In *John Keats: Complete Poems.* Cambridge, Mass.: The Belknap Press of Harvard University Press, 1982. The best edition of the poem to date. Includes commentary on the chronology of composition, Keats's subsequent revisions, textual sources, and an extensive bibliography.

Talbot, Norman. "Porphyro's Enemies." *Essays in Criticism* 38 (1988): 215-231. Argues that Madeline, Angela, and the Beadsman offer only minor resistance to the exploits of Porphyro. Dramatic tension centers on the male protagonist, who fluctuates between romantic hero, hot-blooded opportunist, and religious devotee.

Wasserman, Earl. *The Finer Tone: Keats's Major Poems.* Baltimore: The Johns Hopkins University Press, 1953. A classic introduction to the poem. Discusses the central romance of Porphyro and Madeline in the context of the poem's sensual richness and imaginative intensity.

EVELINA
Or, The History of a Young Lady's Entrance into the World

Type of work: Novel
Author: Fanny Burney (Madame d'Arblay, 1752-1840)
Type of plot: Sentimental
Time of plot: Eighteenth century
Locale: England
First published: 1778

> *Principal characters:*
> SIR JOHN BELMONT, an English nobleman
> EVELINA, Sir John's unacknowledged daughter
> THE REVEREND MR. ARTHUR VILLARS, Evelina's guardian
> MADAME DUVAL, Evelina's grandmother
> LORD ORVILLE, Evelina's husband
> SIR CLEMENT WILLOUGHBY, a gentleman of fashion
> MRS. MIRVAN, Evelina's patroness

The Story:

Abandoned by her father and her maternal grandmother upon the death of her mother, Evelina had been for many years the ward of the Reverend Mr. Arthur Villars, an English clergyman. At last, her grandmother, Madame Duval, wrote from France to say that she would take charge of Evelina, providing proper proof of the child's relationship was forthcoming. Mr. Villars, however, refused to send Evelina to France. He also objected to the invitation of Mrs. Mirvan, who wanted Evelina to join her family in London. He thought that Evelina, having been brought up carefully at Berry Hill in Dorsetshire, should not be exposed to London society life, particularly so since her own father, Sir John Belmont, would not admit his parentage and she was without enough income to permit her to live as the Mirvans did.

After some urging, he finally allowed Evelina to visit Lady Howard, Mrs. Mirvan's mother, at Howard Grove. A short time later, Mrs. Mirvan and her daughter, who were delighted with Evelina, secured permission to have her accompany them to London.

Almost at once, she was swept into fashionable London life. Having grown up in the provinces, the city was a constant joy to her. She soon met Lord Orville, and both were attracted to each other. On several occasions, her lack of London manners caused her embarrassment, and she expressed a desire to return to Dorsetshire. Sir Clement Willoughby was her chief tormentor.

By chance, she met her odious grandmother, the vulgar and presumptuous Madame Duval. On an outing, the Frenchwoman became the subject of ridicule when she was pitched into a mudhole. Evelina met some of her other relations and found them no better than her grandmother.

Madame Duval, attaching herself to the Mirvans, succeeded in making Evelina very unhappy. Evelina went reluctantly to the opera with her relatives and was made miserable by their crudeness. Hoping to escape them, she joined Sir Clement but was only further embarrassed when Sir Clement intentionally delayed his coach while escorting her to her lodging. Evelina was severely scolded by her guardian for the escapade. In a letter to her, he indicated that he lived in daily fear for her honor. He was relieved when he heard that the Mirvans were at last returning with her to Howard Grove.

Lady Howard, urged on by Madame Duval, put forth the plan of forcing Sir John Belmont to acknowledge Evelina as his daughter. Mr. Villars did not approve of this action; he had promised Evelina's mother that the young woman would never know her cruel and unnatural father.

At Howard Grove, Evelina unknowingly participated in a cruel joke planned by Captain Mirvan and Sir Clement. Again made a laughingstock, Madame Duval took to her bed after she had been sent upon a fool's errand and had lost her false curls. When Sir John Belmont refused to admit that Evelina was his daughter, Madame Duval planned to take Evelina to confront Sir John in person and to demand his recognition. Mr. Villars would not listen to her proposal. He did agree, however, to let Evelina spend a month with her grandmother in London. Evelina was unhappy under Madame Duval's chaperonage because her vulgar relations attempted to use her to ingratiate themselves with her fashionable friends. Sir Clement Willoughby visited Evelina while she was staying with her grandmother, but Madame Duval embarrassed everyone by her uncivil remarks to him. She remembered the joke played on her at Howard Grove.

In her London lodgings, Evelina was instrumental in preventing the suicide of Mr. Macartney, an impoverished Scottish poet. Out of pity for his plight, she relieved his need with money from her own purse. At a fireworks display, Evelina was again chagrined, having been discovered by Lord Orville while she was in vulgar company.

Madame Duval announced that she hoped to marry Evelina to the boorish young son of Mr. Branghton, a silversmith. Mr. Branghton was Madame Duval's nephew. Evelina was much distressed, the more so when her grandmother's friends attached themselves to Lord Orville in a familiar manner. When Mr. Branghton asked his lordship's custom for any silver the nobleman might want to buy, Evelina felt ruined forever in Lord Orville's eyes.

In her distress, Evelina wrote to Mr. Villars, who ordered her to return immediately to Berry Hill. From there, she wrote about her London adventures to her friend, Miss Mirvan. A most painful surprise to her was a letter she had received from Lord Orville, to whom she had written to disclaim responsibility for her relatives' crudeness. His reply was so insulting that she became ill and had to be sent to a rest home at Bristol Hot Wells, where she went in the company of Mrs. Selwyn, a neighbor.

At the watering place, Evelina met many of her fashionable London friends, among them Lord Orville. He was so courteous that she had to forgive him for his impolite letter. As Evelina was beginning to feel at home once more among people of wealth and position, Mr. Macartney appeared and embarrassed her with his importunities.

A new arrival at the baths was Miss Belmont, an heiress reputed to be Sir John Belmont's daughter. Mrs. Selwyn, hearing of the young woman's identity, decided to learn more about Miss Belmont. Mrs. Selwyn was convinced that Evelina was the true daughter of Sir John.

Mr. Macartney was trying to return the money Evelina had given him, but she did not want her friends to learn that she had ever known him. She feared that they would suspect her of having had an affair with him. Lord Orville, however, encouraged her to see the unfortunate young poet. From Mr. Macartney, Evelina learned that he believed himself to be an unacknowledged son of Sir John Belmont. Evelina, realizing that she must be the sister of Mr. Macartney, did not reveal her knowledge.

When Sir John Belmont returned to England, Mr. Villars was finally stirred to action against him; for by introducing to society the woman who posed as his daughter, Sir John was indicating that Evelina was an impostor. Determined that Evelina should have her rights, Mr. Villars prepared to force Sir John to acknowledge Evelina as his daughter.

Through the good offices of Mrs. Selwyn and others, the affair was at last untangled. The supposed daughter of Sir John proved to be the daughter of a penniless nurse, who had substituted her own child for Lady Belmont's infant. Evelina, delighted to learn that Sir John's attitude had been the result of error and not neglect, was happily reconciled with her father, who received her warmly. The impostor was treated with great kindness by all concerned as she herself was innocent of the design. She married Mr. Macartney, who was also acknowledged by Sir John. As Sir John's daughter, Evelina was sought after by Lord Orville, to whom she gladly gave her hand in marriage.

Critical Evaluation:

Evelina is Fanny Burney's first and most successful novel. When it was published in 1778, the book's appeal was attributed to its sentimental value, but it has held lasting interest because of the realistic portrayal of eighteenth century English life. In *Evelina*, Burney's attentiveness to the manners and pretentiousness of socialites enabled her to show a culture its foibles. *Evelina* is particularly descriptive of the social position of women.

Sensitively reared by the Reverend Mr. Villars, the heroine, Evelina, has become a kind, compassionate young woman. As she steps into the social life of London, her unblemished perception of society affords both delight at its marvels and disdain for its unscrupulousness and frivolity. Her letters to Mr. Villars convey clear images of London high society.

Evelina first writes with some amazement that London life begins so late that people spend the morning in bed. She adjusts, however, to the nightlife and enjoys the opera, plays, and other events with which she and her company are entertained almost nightly. She is annoyed by audiences who are so talkative throughout the events that the artists cannot be heard, and she quickly realizes that the purpose of the events is more for socializing than for the merit of the performances themselves.

Burney places her heroine with various guardians in a variety of situations in city and country. Evelina's first awkward fortnight in London with the kind Mirvan ladies abruptly contrasts with her second visit in London in the company of Madame Duval and her relatives, the Branghtons. Crude and ill-mannered, they cause Evelina embarrassment by her forced association with them. In her third venture away from her benefactor Mr. Villars, Evelina is again in cultured company under the guardianship of the aggressive Mrs. Selwyn.

In each group, regardless of its social position, Evelina finds individuals of sincerity and those who are masters of divisiveness and deception. Mrs. Mirvan and Maria are sincere and well-mannered. Although uncouth, cruel, and contemptuous, Captain Mirvan is, nevertheless, sincere. He is his own person, honest in his brutal way. Madame Duval shares with her tormentor, Captain Mirvan, the quality of being her own person, disagreeable as she, too, may be.

Evelina readily acknowledges the honorable qualities of Lord Orville and Mr. Macartney. She also quickly perceives the duplicity of Sir Clement, Mr. Lovel, Lord Merton, the Branghtons, Lady Louisa, and Mr. Smith. In lady or silversmith, airs and presumptuousness repel Evelina. Evelina is shocked at the insincerity of those for whom honor and good manners directly relate to dress, immediate company, and situation. Lord Merton ignores Evelina while Lady Louisa is present yet lavishes her with attention at Lady Louisa's absence. Sir Clement is a chameleon whose attention to Evelina is gained at any expense. Lady Louisa acts out roles constantly, purposely ignoring Evelina until she learns that Evelina is to become her brother's wife.

Evelina detects affectation and shows it as being ridiculous. She describes for Mr. Villars an episode from her first dance at which a young man approached her with comically stilted mannerisms and speech. "Allow me, Madam . . . the honour and happiness—if I am not so unhappy as to address you too late—to have the happiness and honour." She confesses that she had to turn away to conceal her laughter.

Evelina is bewildered by the social etiquette that she has had no opportunity to learn at Berry Hill, but her sense of propriety causes her to suffer for her ignorance. She is always aware of her dependent position and constantly relies on her protectors, benefactors, or guardians.

Burney did not intend that Evelina's dependence be read negatively. On the contrary, Evelina was idyllic in her feminine compliance and sensibility. She was a model lady for the times. It is interesting to note, however, how vastly the roles and rights of men and women in the novel differ. Mr. Lovel says, "I have an insuperable aversion to strength, either in body or mind, in a female." Lord Merton echoes a similar view—"for a woman wants nothing to recommend her but beauty and good nature; in everything else she is either impertinent or unnatural."

Burney comments on women's sensibility through her characters. Lady Louisa, whose feigned delicate nature corresponds with her posturing, seems to be the extreme of insincere sensibility. Mrs. Selwyn represents another extreme. She is powerful and aggressive and is disliked by both men and women for her outspokenness. Evelina wishes that Mrs. Selwyn were more sensitive to her needs in awkward situations and finds her lacking in femininity. Evelina writes, "I have never been personally hurt by her want of gentleness, a virtue which nevertheless seems so essential a part of the female character." Lord Orville, the ideal male in the novel, is described by Evelina as "feminine," a compliment to his gentle character. Evelina's description of Mrs. Selwyn as "masculine," however, is definitely a negative criticism.

Given the impropriety of acting independently, Evelina and all gentlewomen must rely upon others for advice. Unfortunately, those counselors are likely to take advantage of women's dependency. Fortunately, Evelina's good sense alerts her to unreliable protectors, but her situation clearly indicates the powerless situation of women who are perpetually rescued or victimized.

Perhaps Mr. Villars' response to Evelina's interference in the attempted suicide of Mr. Macartney best expresses Burney's attitude toward women. "Though gentleness and modesty are the peculiar attributes of your sex, yet fortitude and firmness, when occasion demands them, are virtues as noble and as becoming in women as in men."

Evelina was first published without the name of the author and was generally assumed to have been written by a man. Burney was as dependent as her Evelina in getting the book into publication; a male secret agent smuggled the manuscript to the publisher.

"Critical Evaluation" by Mary Peace Finley

Bibliography:
Bloom, Harold, ed. *Fanny Burney's "Evelina."* New York: Chelsea House, 1988. Includes previously published material, plus Julia L. Epstein's "Evelina's Deceptions: The Letter and the Spirit" and Jennifer A. Wagner's "Privacy and Anonymity in *Evelina*."
Brown, Martha G. "Fanny Burney's Feminism: Gender or Genre?" In *Fetter'd or Free? British Women Novelists, 1670-1815*, edited by Mary Anne Schofield and Cecilia Macheski. Athens: Ohio University Press, 1986. Argues that Burney, as novelist, belongs to the romance tradition rather than the feminist one, except when she undertakes feminism in her last novel.
Cutting, Rose Marie. "Defiant Women: The Growth of Feminism in Fanny Burney's Novels." *Studies in English Literature, 1500-1900* 17, no. 3 (Summer, 1977): 519-530. An early feminist treatment of Burney. Discusses the financial difficulties of her heroines.

Doody, Margaret Anne. *Frances Burney: The Life in the Works*. New Brunswick, N.J.: Rutgers University Press, 1988. Examines all the novels not only as a reflection of but also an indictment of Burney's society's perversities of structure, function, and belief. Discusses Burney's insight into her society's comical and obsessive traits. Judiciously feminist.

Eighteenth Century Fiction 3, no. 4 (July, 1991). Entire issue devoted to *Evelina*. Includes Gina Campbell and David Oakleaf on the heroine's relationship to her father; Margaret Doody on the novel's place in the literature of its time; Julia Epstein on critical contexts; and Susan Greenfield and Amy Pawl on matrilineal and nominal aspects of authorship.

EVERY MAN IN HIS HUMOUR

Type of work: Drama
Author: Ben Jonson (1573-1637)
Type of plot: Comedy
Time of plot: Late sixteenth century
Locale: London
First performed: 1598; first published, 1601; revised, 1605, 1616

> *Principal characters:*
> KNOWELL, an old gentleman
> EDWARD KNOWELL, his son
> BRAINWORM, Knowell's servant
> DOWNRIGHT, a plain man
> WELLBRED, his half brother
> KITELY, a merchant
> CAPTAIN BOBADILL, a cowardly braggart
> DAME KITELY, Kitely's wife
> COB, a water carrier
> TIB, Cob's wife

The Story:

In Hogsden, a conservative suburb north of London's wall, Edward Knowell, a dignified, practical citizen, was somewhat concerned over his son Edward's interest in poetry. Old Knowell was further alarmed that his nephew Stephen, a country simpleton, showed interest in the gentle art of falconry. Old Knowell wished to have his son and his nephew engaged in more practical arts.

One day he was handed a letter meant for his son. The letter, signed by Wellbred, a London gallant, was an invitation to young Knowell to renew his association with a group of young madcaps. Old Knowell, having read the letter, and being convinced that his son was up to no good, had his servant, Brainworm, deliver the letter to the youth in his study, with the directions not to reveal that the letter had been opened. Contrary to orders, Brainworm told his young master that old Knowell had read the letter. The young man, delighted with the prospect of fun in the city, gave little thought to what his father might do.

Meanwhile, in the city, Matthew, an urban fool, called on Captain Bobadill, a spurious cavalier who roomed in the low-class lodgings of Cob, a water carrier. Matthew, his taste having been questioned by Downright, a plain-spoken man, asked for and received instructions in dueling from the braggart, swaggering Bobadill.

In his house nearby, Kitely, a merchant, discussed with Downright the dissolute ways of his brother-in-law, Wellbred, who roomed with the Kitelys. Wellbred had become the leader of a group of scoffers, young men who apparently had no respect for anyone or anything; their greatest sport was to discover fools and make sport of them. Kitely feared that his relation to this sporting crew might endanger his business reputation. In addition, he was jealous of his wife. When Matthew and Bobadill called for Wellbred, Bobadill insulted Downright on Matthew's behalf. Kitely restrained Downright from avenging his honor on the spot.

Brainworm, young Knowell's ally, appeared in Moorfields disguised as a disabled veteran for the purpose of intercepting old Knowell, who he knew would follow young Knowell into

2136

the city to spy on him. Brainworm encountered the old gentleman, who, out of pity, hired Brainworm, who had styled himself Fitz-Sword, as a personal servant.

Inside the city wall, young Knowell revealed to Wellbred that old Knowell had read Wellbred's letter; the pair agreed to make a joke of the situation. Stephen, Matthew, and Bobadill provided rare fun for young Knowell and Wellbred. Stephen assumed a ridiculous air of melancholy, which he thought befitted a lovesick poet; Matthew, a poetaster, reflected this melancholy in what he thought was the urban manner. Bobadill provided entertainment with preposterous lies about his military experiences and with oaths which especially impressed rustic Stephen. Brainworm joined the group, revealed his true identity, and reported to young Knowell that old Knowell had come to the city and was stopping at the house of Justice Clement.

Kitely, meanwhile, obsessed with a growing fear that his wife might be unfaithful to him, decided to forego a profitable business transaction in another part of the city. Later he changed his mind, but before he left home he ordered his servant, Thomas Cash, to report immediately the coming to the house of Wellbred and his companions, or of any stranger. The young gallants came to the house shortly afterward. Cash, in desperation, enlisted Cob to carry the message to Kitely. Having received the message at the house of Justice Clement, where he was doing business, Kitely hurried home, plagued by the imagination of a jealous husband.

In Kitely's house, Downright reproached his sister, Mistress Kitely, for permitting their brother, Wellbred, to use her house as a meeting place for his mad company. Matthew, to the amusement of young Knowell and Wellbred, read bits of stolen verse to Bridget, Kitely's maiden sister. When Downright asked Wellbred and his followers to leave, rapiers were drawn. After Cash and the other servants had separated the antagonists, Bobadill made brave gestures. As Wellbred and his companions left, Kitely entered excitedly and began a search for young Knowell, whose virtues were being praised by Mistress Kitely and Bridget. He feared the women had hidden the young man in the house.

Armed with a warrant and aroused by Kitely's husbandly apprehensions, Cob went by his house to see that all was well with his wife Tib. He advised her to remain indoors and not to admit anyone. Meanwhile Brainworm, as the disabled veteran, returned, at the direction of young Knowell, to inform old Knowell that his son could be apprehended at Cob's house, where an assignation was to take place.

Downright arrived in Moorfields while Bobadill entertained young Knowell, Matthew, and Stephen with unbelievable accounts of his prowess as a swordsman. After Downright disarmed Bobadill easily and thrashed him, Matthew, frightened, ran back to the city. Stephen claimed the russet cloak that Downright left at the scene of the fight.

Back in town, Kitely continued to be tortured by his jealousy. Brainworm, now disguised as Justice Clement's man, Formal, entered and told Kitely that Justice Clement wished to see him immediately. While Kitely again admonished Cash to guard the house against all interlopers, Wellbred conspired with Brainworm for the marriage of young Knowell and Bridget. Wellbred, ever seeking amusement at the expense of others, suggested to Mistress Kitely that perhaps her husband was a philanderer. At this, Mistress Kitely departed to spy on the activities of her husband. Kitely returned to find his wife absent, and when he was told that she had gone to Cob's house he followed, fearful that he had been cuckolded. Wellbred took the opportunity, while neither of the Kitelys was home, to take Bridget to the church.

After their shameful conduct in Moorfields, Bobadill and Matthew met in the city; Bobadill rationalized their cowardice. They encountered Brainworm, still disguised as Formal, and gave him jewelry and clothing to pawn for the price of a warrant to arrest Downright, who they said wore a russet cloak.

The tricks played by Brainworm, young Knowell, and Wellbred began to rebound on the knavish threesome. Old Knowell went to Cob's house, where he was told by the indignant Tib that she knew no Edward Knowell. At the same time, Mistress Kitely appeared and was suspected by old Knowell of being young Knowell's mistress. Kitely arrived next. He and his wife exchanged bitter words of mistrust, for Kitely suspected old Knowell of being his wife's paramour, Mistress Kitely accused her husband of dalliance with Tib. Cob appeared and thrashed his wife for not obeying him. As a result of misunderstandings all around, Kitely insisted that all concerned present themselves before Justice Clement.

In the meantime, Brainworm, having assumed the disguise of a constable, and accompanied by Matthew and Bobadill, arrested Stephen, who was wearing Downright's russet cloak. Brainworm's mistake was quickly recognized, but when Downright himself approached, Matthew and Bobadill departed in haste. Downright, although Stephen had surrendered the cloak, insisted that the matter be explained to Justice Clement.

Practically all of the principals having gathered in the hall of his house, Justice Clement held an investigation of the misunderstandings which had taken place. Brainworm threw off his disguise and explained his part in the confusion of the day. He was forgiven by his master, old Knowell. Young Knowell and Bridget, now man and wife, entered with Wellbred. Kitely and Mistress Kitely, as well as Cob and Tib, were reconciled after explanations had been made. Justice Clement, having seen peace and trust reestablished, dedicated the ensuing evening to celebration and conviviality.

Critical Evaluation:

Ben Jonson substantially revised *Every Man in His Humour* for his 1616 folio publication and added a famous prologue that defends his sort of comedy. He changed the setting of the play from exotic Italy to everyday London, renamed the characters, eliminated extraneous speeches, and particularized general and high-flown speeches of several characters. He writes in the prologue that the play will not utilize the marvelous or the mechanistic such as thunder machines, "But deeds and language such as men do use." He also explains that his comedy will "sport with human follies, not with crimes." *Every Man in His Humour* is thus a lighthearted portrayal of human stupidity, and the medieval theory of the four humors is not very important to the play. For Jonson, the humors were simply the exaggerated and often caricatured manners of people, so that the comedy of humors is really a comedy of manners.

Perhaps more than any other comedy by Jonson, *Every Man in His Humour* is a comedy of noninteraction—in structure and plot, in character and language. By contrast, Shakespearean comedy thrives on close consequence; for example, the resolution of subplot and main plot always results in the plotlines' crossing. What resolution there is at the end of *Every Man in His Humour* is artificial, imposed by Justice Clement, and not strongly felt by the audience to be genuine. The traditional concluding symbols of judgment, marriage, and banquet are arbitrarily imposed on an ending which would otherwise seem hopelessly fragmentary.

Structurally, noninteraction is here very apparent, because the subplots that serve to make up plot seem to be accidental rather than mutually necessary. Meetings between members of different subplots are coincidental and suggest disorder rather than resolution; the meetings in Moorfields and outside Cob's house are good examples. Also, Jonson's characters are each extremely individualistic, almost solipsistic in their belief in the importance of their own existence. This subjectivism produces mazes of misapprehension and nonunderstanding when characters try to communicate. This condition is compounded by the disguises of Brainworm, who casts himself as manipulator of much of the action.

Most of the characters seem unable to practice directness; they resort to communication through go-betweens, thus increasing the possibilities of mistakes and misperceptions. Knowell deals with Edward through Brainworm, who also mediates for Edward with his father. Wellbred conducts Edward's courtship; Kitely tells Cash of his fears about his wife, and Cash then sends Cob with the message to Kitely. Bobadill insults Downright for Matthew, and Justice Clement even relates to a client who is standing before him by means of his assistant. A desire to avoid encounters motivates much of the action: Kitely and Dame Kitely do not speak their minds to each other; Knowell is worried about Edward's and Wellbred's friendship; Brainworm tries to keep apart those he is manipulating. Direct, emotion-filled conversation usually does not occur. Bridget and Edward utter not a single word to each other either before or after marriage, nor does Knowell congratulate Edward. Kitely's feeble remarks to his wife after their reconciliation suggest their essential estrangement. The only place for protestations of real feeling is in soliloquy. The characters are incapable of genuine dialogue.

Noninteraction comes to its logical conclusion in the events which take place before Cob's house (Act IV). Instead of creating a recognition and discovery scene, the characters misunderstand the action and one another because they refuse to go beyond their ossified solipsisms. Thus, Knowell "recognizes" Dame Kitely as Edward's lover; Kitely believes Knowell to be his wife's lover; and Knowell mistakes Kitely for Edward. Justice Clement's plea for reconciliation is not met by any real change in the characters.

In this early Jonson comedy, the debate about poetry that frames the play (Knowell's opening speech and Clement's closing one) does not provide the unity that similar debates do in later Jonson works. The ideal of poetry seems unlikely here to do more than achieve an arbitrary connection with the unity dictated by Clement. Although the characters often speak about poetry, they do not seem to be particularly concerned with it.

As in most Jonsonian comedy, characters' names—be they serious, satiric, or comic—disclose ideas about personality. Justice Clement, as his name suggests, tempers his justice with mercy, but Knowell usually acts the opposite of a knowledgeable father. Some of the characters are recognizable types deriving from Roman comedy, especially that of Plautus: Brainworm, the witty servant; Kitely, the jealous husband; Knowell, the strict father; Wellbred, the man-about-town; Bobadill, the *miles gloriosus*, or braggart soldier. Although Jonson borrowed these typed characters, he made them thoroughly English and assimilated them to his ideas of human follies.

The characters are often connected by contrasts, so that those who appear similar are shown to be different, while those who seem opposed are linked. Thus Matthew, the town gull, supposedly different from Stephen, the country gull, is actually the same sort of person. Both ape fashions in sport (rapier dueling or hawking) and praise a particular fashion in dress; the difference is that the town gull is in style and the country gull is out of style. Similarly, Edward is shown to be essentially different from his friend Wellbred—the one serious and temperate, the other frivolous and extreme. There are also sets of characters that seem to parody each other's behavior: Cob's jealousy burlesques Kitely's, and both reflect Knowell's spying on his son; the relationship of Edward to Wellbred is mimicked by that of Matthew to Bobadill. These contrasts and distorted mirrors help to give a structural balance to the play but do not change its nonrelational quality. Each character is set on a particular course by his personality, a course that is not altered by any collision with another person.

Every Man in His Humour portrays a multiplicity of human aberrations, although here they are more lighthearted follies. Jonson's favorite satiric targets can be found—illusions about education, love, poetry, social place—as a group of characters reiterates each issue. Justice

Clement's plea "to put off all discontent" marks the necessary illusion of change and unity at the end. Only the later Ben Jonson (of *Bartholomew Fair*, 1614) can accept these follies and aberrations as part of human nature.

"Critical Evaluation" by Margaret McFadden-Gerber

Bibliography:
Barton, Anne. *Ben Jonson, Dramatist*. Cambridge, England: Cambridge University Press, 1984. Compares Jonson's and William Shakespeare's treatment of the country and the city as settings. Indicates that contrary to Elizabethan convention, Jonson would not allow sudden conversions in character. Analyzes Jonson's revisions in a later version of the work.
Brock, D. Heyward. *A Ben Jonson Companion*. Bloomington: Indiana University Press, 1983. A valuable resource. Defines key terms. Identifies both real people who were important in Jonson's world and characters who appear in the plays. Selected bibliography.
Dutton, Richard. *Ben Jonson: To the First Folio*. Cambridge, England: Cambridge University Press, 1983. A chapter on the early plays shows how Jonson had to educate his audience to appreciate a kind of comedy different from Shakespeare's because Jonson's comedy relies heavily on neoclassical principles.
Riggs, David. *Ben Jonson: A Life*. Cambridge, Mass.: Harvard University Press, 1989. A chapter on the comedy of humors discusses the theory and the origins of that genre and explains how Jonson's theory of satire differed from Shakespeare's.
Watson, Robert N. *Ben Jonson's Parodic Strategies: Literary Imperialism in the Comedies*. Cambridge, Mass.: Harvard University Press, 1987. The chapter on *Every Man in His Humour*, "The Purging of Monstrous Conventions," shows how "wits supersede the fools," and how satire supersedes the usual plot patterns.

EVERY MAN OUT OF HIS HUMOUR

Type of work: Drama
Author: Ben Jonson (1573-1637)
Type of plot: Comedy
Time of plot: Early seventeenth century
Locale: Probably London
First performed: 1599; first published, 1600

> *Principal characters:*
> MACILENTE, a malcontent
> CARLO BUFFONE, a scoffer
> SOGLIARDO, a wealthy country fool
> SORDIDO, a rural miser
> FUNGOSO, his son
> PUNTARVOLO, a fantastic knight
> FASTIDIOUS BRISK, a courtier
> SAVIOLINA, a lady of the court

The Story:

Macilente, disgusted by the injustices of society, had fled to the country. As he lay idly under a tree he overheard a conversation between the wealthy young farmer, Sogliardo, and Carlo Buffone, a railing cynic whom the rustic bumpkin had chosen as his guide in becoming a gentleman. Macilente winced at Sogliardo's presumption and at Buffone's callous instructions to the foolish Sogliardo. Buffone, seeing Macilente and knowing him to be a malcontent, hurried away with Sogliardo, but in departing he told Macilente that they were going to Puntarvolo's house.

Still musing under the tree, Macilente next listened while Sordido, a miserly farmer, consulted his almanac and hoped for rainy weather in order that his hoarded grain might soar in value. A farmhand delivered to Sordido a note, an official order for him to bring his grain to market. Sordido scorned the order and swore that he would hide his surplus harvest.

In front of Puntarvolo's house, Buffone and Sogliardo talked with the braggart courtier, Sir Fastidious Brisk. The three watched with amazement Puntarvolo's return from the hunt. Puntarvolo, an old-fashioned fantastic knight, was given to extravagances in the form of little homecoming plays which he wrote himself. Assuming the role of a strange knight, Puntarvolo approached his house, inquired about the owner, and heard his virtues praised by his indulgent wife and her women. In another part of the play Puntarvolo wooed his wife in the manner of a knight-errant. Sordido and his son, Fungoso, a law student in the city, appeared. Fungoso was so impressed with the stylish cut of Brisk's clothes that he asked his uncle, Sogliardo, to get him money from Sordido, ostensibly for law books, but actually for a suit of clothes in the latest style. All the while hoping for rain, Sordido reluctantly gave his son money, but not enough.

Reaction varied to Puntarvolo's announcement that he had wagered five thousand pounds at five-to-one odds that he and his wife and their dog could travel to Constantinople and back without a fatal mishap. Buffone saw in this venture material for a colossal joke, while Brisk was interested in investing a hundred pounds in the venture. Fungoso, meanwhile, taken with Brisk's courtly manner and dress, was pleased to learn that his brother-in-law, Deliro, was Brisk's merchant.

2141

The next day Macilente advised his friend Deliro to exercise some control in his doting love for his wife, since this dotage caused the wife, Fallace, to react petulantly to Deliro's affections. Fungoso, wearing a new suit, went to Deliro's house and borrowed money from his sister, Fallace, in order to complete his costume. No sooner had he received the money than Brisk entered in a new suit. Fungoso, frustrated by this new development, wrote his father for more money. Brisk, meanwhile, bragged of his actually nonexistent triumphs at court; he also made arrangements with Deliro for mortgaging his land in the country. Fallace, impatient with her work-a-day husband, admired Brisk's courtliness and dreamed of becoming a court lady.

Buffone, accompanied by Puntarvolo, tried to find two retainers for his newly-arrived gentleman, Sogliardo. Puntarvolo, who had with him a dog and a cat, explained that his wife had withdrawn from the Constantinople venture and that the cat would go in her place.

Brisk promised to take the hopeful Macilente to court if Macilente would purchase himself a fitting suit of clothes. Actually, it was Macilente's purpose to discover Brisk's true standing at the court. Fungoso and his tailor, ever in pursuit of the latest fashion, studied Brisk's clothes as the knight talked to his companions. Sogliardo, who desired to have every gentlemanly attainment, retained a braggart down-at-heels rascal, Shift.

The good weather which prevailed in the country became the despair of Sordido. In desperation, he attempted to hang himself, but he was rescued from that folly by the neighboring farmers, who would save him despite his despicable miserliness. The revelation to him of his evil nature caused him to have a change of heart; he vowed to be a kind and generous neighbor henceforward.

Having dressed themselves in new clothes, Brisk and Macilente appeared at the court, Macilente to observe court life and Brisk's deportment. Macilente marveled at the inane discourse between Brisk and Saviolina, a court lady, and he was amused when Saviolina put Brisk out of countenance for his abominable habit of smoking.

Fallace, meanwhile, dreamed of the virtues of courtier Fastidious Brisk and paid no attention to Deliro's efforts to please her. When Macilente told them of Brisk's folly at court, Deliro was determined to foreclose on the knight. Fallace, shocked at Macilente's disloyalty and eager to help Brisk, sent Fungoso, whom she gave money to buy himself a new suit, to warn Brisk of her husband's intentions.

Brisk failed to keep an appointment at the notary's, where he was to contribute a hundred pounds to Puntarvolo's venture. Not finding Brisk immediately, Deliro had time to reconsider his plan. He decided not to foreclose on Brisk and he renounced Macilente's friendship because Macilente, he felt, had unreasonably urged him to be more realistic in his attitude toward his wife. Sogliardo, meanwhile, was delighted with his man Shift, who pretended to be a former highwayman, but who was, in reality, a shiftless, cowardly indigent. Brisk made his belated appearance at the notary's, with the explanation that he had been detained by ladies of the court. Fungoso, having gone to see his tailor, had failed in his mission to intercept Brisk.

Puntarvolo prepared for his journey to Constantinople with his dog and cat. Sogliardo, persuaded by Buffone and Brisk that the time had finally come, decided to become a courtier. All of his acquaintances conspired to make a fool of him. Fungoso, dressed in what he thought was the latest fashion, discovered Brisk to be wearing a new suit and was unhappy.

At the palace foolish old Puntarvolo put his dog in the care of a surly groom. Macilente privately obtained the dog from the groom and poisoned it. Brisk and Puntarvolo told Saviolina that they were presenting to her an incomparable courtier, Sogliardo, and that this courtier enjoyed playing the part of a country boor. Confronted by clownish Sogliardo, Saviolina insisted that she could detect the gentleman in him; she was appalled to discover that Sogliardo, who was not aware of the joke, was a rude peasant. When Puntarvolo missed his dog, he accused Shift of doing away with the animal and threatened to beat the man. Shift, frightened, confessed, to the disenchantment of Sogliardo, that he had never had the courage to commit even one of the crimes of which he had boasted.

At the Mitre Tavern, Buffone, who could not endure the follies and affectations of court life, greeted his companions. Puntarvolo, dejected by the loss of his dog and the loss of his wager, was teased by Buffone. In a rage, Puntarvolo sealed Buffone's lips with sealing wax. When the police arrived, everyone tried to flee. Brisk was seized. Fungoso, hiding under a table, was discovered and held to pay the reckoning for all the company had eaten and drunk.

Macilente, seeing in the situation a chance to rid Deliro and Fallace of their humors, sent Deliro to rescue Fungoso at the tavern and Fallace to the jail to comfort Brisk. Deliro paid the bill at the Mitre Tavern. Fungoso declared that he was through with fashion forever. Macilente then sent Deliro to the jail to obtain Brisk's release, after telling him that by so doing Deliro would be reconciled to his wife. At the jail Deliro, seeing Fallace's interest in Brisk, was suddenly awakened from his misperceptions. Brisk was doomed to serve a term for his debts. Thus the air was cleared and all who had been taken with a folly were cured.

Critical Evaluation:

Every Man in His Humour (1598) having been a tremendous success, Ben Jonson, possibly urged on by his fellow investors in the theater, wrote *Every Man out of His Humour* as a companion piece to his earlier play. In this play, produced the following year, Jonson over-reached himself: There are too many characters and the plot seems to ramble pointlessly. One explanation for the comparative weakness of the play lies in the fact that at the time of its composition Jonson was actively engaged in the so-called War of the Theaters, a controversy in which rival playwrights employed the stage to satirize each other and to ridicule actors of the rival companies. As a play, *Every Man out of His Humour* is a hodgepodge that manages somehow to work out; as personal satire it no longer holds meaning for the modern audience. Its subject and treatment, however, make it a work of particular interest to historians of literature.

Although intended as a battle in the War of the Theaters, particularly as an attack upon Thomas Dekker and John Marston, *Every Man out of His Humour* is more than that. Jonson's comedy of humors conceived of stage personalities on the basis of a ruling trait or passion, much as Dickens later gave his fictional characters certain dominant traits or characteristics. By placing these typified traits in juxtaposition, the spark of comedy was struck in their conflict and contrast. The result, in *Every Man out of His Humour*, is often funny. Jonson possessed an arrogant, self-righteous personality and he smarted under the satire of his competitors, seeking to get back at them with this play. The satirical picture of contemporary manners, vivid carica-tures, and the witty dialogue carry the play beyond any mere personal attacks. *Every Man out of His Humour* not only satirizes individuals but also levels a general attack upon corruptions.

Jonson could not resist lampooning his enemies, and he raised dramatic lampooning to an art. Marston probably was intended as the character Carlo Buffone, that "public, scurrilous, and profane jester." Asper is undoubtedly meant to be a comic idealization of Jonson himself— wholly admirable and just, "an ingenious and free spirit" and "one whom no servile hope of gain or frosty apprehension of danger, can make to be a parasite."

While John Lyly and others were perfecting the filigree of their prose for courtly audiences, another kind of prose was beginning to be heard in the popular theater, a rough-and-tumble language based on the vernacular. Jonson was among the writers adopting a more abrupt, staccato language, truer to life than the oratorical speeches of most of his contemporaries. The speeches of Carlo Buffone and some of the other characters in *Every Man out of His Humour* simulate the real language of Jonson's time much more closely than had been done before. Carlo's spiteful disposition is chiefly revealed in his penchant for coining scurrilous likenesses, and he leaps in a single speech from the figure of a starved dog to that of scalding oil and fire to that of gunpowder, all to describe Macilente. His speech rhythms trip, stumble, and flicker back and forth between metaphoric and literal abuse.

The characters in this play remain isolated, blocked off from one another, immobilized in their humors. The plot is a kaleidoscopic series of characteristic poses adopted by the personalities; each individual pursues his or her humour, oblivious of everything else. For example, Fungoso, eyes greedily fastened on Fastidious Brisk's suit, makes half-answers to his uncle, while privately calculating how much it will cost him to duplicate the suit. Sogliardo, at the same time, is too engrossed by the prospect of vulgar pleasures in London to notice Fungoso's inattention. Sordido, scarcely aware of the others, gazes into the sky for signs of rain that will raise the value of his wheat.

Jonson's characters rail at one another in a scorching indictment of folly; but they are not mere mouthpieces for their author. Even during the War of the Theaters, Jonson was too much of an artist to use the satiric speeches of his characters merely as clubs. Falling victim to their own imbalance of humors and distempered view of the world, they nevertheless always have their place in a larger design.

Bibliography:
Beaurline, L. A. *Jonson and Elizabethan Comedy: Essays in Dramatic Rhetoric*. San Marino, Calif.: Huntington Library, 1978. Analyzes the rhetorical devices Jonson uses to satirize literary pretensions. The intent of *Every Man out of His Humour* is more "corrective" than its predecessor's, *Every Man in His Humour*, and its occasional roughness derives from its being an experiment.
Brock, D. Heyward. *A Ben Jonson Companion*. Bloomington: Indiana University Press, 1983. A guide to Jonson's life and works and to the literary milieu in which Jonson flourished. Plays are summarized; identifies characters in the works and people in Jonson's life. Defines literary terms and includes bibliography.
Dessen, Alan C. *Jonson's Moral Comedy*. Evanston, Ill.: Northwestern University Press, 1971. Sees Jonson as converting the materials of nondramatic verse satire to the stage in *Every Man out of His Humour*. The characters Macilente and Carlo Buffone replace the satirist of the nondramatic tradition. *Every Man out of His Humour* reveals much about Jonson's aims as a satirist.
Enck, John J. *Jonson and the Comic Truth*. Madison: University of Wisconsin Press, 1957. Useful discussion of the background to the theory of humors and an analysis of Jonson's adaptation of it. Identifies Desiderius Erasmus' *The Praise of Folly* (1509) as a source of inspiration.
Watson, Robert N. *Ben Jonson's Parodic Strategy: Literary Imperialism in the Comedies*. Cambridge, Mass.: Harvard University Press, 1987. Stresses three features of *Every Man out of His Humour*: the indifference to unity in plot and tone; the treatment of literary characters; and the attention to audience attitudes.

EVERYMAN

Type of work: Drama
Author: Unknown
Type of plot: Morality
Time of plot: Indeterminate
Locale: Indeterminate
First extant version: 1508

Principal characters:
GOD
DEATH
EVERYMAN
GOOD-DEEDS

The Story:

One day a Messenger appeared to announce that in the beginning of life, human beings should look to the ending, for they shall see how all earthly possessions avail little in the final reckoning. Sin may look sweet at first, but in the end it causes the soul to weep in pain.

Then God spoke. All living creatures were unkind to him. They lived with no spiritual thought in their worldly possessions. The crucifixion was a lesson they had forgotten. Human beings had turned to the seven deadly sins, and every year their state grew worse. Therefore, God had decided to have a reckoning, lest humankind become more brutish than the beasts.

At an imperative summons, Death came to receive his instructions. He was ordered to search out all human beings and tell them that they had to make a pilgrimage to their final reckoning. Death promised to be cruel in his search for everyone who lived outside God's law.

Spying Everyman walking unconcernedly about his business, his mind on fleshly lust and treasure, Death bade him stand still and asked him if he had forgotten his maker. Death announced that God had dispatched him in all haste to warn Everyman. Everyman was to make a long journey, and he was to take with him his full book of accounts. He was to be very careful, for he had done many bad deeds and only a few good ones. In Paradise, he would soon be forced to account for his life.

Everyman protested that Death could not have been further from his thoughts at the time. Death, who set no store by worldly goods or rank, was adamant; whom he summoned all must obey. Everyman cried in vain for respite. Then he asked if he must go on the long journey alone. Death assured him that he could take any companions who would make the journey with him. Reminding him that his life was only his on loan, Death said he would return very shortly, after allowing Everyman an opportunity to find companions for his journey.

Weeping for his plight and wishing he had never been born, Everyman thought of Fellowship, with whom he had spent so many agreeable days in sport and play. Fortunately, he saw Fellowship and spoke to him. Seeing Everyman's sad countenance, Fellowship asked his trouble. Everyman told him he was in deep sorrow because he had to make a journey. Fellowship reminded him of their past friendship and vowed that he would go anywhere with him, even to Hell. Greatly heartened, Everyman told him of Death's appearance and his urgent summons. Fellowship thought of the long trip from which there would be no return and decided against accompanying Everyman. He would go with him in sport and play, he declared,

2145

or to seek lusty women, but he definitely refused to go on that pilgrimage.

Cast down by this setback, Everyman thought of Kindred. Surely the ties of blood were strong. His Kindred swore that they would help him in any way they could, but when they heard that Everyman had to account for his every deed, good or bad, they knew at once the last journey he had in mind. They refused unanimously to go with him. Everyman appealed directly to his favorite cousin, who said he would have gone willingly if it had not been for a cramp in his toe.

Everyman thought of turning to Goods. All his life he had loved Goods. Goods heard his plea and offered to help him, but when asked to go on the journey to the highest judge of all, Goods promptly refused. Everyman reminded him that money is supposed to right all wrongs. Goods disagreed with him. Anyway, if Everyman took Goods with him he would be the worse off for it, for worldly goods were not given, only lent.

Everyman became ashamed of having sought unworthy companions. Calling aloud to Good-Deeds, he asked again for help. Good-Deeds answered feebly, for he was lying on the cold ground, bound by sins. Good-Deeds already knew of the projected journey and wanted to go along, but he was too weak to stir. Everyman learned that Good-Deeds had a sister, Knowledge, who would stay with him until Good-Deeds could regain strength.

Knowledge promptly offered to go with him and guide him in his great need. Knowledge led him to Confession, who lived in the house of salvation, to ask for strength for Good-Deeds. Confession in pity gave penance to Everyman to shrive his soul. Accepting penance joyfully, Everyman scourged his flesh and afterward Knowledge bequeathed him to his Savior. Thankfully Good-Deeds rose from the ground, delivered from sickness and woe. Declaring himself fit for the journey, Good-Deeds promised to help Everyman count his good works before the judgment throne. With a smile of sympathy, Knowledge told Everyman to be glad and merry, for Good-Deeds would be his true companion. Knowledge gave a garment to Everyman to wear, a garment of sorrow that would deliver him from pain.

Asking Good-Deeds if his accounts were ready, Everyman prepared to start his pilgrimage. Good-Deeds reminded him that three other companions would go part of the way: Discretion, Strength, and Beauty. Knowledge proposed also the Five Wits, who would be his counselors. After Knowledge had called the new companions together, Everyman, now well fortified, set out on his last journey.

Knowledge said that their first stop must be to see the priest, who would give Everyman unction and ointment, for priests perform the seven unctions as intermediaries of God. Surely priests were human beings' best hope on earth, in spite of the many weak and venal people who were often invested with holy orders.

After receiving the last rites from the priest, Everyman prepared to meet Death. Again he was troubled, however, for one by one his companions left him. Even Knowledge refused to go with him into the presence of his maker. Only Good-Deeds stayed with Everyman until the end. So it is with everyone who must die. Knowledge, Strength, Beauty—all the other companions are a help in the journey, but only Good-Deeds can face Death.

The Angel greeted Everyman as an elected spouse of Jesus. Taking him on high, he announced that Everyman was thus exalted by reason of his singular virtue. When Everyman's soul was taken from his body, his reckoning was crystal clear. So shall it be with everyone who lives well before the end.

Finally a Doctor appeared to remind all human beings that on the last journey, Beauty, Strength, Discretion, and the Five Wits forsake everyone at the end; only Good-Deeds avail at the final judgment.

Critical Evaluation:

The morality play, of which *Everyman* is the best extant example, and the mystery play are the two principal kinds of medieval drama. The mystery play is a dramatic recreation of a story from the Bible, its aim being the elucidation of the revelation therein. The morality play, by contrast, is an allegorical form, peopled by personified abstractions such as Beauty, Justice, and Fortitude, and types such as Everyman, Priest, and King. Here the subject matter is admonitory, particularly concerning death. As Albert Baugh has pointed out, it is difficult to discover precise sources for the subject matter or the dramatic method. There are, however, certain parallels with medieval sermons, which often bolstered moral exhortations with allegorical examples. Indeed, allegory is pervasive in medieval literature, as is, for that matter, concern for a happy death. It is not known, however, how these evolved into the particular form of the morality play.

Few morality plays have survived and only *Everyman* remained sufficiently well regarded in later times to be dignified with performance. One reason for the unpopularity of the genre is the limitation of dramatic complication resulting from the static nature of the personifications. The characters are of necessity simple, and there is no possibility of change except perhaps in a central protagonist like Everyman. As a result, there can be little psychological insight and little of the diverse movement that invigorates earlier and later drama.

Like all forms of allegory, the method is essentially intellectual. The active involvement of the spectator is not through emotion so much as it is in the discovery of the meanings of characters and the significance of the configurations in which they are arranged. Allegory engages the mind and *Everyman* succeeds well in representing a complex, highly specific, theological system at the same time that it generates, by juxtaposition and order, sufficient immediacy to give force to the moral exhortation. The structure is elegant and compact. There is no attempt to catalog the deficiencies of Everyman's past life; rather, the play focuses on the poignant hour of death and implies what Everyman is and what he ought to be at that critical moment.

Because of the allegorical method, it is easy to trivialize the significance of the play by reducing it to the identification of the personifications. To do so would be to miss the power of its abstractions and the complex view of life that is represented. A play about the reaction to imminent death, *Everyman* with its configurations of characters implies much about how life should be lived. God initiates the action with the premise that all human beings are to be called to give an account of their actions. As the plot develops, it would perhaps be more accurate to refer to the central character as Anyman, but the use of the name Everyman implies that the experience is not random, not what might happen, but paradigmatic of what will happen and how people ought to respond.

Everyman turns to his valued, habitual companions for comfort on his difficult and danger-ous journey, but the play does not present a pageant of specific sins. Instead, in Fellowship, Kindred, and Goods, we have summary abstractions, which are not particular sins in themselves but rather examples of the distractions that divert people away from positive direction toward God and salvation. Thus Everyman's failures are represented not by a static series of vices but by the vital enticements that have taken too much of his attention. The conception is a Dantescan analysis of sin as a turning away from God.

In the theology of the play, salvation obviously cannot come by faith alone, since it is imperative that Everyman be accompanied to judgment by Good-Deeds. However, Good-Deeds is so infirm because of Everyman's prior misdirection that a prior step is necessary: Everyman is entrusted to Knowledge for guidance. The implication is that knowledge of the institutional Church and its remedies is necessary for the successful living of the good life.

Knowledge first directs Everyman to Confession, one of the tangible means of repentance and regeneration. Once Confession has taken place, Good-Deeds begins to revive, as contrition and amendment free the accumulated merits of past virtuous actions.

Knowledge also summons other attainments, which can travel at least part way with Everyman. Beauty, Strength, Discretion, and Five Wits are all auxiliary human accomplishments that can help and comfort human beings along their way, though none can persevere to the final moment of judgment. As they fall away, one by one, the play presents the process of death. Beauty is obviously the first to depart in this telescoped version of an individual's demise. Strength follows as life ebbs. The last of the attainments to leave is Five Wits, the sensual means through which human beings acquire whatever understanding they gain in life.

In the end, even Knowledge, the representative of the human intellect, which builds on sense and is a higher power than sense, cannot go the whole distance with Everyman. The respect for Knowledge in the play's implied theological system is enormous: Knowledge plays the pivotal role in informing Everyman of the way to salvation. Yet, in the final analysis, only Good-Deeds can descend into the grave with Everyman because it is only the efficacious result of knowledge in right living that merits eternal reward.

An examination of the abstractions and their arrangement in *Everyman* reveals the complex shape of medieval Christianity. The play suggests a means to salvation everywhere consistent with the prescriptions of the medieval Church: There is an ultimate accountability, but human beings have the capacity, through faith and reason, to direct themselves toward God by using the institution of the Church, which enables them to do the good required of all.

"Critical Evaluation" by Edward E. Foster

Bibliography:

Kaula, David. "Time and the Timeless in *Everyman* and *Dr. Faustus.*" *College English* 22 (October, 1960): 9-14. Kaula compares the two morality plays and the kinds of time represented in them. In *Everyman*, astronomical time is finally replaced by moral time with its attendant freedom, in which human beings can control their destiny.

Kinghorn, A. M. *Mediaeval Drama*. London: Evans Brothers, 1968. Examines the plot and themes of the play and its place in the tradition of the morality play.

Kolve, V. A. "*Everyman* and the Parable of the Talents." In *Medieval English Drama: Essays Critical and Contextual*, edited by Jerome Taylor and Alan H. Nelson. Chicago: University of Chicago Press, 1972. Examines the parable as a possible source for the play and includes a close reading of the play and its themes.

Potter, Robert. "The Unity of Medieval Drama: European Contexts for Early English Dramatic Traditions." In *Contexts for Early English Drama*, edited by Marianne G. Briscoe and John C. Coldewey. Bloomington: Indiana University Press, 1989. Examines the relationship between *Everyman* and its Dutch analogues to argue the importance of seeing the larger contexts for early English drama.

Van Laan, Thomas F. "*Everyman:* A Structural Analysis." *PMLA* 78, no. 5 (December, 1963): 465-475. Argues that the play's popularity arises from a structure that accentuates its dramatic qualities. In the first half, there is a falling toward damnation, in the second, there is a rising toward God.

EXILES

Type of work: Drama
Author: James Joyce (1882-1941)
Type of plot: Naturalism
Time of plot: 1912
Locale: Merrion and Ranelagh, Dublin suburbs
First published: 1918; first performed in German in 1919; first performed in English in 1925

> *Principal characters:*
> RICHARD ROWAN, an Irish writer
> BERTHA, his common-law wife
> ARCHIE, their son, eight years old
> ROBERT HAND, a newspaper editor
> BEATRICE JUSTICE, Robert's cousin, a music teacher

The Story:

Richard Rowan and Bertha, unmarried lovers, returned from Italy with their eight-year-old son Archie to Dublin, where, although physically at home, they were in spiritual exile. The two people most involved in their return were Robert and Beatrice, first cousins once engaged to be married. Robert, however, had always been dominated by Richard's ideas and was tenuously in love with Bertha. When he recognized Bertha's love for Richard, he had been gradually drawn to Beatrice, who was in love with him. She too had always been fascinated by Richard, and had found that without him, charming but weak Robert became a mere cipher. Finally, her engagement to Robert had been broken off—a situation from which Beatrice, as she told Richard, was still in emotional recovery.

Richard had thus been the dominant force behind at least three sensitive and intelligent people in their youth. In maturity, his physical passions and his commitment to people still complemented his ideals of freedom and integrity. This fact was demonstrated in a conversation with Robert who, while explaining his eagerness to promote Richard's academic career, had declared that he found in Richard the same faith that a disciple has in his master. Richard answered cryptically that his was a master's faith in the disciple who would eventually betray him. In this fashion he was trying to indicate to Robert, who had uneasily become the editor of a conventional Dublin newspaper, his desire to avoid influencing those he loved while remaining wholly loyal to them.

In somewhat the same fashion Richard desired to be united with Bertha, but not to be bound or to bind, even in love. In Italy, Richard had been absorbed in his writing and Bertha was often sad and lonely. She had remained devoted to him but understood neither his aesthetic standards nor his ethics. In marked contrast was his relationship with Beatrice. She had always understood what he wrote and was fascinated by his unique courage. Through his exile they had corresponded about his writing, and on his return Beatrice came to his house to give piano lessons to Archie. Upon renewed contact, Richard found that there was much in Beatrice's character that he could use in his current novel. This was the most vital bond between them.

Through the perversity of passion Bertha identified herself with Richard and thus saw his relationship with Beatrice as a love affair. Her concern caused her to crystallize her feeling of loss toward him, and she turned to Robert, whom she had always liked because he too looked up to Richard. She subsequently explored Robert's feelings for her and for a time passively accepted his wooing. Once, when Robert visited the house, he brought Bertha roses, a gesture of courtship which confused and moved her. At that meeting they kissed, and Bertha agreed that they must meet somewhere alone and talk together freely. She half-promised to meet Robert at his house that evening.

When Richard questioned Bertha about Robert, she answered willingly. At that time he was distressed neither by her involvement nor by Robert's love for her, but he was angered to learn that she was to meet Robert at the same hour as he, at Robert's arrangement, was to meet the vice-chancellor of the university, where Richard was being considered for the chair of romance literature. He felt that this plan was a betrayal of everything that each of them stood for and that Robert was both a fool and a thief. Richard decided to see Robert himself. His intention infuriated Bertha, who felt that he would simply rob her of their friend's love and respect.

Having expected Bertha, Robert was discountenanced by Richard's arrival; but when Richard explained why he had come, Robert was most eager to talk to him. While they talked, Richard revealed his own fears and doubts. He felt that by refusing to advise Bertha or to ask anything of her he might have neglected her, as she had accused him. The conflict between personal integrity and love for another person was very real to Richard; he realized that it was an inevitable one, yet he felt that his guilt had destroyed Bertha's innocence. He expressed to Robert his willingness to let her go if Robert felt that she would find fulfillment with him. Faced with this need to accept moral responsibility, Robert faltered. Richard feared that he would ultimately desert Bertha as he had other women in the past.

Richard admitted that he had desired some kind of betrayal that would enable him to redeem, through the rebuilding of his soul, his guilt and shame. In answer Robert wildly suggested a duel, but it would be a duel between the ghost of fidelity on one side, of friendship on the other. Richard declared wearily that such had been the language of his youth, expressing emotions of which he was no longer capable. Completely disoriented by Richard's rejection of his heroic pose, and distracted by his emotions, Robert fled when Bertha arrived.

The talk between Richard and Bertha in Robert's cottage led to a partial resolution of their conflict. Bertha was overwhelmed by Richard's apparent lack of faith in her, while he was angered that she was using Robert's love without herself loving him. For the last time she begged Richard to guide her; he merely repeated his statement of faith in her and left the house. When Robert returned, Bertha was uneasy with him and maintained against all persuasion that she could never betray Richard.

Having survived her period of crisis with Robert, Bertha was repossessed by the problem of Beatrice and Richard. After a sleepless night she told Richard that she wished she could meet her lover freely. Only later in conversation with Robert, who planned to leave Ireland, did Richard realize what Bertha had meant, that she wished she could freely revive her former relationship with him. Out of this desire she was able to accept Richard's account of his relationship with Beatrice. Thus they arrived at a point at which they could stay together while continuing to live as independent individuals, self-exiled from the passions and the romantic notions of their youth.

Critical Evaluation:

James Joyce's themes included Irish mores, art, sexuality, and aesthetic integrity. Within this pattern *Exiles* can be considered a part of the continuing development of his genius. The play's importance lies in the fact that it is Joyce's last portrait of the artist. *Exiles* marks a turning point in Joyce's career.

Exiles is also generally regarded as Joyce's least successful work. It has never managed to succeed on the stage, and it has attracted little critical or popular support. Critics have found the play to be inert and dramatically static. One of the problems is the overly diagrammatic portrayal of the characters. Each of them clearly represents an intellectual position, and they are pitted against each other until they come to dramatically unsatisfying resolution.

Joyce described the dramatic form to be the highest to which the artist can aspire. It is to be achieved after passing through the lesser stages of lyric and epic. Joyce, however, does not seem at home in this form; it lacks the narrative voice that he uses with such effect in his fictional works. Without that voice, readers are left with the dogmatic and undramatic dialogue of Richard Rowan and other characters.

The play does have a model, however; it is a version of a problem play by Henrik Ibsen, who was Joyce's earliest master. The play investigates the difficulty of having a relationship between man and woman while preserving the freedom of each. The protagonist, Richard, does not wish to abrogate the freedom of his wife, Bertha. He insists that she be free to accept an invitation to an assignation, even free to have an affair with one of his former friends. Indeed, Richard seems to feel that this betrayal is desirable. As Stephen Dedalus claims in *Ulysses* (1922): "There can be no reconciliation without a sundering." So betrayal is a prelude to a reconciliation and a deeper and closer relationship.

The characters are clearly symbolic; Richard and Beatrice represent the spiritual, and Robert and Bertha represent the physical or material. Richard has been close to Beatrice for years, and their union becomes closer; she will become the inspiration for his art as Beatrice was for Dante Alighieri. Robert tries to instigate a love affair with Bertha. Joyce sees the necessity of contraries coming together for a true relationship. The union of Richard and Beatrice would be sterile, and that of Robert and Bertha debased. So the play ends with Richard's victory in Bertha's affirmation of her love for him; however, he has doubts about her fidelity, a "wound" that debilitates him.

These doubts, like the betrayal, paradoxically enhance rather than diminish the relationship, as Joyce's own doubts about the fidelity of his wife, Nora Barnacle, increased his passion for her.

The play also has an important design in its imagery. Joyce uses images of water, stone, and roses to define the characters' nature. Robert and Bertha are closely associated with water. When Robert meets Bertha at the cottage, he is drenched in the rain, and Bertha spends time swimming in the nearby sea. This image would seem to be a positive one. It is the hydrophobe Richard, however, who seems to have the better of it. He does not sink "like a stone" in water as Robert does but rises up as Joyce suggested in the notes to the play. The "stone" in the play is brought in by Bertha and admired by Robert. They both are closely connected to the lower elements, while Richard is associated with the soaring aspiration of the artist. The "roses" that Robert brings for Bertha are "blown" and corrupted, which identifies both of them with the corruptions of the flesh. Robert is a debased sensualist with no spiritual sense at all.

Freedom is clearly one of the most important thematic elements in the play. Individual freedom, even in marriage, is insisted upon by Richard for Bertha. Bertha seems quite willing to do without that freedom and to re-create her earlier surrender to Richard. Another aspect of freedom is, of course, the freedom of the artist. It is the essential state for any meaningful creation. Stephen Dedalus speaks of flying over the "nets" hindering his freedom to create, and Richard refuses to be tied down to a conventional position of professor that the tempter Robert is offering. In the play, however, what the audience sees is Richard's freedom from things, not his freedom to do anything such as love or create. It seems more of a negative virtue, a refusal. The audience hears of Richard's book, and he is constantly writing something offstage. However, the nature of that work and his status as a creator are unclear.

Another theme is that of exile. Joyce defined himself as an exile, and that condition gave him the perspective to analyze the Ireland that he had left behind. Richard returns from exile—as Joyce did in 1912—but it is uncertain whether he will settle in Dublin. Robert writes a newspaper article on Richard that describes him as an exile who has left Ireland "in her time of need" and is now come back to reap rewards. If Richard were to remain in Dublin he would become a character similar to Gabriel Conroy in "The Dead," a short story in *Dubliners* (1918) that describes a similar situation. Gabriel Conroy is a fussy and sterile professor who learns about an earlier love of his wife, Gretta. This revelation destroys him; he cannot build upon the "betrayal" as Richard Rowan apparently can. Both characters suffer from the paralysis of Dublin.

Although the play has not met with much critical approval, it does have some interesting connections to Joyce's other works. There are parallels between the play and "A Painful Case," another story in *Dubliners*. Stephen Dedalus, who appears in *A Portrait of the Artist as a Young Man* (1914-1915) and *Ulysses*, is an exile and a character who insists on his freedom from family, church, and state. He sees it as the necessary condition for the artist. Leopold Bloom, in *Ulysses*, has an unfaithful wife whose infidelity may lead to a reconciliation and resumption of their sexual relationship. He shares some of the masochistic pleasures in betrayal that Richard Rowan does. *Exiles* has, therefore, an important place in the canon of Joyce's works.

"Critical Evaluation" by James Sullivan

Bibliography:
Bowen, Zack R., and James F. Carens, eds. *A Companion to Joyce Studies*. Westport, Conn.: Greenwood Press, 1984. Devotes an essay to *Exiles*. Includes a textual history.
Deming, Robert H., ed. *James Joyce: The Critical Heritage*. 2 vols. London: Routledge & Kegan Paul, 1970. Pages 130 to 160 in volume 1 contain reviews of *Exiles* by such writers as George Bernard Shaw and Padraic Colum. Useful for tracing the beginnings of critical opinion on the play.
Ellmann, Richard. *James Joyce*. 1959. Rev. ed. New York: Oxford University Press, 1982. References to *Exiles* throughout. Annotations and biographical information provide background on Joyce's artistic intentions in *Exiles*.
Levin, Harry. *James Joyce: A Critical Introduction*. Norfolk, Conn.: New Directions, 1941. A central book in James Joyce studies. A good starting place.
Tysdahl, B. J. *Joyce and Ibsen: A Study in Literary Influence*. Atlantic Highlands, N.J.: Humanities Press, 1968. Pages 87 to 102 discuss *Exiles*. Argues that Joyce's well-known debt to Ibsen can mislead readers into reading *Exiles* as entirely a work of Ibsenesque realism.

THE EXPEDITION OF HUMPHRY CLINKER

Type of work: Novel
Author: Tobias Smollett (1721-1771)
Type of plot: Satire
Time of plot: Mid-eighteenth century
Locale: England, Scotland, and Wales
First published: 1771

Principal characters:
MATTHEW BRAMBLE, a Welsh squire
MISS TABITHA BRAMBLE, his sister
LYDIA MELFORD, his niece
JERRY MELFORD, his nephew
WINIFRED JENKINS, a maid
HUMPHRY CLINKER, a servant, discovered to be Mr. Bramble's natural son
LIEUTENANT OBADIAH LISMAHAGO, an adventurer and sportsman
MR. DENNISON, a country gentleman
GEORGE DENNISON, his son and an actor known as Wilson

The Story:

Squire Matthew Bramble, who owned large estates in Wales, was an eccentric and skeptical gentleman. With him lived his sister, Miss Tabitha Bramble, a middle-aged woman with matrimonial hopes that exceeded probability. Painfully afflicted with gout, the squire set out for Bath, England, to try the waters, but he had few hopes of their healing properties. His sister went with him, as did her servant, Winifred Jenkins, the squire's manservant, and, at the last minute, his orphaned niece and nephew, Lydia and Jerry Melford.

The young Melfords were Squire Bramble's wards. Lydia had been in boarding school, where she had unfortunately fallen in love with an actor named George Wilson, a circumstance Squire Bramble hoped she would soon forget among the gay and fashionable gatherings at Bath. Her brother, who had just finished his studies at Oxford, had hoped to fight a duel with the actor but no opportunity to defend his sister's honor had yet presented itself to his satisfaction.

On the way to Bath, George Wilson made his way into Squire Bramble's lodgings on the pretext of being a Jewish peddler selling glasses. When in a whisper he made himself known to Lydia, she ordered Winifred Jenkins to follow him and talk with him. The maid came back in a great flurry. The actor had told her that Wilson was not his real name, that he was a gentleman, and that he intended to sue for Lydia's hand in his proper character. In her excitement, however, the maid had forgotten Wilson's real name. There was nothing for poor Lydia to do but to conjecture and daydream as the party continued on toward Bath.

Arriving at Bath without further incident, the party entered the festivities there with various degrees of pleasure. Tabitha tried to get proposals of marriage out of every eligible man she met. The Squire became disgusted with the supposed curative powers of the waters that were drunk and bathed in by people with all sorts of infirmities trying to regain their health. Lydia was still pining for Wilson, and Jerry enjoyed the absurdity of the social gatherings. Hoping to raise his niece's spirits, Squire Bramble decided to go on to London.

They had traveled only a short distance toward London when the coach overturned. In the excitement, Miss Tabitha's lapdog bit the Squire's servant. Miss Tabitha made such loud complaint when the servant kicked her dog in return that the Squire was forced to discharge the man on the spot. He also needed another postilion, since Miss Tabitha declared herself unwilling to drive another foot behind the clumsy fellow who had overturned the coach. The Squire hired a ragged country fellow named Humphry Clinker to take the place of the unfortunate postilion, and the party went on to the next village.

Miss Tabitha was shocked by what she called Humphry's nakedness, for he wore no shirt. The maid added to the chorus of outraged modesty. Yielding to these female clamors, the Squire asked about Humphry's circumstances, listened to the story of his life, gruffly read him a lecture on the crimes of poverty and sickness, and gave him a guinea for a new suit of clothes. In gratitude, Humphry refused to be parted from his new benefactor and went on with the party to London.

In London, they were well entertained by a visit to Vauxhall Gardens as well as by several public and private parties. Squire Bramble was disconcerted by the discovery that Humphry was a preacher by inclination and that he had begun giving sermons in the manner of the Methodists. Miss Tabitha and her maid were already among Humphry's followers. The Squire attempted to stop what he considered either hypocrisy or madness on Humphry's part. Miss Tabitha, disgusted with her brother's action, begged him to allow Humphry to continue his sermons.

The family was shocked to learn one day that Humphry had been arrested as a highway robber and was in jail. When the Squire arrived to investigate the case, he discovered that Humphry was obviously innocent of the charge against him; he learned that the charge had been placed by a former convict who made money by turning in criminals to the government. Humphry had made a fine impression on the jailer and his family, and he had converted several of his fellow prisoners. The Squire found the man who supposedly had been robbed and got him to testify that Humphry was not the man who had committed the robbery. In the meantime, Humphry preached so eloquently that he kept the prison taproom empty of customers. No sooner had this become evident, then he was hurriedly released. Squire Bramble promised to allow him to preach his sermons unmolested.

Leaving London, the party continued their travels north, stopping in Scarborough, where they went bathing. Squire Bramble undressed in a little cart that could be rolled down into the sea, so that he was able to bathe nude with the greatest propriety. When he entered the water, he found it much colder than he had expected and gave several shouts as he swam away. Hearing these calls from the Squire, Humphry thought his good master was drowning and rushed fully clothed into the sea to rescue him. He pulled the Squire to shore, almost twisted off his master's ear, and left the modest man shamefaced and naked in full view upon the beach. Humphry was forgiven, however, because he had meant well.

At an inn in Durham, the party made the acquaintance of Lieutenant Lismahago, who seemed somewhat like Don Quixote. The Lieutenant, regaling the company with tales of his adventures among the Indians of North America, captured the heart of Miss Tabitha. Squire Bramble was also charmed with the conversation of the crusty retired soldier and made plans to meet him later on in their journey. The group, especially Winifred, became more and more fond of Humphry as time went on. After a short and frivolous flirtation with Jerry's part-time valet, she settled down to win Humphry as a husband.

The trip continued through Scotland. In Edinburgh, Lydia fainted when she saw a man who looked like Wilson, which showed her uncle that she had not yet forgotten her actor. After visiting several parts of Scotland and enjoying the most gracious hospitality everywhere, the party continued by coach back to England. Lieutenant Lismahago rejoined the party, and Miss Tabitha renewed her designs on him.

Just outside Dumfries, the coach was overturned in the middle of a stream. Jerry and Lismahago succeeded in getting the women out of the water and Humphry staged a heroic rescue of the Squire, who had been caught in the bottom of the coach. They found lodgings at a nearby inn until the coach could be repaired. While all were gathered in the parlor of a tavern, Squire Bramble was accosted by an old college friend named Dennison, a successful farmer of that county. Mr. Dennison had known the Squire only as Matthew Lloyd, a name he had taken for a while to fulfill the terms of a will. When Humphry heard his master called Lloyd, he rushed up in a flutter of excitement and presented the Squire with certain papers he had always carried with him. These papers proved that Humphry was the Squire's natural son. Squire Bramble graciously welcomed his offspring and presented him to the rest of his family. Humphry was overcome with pleasure and shyness. Winifred was afraid that his parentage would spoil her matrimonial plans, but Humphry continued to be the mild religious man he had been before.

The Squire also learned that the actor who had called himself Wilson was really Dennison's son, a fine, proper young man who had run away from school and become an actor only to escape a marriage his father had planned for him. He had told his father about his love for Lydia, but Dennison had not realized that the Mr. Bramble mentioned as her uncle was his old friend Matthew Lloyd. The two young lovers were reunited.

Lieutenant Lismahago asked for Miss Tabitha's hand in marriage, and both the Squire and Miss Tabitha eagerly accepted his offer. The whole party went to stay at Mr. Dennison's house while preparations were underway for the marriage of Lydia and George. The coming marriages prompted Humphry to ask Winifred for her hand, and she too said yes. The three weddings were planned for the same day.

George and Lydia were an attractive couple. The Lieutenant and Tabitha seemed to be more pleasant than ever before. Humphry and Winifred both thanked God for the pleasures he saw fit to give them. The Squire planned to return home to the tranquility of Brambleton Hall and the friendship of his invaluable doctor there.

Critical Evaluation:

The Expedition of Humphry Clinker has often been called the greatest of the epistolary novels, a genre very popular during this time, and an outstanding example of English humor. The novel is also considered by many critics to be the best of Tobias Smollett's works. First published in the year of the author's death, the lively novel was written while Smollett, like his character Matthew Bramble, was in retirement and seeking help for his failing health. Despite the novel's artful treatment of the effect of an individual's health on character and mentality, *The Expedition of Humphry Clinker* caters delightfully to the tastes of its eighteenth century audience. Eighteenth century readers thrived on novels of the exotic, and Smollett focuses primarily on travel and distant societies and manners. At the same time, however, he lent that same exotic excitement to the travels of Bramble and his party through England, Scotland, and Wales. Smollett combined his audience's thirst for the remote with their increasing desire to learn more of history and social structure, particularly their own.

The structure of *The Expedition of Humphry Clinker* is at first glance deceptively simple. As an epistolary novel, it lends itself readily to a straightforward, chronological structure. Dates and locations are given with every letter; even directions are given about where the author will be to receive an answer by return mail. Nevertheless, it is not the passing of time that is important: nothing really changes over time; no one's opinions change; Lydia continues to love Wilson; Jerry continues to despise him; Tabitha continues to hope for masculine attention; Clinker continues to devote himself to a humble way of life; and Matthew Bramble continues to reaffirm his sense of distinct social divisions. Instead, action is of prime importance. Although the conclusion of the novel seems to imply a tremendous change of orientation toward life, this is deceptive. The social structure had been tampered with by chance, but now it has been rectified and all continue to love and despise as before; only the outer semblance of the objects has changed in having been returned to what it should have been in the first place.

The novel also has picaresque aspects in being episodic and treating various levels of society, but the reader is led to ask, who is the picaro? He is not the titular hero, who actually appears long after the novel is under way. The "picaro" is actually Bramble, a type of picaro who appeared often in the eighteenth century. He is neither a criminal with loose morals nor a sympathetic antihero but rather a reflection of the author himself. In his character of Bramble, Smollett is a moralizer, which allows Smollett to unify the novel through humor. Beyond that, however, Smollett-Bramble is that special kind of moralizer, an idealist. According to Bramble's view of humanity, society is to be separated into strict social classes that give society order; with order, humans are essentially safe from the many bothersome problems that would otherwise prevent them from pursuing the style of life to which they feel entitled. Such is the latent subject of the majority of Bramble's letters to his dear Dr. Lewis; but the ironic and humorous vehicle for the moralistic treatises is the description of his encounters with the odd assortment of "originals." While these figures for the most part concur with Bramble's views on society, socially they are not what they seem. Sons of refined blood appear to be lowly; people of adequate means satisfy the richest of tastes; worthy gentlemen are treated ill by life and reduced to impoverished, nearly inescapable circumstances. Most of Bramble's acquaintances are eccentrics and thus "humorous" in the true sense of the word. Each has a master passion that he fervently pursues, often to the point of ludicrousness. Bramble, in his effort to comprehend them magnanimously, creates an equally humorous effect—his endearing desire to help everybody is obviously his own master passion—and the conflict between his head and his heart is never resolved.

In *The Expedition of Humphry Clinker*, humor eventually leads to satire. Smollett is at least partially successful here, though he tends to direct his satire against personal enemies with allusions too obscure to be easily appreciated, One device by which he executes satire more accessibly is by setting up opposites—town versus country, for example, or commoner versus gentleman—where one at first appears clearly preferable to the other. Yet the reader soon sees that Smollett does not present logical alternatives when opposites are in conflict. By their actions and their verbalized reactions, the characters seem to hold common views on propriety, but when the reader tries to reconstruct what these views are, the result is elusive. Although readers know that propriety depends on good favor, a good name, and money, Smollett refuses to spell out what it is these commodities then bring.

The success of *The Expedition of Humphry Clinker* is based on Smollett's reaffirmation of the genuine emotional response. Bramble is presented as someone with sensitivity toward his physical and social surroundings and experiences. He is tempted, for example, to believe that Scotland as he sees it during his trip could provide that ideal way of life he has been searching for and proselytizing; he senses, however, that modernization threatens Scotland with the same laziness and complacency that are seen in England. Smollett also emphasizes how character is shaped by experiences and emotional responses. Bramble's solitary reflections imply that the most intense and meaningful emotions are those an individual does not feel constrained to share in words. In this way, the emotions of Smollett's characters are safe from both the reader's pity and his ridicule.

"Critical Evaluation" by Bonnie Fraser

Bibliography:

Bouce, Paul-Gabriel. *The Novels of Tobias Smollett*. London: Longman, 1976. The best study of the totality of Smollett's fiction. The author, a distinguished French scholar, shows how all of the novelist's interests converge in this last novel. Discusses the formal, thematic, and historical aspects of each of the novels.

Martz, Louis L. *The Later Career of Tobias Smollett*. New Haven, Conn.: Yale University Press, 1942. Relates Smollett's work as compiler and editor during the 1750's to his later creations, particularly *The Expedition of Humphry Clinker*. An advanced and scholarly study, revealing how a gifted writer turned factual dross into fictional gold.

Price, John Valdimir. *Tobias Smollett: The Expedition of Humphry Clinker*. London: Edward Arnold, 1973. A brief and intelligent interpretation of the novel for the beginning student. Discusses many of its elements form a variety of critical approaches, all in a clear, concise manner.

Sekora, John. *Luxury: The Concept in Western Thought, Eden to Smollett*. Baltimore, Md.: The Johns Hopkins University Press, 1977. The most exhaustive book-length study of *The Expedition of Humphry Clinker*, arguing that its politics, history, structure, and characters are informed by the important idea of luxury. Regards the book as "the most successful conservative attack upon luxury written in any genre during the 1750's and 1760's, a pearl in a generation of sand."

Smollett, Tobias. *The Expedition of Humphry Clinker*. Edited by Thomas R. Preston. Athens: University of Georgia Press, 1990. The authoritative source for all levels of student. Provides a definitive text, valuable period illustrations, an elaborate introduction, and exhaustive annotations.

EXPLOSION IN A CATHEDRAL

Type of work: Novel
Author: Alejo Carpentier (1904-1980)
Type of plot: Social realism
Time of plot: 1789-1809
Locale: Caribbean islands and Europe
First published: El siglo de las luces, 1962 (English translation, 1963)

Principal characters:
> CARLOS, the son of a Cuban merchant
> SOFÍA, Carlos' sister
> ESTEBAN, Carlos' and Sofía's cousin
> VICTOR HUGUES, a father figure to Carlos and Sofía
> OGÉ, a Haitian doctor and revolutionary

The Story:

A wealthy Cuban merchant died in Havana, leaving behind an orphaned son and daughter, Carlos and Sofía, and a nephew, Esteban, who had himself been orphaned and who had grown up with Carlos and Sofía. In the absence of paternal authority, the three adolescents were free to pass the time as they wished. They ate and slept at odd hours and transformed the family mansion into a house of "perpetual games," a disorderly labyrinth of unpacked shipping crates. Their harmonious existence in the midst of external chaos was brought to an abrupt end, however, when Victor Hugues, a cosmopolitan businessman from Port-au-Prince, Haiti, arrived one stormy Easter Sunday. Victor, executor of their father's will, restored order to the house and assumed the role of surrogate father. He restored the old values of their deceased father and introduced both Esteban and Sofía into the world of adulthood. He also introduced the young people to the liberal ideas of the Enlightenment and the French Revolution. When Victor, a Freemason, was threatened with arrest by the colonial authorities because of his subversive ideas, Sofía offered the family's country home as a refuge to him and his friend, Ogé, a mulatto doctor from San Domingo. Sofía and Esteban accompanied the two men to the estate. There they became fascinated by heated political discussions about revolution, class war, liberty, and equality.

Although Victor and Ogé used the same language in their discussions about the necessity for social change, Victor, though he upheld the egalitarian principles of the Declaration of the Rights of Man, was primarily concerned with business. For him, the advanced ideas of the New Age were important because they challenged the colonial monopoly of trade in the Americas. He was one of several Creole merchants who set up a contraband organization to circumvent specifically the Spanish monopoly. His mission in Havana was to contact local merchants sympathetic to freemasonry and to form a secret organization to combat the economic tyranny of Spain, but he found little active interest in social issues among the Cubans.

In contrast to Victor, Ogé, though a man of science, espoused a form of revolutionary mysticism that aimed at bringing about change by awakening the transcendental powers of the human spirit. Sofía and Esteban were more attracted to Victor's scientific views of human progress and most of all to his powerful personality as an energetic man of action. When Victor and Ogé were forced to escape the island, they invited Sofía and Esteban to accompany them on a trip to Port-au-Prince. Esteban eagerly joined in the revolutionary adventure that he hoped would be his initiation into manhood. During the sea voyage, Sofía yielded to Victor's sexual advances.

Shortly after their ship docked at Santiago de Cuba, Victor, Ogé, and Esteban left Sofía in that city and proceeded onto Port-au-Prince. There, they found the city in flames and Victor's business establishment burned to the ground. Despite the destruction of his property, Victor felt a sense of freedom, of being on the threshold of a new life. The uprising put an end to his friendship with Ogé, however, whose younger brother had been executed by white settlers in Cap Français. Ogé became bitter toward all whites and warned Victor to leave before he was killed by the black insurgents. Victor and Esteban decided to sail for revolutionary France. In Paris, Victor quickly aligned himself with the new government and began to rise to power as agent of the Revolution of the Americas. Though infected in Paris by the fervor of the early days of the Revolution, Esteban was content to witness rather than participate in the struggle. He perceived it in terms of a stage in the spiritual human progress toward domination over more selfish and violent instincts. After witnessing the Terror, he began to see the contradictions of the revolutionary process and the threat it posed to those who dared to dissent. Esteban grew increasingly disillusioned and returned to Havana.

After her husband died in an epidemic, Sofía sought out Victor and joined him in Cayenne. Sofía's hope of lending herself to an epic struggle that would give meaning to her life failed even more quickly than Esteban's had in France. Victor was transformed from a libertarian to a ruthless tyrant as he led a catastrophic campaign against the rebellious black population in Cayenne. Abandoning Victor Hugues, Sofía sailed for Spain. There she secured release for Esteban, who had been deported from Cuba to Spain for concealing subversive propaganda and who now engaged once more in the revolutionary struggle. Victor Hugues died defending the interests of the new bourgeoisie in Cayenne; Esteban and Sofía joined the first revolution to challenge those values and died anonymously in the streets of Madrid fighting Napoleon's troops.

At the end of the novel, Carlos, who had remained in Havana tending to his deceased father's businesses, reconstructed the last day of Esteban and Sofía in Madrid. He began to carry on what Sofía and Esteban had begun. Wealthy, but with the liberal ideas acquired through his contact with the revolution, he would be the one who would bring about the wars of independence in Cuba.

Critical Evaluation:

In seeking to write about a twentieth century Caribbean culture liberated from both the European conquerors and their allies, the plantation class, Caribbean writers such as Alejo Carpentier selected the drama of history as the terrain of cultural resistance. What is most significant in the Caribbean narrative of history is the form and design of the chronicle and the nature of its subject. In the prologue to his novel *The Kingdom of This World* (1949), Carpentier comments that the American language has yet to exhaust its "mythological mine." He views the history of the Americas as a "chronicle of magic realism." At the heart of Carpentier's notion of magic realism (he originated the term, which was later applied to various writers in the Caribbean and Latin America), is the belief that the West Indian language offers literary forms that resist the rationality and chronology embedded in colonial doctrines of modernism.

In *Explosion in a Cathedral*, the dominant European worldview is transplanted into the Caribbean islands, but its central doctrine, the Enlightenment, is systematically destroyed. The Caribbean intellectual Esteban is placed in the European "circus of civilization," the French Revolution, to test its claim to have ushered society into a previously unknown period of freedom and happiness. He returns home, however, disillusioned with European notions of progress and the idea of modernity itself. As a result, the Caribbean man is forced to turn inward and to search for an American way of interpreting America.

Carpentier's novel focuses on the discontinuity and retardation of European history in the Caribbean and its eventual collapse in the Antilles. The degeneration of European history is here proposed as a precondition for a new Caribbean way of life: At the moment when European models collapse, the colonized writer can rewrite American realities anew.

History is the main topic of Carpentier's fiction, and the history he deals with is that of beginnings. He represents two spiritually contradictory worlds of the Caribbean at the turn of the eighteenth century. Carpentier's narrative subverts the premise that reason liberates the individual and enriches everyday social life. What the Enlightenment casts as a totality of culture is exposed as a fragment suspended in a temporal void somewhere between Europe and the Caribbean.

While most of the monumental changes affecting the Caribbean in the eighteenth century— the French Revolution, the Haitian Revolution, and the Counter-Revolution—are dramatized in the novel, on a deeper level things remain the same. What is important in this context is that both past and future are cast in a new light.

Carpentier's thematic concern with the colonization of the Caribbean is illustrated through the figure of Victor, who functions in the novel as the modern hero. In whatever role he is encountered, whether as liberator, revolutionary or reactionary, Victor is a constant reminder that the central problem of Caribbean culture is the imposition of meanings by the European other. The contradictions that define Victor's relationship with his age are both a reflection of the consciousness of the plantation bourgeoisie as it enters the new age and an indication of the worldview of the eighteenth century. Described as a man of "indeterminate age," Victor is a man who rationalizes nature and attempts to impose a new system of thought in which the conflicting ideologies of the age are formalized into a rational system.

The universalism Victor exhibits throughout the novel is matched only by his desire to secure power over others and to legitimize his image as the new rational man. Victor is also a contradiction in terms, however: Although he owns slaves in Guadeloupe, it is he who introduces the notion of equality of races into the Cuban merchant's house. He also sets out to usurp the position of the dead family patriarch. As the narrative unfolds, Victor's claim to originality is seen to be suspect, his blind revolutionary zeal is exposed as counterfeit, and his actions cast doubt on his integrity.

Victor also draws the reader's attention to the problem encountered by European systems of thought as soon as they are transplanted into the New World economic system. In the novel, there is poignant tension between shattered old beliefs and the new individual who needs to order things to "know" them. Throughout the novel, the shattering of the old is dramatized by the French Revolution, which masquerades as a unique historical event. The shattering gesture has actually already been foreshadowed by the painting "Explosion in a Cathedral," which dominates the text. The painting is variously described as the "apocalyptic immobilization of a catastrophe" and as the "illustration of the End of Time." Yet the people who herald the nineteenth century strive to rationalize, to reorder things, so that they can establish their uniqueness in the precariousness of things.

Ultimately, Victor's belief that revolution restores authority to the individual is questioned rigorously by a narrative voice that constantly contests the hero's revolutionary words and their authority. While Victor and Ogé introduce revolution as a natural and inevitable phenomenon, even Esteban already knows that a gap exists between this "authorized" view of revolution and revolution itself. Esteban joins the revolution to become part of what is regarded as a natural and inevitable process, but he returns merely as a man laden with stories.

The novel underscores the notion that the corruption of the French Revolution actually enables the Haitian Revolution, which recenters Caribbean history. A basic irony, however, is that the revolution is not transferred to the Caribbean to restore freedom to the slaves but to establish a new system of regulation and exchange.

Genevieve Slomski

Bibliography:

Gikandi, Simon. *Writing in Limbo.* Ithaca, N.Y.: Cornell University Press, 1992. This insightful work discusses the work of Carpentier in the context of twentieth century modernism and Caribbean literature.

Gilkes, Michael. *The West Indian Novel.* Boston: Twayne, 1981. Carpentier's work is discussed in the larger context of the historical and cultural environment of West Indian literature. Contains a chronology and bibliography.

Gonzalez Echevarria, Roberto. *Alejo Carpentier: The Pilgrim at Home.* Ithaca, N.Y.: Cornell University Press, 1977. Asserts that the core of Carpentier's fiction lies in the dilemma of what constitutes American history and how to narrate it. Includes a bibliography.

King, Bruce, ed. *West Indian Literature.* Hamden, Conn.: Archon Books, 1979. Excellent overview of the major figures of West Indian literature. Compares and contrasts Carpentier's work with that of other prominent novelists. Contains a bibliography.

Webb, Barbara J. *Myth and History in Caribbean Fiction.* Amherst: University of Massachusetts Press, 1992. This excellent work examines the use of myth and history in the works of Alejo Carpentier, Wilson Harris, and Edouard Glissant. Contains an extensive bibliography.

A FABLE

Type of work: Novel
Author: William Faulkner (1897-1962)
Type of plot: Allegory
Time of plot: 1918
Locale: Western Front in France
First published: 1954

> *Principal characters:*
> THE CORPORAL
> THE MARSHAL, Commander-in-Chief of the Allied Armies in France
> GENERAL GRAGNON, the French Division Commander
> THE QUARTERMASTER GENERAL, the Marshal's former fellow student
> THE RUNNER, a former officer, in sympathy with the Corporal's aims
> THE REVEREND TOBE SUTTERFIELD, a black American preacher
> THE CORPORAL'S WIFE
> MARTHE, the Corporal's younger half sister
> MARYA, the Corporal's feeble-minded half sister
> DAVID LEVINE, a British flight officer
> POLCHEK, a soldier in the Corporal's squad
> PIERRE BOUC, another soldier in the Corporal's squad
> BUCHWALD, an American soldier

The Story:

On a Monday in May, 1918, a most unusual event took place on a battlefield in France. French and German troops faced one another after four years of trench warfare. At dawn, the regiment under the command of General Gragnon refused to attack. Another unbelievable event occurred when the Germans, who were expected to take advantage of the mutiny, did not move either. At noon, the whole sector of the front stopped firing and soon the rest of the front came to a standstill. Division Commander Gragnon requested execution of all three thousand mutineers; he also demanded his own arrest.

On Wednesday, the trucks carrying the mutinous regiment arrived at headquarters in Chaulnesmont, where the dishonor brought on the town aroused the people to noisy demonstration. Relatives and friends of the mutineers knew that a corporal and his squad of twelve, moving in a mysterious way behind the lines, had succeeded in spreading their ideas about peace on earth among the troops. Four of the thirteen men were not Frenchmen by birth; among those only the Corporal spoke French, and he was the object of the crowd's fury.

This situation created uncertainty among the Allied generals because a war ended by mutiny was not reconcilable with military principles. To clarify the confusion, a conference took place to which a German general was invited, and an agreement was reached for continuation of the war. To young Flight Officer David Levine, the unsuspected pause in war meant tragedy. Determined to find glory in battle but realizing that he might miss his opportunity, he committed suicide. To another soldier, the Runner, the truce at the front was a welcome sign. A former officer, he had rejected submissive principles and abuse of authority by superiors, and he had been returned to the ranks. Having heard about the Corporal from the Reverend Tobe Sutterfield, an American black preacher who had arrived under unexplainable circumstances in

France, the Runner tried to show once again the power of the Corporal's ideas. He forced a sentry, who profiteered by collecting fees for life insurance among the soldiers, to leave the trenches and join a British battalion in a peaceful walk toward the German line. When they showed their empty hands, the Germans also came unarmed to meet the French. A sudden artillery barrage by French and German guns killed the sentry and crippled the Runner.

The man to decide the fate of the mutineers was the Commander-in-Chief of the Allied Armies, an aged French Marshal. The orphaned son of a prominent family, he had attended the French military school, St. Cyr. There his unselfish attitude combined with his devotion to studies had made him an outstanding and beloved student. Especially devoted to him was the man who was now his Quartermaster General. After leaving school, the Marshal had been stationed in the Sahara, where he incurred bloodguilt by sacrificing a brutal legionnaire to tribal justice. Later, he spent several years in a Tibetan monastery. In the Middle East, he had met a married woman with two daughters. The affair resulted in the birth of a son in a stable at Christmas. The mother died in childbirth, and Marthe, one of the daughters, cared for the boy. When World War I broke out, the Marshal became the Allied commander and the hope of France.

The mutinous troops were kept in a former factory building while awaiting trial. The Marshal, not surprised by the court proceedings, seemed to anticipate all answers. Marthe and Marya, the Corporal's half sisters, and his wife arrived in Chaulnesmont and, in an interview with the Marshal, revealed that the Corporal was his son. Marthe had married a French farmer, Dumont, and the boy had grown up on her farm. Soon after the outbreak of war, he had enlisted in the army and received a medal for bravery in action. He had married a former prostitute from Marseilles. Again, the old Marshal was not surprised and seemed to know every detail.

On Thursday, a meal was served to the squad during which it became known that soldier Polchek had betrayed the Corporal. Another soldier, Pierre Bouc, denied the Corporal three times. After the meal, the Corporal was called away to meet the Marshal. On a hill overlooking the town, the Marshal tried to explain the futility of his son's martyrdom. When he promised a secret ocean passage to escape the death penalty, the Corporal refused the offer. Later the Marshal made a last attempt to influence his son with the help of an army priest. Recognizing his own unworthiness before the humble Corporal, the priest committed suicide. On the same evening, General Gragnon was executed by an American soldier named Buchwald.

On Friday, the Corporal was tied to a post between two criminals. Shot, he fell into a coil of barbed wire that lacerated his head. The Corporal's body and his medal were buried on the Dumont farm near St. Mihiel. After the burial, a sudden artillery barrage plowed the earth, leaving no trace of the Corporal's grave.

After the war, a unit was sent to reclaim a body to be placed in the Unknown Soldier's tomb under the Arc de Triomphe in Paris. As a reward, they were promised brandy. Near Verdun, they obtained a body and drank the brandy. While they were guarding the coffin, an old woman approached. Having lost her mind because her son had not returned from the war, she had sold her farm in order to search for him. Knowing about the mission of the soldiers, she wanted to look at the body. Convinced that the dead soldier was her son, she offered all her money for the corpse; the soldiers accepted and bought more brandy with the money. They secured another body from a field adjoining the Dumont farm. Thus, the body of the Corporal reached Paris. Four years later, the Runner visited the Dumont farm and picked up the medal.

Six years later, the Marshal's body was carried to the Arc de Triomphe, with dignitaries following the coffin on foot to pay their respects to the dead leader. As soon as the eulogy started, a cripple made his way through the crowd. It was the Runner, who threw the Corporal's medal at the caisson before an angry mob closed in and attacked him. Rescued by the police, he was dragged into a side street, where a few curious onlookers gathered around the injured cripple. While he lay in the gutter, a man resembling the old Quartermaster General stepped forward to comfort the Runner, who declared that he would never die.

Critical Evaluation:

A Fable is probably the most ambitious, although not the most successful, work of one of the twentieth century's most ambitious novelists. By juxtaposing elements of the Passion of Christ against a story of trench mutiny in World War I, William Faulkner attempts to combine two very different types of narrative: an allegorical "fable" and a realistic narrative of war, politics, and personal relationships.

Most of the similarities to Christ's life and death are clear. The Corporal, who was born in a stable and is thirty-three years old, leads a mutinous group of twelve followers, and the events surrounding his capture and execution suggest the Passion: One disciple betrays him for money, another denies him three times; the followers have a "Last Supper"; the Corporal is executed between two thieves in a manner that suggests Christ's crucifixion; he acquires a crown of thorns; he is mourned by women who resemble Mary Magdalene and Mary; and his body vanishes three days after burial. It is necessary, however, to remember that *A Fable* is not the Passion retold in modern dress. Faulkner does not simply update or interpret Christian myth: He alters it. Therefore, any attempt to come to terms with *A Fable* must consider the unique, personal vision that Faulkner presents in his book.

Some critics have faulted the novel on the grounds that the Corporal's personality is insufficiently developed. It is true that he is not strongly individualized, but to present the character in greater detail would risk either the creation of a purely symbolic figure or one too humanized to maintain the Christ parallel. Instead, the Corporal remains a silent, mysterious embodiment of humankind's spiritual side; the concrete presentation of his significance is entrusted to other characters. The most important thing is that, for all the biblical allusions, the Corporal is not the chosen Son of God, but is definitely a son of man—specifically of the Marshal—and the thematic center of the novel is dramatized in the conflict between the Corporal and his father-Marshal antagonist.

In the novel's most powerful and important scene, the final confrontation between the two men, who represent two inimical conditions.

Thus, *A Fable* is not really about one's relationship to God, or to society, but to oneself. Each character stands for one aspect of the human personality, and the conflict between them can be seen in several ways: child versus father, youth versus age, idealist versus realist, common person versus authority, heart versus mind. In short, the major conflict of the book is, in the words of Faulkner's Nobel Prize speech, "the human heart in conflict with itself"—the basic human dualism, which is the major theme of Faulkner's late fiction.

The Corporal is the shadowy incarnation of humanity's spiritual side, but the Marshal, both in his symbolic and his realistic functions, is a much more vivid and complicated character. On the literal level, he is the supreme commander of the Allied Armies in France. He masterminds the Allies' successful military counterstrategy. Symbolically, he is the primary representative of secular power; the Marshal represents everything in human society that denies personal autonomy and spiritual freedom. Any attempt to pin down the Marshal's symbolic import more precisely is very difficult. At times he suggests Satan, at times Pilate or Caesar, or simply military authority, but in the central confrontation scene, his role seems to most closely resemble that of the "Grand Inquisitor," who appears in the greatest of earlier "Second Coming" fictions, Ivan Karamazov's parable in Fyodor Dostoevski's *The Brothers Karamazov* (1879-1880).

Like the Grand Inquisitor, the Marshal faces a Christ surrogate who poses a threat to the established order. Likewise, the Marshal makes an offer to his antagonist of life and freedom in return for betrayal, which he knows in advance will be refused. The Marshal's background also resembles the Inquisitor's in that he, too, began life with a spiritual quest by renouncing the world in favor of the desert and the mountains. Like the Inquisitor—and Christ—the Marshal was tempted and, like the Inquisitor—but unlike Christ—he accepted the temptations and the view of life they represented in return for temporal power.

Thus, although he knows and understands human duality, the Marshal rejects the spiritual and creative side of humanity and accepts the individual only as a mundane, earthbound creature who needs security and control rather than individual freedom and spiritual fulfillment. Further, on the practical level, the Marshal commits himself to the human institution that fixes and formalizes this view of humanity. As does the Inquisitor, the Marshal justifies his actions on the grounds that they are what humanity needs and wants. He taunts his opponent with the notion that he, not the Corporal, is the true believer: "after the last ding dong of doom has rung and died there will still be one sound more; his voice, planning still to build something higher and faster and louder. . . . I don't fear man, I do better: I respect and admire him. . . . Because man and his folly—they will prevail."

These words echo the Nobel Prize speech but differ in one important respect from the novelist's own; in the address, Faulkner went on to add: "He is immortal, not because he alone among creatures has an inexhaustible voice, but because he has a soul, a spirit capable of compassion and sacrifice and endurance." This statement defines the essence of the conflict between the Marshal and the Corporal and their visions.

If the Marshal's view of humankind is correct, then the military hierarchy, the rituals and institutions it supports, and the war itself are things the human race creates for itself and needs for survival. The Corporal's mutiny is, therefore, not only foolish, but even destructive to humanity's well-being. On the other hand, if the Corporal's vision is true, such things are artificial, malevolent restraints on human potential. The mutiny in this context becomes a necessary act in the struggle to cast off the life-denying lies and organizations imposed on him and to fulfill his own human and spiritual capacities by taking control of his own destiny. The immediate secular power belongs to the Marshal, so the earthbound view seems to win, but the question Faulkner raises is whether the impact of the Corporal's actions and martyrdom does not postulate the ultimate triumph of the spiritual vision.

To answer that question, Faulkner attempts to work out the implications of the Corporal's ethic in the actions of several other characters and especially in the attempt of the English Runner to foment a second and wider mutiny. Here lies the primary critical problem of the book: Do these secondary actions establish and elaborate the novel's main thrust, or do they obscure and finally bury it?

Although Faulkner borrows Christian symbolism, he is clearly not presenting a conventionally religious message. He affirms the human spirit, but his attitude toward its ultimate fate is ambiguous. If the Corporal dies a heroic martyr, the other witnesses to the human spirit—the English Runner, the Sentry, the Reverend Sutterfield, the Quartermaster General—suffer dubious or ignominious fates and even the Corporal's death has no clear effect beyond stimulating the Runner's Quixotic gestures. Faulkner postulates hope and faith as vital elements in human fulfillment, but they are presented as ends in themselves; it is unclear as to what humanity should hope for or have faith in.

It seems likely that Faulkner began to write *A Fable* with a number of abstract concepts in mind rather than a special set of human experiences. In his best works, however, the meanings grow out of the concrete situations; in *A Fable*, he tries to impose his meanings on his characters' actions. Consequently, the novel is not completely satisfying on either the realistic or the symbolic level. Yet, even with these problems, *A Fable* is a powerful reading experience. If it fails to fulfill completely Faulkner's most ambitious intentions, it does present separate characters and scenes that are powerful and memorable. If all of Faulkner's concepts are not completely clear, his dramatization of human duality is stimulating and provocative.

"Critical Evaluation" by Keith Neilson

Bibliography:

Brooks, Cleanth. *William Faulkner: Toward Yoknapatawpha and Beyond.* New Haven, Conn.: Yale University Press, 1978. Criticism of the five Faulkner novels that take place outside of Yoknapatawpha County. Finds *A Fable* to be less realistic than other Faulkner novels and therefore weaker.

Butterworth, Keen. *A Critical and Textual Study of Faulkner's "A Fable."* Ann Arbor: University of Michigan Press, 1983. Compares *A Fable* to Faulkner's great novels, then explains the events of the novels and elaborates on the characters and their significance.

Dowling, David. *William Faulkner.* New York: St. Martin's Press, 1989. Includes a chronology and sections outlining the major works completed during different periods in Faulkner's life. Gives considerable criticism of *A Fable* and finds it to be the last great novel written by Faulkner.

Leary, Lewis. *William Faulkner of Yoknapatawpha County.* New York: Thomas Y. Crowell, 1973. A good general guide and introduction to the life of Faulkner. Traces his biography and work with some reference to *A Fable.*

Reed, Joseph W., Jr. *Faulkner's Narrative.* New Haven: Conn.: Yale University Press, 1973. A view of Faulkner's writing technique, form, and thematic devices. Examines his voice and narrative style and the impact of that style on other writers. Useful references to *A Fable.*

A FABLE FOR CRITICS

Type of work: Poetry
Author: James Russell Lowell (1819-1891)
First published: 1848

James Russell Lowell's *A Fable for Critics* appeared in 1848, three years after Edgar Allan Poe's "The Raven" and three years before Hermann Melville's *Moby Dick*. Born the same year as Melville and Walt Whitman, Lowell was twenty-nine years old and had already gained something of a reputation as poet and anti-slavery essayist.

Writing in the age of Ralph Waldo Emerson and Nathaniel Hawthorne, Lowell believed that native American literature had come of age. He argues this in a section of *A Fable for Critics*, echoing Emerson's "American Scholar" address of eleven years earlier and looking ahead to Whitman's famous preface to the 1855 edition of *Leaves of Grass*. "Forget Europe wholly," he advised the American writer.

Eventually, *A Fable for Critics* has come to be read—though rarely all the way through—for its satire. The author flippantly exhibits his contemporaries: Emerson, Henry Wadsworth Longfellow, John Greenleaf Whittier, Richard Henry Dana, Sr., and many lesser-known writers. With his young man's irreverence and capacity for industry, Lowell produced in this 2,100-line poem a number of choice verbal thrusts that have always delighted readers: "There comes Poe, with his raven, like Barnaby Rudge,/ Three-fifths of him genius and two-fifths sheer fudge." Of James Fenimore Cooper he wrote: ". . . the women he draws from one model don't vary,/ All sappy as maples and flat as a prairie."

Lowell often makes acute judgments, as in the quotations above, but the poem has serious defects. It is no systematized essay in verse in the manner of Alexander Pope but, rather, a rambling and digressive caricature. Unfortunately, too, many of the objects of Lowell's satire have so declined in reputation that the point of the satire is lost. Lowell's clattering anapestic tetrameter and his sometimes embarrassing rhymes (as in "philosopher" and "loss of her") prove hard to endure, even in a poem intentionally comic.

The structure of the poem is also problematic. Lowell chose the long way around to get at his satire. Ostensibly the poem merely describes various American writers parading past the not too interested personage of Phoebus Apollo. The writers are in the form of cackling fowls led by "Tityrus Griswold" (Rufus W. Griswold, an influential anthologist of the day). This rather mechanical scheme offers little excitement or sense of direction.

Lowell had precedents for this sort of lampooning. Literary ancestors of *A Fable for Critics* are such works as Pope's *The Dunciad* (1728-1743), Lord Byron's *English Bards and Scotch Reviewers* (1809), and Leigh Hunt's *The Feast of the Poets* (1814), to which it bears the greatest resemblance. Lowell's work itself served as model when a related Lowell, the poet Amy Lowell, decided to produce her own *Critical Fable* in 1922.

Lowell wrote his satire "con amore," to use his term. His high spirits are immediately evident in the title page and the introduction. The elaborate title page, ostensibly no more than an imitation of wordy, old-fashioned book format, is actually the beginning of the rhymed couplets: "Reader! walk up at once (it will soon be too late), and buy at a perfectly ruinous rate *A Fable for Critics*."

In the rhymed introduction that follows, a candid Lowell limits his purpose and forestalls possible censures. The poem, he avers, is a mere "trifle," full of digressions and written in "neither good verse nor bad prose." It is a jeu d'esprit whose verbal portraits are both cynical and faithful. Lowell attached a considerably longer essay in rhyme to the second edition. Here, in the spirit of exuberance that pervades the work from beginning to end, he remarks on the mixed critical reception of the first edition.

Lowell himself narrates the poem throughout, but the first personage encountered is Phoebus Apollo from Greek mythology. Lowell, of course, here uses a favorite device of the fabulist, using setting and characters of other times and other places to add ludicrousness and perspective to his satire on people of his own day.

Apollo, sitting under a laurel tree, has been reading recent poetry and bemoans its mediocrity. Feeling the need to write something himself—to mourn his Daphne—he decides that a lily is needed to set his faculties to work. One of his sycophants, a pedantic bore ("The defect in his brain was just absence of mind"), hastens to fetch it. Apollo meanwhile is "killing the time" when the first of Lowell's real people walks up to him. This is Evert Augustus Duyckinck, editor and critic, who is pictured as a small, muttering, reputation-conscious individual. While he and Apollo exchange barbs, the procession of American authors, which makes up the bulk of the poem, commences with the appearance of Ralph Waldo Emerson, who by 1848 had published his two famous series of essays. It is Apollo who describes the procession, and all descriptions are from his mouth. Lowell's use of the fable device thus allows him to satirize without using his own voice. Emerson has "a Greek head on right Yankee shoulders"; the transcendentalist ". . . sits in mystery calm and intense/ And looks coolly around him with sharp common sense." Two writers who "trod in Emerson's track" then appear: William Ellery Channing, poet and Concord litterateur, and Henry David Thoreau. Both are inferior to Emerson; all they do is pick up the "windfalls" from Emerson's tree.

Fourth and fifth in the procession are Bronson Alcott and Orestes Brownson. Alcott, the Platonic idealist and mystic, avoids the mundane, has "never a fact to perplex him or bore him." Brownson is the New England individualist who turned from Presbyterian to Universalist to Roman Catholic. Amid the satire, Lowell-Apollo speaks commendation: Alcott is a magnificent talker; Brownson writes "transparent and forcible prose." These two vignettes typify Lowell's willingness to compliment as well as to laugh, if compliments are deserved.

Fifty lines characterize the now-forgotten Nathaniel Parker Willis as a foppish and shallow yet delightful and witty poet and playwright. Theodore Parker, Unitarian clergyman and writer, comes next, his doctrinal radicalism satirized as well as his erudite sermons. William Cullen Bryant, the poet of nature, is no William Wordsworth, says Apollo, but perhaps he is a James Thomson or a William Cowper. In any case, he is quiet and cool and as dignified as an iceberg. John Greenleaf Whittier is a pacifist Quaker engaged in militant wars for human rights. In his poetry, there is a major defect: "torrent of verse bursts the dams of reflection." Whittier's human qualities lead Apollo into a general panegyric on all poets who ever "spoke out for the dumb and the down-trodden."

Two lesser-known writers—Richard Henry Dana, Sr., and John Neal, journalist and novelist—continue the procession, followed by Nathaniel Hawthorne, one of the few writers on parade who receive unqualified approval. He is strong, earnest, graceful, good-tempered—"fully and perfectly man." James Fenimore Cooper fares less well in twice as many lines. According to Apollo, he has created one character, the woodsman Natty Bumppo, and has done nothing but copy him ever since. Cooper's virtue is boldness of utterance; he speaks his mind whether people like it or not.

The admirable way in which Cooper "lectures his countrymen gratis" reminds Apollo of several "truths you Americans need to be told," the main one being that they should refuse to be intimidated by England. Americans brag of their New World but do not really quite believe in it and keep looking to England for ideas and literature. Instead, they should reflect their own land and their own century.

After a quick jab at slavery from Apollo, the conversation is interrupted by Miranda (Margaret Fuller), a rather obnoxious egoist "with an I-turn-the-crank-of-the-Universe air." She inspires Apollo to give a digression on bores. Congress is full of them. The parade resumes with a description of the novelist Charles Frederick Briggs, who is amiable, if self-contradictory, followed by the famous vignette of Poe, "who has written some things quite the best of their kind,/ But the heart somehow seems all squeezed out by the mind." This description is interrupted by a spirited defense of Longfellow.

Lydia Maria Child, another forgotten novelist to whom Lowell devotes more than one hundred lines, is succeeded by Washington Irving, who is presented as a man of "warm heart and fine brain." Praise for Irving yields to recognition of Sylvester Judd, a novelist of New England.

At this point Lowell himself enters the poem again, for the purpose of a digressive paean to the state of Massachusetts, the home of workers and industry where the rough new continent was tamed. Here Lowell raises the theme of great art and literature.

Apollo then resumes his commentary on the parade. The vigor, fancy, and fun of Oliver Wendell Holmes receive acclaim, and then comes none other than Lowell himself, "striving Parnassus to climb." After him appears Fitz-Greene Halleck, a minor versifier, followed by figures even more insignificant. Apollo amuses himself by laughing at their self-importance.

Apollo's lily-searchers, who had disappeared at the beginning of the poem, now reenter to lead matters to a conclusion. Before ending, however, Apollo makes some pointed remarks about literary criticism. In the good old days when poets were visionary, free, and prophetic, there were no critics, but now the domain of art is overrun by pedantic and carping critics: "He who would write and can't write can surely review." No sooner has Apollo worked himself into a furious rage however than loquacious Miranda intrudes her opinion. Thereupon, Apollo flees, as does Lowell, and the burlesque comes to an abrupt end.

Bibliography:

Arms, George. *The Fields Were Green: A New View of Bryant, Whittier, Holmes, Lowell, and Longfellow, with a Selection of their Poems.* Stanford, Calif.: Stanford University Press, 1948. Places Lowell and his production in the context of the best popular poetry of the times. Approaches *A Fable for Critics* as an attempt at a series of verse essays that only incidentally contain shrewd critical judgments of Lowell's contemporary authors.

Duberman, Martin. *James Russell Lowell.* Boston: Houghton Mifflin, 1966. Includes a discussion of *A Fable for Critics* that points out the work's weaknesses, especially its hasty composition, forced puns, and digressions. Also emphasizes its many strengths, notably its still valid critical judgments.

Heymann, C. David. *American Aristocracy: The Lives and Times of James Russell, Amy Lowell, and Robert Lowell.* New York: Dodd, Mead, 1980. Sketches early responses to *A Fable for Critics* and compares relevant aspects of the work to Amy Lowell's somewhat similar 1922 work entitled *A Critical Fable.*

McGlinchee, Claire. *James Russell Lowell.* New York: Twayne, 1967. Analyzes *A Fable for Critics* as a demonstration of Lowell's critical acumen and his ability to make dispassionate and lasting judgments about his contemporaries. In particular, praises his perceptive comments on Ralph Waldo Emerson and Edgar Allan Poe.

Smith, Herbert F., ed. *Literary Criticism of James Russell Lowell.* Lincoln: University of Nebraska Press, 1969. Reprints *A Fable for Critics*, accompanied by a detailed introduction and extensive annotations of all persons named, non-English quotations, and difficult literary references and allusions.

THE FABLES

Type of work: Poetry
Author: Jean de La Fontaine (1621-1695)
First published: books 1-6, 1668; books 7-11, 1673-1679; book 12, 1694

While one may be tempted by tradition to think of Jean de La Fontaine's *Fables* as children's stories, such a notion does a disservice to La Fontaine's elegant poetry and down-to-earth, sometimes bitter philosophy and view of life. One point one must keep in mind in reading the *Fables* is that they were written over a period of more than twenty-five years. The first six books of fables were published in 1668, five more books appeared in 1673-1679, and the twelfth and final book was published in 1694. As such, the *Fables* reflect the changes in point of view of a writer who matured and perhaps mellowed as he wrote and published his fable-poems.

To a certain degree, La Fontaine's ideas also reflect social and political problems and philosophical styles in France during the reign of Louis XIV (1643-1715). Many of the early fables seem to comment on specific injustices of Louis XIV's regime, especially as they affected the common people, while the fables from La Fontaine's later years mainly express a spiritual withdrawal that resembles stoicism in certain respects.

As the literary heir of ancient fabulists such as Aesop, Bidpai, and Phaedrus, La Fontaine makes use of a form that was familiar to his readers. Most of his fables feature a story and a moral, the latter often separated from the text of the tale. La Fontaine's verse form varies; he uses eight-syllable lines as a basic structure, but it is to be noted that he often exploits the dignified twelve-syllable Alexandrine form, the verse form identified with seventeenth century French tragedy, when he wishes to express exceptional drama and seriousness.

As for the fables' casts of characters, most of the fables present, as we would expect, familiar characters from the animal kingdom. "I use animals to teach men," says La Fontaine in the poem that serves as a preface to the *Fables*. Some of the fables do, however, feature humans of various social classes and nationalities. In the case of his animal characters, La Fontaine often endows certain creatures with what would be considered traditionally symbolic traits. His lion therefore is always a character who represents royalty and the caprice of absolute power; La Fontaine's wolf is always vicious and violent; the lamb is weak and timid; the fox is clever and insinuating, and so on.

Usually, also, the first fable of each book is especially important because it sets the tone for the fables that follow in that book; similarly, the last fable of each book often sums up or punctuates the themes of the entire book. Indeed, many of the most famous and familiar fables are to be found in book 1. "The Grasshopper and the Ant," which opens book 1 and serves as a passageway to all the fables, is typical of La Fontaine's style. This short fable expresses a peasant or bourgeois wisdom, a practicality which may strike some modern readers as cruel. There are only two characters in this poem, the grasshopper and the ant of the fable's title. The first of these is carefree, a poetess or a singer who has wasted her time singing in the summer when she should have been preparing for the winter to come. As fall approaches, seeing that she will be short of supplies, the grasshopper beseeches her neighbor, the ant, for a loan. The ant, however, is quite unsympathetic, dismissing the grasshopper's airy appeal with curtness. Similarly, the last fable in book 1, "The Oak and the Reed," tells yet another tale of the downfall of the proud and complacent. In this case, the mighty oak tree who mocks the weakness of the reed at the fable's beginning is laid low by a storm at the story's end. The moral of this story is that it is not always best to be strong and rigid; sometimes, being able to bend with prevailing winds is an asset.

"The Fox and the Crow," the second fable in book 1, presents a wily fox who outwits a vain crow. The following fable, "The Frog Who Would Be an Ox," pokes fun at those who want to be something they are not. In this poem, La Fontaine adds a moral that applies what the fable teaches to the world of seventeenth century humans, pointing out that all bourgeois want to be great nobles (in an era when the titles of hereditary nobility could be bought by affluent middle-class people), all petty princes want to have their own ambassadors, and all minor noblemen want to have their own servants. A bit later, "The Wolf and the Dog" suggests that a life of freedom is much better than the life at court which requires the sacrifice of one's dignity. "The Wolf and the Lamb" illustrates the lesson that force gets the best of any argument, regardless of any question of abstract justice.

By the time the reader arrives at the seventeenth fable of the first book, he or she is well conditioned to the author's rather negative outlook on life and its lessons. This poem is in fact "Death and the Woodman," which offers a broad comment on what one ought to do when one discovers that life is not as easy as one would like. The woodman of the fable's title arrives at a point in his existence when he considers that death might offer a good way out of what has proven to be a difficult life of poverty, hard work, and fiscal burdens placed on him by Louis XIV's regime. Once the woodman summons Death himself, however, he reconsiders quickly. The lesson here, says La Fontaine, is that, all things considered, people will usually choose to suffer rather than to die. This expresses one of La Fontaine's fundamental positions, a point he will defend in various forms throughout the *Fables:* One ought not to complain too much, things could always be worse, and one should see that there are some things that can never be changed.

Even though La Fontaine elaborates and modifies certain perspectives in the latter books of the *Fables*, these central texts of the first book set the stage for what he would tell his readers in succeeding books in the years to come. Politics, for example, surfaces again in "The Frogs Asked for a King" (book 3), "The Gardener and the Squire" (book 4), and perhaps most notably in "The Animals Sick of the Plague" (book 7). In the first of these, the race of frogs is so stupid that it has grown weary of democracy. Creatures who make decisions precipitously and without justification are always targets of La Fontaine's ridicule, and here, the frogs who ask Jupiter for a king are devoured in short order by a rapacious crane. Self-interested and uncaring nobles appear in "The Gardener and the Squire," where it is again shown that the best recourse in misfortune is to not complain too loudly. The very moral of "The Animals Sick of the Plague" is that justice is determined by one's social status rather than by true objectivity. In this fable, the lion-king presides over a sham trial, a search for a scapegoat in a time of trouble. The victim turns out to be the ass, an animal who is not really guilty but who is too dim-witted and weak to offer an effective self-defense.

The tone of withdrawal from society and from a life of involvement in the world that we find in the last two books of fables, published when the author was in his early seventies, is well represented by "The Mogul's Dream" (book 11) and by the very last of the fables, "The Judge, the Hospitaler, and the Hermit." The title character of "The Mogul's Dream" dreams of a vizier (a government minister) who finds limitless pleasure in Heaven. In contrast, in the same dream, the mogul sees a hermit who, oddly enough, is tortured by eternal fire. The mogul is confused and seeks out a wise man who interprets his dream by pointing out that in life the minister longed for solitude while the so-called hermit spent his time seeking favor at court. In the fable's extended moral, the narrator says directly that he would like to inspire his reader with a love of peace, quiet, and reflection. If one follows his advice, he suggests, one will escape the contingencies of human passion and caprice. "The Judge, the Hospitaler, and the Hermit" focuses on three saints who try to find salvation in three different ways. The first saint, having been moved by the trials and tribulations he saw in courts of law, decides to be a judge and to try cases equitably and free of charge. The second saint chooses to care for others in a hospital. Both of these men, however, regret their decisions, soon getting their fill of human complaining and discontent. The two saints turn for advice to a third saint. The latter tells his friends that one's greatest obligation in life is to know oneself, which means that one must leave society and take refuge in tranquil places. In the fable's moral, the narrator expands on what has happened in the fable. Since people do go to courts of law and hospitals, the narrator tells the reader, lawyers, judges, and doctors are needed. He adds, however, that one forgets oneself when involved in public pursuits and finds oneself becoming the plaything of the chance, misfortune, and the corruption that mere worldly happiness brings.

With this recommendation, La Fontaine ends his *Fables*, saying in the last words of the collection that he hopes this encouragement to withdraw into oneself and away from society is a lesson that future centuries will learn. He presents this lesson, he continues, to kings and to wise men alike. "Where better end my work than here?" is the final, rhetorical question of the *Fables*.

Ultimately, the reader of La Fontaine's *Fables* has learned about the author's awareness of life's misfortunes, including problems that can be traced specifically to abuses of Louis XIV's political and social system. The poor and socially disadvantaged seem to receive La Fontaine's sympathy up to a point; they are overtaxed and unjustly so, they are the victims of the petty humor of the bourgeoisie, of the nobility, and of the legal system, and they suffer the ills that all men and women suffer: sickness, pain, and death. However, La Fontaine never advises revolt against the political and social abuses that he knows exist. While he sympathizes with human suffering, it is clear that he believes one to be responsible for one's own difficulties. Complaining about life is of no use, the author says, primarily because one can change very little in one's social and political environments. Times change; kings die and are replaced by new kings, but human nature remains essentially the same: a mixture of virtue, vice, flawed values, and vain desires.

Particularly as he grew older himself, La Fontaine began to express that the best way to survive life's travails is to take responsibility only for what can be controlled: one's own state of mind. In making this suggestion, La Fontaine follows the example of such ancient philosophers as Marcus Aurelius Antoninus and Epictetus, who encourage looking to oneself, reflecting on one's own identity, and narrowing one's focus of activity. Only in this way, say Marcus Aurelius, Epictetus, and La Fontaine, can one attain real peace of mind, removed from the transitory nature of life in the world.

Gordon Walters

Bibliography:

Brereton, Geoffrey. *A Short History of French Literature.* New York: Penguin Books, 1960. As the book's title indicates, it places La Fontaine and his *Fables* in the context of French literature.

Cruickshank, John, ed. *French Literature and Its Background.* Vol. 2. New York: Oxford University Press, 1969. This volume contains not only essays on the French seventeenth century but also a fine study of La Fontaine's *Fables* by Margaret McGowan. McGowan deals with both the author's philosophy and how it is relevant to his milieu.

Hollier, Dennis, ed. *A New History of French Literature.* Cambridge, Mass.: Harvard University

Press, 1994. This massive volume, challenging in its unusual perspectives, contains an interesting chapter by Georges Van Den Abbeele on La Fontaine and two other seventeenth century French moralists, Jean de La Bruyère and Jean de La Rochefoucauld. The emphasis in this chapter is on ideas.

La Fontaine, Jean de. *The Fables of La Fontaine*. Translated by Marianne Moore. New York: Viking Press, 1952. An indispensable translation of La Fontaine's *Fables*, rendered by one of America's great poets. Moore's translation preserves the style, point of view, voice, and sense of the *Fables* without straining for rhyme and rhythm at the expense of meaning.

Lough, John. *An Introduction to Seventeenth Century France*. London: Longmans, 1954. It is impossible to understand La Fontaine without an appreciation of his time. Lough's story of the era of Louis XIV contains frequent references to the *Fables*.

THE FAERIE QUEENE

Type of work: Poetry
Author: Edmund Spenser (c. 1552-1599)
Type of plot: Allegory
Time of plot: Arthurian Age
Locale: England
First published: books 1-3, 1590; books 4-6, 1596

Principal characters:
GLORIANA, the Faerie Queene, representing Queen Elizabeth
THE RED CROSS KNIGHT, representing Holiness
UNA, representing Religion
ARCHIMAGO, a magician
DUESSA, representing Roman Catholicism
BRITOMART, representing Chastity
GUYON, representing Temperance
ARTEGALL, representing Justice
PRINCE ARTHUR, legendary English king

The Story:

Gloriana, the Faerie Queene, was holding her annual twelve-day feast. As was the custom, any one in trouble could appear before the court and ask for a champion. The fair lady Una came riding on a white ass, accompanied by a dwarf. She complained that her father and mother had been shut up in a castle by a dragon. The Red Cross Knight offered to help her, and the party set out to rescue Una's parents. In a cave the Red Cross Knight encountered a horrible creature, half serpent, half woman. Although the foul stench nearly overpowered him, the knight slew the monster. After the battle, the Red Cross Knight and Una lost their way. A friendly stranger who offered them shelter was really Archimago, the wicked magician. By making the Red Cross Knight dream that Una was a harlot, Archimago separated Una from her champion.

Una went on her way alone. Archimago quickly assumed the form of the Red Cross Knight and followed her to do her harm. Meanwhile the Red Cross Knight fell into the company of Duessa, an evil enchantress. They met the great giant Orgoglio, who overcame the Red Cross Knight and made Duessa his mistress. Prince Arthur, touched by Una's misfortunes, rescued the Red Cross Knight from Orgoglio and led him to Una. Once again Una and her champion rode on their mission.

At last they came to Una's kingdom, and the dragon who had imprisoned her parents came out to do battle. After two days of fighting, the Red Cross Knight overthrew the dragon. After the parents had been freed, the Red Cross Knight and Una were betrothed. Still hoping to harm the Red Cross Knight, Archimago told Sir Guyon that the Red Cross Knight had despoiled a virgin of her honor. Shocked, Guyon set out to right the wrong. The cunning Archimago disguised Duessa as a young girl and placed her on the road, where she told a piteous tale of wrong done by the Red Cross Knight and urged Guyon to avenge her. When Guyon and the Red Cross Knight met, they lowered their lances and began to fight. Fortunately the signs of the Virgin Mary on the armor of each recalled them to their senses, and Guyon was ashamed that he had been tricked by the magician.

In his travels Guyon fell in with Prince Arthur, and the two visited the Castle of Alma, the stronghold of Temperance. The most powerful enemy of Temperance was the demon Maleger.

In a savage battle Prince Arthur vanquished Maleger. Guyon went on to the Bower of Bliss, where his arch enemy Acrasy was living. With stout heart Guyon overthrew Acrasy and destroyed the last enemy of Temperance. After sending Acrasy back to the fairy court under guard, Guyon and Prince Arthur went on their way until on an open plain they saw a knight arming for battle. With Prince Arthur's permission, Guyon rode against the strange knight, and in the meeting Guyon was unhorsed by the strong lance of his opponent. Ashamed of his fall, Guyon snatched his sword and would have continued the fight on foot.

The palmer, attending Guyon, saw that the champion could not prevail against the stranger, for the strange knight was enchanted. When he stopped the fight, the truth was revealed; the strange knight was really the lovely Britomart, a chaste and pure damsel, who had seen the image of her lover, Artegall, in Venus' looking-glass and had set out in search of him. With the situation explained, Britomart joined Guyon, Prince Arthur, and Arthur's squire, Timias, and the four continued their quest.

In a strange wood they traveled for days, seeing no one, but everywhere they met bears, lions, and bulls. Suddenly a beautiful lady on a white palfrey galloped out of the brush. She was Florimell, pursued by a lustful forester who spurred his steed cruelly in an attempt to catch her. The three men joined the chase, but out of modesty Britomart stayed behind. She waited a long time; then, despairing of ever finding her companions again, she went on alone.

As she approached Castle Joyous she saw six knights attacking one. She rode into the fight and demanded to know why they were fighting in such cowardly fashion. She learned that any knight passing had to love the lady of Castle Joyous or fight six knights. Britomart denounced the rule and with her magic lance unhorsed four of the knights. She entered Castle Joyous as a conqueror. After meeting the Red Cross Knight in the castle, Britomart resolved to go on as a knight errant. She heard from Merlin, whom she visited, that she and Artegall were destined to have illustrious descendants.

Meanwhile Timias had been wounded while pursuing the lustful forester. Belphoebe, the wondrous beauty of the Garden of Adonis, rescued him and healed his wounds. Timias fell in love with Belphoebe. Amoret, the fair one, was held prisoner by a young knight who attempted to defile her. For months she resisted his advances. Then Britomart, hearing of her sad plight, overcame the two knights who guarded Amoret's prison and freed her. Greatly attracted to her brave rescuer, Amoret set out with Britomart.

At a strange castle a knight claimed Amoret as his love. Britomart jousted with him to save Amoret, and after winning the tourney Britomart was forced to take off her helmet. With her identity revealed, Britomart and Amoret set off together in search of their true loves.

Artegall, in search of adventure, joined Scudamour, knight errant. They met Amoret and Britomart, who was still disguised as a knight. Britomart and Artegall fought an indecisive battle during which Artegall was surprised to discover that his opponent was his lost love, Britomart. The two lovers were reunited at last, but in the confusion Amoret was abducted by Lust. With the help of Prince Arthur, Scudamour rescued Amoret from her loathsome captor. He wooed Amoret in the Temple of Love, where they found shelter.

Artegall, champion of true justice, was brought up and well-trained by Astraea. When Artegall was of age, Astraea gave him a trusty groom, and the new knight set out on his adventures. Talus, the groom, was an iron man who carried an iron flail to thresh out falsehood. Irene, who asked at the fairy court for a champion against the wicked Grantorto, set out with Artegall and Talus to regain her heritage. With dispatch Artegall and Talus overcame Grantorto and restored Irene to her throne.

Later Artegall entered the lists against a strange knight who was really the disguised Amazon,

Radigund. Artegall wounded Radigund, but when he saw that his prostrate foe was a comely woman, he threw away his weapons. The wounded Amazon then rushed on the defenseless Artegall and took him prisoner. Artegall was kept in shameful confinement until at last Talus informed Britomart of his fate. Britomart went to her lover's rescue and slew Radigund.

Continuing his quest, Artegall met two hags, Envy and Detraction, who defamed his character and set the Blatant Beast barking at his heels. Artegall forbade Talus to beat the hags and returned to the fairy court. The Blatant Beast, defamer of knightly character and the last remaining enemy of the fairy court, finally met his match. The courteous Calidore, the gentlest of all the knights, conquered the beast and led him, tamed, back to the court of the Fairie Queene.

Critical Evaluation:

The Faerie Queene was the first sustained poetic creation after Chaucer, and its beauty and poetic power made for it a secure place in English literature as soon as it was given to the world. At present it is generally accorded a high place in the history of English literary art. Combined with Spenser's poetic power was his high moral purpose.

Only six books of the twelve planned by Spenser were completed. The fragmentary seventh book was published in 1609, ten years after his death. What he did finish is so great that *The Faerie Queene* is, sad to say, generally more honored than read. The grand conception and execution of the poem reflect both the life of the poet and his participation in the life and ideals of his age. Spenser was committed to public service in the expansive period of Elizabethan efflorescence. A gentleman poet and friend of the great, Spenser never received the preferment he hoped for, but he remained devoted to Elizabeth, to England, and to late sixteenth century optimism. Even during his lifetime, Spenser was honored as a poet by the court and by other men of letters. Spenser's allegorical imagination and his masterful control of language have earned him a reputation as "the poet's poet."

Like other Elizabethan poets, Spenser produced eclogues and a sonnet sequence, but *The Faerie Queene* is his great accomplishment. In a famous letter to Sir Walter Raleigh, Spenser explained the ambitious structure and purpose of his poem. It was to be composed of twelve books, each treating one of Aristotle's moral virtues as represented in the figure of a knight. The whole was to be a consistent moral allegory and the twelve books taken together would describe the circumscribing Aristotelian virtue of magnanimity, which Spenser called Magnificence.

At some point Spenser apparently decided to modify this plan. By the fourth book the simple representation of one virtue in one hero has broken down, though each book still does define a dominant virtue. More significantly, virtues are included which are not in Aristotle. Spenser is true to Aristotle, however, in consistently viewing virtue as a mean between extremes, as a moderate path between many aberrations of excess and defect.

The poem owes many debts to other antecedents. It is filled with references to and echoes of the Bible and the Greek and Latin classics. It is suffused with the spirit and much of the idealized landscape and atmosphere of medieval romance. However, its greatest debts are to the writers of the Continental Renaissance, particularly Ludovico Ariosto. Ariosto's loosely plotted *Orlando furioso* (1516) was the most influential single model and Spenser borrows freely, but where Ariosto was ironic or skeptical, Spenser transforms the same material into a serious medium for his high ethical purposes. Moreover, while allegory is a dimension added to Ariosto by his critics, Spenser's allegorical purpose is unmistakable. In this aim, he is within the Renaissance tradition of writing courtesy books, such as Baldassare Castiglione's *The Courtier* (1528), guides to conduct for the gentleman who would seek excellence in behavior and demeanor. *The Faerie Queene* is a courtesy book turned to the highest of purposes—the moral formation of the ideal Christian gentleman.

Book 1, the story of Red Cross Knight, the Knight of Holiness, is the truest to the original structure intention. Red Cross is assigned to Una to relieve her kingdom of a menacing dragon. Through the book Red Cross's chivalric exploits gradually develop in him the virtue he represents, so that he can ultimately kill the dragon. Book 2 also makes its demonstration in a relatively straightforward way. Sir Guyon, the Knight of Temperance, despite temporary setbacks and failures, eventually gains the knowledge of what true temperance is by seeing how it is violated both by excess and defect, by self-indulgence and by inhuman austerity. Ultimately Guyon can reject the opulent pleasures of the sensuous Bower of Bliss.

In book 3 the allegorical method begins to change, probably because the virtues represented are more sophisticated in concept and more difficult to define. This complexity is mirrored in plot as earlier characters reappear and subsequent characters make brief entries. The result is an elaborate suspense and an intricate definition of virtues by means of examples, comparisons, and contrasts.

Book 3 deals with Chastity, book 4 with Friendship; both incorporate Renaissance platonic notions of love. Chastity is infinitely more than sexual abstinence, because by the perception of beauty and experience of love a person moves closer to divine perfection. The concept of mutuality is emphasized in book 3 by the fact that Scudamour cannot accomplish his quest without Britomart's contribution to his development. Book 4 further explores platonic love by defining true friendship through a series of examples and counter examples which culminate in the noblest kind of friendship, that between a man and a woman.

In book 5, the adventures of Artegall, Spenser develops a summary statement of his political philosophy. Justice is relentless and inexorable; it is not only a matter of abstract principle but also of wise governing. After the stringency of the Book of Justice, book 6 is a softer, more pastoral treatment of the chivalric ideal of Courtesy in the person of Sir Calidore.

Spenser's allegory is enlivened by the meanderings of plot as well as by the fullness and appeal of his personifications. In addition to the well-wrought moral allegory, there is sporadic political allegory, as Elizabeth occasionally becomes visible in Una or Britomart or Belphoebe, or as contemporary events are evoked by the plot. At every point Spenser's style is equal to his noble intentions. The verse-form, the Spenserian stanza, is an ingenious modification of the rhyme royal stanza, in which the last line breaks the decasyllabic monotony with a rhythmically flexible Alexandrine. The diction has often been called archaic, but is perhaps more a capitalizing on all the resources of Elizabethan English, even the obsolescent, in the service of the beauty of sound. Alliteration and assonance also contribute to a consummate aural beauty which not only reinforces sense but also provides a pervasive harmony which is distinctly Spenserian.

"Critical Evaluation" by Edward E. Foster

Bibliography:
Alpers, Paul J. *The Poetry of "The Faerie Queene."* Princeton: N.J.: Princeton University Press, 1967. Attempts to describe the language of *The Faerie Queene* and discusses the nature of Spenser's poetry.
Freeman, Rosemary. *"The Faerie Queene": A Companion for Readers.* Berkeley: University of California Press, 1970. Displays a keen appreciation of Spenser's poetry and the peculiarity of his epic. Part one discusses the poem's origin, structure, and allegory; part two makes a book-by-book thematic analysis.

Graham, Hough. *A Preface to "The Faerie Queene."* New York: W. W. Norton, 1968. A seminal work of Spenser criticism. Relates *The Faerie Queene* to the tradition of the romantic epic. Provides a book-by-book commentary and considers the poem as a whole.

Parker, M. Pauline. *The Allegory of "The Faerie Queene."* Oxford, England: Clarendon Press, 1960. More accessible than other studies of the poem's allegory. Approaches the poem thematically, identifying five major themes that cross the boundaries of individual books.

Sale, Roger. *Reading Spenser: An Introduction to "The Faerie Queene."* New York: Random House, 1968. Speculates that Spenser's transformation from a medieval to a modern poet prevented him from finishing his epic. Also argues that the poem is intentionally "undramatic."

FAHRENHEIT 451

Type of work: Novel
Author: Ray Bradbury (1920-   )
Type of plot: Science fiction
Time of plot: The future
Locale: North America
First published: 1953

> *Principal characters:*
> GUY MONTAG, a fireman
> CLARISSE MCCLELLAN, his young neighbor
> MILDRED MONTAG, Guy's wife
> CAPTAIN BEATTY, the fire chief
> FABER, a retired English teacher
> GRANGER, leader of the "book people"

The Story:

Like all firemen in the future society of the novel, Montag burned books, which were entirely prohibited. One day, while returning home from work, Montag met Clarisse, his mysterious young neighbor. Her probing questions caused him to reflect critically on the purpose of his job. When he entered his house, he found that his wife had taken an overdose of sleeping pills. Montag had to call the emergency hospital to have her stomach pumped.

The next day, however, Mildred failed to recollect the event and returned to her usual life of watching mindless television shows. After talking again to Clarisse, Montag returned to the firehouse. There the Mechanical Hound, a dangerous robotic creature used to track suspects, started acting aggressively toward him. During the following weeks Montag met Clarisse every day, and they discussed the moral and spiritual emptiness of their society, caused by its obsession with frantic consumption and shallow entertainment. One day, however, Clarisse was suddenly gone. Montag now began to asks his colleagues questions concerning the historical origins of book-burning. During the next book-burning raid on an old woman's home, he secretly took a book. The old woman, rather than submitting to be arrested, set fire to herself and her books.

At home, Montag felt increasingly alienated from Mildred. While Mildred was watching her favorite shows on the television screens that covered three entire walls, she casually mentioned that Clarisse had been run over by a car. Montag went to bed imagining he could hear the Mechanical Hound outside his house.

The next day, Montag felt sick and stayed home from work. Shortly afterward, Captain Beatty, Montag's boss the fire chief, arrived at his house and started to explain to him how firemen had become book-burners. According to Beatty, the increasing population pressure caused all entertainment to be leveled down to the lowest common denominator. Furthermore, books were censored in order to avoid offending any particular group in society. In the end, the majority of people preferred happiness to critical awareness, and books were entirely banned.

After Beatty had left the house, Montag confessed his doubts to Mildred and brought out several books he had hidden in the house. He began to read to her, but Mildred simply could not understand his fascination with the printed word. Montag therefore visited Faber, a retired English teacher whom he had once caught reading a book. Faber explained to Montag that books offer a rich texture of life, leisurely enjoyment, and freedom to act on one's ideas—all values despised by the materialistic society around them. Faber believed that the imminent atomic war would soon destroy society. He gave Montag a pair of earphone-transmitters, so that they could stay in permanent radio contact. That night, Mildred's friends arrived to watch television. Montag shattered their complacency by reading a Matthew Arnold poem, "Dover Beach," to them and eventually drove them out of the house.

Montag then returned to the firehouse, where Beatty tried to prove the insignificance of books by citing contradictory passages from world literature. The alarm bell rang, and Montag set off with the team, only to find that Mildred had denounced him and the firemen were going to his own house. After Montag had used the flamethrower to burn the hidden books, he accidentally lost the miniature transmitters Faber had given him. When Beatty threatened to trace the owner, Montag killed him with a blast of the flamethrower. He also managed to incinerate the Mechanical Hound, but not before he had been injured by it.

While Montag was running for his life, he heard that war had been declared. He was almost killed by teenagers in a speeding car but managed to escape and even hide a book in another fireman's house and call in an alarm in order to distract his pursuers. Finally, he reached Faber's apartment. Faber told him to flee toward the open country, where teachers and writers were living as tramps. After changing his clothes to distract the new Mechanical Hound brought in by the police, Montag made a final dash for the river.

After floating down the river, Montag met a group of social outcasts who kept books alive by memorizing them word for word. The book ended with the destruction of the cities by atomic bombs and the hope that civilization, like the mythical Phoenix, would rise again from its ashes. In the meantime, Montag and his newfound friends would remain "living books."

Critical Evaluation:

Fahrenheit 451 was Ray Bradbury's first major novel. His earlier book-length work, *The Martian Chronicles* (1950), was a loosely connected cycle of short stories. In the opinion of many critics, *Fahrenheit 451* remains his only really impressive novel. Appropriately enough for a writer who has generally been considered a master of short fiction, this novel grew out of a story, titled "The Fireman," which Bradbury had published in 1951. *Fahrenheit 451* reached a wide audience through François Truffaut's film adaptation of 1966, which starred Julie Christie as both Mildred and Clarisse and Oscar Werner as Guy Montag.

Bradbury's novel is a classic example of dystopian fiction, a subgenre of utopian literature. Literary utopias, such as Thomas More's *Utopia* (1516), after which the entire genre was named, present fictional depictions of societies that are clearly superior to the one in which the author lives. The societies described in such seventeenth century works as Francis Bacon's *New Atlantis* (1627) and Thomas Campanella's *La città del sole* (1602) are highly structured and static. Utopian novels of the nineteenth and early twentieth centuries (most notably Edward Bellamy's immensely popular *Looking Backward: 2000-1887*, 1888) added the concept of progress, situating their utopian communities in the future rather than in a remote place. Utopian books of that time exhibit a strong belief in the social benefits of advancing technology.

After World War I, however, there was a vehement backlash against the very idea of utopianism, which took the form of dystopian novels. Dystopian novels show that any attempt at establishing utopia will only make matters much worse. The great works of this tradition, such as Evgenii Zamiatin's *My* (1924), Aldous Huxley's *Brave New World* (1932), and George Orwell's *Nineteen Eighty-Four* (1949), establish a pattern that is clearly reflected in Bradbury's *Fahrenheit 451*.

The set of characters in Bradbury's novel closely follows established genre traditions. Like the protagonists of many other dystopian novels, Guy Montag starts out as a loyal member of the future society and only gradually shows signs of disaffection. His progress toward rebellion is aided by a female companion (Clarisse) and an older mentor figure (Faber, and to some extent Beatty also) who provide alternate sets of values.

The most crucial element in the dystopian hero's process of initiation, however, is the discovery of books that help explain the existence of the dystopian society and offer means to overcome it. This is a stock scene in dystopian literature, and it is found in such diverse works as Huxley's *Brave New World*, Orwell's *Nineteen Eighty-Four*, and Ira Levin's *This Perfect Day* (1970). Bradbury developed this standard motif into a spirited defense of literature itself. In Montag's world of state-sponsored book-burning, books are not simply carriers of potentially subversive messages—their very physical existence evokes a rich cultural tradition antithetical to the leveling tendencies of the mass media. Furthermore, Montag, as a lone reader engrossed in a book, symbolizes the ideal of individualism in a society intent on standardizing every aspect of people's lives. Thus, *Fahrenheit 451* takes the genre of dystopia to its logical conclusion by enthusiastically proclaiming the power of the written word against any kind of oppression.

Bradbury's imagery is both vivid and highly ambiguous. The very first paragraph depicts Montag's flamethrower as a "great python spitting its venomous kerosene upon the world." This sets the pattern for a complex juxtaposition of natural and mechanical images that dominates the novel and reflects its central tensions between the country and the city, or culture and technology. Many elements of this future society are portrayed as perverted versions of natural objects: the "beetle" cars used for joy riding, the "seashell" radios that keep people awash in sound, the "cobra-like" stomach pump used on Mildred after her suicide attempt, and, most significantly, the merciless killer robot called the Mechanical Hound. This contrast between the natural and the artificial is also employed in relation to Clarisse and Mildred (both of whom were played by Julie Christie in Truffaut's film version of *Fahrenheit 451*). While Clarisse is associated with trees and the change of the seasons, Mildred is depicted as cold and mechanical.

As the novel progresses, however, Bradbury transcends the static opposition of the natural and the technological and focuses on the ambiguity of his central symbol, fire. Guy Montag is initially fascinated by fire, and this fascination persists, even as his repulsion against the act of book-burning grows. He once compares Clarisse's luminous face to the light of a candle, an image that brings up a nostalgic childhood memory. The first of the many literary quotes that draw Montag inexorably toward forbidden books describes a martyr's death as the lighting of a candle.

The destructive aspect of fire is embodied by Beatty, a true pyromaniac who is constantly playing with fire. For Beatty, fire is the ultimate weapon that allows him to cleanse and purify society by literally incinerating any dissenting voices. When Montag turns the flamethrower on Beatty after having torched his own house, Montag momentarily switches roles with this devil's advocate, and he briefly muses afterward, whether Beatty might not have wanted him to do this.

The ambiguity of fire reaches its climax at the end of the novel, when the cities are destroyed in a nuclear war. Strangely, this scene employs no fire imagery at all and lyrically describes the destroyed cities as briefly floating in the air before they disintegrate. Out of the ashes of the cities, as Granger hopes, the Phoenix of a new civilization will arise, yet the bird Phoenix is also the emblem of the book-burning firemen. Thus, *Fahrenheit 451* at least partially disassociates the reader from the optimism of its protagonists and remains poised between dystopian despair and a utopian belief in the inevitability of the triumph of reason.

Frank Dietz

Bibliography:
Greenberg, Martin Henry, and Joseph D. Olander, eds. *Ray Bradbury*. New York: Taplinger, 1980 . This collection contains several essays discussing aspects of *Fahrenheit 451*. Extensive bibliography.

Johnson, Wayne L. *Ray Bradbury*. New York: Frederick Ungar, 1980. Deals with central themes related to science fiction and fantasy in Bradbury's works.

Mogen, David. *Ray Bradbury*. Boston: Twayne, 1986. Provides biographical background as well as analyses of major works. Sees *Fahrenheit 451* as satire of the McCarthyism of the 1950's, as well as a general attack on totalitarianism.

Spencer, Susan. "The Post-Apocalyptic Library: Oral and Literate Culture in *Fahrenheit 451* and *A Canticle for Leibowitz*." *Extrapolation* 32, no. 4 (Winter, 1991): 331-342. Contrasts Bradbury's more positive view of cultural development with the pessimistic historical determinism of Walter Miller's post-doomsday novel.

Touponce, William F. *Ray Bradbury and the Poetics of Reverie: Fantasy, Science Fiction, and the Reader*. Ann Arbor: University of Michigan Press, 1984. Applies reader-response theories to Bradbury's works. Focuses on *Fahrenheit 451* as a critique of technological rationalism and the contemporary culture industry.

THE FAIR MAID OF PERTH

Type of work: Novel
Author: Sir Walter Scott (1771-1832)
Type of plot: Historical
Time of plot: 1396
Locale: Scotland
First published: 1828

Principal characters:

> HENRY GOW, the smith and armorer of Perth
> CATHARINE GLOVER, the Fair Maid of Perth and his sweetheart
> SIMON GLOVER, her father
> CONACHAR, Simon's apprentice and heir to the chief of Clan Quhele
> THE DUKE OF ROTHSAY, heir to the Scottish throne
> SIR JOHN RAMORNY, his Master of Horse
> ROBERT III, King of Scotland
> THE DUKE OF ALBANY, his brother
> THE EARL OF DOUGLAS, the "Black Douglas"
> OLIVER PROUDFUTE, a Perth burgher, a bonnet-maker, and a friend of
>   Henry Gow
> HENBANE DWINING, Ramorny's physician and a Perth apothecary
> SIR PATRICK CHARTERIS, the provost of Perth

The Story:

As Catharine Glover and her father, Simon, walked to Mass, an unidentified young nobleman, muffled in a cloak, joined them and asked the young woman's permission to come to her window the next morning to take part in the traditional Valentine Day ritual. When she sensibly refused to make any alliance above her social standing, he left her in anger. A welcome guest, Henry Gow, appeared at the Glovers' that evening; he had just returned from a trip on which he had sold armor throughout Scotland. Although Simon approved heartily of Henry's suit for Catharine's hand, she was disturbed by his propensity for quarreling. His fiery spirit led him to rise up vigorously that evening against Conachar, Simon's highlander apprentice, who jealously poured a tankard of beer on the armorer and then tried to stab him.

Henry's martial bent was put to better use the next morning when, coming to present himself to Catharine as her valentine, he discovered a group of men attempting to climb into her room. While fighting them off, he severed the hand of one assailant. Again, a mysterious nobleman was involved. When Simon heard his voice, he sent Henry into his house and freed the other man. In gratitude for Henry's protection, Catharine agreed to be his valentine, but she would not promise to marry him. She assured him that she was not in love with Conachar, who had just returned to his Highlands home, or any other man.

King Robert was discussing the rising power of the Earl of Douglas with his confessor. The earl arrived at the castle just in time to see his son-in-law, the Duke of Rothsay, kiss a traveling entertainer. The "Black Douglas" was infuriated and threatened to kill both the prince and the innocent young woman. The Duke of Albany, King Robert's brother James, and another nobleman calmed the two men. Rothsay committed the entertainer to the care of Henry, who had just entered the courtyard engaged in a scuffle with some of Douglas' men. Although he was reluctant to accept such a charge, especially on the day he had become Catharine's valentine, he took the young woman home with him and sent her on to Dundee the next morning.

The council that followed Rothsay's foolish flirtation revealed the tensions surrounding the weak and easily influenced king. After King Robert had prevented a duel between the arch-rivals, the earls of March and Douglas, March stalked out to join the English. Albany and the prince, too, were struggling for control over king and country. As these personal conflicts smoldered, the men discussed the enmity between the clans Quhele and Chattan and decided to settle it by setting the bravest men from each group against one another in a combat to be fought before the king. After Douglas had gone, the king and Albany questioned the prince about the early morning disturbance at Simon's house, reported to them by Sir Patrick Charteris, the provost of Perth. Confronted with a ring found at Simon's house, Rothsay confessed that he had been present; the ring belonged to Sir John Ramorny, his Master of Horse. Rothsay agreed to dismiss Ramorny, whom both older men regarded as an evil influence over the young prince.

Conachar came back to Perth briefly at Catharine's request that he give refuge to Father Clement, her confessor, who had been accused of heresy. The highlander told her that he was the son of the chief of Clan Quhele and that his real name was Eachin (Hector) MacIan. As he promised protection for Father Clement, he hinted also at his love for Catharine.

Ramorny, whose hand had been cut off in Perth, planned vengeance on his assailant with Henbane Dwining, an apothecary who was jealous of Henry's power and influence. Having gained only a mild revenge by spreading the tale of Henry's association with the itinerant young woman entertainer, he was eager to help Ramorny plot Henry's assassination. That night, as Shrovetide revelers milled about Perth, Oliver Proudfute, a well-meaning but tactless burgher, assured Simon that Henry was not hiding the young woman; he had seen him send her to Dundee. Then, fearing that he had made matters worse, he escaped from a group of taunting masquers and went to Henry to apologize. Proudfute, who liked to think of himself as a hero but who was really a timid soul, avoided the subject of his visit as long as possible. His belated and sheepish confession served only to deepen Henry's depression over his relationship with Catharine; Henry ordered his friend out, after granting the burgher's request for his helmet and jacket to frighten away assailants. Ironically, these garments caused Proudfute's death: As he walked down the street imitating Henry's swagger, he was struck down from behind and killed.

Rothsay, who had been among the masquers, went to Ramorny's to rouse him to join the fun. Rothsay was horrified to learn of Ramorny's missing hand, and Rothsay suspected Ramorny of attempting revenge when Rothsay noticed the surly murderer Bonthron in the room. Ramorny's suggestion that they "allow" Albany to die and force King Robert to abdicate shocked him further. The prince left immediately, vowing to see Ramorny no more and arousing the bitter hatred of his former friend.

The discovery of Proudfute's body the next morning set off a rumor that Henry was dead. Catharine flew disheveled through the streets to see whether he was safe. Henry's joy at this evidence of her affection was marred by the news of the murder and his realization that he must ignore Catharine's feelings and declare himself the champion of Proudfute's widow.

After a brief investigation, the provost suspected that Proudfute's death was the result of the enmity aroused during the Valentine Day encounter between Henry and Ramorny. The council decided to determine the identity of the murderer by an ancient test—the bier-right—based on the superstition that a body bleeds in the presence of its killer. Ramorny's household was later marched by Proudfute's body, with no result until Bonthron refused the test and chose the alternative, trial by combat. Henry defeated the murderer, who, in his confession, followed the instructions of Ramorny and Dwining and laid the principal blame on Rothsay. Albany immediately put the prince in the hands of the high constable to protect him and keep him out of further trouble.

Sir Patrick Charteris came to tell Simon and Catharine that they were to be arrested for heresy. Simon planned to seek asylum with his old friend, Conachar's father, in the Highlands; however, knowing his former apprentice's feelings, he was relieved when the provost offered to take Catharine to Lady Marjory, Duchess of Rothsay.

When he reached his destination, Simon learned that his friend had died, but he was received courteously by the young chief. Conachar confessed to him that he feared the coming combat with Clan Chattan; a coward was not a fit leader for a brave clan. He begged Simon to let him marry Catharine, for he felt that her love would strengthen him. Simon refused, however, to break his word to Henry.

Meanwhile, Ramorny had enticed Rothsay to flee to the former residence of his duchess by telling him that Catharine was coming there. When Catharine arrived, thinking Lady Marjory was still there, the prince at first tried to seduce her but later gave in to her appeal to his honor. He entrusted her to Louise, the itinerant entertainer, whom he had encountered again by chance.

Ramorny and Dwining starved the prince to death, while spreading a rumor that he was ill. Louise and Catharine discovered what was happening, and Louise escaped to bring Douglas to the rescue while Catharine tried to get food to Rothsay. Douglas arrived in time to force Ramorny's surrender and to save Catharine's life; Dwining poisoned himself to avoid his confederate's fate of death by hanging.

Douglas and Albany decided to keep Rothsay's death secret until after the clan combat on Palm Sunday. That morning, Henry volunteered to take the place of a missing Chattan warrior and fought valiantly in order to have a chance to meet Conachar, whom he believed was a rival about to wed Catharine. Conachar's foster father sacrificed his eight sons and himself in an attempt to protect Conachar, but their efforts were useless. When the young leader faced Henry at last, the highlander fled across the River Tay. Late that day, he went to Catharine to tell her of his cowardice before he plunged to his death in the torrent.

Catharine and Henry were married a few months later. Although she was reconciled to her husband's warring impulses, he vowed to take up arms again only in behalf of his country. Their first son had as godparents the Earl of Douglas, Lady Marjory, and Sir Patrick Charteris.

King Robert died soon afterward, brokenhearted by the death of one son and the capture by the English of the other, later James I of Scotland, whom he was sending away to protect him from Albany's power. Albany, acquitted by Parliament of the charge that he was responsible for Rothsay's death, nevertheless did penance for his guilt. His son, who inherited the regency, paid for his father's sins on the scaffold when James I came to the throne years later.

Critical Evaluation:

Sir Walter Scott was one of the greatest novelists of the nineteenth century. His popularity and influence were not limited to Scotland or to the British Isles: He was admired and widely read throughout Europe and the United States. His novels are sweeping historical romances, but underneath the swordplay and the grandeur lies a firm moral underpinning.

Scott was born in Edinburgh, but, when he was less than two years of age, a childhood illness forced the family to send him to live with his grandparents at their home, Sandy Knowe, thirty miles southeast of Edinburgh. He remained there until he was seven or eight years of age. This was border country, a region filled with visual historic landmarks of the long and bloody conflicts with the English. Scott himself was descended from ancient chieftains, as well as from the first Laird of Raeburn. To keep the young Scott entertained, both of his grandparents recounted the oral history of the region and of his own family. Scott grew up immersed in the romance and tragedy of the Jacobite rebellion and the endless skirmishes in which the Scots fought to keep themselves free from British dominion.

Scott retained his childhood fascination with both the history and the landscape of Scotland. It serves as the setting for almost all of his novels. Indeed, this is one of Scott's crowning achievements as a novelist, that he can make history and landscapes breathe with life. Almost all of Scotland's history has been presented in one or another of his novels. *The Fair Maid of Perth*, in which he protrays medieval Scotland, provides an excellent example of this. In its preface, Scott informs us of his fascination with the story of the battle between members of two prominent Highland clans that took place in Perth in 1396, in front of the court of Robert III. Using this incident as a starting point, Scott gives a clear and accurate picture of the period and those who lived then. His portrayal of the weak and ineffectual King Robert III, who is dominated by his treacherous brother, the Duke of Albany, puts a human face on history. Robert's relationship with his son, Rothsay, is recounted in all of its tragedy. History itself proved melodramatic. All of these historic personages are developed clearly and effectively.

Two other historical figures play key roles in the story. Conachar is based on a highland chief who fled the conflict, and Henry Gow on a townsman named Henry Wynd who took part in the battle. Scott also creates a vivid picture of the growing merchant, artisan class that was beginning to have influence in Scotland. The city of Perth teems with bourgeois life. Little more than a century before, Scotland was ruled under a feudal system. In this tale, the newly found merchant class is beginning to exert its power to challenge the nobility. From these varied sources, Scott created the story of *The Fair Maid of Perth*.

Not just history, but also the landscape of Scotland unfolds before the reader. Chapter 1 lovingly describes Perth, noting its importance as far back as the days of the Roman occupation of the land. Chapter 1 even opens with a quote comparing the Tiber with the Tay, the river that will figure so prominently at the novel's end. Scott provides many rich characterizations, quite different from a formulaic romance novel. All three of the suitors for Catharine's hand are unique. Conachar's character is extremely complex. In the city, where he works as an apprentice to Simon Glover, he appears arrogant, feisty, often unlikeable. In the Highlands, however, a new side of Conachar is introduced. He has inherited his father's leadership of the clan Quhele. Behind his flamboyant appearance, however, he has been forced to face the fact that he is a coward. In dealing with this, he becomes a far more compelling figure than a stock warrior. He may not be a totally sympathetic figure, but he is extremely human.

The novel's hero, Henry Gow, also varies from type. His physical appearance is not that of the handsome hero. His moral character, too, falls short of tradition. He has a hot temper and often indulges in battle for the sheer sake of fighting and excitement. He is less than virtuous; only the love of Catharine restrains him from his less-than-perfect behavior.

The theme of *The Fair Maid of Perth* involves contrast. The main conflict lies between violence and pacifism. From the beginning of the novel, Catharine decries the violence and bloodshed in the world around her. While she admires Henry, she is also repelled by his attraction to battle. Henry, the armorer, by trade and by inclination finds fighting both noble and necessary. By the novel's end, however, both Catharine and Henry come to accommodate each other. Catharine has realized that it is not always possible to avoid fighting in a violent world; Henry has had his fill of bloodshed. When the Black Douglas invites him to join his army and become a knight, Henry refuses, noting, "I have shed blood enough already."

Other conflicts also play key roles in the novel. The townspeople are determined to establish their rights and no longer be victimized by the arrogant actions of the nobility. The burghers meet and protest their claims successfully. The traditional enmities appear: between Highlands and Lowlands, between Scotland and England. Scott develops his theme using symbolism, a characteristic that does not occur in many of his novels. Simon is a glover, and from the novel's opening, the importance of the hand and the head are emphasized. *The Fair Maid of Perth*, one of the darkest and most violent of Scott's novels, is also one of the best of his later works.

"Critical Evaluation" by Mary Mahony

Bibliography:
Hart, Francis. *Scott's Novels: The Plotting of Historic Survival*. Charlottesville: University Press of Virginia, 1966. Good introduction analyzes characterization, presenting Henry as a nontraditional hero and noting mythical qualities in both major and minor characters. Discusses theme and symbol.
Johnson, Edgar. *Sir Walter Scott: The Great Unknown*. 2 vols. New York: Macmillan, 1970. Extensively researched biography explores Scott as a man and a writer. Argues that the struggle between courage and cowardice becomes a philosophical discussion of the difficulty of being nonviolent in a violent world; evaluates character and style, paying particular attention to Scott's imagery. An excellent introductory source.
McMaster, Graham. *Scott and Society*. Cambridge, England: Cambridge University Press, 1981. Discusses the novel's disillusion with many aspects of society, revealed in ironic portrayals of characters. Analyzes character, style, and theme.
Sutherland, John. *The Life of Walter Scott: A Critical Biography*. Oxford, England: Basil Blackwell, 1995. Analyzes Scott's use of the fourteenth century story to mirror the political situation in his own time, providing detailed chronology. Asserts that theme centers around weak sons who betray their strong father figures.
Wagenknecht, Edward. *Sir Walter Scott*. New York: Continuum, 1991. Describes this as Scott's darkest and most violent novel, savagely contrasting the differences between the Highlands and the Lowlands, war and peace, the burghers and the ruling class. Argues that Henry Gow is a wild, at times licentious, hero, often out of control, while Catharine is the most saintly of Scott's heroines.

THE FAITHFUL SHEPHERDESS

Type of work: Drama
Author: John Fletcher (1579-1625)
Type of plot: Tragicomedy
Time of plot: Antiquity
Locale: Thessaly
First performed: c. 1608-1609; first published, 1629

Principal characters:
PERIGOT, a shepherd, in love with Amoret
THENOT, a shepherd, in love with Clorin
DAPHNIS, a modest shepherd, in love with Cloe
ALEXIS, a wanton shepherd, in love with Cloe
THE SULLEN SHEPHERD
AMORET, a shepherdess, in love with Perigot
CLORIN, a hermitess, the faithful shepherdess
AMARILLIS, a shepherdess, in love with Perigot
CLOE, a wanton shepherdess

The Story:
Clorin, who had buried her sweetheart in a woodland arbor, vowed to forsake all of the pleasures of a shepherd's life and devote herself to chaste vigil over his grave, relinquishing it only to cure sick people and beasts through her knowledge of the secret virtues of herbs. So great was the power of her virginity that nothing in the woodland could harm her; her mere presence had tamed a rough and brutish satyr, who became her servant. Among the other shepherds and shepherdesses, however, love affairs of various kinds were progressing. The beautiful Amoret agreed to meet her sweetheart Perigot that night in the wood so that they could plight their troth beside a sacred well. Amarillis, a rejected admirer of Perigot, also had plans for the evening. Hoping that Perigot might accept her if he could only be parted from Amoret, she promised the Sullen Shepherd her love if he would break up the meeting. The Sullen Shepherd, who wanted only to satisfy his lust, agreed to carry out any plan she might propose.

Cloe was also seeking a partner for the evening. First she approached Thenot, but he declined her advances because he was in love with the unattainable Clorin. Daphnis, whom she next met, agreed to meet her in the wood, but his modest bearing promised so little that Cloe also made an engagement with Alexis, a youth who was much livelier.

After nightfall, Amarillis and the Sullen Shepherd prepared to deceive Perigot. Following a magical formula, the Sullen Shepherd lowered Amarillis into the sacred well, and when he drew her out again she had taken on the form of Amoret. In this shape, she met Perigot and attempted to seduce him, but he was so offended by her conduct that he attempted to kill her. Seeing her danger, the Sullen Shepherd used another charm to change her back into her true appearance. Perigot rushed off into the dark wood to find and kill the supposedly lustful Amoret.

Cloe, meanwhile, had met Daphnis and found his intentions to be purer than she had hoped. Making an appointment to meet him later at a certain hollow tree, she went in search of Alexis. This swain's desires were in perfect accord with hers, but their embraces were interrupted by the Sullen Shepherd, who attacked and wounded Alexis. Undoubtedly, Alexis would have been killed but for the arrival of Clorin's satyr, who frightened both Cloe and the Sullen Shepherd away and bore Alexis off to his mistress to be healed. Perigot during this time had found the true Amoret, stabbed her, and left her for dead. She was discovered by the Sullen Shepherd who, wishing to make sure of his bargain with Amarillis, threw her into the sacred well to drown. From this fate she was saved by the river god, who also healed her wounds.

Perigot, thinking Amoret dead, was about to take his own life when Amarillis, seeing that things had gone much too far, attempted to explain her deception. In order to convince him, she asked only an hour in which to reappear in Amoret's shape. She had hardly left him, however, when she came upon the true Amoret. Realizing that virtuous love could not be frustrated, she directed the unfortunate shepherdess to the place where Perigot waited; but when Amoret arrived, her sweetheart took her to be Amarillis transformed and, wishing to be revenged, he again stabbed her. Once more the satyr arrived opportunely. As the frightened Perigot fled, the satyr bore Amoret off to Clorin's arbor.

There Clorin had nearly effected Alexis' cure by purging him of lust, but her treatment of Amoret was interrupted because of intemperate influences in the atmosphere. Seeking them out, the satyr found Daphnis and Cloe in the hollow tree. Being innocent of lechery, the young man was dismissed, but Cloe failed the test of chastity to which she was put and was kept for Clorin's ministrations. Perigot, meanwhile, arrived to be cleared of the blood he had shed and to his astonishment found Amoret alive and well. The two were happily reunited. Alexis and Cloe, having been purged of lust, also swore a chaste love to each other.

Critical Evaluation:

John Fletcher's first complete play, *The Faithful Shepherdess* was available in an undated quarto probably in 1609, although it may have been performed by a company of boy actors as early as 1608. In his dedicatory verse to Sir Walter Aston, Fletcher acknowledges the failure of the drama on stage, but he defends its virtues as a poetic "interlude"; in his introduction to the reader, he remarks upon the originality of its concept. A "pastoral tragicomedy," the play is, according to the author's famous definition of the new type, "not so called in respect of mirth and killing, but in respect it wants deaths." Although the play comes close to tragedy, "which is enough to make it no comedy," its conclusion for the characters concerned is sober but not dreadful. As a model of tragicomedy, *The Faithful Shepherdess* is the first in a line of Jacobean dramas that became popular after Francis Beaumont's and Fletcher's *Philaster* (1609) and William Shakespeare's *Cymbeline* (1609-1610).

From a historical point of view, *The Faithful Shepherdess* is interesting as a forerunner of the courtly masque during the period of Caroline (Cavalier) verse drama, 1625-1642. Unlike the more robust Elizabethan masques, notable for their lavish entertainments, rambling forms, and splendid pageantry, Fletcher's play established a more nearly classical model, formally elegant, artificial, and finely structured. Based on Giambattista Guarini's *Pastor Fido* (1589) and Giambattista Giraldi Cinthio's *Egle* (1545), *The Faithful Shepherdess* reduces many of the complicated subplots from the sources to a symmetry of design: the conflict between chaste love and lust.

Fletcher's elaborate presentation of this conflict may appear strained to later audiences. The play celebrates the chief virtue of virginity, and the characters, either virtuous or lewd, become stereotypes either of sexual restraint or of license. Clorin, who has renounced love to preserve her chastity, acts as the agent of redemption for the wanton Cloe and Amarillis, heals Amoret's wounds, teaches Perigot to recognize Amoret's fidelity, and pronounces sentence upon the unrepentant, lascivious Sullen Shepherd. She even tames the satyr, and he becomes her servant in the cause of sexual continence.

Fletcher's emphasis on the theme of virginity as a test of moral conduct may be explained as a retrospective nod to the cult of Queen Elizabeth's chastity, or it may be understood historically as a defense against mounting Puritan attacks on the lechery of the theater. Yet another, more satisfactory explanation is that the subject is treated with such exaggeration that it is intended, for sophisticated patrons of the stage, as a satire. As Helen C. Gilde ably demonstrated in her studies on Elizabethan erotic verse romances, a tradition of that genre is, at least partly, satiric and comic. Read in this light, *The Faithful Shepherdess* is an elegant, static, but witty play that explores with sly delicacy the comedy of sexual pursuit.

Bibliography:

Appleton, William W. *Beaumont and Fletcher: A Critical Study*. London: George Allen & Unwin, 1956. Appleton equivocates about the merits of *The Faithful Shepherdess*, but he shows that this play and other tragicomedies, though being hybrids and reflecting a decadent age, are important forerunners of Restoration heroic drama.

Edwards, Philip. "The Danger not the Death: The Art of John Fletcher." In *Jacobean Theatre*, edited by John Russell Brown and Bernard Harris. New York: Capricorn Books, 1967. Edwards analyzes what he considers the key elements in Fletcher's plays: improbable, elaborately complicated plots; prurience; strong scenes; mystification and disguise; and disputation and persuasion.

Ellis-Fermor, Una. *The Jacobean Drama: An Interpretation*. New York: Vintage Books, 1964. In the chapter on Fletcher and his collaborator Francis Beaumont, Ellis-Fermor treats the tragicomic genre in detail and discusses the strengths and weaknesses of the form in various plays, including *The Faithful Shepherdess*. Declares that this play has a weak plot but some fine poetry.

Finkelpearl, Philip J. *Court and Country Politics in the Plays of Beaumont and Fletcher*. Princeton, N.J.: Princeton University Press, 1990. Looking at the plays as dramatic criticisms of the court and monarch, Finkelpearl links Clorin and Pan in *The Faithful Shepherdess* (which he says is the prototypical Fletcher tragicomedy) with Elizabeth I and James I.

Leech, Clifford. *The John Fletcher Plays*. London: Chatto & Windus, 1962. Analyzes the pastoral form, language, and poetry of *The Faithful Shepherdess*, which distinguish it from other Fletcher plays. Shows that Fletcher's attitude toward human behavior first emerges in this early work. Also discusses similarities between *The Faithful Shepherdess* and William Shakespeare's *The Tempest* (1611).

THE FAKE ASTROLOGER

Type of work: Drama
Author: Pedro Calderón de la Barca (1600-1681)
Type of plot: Farce
Time of plot: Seventeenth century
Locale: Madrid
First performed: c. 1624; first published, 1633 as *El astrólogo fingido* (English translation, 1668)

Principal characters:

MARÍA, a girl of Madrid
JUAN DE MEDRANO, an impoverished young nobleman
DON CARLOS, his friend
DON DIEGO, a wealthy nobleman in love with María
MORÓN, his servant
BEATRIZ, María's servant
LEONARDO, María's father
DOÑA VIOLANTE, a woman in love with Juan

The Story:

Looking from the balcony of her Madrid home, María watched Juan de Medrano ride by, courting her from a distance as he had been doing for two years, and she was moved to confess to her servant Beatriz that she much preferred him to the more aggressive Don Diego. Juan was at last tired of seeing María only at a distance. That afternoon he came to call, with the excuse that next day he was leaving for the wars in Flanders. María postponed their farewells until that night, when Beatriz would bring Juan to her.

Don Diego too had decided on direct action. He arrived with a highly rhetorical demand for her affections. Claiming that she was unable to understand his proposal, María turned him down in the same kind of jargon. Angered, Don Diego directed his servant Morón to try to learn from Beatriz how María might be approached. Though the gift of a gold chain did not open her mouth, Morón knew that Beatriz would in time tell him everything.

Juan wanted his friend Don Carlos to spread the story of his departure for the army, while actually he planned to stay in lodgings in Madrid. As a first step, he sent his farewells to Doña Violante, an errand that Don Carlos performed gladly because, with Juan away, he thought he could win the lady for himself.

The next morning, as she was sneaking Juan out of María's house, materialistic Beatriz reflected on how silly aristocratic ladies were. They would not be seen talking to a man on the street for fear of gossip, but they were prepared to entertain him secretly in their rooms. This time, however, the assignation did not remain a secret. Morón wormed out of Beatriz all the details of Juan's visit and ran with them to his master. Don Diego elaborated on the event as he passed it on to his friend Antonio, and the story grew further as Antonio tried to elicit the true facts. Exasperated and resentful, Don Diego decided to confront María.

When Don Diego mentioned Juan's nocturnal visit, María was sure that her servant had gossiped. To protect Beatriz, whom he loved, Morón explained that Don Diego was an astrologer who could summon up demons and who knew the past and the future. Don Diego did not deny this claim. In fact, when María's father, Leonardo, came up to them, he was predicting an impoverished husband for her. The father, having had experiences with magicians, did not believe in them, and he would have unmasked Don Diego if Morón had not cleverly saved his master from disclosure.

Don Diego's friends, passing on the story, convinced Doña Violante of Don Diego's powers, and she begged him to materialize the absent Juan. To his protest that his power could not cross water, she replied that, according to a letter just delivered by Don Carlos, he was in Zaragoza. At Don Diego's prompting, Doña Violante wrote Juan a letter inviting him to visit her. The note, mysteriously delivered by Don Carlos, brought Juan to her house. There he frightened her and he himself became thoroughly confused, since he knew nothing about the pretended astrologer.

Juan was more eager than ever to see María. Since Leonardo did not know him, he presented himself as a friend of Leonardo's brother, just arrived from Zaragoza. María gave him a ribbon with a costly pin and told him to sell it in order to provide himself with spending money. Then, scheming to bring him back to her, she told her father that the pin had been stolen. Leonardo hurried to consult Don Diego. Since Beatriz had already babbled the new developments to Morón, Don Diego appeared to have miraculous powers, and Leonardo went in search of Juan. When he was discovered, Juan, fearing for María's reputation, confessed to the theft. Angered, Leonardo refused Juan's request to marry María.

His supposed magic prowess brought Don Diego nothing but trouble. Even his servant was claiming a share in his strange powers and trying to send another servant on an aerial journey to his home town. Then Don Diego angered Doña Violante by refusing to give her a spell with which to kill Juan and María. He was, moreover, no further advanced in his own courtship. The conflicting prophecies he had given, hoping that some might come true, caused everyone to turn against him. Finally, when Beatriz explained how he had secured his information, the mock astrologer renounced all claims to magic powers, but not before he had accomplished one good deed. When he revealed the whole truth about the jewel robbery, María and Juan were reunited.

Critical Evaluation:

If Lope de Vega wrote plays at an early age, Pedro Calderón de la Barca was no less precocious. When his *Death, the Best Friend* was published in 1657, it was announced as the work of a nine-year-old boy. In his letter of 1680 to his friend the duke of Veragua, he stated that *Cart of Heaven* was completed when he was thirteen. Very likely he was practicing the art of playwriting before he was graduated from the University of Salamanca in 1619, certainly immediately afterward. One critic has dated *The Fake Astrologer* before 1622 because of its mingling of Tirso de Molina and Lope de Vega, and all critics put it before 1625, when Calderón went into military service. Because of the many pirated copies by publishers and actors, it quickly appeared in several authorized versions before being included, with additional scenes, in part 2 of his *Collected Plays* in 1637, a volume that was reissued posthumously in 1682 by Calderón's friend Juan de Vera Tassis.

In *The Fake Astrologer*, a satire on grifters and impostors, there is no deep philosophy and little beyond a fast-moving farce. The first scene of Act II provides a good sample of the belabored language of Gongorism as Diego pleads his love in baroque style and María replies in language no less flowery and figurative. It takes the servant to bring the speakers down to earth. There is no moral lesson, unless it is Morón's insistence that one cannot trust a woman with a secret.

The Fake Astrologer also satirizes astrology, which had adherents even in devout Catholic Spain of the Golden Age. Calderón, like other literary greats of the time in Spain and Portugal, did not take astrology seriously but sometimes felt compelled to bludgeon it as a pseudoscience that had an unfortunate hold on gullible people. The pretensions of Don Diego to extrasensory talent were typical of the astrological plague that had afflicted Europe sporadically for centuries, despite the opposition of Christianity. As a playwright steeped in Christian theology, Calderón was aware of the biblical injunction against a misuse of astrology and sought to expose the folly of this practice to Spain's dramatic public. Consequently, he lampoons the crude machinations of Don Diego, as well as the simplemindedness of anyone naïve enough to place faith in such deception. The play's basic plot is simple, to which Calderón adds various complications, especially the paralysis of action through a pretense.

The evasion of reality in *The Fake Astrologer*, and Calderón's poetic handling of this flight, has a baroque quality to it. The law of contrast attains maximum effect through the contrast of Don Diego's supposed magic prowess with the empty reality of his true incapacity. Deception governs Don Diego's behavior as he flutters between the two lives of truly being and only potentially being. Typical also of Calderón's dramatic craft is the largeness of Don Diego's role as an antagonist, which symbolizes negation and evil. As protagonist, Don Juan symbolizes the positive and good. Calderón also uses continued contrast, movement, and flight to enhance the mocking of reality; the word *burla* (mockery) or its synonyms are used seventy times in the play.

Some critics feel that Calderón avoided a deep study of his play's personalities because he had an instinctive, baroque aversion to empty and undecorated space and inner emptiness. *The Fake Astrologer* portrays external shapes through its lyric poetry and erudition, which are apparently used deliberately to expose the appearance of learnedness in such personalities as Don Diego, who hollowly crave knowledge without studying.

Even the play's apparently brisk action is more pretense than reality, since decisive action is paralyzed by the dreamy, fictional pretenses of both Don Diego and Juan de Medrano, including the latter's suspended-action courting of Doña María from a distance for two years. Calderón here emphasizes the clash between the world of reality and the world of fiction, and he implies—in a manner so typically Calderónian—that all in this life is truth and that all is a lie.

Bibliography:
Calderón de la Barca, Pedro. *The Fake Astrologer.* Translated by Max Oppenheimer. Lawrence, Kans.: Coronado Press, 1976. The only accessible English edition of the work, with the Spanish and English on facing pages. Contains bibliographical references.
Cohen, Walter. *Drama of a Nation: Public Theater in Renaissance England and Spain.* Ithaca, N.Y.: Cornell University Press, 1985. Good analysis of the differences and similarities between the national theaters of both countries. Discusses the borrowing of plots and characters, which in the case of *The Fake Astrologer* is between Calderón and Dryden by way of Corneille.
Nicoll, Allardyce. *A History of Restoration Drama 1660-1700.* 2d ed. Cambridge, England: Cambridge University Press, 1928. Traces the links between Spanish and British theater. Notes that Charles II was interested in Calderónian theater.
Wardropper, B. W. *Calderón's Comedy and His Serious Sense of Life.* In *Hispanic Studies in Honor of Nicholson B. Adams,* edited John Esten Keller and Karl-Ludwig Selig. Chapel Hill: University of North Carolina Press, 1966. A study by one of the foremost scholars of Calderónian theater, which discusses the playwright's serious purpose lurking behind such comic scenes as in the "clavileño" episode of *The Fake Astrologer.*
Wilson, Margaret. *Spanish Drama of the Golden Age.* Oxford, England: Pergamon Press, 1969. A good starting point for any discussion of Spanish Golden Age theater. Includes detailed footnotes and a list of English translations.

THE FALL

Type of work: Novel
Author: Albert Camus (1913-1960)
Type of plot: Psychological realism
Time of plot: 1950's
Locale: Amsterdam and Paris
First published: La Chute, 1956 (English translation, 1957)

> Principal characters:
> JEAN-BAPTISTE CLAMENCE, formerly a lawyer and presently a judge-
>   penitent
> AN UNIDENTIFIED LISTENER
> THE PROPRIETOR, owner of an Amsterdam bar, called Mexico City

The Story:

In an Amsterdam bar called Mexico City, Jean-Baptiste Clamence was involved in a strange dialogue, strange because he addressed an unidentified silent listener who never answered his questions or commented on his remarks. Clamence, in his forties, talked daily for five consecutive days with the stranger whom he had met in Mexico City bar. The subject of this one-sided dialogue was Clamence, specifically his fall from innocence to sin.

The judge-penitent illuminated his past experiences, clarified the inner motives behind his actions, and imposed his feigned friendliness, his humorous sarcasm, his false humility, his black bitterness, and the cruelty of his lucidity on his listener. Clamence related that at one time he had to feel superior in order to make his life bearable. To relinquish his seat to someone else in the bus, to help a blind person across the street, or to give up his theater seat so that a couple could sit together—all of these incidents created in him a feeling of superiority, resulting in his regarding himself as a type of superman. His sense of superiority kept him in harmony with people around him, with life in general. He attained a certain state of happiness as a mechanical human being who could anticipate what was expected from him and live up to the pleasant image other people had of him. He lived on the surface of a life of words and gestures, but he never touched reality through the people he knew, the books he read, the places he visited, the women he possessed briefly. As a lawyer, he realized that the monotony of modern life had turned human beings into puppets, had made them completely anonymous. Disgusted with their anonymity, they committed crimes, their only means of attracting attention.

Then one evening at the Pont des Arts in Paris, Clamence heard laughter behind him; he turned around but nobody was there. It was Clamence laughing at himself, a sarcastic and triumphant laughter that chilled his existence. Something broke in him; his image of himself was shattered, and he became aware of his double face. He went home to escape from the laughter, but he could still hear it under his window. His existence as he knew it had received a dangerous blow. The same evening, he watched his reflection in the mirror, and it seemed to him that his smile had become double. This laughter started Clamence's fall from innocence to sin. Somehow his usual confidence in himself and his actions had been shattered. The non-existent sarcastic laughter suddenly made his mind lucid, a lucidity that showed him the absurdity of his own existence. The recognition of his lucidity, powerful and convincing, channeled his thinking into a different direction. He gave up his position as lawyer. Human beings pretend to be equal and innocent, but nothing was more natural in them, he concluded, than a constant desire to judge: It makes them feel above others. Clamence left his position as lawyer because he saw the fraud in concepts of innocence and guilt. He soon realized, however, that he was still playing the same game and had only changed his part. Clamence, who had formerly felt in harmony with life and superior to others, fell to the other extreme: He constantly accused himself, insisted on his self-accusations, which elevated him to a new level of superior feeling. He achieved the same satisfaction as before, only from a different, perhaps more cowardly, personal position.

Clamence practiced a kind of Pascalian diversion and self-deception. He used the power of his mind not to get to know himself but to drift away constantly from his authentic self. His desire to maintain a feeling of superiority turned into an existential necessity. Diversion carried him through the recognition of his own absurdity and provided him with moments of ephemeral satisfaction.

Clamence's diabolic laughter menaced his existence. Occasionally, it would creep up behind him and threaten him. Not only the laughter but also the memory of the woman who drowned herself lurked like a lion in the back of his mind. One night in November, two or three years before he heard the laughter, Clamence was crossing a bridge in Paris shortly after midnight and saw the slim figure of a woman bent over the railing. When he had crossed the bridge, he heard a loud splash followed by several cries. He did not return to the bridge, informed nobody about the incident, and avoided the newspapers for several days afterward. In this case again, as always, Clamence had avoided the existential decision. He had closed his ears to the immediate choice and had walked home that evening the same way he always went. Clamence had only one weapon to overcome those moments of despair and failure in the past: the power to forget.

Critical Evaluation:

Albert Camus' death in 1960, at the early age of forty-six, was completely unexpected; it was a great shock to those who had followed his literary and philosophical development from *The Myth of Sisyphus* (1942) and *The Stranger* (1942). Camus had broken with tradition, had engaged himself in a new direction, and had shown vital and promising concepts of his new vision. His sudden death left his oeuvre unfinished. He bequeathed to the world finished works with an unfinished vision. The spiritual wasteland of the modern world was his obsession. He traced the dilemma of modern life back to its absurd roots but offered no new alternative. He died before he could express such an alternative.

Camus had intended to incorporate *The Fall* into a collection of short stories. The story soon outgrew its planned length, however, and was published as a separate novel in 1956.

In *The Fall*, Camus recalls *The Stranger*. Jean-Baptiste Clamence is an intensified Meursault. The themes of *The Stranger* are treated with greater lucidity and bitterness in *The Fall*. The idea of death, the problem of indifference and anonymity in modern life, the notion of guilt and innocence in the individual, the awareness of the absurdity of human actions, and the ambiguous relativity of all traditional values haunt both novels.

In form, *The Fall* is a confession, a philosophical confession of a former lawyer by the name of Jean-Baptiste Clamence, who has become a judge-penitent. His confession differs in tone and attitude, however, from those of St. Augustine and Jean-Jacques Rousseau; there are no sentimental outflows, no softness of language, and, above all, no pity. Clamence makes his confession, reconstructs the past with all of its small incidents, and intertwines it with the present; however, his confession goes beyond the personal realm and assumes the dimensions of a general confession of the modern world, a cruel and dehumanized world where empty words replace life.

Amsterdam represents the stage of this modern world; impersonal and indifferent human beings play their role as lifeless puppets in the narrow-minded, suffocating bourgeois world. Camus even ventures to compare the concentric canals of this city to Dante's circles of hell. Amsterdam and all modern cities turn into a bourgeois hell. The ugliness and forlornness of the modern city build the framework for Camus' novel.

The reader is kept in a constant state of suspense. The reader participates actively in the development of Clamence's thinking and is stimulated to conjecture on the listener's unexpressed responses. Camus reverses the Proustian concept of remembrance. Marcel Proust aims to reconstruct and revive the past; it imparts richness and happiness to the present moment. Clamence fears the past: It becomes a danger to the present. He remembers those moments in which he failed to make the existential choice, and he has to live with the awareness that he will always miss his moment of choice. The novel ends with his expressed realization that he will always be too late—fortunately—to choose.

Camus, attacking the monotony and indifference of modern life, questioned all the usually accepted values and showed their ambiguous and often absurd nature. He revived the concept that nothing can exist without its reverse. Good and evil, innocence and sin exist side by side. Clamence must live with his own duplicity; he has to accept the paradox that in trying not to fool himself, he fools himself. With *The Fall*, Camus opened the way to what came to be known as the New Novel by showing the relativity of traditionally accepted objective values. From Camus, it is only one step to the novels of Alain Robbe-Grillet and Nathalie Sarraute, who destroy the standard notions of what a novel, and by extension, what the world, is supposed to be like.

Bibliography:
Bloom, Harold, ed. *Albert Camus*. New York: Chelsea House, 1989. Collection of critical essays on the writer's career. An article on *The Fall* provides a close analysis of Camus' complex narrative method and reveals the author's concerns about the modern condition of humanity.
Bree, Germaine, ed. *Camus: A Collection of Critical Essays*. Englewood Cliffs, N.J.: Prentice-Hall, 1962. Essays by eminent scholars give an overview of Camus' accomplishments as a novelist and philosopher. One entry focuses on the later novels, including *The Fall*, which is seen as a personal statement by the novelist against a readership who failed to appreciate his earlier work.
Ellison, David R. *Understanding Albert Camus*. Columbia: University of South Carolina Press, 1990. Study of the major works. Includes a detailed study of *The Fall*, concentrating on its setting, structure, and narrative techniques, and commenting on Camus' handling of religion.
Sprintzen, David. *Camus: A Critical Examination*. Philadelphia: Temple University Press, 1988. Critical analysis of Camus' major works, from a philosophical perspective. A chapter on *The Fall* examines the work as a study of modern anxiety and compares it to other novels by the author.
Thody, Philip. *Albert Camus*. London: Macmillan, 1989. General survey of Camus' novels, examining common themes and focusing on his rejection of Christianity in favor of an existential position. A chapter on *The Fall* concentrates on the author's satiric portrait of lawyers as a scourge of modern society.

THE FALL OF THE HOUSE OF USHER

Type of work: Short fiction
Author: Edgar Allan Poe (1809-1849)
Type of plot: Gothic
Time of plot: Nineteenth century
Locale: The House of Usher
First published: 1839

Principal characters:
RODERICK USHER, a madman
MADELINE, his sister
THE NARRATOR, a visitor

The Story:

As the visitor approached the House of Usher, he was forewarned by the appearance of the old mansion. The fall weather was dull and dreary, the countryside shady and gloomy, and the old house seemed to fit perfectly into the desolate surroundings. The windows looked like vacant eyes staring out over the bleak landscape. The visitor had come to the House of Usher in response to a written plea from his boyhood friend, Roderick Usher. The letter told of an illness of body and mind suffered by the last heir in the ancient line of Usher, and although the letter had strangely filled him with dread, the visitor had felt that he must go to his former friend. The Usher family, unlike most, had left only a direct line of descent, and perhaps it was for this reason that the family itself and the house had become one—the House of Usher. As he approached closer, the house appeared even more formidable to the visitor. The stone was discolored and covered with fungi. The building gave the impression of decay, yet the masonry had not fallen. A barely discernible crack extended in a zigzag line from the roof to the foundation, but otherwise there were no visible breaks in the structure.

The visitor entered the house, gave his things to a servant, and proceeded through several dark passages to the study of the master. There he was stunned at the appearance of his old friend. In Usher's cadaverous face, eyes were liquid and lips pallid. His weblike hair was untrimmed and floated over his brow. All in all, he was a depressing figure. In manner, he was even more morbid. He was afflicted with great sensitivity and strange fear. There were only a few sounds, a few odors, a few foods, and a few textures in clothing that did not fill him with terror. In fact, he was haunted incessantly by unnamed fears.

Even more strangely, he was imbued with the thought that the house itself exerted great influence over his morale and that it had obtained influence over his spirit. Usher's moodiness was heightened by the approaching death of his sister, Lady Madeline. His only living relative, she was wasting away from a strange malady that baffled the doctors. Often the disease revealed its cataleptic (muscular rigidity marked by a lack of response to external stimuli) nature. The visitor saw her only once, on the night of his arrival. She had passed through the room without speaking, and her appearance had filled him with awe and foreboding.

For several days, the visitor attempted to cheer the sick master of Usher and restore him to health, but it seemed, rather, that the hypochondria suffered by Usher affected his friend. More and more, the morbid surroundings and the ramblings of Usher's sick mind preyed upon his visitor. More and more, Usher held that the house itself had molded his spirit and that of his ancestors. The visitor was helpless to dispel this morbid fear and was in danger of subscribing to it himself, so powerful was the influence of the gloomy old mansion.

One day, Usher informed his friend that Madeline was no more. It was Usher's intention to bury her in one of the vaults under the house for a period of two weeks. The strangeness of her malady, he said, demanded the precaution of not placing her immediately in the exposed family burial plot. The two men took the encoffined body into the burial vault beneath the house and deposited it upon a trestle. Turning back the lid of the coffin, they took one last look at the lady, and the visitor remarked on the similarity of appearance between her and her brother. Then Usher told him that they were twins and that their natures had been singularly alike. The man then closed the lid, screwed it down securely, and ascended to the upper rooms.

A noticeable change now took possession of Usher. He paced the floors with unusual vigor. He became more pallid, while his eyes glowed with even greater wildness. His voice was little more than a quaver, and his words were utterances of extreme fear. He seemed to have a ghastly secret that he could not share. More and more, the visitor felt that Usher's superstitious beliefs about the malignant influence of the house were true. He could not sleep, and his body began to tremble almost as unreasonably as Usher's.

One night, during a severe storm, the visitor heard low and unrecognizable sounds that filled him with terror. Dressing, he had begun to pace the floor of his apartment when he heard a soft knock at his door. Usher entered, carrying a lamp. His manner was hysterical and his eyes those of a madman. When he threw the window open to the storm, they were lifted almost off their feet by the intensity of the wind. Usher seemed to see something horrible in the night, and the visitor picked up the first book that came to hand and tried to calm his friend by reading. The story was that of Ethelred and Sir Launcelot, and as he read, the visitor seemed to hear the echo of a cracking and ripping sound described in the story. Later, he heard a rasping and grating, of what he knew not. Usher sat facing the door, as if in a trance. His head and his body rocked from side to side in a gentle motion. He murmured some sort of gibberish, as if he were not aware of his friend's presence.

At last, his ravings became intelligible. He muttered at first but spoke louder and louder until he reached a scream. Madeline was alive. He had buried Madeline alive. For days, he had heard her feebly trying to lift the coffin lid. Now she had escaped her tomb and was coming in search of him. At that pronouncement, the door of the room swung back and on the threshold stood the shrouded Lady Madeline of Usher. There was blood on her clothing and evidence of superhuman struggle. She ran to her terrified brother, and the two fell to the floor in death.

The visitor fled from the house in terror. He gazed back as he ran and saw the house of horror split asunder in a zigzag manner, down the line of the crack he had seen as he first looked upon the old mansion. There was a loud noise, like the sound of many waters, and the pond at its base received all that was left of the ruined House of Usher.

Critical Evaluation:

Edgar Allan Poe probably remains, both in his life and his work, America's most controversial writer. Numerous biographical and critical studies have not succeeded in rectifying the initially distorted "myth" of Poe, promulgated by his hostile first biographer, as a self-destructive, alcoholic, almost demoniac creature. Even today, after much serious research and analysis, the true Poe remains enigmatic and elusive. The same is true of his works. Experts as important and varied as D. H. Lawrence, Henry James, T. S. Eliot, Charles Baudelaire, and Aldous Huxley have differed greatly in assessing his works' merits, with opinions ranging from extravagant eulogy to total dismissal. No work of his has excited more diverse opinion or been given more conflicting analyses than his short story "The Fall of the House of Usher."

The problem is that there are many completely different, yet seemingly valid, interpretations of the tale; contradictory readings can explain all of the story's numerous ambiguities. Yet, clearly, as one prominent Poe critic has lamented, the contradictory readings "cannot all be right." Is there any way of choosing between these views or of synthesizing the best of them into a single one? Perhaps the task is not impossible if two important facts about the author are remembered: He was an adroit, conscious craftsman and critic who worked out his ideas with mathematical precision, and yet he was essentially a lyric poet.

These diverse readings can be divided roughly into three primary types: natural or psychological, supernatural, and symbolic. In the first approach, the analysis has usually focused on the "unreliable" narrator as he chronicles Roderick Usher's descent into madness. As an artist, intellectual, and introvert, Usher has become so lopsided that his prolonged isolation, coupled with the sickness of his sister, has driven him to the edge of madness; along with the narrator, the reader sees him go over the edge. Or perhaps the tale is simply a detective story minus a detective; Usher manipulates the narrator into helping him murder Madeline and then goes insane from the emotional strain. The crucial "fantastic" elements in the story—Madeline's return from the tomb and the collapse of the house into the tarn—are "logically" explained in terms of the narrator's mounting hysteria, the resulting hallucination, and the natural destructiveness of the storm.

According to the second general view, the actions of the characters can be explained only by postulating a supernatural agency: The Usher curse is working itself out; the house is possessed and is destroying the occupants; Roderick is a demon drawing vitality from his sister until, as a nemesis figure, she returns to punish him; Madeline is a vampire claiming her victim.

In the third view, the story is seen as an allegory: Roderick as intellect is suppressing sensuality (Madeline) until it revolts; Madeline is a mother figure who returns from the grave to punish Usher-Poe for deserting her and for having incestuous desires; Roderick is the artist who must destroy himself in order to create; the entire story is a symbolic enactment of the Apocalypse according to Poe.

Both as a critic and a writer, Poe was thoroughly aware of the machinery of the gothic, and "The Fall of the House of Usher" is a veritable catalog of devices from the genre—the haunted mansion, the artistic hero-villain, the twins motif, suggestions of vampirism, the dark crypts, the violent electrical storms. It does not follow, however, that because Poe utilizes the conventions of the form, he is also holding himself to the substance of them. It is precisely because he does not commit himself exclusively to either a rational, supernatural, or symbolic reading of the tale that he is able to provoke emotional reactions by indirection and implication that would be impossible if he fixed his meaning more precisely. The technique is essentially that of the lyric poet who uses the power of image, atmosphere, and suggestion to evoke emotions and to produce exactly one emotional, not rational, effect on the reader—which was Poe's stated aim as a short-story writer.

"I feel that the period will sooner or later arrive," says Roderick Usher, "when I must abandon life and reason together, in some struggle with the grim phantasm, FEAR." Thus, Poe underscores "fear" as the central emotion he wishes to provoke, and the story can best be discussed in terms of how he develops this response.

The tale divides into five distinct parts: first, the description of the house and the background of the narrator's relationship to Usher; second, his meeting with Roderick Usher that ends with his glimpse of Lady Madeline; third, the survey of Usher's art, that is, music, painting, the recitation of the poem "The Haunted Palace," Roderick's theory of "sentience," and the description of the library; fourth, Madeline's "death" and entombment; and fifth, her return from the crypt counterpointed against the narrator's reading of "The Mad Trist" story which culminates in the death of the twins, the narrator's flight, and the collapse of the house into the tarn. Each of these phases not only furthers the plot line, but also intensifies the emotions provoked in the reader by means of the narrator's progressive hysteria and the growing distortion of the atmosphere.

The narrator is quickly characterized as a skeptic, who attempts to explain everything rationally, but who is, at the same time, quite susceptible to unexplained anxieties and undefined premonitions. His first glimpse of the Usher mansion provokes "a sense of unsufferable gloom." As he describes it, the house resembles a giant face or skull with "eye-like windows" and hairlike "minute fungi" that almost seem to hold the decayed building together, as well as a "barely perceptible fissure" that threatens to rip it apart. He is even more horrified when he looks into the tarn (a small, stagnant lake in front of the house) and sees the house's inverted reflection in the black water. Thus, in the first paragraph of the tale, readers are introduced to three crucial elements: the subjective reactions of the narrator, which begin with this furtive, general uneasiness and will end in complete hysteria; the central image of a huge, dead, decaying object that is, paradoxically, very alive; and the first of many reflections or doubles that reinforce and intensify the atmosphere and implications of the story.

When the narrator meets his old friend Roderick Usher, the other side of the death-life paradox is suggested. Whereas the dead objects seem "alive," the "live" things seem dead. All the peripheral characters—the two servants, the doctor, the "living" Madeline—are shadows. Roderick, with his "cadaverous" complexion, "large, liquid and luminous eyes," "thin and very pallid" lips, and "hair of more than web-like softness," seems more zombie than human. Moreover, his description mirrors that of the house's exterior: His eyes are like the windows; his hair resembles the fungi.

Roderick does, however, have a definable personality. For all of the spectral hints, Poe never abandons the possibility that Roderick's character and fate can be explained naturally. Although Usher's behavior is violent and erratic, perhaps manic-depressive by modern clinical standards, tenuous rationalizations are provided for everything he does. Nor does Roderick's role as an artist resolve the questions about his character. The extended catalog of his artistic activities may seem digressive in terms of Poe's strict single-effect theory, but it is, in fact, the necessary preparation for the story's harrowing finale. Each of Roderick's artistic ventures conforms to both his realistic personality and the otherworldliness of the situation; they can either signal his descent into psychosis or his ineffectual attempts to understand and withstand the incursion of supernatural forces. His dirges suggest death; his abstract painting of a vaultlike structure previews Madeline's interment. When he recites "The Haunted Palace" poem, he is either metaphorically recounting his own fall into madness, or he is, literally, talking about "haunting." Roderick's statements about the sentience of all vegetable things—that is, the conscious life in all inanimate matter—brings a notion that has previously been latent in the reader's mind to the surface. Finally, Roderick's exotic library, made up almost entirely of books about supernatural journeys, suggests either a perversely narrow and bizarre taste or an attempt to acquire the knowledge needed to defend against demoniac intruders.

Nevertheless, for all of the mounting intensity of suggestion and atmosphere, the actual story does not begin until almost two-thirds of the narrative has been completed. When Roderick announces that Lady Madeline "is no more," the story quickens. It is at this point that the narrator notices the "striking similitude between the brother and sister" and so emphasizes the "twin theme," the most important reflection or double in the tale. As they entomb her, the narrator takes note of the "mockery of a faint blush upon the bosom and the face." Does this suggest a trace of life and implicate Roderick, consciously or unconsciously, in her murder? Or, does it hint at an "undead" specter who, knowing that she will return from the grave, mocks the attempt to inter her?

Nowhere is the value of indirection in the maximizing of suspense more evident than in the last sequence of the story. Having established the literary context of the narrative, Poe then counterpoints the reading of a rather trite medieval romance against Madeline's actual return from the crypt. At the simplest level, "The Mad Trist" tale is a suspense-building device that magnifies the reader's excitement as he awaits Madeline's certain reappearance. Thematically, it suggests a parallel—either straight or ironic, depending on the reader's interpretation—between the knight Ethelred's quest and Madeline's return from the tomb. Reinforced by the violent storm, the narrator's frenzy, and Usher's violence, Madeline's return, her mutually fatal embrace of her brother, the narrator's flight, and the disintegration of the house itself, all fuse into a shattering final effect, which is all that Poe claimed he wanted, and a provocative insight into—what? The collapse of a sick mind? The inevitable self-destruction of the hyperintroverted artistic temperament? The final end of aristocratic inbreeding? Or incest? Or vampirism? Or the end of the world?

Although the meaning of "The Fall of the House of Usher" remains elusive, the experience of the story is powerful, disturbing, and lasting. In the final analysis, the experience of the story is where its greatness lies and why it must be considered one of the finest short stories of its kind ever written.

"Critical Evaluation" by Keith Neilson

Bibliography:

Beebe, Maurice. "The Universe of Roderick Usher." In *Poe: A Collection of Critical Essays*. Edited by Robert Regan. Englewood Cliffs, N.J.: Prentice-Hall, 1967. Discusses the cosmological theory that underlies "Fall of the House of Usher." Claims that an understanding of Poe's *Eureka* helps the reader understand the story as symbolic drama.

Hoffman, Daniel. *Poe Poe Poe Poe Poe Poe Poe*. Garden City, N.Y.: Doubleday, 1972. A personal study of the mind of Poe, containing an extensive discussion of doubling and desire in "The Fall of the House of Usher." Argues that the story is a catalog of all Poe's obsessional themes.

May, Charles E. *Edgar Allan Poe: A Study of the Short Fiction*. Boston: Twayne, 1991. A study of Poe's development of the short story as a genre; discusses "The Fall of the House of Usher" as an esthetic, self-reflexive fable of the basic dilemma of the artist. Also includes an essay with a reader-response approach to the story by Ronald Bieganowski.

Robinson, E. Arthur. "Order and Sentience in 'The Fall of the House of Usher.'" *PMLA* 76 (1961): 68-81. One of the most extensive studies of the story; focuses on its underlying pattern of thought and thematic structure.

Thompson, G. R., and Virgil L. Lokke, eds. *Ruined Eden of the Present*. West Lafayette, Ind.: Purdue University Press, 1981. Contains a debate between G. R. Thompson and Patrick F. Quinn about the psychic state of the narrator in the story.

THE FAMILY AT GILJE

Type of work: Novel
Author: Jonas Lie (1833-1908)
Type of plot: Domestic realism
Time of plot: Nineteenth century
Locale: Norway
First published: Familjen paa Gilje, 1883 (English translation, 1920)

Principal characters:

    CAPTAIN JÄGER, an army officer
    JORGEN, his son
    INGER-JOHANNA, his daughter
    THINKA, another daughter
    MRS. JÄGER, his wife
    CAPTAIN RÖNNOW, another officer
    ARENT GRIP, a student
    GULCKE, the sheriff

The Story:

It was obvious that Inger-Johanna was her father's favorite. He was an army captain, in charge at Gilje. When a fellow officer, Captain Rönnow, stopped at the house, Captain Jäger was delighted because the guest seemed so charmed by Inger-Johanna. Mrs. Jäger was a sister of the governor, and Captain Rönnow told the Jägers that he would petition the governor's wife, with whom he was in favor, to take Inger-Johanna into their home for a year, so that she could learn the ways of society in the city. Gilje was a deserted mountain post and not at all suitable for a young lady of Inger-Johanna's obvious charms.

Captain Jäger wanted his beloved daughter to visit her aunt, but when he learned the cost of the new clothing required, he stormed at his poor wife and could not be quieted. Perhaps his blustering was caused by sorrow at losing his favorite daughter, although he was happy that she would have such a fine opportunity.

Before Inger-Johanna left, she met a student named Arent Grip, the son of an old friend of her father. In spite of his radical ideas, the girl found him interesting and was glad that he too would be in the city.

After the departure of his oldest daughter, the captain's house was desolate, for Thinka, another daughter, had gone to work for a judge in Ryfylke. Poor Jorgen, the only son, and a younger daughter were put through hours of lessons to ease their father's loneliness.

Each letter from Inger-Johanna was read again and again. After her initial shyness had worn off, she loved her life in the city. Parties and balls delighted her. Both Captain Rönnow and Arent Grip were present at many of the functions, her aunt having secured a place for Grip in her husband's office. The aunt also wrote to confide that she secretly hoped a match would develop between the girl and Rönnow, who was advancing rapidly and would be a good catch. The aunt was not fond of Grip. She found him too spirited and unrestrained in expressing his unpopular ideas. Inger-Johanna, however, had completely won over her aunt, who insisted that the girl return home for a visit and then come back to the city for another season.

During his daughter's visit, Captain Jäger was in a delighted mood. Grip called on the family again and arranged to spend time alone with Inger-Johanna. They took a surveying trip into the mountains with her father and Jorgen, and Grip found Jorgen a bright lad who deserved a better education. In his talks with Inger-Johanna, Grip claimed that fundamentals were all that mattered in life, not the external symbols of success. He wanted people to be themselves, not influenced by worldly values.

Inger-Johanna returned to the city before Thinka came home for a visit. The younger daughter had fallen in love with a young clerk in her uncle's office, but when her relative learned of the affair, he fired the clerk, who was poor and without prospects. Thinka often thought of him after her return home, although her parents urged her to forget him.

Sheriff Gulcke called at Gilje and found Thinka attractive. Because his wife had died only three months before, he could say nothing so soon after his loss; but during his stay, he often cast an appreciative eye toward Thinka. In the meantime, Thinka wrote long letters to her sister, to tell of her love for the poor clerk, for whom she had promised to wait. Inger-Johanna, tiring of balls and city life, wrote that she remained only to please her aunt. Grip had changed her way of thinking and had made her see the uselessness of such a life.

Jorgen went to the city to school. Grip tutored him but said that Jorgen should be sent to England or to America to learn a mechanic's trade, because that was the field in which he had great talent. Later Jorgen did sail for England and then to America, a fact which Captain Jäger forever held against Grip.

Thinka was right in her fear that she would never be allowed to marry her clerk. Sheriff Gulcke asked for her hand, and because she was without will to deny her father's wishes, she accepted the older man. After the marriage, she was a good and faithful wife, acting almost as a nurse to her husband. He was kind to her and consented to her every desire, but her heart was sad. Inger-Johanna was dismayed that her sister had no will of her own, and she refused to accept the idea that women were to bend to the will of their fathers and husbands.

Inger-Johanna was soon to be tested. Captain Rönnow wrote her father for her hand. It was the proudest moment of Captain Jäger's life. At first, Inger-Johanna accepted, for Grip had made no proposal and she knew that Rönnow was the man her father desired for her. Before the wedding, however, she returned suddenly from the city. She admitted to herself and to her family that she could love no one but Grip and could not marry Rönnow. Although her father was bitterly disappointed, he could not force his favorite daughter to marry against her will. Sorrowfully, he wrote his old friend his decision.

From that day on, Captain Jäger's health rapidly failed. He suffered dizziness and weakness. He was forced to take a leave of absence from his military duties. One day his carriage did not return home. When the servant went to look for him, he found the horse standing at the foot of Gilje hill, the reins loose on the ground. The captain of Gilje was dead.

Twenty years passed. Mrs. Jäger was dead, and Jorgen was doing well in America. Inger-Johanna, a schoolteacher, taught the children the ideas and ideals she had learned from Grip. Meanwhile, he wandered over the land, a drunkard and an ascetic by turn. He carefully avoided Inger-Johanna but constantly sought news of her. Finally he went to her school and stood by the window to hear the sound of her voice. He saw her face again as she looked out into the night. He left then, sick with pneumonia. When word of his illness reached Inger-Johanna, she went to him and nursed him until his death. Often he was irrational, at times completely lucid. After his death, she knew that he had given her her only reason for living, her spirit for truth and freedom.

Critical Evaluation:

The Family at Gilje is often considered only as a minor Scandinavian classic. It is accorded little significance outside of books of Scandinavian literary history. The novel nevertheless reflects many of the major themes of mainstream European literature of the nineteenth century. One of the most striking commonalities is the theme of the conflict between the individual and various social codes. Very often, this is expressed in terms of romantic love as a metaphor for individual choice. Although Inger-Johanna Jäger is obliged to chose between submission to what her society wants for her and her own desires.

In bringing up Inger-Johanna, the Captain and Mrs. Jäger are faced with a paradox. As members of the relatively prosperous landholding class, they are at the top of the social pyramid, as far as Gilje is concerned, but in the eyes of the wider world they are rural, backward, and, most importantly, culturally impoverished. In sending Inger-Johanna to the city, they try to gain entry for their daughter into social circles that they have not themselves penetrated. The parents find, however, that once the process of Inger-Johanna's acculturation is under way, it can not necessarily be controlled. The reader can sense before it happens that Inger-Johanna will find the charms of the conventional Captain Rönnow lacking and prefer the earnest student Arent Grip. One of Grip's charms is that Inger-Johana's aunt and her parents find him an unattractive candidate for her hand in marriage. As often happens in the nineteenth century European novel, the choice of a spouse is used as a metaphor for self-discovery and the exploration of various philosophical alternatives. Inger-Johanna is exposed to various potential directions in life, and she is encouraged to have the appearance of exploring all her options, but she finds that ultimately her family tries to constrain her freedom.

Although the Jägers are frustrated by Inger-Johanna's willful and headstrong ways, they nevertheless prefer her to the more earthbound Thinka, whose ordinariness illuminates by contrast Inger-Johanna's intellectual and spiritual curiosity. Jörgen Jäger is more like his oldest sister in his ambition and drive. He eventually finds his energies can not be contained by provincial Norway, and ends up immigrating to America, where the traits that threatened to make his life unfulfilled at home assist him in achieving considerable success in America. Being a woman, Inger-Johanna does not really have the option of emigrating alone in the society of her day.

The plot of *The Family at Gilje* surprises by its relative unconventionality. Throughout the first half of the book, the reader is led to think either that Inger-Johanna will elope with Grip and be spiritually and emotionally fulfilled, or that she will marry Rönnow and have her energy and impulsiveness co-opted and reintegrated into the existing structure of social manners and mores. She ends up marrying neither man. Looking beyond the superficial plot contrivance by which Lie secures this outcome, the reader can see that Inger-Johanna's disappointment and renunciation of her once-cherished personal goals provide, for all their depressing limitation, an opportunity for the fulfillment of her spiritual potential. This outcome stands in vivid contrast to that of Thinka, who does not have the backbone to resist the imposition on her of an unwanted husband by her family. Inger-Johanna is aging, alone, and disappointed at the end of the book. Yet, unlike Thinka, she has not only kept her freedom, she has also maintained her personal and moral integrity.

The crucial force in the book's unexpected plot is Grip. Grip is a character type familiar to the nineteenth century novel. He is the idealist who rebels against ingrained social expectations and who advertises vague, radical ideas while also exerting a sort of romantic charisma— a figure highly familiar to European readers of the day. Most of these figures turn out to be either hopelessly shallow and unrealistic or ultimately slack and self-serving, but Grip is different. He has deep beliefs to which he faithfully adheres and by which he lives his life. More important, he is a good man. He is not only intelligent and engaging, but genuinely wants to help others. The crude and backward Norway of his day cannot comprehend these traits, so his life seems a waste. His life is not wasted, however, because he provided Inger-Johanna with the vision of how life should be, how it should have meaning. Even though they see each other only briefly in the twenty years between the time of their failed courtship and that of Grip's death, and although their relationship is never consummated, their relationship has, in spiritual terms, a positive ending. Grip enables Inger-Johanna to glimpse the full beauty of life, even if she never fully experiences it.

Lie's novel thus turns from being a rather conventional chronicle of bourgeois family life toward being a portrait of the imaginative triumphs that the framework of family life can not fully succeed in containing. Lie is not hostile to bourgeois society; he recognizes its necessity and achievements. The Jäger family is a genuinely happy one, and without the kindness of her parents Inger-Johanna could have never achieved her own unusual and winning personality. In a way, Lie argues, all Inger-Johanna was trying to do is take her childhood happiness and reproduce it on a higher, more spiritual plane by marrying Grip; it is only the constraints of society that prevent Inger-Johanna from fulfilling herself within the bounds of family life. After this book, Lie's interest turned much more toward the mystical and the spiritual, toward strange sea tales and ghost stories. *The Family at Gilje*, being his most mainstream work, is the only book of Lie's to have any recognized place in world literature. It holds that status because of the depth of its characters and the importance of its themes.

"Critical Evaluation" by Nicholas Birns

Bibliography:

Gustafson, Alrik. "Impressionistic Realism: Jonas Lie." In *Six Scandinavian Novelists*. Minneapolis: University of Minnesota Press, 1966. Places Lie within contemporary developments in European fiction. Argues that the scrupulous realism of the novel does not preclude formal experiments with tone, character, and symbolism. Examines Lie's stance toward his own characters, especially Captain Jäger.

Larsen, Hanna. "Jonas Lie, 1833-1909." *American-Scandinavian Review* 21 (1993): 461-471. Demonstrates the centrality of *The Family at Gilje* to Lie's career; argues that the rest of his achievement was a falling-off from the clarity achieved in the novel. Examines the role of the town of Gilje and the surrounding landscape in the thematic and symbolic architecture of the novel.

Lyngstad, Sverre. *Jonas Lie*. Boston: Twayne, 1977. The most comprehensive discussion of Lie's work in English. Sees the novel as presenting Norwegian cultural history within the frame of the story of the Jäger family. Examines the differences between Inger-Jonhanna and her sisters and the issues at play between Inger-Johanna and Grip. Comments extensively on the symbolism and values of the book.

_____. "The Vortex and Related Imagery in Jonas Lie's Fiction." *Scandinavian Studies* 51 (Summer, 1979): 211-248. Explores Lie's achievement with a closely textured analysis of Lie's work, focusing on the meaning and integration provided to the novel through its symbols.

MacFarlane, James W. "Jonas Lie." In *Ibsen and the Temper of Norwegian Literature*. London: Harrap, 1960. Compares Lie to later innovators in Norwegian literature such as Ibsen; finds considerable importance in Lie's depictions of bourgeois lifestyles.

THE FAMILY OF PASCUAL DUARTE

Type of work: Novel
Author: Camilo José Cela (1916-   )
Type of plot: Social realism
Time of plot: Early twentieth century
Locale: Extremadura, Spain
First published: La familia de Pascual Duarte, 1942 (English translation, 1946)

> *Principal characters:*
> PASCUAL DUARTE, a convict
> PASCUAL'S MOTHER
> MARIO, his brother
> ROSARIO, his sister
> LOLA, his first wife
> EL ESTIRAO, Rosario and Lola's lover

The Story:

Pascual Duarte was sentenced to death and decided to write a history of his life to serve as a warning to others, or so he implied. Pascual was born to a poor Extremaduran peasant family and was raised in an atmosphere of hate and resentment. Both parents were abusive drunkards and his younger brother Mario was retarded, unable even to walk. The only saving grace of the family was Rosario, his sister, but she had left home to better her situation by becoming a prostitute. She returned home once, ill with fever, but left as soon as she was well. Fifteen years after Rosario, Mario was born. Two days before his birth, Pascual's father, Esteban, was bitten by a rabid dog. The family, afraid of being attacked, locked Esteban in an armoire, where he died on the day of Mario's birth, screaming, driven mad by the disease.

Mario, scorned by everyone except Rosario, crawled and lived on the floor with the pigs and dogs. One day, the pigs ate his ears, and, from then on, it was hard for the family to even look at him. Generally unresponsive, Mario would go into shrieking fits at the sight of pigs. During one of these episodes, Don Rafael, who may have been the boy's father, kicked the child into unconsciousness, blood gushing from the boy's ear cavity. Pascual's mother laughed, but although Pascual, fearing to be called "soft," also did nothing, from that day forward, his active hatred of his mother grew. Shortly afterward, Mario was found drowned in a vat of oil, perhaps murdered by Rafael.

Pascual fell in love with, and raped, Lola. On discovering that she was pregnant, he married her. On their wedding day, their horse injured an old woman, a bad omen that presaged Lola's fall from that same horse on the day they returned from their honeymoon. The fall caused a miscarriage. Pascual was not with her. He had been celebrating with friends in a bar, on a drinking spree that ended in Pascual's seriously wounding a friend who had taunted him.

Pascual had always been given to violence. When he learned of his wife's miscarriage, he blamed the horse and stabbed the animal to death. One day, while sitting in his favorite spot with his only friend, his dog, nearby, he had seemed to read reproach in the animal's eyes and had repeatedly shot the dog to rid himself of that look. Pascual also was tormented by premonitions of ill fortune. When his first child (his wife's second pregnancy) was born, although the baby seemed healthy, he could not rid himself of a sense of foreboding, and the child did die of illness in early infancy. After the baby's death, Pascual could not endure the atmosphere in his home and fled to Madrid. From Madrid, he traveled to La Coruña, hoping to set sail for America. The trip was too costly, however, and after two years of working at odd jobs, Pascual returned home, only to find his wife pregnant with another man's—El Estirao's—child.

El Estirao was the abusive pimp and lover of Rosario who had always delighted in taunting Pascual. His seduction of Pascual's wife maddened the peasant, and, after the effort of confessing the truth to him, Lola had suddenly died in Pascual's arms. When El Estirao returned, looking for Rosario, Pascual killed him, crushing his spine. For this crime he was sent to prison, but was released for good behavior after only serving two years.

When he returned home after his imprisonment, he found no one there to welcome him. Rosario had gone again, and his mother's conduct toward him worsened. He married again, this time to the timid daughter of the local midwife, who had secretly cared for him. His mother's treatment of Esperanza, however, was terrible, and Pascual, now certain that his mother had been and still was the source of all of his trouble, decided he must kill her to survive. Full of loathing, he carefully planned the crime, but at the last moment was unable to strike. He stood paralyzed by her bed until she awoke. After a fierce struggle, he finally subdued and killed her. Earlier, Pascual may also have been responsible for the assassination of the village patriarch, Don Jesús, during an uprising at the start of the Civil War. Pascual was captured and was waiting to be hanged, but whether for the death of his mother or Don Jesús was uncertain.

Pascual, in his memoirs, professed to have come to terms with his fate, but, at the end, he was led kicking and screaming to the scaffold. He did not describe this episode, as one might expect, in his memoirs. Other witnesses reported his shameful end.

Critical Evaluation:

It is now a commonplace to state that Camilo José Cela, who won the 1989 Nobel Prize in Literature, is one of the foremost writers in the Spanish language. In 1942, the publication by a then-unknown writer of the violent *The Family of Pascual Duarte* caused a sensation. Its appearance marked the start of the contemporary Spanish novel and critics and public were shocked by its theme and by the apparent lack of censorship in a Spain where many writers and intellectuals were dead, exiled, or still incarcerated in Franco's prisons.

Narrated in first person, the novel purports to be the life history of an Extremaduran peasant, awaiting execution, who has been mired in a black destiny of heredity and environment. The core of the novel is the question of responsibility. How much influence did Pascual Duarte have on the course of his own life? The bleak answer seems to be: none. Although Duarte states that he is recounting his life so that others may flee from his example and choose other paths, it is evident that Duarte himself believes that his life has been predestined, a fate that he was born into. There are ambiguities and ironies in the text, however, that allow for many interpretations, moral and otherwise.

Pascual's history, after all, is the truth according to Pascual. All the characters are seen through the filter of Pascual's vision of the world. For instance, it becomes clear that Pascual is in some way responsible for the premeditated assassination of Don Jesús, the rich man of the village, but Pascual only hints at this. He wants us to view him as only the victim of his circumstances and to view his actions as the product of spontaneous and understandable rage. In addition, parts of the story are told in unchronological flashbacks so that the motivations that trigger Duarte's responses are often vague and imprecise.

Pascual's defense in a hostile environment is to strike out with violence. It is a measure of the brutishness of the human characters that his attacks on his nonhuman victims—his pet dog, for example—are more appalling than his actions against his fellow human beings. The tenuous line between bestiality and humanity is symbolized by Mario, his pathetic little brother, who lives in filth on the floor and who is treated worse than the pigs who live with him. Pascual's violence accelerates until his hatred centers on the one person he has always hated and blamed for everything and who is never even given a personal name. His mother's death is a symbol to him of freedom, and his first words after her murder are "I could breathe."

This sense of suffocation by society and family is one of the basic themes of the novel. Its images change from the cramped shack in which Pascual lives, to the black circle of grieving women belittling and badgering him after the death of his child, to the graveyard scenes with its high walls, and to Pascual awaiting death in another cramped box.

The shocking murder of his mother is one extreme act in a life characterized by extreme violence. *The Family of Pascual Duarte* is representative of *tremendismo*, a literary movement of the early 1940's that described its protagonists as trapped in an encircling vise of poverty, ignorance, and oppression from which the only escape is violent rebellion. The desired effect is one of shock at the "tremendous" nature of the actions depicted and their resultant consequences.

Nevertheless, although the definition of *tremendismo* can serve equally well as a description of the life of Pascual Duarte, the success of the work, and perhaps its lack of censorship, were due to its being very much within the Spanish narrative tradition. Realism has always been the hallmark of the Spanish novel. Spanish naturalistic writers never shied away from violence, and Pascual Duarte can be seen as a modern-day, although much more negative, successor to the famous *picaro* of the sixteenth and seventeen centuries. Another tribute to the past is Cela's use of the Spanish literary device of a neutral transcriber who just happens to have found the pages of a curious manuscript.

What is purely Cela and what sets the novel apart is the intense blending of environment and atmosphere. The harshness of Extremadura (the name literally joins the words "extreme" and "hard" or "harsh") becomes a character just as real as the people. The grim presence of a brutish superstitious land is in Duarte's description of his village and hovel, in the unpaved roads that all seem to lead to the cemetery, and in the black landscape dimly seen through a dirty train window. It is significant that whenever Pascual Duarte leaves Extremadura, he is treated relatively well. He enjoys his life in Madrid and makes friends; he finds work in La Coruña. Even in prison his jailers see some good in him, and he gains early release, but he returns to Extremadura. His fate seems to be calling him back (he says so in his narrative) and it seems inevitable that it will crush him, just as the death of his mother seems inevitable. His past is always his future.

Charlene E. Suscavage

Bibliography:
Foster, David W. *Forms of the Novel in the Work of Camilo José Cela.* Columbia: University of Missouri Press, 1967. Analyzes Cela's constant tinkering with the narrative structure and intent of his novels and his seeming lack of satisfaction with previous efforts.
Hoyle, Alan. *Cela: La familia de Pascual Duarte.* London: Grant & Cutler, 1994. One of a series of critical guides to Spanish texts, it is a good first introduction to the work. Written in English with Spanish quotations.
Kirsner, Robert. *The Novels and Travels of Camilo José Cela.* Chapel Hill: University of North Carolina Press, 1963. Discusses the narrative techniques used in Cela's novels and trave-

logues in which the line between the two genres is often blurred. A good analysis of the treatment of landscape in *The Family of Pascual Duarte*.

McPheeters, D. W. *Camilo José Cela*. Boston: Twayne, 1969. The best and easiest introduction to the early work of Cela, with special emphasis on *The Family of Pascual Duarte*.

Spires, Robert C. *Mode of Existence and the Concept of Morality in "La familia de Pascual Duarte."* Ames, Iowa: Orrin Frank, 1968. Analyzes the moral climate of the time as well as that of the novel. Good discussion of how Pascual sees the world and how the world sees him.

THE FAMILY REUNION

Type of work: Drama
Author: T. S. Eliot (1888-1965)
Type of plot: Symbolic realism
Time of plot: Twentieth century
Locale: England
First performed: 1939; first published, 1939

Principal characters:
AMY, LADY MONCHENSEY, an old lady
HARRY, her son
AGATHA, her sister
DOWNING, Harry's servant
MARY, Amy's ward

The Story:

Amy, Lady Monchensey, was reluctant to have the lights turned on. She had to sit in the house from October until June, for in winter the sun rarely warmed the cold earth of northern England. Since all she could do was measure time, she hardly wanted to make night come too soon.

The whole family, except her three sons, had gathered to celebrate her birthday, and the sons were expected that evening. The conversation while they waited out the time was tasteless. Gerald and Charles, Amy's brothers-in-law, felt that the younger generation did not accept its responsibilities. Ivy and Violet, her younger sisters, agreed that youth was becoming decadent. When they asked Mary her opinion, as a representative of the new generation, Amy's ward was nettled. Nearing thirty, she had always been poor and had remained unmarried; she thought she belonged to no generation.

Amy lived only to keep Wishwood, the family estate, together. Since her husband's death, she had been head of the house. She knew her family, settled in its ways, was getting older; soon death would come as a surprise for them all. Only Agatha, her older sister, seemed to find a meaning in death. Harry, the oldest son, had been gone eight years. Amy hoped he could drop back into the old routine at the family home, but Agatha was doubtful. The past was over; the future could be built only on the present. When Harry came back he could not take up life where he left off, because he would be a new Harry.

The others began speculating. None had liked Harry's wife, a demanding woman who had persuaded him to take her away from Wishwood. On their travels she had been lost at sea, apparently swept overboard in a storm. Amy said they must feel no remorse for her death.

Harry surprised them by being the first of the sons to arrive. When he seemed upset because the blinds were not drawn, the others reminded him that in the country there was no one to look in. Nevertheless, Harry kept staring at the window. He could see the Eumenides, the vengeful spirits. They had been with him a long time, but only at Wishwood could he see them. He greeted the assembled company with an effort.

Harry became impatient when the relatives began talking of all the old things waiting at home for him. Nothing had ever happened to them; they had gone through life half asleep. Harry, however, was doing some soul searching. In mid-Atlantic he had pushed his wife overboard. Now the Furies were always with him.

Only Agatha seemed to understand him. The others thought him overtired and urged him to go lie down for a while. When he left, they decided to invite Dr. Warburton for dinner so that the family doctor could have a look at him.

Charles and Gerald called in Downing, Harry's servant, to question him. Violet and Ivy objected because they feared scandal. Agatha, however, made no objection, because questioning Downing was as irrelevant as calling in Dr. Warburton. Downing seemed to be frank. He hardly thought Harry's wife had had the courage to commit suicide, and while he was a little distrait, Harry had always appeared normal. The only thing amiss that Downing had noticed was that Harry had always been too much with his wife.

Mary appealed to Agatha for help in getting away from Wishwood. She knew that Amy wanted her to stay on and marry Harry; in that way Amy would have a tame daughter-in-law for a companion. Agatha, however, refused help. Mary should have had the courage to leave earlier; since Harry had returned she could not run away.

When Harry talked with Mary about his fears and doubts, she tried to understand his feeling that change was inevitable. They reminisced about the hollow tree in which they had played as children and about their regret when Amy had it cut down. Harry saw the Furies again in the window embrasure. Startled by his manner, Mary pulled back the curtains to show that nothing was there.

Dr. Warburton came early for dinner to have a confidential talk with Harry. He tried to attack Harry's disturbance indirectly by warning him that Amy's health was very poor and that Harry must take the burden of Wishwood off her shoulders. Harry recalled the unpleasantness of his boyhood when being good meant pleasing Amy. Abruptly, he demanded to know something of his father. The old doctor assured him that there had been no scandal. His father and mother had just agreed to separate, and his father had gone abroad to die.

A police sergeant came to tell the family that John, having suffered a slight concussion in an auto accident, could not be there for the birthday dinner. Although the family buzzed with the news, Harry shocked them with his statement that it hardly mattered because his brother John was unconscious all the time anyway.

A long-distance call came from Arthur, the other brother. He had been in an accident too, and his license had been suspended for drunken driving. Still troubled about his father, Harry pressed Agatha for more details. Agatha remembered his father's feelings, but his mother had complemented his weaknesses. Then Agatha lost her repressions and told the truth. While Amy was pregnant with Harry, her husband had plotted to kill her. Agatha had talked him out of his scheme; she could not bear to think of destroying the new life Amy was carrying.

At that news Harry felt a great release, for the curse of the house seemed clearer. When the Eumenides appeared again, Harry was no longer frightened. He knew at last that the Furies were not pursuing him; he was following them. Harry decided to leave Wishwood.

Amy, furious at the news that Harry was going away, blamed Agatha, the younger sister who had stolen her husband thirty-five years ago and now was taking her son. Mary pleaded with Agatha to stop Harry's departure, but to no avail; Harry had crossed the frontier of reality. Then Mary asked her help in getting a situation, perhaps a fellowship, so she could leave too. As the two women became more confidential, they each revealed that they had also seen the Eumenides. That knowledge was a bond uniting them outside the stifling confines of Wishwood. When they talked with Downing, he confessed he had seen the Furies but he had paid little attention to them; they were Harry's ghosts. Just before she died, Amy began to understand what was happening at Wishwood. Agatha and Mary brought in the birthday cake and blew out the candles as they circled around it. The rest of the family began talking about the will.

Critical Evaluation:

The Family Reunion, T. S. Eliot's second full-length play, is a significant contribution to the world of verse drama. After *Murder in the Cathedral* (1935), Eliot declined all invitations to write more religious, historical dramas. He chose instead to attempt a synthesis of religious and secular drama on a contemporary theme. *The Family Reunion* was his first effort in that direction.

As in most of Eliot's plays, the characters in *The Family Reunion* represent four basic role types: pilgrims or martyrs, witnesses, watchers, and tempters. Harry Monchensey, the play's pilgrim, is the only character to experience growth, or at least a turning point. Harry learns to take the way of self-denial to discover redemption for himself and his community; he learns that he must perfect his will and deny himself the comfortable life of Wishwood, which would prevent him from reaching his spiritual potential. Harry functions as the center of a concentric pattern representing the integration of spiritual values with temporal ones. Harry is surrounded by four witnesses—Agatha, Mary, Downing, and Dr. Warburton—who in various ways aid and reveal Harry's progress. These four characters function like points on the face of a clock on which Harry is the pivotal point, a clock that symbolizes the new order of time he ushers into Wishwood. The walk Mary and Agatha take around the birthday cake at the end of the play portrays this new order.

In contrast to the witnesses, the watchers—Ivy, Violet, Gerald, and Charles—see much on the surface but choose to ignore the inklings of spiritual insight they encounter. They form a second concentric pattern around Amy Monchensey, who represents frozen, lifeless time. In her effort to persuade Harry to sacrifice his life to maintain her illusory world at Wishwood, Amy is the tempter. When the aunts and uncles stand around at the end of the play after Amy's death, they betray their incapacity to move beyond old patterns of merely doing "the right thing."

The characters in Eliot's second full-length drama resemble those in his first, but their pattern of distribution is different. Eliot's most important innovation in characterization is his employment of the Eumenides, or Furies, to function in the double role of haunting the Harry who tries to evade the truth and leading the Harry who seeks enlightenment. Although the Eumenides at first seem like tempters (as in Aeschylus' *Oresteia* of 458 B.C.E., the Greek model for this play), in the end they appear as "bright angels" leading to the "single eye above the desert" where Harry the pilgrim can at last work out his salvation.

The verse in *The Family Reunion* sometimes suffers from artificiality. The choral passages and the lyric duets are particularly difficult to make believable because both types of verse are spoken in a kind of trance during moments broken off from the action of the play. These passages tell rather than show what is happening. The choral passage spoken by the aunts and uncles at the end of the first act illustrates this point well. This passage has poetic qualities but it is encumbered with a self-conscious tone that breaks with the tone employed by the characters in the rest of the play. As Eliot noted in his 1953 lecture "The Three Voices of Poetry," in such instances the poet is speaking rather than the characters. Ideally, the characters should use what Eliot calls the "third voice," which emanates from the persona or character instead of from the writer.

The Family Reunion uses several images from the Christian liturgy and it is indebted to the Eucharistic worship service for its pattern of action. As the title suggests, the play focuses on the reuniting of a family for a special dinner, an activity symbolically similar to the "love feast" of the liturgy. The gathering to which Amy calls her relatives, however, involves little love and even less feasting; the meals take place off stage in a cold and formal ritual. The only visible sharing of food occurs in the opening scene, when the aunts and uncles stand around and complain about the bad habits of the younger generation, including habits of smoking and drinking in which the uncles themselves indulge freely. This unawareness of their own actions illustrates their unawareness of life, as Harry later points out. Because they have never wakened to life, they cannot draw any meaningful pleasure from it or participate in any feast, least of all the Eucharist. Their lives consist of empty rituals.

The drama revolves around a fundamental tension between the empty rituals promoted by Amy's Wishwood and the purposeful rituals sponsored by those who accept a spiritual order of time surpassing that of Wishwood. This tension between rituals is depicted in several varieties of sacrifice, including fruitless sacrifices that result from loveless or self-centered motives. Harry's wife died at sea because the lovelessness, selfishness, and malice of her husband and relations. Amy experiences a tragic end because she is so intent on preserving her illusory Wishwood that she rejects a spiritual life. In contrast, Agatha sacrifices her life for Harry's sake, and Harry sacrifices his life for the benefit of his family. These sacrifices are motivated by love and produce something positive. Although some critics find Harry's quest a cold and selfish one, others point out that his quest is to discover the irreplaceable qualities of love that make of a family more than an association of isolated people joined solely by the accidents of heredity.

"Critical Evaluation" by Daven M. Kari

Bibliography:
Ackroyd, Peter. *T. S. Eliot: A Life*. New York: Simon & Schuster, 1984. A useful biography that includes a discussion of *The Family Reunion*, its genesis, mixed critical reception, and importance to Eliot's early career as a playwright. Ackroyd considers the play to be Eliot's most powerful work because of its use of symbolism.
Evans, Giles. *Wishwood Revisited: A New Interpretation of T. S. Eliot's "The Family Reunion."* Lewes, England: Book Guild, 1991. A subtle analysis of the play, with references to the work of critics and biographers. The author recognizes that the play develops the Christian sympathies and philosophical concerns of earlier works, and he regards it as Eliot's best drama.
Hamalian, Leo. "The Figures in the Window: Design in T. S. Eliot's *The Family Reunion*." *College Literature* 4 (1977): 107-121. A useful analysis of the three levels of consciousness and other patterns that make this play a cohesive and successful whole.
Kari, Daven M. *T. S. Eliot's Dramatic Pilgrimage: A Progress in Craft as an Expression of Christian Perspective*. Studies in Art and Religious Interpretation 13. Lewiston, N.Y.: Edwin Mellen Press, 1990. Considers the play to offer an important experiment in religious verse drama. Examines Eliot's use of characterization, verse techniques, and stagecraft.
Spanos, William V. *The Christian Tradition in Modern British Verse Drama: The Poetics of Sacramental Time*. New Brunswick, N.J.: Rutgers University Press, 1967. One of the most eloquent and insightful treatments of how Christian beliefs have been expressed through modern British verse drama. Excellent discussion of *The Family Reunion* in chapter 6.

THE FAR FIELD

Type of work: Poetry
Author: Theodore Roethke (1908-1963)
First published: 1964

"The Far Field" is the fifth poem in "North American Sequence," which contains six long poems in all and opens Theodore Roethke's last book, *The Far Field* (1964). Therefore, although "The Far Field" is a distinct poem, it must be viewed in the larger poetic context if one is to appreciate its significance. The six poems of this sequence are written in free verse. Roethke expands and contracts the lengths of the lines as though on a journey that requires quick turns, frequent pauses, and long and short strides. The central theme of the work—the individual's quest for spiritual fulfillment—is reflected in the poem's rhythms and structures. The lines lengthen to coincide with the poet's desire to flow like water and to move with a flurry of leaves. The natural world the poet explores and whose center he seeks is portrayed in catalogues of images that depict experiences whose "deep center" becomes his ultimate goal. The poet journeys in search of a self that is at one with the natural world.

In "The Longing," the first poem in the sequence, the poet finds himself in a world that paralyzes the soul and reduces the individual to a creature who stares through empty eyes. This world fills the poet's soul with disgust, even despair. He longs to escape it at the same time that aspects of nature offer him a felicity that sets his soul in motion. The first of his revelations comes to him: "The rose exceeds, the rose exceeds us all." His quest commences: He wants to become like the rose, freed from the emptiness in which the spirit is mired. To do so, he must retreat from the stifling miasma of civilization and rediscover the fresh, vigorous joy of childhood and the expansive energy of the natural world, which is symbolized by flowers in bloom.

He does not wish to escape from the world of the senses. Rather, he longs to escape into it, for the senses are the means by which he can be part of the natural world. Nature is both an experience of the senses and a place where the spiritual and the physical intersect. This initial poem ends on the poet's deliberate commitment to go on a journey. He will take on the nature of the native American, become an explorer:

> Old men should be explorers?
> I'll be an Indian.
> Iroquois.

Ironically, the movement forward begins with an imaginative retreat into the past.

The second poem in the sequence, "Meditation at Oyster River," finds the poet on a rock by a river. The sounds, the sights of undulant waves, dew, salt-soaked wood, fish, snake, bird—he would be with them all. There, flesh and spirit merge, and he discovers a spiritual repose. His experience is that of one just born, yet he has not lost his fear. In sleep he is afraid, and he sees Death's face rise. The river, symbol of the birth of experience and of the onward flow of his exploration, envelopes him with the rhythms of the newborn. The rhythms of morning and of a world that is the "cradle of all that is" bring him a peace otherwise unattainable. As night comes on and the moon rises, he discovers the pervasive nature of light, how it illuminates all within and without.

The title of the third poem in the sequence, "Journey to the Interior," tells where the poet is heading both geographically and psychologically. The opening line ironically speaks of that journey as a journey out of oneself. He must leave some aspect of himself behind as he journeys inward.

He remembers racing along a gravel road, stopping at an old bridge, and discovering that the world all around him is filled with debris, death, and decay. The vision blurs into an awareness of a larger journey, that of the spirit that takes him out of time. In the final section of this poem, the soul observes, the world flows, and in the suspended moment, the poet's senses take on a keenness that enables him to know the heart of the sun and to hear a song in the leaves. He joins the birds, and the spirit of wrath is transformed into the spirit of blessing: "And the dead begin from their dark to sing in my sleep." His journey to the interior has brought him a measure of peace, even bliss.

Where he would be, dreams would no longer bring frightful figures out of the past. One can see how far the poet has come if one recalls what the poet has said in the poem's opening lines, that sleep brings no balm. Even now, he feels the weight of his sensual self. In "The Long Waters," the fourth poem in the sequence, the poet returns to the sea. All he sees enriches his spirit, and the place, filled with life forms, continues to refine his powers of sensuous understanding. His body "shimmers with a light flame," and he is transported out of time and place, becoming "another thing." He loses himself and finds himself. In his newly found largeness, he can embrace the world. Throughout the journey, the poet's relation to the world expands and contracts. At one moment, he is among the stones and leaves; in another moment, he is a river that circles the world or a spirit that embraces it.

Contraction, expansion, ebb and flow, retreating and advancing, going forward and back, finding light in the darkness, a wakeful dream out of a dreaming sleep—these are the rhythms that the poet's journey brings. These elements all come together in "The Far Field," which begins with the poet dreaming of journeys. These journeys, however, are those of the physical man, the untransformed mortal whose car stalls at the end of a road, its wheels spinning futilely. Mired in this physical universe, the poet has reached the end of his journey. His attention turns to the birds, emblems of nature's capacity to rise above the slag-heaps and the effluvia of the degraded city. Throughout his journey, he has admired and felt a spiritual kinship with the birds. They represent nature's ability to confer flight, and the poet wants to be one of them. He imagines himself returned to earth as a bird. Birds are the voices of the land, incarnations of nature's prolific diversity.

The poet's journey to the edge of the city and of his own spiritual perimeters has brought him a triumph over the darkness and has taught him not to fear what lies beyond—death, eternity. He envisions how natural objects rejuvenate themselves and triumph over time and change: "The river turns on itself,/ The tree retreats into its own shadow." The journey inward and outward is a circle that brings the poet back to where he began, only now his discoveries have taken him out of time. He has gained a new insight, a peace with the natural process. Death no longer frightens him. In fact, he is renewed by it, and though he may not yet have found the "deep center," he has come to realize that all he loves is around him, in the earth and air. He has not retreated into a spiritual world. Rather, he has found a spiritual kinship with the world by letting it engulf him and by experiencing it with all of his senses. He sees confluence throughout the natural world and feels a part of it.

The final poem in the sequence, "The Rose," continues the metaphor of the poet's blending with natural objects and events, going beyond himself. The white and red roses the poet remembers seeing in his father's greenhouse beckoned him out of himself even then. They may have been early intimations of his spiritual mission, for he has become something other. He has come out of the whale and into the world, has journeyed to the edge of the field; he has seen the far field and has learned to accept death, not to fear infinity, and to realize that all he desires is here and now, within and without. He has become like the rose, which "Stays in its true place,/ Flowering out of the dark."

The poet, like the rose, has discovered his true place, among the rocks, the places where nature surrounds him and infuses his spirit. In a grove of madronas and half-dead trees, near the rose, the poet finds a culmination of his journey, and an acceptance:

> I came upon a true ease of myself,
> As if another man appeared out of the depths of my being,
> And I stood outside myself,
> Beyond becoming and perishing,
> A something wholly other,
> As if I swayed out on the wildest wave alive,
> And yet was still.
> And I rejoiced in being what I was. . . .

In that revelation—and elevation—the lost man and the final man discover each other, see that they are separate yet of the same spirit. He realizes the spirit unites what before was viewed as irreconcilable opposites. Finally, the poet sees that the lost, wandering man is not lost if he is in his true place, and the final man is not finite man or the last man. Rather, the final man is the culmination of man, even as "the far field" is the culmination of his earthly journey. Language grounds the poet in what he feels and sees; it blends the abstract with the concrete and in that way symbolizes the poet himself. The final man is the final word.

Bernard E. Morris

Bibliography:

Heyen, William, ed. *Profile of Theodore Roethke*. Westerville, Ohio. Charles E. Merrill, 1971. Includes eight major studies of Roethke's work.

Kalaidjian, Walter B. *Understanding Theodore Roethke*. Columbia: University of South Carolina Press, 1987. All the major collections of Roethke's poems are discussed in this book, which begins with an overview and ends with two chapters devoted to *The Far Field*. Excellent bibliography.

Malkoff, Karl. *Theodore Roethke: An Introduction to the Poetry*. New York: Columbia University Press, 1966. Discusses the major themes in Roethke's poetry and the influences of T. S. Eliot, William Butler Yeats, and others, tracing Roethke's poetic development to its conclusion in *The Far Field*.

Roethke, Theodore. *The Collected Poems of Theodore Roethke*. Garden City, N.J.: Anchor Press, 1975. This standard edition contains all the poems from previous books by Roethke except the verse from a book written for children. Previously unpublished poems dating from 1943 to 1962 are also included.

Sullivan, Rosemary. *Theodore Roethke: The Garden Master*. Seattle: University of Washington Press, 1975. Sheds light on the relation of Roethke's personal life to his poetry, and the discussion of "North American Sequence" illuminates the symbols and images of that work.

FAR FROM THE MADDING CROWD

Type of work: Novel
Author: Thomas Hardy (1840-1928)
Type of plot: Psychological realism
Time of plot: 1869-1873
Locale: Wessex, England
First published: 1874

Principal characters:
GABRIEL OAK, a shepherd
BATHSHEBA EVERDENE, the mistress of Weatherbury Farm
SERGEANT TROY, her first husband
WILLIAM BOLDWOOD, her suitor and a farmer and neighbor
FANNY ROBIN, a woman betrayed by Troy

The Story:

Gabriel Oak was a small-scale farmer, but his honesty, integrity, and ability had won him the respect of all of his neighbors. When he heard that a young woman named Bathsheba Everdene had moved into the neighborhood, he went out of his way to see her and fell immediately in love. Gabriel was the kind of man who had to look only once to know that he had found the right woman. After seeing her only a few times, he went to her aunt, for whom Bathsheba worked, and asked for the girl's hand in marriage. Although he was refused, he felt that it was the relative, not Bathsheba, who had denied him.

A short time later, Gabriel's sheepdog became excited and chased his flock of sheep over a cliff, killing them all. Ruined, Gabriel had to give up his farm and go elsewhere to find work. On his way across the country, he passed a burning barn and ran to aid the men fighting the flames. After the fire had been put out, the owner of Weatherbury Farm arrived, and it was suggested that Gabriel be hired as shepherd in return for the fine work he had done. To his surprise, the owner of the farm was Bathsheba Everdene, who had recently inherited the place from her uncle. Gabriel became her shepherd. He was struck by the change in their positions in such a short while. Now Bathsheba was landowner, and Gabriel was the servant.

On his way to his new quarters, Gabriel met a girl standing in the woods. She spoke to him and asked him not to say that he had seen her, and he promised to keep silent. The next morning while working at his new job, he heard that Fanny Robin, one of Bathsheba's maids, had disappeared, and he rightly guessed that Fanny was the girl he had met. It was suspected that she had gone off to meet a soldier who had been stationed in the area a short time before. This suspicion was correct. Fanny had gone to find Sergeant Troy at his new station, for he had promised to marry her if she came to him. A date was set for the wedding, but Fanny went to the wrong church. When she finally found Troy, he refused to make arrangements for a marriage a second time.

Bathsheba was a good manager, and Weatherbury Farm prospered; but she had her caprices. One of these was to send an anonymous valentine to William Boldwood, a conservative, serious man who was her neighbor. Boldwood was upset by the valentine, especially after he learned that Gabriel had recognized Bathsheba's handwriting. The more Boldwood saw of Bathsheba, however, the more deeply he fell in love with her. One day during the sheep washing, he asked her to marry him, but she refused his proposal. Nevertheless, Gabriel and the rest of the workers felt sure that she would eventually marry Boldwood.

About that time, Sergeant Troy returned to the neighborhood. Bathsheba was attracted to him at once. Gabriel knew enough of Troy's character to know that he was not the man for Bathsheba, and he told her so. Not knowing the story of Fanny Robin, Bathsheba was furious at Gabriel's presumption. She and Troy were married soon afterward, and the former Sergeant became the master of Weatherbury Farm. With Troy running the farm, things did not go well. Gabriel was forced to do most of the work of overseeing, and often he was compelled to correct the mistakes Troy made. Troy gambled and drank and caused Bathsheba much unhappiness. Gabriel and Bathsheba were alternately friendly and unfriendly. One day Troy and Bathsheba, riding in a horse cart, passed a young woman walking down the road. Troy stopped the cart and went to talk to her. The woman was Fanny Robin, who was feeble and ill. Troy told her to go on to the next town and wait there for him to come and give her money. As soon as they arrived home, Troy asked Bathsheba for some money. She gave it to him after a quarrel.

Fanny went on to Casterbridge, but she was so weak and ill when she arrived there that she died shortly afterward. When news of her death reached Weatherbury Farm, Bathsheba, unaware that Troy had been the girl's lover, sent a cart to bring the body to the farm for burial. When the body arrived, Gabriel saw scrawled on the coffin lid a message that both Fanny and a child were inside. He erased the last words in his fear that the real relationship of Fanny and Troy might reach Bathsheba's ears; but Bathsheba, suspecting that the coffin concealed some secret, opened the casket late that night. At the same moment, Troy entered the room and learned of Fanny's death and the death of his child. Torn with grief, he told Bathsheba that she meant nothing to him and that Fanny had been the only woman he had ever loved. He had married Bathsheba only for her looks and her money. Bathsheba shut herself up in an attic room.

Troy had a beautiful tombstone put up over Fanny's grave, which he covered with roses and lilies. During a heavy storm that night, water poured from the church roof through the mouth of a gargoyle, splashed on the grave, and ruined all of his work. Troy disappeared from Casterbridge. News came shortly afterward that he had been caught in a dangerous current while swimming in the ocean and had been drowned. Bathsheba did not believe that Troy was really dead; Boldwood, convinced of Troy's death, did his best to get Bathsheba to promise to marry him if Troy did not reappear within seven years, at the end of which time he would be legally declared dead. At a party Boldwood gave for her one night, Bathsheba yielded to his protestations of love and said that after the time had passed, she would marry him. As she was leaving the party, Troy entered. He had been rescued at sea and had wandered slowly back to Casterbridge in the character of a strolling player.

At his entrance, Bathsheba fainted and fell to the floor. Everyone was so concerned for her and surprised by Troy's appearance that they did not see Boldwood when he took down a gun from the wall. Boldwood aimed at Troy and shot him in the chest. Troy died immediately. Boldwood was tried for the murder, but because his mind had given way, he was committed to an institution. Gabriel, who had made every effort to save Boldwood from hanging, had become a leader in the neighborhood. As Bathsheba's bailiff, he managed her farm and that of Boldwood as well. Of her three lovers, he was the only one left.

One day, Gabriel went to Bathsheba and told her that he was planning to leave her service. Bathsheba listened quietly and agreed with all he had to say. Later that night, however, she went to his cottage and there told him, by gesture more than by word, that he was the only person left to her now and that she needed both his help and his love. The farmers of the district were all delighted when Bathsheba became Mrs. Oak, and Gabriel became the master of Weatherbury Farm.

Critical Evaluation:

As the title indicates, Thomas Hardy's first major novel has an isolated setting: rural, remote from the world, and mainly centered upon Upper Weatherbury Farm in Wessex. Unlike that in *Under the Greenwood Tree*, however, this secluded environment at times gives way to the town: the busy corn exchange in Casterbridge, the King's Arms Hotel, the Casterbridge workhouse, the cities of Bath and Budmouth, and the lively Buck's Head Inn on the Casterbridge Road.

Nevertheless, the setting has a timeless quality, accentuated by the round of seasonal activities and the continuity of agricultural life. Major scenes in the novel focus around the sheep shearing, saving of hayricks in the storm, spring sheep washing, and the autumn sheep fair at Greenhill. Nature here, however, is not merely background or a constant factor informing characters' actions and proclivities; it is more powerful, a force vast and indifferent to man's thoughts and actions. This is the nature that in later novels evolved into inexorable fate, before which the individual is helpless and in opposing which he or she comes to destruction. The main characters in this novel who survive are those who succeed in adjusting themselves to nature's laws and often hostile dominance: Gabriel Oak and Bathsheba Everdene.

Far from the Madding Crowd exhibits confident power throughout in its fully developed characters, the imperceptible movements in the various conflicts involving Bathsheba and her three lovers, and in the way these conflicts evolve from their varied personalities. The combination of the four personalities furnishes the most explosive potential for melodramatic situation: Bathsheba's capriciousness and attractiveness to men; Oak's stolid, patient, unswerving loyalty and love for her; Boldwood's composite character with its "enormous antagonistic forces" and "wild capabilities"; Sergeant Troy's impulsiveness, his living only for the present moment, dashing but totally irresponsible; and the simple nature of Fanny, unaffected and victimized. Interactions of these intimately associated characters, in an almost closed environment, engender passionate, at times almost unbelievable, conflicts.

Further complicating the clashes and intricate relationships among these four are the unforeseen, relentless accidents of nature: the initial loss of Oak's sheep, the heavy storm with water that ruins Troy's flowers on Fanny's grave and that precipitates his disappearance, the loss of Boldwood's hayricks in a second storm. The novel progresses in turns, driven headlong by Bathsheba's careless whim of sending Boldwood an anonymous valentine and again by Troy's determination to possess her in spite of all odds. Even Gabriel Oak and Fanny, the two who outwardly seem driven by the impulsive actions of others, unconsciously complicate the plot by their very quiet and uncomplaining natures. Fanny, betrayed by Sergeant Troy, goes down before forces she has no means to combat, although she has a macabre revenge in the scene in which Bathsheba opens her coffin to find Troy's child dead with its mother.

Gabriel, of stronger stuff, endures—like the nature he is so close to and of which he seems an integral part. Although he feels Bathsheba rules his life and the reader may be swept into this illusion, it is the earth and all of its creatures to which he is bound. Only when Bathsheba comes full circle through her marriage to the dissolute, unstable Troy, her half acceptance of Boldwood's position and estate, back to an understanding of the land and its enduring qualities as embodied in Oak, can their marriage be possible. What Gabriel held to in Bathsheba and what she herself did not recognize was the same elemental belonging to the land and its eternal strength.

The language of the novel is bound to the earth; the best example of this is the rural chorus, which is to figure in Hardy's later novels and which provides much of the humor. The habitués of Warren's Malthouse on the Casterbridge Road are intimately involved in the action and contribute to domestic scenes and rural atmosphere. They not only serve to comment on the various episodes but also reinforce the setting, for they, too, belong to the earth. In fact, they form part of the novel's foundation; it is of importance that Gabriel Oak is at home with them and shares their social outlook. When the Malthouse crowd appears at the end of the book to serenade the newly married Gabriel and Bathsheba with their "venerable worm-eaten instruments," Gabriel invites them: "Com in, souls, and have something to eat and drink wi' me and my wife."

In this novel, the reader finds the emerging role of nature, the typical romantic, dramatic situations that will even intensify in later novels, and devices such as the village chorus and rural activities to mark the continuity and coherence of human existence. Also apparent are the chance encounters, series of coincidences, unforeseen accidents, overheard conversations, and secretly observed actions—all of which make up the fabric of a typical Hardy narrative. His plots, because of these devices, share an improbability and sense of the miraculous found in folklore. The coffin scene where Bathsheba finds Fanny and Troy's child is the stuff of which ballads are made. The scene in which Troy woos Bathsheba with a sword exercise, in its bold sexual symbolism, also foreshadows such scenes as the fight between Henchard and Farfrae in *The Mayor of Casterbridge* and the entwined couples at the hay-trusser's dance in *Tess of the D'Urbervilles*.

Although not as carefully structured as his later novels, this work shows Hardy's ability to convey the mental life of his characters, especially that of a complicated woman. He boldly draws his theatrical scenes, exploits his evocative rural settings, and for the first time in his career as a novelist dares give his work amplitude and passion. Not yet, however, does the reader find in this book the intense sense of gloom over a vanishing way of life—a depression that marked much of Hardy's later writing; nor does the story embody humanity's defeat and tragedy that increasingly became Hardy's preoccupation.

"Critical Evaluation" by Muriel B. Ingham

Bibliography:

Buckler, William. *The Victorian Imagination: Essays in Aesthetic Exploration*. New York: New York University Press, 1980. Explores the politics and society of Victorian England as it affects the formal elements (plot, character construction, imagery) and the political and social aspects (gender, class, rural/urban relations) of Hardy's work; specifically addresses *Far from the Madding Crowd*.

Bullen, J. B. *The Expressive Eye: Fiction and Perception in the Work of Thomas Hardy*. Oxford, England: Clarendon Press, 1987. Distinguishes Hardy from other writers of the period by examining his painterly eye and visual accuracy; discussion of Hardy's descriptions of landscapes.

Milligate, Michael. *Thomas Hardy: His Career as a Novelist*. London: Bodley Head, 1971. A full-length study of Hardy's life and his concerns, attitudes, values and problems as they affected his writing and its reception. Offers a fair perspective on Hardy's personal and artistic development.

Shires, Linda M. "Narrative, Gender, and Power in *Far from the Madding Crowd*." *Novel* 24, no. 2 (Winter, 1991): 162-178. Examines the character of Bathsheba Everdene and her feminine power over Oak, Boldwood, and Troy. A feminist analysis that points out Hardy's portrayal of Bathsheba is unusual, in contrast to other heroines such as Eustacia Vye and Tess Durbeyfield.

Swann, Charles. "*Far from the Madding Crowd*: How Good a Shepherd Is Gabriel Oak?" *Notes and Queries* 39, no. 2 (June, 1992): 189-201. Analyzes Gabriel Oak as a character and as a prototype of a Wessex shepherd; addresses Hardy's interpretation of the rural world.

A FAREWELL TO ARMS

Type of work: Novel
Author: Ernest Hemingway (1899-1961)
Type of plot: Impressionistic realism
Time of plot: World War I
Locale: Northern Italy and Switzerland
First published: 1929

Principal characters:
> FREDERIC HENRY, an American serving with an Italian ambulance unit
> CATHERINE BARKLEY, an English nurse

The Story:

Lieutenant Frederic Henry was a young American attached to an Italian ambulance unit on the Italian front. An offensive was soon to begin, and when Henry returned to the front from leave, he learned from his friend, Lieutenant Rinaldi, that a group of British nurses had arrived in his absence to set up a British hospital unit. Rinaldi introduced him to Nurse Catherine Barkley. Between ambulance trips to evacuation posts at the front, Henry called on Miss Barkley. He liked the frank young English girl in a casual sort of way, but he was not in love with her. Before he left for the front to stand by for an attack, she gave him a St. Anthony medal.

At the front, as Henry and some Italian ambulance drivers were eating in a dugout, an Austrian projectile exploded over them. Henry, badly wounded in the legs, was taken to a field hospital. Later, he was moved to a hospital in Milan. Before the doctor was able to see Henry in Milan, the nurse prohibited his drinking wine, but he bribed a porter to bring him a supply which he kept hidden behind his bed. Catherine Barkley came to the hospital, and Henry knew that he was in love with her. The doctors told Henry that he would have to lie in bed six months before they could operate on his knee. Henry insisted on seeing another doctor, who said that the operation could be performed the next day. Meanwhile, Catherine managed to be with Henry constantly.

After his operation, Henry convalesced in Milan with Catherine Barkley as his attendant. Together they dined in out-of-the-way restaurants, and together they rode about the countryside in a carriage. Henry was restless and lonely at nights and Catherine often came to his hospital room. Summer passed into autumn. Henry's wound had healed, and he was due to take convalescent leave in October. He and Catherine planned to spend the leave together, but he came down with jaundice before he could leave the hospital. The head nurse accused him of bringing on the jaundice by drink, in order to avoid being sent back to the front. Before he left for the front, Henry and Catherine stayed together in a hotel room; already she had disclosed to him that she was pregnant. Henry returned to the front with orders to load his three ambulances with hospital equipment and go south into the Po valley. Morale was at a low ebb. Rinaldi admired the job that had been done on the knee and observed that Henry acted like a married man. War weariness was all-pervasive. At the front, the Italians, having learned that German divisions had reinforced the Austrians, began their terrible retreat from Caporetto. Henry drove one of the ambulances loaded with hospital supplies. During the retreat south, the ambulance was held up several times by wagons, guns, and trucks, which extended in stalled lines for miles. Henry picked up two straggling Italian sergeants. During the night, the retreat was halted in the rain for hours.

At daybreak, Henry cut out of the long line and drove across country in an attempt to reach Udine by side roads. The ambulance got stuck in a muddy side road. The sergeants decided to leave, but Henry asked them to help dislodge the car from the mud. They refused and ran. Henry shot and wounded one; the other escaped across the fields. An Italian ambulance corpsman with Henry shot the wounded sergeant through the back of the head. Henry and his three comrades struck out on foot for Udine. On a bridge, Henry saw a German staff car with German bicycle troops crossing another bridge over the same stream. Within sight of Udine, one of Henry's group was killed by an Italian sniper. The others hid in a barn until it seemed safe to circle around Udine and join the mainstream of the retreat toward the Tagliamento River.

By that time, the Italian army was nothing but a frantic mob. Soldiers were throwing down their arms and officers were cutting insignia of rank from their sleeves. At the end of a long wooden bridge across the Tagliamento, military carabiniere were seizing all officers, giving them drumhead trials, and executing them by the riverbank. Henry was detained, but in the dark of night he broke free, plunged into the river, and escaped on a log. He crossed the Venetian plain on foot, then jumped aboard a freight train and rode to Milan, where he went to the hospital in which he had been a patient. There he learned that the English nurses had gone to Stresa.

During the retreat from Caporetto, Henry had made his farewell to arms. He borrowed civilian clothes from an American friend in Milan and went by train to Stresa, where he met Catherine, who was on leave. The bartender of the hotel in which Henry was staying warned Henry that authorities were planning to arrest him for desertion the next morning; he offered his boat by means of which Henry and Catherine could escape to Switzerland. Henry rowed all night. By morning, his hands were so raw that he could barely stand to touch the oars. Over his protests, Catherine took a turn at the rowing. They reached Switzerland safely and were arrested. Henry told the police that he was a sportsman who enjoyed rowing and that he had come to Switzerland for the winter sports. The valid passports and the ample funds that Henry and Catherine possessed saved them from serious trouble with the authorities.

During the rest of the fall and winter, the couple stayed at an inn outside Montreux. They discussed marriage, but Catherine would not be married while she was pregnant. They hiked, read, and talked about what they would do together after the war. When the time for Catherine's confinement approached, she and Henry went to Lausanne to be near a hospital. They planned to return to Montreux in the spring. At the hospital, Catherine's pains caused the doctor to use an anaesthetic on her. After hours of suffering, she delivered a dead baby. The nurse sent Henry out to get something to eat. When he went back to the hospital, he learned that Catherine had had a hemorrhage. He went into the room and stayed with her until she died. There was nothing he could do, no one he could talk to, no place he could go. Catherine was dead. He left the hospital and walked back to his hotel in the dark. It was raining.

Critical Evaluation:

Ernest Hemingway once referred to *A Farewell to Arms* as his version of William Shakespeare's *Romeo and Juliet* (c. 1595). Several parallels exist. Both works are about star-crossed lovers; both show erotic flirtations that rapidly develop into serious, intense love affairs; and both describe the romances against a backdrop of social and political turmoil. Whether *A Farewell to Arms* finally qualifies as tragic is a matter of personal opinion, but it certainly represents, for Hemingway, an attempt to broaden his concerns from the aimless tragicomic problems of the expatriates in *The Sun Also Rises* (1926) to the fundamental question of life's meaning in the face of human mortality.

Frederic Henry begins the affair as a routine wartime seduction, "a game, like bridge, in which you said things instead of playing cards." He feels mildly guilty, especially after learning about Catherine's vulnerability because of the loss of her lover in combat, but he still foresees no complications from the temporary arrangement. It is not until he is wounded and sent to her hospital in Milan that their affair deepens into love—and from that point on, they struggle to free themselves in order to realize it. Yet they are constantly thwarted, first by the impersonal bureaucracy of the military effort, then by the physical separation imposed by the war itself, and, finally, by the biological "accident" that kills Catherine at the point where their "separate peace" at last seems possible.

As Henry's love for Catherine grows, his disillusionment with the war also increases. From the beginning of the book, Henry views the military efforts with ironic detachment, but there is no suggestion that, prior to his meeting with her, he has had any deep reservations about his involvement. Hemingway's attitude toward war was always an ambiguous one. He questioned the rationales for fighting them and the slogans offered in their defense. Like Henry, he felt that "abstract words such as glory, honor, courage, or hallow were obscene." For the individual, however, war could be the necessary test. Facing imminent death in combat, one either demonstrated "grace under pressure" and did the "one right thing" or one did not; one either emerged from the experience as a whole person with self-knowledge and control, or one came out of it lost and broken.

There is little heroism in this war as Henry describes it. The hero's disengagement from the fighting is made most vivid in the extended "retreat from Caporetto," generally considered one of the great sequences in modern fiction. The retreat begins in an orderly, disciplined, military manner. Yet as it progresses, authority breaks down, emotions of self-preservation supersede loyalties, and the neat military procession gradually turns into a panicking mob. Henry is caught up in the momentum and carried along with the group in spite of his attempts to keep personal control and fidelity to the small band of survivors he travels with. Upon reaching the Tagliamento River, Henry is seized, along with all other identifiable officers, and held for execution. After he escapes by leaping into the river—an act of ritual purification as well as physical survival—he feels that his trial has freed him from any and all further loyalty to the Allied cause.

Henry then rejoins Catherine, and they complete the escape together. In Switzerland, they seem lucky and free at last. Up in the mountains, they hike, ski, make love, prepare for the baby, and plan for their postwar life together. Yet even in their most idyllic times, there are ominous hints; they worry about the baby; Catherine jokes about her narrow hips; she becomes frightened by a dream of herself "dead in the rain." Throughout the novel, Hemingway associates the plains and rain with death, disease, and sorrow; the mountains and the snow with life, health, and happiness, Catherine and Frederic are safe and happy in the mountains, but it is impossible to remain there indefinitely. Eventually everyone must return to the plains. When Catherine and Henry descend to the city, it is, in fact, raining, and she does, in fact, die.

Like that of Romeo and Juliet, the love between Catherine and Henry is not destroyed by any moral defect in their own characters. Henry muses that Catherine's fate is the price paid for the good nights in Milan, but such a price is absurdly excessive. Nor, strictly speaking, is the war responsible for their fate, any more than the Montague-Capulet feud directly provokes the deaths of Shakespeare's lovers. Yet the war and the feud provide the backdrop of violence and the accumulation of pressures that coerce the lovers into actions that contribute to their doom. Yet, in the final analysis, both couples are defeated by bad luck—the illness that prevents the friar from delivering Juliet's note to Romeo, the accident of Catherine's anatomy that prevents normal childbearing. Thus, both couples are star-crossed. If a "purpose" can be vaguely ascertained in Shakespeare's version—the feud is ended by the tragedy—there is no metaphysical justification for Catherine's death; it is, in her own words, "a dirty trick"—and nothing more.

Hemingway does not insist that the old religious meanings are completely invalid but only that they do not work for his characters. Henry would like to visit with the priest in his mountain village, but he cannot bring himself to do it. His friend Rinaldi, a combat surgeon, proclaims atheism, hedonism, and work as the only available meanings. Count Greffi, an old billiard player Henry meets in Switzerland, offers good taste, cynicism, and the fact of a long, pleasant life. Catherine and Henry have each other: "You are my religion," she tells him.

All of these things fail in the end. Religion is only for others, patriotism is a sham, hedonism becomes boring, culture is a temporary distraction, work finally fails (the operation on Catherine was "successful"), even love cannot last. Catherine dies; they both know, although they will not admit it, that the memory of it will fade.

All that remains is a stoic acceptance of the above facts with dignity and without bitterness. Life, like war, is absurd. Henry survives because he is lucky; Catherine dies because she is unlucky. There is no guarantee that the luck ever balances out and, since everyone ultimately dies, it probably does not matter. What does matter is the courage, dignity, and style with which one accepts these facts as a basis for life, and, more important, in the face of death.

"Critical Evaluation" by Keith Neilson

Bibliography:

Beversluis, John. "Dispelling the Romantic Myth: A Study of *A Farewell to Arms*." *The Hemingway Review* 9, no. 1 (Fall, 1989): 18-25. Rejecting the common romantic interpretation, Beversluis asserts that this novel explores the problem of self-knowledge. His reading of the character of Catherine is especially interesting. A special *A Farewell to Arms* issue of the journal.

Bloom, Harold, ed. *Ernest Hemingway's "A Farewell to Arms."* New York: Chelsea House, 1987. Offers a representative selection of the best scholarship available on the novel. Includes Bloom's introduction, chronology, bibliography, and index.

Donaldson, Scott, ed. *New Essays on "A Farewell to Arms."* Cambridge, England: Cambridge University Press, 1990. Appropriate for specialists and nonspecialists. The introduction discusses the novel's composition, publication, and reception, as well as its major critical readings from publication to 1990.

Lewis, Robert W. *"A Farewell to Arms": The War of the Words.* Boston: Twayne, 1992. Comprehensive resource. Concludes that the novel is about language—particularly the language by which truth and falsehood are revealed.

Waldhorn, Arthur. *A Readers' Guide to Ernest Hemingway.* New York: Farrar, Straus & Giroux, 1972. A concise, well-written vision of Hemingway and his works, appropriate for specialists and nonspecialists.

THE FATHER

Type of work: Drama
Author: August Strindberg (1849-1912)
Type of plot: Psychological realism
Time of plot: Mid-nineteenth century
Locale: Sweden
First performed: 1887; first published, 1887 as *Fadren* (English translation, 1899)

Principal characters:

THE CAPTAIN, an officer and amateur scientist
LAURA, his wife
BERTHA, their daughter
DR. ÖSTERMARK, the village physician
THE PASTOR, Laura's brother
MARGARET, an old nurse
NÖJD, a soldier

The Story:

When Nöjd got a servant girl named Emma in trouble, the captain sent an orderly to bring Nöjd to face the pastor. The culprit was vague about his affair and hinted that the paternity of the child was uncertain and that it was possible that Ludwig was the real father. The pastor told Nöjd that he would have to support the child, but the soldier claimed that Ludwig should contribute also. The captain declared angrily that the case would go to court. After Nöjd had gone, the captain, who was married to the pastor's sister Laura, berated the pastor for his gentleness. The pastor said he thought it a pity to saddle Nöjd with the support of a child if he were not the real father.

In his house, complained the captain, there were too many women: his mother-in-law, a governess, old nurse Margaret, and his daughter Bertha. The captain, worried about his daughter's education, which was being influenced in all different directions by the people around her, deplored the incessant struggle between men and women.

After the pastor left, Laura entered to collect her household money. Because his affairs were near bankruptcy, the captain asked her to keep an account of the money she spent. Laura asked what he had decided about Bertha's education. Laura objected when he announced his intention to send her to town to board with Auditor Safberg, a freethinker, but the captain reminded her that a father had the sole control of his children. When Laura brought up the subject of Nöjd's affair, the captain admitted that the paternity would be difficult to decide. Laura scoffingly claimed that if such were the case even the child of a married woman could be any other man's offspring.

Laura confided to Dr. Östermark, the new village doctor, her suspicion that her husband was mentally ill. He bought books he never read, and he tried to fathom events on other planets by peering through a microscope. He had become a man who could not stand by his decisions, although he was vehement when he first uttered one. The captain, speaking confidentially with his old nurse, expressed his fear that his family was plotting against him and that something evil was about to happen.

The family quarrel was clearly outlined when Bertha complained to her father that her grandmother was trying to teach her spiritualism and had even told the girl that the captain, who was a meteorologist by profession, was a charlatan. Bertha agreed with her father that she ought to go away to study, but Laura boasted that she would be able to persuade Bertha to stay home. She hinted again that she could prove the captain was not Bertha's father.

Dr. Östermark explained to Laura that she was mistaken about her husband; he had used a spectroscope, not a microscope, to examine the elements on other planets. Still, the doctor said, he would watch the captain for any other signs of insanity. Laura also told the doctor that the captain feared he was not Bertha's father, an idea that Laura had planted in her husband's mind. When he began to worry over his daughter's paternity, old Margaret tried to reassure him.

The captain tried to stop his wife's continued persecution of him. She had intercepted some of his mail, thwarting him in the progress of his scientific ventures. He further accused her of spreading among his friends the idea that he was insane. Afraid that under such provocation he might lose his reason, he appealed to his wife's selfishness. It would be in her best interests for him to remain sane, he said, since insanity might lead to his suicide, which would invalidate her right to collect his life insurance. She could assure his sanity by confessing that Bertha was not his child, a suspicion that was undermining his sanity.

When she refused to admit a sin of which she was not guilty, he reminded her that in doing so she would gain sole control of Bertha's future. The tables were turned. Now the captain began to believe that Bertha was not his child and Laura began to insist that she was. The captain, recalling the circumstances of Bertha's birth, recollected how a solicitor had told Laura that she had no right of inheritance without a child. At that time the captain had been ill. When he recovered, Bertha had been born.

The captain understood the power his wife had held over him. At first he had loved her as he would love a mother; she had loathed him after he became her lover. Laura showed him a letter she had forged, in which he confessed his insanity, and told him that she had sent the letter to court. Boasting that she had employed him only as a breadwinner, she declared that she would use his pension for Bertha's education. In anger, the captain hurled a lamp at her.

Laura succeeded in locking her husband in another room while she examined his private papers. Although the pastor saw through her scheme, she dared him to accuse her. The doctor arrived with a strait jacket shortly before the captain, armed with literary evidence of cases in which a child's paternity had been questioned, burst into the room. His talk was so erratic and his raving about conjugal fidelity so wild that when the doctor told him he was insane, the captain acknowledged his own madness.

Bertha, accusing him of a deliberate attempt to injure her mother, announced that he was not her father if he behaved so badly. The captain, in reply, told her that her soul was in two parts; one was a reflection of his own, and to preserve it he intended to destroy the part that was not his. He seized a revolver but found it empty. Bertha ran out screaming.

Old Margaret soothed the raving man by talking softly to him of his childhood, and when he was off guard she slipped the strait jacket on him. Seeing him seated, helpless and dejected, on the sofa, Laura nearly repented the course she had taken as the captain piteously described his life of torment with mother, wife, and child, all of whom had rejected him. After she had assured him that Bertha was his own child, the captain, calling to old Margaret for comfort, suffered a stroke. As he lay unconscious, Bertha ran to her mother, who caressed her and called the girl her own daughter.

Critical Evaluation:

The plays of August Strindberg have exerted a powerful and pervasive influence on modern drama in both Europe and America. His insights into naturalism, in such early plays as *The Father* and *Miss Julie* (1888), were central in the shaping of that dramatic movement, while his later experiments with expressionism, in such works as *The Ghost Sonata* (1907), *A Dream Play* (1902), and the *To Damascus* trilogy (1898-1904), have profoundly effected nonrealistic approaches to the modern stage. It is virtually impossible to separate Strindberg's life from his works, and this is particularly true in the case of *The Father*. Even Strindberg recognized the close alliance between the two when on November 12, 1887, he wrote to Axel Lundegard: "It is to me as if I were walking in my sleep—as if creation and life were mingled. I do not know whether *The Father* is a creative work, or whether that was my real life."

The relationship between Strindberg's reality and his writing becomes apparent in an examination of *A Madman's Defense* (1893), an autobiographical novel that contains many references essential to an understanding of *The Father*. Written between 1887 and 1888, it chronicles fourteen years of Strindberg's life, including his fateful meeting and marriage to Siri Von Essen. Strindberg intended the work as an exposé of Siri's attempts to confine him for mental treatment, but in reality it presents a clear picture of developing paranoia and acute mental instability.

Strindberg's first-person narrator names his wife Maria and portrays her as suspicious of her husband's sanity from the beginning of their marriage. (Indeed, in 1886 Siri consulted a Swiss doctor about Strindberg's instability, confirming his suspicion that she suspected mental imbalance in him all along and desired to obtain his insurance money or marry again.) Based on her conviction, Maria attempts to provoke behavior from the narrator that can be used as evidence to justify confinement. When she sides with the critics of her husband's book, he calls her a traitor who is responsible for starting rumors about his sanity. When he escapes to Paris to seek comradeship with friends, she follows him and insists on a retreat in Switzerland. Once there, she convinces the doctor, guests, proprietor, and servants that he is, indeed, insane.

Beginning to doubt his own sanity and feeling a persecution mania, the narrator turns his suspicions and hostility on his wife. He studies her behavior and comes to believe that she is an adulteress trying to cover her wrongdoings and gain his insurance money and writings by proving him mentally incompetent. He looks for evidence to prove his theory by rifling through her letters and subjecting her to strenuous cross-examinations. Neither her denials nor the confessions he believes he extracts provide him with convincing answers, but they intensify his agitation and instability. The reader of *A Madman's Defense* cannot help but see the parallels between this autobiographical account and the basic plot of *The Father*, as well as the similarity between the narrator in the novel and the captain in the play. *The Father* becomes almost an adaptation of *A Madman's Defense*.

Along with the fictionalization of the growing paranoia in *A Madman's Defense*, Strindberg's account closely parallels the events that surrounded the publication and subsequent blasphemy trial of the first volume of his *Getting Married* (1884). This collection of short stories deals with the relationship between husbands and wives, drawing for some of the material on Strindberg's early married life and *The Father*. The most important contribution from that collection to *The Father* is in the portrayal of women. Strindberg is scornful toward the "emancipated" woman in marriage, feeling that such a woman wants not equality with her mate but domination over him. The ideal role for the woman, Strindberg believes, is that of wife and mother—anything else can only be destructive.

This view of women had its origins in Strindberg's own background, for he had cause to believe in the evil nature of his mother. Having been unwanted at birth and rejected as a child,

Strindberg grew up a stranger in his own home. What Strindberg sought in a mate (he went through three stormy marriages) was not only a wife but also a substitute mother, a confusion of roles that greatly acerbated his experiences of marriage. Strindberg describes Siri after first meeting her as "a deliciously girlish mother." Even during their trial separation, Strindberg stated that he felt "like an embryo prematurely detached from the umbilical cord." This attitude is echoed by the characters in *The Father*, when Laura tells the captain: "I loved you as if you were my child. But you know, you must have felt it, when your sexual desires were aroused, and you came forward as my lover, I was reluctant, and the joy I felt in your embrace was followed by such revulsion that my very blood knew shame. The son become the lover—oh!"

Strindberg's confusion and disillusion led him naturally into bitter antifeminism, although he was hardly unusual in this respect. His philosophy paralleled that of many contemporaries, particularly those in France—a country he frequented during his exile periods—where the literary atmosphere in the 1870's was extremely misogynistic. The theater had become particularly receptive to the movement, as is especially evident in the character of the femme fatale as popularized by such actors as Sarah Bernhardt. It was felt at the time that people of talent and intellect—particularly men, since they were the more imaginative and talented sex—were being exploited. The female was seen as a parasitic being who lived off of the productivity of the male. As Laura states to the captain: "The mother was your friend, look you, but the woman was your enemy,—for sexual love is strife; and don't imagine that I gave myself; I gave nothing, I only took—what I meant to have."

The source for the question of paternity that is so central to *The Father* is provided by yet another biographical reference. When Strindberg married Siri she was pregnant and had, not long before their marriage, shared the company of her first husband, Baron Wrangel. After Strindberg became actively paranoid, his remembrance of that situation provoked him to harbor active doubts about the paternity of his children. That the suspicion was in his mind was confirmed by his reaction to Henrik Ibsen's play *The Wild Duck* (1884). After its appearance, Strindberg considered suing Ibsen for slander on the grounds that Ibsen had used him as a model for Hjalmar Ekdal, the central character of the play, who doubts the paternity of his child. Strindberg and Siri were also at odds about the future occupations of their two daughters. Siri wished them to become actors, while Strindberg wanted them to be trained as midwives. These two personal conflicts became central issues in *The Father*.

Although Strindberg's own experiences provided the major inspiration for *The Father*, he was also deeply influenced by the literary and cultural milieu of his time. The novels of the Goncourt brothers, with their emphasis on the physiological and psychological approach in human character analysis, and particularly *Chérie* (1884) which was Edmond de Goncourt's last novel, may have directly affected the play. A naturalistic play with the same analytical emphasis, Émile Zola's *Thérèse Raquin* (1873), may also have provided Strindberg with some insight. Before he began writing *The Father*, he studied popular contemporary theories in psychiatric and hypnotic literature, and after finishing *The Father*, he articulated the results of these researches in an essay series entitled *Vivisections* (1887). From their titles alone, two of the essays reveal their influence on *The Father*: "The Battle of the Brains" and "Psychic Murder."

These influences, coupled with "the battle of the brains" and the "psychic murder," connect *The Father* with the school of naturalism. The battle of the brains between Laura and the captain is actually a Darwinian struggle for power, with survival going to the fittest—a central concept in the naturalist school of thought. The captain states that the battle with his wife is "to eat or to be eaten." At one point, the discussion becomes overtly Darwinistic:

CAPTAIN: I feel in this battle one of us must succumb.
LAURA: Who?
CAPTAIN: The weaker, of course.
LAURA: And the stronger is right?
CAPTAIN: He is always right because he has the power.
LAURA: Then I am right.

The amorality of action—with the end justifying the means—the detached scientific tone, the emphasis on the psychological, and the playwright's objectivity strengthen the play's naturalist tendencies.

It was Zola, however, the father of naturalism in the novel, who saw the yet undeveloped aspect of Strindberg's attempt to bring naturalism into the drama. Despite his extremely adequate psychological emphasis and scientific attitude, Strindberg, as Zola pointed out, failed to give the play a "social setting"—that is, he had failed to emphasize the importance of heredity and environment in his characterization. Although attributing the captain's weakness to his feelings of being unwanted when born and to the upbringing given him by a "bad" mother, Strindberg went no further in demonstrating the power of environmental influences on his characters. Despite this weakness, Zola apparently saw Strindberg as his potential dramatic counterpart and encouraged him in his pursuits. After his crucial beginning in *The Father*, Strindberg presented perhaps the first important naturalist drama with his next play, *Miss Julie*. The vital naturalist factors of heredity and milieu are even more explicitly emphasized in this powerful play, which dramatizes the destruction of a willful aristocratic female by her father's brazen valet.

At the time he wrote *The Father*, Strindberg was a man of mental and emotional complexity who stood on the brink of developing one of the most important movements in modern dramatic literature—naturalism. In the third section of his autobiography, covering the period around 1886, Strindberg expresses an awareness of his position in the development of the modern drama. He saw himself as spanning the gap between romanticism and naturalism and being "like the blindworm, which retains rudimentary lizard feet inside its skin." This dependence on his background and his "rudimentary lizard feet" was however no detriment to his dramatic career.

Rather than holding him back, these autobiographical reliances controlled, polished, and became the driving force in his naturalistic writings and, in a different way, were to become the substance of his later experiments with expressionism. His influence was felt throughout Europe as well as in the United States, and he was noted by Eugene O'Neill in his acceptance speech for the Nobel Prize in Literature as one of O'Neill's foremost literary inspirations. Certainly since that time, Strindberg is generally regarded, along with Henrik Ibsen and Anton Chekhov, as one of the three giants most responsible for the shape, direction, and power of twentieth century theater.

"Critical Evaluation" by Phyllis E. Allran

Bibliography:
Brustein, Robert. "Male and Female in August Strindberg." In *Modern Drama: Essays in Criticism*, edited by Travis Bogard. New York: Oxford University Press, 1965. Focuses on Strindberg's paradoxical view of masculine and feminine as reflected in several of his major plays, including *The Father*. Discusses Strindberg's early misogynist views and his recurring fascination with the so-called war between the sexes. Explanatory notes.

Dahlstrom, Carl E. W. L. "Strindberg's *The Father* as Tragedy." *Scandinavian Studies* 27, no. 2 (May, 1955): 45-63. Discusses the classical form and structure of both Greek and Shakespearean tragedy. Contends that *The Father* might not be a tragedy in the classical sense, but that it is a revolt against the mechanistic perspective and therefore, might be the only type of tragedy possible in a mechanistic universe.

Lagercrantz, Olof. *August Strindberg*. Translated by Anselm Hollo. New York: Farrar, Straus & Giroux, 1984. Discusses relevant biographical information concerning many of Strindberg's major plays, including *The Father*. Useful in understanding and interpreting Strindberg's work, which many critics assert is largely autobiographical.

Lyons, Charles R. "The Archetypal Action of Male Submission in Strindberg's *The Father*." *Scandinavian Studies* 36, no. 3 (August, 1964): 218-232. Asserts that the model(s) for male submission within *The Father* might be found in such ancient myths as those of Adam and Eve, Samson and Delilah.

Valency, Maurice. *The Flower and the Castle: An Introduction to Modern Drama*. New York: Macmillan, 1963. A comprehensive discussion of Strindberg's major plays and his contribution to modern theater. Subject index and selected bibliography.

FATHER AND SON

Type of work: Autobiography
Author: Edmund Gosse (1849-1928)
First published: 1907

In chapter 1, Edmund Gosse depicts himself as a small child in a staunchly Puritan, middle-class household where stringent worship takes place daily. As he grew, Gosse enjoyed great freedom during the day, and in the evenings he was lovingly included as an equal third party in his parents' eager, mutually enjoyable discussions of Puritan doctrine.

In chapter 2, Gosse records his life from earliest memory through age six. He emphasized the dichotomous experience of having loving parents who had no sense of the despairing oppressiveness their religious zeal had on their small son. Some escape from the oppressive worship came when, at age six, Gosse discovered a private duality which brought a "consciousness of self, as a force and as a companion," one with whom he secretly conversed during worship.

In chapters 3 and 4, Gosse presents events of his seventh year; chief among them was his mother's death. On her deathbed, she extracted from Gosse's father, Philip, a promise to see that their son Edmund would dedicate himself to their Puritanism. That dedication was to remain an intolerable burden. Adjusting to his mother's death, Gosse realized that the pain it brought had finally allowed his emotions, not merely his intellect, to be stimulated; he felt, for the first time, in touch with his own humanity. His father continued indoctrinating him into Puritan beliefs, leaving no gaps "for nature to fill."

In chapters 5 and 6, Gosse reviews his eighth and ninth years. On his eighth birthday, he and his father, with a new governess, moved to Devonshire. There, his father became a preacher in a Wesleyan church of Cornish people who retained, intact, the traditions of the eighteenth century. His father saw the new scientific works of Charles Lyell, Charles Darwin, Thomas Huxley, and others as attacks on those traditions. A renowned naturalist himself, Philip determined to write a book that would reconcile the account in Genesis of a six-day creation with the new scientific accounts of a slower evolution, thus making compatible his religion and natural science. The book failed. Philip assumed an even stricter faith, an even narrower mind. Pondering this, Gosse believed that his father habitually "mistook fear for love."

In chapters 7 through 9, Gosse relates experiences from his ninth, tenth, and eleventh years, which brought even greater distance between his and his father's spiritual beliefs. Paradoxically, during this period, his father also introduced Gosse to Vergil's classical works. At ten, Gosse suddenly wanted to be all his father expected, and, for diametrically opposed reasons, the father and son successfully instigated the unprecedented inclusion of a child in the adult affairs of a church. Philip wanted his son "saved" before puberty could assail him; Gosse wanted the power and prestige of being a child prodigy.

"Conversion" brought increased religious accountability to Gosse: He was expected to witness daily and to reject all boyish behavior. Despairingly, Gosse was forced to realize that his father expected him to enter the ministry. He saw himself, inevitably, imprisoned for life in the Puritan system. Yet he clung to a "hard nut of individuality," to the duality that allowed him to speak in himself to himself in "inviolable secrecy." Reading more widely, he realized that, unlike his father's "saving" faith, his own had intellectual roots.

At eleven, because of his son's interest in geography, Gosse's father gave him a novel about the sea that he, himself, had enjoyed as a boy. This gift marked a turning point in Gosse's life, as it opened his imagination and taught him the power of words and books. He attributed the continuing "fortitude" of his individuality to his reading of that book.

In chapters 10 and 11, Gosse covers the events of his eleventh through thirteenth years, including his father's marriage to Eliza Brightwen and her positive influence upon his life.

In chapter 12, Gosse presents an account of boarding-school years during his fourteenth through seventeenth years. The very bleakness of his school experience allowed the pursuit of his own "moral and mental development," which taught him to dream, to speculate, and to think for himself. During these years, his father took him to London to an evangelism conference, where a speaker said that William Shakespeare was suffering in hell. Gosse was devastated, for he loved Shakespeare's works but now would not read them if the writer were "lost." After the meeting, his father said he thought the man wrong to so judge Shakespeare, who may well have made a profession of faith before he died. This unexpected observation swept a relieved Gosse with love for his father.

At sixteen, however, while home from school, he confronted the narrow views of his father's faith and his own inability to conceive such a "rigid conception" of God's mercy. He found incongruous his tenderhearted father's belief that God would punish human beings forever because of an intellectual error of comprehension.

He still believed, however, in the apocalyptic return of Christ to the earth, which his father preached. In what he calls the "highest moment" of his religious experience, Gosse stood alone in his room at school, praying expectantly that Jesus would return right then and take him to Paradise. When Jesus did not, Gosse knew Christ was not coming and would never come. Then he felt an initial crumbling of the "artificial faith" he had constructed. He knew his and his father's beliefs would take opposite paths, the "world between [them]."

In the epilogue, Gosse writes of events from his seventeenth through twenty-first years, when he was living on his own in London. His father demanded a constant account of his most private thoughts, rejecting all Gosse's pleas for some small portion of private soul. On a visit home, a final confrontation with his father ended with Gosse's denying that his father was responsible for his "secret, most intimate convictions." Back in London, he received a letter of ultimatum from his father saying that he could make all well between them by repenting and becoming again submissive to his father's will in matters of faith and thought; otherwise, their fellowship would remain broken. Thus challenged, at twenty-one years of age, Gosse says his conscience rejected his father's yoke and took a man's privilege to design his "inner life for himself."

Three central themes weave their way through the tapestry of Edmund Gosse's spiritual autobiography: dualism, the passing of Victorianism, and the faltering faith that heralded modernity. The tapestry itself is what the writer calls, in his preface, an anecdotal documentary. Dualism, the doctrine of a paradoxically divided nature, runs through the pages. Gosse's early dualism separated him into companionable halves that would keep each other company, enabling him mentally to escape long hours of religious study and prayer. His father's dual nature, evidenced variously, is nowhere more significantly shown than by his evident willingness, despite his strict faith, to share forbidden fiction with his son. This sharing introduced Gosse to what became a life's work in literature. This encouragement of his son's literary interests, at significant moments of need, ultimately resulted in the divergence of their respective beliefs.

With his focus on the experience of having the fading religious concepts and practices of Puritanism thrown against his own spiritual development, Gosse reveals himself to be a true child of that transitional, Western age wherein faith went awry as the nineteenth century became the twentieth. Sweeping new scientific "truths" stunned those who were comfortable with the old doctrines. Indeed, Gosse (symbolic of the growing Victorian tendency to embrace Modernity) paralleled his developing, differing, insights with the self-satisfied confidence his father (symbolic of the traditions from which Modernity broke) held toward Puritan dogma.

Of all that lay buried in the passing of the Victorian age, religious faith proved the most traumatic loss. That loss is keenly analyzed in Gosse's autobiography through the schism that grew between father and son as their respective faiths diverged. This schism reflects the rushing changes of Modernity, which swamped people's long-held spiritual belief in absolute, unchanging truths. In this time of the scientific investigations of Charles Lyell and Charles Darwin, the socio-philosophical revolutions of Georg Hegel and Karl Marx, and the psychological insights of Carl Jung and Sigmund Freud, intellectual advancements challenged and frightened those whose understanding was built on an uninvestigated faith of fear.

Unhappily, it was also the period when traditional faith, failing the challenge, gave way in many people's minds—not from new truths but because the old faith was based on a narrow human perspective, fraught with human pride, and could not maintain its limited understanding against those truths. In this, the father proves the son's suspicion that, in spite of his tenderness, his faith in Divine Providence is built on fear, not love. As Modernity/Gosse said, such fearful faith cannot say, simply, "I don't know," yet biblical text confirms that the only answer faith can give to unanswerable paradoxes is exactly that. The faith based on fear falls apart in the face of these paradoxes.

Late twentieth century critics challenged the validity of Gosse's masterpiece, saying perhaps his father had reason to fear his son's lifestyle in London, since he evidently went to parties with young women. Gosse, however, states in the 1907 autobiography that his father never concerned himself with the son's physical actions or attitudes, trusting him implicitly in those areas. Rather, his father was concerned with the matter of "insidious infidelity," which Gosse is careful to connect with his father's fear that new intellectual views which reached fruition in the modern age would lead him astray. His father's worst fears were right, but his son, too, was right: Every person, every generation has the right to grapple with new beliefs, weighing them against the old verities and truths.

Gosse's autobiography is an important work, particularly so for generations at the crossroads of a new century—or a new millennium. The postmodern writer Robert Coover, for example, has said that late twentieth century Fundamentalism's inflexible dogma is the cause of "about 90 percent" of society's "unnecessary pain," because it demands rigid acceptance of its dogma as society's only truth. Such demands were not a new phenomena, even in Gosse's age; the Jews of the first century, likewise, rejected new ideas that did not conform to their rigid interpretation of Scripture.

Having access to all necessary truth, the Jews, the Victorians, and the Fundamentalists evidence the same "congenital lack" of what Edmund Gosse called "that highest modesty," which enables people to admit, "I do not know," when confronted by the wideness of God's many truths of grace. Such inability robs people of imagination and thereby erases the hope of a silencing awe. Such awe, alone, affirms the possibility of the "impossible." As Gosse pointed out, his father could not countenance the potential of truth to have "two forms, each of them indisputable, yet each antagonistic to the other." Such, of course, is the supreme dualism and akin to the age-old, paradoxical question of faith: How can a holy God dwell in human flesh? A saving faith, which must wait to see, really has only the one answer: "I don't know." Certainly, as Gosse concludes, each person has the pertinent right to a mind—and a faith—of his or her own. As his life proves, to deny that right robs a person of what Scripture calls "the substance of things hoped for," which is faith itself.

Jo Culbertson Davis

Bibliography:

Brugmans, Linette F., ed. and trans. *The Correspondence of André Gide and Edmund Gosse, 1904-1928*. New York: New York University Press, 1959. Includes translated letters and introductory explication of the relationship between the two men. Provides a primary source for viewing Gosse through a contemporary's eyes.

Gosse, Edmund. *Ibsen*. New York: Charles Scribner's Sons, 1907. For a researcher working with *Father and Son*, the Ibsen biography is a comparative tool for studying Gosse's use of anecdotes.

Mattheisen, Paul F., and Michael Millgate, eds. *Transalantic Dialogue: Selected American Correspondence of Edmund Gosse*. Austin: University of Texas Press, 1965. Introduction gives insight into Gosse's relationship with American writers. Assorted references to *Father and Son*, including America's favorable response. Extensive index with almost seven pages of autobiographical references.

Thwaite, Ann. *Edmund Gosse: A Literary Landscape, 1849-1928*. Chicago: University of Chicago Press, 1984. Provides a balanced study of the pros and cons on Gosse's life and work. Thwaite began the work to discover what happened after Gosse's twenty-first year, when *Father and Son* ended. Covers Churton Collins' notorious attacks on Gosse's literary criticism. Emphasizes Gosse's far-reaching influence in England.

Woolf, James D. *Sir Edmund Gosse*. New York: Twayne, 1972. A "representative" study of Gosse. Provides an array of Gosse's criticism. Emphasizes Gosse's views on Christianity relative to his religious focus in the early part of *Father and Son*. Provides extensive editorial notes to the text.

THE FATHERS

Type of work: Novel
Author: Allen Tate (1899-1979)
Type of plot: Historical realism
Time of plot: 1860-1861
Locale: Northern Virginia and Georgetown
First published: 1938

Principal characters:
>LACY GORE BUCHAN, the narrator
>MAJOR LEWIS BUCHAN, his father
>SEMMES BUCHAN, Lacy's older brother, killed by George Posey
>SUSAN BUCHAN POSEY, Lacy's sister
>GEORGE POSEY, Lacy's brother-in-law
>JANE POSEY, George's sister, who is loved by Lacy and Semmes
>JOHN LANGTON, George's rival
>YELLOW JIM, George's mulatto half brother, a slave George sells to
>>buy a horse

The Story:

Lacy Buchan, a sixty-year-old bachelor, thought back over the year 1860, when he was fifteen and his mother died. That April, family and friends gathered at Pleasant Hill in Fairfax County, Virginia, for the funeral, the last time they were all together. Among those present were the Poseys, Lacy's sister Susan's in-laws. Susan's husband, George, rode his horse away from the funeral, causing much gossip.

Young Lacy recalled his memories of George, his brother Semmes' friend. During a visit two years before, George had given Lacy a gun. The next day, Lacy had gone to a jousting tournament and stayed with his father's slave, Coriolanus, who talked to some slaves who had just been sold. One was called Yellow Jim; George Posey had sold him and bought a mare.

Riders in the tournament had five tries to take rings from hooks with lances. George and John Langton succeeded each time, and George was awarded the prize for his superior form. When the drunken Langton protested, George threw him to the ground. The victor shared his reward with Lacy's sister, Susan. Langton challenged George to a duel; George shot at a target, then discarded his pistol and punched Langton. Lacy admired his new friend very much.

At the funeral, Lacy's sister-in-law Lucy gave Lacy violets to put in his mother's hands. As he moved from the coffin, Jane, George's sister, took his hand. They left the room, and Lacy kissed Jane. Afterwards, Lacy held a garment belonging to his mother and thought of Jane and of his mother at the same time.

After marrying Susan, George Posey began managing the Buchans' business affairs. Once he sold a family of slaves that Major Buchan had asked him to free, applying the money to one of the Major's debts. George was a practical man, not a principled one like Major Buchan.

During the winter of 1860-1861, the Buchans stayed in Alexandria at the home of Lacy's cousin, John Semmes, who had gone to Washington. Lacy's brother, Charles, and his sister-in-law, Lucy, moved in with the Buchan family. South Carolina seceded from the Union, and other Southern states followed. Lacy's father was a Unionist, but his cousin John favored secession. The Buchans discussed civilly which side they would take in the war, but could not agree.

Charles, who was in the United States Army, drilled with the National Rifles, from which the Unionists had withdrawn. George had supplied the company with firearms. Charles resigned his commission with the U.S. Army because he knew Lincoln would send troops to South Carolina. George told Major Buchan that he sympathized with Unionists, but his loyalty was with Virginia; Colonel Robert E. Lee made the same decision several days later. John Langton became captain of the National Rifles.

Lacy went to stay with the Poseys in Georgetown because his sister sent for him. Her husband, George, was often mysteriously away. In the Posey household were Susan and her daughter, little Jane; George's sister Jane; and Jane and George's mother, uncle, and aunt. Each resident lived in seclusion, and only Susan, Jane, and Lacy dined together.

Northern soldiers kept Washington, D.C., under martial law, and John Semmes was arrested for secessionist activity. When Lacy's brother Semmes became a Confederate, Major Buchan disclaimed the young man.

One night, Lacy heard a noise and went downstairs. The slave Blind Joe (who was not really blind) took him to Yellow Jim, who explained that he had run away and come home. No one was there to send him back to his new owner, so Jim resumed his duties as butler. Jim, who was also George and Jane's half brother, had been Jane's caretaker, but during his three years away, she had grown up and did not need him anymore. In fact, she feared him. Lacy understood her fear, having once see Jim beat a horse who bit him—the very mare George had sold him to buy.

Lacy's brother Semmes proposed to Jane, whom Lacy loved. When Semmes asked Lacy if he loved Jane, Lacy lied. The night after Semmes proposed to Jane, he left. Lacy heard a scream, then a door slam. He ran upstairs and found Yellow Jim crouching in the hall. Susan came from the mother's room and said that the woman had died of fright. Susan and Lacy deduced that the scream had come from Jane, whom they discovered supine on her bedroom floor. They inferred that Jim had raped Jane. Lacy locked him in the basement and sent Blind Joe for George.

The next day, nuns took Jane to a convent. Susan, whose hair had turned white overnight, begged Jim to run away, but he refused. Semmes and George returned and took Jim out to the river; Lacy accompanied them. To avenge Jane, Semmes shot Jim; in reflex, George shot Semmes. Lacy ran ten miles back to the city. He saw that the Confederate flag was no longer flying over Arlington, and Union soldiers told him that the first fatalities of the war had occurred. Lacy, exhausted, headed toward home. By the time he got there, he was ill and delirious. After six weeks, he recovered to learn that his father knew the whole story. The Major forbade him to avenge Semmes' death and accepted some blame for the incident, feeling that he had injured Semmes' pride by denying him.

Lacy's sister, Susan, had gone mad and come home. George came to get her, but she did not seem to recognize him. George donned a Confederate uniform, and he and Lacy left to find General Longstreet's brigade.

They later learned that Union soldiers had come to Pleasant Hill and told Major Buchan to get out. He did not tell them that he was a Unionist; instead, he hanged himself. The soldiers burned the house to the ground. Lacy became a Confederate soldier.

"The Story" by M. Katherine Grimes

Critical Evaluation:

Allen Tate had the misfortune to have *The Fathers* published two years after *Gone with the Wind* (1936) appeared, with the result that his novel soon became a dinghy bobbing in the wake of Margaret Mitchell's overwhelming popular success. The reappearance of Tate's book in a slightly revised version twenty-two years later was an event of considerable importance. *The Fathers*, as *Gone with the Wind* does not, provides an occasion for defining the idea of the South and for critical reflection on the moral significance Tate was able to extract from his social scene and his historical perspective. That the novel failed to evoke any such critical response is shown by the reviews written at the time.

Reading these reviews is an illuminating experience, as much for what they do not say as for what they do. The critics were, on the whole, sympathetic toward the book and generous in their comments, but one takes away the impression that many had not read it carefully and almost none understood the writer's intention. Many readers saw it only as a moving story of one family's tragic collapse during the Civil War; certainly this reading testifies to the richness of the narrative if to nothing else. Others thought that Tate was dramatizing within a family unit the fatal clash of two social orders—that of the traditional society of the South, symbolized by Major Buchan, and that of the industrial society of the North, represented by George Posey, the Major's son-in-law. This conflict was viewed in all its dramatic tensions and implications, but with a feeling on the part of the reviewers that Tate had failed to prove the superiority of the Buchans' ancestral code over George Posey's antitraditional conduct. It is possible to read *The Fathers* in this way, as one can read much of William Faulkner's works in a similar fashion, but to do so is to miss the point, so to speak, of a novel remarkable for its realistic detail, thematic extensions of symbolic reference, moral intensity, and passionate historical sense.

The Fathers presents a philosophical view of society and history within a framework of particular events. It is only natural that these events should center upon the Civil War, for to the Southern writer concerned with the life or culture of his region, the war is central. It is no longer enough to know what happened in that conflict; it is also necessary to know what the conflict meant. For this purpose, the Civil War provides a vast controlling image that gives meaning to the facts of the regional experience, not only to the structure of Southern society but also to the code of morality on which it was based.

Before *The Fathers* appeared, Tate had already defined his position on the South in a series of essays written between 1930 and 1936. In one of these, "Religion and the Old South," he outlines his theory of history in terms of the Long View and the Short View. Within the perspective of the latter, all history reduces to a variety and confusion of images out of which it is possible for readers to make choices in reconstructing the scene or the period. The Long View sees history as idea or concept, not as an account of the particular lives of particular people in a setting that often bewildered them, but as a record of events without accident, contingency, or personal involvement. Tate's own choice between these two ways of historical vision and thinking is as apparent in his fiction as in his poetry. The reviewers who found no real meaning in his novel were looking at history as an abstract concept of principles and causes. *The Fathers* incorporates the Short View.

The novel is spacious in outline, as any work must be which attempts to contain within its limits the picture of a whole society. It is beautifully selective in attention to the detail with which people and places are described, habits of speech and manners are recorded, and the impressions made by events upon the mind of the narrator are carefully noted. Tate achieves his organizational effect, the configuration of theme and structure, by his skillful management of a special point of view. The person telling the story is Lacy Buchan, who as an old man is looking back on events that had happened almost a half century before. As a story retrieved in memory, the novel moves simultaneously on two levels: one, the plane of action conveying with all immediacy the impact of events upon the consciousness of a young boy whose reactions to experience are direct and sensuous; the other, the plane of reflection on which the man, now old, looks back on those happenings and contemplates meanings unperceived at the time of his boyhood. The ease with which Tate moves from past to present and back, setting up a relevant interplay between some event and its significance in retrospect, all the while causing the narrative to expand, its values to join and grow into one another, becomes one of the major triumphs of the novel. What is presented is a deep concern with historical processes and moral issues, but it is all done simply, without resort to the self-conscious or the portentous in association or image. The older Lacy reflects that only in memory and symbol can knowledge of the past be preserved, never in the feelings of the time.

Through all of Lacy Buchan's reflections runs the question of evil; problems of sin, responsibility, and guilt remain shadowy and unresolved. He wonders why life cannot change without entangling many lives; why the innocent, for example, lose their innocence and become violent or evil, thus causing change. He reflects that as people need to recognize the innate aspect of evil in human nature, there is also need to face that evil.

The image at the center of *The Fathers* is the family, the social unit that, with all its widespread connections of kinship, was the foundation of Southern society. The story tells how the Buchan family of Fairfax County, Virginia, is weakened and disrupted by the fierce energies of George Posey, the son-in-law for whom all life—because he cannot recognize, or submit to, the authority that tradition imposes—becomes impulse and motion. In later years, Lacy always thinks of him as a horseman galloping over an abyss, a man of courage and generosity and charm, but doomed because his reckless and irresponsible deeds menaced himself as well as family unity and social order.

Lacy reflects that the Poseys possessed more refinement than the Buchans but were less civilized. This difference is emphasized at the beginning of the novel when Major Buchan, at the time of his wife's funeral, plays the role of the gracious host and not the bereaved husband; he is merely upholding the accepted code of good manners. In much the same way, he leaves his place in his wife's funeral procession to take the hand of Mrs. Buchan's black maid and draw her, immediately behind the coffin, into the line of mourners. George Posey, on the other hand, orders his horse saddled and rides away, unable to face the idea of death. Another trait that he displays is a heartless disregard for others, as when he sells his mulatto half brother in order to buy a blood mare, an act that involves the Buchans and Poseys in a family catastrophe even more devastating than the disunion caused by the Civil War. Before the end of the novel, he has destroyed the Buchans' agrarian economy, killed his brother-in-law Semmes, driven his wife mad, brought about his sister's ruin, and caused his father-in-law's death.

It is important to note that George Posey is neither a villain by nature nor a symbol of Northern capitalism assaulting Southern tradition. He stands for that element in Southern life that was wild and undisciplined from the beginning, just as Semmes Buchan's weakness and John Langdon's violence were a part of the tradition as well. In Tate's view, apparently, the old order was already corrupted from within before the Civil War destroyed it from without. (This is Faulkner's belief as well.) Whether that way of life truly satisfied the needs of those who created it is a matter of relative unimportance. What is important is the fact that the traditional order established sanctions and defined virtues and obligations by which, for a time, people could assume social and moral responsibilities; it set up a concept of truth that made the human effort seem worthwhile. Major Buchan recognizes these sanctions and obligations and acts accordingly, but George Posey does not; therefore, he corrupts or destroys all who come in contact with him.

This is the meaning of the episode in which Lacy Buchan, semidelirious with fever, imagines that he and his dead grandfather are sitting on a pile of fence rails while the old man retells the myth of Jason and Medea. The scene is poetically conceived and morally instructive. Jason's fate, the old man says, was to secure the Golden Fleece or attempt some impossible feat, at the same time becoming involved with the humanity of others whom, in the end, he betrayed not through his intention but through his nature. The old man says that George Posey never really intends to commit evil; his flaw is the lack of will to do good. Thus the only future possible for him is loneliness and the grave.

The Fathers is a novel in which the private life of the family and the public life of action converge upon a decisive moment in history, the outbreak of the Civil War. Its importance as fiction is its power to illuminate, through realistic detail and symbolic extension, the meaning of the past and the shape of the future.

Bibliography:
Carpenter, Lynette. "The Battle Within: The Beleaguered Consciousness in Allen Tate's *The Fathers*." *Southern Literary Journal* 8, no. 2 (Spring, 1976): 3-23. Asserts Lacy Buchan is the central character in Tate's novel and his confused narration is representative of the book's theme: the ambiguity of experience and memory.

Holman, C. Hugh. "*The Fathers* and the Historical Imagination." In *Literary Romanticism in America*, edited by William L. Andrews. Baton Rouge: Louisiana State University Press, 1981. This renowned critic provides a useful review of earlier criticism of *The Fathers*. Discusses the work as a *Bildungsroman* that reviews a family's events through a historical viewpoint.

Law, Richard. " 'Active Faith' and Ritual in *The Fathers*." *American Literature* 55 (October, 1983): 345-366. Posits that part of the novel's greatness lies in its questioning its own thesis: the value of tradition and community. Asserts that it is not a tract, although it represents Agrarianism.

Mizener, Arthur. "*The Fathers* and Realistic Fiction." *Accent* 7 (Winter, 1947): 101-109. Reprinted in *Sewanee Review* 67 (Autumn, 1959): 604-613. Says that Tate's book is "A novel *Gone with the Wind* ought to have been," and that it presents a contrast of public and private life.

Young, Thomas Daniel. "Allen Tate's Double Focus: The Past in the Present." *Mississippi Quarterly* 30 (Fall, 1977): 517-525. This respected scholar asserts that *The Fathers* shows the likelihood that the antebellum South would have destroyed itself even if the Civil War had not occurred. Quotes Tate extensively.

FATHERS AND SONS

Type of work: Novel
Author: Ivan Turgenev (1818-1883)
Type of plot: Social realism
Time of plot: 1859
Locale: Russia
First published: Ottsy i deti, 1862 (English translation, 1867)

> *Principal characters:*
> KIRSANOFF, a Russian gentleman
> PAVEL, his older brother
> ARKADY, his son
> FENICHKA, Kirsanoff's mistress
> BAZAROFF, Arkady's friend
> VASILY, Bazaroff's father
> MADAME ODINTZOFF, a widow
> KATYA, her younger sister

The Story:

At a provincial posting station, Kirsanoff waited impatiently for his son, Arkady, who had completed his education at the university in St. Petersburg. Kirsanoff reflected that Arkady had probably changed, but he hoped his son had not grown away from him entirely. Arkady's mother was dead, and the widower was strongly attached to his son.

At last the coach appeared, rolling along the dusty road. Arkady jumped out, but he was not alone. Lounging superciliously behind was a stranger whom Arkady introduced as Bazaroff, a fellow student. Something in Arkady's manner told Kirsanoff that here was a special attachment. In a low aside, Arkady begged his father to be gracious to his guest.

Feeling some qualms about his unexpected guest, Kirsanoff was troubled during the trip home. He was hesitant about his own news but finally told Arkady that he had taken a mistress, Fenichka, and installed her in his house. To his great relief, Arkady took the news calmly and even congratulated his father on the step. Later, Arkady was pleased to learn that he even had a little half brother.

Kirsanoff soon found he had good reason to distrust Bazaroff, who was a doctor and a clever biologist. Arkady seemed too much under his influence. Worse, Bazaroff was a nihilist. At the university the liberal thinkers had consciously decided to defy or ignore all authority—state, church, home, pan-Russianism. Bazaroff was irritating to talk to, Kirsanoff decided, because he knew so much and had such a sarcastic tongue.

Pavel, Kirsanoff's older brother, was especially irritated by Bazaroff. Pavel was a real aristocrat, bound by tradition, who had come to live in retirement with his younger brother after a disappointing career as an army officer and the lover of a famous beauty, the Princess R——. With his background and stiff notions of propriety, Pavel often disagreed with Bazaroff.

Luckily, Bazaroff kept busy most of the time. He collected frogs and infusoria and was always dissecting and peering into a microscope. He would have been an ideal guest, except for his calmly superior air of belonging to a generation far surpassing Pavel's. Kirsanoff, loving his son so much, did his best to keep peace, but all the while he regretted the nihilism which had so greatly affected Arkady.

Kirsanoff was harassed by other troubles. Soon, by law, the serfs would be freed. Kirsanoff strongly approved of this change and had anticipated the new order by dividing his farm into smaller plots which the peasants rented on a sharecropping basis. With their new independence, however, the peasants cheated him more than ever and were slow in paying their rent.

Arkady and Bazaroff, growing bored with quiet farm life, went to visit in the provincial capital, where they had introductions to the governor. In town, they ran into Sitnikoff, a kind of polished jackal who felt important because he was one of the nihilist circle. Sitnikoff introduced them into provincial society.

At a ball, the two friends met and were greatly taken by a young widow, Madame Odintzoff. Arkady did not dance, but he sat out a mazurka with her. They became friends at once, especially when she found that Arkady's mother had been an intimate friend of her own mother. After the ball, Madame Odintzoff invited the two men to visit her estate.

Arkady and Bazaroff accepted the invitation promptly. In a few days, they settled down to the easy routine of favored guests in a wealthy household. Katya, Madame Odintzoff's young sister, was especially attracted to Arkady. Bazaroff, older and more worldly, became the good friend of the widow. Although Bazaroff, as a good nihilist, despised home and family life, he made a real effort to overcome his scruples; but when he finally began to talk of love and marriage to Madame Odintzoff, he was politely refused. Chagrined at his rejection, he induced Arkady to leave with him at once. The two friends then went on to Bazaroff's home.

Vasily, Bazaroff's father, was glad to see his son, whom he both feared and admired. He and his wife did all they could to make the young men comfortable. At length Arkady and Bazaroff quarreled, chiefly because they were so bored. Abruptly they left and impulsively called again on Madame Odintzoff. She received them coolly. Feeling that they were unwelcome, they went back to the Kirsanoff estate.

Because Bazaroff was convinced that Arkady was also in love with Madame Odintzoff, his friendship with Arkady became greatly strained. Arkady, thinking constantly of Katya, returned by himself to the Odintzoff estate to press his suit of the younger sister. At the Kirsanoff home, Bazaroff became friendly with Fenichka. He prescribed for her sick baby and even for her. Out of friendship, Fenichka spent much of her time with Bazaroff. One morning, as they sat in a garden, Bazaroff kissed her unexpectedly, to her distress and confusion. Pavel witnessed the scene by accident and became increasingly incensed at the strange nihilist.

Although Pavel did not consider Bazaroff a gentleman, he challenged him to a duel with pistols. In the encounter, Pavel was wounded in the leg, and Bazaroff left the house in haste, never to return. Pavel recovered from his wound, but he felt a never-ending shame at being wounded by a low nihilist. He urged Kirsanoff to marry Fenichka, and he returned to his old life. He spent the rest of his days as an aging dandy in Dresden.

Bazaroff stopped briefly at the Odintzoff home. Still convinced that Arkady was in love with Madame Odintzoff, he attempted to help his friend in his suit. Madame Odintzoff ridiculed him, however, when Arkady made his request for the hand of Katya. With a sense of futility, Bazaroff took his leave and rejoined his own family. Vasily was the local doctor, and he eagerly welcomed his son as a colleague. For a time, Bazaroff led a successful life, helping to cure the ailments of the peasants and pursuing his research at the same time. When one of his patients contracted typhus, he accidentally scratched himself with a scalpel he had used. Although Vasily cauterized the wound as well as he could, Bazaroff became ill with a fever. Sure that he would die, he summoned Madame Odintzoff to his side. She came gladly and helped to ease him before his death.

Madame Odintzoff eventually made a good marriage with a lawyer. Arkady was happy managing his father's farm and playing with the son born to him and Katya. Kirsanoff became a magistrate and spent most of his life settling disputes brought about by the liberation of the serfs. Fenichka, at last a respected wife and mother, found great happiness in her daughter-in-law, Katya.

Critical Evaluation:

In *Fathers and Sons*, Ivan Turgenev attempted to examine the forces for change operating, for the most part in isolation and frustration, in mid-nineteenth century Russia. The storm of protest and outrage produced from the moment the novel appeared indicates that he had indeed touched a sensitive nerve in Russian society. In fact, Turgenev never really got over the abuse heaped upon him; his periods of exile in Germany, France, and Italy were all the more frequent and of longer duration after the publication of the novel. One wonders at the excitement occasioned by *Fathers and Sons*, for a cooler reading undertaken more than a hundred years later indicates that Turgenev clearly attempted and achieved a balanced portrait of conservative and revolutionary Russia—a triumphant achievement in political fiction, where the passions of the moment so often damage the artistic effort.

The subtlety and rightness of Turgenev's technique are most clearly seen in the central character Bazaroff. Bazaroff is a pragmatist, a scientist, and a revolutionary idealist. He is put into relationship with every important character, and it is from these relationships that the reader gets to know him and to understand more about him than he understands about himself. A master of literary impressionism, Turgenev liked to do an "atmospheric" treatment of his characters, vividly rendering visual, auditory, and other sense impressions in a nicely selected setting. This technique admits all sorts of lively and contradictory details and prevents the novel—and Bazaroff—from falling into mere ideological rhetoric and political polemic. Most of all, for all of his roughness and bearishness, Turgenev really liked Bazaroff and sympathized with him ("with the exception of [his] views on art, I share almost all his convictions," he wrote).

Bazaroff's chief conflict is with Pavel Kirsanoff, a middle-aged bachelor with refined continental tastes and a highly developed sense of honor. Pavel stands for everything Bazaroff despises: an Old World emphasis upon culture, manners, and refinement, and an aristocratic and elitist view of life. He represents the traditions which Bazaroff vainly struggles to destroy in his efforts to bring a democratic, scientific, and utilitarian plan of action into widespread use. For Bazaroff, "a good chemist is more useful than a score of poets," because the chemist attacks the central problem of poverty, disease, and ignorance. The old humanism represented by Pavel is, for him, a manifestation of ignorance which perpetrates and countenances needless suffering, particularly for the lower classes. His rude and sneering treatment of Pavel is undercut by his participation in the duel, which is an absurd custom of the upper classes he despises. Bazaroff is the loser in the duel and he knows it. His passion, which he tries to cover up with a cold, clinical attitude, leads him into it.

His relationship with Madame Odintzoff shows that Bazaroff is at heart a romantic, though he would hardly admit it. This cool and cultured widow provokes the most ardent response from him—despite his contention that women are mere instruments of amusement and pleasure. With Madame Odintzoff, however, Bazaroff has unfortunately chosen an inadequate object for his passion. She is lovely but cold and detached and is unable to respond to him.

Bazaroff's romanticism, however, is chiefly frustrated in social and political matters. He deeply believes that conditions can be changed and that he and others can work together to that end. When readers look at these "others," they see how painful and tragic his situation is. Arkady, his schoolmate and friend, is a kindly fellow who imitates Bazaroff's revolutionary attitudes. He is in awe of his friend's rough manner, but he does not understand that Bazaroff really intends to follow his ideas to the end. Rather, Arkady is not even dimly aware at first that he is incapable of supporting Bazaroff all the way. Like most men, Arkady is conventional and conforming out of natural adaptability. His marriage to Katya is a model of bourgeois comfort and serves to underline Bazaroff's loneliness and ineffectuality. Like his father before him, Arkady chooses domestic satisfactions and a life of small compromises over the absurd "heroism" of his schoolfellow. The Kirsanoff homestead remains, on the whole, ill-managed and unimproved. No revolution in land management has occurred even though the peasants are about to be freed. Life goes on in a muddle despite the passionate efforts of one or two enlightened persons to reform it.

Bazaroff's curious and potentially violent behavior to Arkady when they are lying in a haystack suggests that he knows that Arkady cannot follow him. Furthermore, this scene reveals that Bazaroff is full of violent distaste for those who pretend to be reformers. He cannot spare them ridicule, and his frustrated energies burst forth in threatening gestures. He is a leader without followers, a general without an army. Nevertheless, he loves his parents, two kindly old representatives of the traditional way of life, for they do not pretend to be anything they are not.

Bazaroff's death is a form of suicide. His willingness to take no immediate steps to prevent the spread of infection after he has carelessly cut himself suggests that he has seen the absurdity of his position and, to some extent at least, given in to it. In his delirium, he states that Russia needs a cobbler, a tailor, a butcher more than she needs him. Nevertheless, for Turgenev, Bazaroff was "the real hero of our time."

"Critical Evaluation" by Benjamin Nyce

Bibliography:
Costlow, Jane T. *Worlds Within Worlds: The Novels of Ivan Turgenev*. Princeton, N.J.: Princeton University Press, 1990. Presents the concept that Turgenev's fourth novel focuses on the structures of human lives, especially on the sense of place. It is also an ideological work dealing with the years in Russia before the 1861 emancipation of the serfs. Turgenev's social resolve is bolstered by his psychological perceptions.

Freeborn, Richard. *Turgenev: The Novelist's Novelist*. London: Oxford University Press, 1960. Chapter 5, "Four Great Novels," explores how Turgenev assimilated the short story form into the novel. The figure of the hero unifies the novel and establishes the tradition of organic form in Russian literature.

Knowles, A. V. *Ivan Turgenev*. Boston: Twayne, 1988. The novel reflects Turgenev's keen interest in politics and his abhorrence of violence. Studies the time frame and construction of the novel, emphasizing its logical progress and sense of inevitability. Also explores character development and theme.

Lowe, David A., ed. *Critical Essays on Ivan Turgenev*. Boston: G. K. Hall, 1989. Lowe's "Comedy and Tragedy in *Fathers and Sons*" suggests the novel's structure is determined by a sequence of trips and a set of confrontations which contribute to its dualism—two parallel but contrasting patterns of tragedy and comedy. Some discussion of other critical readings of the novel are included.

Ripp, Victor. *Turgenev's Russia: From "Notes of a Hunter" to "Fathers and Sons."* Ithaca, N.Y.: Cornell University Press, 1980. Discusses the novel in the light of the Emancipation Act, the contemporary reaction to Turgenev's treatment of his hero, and his impact on his successors. Bazarov absorbs politics into psychology. The novel also develops the theme of a home away from the corrupt world.

FAULTLINE

Type of work: Novel
Author: Sheila Ortiz Taylor
Type of plot: Social realism
Time of plot: 1980's
Locale: Los Angeles, California
First published: 1982

Principal characters:
>ARDEN BENBOW, the main character, a mother of six
>VIOLET GROOT, Arden's high-spirited Aunt Vi
>WHITNEY MALTHUS, Arden's former husband
>WILSON TOPAZ, a gay man who moves in with Arden and Alice
>as a babysitter for the children
>ALICE WICKS, Arden's lover who lives with her

The Story:

Arden Benbow was caught releasing domestic rabbits into a wilderness area outside Los Angeles. She said that owning three hundred rabbits made her look eccentric. She had received a pair of rabbits that multiplied rapidly, so she decided to set them free. Arden was born on the San Andreas fault in Southern California and said that the minor earthquakes she experienced as a child developed her maternal instincts and made her determined to have a large family to counteract her fears of extinction. Arden told the story of her life as an explanation of her present, and other people gave their views of her suitability as a mother.

Arden was an English major in college, and, after her graduation in 1959, she met Whitney Malthus, whom everyone called Malthus. He looked like the actor William Holden and liked to talk about science and how everything worked. Arden was married to him for twelve years during which time they had six children. She came to see Malthus as dull, egotistical, and unfair to women. Malthus gave his view that Arden humiliated him by becoming a lesbian. The mother of his children should not behave in such a way. Mothers should uphold the social standards; lesbians, Malthus believed, were social deviants. He claimed that he should have custody of their children.

Ben Griffin gave Arden the original pair of rabbits and sold her feed for them. He said Arden was a smart woman who paid her bills and that she deserved to raise her children. A man who worked with Malthus said that Malthus treated Arden badly when she fell in love with another woman. A neighbor, Jim Muncey, liked Arden and said she was a dependable person. A receptionist at a veterinarian's office said she got a crank call from a lady asking about birth control for rabbits so she hung up the phone.

Wilson Topaz identified himself as a dancer who could not get many dancing jobs because he was six feet tall, black, and homosexual. He saw the advertisement to work as a babysitter for a lesbian mother, met Arden and her lover Alice and the children, and decided to join their energetic and happy household. He became part of Operation Bunnylift and was there when the police arrived just as the last of the rabbits they had released disappeared into the wilderness.

The Assistant Registrar at Arden's college gave a negative character reference, complaining that Arden had changed her surname from Malthus to Benbow, her grandmother's name, and further annoyed him because she had hired Wilson Topaz, whom the Assistant Registrar had considered a problem when Wilson was a student. The Assistant Registrar then claimed that none of this had to do with homosexuality or race.

Comments were made that Arden had abducted her aunt Violet Groot from a hospital in 1959. Aunt Vi's oppressive husband had placed her there. Aunt Vi arranged a trip to Mexico with the help of an orderly, Maurio Carbonara. His real name was Homer Rice, but Aunt Vi fired his imagination and said he needed a better name. They escaped the institution one night and traveled with Arden in a blue van through Mexico, spending most of their time at Ruby's campground and Trailer Park. Ruby had previously worked as a stripper in a bar in San Francisco and then moved to Mexico to create and run the campground. She liked the trio of visitors and was energized and rejuvenated by Vi and her laughing ways.

Vi's husband hired a detective, Michael Raven, to find his missing wife. Vi decided to let him find and follow her, and Michael became enchanted with the lively group. They continued vacationing in Mexico together and Michael fell in love with Maurio. Aunt Vi was delighted with their happiness, and, as they celebrated with a party, another private investigator showed up, saying Mr. Groot had hired him to find them. Aunt Vi died that night. She had enjoyed the last weeks of her life and had nearly finished writing a gothic romance novel. Arden wrote the last few pages, pondering Aunt Vi's belief that life may end in marriage but never in death. The book became a best-seller; Mr. Groot made all the money. Arden married Malthus because he was persistent, but she came to understand her aunt's statement that marriages can be stifling, killing the spirit in a way that death does not.

A dozen years later, after Arden and Malthus divorced, Allison Honey spoke up for Arden, saying that Arden had fixed her car for her and had found her a job at the catering service Maurio Carbonara and Michael Raven had started in San Francisco. Alice Wicks explained that she had met Arden three years earlier. She too was married. They became friends, fell in love, and started living together permanently. Malthus hired the detective from earlier to spy on Arden and started the child custody dispute. Winnifred Hooper was the social worker who had to be convinced that Arden was a fit mother. Although Winnifred was prepared to dislike them, Arden remembered Aunt Vi's way of taking in the enemy and made friends with her.

Ruby was invited to a big party Arden had planned, and she was excited about seeing Arden and Maurio and Michael again. She went to San Franciso to visit her old bar and then on to Los Angeles for the party, which turned out to be a double wedding ceremony: Arden and Alice, Michael and Mario. It was also a celebration of the thirteenth anniversary of Vi Groot's death, and of the happy conclusion of the custody trial. Arden had invited Jim Muncey; she had learned that Jim had been engaged to Winnifred but that she had run off with another man. The man was gone now, and Jim Muncey wanted Winnifred back. Arden made it clear to Winnifred that she knew something of her past, but, rather than blackmail her, she won her over with happy domesticity. Winnifred had agreed to preside at the "weddings" as well as to support Arden's right to child custody. Jim Muncy was happy to see Winnifred, and she was happy to see him.

Critical Evaluation:

Faultline is a comic novel with a serious message conveyed by example and implication rather than by preaching. Sheila Ortiz Taylor creates a shining cast of characters who speak about their relationships to Arden Benbow as Arden battles her ex-husband Malthus for custody of their six children. Malthus has never considered women equal to men, and his male ego is hurt when Arden prefers living with a woman to staying with him in their dull marriage. He provides the prime example of a person who cannot accept individual differences or see that others have a right to their own lives.

The theme of acceptance of individual differences runs throughout the novel. Malthus is a repeat of Arden's uncle, Mr. Groot, who tries to control his wife in every way. Aunt Vi, however, will not be stifled. She is full of energy and believes that life should be fun and joyful. Mr. Groot has a mistress, and he immediately puts Vi in a hospital when she has a mild stroke. Aunt Vi refuses to end her days in the confining institution. She breaks free and takes Arden to Mexico with her as much for Arden's sake as for her own.

Arden, however, falls into the same marriage trap her aunt did. For example, Malthus refuses to let her go to graduate school; his wife should stay home with the children. It is not until she and Alice Wicks fall in love that Arden can see what her aunt meant about freeing oneself to live fully and to develop the creative spirit within oneself. Alice too has married because that is what society expected of her, but she learns that she must be herself and follow her own spirit.

The faultline of the title refers to the actual geography of the setting in Southern California, but it is also a metaphor for unpredictability and the need for adaptability and acceptance of reality. One chapter is in the words of a professor of geophysics who specializes in plate tectonics, the study of the faultlines where earthquakes happen. "Earthquakes remind us," he says. They are dynamic reactions to changes in the earth's crust that remind people of their mortality and the need to live with enthusiasm. People should not waste their time being prejudiced against others who have their own lives to live. Although he is a scientist, the professor knows—as Malthus does not—that there is more to life than "facts."

The theme of celebrating differences instead of controlling others is shown throughout the novel by characterization. Aunt Vi and Wilson Topaz, for example, have learned to make the most of life despite people who would deny them social opportunities and human rights. Arden Benbow and Alice Wicks become finer people when they acknowledge their love for each other instead of suffering in socially approved but oppressive marriages. Michael Raven and Maurio celebrate their love instead of being dragged down by hostile societal attitudes and proscriptions against homosexual love.

These characters all open their hearts to others and accept them and the changes that occur throughout the years. The characters who are rigid and domineering are shown to be unhappy, whatever material wealth they may have. Malthus will not accept Arden's love for a woman and thus turns his own children against him; they do not want to live with an angry and spiteful father who does not even provide his share of child support. Mr. Groot made money from his late wife's novel, but he never shared Aunt Vi's vitality and sense of play. The pretentious and self-important Assistant Registrar from the college who speaks against Arden is revealed as a sour, unhappy man with no sense of humor and no love for anyone but himself. He cannot accept Arden as a lesbian or Wilson Topaz as an African American gay man; he lives in a prison that cuts him off from reality and from the acceptance of difference.

Faultline emphasizes the need for people to celebrate life rather than to oppress others. Arden Benbow is, after all, not only a fit mother, but an outstanding one who brings to her children and to all around her a sense of fairness and decency and, especially, a joy in living and loving.

Lois A. Marchino

Bibliography:
Bann, Stephen. "Plots." *London Review of Books* 4 (November 17, 1982): 22. Sees *Faultline* as a picaresque novel with an improbable plot. The satire is carefully calculated as part of an almost didactic tone of advocacy. The faultline promises eventual chaos and the rabbits

suggest a family run wild, but Arden shows a new type of family in which various people live together happily in a kind of modulated chaos.

Publishers Weekly. Review of *Faultline*, by Sheila Ortiz Taylor. 221 (January 1, 1982): 48. Lists main characters and considers the novel to be comic and entertaining.

Small Press Review. Review of *Faultline*, by Sheila Ortiz Taylor. 14, no. 3 (March, 1982): 12. Praises novel as zesty, outrageous, and funny. Calls it a lesbian novel that takes the rest of the world in stride.

White, Gail. Review of *Faultline*, by Sheila Ortiz Taylor. *Small Press Review* 14, no. 11 (November, 1982): 1. Sees the novel as a hilarious kaleidoscope exploring Arden Benbow's life through the eyes of a variety of witnesses. States that it is a lesbian novel only in the sense that it features gay characters. White considers the sexuality and politics to be peripheral issues.

FAUST

Type of work: Poetry
Author: Johann Wolfgang von Goethe (1749-1832)
Type of plot: Philosophical
Time of plot: Indeterminate
Locale: The world
First published: Faust: Ein Fragment, 1790 (English translation, *Faust: A Fragment,* 1980); *Faust: Eine Tragödie,* 1808 (English translation, *The Tragedy of Faust,* 1823); *Faust: Eine Tragödie, zweiter Teil,* 1833 (English translation, *The Tragedy of Faust, Part Two,* 1838)

Principal characters:
FAUST, a student of all knowledge
GRETCHEN, a young woman
MEPHISTOPHELES, the devil
WAGNER, Faust's servant
HELEN OF TROY
HOMUNCULUS, a spirit

The Story:
While three archangels were singing in praise of God's lofty works, Mephistopheles appeared and said that he thought conditions on earth to be bad. The Lord tacitly agreed that human beings had their weaknesses but pointed out that His servant Faust could not be swayed from the path of righteousness. Mephistopheles made a wager with the Lord that Faust could be tempted from his faithful service. The Lord was convinced that He could rely on the righteous integrity of Faust, but he knew that Mephistopheles could lead Faust downward if he were able to lay hold of Faust's soul. Mephistopheles considered Faust a likely victim because Faust was trying to obtain the unobtainable.

Faust was not satisfied with all the knowledge he had acquired. He realized the limits of human knowledge and saw his own insignificance in the great macrocosm. In this mood, he went for a walk with his servant, Wagner, among people who were not troubled by thoughts of a philosophical nature. Faust found this atmosphere refreshing, and he was able to feel free and to think clearly. Faust told Wagner of his two souls, one clinging to earthly things, the other striving toward suprasensual things that could never be attained as long as his soul resided in his body. Limited in his daily life and desiring to learn the meaning of existence, Faust was ready to accept anything that offered him a new kind of life.

Mephistopheles recognized that Faust was vulnerable to attack. In the form of a dog, Mephistopheles followed Faust when the scholar returned home. After studying the Bible, Faust concluded that human ability should be used to produce something useful. Witnessing Faust's struggle with his ideas, Mephistopheles stepped forth in his true identity, but Faust remained unmoved by the arguments of his tempter.

The next time Mephistopheles came, he found Faust much more receptive. Faust had decided that, although his struggles were divine, he had produced nothing to show for them. Faust was interested in life on this earth. At Mephistopheles' suggestion that he could enjoy a sensual existence, Faust declared that if ever he could steep himself in sloth and be at peace with himself, or if ever Mephistopheles could so rule him with flattery that he became self-satisfied, then that should be his end. Because Faust had renounced all things that made life worthwhile to most people, he further contracted with Mephistopheles that if ever he found experience so profound that he would wish it to endure, then he would cease to be. This was to be a wager, not the selling of a soul.

Mephistopheles failed to tempt Faust in two trials of debauchery. The next offering he presented was love for a woman. He brought Faust to the Witch's Kitchen, where his youth was restored. Then a pure maiden, Gretchen, was presented to him, but when he saw her in her innocent home, he vowed not to harm her. When, however, Mephistopheles wooed the girl with caskets of jewels that she thought came from Faust, Faust was tempted to return to Gretchen. She surrendered herself to him in fulfillment of her pure love.

Gretchen's brother convinced her that her behavior was shameful in the eyes of society. Troubled by her grief, Faust killed her brother, whereupon Gretchen at last felt the full burden of her sin. Mephistopheles showed Faust more scenes of debauchery, but Faust's spirit had been elevated by contact with Gretchen and he was able to overcome the devil's evil influence. Mephistopheles had hoped that Faust would desire the moment of his fulfillment of love to endure, but Faust knew that enduring human love could not satisfy his craving. He regretted Gretchen's misery and returned to her, but she had killed their child and would not let her lover save her from the death to which she had been condemned.

Mephistopheles brought Faust to the emperor, who asked Faust to show him the most beautiful man and woman who had ever existed—Paris and Helen of Troy. Faust produced the images of these mythological characters; at the sight of Helen, his desire to possess her was so strong that he fainted, and during his swoon Mephistopheles, who was unable to comprehend Faust's desire for the ideal beauty that Helen represented, brought him back to his own laboratory.

With the help of Wagner, Mephistopheles created a formless spirit of learning, Homunculus, who could see what was going on in Faust's mind. Homunculus, Mephistopheles, and Faust went to Greece, where Mephistopheles borrowed from the fantastic images of classical mythology one of their grotesque forms. With Mephistopheles' intervention, a living Helen was brought to Faust. It seemed to Mephistopheles that now, with the supreme joy of having attained Helen's beauty, Faust would ask for the moment to endure. Faust had realized, however, that the enjoyment of transient beauty was no more satisfying than his other experiences had been.

Faust returned to his native land, having gained a new understanding of himself. Achievement now became his goal, as he reaffirmed his earlier pledge that his power should be used to produce something useful. He acquired a large strip of swamp land and restored it to productivity.

Many years passed. Now old and blind, Faust realized he had created a vast territory of land occupied by people who would always be active in making something useful for themselves. Having participated in this achievement, Faust beheld himself standing among free and active people as one of them. At the moment when he realized what he had created, he cried out, wishing that fair moment to remain. Faust had realized that life could be worth living, but in that moment of perception he lost his wager to Mephistopheles. The devil claimed Faust's soul, but in reality he, too, had lost the wager. God was right. Although Faust had made mistakes in his life, he had always remained aware of goodness and truth.

Seeing his own defeat, Mephistopheles attempted to prevent the ascension of Faust's soul to God. Angels appeared to help Faust, however, and he was carried to a place in Heaven where all was active creation—exactly the kind of afterlife that Faust would have chosen.

Critical Evaluation:

Johann Wolfgang von Goethe's masterwork of dramatic poetry, *Faust*, summarizes his entire career, stretching from the passionate storm and stress of his youth through the classical phase of his middle years to his mature, philosophical style. Composition of the work occupied him from the time of his first works in the 1770's until his death in 1832, and each of its various sections reveals new interests and preoccupations, as well as different stylistic approaches. Yet the work possesses a unity that testifies to the continuing centrality of the Faust subject in Goethe's mind.

The first scenes composed, those of Faust in his study and the Gretchen scenes, reflect the twenty-three-year-old Goethe who was still preoccupied with university parodies based on his student experiences but at the same time increasingly interested in titanic projects. In his desire to pursue knowledge and surpass previous limitations, he was typical of other young writers of this period. In fact, *Faust* was originally one of a planned series of dramas about heroic figures who transgress society's rules—among them Julius Caesar, Prometheus, and Götz von Berlich-ingen.

Goethe stresses the tragedy of the scholar whose emotional life is not fulfilled and who seeks for limitless knowledge, only to find himself frustrated by mortal limitations. The scenes with Gretchen provide emotional release but leave Faust with a sense of guilt for the destruction of purity. The theme of the unwed mother was a popular one among young poets of this period, and represented a revolt against traditional bourgeois values, giving occasion for much social criticism. In the Gretchen scenes, Goethe, who as a student himself had romances with young village women, evokes great sympathy for Gretchen, who acts always out of sincere emotion and desires only the good. His theme of the corruption of all human questing, because of the inherent imperfections of human knowledge and will, receives here its first expression, though with no philosophical elaboration. Neither Faust nor Gretchen wills evil, yet evil comes by way of Mephistopheles. The devil, in every utterance the cynic opposed to Faust's idealistic hopes, exposes the coarse reality that in his view is the sole aspect of human life on earth.

Faust was first published in 1790 as a compilation of fragments that dated back to the 1770's. Between 1797 and 1806, with Friedrich Schiller's encouragement, Goethe returned to the work and created the Prologue in Heaven and the pact with Mephistopheles, both of which are crucial to the philosophical aspect of the work. Mephistopheles, no longer the absolute opponent of God, is included in the divine framework; he is a necessary force in creation, a gadfly. The action in the work now becomes a wager between God and Mephistopheles, which God must win. The old blood contract between Faust and Mephistopheles is converted into a wager: Mephistopheles must make Faust deny his very nature by giving up his quest for ever higher satisfactions, by giving him a moment of absolute fulfillment. Damnation, for Goethe, is the cessation of human striving toward the absolute, and this striving is good, no matter what mistakes human beings make in their limited understanding. He makes this clear in the prologue: God recognizes that human beings will err as long as they strive, but He states that only by seeking after the absolute, however confusedly, can they fulfill their nature. Mephi-stopheles sees only the confusion and futility of the results, as well as the coarseness of human life. He is blind to the visionary, poetic quality of Faust that animates his quest. This relation-ship, which is established in the first part, continues until the end of the play. In each episode, Faust begins with an idealistic vision of what he seeks, but he never attains it. Seen externally, Mephistopheles is always right—it is internally that Faust's quest has meaning.

In the original Faust story, Faust meets Helen of Troy, an episode that occupied Goethe in the period of his fascination with the classical world. The third act of part 2 is the union of Faust, the northern, modern, Romantic quester, with Helen, who represents classical harmony and ideal beauty. In this act, Goethe, after imitating the style of Greek tragedy, brings Faust and Helen together in an idyllic realm of fantasy filled with music. This music—Goethe actually wanted an operatic interlude—underlines the purely aesthetic nature of the experience. Helen cannot be the end of Faust's seeking; their relationship can exist only in the mythical Arcadia, where reality, symbolized perhaps by Helen's husband, Menelaus, cannot intrude. The act was subtitled "Classic-Romantic Phantasmagoria," and Goethe followed it immediately with a scene in which Faust sees visions of both Helen and Gretchen and is drawn toward the latter in spite of Helen's ideal perfection. Gretchen, however tragic, is real.

The final sections of *Faust* were composed between 1825 and 1831. In them, Faust's appearances at court are developed and the final scenes of Faust's redemption return to the framework established in the prologue. Faust's last days are still unsatisfied and his quest is as violent as ever; his merchant ships turn to piracy, and a gentle old couple are killed to make room for his palace. His final vision, however, is that of all humanity, which strives to turn chaos to order and seeks a dimly imagined goal represented in the final scene by an endless stairway. Here, on the path toward the divine, Faust continues to strive. His life is redeemed by a divine love represented by Gretchen, who in spite of her crimes is also there, a penitent who prays for Faust. On earth all is transitory and insufficient. Only from the point of view of the divine does all the confused striving attain a meaning that was, in fact, implicit in the stanzas that the three archangels sang at the opening of the play, twelve thousand lines earlier.

"Critical Evaluation" by Steven C. Schaber

Bibliography:

Atkins, Stuart. *Goethe's "Faust": A Literary Analysis*. Cambridge, Mass.: Harvard University Press, 1958. Evaluates *Faust* first and foremost as a drama, showing each section's dramatic as well as symbolic function, and seeks to demonstrate the organic unity of the work. Highly recommended.

Fairley, Barker. *Goethe's "Faust": Six Essays*. Oxford, England: Clarendon Press, 1953. A knowledgeable and well-written set of studies by a preeminent Goethe scholar. Recommended.

Gillies, Alexander. *Goethe's "Faust": An Interpretation*. Oxford, England: Basil Blackwell, 1957. An important and detailed analysis, with lucid, helpful comments. Recommended for the more advanced student.

Goethe, Johann Wolfgang von. *Faust: A Tragedy*. Translated by Walter Arndt and edited by Cyrus Hamlin. New York: W. W. Norton, 1976. Contains introductory essays by both the translator and editor, as well as substantial interpretive notes. Also offers sections on primary sources for *Faust*, Goethe's outlines and correspondence, reactions by contemporaries, twelve essays by modern critics covering different aspects of the work, and a select bibliography. Useful for all levels.

Gray, Ronald. *Goethe: A Critical Introduction*. London: Cambridge University Press, 1967. A discussion of Goethe's life and works, highly useful as an introduction to *Faust*. Two long chapters (7 and 8) discuss *Faust* in detail. Gray also compares the value of *Faust* as literature to Goethe's lesser works. Includes a table of biographical dates, an index, and a select bibliography.

FELIX HOLT, THE RADICAL

Type of work: Novel
Author: George Eliot (Mary Ann Evans, 1819-1880)
Type of plot: Social realism
Time of plot: 1831-1833
Locale: Rural Midland England
First published: 1866

Principal characters:

>FELIX HOLT, the radical, an educated artisan
>HAROLD TRANSOME, the heir to Transome Court and a radical candidate
> for Parliament
>MRS. TRANSOME, his mother
>ESTHER LYON, a refined young woman
>RUFUS LYON, her father and a dissenting minister
>MATTHEW JERMYN, a lawyer
>MR. JOHNSON, another lawyer hired by Jermyn
>PHILIP DEBARRY, a Tory candidate for Parliament
>SIR MAXIMUS DEBARRY, his father and the owner of Treby Manor
>THE REVEREND AUGUSTUS DEBARRY, his brother
>THE REVEREND JOHN LINGON, Mrs. Transome's brother
>HENRY SCADDON (alias MAURICE CHRISTIAN BYCLIFFE), a servant in the
> Debarry household

The Story:

Mrs. Transome, who had long held Transome Court together in spite of financial and legal difficulties and an incompetent husband, eagerly awaited the return of Harold, her younger son. Harold, who had been building up a fortune in Smyrna for the preceding fifteen years, had been called home to take his place as heir to Transome Court after the death of his weak older brother, Durfey. Harold, whose wife was dead, also brought with him a young son.

Mrs. Transome was soon disappointed by Harold. Although he was generous with money and renovated the shabby mansion, he was not willing to respect Mrs. Transome's wishes for a genteel country life, particularly when he announced that he intended to run for Parliament as a Radical candidate. To his mother, he seemed to show a surprising knowledge and shrewdness about contemporary English life. In his campaign, he received the support of his family's lawyer, Matthew Jermyn, and his uncle, the Reverend John Lingon. Neither had thought of deserting the Tory colors before his arrival.

More understandably committed to the Radical cause was Rufus Lyon, the local dissenting minister. One day he received a visit from Mrs. Holt, one of his parishioners, who complained that her son had deliberately stopped the business in patent medicines that she and her late husband had painstakingly established. Her son, Felix, claimed that the business was fraudulent; Mrs. Holt, on the other hand, was convinced that God would not have allowed a fraudulent business to prosper. The minister later sent for young Felix, whom he found highly intelligent, energetic, honest, and independent. Although well educated, Felix was working as a watchmaker in order to feel close to the people. The two men soon became close friends. At the Lyons' home, Felix also met Rufus' daughter Esther, a slight, refined girl educated abroad, who was now teaching the daughters of the rich and reading Byron's poems. The energetic and socially conscious Felix railed at Esther's refinement and at her reading of romantic fantasies, but as time passed, a strange attraction between the two began to grow. Esther, although she did not know it at the time, was not the daughter of Rufus Lyon. Her mother had been a Frenchwoman, alone and destitute, whom Rufus had found wandering the English streets. Her soldier husband had sent for her, but he had died before she could find him. With her child, she was befriended by Rufus Lyon, who gave up a successful post in order to continue to be with her and who later married her.

Harold, beginning his election campaign, left the organizing to his lawyer, Matthew Jermyn. Jermyn hired another lawyer, Mr. Johnson, to go to a workers' pub and stir the men into active support of the Radical candidate. Felix Holt was in the pub at the time. Although a Radical, he objected strongly to the rabble-rousing technique used by Johnson and carried his protest directly to Harold. Although sympathetic to Felix's point of view, Harold felt somewhat indebted to Jermyn, who had helped his mother retain her property through difficult years and an earlier lawsuit. While walking home through the woods, Felix found a purse belonging to Christian, one of the Debarry servants; as a practical joke, the purse had been stolen from his pocket and tossed away while Christian was asleep in the woods. Along with the purse were some papers belonging to Philip Debarry, the Conservative candidate for Parliament.

When Felix took the papers to Rufus Lyon, his friend was amazed to discover evidence that Christian was the first husband of Rufus' French wife and the father of Esther. Through Jermyn, however, Rufus learned that Christian was really a scoundrel named Henry Scaddon who, in order to save himself, had exchanged identities with Maurice Christian Bycliffe, Esther's real father, just before Bycliffe's death. Jermyn also knew that the Bycliffe line established Esther as the real heiress of Transome Court, should an old and senile Transome, who had moved to Treby, die. Although Jermyn kept his information for possible use against the Transome family, Rufus Lyon told his daughter of her origins. Meanwhile, Harold Transome continued campaigning, and the friendship between Esther and Felix grew.

As Felix had feared, the workers rioted on the day of the election. Felix, hoping to quell the riot, led it for a time in a futile effort to lead the workers away from the town. Unsuccessful in his purpose, he was charged with killing a constable. The old Transome was also trampled in the riot. Esther was legally the heiress of Transome Court. Harold Transome, who had lost the election, now turned his attention to Transome Court. Discovering that Jermyn and Johnson, Jermyn's henchman, had been cheating the estate for years, he decided to get rid of Jermyn at once and sue him. Jermyn tried to avoid the suit by telling Harold that the estate really belonged to Esther but that Jermyn would remain silent if Harold dropped proceedings against him. Harold refused the bribe. Later, he and his mother invited Esther to live with them at Transome Court. Both were charmed with Esther, and Harold courted her, partly to regain the estate through marriage.

Meanwhile, Felix's case was announced for trial. Rufus Lyon, Harold, and Esther testified to Felix's attempts to quell the riot, but he had killed a man, although inadvertently, and so he was sentenced to an imprisonment of four years. Esther's plea was so powerful that it moved even the arch-Tory, Sir Maximus Debarry, who helped petition Parliament to grant Felix a pardon. Felix was soon released. In the meantime, Mrs. Transome had been unhappy that Harold had rejected Jermyn thoroughly and was attempting to sue him. Harold, claiming that Jermyn was a thief, intended to carry out the suit. In a final burst of fury, Jermyn told Harold the truth: He was Harold's father and, during his long affair with Mrs. Transome, had saved the estate during several difficult times. Harold was crushed, and only Esther was able to reconcile him to his unhappy mother. Feeling his illegitimacy keenly, Harold told Esther that he could not, as he had intended, ask for her hand. This declaration saved Esther much embarrassment, for she had already acknowledged her love for Felix. To solve problems for all concerned, Esther signed over her rights to Transome Court to Harold, returned to her father's house, and soon married Felix.

Critical Evaluation:

Written amid the hopes and fears of political upheaval before the second major Reform Bill passed in 1867, George Eliot's novel representing conditions accompanying the Reform Bill of 1832 suggests that authentic reform must come by much more than parliamentary legislation. Real reform requires, the novel implies, the slow cultivation of informed minds, class-bridging sympathies, courage, and clear-sighted rejection of personal and class-based delusions. Faithful to her artistic creed of realism—the true-to-life portrayal of human beings, including believably slow development of individuals and the relationships among them—Eliot represents evils that unquestionably urge reform, but she implies that some of these evils derive from human frailties. It is therefore a moral radicalism that would serve the nation best, one that would convert self-serving egotism to altruistic efforts and materialistic obsession to spontaneously creative living.

In a backward-looking introduction, Eliot directs her readers to view social change as a slow process. She returns, after the exotic settings of *Romola* (1862-1863) to the Midland England of her childhood and to the slower-paced life of 1831. Then, as in 1866, the elderly and established feared the rapidity of technological progress and resulting social changes, while progressives attacked blatant social evils. Eliot refers to the social evils of the 1830's as "departed," but the reference is ironic because many of the evils remained in 1866. She argues implicitly for continued reform. She reassures conservative readers of the 1860's that the nation had survived reforming changes and would survive more reform. She also addresses the disappointments of progressives who had hoped too much from the earlier bill. Legislation alone could not instantaneously replace feudalism with democratic capitalism, as if the nation could be "shot, like a bullet" from Winchester to Newcastle, an image that recalls England's long development from its ninth century political center, Winchester, still sleepily agrarian after ten centuries, to the new industrial railway center, Newcastle. Innovation was both inevitable and desirable, however, and Eliot's jabs at those who feared it in 1831 suggest that the author was attempting to quell similar fears in 1866.

Eliot's frequent irony and realistic characterization—her people are neither always heroic nor completely villainous—have obscured for some readers her sympathizing with the reform movement. She saw, however, that expanding the electorate to include hundreds of thousands among the uneducated might lead only to replacing the abuses of a self-interested propertied class with other abuses caused by the short-sighted gullibility and impassioned disorder of the lower classes that she represents in the novel. It is Esther Lyon's personal revolution, beginning with her fantasizing about luxurious vanities, continuing with her awakening to the emptiness of her silken-cushioned despair at Transome Court, and ending with her assertion of freedom to continue growing, that embodies Eliot's vision of authentic reform. Felix too grows with new awareness of his limits after he fails to control the riotous mob—and fails to control himself—and inadvertently causes a death. Felix and Esther prepare to invest their energies in educating others toward the responsibilities of an extended franchise. Ample evidence for this need appears in the rioting miners, in Mrs. Holt's application of divine will to her personal economic plight, and in such corrupt practices as vote-buying, identity-exchanging, and embezzling. All suggest the need for moral, not merely political, reform among all classes.

Eliot was also reforming the fantasy-based fiction popular at the time. She reverses the stereotypical plot of a foundling later identified as gentry and rewarded with wealth and privilege. Instead, Esther, like Eppie Marner, returns to the simpler life of her adoptive father, rejecting the entrapment of Transome Court and affirming the values of useful work and personal freedom. She insists on the freedom to define herself and not be forced into roles governed by outworn feudal property laws or into a subservient relationship with a controlling husband who sees a woman as a means of acquiring and managing property. Eliot also reverses character stereotypes in fiction and political discourse. Mrs. Transome, the privileged, enviable lady, is bereft of power, influence, love, and respect. Her tragedy, cast in the imagery of Dante's underworld of retribution, is the outcome of her having chosen everything Esther rejects. Mrs. Transome's marriage for station and property, touted in popular fiction and practiced in the social world, is revealed as a hellish prison. Mrs. Transome is an object lesson to young woman readers as well as to Esther. Harold Transome—good-looking, competent manager of property and people, "radical" in politics but paternalistic, manipulative, and imperious—is the outward stereotype of a desirable husband. His former wife, however, was a Greek slave that he had bought. Her situation is the parallel of the sexual slavery of English wives. His unthinking, blatant egotism leaves no breathing room for his mother or for Esther. His ego collapses when he discovers his illegitimate birth, suggesting that social status without character is an insubstantial prop.

Eliot's portrayal of Mrs. Transome's powerless despair is a negative example on behalf of the nineteenth century feminist argument that women should be empowered politically and economically. That Mrs. Transome's malaise derives largely from dashed hopes based on her role as a mother is Eliot's pointed reply to a world that prescribed motherhood as the panacea for all female discontents. More broadly, the intricate plot, based on laws of inheritance, is Eliot's argument that generations-old property arrangements prevent national revitalization, just as ties to property preclude vital, spontaneous interpersonal bonds such as those between Esther and Felix. The open, generous nature of Rufus Lyon, who renounces a successful career to save Esther's mother and who can part unselfishly with his much-loved daughter when a better life appears for her, is Eliot's moral ideal, expressed also in Felix's wish to "make life less bitter for a few."

"Critical Evaluation" by Carolyn F. Dickinson

Bibliography:
Carroll, David R. "*Felix Holt:* Society as Protagonist." In *George Eliot: A Collection of Critical Essays*, edited by George R. Creeger. Englewood Cliffs, N.J.: Prentice-Hall, 1970. Develops variations on the theme of rebellion among the characters. Characters move from a condition of illusion to a clearer understanding of reality. Distinguishes vision from illusion and justifies the novel's plot complexity as necessary to its theme.
Coveney, Peter. Introduction to *Felix Holt, the Radical*, by George Eliot. New York: Penguin Books, 1972. Offers a full historical background for the political context of the novel, including legal complexities, parliamentary activities, and many topical allusions.
Horsman, Alan. "George Eliot." In *The Victorian Novel*. Oxford, England: Clarendon Press, 1990. Gives voluminous details that enlighten Eliot's political views and artistic craft; places *Felix Holt, the Radical* in context with Eliot's other works. Bibliography.

Levine, George. "Determinism and Responsibility in the Works of George Eliot." *PMLA* 77 (June, 1962): 268-279. Defines Eliot's sense of the destiny to which human life is subject, comparing it to ideas of John Stuart Mill and distinguishing it from necessitarianism.

Uglow, Jennifer. *George Eliot.* New York: Pantheon Books, 1987. Chapter 11 analyzes the dialectics, figurative language, mythic allusions, connotative imagery, and ironic narrative voice in the novel. Attends particularly to gender definitions and interaction. Bibliography.

THE FELLOWSHIP OF THE RING

Type of work: Novel
Author: J. R. R. Tolkien (1892-1973)
Type of plot: Epic
Time of plot: The Third Age in a remote legendary past
Locale: Middle Earth between the Northern Waste and Sutherland
First published: 1954

Principal characters:

BILBO BAGGINS, the finder of the One Ring and a famous hobbit of the Shire

FRODO BAGGINS, his young kinsman and heir and the chosen Ringbearer

MERIADOC BRANDYBUCK (MERRY), Frodo's cousin from Buckland

PEREGRIN TOOK (PIPPIN), another of Frodo's cousins

SAMWISE GAMGEE (SAM), Frodo's loyal servant and also a hobbit

GANDALF THE GREY (MITHRANDIR), a venerable wizard

ARAGORN (STRIDER), a ranger and the descendant of kings

BOROMIR, the son of Denethor of Gondor and a heroic warrior

GIMLI, the son of Glóin and a warlike dwarf

LEGOLAS, a wood elf and son of King Thranduil of Mirkwood

ELROND HALFELVEN, the ruler of Rivendell

GALADRIEL, the Elf Queen of Lothlorien

SAURON, the Dark Lord, maker of the One Ring, and the supreme agent of evil in the Middle Earth

The Story:

Bilbo Baggins, the most adventurous hobbit of the Shire, planned to celebrate his hundred-and-eleventh birthday. His old friend Gandalf the Grey, a wizard with special control over fire, tried to restrain him from using his magic ring to vanish at the end of the party. Gandalf was disturbed, for he suspected the ring of being the One Ring forged by Sauron, the Dark Lord, in the volcanic fires of Mount Doom. This ring gave long life but corrupted its user. Even Bilbo, who had gained it without losing pity, had begun to show signs of its evil influence. On his departure, however, after his spectacular vanishing, he left his property, reluctantly including the ring, to his nephew Frodo. Gandalf warned Frodo of its dangers and advised that he take it from the Shire.

Frodo left the Shire, accompanied by his loyal servant Sam Gamgee and two of his cousins, Merry and Pippin. Pursued by fearful Black Riders, they narrowly escaped destruction in the Old Forest, but they were rescued by jovial, earthy Tom Bombadil, who proved to be immune to the ring's power. He sent them on their way refreshed.

At Bree, they met a mysterious ranger called Strider and found a letter from Gandalf urging them to go to Rivendell with Strider, whose real name was Aragorn. On their fourth night out of Bree, they were attacked by Black Riders. In terror, Frodo put on the ring and became invisible to his friends but visible and vulnerable to the Riders, Sauron's Ringwraiths, whose leader stabbed Frodo with a weapon that broke off in the wound and melted. Aragorn drove them off with torches, and the company hastened toward Rivendell. Glorifindel, an elf, met them and put Frodo on his horse. At the Ford near Rivendell, the Black Riders tried to intercept him but were thwarted by a flood.

Frodo recovered consciousness to find Gandalf with him and to learn that Elrond of Rivendell had been treating his fearful wound for days. In Rivendell, Frodo found Bilbo and met Elrond, his daughter Arwen Evenstar, and others, including Glóin, an elderly dwarf who had formerly accompanied Bilbo. Elrond called a council to discuss the ring. At the council were Elrond's eleven subjects, as well as a wood elf named Legolas, Glóin and his son Gimli, Gandalf, the five hobbits, Aragorn, and a noble gray-eyed warrior named Boromir of Gondor. Elrond recounted the history of the Rings of Power, which had been made by elvensmiths in the Second Age, and of Sauron's secret forging of a ring to rule and bind all the rest. In that age, Sauron had been overthrown by an alliance of human beings and elves, and Isildur had cut off the Dark Lord's finger and taken the ring, but it had slipped from his finger and betrayed him to the orcs. Years later, it had been found in the river by Deagol, a hobbit whose kinsman Smeagol had murdered him for it and fled underground, becoming the repulsive Gollum. Bilbo had found it underground. Pitying the murderous Gollum, he had not killed him but had merely used the ring to escape. Sauron, though defeated, had not been destroyed. He had gathered an evil host in Mordor and was seeking the ring to make himself ruler of the world. Gandalf told of the treachery of Saruman the White, leader of the wizards, who had imprisoned him. Gandalf had escaped with the help of Gwaihir, the king of the Eagles.

The council decided to send the ring to Mordor to unmake it in the fires of Mount Doom, the only heat that could destroy it. Frodo reluctantly volunteered to remain the Ringbearer. Eight others were chosen to complete the Fellowship of the Ring: Gandalf, Aragorn, Boromir, Gimli, Legolas, Sam, Merry, and Pippin. Aragorn's broken sword, Anduril, was reforged by the elves. Bilbo gave Frodo his elven sword Sting and a coat of mail made of mithril, a precious light metal harder than steel. Frodo wore it under his weather-stained clothes.

The travelers passed through cold barren country and tried to cross over the Misty Mountains, but a blizzard drove them back, and they were attacked by wolves. Gandalf drove away the wolves with magic fire and led the company into the Caverns of Moria, the ancient dwarf kingdom. He told them of Durin, the dwarf king, and his people who delved so deeply for Mithril that they roused a terrible being that destroyed them. Bilbo's old companion Balin had led a company of dwarfs from the Lonely Mountains to retake Moria. The travelers found Balin's tomb and signs of a terrible battle, as well as a bloodstained, tattered book from which Gandalf was able to reconstruct the fortunes of Balin's people to the time when their last battle had begun.

A drum far below signaled an attack by orcs and trolls. The fellowship repelled the first attack, and Frodo was struck down by a spear thrust, but his mithril coat saved him. When they were forced to retreat, Gandalf remained to hold a stone door. Something opposed his will fiercely, and the door shattered. They hastened to a narrow stone bridge across an abyss. A monstrous fire demon appeared. Gandalf opposed him and destroyed the bridge but was dragged into the cleft with the monster. Heavy-hearted, the others followed Aragorn to Lothlorien, home of high elves.

Lothlorien was a haven more wonderful than Rivendell. The ageless beauty of Queen Galadriel charmed them all, especially Gimli, in spite of the ancient enmity between elves and dwarfs. Boromir alone was uneasy in her presence. On their departure, she gave them precious gifts, and the elves supplied them with boats and provisions to continue their journey by water down the Anduin River. They soon learned they were being followed by Gollum, once owner of the ring and now apparently Sauron's spy. They were again attacked by orcs, led by a Ringwraith on a flying mount like a pterodactyl. Legolas gained respite for them by killing the mount with an arrow. After this escape, the evil of the ring corrupted Boromir, who attempted to take it from Frodo. To escape him, Frodo put on the ring and vanished. Boromir returned to the company in a penitent mood. They scattered to look for Frodo.

Alone and invisible, Frodo tried to decide on the right course of action. Suddenly he was aware of an evil eye searching for him, and he was paralyzed with terror; then an inner voice commanded him to take off the ring. He regained control of himself and removed it. A groping shadow seemed to pass over the mountain and to fade away. Frodo decided to take an elven boat and continue his perilous journey alone, but Sam anticipated his decision, discovered him, and begged to be allowed to go along. Frodo accepted Sam's loyal company, and they set out together for Mordor. The Fellowship of the Ring had been broken.

Critical Evaluation:

Samuel Johnson is credited with saying that "A book should teach us to enjoy life or to endure it." J. R. R. Tolkien's trilogy *The Lord of the Rings* teaches both. It also fits the dictum of another writer, Robert Louis Stevenson, who said, "And this is the particular triumph of the artist—not to be true merely, but to be lovable; not simply to convince, but to enchant." Tolkien has been compared with Lodovico Ariosto and with Edmund Spenser. Indeed, he belongs to the tradition of writers of epic and romance going back to the days of Homer. His work is deeply rooted in the great literature of the past and seems likely itself to be a hardy survivor resistant to time. In *The Fellowship of the Ring*, the first volume of *The Lord of the Rings*, Celeborn the Elf King (no doubt speaking for his author) warns against despising the lore that has survived from distant years, for old wives' tales may be the repositories of needful wisdom.

Although *The Lord of the Rings* is a trilogy, each volume of which bears a different title, it is really a single, continuous tale. The author is in complete control of his copious material. He created a consistent world with a sharply realized geography that includes maps; he worked out a many-centuried time scheme and summarized the chronology in an appendix to the third volume, *The Return of the King* (1955). With fertile inventiveness, Tolkien launched an amazing number of well-drawn, believable characters, places, and events. If there are any loose ends in the three volumes, they are so minor as to be negligible. The book has been pronounced an allegory; with equal positiveness it has been pronounced not an allegory. At any rate, it is a gigantic myth of the struggle between good and evil.

The author first presented his invented creatures, the hobbits or halflings, in an early book, *The Hobbit*, to which *The Lord of the Rings* is a sequel, but a sequel with significant differences. Hobbits are small, furry-footed humanoids with a delight in simple pleasures and a dislike of the uncomfortable responsibilities of heroism. They share the world with human beings, wizards, elves, dwarfs, trolls, orcs, and other creatures. Although many of these creatures are not the usual figures of the contemporary novel, the thoughtful reader can find applications to inhabitants and events of their world, which has its share of traitors, malice-driven demidevils, and time-servers, yet is not completely destitute of heroes and individuals of goodwill. Of the three volumes, *The Fellowship of the Ring* has the widest variation in tone: After beginning with comedy and domestic comfort, it moves into high adventure, peril, and sorrow. Occasional verses appear in the pages, but Tolkien's poetry resides in both his prose and his verse.

The Fellowship of the Ring introduces two tales that run side by side throughout the trilogy. One tale is that of the destruction of Sauron and the return of King Elessar to the throne of his fathers; the other is the story of the journey of the hobbits from jolly complacency to unexpected heights of self-knowledge and self-sacrifice. The former gives the work its quality of ancient romance, for the characters are larger than life and speak to one another in elevated language; natural descriptions and expressions of emotion tend to be more formal and ceremonious than realistic. The second tale contains elements of realism; the most realistic, homey, and familiar characters are from Tolkien's invented race, the hobbits.

The major figure in Tolkien's high saga is Aragorn, later King Elessar. He is certainly the most heroic of the characters in the classical sense, but the very elevation of his character has led some critics to see him as inhuman, lifeless, or too good to be true. Actually, however, he is a character of considerable subtlety and complexity; he earns his credentials as a hero honestly. Initially, in his disguise as Strider, Aragorn must use guile and indirection to win the confidence of the hobbits. They understand neither the implications of their situation nor their own personal danger. Aragorn, on the other hand, realizes that he is as frightening to them as any of Sauron's agents. Therefore, he uses their apprehensions toward him to stimulate their sense of danger, after which he ingratiates himself by his wit and finally by Gandalf's letter of identification. When asked why he did not identify himself earlier, he replies that he wants to be accepted for himself. Once the quest begins, Aragorn proves his mettle and worthiness for kingship, not primarily by brute strength or heroic posturing but by his adroit handling of the others and his subtle strategies. A special poignancy and humanity are further given to him by his prolonged and tender love affair with Lady Arwen. Readers may never feel close to Aragorn, but they can understand and feel for him as a human being and admire him as a heroic figure.

Although Aragorn leads the troops to victory in battle, the primary task of the epic falls not to the most heroic of the men but to the mildest of the hobbits, Frodo Baggins. The name of this little race suggests a hob, hobnobbing, a dobbin; it calls up visions of fireside comforts, companionship, patient steadfastness, and good sense. Descriptions of hobbits and hobbit life in the prologue outline the prototype: a steady, plain little person, none too clever.

This impression, however, is belied in the story by the characters of Samwise and Frodo; in developing the character of Sam, Tolkien begins with a collection of those homely virtues that most nations arrogate to their own peasant class and then adds, without loss of credibility, a quirky intelligence that outstrips shrewdness and a fancy for elfish lore. In Frodo, he marries the homely world of the Shire with the high deeds of the Dunedain. In Frodo are combined the best things of both worlds: He is the wisest and most noble of the hobbits and the bravest of the heroes because he is the smallest and most afraid.

It is primarily because of Frodo's unpretentiousness that he is "chosen" for the crucial task of casting the ring into the fire of Mordor. The "large" heroes of the book, Aragorn and Gandalf, refuse the task, not from fear of external dangers but from the knowledge that they would not be able to resist the ring's effect on them—they are too worldly and versed in the ways of power to be immune to the awful temptation to use it. Only Frodo is sufficiently small and humble to withstand its corrupting influence right up to the edge of the fire—where even he weakens and the ring is finally destroyed by powers beyond his control.

Bibliography:

Giddings, Robert, ed. *J. R. R. Tolkien: This Far Land*. London: Vision Press Limited, 1983. A collection of ten essays that discuss Tolkien's world and examine subjects ranging from narrative form and the use of humor to the construction of female sexuality.

Kocher, Paul H. *Master of Middle-Earth*. Boston: Houghton Mifflin, 1972. A critical examination of Tolkien's major fictional works. Focuses on the creation and development of Middle Earth and provides perspective on the different qualities of the races inhabiting the realm. Offers critical insight on Tolkien's notions of choice within a Christian framework.

Penn, Anne C. *One Ring to Bind Them All: Tolkien's Mythology*. Tuscaloosa: University of Alabama Press, 1979. A critical examination of Tolkien's process of mythmaking, moving beyond traditional literary analysis to employ perspectives derived from linguistics, folklore, psychology, and folklore studies.

Tolkien, J. R. R. *The History of Middle-Earth*. Edited by Christopher Tolkien. 12 vols. Boston: Houghton Mifflin, 1988. Edited and fully annotated by J. R. R. Tolkien's son, this series documents the creation of Middle Earth and its mythology in chronological fashion. Volume six, *The Return of the Shadow*, contains the initial drafts of *The Fellowship of the Ring* and demonstrates the painstaking creation of the story in fascinating detail.

Tyler, J. E. A. *The New Tolkien Companion*. New York: St. Martin's Press, 1979. A one-volume encyclopedia of Middle Earth, alphabetically identifying and explaining the characters, peoples, places, languages, religion, and histories that make up Tolkien's world.

FENCES

Type of work: Drama
Author: August Wilson (1945-   )
Type of plot: Domestic realism
Time of plot: 1957-1965
Locale: An American industrial city
First performed: 1985; first published, 1985

> *Principal characters:*
> TROY MAXSON, a fifty-three-year-old garbage collector
> JIM BONO, his friend of thirty years
> ROSE, Troy's wife of eighteen years
> LYONS, Troy's thirty-four-year-old married son
> GABRIEL, Troy's younger brother
> CORY, the teenage son of Troy and Rose
> RAYNELL, the newborn daughter of Troy and Alberta

The Story:

Longtime friends Troy Maxson and Jim Bono were indulging in their typical Friday night drinking ritual on the front porch of the Maxson house. Bono advised Troy not to keep company with Alberta. When Rose, Troy's wife, joined them, Troy showered her with affection. Lyons, Troy's son, appeared, asking to borrow ten dollars. Troy loaned him the money but gave him a hard time for not having a job.

The next morning, Rose and Troy were visited by Gabriel, Troy's younger brother, who had been left mentally deficient by a World War II injury and had a metal plate inserted in his skull. After he left, Rose expressed concern that her brother-in-law might not be eating properly at his new boardinghouse, and she and Troy discussed the possibility of having Gabriel hospitalized again. Troy and Cory were working on assembling the fence that Rose had asked them to put up around the yard when Cory informed Troy that a college football recruiter would be calling on them. Troy's vocal opposition led to an argument between father and son. Troy asserted that he was obligated to feed and clothe Cory because Cory was his flesh and blood, but that he did not feel obligated to like him.

Two weeks later, Cory left the house carrying his football equipment, and Troy and Bono celebrated Troy's promotion to garbage truck driver. When Lyons returned the ten dollars he had borrowed, he reminded Troy that Cory was nearly grown up. Troy, however, was upset that Cory had pretended to be keeping his job at the A&P when he was really sneaking off to football practice without telling his father. When Cory got home, Troy's confrontation with him revealed that Troy had talked to the football coach and had forbidden Cory to play. Troy confided to Lyons that he had been abused by his own father, abuse that had caused him to leave home for good when he was fourteen. He reminisced, too, about meeting Rose, meeting Bono, and learning to play baseball.

The next morning, Rose informed Cory that the police had picked up Gabriel for disturbing the peace. When Troy returned from bailing Gabriel out of jail, he and Bono began to work on the fence. The fence was important to Rose, who saw it as a symbol of keeping her family consolidated and secure within the warm circle of the household. As Bono put it to Troy, "Rose wants to hold on to you all. She loves you." Bono urged Troy not to do wrong by Rose and to get his life in order so that Rose would not have to find out about Troy's love affair with another woman. Troy reminded Bono to do right by his own wife and to buy her the refrigerator for which she had been asking. Bono agreed to buy the refrigerator after Troy finished the fence for Rose.

When Bono left, Troy had an important conversation with Rose, revealing that another woman was pregnant with his child. During their conversation, Gabriel appeared briefly and then exited into the house, interrupting a distressing scene with equanimity and even humor. Rose seemed more baffled than wounded: She simply could not understand why Troy would be unfaithful at this point in their lives—earlier, perhaps, but not after eighteen years. Troy's defense was that he thought he could be a new man with Alberta, who took him away from the pressures and problems of his life. She could make him laugh in a way "that reaches all the way down to the bottom of my shoes," and he did not want to give that up. To Troy's revelation that he felt trapped, as if he had been standing in the same place for eighteen years, Rose retorted that she had been right there standing beside him, willingly giving up whatever hopes and dreams that she could have nurtured to provide a home for him. Her discovery that he was not the finest man in the world only made her hold on to him in love more tightly. At this point, Troy grabbed Rose's arm too tightly, and Cory came to her defense. Troy threateningly declared that Cory now had two strikes against him, and he had better not "strike out."

Six months later, Alberta was in the hospital about to give birth when Rose informed Troy, who could not read, that a paper he had signed in front of a judge had committed Gabriel to an institution and had earmarked half of his money to help pay for the care. A phone call from the hospital interrupted them with the news that Alberta had died giving birth to a healthy baby girl.

Three days later, Troy brought his baby home from the hospital, begging Rose for help. Rose, in a reasonable way, agreed that the child was innocent and should not be punished for the sins of her father, but her assistance carried a consequence: "Okay, Troy . . . I'll take care of your baby for you . . . this child got a mother. But you a womanless man."

When Bono visited Troy two months later, he had bought his wife the refrigerator she wanted, and Troy had ironically completed Rose's fence. Cory and Troy had a final, bitter confrontation in which Troy kicked him out of the house.

Seven years later, Cory, who had become a Marine corporal, returned home for Troy's funeral. Lyons had been jailed for cashing other people's checks, and Troy's daughter Raynell had become the light of Rose's life.

Critical Evaluation:

Fences is one of a series of plays in which August Wilson ambitiously envisioned tapping a well of history more than three hundred years deep, as he sought to compose a cycle of ten plays. He set each one in a different decade of the twentieth century, with each illuminating some unique aspect of the black experience in America. The chronicle is not chronologically composed but begins at a Pittsburgh boardinghouse in 1911 with *Joe Turner's Come and Gone* (1986). It continues in a 1927 Chicago recording session comprising *Ma Rainey's Black Bottom* (1984). Then there is a 1936 dispute over a family heirloom in *The Piano Lesson* (1990). *Seven Guitars* (1995), set among Pittsburgh musicians in the 1940's, is a murder mystery of sorts. *Fences* spans 1957 to 1965. *Two Trains Running* (1992) is set in 1969 and deals with regulars itching for a change at a restaurant scheduled to be torn down as part of urban renewal.

Several important themes and elements stand out as major forces in Wilson's plays. One of these is self-identity—blacks striving for self-definition and focus at a time when they are being exploited by whites. One expression of this theme is manifested by Wilson's use of music, particularly the blues. Wilson emphasizes the value of the blues to black Americans and the inability of whites to fully understand the importance of the blues. The blues, in fact, become a metaphor for differences between blacks and whites. Second, the polarities of loving and dying are offered as elementary powers governing the lives of his characters. Troy Maxson has a rather secular philosophy that allows him, on one hand, to be grateful that he is married to a wonderful woman like Rose but, on the other hand, to satisfy his passions with Alberta because she makes him feel good. Troy finds meaning in his life, to an important extent, through sex. He grapples with death by placing it comfortably within the context of familiar baseball metaphor, thus making it less ominous.

The title *Fences* identifies the major symbol. Rose wants to fence her family members inside the warmth of her love. There are also fences metaphorically between the races. Troy is a baseball player who played in minority black leagues but was barred from all-white major leagues because of his race. At one point in the play, Troy says that he will fence in his yard so that Mr. Death cannot sneak up on him again.

Relationships between fathers and sons are a major motif in Wilson's work. Lyons, Troy's son by a previous marriage, criticizes Troy for not being around when he was growing up. A searingly painful reminiscence describes the abuse that Troy experienced at the hands of his own father, which may explain why Troy is so harsh and demanding with teenager Cory, his son by Rose.

In less than a decade, August Wilson became one of the most significant playwrights in the history of American theater and one of the most important contemporary African American writers. *Fences*, Wilson's second major play, and *The Piano Lesson* (1990), his fourth major play, each won a Pulitzer Prize for drama. Wilson had five Broadway hits, including *Fences*, within eight years, also earning four New York Drama Critics Circle Awards, two Drama Desk Awards, an Outer Critics Circle Award, five Tony nominations, and one Tony (for *Fences*). His plays were called "powerful," "thrilling," and "explosive" by critics. It is particularly remarkable that Wilson has been able to explore and communicate the black experience in America in a way that seems unique and telling of African Americans and at the same time projects a universality to which white theater audiences are also drawn, thus ensuring the commercial success of his plays.

Jill B. Gidmark

Bibliography:
Awkward, Michael. "'The Crookeds with the Straights': *Fences*, Race, and the Politics of Adaptation." In *May All Your Fences Have Gates*, edited by Alan Nadel. Iowa City: University of Iowa Press, 1994. Discusses what happens when a play such as *Fences* becomes adapted into film. Includes Wilson's suggestions concerning directorial qualifications and claim of ownership over language production and representation of blackness.
Gordon, Joanne. "Wilson and Fugard: Politics and Art." In *August Wilson: A Casebook*, edited by Marilyn Elkins. New York: Garland, 1994. Seeks to interpret *Fences* by emphasizing its universal qualities as well as concentrating on the political significance of the piece in terms of the overt political philosophy of white South African artist Athol Fugard.
Henderson, Heather. "Building *Fences:* An Interview with Mary Alice and James Earl Jones." *Theater* 16 (Summer/Fall, 1985): 67-70. Mary Alice and James Earl Jones performed the roles, respectively, of Rose and Troy Maxson when *Fences* opened at the Yale Repertory Theater. In this interview, they discuss the development of their characters, both as directed by Lloyd Richards and as guided by their own spontaneity.

Kester, Gunilla Theander. "Approaches to Africa: The Poetics of Memory and the Body in Two August Wilson Plays." In *August Wilson: A Casebook*, edited by Marilyn Elkins. New York: Garland, 1994. Examines how *Fences* and *Joe Turner's Come and Gone* (1986) highlight the metaphoric relationship between black American history and the black body. Shows how bringing the past into the present often leaves Wilson's characters trapped in a sense of futility.

Shannon, Sandra G. "The Good Christian's Come and Gone: The Shifting Role of Christianity in August Wilson Plays." *MELUS* 16 (Fall, 1989): 127-142. Discusses how some of Wilson's characters, such as Levee (*Ma Rainey's Black Bottom*), Troy Maxson (*Fences*), Herald Loomis (*Joe Turner's Come and Gone*), and Boy Willie (*The Piano Lesson*), impose their authority and overshadow other characters. In their abandonment of Christianity and withdrawal from the religion of their ancestors, they construct their own self-serving and liberating dogma.

FERDYDURKE

Type of work: Novel
Author: Witold Gombrowicz (1904-1969)
Type of plot: Farce
Time of plot: 1930's
Locale: Poland
First published: 1937 (English translation, 1961)

> *Principal characters:*
> JOHNNIE KOWALSKI, a thirty-year-old writer
> T. PIMKO, a professor
> MIENTUS, a seventeen-year-old schoolboy
> MR. YOUTHFUL, an engineer
> MRS. YOUTHFUL, his wife
> ZUTKA, their daughter
> AUNT HURLECKA, Kowalski's mother's sister
> EDWARD, her husband
> ISABEL and
> ALFRED, their children

The Story:

Johnnie Kowalski awoke one morning from a nightmare in which he had reverted to adolescence: The adult in him was mocking the youth and vice versa, and all the ill-fitting parts of his adolescent body were jeering at one another in rude and raucous fashion. The dream had brought back uncomfortable memories of his literary debut and his sense of being doubly trapped, by his own childhood and by the childishness in others' perception of him, "the caricature of myself which existed in their minds." At the moment he had sat down to make a new start, to write a new book that would, this time, be truly identical with himself, the distinguished professor T. Pimko had appeared on his doorstep. As the diminutive but terrible Pimko quizzed him on King Ladislas and Latin grammar, Kowalski felt himself shrinking to schoolboy size. His adult mind knew that the situation was absurd, but his body seemed paralyzed, and when Pimko dragged him off to enroll in school, Kowalski did not resist.

Neither the boys nor the schoolmasters seemed to notice anything odd or unusual, and Kowalski found himself conforming to schoolboy behavior in spite of himself. Like the others, he languished in stultifying classroom sessions where the masters taught that Juliusz Słowacki's poetry was great because Słowacki was a great poet; like the others, he smeared ink on his hands and picked his nose. Only one boy, Kopeida, seemed unaffected by any of this. Kowalski was drawn into a "duel of grimaces" between Siphon, the honorable, innocent Adolescent, and Mientus, the champion of crass, foulmouthed Boyhood. Mientus, on the verge of losing, simply called on his cronies to attack Siphon, and they held him down while Mientus poured all the obscenities he knew into Siphon's ear.

At the very climax of this "violation by the ear," Pimko reappeared and dragged Kowalski away again, this time to the home of the Youthful family, where he was to rent a room. The family consisted of Mr. and Mrs. Youthful (both educated and both earnestly progressive) and their daughter Zutka, who was the embodiment of the modern girl—athletic, unaffected, and absolutely invulnerable. At this point Kowalski became not only unable but also unwilling to reveal his true, thirty-year-old self: All he cared about was what Zutka thought of him. He tried to gain the psychological advantage by annoying her, but drunken Mientus, boasting of his exploits with the housemaid and rambling on about running away to the country to fraternize with honest stable lads, burst in and ruined the moment.

All Johnnie could do was continue his assault on Zutka's perfect, unreflective indifference by playing the fool and knave. He disgusted the Youthfuls with his table manners and invaded their orderly bathroom, where he danced a disorderly dance; he paid a beggar to stand in front of Zutka's window with a green twig in his mouth; and he spied on Zutka through the keyhole and rifled through her desk. There he found love letters from schoolboys, lawyers, doctors, landlords, even Professor Pimko himself. Johnnie decided to lay low both Pimko and the Youthfuls with one stroke: Imitating Zutka's hand, he wrote notes inviting both Pimko and Kopeida to a rendezvous.

At first all went as planned. After Kopeida had climbed through the girl's window, to Zutka's delight, followed by Pimko, to Zutka's consternation, he raised the alarm. The Youthfuls, however, were charmed by their daughter's lack of prudishness—yet another proof that she was thoroughly modern. Pimko, on the other hand, responded less calmly to the situation, and soon the entire group was nothing more than a rolling, punching, kicking, and biting heap on the floor.

As Kowalski was making his escape from the house, Mientus popped up again and announced that he had raped the maid, and he suggested that he and Johnnie make for the countryside, where the real people lived. They trudged through one deserted village after another. Puzzled, they knocked on a door and were greeted by furious barking; they soon discovered that the peasants had turned themselves into dogs. Suspicious of city folk, bureaucrats, and "stitizens wi'eir intentions," the snarling pack of villagers set upon Mientus and Johnnie. Suddenly a car drove right into their midst; it was Kowalski's aunt on her way home to the country estate where he had been raised. Clucking and chiding, she whisked both "boys" into the car. On the way, she tallied up events and birthdays to come up with Kowalski's true age, but it didn't matter. For her he would always be ten years old.

At the estate lived Uncle Edward, cousins Isabel and Alfred, many servants, and a multitude of hunting dogs. The masters sleepily ate, played cards, and discussed the various family ailments and their cures. Mientus discovered his ideal of a stable boy in the person of Bert, a young servant. The family therefore assumed he was either a homosexual or a communist, but they were not disturbed until Mientus resolved to show his solidarity with the common folk by goading Bert into hitting him in the face. Servants and masters alike were scandalized. Kowalski felt the atmosphere growing thick and poisonous, and once again plotted his escape, resigning himself to taking Bert at least part of the way because Mientus refused to leave without him. It occurred to Kowalski that abducting his cousin Isabel would be more logical than abducting a stable boy, but he discarded the idea.

The boys were discovered, and Uncle Edward's attempt to reestablish his feudal prerogatives by beating Bert into submission backfired. Bert hit back, and soon Bert, Mientus, Alfred, Edward, and the aunt were engaged in the fray. Johnnie left the pile of wriggling bodies and made for the gates, where cousin Isabel found him. Rather than explain the whole absurd situation to Isabel or some later audience, Kowalski declared his passion for the girl; she eagerly fell in with all the conventional expectations about runaway lovers and elopements. As Isabel clung to him, the sun, the "arch-bum," rose over the forest, and Johnnie, knowing flight was useless, fled.

Critical Evaluation:

Many a Polish writer has ended up in exile, but the ironies of Witold Gombrowicz's situation are nearly as fantastic as some of his plots. In the summer of 1939, he set out on what was to be a leisurely transatlantic cruise to South America and back. By the time the ship docked in Argentina, Nazi Germany and Soviet Russia had invaded Poland and World War II had begun. Gombrowicz spent the next ten years contending with poverty and isolation, clerking by day and writing by night, until translations into Spanish and publications abroad again brought him some renown. Belligerently apolitical, Gombrowicz maintained ties with both the emigré press and the press in Poland, and he refused to take part in any ideological exercises. In his homeland, however, his earlier works were not reprinted, nor were his newer ones published until "the Polish October" of 1956-1958, a period of relative liberalization. The 1957 edition of *Ferdydurke* sold out in a matter of days, Gombrowicz's plays were staged, his correspondence was published, and he stood at the very center of debate on Polish literary and cultural life. His absolute rebellion against all fixed expectations of behavior, however, whether social, cultural, ideological, or national, made him too volatile an element in an atmosphere of forced stability and stale dogma. In 1958, his name and works virtually disappeared from print again, but he continued to exert a tremendous influence on Polish writing and thought.

Gombrowicz was a provocateur in life and in letters; it was his method of confronting reality, his style of existence. Paradox lies at the foundation of his work, in which he aimed to provoke, amuse, confound, and finally leave the reader nose to nose with some highly unpleasant psychological and philosophical truths. *Ferdydurke*, with its three acts and two intermezzos, resembles theater more than it does the traditional novel, and its characters are more puppet than human. Its language is playful and inventive, and its very title is a fantastic, meaningless word. In fact, Gombrowicz claimed to be bored by readers' constant questions about "meaning," and he wrote in his diary: "Come, come, be more sensuous, less cerebral, start dancing with the book instead of asking for meanings. Why take so much interest in the skeleton if it's got a body? See rather whether it is capable of pleasing and is not devoid of grace and passion."

Grace and passion might not be the reader's first impression of *Ferdydurke*, but the body can hardly be missed. Beginning with Kowalski's dream and ending with his futile flight from "the arch-bum," Gombrowicz's imagery grows out of the human form. The narrator-hero's "childish, idiotic little behind" is what glues him to his chair as Pimko talks, and he sees that everyone around him is ruled by "the tyranny of the backside." Kowalski cannot run from the classroom because he has stuck his finger into his shoe. Zutka's calves stand for an entire generation. The conflict between masters and servants comes down to the collision of faces and fists. "Philifor Honeycombed with Childishness," one of the two nonsensical fables with which Gombrowicz punctuates Kowalski's story, begins with a philosophical dispute and ends with a hail of gunfire and flying body parts, and each stage of Kowalski's own adventures ends with a welter of bodies writhing on the floor.

For Gombrowicz, observes fellow Polish writer Czesław Miłosz, these heaps may be an image of the only authentic form of human contact. All other contact, all other behavior is shaped by convention—by groups, not individuals. Ultimately there may be no such thing as an individual self, and when Kowalski sits down to write his new book, his new self, he takes on an impossible task. He wants to escape his own "greenness," his own inferiority, but the alternatives are even worse. Pimko, himself a collection of clichés, imposes his notion of boyhood on Kowalski; the schoolboys are also ruled by the expectation that "boys will be boys"; the Youthfuls' supposed frankness and liberality is merely another fixed form, as are Mientus' romantic notion of the rustic stable boy, the family relationships so dear to Kowalski's aunt, and the feudal ones so dear to his uncle. Underlying all of this is a fixed notion of what it is to be Polish. Every attempt at escaping one pattern simply leads to another, and the only thing that seems to break the form, at least temporarily, is a ridiculous or violent gesture—a green twig in a beggar's mouth, or a bite just below the knee.

Jane Ann Miller

Bibliography:

Gombrowicz, Witold. *Diary, Volume 1*. Edited by Jan Kott and translated by Lillian Vallee. Evanston, Ill.: Northwestern University Press, 1988. Gombrowicz himself provides some of the best insight into the novel in this first volume of his diaries, which he began in 1953 for serial publication in the Polish emigré press.

Gőmőri George. "The Antinomies of Witold Gombrowicz." *Modern Language Review* 73 (January, 1978): 119-129. A brief but essential introduction to Gombrowicz's major themes, with special attention to Ferdydurke, and emphasis on his use of paradox.

Holmgren, Beth. "Witold Gombrowicz in the United States." *The Polish Review* 33, no. 4 (1988): 409-418. Gombrowicz has remained a rather obscure figure in the United States, and this article addresses some of the reasons why. Also gives a thorough overview of work on Gombrowicz in English.

Longinovic, Tomislav. *Borderline Culture: The Politics of Identity in Four Twentieth-Century Slavic Novels*. Fayetteville: University of Arkansas Press, 1993. Discusses the conflict of identity and ideology in *Ferdydurke*, and argues that it is a parody of the entire Western metaphysical tradition.

Thompson, Ewa. *Witold Gombrowicz*. Boston: Twayne, 1979. An excellent introduction to Gombrowicz, a straightforward discussion of his life and works. Includes a bibliography.

FÊTES GALANTES AND OTHER POEMS

Type of work: Poetry
Author: Paul Verlaine (1844-1896)
Principal works: Poèmes saturniens, 1866; *Fêtes galantes*, 1869 (*Galant Parties*, 1912); *La Bonne Chanson*, 1870; *Romances sans paroles*, 1874 (*Romances Without Words*, 1921); *Sagesse*, 1881; *Jadis et naguère*, 1884; *Amour*, 1888; *Parallèlement*, 1889, 1894; *Femmes*, 1891; *Bonheur*, 1891; *Chansons pour elle*, 1891; *Liturgies intimes*, 1892; *Odes en son honneur*, 1893; *Élégies*, 1893; *Dans les limbes*, 1894; *Épigrammes*, 1894 (English translation, 1977); *Chair, dernière poésies*, 1896; *Invectives*, 1896; *Hombres*, 1903 (English translation, 1977); *Selected Poems*, 1948; *Femmes/Hombres*, 1977 (includes English translation of *Femmes* and *Hombres*).

The importance of literary groups or schools has always been greater in France than in England or America, and much of French literary history can best be understood through the reaction of one school against another. After the great wave of Romanticism in the 1830's and 1840's, a counterwave was inevitable. This originated in the group known as the Parnassians, which first made itself known in 1866 and was led by Leconte de Lisle (1818-1894) and continued by José-Maria de Heredia (1842-1905). The members of the school had two objectives. They wanted the reformation of the loose metrical methods of the disciples of Victor Hugo and Alphonse de Lamartine and a return to something like the traditional strictness of French prosody. More important, they were reacting against the excessive subjectivity and emotionalism of Romantics like Alfred de Musset, who exploited his famous love affair with George Sand in his verse. Poetry, according to the Parnassians, should aim at an "abstract beauty" and avoid the cultivation of "private sorrows and their lamentation"; it should be cold and aloof, purely objective. In the famous "Les Éléphants" by de Lisle, for example, the great beasts solemnly march across the desert of red sand and as solemnly disappear; "and the desert resumes its immobility." As James Elroy Flecker, one of the group's few English disciples, wrote, Parnassians considered it abhorrent "to overlay fine work with gross and irrelevant egoism," as Hugo had done; had the movement existed in England, Alfred, Lord Tennyson "would never have published 'Locksley Hall.'"

It was in this spirit that Paul Verlaine wrote his early poems. He was, however, never a thoroughgoing Parnassian; occasionally, as in "Un Dahlia," he achieved something of the desired objectivity, but even in his first volume there were hints of the much more characteristic manner that was to develop three years later in *Fêtes galantes*. In such a poem as "Nuit du Walpurgis classique," with its description of the "correct, ridiculous, and charming" garden designed by Le Nôtre, there is a distinct foreshadowing of the eighteenth century fantasies of his subsequent volume. Also included in this first book was what became one of his most famous poems, "Chanson d'automne," one of those almost wordless little songs associated with his later manner.

The publication, between 1857 and 1875, of three books by Edmond and Jules de Goncourt on various aspects of life and art during the eighteenth century marked another sharp break with the Romantics. As had happened earlier in England, the French Romantics had turned violently against the preceding century, detesting what they considered to be its coldness and artificiality. Yet as a result of this latest turn of the wheel of taste, this very artificiality became the eighteenth century's greatest charm; some writers were fascinated by the brilliant, stately society that their grandfathers had overthrown. Verlaine's *Fêtes galantes*—probably his best-known book outside

France—belongs to this pattern; in it, as Holbrook Jackson said, "Watteau became literature." It is an evocation of the world of François Boucher and Jean-Honoré Fragonard, with its formal gardens, silks, fluttering of fans, and tinkling of mandolins in the eternal twilight or moonlight, while abbés, shepherdesses, Pierrot, and Columbine stroll along paths beside the fountains.

This kind of eighteenth century bric-a-brac, while very charming, does not represent Verlaine's most important contribution to French poetry. His chief literary significance lies in his connection with the Symbolist movement, which began as an unconscious protest against what has been called the Spartan creed of the Parnassians and which had links with the work of the Impressionist painters. Arthur Symons, who knew many of the writers involved and who translated a few of Verlaine's pieces, called the whole body of late nineteenth century French literature the Decadent movement, which he then divided into Impressionism and Symbolism. It is difficult and perhaps unnecessary to make a distinction between the two. According to Symons, Impressionism gives the truth "of the visible world to the eyes that see it"; Symbolism, "the truth of spiritual things to the spiritual vision." Yet Symons himself cited Verlaine's *Romances sans paroles*, the book that is usually considered the beginning of the poet's Symbolist period, as an example of Impressionism.

It was the effort of the Symbolists to see through outward appearances to inward reality by trying to express "the secret affinities of things with one's soul." It is generally thought that the germ of this point of view is to be found in Charles Baudelaire's poem "Correspondences." That poet saw nature as a "forest of symbols" where "perfumes, colors, and sounds answer one another," a point of view that resulted in poetry in which the subject becomes unimportant or disappears altogether. The meaning of the poem is of no more significance than in a musical composition. A remark of Walter Pater's is frequently quoted in this connection: "All art constantly aspires towards the condition of music; and the perfection of poetry seems to depend in part on a certain suppression of mere subject, so that the meaning reaches us through ways not distinctly traceable by the understanding." "Music before everything," Verlaine said in his "Art poétique." He also declared: "no color, only the nuance," for it is this nuance that weds "the dream to the dream." His later poems became almost literally songs without words, in which the content consists only of half hints and vague suggestions.

In France, this kind of poetry led to the work of Stéphane Mallarmé, who composed poems filled with symbols within symbols, in which hardly a word is meant to be taken in its customary sense; the French claim that his verse is better understood by foreigners. In England, Verlaine was much admired by the minor poets of the 1890's, several of whom—among them Symons, John Gray, and Ernest Dowson—translated some of his poems. It is certainly possible to see his influence, or that of his school, on some of the early poems of William Butler Yeats.

Although Verlaine experienced a religious conversion that found expression in many of the poems in *Sagesse*, his life was a tragic one. He has been called a modern Villon. Almost everyone who wrote about him has referred to his childlike qualities. François Coppé said: "Alas, like a child he was without any defense, and life wounded him often and cruelly. But suffering is the ransom paid by genius, and this word can be uttered in speaking of Verlaine, for his name will always awaken the memory of an absolutely new poetry which, in French literature, has acquired the importance of a discovery."

Bibliography:
Adam, Antoine. *The Art of Paul Verlaine.* Translated by Carl Morse. New York: New York University Press, 1963. A classic psychological study of the author's works. Provides considerable analysis of Verlaine's oeuvre in the context of the period.

Balakian, Anna. *The Symbolist Movement: A Critical Appraisal*. New York: New York University Press, 1977. Explores Verlaine's role in the European Symbolist movement. Balakian proposes that *Fêtes galantes*, with its suggestive emotional nuance, musicality, and attentiveness to color, marked the inception of Verlaine's Symbolist poetry.

Carter, A. E. *Paul Verlaine*. New York: Twayne, 1971. Provides a chronological overview of Verlaine's life and works. Concludes that melancholy and alienation reside beneath the musicality and light manner of the poetry.

Richardson, Joanna. *Verlaine*. London: Weidenfeld and Nicolson, 1971. Standard biography of the author in English. Richardson evaluates Verlaine's poetry as an event in his personal development.

Taylor-Horrex, Susan. *Verlaine, "Fêtes galantes" and "Romances sans paroles."* London: Grant & Cutler, 1988. Analyzes individual poems as well as prominent themes unifying the collections. Emphasizes the coherence of the collections as landscapes of the soul and cites the concepts of love and passivity as being primary to the poetry. Also discusses several possible sources of influence.

FICCIONES, 1935-1944

Type of work: Short fiction
Author: Jorge Luis Borges (1899-1986)
First published: 1944 (English translation, 1962)

One of the most innovative Latin American writers in the twentieth century, Jorge Luis Borges is considered by many to have exerted a powerful force in reforming the Spanish language. His prose is precise, compact, and direct; it is at times deceptively simple yet abounds in psychological and philosophical subtlety. The author of essays and poetry, Borges is known primarily for two volumes of short stories, *Ficciones* (1944) and *El Aleph* (1949). *Ficciones* is an anthology of short stories in two parts entitled "The Garden of the Forking Paths" and "Artifices." Whereas part 1 had been published separately several years earlier in Buenos Aires, part 2 contains a number of stories published for the first time.

Throughout his long career, Borges remained interested in a number of topics. He had a lifelong love of things Argentine, including a fascination with the country's great stark plains, the Pampa, and their violent and elemental cowboys, called gauchos. His broader attraction to Argentine life and literature found its focus in Buenos Aires, a city he loved and knew intimately and where he spent much of his life. Borges' second enduring interest can be classified as philosophical, though his thought and knowledge range widely over metaphysics, history, religion, art, and literature. Early in his life, Borges gained a reputation as a difficult writer, one who wrote not for the masses but for a select few scholars and literary critics. Yet particularly his short stories—which allow insight into one of the most creative literary minds of the twentieth century—are readily accessible to those willing to approach them with patience.

The stories center around themes (destiny, time, infinity) that recur throughout the entire corpus of his work. Borges avoids, however, merely clothing ideas in literary form; rather, he carefully constructs plots that flow relentlessly to their conclusion. His elegant integration of complex philosophical concerns and the striking artistic unity of his stories are testimony to his skill as a writer.

In "Tlōn Uqbar, Orbis Tertius," Borges envisions the possibility of a world constructed according to the idealist tenets of the English philosopher Bishop Berkeley. Although Borges often insisted that he was not a philosopher in the traditional sense, he had a tendency to favor idealism, the proposition that thought is primary to matter. "Tlōn, Uqbar, Orbis Tertius" begins with the narrator, Borges himself, stating that he owes "the discovery of Uqbar to the conjunction of a mirror and an encyclopedia," an opening that hints more at a detective tale than a metaphysical one. Borges' friend and dinner companion, Bioy Casares, responds that the mirror is abominable, as is copulation, "since both multiply the numbers of man," a quote not from Casares himself but from an article on the country of Uqbar in the *Anglo-American Encyclopedia*. Narrator Borges and Casares are puzzled, however, to find that they are able to locate the article on Uqbar in only one set of the *Anglo-American Encyclopedia*, a fact made even more inexplicable by the mysterious inclusion of several additional pages in the volume containing the article. The story plays out in detective fashion. The narrator later accidentally discovers volume 11 of *A First Encyclopedia of Tlōn*, a source of information about an imaginary land in the literature of the imaginary country Uqbar. Oddly enough, the nations of Tlōn are "congenitally idealist"; their language, religion, literature, and metaphysics all reject any suggestion of materialism. There are, for example, no nouns in the language of Tlōn but only sentences constructed of verbs and other parts of speech, which validates the idealist basis of life on Tlön. The seemingly impossible takes place when certain thinkers on Tlön attempt to demonstrate the validity of materialism, an undertaking that causes considerable unease.

Borges' fascination with idealism and its implications plays out in the final third of the story when, first inexplicably, then ominously, objects from Tlön begin to appear in the world of the narrator. The story, a finely crafted philosophical tale, may be a parable of the effects of thought on the formation of the world. Tlön, an imaginary planet in the literature of an imaginary country, which is itself created by a mysterious brotherhood, slowly permeates and dissolves the world and replaces it with Tlön itself. "The world," according to Borges, "will be Tlön."

As in "Tlön, Uqbar, Orbis Tertius," the central premise of "The Circular Ruins" revolves around the notion that "all is mind" and that the construction of a world in accordance with this tenet must conform to certain idealist strictures. In this story, a ragged wizard is instructed by an unknown god to dream a disciple, only to discover that he too, the dreamer, is the dream of another. "The Circular Ruins," shorter than "Tlön, Uqbar, Orbis Tertius," is compact in structure and dense with possible meanings. The story is set in a thick jungle, in an imaginary land of Borges' invention made eerily familiar by the mention of Greek, which had not "contaminated" the Zend language. As in many of his other tales, Borges places a mystery at the core of his narrative whose solution provides the reader an epiphany or moment of realization in which certain aspects of reality can be examined. In "The Circular Ruins," the ending suggests that the reader may be the fiction or dream of another being.

"The Garden of the Forking Paths" is perhaps the best example of Borges' artful blending of the detective story and the philosophical tale. In "The Garden of the Forking Paths," one of his most complex, detailed, and thought-provoking stories, Borges incorporates notions of time, infinity, and destiny. The tale is narrated by Yu Tsun, a German spy and great-grandson of Ts'ui Pên, the governor of Yunnan and author of the mysterious novel *The Garden of the Forking Paths*. The plot of the detective story revolves around Yu Tsun's efforts to relay a message to his superiors in Berlin, whom he despises. Borges weaves a parallel tale of Tsun's enigmatic ancestor, who set out to write a novel "with more characters than there are in the *Hung Lou Mêng*, and to create a maze in which all men could lose themselves." Tsun later discovers that the maze and the novel are one and the same. A hunted man, Tsun momentarily forgets his destiny—that he be tried and executed as a spy—as he meditates on his ancestor's curious project. Oddly, yet inexorably, Yu Tsun is drawn toward a destiny that somehow merges with that of his ancestor of the labyrinthine novel. Ts'ui Pên's novel, which splits in time and creates multiple possibilities for the future, allows for a dizzying proliferation of scenarios. In one future, a man may be murdered by an assassin, while in another he himself may be the murderer of that man. In still a third, the two men may be friends. *The Garden of the Forking Paths*, writes Borges, "is an enormous guessing game, or parable, in which the subject is time," and it is in time, or in its bifurcation, that all men exist and find their destiny. It is Yu Tsun's destiny to be hanged as a spy, which he accepts with resignation, sadness, even joy.

Borges' fascination with time and destiny also forms the core of "The Secret Miracle," which takes place in Prague, 1939, during the German occupation. In this tale, Jaromir Hladík, author of an unfinished tragedy *The Enemies*, *a Vindication of Eternity*, and "an inquiry into the indirect Jewish sources of Jakob Boehme," falls into the hands of the Germans, who promptly sentence him to death. Although his life is filled with creative activity, Hladík nevertheless considers his life wasted because he has never written anything of lasting value, nothing that would justify him in the face of eternity or in the eyes of God. In "The Secret Miracle," as in other stories of Borges, a man's destiny depends on one task he must complete before his death.

Often this is an action that in some way involves the protagonist in death itself. Moments before he is cut down by a German firing squad, his wish seems to have been granted, for the awesome machinery of time grinds to a halt. As a drop of rain grazes one of Hladík's temples and rolls down his cheek, he is catapulted into a timeless, productive limbo where he works to complete his unfinished tragedy.

Hladík cannot escape his destiny. He dies by firing squad exactly one year (in his mind) after standing before the German soldiers. The reader understands that nothing appeared to be out of the ordinary and that to an observer a mere second has passed. Yet for Hladík, as for Borges perhaps, the enigmas of time and death leave room for the unexpected. Hladík, in making peace with himself and God in the moment before his death, has apparently achieved a measure of liberty in the face of an irrevocable and ironclad destiny.

"The South," Borges' final story in *Ficciones*, explores the destiny of a man dying of septicemia in a hospital bed, who dreams a destiny for himself not unlike that of his soldier grandfather. Here Borges skirts the shadowy borders of dream and reality, where it is not clear what is actual and what is not. The protagonist's destiny cannot be revoked or even truly changed, yet Borges suggests that the perception of that destiny may be all. Juan Dahlmann, secretary of a municipal library in Buenos Aires and grandson of a German immigrant and a native Argentinean who died defending Buenos Aires from Indians, chooses to die the honorable death of his grandfather. Avoiding a shameful, perhaps meaningless death in a hospital, Dahlman's delirium carries him to the South, into the brutal, elemental world of the Pampa. Though Dahlman's apparent recovery from his illness and trip to the South are presented in realistic fashion, Borges injects subtle hints that Dahlmann is actually dying in his bed, a fact that may be less important than Dahlman's choice of a death that embraces his romantic vision of his own destiny.

With the publication of *Ficciones*, Jorge Luis Borges attracted the attention of critics and general readers alike in the Spanish and non-Spanish speaking worlds. His work has been translated into many languages. Always thought-provoking, his juxtaposition of the familiar and the unusual make reality itself seem strange, a strangeness that causes the reader to perceive the familiar in new ways. Through his complex and subtle art, Borges aims both to entertain and to motivate readers to question the world and themselves. The pages of his tales become the impetus to complete the journey he started.

Howard Giskin

Bibliography:
Alazraki, Jaime, ed. *Critical Essays on Jorge Luis Borges.* Boston: G. K. Hall, 1987. A collection of articles and reviews by literary critics and writers that aims at a contemporary assessment of the range and scope of Borges' work.
Barrenechea, Ana María. *Borges: The Labyrinth Maker.* Translated and edited by Robert Lima. New York: New York University Press, 1965. A thorough treatment of Borges' philosophy, covering such topics as his use of infinity, pantheism, and time.
Bell-Villada, Gene H. *Borges and His Fiction: A Guide to His Mind and Art.* Chapel Hill: University of North Carolina Press, 1981. Focuses on Borges' stories and essays and provides detailed discussion of a number of works. Part 1 includes introductory chapters that examine Borges' place in Argentine and world literature. In part 2, Bell-Villada classifies Borges' works according to theme and topic.
Rodriguez Monegal, Emir. *Jorge Luis Borges: A Literary Biography.* New York: E. P. Dutton,

1978. A detailed account of the evolution of Borges the man and his art. Monegal draws extensively on interviews with Borges.

Stabb, Martin S. *Jorge Luis Borges.* New York: Twayne, 1970. A useful introductory treatment of Borges the poet, essayist, and writer of fiction. Chapter 1 is a biographical sketch that focuses on the development of Borges' art.

THE FIELD OF VISION

Type of work: Novel
Author: Wright Morris (1910-   )
Type of plot: Psychological realism
Time of plot: Mid-twentieth century
Locale: Mexico
First published: 1956

> *Principal characters:*
> WALTER MCKEE, a middle-aged American
> LOIS MCKEE, his wife
> GORDON MCKEE, their son
> GORDON BOYD, a failed playwright
> DR. LEOPOLD LEHMANN, a psychiatrist
> TOM SCANLON, Lois McKee's father

The Story:

Vacationing in Mexico in the 1950's, Walter McKee ran into his best friend Gordon Boyd, whom he had not seen for fifteen years. Without any introduction, Boyd said, "How's the little woman?" McKee replied that he and his wife could not be happier, which irritated Boyd, who instead of settling down like his friend McKee had spent his life on the road, wandering wherever fate took him. McKee had made money and become a success, although years earlier he had stood on his fiancée's front porch while Boyd gave Lois her first kiss.

At a bullfight to which they all went, Lois McKee was busy supervising her elderly father and her young grandson. Both wore coonskin caps reminiscent of Davy Crockett and of the old man's solitary life on the Midwestern plains. Mrs. McKee had been alarmed when she heard that her husband had met Boyd for she wished to conceal from the world that Gordon Boyd was the only man who had ever excited her. Afraid of the desire he had roused in her that day on the porch, she had instead married the steady but boring McKee, who annoyed her with his overbearing manner and his habit of chewing such things as burnt matches, cigars, even things he picked up in the street. Above all, she disliked the fact that her husband worshipped Boyd. Running into Boyd when they were on vacation struck her as bad luck.

Boyd had suggested to McKee that they all go to a bullfight together, explaining that he would also be bringing his psychiatrist, Dr. Lehmann, who was treating him for depression. None of Boyd's youthful dreams had been fulfilled. Instead of becoming a successful play-wright, he had ended up eking out an existence in New York. His namesake and McKee's son, Gordon, had been dissuaded from pursuing a career in the theater when he had seen Gordon's dingy apartment and lonely life.

Mrs. McKee had not liked the idea of a bullfight, but since Boyd had invited them and clearly expected her to decline, she decided to attend. As for her grandson, Boyd assured her that children liked blood. McKee pretended to look forward to the bullfight until Dr. Lehmann informed him that more than one bull would be killed. To comfort herself, Mrs. McKee read a book entitled: *Toros Without Tears.*

After they took their seats on the shady side of the bullring, where it was cold and made them wish they had gotten seats in the sun, the first bull entered. McKee thought he looked small. Up to his old clowning days, Boyd called the bull over to the edge of the ring, shook up a bottle of soda pop and squirted the little bull in the face. The bull licked it off and the crowd laughed.

Boyd took a bow and McKee was thrilled, but his wife was embarrassed. Gordon Boyd still had not grown up and it appeared he never would. She was reminded of the time he had torn the pocket of baseball legend Ty Cobb's pants as he rounded third at an exhibition game; in all the years that had gone by, that dirty piece of cloth was the only thing Boyd had managed to keep. Much to her amazement, Mrs. McKee had seen it in Boyd's apartment in New York.

McKee tried to explain to his wife that Boyd was special, that once he had even tried to walk on water at a sand pit where he had nearly drowned, but Mrs. McKee remained unconvinced. Boyd was an interesting and aging con man and nothing else. She had to admit, however, that she still found him exciting.

Only Dr. Lehmann was not fooled. During the bullfight he caught Boyd's eye while Boyd was fooling around, to show him that as his physician he understood why Boyd was acting up. Dr. Lehmann forced his patient to confront the truth about himself: that his life had not worked and that he had even failed at failure.

At the end of the bullfight, Boyd threw Gordon McKee's coonskin cap into the ring. When the boy chased after it, Boyd muttered, "touch bottom" and felt himself push off against it. At that moment, he realized that he must transform himself or perish. Reaching down, he rescued the boy and retrieved his cap. Then he silently vowed to renew his quest for truth and beauty and to turn his back on deterioration and failure.

Critical Evaluation:

Wright Morris worked in a variety of literary genres, including novels, short stories, and essays, and he was also a photographer. His award-winning novels focus on the interpersonal relationships between men and women, the effect of the past on people's lives, the pursuit of wealth and the American Dream, and the quest for an authentic identity. Many of Morris' characters come from the Midwest, an endless plain that forms the backdrop for the emotional lives of his ordinary men and women. For revealing them in their quests for meaning and love and for the humor and originality of his technique, Morris gained far-reaching critical success, but his popular acclaim remained comparatively small. The reason for his relative obscurity may lie in the fact that he does not use a traditional, linear plot. This accounts for certain difficulties in his works, yet their complexity is tempered by vivid characterization, country charm, and wit. Morris writes in the vernacular, playing off the peculiar rhythms and hidden meanings that infuse everyday speech. It is actually the author's colloquial jokes and startling images that form the texture of the novel.

In terms of structure, Morris' technique is sophisticated, if not avant-garde. As its title suggests, *The Field of Vision* is about point of view. More specifically, the novel poses the question, How do we know what we know? The answer is that all truth is subjective. At the bullfight, for example, there are as many bullfights as there are spectators. Nobody sees the same bullfight, because every individual's experience of the present is colored and shaped by memory of the past. Personal history is the lens through which each individual views the world. The form of Morris' novel reflects its content: Each chapter bears the name of the character whose perceptions filter the events of the narrative and act as channels for the reader.

Each character sees things differently. Consequently, the real bullfight disappears and the reader is left with contrasting impressions of the same event. After the moment when Boyd shakes up his soda pop and squirts it into the bull's face, Boyd sees himself as the clowning hero, the show-stealer, and life of the party. His friend McKee sees him as the same old joker, as the man who said he could walk on water and who persuaded McKee to believe him. Mrs. McKee sees Boyd as the foolish braggart who once stole her heart but has idiotically refused to grow up. Her father, Tom Scanlon, simply sees him as an ass, and Boyd's psychiatrist, Dr. Lehmann, views him as a brilliant visionary who has not even come close to touching the rock bottom he mistakenly believes himself to have encountered.

Central to *The Field of Vision* is the problem of charisma, hero worship in general, and, specifically, the domination of one personality over another. Gordon Boyd is a charmer, a lady's man with the gift of gab. Mrs. McKee cannot forget that Boyd was the first man to kiss her, and she is haunted by a sensual memory of youth and happiness even while despising her husband for catering to Boyd's vanity. Boyd is always in need of an audience; he has to be center stage, and this need has different effects on different people.

McKee has been enamored of Boyd ever since they were boys, and he sees nothing wrong with his infatuation; indeed, he is hardly conscious of it, going so far as to allow his own son to be named after Boyd. Symbolically, then, he relinquished his paternity and masculinity just as he did when he allowed Boyd to kiss his fiancée. At the close of the novel, though, McKee undergoes the transformative experience that is central to Morris' work. When Boyd lowers McKee's son into the bullring, McKee finally stands up to him: " 'If something should happen to that boy—' said McKee, but it left him speechless, just to think of it. 'Gordon—' he said, waving his arm, 'you get in there and get that boy.' " Thus McKee regains his identity and reasserts himself as a patriarch, the solid family man in contrast to the single, childless, and unhappy loner. McKee no longer wants Boyd in his life and realizes that this man is no friend. He does, however, accept that Boyd's hold over him—that is, Boyd's charisma—will never entirely disappear. The author poses the question whether the power of charisma is to be desired or feared, whether its effects are constructive or destructive. The McKees, for example, expose themselves to extreme psychological states when they encounter the likes of Boyd, but that may be precisely why they do it—to feel something, even pain, in the ordinariness of their lives.

Boyd's charisma causes pain to himself as well. Indeed, thinking Boyd was just another bum on a park bench feeding his last crust of bread to a squirrel, a photographer took a picture that ended up in a national magazine. Boyd was unable even to fail at failure. For Morris, however, he remains a kind of hero. For Boyd acts with dash and audacity; he refuses to accept the harsh precepts of society and would rather make his own way, even if that way is more difficult. His individualism is of the self-reliant but rebellious variety. Boyd is just clever enough to get by, without really joining society. Morris raises the question whether that is enough, and what an individual is to do with some, but not sufficient, talent.

The answer lies in the potential of transformation of character. Although an individual's field of vision may be limited to a particular perspective, this does not imply paralysis. On the contrary, even as Boyd believes himself to be hitting rock bottom he is rebounding. As Dr. Lehmann points out, rock bottom lies a lot further down than he has ever reached. Indeed, it is Dr. Lehmann who becomes the scientific, rationalistic, and good-hearted conscience of the novel. Without becoming sweetly sentimental or subscribing to established religious dogma, Dr. Lehmann speaks for the author when he offers a way out: "He saw it take place. Before his eyes, the commonplace miracle of everyday life. You can begin with a will, a way, and you end up with something else. The human thing to do was transform something, especially yourself."

David Johansson

Bibliography:
Hicks, Granville. Introduction to *Wright Morris: A Reader*, by Wright Morris. New York: Harper & Row, 1970. Discusses recurrent themes in Morris' work, such as setting and its

effect on identity. Also examines his place in American literary history. Includes an overview of the reasons for Morris' popular and critical neglect.

Knoll, Robert, ed. *Conversations with Wright Morris: Critical Views and Responses*. Lincoln: University of Nebraska Press, 1977. Covers a wide range of critical evaluation, including New Criticism and structuralism. Examines the author's postmodern use of point-of-view and investigates the absence of a traditional narrative structure.

Updike, John. "Wright on Writing." *The New Yorker*, April 14, 1975, 124-127. Examines the characters and regions that are most prevalent in Morris' novels. The landscape of the Midwest is discussed in terms of its effect on character development.

Wilson, J. C. "Wright Morris and the Search for the 'Still Point.'" *Prairie Schooner* (Summer, 1975): 154-163. Examines the motif of the quest for identity in Morris' fiction and the pressure of past events on characters' present-day lives.

Yardley, Jonathan. "The Achievement of Wright Morris." *Book World—The Washington Post*, February 3, 1985, 3, 13. Examines the arc of Morris' literary career. Includes a discussion of his work in various genres, covering photography, journalism, and autobiography.

FIESTA IN NOVEMBER

Type of work: Novel
Author: Eduardo Mallea (1903-1982)
Type of plot: Social realism
Time of plot: Mid-1930's
Locale: Buenos Aires, Argentina
First published: Fiesta en noviembre, 1938 (English translation, 1942)

Principal characters:
EUGENIA RAGUE, a society leader born in England
GEORGE RAGUE, her wealthy husband
MARTA, their bored daughter
BRENDA, their younger daughter
SEÑOR RAÍCES, an Argentine financier
LINTAS, an artist
A POET, a political victim

The Story:

A young poet was writing a poem on love on a scrap of paper. The time was eleven o'clock at night. Suddenly a violent, protracted rapping sounded on the door. As he went to answer the pounding, he took with him a piece of bread. Opening the door, he was confronted by the leader of a patrol of armed men in dirty uniforms. The leader stated that they had come for him.

At eight o'clock on a warm springlike evening in November, Eugenia Rague came down the stairs for a final inspection of the setting for her fiesta. English by birth but Argentine by adoption, she dominated her aristocratic surroundings as Cardinal Wolsey, whose portrait adorned her salon, had dominated his. There passed through her head the memory of the lack of respect shown her by Lord Burglay and Lady Gower during her visit to London. She had, however, to concentrate on her guests about to arrive.

Others in the house were reacting differently to the hot evening. In another room, her husband, George, was trying to concentrate on acquiring culture through a phonograph record, but he kept thinking of how he could persuade Señor Raíces, after dinner, to sign a profitable stock purchase. Should delays result, he might lose everything. Intruding into these thoughts came those of his treadmill life, his wife's incessant pressure, and his own desire to relax and perhaps to dream. The arrival of the butler with the afternoon mail interrupted and infuriated him. Then it was time for him to prepare for the party. Marta, the older daughter, lay naked on her bed, wondering why she had spurned a highborn lover.

At nine, the lights were turned on, the orchestra tuned up, and the first guests arrived, the elite of Argentine society. Their conversation was frivolous: the latest scandalous behavior of some politician, the proposal to exterminate the unimportant lower class. The reception, with its empty conversation and the borrowed phrases from the world of ideas revealed the waste of these people's lives.

Meanwhile, Marta made her entrance, prepared for a boring and perhaps detestable evening among unexciting people she had fully comprehended several years earlier. Several young men brought her drinks, and her father welcomed her assistance in his social duties. When Raíces appeared, Rague gave the signal to proceed to the dining room.

In perplexity, the poet questioned the armed men, asking what they could possibly want with him.

At the reception the painter, Lintas, rushed in, late as usual, but in time for the chilled consommé. As he drank it, he became attracted to Marta. Her sudden smile showed her reaction to him, but a pseudophilosophic discussion prevented any words. Lintas noticed her distraught expression when her mother mentioned the fact that Brenda was not there. Only Marta knew of the appeal from Brenda to come immediately to give her assistance. While dismissing her curiosity about the identity of the man across the table from her, she tried to imagine what help her sister could need. The characters became involved in their own thoughts.

After the meal, dancing began in the garden. Lintas found himself dancing with Marta as though they were enemies. Later, more friendly, they discussed some of his paintings. Then she remembered Brenda and without a word of explanation she left. Meanwhile, the leader of the patrol began to lose patience. His men glared at the young man who was wasting their time. They prepared to march their prisoner away.

Marta's flight took her to a shabby house and into a stench-filled room, where she found Brenda recovering from an abortion. Brenda needed her sister's help to conceal her situation from her parents and to supply additional money for the operation, which had cost more than the previous one. Marta left the house and headed for home.

At the fiesta, no one had noticed Marta's absence. Rague and Raíces were discussing stock, and Raíces was trying to explain why he did not want to rush into the transaction. Eugenia Rague had maneuvered Lintas into visiting her art gallery to pass judgment on some new purchases. Amid a group of interested guests, he pronounced them fakes. Lintas knew that he had created a conflict because Eugenia would have preferred a comfortable lie to the unpleasant truth. Marta, returning as Lintas was leaving the fiesta, offered to take him home.

Through the door, the poet saw a fighting cock belonging to a neighbor. He tried to imagine what was going to happen to him. He was suddenly frightened.

In the car, Marta felt impelled to talk. She protested against the sterility of the civilized universe and the difficulty people find in trying to communicate. When they reached his home, he invited her in. The screams of a neighboring woman started him on the story of his life. Poverty had engendered in him a hatred for people like her. He told her of a gang of ruffians who had beaten up an old bookseller because he was foreign and was selling "subversive books." It was his widow who had screamed. This atrocity, making him feel for the first time involved in humanity, had increased his loathing for the governing class that permitted such crimes to go unpunished. They continued their discussion during a walk at dawn through the woods. As she left, they realized that neither had convinced the other of his or her beliefs.

The prisoner asked for permission to get his hat. What he really wanted was time.

Marta hated to go home. Brenda would be in a troubled sleep; her father would be snoring, and her mother would be sneaking down to the kitchen for a snack. Marta knew that in other parts of the world vigils more painful than hers were going on. She now realized that her trouble was a hatred of herself because of an unsatisfied yearning for something. Suddenly, the thought came to her that she, who had always been served, ought to serve others. She paused at a church, but it offered no promise of relief. She stopped next at a coffee shop. Though sensing herself out of place among the customers, eventually she began to feel a comprehension of them and a oneness with them all. She went home. In her room, she took stock of herself. She felt a resemblance to her country with its variety and abundance. Before she fell asleep, she decided that a true change from the horrors of life must come from the tormented people themselves.

The poet's cousin had already been arrested and shot, and his family had been denied permission to bury him. The poet joined the patrol, protesting, but the only reply was rifle butts in his face. When they reached a deserted house and an open space, he tried to run. The patrol fired after him. He fell to the ground and blood soaked the piece of bread he dropped. One of the men turned over the body to make sure the poet was dead. The patrol, leaving him lying on the ground, walked away, loathing one another.

Critical Evaluation:

In a graceful style, rich with vivid, precise images, neither pretentious nor overly decorated, Eduardo Mallea tells the moving story of two people struggling to communicate with each other while lost in the midst of a shallow, violent world. Although the painter Lintas and Marta Rague are the two most sympathetic characters in this short novel, both are held back by their pride from the honesty and openness that would liberate them and enable them to achieve an authentic relationship. They are the only individuals in *Fiesta in November* who even care about moral concerns, except for the poet, unnamed and doomed, whose brief story alternates like an almost subliminal theme with the main body of the story, illuminating and commenting upon it.

The two fiestas, one social, the other of blood, are linked thematically by Lintas' account to Marta of the fatal beating of a Jewish bookdealer in Buenos Aires by a group of Argentine Fascists. An undercurrent of violence also lies behind the conversation and actions of the guests in the house of Marta's mother, Eugenia Rague. The fragments of the condemned poet's story are in italics, a sign of emphasis, suggesting that in spite of its shorter length, this narrative is the more important of the two.

The opening arrest of the poet could be that of Joseph K. in *The Trial* (1925). There are more than casual similarities between the work of Kafka and this novel. The contrast between the scene with the poet and the luxurious setting of Eugenia Rague's home is shocking. Eugenia is a vain, acquisitive character. Her only passions are for her collection of objects from the past and for power. "Power is power," she thinks, "and damn all the rest." She detests sentiment and everything connected with it, so it is not surprising that she is completely alienated from her two daughters. Her husband George, despite his wealth, feels no fulfillment or peace.

A sultry, perfumed lushness pervades the novel, the heat of summer and passion—and of violence. Objects seem to have lives of their own. The opening picture of the dinner party is a devastating glimpse of empty lives and futile social ritual. The characters are struggling with an inner tyranny, a psychic trap more terrible than the cruelty of society, if they only realized it. "All art," thinks Lintas, "is a great and terrible demand for response." Indeed, this unusual novel demands a response from the reader.

Lintas appears on the scene like a breath of fresh air in the stale world of the Rague mansion. Mr. and Mrs. Rague and their guests would be lost without their ceremonies, but Lintas deliberately walks over their carefully plotted maneuvers. Marta and Lintas recognize each other from the beginning as two of a kind—exiles in a world they detest. Marta, at age twenty-seven, still is filled with a passionate curiosity, still is eager to experience life. Human beings, she reflects, only seek their own private ends, only hope to satisfy their appetites. Marta hates the pretense of society, the constant betrayal of her own nature. A dream—unknown but tragic—burns in the depths of her spirit, stifled by daily compromises.

Mirrors and windows and polished surfaces constantly reflect faces, oblique views of people, staring eyes. The reflected images seem more real than many of the actual figures and faces. Mallea seems to be asking, what is the reality and what is false?

Brenda Rague, Marta's sister, is having an abortion while her mother's fiesta is in progress. This revelation causes Marta to think in a new way about their lives, and her meeting with Lintas continues to stimulate her chain of thoughts. Lintas himself was made suddenly aware by the episode of the brutal beating of the bookseller. Are there social castes, they ask, or only moral castes? Where is the moral answer? The word "serve" appears to Marta as she walks down the empty city streets before dawn. What does it mean? Could it be the answer for her? She realizes that each individual must be heroic, walk alone, bravely, honestly, toward fate.

The inner dramas of the novel are not resolved. They move from climax to climax, cumulatively, charged with great lyric tension. Seemingly insignificant individual lives are transformed by Mallea into the essence of the human condition. *Fiesta in November* is an extraordinary novel by a great author. It is a book that haunts the reader, as Mallea intended, for the questions that it raises are not easily answered.

Mallea's view of life is religious and moral. His works often suggest the European Existentialists, although most of his writing anticipated their novels and dramas. He was descended from an old Creole family and attended an English school in Bahia Blanca, where the majority of his classmates were the sons of immigrants. (He has never lost sight of the fact that Argentina is a melting pot.) At the age of thirteen, he moved to Buenos Aires with his family. The city was a revelation for the withdrawn adolescent. His first published stories won immediate attention, and he eventually became an acclaimed public figure. In the 1930's and 1940's, he was director of some of the most influential literary publications in Latin America. He was a steadfast opponent of the Perón regime. After the revolution that overthrew the Perón dictatorship, he was named ambassador to the United Nations Educational, Scientific, and Cultural Organization (UNESCO) in Paris. Subsequently, he returned to private life to devote himself exclusively to writing. He has lectured in Europe and the United States. *Fiesta in November* and other novels and stories have established Mallea as one of Latin America's greatest writers and one of the outstanding prose stylists in the world.

"Critical Evaluation" by Bruce D. Reeves

Bibliography:
Belloni, Manuel. "The Inner Silence of Eduardo Mallea." *Américas* 19 (October, 1967): 20-27. Discusses Mallea's technique and theme of reaching the essential by means of describing the nonessential.
Flint, J. M. "The Expression of Isolation: Notes on Mallea's Stylistic Techniques." *Bulletin of Hispanic Studies* 44 (1967): 203-209. Another discussion of Mallea's masterful style.
Lewald, H. Ernest. *Eduardo Mallea*. Boston: Twayne, 1977. A good starting place in the study of Mallea and his work. Bibliography.
Petersen, Fred. "Notes on Mallea's Definition of Argentina." *Hispania* 45 (1962): 621-624. Brief, cogent description of an important aspect of Mallea's moral vision.
Polt, John Herman Richard. *The Writings of Eduardo Mallea*. Berkeley: University of California Press, 1959. Critical survey of Mallea's works. Notes and bibliography.

THE FIFTH HORSEMAN

Type of work: Novel
Author: José Antonio Villarreal (1924-   )
Type of plot: Historical realism
Time of plot: 1893-1915
Locale: The north of Mexico
First published: 1974

Principal characters:

HERACLIO INÉS, a horseman and a revolutionary
DAVID CONTRERAS, his boyhood friend turned mortal enemy
CARMEN BECERRA, the patrón's daughter
PANCHO VILLA, bandit turned rebel leader
MARCELINA ORTIZ, Heraclio's devoted wife
XÓCHITL SALAMANCA, Heraclio's mistress

The Story:

After Heraclio Inés' mother died while giving birth to him and his father died while attempting to tame a wild stallion five years later, he was sent to be a lowly shepherd on the Hacienda de la Flor, even though his family enjoyed the protection of the patrón, Don Aurelio Becerra, who was also his godfather. Heraclio left behind his fellow pastor, the young but already embittered David Contreras, Don Aurelio's illegitimate son by María Contreras, who was thought to be a witch. Heraclio's brothers treated him cruelly in his new home, forcing him to break horses as they had once done and to be brave beyond his years. Under the threat of a lashing should he return home on foot, the brothers left Heraclio, the proud and diffident fifth horseman, to tame a wild stallion thirty kilometers away from the hacienda.

When Heraclio was rude to the patrón's children, Crispín and Carmen Becerra, Don Aurelio did not rebuke him because Don Aurelio was inordinately fond of his godson and only asked that he provide the two with riding lessons. For the haughty Carmen, these occasions soon turned into opportunities for sexual encounters that all would have frowned upon for their scandalous violation of the church's moral teachings, as well as for their violation of society's strict class boundaries. Heraclio's discovery of their irreconcilable worldviews concerning the future of Mexico led him to tell Carmen about her father's sexual exploitation of the native women living on the Hacienda de la Flor; he disclosed this before she and her brother left to attend the university in Seattle. In their absence, Carmen's dissolute cousin from Spain, Domingo Arguiú, arrived to fulfill a contract to unite in marriage the Becerra fortune with the noble name of his family. Heraclio took an immediate dislike to his dandified elitism, but perversely thought that Domingo might make a suitable husband for Carmen.

Some time later, the patrón organized a fiesta to welcome home his children from the United States. Carmen, more eager than Heraclio to continue their illicit relationship, eventually disclosed the situation to her parents. The knowledge prompted Don Aurelio to plan a hasty marriage for the boy. Meanwhile, Crispín vowed never to succeed his father as patrón in such an oppressive social order, and he went to the United States with his American wife. After the Inés brothers dominated the hacienda's equestrian competition, winning and sharing prizes in every category of horsemanship, Heraclio killed the patrón's contador, Juan Vásquez, who had come upon him making love to Carmen. He thereupon fled to the hills, where he joined a bandit group that included his childhood friend David Contreras.

The aged Ysabel Pulido, leader of the thieves who redistributed their booty among the rural poor, was taking his men to join forces with the emerging rebel hero, Pancho Villa, when he died suddenly in his sleep. Though he was still a teenager, Heraclio declared himself the new leader of this rebel band, much to the envy of David and to the amusement of Villa. David tried to shoot Heraclio in the back at Juárez. Upon his return to the hacienda during a lull in the fighting, Heraclio married the saddlemaker's daughter, Marcelina Ortiz, and spent the night with María Contreras. David's robbery and murder of a merchant sealed his fate as an outlaw. Soon, though, Heraclio was called to rejoin the ever more powerful and seemingly unstoppable Villa, who was celebrating victories in Jiménez and Chihuahua. Villa set up his revolutionary headquarters in Chihuahua, and he passed the virginal Indian circus performer Xóchitl Salamanca on to Heraclio to be his mistress; she had innocently declared that she would prefer to be violated by the more handsome of the two men. Decisive rebel victories followed at Torreón and Zacatecas, where the foolish Domingo perished during a bandit attack; Domingo had gone against Heraclio's advice not to surrender.

After a variola plague in Zacatecas killed off the devoted Xóchitl, Heraclio lost his revolutionary fervor and returned to resume his family life on the Hacienda de la Flor, where he expressed his condolences to the widowed Carmen. In a brutal attack that had been seething inside him since the night his revered Ysabel Pulido died, David killed Heraclio's baby daughter and raped Marcelina, who also died. This forced Heraclio to murder David in revenge. Heraclio refused Carmen's suggestion that he marry her and become patrón. Instead, he traveled a great distance by train to kill the traitorous General Celestino Gámez. He decided against wedding his brother Concepción's widow, Otilia, for whom he had always felt a great affection, and fled into California to begin a life in exile. Villa's decimated Division of the North headed for sure defeat.

Critical Evaluation:

The Fifth Horseman is the second of José Antonio Villarreal's three influential novels about the Mexican American experience that helped define the parameters of Chicano literature. Although particularly notable for its stark depiction of the social inequalities leading up to the Mexican Revolution (1910-1920), this work ends promisingly with the protagonist's flight into the United States as one of a wave of refugees who were the first to embody the problematics of Chicano identity that lie at the core of all subsequent Mexican American works. Villarreal's *Pocho* (1959), by contrast, treats the coming of age of Richard Rubio, whose conflicts with his Old World parents in the more progressive social milieu of the United States lead him to join the military in World War II to fight for his adopted country, thus forging for himself a coherent sense of cultural belonging. *Clemente Chacón* (1984) presents a similar American-Dream saga, this time of a successful Mexican immigrant who feels no need to deny either his heritage or his newfound nationality; he proudly declares himself a Chicano.

An amalgam of two literary genres, *The Fifth Horseman* displays the influences both of American historical novels and of Mexican novels of the revolution, including Mariano Azuela's *The Underdogs* (1916), Agustín Yáñez's *The Edge of the Storm* (1947), and Juan Rulfo's *Pedro Páramo* (1955). Villarreal largely eschews the more technically innovative styles of later novels of this type, such as Carlos Fuentes' *The Death of Artemio Cruz* (1963), and employs instead a realistic mode of narration. He describes the oppression and abuses of the prerevolutionary system of the hacienda, where native Mexican peons lived at the mercy of their patrons' whims, forever in their debt because of the inflated prices of provisions at their supply stores.

Villarreal's seamless blending of fact and fiction depicts Heraclio's developing political tendencies against the backdrop of the period's turbulent history. There were no less than ten changes in Mexican leadership over a span of twenty years. Villarreal also portrays the unique cultural flavor of the northern Mexican countryside, indulging in a spirited *costumbrismo* that includes the upper-class social world of the hacienda as well as the contests of daring horsemanship native to the region. The novel includes descriptions of the lavish ball thrown to welcome home the patron's children and of the brothers Inés as they engage in the so-called ride of death. In keeping with his naturalist bent, Villarreal throughout the novel uses an English style characterized by Spanish syntactical structures. It is as if he is reminding his readers at every turn of the linguistic crossroads at the heart of the Chicano experience.

Heraclio's escape into California in the novel's conclusion, an apparent abandonment of his past revolutionary goals, aptly reflects the uncertainty of his motivations and involvement in the conflict. Does he embody as an individual the momentous change in historical consciousness that rejected the autocratic oppression of the hacienda system and occasioned the inevitable bloodletting of the revolution for the sake of a greater social equality, or can his rebelliousness be more simply and readily explained by his naturally arrogant disposition? After all, from a young age, Heraclio openly flouts his brothers' authority, and he decides that he will do only occasional work on the hacienda and shows little inclination to bow to the authority of the patron or his family. Heraclio's determination to uphold the ideals of the revolution stands in stark contrast to the fatalistic belief in destiny that so many other characters in the novel hold. Whereas a number of *The Fifth Horseman*'s ruling-class Mexicans and peons see no possibility of or express scant sympathy for significant political change in their country, Heraclio takes history into his own hands and risks his life for what he believes will be a more socially just existence for all Mexicans.

Yet disillusionment with the course of the conflict gripping the nation gnaws at Heraclio. He has trouble deciding whether the plundering rapist and murderer Pancho Villa is really anything more than the marauding fugitive he was at the start, or whether this master strategist and tactician perhaps represents the revolution's high-minded quest for greater social equality. Time after time, Heraclio heeds the call to return to battle from civilian life; on each occasion he reports dutifully to Villa, whom he considers the only true nationalist among the revolution's bickering generals and politicians. It is telling of the nebulous duality to his actions and motives, though, that Heraclio's loss of faith in the bloody, hard-fought campaign ultimately follows upon Villa's decision to isolate in Zacatecas those unfortunates afflicted by the variola plague—the order essentially seals the fate of the stricken Xóchitl, who dies from lack of medical attention. Heraclio's behavior seems at least partially contingent on personal factors—the disaffection with Villa's callousness and the disheartening blow of his mistress' death—and not sheer political partisanship. With seemingly little left to fight for, Heraclio leaves his life as a ranch worker in order to kill a general who had been disloyal to Villa: He risks his life one last time for the revolution's elusive ideals before fleeing into California and permanently renouncing the fighting and its muddled objectives.

Gregary J. Racz

Bibliography:
Jiménez, Francisco, ed. *The Identification and Analysis of Chicano Literature*. New York: Bilingual Press, 1979. A comprehensive collection of scholarly essays that chronicle the history of the rise of Chicano literature, with an emphasis on current critical approaches to

Chicano literary texts. Provides detailed analysis of important trends, the role of women, and the issue of Mexican American identity.

Rocard, Marcienne. *The Children of the Sun: Mexican-Americans in the Literature of the United States.* Translated by Edward G. Brown, Jr. Tucson: University of Arizona Press, 1989. Examines the forging of Chicano identity from both the Anglo and the Hispanic perspective. The work is notable for its careful tracing of the progression of Chicano cultural attitudes and their influence on self-representation.

Shirley, Carl R., and Paula W. Shirley. *Understanding Chicano Literature.* Columbia: University of South Carolina Press, 1988. Considers the canon of Chicano literature largely along generic lines and contains a separate section on *literatura chicanesca*, works about Chicanos by non-Chicano authors. Provides thumbnail sketches of Villarreal's three novels.

Sommers, Joseph, and Tomás Ybarra-Frausto, eds. *Modern Chicano Writers: A Collection of Critical Essays.* Englewood Cliffs, N.J.: Prentice-Hall, 1979. An excellent volume of diverse essays exploring the historical and cultural influences on contemporary Chicano literature, from indigenous folkloric traditions to the impact of the Mexican-American War. A narrative section focuses on Tomás Rivera.

Tatum, Charles. *Chicano Literature.* Boston: Twayne, 1982. Places Villarreal among the pioneer novelists of Chicano literature. While critical of the author's black-and-white portrayal of good versus evil, the study praises his evocative depiction of Mexico's exploitative prerevolutionary social order centered around the hacienda.

IL FILOSTRATO

Type of work: Poetry
Author: Giovanni Boccaccio (1313-1375)
Type of plot: Love
Time of plot: c. 1200 B.C.E.
Locale: Ancient Troy
First transcribed: c. 1335

> *Principal characters:*
> PRIAMO, King of Troy
> TROILO and
> HECTOR, his sons
> PANDARO, Troilo's friend
> GRISEIDA, his cousin
> CALCHAS, her father
> DIOMEDE, a Greek commander

The Story:

When Troy was besieged by Greeks who had come to avenge the abduction and rape of Queen Helen by Paris, son of Priamo, Calchas, a Trojan priest, foresaw the fall of Troy and fled to the Greeks, leaving behind his widowed daughter, Griseida. When the Trojan people heard of Calchas' treachery, they assembled to burn her house, but they were stopped by Hector, who said she could remain in Troy.

Some days later Troilo happened to see Griseida at a religious festival and, overcome with her exquisite beauty, he immediately fell in love with her. In order to keep his love secret, however, he made remarks about the stupidity of love. In private he would praise Griseida's beauty and his love for her. Soon he began to fight fiercely against the Greeks in the hope that his feats would be pleasing to her, but she showed no signs of recognizing his love. With each day his pining for her grew worse until he could not eat or sleep, but spent his time imploring Love to tell Griseida of his pain.

Pandaro found Troilo in this condition and asked what had caused his grief. Pledging Pandaro to secrecy, Troilo told of his unrequited love for Griseida. Pandaro, agreeing that Griseida was worthy of such love, assured Troilo that he would, with his cunning, find a way to win the girl for him.

Pandaro left Troilo and went immediately to Griseida's house to tell her that she was greatly loved by a noble and virtuous man of Troy. After considerable teasing Pandaro revealed Troilo's name to her. Though she considered Troilo worthy, Griseida still grieved for her dead husband, and she told Pandaro that Troilo's love would pass. Pandaro persisted in telling her of Troilo's miserable state, and at last she was convinced.

After Pandaro had accomplished his mission, he returned to Troilo and told him of his success. Troilo was overcome with joy. After praising Venus, he went with Pandaro to behold Griseida's beauty.

For a time Troilo was satisfied with the knowledge that Griseida acknowledged his love, but as his passion increased he desired more than brief glimpses of her. His grief soon returned. When he told Pandaro of his frustration, his friend suggested that he write a letter which Pandaro would take to Griseida.

The heartrending letter was written and carried to Griseida. Again she was hesitant, fearing that if she answered the letter she would appear immodest. Again Pandaro convinced her, and she wrote a letter telling Troilo that she desired to meet him; but once more her better judgment restrained her. Pandaro returned to Griseida after delivering the response and told her that mere words were not sufficient. After some argument he assured her that her reputation would not be injured, as the matter would be kept secret.

When Griseida consented to meet Troilo in a secret room in her house, Pandaro cautioned Troilo to be prudent. The young lover went to Griseida's house. Upon meeting, the two lovers embraced and after a few words went to her bed chamber where they passed the evening in physical delight.

A few days later the two lovers had another opportunity to be together. Troilo again met her in the secret chamber, and once more they made love. They cursed the morning which ended their meeting and planned to meet again when they could. The consummation of his love completely changed Troilo. He became even more fierce as a soldier, and he continually praised Love and the happy state of those who share its bounties.

Meanwhile, after some savage fighting, the Greeks had taken many of the best Trojan warriors as prisoners. Priamo was granted a truce, however, and an exchange of prisoners took place. Calchas, hearing of this exchange, asked the Greeks to give him one of the Trojan warriors to exchange for his daughter Griseida. He was given the mighty Antenor.

During the negotiations Troilo heard that Griseida would be exchanged, and, heartbroken that he might lose her, swooned. When he recovered, without revealing the cause of his consternation, he returned to his palace. There he remained, desolate and sick, reviling Fortune for permitting such a loss to occur. Eventually he summoned Pandaro, who consoled him by saying that Griseida was not the only beautiful woman in Troy and that a new love would drive away the memories of the old one. Troilo, failing to respond to Pandaro's words, wished only for death. At last Pandaro suggested that Troilo abduct his love from the Greeks, a plan to which Troilo agreed, provided Griseida would consent.

That night Troilo visited Griseida and the two bemoaned their fate. Griseida suggested that the war might end soon and she could return, or, at the least, they could see each other during the truces. Troilo, not convinced, suggested that they run away. Fearing the loss of her honor, Griseida rejected this proposal. She told Troilo to wait patiently for her return, which she would arrange within ten days.

After a tearful farewell, Griseida was delivered to Diomede in exchange for Antenor. Troilo passed the following days lamenting his loss until, at the suggestion of Pandaro, he went with his friend to a feast in order to make the time pass more quickly.

In the Greek camp, meanwhile, Diomede had discovered Griseida weeping. Upon learning the cause of her sorrow, he convinced her that Troy would fall and her love for Troilo was unwise. Eventually Griseida was overcome by his arguments and his suit of love, and her feeling for Troilo lessened.

On the tenth day Troilo and Pandaro went to the city gate. There they waited expectantly for Griseida's return, but she did not appear. For the next six days Troilo hopefully waited at the gate. Soon he began to lose his strength and became sickly. Then, in a dream, he saw Griseida being ravished by a wild boar that he believed represented Diomede. Overcome by the vision, Troilo attempted to kill himself, but he was stopped by Pandaro, who told him to verify the dream by writing to his love. He wrote as Pandaro had suggested, requesting that she return or quell his fears, but he received no answer.

For a time he vented his anger in battle. Then he received an answer from Griseida, reaffirming her love. Troilo, still believing that she was being held in the Greek camp against her will, sent numerous messages to which she responded favorably. During a battle, however, a Trojan soldier wounded Diomede and took from him a brooch which Troilo identified as a gift he had given Griseida. Feeling now that his suspicion had been true, he sought out Diomede in battle and the two fought fiercely, but neither was able to overcome the other. One day, after Troilo had killed many Greeks, Achille slew Troilo and thus ended the ill-conceived love between Troilo and Griseida.

Critical Evaluation:

Giovanni Boccaccio took a minor incident in the story of the Trojan War and made it the center of his story. Geoffrey Chaucer is indebted to Boccaccio for Chaucer's *Troilus and Criseyde* (1382). Though *Il Filostrato* contains none of the psychological portraiture of Chaucer's work, it has great literary merit and is probably superior to Chaucer's work in its directness and passionate intensity.

Il Filostrato, a word coined by Boccaccio meaning "the one who is vanquished by love," contains many of the traditional courtly love elements found in medieval romance but also develops a worldview based upon moral standards that are new to the genre. It can thus be seen as a transitional work, bridging the medieval and Renaissance periods.

One factor distinguishing Boccaccio from earlier writers of medieval romance is that he represents the bourgeois class that was so decisive a force in the dissolution of the Middle Ages. His attitude toward courtly love is thus quite different from the mystical orientation of such writers as Dante Alighieri or the aristocratic tradition of the writers of French romances such as Chrétien de Troyes.

An indication of the new manner in which Boccaccio approaches courtly love can be found in the particular way in which he transforms the tale of Troilus and Cressida as originally found in the *Roman de Troie* of Benoît de Saint-Maure, who lived during the twelfth century. The story as narrated by Benoît was within the tradition of the medieval epic and represents a masculine and military orientation in which the prowess of arms plays the primary role. Women and love, if they appear at all, are of only secondary importance. When Benoît describes love, his emphasis is on Troilus and Diomede, and not on Cressida. Indeed his story appears to be that of Diomede rather than of Troilus. Boccaccio took the basic plot of Benoît and transformed it for his own purpose.

This purpose is related in the poem to *Il Filostrato*, in which Boccaccio indicates that he will narrate the suffering of Troilus so that the lady to whom the poem is addressed will understand that Boccaccio himself is suffering as Troilus had suffered. This lady is generally acknowledged to have been Maria d'Aquino, the natural daughter of the King of Naples, who had absented herself from Naples where Boccaccio was then residing. *Il Filostrato* was designed to function as a love letter. This may have been an extraliterary reason for Boccaccio's amplification of the role of Pandarus. The purpose of the work was to seduce Maria (and cause her to return to Naples) as Pandarus helps to seduce Cressida.

Superficially, *Il Filostrato* appears to be a conventional tale of courtly love, and many familiar conceits associated with the tradition of courtly love are in evidence. The work opens in a courtly setting with the presentation of questions in a court of love. Love enters through the eyes in "the fair season." Cressida is described as being "so fair and so like an angel." Troilus is depicted as being ennobled by love; he becomes a more fierce and vigorous fighter against the Greeks because of the love bestowed upon him by Cressida. Troilus suffers (in this respect Boccaccio exceeds himself; he is supposedly basing his descriptions of anguish upon his own experience); he is pale, lacks appetite, loses sleep, becomes weak.

Boccaccio places particular emphasis on the courtly love doctrine of nobility as residing not in noble birth but in a noble heart. Since Boccaccio was a member of the bourgeoisie and was attempting to make his way in the royal court of Naples, this view was of personal interest. Nobility is depicted as based upon virtue, not power. Although of a lower social rank than Troilus, Cressida is considered worthy of his love because of her "proud and noble bearing . . . high worth and courtly speech . . . manner more courteous than those of other ladies."

Despite the presence of these traditional courtly love elements, other aspects of the tradition are contradicted within the poem. For example, the purpose of love is not ennoblement but satisfaction of Troilus' "hot desire." Cressida understands (as Boccaccio hoped Maria would understand) the true purpose of the courtship. She is outside the courtly love tradition, not merely for her later betrayal, but because of her easy seduction. The danger and barriers that confound the lover in a typical medieval romance are missing. Troilus, unlike the heroes of the medieval romances of Chrétien de Troyes, does not have to prove himself by submitting himself to constant danger. His love is unearned and too easily won. Troilus recognizes this when he states that "what I crave has not been earned by my service."

Boccaccio is not concerned with ennobling Troilus, however, but with telling of his passion. He wishes Maria to understand from the tale "how great and of what sort my desires are, what is their goal, and what beyond all else they crave." Like Troilus, Boccaccio is concerned with making his love known to his lady and drawing her to him. If his lady should fail to understand, he addresses her directly in the invocation to canto 3 and requests that she "refuse not my high desire; graciously grant that which I ask."

Not only is the noble purpose of courtly love lacking, but the moral lesson is as well. Boccaccio makes no distinction between earthly love and heavenly love. Boccaccio's salvation will come from his lady and not from heaven. The song of Troilus, dedicated to Venus, reinforces one's recognition that Boccaccio is not conflating earthly and heavenly love. He is not rejecting religious values; they merely have no place within the context of his work.

The lack of a palinode in *Il Filostrato* is thus not surprising. (The palinode was the recantation of earthly love and the reassertion of the supreme value of heavenly love found at the conclusion of many traditional medieval romances. Its purpose was to remind the reader that although courtly love may be supreme on this earth, heavenly love was always preferable. Courtly love was, therefore, generally placed within a framework of religious values.) Since Boccaccio's narrative is based solely upon worldly values, there is no need to recant. Boccaccio's only warning to the reader is presented, not as a moral lesson, but as a practical lesson, in keeping with the practical tone of his poem. He advises young men to place their love in ladies of true nobility, that is, ladies who will not betray them.

Although Boccaccio in *Il Filostrato* is utilizing the conventions of courtly love for a purely sensual end, this should not suggest that he could not write tales completely within a courtly tradition. One has only to turn to the fifth day of *The Decameron* to realize with what seriousness Boccaccio could write of courtly love. In *Il Filostrato*, however, Boccaccio can be seen as a transitional figure, already drawing away from the values of the Middle Ages, but not completely caught within the values of the Renaissance.

"Critical Evaluation" by Phyllis Mael

Bibliography:
Bergin, Thomas G. *Boccaccio*. New York: Viking Penguin, 1981. Devotes a chapter to *Il Filo-*

strato, summarizing the plot, examining the work's literary origins, and analyzing its themes. Notes the importance of the work to Chaucer's *Troilus and Criseyde*.

Boccaccio, Giovanni. *Il Filostrato*. Italian text edited by Vincenzo Pernicone, translated by Robert P. apRoberts and Anna Bruni-Seldis. New York: Garland, 1986. In a comprehensive introduction, the translators trace the history of the Troilus story, examine the autobiographical elements (including the now-discarded identifications of the woman to whom Boccaccio supposedly wrote his work), review Boccaccio's ideas about courtly love, and tell of the appearance of the story in English literature.

Dean, James. "Chaucer's *Troilus*, Boccaccio's *Filostrato*, and the Poetics of Closure." *Philological Quarterly* 64, no. 2 (Spring, 1985): 175-184. Examines the difference between the two versions of the tale, with particular attention to their endings. Concludes that Chaucer's tale is more philosophical.

Kearney, Milo, and Mimosa Schraer. "The Flaw in Troilus." *Chaucer Review* 22, no. 3 (1988): 185-191. Compares Chaucer's work to Boccaccio's, examining the scene in which Pandarus encourages Troilus to find other women if he cannot have Criseyde. Troilus' failure to defend his love exemplifies several situations in which Chaucer makes his hero more passive than Boccaccio's.

Serafini-Sauli, Judith Powers. *Giovanni Boccaccio*. Boston: Twayne, 1982. Examines *Il Filostrato* with reference to its use of courtly love, character development, and Griseida's betrayal of her lover.

FINAL PAYMENTS

Type of work: Novel
Author: Mary Gordon (1949-   )
Type of plot: Domestic realism
Time of plot: Early 1970's
Locale: New York
First published: 1977

> *Principal characters:*
> ISABEL MOORE, a thirty-year-old woman
> JOSEPH MOORE, Isabel's father and a devout Catholic
> ELEANOR, Isabel's best friend
> LIZ, Isabel's close friend
> MARGARET CASEY, the former housekeeper for Isabel and her father
> HUGH SLADE, Isabel's lover

The Story:

Isabel had been devotedly caring for her father, Joseph Moore, for eleven years until he died, believing that it was her penance for having betrayed him. When she was nineteen, he had found her in bed with his student, David Lowe. Three weeks later, he had suffered his first stroke. Many years earlier, the housekeeper, Margaret Casey, had wanted to marry Joseph Moore. Isabel, then thirteen years old, had jealously despised Margaret and had done what neither her authoritarian father nor their loyal parish priest, Father Mulcahy, would do—she had fired Margaret. When Isabel saw Margaret at her father's funeral, she felt the same revulsion she had felt sixteen years earlier.

Isabel and her two childhood friends, Eleanor and Liz, had maintained their friendships. All three women had given up Catholicism. With her new-found freedom and the support of her friends, Isabel rapidly began to change her life. She bought stylish, comfortable clothes with Eleanor; she spent a weekend in Ringkill with Liz, Liz's glamorous but oafish husband, John, and her children. Liz introduced Isabel to her beautiful, young lover, Erica. John, whom everyone, including his wife, knew to be a womanizer, offered Isabel her first job, a six-month pilot program involving home care for the aged. She gratefully accepted.

Isabel returned to Queens, sold her father's house, endured the painful insertion of an IUD, and moved upstate. She found her own apartment and began her job. At the first social gathering with her young colleagues, Isabel, out of anxiety, drank too much; after the party, she allowed John to have sex with her. Isabel craved affection but this left her feeling wrong, dirty, and out of control. Liz was angry with Isabel for having allowed John to seduce her and out of spite and curiosity she introduced Isabel to another married man, Hugh Slade, a cool rationalist who described Isabel's Catholic upbringing as "barbarous." Isabel decided that she would be Hugh's lover, although John continued to pursue her.

It was Isabel's job to visit private homes where elderly people received care and to judge the caretakers and the living conditions. She was often deeply moved by the individual stories she heard as she visited the homes, but they confirmed her belief that there was no way to control what makes people happy.

One day, on a hike with Hugh, Erica, and Liz, Isabel was quick to tire and became infuriated with the patronizing tolerance with which the others treated her. When she finally reached the end of the climb and Hugh told her for the first time that he loved her, she felt both the richness of the moment and the first foreboding that what she valued now was impossible to guarantee.

John continued to pursue her. Isabel had to fend off his advances by punching him in the eye. He left her alone after that, but not without threatening to pay her back. When Hugh came to eat a dinner she had lovingly prepared, he scolded her for living in filth when he found a moldy coffee cup in her living room. His words made Isabel realize that he could not be trusted with her new and shaky womanhood.

Some weeks later, Hugh told her he was considering leaving his wife, Cynthia. At a party Cynthia verbally accosted Isabel, calling her "the little bitch." John had maliciously told Cynthia a great deal about Isabel, and on the basis of that knowledge Cynthia knew exactly what to say to hurt Isabel, telling her she was selfish, perverted, and that she had been impatient for her father to die. Cynthia's words crumbled Isabel's illusions and all semblance of equilibrium. Completely distraught, she withdrew, believing she was utterly alone and inexorably guilty. She broke off her relationship with Hugh, telling him to return to Cynthia.

Out of an irrational need to stop causing others pain, to do penance, and to cast her life back in the role that was safe, Isabel went to take care of Margaret. Margaret treated her hatefully, but Isabel persevered. As she cooked and cleaned, she ate and gained weight, with her dress size increasing from ten to sixteen. When Margaret insisted, she had her long, lovely hair cut into a "bubble." Father Mulcahy's visit gave her an evening of respite, but when Margaret insulted him, Isabel finally saw that what she was doing in this ugly house with a mean-spirited woman was to try to give up all that she loved so as never to have to lose it.

Having realized this, Isabel could write to Hugh and ask him to wait for her while she healed and to call Eleanor to come for her. To free herself from Margaret, she had to make her final payment: She gave her all the money she possessed, the $20,000 she had received from the sale of her father's house. Eleanor and Liz came to get her late that night and, exhilarated and free, they drove off into the dawn.

Critical Evaluation:

Isabel's new life is an absolute transformation from the one in which her father and her father's bed had served as her center. She emerges as if from a cocoon after her years of all-consuming caregiving. She has lived on the perimeter of a decade, and her marginality makes her feel like a blundering outsider. Always having defined herself as her father's devoted daughter, it was impossible for her to be an adult as long as he was alive. With his death, she no longer has his authoritarian certitude of right and wrong, nor does she know how to define herself with only herself to go by. She therefore continues to look to others for self-definition and self-confirmation, a dependency that leaves her especially vulnerable.

Although Liz tries to persuade her that her past has nothing to do with her new life, Isabel knows that it has a great deal to do with it. Even though it may seem that she is starting fresh, she has brought demons with her into her present, especially her ineradicable feelings of guilt and self-condemnation. Her sexuality, on hold for eleven years, once again proves to uncenter her. She has long believed that her father's first stroke was caused by his discovery of David Lowe and her having sex. Her sexual encounters with John are unsatisfactory, yet her body wants to be warmed, filled, rested. Caught in this web of desire and guilt, she luxuriates in her passionate affair with Hugh but believes Cynthia's accusation that she is selfish and sick. When Isabel sees her sexual desire as a disease, she believes that the only way to protect herself against it is to bury herself in Margaret's house and overeat until she has hidden her beauty.

Isabel's inability to keep a clean, orderly house is another source of irrational guilt. When at thirteen she fired Margaret, she was completely unequipped to take on the responsibilities of housekeeping, and she never truly learned how to do so. When Hugh cruelly insists that he could never live with a woman "who could live in such filth," Isabel accepts his criticism as confirmation of her unwomanliness. She feels so much shame that she compares it to discovering the beginnings of a beard on her face. Overwhelmed, she is unable to control either the demands of her body or those of her home and at the same time unable to find order beneath the chaotic surface of everyday life.

Through her work and sifting through her past, Isabel comes to the conclusion that what everybody wants is "to be loved alone," but that most do not get that. When Hugh tells her that he loves her, she becomes aware not only of the impoverishment of her previous life but also of the danger of loss that love brings with it. As she waits for him to leave his wife, she realizes she has again made herself subject to a man's power; now her happiness depends on Hugh just as it had once depended on her father.

When confronted with Cynthia's condemnation, Isabel is powerless to offer an alternative interpretation. Instead, she is wrenched from the sanctuary that being the "good daughter" had offered. When Cynthia suggests she could not wait for her father to die, Isabel agrees and goes even further by holding herself accountable for his death. After that, it is only by devoting herself to Margaret that she can return to the safety offered her by the self-sacrificing role of caretaker, believing she will "get more, far more, by giving up life than by embracing it."

Yet in her despair and isolation in Margaret's home, Isabel begins to heal and to think that by giving reasonably of herself she might after all be able to have love, work, and friends. By the time she accepts that the greatest love also carries with it the greatest danger, she is no longer defeated; instead, she sees ways she might be able to receive refreshment and sustenance despite the danger of loss. She can see Margaret as an exhausted and frightened old woman whom she can help by giving her money. With self-understanding, a new-found courage and faith in human beings, and the nurturing loyalty of Liz and Eleanor, who ask nothing of her but that she be Isabel, she can go back into the miraculous though risky world of real and possible existences.

Janet Mason Ellerby

Bibliography:

Cooper-Clark, Diana. "An Interview with Mary Gordon." *Commonweal* 107 (May 9, 1980): 270-273. Gordon addresses *Final Payments* at length, discussing Isabel as one who sees everything in metaphors of Catholicism even though her path of self-identification is not a religious one. Gordon also discusses her debt to Virginia Woolf, about whom she was writing her dissertation while working on *Final Payments*.

Gordon, Mary. "More Catholic than the Pope: Archbishop Lefebvre and a Romance of the One True Church." *Harpers* 257 (July, 1978): 58-69. Gordon discusses her own Catholic up-bringing and her visit to the Society of St. Pius X, radically conservative followers of Archbishop Lefebvre. She writes of having sought "miracle, mystery, and authority" but finally being disillusioned.

Neary, John M. "Mary Gordon's *Final Payments:* A Romance of the One True Language." *Essays in Literature* 17 (Spring, 1990): 94-110. Neary focuses on Isabel's central crisis, which he sees as a realization that the human world cannot provide an absolute presence of God, of parent, or of an ordered world.

Schreiber, Le Anne. "A Talk with Mary Gordon." *The New York Times Book Review* 86 (February 15, 1981): 26-28. Gordon points out that a central issue for her is the phenomenon of women who could be very powerful in their own lives and in their outside accomplishments but instead buckle under the authority of men.

Ward, Susan. "In Search of 'Ordinary Human Happiness': Rebellion and Affirmation in Mary Gordon's Novels." In *Faith of a (Woman) Writer*, edited by Alice Kessler-Harris and William McBrien. New York: Greenwood, 1988. Ward addresses three themes that run through Gordon's work: Self-assertive, intelligent young women must rebel against any code they were raised to obey unthinkingly; fathers are often dominant influences and growing up must involve replacement and reconciliation with the father; and patriarchal institutions offer little hope to modern women.

THE FINANCIER

Type of work: Novel
Author: Theodore Dreiser (1871-1945)
Type of plot: Naturalism
Time of plot: c. 1850-1874
Locale: Philadelphia
First published: 1912; revised, 1927

> *Principal characters:*
> FRANK A. COWPERWOOD, the financier
> LILLIAN SEMPLE COWPERWOOD, his wife
> EDWARD BUTLER, a contractor and politician
> AILEEN BUTLER, his daughter
> HENRY COWPERWOOD, Frank's father

The Story:

From the time he was young, Frank Cowperwood was interested in only one thing—making money. When he was still in his teens, he made his first successful business transaction: Passing by an auction sale, he successfully bid for a lot of Java coffee, which he sold to a grocer at a profit of one hundred percent. His family marveled at Frank's ability, and his wealthy uncle, Seneca Davis, encouraged him to go into business as soon as possible. Through several well-paying positions and shrewd speculation, Frank acquired enough money to open his own brokerage house. Within a short time, he was one of the most enterprising and successful young financiers in Philadelphia.

One day he met Lillian Semple, the wife of a business associate. About a year later, her husband died, and Frank married the widow. By that time, he had accumulated a large fortune, and he was familiar with local and state politicians, among them Edward Butler, who had risen from being a garbage collector to a leading position in local politics. Through Butler, Frank met many other influential people, and his business and popularity increased.

Frank and Lillian had several children, but the youngsters did not particularly interest him, for his sole interest remained his business. When his father, Henry Cowperwood, finally became president of the bank in which he was employed, both Cowperwoods built expensive houses and furnished them luxuriously. Frank bought fine paintings and rare objects of art.

His home life was not satisfactory, since Lillian was older and more passive than he was; moreover, her beauty had almost disappeared. By contrast, Edward Butler's daughter Aileen was young, beautiful, and high-spirited. Frank fell in love with her, and she, in spite of her strong religious training, became his mistress. He rented a house where they met and furnished it with his paintings and statues.

Because Frank had become one of the financial powers in Philadelphia, he had to plan and scheme continually in order to thwart more powerful monopolists. He managed to acquire large sums from the state treasury through local politicians. The city treasurer, Stener, proved amenable in many ways, and he and Frank became involved in many shady transactions. Frank bought shares in railroads and local streetcar properties. After the great Chicago fire, some of Frank's investments were in a perilous state. He went to friends and associates and urged them to stand together in order to avoid losses. So widespread were the effects of the fire, however, that the manipulations of the city politicians were certain to be discovered on the eve of an election. Something had to be done to satisfy indignant reform groups who were sure to demand action when they discovered what had occurred.

In the meantime, someone had sent an anonymous note to Edward Butler, telling him that Frank and Aileen were living together. When Frank went to Butler and the contractor refused to help him, Frank knew that he must have discovered his relationship with Aileen. Butler became his enemy and urged the other politicians to make Frank the scapegoat for everyone's dishonest dealings.

As a result, Frank and Stener, the city treasurer, were indicted on charges of embezzlement and grand larceny and Frank was ruined financially. He pleaded not guilty, but the jury convicted both him and Stener. He appealed and posted bail to avoid jail, but the appeal was denied, although the judges were not united in their decision. As soon as the appeal was denied, the sheriff was supposed to take Frank to jail until sentencing, but Frank bribed the sheriff and had a few more days of freedom. His property was sold to pay his debts, and his father resigned his position at the bank.

Frank and Aileen had given up the house where they used to meet. Their meetings now took place at a house in another part of town. Determined to put an end to the affair, Butler and Pinkerton detectives entered the house and confronted the couple. Butler tried various schemes to make Aileen leave Philadelphia, but he was unsuccessful once Aileen learned that he had hired detectives to trail her.

Frank was sentenced to four years and nine months in the penitentiary. Aileen remained faithful to him. When Lillian went to visit him, Frank asked her for a divorce, but she refused.

After Edward Butler died, Frank's friends managed to get him a parole. At the end of thirteen months in jail, in March, 1873, he was freed. Through Wingate, a friend and business associate, he succeeded in rebuilding his business, and he kept a bachelor apartment where Aileen visited him. Though he was ostensibly still living with his wife, everyone had long ago learned of his relationship with Aileen.

In September, 1873, there was a panic. Frank, who had bought stocks cheaply, made a fortune. Several months later, he went with Aileen to Chicago, where he planned to reestablish himself. Lillian got a divorce but remained friendly with the Cowperwood family. She lived luxuriously, since Frank, to buy his own freedom, had provided handsomely for her and the children.

Critical Evaluation:

Two symbolic passages concerning sea predators, one early in the novel and one at the conclusion, provide important clues to understanding Theodore Dreiser's theme in *The Financier*. As a boy, Frank Cowperwood stoically observes an unequal contest in a large fish tank between a lobster and a squid. The lobster, certain of victory, bides his time and slowly devours the defenseless squid. In the context of Dreiser's social metaphor, the strong destroy the weak, whether with sudden terrible force or gradually and relentlessly, like the lobster. The final symbolic passage, crudely added as an epilogue to the novel, treats the *Mycteroperca bonaci* (or black grouper), which, chameleonlike, changes its colors to avoid danger or to strike out at a weaker adversary. From Dreiser's point of view, the black grouper represents an element of "subtlety, chicanery, trickery" that is also part of the human condition. The fish is no more responsible, in a Godless universe, for its trickery than humans are morally responsible for using deception as a means of power. In *The Titan* (1914), Dreiser continued the theme embodied in Cowperwood's rise to wealth and influence, an ascent that is determined by what the author understands as the laws of social Darwinism, as well as the theme of his socially conditioned fall from power. In *The Financier*, Dreiser details, with a naturalistic concern for inductive evidence, the causes both for Cowperwood's success and his eventual failure, just as a scientist might describe the behavior of a fish in an aquarium.

However, unlike a true scientist who observes phenomena objectively and dispassionately, Dreiser views the activities of his hero from the vantage point of his socialist philosophy. With that bias, the ruthless financier Cowperwood ought to serve as an object lesson on the corruption of the capitalistic system. Yet Dreiser, despite the Marxist determinism at the center of his economic philosophy, obviously admires Cowperwood as a man if not as a social creature. He sympathizes with his hero's single-minded ambition to succeed, his contempt for intellectual inferiors, his violent sexual passions, and his stubborn, egoistical will. Although Dreiser's early view of Cowperwood may have been satirical, he treats him ultimately as a Nietzschean superman, advanced beyond the conventional feelings of petty morality, beyond remorse, pity, or loyalty for anyone but Aileen Butler, whose iron will and courage match his own. Even in Cowperwood's love for Aileen there is, however, a measure of selfishness, for, quite simply, she satisfies his needs. Unlike many of the protagonists of Dreiser's other novels—among them Carrie Meeber, Jennie Gerhardt, Clyde Griffiths, Eugene Witla—Frank Cowperwood is a strong, magnetic, self-assured character, more the predatory lobster than the pitiful squid. Because Dreiser's attitude toward Cowperwood is ambivalent—he admires the man but is contemptuous of his capitalistic endeavors—the message of the novel is correspondingly ambiguous.

The Financier had other weaknesses, including a sometimes careless use of language. In the major scenes, however, Dreiser sustains a powerful, honest sense of realism. The author is at his best in analyzing Cowperwood's tangled love affair with Aileen. The trial scene is masterly, as are the prison scenes. Without sentimentality, Dreiser touches life. In spite of its ambiguous theme and some stylistic weaknesses, *The Financier* is a novel of massive integrity that continues to move readers.

Bibliography:

Dreiser, Theodore. *The Financier*. New York: New American Library, 1967. After publishing *The Financier* in 1912, Dreiser in 1927 published a revised, shortened version, to which Larzer Ziff wrote a new afterword.

Gerber, Philip L. *Theodore Dreiser Revisited*. New York: Twayne, 1992. This recently revised reference work contains background on Dreiser's life and novels. Includes a chapter on Dreiser's *Trilogy of Desire*, of which *The Financier* is the first volume.

Lingeman, Richard R. *An American Journey, 1908-1945*. Vol. 2 in *Theodore Dreiser*. New York: Putnam, 1986-1990. Provides biographical information and analyzes Dreiser's fiction. Includes bibliographical references and indexes.

Michaels, Walter Benn. *The Gold Standard and the Logic of Naturalism: American Literature at the Turn of the Century*. Berkeley: University of California Press, 1987. In a chapter titled "Dreiser's *Financier*: The Man of Business as a Man of Letters," Michaels argues that instead of attacking the excesses of the marketplace, as most critics have claimed, Dreiser and *The Financier* participate in and promote consumer capitalism.

Pizer, Donald. *The Novels of Theodore Dreiser: A Critical Study*. Minneapolis: University of Minnesota Press, 1976. Donald Pizer, a recognized authority on Dreiser and naturalism, offers both a solid reading of *The Financier* and important background information on the novel.

FINN CYCLE

Type of work: Poetry
Author: Unknown
Type of plot: Folklore
Time of plot: Third century
Locale: Ireland
First transcribed: Possibly eleventh century

Principal characters:
> FINN, the leader of the Fianna Erinn
> OISIN, Finn's son
> OSCAR, Oisin's son
> GOLL MAC MORNA,
> DERMOT,
> KEELTA, and
> CONAN THE BALD, Finn's men
> NIAM, Oisin's fairy mistress
> GRANIA, King Cormac's daughter

The Story:

Long ago in Ireland, Cumhal was the leader of the Fianna Erinn, the king's warriors. A rival clan in this group grew envious of Cumhal, took up arms against him, and slew him at the battle of Castleknock. Cumhal's wife, Murna, gave birth to a boy shortly thereafter. Fearing for the child's life now that Goll Mac Morna was in power, she gave him to two wise women to rear.

Under these two women, the child grew to be a handsome lad. He learned to run faster than the rabbit, to kill deer without hounds, and to bring down birds with his sling. One day, while roaming in the fields, he found a group of boys playing. He joined them, and it was soon obvious that he was a match for all of them. In envy, the boys tried to kill him, but he overcame seven of them and chased the rest home. From that day, he was called Finn, meaning the fair. His two nurses felt that because the warriors of the Morna clan would kill him if they found him, he must start off on his own.

Finn gathered a group of youths about him and began to seek adventure. His first exploit was to avenge a woman whose son had been killed by the lord of Luachar. Finn and his companions stormed the ramparts of the chieftain's castle, recovered jewels Cumhal had lost in battle, and slew the lord of Luachar and his men. Finn then returned the jewels to the old men who had fought with his dead father in battle.

Finn set out to learn wisdom and the art of poetry from the sage Finegas. While he was with the sage, he caught the salmon of wisdom and accidentally tasted it. Having learned wisdom and the art of poetry, Finn composed a song in praise of May and then set out to become the leader of the Fianna Erinn.

At that time, Conn was the ruler of Ireland. He held an annual banquet at which peace was declared among the various clans. When Finn entered the banquet hall, Conn asked him who he was. The king accepted him immediately because he was the son of an old friend. Soon Finn inquired whether he would become captain of the Fianna Erinn if he rid the royal town of the goblin that now haunted it. The king agreed, and Finn set out with a magic spear to slay the goblin. The goblin appeared with his magic harp and enchanted Finn with the music, but with the aid of his spear, Finn slew the spirit and returned victorious. Conn kept his word, and Finn was made captain of the Fianna Erinn. Faced with the choice of serving his clan enemy or leaving Ireland, Goll Mac Morna chose to serve Finn, and the rest of his men followed him.

Finn was a strong, generous, and wise captain who drew the best poets and warriors of Ireland around him. Oisin was his gallant son, one of the finest fighters and poets; Oscar, Oisin's son, was the fiercest fighter of the group; Goll Mac Morna was strong and loyal; Dermot of the Love Spot was the fair ladies' man of great endurance and agility; Keelta was another strong warrior and fine poet; Conan the Bald was full of trickery, gluttony, and sloth; and there was also Mac Luga, whom Finn instructed in the art of courtesy, and many other brave warriors. Finn was generous to all. It was necessary to pass extremely rigorous tests of strength, skill, poise, and poetic ability to enter the Fianna Erinn.

One day, Finn and his companions gave chase to a doe. The doe far outstripped everyone but Finn and his two hounds. When Finn reached the doe, he found his two hounds playing with her, and he gave orders that no one should hurt her. That night, Finn awakened to find a beautiful woman standing by his bed. She informed him that she had been changed into a deer by the Dark Druid because she had refused to give him her love and that Finn had restored her to her original form. Finn took her to live with him as his wife. After a few months of happiness, Finn was called away to fight the Northmen. Returning victorious, he found his new wife gone; the Dark Druid had come for her in the shape of Finn, and when she had rushed to greet him he had taken her away. For three days, Finn mourned before returning to his band. Seven years later, Finn found a brave young man fighting off a pack of hounds. On calling off the dogs and questioning the boy, Finn learned that this was the son he had had by his wife before the Dark Druid had come again and taken her away forever. Finn took his son and trained him to be a great warrior-poet.

Finn and his men were hunting one day, when the giantess Vivionn came seeking Finn's protection from a lover she had scorned. While she was talking, her lover appeared and thrust his spear into her breast. Finn and Goll stayed by the dying giantess, and the rest of the company set out after the giant. They chased him over hill and plain to the sea, where he escaped after they had gained his sword and shield. Returning, they found the giantess dead. They buried her and mourned her death.

Once when Finn and his companions were hunting, they saw an ugly, clumsy giant coming toward them with an equally ugly old nag. In an unmannerly way, the giant told Finn that he wanted to join his band, and Finn reluctantly agreed. Finn's companions turned the giant's horse out to pasture with the other horses, but it immediately began injuring them. Finn told one of his men to ride the nag to death. When the animal refused to move, thirteen men got on its back in jest. Seeing that they were making fun of him, the giant ran off in fury, and his nag followed with thirteen of Finn's men on its back. Finn and the rest of his men followed, but they were outdistanced when the giant and his nag crossed the ocean.

Finn thereupon outfitted himself and his men with a ship, food, and gold and set out across the sea in search of his missing men. At last, they came to a huge, slippery cliff. Because Dermot was the ablest, he was sent to investigate the land. Before long, Dermot came to a woodland pool where for three days he fought an armed warrior. On the third night, he dived into the pool with the warrior and found himself in a land of wonders. He was beaten by the men of this land and left for dead. Eventually, Dermot was awakened by a man who led him into a friendlier kingdom. There he was welcomed by the king, who himself had served in the Fianna Erinn under Finn. Meanwhile, Finn and his men had entered the underground kingdom by another route, and he and his warriors were reunited. They learned that they had been brought there to fight in the service of the underground king against the king of the Well and his allies. In battle, Finn and his men proved matchless. After winning the enemy king's daughter, Finn defeated the foe and restored peace to the land. Finn asked for no reward from the king, but when Conan made a jest, the king transported the band back to the Irish hills in the space of a second. The whole adventure seemed like a dream.

One day the old feud between Finn's clan and Goll's clan reawakened over a dispute about booty. A battle started in the hall, and blood was shed until Fergus, the minstrel, awoke and reminded them with his music of the dangers they had shared. So peace was restored.

For many years, Finn and his men passed their lives in adventures, hunts, and enchantments. There came a time, however, when the Fianna Erinn began to disintegrate, when Finn's men became dishonest and unruly, and when Finn lost his honor through treachery.

When Finn was an old man, he planned to marry Grania, daughter of the king of Ireland. Grania fell in love with Dermot, the ladies' man, however, and begged him to run away with her. Dermot was extremely reluctant to do so, but Grania bound him by the laws of Fian chivalry, and he was forced to abduct her on her wedding night. Finn jealously chased the pair over Ireland. At length, Dermot made peace with Finn. While Finn and Dermot were hunting one day, a boar fatally wounded Dermot. The only way to save Dermot was for Finn to bring him water. Remembering his hurt pride, Finn let the water fall, and Dermot died. The king of Ireland then ordered the Fianna Erinn to disband forever. The final blow to the company came at the battle of Gabhra, in which Oscar, Finn's grandson, was killed and the Fenians were all but wiped out.

Niam, a fairy princess, then came to take Oisin to an enchanted land where all wishes came true. She sang a magic song to him, and he bade farewell to his companions forever. In this land, Oisin could love, hunt, and fight without growing old. The time came, however, when he longed to return to Ireland to see his old companions. Niam tearfully let him go but warned him not to set foot on the soil. On returning to Ireland, he found a degenerate race that was both smaller and weaker than the lowliest men of his time. Impetuously, Oisin dismounted from his horse to help the weaklings move a stone, whereupon he immediately became an old man. He soon learned that his companions had been dead for three hundred years. Oisin was taken to Saint Patrick. At first, there was strong distrust between the two men, but gradually the saint grew to love Oisin's tales of the Fianna Erinn and he recorded them. Oisin, for his part, was baptized into the Church.

Critical Evaluation:

Finn Cycle, which is also known as the Fenian Cycle, is a series of ballad tales celebrating the deeds of Finn, a third century Irish hero, and his band of warriors. Their organization, known as the Fianna Erinn, fought and hunted under service to the king of Ireland, and the warriors enjoyed privilege and wealth. The tone of these ballad stories is romantic, and the stories show a delight in sensuous details and a deep feeling for the Irish countryside and glen. Finn himself stands out as a strong, courageous leader who inspired devotion in his men, but he is not without a touch of cunning and treachery. In many respects, he is like Robin Hood and King Arthur— a bold hero, capable leader, and tender lover. Like them, he witnesses the passing of his strength, the dissolution of his band, and the waning of a heroic era.

The audience for whom *Finn Cycle* was composed was naïve, socially young, and intellectually credulous, although it had a definite protocol and a certain dignified etiquette. This audience demanded stirring words from the storyteller, as well as a stimulating imagination. Although these tales were very popular in the eleventh and twelfth centuries, the stories of Finn,

Oisin, and the others had existed among the people for many centuries. A note of nostalgia for a past glory and a longing for a heroic period exist in the stories. There is perhaps a contrast between the old hierarchical society of the legends and the society telling them, a society facing a rapidly changing and hostile world. The old ballad system was breaking down by this time, and these tales were the beginnings of a new, popular literature in Ireland and Scotland. As the literature passed into the hands of the people, the versification became easier and the meters drastically simplified.

Most, although not all, of the ballads and prose of this period are concerned with Finn, the hero, and his war band, or fian (hence, the word "Fenian"). The original meaning of the word fian was "a driving, pursuing, hunting," but eventually it came to mean a band of warriors on the warpath. In a stricter sense, fian meant a band of roving warriors who had joined together for the purpose of making war on their own account. They were not, however, mere robbers or marauders. They were often men who had been expelled from their clan, landless men, the sons of kings who had quarreled with their fathers, or men who seized this way of avenging some private wrong. They were the only professional soldiers in Ireland in the old times, apart from mercenaries, who were often foreigners. For this reason the word fian was often used, especially in poetry, to refer to any war band. The various fianna were held together by discipline and had their own organization and customs; as is shown in *Finn Cycle*, men who wished to join the ranks had to pass a test of skill or bravery. The various fianna took their names from their leaders. From their roving life, adventures, and exploits, the various fianna and their chiefs naturally evolved into the early subjects of storytelling. Probably, many such stories and ballads have been lost.

In later times, the word fianna came to be used exclusively for the war band headed by Finn, or Mac Cumhal, as he came to be called, for the development of this legend overshadowed all the others. Even as late as the tenth century, however, Finn and his fianna were only one among several well-known similar bands. In popular imagination, the figure of Finn overpowered other heroes and attracted to itself, from century to century, exploits originally attributed to others. *Finn Cycle* absorbed much of the legendary lore of the older cycles, until all of Ireland held up Finn as the supreme heroic leader.

The popular imagination blended the tales and made them into the kind of legend the people needed and wanted. People were close to the earth and nature, and this is reflected in the tales of Finn, which refer to a time when wild woods were giving way to pasture and tillage and people no longer had reason to consider every wild cry of the night, to ponder each call of the birds and beasts. For Finn, the battles were only interruptions in the life of hunting. The ballads speak of his delight in the cackling of ducks, the bellowing of the oxen, and the whistle of the eagle. Many metaphors and allusions in the tales draw upon nature and animals, as when the women, sorrowing, feel sympathy for the wild birds and beasts that are like themselves.

Finn himself seems to transcend the world of which he is a part; certainly he is larger than his moment in history. When the Fianna are broken up at last after hundreds of years of hunting and fighting, it hardly seems that he dies. More likely, he comes back repeatedly in different shapes, and his son, Oisin, is made king over a divine country. In these tales, Finn is not so much an individual man as he is a force of nature, a part of the universe like the clouds or the gods that shape and reshape the clouds. Seer and poet, king and druid, Finn was a mortal who became immortal. He was a better fighter and hunter and infinitely wiser than any other mortal. Quiet in peace, the ballads say, but angry in battle, Finn was the perfect leader.

The men in the stories are warriors, men of action rather than thought. Their existence is devoted to love and companionship, and they can imagine no higher consideration. There is none of the philosophical worrying of Arthur and Merlin in these ballads. The men here do not speculate on eternity; they are sure of their simple values and fight to defend them. The brotherhood of the warrior is all. It is based on their hard and vigorous way of life and on their few necessary belongings; running through the ballads is a strong sense of material possession, of the things that people use to live. A feeling of the matter-of-factness of life colors the ballads and the attitudes of the characters.

The structure of *Finn Cycle* is loose and rambling, and it lacks the tightly woven pattern of the great epics. The many incidents that compose the cycle are a succession of detached episodes rather than a continuing story, such as that of the *Iliad* (c. 800 B.C.E.) or the legends of King Arthur. The people who imagined the cycle were unsophisticated and childlike and did not comprehend a large, encompassing design. Their stories wander without aim, each adventure independent of the previous one and the one that will follow. Cumulatively, however, the ballads of the cycle tell vividly of the heroic life, of the strength necessary to survive in a young and hard world, and of the codes of honor and companionship that make survival worthwhile.

"Critical Evaluation" by Bruce D. Reeves

Bibliography:
Gregory, Isabella Augusta. *Gods and Fighting Men*. 2d ed. Gerrard Cross, England: Colin Smythe, 1976. A reprint of Lady Gregory's 1904 retelling of Irish legends. Includes an introduction to the influence of Irish myth by W. B. Yeats and a preface. Most of the book represents stories from *Finn Cycle* with some explanation. Includes interesting notes.

Mac Cana, Proinsias. *Celtic Mythology*. New York: Peter Bedrick Books, 1985. An excellent introduction to Celtic mythology and *Finn Cycle*. A perfect source for beginners. Includes index.

Matthews, John. *Celtic Battle Heroes: Cuchulainn, Boadicea, Fionn MacCumhail, Macbeth*. Poole, Dorset, England: Firebird, 1988. An informative and accessible supplement that provides information on all essential elements of *Finn Cycle*. Examines the legend's thematic relation to contemporary ideas.

Rolleston, T. W. *Celtic Myths and Legends*. 1911. Reprint. New York: Dover Publications, 1990. An exhaustive study of Irish and Welsh myths within a historical, literary, and religious setting. A solid, often enjoyable retelling of the stories. Includes drawings, a copious index, and glossary.

Sutcliff, Rosemary. *The High Deeds of Finn Mac Cool*. New York: Dutton, 1967. An enjoyable retelling of the legends surrounding *Finn Cycle*. Drawings enhance the text. Includes an interesting introduction to the project.

FINNEGANS WAKE

Type of work: Novel
Author: James Joyce (1882-1941)
Type of plot: Fantasy
Time of plot: Early twentieth century
Locale: Chapelizod, Dublin, Ireland
First published: 1939

Principal characters:
> HUMPHREY CHIMPDEN EARWICKER, an innkeeper
> ANNA LIVIA PLURABELLE, his wife
> SHEM, their artistic son
> SHAUN, his philistine brother
> ISSY, their sister

The Story:
Finnegans Wake is an expression of the dreaming collective psyche as it relives the major conflicts of myth and history. This psyche is divided into the two sexual principles, the major representations of which are Humphrey Chimpden Earwicker (HCE) and Anna Livia Plurabelle (ALP). As the archetypal husband-father, HCE (Haveth Childers Everywhere/Here Comes Everybody) is burdened with guilt over an indiscretion in Dublin's Phoenix Park. This obscure event is central to the entire dream. A lone man encountered two girls and performed an obscure offense, an incident witnessed by three soldiers or boys, and news of it spread by the gossipy Four Old Men. The retellings through rumor, gossip, and popular song rendered everything about this Original Sin unreliable, except that it happened. Protesting his innocence, HCE goes to sleep. In his dreams, however, he encounters previous versions of his crime, which, encrusted with sexual and scatological innuendo, further cloud the precise nature of the offense.

News of this sin is carried throughout the dreambook of history through rumors and documents, lectures and arguments, accusations and recriminations. Interrogators appear in fours, accompanied by twelve bystanders: variously jurymen, apostles, mourners, and drinkers. As HCE is identified with the Dublin landscape—from Chapelizod to "Howth Castle and Environs"—his wife is the personification of the River Liffey (Livia) flowing through that landscape. She is the universal wife-mother, and like all the rivers of the world, constantly in flux.

The three soldiers and their familial equivalents, Shem and Shaun, represent the younger generation taking advantage of HCE's and ALP's age to displace them. Yet even while so doing, Shem and Shaun, the contrary twins, in their various manifestations, represent the contention between opposite character types: introvert and extrovert, artist and man of affairs, relativist and dogmatist. While Shem is an irresponsible bohemian and exile, Shaun is a dull, bourgeois hypocrite. Their sister Issy is the divisive ingenue of *Finnegans Wake*, in contrast with her mother, whose influence is unitive.

Finnegans Wake progresses through four books, following the structure of human history according to Giambattista Vico's theory in *Principi di scienza nuova d'intorno alla comune natura delle nazioni* (1744; *The New Science*, 1948), the four phases of theocratic, aristocratic, democratic, and anarchic, and thence through a *ricorso* to a new cycle. In the course of the nighttime of *Finnegans Wake*, the five principal "characters" undergo a series of metamorphoses as they pass through these four phases of history, representing the totality of indvidual and collective development. Through a vast exfoliation of such metamorphoses, James Joyce structures and populates his universe.

Thus while HCE the Protestant innkeeper is a current manifestation of the collective unconscious, the principle he represents appears in many other forms in the course of the night: Jarl van Hoother, Festy King, the Norwegian Captain, the Russian General, Persse O'Reilly, and Mr. Porter. As opposite aspects of Earwicker's personality, Shem and Shaun are sometimes identified (as Butt and Taff) but are usually at odds: as the Mookse and the Gripes, Chuff and Glugg, Kev and Dolph, the Ondt and the Gracehoper, Jaun and Dave, or Kevin and Jerry. In sum, these characters represent major thematic and structural principles, as, for example, in the argument between St. Patrick and the Archdruid Berkeley: whether reality is best described as white light (unity) or the spectrum of colors (diversity).

In broad outline, the first book (3-216), composed of eight chapters, corresponds to Vico's divine age. Dominated by the two parental figures, it represents the male and female cycles. First, the mythic Finnegan fell and was replaced by Earwicker. His primal transgression was enacted in the trial of Festy King. Meanwhile, following Earwicker's death, ALP entered the universe through the resurrection of her letter, and her sons Shem and Shaun engaged in a duel of wits. Sharing the responsibility for her husband's sins, ALP made her exit as the River Liffey diluted in Dublin Bay.

In book 2 (219-399) the children replace their parents, both in their heroic quest for knowledge and in their usurpation of their authority; they then reenact their transgressions. Thus, while ostensibly studying grammar, history, and mathematics, they are actually investigating their parents' identities and their relationships with them. Earwicker, having closed up the bar, falls asleep on the floor and in a dream concedes to his children under various personas: the Norwegian Captain, the Russian General, Fionn Mac Cool, and Roderic O'Conor. This disintegration of his psyche takes the form of the disagreement between the Four Old Men about the departing loveship of Tristram and Iseult.

The four chapters of book 3 (403-590) represent the future, civil age, and center on Shaun, Earwicker's heir. With HCE and ALP in bed at midnight, Shaun the Postman enters the dreamer's vision. Having heard the fable of the Ondt and the Gracehoper, Shaun attacks it and, claiming equal literary ability with Shem, denounces his father and vilifies his brother. Under a succession of personae (Jaun, Juan, Yawn), he degenerates until, tumbling into a barrel, he rolls backward down the river. Issy and all of Ireland mourn him, but his return is assured.

Book 4 (593-628), a recapitulation of the whole book, takes place in an instant between death and resurrection. As dawn approaches, the sleep of the Porter family (another manifestation of the archetypal family) is interrupted by the child Jerry's cry. As the new era begins, the newspapers tell of HCE's indiscretion, St. Kevin is seen meditating in his bathtub-altar, Muta and Juva watch the encounter between St. Patrick and the Archdruid, and ALP's letter is in the morning mail. Finally, Anna Livia soliloquizes resignedly as she flows out to sea.

Critical Evaluation:

Finnegans Wake sets out to render the collective unconsious in appropriate form and language. Thus, it encompasses all of human experience through the millennia in a cycle or recurring forms through a universal language, the language of dreams. To this end, it employs a language with simultaneous references to multiple tongues, expressing the major theme of the cyclical nature of history.

Thus, *Finnegans Wake* is not a novel with characters and plot, nor is it a narrative with mythic overtones. Earwicker and his family are perhaps best understood as contemporary, local instances of a great allegory. In reading *Finnegans Wake* readers confront the anxiety and confusion of their own dreams. No character exists as an independent, stable personality. Similarly, perspectives are continuously shifting between various aspects of the collective unconscious. Thus Earwicker is a kind of Everyman. He can be identified with all the characters to some extent, but whereas he can be called Adam in the biblical system, the Finn Mac Cool of Irish myth, the Tim Finnegan of popular song, or a concession to the bias of his living readers, his identity is most easily comprehended as the Chapelizod pubkeeper Earwicker.

The major themes of *Finnegans Wake* are death and resurrection, the Fall, guilt, family relations, generational conflict, sexual identity and desire—all marshaled under a quasi-Jungian concept of collective identity. Similarly, following Vico, Joyce presumes that all aspects of a culture—its government, religion, language, and other institutions—are related to one another and that all have a profound impact on the way that individuals within that culture view themselves and their world, since Joyce planned to portray his hero, Earwicker, as inseparable from the cultural matrix of his society. All the figures in this dream-vision are fluid composites involving an unconfined blur of myths and fictitious characters as well as nonhuman elements. This vision is structured in cyclic form, establishing intricate parallels between the broad patterns of historical development and the events and conflicts in the life of an ordinary Irish family. In *Finnegans Wake*, imagination subsumes the events it describes, radically destabilizing language, identity, and narrative. In these ways it constitutes a clear break with the mainstream of English literature.

Fifty years of attempts to explicate *Finnegans Wake* appear to confirm Joyce's prediction that the work would keep the professors busy for centuries. A general opinion among those who take the work seriously is that as a dreambook and a leading expression of the twentieth century worldview, it is indeterminate, untranslatable, irreducible. It is a work in which every single element has a function; it contains no nonsense yet is finally beyond explication. Critical analyses of *Finnegans Wake* have been either macrocosmic or microcosmic, emphasizing its overall design (by reference to Vico, dream theory, and other systems) or attempting to gloss particular passages (the Pranquean episode or the Encounter with the Cad, for example). Thus while *Finnegans Wake* is generally well understood, specialized studies from either of these perspectives continue to appear.

The apparent impenetrability of *Finnegans Wake* is an essential aspect of its intention: to give adequate shape to the sleeping experience. Thus although it stands up to literal scrutiny, it should not be read in a literal-minded way. Wordplay in *Finnegans Wake* is multilingual, etymological, associative, and acoustic. Therefore it is best read aloud, and in an open-minded way, the inferences shared and sifted among a group of simultaneous readers. This helps each reader best appreciate the "collideorscape" of its language, figures, moods, and themes, preventing any single reading from becoming unduly dominant.

Finnegans Wake is a virtuoso production: Drawing on more than thirty languages, it has a cast of hundreds from every phase of world history and digests an encyclopedia of information. It is a book of many moods, of many degrees of opacity, a book of many exits and entrances. Some sections are relatively clear set pieces, such as the portrait of Shem (169-170) or the fable of the Ondt and the Gracehoper (414-419)—immediately delightful to the new reader. Others, such as the opening chapter, are extremely dense and daunting to first-time readers. Yet others are poetic prose of supreme beauty, notably ALP's departure (212-216), which was made available in an audio recording of its author's own voice.

Finnegans Wake is Joyce's most ambitious literary endeavor. Within the narrow confines of immediate family relations he aimed to encompass all human experience, mythic and historical. Drawing on the traditions of intellectual and popular culture, he forged a literary language that was both highminded and lowbrow. He anticipated, yet underestimated, the difficulties his readers would encounter and was disappointed that so many of those who acclaimed *A Portrait of the Artist as a Young Man* (1916) and *Ulysses* (1922) as supreme expressions of modernity were unprepared to pursue his explorations to the limits of language in *Finnegans Wake*.

Cóilín D. Owens

Bibliography:
Bishop, John. *Joyce's Book of the Dark: "Finnegans Wake."* Madison: University of Wisconsin Press, 1986. Joyce's determination to represent noctural experience accounts for the form, shape, direction, and language of *Finnegans Wake*. Relates *Finnegans Wake* to dream theory and interpretation, thanatology, optics and phonetics, embryology and gender, sexuality and power.
Ellmann, Richard. *James Joyce*. Rev. ed. New York: Oxford University Press, 1982. Elegant and authoritative biography providing valuable information on the writing of *Finnegans Wake*, Joyce's intentions, his methods, and the difficulties he encountered.
McCarthy, Patrick A, ed. *Critical Essays on James Joyce's "Finnegans Wake."* New York: G. K. Hall, 1992. Twenty essays surveying past criticism and broad concerns: studies of structure, voice, narration, language, and interpretation, analyses of important themes, and readings of passages in ways that pose crucial questions about *Finnegans Wake* as a whole. Shows how enjoyable an experience reading *Finnegans Wake* is.
McHugh, Roland. *Annotations to "Finnegans Wake."* Rev. ed. Baltimore: The Johns Hopkins University Press, 1991. A line-by-line explication of foreign words, English overtones, place names, personal names, phrases parodied, song titles and quotations, literary sources, historical events. Basic reference tool, designed to be consulted in tandem with a reading of *Finnegans Wake*.
Rose, Danis, and John O'Hanlon. *Understanding "Finnegans Wake": A Guide to the Narrative of James Joyce's Masterpiece*. New York: Garland, 1982. A section-by-section synopsis of *Finnegans Wake*. Very useful companion for the beginning reader, it clarifies the main techniques and themes in the form of a running commentary.

THE FIRE NEXT TIME

Type of work: Essays
Author: James Baldwin (1924-1987)
First published: 1963

James Baldwin's *The Fire Next Time*, according to writer William Styron, is "one of the great documents of the twentieth century." It articulates the anger, frustration, and hope felt by African Americans during the 1960's. The two essays composing this work were published in 1963, selling over one million copies, making Baldwin—according to *The New York Times*—the widest read African American writer of his time. The book is Baldwin's response to the social and racial injustice he witnessed in America. Having lived in Europe for almost twenty years, Baldwin felt compelled to return to America to participate in the Civil Rights movement. He offered *The Fire Next Time* as "a kind of plea" because "we, the black and the white, deeply need each other here if we are really to become a nation."

The first short essay, "My Dungeon Shook: Letter to My Nephew on the One Hundredth Anniversary of the Emancipation," is Baldwin's diagnosis of America's racism as well as his prescription for his young nephew's survival in such a diseased society. As a man who has seen America at its worst, Baldwin warns his nephew of the dangers threatening a young black man. He also offers him a challenge: to be a catalyst of change. Baldwin contends that the fates of black and white Americans are inextricably intertwined, that for America to fulfill its promise, both must acknowledge the need for the other. White America holds fast to ideals that are not actually practiced. This failure to practice its ideals is proven in its steadfast denial of the value of black lives. Baldwin tells his nephew that American society has narrowly circumscribed his world so that his dreams will never move beyond the street corner of the Harlem ghetto.

Baldwin offers hope to all African Americans, but it comes with great responsibility. He maintains that because white America insists on its innocence, on the ideal image it has created of itself, it cannot initiate change. Baldwin observes that "these innocent people have no other hope. They are, in effect, still trapped in a history which they do not understand; and until they understand it, they cannot be released from it." African Americans must force white America to examine itself. African Americans, Baldwin predicts, "can make America what America must become." Neither white America nor black America, however, can find freedom or justice apart from each other. Their fates are necessarily and inextricably connected.

The second much longer and more substantial essay, "Down at the Cross: Letter from a Region in My Mind," can be divided into three sections. The first discusses Baldwin's growing up in the Harlem ghetto and the influences that led to his involvement in the church. The second is a reflection on the black nationalism (advocated by the Black Muslims) occasioned by Baldwin's meeting with Elijah Muhammad of the Nation of Islam. The third part proposes as much of a solution to the racial conflict existing in America as Baldwin can offer.

James Baldwin tells the story of his childhood in his autobiographical novel, *Go Tell It on the Mountain* (1953), and in his famous essay, "Notes of a Native Son" (1955). The additional account in *The Fire Next Time* proves an argumentative point—that the racism experienced daily by African Americans is overwhelming and devastating. Baldwin describes the overwhelming fear that permeated his life from his earliest memory, a fear affecting every aspect of his life. He reports that every black child is raised not only to fear his parents' punishment, but also white people's judging his every word and action. He sees the terror in his parents' eyes lest he should say or do something in the presence of white people that could lead to his demise.

Baldwin's own dreams of finishing high school and becoming a writer drew down the wrath of his father. Better to beat such dangerous aspirations from the child early than to have him beaten or killed in the hostile white world.

In the ghetto, a child had to have a gimmick, Baldwin claims, a method that would save him from the constant humiliation that was his life. The street's alcohol, drugs, and sex offered one kind of escape—a carnal seduction. The church held out to him a "spiritual seduction." The woman minister who led him to his salvation asked fourteen-year-old Baldwin, "Whose little boy are you?" It was a question asked of him everyday on the street by pimps, pushers, and prostitutes. He wanted to be someone's little boy; he wanted to escape the sense of alienation and self-hatred that had been a condition of his life from his earliest memory. The church spoke to that state. For three years, Baldwin was a boy preacher. He soon became disillusioned. The church was a human institution, and he came to recognize its flaws. He saw the church as theater and himself as a mere performer able to work the congregation for an emotional or financial response. His "redemption" did not alleviate his sense of self-loathing. Christ could not change the color of his skin.

His experience in the church, however, led Baldwin to further revelation: Despite its claims of love, hope, and charity, the church's fundamental principles were "Blindness, Loneliness, and Terror." After a year in the pulpit, Baldwin realized that he was preaching a gospel written by white men and that their revelation could not change the basic fact of his life and the cause of his sense of worthlessness and alienation: his blackness. He also came to see that "there was no love in the church. It was a mask for hatred and self-hatred and despair." The loving kindness of Christ's words, it seemed, applied only to those who believed as the church members did and to white people not at all. Baldwin came to question his salvation and the love of God if it did not permit him to love others, including white people. He concludes the first section of this essay with the observation, "If the concept of God has any validity or any use, it can only be to make us larger, freer, and more loving. If God cannot do this, then it is time we get rid of Him." James Baldwin left the church. In the 1960's, many African Americans sought answers from another source—the Nation of Islam.

The second part of "Down at the Cross" examines the appeal for African Americans of the Nation of Islam. Baldwin himself was never attracted to Muslim teaching. Police inaction in protecting black people and the radical life changes in the followers of Islam, however, prompted Baldwin's curiosity. He found in Elijah Muhammad a quiet but confident man who offered his young followers an explanation for and an alternative to the society that rejected them. Baldwin asserts that the times were ripe for the Muslim message. World War II convinced African Americans that white Christian culture had nothing to offer them. The Third Reich, emblematic of white Christian "civilization," may have shocked the world, but it did not surprise African Americans, who had long known the cruelty and the inhumanity of which white Christians are capable. Germany's actions only confirmed what they had experienced, in the United States and elsewhere, for hundreds of years. Returning "home" after risking their lives in defense of their country, black soldiers faced a segregated society that had treated German prisoners of war with more respect than it did its own black citizens. They found in foreign countries more acceptance than they did in their own homeland. A white God and Christianity was proven void; Allah and Islam provided another alternative.

Baldwin identifies some key ideas promoted by the Nation of Islam. First, Elijah Muhammad claims that all white men are devils, that they were the results of experiments by black scientists thousands of years ago, and that their period of dominance is now over. There is simply "no virtue in white people." Second, he offers an explanation of black people and culture that obviates white culture altogether. Third, Elijah Muhammad gives African Americans hope in proposing a separate black American nation with its own separate economy that is independent of white sources of wealth and in which black people will own land. Finally, Islam replaces the white God with a black one. Baldwin writes, "The white God has not delivered them; perhaps the Black God will."

Baldwin's critique of the Nation of Islam is uncompromising: just as white America cannot change until it acknowledges and embraces black America, black America cannot change until it acknowledges the fact that it has been shaped and formed by white America. Both black and white Americans, Baldwin insists, need each other if they are ever to come to terms with themselves. Baldwin states that Black Muslims have invented a past that helps them to explain the suffering and the humiliation African Americans have had to endure at the hands of the white people. Conversely, white Americans have held onto their notions of "innocence" and their American Dream, neither of which accurately describes real life. African Americans must face the fact that their identities have been formed in America, not Africa. They must accept their true past, he insists, not invent a more favorable one.

In the final section of the essay, Baldwin proffers an answer to the radical conflict dividing America. Literary critic Nick Aaron Ford has remarked that *The Fire Next Time* "offers no new solutions to the problem of race relations in America. Indeed, its basic solution is as old as the Holy Bible and as simple as the Sermon on the Mount." Baldwin insists that there will be no progress in this nation without radical social and political change. In his now famous conclusion, he prescribes what must be done to heal the racial rift in the country:

> If we—and now I mean the relatively conscious whites and the relatively conscious blacks, who must, like lovers, insist on, or create, the consciousness of the others—do not falter in our duty now, we may be able, handful that we are, to end the racial nightmare, and achieve our country, and change the history of the world. If we do not now dare everything, the fulfillment of that prophecy, re-created from the Bible in song by a slave, is upon us: *God gave Noah the rainbow sign, No more water, the fire next time!*

With the publication of this book, Baldwin became—as African American literary critic Henry Louis Gates, Jr., states—"exalted as *the* voice of black America. . . . Perhaps not since Booker T. Washington had one man been taken to embody the voice of 'the Negro.'" It was a voice heeded by both black and white America. *The Fire Next Time* was the text to which America listened.

Laura Weiss Zlogar

Bibliography:
Baraka, Amiri. "Jimmy! (Eulogy for James Baldwin, 1987)." *The LeRoi Jones/Amiri Baraka Reader*. Edited by William J. Harris. New York: Thunder's Mouth Press, 1991. Delivered on December 8, 1987, Baraka's eulogy praises Baldwin's contributions to the Civil Rights movement and to African American aesthetics.
Gates, Henry Louis, Jr. "The Fire Last Time." *The New Republic* 206 (June, 1992): 37-43. An insightful reflection on the career and reputation of James Baldwin, the important role he played during the 1950's and 1960's as spokesperson of the Civil Rights movement, and the critical disfavor he experienced during the 1970's and 1980's.
Gibson, Donald B., ed. *Five Black Writers: Essays on Wright, Ellison, Baldwin, Hughes, and LeRoi Jones*. New York: New York University Press, 1970. Includes four essays on the works of Baldwin.

Standley, Fred L., and Nancy V. Burt. *Critical Essays on James Baldwin*. Boston: G. K. Hall, 1988. A collection of essays on the major works of James Baldwin. Included are a review of *The Fire Next Time* and an essay on Baldwin and the 1960's.

Thorsen, Karen, dir. *James Baldwin: The Price of the Ticket*. San Francisco: California Newsreel, 1989. An excellent videotape on the life and career of James Baldwin. Included are interviews with family members, friends, writers, and critics. Provides a thorough understanding of Baldwin's literary and political contributions.

THE FIREBUGS
A Learning-Play Without a Lesson

Type of work: Drama
Author: Max Frisch (1911-1991)
Type of plot: Absurdist
Time of plot: Post-World War II
Locale: House of Gottlieb Biedermann, in an unidentified city
First performed: Biedermann und die Brandstifter, 1953, as a radio play; first published,
  1958 (English translation, 1959)

Principal characters:
GOTTLIEB BIEDERMANN, a manufacturer of hair tonic
BABETTE, his wife
ANNA, their maidservant
SEPP SCHMITZ, a wrestler
WILLI EISENRING, a waiter
MRS. KNECHTLING, widow to Biedermann's former employee
PH.D., a professor
POLICEMAN
CHORUS OF FIREMEN

The Story:

Gottlieb Biedermann, a businessman, while on his way home, lit a cigar and witnessed the Chorus of Fireman setting their watch. Afterward, at home, seated in his living room, reading the newspaper, Biedermann vented his disgust with the arsonists plaguing his city, convinced that they should all be hanged. He was interrupted by Anna, his servant, who informed him that a peddler waited to see him. Biedermann told her to get rid of the man, but the intruder entered unbidden, identifying himself as Sepp Schmitz, a circus wrestler. The astonished Biedermann, nonplussed by the stranger's sudden appearance, invited the ingratiating Schmitz to have some bread, which the visitor managed to parlay into a substantial snack through flattery and self-deprecation mixed with quiet but insistent demands. Their discussion was briefly interrupted when Herr Knechtling, a former employee released by Biedermann, came to the door seeking an audience. His request outraged Biedermann, who directed Anna to send him away. He then took Sepp to his attic, where the visitor was invited to stay on the condition that he swear that he was not an arsonist—one of the firebugs. Sepp only laughed, but Biedermann, satisfied, permitted Schmitz to stay.

The next morning, after Biedermann's wife, Babette, had spent a troubled night, fearful that there might be a firebug in the attic, Biedermann introduced her to Schmitz before leaving for work. Although Babette was determined to send the wrestler away, she fed him breakfast while searching for a tactful way of doing so. Sepp played on her kindness, preparing her to receive the next suspicious guest, Willi Eisenring, an unemployed waiter. The next day, Biedermann, set on throwing both men out, went to his attic, where Schmitz and Eisenring had just finished stacking up some large drums. Biedermann's anger was soothed by Willi, who admonished Sepp for his lack of manners and insensitivity to Biedermann's feelings. Biedermann spotted the drums and became alarmed. The labels clearly revealed their contents:

gasoline. He then threatened to call the police, but a policeman had already arrived to tell Biedermann that Herr Knechtling had committed suicide the previous night. Oddly, when the policeman asked what was in the drums, Biedermann told him it was only Hormotone, the hair tonic made by Biedermann's firm. After justifying his behavior to the Chorus of Firemen, arguing that one had to maintain trust in people, Biedermann explained to Babette that even if the two men were firebugs, it was best to treat them as friends. He then told her to include them for dinner.

Somewhat later, in the attic, Eisenring explained to the increasingly officious Biedermann that Sepp was out on an errand, looking for sawdust to help spread the fire. He also explained that he was a former prisoner and told Biedermann that he was looking for a detonator cap. Biedermann took these bald admissions as a joke, and Eisenring confirmed that a joke was a good camouflage but that the truth was even better. He then tactfully advised Biedermann to extinguish his cigar and asked him to help wire the detonator and fuse. Unshaken, Biedermann revealed that he had come to invite Eisenring and Schmitz to dinner. After Biedermann left, Eisenring told the professor, a Ph.D., to come out from the pile of gasoline drums, to keep guard while he and Sepp went to the dinner. The Professor tried to warn Babette about the arsonists, but Babette, who accepted Biedermann's idea that they should not offend Eisenring and Schmitz, did nothing.

Before the dinner, Biedermann directed Anna to remove the table finery she had laid out. Then, after a funerary wreath was delivered that mistakenly identified Biedermann rather than Knechtling as the deceased, Biedermann left the room with instructions to Anna that she should also dress simply and not serve in a formal fashion. When Eisenring and Schmitz entered, Anna left the two men alone. In their talk, they realized that, after dinner, they would have to ask Biedermann for matches. The dinner proved a disaster. It began in laughter, with Biedermann explaining Willi's "joke" that oil waste was a better incendiary than sawdust and upbraiding Babette for her lack of humor. As the fine food and excessive quantities of good wine were consumed, Eisenring and Schmitz admitted that they had a taste for expensive things, despite their humble backgrounds. They even mentioned specific items, like damask tablecloths, good crystal, finger bowls, and knife rests. Biedermann then ordered Anna to bring back the elegant tableware that he earlier had ordered her to remove, including the damask tablecloth and a silver candelabra. Eisenring next told how the restaurant where he worked had burned to the ground and how he had met Schmitz at the station where the police had taken him after his arrest. Schmitz then explained that he had briefly been an actor, specializing in ghosts, and began acting out a parody of the morality play *Everyman*, drawing Biedermann into the title role. The spoof abruptly ended when Schmitz identified his part as the ghost of Knechtling, causing Babette to scream. Seemingly drunk, the two men started singing, and were joined by Biedermann, who also handed out cigars. Then, while fire sirens wailed in the distance, the two men confessed that they were firebugs and that they had to leave. Biedermann, still unwilling to face the truth, tried to mollify the pair with a final toast to their friendship. They begged matches of him, then left.

As the sky began turning an ominous red, the Professor entered to tell the Biedermanns that although he had known what the firebugs were up to in the attic, he had not known that they were doing it simply for fun. He then exited, and Babette asked Biedermann what he had given Schmitz and Eisenring. He admitted that he had given them matches, then attempted to allay her concern with the argument that if they had been firebugs, they surely would have had their own. At the end, the Chorus of Firemen lamented the burning of the gas works as the sounds of explosions and crashing buildings announced the imminent destruction of the whole city.

Critical Evaluation:

Biedermann und die Brandstifter, variously translated from the German as *Biedermann and the Firebugs, Biedermann and the Fire Raisers*, or simply *The Firebugs*, bears the subtitle *A Learning-Play Without a Lesson*. It is easy to interpret as a modern allegory or parable, with a lesson. In a general sense, it seems aimed at people's irredeemable folly, their perverse tendency to act contrary to what is clearly in their own best interest. Barbara Tuchman has shown in *The March of Folly* (1984) that history offers plenty of examples of incredible wrongheadedness; people do not seem able to learn from past mistakes. For Max Frisch, the political appeasements that led to the pre-World War II rise of Nazism and postwar takeover of Czechoslovakia by communists were the specific political analogues, but his allegory, a secular morality play, is really timeless.

The long one-act play utilizes techniques that help convey a sense of that timelessness. Although the setting is modern, the action is not localized to any specific time or place. As with many absurdist plays, there is only a metaphysical present, a now, as opposed to a past or future. The details about things mentioned or used in the play are all generic, found everywhere, and, therefore, nowhere in particular. Biedermann is himself a kind of Everyman, with whom, during the play, he is specifically identified. He exhibits, too, the "empty good-naturedness" that, according to Martin Esslin, prevents the absurd antihero from distinguishing what is of value from what is not. His decency is tragically misplaced.

Frisch, who denounced the absurdist playwrights as purveyors of nonsense, is not interested in metaphysical conundrums. Unlike most of the plays of absurdist playwrights (those of Samuel Beckett and Eugène Ionesco, for example), *The Firebugs* is very transparent and logical. Biedermann's kind and deferential treatment of Schmitz and Eisenring can be interpreted as displaced guilt, a kind of compensation for his wretched treatment of his former, loyal employee, Herr Knechtling. His guilt is clearly what the firebugs trade on, as Eisenring confirms when, in scene iv, he and Schmitz stack up the cans of gasoline. He tells Schmitz, worried that Biedermann might call the police, not to fear, for "above a certain income every citizen is guilty one way or another." Thus, as obtuse as Biedermann seems to be, his behavior is psychologically validated.

The Firebugs has a causal pattern and a logic of structure that most classic examples of absurdist drama deliberately lack. When there is such a pattern, as in Ionesco's *Rhinoceros*, the work, like *The Firebugs*, usually lends itself to interpretation as an existential parable. The focus may be on some personal choice the protagonist has to make in a world devoid of moral certainty or purpose. In Frisch's play, the firebugs triumph over the shallow and short-sighted decency of Biedermann not so much because he lacks a moral rudder as because they lack all principle. As the professor explains, they are anarchists for fun, and their violence against the city is gratuitous and wholly senseless.

If not purely absurdist, *The Firebugs* is also a far cry from realism. It uses devices atypical of problem plays written from Ibsen forward. For example, it employs a chorus, whose lyrics, like the choric odes of Greek tragedy, have antiphonal exchanges between the leader and the rest of the chorus, in this case the firemen. In scene vii, Frisch has Biedermann address the audience directly, asking its advice as to how he should proceed. That is, of course, a common device used to shatter the conventional, invisible fourth wall of realistic theater.

Finally, *The Firebugs* has the pronounced tragicomic, farcical tone of much absurdist drama. There is, for example, the grimly comic appearance of the memorial wreath, sent to the Biedermanns' house, with Biedermann's name on it, identified as the deceased. There is also a sense of angst, of apprehension, and a skewing of common sense. In general, too, the characters' speeches have some of the inane and mechanical features of Ionesco's dialogue. Language proves ineffectual, vacuous, pointless. Thus, given the anarchistic and insane world of the firebugs, language, reason, and human decency are completely inadequate tools of survival. That is a terrible, darkly comic conclusion that Frisch and the absurdists seem to share.

John W. Fiero

Bibliography:
Butler, Michael. *The Plays of Max Frisch.* New York: St. Martin's Press, 1985. Most readable and succinct English introduction to Frisch's plays, recommended for further study. Discusses *The Firebugs* as a parable play and analyzes its language, using translated passages in German.
Pickar, Gertrud B. *The Dramatic Works of Max Frisch.* Frankfurt, Germany: Lang, 1977. The most comprehensive and insightful English-language study of Frisch's dramatic canon.
Probst, Gerhard F., and Jay E. Bodine, eds. *Perspectives on Max Frisch.* Lexington: University Press of Kentucky, 1982. A sampling of critical articles, including "The Drama of Frisch" by Manfred Jurgensen. Extensive international bibliography.
Subiotto, Arrigo. "The Swiss Contribution." In *The German Theatre: A Symposium,* edited by Ronald Hayman. New York: Barnes & Noble Books, 1975. Relates the dramatic works of Frisch and Friedrich Dürrenmatt to the larger framework of modern German theater and post-World War II European politics.
Weisstein, Ulrich. *Max Frisch.* New York: Twayne, 1967. A useful critical biography with a chronology and guide to selected sources. Contrasts *The Firebugs* with absurdist drama.

FIRST POETIC WORKS and NEW POETIC WORKS

Type of work: Poetry
Author: Alfred de Musset (1810-1857)
First published: Poésies nouvelles, 1840; *Premières poésies*, 1840; definitive edition, 1852
   (English translation, 1905)

In 1852, the whole body of Alfred de Musset's poetry was gathered into two volumes and published as the *First Poetic Works* and *New Poetic Works*. The first volume is made up of *Romances of Spain and Italy* (1829) and *A Show from an Easy Chair* (1833). The second collection contains pieces written after 1833. It is worth recalling that by 1840, when the poet was thirty years old, Musset's creative talents were virtually exhausted. A complete explanation of this premature exhaustion should not be sought in the character of Musset's poetic doctrine. However, in the light of Musset's stated belief that the greatness of verse was commensurate with the magnitude of the poet's suffering, the intensity of his emotion, it will be readily understood that his creative talent was likely to fade relatively early.

Only a handful of people turned up for Musset's funeral in 1857. This seems remarkable now, in the light of Musset's continuing popular appeal both as poet and dramatist. It is all the more remarkable in view of the enthusiastic welcome given him by the members of the Romantic *Cénacle* when he first joined the group in 1828. His precocious poetic talent and dazzling wit could not, and did not, fail to impress its members.

Musset's *Romances of Spain and Italy* was written after the first collected works of Victor Hugo had become available. Just as it is of little moment that Victor Hugo's *Poems of the Orient* (1829) was inspired by his watching the sun set over Paris, so it matters little that when Musset's collection first appeared, he was not familiar with either Spain or Italy. The brightness and color of these countries, remembered or imagined, appealed to the young Romantics seeking a vivid contrast with the drabness of France in their day; a rich backcloth in front of which intense passion could be appropriately represented.

The poems for which Musset is best known are the series of four "Nights": "The Night of May," "The Night of December," "The Night of August," and "The Night of October." All four relate directly to his turbulent, unhappy love affair with the novelist George Sand. Although it is easy to exaggerate the effect of this liaison on Musset, it does seem certain that he was deeply marked by it and that subsequent affairs even served to remind him of it.

The four "Nights" contain some of the finest lyrical passages that may be found in French verse. They take the dramatic form of dialogues between the poet and his Muse, with the latter acting as a confidante who listens, advises, and consoles.

In "The Night of May," the Spring Muse vainly begs the poet to give form to his suffering in a work of art; by so doing, he will be participating in the rites of creation and eternal renewal taking place around him. At first, the poet thinks he is only imagining the voice of the Muse, but little by little it grows louder and more urgent, and he clearly makes out the words "Poet, take thy lute." The Muse despairs of banishing the poet's indolence, after insisting, however, that his very unhappiness would have been a guarantee of the beauty of his verse: "The most desperate songs are the most beautiful;/ I know some immortal ones that are pure sobs." The poet breaks his silence to claim that the weight of his grief is such that no form of expression could bear it:

> But I have suffered a hard martyrdom
> And the least I might say about it,

> Were I to try it on my lute,
> Would break it like a reed . . .

"The Night of December" presents, beside the poet, a mysterious companion who follows him through all the stages of his life. This brother reveals himself to be the image of loneliness. In "The Night of August" a happier note is struck, for the work is a hymn of praise to the forces of life that allow human beings to recover from the setbacks in life. However, "The Night of October" contains a return to anguish for the poet. He knows once more wrath and despair; he realizes that he has not in fact recovered from his unhappy love affair.

In his series of "Nights," Musset seems to have moved away from the mainstream of the nineteenth century Romantic movement. Yet in doing so, he renews contact with some of the resources of Romanticism in its ageless aspects. For here the poet places himself at the center of his poetic meditation and, in representing himself as sincerely and directly as possible, admits the reader to a position of privileged intimacy. The reader feels in sympathy with the poet. Musset's sincere, lyrical laying bare of the emotions in the form of confidential poetry was to be imitated frequently in the course of the nineteenth century.

The emotion that recurs most frequently in Musset's verse is love, which is generally associated with suffering and a form of regret. A partial explanation of Musset's considerable popularity may doubtless be sought in the lucidity with which he was able to analyze his sufferings and their causes. It is this lucidity and the regret that it provokes that make Musset's unhappiness especially poignant. One of the most moving illustrations of this sincere self-analysis, from which all trace of oratory or rhetoric is excluded, may be found in the short piece entitled "Sadness." This sonnet, collected in the *New Poetic Works*, was written in June, 1840. It is a confession of failure in life: a loss of pride, a wasting of energy, and a sense of shame about the whole situation:

> I have wasted my strength and my life,
> I have lost my friends, my gaiety;
> I have even lost my pride
> Which gave confidence in my genius.

The simplicity of the language, its power to suggest the repentance of the sinner, reminds the reader of similar confessions by François Villon four hundred years earlier.

In Musset, the dramatist often coexists with the poet, and it is difficult to separate the two. This is readily evident in the dramatic dialogue employed in the "Nights." Regrettably, it also shows up in oratorical aspects of these poems. The double role of poet and dramatist seems part of a greater dualism and even dichotomy in Musset. On the one hand he was truly a child of his century, containing within himself many of its contradictions, much of its anguish. On the other, he was an admirer of the great French classics, too aware of the tradition of French letters ever to subscribe completely to the doctrines of the Romantic *Cénacle*. Some of the distrust with which he came to be viewed by members of the group may be explained by his mischievously parodying some of their excesses. If it is valid to talk of Musset as a poet aiming at a free transfer of emotion from himself to his reader, it is yet necessary to remark that irony and whimsical, critical detachment are also components of Musset's poetic repertory.

"A Wasted Evening"—a poem about an evening at the theater—is one of Musset's finest poems. It has the tone of a conversation. Whereas in other pieces by Musset one might regret the absence of those elements of density and surprise often held to be essential to a poem, here they are much in evidence. The poem is related to a precise circumstance in his life: a performance of Molière's *The Misanthropist* (1666) in Paris in 1840. Musset proceeds from an ironic, effective treatment of current tastes in the theater:

> I was alone, the other evening, at the Théâtre-Français,
> Or almost alone; the author had but little success.
> Of course, it was just Molière. . . .

Then, in masterly fashion, he weaves in a new theme: the glimpse of a girl in the theater brings to mind a phrase from the poet André Chénier. This is enough to distract the poet from the task he had set himself: to rehabilitate, and imitate, the talent of the seventeenth century dramatist. Musset succeeds admirably here in calling to life an atmosphere and in making a concise, critical commentary on the tastes of men of his day. Moreover, he shows up strikingly the problem of his personal, artistic indolence.

That flippancy and irony were a studied technique becomes obvious in a piece such as "Upon Three Steps of Marble," a poem composed in 1849. The title refers to the stairs of the terrace of the *Orangerie* at Versailles. The beginning of the poem is a disrespectful description of the palace and park of Versailles:

> I do not believe that there is on earth a place
> .   .   .   .   .   .
> More described, more lauded, more sung
> Than the boring park of Versailles.

The flippant beginning, with its implicit criticism of descriptive poetry, gives way, however, to a magnificent evocation of the century of Louis XIV, with which Musset patently feels considerable spiritual affinity.

When Musset's name is mentioned, regret is often expressed. It is felt by many readers that with a more sustained effort, he could have accomplished far more than he did, that his life of dissipation must be deplored. Some have the impression that in his emotional development Musset never did seem to move far beyond adolescence. The poet himself hints at this possibility in an address to the reader in the *First Poetic Works*:

> My first poems are those of a child
> The second of an adolescent
> The last scarcely of a man.

Even if this is true, and it seems possible, it is to be remembered that Musset is in good company. It could perhaps be shown that many great poets, although they did not write during their actual adolescence, frequently referred to it, consciously or unconsciously, as their primary source of inspiration.

Bibliography:
Barine, Arvède. *The Life of Alfred de Musset.* Translated by Charles Conner Hayden. New York: Edwin C. Hill, 1906. Important early work on the writer, still highly useful for scholars and general readers. Describes the young Musset's growing awareness of his poetic talents and discusses the production of works that would be included in his two collections.
Denomme, Robert T. "Alfred de Musset and the Poetry of Experience." In *Nineteenth-Century French Romantic Poets.* Carbondale: Southern Illinois University Press, 1969. Discusses the significance of human love as an informing principle in Musset's poetry. Focuses on the

poet's attempts to capture the intensity of experience in his art.

Grant, Elliott M. *French Poetry of the Nineteenth Century*. 2d ed. New York: Macmillan, 1962. Briefly outlines the composition process for poems included in these volumes. Reproduces selected poems and explicates them for general readers, focusing on technical and thematic issues.

Haldane, Charlotte. *Alfred: The Passionate Life of Alfred de Musset*. New York: Roy Publishers, 1961. Offers sensitive commentary on Musset's poetry. Explains the genesis for many of Musset's poems and interprets a number of them in detail.

Sedgwick, Henry Dwight. *Alfred de Musset 1810-1857*. 1st ed. Indianapolis: Bobbs-Merrill, 1931. A detailed study of the writer's life that interweaves commentary on the poems into the biographical narrative. Explains the source of Musset's inspiration for a number of the works included in his collections.

THE FISHER MAIDEN

Type of work: Short fiction
Author: Bjørnstjerne Bjørnson (1832-1910)
Type of plot: Pastoral
Time of plot: Early nineteenth century
Locale: Norway
First published: Fiskerjenten, 1868 (English translation, 1869)

> *Principal characters:*
> PETRA, the fisher maiden
> GUNLAUG, her mother
> PEDRO, her father
> HANS ODEGAARD, the pastor's son

The Story:

Pedro Ohlsen, the son of Peter Ohlsen and the grandson of old Per Ohlsen, was not like either his father or his grandfather. They had tended to their businesses like the shrewd, practical men they were. Pedro, in contrast, was a dreamer. Scolded from morning to night by his father and his schoolfellows, he began to seek out the poor children in the community for companions, among them a spritelike girl named Gunlaug, whom people called the fisher maiden.

When Peter died, he left enough money for his widow and Pedro to live quietly without working. Pedro devoted his time to flute playing. He and the fisher maiden separated after a quarrel; she thought him a weakling and left the town. Nine years later, she returned with a child, Petra, a little girl who also became known as the fisher maiden.

One day Petra, who was as audacious as her mother had been, went to steal apples from a tree belonging to Pedro Ohlsen. He caught her and identified her as the child of his lost love. When Petra escaped, she told her mother of the encounter. Gunlaug told her never again to speak to Pedro Ohlsen.

Hans Odegaard, the pastor's son, asked permission to teach Petra to read, and she learned rapidly under his guidance. A tragedy befell Hans's best friend and in his grief, Hans could not be persuaded to take up his career. His indifference was a bitter thing for his father, the old pastor. Petra wept when Hans left the village.

Young men came to woo Petra, among them Gunnar, the sailor, and a stranger who kept his name from her and mystified her with strange songs and tales. Finally, he gave her a gold chain and told her his name was Yngve Vold. Unlike Gunnar, who was poor, Yngve Vold owned his own ship. Both went suddenly to sea. When Yngve returned, he told her that he intended to marry her. He was the richest man in the town, which frightened Petra, for she knew that many of the townspeople would not approve of the wealthy shipowner marrying the fisher maiden.

Gunnar too sent her a ring and a love letter. Before she could decide between her two suitors, however, Hans Odegaard returned, and she realized that he was the man she loved best. The next day, Hans beat Yngve with his cane for announcing his plan to marry Petra. Hans then told Petra that his life was ruined, for she had betrayed him. Gunnar returned, and he, too, beat Yngve Vold. The whole town buzzed with the gossip that Petra had three men engaged to her, all at the same time. A mob went to Gunlaug's house and threw stones through Petra's window. Gunlaug helped her daughter to escape from the town by dressing her as a sailor, and Pedro rowed her out to a boat that would take her to Bergen, where she was unknown.

In Bergen, Petra was greatly humiliated. The theater attracted her, but because she was awkward and unlettered, no theater manager would hire her. At last, she left Bergen and made her home among shepherds to the north. A pastor took her in for a time, and when he learned that Petra knew Hans Odegaard, he permitted her to stay in his household. There, for the next three years, she studied the great plays under the pastor and his daughter Signe. Eventually, however, the pastor became suspicious of Petra and suspected that she was artfully concealing secret admirers. Suddenly, Hans arrived. Signe had written him, gently explaining how much Petra had suffered.

He forgave Petra for the harm she had done him and encouraged her to go on the stage. When Pedro Ohlsen died, he left Petra enough money to begin her career. Drawing on her experience of suffering and her knowledge of life, Petra followed her greatest desire, happy at the same time to know that Signe was going to marry Hans Odegaard.

Critical Evaluation:

Much of Bjørnstjerne Bjørnson's writing was characterized by a Whitmanesque expansiveness and a generosity of spirit as notable for its elemental energy as for its moral fearlessness. Bjørnson was concerned with the issues underlying the fundamental connection between love and power. In *The Fisher Maiden*, he provided fascinating insights into some of the key elements involved in the genesis of the Scandinavian feminist movement. This movement flourished because of the social criticism and remarkable insights of such contemporaries as Camilla Collett, Alexander Kielland, Jonas Lie, Henrik Ibsen, and Bjørnson himself.

The Fisher Maiden is more than a novella and something less than a complete novel. It describes in both idyllic and Darwinistic terms the experiences of a young heroine, Petra, who is compelled to move from the country to the city, where her ambitions are realized in the theater. Petra is a woman of considerable genius, and she becomes entangled in a series of capricious affairs involving a succession of lovers who are utterly enchanted by her reveries. Yet Petra is not truly in love with any of her suitors, and any relationship beyond the fanciful and the theatrical can serve only as a prop for her romantic genius and her artistic nature. Thus Bjørnson presents an elemental crisis that pits career against nuptial fulfillment. In Petra's case, the nuptial element is subordinated to the dramatic and creative. The result is a nineteenth century portrait that questions a woman's place at the hearth and the role of marriage as the mainstay of her fulfillment or salvation.

Bjørnson recognized an unbroken connection of his time to the beliefs, courage, and values of the Viking past, which all Norwegians cherished. At the same time, he was concerned with the problems of human estrangement and reconciliation, particularly in the relationship of the sexes. Throughout his literary career, Bjørnson advocated women's emancipation with oratorical fervor, and much of his work serves as a profound commentary on the degradation of women living in a society dominated by men. In *The Fisher Maiden*, he makes it clear that happiness and productivity are not necessarily attained only through marriage and that an immoral marriage involving abuse and subordination must be terminated. Bjørnson also felt that love was only one of many strands woven into the fabric of life, and he advocated that women's equality be founded on the dissolution of the double standard.

For Petra, no amount of saintly condemnation by the village bigots who will not countenance music and dancing can destroy her spirit; nor can that condemnation force her to seek refuge in marriage. Indeed, she has very little regard for the village ideas regarding the ethic of courtship, and she is not so overwhelmed by the supposed anguish of her suitors as to be overcome with pity. She refuses to be, like her mother, compelled to live in contempt and fervent regret because of an unfortunate affair or a momentary weakness. Petra feels destined to become an actress, and she does so despite the pressures and moral indignation of a society that would have her choose otherwise.

Bjørnson felt nothing but contempt for innocence predicated on ignorance and superstition. He believed that growth could not be manifested in the miraculous and the supernatural; rather, its fundamental tenet was based on reason, law, and political and social evolution. In many ways, Bjørnson presented the moral, spiritual, religious, and political crisis of orthodox Christianity in its support of traditional sociopolitical beliefs regarding women. As an aggressive radical, he believed that life must supersede religion, most especially when the two conflicted. As the pastor says to the village saints: "Spiritual life thrives but poorly in your mountain home, and partakes of the gloom of the surrounding vegetation. Prejudice, like the cliffs themselves, overhangs your life and casts a shadow upon it."

For Petra, as for so many of Bjørnson's fictional characters, guilt serves as a driving force of human motivation. It underlies much of the struggle for power; it is the primary consideration in the struggle for control; and in matters of personal fulfillment it has an extraordinary potential for confusing and undermining the relationships between the sexes.

Petra ultimately gains courage and wisdom from her suffering and from the betrayals, duplicity, and chicanery of the society that had driven her from her home. That wisdom is sufficient to support her in her dedication to the theater. Bjørnson questions whether it is reasonable to impose blame for certain forms of behavior or feeling without regard for the extent of provocation.

Indeed, he suggests the possibility of mutual culpability in certain situations involving attraction and seduction, and it seems that he also insists on some element of feminine responsibility. He poses difficult moral questions in *The Fisher Maiden* and appears to permit no easy answers.

The Fisher Maiden is a novel of remarkable lyric power, implicit optimism, and visionary fervor. By establishing a series of polarities and contrasts in the characters of Petra, Gunlaug, Hans Odegaard, and Pedro, Bjørnson entertains and educates the reader with a story that is supported by a curious blend of mysticism and rationalism. That blend serves as an extraordinary means for revealing the fundamental egalitarianism of the Norwegian character.

"Critical Evaluation" by Matts Djos

Bibliography:
Brandes, Georg. "Bjørnstjerne Bjørnson." In *Henrik Ibsen: A Critical Study—with a 42 Page Essay on Bjørnstjerne Bjørnson.* 1899. Reprint. New York: Benjamin Bloom, 1964. A firsthand biographical and critical portrait of Bjørnson's literary and political career. Notes that his daring apostasy of the Norwegian cause was implicitly optimistic, idyllic, and distinctively feminist.
"The Bravura of Bjørnson." *The Times Literary Supplement,* June 20, 1958, p. 344. Describes Bjørnson's literary career, especially as it related to his public image.
Kepos, Paula, et al., eds. "Bjørnstjerne Bjørnson." In *Twentieth-Century Literary Criticism.* Detroit, Mich.: Gale Research, 1991. An excellent biographical and critical overview of the author's work. Includes a comprehensive bibliography of his principal works and reprints of critical reviews of the author, including those of Max Beerbohm, William Payne, and Edwin Bjørkman, and an excellent contemporary analysis of *The Fisher Maiden* by William Dean Howells.

McFarlane, James Walter. "Bjørnstjerne Bjørnson." In *Ibsen and the Temper of Norwegian Literature*. New York: Octagon Books, 1979. A general survey of the work of this poet, dramatist, novelist, and national hero. Describes his talents in theater and as a writer and critiques his role as a public figure and passionate advocate of women's rights.

Rottem, Oystein. "The Multifarious Bjørnson." *Scandinavica* 24, no. 1 (1985): 59-64. Reviews a five-volume jubilee edition of Bjørnson's works, published in Norway to commemorate the 150th anniversary of Bjørnson's birth.

FIVE WOMEN WHO LOVED LOVE

Type of work: Short fiction
Author: Ihara Saikaku (Hirayama Tōgo, 1642-1693)
Type of plot: Love
Time of plot: Seventeenth century
Locale: Japan
First published: Kōshoku gonin onna, 1686 (English translation, 1956)

> *Principal characters:*
> SEIJŪRŌ, an apprentice
> ONATSU, his master's younger sister
> OSEN, a young wife
> THE COOPER, her husband
> CHŌZAEMON, a yeast maker
> CHŌZAEMON'S WIFE
> OSAN, a merchant's wife
> RIN, her maid
> MOEMON, the merchant's clerk
> OSHICHI, a young woman
> HER MOTHER
> ONOGAWA KICHISABURŌ, a young samurai
> GENGOBEI, a Buddhist monk, formerly a pederast
> HACHIJŪRŌ, Gengobei's former lover
> OMAN, a young girl

The Stories:

The First Story. Seijūrō, a handsome, gallant young man disowned by his wealthy father for his profligacies, apprenticed himself to a shopkeeper and proved hardworking and reliable. When Onatsu, his master's younger sister, fell in love with him, he, after some reluctance, at last fully returned her affection. As an apprentice, he was far from an eligible suitor, and so the lovers were forced to elope. Seven hundred gold pieces disappeared at the same time. When the lovers were discovered, Seijūrō, condemned for theft as well as for seduction, was executed. The gold was later found where it had been mislaid. Onatsu went mad for a time. Later, she entered a nunnery.

The Second Story. Osen, a country woman, was married happily to a cooper. When Chōzaemon, the yeast maker, was planning to celebrate the fiftieth anniversary of his father's death, Osen offered to help in the preparations. While she was arranging sweetmeats, Chōzaemon accidentally dropped a bowl on her head, disarranging her hair. Chōzaemon's suspicious, jealous wife accused Osen of adultery. Because she had been unjustly accused, Osen impulsively decided to revenge herself on the wife by truly making love to Chōzaemon, although she cared nothing for him. When her husband, the cooper, discovered the lovers, Osen committed suicide and Chōzaemon was executed.

The Third Story. Osan's husband had gone to Edo on business. Her maid, Rin, was in love with Moemon, a clerk. Moemon, however, felt coldly toward Rin and only reluctantly agreed to visit her bed. Together, Rin and Osan decided to punish him, and Osan took Rin's place in

2327

the bed. The trick had other results, however, when Osan and Moemon found themselves hopelessly in love. After pretending to commit suicide together, they hid in a faraway village for a time. Eventually, they were discovered and executed.

The Fourth Story. Oshichi, an innocent young woman, was taken by her mother to find refuge in a temple after their house had burned down. There she met and fell in love with Onogawa Kichisaburō, a young samurai. When Oshichi and her mother returned to their home, the lovers were not able to meet in secret. Oshichi, remembering how she first met her lover, decided to start another fire, but she was discovered, arrested, exposed to shame, and burned at the stake. Kichisaburō, who had been ill, did not know of her death until he accidentally saw her gravestone. At first, he planned to commit suicide, but he was persuaded to delay his plan until after a talk with his mentor and sworn brother. As the result of his friend's advice, Kichisaburō decided to become a monk.

The Fifth Story. Gengobei, a pederast, took priestly vows after the death of Hachijūrō, his lover. Later, he fell in love with another boy who returned from the dead to see him again. In his grief, Gengobei retired to a mountain hut. Meanwhile, a girl, Oman, had seen and fallen in love with Gengobei. Determined to win him, she disguised herself as a boy and visited his retreat. There she succeeded in winning Gengobei's love, even after her sex had been revealed. Gengobei left the priesthood, and the lovers lived in great poverty together until Oman's parents finally found her. Rejoicing at her recovery, her parents decided to have the two lovers marry and then give their family fortune to Gengobei. Oman's love story, therefore, came to a happy ending.

Critical Evaluation:

The Japanese writer Ihara (sometimes Ibara) Saikaku was both a poet who wrote a prodigious number of seventeen-syllable *haiku* and the leading novelist of the Genroku Period (1600-1868) in Japan. The subjects of his fiction fall chronologically into three distinct types: those dealing with matters of love and the pleasure quarter; those dealing with life among the warrior class; and those dealing with the lives of the merchant class. *Five Women Who Loved Love* belongs to the first group, and all five of the short novels of which this work is comprised are based on actual happenings. The work was first published in 1686.

In order to appreciate fully the prose fiction of Ihara, it is necessary to understand the nature of Japanese society during the latter half of the seventeenth century. Although Edo (Tokyo) was still the feudal capital (the residence of the shogun and the source of the real power), and Kyoto was still the residence of the mikado (the nominal ruler), Osaka witnessed the rise of a merchant class; but because of the rigid class distinctions and feudal laws maintained by the shogun and samurai, the merchants were unable to convert their economic power into political or social power. The official religion was Confucianism, and the ensuing laws ensured the maintenance of a rigidly stratified society with a hierarchy of classes, making it punishable by death to attempt to move from one class to another. The merchants thus sought an outlet for the frustration of their thwarted power and for their money in the *ukiyo* (floating world).

Ukiyo originally had a Buddhist meaning of the transitory life, death, and decay, and the works of Ihara always retained some of this original meaning. In the seventeenth century, however, the *ukiyo* became the term for the diverting quarters of town or the theater. The new heroes of this society were the actors and courtesans; the new values were love and money.

The five stories of *Five Women Who Loved Love* are linked by a common theme: the transgression of the social code for love. Each tale is divided into five parts or chapters, perhaps because of the five-act division of the drama, and the third part depicts a journey (also borrowed from drama). The plots are simple and, with one exception, tragic. The strength of the work lies in its evocation of character and subject. Each tale is linked to a particular locale, three to the major cities of Edo, Kyoto, and Osaka, and two to outlying provinces. In the first four tales, the transgression of the feudal law leads to death; in the fifth tale, however, the lovers live because they are both of the same social class. The five heroines are not languishing, leisurely ladies but rather women of character who have a part in creating their tragedies instead of being helplessly fated. Only Oman, the heroine of the last story, is allowed to live happily ever after, and she, in her charming determination to win her love, resembles in some respects William Shakespeare's Rosalind. Throughout the work, Saikaku seems to imply that there should be no conflict between love and society, especially one made along class lines. The conflict exists, however; the heroines choose love and accept the consequences without despair.

Bibliography:
Kato, Shuichi. *The Years of Isolation.* Vol. 2 in *A History of Japanese Literature.* New York: Kodansha International, 1983. Pages 104-112 deal primarily with the third story in the collection, is related to Chikamatsu Monzaemon's dramatic version of the same episode.
Keene, Donald. *World Within Walls: Japanese Literature of the Pre-Modern Era, 1600-1867.* New York: Holt, Rinehart and Winston, 1976. Pages 167-215 discuss *Five Women Who Loved Love* in relation to Saikaku's other works, particularly *Life of an Amorous Man* and *Life of an Amorous Woman.*
Kirkwood, Kenneth P. *Renaissance in Japan: A Cultural Survey of the Seventeenth Century.* Rutland, Vt.: Charles E. Tuttle, 1970. Pages 192-223 provide a general biographical sketch of Saikaku, including his work as a poet, playwright, and writer of fiction. It comments particularly on the Osaka cultural milieu.
Morris, Ivan. *Life of an Amorous Woman and Other Writings.* New York: New Directions, 1963. Pages 3-51 deal with Saikaku and his cultural and historical context. Comments as well on elements of literary style and on illustrations.
Rimer, J. Thomas. *A Reader's Guide to Japanese Literature from the Eighth Century to the Present.* New York: Kodansha International, 1988. Pages 66-69 contain a brief discussion of one of the five stories in the collection. Also comments on Saikaku's literary background.

THE FIXER

Type of work: Novel
Author: Bernard Malamud (1914-1986)
Type of plot: Historical realism
Time of plot: Shortly before World War I
Locale: Around Kiev, in the Ukraine, Russia
First published: 1966

>   *Principal characters:*
>   YAKOV BOK, a handyman (the fixer of the title)
>   BIBIKOV, the investigating magistrate
>   NIKOLAI MAXIMOVITCH LEBEDEV, brick factory owner
>   ZINAIDA NIKOLAEVNA, daughter of the brick factory owner
>   SHMUEL RABINOVITCH, father-in-law of Yakov Bok
>   RAISL BOK, wife of Yakov, daughter of Shmuel

The Story:

Yakov Bok, a fixer, decided in his thirties to leave his native village and go to the big city of Kiev, in search of a better life. His father-in-law, Shmuel, came to see him off. They talked, a bit gingerly, about the fact that his wife, Raisl, daughter of Shmuel, had left him a couple of months earlier and run off with a stranger. Yakov felt humiliated by this, because he was the laughing-stock of the village. Yakov reminded Shmuel that his daughter was also barren, for in the nearly six years they lived together she had failed to give him a child. Yakov was also pessimistic about the village's economic future; he was finding it harder and harder to make a living there as a fixer, and feared there were likely soon to be pogroms in the area.

Shmuel had given Yakov his horse and wagon in exchange for Yakov's cow, which he hoped would prove more profitable. His parting advice to his son-in-law was to recall that it was illegal for Jews to live in Kiev, except in specified Jewish districts, and to advise him to settle in the Jewish district near the synagogue, because without spiritual support a Jew would be vulnerable in a hostile world. Soon after Yakov set out, his wagon failed him. A wheel broke, and even the fixer could not repair it. He continued on horseback as far as the sickly horse could take him, then sold the horse as meat and completed his journey on foot. He did settle in the Jewish district, but found no adequate housing there, and too little work as a handyman. He concluded that he ought to try other districts and ventured into the larger city in search of better luck. Winter had come. One cold evening he came upon an elderly man lying face down in the snow. The man, who appeared drunk, wore a button with the two-headed eagle of the Black Hundreds, a notorious anti-Semitic group. Nevertheless, Yakov felt obligated to help the man. He was joined by a young woman with a crippled leg, who said the man was her father. Yakov helped her carry the man to their nearby house, and as Yakov was leaving, the young woman urged him to return the next morning so that her father, Nikolai Maximovitch Lebedev, could thank him properly.

Yakov worried about going back to the home of an anti-Semite, but, hoping for a reward for his good deed, he went anyway. The result was that Yakov was offered the job of manager of the brick factory the old man owned. With the job came living quarters right in the factory. Yakov gave a false name, realizing it would be illegal for him to live in an area forbidden to Jews. Noting that the old man did not ask for his passport, Yakov decided to take the job and risk the consequences. To complicate his situation even more, Zinaida Nikolaevna, the old man's daughter, invited him to dinner, then tried to seduce him. He refused, for fear of the discovery that would result, more than anything else, and knew that he had made an enemy of her.

Through the winter and early spring, Yakov worked as a manager, overseeing the making and shipping of bricks, and trying to prevent theft by his workmen. One day, he read in the newspaper that a twelve-year-old boy had been found dead in a cave near the brick factory. It was said the boy had dozens of stab wounds all over his body, which had been bled white. The newspaper article hinted at ritual murder. Yakov anxiously watched the boy's funeral from a distance and saw that anti-Semitic pamphlets were distributed, blaming the boy's death on the Jews. He decided it was time to flee, since a pogrom was brewing, but as he gathered his belongings, he was arrested.

Yakov was first interrogated in the courthouse and held there in a cell. After many weeks, he was sent to a prison, where relentless interrogation continued, and he was kept in solitary confinement for eighteen more months. The one glimmer of light for Yakov was his frequent sessions with the investigating magistrate, whose name was Bibikov, who proved to be a man of integrity and compassion. Bibikov and Yakov even had one long discussion about Spinoza (whose autobiography Yakov had read, in a volume he had found in a junk shop). In his simple way, Yakov, untrained in philosophy, understood that Spinoza's main concern was how a man may be free, and Bibikov, impressed, helped Yakov understand a bit more by explaining some of Spinoza's complex ideas to him. Bibikov was the only person in authority who treated Yakov humanely during all the nearly two years Yakov was in custody. One day, Yakov had the horrible experience of passing a jail cell in which a man had hanged himself with his belt. The man was Bibikov.

During Yakov's long travail in prison, he was abused every day by humiliating body searches and even served poisoned food. The purpose of the cruelty was to try to force him to confess to the murder, since the prosecutors had been unable to obtain any positive proof against him. Yakov had no way to prove his innocence, either, since the evidence against him was vague and circumstantial. While in prison he had two especially painful visits. One was from Shmuel, who showed great sympathy, but made the empty promise to try to get him some help. The other was from his wife Raisl, who wanted him to sign a paper acknowledging her illegitimate child as his, so the boy would not be stigmatized as a bastard. Yakov wearily agreed. It was announced that Yakov had been formally indicted, and he was led out of the prison and marched through the crowd-lined streets. Much shouting, some hostile, some friendly, accompanied him on his way to the courthouse to be tried for ritual murder.

Critical Evaluation:

Bernard Malamud readily acknowledged that *The Fixer* is a fictionalized adaptation of a notorious historical event. Jewish brick factory manager Mendel Beilis was accused of murdering a twelve-year-old Christian boy and of draining the boy's blood for use in making matzos for Passover. The arrest took place in 1911 in Kiev, and for two years afterward, while the Russian authorities strove to manufacture a believable case against Beilis, the accused languished in jail. A public outcry arose, both inside and outside Russia, at the spectacle of a state system of justice relying, for its case against a Jew, on an absurdly superstitious legend, circulated by anti-Semites, that Jews practiced ritual murder. When Beilis was finally brought to trial in 1913, the court returned a verdict of not guilty.

Malamud takes several significant liberties with the historical truth. For example, Malamud's victim is a handyman, unlike Beilis, and the owner of the brick factory where Yakov is employed is a Christian anti-Semite, rather than a Jew, as was Beilis' boss. It is far more important to note how closely Malamud adheres to the main facts of the historical case. One of the finest achievements of the novel is the care and accuracy with which it evokes the atmosphere of czarist Russia in the years before World War I, including the restricted life imposed upon Jews and the horrors of its inhumane prisons and system of justice. As literature *The Fixer* is, more than anything else, a vivid exercise in historical realism. About three-fourths of the novel focuses on detailed description of what Yakov Bok endures at the hands of prosecutors and prison officials.

An essential feature of the novel is that, while the novel is a third-person narrative, Malamud has contrived to filter all of the novel's action through the consciousness of Yakov Bok, giving the novel the effect of a first-person narrative. The point of view in the novel is steadily and unequivocally that of the protagonist. As a result, the reader sees the world as Yakov Bok sees it, and that perspective is extremely pessimistic and cynical. Yakov always expects the worst to happen because his life has been an unbroken series of hard blows, beginning with the death of his father in a pogrom when Yakov was an infant. The death of his mother came soon after, which forced him to spend his lonely childhood and youth in an orphanage. The humiliating disaster of his marriage and the hapless journey to Kiev in which everything went wrong force from Yakov's mouth the phrase, "Who invented my life?" This is Yakov's veiled attack on the God he could not quite believe in but worshiped anyway.

Malamud chose the name "Bok" for his protagonist because it defines his role perfectly. In Yiddish and in German *Bok* means a he-goat, the traditional image of the outcast and surrogate victim. Bok is the scapegoat. Yakov Bok is a born victim, to be blamed for whatever evils befall society and to be cast out of society, taking those evils with him, so society can be cleansed. It is a universal type that Malamud has in mind, to be found in every society, big or small, and in every age. That is why Bok is a handyman, familiar to everyone yet living on the margins of society, an outsider who is easy to blame for bad times. Malamud seems to have intended Yakov Bok to be an itinerant Everyman, a stranger everywhere, always viewed with suspicion, whose destiny is to bear the burdens of suffering for everyone else when trouble comes. The novel may be read as a protest against society's tendency to victimize the poor and helpless.

This universal scapegoating impulse, which Malamud saw as the essence of the Beilis case, may explain why Malamud chose to end his novel just as the trial of Yakov Bok was about to begin. Critics have accused Malamud of a failure of nerve in refusing to conclude his novel with the exoneration of the intended victim. Surely Malamud wished to make the point that eventual exoneration, however welcome, can not cancel the victim's suffering. By stopping his novel before the trial begins, Malamud forces his reader to focus on the real injustice against which he is protesting, namely, the scapegoating itself, and does not allow the reader the false comfort of one isolated happy ending.

Murray Sachs

Bibliography:
Ducharme, Robert. *Art and Idea in the Novels of Bernard Malamud: Toward the Fixer*. The Hague: Mouton, 1974. Argues that the theme of the tension between suffering and responsibility runs through all Malamud's work and provides a key to *The Fixer*.
Field, Leslie A., and Joyce W. Field, eds. *Bernard Malamud: A Collection of Critical Essays*. Englewood Cliffs, N.J.: Prentice-Hall, 1975. Excellent choice of essays, prefaced by a revealing interview with Malamud.

Hershinow, Sheldon J. *Bernard Malamud*. New York: Frederick Ungar, 1980. Good general study of Malamud's work, identifying his main themes.

Salzberg, Joel. *Bernard Malamud. A Reference Guide*. Boston: G. K. Hall, 1985. A comprehensive listing of books, articles, and reviews of Malamud's writings, with a brief summary of the content of each item.

THE FLIES

Type of work: Novel
Author: Mariano Azuela (1873-1952)
Type of plot: Historical realism
Time of plot: Early twentieth century
Locale: Mexico
First published: Las moscas, 1918 (English translation, 1956)

> *Principal characters:*
> MARTA REYES TÉLLEZ, a widow in her sixties
> RUBÉN,
> ROSITA, and
> MATILDE, her son and daughters
> DONACIANO RÍOS, a government officer
> GENERAL MALACARA, an army officer opposing the revolutionary leader
> VENUSTIANO CARRANZA, a revolutionist and military leader
> MORALITOS, a government officer
> SEÑOR DOCTOR, the town physician
> RODOLFO BOCANEGRA, a lawyer
> DON SINFOROSO, a former lieutenant in the federalist army

The Story:

In his struggle to wrest the Mexican presidency from Victoriano Huerta, Venustiano Carranza laid siege to Querétaro, a town to the north of Mexico City. Querétaro was in chaos. People fled to the train station, hoping to escape Carranza's squadrons. Among those thousands, Marta, her two daughters, and her son sought space on the train; however, their efforts were fruitless. The crowd separated them until Rosita's voice caught Marta's and Matilde's attention. Rosita and Rubén managed to convince a doctor to allow them to travel in the medical car. The doctor opposed Marta's and Matilde's traveling with them, but Matilde declared that she had permission from General Malacara, an officer in charge.

Marta and her family told her fellow passengers about the siege by Carranza's army; the army had taken over the best houses, schools, and even the churches for military use. The cathedral was stripped of all valuables and was turned into a hospital. Everyone agreed that greed was the worst enemy of the revolution—and the reason for its failure. The conversation was interrupted by the arrival of General Malacara, who, to Rosita's surprise, came with two women. General Malacara had been flirting with Rosita; she had felt that his attentions were serious.

The train traveled all night with no problems, but almost everyone feared an attack by Carranza's forces. Marta and her daughters prepared breakfast for the doctor; they believed that he was an important man, or at least one with money. The men continued their political discussion. The train suddenly stopped near Irapuato, a town southwest of Mexico City. During an attempt to learn why the train had stopped, don Sinforoso insulted a soldier, who threatened the old man with a rifle. Don Sinforoso's friends took him away from the soldier.

Rosita flirted with the doctor, who, surprised by her friendliness, confronted her with the rumor that General Malacara had courted her. Malacara assured Marta that his young women companions were distant relatives. Their conversation was interrupted by news about reasons for the delay: The northbound trains had been derailed by a blockade, and hundreds of boilers were burning. General Malacara invited Marta and her daughters to an automobile ride around town. To his surprise, Marta declined the invitation, claiming that the doctor had already invited the women.

The doctor did not own a car; instead, he owned a horse cart. The women displayed their displeasure. They climbed up into the cart only when they were sure that General Malacara could not see them. At Irapuato, people were evacuating the town because they feared that Pancho Villa had lost the battle to Carranza. Rubén left to find Quiñones, a friend connected to Obregón, Carranza's strongman. The women bought food with the doctor's money, and they promised to pay him back when Rubén returned from looking for his friend. They also made him pay for boots for Rosita. When Matilde also wanted boots, the doctor showed them his empty wallet. Marta took that action as an insult, and she left the doctor behind, with a promise that they would pay him later.

They saw General Malacara's car approaching. Rosita again flirted with Malacara, denying any sentimental interest in the doctor. The women wanted Malacara to introduce them to Villa, who had a reputation for kindness. They planned to ask Villa for money, food, and passes to Juarez City. If Villa lost power, the women would have spent the money, while Rubén, aided by Quiñones, would be working on Carranza's side. Malacara promised to arrange an interview with Villa, and he took them to buy shoes. While they were in the store, Rubén arrived with good news; Rubén had seen Quiñones, and Quiñones could help them. Rubén claimed that he had left his wallet behind, so Malacara also bought shoes for Rubén. On their way back to the train, Marta asked Malacara to take them to the governor's personal car, claiming that the doctor had flirted with Rosita.

Dissension among the supporters of Villa took place. Men who had sworn loyalty to Villa decided to stay in Irapuato, so that the people from the town would think that they belonged to the Carranza forces, and the Carranza men, when they came, would think that they were local citizens.

Marta and children arrived at the train station in search of Malacara. They were accompanied by Quiñones, who made loud comments against Villa. A soldier overheard them and, by mistake, arrested Rubén, who was released when the women showed proof that they were Villa followers; the proof was passes and Villa currency, presumably given to them by Villa. After the incident, they could not find Malacara, but they found the doctor and again pretended friendship. Once in the hospital car, it was decided that Rubén should stay in the town in order to proceed with their plans. As the train rolled away from the town, military police suddenly climbed into the wagons, as if escaping.

Critical Evaluation:

Considered the initiator of the literary movement known as the Novel of the Mexican Revolution, Mariano Azuela offers in his works an eyewitness account of historical incidents in the Revolution of 1910. A revolutionary ideologue, Azuela was an army surgeon in Francisco (Pancho) Villa's guerrilla forces from 1910 to 1920. His writing depicts his experiences as a doctor and as a revolutionary. In 1941, Azuela received a national award for his literary craft. His active participation in the political arena won for him a reputation as a founding father of modern Mexican society. He was buried with other heroes of the revolution in an official ceremony in Mexico City.

Azuela's novel of the Mexican Revolution belongs to the literary trend of realism, which sometimes offers a photographic depiction. Azuela presents the revolution's struggle against oppression by the former power structure. His simple, direct literary style documents the revolution as the first Latin American armed movement of the twentieth century. Aware of the fact that the revolution produced radical changes in the social core of Mexican life, Azuela presents the movement in a positive light. His characters are representative of those involved in the political reorganization that leads to a new group in power as the economic center shifts from millionaire landowners to the peasant class.

The new literature of writers such as Azuela incorporates the political themes reflected in the motto "land for all." These writers propose an examination of the new ruling class' role in the shaping of contemporary Mexican society. Their works also offer harsh criticisms of the revolution, and they constantly monitor the movement, praising its successes, but also denouncing its irregularities.

Azuela assumes the tasks of documenting, acclaiming, or censuring the revolutionary events that he has witnessed. His analysis differs from that of other writers, however, as he is clearly inspired by socialist political theories of justice for the working masses. With the rational precision of a scientist, Azuela conducts a detailed observation of the characters involved in the reshaping of Mexican society, as promoted by the revolution. Azuela documents these changes, which are diverse and controversial, especially those related to landowners' loss of power (political and economic). Azuela accomplishes this by becoming a newspaper reporter. His numerous articles published in Mexican and Spanish newspapers in the United States are the work of an eyewitness.

Azuela is not, however, a historian. His training as a reporter provides him with material for documentation of scenes of the revolution in a literary form known as "*costumbrismo*," an early genre of realist literature that reproduces everyday customs and incidents of historical relevance that create the spirit of an age. By means of careful reproduction of revolutionary times, Azuela aims to achieve a twofold purpose: to explore the significance of the revolution as a historical occurrence of worldwide importance, and to bring in fresh literary material which offers a metaphorical exploration of human behavior.

The Flies brings together a collection of stories at the moment when Francisco Villa and Venustiano Carranza, two legendary revolutionary leaders, were fighting for political power. Although these men do not appear in the text, their presence is strongly portrayed by characters who represent their leaders' political platforms. For instance, characters who take advantage of others (such as Marta and her children) reflect Carranza's ruthless ambitions for the Mexican presidency—in clear disregard of Villa's and other revolutionary leaders' services in deposing the brutal Victoriano Huerta.

The plot, although simple, reflects the strong personalities involved in the revolutionary fighting. *The Flies* exposes those who oppose the revolution solely because of their loss of wealth and social prestige. By contrast, the lower classes, in search of a better life, illustrate Francisco Villa's strong ethical values. Although the characters of the lower classes are scarce in *The Flies*, they are true heroes because they stand for positive moral values. On the other hand, the upper-class protagonists are parasites and opportunists. These formerly respected individuals are compared to flies, hanging together in a desperate attempt to survive by means of their old tricks.

Azuela's characters are not, however, caricatures. They are clearly Mexicans bound to a particular historical movement who, by their relation to that movement, would help or hinder the creation of a new society. His well-researched literary works promote the revolution as a key movement in the shaping of the modern Mexican psyche.

Rafael Ocasio

Bibliography:
Clive, Griffin. "The Structure of *Los de abajo.*" *Revista Canadiense de Estudios Hispánicos* 6, no. 1 (Fall, 1981): 25-41. Azuela's best-known novel is analyzed within the context of the literary movement of the Mexican Revolution. Emphasizes Azuela's literary craft as a departure from older patterns.

Dean, James Seay. "Extreme Unction for Past Power and Glory: Four Fictions on the Mexican Revolution." *Revista de Estudios Hispánicos* 17, no. 1 (January, 1983): 89-106. A comparative study of Azuela's novels and of novels by Malcolm Lowry, Luis Martín Guzmán, and Graham Greene, all of whose works are deeply influenced by historical events surrounding the Mexican Revolution.

Herbst, Gerhard R. *Mexican Society as Seen by Mariano Azuela.* New York: Abra Ediciones, 1977. Azuela's novels of the Mexican Revolution are studied for historical, eyewitness accuracy. Focuses on Azuela's use of realist techniques in his descriptions of key historical incidents of the revolution.

Leal, Luis. *Mariano Azuela.* New York: Twayne, 1971. An excellent starting point to Azuela's life and works. Offers an analysis of his works and a strong biographical and historical background.

Martínez, Eliud. *The Art of Mariano Azuela: Modernism in "La malhora," "El desquite," "La luciérnaga."* Pittsburgh: Latin American Literary Review Press, 1980. Azuela is considered a precursor of Latin American modernism, one of the first literary movements of the twentieth century. Modernist analysis of three representative novels focuses on Azuela's interest in the Mexican Revolution.

THE FLIES

Type of work: Drama
Author: Jean-Paul Sartre (1905-1980)
Type of plot: Existentialism
Time of plot: Antiquity
Locale: Argos, Greece
First performed: 1943; first published, 1943 as *Les Mouches* (English translation, 1946)

> *Principal characters:*
> ORESTES, Agamemnon's son and heir to the throne of Argos
> ELECTRA, his sister
> CLYTEMNESTRA, his mother
> AEGISTHEUS, the ruler of Argos after Agamemnon's death
> THE PEDAGOGUE, Orestes' tutor
> ZEUS, the king of the gods
> THE ERINYES, the Furies

The Story:

Fifteen years had passed since the slaying of Agamemnon. Orestes, Agamemnon's son, arrived in Argos with his tutor. He traveled under another name, for Aegistheus, who had ruled in Argos since killing Agamemnon, had ordered him killed while he was still a young child. Orestes, however, had been saved, and reared by wealthy Athenians. Orestes was anxious to visit Argos, for his mother, Clytemnestra, now shared the throne with Aegistheus. His sister Electra was also still in Argos. Orestes arrived, not as one seeking vengeance, but as a tourist. Young, rich, handsome, and well educated, he was free of obligations or commitments, light as air, and apparently reasonably happy to be so. He found a city in which the atmosphere was leaden and oppressive. He received no answer to his requests for directions, and the first person to address a word to him was an idiot. It was as though a conspiracy existed to exclude him from the affairs of the city.

The truth was that the people of Argos were so involved with their own problem that they were quite incapable of seeing beyond it. The problem from which they suffered was that they had assumed a burden of collective guilt. Fifteen years before, they had done nothing to prevent Agamemnon's death; instead of admitting their responsibility, they wrapped themselves up in remorse. This uniform pattern of behavior suited the god Zeus, since it held Aegistheus' subjects in check and left little scope for personal initiative. Another sinister, persistent presence was that of swarms of flies, sent by the gods to plague the populace as a constant reminder of their guilt. Death seemed to be curiously intermingled with life in this city of frightened people. Repentance had even been institutionalized. Once a year, on the anniversary of Agamemnon's death, the "day of the dead" was announced.

One person in Argos, however, remained independent and defiant. Electra, though treated as a slave by her mother and Aegistheus, was rebellious. Contemptuous of the general fear and superstition, she let it be known to Orestes, who had not as yet revealed his true identity, that she lived only for the day when her brother would come to seek vengeance. At the same time, however, Electra was pathetic and occasionally childlike. While she vilified Zeus with all her might, she also betrayed her longing for warmth and affection in her questions about other cities of Greece. When Orestes asked her if she had ever thought of fleeing, she only answered that she lacked the courage to do so because she would be afraid on the roads by herself. Electra, however, also had a fixed attitude. She felt a thirst for vengeance which did not ring true or confident when set alongside her gentleness in other matters. As was foreseeable, Orestes became sufficiently curious about the city, or sufficiently interested in the plight of his sister, to decide to remain a little longer in Argos.

At the beginning of the second act, the scene changed from Argos to a mountain slope outside the city. The people were gathered for the rites of the "day of the dead" and for the release of the dead from the underworld, for it had been made known that a rock on the mountainside concealed the entrance to the underworld. Once a year, this rock was rolled back, and dead acquaintances of the people of Argos came back to torture the city's conscience. On this occasion, Aegistheus arrived late for the ceremonies, which he himself had instituted. The solid, impenetrable fear of the crowd began to give way to blind panic, as they felt quite helpless without some leadership when facing the presence of the dead. After Aegistheus appeared and the stone was rolled back, the crowd, men, women, and even children, begged for pity and asked forgiveness for being alive.

Into this uncanny, grotesque, hysterical atmosphere stepped Electra. Fired by what Orestes had told her about happy, sunny towns elsewhere in Greece, she told the crowd to throw off its burden of guilt. For a brief time, the assembled people listened hopefully. She, however, was no match for Zeus. Displaying his divine powers, he sent the stone that was supposed to bar the entrance to the underworld crashing against the steps of the temple built on the mountainside. Awed, the crowd turned against Electra.

In this sclerotic society, whose organization had, for fifteen years, been hardened from above, no change from inside seemed possible. Through contact with Orestes, Electra became enterprising enough to attempt a change. Electra's only weapon, however, was words, and her effort, though noble, was inevitably futile. It was to a considerable extent through Electra that Orestes became fully involved in the affairs of Argos and committed himself to a course of action. He revealed his identity to her. Electra, bewildered by the disproportion between her expectations and the Orestes she saw before her, could not conceal her disappointment. The change was not sudden, but, more than ever, Orestes was conscious of his meaninglessness in Argos and elsewhere. Bitterly regretful, he said that he barely existed, for he was ignorant of the deep passions of living men and women.

He affirmed that he wanted to belong fully to the town, that he wished to draw it to him. Still unsure of himself, however, he tried to appeal to a higher authority. Zeus, lurking in the background, was only too glad to suggest that Orestes continue in the path of humility. At this, Orestes rebelled; he realized that he must commit himself, that it was he who must make a decision. He decided that, in the circumstances, there was only one course which could be followed. He planned and executed the killing of Aegistheus and Clytemnestra.

In the end, in a speech to the people of Argos, Orestes claimed that he had killed for their sake, to free them. He proclaimed that he had taken over their guilt and that they need no longer be afraid. Taking the burden of guilt from the city, Orestes fled Argos. Electra, however, did not have the strength to follow Orestes. It was as though, in slaying Clytemnestra and Aegistheus, Orestes had taken away her one reason for living, her desire for vengeance. Zeus did not have much trouble in winning her over to the side of those who spend their lives in atonement. At the end of the play, Electra had become credulous, tractable, repentant. Once Orestes had fled, no explanation was offered of where Orestes went or of what happened to Argos.

Critical Evaluation:

The Flies, the first play by Jean-Paul Sartre to be presented to the public, was well received when it was acted in occupied Paris. If one bears in mind that it is concerned with the problem of liberty, and that many of its references must have been pointedly topical in 1943, the interest it aroused is scarcely surprising. On the other hand, although *The Flies* has lost some of the immediacy of its appeal, the problem of liberty is not, of course, exclusive to any particular time period, and this play is still popular and frequently staged.

For Sartre, it is nonsense to speak of a universal human nature; only the situations in which human beings may find themselves can be universal. Indeed, all of his theater involves a character moving toward a choice or decision in relation or in opposition to a given situation. The success of Sartre's theater resides, at least in part, in his leaving his principal character or characters a considerable amount of freedom to develop in the course of the action. Moveover, he has successfully created situations that audiences often find familiar.

If his philosophical writings, such as *Being and Nothingness* (1943), are difficult to understand, Sartre was nevertheless able to bring a wide audience to espouse the philosophical theory of existentialism. He accomplished this through striking statements and illustrations of his philosophy in both fiction, as seen in *Nausea* (1938), and theater. *The Flies* contends, through the hero's own discoveries, that existence and freedom, along with the need to act, constitute the existence of an individual.

The story of Orestes and Electra has been told many times in the theater, always from a different point of view. The Homeric myth of Orestes, driven by the Delphic oracle and by his sister, Electra, to avenge the murder of their father by killing their mother and her lover, is found in stylized form in the Greek tragedies of Aeschylus, Sophocles, and Euripides. Sartre, like other modern dramatists, draws variously on all three by freely adapting the myth to suit his purposes.

The Flies represents a moment of crisis and decision, since the central conflict consists of different ethical positions. In view of the fact that an existentialist situation must offer individuals the opportunity to make meaningful choices that will determine their acts, the problem of action is not merely the problem of what happens and why it happens, but the problem of commitment to a choice.

In the original myth, Orestes' actions were divinely ordered or forbidden, hence his dilemma as a thinking man confronted by religious power and arbitrariness as he tried to reconcile his relationship with the gods and to arrive at a possible meaning for human existence. The atheist Sartre, however, transforms these plays of fatality into a drama of choice that negates Judeo-Christian beliefs. No oracle is present to predict destiny and no divine hand guides human events.

Before returning to Argos, Orestes led a life devoid of interest, devoid of purpose. Existentialism, however, posits that one's past has no influence on one's future because there is no cosmic time. The present is important, since it is a time of anguish and of choice—what Sartre calls respectively "nausea" and "commitment." When Orestes understands that he is free, he must act, but the act must represent the man he is committed to being. He performs a heinous crime, real, bloody, and horrible. The author provides his protagonist with a motive (to avenge his murdered father), but the real reason he kills is to validate his freedom. If, instead, he had killed out of vengeance, he would have acted in bad faith and found himself even more imprisoned.

Zeus appears in Argos to drive Orestes out of the city before he becomes aware of his true freedom to act, for Zeus knows that freedom destroys the power of the gods over humans. To Orestes, now liberated from social, moral, religious, and political barriers, Zeus can only show his power on objects. By transferring justice to earth, Sartre makes the myth more human, even humanistic, when Orestes asserts that Zeus is "not the king of man."

In the beginning of the story, Orestes was a stranger in his own country. However, through his willed double murder and his assumption of responsibility for it, he not only shows supreme love for the citizens of Argos by giving them freedom and by voluntarily offering himself to be punished in their place, but his metaphysical exile disappears. He understands at last that his acts are his and only his, since human beings are what they make of themselves. Furthermore, because they are irreversible, such acts are foreign to the traditional notions of good and evil.

It is significant that Sartre does not explore the dramatic potential of a confrontation between Orestes and Aegistheus, the murderer of his father. Instead, Sartre concentrates on the commitment Orestes makes in his decision to kill Aegistheus and Clytemnestra. This decision presents one of the main points of Sartre's philosophical theory. In choosing an action, Orestes defines himself. Existence, to Sartre, is the sum of one's actions, and Orestes begins to exist only when he involves himself in action. Being the only person responsible for his action and its consequences, Orestes cannot appeal to any higher authority for a justification or an excuse for the murders.

By means of a scene in which Jupiter warns Aegistheus of the danger to his life, Sartre also lays bare the workings of Aegistheus' mind. Aegistheus, though a ruler, is a victim of the image he has created for himself. Motivated by a love of order, all his actions have tended in that direction. Now, old and weary, prey to some of the fears and superstitions for which he was himself responsible, he looks forward gladly to death. The thought, however, that Orestes knows himself to be free can rouse Aegistheus to indignation, for this freedom constitutes a threat to order.

Set against this backdrop is Electra, Orestes' loyal and devoted sister. At first, she is passionately against her stepfather's reign and even suggests to Orestes the possibility of making a choice of action, but not an existentialist choice, since the choice of which she speaks is only one between retreat and vengeance. Understandably, after Aegistheus' death, she denies her participation in the assassination and accepts remorse and divine retribution: "I will be your creature and your slave. . . . I repent, Zeus, I bitterly repent." In this way, her conduct shows the worst example of bad faith.

The citizens are also not authentic in the existentialist way. While Electra wrongly believes that she was misled by Orestes, the citizens play at public confessions in blind conformity to collective remorse and in superstitious fear of words. They are told, but refuse to admit, that the plague is in fact no more than the imposition of responsibility on themselves from the outside, from the gods or from Aegistheus, and that they have the power to reject this allegedly superior order in recognition of humanity as the one and only value.

Besides a literary exposition of Sartre's philosophical ideas, *The Flies* can also be interpreted as a reference to the situation in France during the Nazi era. In this context, the flies represent the German occupiers; Zeus, as their leader trying to enforce his arbitrary rule on the French citizens through Aegistheus, obviously portrays Marshal Philippe Pétain, France's main collaborator with Adolf Hitler. That the French are willing to tolerate abuse and moral shame to survive is evident by their acceptance of the political status quo. Only Orestes and Electra are eager to resist the new order, although Electra is ultimately unable to withstand the physical and mental torture inherent in such a regime. For his part, Orestes proves by his actions that people are free and that dictators remain in power solely when no one rises to question their authority. In posing the central question of commitment, this drama foreshadows much of Sartre's postwar fiction.

"Critical Evaluation" by Pierre L. Horn

Bibliography:

Champigny, Robert. *Sartre and Drama*. Birmingham, Ala.: French Literature Publications, 1982. After first developing a critical discussion based on Sartre's dramatic theories, this brief but well-argued monograph shows, by examining individual plays, that Sartre did not always put theories into practice in his plays.

Contat, Michel, and Michel Rybalka, eds. *Sartre on Theater*. Translated by Frank Jellinek. New York: Pantheon Books, 1976. A handy anthology of various documents written by Sartre about the theater. Included, along with the jacket copy for the French publication of *The Flies* in book form, are excerpts of press interviews and articles pointing out the political content of this work.

McCall, Dorothy. *The Theatre of Jean-Paul Sartre*. New York: Columbia University Press, 1969. An excellent overview of Sartre's dramatic works with special emphasis on their philosophical, literary, psychological, and sociological ideas and values. Useful bibliography.

Schilpp, Paul A., ed. *The Philosophy of Jean-Paul Sartre*. La Salle, Ill.: Open Court, 1981. Intelligent and scholarly presentation of the different aspects of Sartrean philosophy. Of particular interest to readers of *The Flies* are the chapters concerned with bad faith, authenticity, freedom, essence, and commitment.

Spoerri, Theophil. "The Structure of Existence: *The Flies*." In *Sartre: A Collection of Critical Essays*, edited by Edith Kern. Englewood Cliffs, N.J.: Prentice-Hall, 1962. An imaginative and penetrating interpretation exploring not only the play's main themes and characters but also the difficult obstacle of reconciling Orestes' ethical revolt with his love for his people.

THE FLOATING OPERA

Type of work: Novel
Author: John Barth (1930-   )
Type of plot: Psychological realism
Time of plot: 1930's
Locale: Maryland's eastern shore
First published: 1956; revised, 1967

> *Principal characters:*
> TODD ANDREWS, narrator of the novel and lawyer in the town of
>   Cambridge, Maryland
> HARRISON MACK, Todd's friend
> JANE MACK, Harrison's wife and Todd's mistress
> JEANNINE MACK, the Macks' child and possibly Todd's daughter
> CAPTAIN OSBORN JONES and
> MISTER HAECKER, roomers at the hotel where Todd lives

The Story:

The 1956 version of *The Floating Opera* was heavily edited by the original publisher; the account that follows refers to John Barth's revised 1967 version.

Todd Andrews, narrator of *The Floating Opera*, began in 1954 to write the story of one important day in his life, June 21 or 22, 1937 (he could not remember exactly which), the day he finally decided not to kill himself. *The Floating Opera* was not only the name of Todd's account of that day but also an important part of the narrative and a metaphor for the organization of the book. Todd imagined a kind of showboat that would drift up and down a waterway, moved by the currents and the tide. The boat would carry actors who would put on a show for the people along the shore. The boat would be moving, so people would only be able to see and hear pieces of the show. Todd wrote that life is like that, and so was his book. Such a showboat, also called *The Floating Opera*, figured in the climax of the book, for Todd originally planned to blow up himself and all the people on the boat during a performance.

Todd was a lawyer who lived in a hotel, where he sometimes had visits from his lover, Jane Mack, the wife of one of his friends and clients, Harrison Mack. The affair had begun some years earlier when Harrison and Jane wanted to prove that they had a liberal marriage by coercing Todd into sleeping with Jane. After the affair began, Harrison found that he did not feel as casual about sharing his wife with another man as he had thought that he would, and Jane also felt guilty, but the relationship between Todd and Jane continued in a haphazard manner for years. Jane had a daughter, Jeannine, who may have been Todd's daughter; no one was sure. On the morning of Todd's important day, Jane had visited him in his room.

After visiting with two other roomers in the hotel, Captain Osborn Jones and Mister Haecker, Todd paid his rent for one day at the hotel desk as he always had. Todd had lived at the hotel for years, so there was no apparent reason for paying his rent one day at a time, but Todd did so to remind himself each day that it might be his last. There would be no point in paying for more than one day. In fact, Todd had much evidence in his life that death could overtake him at any time. He remembered his father chopping the head off a chicken and then handing the carcass to Todd to help prepare for supper. He had been in World War I and shared a frightened night in a foxhole with a German soldier. As morning approached, although Todd had felt a renewed sense of humanity from his contact with the German, Todd killed the other soldier. During a service physical Todd found that he had a weak heart that might fail at any moment.

The most stunning reminder of the closeness of death was the suicide of Todd's father, who had been despondent over his business failures. Todd's attempt to make sense of his father's death was the purpose of the manuscript on which Todd labored at night, the *Inquiry*. Although the *Inquiry* was supposed to be an explanation of the reasons behind Todd's father's suicide, it had expanded to cover a number of related topics and filled several large containers in Todd's room. Todd also worked from time to time on a boat that he was as likely to finish as the *Inquiry*. He considered his work on the boat and on the *Inquiry* to be as hopeful as his paying his rent one day at a time was not; his life might end at any time, but it also might go on for a long time. No one could know which.

On Todd's important day, he decided that after years of living and thinking, he could find no reason why any course of action was better or worse than any other. Therefore, there was no reason to live, so he resolved in the morning to live the day ahead as he would any other and then to kill himself at its conclusion. This action was gratuitous, but Todd had a history of gratuitous behavior. Besides the killing of the German soldier, which might have made some sense because both men were participants in a war, Todd had also given five thousand dollars to wealthy Colonel Morton, an action so unusual that it bedeviled the Colonel. To vary his regular activities would suggest that there was some reason for his suicide, so Todd continued to conduct the business of his law firm.

At the end of the day, there was a performance on *The Floating Opera* at the harbor, which Todd and the Macks attended. Todd arranged his suicide by turning on the gas jets in a cabin on the boat and waiting for the explosion that would kill him and everyone else on board. After a time, during which there should have been an explosion but nothing happened, Todd gave up and left the boat, along with the rest of the audience. Someone perhaps had come along and closed the gas jets; Todd never found out why the boat did not blow up. The event made him rethink his reasons for choosing suicide. If there was no reason to do anything, there was no reason to kill oneself. One may as well go on living.

Critical Evaluation:

The Floating Opera is simultaneously funny, with a laugh on every page, and depressing, with a somber background that is difficult to dismiss even in the novel's most comic moments. Its narrator is a man who at one point in his life decided that he did not want to live and acted to kill himself. The day is shadowed over with dread as he moves toward that tragic conclusion. The dread is felt by the reader, not by Todd, who carries on as if the day were like any other. The reader knows that Todd did not kill himself, because he survived to write his narrative. Furthermore, Todd Andrews announces early in his story that the key day is really the day that he decided not to kill himself, although the day began with the decision to commit suicide. Throughout the book Todd presents his reasons for self-destruction, yet the reader is held in psychological suspension, knowing that all the reasons Todd advances, with the attention to detail characteristic of a lawyer, will somehow be swept away. There is hope in the despair and laughter in the tears.

One of the literary antecedents of *The Floating Opera* is Laurence Sterne's novel *Tristram Shandy* (1759-1767), in which a first-person narrator, Tristram Shandy, sets out to tell the story of one day in his life—the day he was born. As Tristram begins to describe his mother, his father, and his uncle in order to explain the circumstances of his birth, he digresses to incidents before his birth and during his life to fill out the history of these other characters. After several hundred pages, in the course of which the reader finds out what kind of a person Tristram is, he is still no closer to his announced purpose than when he started. The general effect and most of the digressions are comic, but the novel makes a serious point about time, which is that time is not outside but inside. Each human being contains all the moments of his or her life. Many of the moments of one's past may have more impact on one's life than what is occurring in the present. *The Floating Opera* uses the same rambling, digression-filled approach to make the same point.

A profound moment for Todd was his father's suicide. Todd found his father's blackened, bulgy-eyed hanged body, cut it down, and carried it to a bedroom. Although Todd presents these details with the same kind of control that characterizes his handling of the rest of the novel, this event obviously has had a powerful impact upon him. It is an example of the past's dominance over the present. One's first source of love and assurance is one's parents, and when a parent commits suicide, a child feels the ultimate withdrawal of love and experiences the worst act of rejection. Todd had, even before his father's death, come to think of sex as little consolation. While making love for the first time with his high school friend Betty June Gunter, Todd looks in a mirror, sees how ridiculous the two of them look, and begins laughing.

Sex does not distract Todd; friendship and love do not help deter Todd from his goal of suicide either. When Jane Mack broke off their affair in the past, this disruption caused Todd no particular grief, and he resumes their relationship with the same indifference. He shows no special regard for Jeannine, the little girl whose father he might be. This point marks an important difference between the first version of the novel and the second. In the second version, Todd arranges for not only his own death but almost takes seven hundred people with him. The original publishers thought that readers would reject a mass murderer, so they had Barth change the ending to one in which Todd plans to destroy only the part of the boat that he is in. Moreover, he is interrupted by a crew member who finds him and turns off the gas jets, giving Todd the news that Jeannine has become ill. Thus, Todd, prior to his attempted suicide, is concerned about the lives of others and is brought back from the brink of death by ordinary human concern for his possible daughter. Some of the reviewers of the first version of *The Floating Opera* thought that ending to be sentimental, unconvincing, and inconsistent with Todd's character.

The ending that Barth preferred all along and that he used in the second version fits Todd better. He is not interested in people and emotions, but in ideas. If nothing has any ultimate meaning, then there is no reason for Todd to try to preserve the lives of the hundreds of people on the boat, any more than there is a reason for him to preserve his own. The absence of the explosion in both versions gives Todd a chance to make a further observation. If nothing has any ultimate meaning or value, there is no point in choosing a course of action based on negativity, be is asceticism, cynicism, or suicide. To choose such a course of action would be to impute ultimate meaning to the theory that there is no ultimate meaning. It is reasonable, even logical, to go on living in the midst of the mystery of life.

Jim Baird

Bibliography:
Bowen, Zack. *A Reader's Guide to John Barth*. Westport, Conn.: Greenwood Press, 1994. Contains a chapter on *The Floating Opera* with emphasis on the book's relationship to twentieth century philosophical and artistic concerns.
LeClair, Thomas. "John Barth's *The Floating Opera*: Death and the Craft of Fiction." *Texas Studies in Literature and Language* 14, no. 4 (Winter, 1973): 711-730. Focuses on Todd

Andrews as narrator of his story and how his storytelling ultimately helps to save him from suicide.

Morrell, David. *John Barth: An Introduction*. University Park: Pennsylvania State University Press, 1976. The chapter on *The Floating Opera* notes carefully the differences between the two versions and comments on the philosophical values expressed in the novel.

Schickel, Richard. "*The Floating Opera*." *Critique* 6, no. 2 (Fall, 1963): 53-67. This essay appeared before the second version of the novel, and it assesses the weaknesses of the first version, which the second version corrected.

Walkiewicz, E. P. *John Barth*. Boston: Twayne, 1986. A brief introduction to all of Barth's work, with sections on *The Floating Opera*.

FLOWERS OF EVIL

Type of work: Poetry
Author: Charles Baudelaire (1821-1867)
First published: Les Fleurs du mal, 1857; revised, 1861; definitive edition, 1868 (English translation, 1931)

Flowers of Evil, Charles Baudelaire's most famous work, is classical in its clarity, discipline, and form, yet Romantic in its subjectivity, spirit of revolt, and macabre elements. Baudelaire's collection contains none of the historical or narrative poems typical of contemporaneous poetic works. The poems of *Flowers of Evil* were written at various dates, but their grouping and emotional tenor lend coherence and heighten intertextual relation. In the enlarged second edition, the book opens with "Benediction," describing the poet's birth, and closes with a vision of death and promise of rebirth in "The Voyage." The punning title suggests the poems are products of evil and illness (both meanings of the French word *mal*). At the same time, they adorn evil. True poetry, like a flower, beautifies whatever it touches.

In the first and largest section, *Spleen and Ideal*, the poet discards previous criteria of ideal beauty and instead finds poetry in the hideous realities of everyday life. Although entitled *Spleen and Ideal*, the cycle tends more toward the ideal. The first twenty-one poems are all related to the problems facing the artist and to the nature of beauty. Within these poems, there are two subcycles: One considers the grandeur, the misery, and the ideal of beauty; the other considers the three women important to Baudelaire and different permutations of love.

"Benediction" depicts the poet persecuted by society and redeemed by posthumous fame. "The Albatross," one of the most famous poems of the collection, treats the Romantic theme of the poet's isolation. The poem builds the traditional antithesis between the genius of the poet and his inability to adapt to an indifferent society. "Correspondences" evokes Platonic correspondences between visible forms and higher reality, as well as those between the senses. "Beacons" delineates the work of eight writers and artists as proof of humankind's dignity. "A Former Life" revels in the sensuous pleasure of exotic beauty. "Beauty" suggests true beauty is passionless, while passion is animal. "The Ideal" and "The Giant" reveal that beauty is always strange and monumental. In "Hymn to Beauty," art results from attraction to good and evil simultaneously. In the end, beauty's chief value is its power to satisfy a longing for the infinite and an escape from the misery of the human condition.

The love poems in *Spleen and Ideal* divide into three groups, each devoted to a particular woman and the type of beauty she represents. Memory is both Baudelaire's theme and method in the love poems. His emotions reveal a mingling of love and hate, loathing of his own weakness and of his mistress' cruelty. The poems celebrating Jeanne Duval evoke physical passion and despair aroused by a woman incapable of appreciating his art or love. The sensuality of "The Jewels" is both cerebral and aesthetic. "Exotic Perfume" and "Her Hair" are both inspired by scent, which offers an exotic escape from reality. Baudelaire sees himself as a victim of desire in "The Vampire" and compares his tormentor to a cold, aloof feline in "The Cat." "The Balcony," however, traces feelings of nostalgia and anticipates a reconciliation. Madame Sabatier's cycle of poems parallels the sequence of experiences in the cycle devoted to Jeanne. The poems begin with a celebration of the blonde Venus' grace and end with contradictory emotions of love and hate. In "Evening Harmony," the poet's ecstasy is expressed in terms of religious adoration. The cycle of Marie Daubrun associates her beauty with autumn's misty skies. "The Invitation to a Voyage," another of Baudelaire's famed verses, returns to a lost Eden that he shares with his beloved. The cycle of Marie ends with a baroque poem, "To a Madonna," that combines love, hate, jealousy, and revenge in a rich, ornate style.

The rest of the poems in *Spleen and Ideal* first adopt a lighter tone before yielding to a somber mood, enhancing the irony that Baudelaire felt was fundamental to literary creation. Spleen is a metaphysical malady, a paralysis of emotions, a feeling of isolation, a lack of desire. Nature reflects his fear in "Obsession." "The Thirst for Nothingness," one of the better known *Spleen and Ideal* poems, reflects the utter despair of the poet by images of absence. The most sadistic of the poems, "The Self-Torturer," seems an ironic commentary on his lover's deception, but also seems to refer to his own self-deception.

In the next section, *Parisian Scenes*, Baudelaire finds inspiration in the streets of Paris, lingering in the mystical acuity of sensation. He added the Parisian poems in 1861 to create a cityscape. In "Landscape," which opens the new section, Baudelaire combines personal impression with realistic description. "The Swan" expresses the feelings of exile that he shares with other city dwellers. "The Blind," like the poet himself, wander through the city in bewilderment and despair. The poet, however, has no hope, while the blind, eyes heavenward, have faith. In "To a Passerby," the poet encounters a woman who, as she disappears from sight, brings a realization of a love that might have been. In "Parisian Dream," Baudelaire envisions a futuristic city without nature, sound, or light. The dream he recounts, induced by drugs, marks a preference for the artificial. In "Twilight" and "Dawn," he celebrates the city rather than nature. Baudelaire endows the cityscape with mystery and tragedy.

In the sections *Wine* and *Flowers of Evil*, the poet turns to wine and sadism as an artificial paradise. In the 1861 edition, wine and narcotics symbolize vices that ultimately lead to humanity's destruction. There are only five poems in the section *Wine*, and these are among the least successful in the collection. In *Flowers of Evil*, he indulges in sadistic dreams of torture and violence to stimulate his senses and enliven dead emotions. The opening poem, "Destruction," depicts a struggle between extreme sensuality and spiritual longing. Throughout the cycle, Baudelaire emphasizes the deceptive charm of evil and its disastrous consequences. In "A Martyr," the beauty of an ornate room redolent with decaying flowers frames the sight of a woman's decapitated body, rendering the horrible beautiful. "The Damned Women," which was banned in the 1861 edition, evokes compassion for those who ignore custom and law. Baudelaire, in the poems on lesbianism, pities those who suffer torment from pleasure. "Lesbos" looks back nostalgically to Sappho's time. "A Voyage to Cythera," one of the finest poems in the collection, is an ironic allegory of idealized love.

In *Revolt*, the poet rejects his illusions and revolts against an imperfect world. While admitting Christ's divinity and remembering his suffering, he reproaches his failure to seek reform through positive action. "The Denial of Saint Peter" encourages human struggle against pain and evil. "Abel and Cain" focuses on Cain, who rejects society and an unjust God, whereas Abel is smugly content. "The Litanies of Satan" are based on the Catholic liturgy. The prayers are directed to the Romantic Satan, who was a symbol of revolt and heroic energy. Since God is evil and Christ has failed, Satan comforts by offering revolt against the injustice of social order.

In the cycle entitled *Death*, the poet longs for the discovery of another world. Death is welcomed as the only hope in "The Death of the Poor." In "The Death of Artists," death brings fruition to their dreams. "The Voyage" brings the collection to a logical conclusion by reintroducing the taste for the infinite, the desire to escape, the quest for the unknown, the prevalence of sin, and a disbelief in progress. The dramatic use of monologue and dialogue, the change of tone from casual to sweeping, alternations in mood from ironic to exalted, and inventive imagery mark the culmination of Baudelaire's poetic creation.

The conflict between good and evil, spleen and ideal, dream and reality, unify the six sections. Obsessed with a belief in Original Sin and the duality of human nature, Baudelaire examines the spiritual problems of his age with a brutal self-analysis that distinguishes him from predecessors. The poems are morally neutral, recording obsessions, fantasies, delinquency, inertia, and despair in a claustrophobic atmosphere. His sympathies for his fellow beings is selective, but he champions those on the margins of society, both meek victims and defiant rebels. Descriptions of nature are virtually absent from his poetry; instead, the city is invoked as a concentrated arena of human distress and vitality.

Among Baudelaire's chief innovations are correspondences on a transcendental level between the visible and invisible worlds, and between exterior nature and inner thoughts and feelings. He finds symbols in exterior reality that correspond to his inner thoughts and feelings. Human beauty is a terrestrial experience, which finds its double in transcendent experience. This type of symbol not only gives concrete form to abstraction but helps Baudelaire to achieve an indispensable obscurity that allows the reader's participation. Baudelaire also introduces correspondences between the senses in a synaesthetic mixture of sounds, colors, and perfumes. Perfumes, colors, and sounds, in turn, suggest feelings and moods.

Baudelaire prefers analysis to pure exoticism. His poetry introduces the crude or prosaic image in the midst of highly poetic style, and treats sordid reality without losing poetic elevation. Allegorical personifications dominate his poetry. Emotional and intellectual states are featured as characters, like Pleasure or Bitterness, and recall Baroque poetry. Irony, including puns, paradox, and antithesis, is the most common feature of expression. Images of infinity contrast with those of immobility throughout the collection. The very ideal of Beauty is absolute immobility. For all of Baudelaire's innovation in poetic expression, he does not experiment with prosody. The structure of his lines and stanzas are firmly entrenched in the classical French tradition.

Flowers of Evil spiritualizes both memory and sensuous fulfillment. The majority of the poems are marked by recollection. Baudelaire was among the first poets to explore the full potential of olfactory images and their association with memory. Memory heightens the contradiction between desire for the infinite and for the sensual and concrete. The love poems also turn to a past more strongly desired than the present. Love poems, which serve as tributes to the physical and moral attributes of women, examine psychological as well as physical moments of intimacy. The relationships move from passion to tenderness to disenchantment. As the poet moves from past to present, love evolves into obsession mingled with contempt, degradation, and torment.

Baudelaire was well aware that he risked prosecution for blasphemy and offenses against public morality on the publication of *Flowers of Evil*. The defense offered at the trial claimed that book should be taken as a whole. Blasphemous or obscene poems must be set against others of spiritual beauty and platonic love. His Satanism and rebelliousness reflect Romantic developments, while his subject matter resembles that of the Realists, and his love poetry revives Renaissance traditions of gallantry. His exploration of the associative powers of language also anticipates Surrealism. Baudelaire not only synthesized traditions, but also created innovative verse through the intensity and detail of his self-analysis, the emotional ambivalence that confuses hate and love, and an eye for the teeming pathos and mystery of city life.

Pamela Pavliscak

Bibliography:

Benjamin, Walter. *Charles Baudelaire: A Lyric Poet in the Era of High Capitalism.* Translated by Harry Zohn. London: New Left Books, 1973. Looks at literature in its social context and finds Baudelaire to be emblematic of his times. Discusses Baudelaire as a chronicler of Parisian city life, and a critic of industrialization and the advent of materialist culture.

Houston, John Porter. *French Symbolism and the Modernist Movement: A Study of Poetic Structures.* Baton Rouge: Louisiana State University Press, 1980. Presents *Flowers of Evil* as the foundation of French Symbolism and European Modernism. Focuses on the self-reflexive quality of Baudelaire's poetry and his demoniac persona.

Hyslop, Lois Boe. *Charles Baudelaire Revisited.* New York: Twayne, 1992. Excellent overview of the poet's life and works. The chapter devoted to *Flowers of Evil* examines the poems in their respective groupings, followed by a consideration of overarching themes. Suggests its continuity with Baudelaire's other works.

Leakey, F. W. *Baudelaire: "Les Fleurs du mal."* Cambridge, England: Cambridge University Press, 1992. Extensive evaluation of each edition of *Flowers of Evil.* Analyzes the differences between the different editions; elaborates on the coherence of each section and the collection as a whole. Discusses the main themes and stylistic features of the verse.

Peyre, Henri, ed. *Baudelaire: A Collection of Critical Essays.* Englewood Cliffs, N.J.: Prentice-Hall, 1962. Eleven important articles written by eminent Baudelaire scholars. Spans a wide range of topics, including an exploration of imagery, the poet's persona, public reaction, and Baudelaire's influence on contemporaries.

THE FOLKS

Type of work: Novel
Author: Ruth Suckow (1892-1960)
Type of plot: Domestic realism
Time of plot: Early twentieth century
Locale: Iowa
First published: 1934

> *Principal characters:*
> FRED FERGUSON, a husband and father
> ANNIE FERGUSON, his wife
> CARL WILLIAM FERGUSON, their older son
> MARGARET "MARGOT" FERGUSON, their older daughter
> DOROTHY FERGUSON, their younger daughter
> BUNNY FERGUSON, a son, their youngest child

The Story:

On a beautiful September morning, Fred Ferguson got up early and strolled around his yard. Although he was proud of his comfortable home and his position in the small town of Belmond, Iowa, where he lived, Fred felt burdened by his responsibilities. So many people seemed to depend on Fred: his family, his coworkers at the bank, his fellow Presbyterians, in fact, the whole community. When Fred's wife, Annie, got up, she thought briefly about her dead parents and the inevitability of change. Then she began her day's work. At breakfast, their daughter Margaret was generally nasty, causing Annie to wonder why this middle child was so different. As usual, Fred was obtuse; as usual, Annie tried to please him. After everyone had left, she brooded about how tired she was of pretending and how much she resented having to placate Fred's hypercritical mother and sister.

Life went on. Margaret disobeyed her mother and had to be punished. The Fergusons went to dinner at the home place. The Monday Club met with Annie, and for the first time the frugal Fred let his wife hire someone to help her. That night, Annie amazed Fred by telling him of her feelings about the family. Although he assured her of his love, he still did not understand.

The children were growing up. Still playing his part as the good son, Carl was a star football player and a student leader of his high school. He was admired by everyone, especially his little brother, Bunny, and his girlfriend, Lillian White. At the Presbyterian college he attended, Carl was fascinated by livelier girls, but after graduation he married Lillian. They had two sons. Carl became a school principal, then a superintendent. Bored by his work and frustrated by Lillian's sexual passiveness, Carl sought the company of more vivacious women. The crisis came when he told Lillian that they were moving to Philadelphia, where one of his women friends had found him a new position. Upset about her pregnancy and certain that her husband did not love her, Lillian tried to kill herself, but Carl stopped her in the nick of time. Turning down the Philadelphia offer, Carl became superintendent of schools in a town near Belmond. Although Lillian lost her baby, she was now secure in their marriage. Carl, however, had lost his faith in himself. He now knew that he was nothing special after all.

On Dorothy's wedding day, everything seemed perfect. Her handsome fiancé, Jesse Woodward, liked her family and her little town. He had even been nice about going with her to be introduced to old family friends. Dorothy and Jesse had a shiny new roadster, their wedding gift

2351

from Jesse's wealthy grandfather. Almost before she knew it, Dorothy was putting on her bridal dress and hearing the familiar words. Suddenly the ceremony was over, and the two young people drove off to start their life together.

Margaret helped a friend elope, and so was expelled from college and sent home, where she proceeded to inflict her own unhappiness on everyone around her. She could foresee spending her life working at the Belmond public library, but it was her library job that enabled her to escape. Fred permitted Margaret to go to New York in order to take a library course. Once there, Margaret quit school and left the family with whom her father had deposited her. Encouraged by her new, artistic friends, Margaret renamed herself Margot, cut her hair, and moved into a Greenwich Village apartment, supporting herself by working as a waitress.

When she met Bruce Williams, an older, married man, Margot abandoned the Bohemian life. She had always dreamed of a grand passion, and she was sure that this was it. When she set off on a long trip to the West with Bruce, Margot could not have been happier. Bruce kept thinking about his wife and his children, however, and eventually he returned home. Devastated, Margot went back to Belmond, only to find that she was now regarded as a temptress. Determined to make a career for herself, Margot went back to New York. Then Bruce telephoned, and Margot took him back on his own terms.

Just when Annie was thinking that at least she still had Bunny, he came home with a wife. The former Charlotte Bukowksa did not like her new family any more than they liked her. Annie thought her rude and sullen. Charlotte, who was a Marxist, classified the Fergusons as hopelessly bourgeois. When the couple left Belmond for Chicago, it did not seem likely that they would be back soon.

When Fred retired, he agreed to take Annie on the trip she had always dreamed about, and the two set off for California. When they got to San Diego, they found that Dorothy and Jesse were so hard-pressed financially that they had rented out their big home and were camping out in a tiny house with no room for guests. Living in a small apartment they rented, Fred and Annie could not help wishing they were back home. On their way home, they stopped at the luxurious home of Annie's sister Louise, but Annie found that she and her sister had lost their old closeness.

Back in Belmond, at first Fred and Annie felt displaced. Fred's church had closed, and his bank was in difficulty. Fred soon found that there were people who needed his help, and once again he had a reason for living. As for Annie, now that she had finally had her trip, she began to feel her old tenderness toward Fred. Whatever the future held, they both realized, they could face it together.

Critical Evaluation:

When it was published, *The Folks* was hailed as, if not the great American novel, at least the best novel about the Midwest that had ever been written. Unlike contemporaries like Sinclair Lewis, who in *Main Street* (1920) and later novels pictured Midwestern small towns as stifling, their inhabitants as pretentious and hypocritical, Ruth Suckow had produced a book that critics called truly realistic. Although to outsiders Belmond may seem serene and even dull, its people have their share of inner conflicts and of uncertainty about the future.

In *The Folks*, the Ferguson home place represents the agrarian life and traditional values. At the beginning of the novel, Fred's aging parents still live in the old family home, which is appropriately called the rock house. Just across the road is the new house, built by Fred's sister and her husband, who works the farm. When they are young, all of Fred's children like to go out to the home place. As adults, however, Margaret finds her place in the city, Dorothy in the suburbs. Even for Carl, living on the farm is never a real option. During his mid-life crisis, Carl daydreams about becoming a farmer, but he lacks the will to make any drastic change in his life. Perhaps what Carl really wants is not a new vocation but a return to his youth.

By the time Bunny takes his new wife out to the home place, his grandparents are dead, the rock house is deserted, and the farm itself is being worked by renters. Bunny speaks about spending a summer in the rock house; however, Charlotte feels a revulsion toward any land that is privately owned. Her aim is to move to Russia and work in an agricultural commune.

In *The Folks*, Americans are shown to be losing a system of values, along with their ties to the land. Annie may be correct in blaming Fred's frugality on his Scottish ancestry, but his sense of obligation to his church and to the less fortunate in his community reflect the ethical and religious standards of an earlier time, not of a particular national background. Fred always tries to do what is right, not what is convenient, but none of his children possesses the father's sense of moral certainty. Dorothy drifts along with Jesse, and Bunny, troubled by social injustice, meanders toward Marxism. The rebellious Margaret easily discards her parents' standards of sexual morality and embarks on her own pursuit of happiness. One might think that Carl, at least, is impelled by principle when he renews his commitment to Lillian. In fact, Carl is only too aware that his remaining with his wife is the result of his weakness, rather than of any moral strength. Carl is not, like Fred, a man of conviction; he is simply a conformist, still trying to fit into the role of the good son that he had assumed in childhood.

Despite Fred's goodness, he is too much a man of his time to comprehend the frustrations of his own wife. Annie loves Fred and wants to be a good wife to him; however, society defines that role as one of total submission. It is not just that Fred buys the cars and decides when the house should be remodeled, or even that he assumes Annie will attend his church. Even her smallest decision is designed to avoid criticism from him or from his family. When she runs out of eggs and needs to do some baking, Annie cannot just get what she needs from the store, for her thrifty husband would want her to wait for the free eggs from the farm. Even her treasured time alone, after everyone has finished breakfast and left the house, has to be cut short because someone from Fred's family might stop by, see that the dishes had not yet been washed, and report Annie's slothfulness to her husband.

Annie blames Fred and his obtuseness for her occasional unhappiness. Like most of the women of Belmond, Annie has no idea that society could be structured other than as a patriarchal system. Suckow sees change coming even in the area of gender roles; ever the realist, she does not see the new independence of women as an unmixed blessing. Thus Margaret, who scorns docile women like her mother and her sister, in fact gives up her freedom, as well as her future, when she agrees to be the mistress of a married man. Ironically, the most independent woman in the novel, Charlotte, is also one of the most unpleasant.

At the end of *The Folks*, even Fred sees that his era is over and that his children will lead lives much different from his. With her characteristic honesty, Suckow stops there. The future, she implies, must speak for itself.

Rosemary M. Canfield Reisman

Bibliography:
Herron, Ima Honaker. *The Small Town in American Literature.* New York: Haskell House, 1971. Classifies Suckow as a fair, dispassionate, and accurate observer of small town life in the Midwest. *The Folks* is also the story of rapidly changing times and a changing American society.

Kissane, Leedice McAnelly. *Ruth Suckow*. New York: Twayne, 1969. Major book-length study of the author. In a lengthy analysis of *The Folks*, which she considers Suckow's best work, Kissane considers style, theme, and characterization. Chronology, extensive notes, and annotated bibliography.

Omrcanin, Margaret Stewart. *Ruth Suckow: A Critical Study of Her Fiction*. Philadelphia: Dorrance, 1972. A topical analysis of Suckow's works. References to *The Folks* are scattered through chapters on setting, social significance, and universal themes. Appendices contain chronological bibliography of Suckow's writings and comprehensive list of secondary sources.

Tomkinson, Grace. "Cycle of Iowa." *The Canadian Forum* 15 (December, 1934): 119-120. Praises Suckow's skill, her honesty, her penetrating characterization, and her gentle satire. Although called "the great Middlewestern novel," in fact *The Folks* has a universal appeal.

Van Doren, Dorothy. "Real People." *The Nation* 139 (October 17, 1934): 454-455. An interesting contemporaneous review. Argues that the novel is about the failure of an old order and the birth of a new, "as inevitable as it is unsatisfying." Despite some technical imperfections, *The Folks* is "warm with the breath of life."

FOMA GORDEYEV

Type of work: Novel
Author: Maxim Gorky (Aleksey Maksimovich Peshkov, 1868-1936)
Type of plot: Psychological realism
Time of plot: Late nineteenth century
Locale: Russia
First published: 1899 (English translation, 1901)

Principal characters:
> FOMA GORDEYEV, a young man of the merchant class
> IGNAT, his father
> ANFISA, his aunt
> MAYAKIN, his godfather
> EZHOFF, a brilliant youth
> LIUBOFF, Mayakin's daughter

The Story:

Ignat began as a water pumper, but, by the time he was forty years old, he was a rich owner of barges and tugs and a determined and ruthless trader. At times, however, he was subject to fits of depression and he would carouse with the dregs of the city; sometimes, he would exult fiercely when one of his barges burned. He was a huge man with boundless energy. His greatest disappointment was that he had no son; his wife had borne only daughters who died in infancy. When he was forty-three years old, his wife suddenly died, and, within six months, he had found a young bride. Natalya was tall and handsome, dutiful but mysterious. Although ordinarily submissive, she had strength of character which made boisterous Ignat afraid to beat her. She died after the birth of Foma, Ignat's long-desired son.

Until he was six years old, Foma was reared in his godfather Mayakin's house. Under the watchful, stupid eye of a female relative, he played unimaginatively with Liuboff, Mayakin's daughter. Ignat then took back his son, and Foma's Aunt Anfisa looked after him. Anfisa told him many fanciful tales which whetted the young boy's imagination.

At the age of eight, Foma discussed the family business with Ignat and was disappointed that his father was only a river merchant instead of a pirate. To clear up his misapprehensions, Ignat took the boy on a business trip down the river. Foma got along well with the peasants until he told his father how one worker had been uncomplimentary to the capitalistic class. Ignat struck the worker. This incident always seemed brutal to the boy.

At school, Foma made two friends: Smolin, a fat, rich boy, and Ezhoff, a quick-thinking poor boy. Foma progressed well in his classes because Ezhoff helped him study and prompted him during recitations. In and out of school pranks, Foma was a daring leader. His courage was due in part to his father's wealth, but he was also truly honest and fearless. As he grew up, Liuboff was the only girl he knew. Mayakin hoped that they would marry and unite the two family fortunes.

When Foma was not yet twenty, Ignat put him in charge of a trading expedition and told the tug captain to keep an eye on the young man. Foma quickly established his superiority over the older captain and took complete command. He did quite well, except that he was often too generous in giving grain to the peasants. He noticed on deck one night a peasant woman with attractive eyes. Although she was older than he, Foma desired to meet her, and the captain arranged to have her come to Foma's cabin at night. The woman was thirty years old, delightfully mature to the naïve Foma. He left her with regret when Mayakin sent a message requiring him to come home as soon as possible.

Mayakin told Foma that his father was in the clutches of a conniving woman who had already gotten large sums of money from him. At first, Foma was afraid that Ignat had taken a mistress. To Mayakin, the situation seemed even worse; Madame Medynsky had induced Ignat to give liberally to charity. Mayakin had no use for charity. The merchant class, he thought, should use its money to make more money. For a time, Foma helped his father and faithfully attended to business. It was hard work for him, although he was far from stupid. He could see no point in trading, no excuse for amassing a fortune. Liuboff confused him when he talked with her. She read books, to Foma a foolish pastime, for in them he found no answers to his questions. Foma never read much; in polite society, he was always ill at ease.

When Ignat died, Foma felt more insecure. Attending a public gathering to dedicate a building to which his father had contributed, he had to leave before the ceremony was over. Nevertheless, he was greatly interested in Madame Medynsky, the moving spirit in his father's philanthropies. He visited her often, and she was very gracious to him, for he was handsome as well as rich. All the while, however, Foma felt troubled, for she seemed to play with his affections. When Foma heard she was an abandoned woman, he refused to believe the tales. In fact, one night he soundly thrashed an official who spoke slightingly of her chastity.

When Mayakin tried to quiet the affair and set Foma back in the path of commercial rectitude, Foma rebelled. He went on a spree with several others and finally wound up on a raft in company with coldly attractive Sasha. Drunk enough to be affected greatly by Sasha's duets with her sister, he cut the mooring lines. As the raft floated away, Sasha swam to shore. She and Foma laughed immoderately as the others in the party floated helplessly down the river.

After some days, he and Sasha came upon one of his barges, and Foma forced the captain to let him take command. He promptly steered the barge into a collision, and the craft sank. It was an expensive and scandalous business to raise it. In the midst of their liaison, Sasha left Foma. She could not stand his continual questioning as to the purpose of life. When Mayakin heard what had happened to the barge, he took a power of attorney and left Foma to his own devices.

By chance, Foma encountered Ezhoff, now a brilliant, satirical journalist. Fascinated by his former schoolmate, he was puzzled because Ezhoff had had so little worldly success. Once he went with Ezhoff when the journalist made a revolutionary speech to a gathering of printers, but mostly the two drank together. At last, Foma went home, soberer but scarcely wiser. There he learned Liuboff had become engaged to Smolin, who had turned into an unctuous, polished trader. Mayakin, still hoping to redeem Foma, took him to a ship launching. As he listened to the laudatory speeches and heard the blatant congratulations to the owner, Foma lost control of himself. He compelled the rich businessmen to listen as he probed beneath their smug shells of respectability. One man had barely escaped trial for seducing a little girl; another had falsely accused his mistress and had her sent to prison; a third had turned out his nephews to starve; still another had owned a brothel. As Foma bawled out his terrible accusations, the men fell on him and bound him. His godfather had him confined in an asylum. Years later, he could be seen in the streets of the town, shabby, half-witted, and intoxicated. He lived in a little wing off Liuboff's courtyard.

Critical Evaluation:

Foma Gordeyev is Maxim Gorky's first novel. Some see in it the ebullience of a young writer flexing his wings, exhibiting shortcomings typical of a novice; others see it as his best novel. Interestingly, this early work harbors both Gorky's favorite themes as well as the main characteristics of his style. It can be said that the changes in Gorky's artistic style after this work were only a matter of degree.

From the onset, Gorky was preoccupied with social themes. At the end of the nineteenth century, Russia found itself in the throes of a rapid rise of the merchant class and of industry, while the huge peasant and working masses sank deeper and deeper into poverty and despair. This development led straight to the revolution of 1917 and to Communist rule for seven decades. Intellectuals played a significant role in this, and Gorky was one of the leading writers with revolutionary and Marxist leanings. He was determined to help right the wrongs and to bring about a better life for all people, especially the downtrodden. He chose the pen name, Gorky ("bitter"), to underscore the intensity of his feelings. He was basically an idealist, a humanitarian who wanted to achieve his altruistic goals with love and kindness, not with fire and sword. His moderate attitude often brought him in conflict with the less forgiving revolutionaries, although he remained a supporter of the revolution to the end.

All this was to come later in his life. In 1899, his revolutionary development had just begun. For that reason, *Foma Gordeyev* lacks the purposefulness of his later works, yet the contours of his ideological profile are discernible already. The novel deals with the rise of the merchant class, embodied in Ignat Gordeyev and his son Foma. The two will eventually evolve into opposing poles. Ignat, an owner of boats and barges on the Volga River, is a powerful, ruthless, volcanic man, whose brutal strength and merciless treatment of people under him enabled him to amass great wealth. Even a seven-year-old Foma seems to understand his father's true nature when he asks, "But you are a robber, aren't you, father?" Although Foma admired his father's success, he also felt sorry for him because success did not bring him happiness.

Foma developed into the opposite type of person. He grew into a reserved, taciturn young man, self-confident, upright, with a fine sense for justice. After his father's death, he gradually brought on a demise of the family fortunes, despite the efforts of his godfather, Mayakin, to steer him in the "right" direction. Foma's greatest obstacle toward success was his idealization of the working class and his tendency to look for compassion in people. The end result was Foma's failure in the eyes of the merchant society and his descent into the limbo of a displaced, superfluous man, who was declared insane and who spent the rest of his life roaming the streets in rags. In some ways, Foma echoes Gorky's own thoughts and desires, especially his hope that life can be changed for the better with love and understanding.

Gorky tells his tale in the fashion that would become his trademark: straightforward realism, buoyed by warmth and concern for every human being. He creates credible scenes, in which characters unburden themselves of their concerns freely. Gorky's proverbial gift of observation, seen perhaps at its best in his recollections of Leo Tolstoy and Anton Chekhov, enlivens the descriptions and dialogues. On the debit side, the novel is burdened by some of the notorious weaknesses of Gorky's writing habits. His characters philosophize too much, talk profusely, state the obvious repeatedly. Even his realism sometimes slides into romanticism and sentimentality. The characters are frequently so concerned with their own thoughts that they seem to lose touch with others. Unlike the economy of words in his short stories, the descriptive profusion in Gorky's novels dilutes the overall striking effects that abound in the novel.

Despite these shortcomings, Foma Gordeyev is a colorful novel, with powerful characterization and with a vivid picture of the life in Russia at the turn of the century and of the merchant class that was the backbone of the Russian society just before the revolution. Some chapters offer the best pages Gorky has written and a few characters, such as Foma, his father

Ignat, his godsister Liuboff, his aunt Anfisa, and the firebrand intellectual Ezhoff, are indeed unforgettable.

"Critical Evaluation" by Vasa D. Mihailovich

Bibliography:

Borras, F. M. *Maxim Gorky the Writer: An Interpretation*. Oxford, England: Clarendon Press, 1967. One of the more astute interpretations of Gorky's works, especially his novels and plays. Unlike many other books which concentrate either on biography or political issues, Borras emphasizes Gorky's artistic achievements. *Foma Gordeyev* is discussed in passing.

Hare, Richard. *Maxim Gorky: Romantic Realist and Conservative Revolutionary*. London: Oxford University Press, 1962. A substantial study of Gorky, including some interesting observations obtained from people who knew Gorky well. *Foma Gordeyev* is also discussed.

Holtzman, Filia. *The Young Maxim Gorky, 1868-1902*. New York: Columbia University Press, 1948. A detailed survey of the first half of Gorky's life, describing his formation as a writer. Reliable but of limited coverage.

Levin, Dan. *Stormy Petrel: The Life and Work of Maxim Gorky*. New York: Appleton-Century-Crofts, 1965. Another general book, covering Gorky's entire life. Written in a lively manner. *Foma Gordeyev* is discussed.

Muchnic, Helen. "Maxim Gorky." In *From Gorky to Pasternak*. New York: Random House, 1961. An extensive study of Gorky the man and the writer. Discusses his works, including *Foma Gordeyev*.

Weil, Irwin. *Gorky: His Literary Development and Influence on Soviet Intellectual Life*. New York: Random House, 1966. The most scholarly book on Gorky in English, skillfully combining biography with critical analysis, including *Foma Gordeyev*. Valuable especially for the discussion of Soviet literary life and Gorky's connection with, and influence on, younger Soviet writers.

FONTAMARA

Type of work: Novel
Author: Ignazio Silone (Secondo Tranquilli, 1900-1978)
Type of plot: Social realism
Time of plot: Early 1930's
Locale: The Abruzzi region in southern Italy
First published: German edition, 1930; Italian edition, 1933; revised, 1958 (English translation, 1934, 1960)

> *Principal characters:*
> BERARDO VIOLA, the strongest Fontamaran peasant
> GIOVÀ (also GIUVÀ), a peasant
> MATALÈ, his wife
> THEIR SON
> THE CONTRACTOR, a wealthy landowner
> DON CIRCONSTANZA, a lawyer
> DON ABBACCHIO, a priest
> THE MYSTERY MAN, a revolutionary

The Story:

The hillside town of Fontamara was without electricity. While several *cafoni* (a common term for southern Italian peasants) were seated in front of Marietta Sorcanera's bar, a government bureaucrat named Pelino arrived on the scene with blank papers that the *cafoni* were asked to sign. The peasants balked at the idea, but they acquiesced when they were assured that no new taxes were involved. The official left with the signatures, some authentic, some forged; he threatened the peasants for having cursed the Church and the state. Perplexed, the Fontamarans returned home in the dark. On the way, Giovà passed Berardo, who was intent on breaking the electric lamps no longer of use.

The next morning, a crew of roadmen began to divert the stream which irrigated the peasants' soil. It was decided that the women would go to the town and complain to the mayor. At the town hall, the women were told that there was no longer a mayor, but, instead, there was a new *podestà* (a term for mayor, used during the Fascist period). The police escorted the women to the home of the *podestà* where, to their surprise, they learned that he was the rich and powerful Contractor, a newcomer who had "discovered America" in southern Italy.

The women tried in vain to speak to the Contractor. Out of desperation they turned to Don Circonstanza, a lawyer and self-proclaimed "Friend of the People" who was dining at the Contractor's house. Don Circonstanza solved the problem; the Contractor would receive three-quarters of the stream's water, and the Fontamarans would receive three-quarters of the remaining water. Confused, the women signed a hurriedly produced paper, once they were assured that there would be nothing to pay.

The next day, the digging continued as the quarrels among the peasants became more frequent and more furious. Don Abbacchio, the town priest, arrived in Fontamara and urged the peasants not to oppose the Contractor who, he said, was the devil incarnate. The peasants noticed, however, that Don Abbacchio had arrived in a coach owned by the Contractor.

The Fontamarans were later summoned to Avezzano, where they would learn the decisions made by the new government concerning the redivision of the fertile Fucino plain. The *cafoni* were herded into a large square and were ordered to stand and cheer on cue as local administrators paraded past amid myriad black flags marked with skulls and crossbones. Fortunately, the peasants did not allow themselves to be influenced by a police informant who would have incited them to violence and then would have had them arrested.

A wooden fence was soon built around the community grazing ground in Fontamara. The Contractor had apparently appropriated the land which had been common property for thousands of years. After the fence had been burned, rebuilt and then burned a second time, several trucks arrived in the village while the men were in the fields. Gunshot from the trucks broke the church windows. Two hundred armed men descended upon the homes of the peasants and destroyed everything in their path; they also raped the women. The ringing of the church bells caused the violence to cease. The frightened men, departing hastily, did not see the tree trunks placed across the road, and many of them were injured.

In the meantime, Berardo, having returned to the village from the fields, learned that Elvira had fainted atop the belltower. He picked her up in his arms and carried her to her home. The next day, it was rumored that Berardo and Elvira would marry. Berardo, who owned no land, had to find work. Don Circonstanza tricked him into working for a pittance, and Berardo's only consolation was a letter of recommendation which the lawyer sent to a friend in Rome.

The Contractor returned to Fontamara—this time with a hundred policemen—in order to resolve the issue of the diverted stream. Again Don Circonstanza came to the aid of his "beloved" Fontamarans by proposing that the three-quarters of the water would belong to the Contractor for only ten lusters, rather than for fifty years. The uneducated peasants, unaware that ten lusters is fifty years, accepted his proposal.

The ensuing shortage of water caused the peasants great hardship. The crops were not growing, and the peasants faced a terrible winter. Disillusioned with Don Circonstanza's help, the men talked of taking matters into their own hands. Berardo, however, would not hear of the revolt. He was going to Rome, where the lawyer's letter of reference would enable him to find work.

That next morning, accompanied by Giovà's son, Berardo took the train to Rome. The two men stayed in a modest inn where they met Don Achille Pazienza, a lawyer who extorted money from them by promising to find them work. Thrown out of the inn because they could not pay their bill, Berardo and Giovà's son ran into the stranger from Avezzano; the stranger bought them something to eat. Shortly thereafter, the three men were arrested for allegedly leaving in the café a parcel of clandestine newspapers which attacked the Fascist regime.

At that time, the police were looking for a suspect called "the Mystery Man" who was responsible for spreading anti-Fascist literature in the city. While he was being interrogated at the police station, Berardo declared that he was the Mystery Man. The real Mystery Man was released while Berardo was subjected to numerous tortures. As he was about to inform on his friend, Berardo found a newspaper which reported Elvira's death. He changed his mind. Berardo soon died in prison after repeated beatings. His death was reported in the newspapers as a suicide.

Giovà's son was released from prison after he signed a statement attesting Berardo's "suicidal tendencies." He returned to Fontamara, where the Mystery Man had already told the true story of Berardo's death and had left a duplicating machine. The peasants were busy selecting a title for their newspaper.

Shortly after the first edition of the newspaper was distributed, gunfire broke out in Fontamara. Most of the peasants were killed. Among the few survivors were Giovà, Matalè, and their son who, with the help of the Mystery Man, were able to flee to Switzerland.

Critical Evaluation:

Ignazio Silone was born in Pescina, a small town in the Abruzzi region of southern Italy; the town served as a model for Fontamara. Silone was the son of small landowners, and spent much of his youth among the impoverished peasants of the area. He witnessed the social injustices and economic hardships to which the *cafoni* were subjected.

It was Silone's sympathy for the peasants that led him to turn to political action as a vehicle for social and political change. He envisioned a society founded on the socialist concepts of solidarity and equality and the Christian virtue of charity. As a young activist, Silone joined the Socialist Youth League and, in 1921, he helped to found the Italian Communist Party. In 1930, sought by the Fascist police for his involvement in the underground movement against Mussolini's regime, he was forced to flee from Italy.

Fontamara was written while Silone was in exile in Davos, Switzerland. In the novel, he has three refugees from Fontamara—Giovà, Matalè, and their son—visit him in exile in order to relate the tragic story of their hometown. Giovà is the first to narrate, and within the narration, the other *cafoni* speak for themselves. This technique creates the impression of a choral narrative and appropriately so, for *Fontamara* is the story of all suffering peasants and oppressed people in the world.

Within Giovà's narration, one of the *cafoni*, Michele Zompa, relates a dream he has had concerning the lice that plague the townspeople. In the dream, Christ told the Pope that he wished to celebrate the Concordat of 1929 between the church and the Fascist state by granting the *cafoni* a favor such as a gift of land, an exemption from taxes, or an abundant harvest. The Pope rejected Christ's proposals because such favors, he argued, would damage the interests of rich landowners and government officials. The Pope chose as a gift for the peasants a new and vicious strain of lice which would cause them to scratch fiercely, thus distracting them from their misery. The fable-like quality of the dream stands in sharp contrast to the biting realism of its implications—the church's complicity with the oppressive Fascist government and the church's blatant insensitivity to the plight of the peasants—recurrent themes in the novel, which are personified by the figure of a corrupt priest, Don Abbacchio.

Forsaken by the church, the *cafoni* remain the helpless victims of Fascist oppressors; they are mercilessly burdened by government taxes, and they are repeatedly swindled by the Contractor and by Don Circonstanza. As Matalè relates in the second chapter, however, such treatment is to be expected, for the *cafoni* are looked upon by the rich and the middle class as "flesh used to suffering." Since time immemorial, the peasants of Fontamara have been resigned to the economic deprivation and the social injustices perpetuated by government officials.

Only Berardo Viola's anarchic acts of violence offer some resistance to government oppression. Berardo destroys the electric lamps, burns the Contractor's fences, and places a tree trucks in the path of the fleeing Fascist henchmen. Ironically, the *cafoni* are driven by desperation to active revolt against the state at the time when Berardo decides to conform—to work and set aside a small sum of money—so that he can marry Elvira.

Elvira's death transforms Berardo's social consciousness so deeply that he emerges as a Christ-figure. Giovà's son narrates the most poignant part of the novel in which Berardo sacrifices himself for the love of his fellow men—for their socioeconomic redemption—his confession will enable the Mystery Man to go to Fontamara and incite the *cafoni* to revolt.

The novel ends as the three narrators ask: "What are we to do?"—a question that echoes the title of the clandestine newspaper that caused the destruction of Fontamara and its inhabitants. The novel ends on a positive note, however, and this note is consistent with Silone's faith in socialist ideals. Berardo Viola, the first peasant to die for the love of his fellows, has pointed the way to the establishment of a society rooted in Christian brotherhood and charity, a society in which freedom, social justice, and equality will prevail.

Lucille Izzo Pallotta

Bibliography:
Brown, Robert McAfee. "Ignazio Silone and the Pseudonyms of God." In *The Shapeless God: Essays on Modern Fiction*, edited by Harry J. Mooney, Jr., and Thomas F. Staley. Pittsburgh: University of Pittsburgh Press, 1968. A study of Silone's novels as a quest for a "shapeless God" seen in such forces as socialism, revolution, and brotherly love. Discusses the salient events in the author's life which influenced Silone's writing.
Caserta, Ernesto G. "The Meaning of Christianity in the Novels of Silone." *Italian Quarterly* 16, nos. 62-63 (1972): 19-39. The character of Berardo Viola is studied as an expression of Silone's ethical and religious search for a solution to the social problems of southern Italian peasants.
Hanne, Michael. "Silone's *Fontamara*: Polyvalence and Power." *MLN* 107 (January, 1992): 132-159. A well-documented study of *Fontamara* based on Hanne's premise that the novel is not a historically accurate account of Fascist oppression and peasant resistance in southern Italy, but, rather, a text of universal significance.
Lewis, R. W. B. "Ignazio Silone: The Politics of Charity." In *The Picaresque Saint*. Philadelphia: J. B. Lippincott, 1959. A detailed account of the author's life precedes this study of *Fontamara*, which is viewed as the first stage in Silone's "conversion from politics to love." Includes a discussion of the language, the humor, and the narrative devices used in the novel.
Scott, Nathan A. "Ignazio Silone: Novelist of the Revolutionary Sensibility." In *Rehearsals of Decomposure*. New York: King's Crown Press, 1952. Sees *Fontamara* as the initial statement of major themes developed in Silone's later novels; these themes include the corruption in the government and the dichotomy between the middle class and the proletariat.

FOOL FOR LOVE

Type of work: Drama
Author: Sam Shepard (Samuel Shepard Rogers, 1943-   )
Type of plot: Hyperrealism
Time of plot: Late twentieth century
Locale: A low-rent motel room on the edge of the Mojave Desert
First performed: 1983; first published, 1983

> *Principal characters:*
> MAY, a young woman
> EDDIE, a young man
> MARTIN, May's date
> THE OLD MAN, a presence in the motel room

The Story:

The shabby old man sat in a rocking chair drinking whiskey. He existed only in the minds of Eddie and May. May sat on the edge of the bed, staring at the floor. Eddie sat at the table facing May, working resin into his bucking glove. He tossed the glove on the table and insisted to May that he was not leaving. She would not look at him. He moved closer to stroke her hair. She squeezed his legs, then pushed him away. May said he smelled like he had been with another woman. Eddie said it was the horses.

Eddie left, disgusted. May screamed for him not to go, grabbed a pillow and threw herself on the bed, moaning and moving around on it. Eddie returned, slamming the door. May backed herself into a corner and said she would kill the countess he had been with, and then she would kill Eddie. Eddie told her how many miles he had ridden to see her. He lowered his eyes and said he missed her neck. Eddied insisted he had it all figured out this time, but May did not want to hear it. She said she had her own job and life now. When Eddie seemed ready to accept that May wanted him to leave, they came together for a long, tender kiss. Then May kneed him in the groin. Eddie doubled over and dropped to the floor. May went into the bathroom and slammed the door. The old man pointed to a picture of Barbara Mandrell and claimed he was married to her in his mind, and it was important that Eddie understand the difference between being married in his mind and being married in real life.

May came out of the bathroom carrying a sleek red dress and heels. As she changed into the sexy clothes she said numbly that she hated Eddie. Eddie said he would go. May said he had better, since someone was coming over to see her. Eddie wanted to know how long this had been going on, and then he left suddenly. May yelled after him, and then grabbed a suitcase from under the bed and started packing. When she heard Eddie returning, she shoved it back under the bed, and began brushing her hair. Eddie returned with a shotgun and a bottle of tequila. He took a long drink from the bottle. May asked Eddie why he always messed her up like this. Eddie said nothing would ever separate them, and May told him to get out. Eddie went out the door carrying the shotgun.

May threw herself against the door and wept. The old man told a story about when May was a baby and would not stop crying. May crawled slowly to the bed, grabbed a pillow, and rocked herself. Suddenly she stopped grieving, sat at the table, and took a long drink of tequila. Eddie returned with steer ropes. They ignored each other. Eddie looped the bedposts, and said he did not believe there was any guy coming over.

May said there was no point in trying to impress her because it was all over. She tried to leave, but Eddie dragged her, kicking and screaming, back into the room. Headlights shined through the window. May opened the door, and saw a woman in a Mercedes Benz. Just as Eddie slammed the door shut and pushed May out of the way, a pistol shot ripped through glass outside. May was furious, and she struggled to get away from Eddie but he rolled on top of her to keep her down on the floor.

The countess had blown the windshield out of Eddie's truck. He wanted to keep the lights off or leave, but May would not do either. The old man said he could not see himself in either one of them, and that it was a good thing that he had gotten out when he did. Eddie insisted May would never get rid of him, and May wanted to know why she should believe this time was any different from the others. She opened the door and challenged the countess. Instead, her date, Martin, came crashing in and tackled Eddie, believing he had been trying to hurt May. May told him it was okay since Eddie was her cousin. Eddie said May was lying. May went into the bathroom.

Eddie told Martin he and May were half brother and sister. Their father, the old man, had fallen in love twice but neither family had known about the other until May and Eddie had already met in high school and fallen in love. The old man drank with Eddie and Martin during the story, and commented occasionally on what Eddie was saying. Eddie described going on a long walk one night with his father which ended up at the house where May and her mother had lived. Eddie then realized his father had two lives, and that May was his sister.

May returned to the room, saying she had heard every word. May claimed Eddie was not telling the whole truth, and insisted on going to the movies, but Eddie would not let them leave, so May decided to tell Martin the rest of the story. She said she and her mother had tracked her missing father down and had discovered him eating dinner with his other family, Eddie and his mother. After that incident, the old man had disappeared forever. Her mother had grieved terribly. May said she had been so much in love with Eddie at the time that they were both sick when they could not be together. Her mother had begged them not see each other anymore. She had gone to Eddie's mother with the truth. Eddie's mother had shot herself in the head as a result.

The old man protested this version could not have possibly happened, but Eddie calmly tells him that his own shotgun was the one his mother had used to kill herself. May and Eddie met and locked gazes. The old man tried to part them, but Eddie and May ignored him. They embraced tenderly. A loud explosion and the sound of shattering glass was heard outside. A gasoline fire burned, and horses screamed and galloped away. Martin told Eddie his horses were loose. Eddie decided to go check on them, and told May he would be back in a minute. May stared at the door as Eddie went through it, then turned to get the suitcase. Martin asked her if she was going with Eddie. May straightened herself up and stared at Martin. She told him Eddie had already gone, and then she left the room herself, suitcase in hand, without closing the door. The old man pointed to an imaginary picture, claiming it was the woman of his dreams, and began to rock slowly in his chair.

Critical Evaluation:

Sam Shepard began writing plays in the 1960's and had many of them produced in New York before the age of thirty. *Fool for Love* shares the one-act structure and relentless pace of earlier plays such as or *Operation Sidwinder* (1970) or *Cowboy Mouth* (1971), but it is written after Shepard's longer "family plays," such as *Curse of the Starving Class* (1976) or *Buried Child* (1978), which won the Pulitzer Prize in drama 1979. It combines the wild urgency of some earlier plays with more complex character development. The most significant innovation in *Fool for Love* is that many critics consider it the first Shepard play in which a woman's character, May, is as fully and interestingly drawn as a man's.

The term "realistic," however, is not an accurate way to describe Shepard's rendering of May, or any other of his characters, if by "realistic" one means objectively consistent. Neither is May's character "absurd" in the traditional sense of that term, since the motivation for her actions is uncovered in the course of the play. Shepard's style of drama is hard to define according to existing, traditional formulas. A director who has worked with Shepard, has made an interesting case for labeling Shepard's work "hyperrealism." What makes Shepard's characters "hyperreal" is their awareness of what others consider "realistic" at the same time they have abandoned attempts to project an objective presentation of themselves. The audience meets all of them at a place well beyond the breakdown of objective pretense as a façade. All that the characters say and do comments on the discrepancy between the audience's conventional concept of how they should behave and the way their own obsessions motivate them.

May's character is an example of this dynamic. She is a pragmatist, a scathing foil to Eddie's stock Shepard-style male caricature, whose occupation is that of a "cowboy," "who dreams things up." Unlike the women in earlier plays, May talks openly and frankly about her own emotional landscape and all its contradictory passions. The audience quickly learns that Eddie's attempt to pacify her with fantasy during his long absences (a pile of fashion magazines) has sent her packing in search of her own life. The play's imperative to dramatize her reality is seen most strikingly when she tells Martin the rest of the story about her and Eddie, and, against the old man's protests, Eddie quietly corroborates her version as the truth.

Another significant way in which Shepard plays with dramatic conventions in *Fool for Love* is his usual attention to dramatization of images rather than ideas. Often the most significant, climactic moments are underscored by stage images rather than dialogue. Dialogue is part of the image being performed, and is used for emphasis of these images. There are many examples of this in *Fool for Love*, among them the long, motionless opening position of May on the bed, unresponsive to Eddie's coaxing, and the way Eddie and May physically back themselves up against and slam against the walls of the motel room as they argue. In this way stage directions place the dialogue in the visual context of the play more than the speeches themselves direct the action.

Although some contend the monologues in this play are prosaic by comparison to those in Shepard's other plays, the images they evoke are still memorable. The presence of animal instinct as an overriding motivator, for example, is present in the old man's speech about how he got May to stop crying one night by taking her unawares out into a herd of cattle neither of them could see. In other places, the clipped conversational style of the speeches emphasizes the physical settings each interaction dramatizes. Shepard uses words like paints or musical notes, rather than as carriers of ideas. In *Fool for Love*, the fiery, tortured image of Eddie and May in the grips of incestuous love exhibits the contradictory way the American myth of masculinity has defined love, and the effect it has on American women.

Maria Theresa Maggi

Bibliography:
Hart, Lynda. *Sam Shepard's Metaphorical Stages*. Westport, Conn.: Greenwood Press, 1987. In the section of her book about Shepard's brand of realism, "Realism Revisited," Hart devotes several pages of discussion to the staging of *Fool for Love*.

Londre, Felicia Hardison. "A Motel of the Mind: *Fool for Love* and *A Lie of the Mind*." In *Rereading Shepard*, edited by Leonard Wilcox. New York: St. Martin's Press, 1993. An interesting discussion of motels as metaphors for states of mind and heart in Shepard's plays.

Marlowe, Joan, and Betty Blake, eds. *New York Theatre Critics' Reviews* 44, no. 19 (1983): 212-216. Six reviews from New York papers. Gives a wide range of interpretive opinions about the original Shepard-directed production.

Tucker, Martin. *Sam Shepard*. Literature and Life: American Writers. New York: Continuum Press, 1992. Contains an interesting discussion of *Fool for Love* that speculates about possible autobiographical links to the romantic and family dynamics explored in the play.

Wetzsetson, Ross. Introduction to *Fool for Love and Other Plays* by Sam Shepard. New York: Bantam Books, 1984. An insightful and readable description of Shepard's dramatic sensibility, with special attention to *Fool for Love*.

THE FOOL OF QUALITY
Or, The History of Henry, Earl of Moreland

Type of work: Novel
Author: Henry Brooke (1703?-1783)
Type of plot: Didactic
Time of plot: Eighteenth century
Locale: England
First published: 1765-1770

> *Principal characters:*
> HENRY CLINTON, Earl of Moreland
> MR. FENTON, his foster father
> NED, Henry's friend
> FANNY GOODALL, Mr. Fenton's cousin
> ABENAIDE, princess of Morocco

The Story:

Put out to nurse when he was a baby, Henry Clinton, second son of the Earl of Moreland, saw little of his noble parents and their favorite older son. At the age of five and a half, young Harry, as he was called, made the acquaintance of Mr. Fenton, an old man of the neighborhood. The old gentleman was so impressed by the innate goodness of Harry's nature that he stole the boy away from his nurse, after leaving a note for the parents telling them that he would one day return their son. It was Mr. Fenton's purpose to train young Harry to become the most accomplished and perfect of men. The parents grieved for a short time but soon forgot the boy in favor of his older brother.

Mr. Fenton took Harry to a mansion at Hampstead. With them they took Ned, a beggar lad whom Harry had befriended. There, Harry's education began. Mr. Fenton, a very wealthy man, gave Harry large sums of money and hundreds of garments to distribute to the deserving poor. It was Harry's task to learn to distinguish the deserving from the rascals. At the same time, the boys were instructed in academic subjects, bodybuilding, and other suitable lessons. Ned had irrepressible spirits, and he constantly tormented his teachers. Sometimes Harry joined in the fun, but he was such a good boy that he immediately performed a favor for anyone who might have suffered because of Ned or himself.

Harry was so tenderhearted that he frequently brought whole families to live at the mansion and gave them money, clothing, and work. Mr. Fenton was highly pleased with the boy, who had purity of heart and a willingness to be instructed in all phases of life. The old gentleman taught him theology, principles of government, moral rules, and many other forms of philosophy.

Harry became the champion of all those who were tormented by bullies, even though the ruffians were often larger and stronger than he. He soundly thrashed many boys and men and then immediately helped them to their feet and became their friend. Once he trounced the son of a nobleman. The mother, not knowing Harry was also an earl's son, would have had him severely punished, but the father saw Harry's good character and defended the lad. Most of the people Harry thrashed became his devoted servants, seeing and loving the nobility of character he possessed.

One day, Mr. Fenton called on a lady who had issued several invitations to him. He was delighted to learn that the woman, now Lady Maitland, was his cousin Fanny Goodall. In their youth they had loved each other, but he was many years older than Fanny. Recognizing Mr. Fenton, Fanny now called him Harry Clinton. He was the brother of young Harry's father, the Earl of Moreland; thus, he was Harry's uncle. Cast out with a small inheritance as was the custom with younger sons, he had made his fortune as a merchant, married a wealthy woman, and prospered still more, but his beloved wife, his children, and his dear father-in-law all died, leaving him bereft of any emotion but sorrow. Although he gained a great fortune on the death of his father-in-law, he considered himself the poorest of men. Fanny was also a widow, and the two friends comforted each other as they talked of their sad lives. Mr. Fenton saw that Fanny was almost overcome with grief and promised to tell her the rest of his story later, but the good lady was called away before she could hear more.

Harry's education continued. Mr. Fenton, as he was known to all but Fanny, sent him to the prisons to pay the debts of deserving persons and to secure their release. He continued to take unfortunates home with him, much to the joy of Mr. Fenton. Ned, too, was improving, although he still did not have the nobility of character that Harry possessed. One day, Ned's parents were found. Harry had helped some people who had suffered an accident nearby, and these people became friends of the household. By a scar that his old nurse recognized, Ned was known to her and then to his parents. The boy had been stolen in infancy. It was with great joy that the parents greeted their son. Although Ned was saddened to leave Mr. Fenton and his beloved friend Harry, he went joyfully with his rightful parents.

Countless numbers of people became Harry's friends because of his concern for their well-being. Mr. Fenton sent him and his tutor, one of Harry's charities, to London to learn the ways of the city and the court. Even the king was impressed by the lad. Harry retained his modesty through all the adulation he received, a fact which added to his popularity. The queen and other noble ladies sought his company, but he eluded them all, making them better, however, for having known him.

When Mr. Fenton learned of the death of Harry's mother and brother, he returned the boy to his father, the Earl of Moreland, who was overjoyed at finding his lost son. When he learned that the child's abductor had been his own brother, thought dead, the Earl was filled with remorse for having treated his brother so badly many years before. The brothers were united publicly, and everyone learned that Mr. Fenton was in reality the second son of the house of Moreland. The Earl was grateful to his brother for stealing the boy and making a perfect man of him.

Mr. Clinton, as Mr. Fenton was called from then on, told the rest of the story of his life. After the death of his loved ones, he lived in sorrow for many years. Then he married again after almost losing his life in his suit of the girl he loved, Louisa d'Aubigny. They had a lovely daughter named Eloisa. Sorrow, however, again haunted Mr. Clinton, for Louisa died from a fall and Eloisa was washed from a ship and seen no more. The bereaved man had lived in solitude and misery until he had met and abducted Harry.

Not long after learning his brother's story, Harry's father died, and the boy became the Earl of Moreland. He now had a huge fortune to spend for charity, and he spent wisely so that those who received would profit from the money in all ways.

Before long, Mr. Clinton learned from his dead wife's brother that he was coming to England, accompanied by Fanny Goodall. Fanny had married Louisa's brother and thus had become Mr. Clinton's sister-in-law. The old friends rejoiced at their reunion. Fanny was accompanied by a dark Moorish page to whom Harry was instantly attracted. The boy told Harry that he had a sister Abenaide, as fair as he himself was dark. She would soon accompany their father, the emperor, who was coming to England with his wife. The boy had been sent ahead as a page to be trained in genteel conduct. When the girl arrived, Mr. Clinton found her to be the daughter of his own supposedly dead Eloisa. Saved from the sea, Eloisa had married the Emperor of Morocco. To Harry's extreme surprise, the Moorish princess was the same page whom he had loved so dearly. She had been in disguise to escape an unwanted royal lover and had continued the deception in order to tease Harry. The Princess Abenaide and Harry were married, their wedding being blessed with the prayers of the hundreds the perfect young man had befriended.

Critical Evaluation:

With a text that exceeds three hundred thousand words, about five times as long as an average modern novel, *The Fool of Quality* was originally published by installment in five volumes. Although it achieved success in its original form, the book became better known through a single-volume abridgment by John Wesley. It is a didactic work that does not readily fit any traditional category. It most nearly resembles the sentimental novel, a form pioneered in English by such writers as Samuel Richardson, Laurence Sterne, and Henry Mackenzie. On the other hand, its loosely knit, episodic plot, its sporadic exotic adventures, and its idealistic theme of constantly righting wrongs link it with the picaresque tradition, specifically with Miguel de Cervantes' *Don Quixote* (1605, 1615).

The preface establishes a tone of satire; Brooke assails his society for its self-indulgence, luxury, and greed, and denounces these vices as threats to the nation. Although the novel includes little direct satire, occasional character names such as Lord Freelove, Mr. Sneer, Lady Cribbage, and Miss Trinket suggest satire against the vanity and superficiality of the upper class. Despite the novel's profession of egalitarianism, however, most of the commoners turn out to be gentle folk whose true identities have been either lost or concealed. In the end Brooke has his protagonist marry a Moroccan princess who, he has just learned, is his cousin.

In a general sense, the account of the hero's education follows the course laid down by Jean-Jacques Rousseau in *Emilius and Sophia: Or, A New System of Education* (1762). Unschooled in the vanity and hypocrisy that pervade aristocratic society, Henry Clinton receives the ironic epithet "fool." As the second son of an earl, Henry is a man of quality, yet his father expects that he will have no aristocratic responsibility. He is thus sent from home to be reared in a modest rural setting by the family of his nurse. The simplicity and beauty of nature plus the kind treatment by his foster family lay the foundation for his education in right conduct. Removed by his uncle, Mr. Fenton, Henry gains further advantage through continuing his education by acquiring sound moral principles. Mr. Fenton's seemingly unlimited wealth enables Henry to learn the importance of compassion and charity in dealing with those less fortunate. An underlying theme, illustrated in the story of the wealthy Mr. Fenton, is that virtue is the road to wealth and power. The middle portion of his education—by the kindly Mr. Clement, a tutor hired by Mr. Fenton—guides the youth in charitable activities.

Mr. Fenton himself directly educates Henry in matters of government, clarifying the English constitution in a lengthy lesson. In addition to a conservative, straightforward account of political entities, the lesson incorporates Rousseau's principles of popular sovereignty and consent of the governed. With the further assistance of a clergyman, Mr. Meekly, Mr. Fenton educates the young man in religion, their discourse upholding the rational Christianity widely accepted in eighteenth century England. Relying heavily on biblical passages, the account endorses the providential view of history. The unexpected death of Henry's brother assures that Henry inherits the title and becomes able to apply all his lessons in virtue and practical power.

Henry's coming to maturity thus portrays Rousseau's educational philosophy as beneficial and feasible.

As a sentimental novel, the work employs a narrative technique that makes it somewhat less successful than its predecessors. It offers an abundance of emotion, with mature characters fainting, blushing, bursting into tears, or freely embracing—reactions that serve to reinforce Rousseau's message that emotion is good. The most poignant parts of the narrative, however, are presented from the point of view of a character relating his or her past. Typically, these tales feature pitiable details of suffering, but the reader does not see the wretchedness firsthand through the narrator's eyes—as happens, for example, in Sterne's *A Sentimental Journey Through France and Italy* (1768), in which the plight of Maria is indelibly impressed on the memory. Brooke's method of narration distances the most moving events from the reader and thus reduces their emotional impact. Another narrative technique results in a further disruption of the already slow narrative pace. At the end of most chapters, Brooke includes a dialogue between the Author and Friend, who usually questions the author about the narrative and its themes.

In support of the theme of charity, the plot incorporates astounding coincidence and extravagant improbabilities. Long-lost relatives are recognized and reunited with family members, people live for years under assumed names until their true identity can be revealed, characters disguise themselves to take part in unlikely adventures, and astounding escapes are brought about. For example, as Mr. Fenton is narrating his life to Fanny Goodall, he includes the story of his wealthy servant John. Approaching his death without any living relatives, John resolved to leave his fortune to the next needy person who came to Mr. Fenton's door. The next arrival was a woman who asked for charity, and a small initial promise elicited her story. Her misfortune came about because her husband, in a fit of jealousy, had mistaken her long-lost brother for a lover and, after stabbing him, had fled. It was learned that the dying John was the husband, formerly Barnaby Tirrell, and the reunion was appropriately tearful. When another recipient of Mr. Fenton's bounty, Homely, narrates his unfortunate life, it is discovered he had saved Fenton from drowning twenty years earlier.

Its length, heavy didacticism, and departures from realism make *The Fool of Quality* an unlikely candidate for popular revival. From the standpoint of literary history, however, the work remains significant for its standing as a novel of sentiment, a precursor of the novel of reform.

"Critical Evaluation" by Stanley Archer

Bibliography:
Baker, Ernest A. *The History of the English Novel.* Vol. 5 in *The Novel of Sentiment and Gothic Romance.* 10 vols. New York: Barnes & Noble Books, 1924-1939. Classifies the novel as sentimental and devotes discussion to its literary allusions and inset stories. Praises the work as the first novel that presents a full and sympathetic account of a boy growing to maturity.
Foster, James R. *History of the Pre-Romantic Novel in England.* New York: Modern Language Association of America, 1949. Summarizes portions of the novel and points out incongruities in Brooke's narrative. An unsympathetic analysis draws attention to the book's exaggerations.
Probyn, Clive T. *English Fiction of the Eighteenth Century, 1700-1789.* London: Longman, 1987. Suggests that Brooke drew upon Henry Fielding's *Joseph Andrews* (1742) and *Tom Jones* (1749). Argues that the excesses of sentimentalism and idealism mar Brooke's didactic purpose.

Scurr, Helen Margaret. *Henry Brooke*. Minneapolis: University of Minnesota Press, 1927. Represents the only comprehensive and detailed examination of Brooke's life and career. The chapter on the novels centers on *The Fool of Quality*, treating it as a flawed narrative that exerted a measurable influence on subsequent fiction.

Shroff, Homai J. *The Eighteenth Century Novel: The Idea of the Gentleman*. London: Edward Arnold, 1983. Links Brooke with Henry Mackenzie, demonstrating how both differed from Rousseau's ideas about the essentials of education for the gentleman. Points out that despite its seeming egalitarianism, the novel usually portrays worthy characters as members of the gentry.

FOOLS CROW

Type of work: Novel
Author: James Welch (1940-   )
Type of plot: Historical realism
Time of plot: 1868-1870
Locale: Montana Territory
First published: 1986

Principal characters:

FOOLS CROW (formerly WHITE MAN'S DOG), a Pikuni Blackfeet youth
RIDES-AT-THE-DOOR, his father
FAST HORSE, Fools Crow's boastful friend
YELLOW KIDNEY, a respected warrior
RUNNING FISHER, Fools Crow's younger brother
FEATHER WOMAN, a legendary Pikuni woman

The Story:

White Man's Dog, an unlucky youth of the Lone Eaters band of Pikuni Blackfeet, was invited by his friend Fast Horse to join a winter horse-riding party on the Crow camp, to be led by the wise warrior Yellow Kidney. Most of the men were young and inexperienced; Yellow Kidney watched Fast Horse carefully, believing him to be too boastful and reckless.

Once at the great Crow camp of Bull Shield, White Man's Dog and three others were able to separate more than a hundred horses from the large herd and safely escape with them. Only Yellow Kidney, who with Fast Horse had gone into the camp to steal the powerful horses of the Crow chiefs, failed to return. Fast Horse reported that he had last seen Yellow Kidney in the camp, and they feared he was dead.

After a period of mourning, Yellow Kidney's wife requested that she be allowed to be the Sacred Vow Woman for the next Sun Dance ceremony. She offered this sacrifice to ensure the safe return of her husband. Meanwhile, White Man's Dog, gaining courage and power with the help of the healer Mik-api, supplied her family with meat and prepared to marry her daughter.

Months later, a weak and mutilated Yellow Kidney returned to the Lone Eaters camp. He related how the Crows had captured him after being alerted by the loud, foolish boasts of Fast Horse. Bull Shield had cut off Yellow Kidney's fingers, a humiliation that would prevent him from hunting and providing for his family ever again. Then he was tied to a horse and sent into the snow. He had been found and cared for by the Spotted Horse (Cheyenne) people. When the Lone Eaters council heard Yellow Kidney's story, they agreed to banish Fast Horse for his lies and for causing harm to come to this brave warrior. Fast Horse fled to a renegade band of Pikuni raiders headed by Owl Child.

The Pikunis massed to send a war party of three hundred to avenge the mutilation of Yellow Kidney and punish Bull Shield. White Man's Dog had the honor of striking the enemy first on behalf of his father-in-law Yellow Kidney, and he managed to kill and scalp Bull Shield. His exploits earned him a new name, Fools Crow. His brother Running Fisher, on the other hand, lost courage and spirit.

A wounded Fast Horse returned to the Lone Eaters camp, gut-shot by a white settler whom he had attacked. Fast Horse's father urged Fools Crow to speak with him, and when a sullen Fast Horse left the camp again, Fools Crow was sent after his friend to convince him to return.

Fools Crow knew his attempt would be useless because Fast Horse refused to accept responsibility for his betrayal of Yellow Kidney. Meanwhile, Yellow Kidney, who saw himself now as a nothing-man, determined to leave the camp and return to the Spotted Horse people. While he rested in an empty war lodge, he was found and killed by a vengeful white man in retaliation for the murders committed by Owl Child and his raiders.

A scout arrived at the Lone Eaters camp to call the chiefs to a council with the seizer (United States Army) chiefs. Most of the Pikuni chiefs refused to attend. Only the peace chief Heavy Runner, a good man but too trusting, and three others agreed to go, along with Fools Crow's father, Rides-at-the-door, who understood English and had been asked to speak for the Lone Eaters. The seizer general was not pleased that so few came to this council, and he made demands that the chiefs knew they could not meet. Heavy Runner agreed not to make war upon the whites, but when the men's societies' chiefs met afterward, they were unable to decide what to do.

Fools Crow feared that his people were helpless. Nitsokan, Dream Helper, told him to journey for three days and three nights without stopping, in a quest for answers. When he came to a strange valley between sky and earth, he found Feather Woman, a figure from Pikuni legend. Her marriage to Morning Star, the child of Sun and Moon, had resulted in the birth of her son Scarface, who brought the Sun Dance ceremony to the Pikunis. Feather Woman had dug a sacred turnip out of the sky, creating a hole, so she had been banished to this place, where she mourned for her lost husband and son.

For Fools Crow, she painted prophetic scenes upon a yellow skin—visions of the fate of his people. Feather Woman told him that he could aid them best by preparing them for the hard times to come. When he returned, the dreaded white-scabs (smallpox) had already invaded the Lone Eaters camp, and he struggled to help the sick.

After two weeks, those men who were still healthy rode out in search of meat. They met eight wounded Pikunis, survivors of Heavy Runner's peaceful band, which had been attacked by the seizers. Fools Crow went on alone to the massacred camp to witness the horribly burned bodies. This had become his role, knowing that, like Feather Woman, he was "burdened with the knowledge of his people." He also knew from his visions that his people would ultimately survive.

Critical Evaluation:

Combining history, fiction, and legend, *Fools Crow* received the Pacific Northwest Booksellers Association Book Award in 1987. Perhaps the novel's outstanding achievement is its evocation of the daily life and worldview of the Pikuni Blackfeet people. James Welch, who is of Blackfeet, Gros Ventre, and Irish ancestry, had to research details of custom and ceremony. He translates names and idioms literally to suggest the flavor of Pikuni speech. For example, the moon is called Night Red Light; Fools Crow's power animal is Skunk-bear (wolverine); and the white soldiers become the seizers.

The novel culminates in the historic Marias River Massacre of January 23, 1870, in which 173 Blackfeet, mostly old people, women, and children, were attacked and killed by United States troops. The dead were members of the Pikuni band led by Heavy Runner, a chief friendly to the whites, who had been given written assurance of safe conduct by General Alfred H. Sully. Welch's own great-grandmother, Red Paint Woman, was a survivor of this terrible event. This massacre of peaceful civilians had been ignored or forgotten in the annals of the American history. The "massacre" six years later of General George Armstrong Custer's 210 armed troops, who were making war on the Indians, by a much larger force of Sioux and Cheyennes, however, has not been. Welch brings a different perspective, that of the Native American, to United States history.

In the world of *Fools Crow*, there is a blurring of the line between the truth of everyday reality and the truth of dream and legend. A dream may serve as a source of power; a myth offers an alternate perception of the world. Welch's characters readily accept both. Fools Crow's repeated dream of the white-faced girl who beckons to him makes him uneasy. He is horrified when he realizes that he has dreamed of the white-scabs death lodge into which Yellow Kidney later stumbles, and he feels guilty that he did not warn Yellow Kidney of his dream. At the same time another youth has dreamed of a blind white pony with streaks of blood across its back—a death horse and an omen. Dreams are even shared: Both Fools Crow and his father's young third wife dream simultaneously of consummating their guilty passion beside a white, unknown river.

The novel's loose structure lends itself to digression. Action slows in order to introduce a legend, such as that of Feather Woman, the Pikuni woman who married Morning Star and lived with him in the sky. She brought to her people the sacred medicine bonnet and digging stick. Her son Scarface taught the Pikunis the Sun Dance so that they could honor his grandfather.

Magical Realism, an element in the literature of Latin America, is also integral to Native American literature. When the young Fools Crow seeks his power animal in the mountains, he follows a raven. When they come to a clearing, the bird speaks: "It surprises you that I speak the language of the two-leggeds. It's easy." Raven helps him to find his power animal.

The last part of the novel involves the final quest that Fools Crow undertakes, wearing the painted face of death and riding through the snow to help his people. He must go as a supplicant, without weapons or belongings, to find his vision. When he arrives at the mysterious valley, it is summer. A woman in a white doeskin dress approaches him. At first she seems old but appears younger as she comes closer, wearing the short hair of one in mourning. Feather Woman tells Fools Crow that she has brought misery on her people, but that one day she will be allowed to return to her husband and son, and then the Pikunis will be happy.

Feather Woman paints for him the terrible visions on the yellow skin. He sees the Pikunis dying from the white-scabs. He sees hundreds of seizers riding out from their fort, heading north to Pikuni country. He sees starving people and a prairie barren of game. Nitsokan has chosen him to see what is to come, and he is afraid. Then he hears children laughing and sees Indian children at a government school, and he is comforted. Somehow, the Pikunis will survive. For Fools Crow, dreams are real, animals speak, and one can see the future.

Joanne McCarthy

Bibliography:
Barry, Nora. "'A Myth to Be Alive': James Welch's *Fools Crow*." *MELUS: The Journal of the Society for the Study of the Multi-Ethnic Literature of the United States* 17, no. 1 (Spring, 1991-1992): 3-20. An examination of Fools Crow's role as character and mythic hero. Links him to the legend of Scarface, the unpromising hero, contrasted with the failed heroes Fast Horse and Running Fisher.
Gish, Robert F. "Word Medicine: Storytelling and Magic Realism in James Welch's *Fools Crow*." *American Indian Quarterly* 14, no. 4 (Fall, 1990): 349-354. An excellent discussion of the multiple levels of storytelling and language, dreams and Magical Realism present in the novel. Suggests that Native American literature establishes a crucial link between primitive and modern worldviews.

Murphree, Bruce. "Welch's *Fools Crow*." *Explicator* 52, no. 3 (Spring, 1994): 186-187. Applies the legend of Seco-mo-muckon and the firehorn to the relationship between Fast Horse and Yellow Kidney during the horse-stealing raid on the Crow camp. Underscores the importance of tribal unity apparent in both legend and novel.

Ramsey, Jarold. "*Fools Crow*." *Parabola* 12, no. 1 (February, 1987): 108, 110-112. Praises the novel as a "magnificent" blending of historical accuracy and tribal myth, at the forefront of Native American literature.

Wild, Peter. "Visions of a Blackfoot." *The New York Times Book Review*, November 2, 1986, 14. Explores the new direction taken by Welch in this novel. Notes how the spiritual and cultural implications of Fools Crow's coming-of-age weave this world and the world of visions together.

FOR COLORED GIRLS WHO HAVE CONSIDERED SUICIDE/ WHEN THE RAINBOW IS ENUF
A Choreopoem

Type of work: Drama
Author: Ntozake Shange (Paulette Williams, 1948-   )
Type of plot: Social realism
Time of plot: Twentieth century
Locale: Outside the cities of Chicago, Detroit, Houston, Baltimore, San Francisco, Manhattan, St. Louis
First performed: 1976; first published, 1977

Principal characters:

LADY IN BROWN, pays the drama's only positive tribute to a black man
LADY IN RED, describes the methods she uses to get a man to love her
LADY IN YELLOW, summarizes the predicament of black women
LADY IN PURPLE, chooses companions who can not comprehend her as a means of avoiding hurt
LADY IN GREEN, squanders her love on an indifferent man
LADY IN BLUE, a victim of emotional and physical abuse
LADY IN ORANGE, tries to use music to cure her pain

The Story:

All the ladies came onto the stage and froze in positions of distress. The lady in brown called upon the others to sing a black girl's song, to give her words and to bring her out of herself. Each lady declared her origins—the lady in brown outside Chicago, the lady in yellow outside Detroit, the lady in purple outside Houston, the lady in red outside Baltimore, the lady in green outside San Francisco, the lady in blue outside Manhattan, and the lady in orange outside St. Louis. Then they began to sing songs of infancy and childhood: "Mama's Little Baby Likes Shortnin Bread" and "Little Sally Walker."

The lady in yellow told the story of graduation night when she was the only virgin in the crowd. She drank and danced and went out to the parking lot with Bobby, where she made love to him in the back seat of a Buick. The lady in blue then related how, pretending she was Puerto Rican, she had run away at sixteen to the South Bronx to dance with Willie Colón, the famous salsa musician. When he did not show up at the dance hall, she got mad, refused to dance with anyone, and started yelling in English. Later she was possessed by the subtle blues of Archie Shepp, and she recited her poem as a thank-you for music which she loved "more than poem."

The lady in red recited a note attached to a plant she gave to her lover when she ended the affair. She had loved him for eight months, two weeks, and a day, had been stood up four times, had left him presents, poems, and plants, had driven miles to see him before work, and had finally decided that her experiment of debasing herself to gain love was a failure. All of the ladies then danced to Willie Colón's "Che Che Cole"—they danced to keep from crying and to keep from dying.

A sudden light change stopped the dancing, and the ladies in green, yellow, orange, and brown left the stage. The ladies in red, blue, and purple discussed how difficult it was to press rape charges against someone you had known, someone who had taken you out to dinner or had made dinner for you and then had beaten you and betrayed you. The nature of rape had changed;

2376

it haunted the places and people where companionship was sought. When the light again changed, the ladies were hit by an imaginary slap. The ladies in red and purple exited. The lady in blue revealed her experience of a lonely abortion. She went alone because she did not want anyone to see her or to know that she was pregnant and ashamed. After her monologue, she exited the stage.

Soft, deep music was heard and voices called "Sechita." The lady in purple entered and described the quadroon balls in St. Louis and the gambling boats on the Mississippi. She narrated the story of Sechita, as the lady in green danced her life. Sechita danced in a creole carnival after the wrestlers had finished their match; she danced the dance of Nefertiti, of the Egyptian goddess of love and creativity, of the rituals of the second millennium, and then she left the stage. Portraying an eight-year-old girl in St. Louis, the lady in brown explained how she was disqualified from a library reading contest because she reported on a book from the Adult Reading Room. The book, a biography of Toussaint L'Ouverture, the liberator of Haiti, introduced her to her first black hero, and she fell in love with him and decided to run away to Haiti. When she got down to the docks, she met a little boy whose name was Toussaint Jones, and she decided that they might be able to move some of their own spirits down by the river in St. Louis, 1955.

The lady in red followed with the tale of a dazzling coquette who lured men to her bed and made divine love to them. At 4:30 A.M. she arose, bathed, and became herself, an ordinary brown-braided woman who chased the men from her bed, wrote accounts of her exploits in a journal, and cried herself to sleep.

The lady in blue explained how she used to live in the world until she moved to Harlem, and that she felt her universe constricted to six blocks and a tunnel with a train. The ladies in purple, yellow, and orange entered and represented the strangers that the lady in blue feared. In another tone, the lady in purple told the story of three friends all attracted to the same man, who dated one and flirted with the other two. When the first romance waned, he sought out one of the others, who told her friend that he claimed the relationship was over. The two found him with another woman, and the friends comforted each other.

A quartet of the ladies in blue, purple, yellow, and orange sang of their lost loves and pain until they were joined by the ladies in red, green, and brown, who chanted with them an affirmation of their love, dancing until they were full of life and togetherness. The lady in green then celebrated the recovery of all of her stuff which "somebody almost walked off wid." After the ladies had recited the excuses and apologies men had given them, the lady in blue asserted her right to be angry and accept no more apologies.

The last story of Crystal and Beau Willie was told by the lady in red. Beau Willie, a Vietnam veteran, had come home "crazy as hell" from the war. When he tried to go to school, he was put into remedial classes because he could not read, so he drove a gypsy cab that kept breaking down. His girlfriend Crystal had a baby that he was not sure was his while he was in Vietnam; she got pregnant again when he returned, so Beau Willie had two children, a girl and a boy. When Crystal refused to marry him, he got drunk and started swinging chairs at her, including the high chair with his son. Having almost died, Crystal got a court order to keep Beau Willie away. He went to Crystal's to try to convince her to marry him; when she would not open the door, he broke it down. He coaxed the children into his arms. When Crystal again refused to marry him, he held the children out of the fifth-story window and dropped them.

The ladies came out and chanted how each had missed a "layin on of hands" until "i found god in myself & i loved her/ i loved her fiercely" arose as a song of joy to each other and to the audience.

Critical Evaluation:

Ntozake Shange calls *for colored girls who have considered suicide/ when the rainbow is enuf* a choreopoem; it is a performance piece made up of twenty-three poems that are chanted, sung, and danced to the accompaniment of music by seven women. Originally performed in improvisational style in Berkeley, California, in 1974, the play was picked up in an expanded form by the New York Shakespeare Festival, which first presented it in an Obie Award-winning production in 1976 at the Henry Street Play House and then moved it to the Booth Theatre on Broadway, where it had a long, successful run.

Shange is considered a pioneer both for the collage-like techniques of her drama and for her subject matter: the anger of African American women at their double subjugation at the hands of white America and black men. While some critics were disturbed at what they saw as her generally negative depiction of black males and her disconnection from traditional black political concerns, others saw in *for colored girls who have considered suicide/ when the rainbow is enuf* an attempt to find new solutions to the reality of the lives of African American women. Shange's work may be considered, along with that of Margaret Walker, Toni Morrison, and Alice Walker, a harbinger of the African American cultural renaissance that began in the early 1980's.

This emergence of African American culture into the mainstream of American life signifies the culture's transition from being an attack on the obstacles of black self-realization to what has been called "the moment of becoming." The possibilities of what that moment of change may mean open up numerous potential paths, some traditional, some not. Shange, in interviews, has identified herself with not only the North American black community but with women's culture and with the culture of the Third World. She sees herself as a "child of the new world," who must help forge a new language in order to function fully and to express the experience of that new world. Fluent in French, Spanish, and Portuguese, Shange has been able to cross communication boundaries in American, African, and European cultures. Brought up as a Presbyterian, Congregationalist, and Unitarian, she practices Methodist Episcopalianism and *santería*. Raised in the jazz culture and race politics of the 1950's, educated at Barnard and the University of Southern California (USC), she participated in the Civil Rights movement of the 1960's and the communal feminism of the 1970's. While a graduate student at USC, she adopted the names "ntozake," "she who comes with her own things" and "shange" "she who walks like a lion."

In *for colored girls who have considered suicide/ when the rainbow is enuf*, this complex of influences reveals itself. Praised for its faithful replication of black women's speech and movement that transcended stereotypes, the piece reflects the call-and-response pattern of the African American church in its use of monologue against a chorus of voices. Its incantatory use of music, language, and dance is a reflection of *candomblé* and *santería*. The language in the play ignores standard grammar and punctuation in an effort to re-create the music of African American storytelling. Shange attempts both to confront the issues of black women's sexuality and exploitation and to transcend that exploitation in an exploration of the possibilities of re-creation of the self that is grounded in the life-giving forces of nature and sisterhood.

Jane Anderson Jones

Bibliography:
Christ, Carol P. " 'I Found God in Myself . . . & I Loved Her Fiercely': Ntozake Shange." In *Diving Deep and Surfacing: Women Writers on Spiritual Quest*. Boston: Beacon Press, 1980.

for colored girls who have considered suicide / SHANGE

Describes how the women in the play come to an affirmation of themselves by envisioning a new image that acknowledges their history and moves beyond it to "the ends of their own rainbows."

Flowers, Sandra Hollin. " 'Colored Girls': Textbook for the Eighties." *Black American Literature Forum* 15, no. 2 (Summer, 1981): 51-54. Discusses how the play reveals the crisis in love relationships and communication between black men and women.

Richards, Sandra L. "Conflicting Impulses in the Plays of Ntozake Shange." *Black American Literature Forum* 17, no. 2 (Summer, 1983): 73-78. Sees Shange's sources in new world African religions such as *santería* and in two traditions of contemporary theater: Bertolt Brecht's epic theater and Antonin Artaud's theater of cruelty.

Rushing, Andrea Benton. "For Colored Girls, Suicide or Struggle." *The Massachusetts Review* 22, no. 3 (Autumn, 1981): 539-550. Rushing argues that the play is rooted in Shange's experience as a middle-class, geographically rootless, highly educated black woman who came of age in the 1960's and who had attempted suicide at least twice. She claims Shange is alienated from the two traditional support systems of black womanhood: the extended family and the black church.

Vandergrift, Kay E. "And Bid Her Sing: A White Feminist Reads African-American Female Poets." In *African-American Voices: Tradition, Transition, Transformation*, edited by Karen Patricia Smith. Metuchen, N.J.: The Scarecrow Press, 1994. Emphasizes the power of the song elements in the play, showing how bebop and jazz rhythms combine with literary, socio-political, and popular culture references in the poems.

FOR THE UNION DEAD

Type of work: Poetry
Author: Robert Lowell (1917-1977)
First published: 1964

Born to a prominent New England family noted for its contributions to American literature, Robert Lowell blends personal and cultural histories in his work. By the time the thirty-five poems of *For the Union Dead* appeared, Lowell was at the height of his powers, having won the Pulitzer Prize in poetry for *Lord Weary's Castle* in 1947 and the National Book Award for *Life Studies* in 1959. Most readers consider *Life Studies*, which includes a lengthy prose memoir of his dysfunctional family, to be his best book.

In 1949, Lowell was institutionalized for a nervous breakdown, and he suffered attacks of manic-depressive disorder for the rest of his life. In 1948, he divorced his first wife, novelist Jean Stafford, and the next year he married Elizabeth Hardwick, from whom he was divorced in 1972. "Old Flame," the second poem in the collection, concerns his first wife; the first poem, "Water," is a reminiscence of his relationship with the poet Elizabeth Bishop, whom he met in 1946 and who was to remain a lifelong friend.

Lowell is widely recognized as the "father" of the confessional movement in post-World War II American poetry, having taught both Sylvia Plath and Anne Sexton while at Boston University in the late 1950's. In general, the confessional poets, many of whom went through psychoanalysis, place themselves, and often their parents, at the center of their work, as Lowell does in "Middle Age," the third poem in this book, where, at forty-five, he claims to have met his father (who died in 1950) on the "chewed-up streets" of New York and asked him to "forgive me/ my injuries,/ as I forgive/ those I/ have injured!" The religious echo is common in Lowell's poems.

Typically, confessional poets work through pain and anger, even outrage, sometimes appearing self-analytical and harsh in their judgments on themselves, sometimes self-pitying and morbid. The self or ego is so prevalent in Lowell's poems that when the third person appears, as in "The Mouth of the Hudson," the reader may accept the third person as an alter-ego, or another side of Lowell. In that poem, the man is isolated in an industrial wasteland, and he has "trouble with his balance" (both mental and physical). The poem ends with an image referring to "the sulphur-yellow sun/ of the unforgivable landscape." It is a curiosity, if not a symptom, of confessional poetry that the confessions rarely lead to a sense of healing forgiveness.

The title of the opening poem is "Water," and water is a conventional symbol of life or purification, but the lovers discover at the end that "the water was too cold for us." In "Eye and Tooth," which echoes the biblical "eye for eye, tooth for tooth," the myopic poet (Lowell's vision had been bad since boyhood) sees the cycle of life during a "summer rain" as "a simmer of rot and renewal." (The sound play between "summer" and "simmer" and the alliterative 'r' sounds typify Lowell's acute ear.) At the end of that poem he declares, "I am tired. Everyone's tired of my turmoil."

One way of looking at *For the Union Dead* is that the poems show Lowell struggling against the limitations of his own subjectivity, not by rejecting the potential of the inner self, but by forcing the self out of its shell and into contact with the outer world of time and history. In "Fall 1961," for example, he confronts time, which he portrays as "the orange, bland, ambassadorial/ face of the moon/ on the grandfather clock." The talk of nuclear war during that time of the Cuban Missile Crisis created an apocalyptic anxiety, in which the speaker feels like a fish in an aquarium: "I swim like a minnow/ behind my studio window." Similarly, the state seems helpless, like "a diver under a glass bell." As "Our end drifts nearer,/ the moon lifts,/ radiant with terror," so that the symbol of romance is transformed into one of fear. Note Lowell's rhyming of "drifts" and "lifts" and his slant rhyming of "nearer" with "terror."

The father who appears in "Fall 1961" is not his own "dinosaur" father of "Middle Age," but himself: "A father's no shield/ to his child." Lowell's daughter was then four years old. In a simile that may reach back to a sermon entitled "Sinners in the Hands of an Angry God," by the eighteenth-century Calvinist minister Jonathan Edwards (himself the subject of a poem later in the book), Lowell writes: "We are like a lot of wild/ spiders crying together,/ but without tears." At the conclusion of the poem, as the clock ticks tediously, the speaker retreats to his "one point of rest," which is an oriole's nest. He remains unready to face the threatening external world.

The references to fish, dinosaurs, birds, and spiders, and to other nonhuman forms of life accumulate throughout this book, sometimes, as with the spiders, identified with humans, and sometimes depicted as victims of what humans are making of the world. In "The Public Garden," even in its title an effort to reach out from the self and into the world of current realities, the speaker first declares that "all's alive" as he watches children "crowding home from school at five." Then he sees that the swanboats are a "jaded flock" and the park is drying up so that "the heads of four stone lions stare/ and suck on empty faucets." The moon appears again as a perverse symbol, "always a stranger!" At the end the speaker remembers summer but sees people as "drowned in Eden," and in the closing lines, heavy with alliterative *f* sounds, he sees no spark of life or inspiration: "The fountain's failing waters flash around/ the garden. Nothing catches fire."

Near the center of the collection, however, in the poem entitled "Returning," even though the speaker sees the outer world as "rather a dead town," the poem may hold out some promise for reconciliation. The speaker remembers the world's "former fertility,/ how everything came out clearly/ in the hour of credulity/ and young summer." Religious overtones in this poem suggest that Lowell is looking back wistfully at his conversion to Roman Catholicism in 1940, but the "venerable elm," (the Church, presumably), now sick, "gave too much shelter."

In "The Drinker," Lowell, who had a serious drinking problem himself, resorts to the objectifying distance of the third person. The man in the first line is "killing time." Despite some ugly images ("the cheese wilts in the rat-trap"), the poem closes on a positive note, reversing the initial assertion into a question: "Is he killing time?" Lowell follows with an image of "two cops on horseback" in the April rain checking parking meters, "their oilskins yellow as forsythia."

The next two poems, in which Lowell reflects on historical personages (the nineteenth century American writer, Nathaniel Hawthorne, and Jonathan Edwards), concern cultural history. In "The Neo-Classical Urn" the speaker compares himself to the turtles that he caught as a boy, but which died in captivity. Lowell may intend the reader to think of English poet John Keats's "Ode on a Grecian Urn," but if so, the relationship between the poems is ironic, for Keats sees the urn as representative of timelessness and immortality, whereas the turtles die. Lowell's vision at the end is complex. As a man he can see that turtles have no mind or will; they are "nothings." When he rubs his head, he describes it as "that turtle shell," and he breathes in their "dying smell"; that is, he identifies himself with their mortality and with their place in "history," at least with his personal history.

The following poem, "Caligula," refers to the tyrannical Roman emperor whose name was the source of Lowell's nickname from prep school days, "Cal." So, in that poem, too, he continues to expand from the confined self into the outer world. "Beyond the Alps," in fact, opens up both historically and geographically, and the next several poems continue that expansion: "July in Washington," "Buenos Aires," "Dropping South: Brazil," "Soft Wood" (in which the speaker, in Maine, regards his cousin dying in Washington, D.C.).

The compelling title poem, which concludes the book, moves from at least two historical vantage points (one personal and the other cultural) to make perhaps the most powerful political statement Lowell had made to date. (A critic of the war in Vietnam, Lowell was much involved with writers' protests after 1965.) The poem, in quatrains of varying line lengths, begins with Lowell's memory of himself as a boy at the South Boston Aquarium, now boarded up. Once his "hand tingled/ to burst the bubbles" of the "cowed, compliant fish," but now he draws back and yearns for "the dark downward and vegetating kingdom/ of the fish and reptile." He emerges from this reverse evolution, however, into the historical present of "one morning last March."

In the world at hand, he finds that the dinosaurs, in the form of steamshovels, still exist, gouging an "underworld garage." The "heart of Boston" is being crowded by luxuries in the form of parking spaces, and the Puritan legacy of the "tingling Statehouse" shakes with the "earthquake" caused by the construction. (Several words and images, such as tingled/tingling and bubbles, echo throughout the poem.) Lowell moves from the personal past to the cultural present in the third quatrain, but with the sixth stanza, which introduces the statue of Colonel Robert Shaw and the 44th Massachusetts Negro regiment, he moves into the cultural past. (The regiment's disastrous assault on Fort Wagner in 1863 is dramatized in the film *Glory*, 1989.)

Lowell examines the impact of the cultural past on the present, which involves the Civil Rights movement. South Boston was notorious for its racism in the early 1960's. "Their monument sticks like a fishbone/ in the city's throat." Unlike Lowell, the colonel is "out of bounds now," free of time and change. The heroism of Colonel Shaw is implicit in his choice of "life and death," which the churches of New England at least appear to commemorate. Shaw's choice of life and death constitutes the ultimate triumph of free human will.

In the thirteenth quatrain, Lowell says Shaw's father wanted no such monument. He was content with the "ditch," or mass grave, in which his son and his men were buried. (Lowell's mention of the word "niggers" in this stanza should not be ascribed to Shaw's father, but to racists generally, in 1863 and 1960.) In the last four stanzas, Lowell returns to the present: "The ditch is nearer." He concludes with a warning against nuclear war and racism, depicting Shaw "riding on his bubble" and waiting for it to pop, and in the last quatrain he indicts the society that he sees as greedy in its desire for luxury cars and insensitive to the value of such an institution as the city aquarium:

> The Aquarium is gone. Everywhere,
> giant finned cars nose forward like fish;
> a savage servility
> slides by on grease.

The phrase, "savage servility," an oxymoron, encapsulates Lowell's condemnation of a materialistic culture, servile as, for example, a salesman and savage in its war and racism (which a salesman would also support and participate in).

Out of its own dark turmoil, the troubled self detects a frightening and vicious world given over to greed and violence. It should be no wonder that when such poets move to a political voice, its tones will be apocalyptic.

Ron McFarland

Bibliography:

Axelrod, Steven Gould. *Robert Lowell: Life and Art.* Princeton, N.J.: Princeton University Press, 1978. Comments on movement between past and present; explores the poems as a sequence. Offers valuable contexts for title poem.

Fein, Richard J. *Robert Lowell.* 2d ed. Boston: Twayne, 1979. Surveys poems and remarks on animal imagery. Close reading of title poem.

Mazzaro, Jerome. *The Poetic Themes of Robert Lowell.* Ann Arbor: University of Michigan Press, 1965. Reflects on solipsism and narcissism in the poems; Lowell often slips into self-pity.

Rudman, Mark. *Robert Lowell: An Introduction to the Poetry.* New York: Columbia University Press, 1983. Argues that the poems "progressively" darken, that the subject of the book is "pain."

Yenser, Stephen. *Circle to Circle: The Poetry of Robert Lowell.* Berkeley: University of California Press, 1975. Finds Lowell's poems sometimes "excruciatingly introspective." Comments on most of the poems.

FOR WHOM THE BELL TOLLS

Type of work: Novel
Author: Ernest Hemingway (1899-1961)
Type of plot: Impressionistic realism
Time of plot: 1937
Locale: Spain
First published: 1940

> *Principal characters:*
> ROBERT JORDAN, an American fighting with the Spanish Loyalists
> PABLO, a guerrilla leader
> PILAR, his wife
> MARIA, the beloved of Jordan
> ANSELMO, another guerrilla

The Story:

At first, the only important thing was the bridge. Robert Jordan was a young American teacher who was in Spain fighting with the Loyalist guerrillas. His present and most important mission was to blow up a bridge that would be of great strategic importance during an offensive three days hence. Jordan was behind the Fascist lines, with orders to make contact with Pablo, the leader of a guerrilla band, and with his wife, Pilar, who was the strongest figure among the partisans. Pablo was a weak and drunken braggart, but Pilar was strong and trustworthy. She was a swarthy, raw-boned woman, vulgar and outspoken, but so fiercely devoted to the Loyalist cause that Jordan knew she would carry out her part of the mission regardless of danger to herself.

The plan was that Jordan study the bridge from all angles and then finalize the plans for its destruction at the proper moment. Jordan had blown up many bridges and three trains, but this was the first time everything had to be done on a split-second schedule. Pablo and Pilar were to assist Jordan in any way they could, even in rounding up other bands of guerrillas if Jordan needed them to accomplish his mission.

At the cave hideout of Pablo and Pilar, Jordan met a beautiful young girl named Maria, who had escaped from the Fascists. Maria had been subjected to every possible indignity, having been starved, tortured, and raped, and she felt unclean. At the camp, Jordan also met Anselmo, a loyal old man who would follow orders regardless of his personal safety. Anselmo hated having to kill but would do so if necessary.

Jordan loved the brutal, shrewd, desperate, loyal guerrillas, for he knew that their cruelties against the Fascists stemmed from poverty and ignorance. The Fascists' cruelty, however, he abhorred, for the Fascists came largely from the wealthy, ambitious class. The story of Maria's suffering filled him with such hatred that he could have killed a thousand of them, even though he, like Anselmo, hated to kill.

The first night he spent at the guerrilla camp destroyed his cold approach to the mission before him, for he fell deeply in love with Maria. She came to his sleeping bag that night, and although they talked little, he knew after she left that he was no longer ready to die. He told Maria that one day they would be married, but he was afraid of the future, and fear was dangerous for a man on an important mission.

Jordan made many sketches of the bridge and laid his plans carefully, but the night before the bridge was to be blown up his work was almost ruined by Pablo, who deserted after stealing and destroying the explosives and the detonators hidden in Jordan's pack. Pablo returned repentant on the morning of the mission, but the loss of the detonators and explosives meant that Jordan and his helper would have to blow up the bridge with hand grenades, a much more dangerous method. Pablo had tried to redeem himself by bringing another small guerrilla band and their horses with him. Although Jordan despised Pablo by that time, he forgave him, as did Pilar.

At the bridge, Jordan worked quickly and carefully. Each person had a specific job to do, and each did his work well. First Jordan and Anselmo killed the sentries, then Pablo and his guerrillas attacked the Fascist lines approaching the bridge, so as to prevent their crossing before the bridge was demolished. Jordan had been ordered to blow up the bridge at the beginning of a Loyalist bombing attack over the Fascist lines. When he heard the thudding explosions of the bombs, he pulled the pins and the bridge shot high into the air. Jordan got to cover safely, but Anselmo was killed by a steel fragment from the bridge. As Jordan looked at the old man and realized that he might be alive if Pablo had not stolen the detonators, he wanted to kill Pablo. Yet he knew what his duty was and ran to the designated meeting place of the fugitive guerrillas.

There he found Pablo, Pilar, Maria, and the two remaining gypsy partisans. Pablo, herding the extra horses, said that all the other guerrillas had been killed. Jordan knew, however, that Pablo had killed the men so that he could get their horses. When he confronted him, Pablo admitted the slaughter, but shrugged his great shoulders and said that the men had not been of his band.

The next problem before them was to cross a road that could be swept by Fascist gunfire. Jordan knew that the first two people would have the best chance, since they would probably be able to cross before the Fascists were alerted. Because Pablo knew the road to safety, Jordan put him on the first horse. Maria was second, for Jordan was determined that she should be saved before the others. Pilar was to go next, then the two remaining guerrillas, and, last of all Jordan. The first four crossed safely, but Jordan's horse, wounded by Fascist bullets, fell on his leg. The others dragged him across the road and out of the line of fire, but he knew that he could not go on and was too badly injured to ride a horse. Pablo and Pilar understood, but Maria begged to stay with him. Jordan told Pilar to take Maria away when he gave the signal; then he talked to the girl, telling her that she must go on, that as long as she lived, he lived also. When the time came, she had to be put on her horse and led away.

Jordan, settling down to wait for the approaching Fascist troops, propped himself against a tree, with his submachine gun across his knees. As he waited, he thought over the events that had brought him to that place. He knew that what he had done was right, but that his side might not win for many years. He knew, too, that if the common people kept trying, they would eventually win. He hoped they would be prepared when that day came, that they would no longer want to kill and torture but would struggle for peace and good as they were now struggling for freedom. He felt at the end that his own part in the struggle had not been in vain. As he saw the first Fascist officer approaching, Robert Jordan smiled. He was ready.

Critical Evaluation:

In 1940, Ernest Hemingway published *For Whom the Bell Tolls* to wide critical and public acclaim. The novel became an immediate best-seller, erasing his somewhat flawed performance in *To Have and Have Not* (1937). During the 1930's, a time when Hemingway enjoyed great publicity, he went on the African safari that produced *Green Hills of Africa* (1935) and his column in *Esquire* (1933-1936). In 1940, he was divorced by his second wife, Pauline Pfeiffer, and married Martha Gellhorn. He set fishing records at Bimini in marlin tournaments, hunted in Wyoming, and fished at Key West, Florida, where he bought a home. In 1937, when the Spanish Civil War broke out, Hemingway went to Spain as a correspondent with a passionate devotion to the Spain of his early years. Not content merely to report the war, he became actively involved with the Loyalist Army in its fight against Franco and the generals. He wrote the script for the propaganda film *The Spanish Earth* (1937), which was shown at the White House at a presidential dinner. The proceeds of the film were used to buy ambulances for the Loyalists. In 1939, with the war a lost cause and just as World War II was beginning its course of destruction, Hemingway wrote *For Whom the Bell Tolls*.

To understand Hemingway's motive in writing the book, it is helpful to study the quotation from John Donne, from which Hemingway took his theme, "any mans death diminishes me, because I am involved in Mankinde; And therefore never send to know for whom the bell tolls; It tolls for thee." Hemingway wanted his readers to feel that what happened to the Loyalists in Spain in 1937 was a part of the twentieth century world crisis in which everyone shared.

Even more than in *A Farewell to Arms* (1929), Hemingway in *For Whom the Bell Tolls* focused the conflict of war in the experiences of a single man. Like Frederic Henry, Robert Jordan is an American in a European country fighting for a cause that is not his by birth. Henry just happened to be in Italy when World War I broke out; he had no ideological commitment to the war. Robert Jordan, however, came to Spain because he believed in the Loyalist cause. He believed in the land and the people, a belief that ultimately cost him his life. Yet Jordan's death is an affirmation and the novel a clear political statement of what a human being must do under pressure.

For Whom the Bell Tolls is a circular novel. It begins with Robert Jordan in a pine forest in Spain, observing a bridge he has been assigned to destroy, and it ends with him in snow that covers the pine needles carefully sighting on an enemy officer approaching on horseback. Between the opening and closing paragraphs is a time period of only seventy hours, and at the center of all the action and meditation is the bridge, the focal point of the conflict to which the reader and the characters are repeatedly drawn.

In what was at that point his longest novel, Hemingway forged a tightly unified plot, with a single place, a single action, and a brief time—the old Greek unities. Jordan's military action takes on other epic qualities associated with the Greeks. His sacrifice is not unlike that of Leonidas at the crucial pass of Thermopylae, during the Persian Wars. There, too, heroic action was required to defend an entry point, and there, too, the leader died in an action that proved futile in military terms but became a standard measure of courage and commitment.

Abandoning somewhat the terse, clipped style of his earlier novels, Hemingway makes effective use of flashbacks to delineate the major characters. Earlier central characters seemed to exist without a past. Yet if Robert Jordan's death was to "diminish mankind," then the reader had to know more about him. This character development takes place almost within suspended time, and Jordan and Maria try to condense an entire life into those seventy hours. The reader is never allowed to forget time altogether, for the days move, light changes, meals are eaten, and snow falls. Everything moves toward the time when the bridge must be blown up, and life, love, and death are compressed into those seventy hours. The novel becomes a compact cycle suspended in time.

In the gypsy camp, each person becomes important. Pilar is often cited as one of Hemingway's better female characters, just as Maria is often criticized as being unbelievable. Yet

Maria's psychological scars are carefully developed. She is just as mentally unstable as are Brett Ashley and Catherine Barkley. Jordan, too, is a wounded man. He lives with the suicide of his father and the killing of his fellow dynamiter. The love of Jordan and Maria makes them both temporarily whole again.

The destruction of the bridge is meaningless in military terms. Seen in the larger political context, Jordan's courage and death were wasted. However, the bridge was important for its effect on the group, giving them a purpose and a focal point and forging them into a unity, a whole. They can take pride in their accomplishment despite its cost. Life is ultimately a defeat no matter how it is lived; what gives defeat meaning is the courage that a human being is capable of forging in the face of death's certainty. One man's death does diminish the group, for they are involved together, but Jordan's loss is balanced by the purpose he has given to the group.

Just as the mountains are no longer a place safe from the Fascists with their airplanes, Hemingway seems to be saying that no person and no place are any longer safe. It is no longer possible to make a separate peace as Frederic Henry did with his war. When Fascist violence is loose in the world, people must take a stand. Jordan does not believe in the Communist ideology that supports the Loyalists, but he does believe in the earth and its people. He is essentially the nonpolitical man caught in a political conflict that he cannot avoid, and he does the best he can with the weapons available to him.

"Critical Evaluation" by Michael S. Reynolds

Bibliography:

Bloom, Harold, ed. *Ernest Hemingway*. New York: Chelsea House, 1985. Although no essay in this collection deals exclusively with *For Whom the Bell Tolls*, the novel is mentioned in many of them. Of particular interest may be Robert Penn Warren's discussion of irony in *For Whom the Bell Tolls*. Includes a good index.

Josephs, Allen. *"For Whom the Bell Tolls": Ernest Hemingway's Undiscovered Country*. New York: Twayne, 1994. Considers the literary and historical context for the novel and gives a detailed reading. An interesting and accessible discussion. Includes an excellent annotated bibliography.

Reynolds, Michael. "Ringing the Changes: Hemingway's Bell Tolls Fifty." *Virginia Quarterly Review* 67 (Winter, 1991): 1-18. In this good general reference, Reynolds presents the novel in historical context and suggests ways in which it can be seen to transcend its own time.

Rovit, Earl, and Gerry Brenner. *Ernest Hemingway*. Rev. ed. Boston: Twayne, 1986. Focuses on the totality of Hemingway's fiction rather than on individual works. A useful and accessible source, with fairly detailed explication of *For Whom the Bell Tolls*. Also includes an index.

Sanderson, Rena, ed. *Blowing the Bridge: Essays on Hemingway and "For Whom the Bell Tolls."* New York: Greenwood Press, 1992. A collection of twelve essays that take a fresh look at Hemingway and his most neglected major novel. The introduction gives an overview of the novel's composition and critical reception and offers a reassessment fifty years after publication.

THE FOREIGN GIRL

Type of work: Drama
Author: Florencio Sánchez (1875-1910)
Type of plot: Comedy
Time of plot: Early twentieth century
Locale: Pampas near Santa Fe, Argentina
First performed: 1904; first published as *La gringa*, 1910 (English translation, 1942)

> *Principal characters:*
> DON NICOLA, an ambitious Italian immigrant farmer
> MARÍA, his wife
> VICTORIA, their daughter
> HORACIO, their son
> DON CANTALICIO, an easygoing, native-born farmer
> PRÓSPERO, his son, who is in love with Victoria

The Story:

Don Nicola was an immigrant landowner who worked hard on his farm and expected his laborers to do the same. Privately, his workmen and less ambitious neighbors criticized him because he made his wife and children get up at two o'clock in the morning to begin their daily chores.

One of his neighbors was Don Cantalicio, an easygoing creole farmer deeply in Don Nicola's debt. Próspero, his son, worked for Don Nicola and cast many languishing glances in the direction of Victoria, his employer's pretty daughter. Early one morning, coming to breakfast with the other laborers, Próspero found Victoria at her work and seized the chance to kiss her. She offered little resistance to his embrace. Later, one of the boys reported that he had seen the Italian's white ox in old Cantalicio's pasture. Próspero was forced to defend his father against a charge of thievery.

With a payment of a loan of forty-five hundred pesos about to fall due, Cantalicio begged his neighbor for a year's extension of credit. Don Nicola said that he intended to foreclose on Cantalicio's property because his son Horacio, then studying in Buenos Aires, wanted the land for a farm. Cantalicio was unable to pay the debt, but he refused to give up the property. When Próspero commented that his father should have planted wheat instead of trying to pasture cattle, Cantalicio turned on his son and accused him of becoming a gringo—a despised foreigner.

Not long afterward María, Don Nicola's wife, discovered Próspero hugging her daughter. When she told her husband, he discharged the young man. It did no good for Próspero to ask for Victoria's hand. Don Nicola told him that he was not making money for a creole son-in-law to squander.

A few days later, the customers in a nearby tavern were drinking and teasing the waitress when a call came for the doctor to attend a sick but penniless peon. The doctor refused to leave until some of the loiterers offered to pay his fee. Into the tavern to gossip with the manager's wife came María and Victoria, who had been shopping in town while Don Nicola was with his lawyer discussing the confiscation of Cantalicio's property. Próspero also arrived, about to leave Santa Fe. He would not listen when Victoria pleaded with him to stay. He quarrelled again with his father, who again accused him of taking the side of foreigners against those of good Argentineans.

Once Cantalicio lost the lawsuit he had brought in an attempt to keep his property, he, too, prepared to leave the district. He complained bitterly that the immigrants were taking over all the land. When Don Nicola appeared at the tavern to pay him the cash difference between the amount of the debt and the value of the farm, Cantalicio refused to accept a note for a part of the settlement, even though the priest promised to see that the note was made good. The ruined creole trusted no one, and he wept as he declared that everyone was against him.

Two years later, many changes could be seen on the farm that Don Nicola had taken over. To make room for a new building, he now planned to have the workmen chop down the ancient ombu tree, symbol of the old-time Argentine gaucho. Horacio, who was settled on the farm, was explaining to his father the use of gravity in connection with a new reservoir when Victoria appeared. She was listless and showed no interest in anything, not even in plans for her own room in the new house.

Old Cantalicio turned up unexpectedly. He was now working for others and driving oxen to a nearby town, and he stopped to see what his old home looked like. Every change saddened him, but he reacted most strongly to the cutting down of the ombu. Don Nicola had no right to touch the tree, he asserted; it belonged to the land.

Victoria kept trying to tell him something, but all she could bring herself to say was that she had been in Rosario for several months. There she had seen Próspero, who missed his father. She let slip the fact that she was receiving letters from him. Horacio reported that Mr. Daples, an agent for farm machinery in Rosario, regarded Cantalicio's son as his most valued employee. The brother and sister offered to take the old man around the farm. Still resentful, he refused and hurriedly mounted his horse.

At that moment, the automobile of the man who was building the new house chugged over the hill. That symbol of modern progress frightened Cantalicio's horse, who bolted and threw his rider in front of the car. Refusing the aid of everyone except Victoria, the hurt man begged her to help him to the ombu; he wanted to die when it fell. He cursed Don Nicola, calling him a gringo.

Several weeks later, everything was going well on the renovated farm. Buyers were offering bonuses to get Don Nicola's clean wheat as soon as the thresher arrived to harvest it. Don Nicola told Horacio that the contractor wanted to marry Victoria and had asked for an answer before he left that night. The father was anxious to consult her as to her choice, but she was spending most of her time looking after Cantalicio, who had lost his right arm through his accident. Some of the household thought that he would be better off in a hospital.

Overhearing their discussion, Cantalicio announced that he would leave the farm at once, on foot if they would not lend him a wagon. Victoria refused to hear of his leaving, however. Breaking down, she insisted that she needed him, for she was carrying Próspero's child.

Mr. Daples sent Próspero to the farm to run the threshing machine. Great was María's dismay when she again caught him embracing her daughter. When she called for her husband to come and drive Próspero off the place once and for all, Don Nicola remarked on the young man's industry and calculated that if the boy married into the family they could get their threshing done for nothing. Even Cantalicio became reconciled to the gringos—at least to one of them—and let drop the announcement of his expected grandchild. All were excited. Don Nicola however was never one to waste time, even for such a reason. He declared that Próspero could wed Victoria, but meanwhile there was the threshing to be done. Grandchild or no grandchild, work must come first.

Critical Evaluation:

Born in Montevideo, Uruguay, to Argentine exiles, Florencio Sánchez was brought up in a poverty that made him closely acquainted with an emerging working class that flooded such major Latin American cities as Montevideo and Buenos Aires before World War I. Himself the child of immigrants, Sánchez showed a marked interest in the migration of thousands of foreigners to the cities. In *The Foreign Girl*, he shows the animosity and discomfort of the local population, especially the local peasant class, who felt displaced by an aggressive foreign working class.

The Foreign Girl also raises another important issue: What local traditions should be preserved despite the tremendous changes experienced in the area as the result of worldwide technological advances? Sánchez answers this question in the various types of characters he uses to define the social groups involved in the controversy.

As a newspaper reporter, Sánchez became an indefatigable traveler, which allowed him to witness local traditions representing the Argentine identity. Since much of that local folklore belonged to the lower social groups, he also got to know intimately the problems faced by those marginalized classes. Sánchez's characters represent genuine types of people, and his play *The Foreign Girl* is a realistic portrayal of life at the turn of the century. In fact, Sánchez' total production could be labeled a reliable reproduction of rural life in the outskirts of Southern Cone urban centers.

The Foreign Girl's main character, Victoria, represents the new Argentine of the twentieth century: a first-generation country girl of Italian parents. Her derogatory nickname, Gringa, reflects local animosity against foreigners. In the play, Victoria has the positive, sympathetic role of a hardworking young woman, who is well liked in the neighborhood because of her kindness and consideration toward all around her, including her Argentine neighbors. She considers herself an Argentine and displays deeply rooted attachment to the land.

Her father, Don Nicola, is her opposite: an abusive father and husband who forces his daughter and wife to do long hours of heavy farm labor. This strong Italian man has no connection to the land, from which he tries to force optimal productivity, showing no concern for environmental damage. Don Nicola keeps himself apart from the Argentine community, a fact that brings further resentment from the local inhabitants.

Sánchez' social views rescue the play from being inflammatory antiforeigner propaganda. His stand is clear: The conflict between Don Nicola and Don Cantalicio is not due to one man's being more hardworking than the other, but to Don Nicola's exploitation of the land and his lack of attachment to the country. Such lack of connection to the host country is not shared by the first generation born in Argentina, represented in the play by Victoria and Horacio, Don Nicola's son. Horacio, a university-trained land surveyor, instructs his father on more efficient ways to cultivate the land and warns him about the dangers of overworking the land. Some of this advice had already been offered by Don Cantalicio to Don Nicola.

In a dramatic turn of events, Don Cantalicio is also taught a lesson by his son, Próspero, who blames his father for losing his farm to Don Nicola because Don Cantalicio had not rotated his crops to revitalize the aging soil. Having fallen in love with Victoria, Próspero sets out to prove to her that he is a worthy, hardworking, intelligent man. He transforms one of the nearby farms into one of the most productive in the area. Final recognition of Próspero's knowledge of agricultural matters comes from Horacio, who seeks Próspero's advice for his father's farm, of which Horacio is now overseer.

The Foreign Girl's happy ending—Victoria and Próspero getting married with their parents' permission—reflects Latin American society's positive attitude at the time toward the twentieth century. Sánchez expresses a widespread belief that Latin America's entrance into the twentieth century began when its people accepted foreign help in the shaping of their society. Sánchez recognizes, however, that native values are in jeopardy, and he urges that modern Latin American society observe a balance between the ancient, local South American customs and the ideas of European industrialism.

Sánchez' contribution to Latin American theater lies in his concrete expression of social ideas. His characters, presented in photographic detail, prove that rural life with its many problems and joys is material worthy of the drama. Sánchez' aim to educate by means of simple plots and real characters makes him a precursor of the popular theater.

"Critical Evaluation" by Rafael Ocasio

Bibliography:
Dorn, Georgette M. "Florencio Sánchez." In *Latin American Writers*, edited by Carlos A. Solé and María Isabel Abreu. Vol. 2. New York: Charles Scribner's Sons, 1989. Presents an overview of Sánchez' literary production. An ideal introduction to Sánchez' best known works.
Foster, David William. "Ideological Shift in the Rural Images in Florencio Sánchez's Theater." *Hispanic Journal* 11, no. 1 (Spring, 1990): 97-106. A detailed study of Argentina's rural life at the turn of the century. Compares two plays, *The Foreign Girl* and *Down the Gully* (1905) and emphasizes Sanchez' treatment of European immigration to Argentina.
Foster, David William, and Virgina Ramos Foster. "Sánchez, Florencio." In *Modern Latin American Literature*. New York: Frederick Ungar, 1975. Offers a survey of Sánchez' production by providing excerpts form critical studies by various critics.
Muñoz, Vladimiro. *Florencio Sánchez: A Chronology*. Translated by W. Scott Johnson. New York: Gordon Press, 1979. Traces Sánchez' life and places his works within the context of his many trips and political confrontations.
Richardson, Ruth. *Florencio Sánchez and the Argentine Theater*. New York: Instituto de las Españas en los Estados Unidos, 1933. Traces Sánchez' contributions as a founding father of contemporary Argentine theater, and the status of the national theater.

THE FORSYTE SAGA

Type of work: Novel
Author: John Galsworthy (1867-1933)
Type of plot: Family
Time of plot: 1886-1920
Locale: England
First published: 1922: *The Man of Property*, 1906; *In Chancery*, 1920; *To Let*, 1921

> *Principal characters:*
> SOAMES FORSYTE, a man of property
> IRENE, his wife
> OLD JOLYON FORSYTE, his uncle
> YOUNG JOLYON, Old Jolyon's son
> JUNE, Young Jolyon's daughter
> PHILIP BOSINNEY, an architect engaged to June
> ANNETTE, Soames's second wife
> FLEUR, their daughter
> JON, Irene and Young Jolyon's son
> WINIFRED DARTIE, Soames's sister and Monty Dartie's wife

The Story:

In 1886, all the Forsytes gathered at Old Jolyon Forsyte's house to celebrate the engagement of his granddaughter, June, to Philip Bosinney, a young architect. Young Jolyon Forsyte, June's father, was estranged from his family because he had run away with a governess, whom he had married after June's mother died.

Old Jolyon complained that he saw little of June. Because he was lonely, he called on Young Jolyon, whom he had not seen in many years. He found his son working as an underwriter for Lloyd's and painting watercolors. He had two children, Holly and Jolly, by his second wife.

The family knew that Soames had been having trouble with his lovely wife, Irene. She had developed a profound aversion for her husband and had recently reminded him of her premarital stipulation that she should have her freedom if the marriage were not a success. Desperate to please her, Soames planned to build a large country place at Robin Hill and hired June's fiancé to design and build the house.

When Soames suggested alterations to the plans, Bosinney appeared offended, and in the end, the plans remained as they had been drawn. As work on the house proceeded, the two men argued over the costs, which were exceeding the original estimate. One day, when Soames's uncle, Swithin Forsyte, took Irene to see the house, she met Bosinney there. While Swithin dozed, the architect and Irene talked and fell deeply in love with each other. From that point on, Irene's already unbearable life with Soames became impossible. She asked for a separate room.

Problems over the house continued. Bosinney had agreed to decorate it but only if he could have a free hand, to which Soames finally agreed. Irene and Bosinney began to meet secretly. As their affair progressed, June became more unhappy and self-centered. Finally, Old Jolyon took June away for a holiday. He wrote to Young Jolyon, asking him to see Bosinney and learn his intentions toward June. Young Jolyon talked to Bosinney, but the report he made to his father was vague.

When the house was completed, Soames sued Bosinney for exceeding his highest estimate. Irene refused to move to Robin Hill. When the lawsuit over the house came to trial, Soames won his case without difficulty. That same night Bosinney, after spending the afternoon with Irene and learning that Soames had forced himself on her, was accidentally run over and killed. Irene had left her husband on the day of the trial, but that night she returned to his house because there was nowhere else for her to go. June persuaded her grandfather to buy Robin Hill for Jolyon's family.

A short time after Bosinney's death, Irene left Soames permanently; she settled in a small flat, and started giving music lessons to support herself. Several years later, Irene visited Robin Hill secretly and there met Old Jolyon. She won him over with her gentleness and charm, and during that summer, she made his days happy. Late in the summer, he died quietly while waiting for her.

After his separation from Irene, Soames devoted himself to making money. Then, still hoping to have an heir, he began to court a young French woman, Annette Lamotte. His sister Winifred was facing difficulties about that time. Her husband, Monty Dartie, stole her pearls and ran away to South America with a Spanish dancer. When Soames decided to marry Annette, he went to Irene to see if she would provide grounds for a divorce. He found that she had lived a very quiet, model life. Soames realized that he still loved her and tried to persuade her to come back to him. When she refused, he hired a detective to get evidence with which to divorce her.

Old Jolyon had left a legacy to Irene in his will, and Young Jolyon, now a widower, had been appointed trustee. When Soames annoyed Irene, she appealed to Young Jolyon for protection. Irene went to Paris to avoid Soames; shortly afterward, Young Jolyon joined her. Her visit was cut short by Jolly, who announced that he had joined the yeomanry to fight in the Boer War. Holly had in the meantime fallen in love with Val Dartie, her cousin. When Val proposed to Holly, he was overheard by Jolly, who dared Val to join the yeomanry with him. Val accepted. June then decided to become a Red Cross nurse, and Holly went with her. Monty Dartie reappeared unexpectedly. To avoid further scandal, Winifred decided to allow him to come back.

Soames went to Paris in a last effort to persuade Irene. Frightened, Irene returned to Young Jolyon. Before they became lovers, they were presented with papers by Soames's lawyer. They decided to go abroad together. Before their departure, Young Jolyon received word that Jolly had died of enteric fever during the African campaign. Later, Soames secured his divorce and married Annette. To the discomfiture of both branches of the family, Val married Holly.

Irene presented Jolyon with a son, Jon. When Annette was about to give birth to a child, Soames had to choose between saving the mother or the child. Wishing an heir, Soames chose to save the child. Fortunately, both Annette and the baby, Fleur, lived. Little Jon grew up under the adoring eyes of his parents. Fleur grew up spoiled by her doting father.

Years passed. Monty Dartie was dead. Val and Holly were training racehorses. One day in a picture gallery, Soames impulsively invited a young man, Michael Mont, to see his collection of pictures. That same afternoon, he saw Irene and her son Jon for the first time in twenty years. Fleur and Jon met by chance. Having decided that he wanted to try farming, Jon went to stay with Val Dartie. Fleur also appeared to spend the week with Holly. Jon and Fleur fell deeply in love.

They had only vague ideas regarding the cause of the feud between their respective branches of the family. Later, Fleur learned all the details from Prosper Profond, with whom Annette was having an affair, and from Winifred Dartie. She was still determined to marry Jon. Michael Mont had received Soames's permission to court Fleur. When Soames heard of the affair between Annette and Prosper, she did not deny it but promised there would be no scandal.

Fleur tried to persuade Jon into a hasty marriage. She failed because Young Jolyon reluctantly gave his son a letter revealing the story of Soames and Irene. After reading the letter, Jon realized that he could never marry Fleur. His decision became irrevocable when his father died. He left England at once and went to America, where Irene joined him. Fleur, disappointed, married Michael Mont. Timothy was the last of the old Forsytes; when he died, Soames realized that the Forsyte age had passed. Its way of life was like an empty house that was to let. He felt lonely and old.

Critical Evaluation:

The Forsyte Saga won the Nobel Prize in literature for John Galsworthy in 1932. Its initial immense popularity subsided for a time but was revived again in the 1970's, partly as a result of a televised dramatization by the British Broadcasting Corporation in 1969. The three novels that make up the trilogy—*The Man of Property*, *In Chancery*, and *To Let*—are sequences in the history of a wealthy, middle-class English family, the Forsytes, who are conscious of their social position and eager to keep it. Their pettiness in matters of decorum is typical of the wealthy bourgeoisie of the times.

The differences among the various members of the Forsyte clan are to a great extent due to generational misunderstanding. The older members of the family, such as Uncle Swithin and Old Jolyon, lived in a different world, both chronologically and psychologically, from that of such young Forsytes as Fleur and Jolly. Those two worlds were straddled by Soames and Winifred, products of the tranquil Victorian period but now faced with disturbing societal changes that made them cling to the old familiar ways and fear acceptance of new ideas and new people. The transition from the old world into the new is one of the major strengths of the novel, and John Galsworthy draws readers into the lives of the Forsytes in such a way that they feel they are actually living through this time of change.

Perhaps the greatest merit of *The Forsyte Saga* is the fact that while its overall aim is one of social criticism, the characters are not sacrificed to this end but used to illuminate the comments. Although critics have claimed that most of the characters are incomplete, the mystery in each of the main characters, especially Irene and Bosinney, proves immensely engrossing.

The novel is a period piece, but it can be appreciated by readers not primarily interested in that historical age because the turns of fortune in the lives of the main characters address universal human concerns. The first episode of the story, the festive occasion of a party celebrating the engagement of young June to Philip Bosinney, is a case in point. The setting is that of a large family gathering intended to evaluate the worthiness of a prospective new member of the family. The conversation may at times have a uniquely Victorian flavor, but the setting and mood are ageless.

The complications among the characters are likewise ageless. Irene hopes to help June obtain family acceptance for Bosinney, but she falls in love with him herself. Soames tries to gain Irene's love by building a beautiful house for her, but he only succeeds in forcing her to leave him, which in turn makes him even more the distasteful "man of property" than he had been. This hardening of Soames's character is one of the things that makes him more a tragic character than a bad one.

Using an episodic structure in the novels, Galsworthy succeeds in portraying the thoughts and actions of an age in transition from the staid and superficially tranquil Victorian age to the bustling, confused early twentieth century. By using a large family as the base of the novel, he is able to introduce a representative variety of events and individuals. He uses many types of personality, among them Soames, the lonely businessman; Young Jolyon, the man who renounces his family to pursue a career as an artist; Fleur, the archetypal flapper of the post-World War I era. These and other characters play important roles in the progress of the story, but beyond that they are representative of the times. It is for these characterizations and for the overall view of the period that this trilogy will retain its position in literature.

"Critical Evaluation" by Patricia Ann King

Bibliography:

Gindin, James. "Ethical Structures in John Galsworthy, Elizabeth Bowen, and Iris Murdoch." In *Forms of Modern British Fiction*, edited by Alan Warren Friedman. Austin: University of Texas Press, 1975. Concludes that the central concern of the Galsworthy trilogy is ethical and explores what it is that people do to themselves and others. The main struggle is often between property and beauty.

Johnson, Pamela Hansford. "Speaking of Books: *The Forsyte Saga.*" *The New York Times Sunday Review of Books*, March 12, 1967, pp. 2, 36. Discusses the reception of Galsworthy's trilogy and the fact that the writer's reputation had fallen but was on the rise because of the television production of *The Forsyte Saga*.

Sternlicht, Sanford. *John Galsworthy*. Boston: G. K. Hall, 1987. Chapter 3 describes *The Forsyte Saga* as Galsworthy's crowning achievement, an ironic account without heroes or epic battles and a fine portrait of the passing from power of England's upper middle class.

Stevens, Earl. "John Galsworthy." In *British Winners of the Nobel Literary Prize*, edited by Walter Kidd. Norman: University of Oklahoma Press, 1973. Concludes that *The Forsyte Saga* alternates between satiric novel and lyric interlude and that Galsworthy seeks to teach readers to see the world more completely.

Stevens, Ray. "Mrs. Woolf and Mr. Galsworthy, and the Queer Case of *Beyond*." *English Literature in Transition* (1985): 65-87. Reexamines Virginia Woolf's criticism of Galsworthy and shows the nuances in the relationship between them, as well as their relationships with Arnold Bennett and H. G. Wells.

FORTUNATA AND JACINTA

Type of work: Novel
Author: Benito Pérez Galdós (1843-1920)
Type of plot: Social chronicle
Time of plot: 1869-1875
Locale: Madrid, Spain
First published: Fortunata y Jacinta, 1886-1887 (English translation, 1973)

Principal characters:
    FORTUNATA, a woman of the lower class
    JUANITO SANTA CRUZ, her lover
    MAXIMILIANO RUBÍN, her husband
    JACINTA, Juanito's wife
    MORENO ISLA, her admirer
    COLONEL EVARISTO FEIJÓO, Fortunata's protector

The Story:

The Santa Cruz dry-goods store in Madrid, established in the eighteenth century, provided an income for Juanito Santa Cruz. Having graduated from the university at the age of twenty-four, he was not yet ready to take his place in the family business. He wanted to enjoy life, and Barbara Santa Cruz, his mother, spoiled him. Her chief adviser was a former clerk, Placido Estupiñá, who smuggled goods into the city in his spare time.

At the home of a fellow student, Juanito met the attractive Fortunata and took her as his mistress. Shortly afterward, Estupiñá found out about the affair, and Juanito's mother contracted for him a marriage with his beautiful but passive cousin, Jacinta. They were married in May, 1871. When the couple returned from their honeymoon, Fortunata had left Madrid.

Jacinta discovered in the passing years that she could not have children. Learning some details of her husband's earlier affair with Fortunata, including the fact that his mistress had borne him a son nicknamed Petusin, she wondered whether it was her duty to take care of the child. In the meantime, Juanito had been told that Fortunata was back in Madrid. He immediately began to look for her, but his search ended when a lung infection made him an invalid for a long time.

Among Fortunata's admirers was the ill-favored and schizophrenic Maximiliano Rubín, the orphan of a goldsmith, who, like his two brothers, was subject to violent headaches. Thin and weak, he had been reared by his Aunt Lupe, who allowed him to live in a world of his own imagination. While studying to become a pharmacist, he met Fortunata at a friend's house. Her poverty afforded her the opportunity to overlook his ugliness and date him. When she confessed her past, he proposed marriage in order to redeem her.

Hearing of his plan, Aunt Lupe sent one of his brothers, a priest, to talk to Fortunata. The woman said frankly that Maximiliano was the only one of her lovers—except one now married—for whom she had ever cared. The priest proposed that she spend some time in a home for wayward girls; if she benefited by the experience, he would agree to the marriage. After a term in the institution, Fortunata married Maximiliano on a day when he was suffering from one of his worst headaches.

Having known beforehand of the proposed marriage, Juanito had taken a room in the boardinghouse that Fortunata and her husband were to occupy. At first he had intended only to see Fortunata again, but on the night of the wedding her husband was ill, and they resumed their old intimacy. Maximiliano, finding out about the affair, quarreled with Juanito, who overpowered the puny pharmacist and sent him to the hospital with an injured larynx. Then Fortunata packed her belongings and left her husband.

Juan Pablo, the second of Maximiliano's brothers, spent his afternoons in one café or another with his cronies, among them the elderly Colonel Evaristo Feijóo. While watching the parade marking the restoration of the monarchy in 1874, one of the loiterers saw Juanito and Fortunata sharing a balcony. Through gossip, Jacinta learned of her husband's infidelity. When she accused him, he aroused her sympathy for Fortunata by telling how badly she had been treated by her husband. Nevertheless, he did promise to break off relations with the woman. His farewell message, with an enclosure of one thousand pesetas, so angered Fortunata that she went to his house in order to create a scandal. The sight of Jacinta's gentle beauty tempered her anger, however, and while she was trying to decide what to do she saw Colonel Feijóo. He pointed out that, untrained as she was for any career, she had only three choices: go back to her husband, accept the attentions of any man with money to pay her, or take him as her protector.

She chose Feijóo as her lover, at the same time planning to make her future secure after his death and to reinstate herself in the good graces of the Rubín family. On one occasion, Fortunata came face-to-face with Jacinta, who did not know what her husband's former mistress looked like. Torn between a realization of Jacinta's beauty and goodness and her hatred for her as Juanito's wife, Fortunata blurted out her identity, much to Jacinta's confusion.

Only one woman present during the encounter knew what to do. Guillermina Pacheco asked Fortunata to come to see her the next day to discuss the situation. The frank conversation between the two women was overheard by Jacinta, who was in the next room. The cruelest blow to Jacinta was Fortunata's insistence that Juanito needed her, since she had given him the son his wife could never bear him. When Fortunata discovered the eavesdropper, her angry words showed that she was still essentially of the lower class.

Later, Fortunata had a scene with Maximiliano, who was gradually losing his mind. At last he drove her out of the house. Before long, she and Juanito once again became lovers. Maximiliano tried to earn a living by working in a drugstore, but his mental state caused him to make dangerous mistakes in mixing drugs. His employer had two daughters. One was Aurora, the thirty-three-year-old widow of a Frenchman killed while fighting the Prussians in 1870. She wore clothes with a Parisian flair and soon caught the eye of Juanito, as Fortunata learned to her dismay.

In the meantime, Moreno Isla had fallen violently in love with Jacinta. He and Guillermina Pacheco, bribed by Moreno, tried to convince her that her husband would never be faithful, but Jacinta gave Moreno no encouragement. At the same time Aurora, for her own purposes, tried to convince Juanito that his wife was in love with another man.

Fortunata was pregnant and was therefore afraid to live with Maximiliano any longer. He talked constantly of a philosophy of death; afraid, she hid herself at Aunt Lupe's house. While looking for her, Maximiliano discovered proof that Juanito and Aurora were having an affair. He finally discovered his wife's hiding place after Estupiñá took the news of Fortunata's baby son to the Santa Cruz household. No longer wanting to kill her, Maximiliano forced his way into Fortunata's room, where he told her what he knew about Juanito and Aurora. Although the doctor had ordered her not to leave her bed, Fortunata rushed out to revenge herself on Jacinta's enemy and her own. The exertion caused her death. Before she died, she sent a letter by Estupiñá to Jacinta. In the letter, she asked Jacinta to care for Juanito's son.

Being compelled to acknowledge his paternity was a blow to Juanito, for it lost him his wife's remaining esteem. He realized sadly that his philandering had brought him to old age in spirit while he was still young in years, with nothing but an empty and unhappy future before him.

Critical Evaluation:

Considered by some to be the greatest Spanish novelist after Miguel de Cervantes, Benito Pérez Galdós is known for his numerous historical novels and his treatment of nineteenth century Spain. In his contemporary novels, Pérez Galdós attempts to capture the flavor of Spanish life during a period of great turmoil and political change. In addition to a complex portrayal of nineteenth century Spanish life, Pérez Galdós' novels are rich in characterization and psychological subtlety. They are matched by few other novels of the time.

Pérez Galdós spent his childhood in the Canary Islands, where he was the youngest in a well-to-do family. In 1863, Pérez Galdós left for Madrid to study law at the University of Madrid. He failed, through lack of interest, his law course, but Pérez Galdós took an intense interest in the daily life of Madrid. An astute observer of life, he set out to pursue his interest in writing, which led him to work for a newspaper after his university days. He published his first novel in 1870, the start of a long and immensely productive career as a writer.

Fortunata and Jacinta is a massive novel in four volumes, which focuses on the lives, sufferings, and eventual reconciliation of two women of very different background and social status. The women are the lover and the wife of Juanito Santa Cruz. Both vie for his attention and loyalty. While *Fortunata and Jacinta* overflows with finely portrayed characters from nearly all strata of nineteenth century Spanish society, the core of the novel focuses on the subtly idealized, yet flesh-and-blood portrayal of the female protagonists as representatives of two opposing ideals. This opposition is set in a Christian framework, in which charity, compassion, and forgiveness are seen as the highest principles of a spiritual life.

Many of the characters in the novel are portrayed with great complexity and depth, but their purpose is primarily to act as foils for Fortunata and Jacinta. Probably the most complex character besides the two female protagonists is Maximiliano Rubín, or Maxi, who, despite his mental and physical weakness, appears to embody certain philosophical and ethical concerns of Pérez Galdós. These concerns are the overbearing effects of environment and heredity on a person's life. Maxi strives to overcome his inherited weaknesses, but he is fated to be thwarted at every turn by bad health and mental instability. Juanito, in contrast, is a character of little emotional depth, who lacks intelligence, sensitivity, or insight, and whose main function in the novel is to further the character development of the two protagonists.

The narrative complexity of *Fortunata and Jacinta* is typical of nineteenth century realist novels, whose aim is to provide the illusion of a complete vision of the actual life of the time and place portrayed. This aim accounts for the extensive background material presented in volume 1 of the novel. Readers may feel this material to be excessive, but should take into consideration the fact that family history, references to actual events, political figures, places, streets, names, and other detailed information are all meant to provide the sense that readers are getting a true glimpse into Spanish society. These details also set the stage for the further development of the characters. Pérez Galdós, for instance, meticulously portrays Juanito as the indolent and spoiled child of doting upper-class parents. All his actions during the early chapters of volume 1 confirm that his behavior will cause suffering to Fortunata and Jacinta, although the relative flatness of his character prevents readers from assigning him anything but cursory blame for their pain.

The final chapter of volume 4 brings together the many tributaries of Pérez Galdós' tale, uniting Fortunata and Jacinta with a bond of love, understanding, and forgiveness. Fortunata's suffering ends in death, as readers suspect it must, while the barren Jacinta inherits the infant Fortunata has had by Juanito. Despite the continual sufferings of both women they are redeemed, at least partially, by the resolution of their circumstances. As she nears death, Fortunata is seen to be capable of deep sympathy as well as compassion for those who have caused her to suffer, and seems also to transcend her earthy nature.

On her deathbed, she accepts Jacinta's message of thanks through Guillermina, forgives even Juanito, then finally, in a delirium that resembles religious ecstasy, declares herself to be an angel, an "angel face," just like her infant.

With Jacinta's adoption of the infant after Fortunata's death, Jacinta at long last finds the joy that has escaped her. She had effectively borne a child, although through the womb of another woman. An association of Fortunata with the Christ figure is not out of the question, for in dying she brings life and hope. The final message of *Fortunata and Jacinata* appears to be a positive one in which disparate, often conflicting personalities and beliefs are reconciled under the veil of a somewhat mystic ethic of compassion. The two former enemies, with death separating them, "one of them in visible life and the other in invisible life . . . may possibly have looked at each other from opposite banks and wished to embrace." Juanito, as obtuse as ever, finally receives his due from Jacinta, who consigns him to the role of a nothing, a husband who has lost all respect from and influence over his wife. He becomes utterly superfluous, an appendage to his wife's existence.

The novel ends with Maxi having finally been placed in an asylum for the insane. Even in this end there is hope, for it is in his confinement that Maxi, like all the others who have suffered in Pérez Galdós' story, finds rest in the submission of his will "to whatever the world wishes to do with me." He, as have Fortunata and Jacinta, makes his peace with the world.

"Critical Evaluation" by Howard Giskin

Bibliography:

Gullón, Agnes Money. "The Bird Motif and the Introductory Motif: Structure in *Fortunata y Jacinta*." *Anales Galdosianos* 9 (1974): 51-75. Describes a "bird motif" as it appears in its various manifestations throughout the novel, as well as an "introductory motif" at the head of each of the novel's four parts. Explores the novel's intricate structural components.

Pattison, Walter T. *Benito Pérez Galdós*. Boston: Twayne, 1975. A concise and informative biography of Pérez Galdós. Chapter 7 dwells rather extensively on *Fortunata and Jacinta*.

Ribbans, Geoffrey. "Contemporary History in the Structure and Characterization of *Fortunata y Jacinta*." In *Galdós Studies*, edited by J. E. Varey. London: Tamesis Books, 1970. Elucidates Pérez Galdós references to specific historical, political, and social events in nineteenth century Spain. Discusses the manner in which Pérez Galdós integrates fact and fiction.

Shoemaker, William H. *The Novelistic Art of Galdós*. 2 vols. Valencia: Albatros Ediciones Hispanofila, 1980. Volume 1 of this work is a broad literary critique of Pérez Galdós' novels in their entirety. Volume 2 examines each of the novels in turn.

Turner, Harriet S. *Fortunata and Jacinta*. Cambridge, England: Cambridge University Press, 1972. Thorough introduction to the novel. Detailed discussions of the sociohistorical, structural, and metaphorical aspects of Pérez Galdós' masterwork.

THE FORTUNES OF NIGEL

Type of work: Novel
Author: Sir Walter Scott (1771-1832)
Type of plot: Historical
Time of plot: Early seventeenth century
Locale: England
First published: 1822

Principal characters:

NIGEL OLIFAUNT, the lord of Glenvarloch
RICHARD MONIPLIES, his servant
GEORGE HERIOT, a goldsmith and friend of Nigel's father
MARGARET RAMSAY, Heriot's goddaughter
THE EARL OF HUNTINGLEN, an old nobleman
LORD DALGARNO, his son
LADY HERMIONE, a relative of Nigel
DAME SUDDLECHOP, a gossip
TRAPBOIS, a usurer
MARTHA TRAPBOIS, his daughter
JAMES I, the king of England

The Story:

The threatened loss of his family estates in Scotland sent Nigel Olifaunt, the lord of Glenvarloch, and his servant, Richard Moniplies, to London. Their mission there was to petition King James I for the repayment of large loans made to the crown by Nigel's late father. After Richie Moniplies had made an unsuccessful attempt to deliver his master's petition, he was followed from the court by George Heriot, the royal goldsmith, who went to Nigel and offered to help him gain favor with the king. Heriot gave his friendship with Nigel's late father as his motive. He succeeded in presenting Nigel's petition to the king. King James, in royal good humor, ordered Heriot to provide Nigel with money needed to outfit himself properly for an appearance at court, so that he could speak in his own behalf. The king gave Heriot a small crown of jewels with instructions that the gems were to remain in Heriot's possession until the state repaid him for the money he would lend to Nigel. The state's finances were seriously depleted, and the king was forced to do business by warrant.

While dining at Heriot's house the next day, Nigel met Margaret Ramsay, Heriot's godchild and the daughter of David Ramsay, the royal clockmaker. Margaret promptly lost her heart to Nigel, but because he was a nobleman, she was too shy to talk with him. That same night, however, she commissioned Dame Suddlechop, a local gossip, to investigate Nigel and his business. The Dame already knew that Nigel had powerful enemies in court, who were interested in seeing that he was prevented from taking rightful possession of his estates. On the promise of more money in the future, the old gossip agreed to learn all she could about Nigel and his affairs.

Dressed in clothing bought by money advanced by Heriot, Nigel went to the king with his petition. At first, he had difficulty in gaining admittance, but at last, he managed to see the king. The king confessed that there were no funds available for the debt, but he made a notation on the petition to the Scottish Exchequer and told Nigel that perhaps he could borrow from moneylenders on the strength of the royal warrant. Nigel left the court with Heriot and the earl of Huntinglen, who had also befriended him because of his father's name.

Anticipating a session with the moneylenders, the three decided to have a paper drawn up, a document that would allow Nigel ample time to redeem his estates by means of the king's warrant. Trusting Heriot and the old earl to handle his business, Nigel devoted himself to becoming acquainted with the earl's young son, Lord Dalgarno. Pretending friendship, Dalgarno in reality began a campaign to undermine Nigel's character and reputation and complete his financial ruin. Dalgarno himself hoped to gain possession of Nigel's estate.

Dalgarno took Nigel to gaming houses and other questionable places until Nigel's reputation began to suffer in the city and at court. At last, even faithful Richie asked for permission to leave his service and return to Scotland. Immediately after Richie's departure, Nigel received an anonymous note, telling him of Dalgarno's plot to ruin him. At first, Nigel refused to consider such a possibility, but at length, he decided to investigate the charges. When he confronted Dalgarno in the park and accused him of knavery, Dalgarno was so contemptuous of him that Nigel drew his sword and struck Dalgarno. The young courtier was not injured. There was a severe penalty for drawing swords in the park, however, and Nigel was forced to flee in order to avoid arrest. He was befriended by a young man he had met in a gaming house and was hidden in the house of an old usurer named Trapbois. His refuge was in Whitefriars, known as Alsatia, the haunt of bravos, bankrupts, bullyboys, and thieves.

Meanwhile, Margaret Ramsay was trying to help the young Scottish lord. A mysterious lady stayed apart in a secluded apartment in Heriot's house. She had seen Nigel once during his first visit at the house. This lady was Lady Hermione, who was in seclusion in Heriot's house following a tragic affair of the heart. Because she was extremely wealthy, Margaret begged her to help Nigel out of his difficulties. Lady Hermione revealed to Margaret that she was of the House of Glenvarloch and thus a distant relative of Nigel's. When Margaret told her of Dalgarno's plot to ruin Nigel, Lady Hermione gave her the money but warned her not to lose her heart to Nigel, for he was too highborn for a clockmaker's daughter.

Margaret arranged with an apprentice for Nigel's escape. The apprentice was willing to aid her because he was in love with Margaret and had been advised by old Dame Suddlechop that he might win the girl's heart by helping Nigel. In the meantime, Nigel killed one of two Russians who had murdered Trapbois. Nigel took Trapbois' daughter Martha with him when he escaped from Alsatia with the help of the apprentice sent by Margaret.

Nigel sent Martha to the house of a ship chandler with whom he had lodged for a time and then set out to find the king and present his own account of the quarrel with Dalgarno. Martha had difficulty in gaining admittance to the house where Nigel had sent her, for the ship chandler's wife had disappeared. She was discovered and protected by Richie Moniplies, who had returned to London to look for his master and try to help him. Nigel, in the meantime, tried to approach the king. James, believing that Nigel wanted to kill him, called out for help. His attendants seized Nigel and carried him off to the Tower. Dalgarno, one of the royal party, was only too glad to see Nigel imprisoned.

In his cell, Nigel was accused by Heriot of adultery with the ship chandler's wife and of duplicity in the disappearance of Martha Trapbois. Nigel denied his guilt in either of these affairs. Heriot, while refusing to believe him, nevertheless said that he would again try to help Nigel for his dead father's sake, and he asked Nigel for the royal warrant. His plan was to collect the money from the state and satisfy the moneylenders who were pressing for the repayment of Nigel's loan. Nigel was in despair when he discovered that the royal warrant had been taken from his baggage.

Through a noble friend, Nigel was cleared of the charge of treason—that is, his supposed attempt on the king's life. Nevertheless, he still had to stand trial for drawing his sword against Dalgarno. Richie went to Nigel in his cell and promised to help his master out of his troubles.

In the meantime, the king received a letter from the Lady Hermione, in which she charged that Dalgarno was the man who had betrayed her. In an attempt to amend the wrongdoing, the king forced Dalgarno to marry Lady Hermione; after the ceremony, however, Dalgarno informed the king that he now possessed his wife's wealth and through her a claim upon the Glenvarloch estates. He announced that if the redemption money were not paid by noon of the following day, he would take possession of Nigel's property. Convinced at last that Nigel was the injured party in the affair with Dalgarno, the king informed Richie that his master would be restored to royal favor. Richie, armed with money given to him by Martha Trapbois, paid the mortgage on Nigel's estates. After trying to show that the redemption papers were gained unlawfully, Dalgarno proceeded on his way to Scotland to claim the property; but on the way, he was killed by the same ruffian he had hired to murder Trapbois some time before. His death restored to Lady Hermione the fortune that Dalgarno, as her husband, had claimed. She gave a large portion of her wealth to Margaret and the rest to Nigel, her kinsman. Nigel and Margaret declared their love for each other and were married. During the ceremony, Richie appeared with Martha Trapbois, whom he had married. Martha told Nigel that her father had stolen his royal warrant, and by returning the paper to him, she made his estates secure. In gratitude to Richie for his part in restoring honor in the court, the king made the faithful servant a knight of the land.

Critical Evaluation:

In *The Fortunes of Nigel*, Sir Walter Scott surpassed even his former efforts to introduce dozens of characters and plots into one novel. Although the multiplicity of people and events and the use of Scottish dialect may make this novel a difficult one for some readers, the reward in the end is worth the effort. This novel is an exciting tale of intrigue and mystery, one of the great adventure stories in the language. As is also common in stories by Scott, the novel takes much of its romantic atmosphere and dramatic vigor from the author's use of many characters drawn from the lower levels of society. To balance these, Scott also presents in the figure of James I, king of England and Scotland, his finest historical portrait.

Since most of Scott's important work was completed in the first twenty-five years of the nineteenth century, he is often considered part of the Romantic literary movement. Rebelling against the formalism of the eighteenth century, this literary impulse advocated the natural expression of feelings, the value of nature against artifice, and the possibilities of life beyond the strict confines of rationalism. The diverse intellectual and literary trends within the Romantic movement make the classification of most authors problematic; there was a coherent movement, however, and it did stand for certain modes of expression and ideas.

Clearly, many of the features of Scott's novels and of *The Fortunes of Nigel* can be considered Romantic. Although he did not always succeed, he was interested in preserving and presenting the rhythms of the natural speech of his countrymen. His willingness to portray all the ranks of society, the loosely knit structure of the novel, the use of the past, the idealization of women, the intense sentiments—all these can be taken as Romantic features in Scott's work in general and in *The Fortunes of Nigel* in particular. At the same time, however, there are clearly principles of rationalism, neoclassicism, and literary Realism apparent in *The Fortunes of Nigel*. First, in the "Introductory Epistle" Scott attached to his novel, there is a defensive essay (written, significantly, in the form of a dialogue) that supports the didactic views of the literature of neoclassicism.

In fact, Scott's work stands at one of those junctures in the history of literature where various traditions meet, in mixtures of unpredictable and varying quality, only to separate again as historical and literary circumstances change; it can be said that realists and Romantics may claim Scott with justification. Alexandre Dumas, *père*, and James Fenimore Cooper were profoundly influenced by him, but so were Honoré de Balzac and Leo Tolstoy. In short, whatever the value of Scott's novels (and there has been much disagreement on that score), Scott is a seminal figure in literary history. Therefore, *The Fortunes of Nigel* can be judged not only as a historical novel but as a work influential in the history of the novel.

Scott's literary production may be divided into four parts: the early poetry, the initial group of the Waverley series, the later group of historical novels, and the novels after his financial collapse in 1826. It was during the middle period of the Waverley novels and the years immediately following that Scott did his best work. *The Fortunes of Nigel* falls into the late Waverley period. *The Fortunes of Nigel*, like the early Waverley novels, was highly successful. Although the book was priced out of the reach of the ordinary reader, it nevertheless sold ten thousand copies in the first printing.

In a manner characteristic of the Waverley series, *The Fortunes of Nigel* abounds in realistic detail. There is little of the excess and abstraction typical of the Romantic novel. In *The Fortunes of Nigel*, for example, an enormous variety of social strata are presented, the details of the characters' lives revealed, and their connections with other social groupings and classes dramatized. This sort of description is more exemplary of the realistic novel than of the Romantic. What separates *The Fortunes of Nigel* from the earlier Waverley group is the setting, which Scott moves from Scotland and the Scottish border to England. Although earlier readers and critics seem to have preferred the original setting, Scott's portrait of James I won for him a much expanded audience south of the border.

Although the setting differs, the substance of the novel is similar to Scott's other work. *The Fortunes of Nigel* is about history—the social, personal, and political forces that compose history; the plot in *The Fortunes of Nigel*, however, is less vivid than the scenes of life, of social contrasts and collisions, which appear throughout the book. Since Nigel is exceedingly passive and is more an observer of the action surrounding him than an active principal in it, he shares the plot's comparative weakness. The weakness of this character and the incidental nature of the plot led some contemporary critics of Scott, in reviewing *The Fortunes of Nigel*, to summarize its stereotyped features. In 1822, the *Quarterly Review* remarked: "The poor passive hero is buffeted about in the usual manner, involved, as usual, in the chicaneries of civil process, and exposed to the dangers of a criminal execution, and rewarded by the hand of the heroine, such as she is, and the redemption of the mortgage on the family estate."

It is certainly true that Scott repeated himself from novel to novel. He wrote very rapidly, almost never reviewed or rewrote his own work, and was frequently guilty of poor and careless writing. At the same time, however, Scott was a master of describing social and historical clashes. Above all, he was concerned with the process of history—the confrontation between the old and the new. For example, in the opening pages of *The Fortunes of Nigel*, Scott draws a picture of the construction of a new palace by James I. As critics have remarked, the passage is designed to show the position of James I, a monarch poised between feudalism and mercantile capitalism, between Scotland and England, between the past and the present.

Scott was also highly sensitive in some cases to the English language and especially to the social and cultural contexts of dialect. In *The Fortunes of Nigel*, for example, Scott was able to switch fluently from Scots to English. Heriot, who uses formal English in his business transactions, finds himself speaking Scots when another character reminds him of home. The king himself uses an ornate, Latinized form in one social setting and then, for purposes of political image or personal satisfaction, returns to Scots or part Scots and part ornamented English.

The reputation of Sir Walter Scott has suffered an eclipse. Scott himself, in his introduction to *The Fortunes of Nigel*, shows an awareness of questions of his less-than-careful writing style—raised even in his own day—and tries to defend himself and his method of composition. Other critics, however, such as the Marxist George Lukacs, argue that Scott was a great novelist. The introduction of history into the writing of novels, the vivid portrayal of social types, and the depiction of profound social and historical conflict outweigh the stylistic and compositional faults of the novels, according to Lukacs. Nor can one ignore Scott's impact on his contemporaries and on the history of fiction.

"Critical Evaluation" by Howard Lee Hertz

Bibliography:
Johnson, Edgar. *Sir Walter Scott: The Great Unknown*. 2 vols. New York: Macmillan, 1970. The fullest biography of Scott. Contains one chapter on *The Fortunes of Nigel*. Notes, index, and bibliography.
Lauber, John. *Sir Walter Scott*. Rev. ed. Boston: Twayne, 1989. A good starting place for study of Scott. Bibliography and index.
Shaw, Harry E. *The Forms of Historical Fiction: Sir Walter Scott and his Successors*. Ithaca, N.Y.: Cornell University Press, 1983. Begins with an excellent analysis of historical fiction as a genre. There is a thoughtful discussion of some of Scott's problems with his characterization. Bibliography and index.
Sutherland, John. *The Life of Walter Scott: A Critical Biography*. Cambridge, Mass.: Blackwell, 1995. Puts Scott's poetry and fiction in their biographical and historical context. Links *The Fortunes of Nigel* to Scott's visit to the coronation of 1821 in London and to Scott's growing indebtedness. Biography and notes.
Wilt, Judith. *Secret Leaves: The Novels of Sir Walter Scott*. Chicago: University of Chicago Press, 1985. Not an easy book, but with genuine insights into the hidden psychological mainsprings to Scott's fiction. Notes the fondness for changeling stories, and brings out the variety and richness of his emotional portrayals.

THE FORTY DAYS OF MUSA DAGH

Type of work: Novel
Author: Franz Werfel (1890-1945)
Type of plot: Historical
Time of plot: 1915
Locale: Near Antioch, Syria
First published: Die vierzig Tage des Musa Dagh, 1933 (English translation, 1934)

> *Principal characters:*
> GABRIEL BAGRADIAN, an Armenian patriot
> JULIETTE BAGRADIAN, his wife
> STEPHAN BAGRADIAN, their son
> TER HAIGASUN, an Armenian priest of the village of Yoghonoluk

The Story:

After twenty-three years spent in Paris, Gabriel Bagradian returned with his wife and child to his ancestral village of Yoghonoluk. He had gone back to Turkey to settle the affairs of his dying brother, and after his brother's death, he had stayed on in the village to await the end of European hostilities.

One Sunday, his son's tutor told him that officials had been through the village collecting all passports. To learn what had happened, Bagradian saddled a horse and started for Antioch. There the Kaimakam, or governor, gave only evasive answers about the passport incident. In a Turkish bath, Bagradian heard that the Turkish war minister had ordered all Armenians disarmed and given menial work. From his Mohammedan friend Agha Rifaat Bereket, Bagradian learned that rich and prominent Armenians would soon be persecuted.

Gabriel was worried. On his return to Yoghonoluk, he began to collect data on the number of men of fighting age in the vicinity. Ter Haigasun, the Gregorian priest, told him one day that there had been a mass arrest in Antioch. Bagradian began a survey of Musa Dagh, a mountain that lay between the Armenian villages and the Mediterranean Sea. After having maps drawn of the terrain, Bagradian knew that the plateau with its natural fortifications offered a refuge for his people.

One day, a friendly Turkish policeman confided to Bagradian that in three days the village would be ordered to prepare for its trip into exile. Bagradian called a meeting of the people. The Protestant pastor, Nokhudian, and his congregation voted to accept banishment, the rest of the population to defend Musa Dagh. Ter Haigasun was elected leader. The next morning, the young men under Bagradian's directions began the construction of trenches and other defenses on Musa Dagh, and at night the people carried provisions up the mountain. Unfortunately there were not enough rifles to go around and very little ammunition, but the men of the village were augmented by army deserters who drifted in from the desert. Eventually, there were sixty armed men in the community. On the third day, the convoy escort arrived. The village pretended to busy itself with preparations for the trip, but that night everyone but Pastor Nokhudian's flock secretly departed for Musa Dagh.

It took five days for the Turks to discover Bagradian's mountain retreat, for the woods were so thick and the trenches dug so cleverly that the encampment was not visible from below. During that time the trenches were completed, posts assigned, and patterns for daily living established. Everyone was given a task, and the food of the community was held in common so that all might be treated fairly.

The first sortie ended in a victory for the holders of Musa Dagh. The four hundred regulars and gendarmes who attacked without even seeking cover were quickly routed, and substantial booty of badly needed ammunition, boots, and uniforms was recovered. The second attack came several days later. Turkish howitzers managed to do considerable damage, wounding six noncombatants in the town enclosure and setting the grain depot on fire. Sarkis Kilikian, commander of the south bastion, rigged up a catapult to hurl stones at the attackers. These caused a landslide, which killed or maimed half the Turkish force. Young Stephan Bagradian and his friend Haik raided the Turkish gun emplacements. Sixteen of the defenders were killed.

Three days later, there were again signs of activity in the valley. The Kaimakam had imported families of Arabs to take over the Armenian houses and farms. On Musa Dagh, a Greek American adventurer, Gonzague Maris, who had fled with the Armenians and who had since seduced Juliette Bagradian, tried to persuade her to flee with him under the protection his passport afforded. She was undecided. She and her husband, Gabriel Bagradian, had grown apart in those troubled times; he was burdened with military duties, and she seemed indifferent to his fate. Bagradian found his only companionship in Iskuhi, a refugee from Zeitun.

The next attack was carried out by two thousand trained Turkish soldiers. In fierce fighting, they captured the first line of trenches below the southern bastion. That night Bagradian ordered his troops to counterattack, and the trenches were retaken. The defenders also set a fire that raced down the mountain, driving the Turks into the valley. Musa Dagh had again been saved.

Gonzague Maris begged Juliette several times to go away with him, but she did not have the courage to tell her husband that she was leaving him. Then Bagradian discovered the lovers together and took his wife, half-unconscious with a fever, back to her tent. Gonzague Maris disappeared.

That same night, Stephan Bagradian left Musa Dagh without permission to accompany his friend Haik, who was being sent to the American consul in Aleppo to ask for intervention on behalf of his people. Haik made his way safely to Aleppo, but Stephan developed a fever and had to start back to the mountain. On the way, the Turks captured and killed him. His body was thrown into the cemetery yard in Yoghonoluk where it was found by some old women who took it to his father. The last of the Bagradians was buried on Musa Dagh.

The next day, flocks grazing beyond the fortifications were captured by the Turks. There was now only enough food to last three or four more days. On the fortieth day on Musa Dagh, the people were suffering. It was their third day of famine. Gabriel had planned one last desperate attack for that night, an attempt to reach the valley with his men, capture some high officials as hostages, and return to the mountain. That afternoon, however, as Ter Haigasun held a service to petition God for help, Sarkis Kilikian and his deserters broke into the town enclosure to steal ammunition and food. As they fled, they set fire to the buildings to cover their escape. The Turks took advantage of their desertion to capture the south bastion. Kilikian was brought back by deserters who felt it would be better to die with their own people than to be captured by the Turks. He was put to death.

As the Turks prepared to advance at dawn, a French cruiser dropped its first shell into the valley. Its commander had seen the fire in the town enclosure the day before. Approaching to investigate, he had seen the enormous flag the Armenians were using as a distress signal. The Turks retreated into the valley. Bagradian led the weary defenders to the coast and saw them safely aboard a cruiser and a troopship. Then he started back up the mountain for a last view of his son's grave. Exhausted by his ordeal, he fell asleep halfway up the mountainside. When he awoke, the ships were already standing out at sea. He started to signal them but changed his mind. He felt that his life was now complete. Up he climbed until he reached his son's grave.

There a bullet from a Turkish scout caught him in the temple. He fell on his son's grave, Stephan's cross on his heart.

Critical Evaluation:

When Franz Werfel arrived in the United States as an exile from Nazi Germany, his fame there had been established, based largely on the popularity of *The Forty Days of Musa Dagh*, a 1934 Book-of-the-Month Club selection. Arguably Werfel's most powerful prose work, the Hollywood studio Metro-Goldwyn-Mayer acquired an option on making a film of the novel; the project was eventually abandoned, purportedly because of pressure exerted by the Turkish government.

For the Armenian people, *The Forty Days of Musa Dagh* became something of a national epic. An Armenian priest in New York is recorded to have preached that the novel invested his people with a soul. The financial assistance of the Armenian community in the United States made possible the transfer of Werfel's remains from Hollywood to Vienna in 1975, as well as, that same year, the holding of a Werfel symposium and the publication of a volume of his occasional writings.

The Forty Days of Musa Dagh almost single-handedly publicized the genocide of Turkey's Armenian population during World War I. Werfel had planned to write about the crime when he first learned of it while serving at the military press bureau in Vienna. Yet it was not until 1930, when he encountered young Armenian refugees laboring in a carpet factory in Damascus, that the abstract number of more than one million victims became a disturbing reality for the novelist. Werfel immersed himself for two years in research, including a study of first-hand accounts, that resulted in the particular blend of historical re-creation and imaginative invention that marks *The Forty Days of Musa Dagh.*

The defense of Musa Dagh in 1915 was an actual event, and some of the novel's peripheral characters, such as the Turkish official Enver Pascha, were historical figures. Werfel's drawing on reality and the wealth of descriptive details, ranging from architecture to children's games to farming methods, lend the novel a compelling aura of authenticity.

As a creative writer, Werfel occasionally suited facts to his purposes. Sources differed, for example, on whether the Armenian contingent spent fifty-three or thirty-six days on the mountain. By indicating that the sojourn lasted forty days, Werfel links the incident to biblical events: the forty days of the flood, the forty days that both Moses and Jesus fasted, and the forty years the Hebrews wandered in the desert following their liberation from bondage in Egypt. Other biblical associations in the novel include the destiny of Gabriel Bagradian to die, as did Moses, within sight of, though not actually entering, the promised land. Bagradian is a type modeled on Moses: an individual assimilated to a foreign culture and estranged from his own people who, through circumstance, reunites with them to guide them out of captivity. Significantly enough, Musa Dagh translates to "Mount of Moses." The piety of the Armenians of Musa Dagh is emphasized by their placing an altar at the center of their settlement.

Given the preponderance of biblical allusions in the novel, it is not surprising that the solutions to the political issues it raises are invariably spiritual ones. Werfel suggests that sacrifice—particularly that of father and son—is supremely efficacious. Some have criticized Werfel's symbolism as heavy-handed, for instance, in invoking the crucifixion in the deaths of Gabriel and Stephan Bagradian.

The fundamental conflict in the novel is evidently between godliness, signified by commitment to a transpersonal and transnational entity, and godlessness, an amoral and reductionistic pragmatism. An apocalyptic note—signifying the Day of Judgment and its separation of the "wheat," or the godly, and the "chaff," or the ungodly—is sounded by the titles of the novel's three parts, which are taken from the Book of Revelation. It has been pointed out that Gabriel Bagradian is another example of the prodigal son in Werfel's writings: From an alienated life of worldly sophistication, he returns to his people and his roots and, in suffering and self-transcendence, ultimately finds fulfillment. Bagradian's personal drama is, moreover, played out in the context of the persecution of a religious minority by an atheistic political regime in the relentless pursuit of modernity, which, for Werfel, meant nationalism, racism, and progress merely for progress' sake. The "progress" promoted by the Young Turks, in Werfel's view, raised expectations among the Turkish people that could not be satisfied without violence.

Much of the attention *The Forty Days of Musa Dagh* has attracted concerns its foreshadowing of the Holocaust. Parallels between the mass murder of the Jews by the Third Reich and that of the Armenians as presented in the novel are striking: the clinical, bureaucratic nature of the Turkish execution of policy; the reluctance of Armenians to recognize their peril; and the acceptance of the official lie that the government's plan was one of resettlement. Nevertheless, critics debate the extent to which Werfel intended to be a prophet of the fate of his own people, the Jews.

Those who stress the topicality and prophetic nature of the novel claim that Werfel revealed his premonition when, on a lecture tour in Germany in 1932, pending the book's publication, he chose to read from it a chapter that included a plea by a German pastor on behalf of the Armenian people. Some have argued that there is no empirical evidence for Werfel's having gauged early on the extent of danger to European Jewry; they point to the fact that the novelist did not flee Europe until as late as 1940. Many consider the implications of Werfel's insights all the richer for their not having been calculated. In any case, critical consensus maintains that as an investigation into the historical phenomenon of genocide, *The Forty Days of Musa Dagh* is a novel of fundamental significance.

"Critical Evaluation" by Amy Adelstein

Bibliography:

Jungk, Peter Stephan. *"Die vierzig Tage des Musa Dagh."* In *Franz Werfel: An Austrian Writer Reassessed*, edited by Lothar Huber. New York: St. Martin's Press, 1989. A dramatic, well-detailed account of the genesis of the novel. Portrays Werfel in a positive light. Jungk scripted and directed a film on Werfel for German television.

Keith-Smith, Brian. "The Concept of 'Gemeinschaft' in the Works of Franz Werfel and Lothar Schreyer." In *Franz Werfel: An Austrian Writer Reassessed*, edited by Lothar Huber. New York: St. Martin's Press, 1989. Elaborates on the importance of community in Werfel's work. Knowledge of German not essential but would be helpful.

Michaels, Jennifer. *Franz Werfel and the Critics*. Columbia, S.C.: Camden House, 1994. Identifies aspects of Werfel's work that have attracted critical interest. Also shows how various trends in criticism have shaped Werfel's reputation as a writer. A clear and comprehensive presentation.

Steiman, Lionel B. *Franz Werfel: The Faith of an Exile from Prague to Beverly Hills*. Ontario, Canada: Wilfrid Laurier University Press, 1985. A penetrating analysis of Werfel's political and theological development in historical context. Generally critical of his faith and work.

Wagener, Hans. *Understanding Franz Werfel*. Columbia: University of South Carolina Press, 1993. Assesses Werfel's work from a literary as well as historical perspective. Readable and concise.

THE FOUNTAINHEAD

Type of work: Novel
Author: Ayn Rand (Alice Rosenbaum, 1905-1982)
Type of plot: Parable
Time of plot: 1922-1930's
Locale: New York City
First published: 1943

>   *Principal characters:*
>   HOWARD ROARK, an architect
>   PETER KEATING, an architect
>   ELLSWORTH TOOHEY, a writer and social reformer
>   CATHERINE HALSEY, Keating's girlfriend and Toohey's niece
>   GUY FRANCON, the principal partner of the firm where Keating works
>   DOMINIQUE FRANCON, his daughter
>   GAIL WYNAND, a newspaper publisher

The Story:

Howard Roark was expelled from architectural school because he had no respect for copying the past. Peter Keating, one of the favorite students at the school, frequently persuaded Roark to help him with his assignments. Roark decided to go to New York City to work for Henry Cameron, a once-respected but now renegade architect who shared Roark's ideals. Keating took a job with the firm of Guy Francon, a powerful and influential architect who believed in copying classic buildings. After Cameron's business failed, Keating hired Roark, but the job did not last long. Francon fired Roark for his failure to draft an adaptation of one of Cameron's buildings; Roark continued to refuse to copy others' work.

Dominique Francon, Guy's daughter, visited the office. Her beauty immediately impressed Keating, and he remained interested in her even after discovering that she had written a newspaper column in Gail Wynand's *Banner* in which she criticized one of his building designs. They later began dating. Keating's longtime girlfriend, Catherine Halsey, announced that she wanted to get married immediately; however, she agreed to wait. Keating knew that Halsey was the niece of Ellsworth Toohey, a *Banner* columnist who wrote about architecture and many other topics. He refused to use his relationship with Halsey to gain influence with Toohey.

Roark took a job with another firm but learned that his designs would be combined with those of others. His employer used most of Roark's drawing in a draft presented to one client, who said that it was the best of many designs that he had seen but that it was somehow wrong. Roark seized the drawing and marked over it, restoring his original work. The client hired Roark, inspiring Roark to start his own firm.

In an attempt to cement his position, Keating attempted to blackmail Lucius Heyer, Francon's partner, who did almost no work in the firm and was not respected by the employees. Heyer died, leaving Keating his share in the firm because Keating had once been kind to him. Keating won a worldwide design contest, after getting Roark's assistance. He attempted to bribe Roark to remain silent about working on the design, but Roark said that Keating would be doing him a favor by not mentioning his assistance.

Roark's business failed because he was too selective in accepting commissions; he preferred not to work at all than to design buildings he did not believe in. He took a job in a granite quarry owned by Guy Francon. Dominique saw him working in the quarry and was struck by his beauty and by the way he approached his work. She purposely damaged a piece of marble in her house and had him assess the damage. She then hired him to come back and repair the damage; however, he sent another worker. Later, he returned and raped her. Soon thereafter, Roark received a letter of inquiry from Roger Enright about designing a house, whereupon he left the quarry job.

Toohey wrote a favorable column about Keating's work and asked to meet him, then suggested that Keating head a group of young architects. He also acknowledged Keating's engagement to Halsey. Dominique Francon told Keating that she no longer wanted to see him because he was the best of what there was, and she did not approve of perfection. She saw plans for the Enright house, not knowing it was Roark's work or even that Roark was an architect, and told Toohey that the man who designed it should not allow it to be built because it would not be appreciated. Roark agreed to go to a party because he knew that Dominique would be there and would not expect to see him. They pretended not to know each other. Afterward, she wrote a column disparaging the Enright house, having found out that it was his design. She also convinced a potential client not to hire him. She went to Roark's office and told him that she would continue to try to destroy him. She wanted him to own her, however, and she told him that she would come to him every time she had beaten him. She continued to denigrate his work in her newspaper columns, and she convinced clients to use Keating, instead.

Toohey convinced multimillionaire Hopton Stoddard to let Roark design an interdenominational temple for him and to give Roark a completely free hand in the design. Stoddard, a traditionalist, did not see the building until it had been completed; he then refused to open it. Stoddard saw it as inappropriate for a temple, in part because of the nude statue of Dominique that Roark had commissioned for it. Toohey persuaded Stoddard to sue Roark; Toohey's plan all along had been to destroy Roark's reputation. Stoddard won the lawsuit, and Dominique was fired for testifying at the trial that the building should be destroyed, not because it was faulty but because it was too good.

Keating proposed marriage to Halsey, but Dominique Francon proposed to him later that day and he accepted. Dominique told Roark that she believed that he would be destroyed because he was too near perfection and that she would destroy herself before she was destroyed by others. About a year later, she agreed to sleep with the newspaper publisher Gail Wynand to get a commission for her husband, Keating. She and Wynand took a trip to Wynand's yacht, but they began talking before they had slept together. They discovered that they had similar ideas and agreed to be married.

Toohey assembled mediocre workers in various professions and promoted their work because he believed in the value of the average. Keating's business declined. When he complained that Toohey had promoted another architect, Toohey claimed that Keating and the others were interchangeable. Desperate for work, Keating hired Roark to design a low-income housing project so that Keating could submit the plans to the government. Roark undertook the project for the challenge; he knew that with his reputation he could never land a government contract. He made Keating agree to construct the buildings exactly as designed.

Wynand and Dominique recognized the new project as Roark's work. Wynand and Roark became friends, and they took a trip on Wynand's yacht. When they returned, Roark saw that other architects had been brought onto the housing project. When he saw that the buildings were different from his plans, he dynamited them, with Dominique's help. Wynand did everything he could to help Roark at his criminal trial, even though he knew that Roark's victory would cost him Dominique. Toohey managed to get a column opposing Roark into print. Wynand fired him, prompting a strike at the paper.

Dominique arranged for news of the affair between her and Roark to become public, and Wynand agreed to file for divorce. Roark won his acquittal. Wynand closed the newspaper and then hired Roark to design a building for him; Wynand did this to symbolize his new freedom from trying to please people with his publications. Roark and Dominique were married.

Critical Evaluation:

Ayn Rand wrote *Atlas Shrugged* (1957) as a more complete exposition of the principles and ideas espoused in *The Fountainhead*. Both novels illustrate her philosophy of positive rational egoism, morality based on self-interest rather than on compassion for others. *The Fountainhead*'s heroes, including Roark, Dominique Francon, and, eventually, Gail Wynand, stand for their principles and refuse to conform. Wynand at first tries to offer what people want in his newspaper but later refuses to submit to Toohey and others, who want to promote the ideas of selfless service to others and lack of personal responsibility. Toohey and Keating are the primary antagonists. Toohey appears noble in his deflection of attention from himself; however, he seeks absolute power through manipulation of public opinion. He tells Halsey that people should not think; they should merely believe and serve others. Keating represents conformity for its own sake and pandering to popular opinion, values Rand clearly opposes.

As in *Atlas Shrugged*, the heroes are attractive: tall, physically fit, with strong faces. Roark and Dominique Francon receive glowing descriptions of their physical beauty. Roark's ideals are clear; Francon's are somewhat more puzzling. Her short speeches describing her goals are unclear, perhaps as Rand intended. Francon claims to admire perfection, but at the same time she hates it because it is not appreciated by others; she buys artworks and destroys them.

The Fountainhead is a sweeping drama, drawing in a large number of characters with large roles and covering an array of events. Rand shifts her attention between characters, allowing various individuals to come forth at appropriate moments. Dominique Francon, perhaps the most perplexing character, draws the others together. Her actions play off those of other characters and offer contrasts. She brings out the best in Peter Keating, making him doubt the value of conformity and also making him realize what Roark has to offer. She also aids Wynand in his journey toward fulfilling his personal ideas, rather than simply producing newspapers that cater to the lowest common denominator. In some ways she destroys the people with whom she comes in contact, but it is a creative destruction, allowing them to emerge stronger than before. She deliberately tries to ruin Roark because he is too good for an imperfect world, but her efforts against him, as she intends, make him stronger. Inevitably they end up together.

Rand uses various plot lines to make her points in a novel clearly intended more as a social message than as literature. Toohey is her primary villain. He appears benevolent and caring but promotes selflessness, which Rand sees as ultimately harmful because it teaches reliance on others. The result can only be mediocrity; in fact, Toohey deliberately promotes the work of mediocre artists, architects, and others. Catherine Halsey is a relatively minor character, but she is important for her frank admission that, in her job as a social worker, she has come to resent people who can improve themselves without her help. She also provides a foil for Keating and his personal ambition. Keating wants to be considered a great architect more than he actually wants to be one; Halsey appears selfless. Each time Keating gets close to Halsey, Dominique draws him away, thus helping him in his personal development by removing Halsey's influence on him.

The Fountainhead has been praised as a novel of ideas. In the 1940's, publication of such a novel by an American woman was relatively uncommon. Rand later abandoned the novelistic form, choosing instead to write directly on what she called the morality of reason. Rand had grown up in Russia and lived through the Bolshevik Revolution; this background led to her becoming a champion of capitalism in its purest forms. Her heroes are self-interested individuals who oppose the social reformers claiming to work for the public good.

A. J. Sobczak

Bibliography:

Baker, James T. *Ayn Rand.* Boston: Twayne, 1987. An objective study of Rand's career. Includes brief descriptions and analyses of her major works of fiction and drama. One chapter succinctly describes the main themes and ideas expressed in her written work.

Gladstein, Mimi. *The Ayn Rand Companion.* Westport, Conn.: Greenwood Press, 1984. Offers concise notes helpful in reading all Rand's fiction, including *The Fountainhead.*

Peikoff, Leonard. *Objectivism: The Philosophy of Ayn Rand.* New York: E. P. Dutton, 1991. Based on a set of the author's lectures on Rand's philosophy, which were authorized by Rand. Understanding Rand's philosophy is vital to understanding *The Fountainhead.*

Rand, Ayn. *For the New Intellectual: The Philosophy of Ayn Rand.* New York: Random House, 1961. Provides Rand's introduction to her philosophy. Separate chapters on individual works of fiction give excerpts from those works that illustrate her philosophy.

_____. *Philosophy: Who Needs It?* Indianapolis, Ind.: Bobbs-Merrill, 1982. Essays range in content from the basics of Rand's philosophy to its applications in social policy. Most were written between 1970-1975 and reflect contemporary events, her philosophy, and thoughts on her fiction.

THE FOUR HORSEMEN OF THE APOCALYPSE

Type of work: Novel
Author: Vicente Blasco Ibáñez (1867-1928)
Type of plot: Historical
Time of plot: Early 1900's
Locale: Argentina, Paris, and the front lines of World War I
First published: Los cuatro jinetes del Apocalipsis, 1916 (English translation, 1918)

Principal characters:

JULIO MADARIAGA, the intrepid owner of a successful cattle ranch in
    Argentina
MARCELO DESNOYERS, a French immigrant to Argentina who had
    married Madariaga's daughter, Luisa
JULIO DESNOYERS, Marcelo's son and heir
MARGUERITE LAURIER, Julio's lover
ÉTIENNE LAURIER, Marguerite's husband

The Story:

    Julio Desnoyers' father, Marcelo, angered by his nation's participation in the Franco-Prussian War (1870-1871), had immigrated to Argentina. There he helped a vital Spaniard named Julio Madariaga (nicknamed the Centaur because of his lust for life and his many illegitimate offspring), carve a ranch out of a wilderness. In the process, they had had to defeat or win over the Indians, but eventually they built an empire and made a fortune. Desnoyers experienced the splendor of turn-of-the-century Argentina, with its multicultural population and its potential for growth and development. Eventually, Desnoyers married Madariaga's daughter, Luisa, and oversaw the financial management of the estate, converting where possible Madariaga's intensely personal and erratic methods to more methodical and efficient ones. The accidental death of Madariaga's only legitimate son left Desnoyers as Madariaga's principal heir, with a fortune at his disposal. His German brother-in-law, Karl Hartrott, had eloped with Madariaga's second daughter, Elena, much to her father's consternation; after a period of ostracism, Karl had finagled his way back to the ranch and into an inheritance. When Julio Madariaga died, the German and French sides of his family decided to return to Europe. Desnoyers did so under pressure from his wife, who was disturbed that their daughter Chichi was growing up a wild savage, riding the range alongside her grandfather as if she were the son he had lost.

    The Hartrotts ingratiated themselves with the German nobility and assumed the haughtiness and pretensions of the German aristocracy, while the Desnoyers became an established part of Parisian society. A visit to their German relatives confirmed the Desnoyers' negative feelings about them. Desnoyers wasted a fortune on grand antiques sold at bargain prices in auctions and filled up a castle with ostentatious wealth, including a solid gold bathtub. His son Julio became a known roué and was invited to the best homes because of his skill at the tango, the most popular dance of the time; he was also the adulterous lover of many an aficionado of the tango. When, however, he met Marguerite Laurier, everything changed, and Julio's artist's studio became the scene of a romance that promised to blossom into marriage, once a messy divorce was past.

Returning from a business trip to Argentina, Julio was disturbed at the dinner table conversations of the German travelers who looked forward to war and blamed others as the aggressors. He also noticed that the personnel of the German ship had changed; instead of being courteous and eager to please, they had become arrogant and commanding. Back home in Paris, he was disturbed that Marguerite was impressed with the good reports he had earned as a fearless soldier; she could not understand Julio's reluctance to join what for him was a foreign army.

Julio's father, Marcelo Desnoyers, disapproved of his son's profligate life and his affair with Marguerite, especially because her husband, Étienne Laurier, was one of his good friends. When news came that Étienne had been seriously injured, possibly blinded in battle, Marguerite abandoned Julio and Paris. Later, when Julio traced her to a convalescent home, he found her nursing her husband. Though she could not deny her continued love for Julio, she had found a deeper commitment to a brave patriot who loved her dearly and whose sacrifice for his country demanded her courageous support. Desnoyers was pleased that the affair was over, but Julio, distraught, joined the French army and flung himself into conflict with an abandon that won him the hearts of his comrades and the respect of his superiors.

When the rich of Paris fled south to escape the invading Germans, Marcelo Desnoyers traveled north to protect his castle from looting. He assumed that civilized rules of confrontation would be in force and that civilians would go unmolested. Instead, he found Germans executing civilians, raping young women, shooting babies, burning villages, defacing property, and engaging in wholesale looting. An encounter with a Hartrott offspring saved Desnoyers from certain death, but could not prevent him from having to endure German officers disporting themselves lewdly, defecating on his valuable furnishings, and participating in acts of perversion and sadism. As a landowner and victim, Desnoyers cheered the French resurgence at the Battle of the Marne and made his way safely back to Paris and security. Later, his growing pride in his son's heroism made him seek out Argensola, his son's companion and manservant, and look with greater forgiveness on the indiscretions of Julio's youth. Through the influence of Senator Lacour, whose son René was engaged to his daughter Chichi, Desnoyers visited Julio in the trenches and observed the nightmare of trench warfare at first hand. News of his son's injury made him fear for Julio's life, and only shortly thereafter he received news of his death. The old man's final trip to the front was toward the close of the war, as he sought his son's name on a mass grave near the spot where he died. Desnoyers realized the futility of his wealth, for it had not been able to prevent the loss of his son. His grief was mirrored in that of his sister-in-law, Elena, whose strong, unquestioning support of the German cause had resulted in the loss of two sons and injury of a third. Only the young, among them Desnoyers' daughter, Chichi, could look to the future with confidence.

Critical Evaluation:

Vicente Blasco Ibáñez is among the most widely read Spanish novelists, and *The Four Horsemen of the Apocalypse* is one of his most popular works. The 1921 Rudolph Valentino film and a 1962 World War II adaptation starring Glen Ford further popularized the book. Its multicultural perspective, its warnings about the dangers of racism and of twisting logic to defend the indefensible, its prescience about World War II and the causes of modern conflagrations, and its antiwar sentiments based on realistic portraits of the horrors of war make *The Four Horsemen of the Apocalypse* relevant to ages beyond its own. Its underlying picaresque conventions, roguish young hero, and competent, yet somehow innocent, older hero lend it charm and interest, and its character studies of the way in which war transforms individuals and instills a spirit of self-sacrifice and fortitude are psychologically convincing.

The book's title is derived from the biblical book Revelation, which describes the four scourges that will afflict humanity at the end of time: Disease, War, Famine, and Death. Part 1 of the novel treats the life of the Desnoyers family before the onset of World War I; it ends with the Russian Tchernoff, the French-Argentine Julio Desnoyers, and the Spaniard Argensola discussing the suicide of a German woman and seeing her death as the beginning of the end. Drawing on memories of the famous engravings by Albrecht Dürer, they envision an apocalyptic beast, a blind force of evil, rising from the depths of the sea and threatening to engulf all humanity, with the four horsemen that signal its arrival brutally sweeping the earth ahead of it and bringing agony in "their merciless gallop of destruction."

In parts 2 and 3, Blasco Ibáñez demonstrates the fulfillment of that prophecy as war sweeps across Europe. Part 2 is a graphic and memorable portrait of the Battle of the Marne and of German brutality, which is lent added force from the description of the aging Marcelo Desnoyers' incredulity at what he is witnessing. The details of slaughter, inhumanity, and torture are convincingly realistic, yet the point of view adds a touch of the surreal. Part 3 provides a closer look at twentieth century trench warfare, with its intricate maze of trenches, the horror of the mud and the rats, the insidiousness of the gases blown across from enemy lines, and the buzzing of bullets overhead. Again the description is intensified by the drama of a determined father braving the nightmare for a brief glimpse of his beloved son.

Blasco Ibáñez had been a political activist ever since his university years, and he endured imprisonment and exile for his outspoken political statements. *The Four Horsemen of the Apocalypse* is in keeping with this spirit of protest. The novel is a condemnation, not only of the World War I German military establishment and its barbaric methods of conducting warfare but also of the German people's inflated sense of superiority and the intellectuals and artists who perpetuated that myth of superiority and right to power. The novel was condemned as a heavy-handed tract by critics who disapproved of Blasco Ibáñez's life and politics and envied his financial success, but the work also reflects a deeply felt revulsion for war and a frighteningly accurate prophecy of the horrors of Nazism.

Blasco Ibáñez sets up a compelling contrast between the inhumanity of the war machine that leaves chaos, destruction, and despair in its wake and the constructive fervor of the lively, impassioned Spaniard Madariaga, who helps transform the Argentine pampas into thriving ranch land and whose prodigious reproductive powers reflect a love of life. Blasco Ibáñez also establishes the contrast between war and the civilized, cultured life of Paris, where artists and lovers thrive, and conflicts of opinions lead only to good-natured arguments over a bottle of wine. Against these life-affirming regions and peoples, the scenes of conquest and destruction seem completely senseless. Blasco Ibáñez has been praised for the realism of his portraits of war, but it is his portrait of peace that makes his images of war so horrifying.

Gina Macdonald

Bibliography:

Day, A. Grove, and Edgar Knowlton. *V. Blasco Ibáñez*. New York: Twayne, 1972. A survey of Blasco Ibáñez's life and canon that includes a discussion of his revolutionary influences, cosmopolitan experiences, interest in social protest and human psychology, glorification of Spain, and intense dislike of Germans.

Howells, William Dean. "The Fiction of Blasco Ibáñez." *Harpers* 131 (1915): 956-960. Howells praises Blasco Ibáñez's literary skill.

Swain, James Q. *Vicente Blasco Ibáñez: General Study—Special Emphasis on Realistic Tech-*

niques. Knoxville: University of Tennessee Press, 1959. One chapter focuses on the realistic images of war in *The Four Horsemen of the Apocalypse*.

Wedel, Alfred R. "Blasco Ibáñez's Antipathy Toward Germans." *Revista de Istorie si Teorie Literara* 35 (July-December, 1987): 3-4, 192-200. Discusses the negative portrait of Germans in *The Four Horsemen of the Apocalypse*.

FOUR QUARTETS

Type of work: Poetry
Author: T. S. Eliot (1888-1965)
First published: 1943

Four Quartets is T. S. Eliot's last book of nondramatic poetry. Each of the quartets, which were written over a period of eight years and published separately, has the same structure and helps develop cumulatively the same themes. Eliot said that transitions in poetry can be similar to those in a symphony or quartet, and that these quartets are written in a five-movement sonata form.

The personal and historical significance of the place names in the poems' titles are the points of departure for the themes developed in the first part of each quartet. The theme of "Burnt Norton"—an old Gloucestershire house—is the nature of time and personal memories and experience. "East Coker," which is the name of the English village from which Eliot's ancestor left for America in the seventeenth century, is a consideration of the meaning of history and an explanation of the idea of spiritual rebirth. "The Dry Salvages," a group of rocks off the coast of Massachusetts, which Eliot knew as a boy, continues the meditations on time and history and includes reflections on human endeavor and the nature of experience. These themes are all also present in "Little Gidding," whose title refers to an Anglican lay community founded by Nicholas Ferrar.

All the themes are present in each quartet with different emphases, and the subsidiary themes are directly related to the major ones. What distinguishes these poems from Eliot's earlier verse is that, in addition to the elements of surprise and rapid transition that mark his earlier works, these include transitional passages. The same symbols also occur in each of the quartets, and their multiple and shifting meanings are resolved in "Little Gidding."

In "Burnt Norton," Eliot writes "What might have been and what has been/ Point to one end which is always present." Here there is no placing of experience in time ("do not call it fixity"); it is instead a "stillness," a point beyond experience "into the rose garden." To reach it requires the negation of flesh and spirit. Eliot repeatedly considers this way of purgation, which requires release from desire and compulsion. Meaningful experience is both in and out of time, but life is too full of distraction for this to be often attained. The description of that distraction is a vivid realization of the contemporary predicament: "Only a flicker/ Over the strained, time-ridden faces/ Distracted from distraction by distraction." The passage following these lines presents "the way down" toward the dark night of the soul, "desiccation of the world of sense." Yet there are times in the realm of art when the moment can be prolonged "as a Chinese jar still/ Moves perpetually in its stillness." A further theme in the quartets, the nature and difficulty of poetic creation, creates a contrast to the image of the jar. The struggle with words that "decay with imprecision" introduces the Word, which is subject always to temptation. "Burnt Norton" ends with a repetition of the vision of hidden children laughing in the rose garden, a motif from the first movement. Such immediacy is contrasted with the usual bleakness of existence.

Time in "East Coker" involves the consideration of human history. This, the most despairing of the quartets, approaches complete and unredeemed bitterness. Eliot stresses the cyclic nature of life and experience. Fields give way to factories that crumble to dust, and the life cycle of humans and the earth is presented as if in a vision after the poet has gone down the dark lane into the somnolent village. The second section begins with a lyric on November, which is followed by a characteristic reversal: "That was a way of putting it . . ./ A periphrastic study in a wornout poetical fashion." The theme of the bitterness and deception of time mentioned in "Burnt Norton" is expanded here; the wisdom of old men is really folly, and "The only wisdom we can hope to acquire/ Is the wisdom of humility." The concrete description, which in these poems always either immediately follows or precedes the abstract thought, is here that of the descent into subways that had been used as air-raid shelters during World War II. Thus negation and stillness are combined, and the necessity for "waiting" is introduced.

The fourth movement is a lyric on the Christian paradox of life in death and death in life. The symbols are those of a hospital with a wounded surgeon and a dying nurse, "Wherein, if we do well, we shall/ Die of the absolute paternal care." Fire and roses are multiple symbols of destruction and salvation, purgation and resurrection. After the cold fever of death there is purgatory, "Of which the flame is roses, and the smoke is briars." In the fifth section, Eliot despairs of poetic creation, which, at "every attempt/ Is a wholly new start" because the difficulties once conquered are no longer those that face the poet. The resolution of this dilemma is similar to that for the soul: "For us there is only the trying." The conclusion inverts the opening statement—"In my beginning is my end"—to become "In my end is my beginning."

The superb pictures of the Mississippi River and the Atlantic Ocean in "The Dry Salvages" show an increase in the music of the verse, which is sustained in "Little Gidding." The river is "a strong brown god" and the sea has "Many gods and many voices." The sea time "is not our time"; "time stops and is never ending." The lyric in section 2 speaks of the grief of shipwreck and of those things thought "most reliable" that are "therefore the fittest for renunciation." There is no end to this pain, only the possibility of prayer.

The pattern of the past with its content of meaningful experience is seen here in its historical perspective: "And approach to the meaning restores the experience/ In a different form, beyond any meaning/ We can assign to happiness." This passage connects with the reference to Krishna in section 3, one of the many allusions to and quotations of other authors in the *Four Quartets*. The theory of time is drawn from the philosopher Heraclitus and part of the conclusion of "Little Gidding" from Dame Julian of Norwich. The rose and fire symbolism is reminiscent of Dante, whereas the conception of the dark night of the soul is that of St. John of the Cross. While awareness of these sources adds considerably to the enjoyment of the poems, Eliot integrates them so completely and controls their place in the poetry so perfectly, placing them where they have an exact significance, that the poems can be appreciated and understood without knowledge of source or influence. The poet Krishna is mentioned by name, however, and his words, "fare forward, voyagers" instead of "fare well" are important, as they indicate the essential release from desires and are an exhortation to unselfishness or selflessness.

Section 5 contains the meaning of the explanation of time's paradoxical aspects: ". . . But to apprehend/ The point of intersection of the timeless/ With time, is an occupation for the saint." The images of flowers, sunlight, and music, which have recurred throughout these poems, symbolize ordinary human experiences that, although fragmentary, nevertheless are "hints of grace": "The hint half guessed, the gift half understood, is Incarnation."

The resolution of themes in "Little Gidding" is accomplished by semirepetitive exposition and further development. The chapel at Little Gidding is a place "where prayer has been valid." T. S. Eliot also explains the many allusions to writers and saints and saints who were writers as ". . . the communication/ Of the dead is tongued with fire beyond the language of the living." The death of the four elements in section 2 opens the way to spiritual resurrection. This lyric is followed by the poet's meeting, after an air raid, with a "familiar compound ghost"—the shade of all his past teachers—who tells him of the grief and failure of old age ". . . unless restored by that refining fire/ Where you must move in measure like a dancer." The historical theme is restated in the relationship of the present and the past as a reconciliation of opposites: "History may be servitude,/ History may be freedom," while "Whatever we inherit from the fortunate/ We have taken from the defeated." The solution of the dilemma of the burden of divine care for humanity, so bleakly felt in "East Coker," is here seen to be love, which binds us in our desires and alone is able to give the essential release from them.

The end of exploration, of the struggle with words and of all human actions "Will be to arrive where we started/ And to know the place for the first time." The moments of personal and historical experience are never lost:

> The moment of the rose and the moment of the yew tree
> Are of equal duration. A people without history
> Is not redeemed from time, for history is a pattern
> Of timeless moments.

The way of purgation, which requires the whole being, has led to "complete simplicity" where "the fire and the rose are one."

For all its complexity, *Four Quartets* contains Eliot's most explicit poetry. The poems are specifically Christian, recording the progress of the soul toward salvation. The way in which the themes are at various levels interwoven to augment and illuminate one another, the control of language and rhythm, and the beauty and precision of the images have led some critics to call these quartets Eliot's finest achievement.

Bibliography:
Gardner, Helen Louise. *The Art of T. S. Eliot.* London: Cresset Press, 1949. A skillful and informative analysis of the poetry and verse dramas of Eliot. The chapter treating the *Four Quartets* offers a helpful interpretation of the poem as a musical work.
_____. *The Composition of "Four Quartets."* New York: Oxford University Press, 1978. Easily one of the best critics of Eliot's poetry, Gardner employs her ample resources in examining his process of composition. Gardner's work is a helpful summary of primary documents and includes many notes on versions of the text.
Lobb, Edward, ed. *Words in Time: New Essays on Eliot's "Four Quartets."* Ann Arbor: University of Michigan Press, 1993. A fine collection of ten essays by authors such as Denis Donoghue, Lyndall Gordon, and Louis L. Martz, which expands the discussion of Eliot's *Four Quartets.* Useful for new readers and scholars alike.
Smith, Grover Cleveland. *T. S. Eliot's Poetry and Plays: A Study in Sources and Meaning.* 2d ed. Chicago: University of Chicago Press, 1974. A detailed and probing exploration of Eliot's clever use of allusions and quotations to express his spiritual and philosophical concerns. This book remains a standard critical work on Eliot's poetry, a good sourcebook for scholars.
Traversi, Derek Antona. *T. S. Eliot: The Longer Poems: "The Waste Land," "Ash Wednesday," "Four Quartets."* London: Bodley Head, 1976. A scholarly, objective analysis of the *Four Quartets.* Traversi sees Eliot's poetry as a continuous whole and offers a detailed study of these poems on their own terms rather than primarily as expressions of a given ideology, Christian or otherwise.

FRANKENSTEIN
Or, The Modern Prometheus

Type of work: Novel
Author: Mary Wollstonecraft Godwin Shelley (1797-1851)
Type of plot: Gothic
Time of plot: Eighteenth century
Locale: Europe
First published: 1818

Principal characters:
ROBERT WALTON, an explorer
VICTOR FRANKENSTEIN, an inventor
ELIZABETH, his foster sister
WILLIAM, his brother
JUSTINE, the Frankensteins' servant
CLERVAL, Victor's friend
THE MONSTER

The Story:

Robert Walton was an English explorer whose ship was held fast in polar ice. As the company looked out over the empty ice field, they were astonished to see a sledge drawn by dogs speeding northward. The sledge driver looked huge and misshapen. That night, an ice floe carried to the ship another sledge, one dog, and a man in weakened condition. When the newcomer learned that his was the second sledge sighted from the ship, he became agitated.

Walton was greatly attracted to the man during his convalescence, and as they continued fast in the ice, the men had leisure time to get acquainted. At last, after he had recovered somewhat from exposure and hunger, the man told Walton his story.

Victor Frankenstein was born into an aristocratic family in Geneva. As a playmate for their son, the parents had adopted a lovely little girl of the same age. Victor and Elizabeth grew up as brother and sister. Much later another son, William, was born to the Frankensteins.

At an early age, Victor showed promise in the natural sciences. He devoured the works of Paracelsus and Albertus Magnus and thought in his ignorance that they were the real masters. When he grew older, his father decided to send Victor to the university at Ingolstadt. There he soon learned all that his masters could teach him in the field of natural science. Engaged in brilliant and terrible research, he stumbled by chance on the secret of creating life. Once he had gained this knowledge, he could not rest until he had employed it to create a living being. By haunting the butcher shops and dissecting rooms, he soon had the necessary raw materials. With great cunning, he fashioned an eight-foot monster and endowed him with life.

As soon as he had created his monster, however, he was subject to strange misgivings. During the night, the monster came to his bed. At the sight of the horrible face, he shrieked and frightened the monster. Overcome by the horror of his act, he became ill with a brain fever. His best friend, Henry Clerval, arrived from Geneva and helped to nurse him through his illness. He was unable to tell Clerval what he had done.

Terrible news then came from Geneva. William, Victor's young brother, was dead by the hand of a murderer. He had been found strangled in a park, and a faithful family servant, Justine, had been charged with the crime. Victor hurried to Geneva.

At the trial, Justine told a convincing story. She had been looking for William in the countryside and, returning after the city gates had been closed, had spent the night in a deserted hut; she could not, however, explain how a miniature from William's neck came to be in her pocket. Victor and Elizabeth believed the girl's story, but despite all of their efforts, Justine was convicted and condemned.

Depressed by these tragic events, Victor went hiking over the mountainous countryside. Far ahead on the glacier, he saw a strange, agile figure that filled him with horrible suspicions. Unable to overtake the figure, he sat down to rest. Suddenly, the monster appeared before him. The creature demanded that Victor listen to his story. The monster began to tell him that when he left Victor's chambers in Ingolstadt, everyone he met screamed and ran from him. Wandering confusedly, the monster finally found shelter in an abandoned hovel adjoining a cottage. By great stealth, he remained there during daylight and, at night, sought berries for food. Through observation, he began to learn the ways of humankind. Feeling an urge to friendship, he brought wood to the cottage every day, but when he attempted to make friends with the cottagers, he was repulsed with such fear and fury that his heart became bitter toward all people. When he saw William playing in the park, he strangled the boy and took the miniature from his neck. Then during the night, he came upon Justine in the hut and put the picture in her pocket.

Presently, the monster made a horrible demand. He insisted that Victor fashion a mate for him who would give him love and companionship. The monster threatened to ravage and kill at random if Victor refused the request, but, if Victor agreed, the monster promised to take his mate to the wilds of South America, where they would never again be seen by humankind. It was a hard choice, but Victor felt that he must accept.

Victor left for England with his friend Clerval. After parting from his friend, he went to the distant Orkneys and began his task. He was almost ready to animate the gross mass of flesh when his conscience stopped him. He could not let the two monsters mate and spawn a race of monsters. He destroyed his work. The monster was watching at a window. Angered to see his mate destroyed, he forced his way into the house and warned Victor that a terrible punishment would fall upon the young man on his wedding night. Then the monster escaped by sea. Later, to torment his maker, he fiendishly killed Clerval.

Victor was suspected of the crime. Released for lack of evidence, he went back to Geneva. He and Elizabeth were married there. Although Victor was armed and alert, the monster got into the nuptial chamber and strangled the bride. Victor shot at him, but he escaped again. Victor vowed to follow the monster and kill him.

Weakened by exposure, Victor died on the ship in the ice with Elizabeth, William, Justine, and Clerval unavenged. Then the monster came to the dead man's cabin, and Walton, stifling his fear, addressed the gigantic, hideous creature. Victor's was the greater crime, the monster said. He had created a man, a man without love or friend or soul. He deserved his punishment. After his speech, the monster vanished over the ice field.

Critical Evaluation:

So much is amazing about *Frankenstein.* Perhaps most remarkable is this early nineteenth century novel's continued fame. The novel was not interpreted as serious literature until the latter part of the twentieth century; since that time, *Frankenstein* has been viewed from many critical perspectives, whether it be feminist, psychoanalytical, Marxist, or any one of a number of other possible interpretations. The range and depth of the criticism are proof of the richness of the novel.

Frankenstein was first published anonymously, and some nineteenth century readers at first credited Mary Shelley's husband, the famous Romantic poet Percy Bysshe Shelley, with writing the work. Readers today are as surprised as Shelley's contemporaries to find that this combination of gothic horror and science fiction was written by a nineteen-year-old woman. Much has been made of the connections between Shelley's life and the novel. For example, mothers are noticeably absent from the novel, as Shelley's mother, having died shortly after Mary's birth, was absent from her daughter's life. In the novel, Victor's mother dies early, leaving a painful void in his life. Perhaps more interesting is that the creation of the monster by Victor, "the pale student of unhallowed arts," is essentially a motherless birth.

One could also examine the theme of "doubles" in this work. The explorer, Walton, is fascinated by Victor and, in effect, serves as his double. Like Victor, Walton is obsessed with exploring dangerous areas heretofore unknown to humanity: Walton is attempting to explore the northernmost regions of the world, while Victor has dabbled in the creation of life. It is too late for Victor, and he agrees to tell his miserable tale as a type of warning. For Walton, it is not too late to change his course. Victor has been somewhat isolated for most of the novel until, after the creature's revenge, he is left utterly alone in the world. Walton is also lonely and writes to his sister that he "bitterly feel(s) the want of a friend."

Some controversial psychoanalytic criticism suggests that the creature serves as a sort of double for Victor, too, or perhaps as another side of him. In Freudian terms, the creature is like Victor's id, acting out all the terrible fantasies Victor has perhaps entertained. Along this same line of thinking, Elizabeth and Clerval can be seen, then, as Victor's superego, consistently trying to appeal to all that is moral and upright in Victor.

Elizabeth seems to double as Victor's mother after the older woman's death. Later in the novel, Elizabeth is symbolically tied to the mate Victor begins to construct for the creature. Victor destroys the creature's mate, which results in Elizabeth's death at the hands of the creature.

The novel also contains biblical symbolism, particularly the theme of the outcast and the story of creation. The creature is bitter and dejected after being turned away from human civilization, much the same way Adam was turned out of the Garden of Eden. One difference, though, makes the monster a sympathetic character, especially to contemporary readers. In the biblical story, Adam causes his own fate by sinning. The creature's hideous existence, however, is caused by his creator, Victor, and it is this grotesqueness that leads to the creature's being spurned. Only after he is repeatedly rejected does the creature become violent and decide to seek revenge. This creation allegory is made clear from the beginning with the epigraph from John Milton's *Paradise Lost* (1667) which begins the novel:

> Did I request thee, Maker, from my clay
> To mould Me man? Did I solicit thee
> From darkness to promote me?

Again, any discussion of Frankenstein inevitably leads back to aspects of its author's life. Perhaps more interesting than Shelley's marriage to the poet Percy Bysshe Shelley is her literary and biological parentage. She was the daughter of the revolutionary feminist writer Mary Wollstonecraft and the radical philosopher William Godwin, who was nearly arrested for supporting the French Revolution. The political views of Shelley's parents often led to their being considered outcasts by "proper" society, a role their daughter would later repeat by running off with the married poet. Ironically, the political views of Wollstonecraft and Godwin were often at odds with the choices they made in their personal lives; for example, both were philosophically opposed to the institution of marriage but married as soon as Wollstonecraft became pregnant.

Mary Shelley studied the writings of both her parents but never adopted extreme philosophies. Her own politics seemed to be based on a realistic view of the world, tempered by compassion. In other works, Shelley wrote sympathetically of the poor and saw the need for reform, but she also feared the violence of a revolution of the underclass. Readers of Frankenstein feel the same ambivalence about the creature. While sympathizing with him and recognizing the injustice of his plight, the reader, like Victor, also begins to fear the creature's revenge.

As mentioned, the endurance of *Frankenstein* may be the most remarkable aspect of the novel. The story has captured not only the literary imagination of the twentieth century but the popular imagination as well, which is perhaps most evident in the number of popular films based on the story. Many films stretch and radically change the original story, although some have attempted to follow the book closely. One interesting fact is that films have traditionally made the most of a scene that was not even included in the novel: the creation of the monster.

It may seem trite to say that Shelley's perspective was ahead of her time when she wrote *Frankenstein*, but that certainly is the case. This short novel predates the modern horror novel as well as the modern science-fiction novel. *Frankenstein* also seems to be a precursor to the twentieth century fear of scientific experiments gone out of control; one could find numerous parallels to the creation of the monster in modern times. Though there is much to analyze and appreciate in this intricately woven tale, the final note may be that the story of Frankenstein's monster is, ironically, human enough to have fascinated readers for years and continues to do so.

"Critical Evaluation" by Bonnie Flaig

Bibliography:
Bloom, Harold, ed. *Mary Shelley's "Frankenstein."* New York: Chelsea House, 1987. Offers a wide variety of critical essays on the novel.
Grylls, R. Glynn. *Mary Shelley: A Biography.* London: Oxford University Press, 1938. Includes extensive discussion of events surrounding the writing of *Frankenstein*.
Levine, George, and U. C. Knoepflmacher, eds. *The Endurance of Frankenstein: Essays on Mary Shelley's Novel.* Berkeley: University of California Press, 1979. Collection of essays focusing more on the endurance of the story of Frankenstein rather than the novel, most notably "The Stage and Film Children of Frankenstein: A Survey," by Albert J. LaValley.
Mellor, Anne K. *Mary Shelley: Her Life, Her Fiction, Her Monsters.* New York: Routledge, 1988. Combines critical analysis of the novel with biographical material from Shelley's life.
Shelley, Mary W. *Frankenstein.* Edited by Johanna M. Smith. Boston: Bedford Books, 1992. Complete, authoritative text with biographical and historical contexts, critical history, and essays from five contemporary critical perspectives.

FRANNY AND ZOOEY

Type of work: Novel
Author: J. D. Salinger (1919-   )
Type of plot: Domestic realism
Time of plot: November, 1955
Locale: Princeton and Manhattan
First published: "Franny," 1955; "Zooey," 1957; novel, 1961

> *Principal characters:*
> BESSIE GALLAGHER GLASS, the mother of seven children
> FRANNY, her youngest daughter, a college student
> ZOOEY, Franny's older brother, a television actor
> BUDDY, the oldest living child, a writing professor

The Story:

Franny Glass, a twenty-year-old college student, met her weekend date, Lane Coutell, at the train station. She had come to town for the big Yale football game at an unidentified eastern Ivy League college where Lane was an undergraduate. She greeted him enthusiastically, despite his spurious, narcissistic detachment. They immediately went to a trendy restaurant for lunch, where Lane dug into snails and frog legs and Franny left her chicken sandwich untouched. They smoked incessantly, while Lane spoke at length and with scarcely veiled pomposity of a recent paper he had written on Gustave Flaubert. Franny grew paler as she tried to listen attentively. She finally exploded in a hushed rant against pedants, section men, pseudointellectuals, and shallow humanity in general. She told him that she had quit the theater group at school, which had been her one great love, because she was so fed up with ego. Feeling undone, she fled to the ladies room where, secluded in a vacant stall, she sobbed freely for five minutes. She stopped abruptly and clutched to her chest a small green book she was carrying, as if it were her security blanket. She returned to the table determined to apologize and salvage the weekend, but Lane noticed her little book, *The Way of the Pilgrim*, and engaged her in a discussion about it. Trying to appear casual, Franny told him about the pilgrim's quest for enlightenment through praying without ceasing. Lane responded with condescending skepticism, which made Franny angry again. As she again made her way to the ladies room, she fainted.

Buddy Glass, the oldest living child of the Glass family and a rather eccentric writer and professor, related the events of Franny's return home after her nervous collapse. He had not been there but told the story as a sort of "prose home movie" as gleaned from the primary players. Zooey Glass, Franny's twenty-five-year-old brother, sat in the tub in the Glass house in midtown Manhattan. He read a four-year-old letter from his brother Buddy, which concerned Zooey's acting career, and whether or not he could tolerate the inherent phoniness of the trade. After Zooey had finished reading, he picked up a television script and studied it. He was soon interrupted by his mother, Bessie, who wanted to give him something. Zooey grudgingly let his mother in and finished dressing for an afternoon appointment while carrying on a long, at times excruciatingly tense, conversation with her about Franny's breakdown. After much squabbling over that and other relatively inconsequential practical matters, Bessie left the bathroom with nothing having been decided except that a neighbor's psychologist would not be called in.

Franny had come home after the fainting incident and taken over the living room sofa, where she cried, refused to eat, and continued to murmur the prayer "Lord Jesus Christ, have mercy on me." Zooey, at his mother's request, went in to see Franny and made a long, unsuccessful attempt to rouse Franny from what seemed to be a nervous breakdown. He rantingly spoke of religion and Jesus, the search for enlightenment, the Glass family's brilliance, and the need for Franny to pull herself together and appreciate the nice things in the world. He advised her to strive for perfection on her own terms instead of criticizing the world or retreating into religion as a haven from it. He described himself and her as spiritual freaks, which he blamed on the religious teachings they had received from their oldest brothers at a very early age. They were too aware to live in ignorant bliss as did the masses, but live among them they must.

His tactless tirade sent Franny into an even deeper fit of sobbing. With a halfhearted apology, Zooey left the room and entered the bedroom that his oldest brother Seymour had shared with Buddy. It was the first time Zooey had entered the room since Seymour's suicide seven years earlier. On the back of the bedroom door were quotations from many of the world's most enlightened religious thinkers. After pondering those words for some time and reading a portion of Seymour's old diary, he rang Franny on Seymour's old private phone, pretending to be Buddy. A slip caused Franny to catch on that it was Zooey, but by that time he had told her that as an actress she must act on her own terms and disregard those of the ever-present, ignorant audience. Zooey used the same metaphor of performing for the fat lady that Seymour had used when they were children to inspire them to do their best. Carrying this metaphor further, Zooey told Franny that everyone is that fat lady and that the fat lady is Jesus Christ. This revelation of interconnectedness allowed Franny to find peace, and she fell into the deep sleep of renewal.

Critical Evaluation:

J. D. Salinger is generally regarded, whether critically or reverentially, as the preeminent literary force from the Beat era to capture the spirit of and speak to young Americans. Salinger's technique of presenting twentieth century American family relationships has been compared with the work of such authors as William Faulkner, Ernest Hemingway, and F. Scott Fitzgerald. Salinger was known primarily as a short-story writer when the novel *Franny and Zooey* was first published in two parts in *The New Yorker*. Salinger wrote "Franny" as a wedding gift for his wife, upon whom the title character is based. "Franny" also marked the beginning of what became Salinger's obsession with the Glass family.

Franny and Zooey are the youngest of seven brilliant children sired by a successful vaudevillian couple from the 1920's, Les Glass, who was Jewish, and his wife, Bessie Gallagher, who was Irish. The oldest and most brilliant of the children, Seymour, killed himself while on his second honeymoon, presumably because of an inability to reconcile childhood innocence with adulthood. The heir to Seymour's role as guru is Buddy, an author and writing instructor at a small college, who lives in modified, self-imposed hermitage. The character of Buddy has often been identified as the alter-ego of Salinger, who is known to be a heavily autobiographical writer, and who has been accused of being self-indulgent and preachy, especially in the later works introduced by *Franny and Zooey*.

With this novel, Salinger took a marked turn from focusing on action, structure, and humor to a preoccupation with monologue, character development, and seriousness. The shift is underscored by a change from the omniscient third-person narrative voice in "Franny" to the first-person voice of Buddy, who tells the "Zooey" portion of the novel. It is here that discourse and extensive detail take the place of plot and structure. More than one-third of the novel takes place in bathrooms, and both stories cover only a very few hours of time. "Zooey" proceeds as if the narrator were looking through a randomly roving and pausing camera lens. By paying minimal attention to plot and attempting to present all objects with equal emphasis, Salinger tries gradually to reveal the complex nature and interconnectedness of otherwise static characters.

Salinger's work is mostly concerned with the various trials of adolescence: alienation, loss of innocence, the obscenity of modern life, the search for meaning, and the redeeming power of love. Franny is a typical Salinger character seeking enlightenment, struggling against an onerous ego, and isolated by a hypersensitivity to her own shortcomings and those of others. There are differences, however, between Franny and Salinger's earlier protagonists, the most obvious being that Salinger for the first time uses a female character as spokesperson for this battle. The strong Judeo-Christian element in *Franny and Zooey* is a departure from Salinger's previous Zen-Buddhist point of view. Salinger appears to be taking a more general view of religion, not as a solution to the world's problems but rather as a means of learning to live with them and with oneself.

The overall theme of the novel is one of renewal, which is attained when the characters realize the unifying principle or interconnectedness of the universe. This realization is dependent on a dissolution of such opposites as phony and nice, bad and good, adulthood and childhood, knowledge and naïveté, boy and girl, us and them. The recurrent symbol of the little girl—which makes epiphanous appearances in Seymour's, Buddy's, and Zooey's lives, and whom Franny turns into as she makes her journey down the corridor to receive the ostensible Buddy's phone call—represents innocence and beauty. It is the loss of this innocence as they strive to connect with the unbearably ugly adult world that causes all of the Glass children in turn to go through a spiritual crisis. Seymour's fat lady—for whom he told Zooey to shine his shoes and Franny to sing when they were child radio stars—is supposed to represent that spiritual singleness of the universe. The fat lady is Everyman, and Everyman is Jesus Christ, or God, or Buddha, or Brahman. It is this realization that allows Franny to reconcile her views of self, ego, and the world and to resolve her spiritual crisis.

Some critics have thought that the resolution rings false and that when Salinger sets the Glasses apart from the rest of the world—in describing them as handsomer and more brilliant and spiritually aware than other people—he is implying that only those with their intellectual and spiritual potential can search for the true way.

Beyond being impressively crafted and philosophically uplifting, *Franny and Zooey* presents Salinger's belief in the importance of spiritual seeking. As Zooey says in the closing scene, "the artist's only concern is to shoot for some kind of perfection, and *on his own terms*, not anyone else's."

Leslie M. Pendleton

Bibliography:
French, Warren. *J. D. Salinger*. New York: Twayne, 1963. One of the few attempts critically to evaluate Salinger's writing by focusing on its effects on young readers rather than on Salinger's personal psychological and spiritual underpinnings. The result is an insightful explanation of the portrait of adolescence in Salinger's work and why it has been so heartily embraced by American youth.
Laser, Marvin, and Norman Fruman. *Studies in J. D. Salinger: Reviews, Essays, and Critiques of "The Catcher in the Rye" and Other Fiction*. New York: Odyssey Press, 1963. A wonderful and diverse collection of analyses written at the time of Salinger's publications by some of the most recognized contemporary critics.

Lundquist, James. *J. D. Salinger.* New York: Frederick Ungar, 1979. A so-called New Criticism analysis that conflates Salinger's life with the lives of his characters and stories. The thorough chronology is very useful in this context.

Miller, James E., Jr. *J. D. Salinger.* Minneapolis: University of Minnesota Press, 1965. Number 51 of a series of pamphlets written on American writers. A concise, succinct, and accessible synopsis of Salinger's writing.

Ranchan, Som P. "Zooey and Franny" and "Bessie." In *An Adventure in Vedanta (J. D. Salinger's The Glass Family).* Delhi, India: Ajanta Publications, 1989. An interesting but very narrow reading of his works. Interprets both Salinger's personal life and his stories in light of the Vedantic vision, which entails a spiritual quest for that universal truth said to be found in all religions.

FREE FALL

Type of work: Novel
Author: William Golding (1911-1993)
Type of plot: Bildungsroman
Time of plot: 1917-c. 1950
Locale: Southeast England
First published: 1959

> *Principal characters:*
> SAMMY MOUNTJOY, a painter
> BEATRICE IFOR, a former girlfriend of Sammy
> ROWENA PRINGLE, a teacher
> NICK SHALES, a teacher
> MA, Sammy's mother
> FR. WATTS-WATT, a clergyman, Sammy's guardian
> PHILIP ARNOLD, a schoolfriend
> JOHNNY SPRAGG, a schoolfriend
> DR. HALDE, a member of the Gestapo
> TAFFY, Sammy's wife

The Story:

Sammy Mountjoy, a well-known painter, needed to review his past life, to discover where his sense of guilt had begun and his innocence lost. He was convinced there was a moment of fall, when a choice had been freely made that had cost him his subsequent freedom of action. Several sites of possible moments are examined, until a defining moment is discovered.

Sammy first examined his infancy. Born illegitimately, he lived with his obese, dirt-poor mother in a rural slum in Kent. It was an animal existence, however warm and sensuous. He enjoyed his infants' school, where his talent for drawing was first noticed, and then the boys' elementary school. Here he became a gang leader, vying against Johnny Spragg's gang. Aided by a manipulative friend, Philip Arnold, he set up a playground extortion racket that was soon discovered. Philip attended the local Church of England, and dared Sammy to desecrate the altar by urinating on it. Sammy could only manage a weak spit, but even then was promptly pounced on by the verger, who hit him violently round the ear. As a result, Sammy needed hospitalization, during which time his mother died. The vicar, Father Watts-Watt, perhaps as a sign of atonement, became his guardian. For all his naughtiness, Sammy did not believe he had lost his innocence during this period.

He analyzed next his time as an art student in London just before the outbreak of World War II. He had become infatuated with Beatrice Ifor at school. She was also in London at a teacher training college; he determined to seduce her. His violent, obsessive nature frightened her, but eventually she yielded. Sammy was disappointed: He could find no personality in her, let alone the mystery he had been seeking. Their lovemaking was disappointing and he soon tired of her, although she was emotionally dependent on him. In the end he met Taffy at a Communist Party meeting, fell instantly in love with her, and abandoned Beatrice. In reviewing this part of his life, Sammy realized his compulsive behavior was a sign that he had already lost his freedom: he was a driven man.

He then explored a defining moment of insight that he had had as a prisoner of war in a German prisoner of war camp. He was being interrogated by Dr. Halde about certain escape plans. Dr. Halde, a psychologist, was working for the Gestapo. Sammy did not know any of the details of the plan, but Dr. Halde knew that as an artist Sammy would have had intuitive insights and not be held by any strict morality. Before Sammy could articulate any such intuitions, he was placed in a completely dark cell. Sammy had been terrified of the dark since living at Fr. Watts-Watt's vicarage, and he was on the point of panic. He measured the cell to keep his sanity, but all the time his imagination was running riot. When he touched a wet soft mass in the center of the cell, he imagined it to be human organs, left perhaps when the ceiling had descended and crushed a former inmate. At that point he broke down completely, crying "Help me! Help me!" This expression of utter helplessness and hopelessness became a death experience. When he was released, he felt resurrected, seeing everything quite differently. Life became a glory to him; his old self-centeredness had been broken.

This revelation enabled him to regain his schoolboy faith in the spiritual and to reject scientific materialism as a full explanation of life. He now examined the powerful influence of two teachers in his losing faith. Miss Pringle had taught religious education, and her lessons on the miraculous and transcendent events of the Bible thrilled him, but her attitude toward Sammy seemed to deny what she said. By contrast, Nick Shales, the science teacher, expressed a strictly logical and material view of life, and his kindness and generosity to his pupils had won Sammy over. Sammy, however, felt that neither teacher had touched a still-existing innocence within him.

One other episode at school was examined. During an art class, Sammy had managed, almost by accident, to capture the inner character of one of the students sitting as a model, Beatrice. From then on Sammy's infatuation grew as he tried to recapture, unsuccessfully, that moment of artistic insight. On graduation day, the headmaster had told Sammy he could achieve anything if he were willing to pay a high enough price, even though he would always be disappointed by what he got. As he went swimming that day, he made a conscious decision to have Beatrice. There lay the moment of fall and the loss of innocence.

Once the war ended, Sammy revisited Beatrice, Miss Pringle, and Nick, in the hope of communicating his new vision and perhaps to set the record straight. None of the three visits was successful. Beatrice had become incurably insane and merely urinated over his shoes; Nick was dying; Miss Pringle had rearranged her own reality to see herself as an early patron of Sammy. The past could not be undone. Sammy's final memory was the final glimpse he had of the dark prison cell. He had been in a broom cupboard, the wet mass a floorcloth. The Camp Commandant apologized for Dr. Halde's behavior: "The Herr Doktor does not know about peoples."

Critical Evaluation:

Free Fall is the fourth novel of Sir William Golding. It is written not only in the genre of the novel of personal development, but also in that of the *Künstlerroman*, the novel about artistic development and personality. As most of Golding's earlier novels, it is written in conscious dialectic to some other narrative, in this case Albert Camus' *La Chute* (1956; *The Fall*, 1957). Camus sees no possibility of regeneration or redemption after a fall; Golding does. There are other literary influences. Joyce Cary's *The Horse's Mouth* (1944) also is a first-person narrative by a painter; Golding's style is at times reminiscent of Cary's. L. P. Hartley's prizewinning novel *The Go-Between* had been published only a few years previously (1953) and also dealt with a boy's loss of innocence through sexual knowledge, though Leo is a much more passive protagonist than Sammy. Another influence is the great French text *À la recherche du temps perdu* (1913-1927; *Remembrance of Things Past*, 1922-1931) by Marcel Proust, a model for Sammy's search for significant moments of time buried in half-conscious memory.

The title suggests that the novel stands in a central literary tradition of exploration of the limits of freedom. Golding's achievement is to be able to restate such traditional material, often of a theological nature, in the language and thought of the post-World War II Western world. The novel also describes moments of revelation that define one's view of reality, the futility of material life without a spiritual or transcendent dimension, the nature of evil, and the correspondence of personal to social integration or disintegration. Perhaps new to this novel, for Golding, is an exploration of the relationship of guilt to forgiveness, and the way that conviction of guilt and the ability to forgive need conversion experiences. Golding seems to suggest that redemption can only be partial. Beatrice remains insane, with no hope of recovery. Sammy has to bear some, though not all, the guilt for this. Past time can be examined to find truth, but it cannot be remade.

Although Sammy is an artist, the novel's style is not altogether painterly. Much of the imagery is, in fact, religious and is Golding's way of expressing traditional theological concepts in contemporary concerns. Fire is one such example. In the novel, it has its traditional symbolism of Pentecostal fire, the bringing of new spiritual life; less frequently it refers to hell. Fire is also related to the burning bush of Moses, both as miracle and as glory, and to Nick's placing a candle in a bell jar, symbolizing rationality, but also confinement, the death of the spirit. Other recurring religious images are of paradise, water, "fear and trembling," altars and temples, and Christ's temptations. The other image that is central to the novel and to all of Golding's fiction is that of darkness—from the dreadful panic of the cell to the "warm darkness" of Ma. Images of sickness, captivity, and cells/cellars can also be traced.

Episodes take on symbolic value as enacted images: the cell, the desecration of the altar, Sammy's waiting at red traffic lights on the way to Beatrice, for example. Surprisingly, only a few of Sammy's drawings are seen as images, the most obvious being the few hurried, uncredited lines that somehow capture the essence of Beatrice in a way no seduction could ever do. Names also take on symbolic force: Beatrice echoes Dante's inspirational love, but her surname, "if/or" suggests dislocation, lack of result. "Mountjoy" is ironic until his cell experience, where for the first time he does discover joy, but only by going through the depths.

Golding also uses little catch phrases, or leitmotifs, to encapsulate symbolic force—"the taste of potatoes" is one such, symbolizing the authenticity of felt experience. Another is "blue cornflowers." Both are clearly memory fragments.

Golding's narrative method is not to conduct a simple autobiographical plotline. Although he covers much of Sammy's life, there are numerous omissions. The novel is more an excavation, starting at the most obvious places. It is also like a treasure hunt, in which what is buried is only to be found at the end. One may guess where the treasure lies, but not predict the actual moment of discovery. The reader explores with Sammy. Perceptions are partly those of the adult Sammy looking back, partly those of Sammy as a child. Sammy the innocent, the unregenerate, and the regenerate are all represented. This helps Golding elicit a response from the reader that is neither too sympathetic nor too hostile to Sammy.

David Barratt

Bibliography:
Babb, Howard S. *The Novels of William Golding.* Columbus: Ohio State University Press, 1970. One chapter is given to each novel. Babb's strength in writing on *Free Fall* is his introductory analysis of Golding's style.
Boyd, S. J. *The Novels of William Golding.* New York: St. Martin's Press, 1988. Boyd's volume

is contemporaneous to the later novels of Golding, and thus able to look back on the earlier ones with some hindsight. The quality of Sammy's love is central to Boyd's analysis.

Gindin, James. *William Golding*. New York: Macmillan, 1988. Sees Golding relating sinfulness to "becoming" in *Free Fall*. An economic, well focused thematic discussion.

Kinkead-Weekes, Martin, and Ian Gregor. *William Golding: A Critical Study*. 2d ed. Winchester, Mass.: Faber & Faber, 1984. Anticipates later criticisms of the novel's being too reductionist by arguing that such criticisms are misconceived.

Redpath, Philip. *William Golding: A Structural Reading of His Fiction*. New York: Barnes & Nobel Books, 1986. Examines the circular structure of *Free Fall* and other novels of Golding.

FREEDOM OR DEATH

Type of work: Novel
Author: Nikos Kazantzakis (1883-1957)
Type of plot: Historical
Time of plot: 1889
Locale: Meghalo Kastro, Crete
First published: Ho Kapetan Michales, 1953 (English translation, 1956)

Principal characters:
    CAPTAIN MICHALES, the principal rebel
    NURI BEY, a Turk, Michales' "blood brother"
    KOSMAS, Michales' nephew
    CAPTAIN POLYXIGIS, a rival Cretan
    EMINÉ, Nuri's wife and later Polyxigis' wife
    SEFAKAS, Michales' father
    NOEMI (CHRYSULA), Kosmas' wife
    TITYROS, Michales' brother
    VANGELIO, Tityros' wife
    MANUSAKAS, Michales' brother
    THE PASHA OF MEGHALO KASTRO, leader of the Turks
    THE METROPOLITAN OF MEGHALO KASTRO, Greek religious leader

The Story:

Captain Michales was obsessed with the ideal of freedom. He did not listen to his wife or to the elders of Meghalo Kastro. Turks, with the exception of Michales' boyhood friend Nuri Bey, were Michales' natural enemies. Counterbalancing this obsession was Michales' attraction to Nuri's wife, Eminé. He was enraptured by her beauty and enchanting voice, but he realized that this attraction interfered with his total dedication to the liberation of Crete. Another problem was his heavy drinking bouts, which were usually followed by senseless cruelty toward Turks.

In the same gathering at which Eminé first captivated Michales, another Cretan fighter, Captain Polyxigis, also fell under her spell. It was Polyxigis who eventually won Eminé's heart and became her lover. Michales was jealous of Polyxigis, although he respected him as a comrade in arms.

Polyxigis' success in winning Eminé did not stop Michales from trying to impress her. In a contest of strength, Michales won a match over Nuri, who was devastated and felt ineffectual in the eyes of Eminé. Nuri became further humiliated in a fight with Michales' brother Manusakas. Although he managed to kill Manusakas, Nuri was permanently emasculated by a knife wound.

Michales, hearing of his brother's murder, renounced his childhood friendship with Nuri and vowed revenge. When the opportune moment came, however, he found Nuri in a pathetic condition and relented. Nuri, who had wanted to die in battle, had lost his manhood, his wife, his friend, and his honor. He committed suicide. Nuri's death saddened Michales but emboldened Polyxigis to propose marriage to Eminé. He succeeded in converting her from Islam to Christianity.

The war had intensified. The Turks made major advances and pillaged many towns, slaughtering the inhabitants. Michales with two hundred rebels and sixty-five monks defended the monastery of Arkadi for two days and nights against fifteen thousand Turks. In the midst of the fighting, Michales received word that Eminé had been captured by Turks. He and a group of his men rushed off to rescue her. By the time he returned, the monastery was on the verge of collapse. He felt guilt and shame. He refused to surrender in spite of the odds. All other officers and troops had retreated except Michales and a few of his devoted followers.

Michales' dedication was infectious and could transform others. His brother Tityros, an ineffectual school teacher, had been involved in petty domestic rivalries that resulted in his killing his brother-in-law. His wife Vangelio, heartbroken over her brother's death, had killed herself. These events and his brother's influence wrought a spiritual transformation in Tityros. He became a revolutionary.

Another transformation took place in Kosmas, Michales' nephew. Kosmas was an intellectual who had been studying at a German university. He surprised his family by coming home with Noemi, a Russian-Jewish wife. Upon their arrival, Sefakas, Kosmas' grandfather, died. The family thought it was time for Michales to retreat and come home. Kosmas volunteered to go to the mountains to persuade his uncle to return. He carried letters from the family and from the elders of Crete that accepted failure of the revolt and requested Michales' return.

When he entered the trenches where Michales was valiantly fighting the Turks, Kosmas was strongly affected by his uncle's idealism. Instead of trying to persuade him to come back, he joined in the fighting. Shortly afterward, the young freedom fighter was captured and beheaded by the Turks.

When the Turks finally rammed through the gate of the monastery, a Cretan fighter fired his pistol into an underground powder vault where six hundred women and children were hiding. All perished, together with everyone at the monastery, including the hundreds of Turks who had already entered.

Michales grabbed his nephew's severed head by the hair and, raising it like a banner, charged the enemy roaring, "Freedom or . . ." Before he could finish the famous Cretan slogan, the Turkish bullets found their target.

Critical Evaluation:

Freedom or Death is a colorful story full of symbolic motifs. In it, Nikos Kazantzakis depicts his own experiences as a child in Meghalo Kastro. He recalls that in 1889, Christians in his village killed a prominent Turkish dignitary, which triggered a new Turkish massacre of Cretan civilians. "My mother, my sister, and I sat glued to one another," Kazantzakis recalls, "barricaded within our house." Turks outside cursed, broke down doors, and slaughtered Christians. His father, standing with a loaded musket and his long knife unsheathed, told the family he planned to slaughter them before they fell into Turkish hands.

Kazantzakis altered much of his personal history, yet many characters and episodes match real persons and events, and the character of Kosmas embodies Kazantzakis' politics and experiences as an expatriate. Kosmas, like Kazantzakis, studies in Germany, travels throughout Russia, and marries a Russian-Jewish girl. Like Kazantzakis, he is a follower of Bergson and Nietzsche and has Marxist tendencies.

Kazantzakis' central plot is derived from a famous Cretan folk song about a 1770 revolt led by a teacher named Dhaskaloyannis. With a band of eight hundred Sphakians, the hero held off twenty-five thousand Turkish regulars for several weeks. Both in the 1770 revolt and in the revolt of 1889 chronicled in *Freedom or Death*, the Russians promised assistance that they never delivered. Dhashkaloyannis surrendered but refused to sign a truce, stoically accepting torture and death.

In *Freedom or Death*, past and present, fact and fiction, art and life, and dream and reality are often indistinguishable. This is a reflection of both the Cretan sense of history and Kazantzakis' own interest in Freudian and Jungian conceptions of the interrelationship between the conscious and the unconscious. Characters in the novel may seem exaggerated, scenes overly dramatic, and people and events inflated, unreal, and larger than life. In this, the work reflects Cretan sensibility, a synthesis of mythology and reality. Greek mythology by its nature is a colorful and fantastic reflection of Greek views of humans, God, nature, and death. These are the primitive forces that generate mythology to inspire hope and relieve anxiety. Kazantzakis' *Freedom or Death* was created within that tradition.

Anthropomorphic and metaphorical characterization such as animal imagery is dominant in the novel. Michales is referred to as wild boar, dragon, lion, bull, and minotaur. Kazantzakis describes various characters and situations in naturalistic terms, giving them animal vitality and raw qualities. Spring "leaps" onto the village like a man falling onto a woman, allowing no sleep. Michales is like an "earthquake" or "hard, knotty tree." His father Sefakas is like a "great oak tree." Kosmas is like a Cretan "rock."

A Christ metaphor is used in Crete. It is Crete that is crucified like Christ. The return of Christ is intimately associated with the prospect of a Crete free of Turkish domination. There are visions of the Greek king's son coming by sea to free Crete, like Christ coming on a cloud to establish his rule on earth. Michales on the mountain top calls out to his few remaining followers that whoever dies for the Immortal Crete is dying for Christ and will return with Christ to regenerate the island.

Kazantzakis presents a genre of sacrifice and martyrdom that does not come out of Marxist dialectics or intellectual inspiration but out of vital, sensual forces similar to the Christian faith. Kosmas, a socialist, dies not for an intellectually reasoned purpose but for a raw and visceral prompting of his soul, for the mythical Crete. Michales scorns the education of his nephew and brother. Yet this anti-intellectualism is not an idiosyncratic characteristic; rather, it is a Cretan resentment of any activity that might diminish or call into question the individual's love affair with Crete.

By offering a visceral philosophy of action, Kazantzakis in a sophisticated manner leans toward a naturalistic free will as opposed to the Turk's Islamic fatalism. Pasha tells Michales to surrender because everything that happens in a war is already predestined. Michales however believes that human beings always win over fate if they persist to the death. Even when defeated they are ennobled, not degraded.

Michales is an individualistic, primitive, culture-bound, and primitively Christian being. Kazantzakis was able to blend such an odd number of sensibilities into one unified character because he was influenced by a variety of Western and Eastern philosophies, among them Marxism, Freudian psychoanalysis, the Jungian collective unconscious, and Buddhism's Nothing.

Dreams play an important part in *Freedom or Death* in shaping the reality of the townsfolk of Meghalo Kastro. Dreams are a means of justification for their personal beliefs, aspirations, and actions. The tavern keeper Vendusos dreams of the wine goddess who turns out to be the Virgin Mary. Efendina, a devout Muslim, dreams of pork and wine. Michales dreams of Eminé, the liberation of Crete, and his father.

Kosmas' dead father appears in his dreams to chastise, advise, and uplift his spirits, as well as to order him to take revenge on the Turks. Noemi, Kosmas' pregnant wife, dreams that grandfather Sefakas does not want her to have the baby; he kicks her in the stomach and she wakes up in a pool of blood after suffering a miscarriage. Indeed, there is a dreamlike quality to the novel. Dreams and harsh realities imperceptibly mingle. Ultimately, all dreams seem to originate from one spiritual source, the Cretan slogan of "Freedom or Death."

The similarity of dreams among the Cretans suggests the influence on Kazantzakis of Jung's belief in the collective unconscious underlying the history of struggle and oppression. Primitive ancestors, with all of their beastlike grandeur, stir within Michales and Kosmas and goad them to extraordinary sacrifices. The Cretan martyrs of past revolutions whisper in Cretan ears and recruit a fresh army of superhumans.

Cretans can easily become heroes, but these are not such antiheroes as James Joyce's Leopold Bloom, Franz Kafka's K., or Thomas Mann's Hans Castorp. Kazantzakis' insignificant characters become heroes because they are intoxicated with an ideology and play out their madness to its ultimate degree. They are not ruled by history or fate. They may die but are never defeated. These heroes possess the qualities of positive humanism. They are quintessentially free because they believe in a myth.

Chogollah Maroufi

Bibliography:

Anton, John. "Kazantzakis and the Tradition of the Tragic." *Journal of the Hellenic Diaspora* 10, no. 4 (Winter, 1983): 53-67. A clear exposition of Kazantzakis' understanding and use of the ancient notions of tragedy, which are discussed as they relate to his novels, including *Freedom or Death*.

Bien, Peter. "O Kapetan Mihalis, an Epic (Romance?) Manqué." *Journal of Modern Greek Studies* 5, no. 2 (October, 1987): 153-173. A delightful and well-written analysis of the character of Captain Michales in *Freedom or Death*. Bien discusses the notions of romance in the novel.

Block, Adele. "Mythological Syncretism in the Works of Four Modern Novelists." *International Fiction Review* 8, no. 2 (Summer, 1991): 114-118. A useful analysis of the method by which Kazantzakis in *Freedom or Death* synthesizes various mythological motifs in a workable and unified system.

Gilevski, Paskal. "From Homer to Kazantzakis." *Macedonian Review* 22, no. 2 (1992): 147-150. An interesting review and analysis of the connection between Kazantzakis' tragic hero Michales and the tragic mythological heroes of Homer's epics.

Levitt, Morton P. "*Freedom or Death* and Rebellion on Crete." In *The Cretan Glance: The World and Art of Kazantzakis*. Columbus: Ohio State University Press, 1980. An excellent exposition and evaluation of *Freedom or Death*. Levitt looks at this novel from historical, social, cultural, and philosophical perspectives.

THE FRENCH LIEUTENANT'S WOMAN

Type of work: Novel
Author: John Fowles (1926-   )
Type of plot: Symbolic realism
Time of plot: 1867
Locale: Lyme Regis, Dorset, England
First published: 1969

Principal characters:

> SARAH WOODRUFF, a mysterious seduced-and-abandoned governess
> CHARLES SMITHSON, a thirty-two-year-old London gentleman and
>   amateur paleontologist
> ERNESTINA FREEMAN, his twenty-one-year-old fiancée
> AUNT TRANTER, a kindly spinster with whom Ernestina is staying
> MARY, Aunt Tranter's maid
> SAM, Charles's manservant
> MRS. POULTENEY, a self-righteous prude who takes Sarah in to
>   demonstrate her charity
> DR. GROGAN, a scholarly bachelor physician
> THE NARRATOR, the unnamed and mysterious spy who observes the
>   events of the story and describes them to the reader

The Story:

Charles Smithson, a London gentleman on vacation in the South of England, went for a walk with his fiancée Ernestina Freeman on the sea ramparts in Lyme Regis on the Dorset coast. They saw a woman in a black coat and bonnet staring seaward from the very end of the quay, who, when warned of the danger, turned and gave Charles such a look of sadness that he never forgot it. He was further fascinated when Ernestina told him the story of the woman, Sarah Woodruff, who, it was rumored, had been seduced and abandoned by a shipwrecked naval officer she had nursed back to health. Since then, she was called "Tragedy" or the "French Lieutenant's Woman," a euphemism for "whore."

The next day, while Charles, an amateur paleontologist, was looking for fossils in an area known as the Undercliff, he once again saw Sarah, sleeping on a ledge beneath the path where he walked, and was struck by her appalling loneliness. When she suddenly woke up, startled, he could only apologize for his intrusion. After she ran away, he followed her and offered to walk her to town, but she refused. On the following day, Charles saw Sarah again when he visited Mrs. Poulteney's, where Sarah had been taken in as a kind of charity case. They shared a look of understanding but did not indicate that they had met.

Later, Charles encountered Sarah on the Undercliff again and offered to help her get away from the self-righteous Mrs. Poulteney, but Sarah refused, leaving Charles puzzled as to what kept her in Lyme Regis. Charles talked to his physician and friend Dr. Grogan about his interest in Sarah, justifying it as only humanitarian, but Dr. Grogan thought it was something more. The next time Charles met with Sarah, she told him that she had not been seduced by the French Lieutenant but had willingly given herself to him in order to free herself from the restraints of Victorian expectations of women. Charles, disillusioned with Ernestina's simplicity and conformity to Victorian conventions, found Sarah puzzling and irresistible.

Sarah asked Charles to meet her one more time. She then purposely got herself discharged by Mrs. Poulteney. When Charles met with Dr. Grogan again and talked to him about Sarah, Dr. Grogan warned him about Sarah's possibly trying to entrap him. Although Charles agreed with Dr. Grogan's advice that Dr. Grogan meet her instead of Charles, he left ahead of Grogan and found Sarah in a barn. Interrupted by his manservant Sam and the maid Mary just as he was about to kiss Sarah, Charles gave her money on which to live. Sarah went to Exeter, took a hotel room, and sent Charles her address. Charles went to London, got drunk, and visited a prostitute, but got sick and vomited when she told him her name was Sarah.

On the way back to Lyme Regis, Charles decided to forget Sarah and return to Ernestina. Charles and Ernestina got married, Charles became a businessman, the couple had children, and Sarah was never heard from again. The narrator says, however, that this is not the real ending of the novel but the one that Charles imagined and the most conventional one according to Victorian standards. What really happened, the narrator says, is that Charles stopped at Exeter and went to Sarah's hotel, where she was expecting him. Sarah subtly seduced Charles into her bed, and he discovered that she had not given herself sexually to the French Lieutenant but was a virgin. Sarah admitted it, telling Charles it was part of her plan to exile herself from conventional expectations, and sent him away. Charles went to a church and suddenly had an insight about Sarah as a real person, not as an ideal.

Charles wrote a letter to Sarah telling her he wanted to marry her, but his servant Sam did not deliver it. Charles broke his engagement with Ernestina and went back to the hotel, only to find Sarah gone. Barely escaping a disastrous legal revenge by Ernestina's father, Charles looked everywhere for Sarah, even going to America, which he discovered was more suitable to his new sense of freedom than England. After a few years of searching, he received word from Sam (who married Mary, worked in a shop, and felt guilty for not having delivered Charles's letter) that Sarah was living in London. Charles found Sarah working as a secretary and model to the famous artist Dante Gabriel Rossetti. Sarah told Charles that she would never marry him, but when he turned to leave, she introduced him to their daughter, Lalage, and they all embraced. The narrator of the novel, who had been watching from across the way, set his watch back fifteen minutes. The reader witnesses, for a second time, the meeting of Charles and Sarah. This time, there was no daughter to reunite them. Although Sarah offered Charles an unmarried relationship, he left her to start his life over again.

Critical Evaluation:

The French Lieutenant's Woman became a best-selling novel both in England and America when it was first published. It was also the novel that made John Fowles's work of interest to academic critics because of its experimentation with narrative structure and style. The book is not only a historical novel, it is also a self-reflexive work about the Victorian novel, on which it is patterned. Although the primary action focuses on a triangle love relationship taking place in 1867, it is clear from the beginning that the narrator of the novel is a twentieth century man familiar with the conventions of the late nineteenth century novel genre as well as the cultural and intellectual changes that have taken place in the one hundred years between 1867 and 1967, when Fowles began writing the novel. Exploiting this historical perspective, the narrator, who places himself within the novel's action, parodies the conventions of the Victorian novel and creates a tension between the past and the present as well as between the nature of reality and the nature of fiction.

Much of the importance of this novel depends on its parody and play with novelistic conventions, including the many asides in which the narrator interferes with and comments on the action. A plot summary of the novel's nineteenth century story does not truly reflect its multilayered structure and sophisticated point of view. Not only does the narrator refer to the action from the perspective of having known such twentieth century figures as Sigmund Freud, Adolf Hitler, and Marshall McLuhan, he purposely places himself—a twentieth-century man— within the story as an observer-voyeur, beginning with the first chapter, when he appears as a spy, looking through a telescope at Charles and Ernestina walking on the quay, and continuing to the last chapter when he sets his watch back fifteen minutes and creates an alternate ending to the novel, so that the book ends both conventionally and unconventionally. At one point in the novel, he even justifies his breaking of the illusion of reality by reminding readers that reality is not so real as they think; they do not even believe that their own past is quite real, he says, for it is dressed up, censored, fictionalized, and put away on a shelf. He concludes that the basic definition of human beings is that they are all in flight from reality.

In addition to the two alternate endings in the last two chapters, the novel also has a third possible ending that occurs in chapter 44, over a hundred pages before the actual conclusion of the book. In this first ending, Charles does not go to Sarah's hotel and end up in her bed. Instead, he goes back to Ernestina and they get married and Charles never hears of Sarah again. The narrator says that although this may be a very traditional ending, it is not what "really" happened, only what Charles imagined happened. Indeed, this first ending is the most conventional ending, satisfying all the Victorian expectations of morality and social responsibility.

The central figure in *The French Lieutenant's Woman* is the mysterious Sarah, although Charles is the character caught in a moral, ethical, and social conflict. The basic question the narrator poses about Sarah is: "Who is Sarah? Out of what shadows does she come?" He says Charles is attracted to her not for herself, but for some emotion or some possibility that she symbolizes, that Sarah is more like a figure from myth than from actuality. Sarah is a symbol of the kind of woman who was not allowed to exist in the Victorian novel or Victorian society, or rather she embodies a kind of wish for a freedom that was not permitted. Sarah creates a fiction in which she may live a reality radically different from that in which society would force her to live. She transforms herself from the conventional Victorian female to a modern woman, cutting herself loose from society by a single act of defiance—an act that is a supreme bit of fiction. She was not, in fact, seduced. Realizing that she has transformed herself from human being to mythic and symbolic embodiment, Sarah says, "I am hardly human any more."

What Sarah symbolizes to Charles is the tension between desire and renunciation. She carries the promise of existential freedom long before Jean-Paul Sartre made that notion a popular one in twentieth century philosophy. The narrator provides an important clue to the basic tension in the novel when he says that Robert Louis Stevenson's *The Strange Case of Dr. Jekyll and Mr. Hyde* (1886) is the guide book for the Victorian period. Conflict between physical desire and social expectations (between what Freud called the id and the superego) is the central theme of the novel. *The French Lieutenant's Woman* is, by extension, also about the unraveling of Victorian society and the beginnings of the modern period. The novel moves thematically from the biological sources of life in the fossils for which Charles searches in the Undercliff to the modern period's remaking of reality by the aesthete as suggested by Sarah's becoming a model for Dante Gabriel Rossetti. In this sense, Sarah is the first modern woman, one who insists on escaping biology and society and making herself in her own image. Similarly, Charles is the first modern man, caught in an existential dilemma before the word "existentialism" was ever coined.

Charles E. May

Bibliography:

Conradi, Peter. *John Fowles*. New York: Methuen, 1982. A general introduction to Fowles's fiction. Brief discussion of the novel's technique and themes.

Huffaker, Robert. *John Fowles*. Boston: Twayne, 1980. A general introduction to Fowles's fiction. Focuses on the intrusive author, the novelist as character, and the alternative Victorian and modern endings of the book.

Olshen, Barry N. *John Fowles*. New York: Frederick Ungar, 1978. An introduction to Fowles's fiction, focusing on the basic themes in *The French Lieutenant's Woman*, including that of the breakup of Victorian culture and the rise of existential modernism.

Palmer, William. *The Fiction of John Fowles: Tradition, Art, and the Loneliness of Selfhood*. Columbia: University of Missouri Press, 1974. Brief discussion of Fowles's fiction, focusing on technique and the novel tradition.

Wolfe, Peter. *John Fowles: Magus and Moralist*. Cranbury, N.J.: Bucknell University Press, 1976. Provides a useful summary of the critical reception of the book and discusses how the mystery of Sarah is crucial.

THE FRENCH REVOLUTION

Type of work: History
Author: Thomas Carlyle (1795-1881)
First published: 1837

Principal personages:
KING LOUIS XV
KING LOUIS XVI
QUEEN MARIE ANTOINETTE
DANTON
MARAT
ROBESPIERRE
TURGOT
NAPOLEON BONAPARTE
COUNT FERSEN, Swedish admirer of Marie Antoinette

The French Revolution is a landmark in the history of nineteenth century English literature, the work that, after the comparative public failure of *Sartor Resartus* (1833-1834), helped to establish Thomas Carlyle. In its dramatic picture of the French Revolution it offers the reader an estimate of an event that had disturbed and shocked the consciences of Carlyle's grandparents. It offers a measure of revolutionary and socially disruptive narrative but it is neither optimistic and blindly trustful of progress (here Carlyle differed from Utilitarian friends) nor pessimistic and horrified, as Edmund Burke had been at the time of the revolution. Finally, and perhaps most important for readers, *The French Revolution* is a more successful self-realization for Carlyle than the comparatively nebulous explorations of ideas in *Sartor Resartus*. That earlier work presents Carlyle's ideas in a kind of cloud formation that conceals whatever terrain of fact and real human experience they float over; *The French Revolution* presents the same ideas brought into relation to and supported by a bewilderingly rich body of facts: the day-by-day events of the disturbing French years.

Impressive as Carlyle's method of digesting and arranging the body of facts is, still more memorable is the way he musters them in a readable narrative. Like an Old Testament prophet, Carlyle rides the hurricane and directs the storm of the fall of absolute monarchy in France. He produces not simply another history of a vexed period, full of rationalized information. It is true of Carlyle that his view of one period of history is always on the verge of becoming a vision of all human history. The French women who march on Versailles stand for the passionate outbreak of all oppressed human beings, and the sorrows of Marie Antoinette in the Conciergerie stand for the agonies of all trivial human beings carried to their doom by forces they cannot control.

It is possible to indicate some of the means that Carlyle employs to create his apocalyptic vision—a vision, not of last things, but certainly of the forces that combine to drive history onward. The arrangement of the facts is rigorously chronological. The book begins with the death-pangs of King Louis XV; these are represented as the death-throes not simply of one aged monarch but of a regime that once justified itself but that has become a hollow shell. The book continues with an account of the suicidal follies of the young king, Louis XVI, and his pretty and thoughtless wife, Marie Antoinette. It notes the efforts of some of the king's ministers, Necker, Turgot, and others, to stem the advancing tide: to restore financial soundness and yet provide money for all who thought they had a right to spend it. Carlyle, often with a somewhat uneven pace, one that permits him to stop for angry or compassionate meditation when he wishes to point out the "inevitable" chain of disaster and struggle, continues his year-by-year and month-by-month account. He tells of the meeting of the Estates General, the Tennis Court Oath, the march on Versailles, the various attempts to frame a constitution, the degeneration of the relation between the royal couple and the Revolutionary Government, the royal family's attempted escape to Varennes, the successive decapitations of king and queen, the succession of leaders who could not lead but had to dictate by harangue and outright terror, and, finally, the end of the revolution at the hands of Napoleon Bonaparte, who brought order with a "whiff of grapeshot."

Carlyle, at the end of his work, speaks of a ship that finally is over the bar after much labor and peril from counter winds; and this is certainly the effect of his narrative. Despite its complexity, his story is the single account of a set of events that gives a full demonstration of the glories and horrors of revolution, a period of history that was inevitable but not, because of its inevitability, admirable.

In dramatizing a mighty and perilous passage that involved not the French nation alone but all humanity, Thomas Carlyle was able to transform his account of actual events into an apocalyptic statement about humanity that does not seem to belong to any particular time at all. He did so by means of his style of presentation and by passages of direct, explicit interpretation. Perhaps it is the style that is most decisive. Never before or since has a historian writing in English written a book like this history of Carlyle's. The narrative is couched in the present tense, wearing but hortatory; what occurs happens not in a safely distant past, but here and now. The sentimentality of the French philosophes and the ignorant and brutal enthusiasms of the mob threaten us the readers, as Carlyle drags readers through mountains of detail and event. Moreover, Carlyle frequently interrupts the forward movement of the narrative to harangue some of the chief actors in his story—Danton, Mirabeau, Marie Antoinette—and as readers read it seems possible that they may listen to him and escape what readers well know was their historical fate. Some of the harangues, of course, speak not to the historical personages but to readers and suggest that readers (even more than a century after the appearance of the book) may escape their historical fate, whatever it may be, if readers will but listen to Thomas Carlyle. Or if readers may not escape it, readers will understand it better after reading *The French Revolution.*

Implication becomes explicit in innumerable passages like the following brief one:

> Or, apart from all Transcendentalism, is it not a plain truth of sense, which the duller mind can even consider as a truism, that human things wholly are in continual movement, and action and reaction; working continually forward, phasis after phasis, by unalterable laws, towards prescribed issues? How often must readers say, and yet not rightly lay to heart: The seed that is sown, it will spring! Given the summer's blossoming, then there is also given the autumnal withering: so is it ordered not with seedfields only, but with transactions, arrangements, philosophies, societies, French Revolutions, whatsoever man works with in this lower world.

A great body of French fact attests what the drifting clouds of *Sartor Resartus* suggested. It is the law of life that social forms become old clothes unless they are worn by the people who have some kind of faith: faith in duty, faith in silent work, faith in, finally, the transcendental, self-realizing movement of some force, some kind of deity which is realizing itself in the movements of human history and particularly in the great persons who rise above themselves and command the attention of the rest of humanity, pointing a finger to show the way all should go.

Carlyle devoted later books to such demonstration. Oliver Cromwell, Frederick the Great, and a whole company of great men in *On Heroes and Hero-Worship* (1841)—all of these so exhort. The essential tragedy of the French Revolution, as Carlyle saw it, was that in it was a congeries of events that cried out for a hero and found only destruction and social chaos. It lacked, among other things, a contemporary such as Carlyle to annotate that chaos. The French people's loss, however, is the readers' gain. Upon their agonies Carlyle rests a view of history as a scroll of events always on the verge of parting and revealing to readers—in the heavens or in the depths of their beings—the essential divine plan.

Bibliography:

Clubbe, John. "Carlyle as Epic Historian." In *Victorian Literature and Society*, edited by James R. Kincaid. Columbus: Ohio State University Press, 1984. Carlyle's reading of the *Iliad* in 1834 transformed his vision of what history could become. *The French Revolution*, subsequently, was envisioned as an epic.

Rosenberg, John D. "Carlyle and Historical Narration." *The Carlyle Annual* 10 (Spring, 1989): 14-20. Treats *The French Revolution* as an experiment in narrative form, an attempt to create a relevant literary structure.

Roy, G. Ross. "The French Reputation of Thomas Carlyle in the Nineteenth Century." In *Thomas Carlyle 1981: Papers Given at the International Thomas Carlyle Centenary Symposium*, edited by Horst W. Drescher. Frankfurt: Lang, 1983. Carlyle's relationship with Germany is well known, but his book on the French Revolution brought him to the attention of French readers. It was the first of his books to be translated.

Ryals, Clyde de L. "Carlyle's *The French Revolution*: A 'True Fiction.'" *English Literary History* 54, no. 4 (Winter, 1987): 925-940. Scholars have had trouble deciding on *The French Revolution*'s genre. Some see it as an epic, some as a tragedy. Argues that the work is romantic, with many genres intermingled.

Timko, Michael. "Splendid Impressions and Picturesque Means: Dickens, Carlyle, and the French Revolution." *Dickens Studies Annual* 12 (1983): 177-195. Examines the influence of *The French Revolution* on Dickens. Shows the dominance of Carlyle's notions of history as prophecy and history as vignettes of the lives and characters of individuals.

FRIAR BACON AND FRIAR BUNGAY

Type of work: Drama
Author: Robert Greene (1558-1592)
Type of plot: Historical
Time of plot: Thirteenth century
Locale: England
First performed: c. 1589; first published, 1594

> *Principal characters:*
> HENRY III, king of England
> EDWARD, prince of Wales
> LACY, earl of Lincoln
> ROGER BACON, a Franciscan friar
> BUNGAY, a Suffolk conjurer
> JAQUES VANDERMAST, a German conjurer
> ELINOR, princess of Castile
> MARGARET, daughter of the Keeper of Fressingfield Park

The Story:

When Prince Edward returned from hunting in a downcast mood, Lacy remarked on his lord's temper. It remained for Ralph, the court fool, to hit on the truth. The hunting party had stopped for refreshments at the keeper's lodge in Fressingfield Park, and Prince Edward had fallen in love with Margaret, the keeper's daughter.

Plans were laid to win Margaret's love for Edward, but the maid was modest and would keep her virtue for her husband. Ralph proposed that Edward should dress in the jester's motley, and Ralph should dress as the prince. They would then go to Oxford and enlist the help of Friar Roger Bacon, since only magic would win over the girl. Lacy was to go to the fair at Harleston to spy on Margaret there and to press a suit on behalf of the prince.

At Oxford, Friar Bacon and his poor scholar Miles received a deputation of learned doctors. Burden, their spokesman, asked about certain rumors they had heard. It was said that Friar Bacon had fashioned a great head of brass and with it he was going to raise a wall of brass around all of England. Bacon admitted that he planned such a project. Burden doubted whether even Friar Bacon could accomplish such a mighty deed.

To demonstrate his power, Friar Bacon had a devil bring a tavern hostess from Henley, a woman with whom Burden had spent the previous day. Thus the doctors were convinced of Bacon's powers. At Harleston, Lacy approached Margaret. Although the earl was dressed as a farmer, his manners were so elegant that Margaret was attracted to him. Lacy had a mind to press a suit in his own behalf.

At court, meanwhile, King Henry received the king of Castile, his daughter Elinor, and the Emperor of Germany. Negotiations were under way to betroth Elinor to Prince Edward. The princess, having seen a portrait of Edward, was much inclined to love the prince. The emperor had brought with him a German conjurer, Vandermast, to test his powers against the wise men of England. The royal party departed for Oxford to find Friar Bacon.

With the jester disguised as the prince and Edward disguised as a gentleman in waiting, the prince's party met the friar and Miles at Oxford. An argument developed between Miles and the others. To save his scholar, Friar Bacon froze Edward's sword in its scabbard. After rebuking the prince for trying to disguise himself, he invited Edward into his cell. There he let the prince look into a magic glass which showed Margaret and Lacy at Fressingfield.

Friar Bungay was revealing the secret of Lacy's identity to Margaret as Edward watched from afar. Margaret was troubled, for she had fallen in love with Lacy. When Lacy entered, he declared at once his desire to wed Margaret. Friar Bungay was about to perform the ceremony on the spot, but the anguished prince called on Friar Bacon to stop the wedding. The friar obliged by striking Bungay mute and whisking him away to Oxford.

Edward, posting to Fressingfield in great haste, charged Lacy with treachery and threatened to kill him. Lacy admitted his guilt and prepared to submit, but Margaret pleaded valiantly for the cause of true love and begged Edward to kill her instead. Edward, marveling at his own weakness, changed his mind and gave his permission for Lacy to marry Margaret.

At Oxford, the emperor of Germany had Vandermast dispute with Friar Bungay. Bungay conjured up the tree that guarded the Garden at Hesperides. In return Vandermast brought in Hercules and commanded him to tear the branches from the tree. Triumphantly the German challenged Friar Bungay to make Hercules stop, but Bungay had to admit that he was vanquished. When Friar Bacon arrived, Hercules, to the emperor's chagrin, ceased his task immediately for fear of Bacon. To demonstrate the eminence of Oxford, Friar Bacon then forced Hercules to transport Vandermast back to Hapsburg.

Two squires came to seek the hand of Margaret. Both were wealthy and insistent, and the keeper asked his daughter to choose between them. Margaret was evasive and put off her answer for ten days, because she was sure Lacy would return by that time. After the squires left, a messenger came with a letter and a sack of gold. In the letter Margaret read that Lacy had chosen to marry a Spanish lady-in-waiting to Princess Elinor, and he sent the gold as a dowry for her own wedding. In great grief, Margaret gave the gold to the messenger and vowed to enter a convent.

Working in his cell, Friar Bacon was at the climax of his experiments, for he had completed with much labor the brazen head. Tired from wrestling with spirits, he lay down to sleep. Miles was to watch the head and wake his master as soon as it should speak. During the night the head made a great noise and said, "Time is." Thinking those words unimportant, Miles rested on. The head made more noise and said, "Time was." Again Miles did not arouse the friar. A third time the head spoke: "Time has been." Lightning flashed and a great hand appeared and broke the head with a hammer.

Then Miles awoke Friar Bacon, who knew at once that the blundering Miles had ruined his work. No wall of brass would ever surround England. In his wrath the friar sent Miles to wander homeless with a devil to torment him. After he left Oxford, however, Miles made the best of a bad situation. He got on the devil's back and went with him to Hell, where he was engaged as a tapster.

King Henry and the king of Castile were both pleased that Elinor and Edward had made a match. Lacy, thinking still of Margaret, spoke so persuasively of her beauty that the king sanctioned their marriage as well. Elinor was particularly gracious in suggesting a double wedding. The happy Lacy set out for Fressingfield to seek his bride.

Friar Bacon broke the sad news of the brazen head to Friar Bungay. As he finished his tale, two young scholars came in to ask permission to look into Friar Bacon's glass; they wanted to see what their fathers were doing. The fathers, who were the two squires seeking Margaret's hand, were fighting a duel. As the sons watched, the squires were stabbed to death. The sons then fought and each mortally wounded the other. In sorrow, Friar Bacon broke his magic glass.

In spite of her father's remonstrances, Margaret was preparing to enter a nunnery when Lacy rode up to claim his bride. Reproached for his cruel letter, he explained he had written it to test her constancy. Margaret, yielding to his entreaties, accompanied him back to court. The double wedding was solemnized with royal pomp. Before the wedding feast Friar Bacon made a prophecy of the future of England. He foresaw a period of triumph and peace under a fair ruler who would exalt the glory of England over all other nations. Not understanding that reference to Queen Elizabeth, Henry called the prophecy mystical and led the guests to the dining hall.

Critical Evaluation:

Friar Bacon and Friar Bungay, a comical history play by Robert Greene, is his most enduring work. It combines the romanticism and realism that are his hallmarks. The precise date of the play (although 1589-1590 is most likely) is unknown, so the play's relationship with Christopher Marlowe's *Doctor Faustus* (1604) is unclear. Was Greene or Marlowe the borrower who drew upon the recent success of a fellow dramatist's conjuring play? Whichever came first, both works cater to the Elizabethans' curiosity about magic and sorcery, delight in theatrical horseplay, and pleasure in seeing ordinary people rise to power and influence. *Friar Bacon and Friar Bungay*, like *Doctor Faustus*, was frequently revived in the 1590's, two of many conjuring plays of the period.

Greene's main source was a mid-sixteenth century anonymous prose romance. The events in his drama of thirteenth century England are fictional, but there actually was a Roger Bacon at that time who allegedly practiced black magic at Oxford University (Greene's alma mater) and around whom legends developed. Despite Bacon's title, Bacon does not function as a churchman in the play, but is more like Merlin, the patriotic Arthurian sorcerer. Bacon's repentance speech late in the play reflects prevailing Elizabethan beliefs. Bacon's dalliances, however, unlike those of Faustus, are not frightening and do not lead to damnation, although they do cause deaths.

Noteworthy about *Friar Bacon and Friar Bungay* is how it brings together royalty, nobility, and commoners, preserving some traditional class barriers but breaking through others. Greene's idealistic portrait of a benevolently democratic aristocracy may reflect the outburst of patriotism in England following the 1588 defeat of the Spanish Armada. Also indicative of this national-istic theme are Bacon's plan to build a protective brass wall around England and his humiliation of the German emperor's necromancer Jaques Vandermast.

Multiple plots are commonplace in Elizabethan comedies, and Greene's play is typical in this regard. Half of it is devoted to a presentation of Bacon's prodigious powers, which his foolish servant Miles partially thwarts. In his first appearance, with the visiting group of doubtful scholars, Bacon boasts of his skills. This prideful display announces his later troubles, but the magician does prove himself by evoking the devil and transporting the hostess of a pub to his cell. Later, he strikes his rival Bungay mute (to prevent him from marrying Lacy and Margaret). Then Bacon joins with Bungay in a conjuring contest against foreigners and commands the spirit of Hercules to carry Vandermast back to Germany. Bacon's one act of damnation is directed at Miles after the servant's ineptness destroys the friar's life work. When the devil comes for him, Miles, rather than being afraid, delights in the singular experience. The other half of the play revolves about the fair maid Margaret of Fressingfield, her multiple suitors, her loyalty to her love, and Prince Edward's magnanimity.

Edward at the start of the play is lovesick for Margaret, but seduction, not marriage, is his aim. Inhibited by his royal position, he relies upon his fool, Ralph, and friend, Lacy, to advance his cause. When the plan fails, Edward denounces Lacy and Margaret but almost immediately reverses himself, recognizing his royal position and offering to give away Margaret in a wedding that will make her countess of Lincoln.

Friar Bacon and Friar Bungay is not as formless as it sometimes is said to be. The halves are linked by the presence of Bacon in both plots, but there are other, more important, parallels. The love story moves from joy through sadness to happiness, and the Bacon plot progresses from great heights to disaster and tragedy (the deaths of the suitors and their fathers) but again to joy. Further, in both plots, exceptional gifts (Bacon's magical abilities and Margaret's outstanding beauty) lead to misery which causes each to renounce the gift (he forsakes his magic, and she joins a convent). The play is a comedy, however, so everyone eventually is reconciled, and the last scene celebrates a double marriage and restoration of the natural order.

The critical assessment that Margaret is the first realistically portrayed and thoroughly believable female character in English drama has been superseded by the judgment that she is little more than a patient Griselda type. As such, substantive development of her personality would have been superfluous. She remains an interesting character. Her father respects her judgment regarding Lacy, deferring to her when the rival suitors—Lambert and Serlsby—ask him for her hand in marriage. She buys time with the rivals but later acts quickly—deciding to become a nun—after receiving Lacy's letter with news of his intention to marry another. When he comes to the convent, reveals that he only meant to test her, and asks her to marry, she renounces her vocation and agrees. Margaret's impulsiveness and the prince's sudden turnabout are not wholly credible, but these actions are in harmony with the rest of *Friar Bacon and Friar Bungay*, a romantic, not realistic, comedy.

"Critical Evaluation" by Gerald H. Strauss

Bibliography:

Clemen, Wolfgang. *English Tragedy Before Shakespeare: The Development of Dramatic Speech.* Translated by T. S. Dorsch. New York: Barnes & Noble Books, 1961. Concludes that the playwright does not maintain a "free and easy style," though he does praise the language of Miles and Simnel as being "robust and realistic."

Empson, William. *Some Versions of Pastoral.* New York: New Directions, 1974. This classic study shows that through the characterizations of Bacon and Margaret the playwright succeeds in developing a literary metaphor that likens magic and beauty and thus unifies the two plots.

Greene, Robert. *Friar Bacon and Friar Bungay.* Edited by Daniel Seltzer. Lincoln: University of Nebraska Press, 1963. Deals with such matters as the problem of dating the play, Greene's use of his source, and occult science in the Renaissance.

Muir, Kenneth. "Robert Greene as Dramatist." In *Essays on Shakespeare and Elizabethan Drama in Honor of Hardin Craig,* edited by Richard Hosley. Columbia: University of Missouri Press, 1962. Thinks Greene excelled as a prose writer, but respects the plotting of the play and shows how magic unifies it.

Parrott, Thomas Marc, and Robert Hamilton Ball. *A Short View of Elizabethan Drama.* New York: Charles Scribner's Sons, 1943. An analysis of *Friar Bacon and Friar Bungay* that subsequent criticism has not yet superseded.

FRITHIOF'S SAGA

Type of work: Poetry
Author: Esaias Tegnér (1782-1846)
Type of plot: Epic
Time of plot: Eleventh century
Locale: Scandinavia
First published: Frithiofs saga, 1825 (English translation, 1835)

Principal characters:
FRITHIOF, a Viking adventurer and fighter
INGEBORG, a noblewoman loved by Frithiof
HELGE and
HALFDAN, brother kings in Scandinavia
HRING, a petty king married to Ingeborg

The Story:

In the ancient days of Scandinavia there was a king named Bele, who had two sons, Helge and Halfdan. King Bele also had a daughter, Ingeborg, who was very beautiful. As King Bele grew old and near death, he called to him his friend of former days, Thorsten Vikingsson, who had been loyal to the king in peace and battle for many years and who was also near the end of his days. The king told his sons of the help that Thorsten Vikingsson had given him in past days and warned his sons to keep the friendship of Thorsten's son, Frithiof.

Frithiof had grown up with the companionship of King Bele's daughter Ingeborg and her brothers. After the deaths of King Bele and old Thorsten, who were both laid to rest in burial mounds overlooking a fjord, the sons of Bele forgot the warning that their father had given them, and their friendship toward Frithiof cooled. When Frithiof, who had long loved Ingeborg, sued for her hand from her brothers, they refused his request. Frithiof, angered and humiliated, vowed that he would find his revenge and that he never would carry out his father's request to help the brother kings.

Not long thereafter, when King Hring made war upon the brothers, they sent for Frithiof to help them. Frithiof, remembering his vows, continued to play at chess and ignored their summons. King Hring, successful in his campaign against the sons of Bele, made them promise to give him Ingeborg as his wife. Meanwhile, Ingeborg had taken refuge in the temple of Balder. Frithiof, disdainful of the sanctity of the temple, had visited her there, where they exchanged rings. Frithiof thus ran the risk of Balder's wrath.

To punish him for violating the temple, the brother kings sent Frithiof to collect tribute from the inhabitants of the Faroe Islands. Frithiof, with his foster brother, set sail for the Faroes in *Ellida*, the best ship in the North country. It was said of *Ellida* that it could even understand human speech.

During the trip a violent storm came up and the ship almost foundered. Frithiof broke the ring he had received from Ingeborg and gave the shards to his men, so that none of the crew might enter the kingdom of the sea-goddess without gold. When the storm subsided, as it did after the men had conquered a pair of sea-spirits who rode against them on the backs of whales, the ship reached the Faroe Islands in safety. Yarl Angantyr, ruler of the islands, let the tribute be collected, and then Frithiof departed again for his homeland in Scandinavia.

Upon his return Frithiof heard that the brother kings had burned his hall. Learning that the kings were celebrating the midsummer feast at the grove of Balder, he went there to confront them. Upon his arrival he found few people, but among them were Helge and his queen, who was anointing the image of the god.

Frithiof threw the purse with the tribute money into Helge's face with such force that Helge's teeth were knocked out. As Frithiof turned to leave, he saw on the arm of Helge's queen the great ring of gold he had given to Ingeborg when they had exchanged vows. Frithiof snatched the ring from the queen's arm, and when she fell to the ground because of his violence, the god's image overturned into the sacred fire which, blazing up, destroyed the temple.

Helge pursued Frithiof to punish him, but pursuit was impossible because the royal ships had been damaged by Frithiof and his men. In his anger Frithiof pulled with such might upon the oars of his ship that its powerful oars broke like kindling. Frithiof's violence against Helge and his queen and the profanation of Balder's temple made the warrior an outcast from his homeland. A true son of the Vikings, he took to the sea and battled with haughty sea-kings, whom he slew. In spite of his outlawry he permitted traders to travel the seaways unmolested. When he earned great glory as a fighter and much gold through his exploits, Frithiof sought once again to return to his homeland in the North.

Disguising himself as a salt-burner, he visited the land of the brother kings' enemy, King Hring, who had long since married Ingeborg, Frithiof's beloved. Hring, recognizing Frithiof but not mentioning it, commanded that the warrior be seated next to him at the head of the table. Frithiof remained in the hall of King Hring. Ingeborg, who also recognized Frithiof, spoke but little to him, because she was now the wife of another man. She remembered that she and Frithiof had once exchanged rings, and she was still in love with him.

During his stay with Hring, Frithiof saved the king and Ingeborg from death when their sleigh fell through the ice and went under the water. Frithiof dragged the sleigh, with its occupants and horses, back onto the surface of the ice. One day, while he and the king were alone in the woods, Frithiof was tempted to kill Hring while he slept, but he conquered his temptation and threw away his sword. Awaking, the king told Frithiof, who was still disguised, that he had known from the first night who his guest was.

Frithiof wished to leave the household of Hring, but the good king would not allow him to depart. Instead, Hring gave up Ingeborg to Frithiof and made the warrior guardian of the kingdom. Soon afterward Hring died and Frithiof was named to follow him upon the throne. When Helge and Halfdan, the brother kings, went to war against their old enemy, they were defeated. Helge was slain in battle by Frithiof, and Halfdan was made to swear fealty to his conqueror.

Critical Evaluation:

A tale of ancient Scandinavia, *Frithiof's Saga* is told in a modern spirit by Esaias Tegnér. The old story is in a narrative poem of twenty-four cantos, each canto done in a different meter. Frithiof himself is more akin to a modern hero than he is to the great warriors of other Scandinavian tales. Tegnér's effort is similar to that of Tennyson, in that he attempts to shape the epic material of an ancient Norse story into nineteenth century poetic form. Although the poem lacks the simplicity and power of old Norse poetry, the imagery is memorable and the lyricism sweet and beautiful. Tegnér's long narrative poem displays an odd sort of virtuosity: The poem remains faithful to its ancient ancestor in theme and narrative detail, yet it is made up of a curious blend of Scandinavian and English images and rhetorical devices, in twenty-four different meters.

Through forces beyond their control, Frithiof's beloved marries another, King Hring. The hero gallantly respects the marriage, and the king to whom his beloved is married, by maintaining the proper courtly distance. However, *Frithiof's Saga* does not end tragically. Through Hring's benevolence, Frithiof and Ingeborg are reunited and Frithiof satisfies his pride against the brother kings. The magnificent reconciliation canto, rendered by Tegnér in blank verse, evokes the grandeur of Norse mythology and the theme of atonement.

Frithiof's Saga provided Tegnér with the opportunity to employ a pastiche of images and rhetorical devices. His rendering of each canto in a different meter demonstrates both virtuosity and preoccupation with the surfaces of poetry. Virtuosity for its own sake is no virtue, and it is regrettable that Tegnér did not choose to render his poem in a less obtrusive and more unified manner, for he elevates style at the expense of content. Tegnér's use of imagery raises further concerns. For example, readers find the Norse blood-and-guts warrior amid Elizabethan roses and the lilies, nightingale, and vanished dreams of the English Romantics. There are two or three obvious thefts from William Shakespeare, and perhaps another from Percy Bysshe Shelley. It may be that the Swedish poet wished to align his narrative poem with the English literary tradition. *Frithiof's Saga* was enormously successful, becoming something of the poem of Swedish people. It has been translated and read around the world.

Bibliography:
Brandes, Georg Morris Cohen, and Rasmus Bjorn Anderson. *Creative Spirits of the Nineteenth Century.* New York: Thomas Y. Crowell, 1923. Pages 107-183 provide a somewhat dated but accessible discussion of Tegnér and his works. Places *Frithiof's Saga* in its literary context.
Hilen, Andrew R. *Longfellow and Scandinavia: A Study of the Poet's Relationship.* New Haven, Conn.: Yale University Press, 1947. Explains the relationship of Henry Wadsworth Longfellow and Tegnér. Argues that Tegnér was influential in the development of Longfellow's poetry.

THE FROGS

Type of work: Drama
Author: Aristophanes (c. 450-c. 385 B.C.E.)
Type of plot: Satire
Time of plot: Fifth century B.C.E.
Locale: Underworld
First performed: Batrachoi, 405 B.C.E. (English translation, 1780)

Principal characters:
  BACCHUS, the god of wine and revelry
  XANTHIAS, his slave
  HERCULES, the mythological hero
  CHARON, the ferryman of Hades
  EURIPIDES, a famous Greek playwright
  AESCHYLUS, another Greek dramatist

The Story:

Wishing to visit the underworld, Bacchus set out with his slave, Xanthias, to visit Hercules, from whom the god of wine hoped to get directions for his visit to the lower regions. On the way, Xanthias grumbled and moaned about his many bundles. Xanthias was actually being carried on a donkey, but he complained until Bacchus lost patience and suggested that perhaps Xanthias would like to carry the donkey for a while.

Hercules, when consulted, suggested that Bacchus allow himself to be killed in order to arrive in the land of the dead. Bacchus wanted to go there alive because he was anxious to see and talk to the great playwrights; the critics had told him that all good writers were dead and gone. He was particularly anxious to meet Euripides. Hercules advised him to be content with the playwrights who were still alive. Bacchus argued that none of them was good enough. After getting directions from Hercules, he started out, Xanthias still complaining about his bundles.

They came to the River Acheron and met Charon, who ferried Bacchus across, insisting, however, that Bacchus row the boat; Xanthias had to walk around the margin of the stream because he had dishonored himself by not volunteering for a naval victory. Xanthias tried to excuse himself on the grounds that he had had sore eyes, but Charon refused to listen.

While Bacchus and Xanthias talked to Charon, a chorus of frogs set up a hoarse croaking, imitating the noisy plebeians at the theater with their senseless hooting. Bacchus sprained his back with his rowing and the frogs thought his groans quite amusing.

Safely on the other side, Bacchus paid his fare and joined his slave. The two met a monster, which Bacchus took care to avoid until it turned into a beautiful woman. With difficulty, they found their way to the doorway of Pluto's realm, Xanthias still grumbling because of his heavy bundles.

At the entrance to Hades, Bacchus foolishly pretended to be Hercules—a mistake on his part, for Aeacus, the doorman, raised a clamor over the theft of Cerberus, the watchdog. When Aeacus threatened all sorts of punishments, Bacchus revealed who he really was. Xanthias accused him of cowardice, but Bacchus stoutly denied the charge.

Bacchus and Xanthias decided to change characters. Xanthias pretended to be Hercules and Bacchus took up the bundles his slave had carried. When, however, servants of Proserpine entered and offered Xanthias a fine entertainment, Bacchus demanded his legitimate character back.

Aeacus returned, eager to punish someone, and Xanthias gave him permission to beat Bacchus. Bacchus said that he was a deity and that he should therefore not be beaten. Xanthias countered by saying that since Bacchus was an immortal he need not mind the beating. Aeacus decided they both should be beaten soundly, and he finally decided to take them both to Pluto and Proserpine, to discover who was the deity. Aeacus said Bacchus was apparently a gentleman, and Xanthias agreed wholeheartedly, saying Bacchus did not do anything except dissipate and carouse.

In Pluto's realm, they found two dead dramatists, Aeschylus and Euripides, fighting for favor. The rule in Hades was that the most famous man of any art or craft ate at Pluto's table until some more talented man in his field died and came to Hades. Aeschylus had held the seat Euripides was now claiming.

Aeacus said that the dramatists intended to measure their plays line for line by rules and compasses to determine the superior craftsman. The quarreling dramatists debated, accusing each of the other's faults. Aeschylus said he was at a disadvantage because Euripides' plays died with him and were present to help him, whereas his own plays still lived on earth.

Bacchus offered to be the judge, whereupon each dramatist began to defend himself. In the midst of their violent quarrel, Pluto appeared. Bacchus ordered each to recite from his own works. Euripides seemed to have the worst of this contest, but Bacchus wisely refused to judge so as not to make either playwright angry with him. Pluto wearily insisted that he pick one winner and take his choice back with him to the upper world in order to stop needless rivalry in Hades.

At last, Bacchus voted for Aeschylus. Euripides complained at the choice. He was consoled, however, when Pluto said he might be sure of a good meal in the underworld, while Aeschylus would be burdened forever with the task of earning his living by his attempts to reform folly and evil in the world above.

Critical Evaluation:

The Frogs is deservedly one of the best-known plays of Aristophanes. It took the first prize for comedy on first being presented, and continued over the centuries to retain much of its freshness and exuberance. As a depiction of the foibles and follies of men and gods alike, the play is great satirical fun. The high point of the comedy, however, is the witty debate between Aeschylus and Euripides as to which of them produced the better tragedies. Some knowledge is desirable of Aristophanes' opinions and the times in which he lived, of the Athenian crisis at the end of the Peloponnesian War, and of Aeschylus and Euripides.

The play starts with the absurdity that Bacchus braves the terrors of the underworld to bring Euripides back to life. On this conceit Aristophanes builds a farcical sequence of situations all of which defy reason or probability. It is important to know that shortly before Aristophanes wrote *The Frogs*, *The Bacchae* (405 B.C.E.), Euripides' last play, was produced, in which Euripides portrayed Bacchus (Dionysus), who is both the god of wine and the god of the theater, as a powerful, mysterious, fearless, and vengeful being. It is therefore all the funnier that Aristophanes shows him as a weak, pedestrian, cowardly, and pacific god who is obviously flattered by Euripides and wants him brought back to life to continue the praise. The humor of the first half of *The Frogs* is devoted to exposing Bacchus as a fraud and, by implication, Euripides himself. *The Bacchae* was awarded first prize, posthumously; and the chorus of frogs in Aristophanes' comedy represents the popular clamor that greeted Euripides' play.

Having thoroughly routed Bacchus, Aristophanes brings Euripides and Aeschylus on stage to engage in comic debate. Euripides is depicted as an upstart in Hades. Recently dead, he tries to wrest the chair of honor from Aeschylus. Obviously, Aristophanes regarded Euripides as a base-born upstart in life as well, for the tragedian also appeared as a farcical character in *The Acharnians* (425 B.C.E.) and *The Thesmophoriazusae* (411 B.C.E.), and he was made the butt of numerous jokes in other plays. The antagonism was largely due to Aristophanes' snobbery and conservatism, for he prided himself on coming from landed gentry.

Aristophanes thought that Euripides was partly responsible for the decline in Athenian politics and morality. There is no question that Euripides used tragedy to turn a light on current social issues and effect changes. This is the heart of the matter: The comic poet propagandized for conservatism, while the tragic poet urged reform. The importance of drama in Athenian life cannot be overemphasized. Public oratory and the theater were the only media, the only means of conveying propaganda to large audiences. Aristophanes' comments against Euripides are far more than mere fun or the prejudices of a clever conservative; in actuality they were part of a battle to control public opinion.

Some of the charges Aristophanes makes against Euripides in *The Frogs* could be leveled at himself as well. Impiety, near-colloquial verse, sordid passions, and characters who reasoned sophistically without any sincerity are all a part of his comic art. What Euripides had done in essence was to lessen the difference between tragedy and comedy; but what Aristophanes could not forgive was that Euripides tended to be a left-wing social reformer, tearing away at established institutions.

The truth is that Athenian politics and life did degenerate during Euripides' long career, but it would be as foolish to blame it on him as on Aristophanes. The real villains were those who initiated the Peloponnesian War and kept it going for twenty-seven years.

The Frogs can be read as a literary, social, or political tract by a very amusing dramatist. On the literary level, Euripides pokes fun at Aeschylus' bombast and theatricality, while Aeschylus ridicules Euripides' commonness of diction. When Aeschylus' lines of poetry are weighed against those of Euripides, the latter is shown quite literally to be a lightweight talent. Socially, Aeschylus is made to represent the old, heroic, patriotic virtues of Athens, whereas Euripides stands for the degenerate contemporary society. Aristophanes hints that Euripides comes of lower-class people, and he states openly that his audience in Hades consists of felons, who love his sophistries.

Nevertheless, it is on the political plane that Aristophanes really indicts Euripides, suggesting that the demagogues learned their twisting logic from Euripides. In fact, the contest between Aeschylus and Euripides is finally settled over who offers the best advice politically. In this, Aeschylus wins hands down, and he is taken back to earth by Bacchus to teach the Athenians virtue. Aristophanes had no intention of playing fair. To him Euripides represented everything corrupt in Athenian society. Moreover, *The Frogs* was written in a time of crisis, when it was clear to many that Athens either had to make peace with Sparta or be ruled by her. The Peloponnesian War had yet one more year to go. In the middle of the play, Aristophanes makes a direct political plea to the audience, trying to convince Athenians so that they might avoid defeat. The wonder is that, given the author's bias and the times in which it was written, *The Frogs* should be one of the most delightful comedies of any age.

"Critical Evaluation" by James Weigel, Jr.

Bibliography:
Bowie, A. M. *Aristophanes: Myth, Ritual, and Comedy.* New York: Cambridge University Press, 1993. Presents criticism and interpretation of the mythic and ritualistic content of

Aristophanes' comedies. Drawing from examples such as Dionysus' and Heracles' presence in *The Frogs*, Bowie considers the importance of mythology in Aristophanes' comedic plays in particular and in Greek drama in general.

Dover, Kenneth, ed. Introduction to *The Frogs*. New York: Oxford University Press, 1993. Dover's essay and commentary, which accompany Aristophanes' original text, offer a comprehensive overview of the structure and significance of the play.

Harriott, Rosemary M. *Aristophanes, Poet and Dramatist*. Baltimore, Md.: The Johns Hopkins University Press, 1986. Offers criticism and interpretation of Aristophanes' poems and plays. Sets *The Frogs* in the context of such other works as *The Clouds* (423 B.C.E.), *The Knights* (424 B.C.E.), and *The Birds* (414 B.C.E.).

Littlefield, David J., ed. *Twentieth Century Interpretations of "The Frogs": A Collection of Critical Essays*. Englewood Cliffs, N.J.: Prentice-Hall, 1968. A collection of analytical papers examining Aristophanes' *The Frogs* in terms of style, characterization, dramatic theory, symbolism, and structure. Provides a spectrum of interpretations on the work's position in literature from classical times to the present.

Whitman, Cedric Hubbell. *Aristophanes and the Comic Hero*. Cambridge, Mass.: Harvard University Press, 1964. Explores Aristophanes' construction of heroes in his comedic plays and provides an overview of Aristophanic comedy. Considers the dramatist's lampooning of such contemporary figures in Greek society as the playwrights Euripides and Aeschylus in *The Frogs*.

THE FRUIT OF THE TREE

Type of work: Novel
Author: Edith Wharton (1862-1937)
Type of plot: Social realism
Time of plot: Late nineteenth century
Locale: United States
First published: 1907

> *Principal characters:*
> JOHN AMHERST, an assistant mill manager
> BESSY WESTMORE, his first wife and owner of the mills
> JUSTINE BRENT, his second wife
> MR. LANGHOPE, Bessy's father
> DR. WYANT, Justine's former suitor

The Story:

When Justine Brent, a nurse who was visiting Mrs. Harry Dressel at Hanaford, volunteered to care for Dillon, an operator who had been injured at Westmore Mills, she was approached by John Amherst, the assistant manager of the mills. Amherst deplored the miserable living and working conditions of the mill workers and, since Dillon's accident had been the result of these conditions, he wanted to use his case to show the need for improvement to Bessy Westmore, the newly widowed owner of the mills who was due to make an inspection tour the following day.

The next day, Amherst conducted Bessy Westmore through the mills. Bessy, touched by Dillon's case, decided to stay at Hanaford for a while. She recalled that she and Justine had attended school together before Justine's parents had lost their wealth.

Bessy and Amherst made plans to improve the living conditions of the workers, and this association finally led to their marriage. Amherst, hoping to make Westmore Mills a model of humanitarianism, was disillusioned to learn that Bessy was not willing to sacrifice the time or the money to accomplish this end.

Some time later, Justine came to Lynbrook, the Amherst country house, to be a companion to Bessy, who was not feeling well. Amherst, meanwhile, spent most of his time at the mills in Hanaford. Bessy, to compensate for Amherst's long absences, began to entertain lavishly, at the same time confiding her bitterness and loneliness to Justine. Later, Amherst decided to manage a friend's cotton mill in the South.

Justine wrote to Amherst saying that Bessy needed him. Amherst replied that he would not return and, in a postscript, asked her not to permit Bessy to ride a particularly spirited horse they owned. Bessy, learning of his request, later took the horse out into the frost-covered countryside. There Bessy suffered an accident that seriously injured her spinal cord. She was taken home and looked after by Dr. Wyant, a local doctor whose proposal Justine had refused some time before. A surgeon and various other consultants were also summoned. Bessy remained paralyzed after an operation; Justine knew that the sick woman would never recover. By this time, Amherst was on a business trip into a remote part of South America, and Bessy's father was in Europe.

One day, while Justine was caring for her alone, Bessy regained enough consciousness from her opiated state to plead with Justine to relieve her pain. Justine, convinced that she was doing the right thing, later gave Bessy an overdose of morphine. When Dr. Wyant came into the room, Justine told him that Bessy was dead. Dr. Wyant seemed to sense what had happened.

A year and a half later, Amherst was back at the Westmore Mills. Bessy had left half her fortune to Cicely, her daughter by her first marriage, and the other half to Amherst. He lived at Hanaford and continued his plans of reconstruction. In the meantime, Justine was taking care of Cicely and an intimate friendship developed between the two. Later, when she went to visit Mrs. Dressel in Hanaford, Justine met Amherst again, a romance developed between them, and they were married. Cicely went to live with her grandfather. Justine took an active part in Amherst's work.

Dr. Wyant, who had left Lynwood and married, now needed money, and he came to Justine and threatened to expose her mercy killing of Bessy unless she arranged to have Amherst write him a letter of recommendation to Mr. Langhope, who could give him a responsible hospital post. Justine, realizing that Dr. Wyant had become a narcotics addict, could not in her conscience arrange a recommendation for him. When she went out of the room, Amherst came in. Learning that Dr. Wyant was in financial straits, Amherst wrote him a letter of recommendation in gratitude for his services to Bessy. On her return, Justine told her husband that Dr. Wyant was not qualified for the hospital post. Dr. Wyant, in retaliation, charged Justine with the mercy killing and left. Intellectually, Amherst approved of Justine. Emotionally, he was horrified at what she had done. Their relationship became strained.

When Dr. Wyant was appointed to the hospital post, Amherst remembered the letter of recommendation. He knew that if Mr. Langhope were told about Dr. Wyant's addiction to narcotics, the doctor would in turn disclose Justine's crime. Amherst told Justine that if Mr. Langhope thought that she had been in love with Amherst when she killed Bessy, he and Justine would have to give up the mills, go away, and start a new life. Justine secretly went to New York to see Mr. Langhope and told him the truth about Dr. Wyant and herself. She then promised to disappear if Mr. Langhope would continue on his former terms with Amherst. Mr. Langhope agreed.

Justine, returning to Hanaford, told Amherst that Mr. Langhope had taken the news very well. In the course of the following months, Amherst's horror of Justine's crime caused their relationship to deteriorate even more. At last, Justine went to Michigan to resume her nursing career, thus fulfilling her promise to Mr. Langhope.

A year later, Cicely became ill. Mr. Langhope, realizing that she needed Justine's love, asked Justine to come back to Amherst so that she could be close to Cicely. When Amherst learned why Justine had left him, he felt love for her and remorse for his attitude. They continued, however, to feel somewhat estranged.

About a year later, Amherst, speaking at the dedication of the mill workers' new recreational center, gave a stirring tribute to Bessy who, he said, had drawn up the plans herself. Justine realized that Amherst was referring to the plans for a gymnasium that Bessy had intended for her own pleasure at Lynbrook, in open defiance of Amherst's wishes. Although angry, Justine kept Bessy's secret.

As they left the dedication, Amherst told Justine how good he felt over improved conditions at the mill. They walked away hand in hand.

Critical Evaluation:

It is clear from its opening scene that *The Fruit of the Tree* is about class conflict in the era of industrialization at the time around the beginning of the twentieth century. The novel opens with John Amherst, the idealistic assistant manager of the Westmore mills, standing over the hospital bedside of an injured worker. Amherst is determined to show the mills' new owner, Bessy Westmore, that this latest accident is the result of the brutality inherent in a factory system fueled by a profit motive. He wants to "awaken" Bessy, a pampered, unthinking member of a leisure class that wants generous profits supplied as unobtrusively as possible. Edith Wharton brings together the two classes, embodied in Amherst and Bessy, in a struggle over the improvement of the lives of the mill workers.

In depicting this class struggle, Wharton also brings together two kinds of narrative: social realism and love. Bessy is first drawn into Amherst's world. She comes to the ugly mill town; she tours the noisy, dirty mills; she weeps at the plight of the ill-treated, malnourished, and exhausted workers. Her sympathetic reactions, as well as her plans for a nursery and a night school, promise future reforms. The novel begins with Amherst guiding Bessy through rows of pounding machines, but it subtly turns its focus to the relationships between individual hearts and minds. Amherst is attracted to Bessy's physical beauty and charm, which he interprets as outward signs of her moral and spiritual beauty. He marries her, but this action pulls him away from Westmore more than it connects Bessy to it. Amherst's work at Westmore, although it is described as his life, takes place out of sight, away from and in conflict with his personal and domestic concerns at Lynbrook, Bessy's home.

Amherst attempts to resist Bessy's world of luxury, keeping himself aloof from her party guests and encouraging her to trim her expenses so that money can go into the mills. He views himself as caught between "sacrificing" the mills to his wife's need for luxury and "sacrificing" his wife to the mills. When they are not in the forefront of the novel, the Westmore mills serve as the influential backdrop for the rest of the story. The novel evolves into a troubled mixture of love story and social realism. The mills and the mill workers become little more than an abstraction, a point of contention between husband and wife, the yardstick by which they measure their failing marriage. Even after Bessy's death and Amherst's marriage to Justine Brent, a nurse whose heart and mind are more attuned to his, the work of improvement at Westmore has an abstract quality, uniting the two in the chill atmosphere of high principles.

Wharton uses the imagery of hands and machines to emphasize the dehumanizing atmosphere of the worlds of both the working and the leisure classes. The mill hands, like Dillon's arm, are merely objects caught up in the great machine of industrialization. Bessy's world is equally mechanical and empty, despite its glittering sophistication and luxury. Amherst sees her world of ease as "mental and spiritual bondage," fearing that it "might draw him back into its revolutions as he had once seen a careless factory hand seized and dragged into a flying belt." Justine Brent, too, recognizes the mechanical quality of Bessy's household, getting "a queer awed feeling that, whatever happened, a machine so perfectly adjusted would work on inexorably," despite Bessy's crippling injury. Existence itself becomes "the machinery of life."

John Amherst is transformed from a truly revolutionary thinker viewed with suspicion by the upper class into a bland paternal figure who has settled "down into a kind of mechanical altruism" and who stands within the confines of the rich as he surveys the little kingdom that he has created. Early in the novel, Justine wonders about the "wings" that one sprouts "when one meets a pair of kindred shoulders," and wonders how well Amherst's are doing under the constrictive clothing of his new social position. By the end of the novel, Wharton reveals how much those wings have atrophied. When Amherst hears how Justine killed Bessy out of a sense of love and respect, a truly radical defiance of science and religion, he is horrified. His wings of mercy and radicalism have atrophied. He exacts a high price from Justine. His unspoken censure of Justine and his conveniently revisionist memory of a saintly Bessy are moral failings.

Despite the novel's sometimes radical critique of the factory world as brutalizing and the leisure world as empty and dehumanizing, the social import of *The Fruit of the Tree* is ultimately conservative. The narrative operates with a dual movement: It recognizes class conflict, but at the same time it attempts to efface that conflict. Real, and largely irreconcilable, social conflict is hidden behind the trappings of a love story in the same way that the real conditions of labor at Westmore are finally hidden behind flower beds and fresh paint for the dingy houses that line the grim streets of the mill town. The final irony of the novel is that Amherst mistakenly believes that Bessy was planning to build a "pleasure-house" for the mill workers when what she really wanted was an extravagant gymnasium for herself.

In this novel, Wharton responds to social concern about industrialization in America by turning polemic into fiction and using it not only to reflect that concern but also to manipulate it. She takes on the important but potentially dangerous subject of factory reform, and then successfully transforms that material into something that will please the greatest number of people—a romance and a success story. She rewards Amherst with the fulfillment of his dreams, and she gives material improvements to the factory workers in return for their patient silence. The upper class, too, is happy. Its members have new outlets for their self-important philanthropic endeavors. The brutal factory system described so graphically at the beginning of the novel becomes a kind of extended family at the end. The happy ending for the Westmore workers helps to assuage the anxieties of a public increasingly aware of horrible factory conditions. The problems inherent in the new wealth of industrialization thus become more acceptable in the glow of upper-class philanthropy, love, and duty.

"Critical Evaluation" by Judith Burdan

Bibliography:

Ammons, Elizabeth. *Edith Wharton's Argument with America.* Athens: University of Georgia Press, 1980. Comprehensive study of Wharton's fiction with the focus on women. Reads the novel as an attack on patriarchal power.

Carlin, Deborah. "To Form a More Imperfect Union: Gender, Tradition, and the Text in Wharton's *The Fruit of the Tree.*" In *Edith Wharton: New Critical Essays,* edited by Alfred Bendixen and Annette Zilversmit. New York: Garland, 1992. Analyzes Miltonic echoes and Edenic allusions. Describes the way in which Wharton uses marital incompatibility to examine various other irreconcilable social issues.

Goodwyn, Janet. *Edith Wharton: Traveller in the Land of Letters.* New York: St. Martin's Press, 1990. Discusses Wharton's use of specific landscapes and explores her consistent concerns with ideas of place. Argues that the number of contentious issues Wharton covers in the novel leads to a confusion of aim and direction.

Wershoven, Carol. *The Female Intruder in the Novels of Edith Wharton.* Rutherford, N.J.: Fairleigh Dickinson University Press, 1982. Focuses on Wharton's disruptive and often defiant heroines. Sees two intruders in the novel who link the work's different subjects.

Wolff, Cynthia Griffin. *A Feast of Words: The Triumph of Edith Wharton.* New York: Oxford University Press, 1977. A superb psychological study of Wharton's life and artistic career. Perceives Justine's need to find fulfillment as a woman as a core issue of the work.

GABRIELA, CLOVE AND CINNAMON

Type of work: Novel
Author: Jorge Amado (1912-   )
Type of plot: Social realism
Time of plot: 1925-1926
Locale: Ilhéus, Bahia, Brazil
First published: Gabriela, cravo e canela, 1958 (English translation, 1962)

> *Principal characters:*
> GABRIELA, a beautiful young mulatto
> NACIB SAAD, the Syrian-born proprietor of the Vesuvius Bar
> MUNDINHO FALCÃO, a young cacao exporter and rising political reformer
> COLONEL RAMIRO BASTOS, the rugged old political boss of Ilhéus
> COLONEL MANUEL OF THE JAGUARS, a planter from the outlands
> COLONEL JESUÍNO MENDONÇA, a cuckold
> COLONEL AMÂNÇIO LEAL, a former bandit chief
> PROFESSOR JOSUÉ, a young teacher
> TONICO BASTOS, the most elegant man in Ilhéus and a ladykiller
> COLONEL CARIOLANO RIBEIRO, a wealthy plantation owner
> GLORIA, his mistress
> FATHER BASÍLIO CERGUEIRA, a worldly priest
> JOAO FULGÊNCIO, a good-natured skeptic
> QUINQUANA and
> FLORZINHA DOS REIS, the spinster sisters of an old Ilhean family
> DONA ARMINDA, Nacib Saad's neighbor and a widow

The Story:

In the mid-1920's, the Brazilian provinces were suffering under the political, social, and economic dominance of the *coroneis*. These "colonels," who ran the local organization of both major political parties unchallenged, who dictated at whim all manners and morals, and who held, often by violence, the huge estates that supplied the money upon which all provincial life depended, were the direct administrators of a feudal society. They ruled vast territories through a complicated system of allegiances built upon favors, kinship, and power. In the country around Ilhéus, a seacoast town in the province of Bahia, the grip of the colonels, given sinews by a boom in the international market for cacao, had remained anachronistically strong. A challenge came to that feudal order, as represented by the colonels, in the person of Mundinho Falcão, a rich, energetic, progress-minded young man from Rio de Janeiro.

Unlike most of the colonels, who were self-made men, Falcão was the son of an illustrious family whose influence extended into the highest reaches of the national government. He had exiled himself from the high life of Rio de Janeiro for three reasons: to make his own fortune, to forget a woman, and to accomplish needed social reforms. One of the colonels had recently murdered his wife and her lover. The fact that she had had a lover at all revealed some cracks in the old order. That no effort was made at first to punish the colonel, in observance of the region's unwritten law, indicated that, for the time being at least, the old order survived as an effective force.

2458

Meanwhile, Nacib Saad, a fat, gentle Brazilian from Syria and the owner of the Vesuvius Bar, had recently lost his cook, whose appetizers and tidbits had largely accounted for his considerable success. Fortunately for him, however, a continuing drought in the backlands brought a steady stream of homeless migrants to Ilhéus looking for work. Nacib was becoming desperate when he discovered among them Gabriela, whose cinnamon-colored skin and scent of clove enhanced her equal and prodigious talents for cooking food and making love. Gabriela represented a way of life that was older and more essentially Brazilian than any of the ways represented by either the colonels or Mundinho Falcão. She embodied the idea of *convivência*—of varied and mingling races and classes mutually dissolving and living together in harmony and absolute democracy—that was a Brazilian tradition and ideal.

Mundinho Falcão sought to operate upon the body of society, rechanneling its old systems into new ones, but Gabriela unconsciously operated upon its soul. Every man in town adored her and few of the women were jealous. When election time arrived, the colonels found their influence whittled away to the vanishing point. In a last attempt to save their ascendancy, the more reactionary of them attempted to arrange the assassination of a powerful political chief who had defected to Falcão. The attempt failed, and Falcão's forces of reform were swept into office, not without his privately acknowledging, however, that his promised reforms were only temporary and had to lead to even greater changes.

Nacib Saad's attempt to transform Gabriela into a married and respectably shod little bourgeoise ended in the discovery that her love was as naturally democratic as her ancestry. She had slept with any man in Ilhéus lucky enough to be handsome. As her husband, poor Nacib was shocked, but not for long. Gabriela still loved him, and he learned, too, in the course of a short estrangement that was disastrous for the business of the Vesuvius Bar, that he likewise still loved her. Wild and free, the mulatto woman was as unregimentable as she was desirable, as indomitable as she was beautiful. She found herself no longer his unhappy wife but once again established as Nacib's happy cook and mistress. All other factions—the colonels' and Falcão's—were reunited in freedom to celebrate new prosperity and progress for Ilhéus. The colonel who had shot his wife was sent, as testimony to a new reign of law, to prison.

Critical Evaluation:

Gabriela, Clove and Cinnamon is a complex novel that marks an important change in the direction of Jorge Amado's writing. The new direction that Amado began to follow may be seen as representing a fresh, invigorating movement in twentieth century fiction in general. Earlier in his career, Amado favored novels in a political vein written in the mode of gritty realism. Starting with *Gabriela, Clove and Cinnamon*, however, Amado's fictive canvases become brighter in tone, his plots more wildly imaginative (including frequent use of the supernatural), and his characters more varied and colorful. So too in twentieth century fiction in general, the development of the novel of realism, from Miguel de Cervantes through the great nineteenth century realists such as Leo Tolstoy and Gustave Flaubert, seemed to have reached a climax with the modernists—Marcel Proust, James Joyce, and William Faulkner prominent among them. Thereafter, in the eyes of many readers and critics, a stagnation set in, not relieved until the appearance of the great Latin American Magical Realists such as Jorge Luis Borges and Gabriel García Márquez. Jorge Amado has earned a place among this latter group.

Describing *Gabriela, Clove and Cinnamon* as a complex novel should not be taken to imply that it is necessarily difficult reading. In contrast to many of the modernists, who often deliberately designed forbiddingly inaccessible fictive structures, most Magical Realists seem to take as a primary goal the ancient one of delighting and entertaining the reader. Any critical analysis is flawed that neglects to note that *Gabriella, Clove and Cinnamon* is from beginning to end a great joy to read. One senses that Amado is writing in much the same spirit as the authors of the chivalric romances that Cervantes so entertainingly parodies. Rather than Magical Realism—a term borrowed from art criticism and often misleading when applied to literature—the term "romance" better prepares readers for the style and technical strategies of Amado's later novels.

Gabriela is within the romantic tradition. As a fictive creation she would be out of place in a novel of traditional realism. In such a work, the author would try to emphasize her ordinariness. Amado's Gabriela, however, is extraordinary to the point of mythic proportions. Gabriela does not walk but "glides." She is not simply a capable cook and lover but is "perfect" as both. When she enters a room and smiles, the whole room smiles with her; when she is unhappy, the whole world seems to lose its zest for life. Professor Josué maintains that a prospective lover should not write a sonnet—a sophisticated, polished, and studied from—for her but a ballad, with its implications of raw emotions, passion, and violence. A major subtheme of the novel is adultery, jealousy, and violent reprisal, the stuff of ballads and romances.

Gabriela, Clove and Cinnamon is not simply an updated romance; it is a romance novel. Gabriela's often almost melodramatic story is only one of the plot lines. The novel is divided into chapters that alternate between the many romantic crises of Gabriela and her associates and the political crises faced by Mundinho Falcão as he attempts to invade the entrenched power structure of Ilhéus. The principals in this latter plot line—Mundinho, Colonel Ramiro Bastos, and Colonel Cariolano Ribeiro—are based, if not on specific historical individuals, on actual historical types. Amado provides richly detailed backgrounds for these characters, along with astute analyses of the economic, cultural, and political forces that shaped them. This focus on historical realism shows Amado the realistic novelist adding to his romantic work. *Gabriela, Clove and Cinnamon* is, ultimately, every bit as political as the novels from the earlier phase of his career. In *Gabriela, Clove and Cinnamon*, however, Amado has found that he can have it both ways: He can teach readers important political lessons while amusing them.

The two plot lines and the two goals—to teach and to entertain—are not mutually exclusive. Mundinho is not part of a distant political establishment of which Gabriela and the denizens of her world are only vaguely aware. Mundinho knows Gabriela and her husband, Nacib Saad, personally. More importantly, Mundinho is touched by Gabriela's world of emotion and romance. How much of Mundinho's drive to succeed, the readers might well ponder, derives from the fact that he fled to Ilhéus to make his fortune after an unhappy love affair? Is Colonel Bastos' stubborn clinging to power based on genuine convictions or on the same sort of irrational, ingrained self-centeredness that drives men to see their wives as property and to murder suspected adulterers?

Just as the actors in the political plot line are caught up in the same passions of the romance plot line of Gabriela, Gabriela is also affected by currents in the realistic political world. She makes her way to the city, for instance, as part of the historical movement of peasants from the countryside to urban areas, where they too often find their old mores and customs eroded. Hence, Gabriela begins to lose her zest for life—and the world around her seems accordingly to lose its zest—when her husband insists that she wear shoes.

The action in the novel covers exactly one year, implying the cyclical nature of the changes besetting Gabriela's and Mundinho's world. All are victims of change, just as all are in various ways instigators. The only sure victors are the readers of Amado's marvelous novel.

"Critical Evaluation" by Dennis Vannatta

Bibliography:

Chamberlain, Bobby J. "Escape from the Tower: Women's Liberation in Amado's *Gabriela, cravo e canela.*" In *Prismal/Cabral: Revista de Literatura Hispanica/Caderno AfroBrasileiro Asiatico Lustitano* 6 (Spring, 1981): 70-86. Discusses feminist issues in the novel. Sees Gabriela as a victim of male power and a source of liberation.

Ellison, Fred P. *Brazil's New Novel.* Berkeley: University of California Press, 1954. Discusses the political impulse of Amado's early novels. Useful for judging the change in Amado's writing represented by *Gabriela, Clove and Cinnamon.*

Hall, Linda B. "Jorge Amado: Women, Love, and Possession." *Southwest Review* 68 (Winter, 1983): 67-77. Discusses male and female relationships in *Gabriela, Clove and Cinnamon* and other Amado novels.

Keating, L. Clark. "The Guys and Dolls of Jorge Amado." *Hispania* 66 (September, 1983): 340-344. Discusses *Gabriela, Clove and Cinnamon* in the context of other Amado novels in which the author's ultimate aim is to reform society. Amado's most frequent strategy is the use of heavy irony.

Martin, John, and Donna L. Bodegraven. "Mythical Patterns in Jorge Amado's *Gabriela, Clove and Cinnamon* and Bruno Barreto's Film *Gabriela.*" In *Film and Literature: A Comparative Approach to Adaptation*, edited by Wendell Aycock and Michael Schoenecke. Lubbock: Texas Tech University Press, 1988. Focuses on the characterization of Gabriela and Nacib and the novel's sources in classical myth.

GALILEO

Type of work: Drama
Author: Bertolt Brecht (1898-1956)
Type of plot: Historical
Time of plot: 1609-1637
Locale: Florence, Padua, Rome, and Venice
First performed: Leben des Galilei, first version, 1943; second version (in English), 1947; third version (in German), 1955; first published, 1952; third version, 1955; revised, 1957 (English translation, 1960)

> *Principal characters:*
> GALILEO GALILEI, an astronomer and professor of mathematics at Padua
> VIRGINIA, his daughter
> LUDOVICO MARILI, Galileo's pupil and later Virginia's fiancé
> MRS. SARTI, Galileo's housekeeper
> ANDREA SARTI, her son and Galileo's apprentice
> PRIULI, a curator
> SAGREDO, Galileo's friend
> PHILOSOPHER, later the rector of the University of Padua
> LITTLE MONK, Galileo's disciple
> FEDERZONI, assistant to Galileo
> CARDINAL BARBERINI, later Pope Urban VIII

The Story:

In 1609, the forty-six-year-old Galileo Galilei, a professor of mathematics at the University of Padua, Italy, was forced to live frugally and in humble surroundings, despite his taste for luxury and good food, which matched his enthusiasm for his studies. When his housekeeper's son, Andrea, brought in a model of the geocentric universe based on the ancient Ptolemaic system, Galileo demonstrated how the earth orbited around the sun, as had been hypothesized by the Polish astronomer Nicolaus Copernicus. A young aristocrat named Ludovico arrived, seeking a tutorship under Galileo. He explained that he had seen primitive telescopes in Amsterdam, where they were being sold in the streets. Galileo sent Andrea out to purchase lenses for his own experiments with the device. He promised Priuli, the curator, that he had something practical to offer the authorities in Venice.

Some time later, Galileo gave a demonstration of his own improved telescope to the Venetian senators and arsenal artisans; afterward, he had his fourteen-year-old daughter Virginia present it to the city as a gift, to be copied and openly sold. Priuli told Galileo that the gift would improve Galileo's financial situation. On January 10, 1610, however, the curator visited Galileo and his friend Sagredo to complain that Galileo had deceived the city fathers. A ship from Holland had arrived in Venice and was about to unload a shipment of telescopes that would be hawked cheaply on every street corner. After the curator's indignant exit, Galileo explained to Sagredo what his improved telescope had revealed to him: evidence that there was movement in the previously believed fixed and rigid crystalline spheres of the universe. To Virginia and Sagredo, Galileo announced his resolute intention of moving to Florence to seek patronage and protection under the de Medicis.

In Florence, Galileo was quickly disappointed by the cautious and politic courtiers of Cosimo de Medici, who was then but a boy of nine. However, he earned a temporary victory when

Christopher Clavius, the chief astronomer at the Papal College in Rome, confirmed Galileo's findings. Soon after, in 1616, Galileo encountered Cardinal Barberini at a masked party and dinner at the home of Cardinal Bellarmin. Barberini, who later became Pope Urban VIII, took a practical view of Galileo's findings, which led Galileo to believe that he had a strong ally at the Papal Court, despite the guarded manner in which Barberini expressed his support. At the same party, another churchman, an inquisitor, urged Virginia to look after her father's spiritual well-being, with a veiled hint that she should spy on him.

Galileo's growing renown won for him many converts, including the Little Monk, who, when first confronting Galileo, strongly argued a humanitarian's case for not disseminating Galileo's sun-centered theory of the solar system. The Little Monk's thirst for truth proved too powerful, however, and he was soon drawn into Galileo's inner circle.

Between 1616 and 1624, Galileo remained content to study without publishing his findings. Then, just as his sight began to fail from having repeatedly looked at the sun in his telescope, Galileo grew bolder. Word came that the pope was dying and that his most likely successor would be Cardinal Barberini, which gave Galileo hope that the Church would be more receptive to his ideas. Galileo soon began to pay a price for his dedication and relentless pursuit of evidence to prove his theories. His daughter was the first to suffer, when Ludovico, with warnings to Galileo about his revolutionary concepts, broke off his eight-year engagement to her.

By 1632, Galileo's ideas had became common knowledge in Italian streets, where ballad singers spread what the authorities considered dangerously heretical and seditious notions. Friends and supporters, like Matti, an iron founder, tried to warn Galileo, then gradually deserted him. Under pressure from the Church, Cosimo de Medici withdrew his protection, as did Pope Urban VIII, the former Cardinal Barberini, who allowed his Cardinal Inquisitor to threaten Galileo with torture in order to exact a confession of heresy and a recantation.

To the dismay of his close followers, who awaited him at the Florentine ambassador's house in Rome, Galileo recanted on June 22, 1633. Already almost blind, he was unwilling to martyr himself for his theories. The news was announced to his family and friends by the church bells of Saint Marcus, followed by the town crier's reading of the text of the recantation. Feeling betrayed, his disciples turned away from him. Only Virginia, who was becoming a pious old maid, believed that her father had done the right thing and that he had saved himself from damnation.

Thereafter, until his death in 1642, Galileo remained a prisoner of the Inquisition, under house arrest, and under the care and watchful eye of Virginia. Secretly, he worked at night on his scientific opus, the *Discorsi*. He hid his papers inside a globe and was able to get his work to the outside world after Andrea visited him, reluctantly, to ask after his health. After admitting that he had recanted from a fear of torture, Galileo gave the manuscript to Andrea, who, in 1637, conveyed it across the Italian frontier on his way to Amsterdam, where it could be published and circulated without reprisal from the Church.

Critical Evaluation:

Galileo, created during Bertolt Brecht's exile in America, exists in a number of versions, the first written in German, the second in English. That version took shape in close collaboration with the great English actor Charles Laughton, and it is the version considered here. A third, expanded version, in German, was in production at the time of Brecht's death in 1956.

Galileo is a chronicle play that in structure and technique is reminiscent of the history plays of the English Renaissance. Brecht had freely adapted and produced one of these, Christopher

Marlowe's *Edward II* (1592), in 1924. To some extent, *Galileo* also resembles Brecht's epic theater pieces, but it is Brecht's only major and original example based on the life of an actual person, one of the world's great scientists and revolutionary thinkers.

The play is divided into fourteen scenes or vignettes that cover a period of several years, from 1609 to 1637, six years before Galileo's death in 1643. In the manner of the chronicle play, these vignettes are isolated episodes, not always linked in a causal way. Although the plot advances in chronological order, it is thus more like a composite or montage than a piece structured from logically interrelated parts. As in other epic theater plays, most of the individual vignettes contain a *gestus* or dramatic kernel, sometimes a line or phrase, around which the scene is built.

Galileo contains other devices characteristically used by Brecht to achieve an effect of *Verfremdung* or alienation, the core of his didactic, anti-illusionistic theory of drama. Alienation emotionally distances an audience by repeatedly reminding them that they are watching a play. To achieve that end in his epic theater plays, Brecht calls for minimalist sets, a panoramic sweep of action, a large number of characters, and a variety of such devices as narrative frames, snippets of poetry and song, and placards announcing the action line of each scene. In *Galileo*, Brecht uses some of these devices, but he does so rather sparingly.

The play mingles different styles and techniques. Some of the scenes do very little to dispel the conventional illusion of reality that Brecht in theory deplored, whereas other scenes are more symbolic and expressionistic. Although Brecht himself complained that the play throughout was too traditional in technique, these vignettes are both unconventional and highly imaginative. In scene xii, for example, during the investiture of Cardinal Barberini as Pope Urban VIII, Barberini, dressed in the outsized papal clothing, listens to the Cardinal Inquisitor who wants to silence Galileo as a heretic. By the time he is buried under the heavy clothing of his new office, Barberini's open-mindedness has become equally buried under the papal panoply, and he permits the Inquisitor to proceed against Galileo. Throughout the brief scene, to the growing annoyance of Barberini, there is a persistent offstage shuffling of feet that the Cardinal Inquisitor claims belongs to a select gathering of the faithful; it also, however, suggests the aimless shuffling of a humanity as ubiquitous and ignorant as locusts.

Other expressionistic passages occur in scene ix, in which a ballad singer spreads Galileo's theories to a carnival gathering, and, to a lesser extent, in scene vi, which occurs during a masquerade dance and dinner at the house of Cardinal Bellarmin. In both scenes, Brecht uses symbolic devices charged with implications for the protagonist. In scene vi, Cardinals Bellarmin and Barberini wear masks, which they raise or lower as the situation requires; their actions suggest that they are astute and pragmatic politicians, quite capable of masking their true beliefs as the winds of necessity dictate. However, Galileo, as Barberini remarks, has no mask to hide behind; he deals not with policy with but scientific truth, which makes him both vulnerable and defenseless. In scene ix, after the ballad singer has given a narrative account in song of the impact of Galileo's theories on the Church and society and after much riotous and irreverent behavior by many characters, a procession begins, led by a float supporting a huge figure of Galileo. The effigy holds a Bible with pages crossed out and mechanically turns its head from side to side to deny the infallibility of scripture. A voice then proclaims "Galileo, the Bible killer!" prompting the people to laugh with loud delight. It is a scene full of spectacle, unlike anything else in the play.

These two scenes are sandwiched among much more realistic vignettes, including the opening and closing scenes of the play, where the dialogue tends to be more conventional and conversational. Scene xiv, however, the final vignette, builds on a *gestus* analogous to Plato's allegory of the cave. When Andrea shows some children that they have falsely accused a woman of being a witch, they reject the evidence and cling to their destructive, superstitious ignorance. The scene is the dramatist's own allegorical indictment of humankind.

Reportedly, Brecht felt even more ambivalent toward Galileo, believing that, in recanting, the scientist had betrayed a great trust and that, in fact, he should have martyred himself for his beliefs. To what extent this is consistent with the writer's Marxist philosophy is unclear. In fact, the main character in *Galileo* seems much more engaging and sympathetic than Brecht may have intended, and rather than condemn Galileo as a sensualist and moral coward, his lust for life and his desire to avoid pain, if not admirable, at least seem wholly human and ultimately forgivable.

John W. Fiero

Bibliography:

Esslin, Martin. *Brecht: The Man and His Work*. Rev. ed. Garden City, N.Y.: Anchor Books, 1971. A seminal study of Brecht that remains significant because of its insights into Brecht's own theories of drama and the relationship of his works to Communist ideology.

Fuegi, John. *Bertolt Brecht: Chaos, According to Plan*. Cambridge, England: Cambridge University Press, 1987. Offers a very detailed chronology and reviews the production problems of the 1947 staging of the play with Laughton in the title role. Useful selective bibliography.

Gray, Ronald. *Brecht: The Dramatist*. Cambridge, England: Cambridge University Press, 1976. An excellent introduction to Brecht, focusing exclusively on his plays, his dramatic theory, and his theater.

Hayman, Ronald. *Bertolt Brecht: The Plays*. Totowa, N.J.: Barnes & Noble Books, 1984. A short, succinct study by a major Brecht biographer. An excellent starting place for further study of Brecht's plays. Relates *Galileo* to Brecht's Marxist ideology and his practical reasons for writing the play.

Hill, Claude. *Bertolt Brecht*. Boston: Twayne, 1975. A good critical introduction to Brecht, with a chronology and bibliography. Focuses in the discussion of *Galileo* on Brecht's artistic intention in the different versions of the play.

THE GAMBLER

Type of work: Novel
Author: Fyodor Dostoevski (1821-1881)
Type of plot: Psychological realism
Time of plot: Mid-nineteenth century
Locale: German watering places
First published: Igrok, 1866 (English translation, 1949)

Principal characters:
ALEXEY IVANOVITCH, a young gambler
THE GENERAL, a Russian aristocrat
POLINA, his stepdaughter
MADEMOISELLE BLANCHE, a French adventuress
THE MARQUIS DE GRIEUX, a factitious French nobleman
ASTLEY, a young English capitalist
ANTONIDA TARASEVITCHEVA, the General's wealthy old aunt

The Story:

Alexey Ivanovitch returned to Roulettenburg, a German resort, after two weeks in Paris. He was tutor in the family of a Russian general who had come to the resort to repair his dwindling fortune. The General wooed an apparently wealthy young Frenchwoman, Mademoiselle Blanche. Polina, the General's stepdaughter, was attracted to Mademoiselle Blanche's alleged distant relative, the Marquis de Grieux. Alexey was Polina's creature; he loved her and accepted any humiliation at her hands.

Alexey went to the casino with money Polina had given him. After winning a tidy amount, he felt that his stay in Roulettenburg would affect his life seriously. Believing that he could not lose at the gambling tables, Alexey told Polina that hereafter he would gamble only for himself. Polina, however, aware of her power over Alexey, easily persuaded him to share his winnings with her.

An affluent young English capitalist, Astley, came to Roulettenburg and, much to the General's discomfort, diverted the attentions of Mlle Blanche, who was growing tired of waiting for the General's old aunt to die. The General telegraphed Moscow every day to inquire about the condition of the old lady, who, he was sure, would leave him a fortune.

It was soon evident that Astley was in love with Polina. Alexey, suspecting the French pair to be impostors, wanted to get away from the machinations of Roulettenburg existence, but his love for Polina held him. At the casino he lost a large amount of Polina's money; his possession of the money aroused renewed interest in the General on the part of Mlle Blanche. The General, it seems, was deeply in debt to de Grieux.

Unable to win with Polina's money, Alexey offered to win with his own and to lend her whatever she wanted. Alexey hoped that he could win Polina's love by becoming wealthy through gambling. He confessed his ardent love for her, and when he told her that he could even commit murder for her, she impishly ordered him to speak in French to a stuffy German baroness who was passing by with her husband. After Alexey brashly insulted the Germans, he was discharged by the General, despite his plea that he was mentally aberrant during the escapade. Alexey managed to maintain his self-respect when he told the General, who had apologized to the baron for him, that he was capable of making his own apologies, that as the son of a nobleman he objected to the General's patronizing treatment. The General, fearful of the consequences of Alexey's further impetuosities, unsuccessfully tried to mollify the youth.

De Grieux, as mediator, told Alexey that any further indiscretion on his part might spoil the chances of the General's marriage to Mlle Blanche. He also promised that the General would reemploy Alexey soon and would continue, meanwhile, to pay him his salary. Alexey, however, chose Astley to be his second in a duel with the baron. De Grieux then produced a letter from Polina asking Alexey to drop the matter. The young man obeyed, although he knew for certain that Polina loved de Grieux.

Astley indirectly confirmed Alexey's suspicions that Mlle Blanche and de Grieux were adventurers. During previous exploits at Roulettenburg, Mlle Blanche had made advances to the baron and, at the direction of the baroness, had been escorted out of the casino by the police. Alexey suspected the General of being indebted somehow to Mlle Blanche, and Polina of being involved with the French couple.

The General's old aunt, Antonida Tarasevitcheva, arrived from Moscow with a large retinue. Quite alive, she wickedly chaffed the General on his urgent solicitations and criticized him for squandering his children's inheritance. The General was visibly shocked by her arrival. Accompanied by the General's party, the old lady visited the casino and won fabulously at the gaming tables. In her triumph she gave money to her servants and to beggars.

Polina became more of an enigma to Alexey when she had him deliver a letter to Astley. Despite the General's pleas to the young tutor to prevent Antonida from gambling away her fortune, Alexey and the old lady frequented the casino together. Obsessed with the fever to win, she lost heavily. When she prepared to return to Moscow, she invited Polina to return with her, but Polina declined. Antonida, unable to resist one last try at the gambling tables, again lost heavily. She converted bonds into cash and again lost. The old lady now possessed nothing but land and the houses on it; she borrowed money from Astley in order to return to Moscow.

The General's inheritance having been lost at roulette, Mlle Blanche and de Grieux broke off relations with him and prepared to leave Roulettenburg. The General was a ruined man. Polina was distracted by her impending loss of de Grieux, but she was shaken out of her infatuation when de Grieux offered her consolation money from the proceeds of the General's property, which was mortgaged to de Grieux. In distress, Polina turned to Alexey, who went to the casino and won a fortune for her to hurl in de Grieux's face. She spent the night with Alexey in his hotel room. The next morning she took his money, then threw it in his face. She fled to Astley. Alexey went with Mlle Blanche to Paris, where he lived with her while she spent his winnings. Tired of the life of an adventuress, Mlle Blanche, persuaded by Alexey, decided to marry the General.

Now a confirmed gambler, Alexey returned to the gambling tables of the German resort towns. Once he went to jail for debt. In Homburg he saw Astley, who told him that Polina, recuperating from an illness, was in Switzerland with Astley's family. Meanwhile the General had died of a stroke in Paris, and Mlle Blanche had received his inheritance from Antonida, who had died in Moscow. Alexey regretfully reminded Astley of Polina's infatuation for de Grieux and was momentarily hopeful when Astley told him that Polina had sent him to Homburg to bring Alexey back to her. Alexey knew that he had no choice, really—he had given his heart and soul to gambling.

Critical Evaluation:

Fyodor Dostoevski was every bit as erratic, volatile, irresponsible, and contradictory in his personal life as any of his fictional characters. He created most of his works in the face of extreme pressures and adversities which, more often than not, were the product of his own actions. *The Gambler*, a novel he probably never wanted to write, resulted from such a self-created pressure, a situation as pathetic and comic as the book itself.

In 1865, in severe financial difficulties (a frequent condition), Dostoevski signed a contract with Stellovsky, an unscrupulous publisher, in which he agreed to furnish a new novel by November 1, 1866, or else grant Stellovsky the right to publish all of his works royalty-free for nine years. As of October 1, Dostoevski had nothing on paper. In desperation he hired a stenography student and began to dictate. It was one of the most important decisions of his life. Prodded by the shy, awed, but firm and sensible young lady Anna Grigorievna Snitkina, Dostoevski completed the novel in less than a month and salvaged his financial future. He also acquired, in Anna, a second wife who put an efficiency and order into his life that considerably eased his last years and freed him to concentrate on the writing of his greatest works.

The intense pressure under which *The Gambler* was composed is no doubt one reason why, except for *Notes from the House of the Dead*, it is the most directly personal, even autobiographical, of his works of fiction. The primary motifs in *The Gambler* are frustrated love and compulsive gambling, two conditions that dominated Dostoevski's life in the years immediately preceding its writing. The book's narrator, Alexey Ivanovitch, resembles the Dostoevski of that period in many ways, and Polina Alexandrovna is a thinly disguised re-creation of Polina Suslova (note the names), a student half his age, whom he met in 1862 while on his first European visit. It was on this same tour that he also began to gamble. Thus, Alexey's experiences in Roulettenburg are loosely based on a confused and traumatic trip the novelist took with Polina Suslova in 1863. Consequently, the passions of love and gambling were inextricably bound in Dostoevski's mind and, in *The Gambler*, he renders them in all of their complexity.

These motifs, however, do not actually become central until quite late in the book. The first two-thirds of the novel concentrates on the seriocomic machinations of the general's party as they vie with one another and with old "Granny" Antonida Tarasevitcheva. Except for the narrator and Polina, the characters, even the colorful old lady, are one-dimensional, almost caricatures. The general is a sophisticated Russian quasi-aristocrat who, cut off from his native roots, is the easy, pathetic victim of all West European temptations. De Grieux is the stock French adventurer: stylish, cultivated, shallow, and corrupt. The Englishman, Astley, is likewise a national type: stolid, laconic, honest, and dull. Mademoiselle Blanche is the French seductress: beautiful, coaxing, playful, free with sex and other people's money but essentially selfish and shrewd (it is she who finally ends up with Granny's money). Even Antonida is a stereotype: the headstrong, obstinate, outspoken, outrageous old woman.

If individually the characters are little more than clichés, however, collectively they provoke a colorful sequence of comic situations that make the first two-thirds of the novella exciting and amusing. Then, as Dostoevski comes to focus the book more intensely on Alexey and Polina, the other characters retreat into the background but continue to provide a grotesque comic counterpoint to the more serious antics of the principals.

The association of Alexey's love for Polina with his addiction to gambling is made early in the novel when she asks him to play roulette for her. Thus, from the beginning, Polina shows a dependence on Alexey, but, at that point in the novel, there is little he can do to help her. One of the most important, if subtle, movements in the book is the manner in which Alexey gradually ascends from the position of a disdained inferior to that of a sought-after superior who gains powers over the others—the general, de Grieux, and finally Polina—and then rapidly loses it all.

Ostensibly, Alexey's power derives initially from his role as the old woman's "adviser" and then from the fortune he wins gambling, but the real source of it probably lies in his lack of identity and commitment. Because he has little interest in appearances and social postures, he has a great advantage over the others. As they strive to protect and enhance their social, financial, and romantic positions in the group, Alexey moves around freely and unobtrusively, capitalizing on his associates' failures and weaknesses. He becomes progressively absorbed by his two passions, Polina and gambling; however, he cannot translate his advantages into permanent victory but must ultimately destroy himself pursuing these addictions.

Polina is a fascinating mixture of femme fatale and passionate victim. She loves Alexey yet feels a need to demean him. When he seriously expresses a willingness to kill himself for her, she reduces it to the comic by suggesting that he insult a German baron. She mocks his vow to "kill her" but is excited by it. She fears being in his power but comes to him in her hour of need. In the novel's enigmatic climax, when she offers herself to him, her behavior is erratic, volatile, almost hysterical; she rapidly alternates between abjectly demeaning herself, stridently justifying her behavior, belittling and berating Alexey, and proclaiming her lasting love for him. Then, after spending the night with him, she flings the money into his face and flees.

Alexey is perhaps even more puzzling. He both loves and hates Polina. He abjectly submits to her every whim, yet he also wants dominance, perhaps both at the same time. His feelings for her are inevitably bound up with his gambling compulsions. At the point when she offers herself to him, he feels the need to rush out to the gaming table. As he feverishly plays, he forgets about her. After he wins, he hurries back and empties his pockets before her almost as an integral part of the lovemaking ritual. When she leaves him, he casually enters into an unexpected affair with Mlle Blanche and gives her free reign to dissipate his modest fortune, which she quickly does. Many critics have seen this sudden shift in his character as unlikely and, after considering the pressures on the author, have dismissed it as a quick and easy resolution to the story.

However, in the light of Dostoevski's association of Alexey's compulsive gambling with his love for Polina, the ending makes definite psychological sense. Rationally, the hero's love for Polina has as its object the consummation of the affair; the gambling is a way of quickly procuring the money necessary to support the romance. Alexey, however, is not essentially a rational creature but one driven by needs and emotions that he does not fully comprehend. It is the intensity of the experience of pursuing Polina, not the physical actuality of the woman, that really enraptures Alexey, and, likewise, it is the excitement and danger of gambling, and not the monetary outcome, that captivate him. It is even possible that, given his taste for self-humiliation, Alexey gambles to lose rather than to win. Having "won" Polina, he casts money at her to provoke her rejection of him; having won the fortune, he subconsciously wants it taken from him.

Thus, in *The Gambler*, Dostoevski not only explores frustrated love and compulsive gambling, but he also analyzes the dynamics of psychological self-destruction, creating in Alexey a character type that was to become central in his most powerful novels.

"Critical Evaluation" by Keith Neilson

Bibliography:
Frank, Joseph. *Dostoevsky: The Miraculous Years, 1865-1871*. Princeton, N.J.: Princeton University Press, 1995. The fourth book of a five-book series on Dostoevski. Contains extensive biographical information and readings of the novels and most of the work.

Hlybinny, Uladzimer. *Dostoevski's Image in Russia Today*. Belmont, Mass.: Nordland, 1975. Traces Dostoevski's life from childhood onward. Covers what is mostly unknown in Dostoevski's writing as well as what is popular. A large and complete book.

Jackson, Robert Louis. *The Art of Dostoevsky: Deliriums and Nocturnes*. Princeton, N.J.: Princeton University Press, 1981. An authority on Dostoevski examines the novels written in Dostoevski's last twenty years. Links the themes of these most important novels and gives an extended character description of Polina from *The Gambler*.

_____. *Dostoevsky's Quest for Form: A Study of His Philosophy of Art*. 2d ed. Bloomington, Indiana: Physsardt, 1978. Considers the contradiction between Dostoevski's working aesthetic and his higher aesthetic of true beauty. A mature and helpful study for the serious Dostoevski reader.

Mackiewicz, Stanislaw. *Dostoyevsky*. Maryknoll, N.Y.: Orbis Books, 1947. Discusses the characters and circumstances of *The Gambler* and several other novels. Examines the women characters and their relevance to the loves of Dostoevski's life. Biographical information and critiques of the novels.

THE GARDEN PARTY AND OTHER STORIES

Type of work: Short fiction
Author: Katherine Mansfield (1888-1923)
First published: 1922

Katherine Mansfield revolutionized the short story genre by ending the predominant reliance upon traditional plot structure, instead relying more on a specific moment in time, expressed through image patterns. By doing this, Mansfield carried the short story genre away from formalistic structuring and helped to establish its credibility as a literary form.

This collection of short fiction contains the following stories: "At the Bay," "The Garden Party," "The Daughters of the Late Colonel," "Mr. and Mrs. Dove," "The Young Girl," "Life of Ma Parker," "Marriage à la Mode," "The Voyage," "Miss Brill," "Her First Ball," "The Singing Lesson," "The Stranger," "Bank Holiday," "An Ideal Family," and "The Lady's Maid."

The Garden Party and Other Stories centers around female protagonists and the roles they play in family and social structures. These female characters differ in both age and class, ranging between the ages of six and sixty-five years and belonging to lower-, middle-, and upper-class social groups. For example, in "The Garden Party," the collection's title story, the female protagonist is approximately sixteen and is a member of aristocratic society, whereas in "Life of Ma Parker," the title character, a maid, belongs to the lower class and is perhaps fifty.

Not only does Mansfield like to juxtapose differences in class and differences in age, she also likes to position fictional elements against one another. Characters, settings, and themes are juxtaposed in her short fiction. In "The Garden Party" two classes are juxtaposed: On one hand there is the affluent and aristocratic Sheridan family celebrating the new flowers in bloom, and on the other hand there is the poor family, less than two miles away from the Sheridan estate, that has just suffered the father's untimely death.

A feminist, Mansfield juxtaposes the roles of men and women in "At the Bay." She uses the character of Linda to address the idea that women need more to fulfill their lives than a husband and children. The story's narrative depicts Linda's growing realization that there is more to life than wifely and motherly duties. Increasingly evident within the story is her desire to take an active role in her own life.

Mansfield is a master of utilizing and implementing many literary techniques. A striking use of metaphor is apparent in Mansfield's short fiction. Her stories also tend to operate by means of the implied rather than the direct. Furthermore, she uses a voice that is influenced by the characters, experiments with point of view, employs the use of natural elements, and begins stories in medias res.

Mansfield uses voice to present a character accurately. If a character is a young woman or an adolescent, for example, voice conveys the character's young or adolescent feelings. If the narrator speaks from the consciousness of a young child, the words are short, to the point, and not complicated, like the language and speech patterns of an actual child. Thus does narrative voice help to give the reader a realistic impression of the character.

Mansfield also experiments with point of view. She uses first and third person viewpoints, standard to short fiction, yet she has also created a point of view peculiarly her own that seemingly derives from her gift of impersonation. Her early mimicking of family and acquaintances carries over in her fiction to her use of a multipersonal perspective. Writing from a multipersonal point of view also allows Mansfield to give readers an extended sense of time, both in a historical and an immediate sense. This point of view also allows Mansfield to extend the viewpoint of a story from that a single character to that of an entire group. In "The Garden Party," the beginning viewpoint is that of Laura Sheridan; however, at the end of the story, the viewpoint has shifted to be inclusive of the entire family.

The use of natural elements is an essential component of Katherine Mansfield's narrative craft. She believes that natural elements, such as air, sea, and gardens help to create one's existence. In "Bank Holiday," for example, the use of the wind is important. The characters are pushed by the wind and do not realize the role played by the wind in moving them to their ultimate destination. Another use of natural elements is in "The Voyage." During the night, the young girl Fenella is taken by sea from a place that is familiar to her and emerges in a new place at the beginning of a new day.

Another characteristic device used by Mansfield is beginning stories in medias res, for example, in "The Voyage" and "The Daughters of the Late Colonel." In "The Voyage," Fenella is whisked away from her father, and readers do not understand why until near the end of the story. Similarly, when "The Daughters of the Late Colonel" begins, the father has died and the daughters are indecisive as to how to behave. These in medias res beginnings emphasize endings in a way that typical plot structure does not.

Not only are Mansfield's short stories characterized by female protagonists, each story addresses a social or psychological issue, including class, loneliness, or despair. "Miss Brill," "The Voyage," "Life of Ma Parker," and "The Lady's Maid" are representations of different women's existences and their varying relationships with those around them. In "Miss Brill," for example, Mansfield brings to the reader's consciousness the struggle between the young and the old. Miss Brill is elderly and alone, so she is forced to become "an actress" in the lives of those around her. She is no more than an observer in the conversations and lives of others who are also in the park, and at the end of the story she is compelled to realize this. The mean and hurtful words of the young couple she encounters force her to recognize that she is an outsider and unappreciated. Upon her return home, Miss Brill begins returning her fur stole to its box and then seems to hear the fox whimpering. In actuality, Mansfield suggests that it is Miss Brill herself who is crying because she is not only alone but also without hope of ever being more than "an actress" in the lives of others.

Both female protagonists in "The Lady's Maid" and "Life of Ma Parker" exemplify women who have an undying commitment to those who surround them. Ellen in "The Lady's Maid" has previously declined a marriage proposal she received as a young girl in order to fulfill her obligation to her "lady." Ellen wanted to marry but realized unselfishly that it would not be such a good idea to leave a lady alone who could not adequately take care of herself. Along with Ellen, Ma Parker also demonstrates a sense of commitment. She never once sheds a tear or thinks of herself when her husband dies of consumption or when seven of her thirteen children die. She exemplifies strength and a strong commitment to others. Eventually, she realizes that she needs to release her pent-up emotions and begin healing from the pain she has experienced over the years.

Other themes and issues brought forth by Mansfield in *The Garden Party and Other Stories* include those of suffering, loneliness, abandonment, denial of self-fulfillment, and, most important, death's effect on human consciousness.

The effect of death on human consciousness is the thread that connects most of the stories. According to Saralyn R. Daly, death is relevant to the human condition: "In each instance the characters are affected by a death, but it becomes clear that death is not central in the author's mind." In "The Stranger" and "Marriage à la Mode," the death that occurs is not to a human being but to a relationship. In both stories, the bond between husband and wife falls apart for one reason or another. In "The Stranger," the relationship deteriorates because Janey Hammond has emotionally shut herself off from her husband. In "Marriage à la Mode," the relationship falls apart because there is a communication gap between William and Isabel. In the early years of their marriage William was content and Isabel was not. They decide to move to appease her, and then the roles are reversed. William is unhappy and Isabel is ecstatic. Their relationship falls apart because they have failed to express their feelings to each other. What each of these stories suggests is that death comes in all forms and is capable of affecting everything and everyone. In many of Mansfield's stories, relationships die because people fail to acknowledge the needs of others.

To Mansfield, death is the beginning of a self-awakening process. In "The Daughters of the Late Colonel," the father's death leads the sisters to the discovery of how desperate their lives have been up to that point. As a result of the colonel's death, the sisters realize that they have been excluded from others and are lonely for companionship. After their father's death they are not able to communicate or socialize independently. Everything has been organized and dictated to them by their father, and now there is no one to tell them what to do.

All of the stories that belong to *The Garden Party and Other Stories* suggest that life needs to be examined and that everyone needs to pursue some sort of happiness, whether it be alone, in a relationship, or in practicing everyday rituals such as going to the park and listening to music. Each story presents a moment in which such happiness is either missing or attained, and together these tales reinforce the value of such moments by presenting them vividly and convincingly.

Tara Y. Carter
Mary Rohrberger

Bibliography:

Bell, Barbara Currier. "Non-Identical Twins: Nature in 'The Garden Party' and 'The Grave.'" *The Comparatist* 12 (May, 1988): 58-66. Examines the meaning of nature in both short stories. Provides insight into Mansfield's use of nature in most of her short fiction.

Boddy, Gillian. *Katherine Mansfield: The Woman and the Writer.* New York: Penguin Books, 1988. An extensive biography of Mansfield. Discusses her life in the context of her writings and experiences.

Daly, Saralyn R. *Katherine Mansfield.* New York: Twayne, 1965. Chapter 6 is the most useful in terms of understanding themes and meanings; however the entire book lends insight into Mansfield as a writer.

Kaplan, Sydney Janet. *Katherine Mansfield and the Origins of Modernist Fiction.* Ithaca, N.Y.: Cornell University Press, 1991. Chapter 8 offers another tool for analysis of Mansfield's characters. Stresses that a feminist approach is applicable to the interpretation of her works.

Rohrberger, Mary. *The Art of Katherine Mansfield.* Ann Arbor, Mich.: University Microfilms International, 1977. Chapters 4, 5, and 6 are principally concerned with explaining the themes and techniques used in *The Garden Party and Other Stories* and other short stories. Extensive bibliographic notes and index.

THE GARDENER'S DOG

Type of work: Drama
Author: Lope de Vega Carpio (1562-1635)
Type of plot: Comedy of manners
Time of plot: Late sixteenth century
Locale: Naples
First published: El perro del hortelano, 1618 (English translation, 1903)

Principal characters:
> DIANA, the countess of Belflor
> TEODORO, her secretary
> FABIO, a gentleman of Naples
> MARCELLA,
> DOROTEA, and
> ANARDA, ladies-in-waiting
> COUNT FEDERIGO, in love with Diana
> THE MARQUIS RICCARDO, also in love with Diana
> COUNT LODOVICO, an old nobleman
> TRISTAN, Teodoro's lackey

The Story:

The countess Diana was enraged when she heard that a man had been seen leaving the upper chambers of the palace. He had thrown his cap at the candle, snuffing out the only light so that he could not be identified. Diana sent for her ladies-in-waiting and questioned them to learn who had been visited by a lover during the night. Dorotea and Anarda pleaded innocent but whispered to Diana that Marcella had a lover in the palace. He was Teodoro, secretary to the countess Diana herself. Marcella confessed her love but protested that it was a pure love. Teodoro wanted to marry her. Diana gave her consent to the marriage but cautioned Marcella to stay away from Teodoro until the wedding day; otherwise passion might consume honor. After her ladies had left her alone, Diana realized that she too loved Teodoro, but since he was not highborn she could not proclaim her love.

Teodoro, who had indeed been the man involved in the midnight escapade, feared that he would be found out and banished or executed, but he could not get Marcella out of his heart. Tristan, his lackey, begged him to forget Marcella and never see her again lest Diana punish them; it was Tristan who had thrown the cap and snuffed out the candle so that his master would not be recognized while escaping. Soon afterward, Diana tricked Tristan into revealing his part in the affair; she also sent for Teodoro and subtly hinted at her love for him in a letter she feigned was intended for someone else.

Marcella went to Teodoro and told him that Diana had blessed their betrothal. Confused, Teodoro took Marcella in his arms just as Diana appeared. When he thanked her for giving Marcella to him, their capricious mistress ordered Marcella locked in her room to await her decision concerning the wedding. Then Diana again hinted to Teodoro that she loved him, whereupon he renounced Marcella. He regretted rejecting Marcella, but he could not put aside the lure of wealth and power that would be his if Diana took him for a husband. After Marcella was released from the locked room, Teodoro, meeting her, spurned her love and disgraced her. Marcella swore revenge on him and on Anarda, who had, as she had learned, betrayed her and Teodoro to Diana because Anarda thought Marcella had been encouraging Fabio, a gentleman with whom Anarda was in love. Marcella, meeting Fabio, offered him her love and greatly confused that poor man by her words and actions.

When two noblemen, the Marquis Riccardo and Count Federigo, both begged for Diana's hand, she sent Teodoro to tell Riccardo that she chose him for her husband. Deserted by the lovely countess before she was really his, Teodoro turned back to Marcella and told her that he loved only her. At first she spurned him and declared she would marry Fabio, but at last love won over jealousy. Falling into Teodoro's arms, she made him forswear Diana forever. The lovers called their mistress a devil, an ass, and a bore, not knowing that Diana and Anarda were hidden nearby and listening to their conversation. When they suddenly appeared, they frightened the lovers almost to death. Diana dictated a letter to Teodoro, in which she stated that if a noble lady loved a man, he dared not love another. When she cautioned him to interpret its meaning correctly, Teodoro again renounced Marcella and told her to marry Fabio so as to please Diana.

Riccardo, appearing in answer to the summons from Diana, was told that Teodoro had misunderstood her words and that she had not intended to marry him. Teodoro, believing then that his mistress truly loved him, declared his love for her. Instead of listening to his pleas, Diana berated him for daring to speak of love when he was lowborn and she a lady. As she did not intend to have him herself, he thereupon asked her for Marcella. Like the gardener's dog who would allow no other dog to eat what he himself did not want, she refused to let Teodoro have Marcella. Instead, she struck at Teodoro with her knife. He half-believed that she had wounded him because she loved him, and, when she returned and wiped the blood from his wound, he was sure that it was love that made her cruel to him.

Count Federigo and the Marquis Riccardo, hearing that Diana had wounded Teodoro, were convinced that he had threatened her honor, and they decided to have him killed. For their assassin they hired Teodoro's faithful lackey, Tristan, who took their gold and then informed Teodoro of their plot. Tristan had other plans for helping his master. He had learned of one Count Lodovico, who had lost a son named Teodoro twenty years before. The boy had been captured by the Moors and was never heard of again. Tristan planned to convince the old count that Teodoro was his long-lost son. Then Teodoro would have a family of birth and wealth and would be good enough to wed Diana. Teodoro, too honorable for such knavery, went to Diana and told her that he was going to Spain, to avoid both the death planned for him by her suitors and the torture he endured while in her presence. Diana, not knowing her own mind, alternately told him to leave and to stay. When Marcella went to Diana and asked for permission to accompany Teodoro to Spain, Diana told the girl that she must marry Fabio.

Meanwhile Tristan carried through his plot to make Count Lodovico think Teodoro his lost son, and the old man was delighted at the prospect of having his child returned to him. Before the old count saw Teodoro, Diana, knowing that her true love was to leave her, told him at last that she loved him. Still she refused to marry him because of his humble birth. When Count Lodovico appeared with the announcement that Teodoro was his son, Diana opened her arms to Teodoro and said that they would be married that very night. Marcella, finally realizing that she could never have Teodoro, agreed to marry Fabio.

Teodoro, in one last attempt to save his honor, confessed to Diana that Tristan had tricked the old nobleman into believing Teodoro his own missing son. By that time, however, Diana had learned that love did not respect position. She declared that they would marry anyway and keep the secret between themselves and Tristan. Federigo and Riccardo confessed their plot to have Teodoro killed, and Diana gave Dorotea to Tristan as his bride. So all ended well, with honor saved and love triumphant. The gardener's dog had made a final choice.

Critical Evaluation:

The Gardener's Dog has often been called Shakespearean in the style and manner of its seriocomic treatment of love. Indeed, this play is, perhaps, Lope de Vega Carpio's *A Midsummer Night's Dream*. A dreamlike quality suffuses the action, as love turns into hate and back into love, affection turns to scorn, indifference turns to desire, sweet heroines turn vindictive, courtly lovers turn would-be murderers, lovers change partners, and confusion reigns supreme. Both audience and characters wonder what will happen next.

If, however, the treatment of love is Shakespearean, the treatment of illusion versus reality is closer to Luigi Pirandello. The play's conclusion hints that perhaps Teodoro becomes an actual count because everyone believes him to be one. The situation is an interesting reversal from that in Pirandello's *Henry IV* (1922), where a character in his madness believes he is a king, while everyone around him, knowing him for what he really is, simply humors him. In Vega Carpio's play, only Teodoro, Tristan, and Diana know the facts of the matter, while the rest of the world believes it is paying court to a true count. The practical result in both cases is the same, however, whereby Vega Carpio may perhaps be suggesting that nobility is nothing more than a social convention and has no other basis than that people agree to honor its credentials, no matter how spurious.

This proposition may be self-evident to later ages, but in early seventeenth century Spain it was an assumption that struck at the heart of the social order, though admittedly, in not quite so revolutionary a manner as Vega Carpio's *The Sheep Well* (1619). In fact, Teodoro's instant pedigree may have been less a social statement than simply a convenient dramatic device to bring Diana, the countess of Belflor, and her secretary together at last. For centuries, writers of comedy and romance have solved the problem of love between highborn and lowborn by revealing that the lowborn hero or heroine was actually highborn (having been, like the baby in Tristan's story, stolen in childhood by pirates, or else, inadvertently mixed up with another baby). Vega Carpio's dramatic resolution is an interesting variation of this theme; nevertheless, he seems to accept the underlying premise that highborn and lowborn must not marry in defiance of convention.

For all the intriguing questions of reality and appearance in the play, the main focus is on the nature of love, on just what this universal yet incomprehensible phenomenon is. In the first act, Marcella sighs that love causes people to mount as if to heaven; in the second, she calls love "god of envy, god of hate!" As the play progresses, it dramatizes the often-asked questions as to how love originates, how it is affected by jealousy, how it causes people to behave, how it is affected by absence, what happens when it is frustrated by power or social convention, and how it affects a person's natural temperament.

The air of questioning and confusion that pervades the work is set at the very beginning of the first act. (The second line of the play, "Who's there?" echoes the first line of *Hamlet* [1600-1601], a play also suffused with doubt and ambiguity of motive.) Roused in the middle of the night by a mysterious noise, Diana and her ladies-in-waiting dash in and out and scurry around the stage, with only shadows and feathers as solid evidence of intruders. Was the disturbance a dream? Two figures were seen on stage on some unknown mission at the outset, but they disappeared after breathlessly delivering only four short lines.

As the action progresses, more questions press for answers. Is it possible that Diana had no inclination at all toward Teodoro until she learned that he loved and was loved by Marcella? How much of Teodoro's love for Diana is based on true passion, and how much on his greed for wealth and station? If the latter is his predominant motivation, then how much sympathy does he deserve? Teodoro complains at great length of the extremities to which Diana's passions run and of her cruelty to him, yet his own treatment of Marcella is crass and heartless. He adores her at the beginning, shifts his love to Diana when the countess suggests her interest in him, comes whining back to his first love when Diana's attitude seems to change, and then unfeelingly spurns Marcella a second time when the wind of love once more blows his way. When, at the conclusion, Diana expresses some concern that her former secretary may have some lingering feelings for Marcella, the "count" loftily assures her, "Noblemen know no maidservants."

To help him develop his ideas on the range of love, Vega Carpio uses an unconventional dramatic device: a series of sonnets interspersed through the action and spoken by either Diana, Teodoro, or Marcella. Each sonnet develops a different aspect of love: Diana's first sonnet deals with the passion, jealousy, and frustration of love; Teodoro's deals with the nature of new love and with the conflicting feelings of affection, ambition, conscience, and cynicism it arouses; Marcella's deals with the constancy and permanency of love, despite all barriers and reverses. Other sonnets treat love's violence and cruelty, its cautions and terrors, and its black moments of despair. Counterpointed to these sonnets are other set speeches on love. In the Marquis Riccardo's speech to Diana, for instance, we hear the conventional high-flown rhetoric of courtly love, as splendid as it is artificial: "Did I command gold . . . or the frozen tears of heaven . . . or mines of oriental gems whose gleam has ploughed a furrow through the heaving hillocks of the sun, I would lay them at your feet, and delve beyond the confines of the light." Earlier in the play, Teodoro reveals that his love for Marcella is based on an idealized view of woman: "pure serenely crystallized, transparent like glass." Tristan, who often acts like Lear's fool in throwing the cold water of common sense on these romantic illusions, responds with a more realistic picture of women, one that emphasizes their defects instead of their glories. (Like many a fool, Tristan is resourceful, shrewd, and basically decent—he rebukes Teodoro for his treatment of Marcella—though he ultimately lacks the nobility that elevates his master at the end.)

In its overall conception, *The Gardener's Dog* is a highly mature example of dramatic art. Unlike the majority of contemporary plays, including Vega Carpio's own, it does not rely on villainous antagonists for its plot complications, but rather on the vagaries of love and the effects of this ennobling and exasperating passion. All of the important characters are drawn with a high degree of sympathy, though the playwright is not afraid to look unflinchingly at their defects. As long as the focus remains on love, the play remains a work of art. The quality begins to decline markedly in the third and final act when character development begins to slacken and the standard mechanics of plot contrivance take over. Yet it would be charitable to forgive the prolific Vega Carpio for the absurdities of his dramatic resolution, for seldom have the many faces of love been presented so subtly and at the same time so entertainingly.

"Critical Evaluation" by Laurence Behrens

Bibliography:

Dixon, Victor. Introduction to *The Dog in the Manger*, by Lope de Vega Carpio. Ottawa: Dovehouse Editions, 1990. Extensive examination of the sources, structure, and characterization of the work. Explicates the action and discusses the complexity of plotting; reviews Vega Carpio's intriguing resolution of the comedy.

Hayes, Francis C. *Lope de Vega.* New York: Twayne, 1967. Suitable for general readers, with separate chapters providing a brief biographical sketch, analysis of the writer's plays and nondramatic works, and commentary on the status of drama in Vega Carpio's lifetime. Classifies *The Gardener's Dog* as one of several works in which Vega Carpio uses stock devices to achieve humor.

Pring-Mill, R. D. F. Introduction to *Lope de Vega: Five Plays*, translated by Jill Booty. New York: Hill & Wang, 1961. Brief but insightful commentary on the play, highlighting Vega Carpio's use of irony, especially in the ending, where he reveals that honor as portrayed by the protagonists is no more than a sham.

Rennert, Hugo A. *The Life of Lope de Vega.* New York: G. E. Stechert, 1904. Though Rennert does not have the benefit of twentieth century scholarship, this volume contains useful information on *The Gardener's Dog* and other works; especially helpful for understanding the place of individual dramas within Vega Carpio's canon.

Vega Carpio, Lope de. *Four Plays.* New York: Charles Scribner's Sons, 1936. Includes an introduction by John Garrett Underhill and a critical essay by Jacinto Benavente, in which a practicing artist discusses technical aspects of *The Gardener's Dog* and Vega Carpio's accomplishments as a dramatist.

GARGANTUA AND PANTAGRUEL

Type of work: Fiction
Author: François Rabelais (c. 1494-1553)
Type of plot: Mock-heroic
Time of plot: Renaissance
Locale: France
First published: Gargantua et Pantagruel, 1567 (first complete edition); *Gargantua,* 1534
   (English translation, 1653); *Pantagruel,* 1532 (English translation, 1653); *Tiers livre,*
   1546 *(Third Book,* 1693); *Le Quart Livre,* 1552 *(Fourth Book,* 1694); *Le Cinquiesme
   Livre,* 1564 *(Fifth Book,* 1694)

> *Principal characters:*
> GRANGOSIER, a giant king
> GARGAMELLE, his wife
> GARGANTUA, their son
> PANTAGRUEL, the son of Gargantua
> PANURGE, a clever rascal
> FRIAR JOHN OF THE FUNNELS, a lusty monk

The Story:
   Grangosier and Gargamelle were expecting a child. During the eleventh month of her pregnancy, Gargamelle ate too many tripes and then played tag on the green. That afternoon, in a green meadow, Gargantua was born from his mother's left ear. Gargantua was a prodigy and, with his first breath, he began to clamor for drink. To supply him with milk, 17,913 cows were needed. Tailors used 900 ells of linen to make his shirt and 1,105 ells of white broadcloth to make his breeches. Eleven hundred cowhides were used for the soles of his shoes.
   At first, Gargantua's education was in the hands of two masters of the old school, Holofernes and Joberlin Bride. When Grangosier observed that his son was making no progress, however, he sent him to Paris to study with Ponocrates. Aside from some mishaps, as when he took the bells from the tower of Notre Dame to tie around his horse's neck, Gargantua did much better with his studies in Paris.
   Back home, a dispute arose. The bakers of Lerne refused to sell cakes to the shepherds of Grangosier. In the quarrel, a shepherd felled a baker, and King Picrochole of Lerne invaded the country. Grangosier baked cartloads of cakes to appease Picrochole, but to no avail, for no one dared oppose Picrochole except doughty Friar John of the Funnels. Finally, Grangosier asked Gargantua to come to his aid. Gargantua fought valiantly. Cannonballs seemed to him as grape seeds, and when he combed his hair, cannonballs dropped out. After he had conquered the army of Lerne, he generously set all the prisoners free.
   All of his helpers were rewarded well, but for Friar John, Gargantua built the famous Abbey of Theleme, where men and women were together, all could leave when they wished, and marriage and the accumulation of wealth were encouraged. When he was more than four hundred years old, Gargantua had a son, Pantagruel. A remarkable baby, Pantagruel was hairy as a bear at birth and of such great size that he cost the life of his mother. Gargantua was sorely vexed, between weeping for his wife and rejoicing for his son.
   Pantagruel required the services of forty-six hundred cows to nurse him. Once he got an

arm out of his swaddling clothes and, grasping the cow nursing him, ate the cow. Afterward, Pantagruel's arms were bound with anchor ropes. One day, the women forgot to clean his face after nursing, and a bear came and licked the drops of milk from the baby's face. By a great effort, Pantagruel broke the ropes and ate the bear. In despair, Gargantua bound his son with four great chains, one of which was later used to bind Lucifer when he had the colic. Pantagruel, however, broke the five-foot beam that constituted the footboard of his cradle and ran around with the cradle on his back.

Pantagruel showed great promise as a scholar. After a period of wandering, he settled down in Paris. There he was frequently called on to settle disputes between learned lawyers. One day he met Panurge, a ragged young beggar. On speaking to him, Pantagruel received answers in twelve known and unknown tongues. Pantagruel was greatly taken by this fluent beggar, and the two men became great friends. Panurge was a merry fellow who knew 63 ways to make money and 214 ways to spend it.

Pantagruel learned that the Dipsodes had invaded the land of the Amaurots. Stirred by this danger to Utopia, he set out by ship to do battle. By trickery and courage, Pantagruel overcame the wicked giants. He married their king, Anarchus, to an old lantern-carrying hag and made the king a crier of green sauce. Now that the land of Dipsody had been conquered, Pantagruel transported a colony of Utopians there, numbering 9,876,543,210 men, plus many women and children. All of these people were very fertile. Every nine months, each married woman bore seven children. In a short time, Dipsody was populated by virtuous Utopians.

For his services and friendship, Panurge was made Laird of Salmigondin. The revenue from this lairdship amounted to 6,789,106,789 gold royals a year, but Panurge managed to spend his income well in advance. Intending to settle down, Panurge began to reflect seriously on marriage, and he consulted his lord Pantagruel. They came to no conclusion in the matter because they got into an argument about the virtues of borrowing and lending money. Nevertheless, the flea in his ear kept reminding Panurge of his contemplated marriage, and he set off to seek other counsel.

Panurge consulted the Sibyl of Panzoult, the poet Raminagrobis, Herr Tripa, and Friar John. When all the advice he received proved contradictory, Panurge prevailed on Pantagruel and Friar John to set out with him to consult the Oracle of the Holy Bottle. From Saint Malo, the party sailed in twelve ships for the Holy Bottle, located in Upper India. The Portuguese sometimes took three years for that voyage, but Pantagruel and Panurge cut that time to one month by sailing across the Frozen Sea north of Canada.

The valiant company had many adventures on the way. On the Island of the Ennasins, they found a race of people with noses shaped like the ace of clubs. The people who lived on the Island of Ruach ate and drank nothing but wind. At the Ringing Islands, they found a strange race of Siticines who had long ago turned into birds. On Condemnation Island, they fell into the power of Gripe-men-all, Archduke of the Furred Law-cats, and Panurge was forced to solve a riddle before the travelers were given their freedom.

At last, they came to the island of the Holy Bottle. Guided by a Lantern from Lanternland, they came to a large vineyard planted by Bacchus himself. Then they went underground through a plastered vault and came to marble steps. Down they went, a hundred steps or more. Panurge was greatly afraid, but Friar John took him by the collar and heartened him. At the bottom, they came to a great mosaic floor on which was shown the history of Bacchus. Finally, they were met by the priestess Bacbuc, who was to conduct them to the Holy Bottle. Panurge knelt to kiss the rim of the fountain. Bacbuc threw something into the well, and the water began to boil. When Panurge sang the prescribed ritual, the Holy Bottle pronounced one word, "trinc." Bacbuc looked up the word in a huge silver book. It meant drink, a word declared to be the most gracious and intelligible she had ever heard from the Holy Bottle. Panurge took the word as a sanction for his marriage.

Critical Evaluation:

Partly because France's greatest comic prose writer was a legend even in his own lifetime, most of the facts of François Rabelais' life remain hazy. A monk, doctor of medicine, and writer, Rabelais transferred from the Franciscan to the Benedictine order with the Pope's express permission, because the latter order was more tolerant and more scholarly. The year 1532 found him in Lyons, at that time the intellectual center of France, where he published his first creative work, *Pantagruel*. As a satirist and humanist, Rabelais labored between the two religious extremes of Roman Catholicism and Genevan Protestantism; he had the mixed blessings of being attacked, alike, by Julius Caesar Scaliger, St. Francis of Sales, and John Calvin. All of them warned against his heretical impiety. Rabelais was, first and last, an iconoclast, but he attempted to be moderate in his views and writings. This may have made Rabelais unpopular with his more radical contemporaries, such as Martin Luther and Ignatius Loyola, but it also made him one of the most durable and most humane comic writers. As indecorous as his writings are, they also reveal a relatively conservative spirit; they show a sense of proportion and of human limitation in outraging both.

In Rabelais, the spirit of comedy blends with the spirit of epic to produce a novel work without parallel or close precedent. The chronicles are quite inclusive, expressing the Renaissance ambition to explore and chart all realms of human experience and thought. The mood of the narrator matches the scope of the narration. Rabelais attributes his infinite exuberance to his literal and symbolic inebriation, which he invites his readers to share. His curiosity, interest in the things of this world, joy, and unpredictability are greatly enjoyable, as long as the reader is willing to be intoxicated by a distillation of strong wit and language. As a genre, the chronicles may be compared to other books of instruction so popular during the Renaissance (such as Niccolò Machiavelli's *The Prince*, 1532; Baldassare Castiglione's *The Courtier*, 1528; Roger Ascham's *The Schoolmaster*, 1570). They also have been considered a parody of medieval adventure romances. *Gargantua and Pantagruel* includes history, fable, myth, drama, lyric, comedy, burlesque, novel, and epic. Its sources include sculpture, jurisprudence, pedagogy, architecture, painting, medicine, physics, mathematics, astronomy, chemistry, theology, religion, music, aeronautics, agriculture, botany, athletics, and psychological counseling. All of these elements are thrown together with flair and abandon.

It is a consistency of mood that holds together this diverse and variegated work. That mood is not one of thoughtfulness, for Rabelais is no great thinker. The unifying idea, eternal in its simplicity, is the philosophy of Pantagruelism: "Do As Thou Wilt." The world of Pantagruel is a world in which no restrictions on sensual or intellectual exploration can be tolerated; excessive discipline is regarded as evil and inhuman. In true epicurean fashion, Rabelais has no patience for inhibitions. People live for too brief a time to allow themselves the luxury of denial. The Abbey of Theleme is the thematic center of the work, with its credo that instinct forms the only valid basis for morality and social structure. Rabelais ignores the dangers of the anarchy this credo implies; he is talking about the mind, not the body politic. The dullest thing imaginable is the unimaginative, conforming mind. His satirical pen is lifted against all who lessen freedom of any kind in any fashion: hypocrites, militarists, abusers of justice, pedants, and medieval scholastics.

The reader of these gigantic chronicles, then, must not expect a plot. Anything so regular is anathema to Pantagruelism. Readers also should realize that the characters themselves are not the focus of the author's art but are largely indistinguishable. One of the most amusing elements of the book is that they are also indistinguishably large; Pantagruel's mouth, described in book 2, chapter 32, one of the finest chapters in European literature, is, at times, large enough to contain kingdoms and mountain ranges, at other times, no larger than a dovecote. The exception is Panurge, the normal-size man. He is an unforgettable character who makes so strong an impression, even on the author, that he cannot be forgotten. The third, fourth, and fifth books, in fact, are based on his adventures—just as William Shakespeare's *The Merry Wives of Windsor* (1600-1601) was written to exploit the beloved character of Falstaff. Panurge is the heroic companion of Pantagruel, in the best epic tradition; he also has the cunning of Ulysses, the drunken mirth of Falstaff, the roguishness of Jack Wilton and Tyl Ulenspiegel (his numerous pockets filled with innumerable tricks), the cynical but lighthearted opportunism of Geoffrey Chaucer's Pardoner, the magic powers of Shakespeare's Puck or Ariel. He is the wise fool of Erasmus and King Lear, and a Socratic gadfly who bursts the pretensions and illusions of all he encounters. The chapter entitled "How Panurge Non-plussed the Englishman Who Argued by Signs" is a literary tour de force, concentrating into one vivid, raucous chapter the comic spirit forever to be known as Rabelaisian. Important in other ways are "How Pantagruel Met a Limousin Who Spoke Spurious French," for its attack on unfounded affectation; and Gargantua's letter to Pantagruel, expressing the entire range of Renaissance learning, juxtaposed with the chapter introducing Panurge, who personifies Renaissance wit.

Rabelais' chaotically inventive style, filled with puns, wordplay, and synonyms, as well as with neologisms of his own creation, makes him difficult to translate accurately. His language reflects the rich variety of sixteenth century France; as the first to observe invariable rules in the writing of French prose, he has been called the father of the French idiom. His syntax is flexible, supple, expansive, sparkling with vitality and the harmony of an ebullient character, complex, and original. Rabelais does for French vocabulary what Geoffrey Chaucer did for English, fortifying it with eclectically selected terms of the soil, mill, tavern, and market, as well as scholarly terms and phrases gleaned from nearly all languages. As his comic theme reflects the universal as well as the particular, Rabelais' language combines the provincial with the popular in a stew fit for the mouths of giants.

"Critical Evaluation" by Kenneth John Atchity

Bibliography:
Chesney, Elizabeth A., and Marcel Tetel. *Rabelais Revisited*. New York: Twayne, 1993. Contains a good general introduction to the four novels definitely written by Rabelais and an annotated bibliography of important critical studies on Rabelais. Explores relationships between male and female characters in Rabelais' novels.
Febvre, Lucien. *The Problem of Unbelief in the Sixteenth Century: The Religion of Rabelais*. Translated by Beatrice Gottlieb. Cambridge, Mass.: Harvard University Press, 1982. Explores the many different representations of religious belief in Rabelais' writings. Demonstrates the need for modern scholars to avoid anachronistic interpretations of Renaissance treatments of religious topics.
Frame, Donald. *François Rabelais: A Study*. New York: Harcourt Brace Jovanovich, 1977. Clear, well-documented biography of Rabelais' life as a monk, medical doctor, and novelist. Summarizes general trends in the critical reception of Rabelais' works since the sixteenth century.

Greene, Thomas. *Rabelais: A Study in Comic Courage*. Englewood Cliffs, N.J.: Prentice-Hall, 1970. Thoughtful analysis of the coexistence of farce and high comedy in Rabelais' writings. Explains clearly how Rabelais uses laughter as an effective weapon for discrediting unsympathetic characters.

Screech, Michael A. *Rabelais*. Ithaca, N.Y.: Cornell University Press, 1979. Insightful, thorough study of Rabelais' four books. Discusses Rabelais' work in the light of Renaissance philosophy and theology, and examines his creative imitation of biblical, classical, medieval, and Renaissance sources.

THE GAUCHO MARTÍN FIERRO

Type of work: Poetry
Author: José Hernández (1834-1886)
Type of plot: Adventure
Time of plot: Nineteenth century
Locale: Argentina
First published: part 1, *El gaucho Martín Fierro*, 1872; part 2, *La vuelta de Martín Fierro*,
   1879 (English translation, 1935)

> *Principal characters:*
> MARTÍN FIERRO, the gaucho
> CRUZ, his friend
> PICARDIA, Cruz's son
> TWO SONS OF MARTÍN FIERRO

The Story:

Martín Fierro was a gaucho, born and raised on the rolling plains of Argentina. A gaucho was a mixture of the Spaniard and the Moor, transplanted to South America and mixed again with aboriginal Indians. He was God-fearing, brutal, superstitious, ignorant, lazy, and kind. His type was a passing one, but while he roamed the plains he became a legend. Martín Fierro played his guitar and sang his songs, songs that told of his unhappiness and the sorrows of the gaucho all over the land.

There was a time when Martín had a home and a wife and children to comfort him. He had owned land and cattle and a snug house. He rode the plains and lived in peace with his neighbors. Then officers appeared to take Martín and his neighbors away from their homes and families to serve the government in wars with the Indians. Martín was among those chosen because he had not voted when the judge was up for election, and the judge said that those who did not vote helped the opposition. The government promised that the gauchos would serve only six months and then be replaced. Martín took his horse and clothes and left his wife and children.

The men lived in filth and poverty. Complaints brought a staking out and lashes with leather thongs. There were no arms; the colonel kept the guns and ammunition locked up except when the Indians attacked. The Indians came and went as they pleased, killing, plundering, and taking hostages. They pulled babies from mothers' arms and killed them for sport. The Indians were not much worse than the officers, however. The men had no pay, no decent food. They wore rags, and rats crawled over them while they slept.

At last, Martín escaped and returned to his home. There he found his wife and sons gone, the house destroyed, the cattle and sheep sold by the government. Martín swore revenge and set out to find his sons. He was soon in more trouble. He killed a black man in a fight. Another swaggering gaucho picked a quarrel and Martín killed him. These killings brought the police after him. They had tracked him down and were about to kill him when one of their number joined him in fighting the others. Cruz, his new friend, fought so bravely that the two of them drove off or killed their attackers.

Cruz, telling Martín his story, sang it like a true gaucho. He had lost his woman to the *commandante* of the army and so had left his home. He, too, had killed a man and been hunted by the law before an influential friend got him a pardon and a job with the police, but Cruz had no heart for the police. Seeing Martín prepared to fight against great odds, he had decided to join him. The two resolved to leave the frontier and go to live among the Indians.

Martín and Cruz traveled across the desert to the land of the savages. Before they could make friends and join a tribe, they were captured by a raiding party. For two years, they suffered tortures inflicted by the Indians; then they were allowed to pitch a tent and live together, still under guard. They had to ride with the savages on raids against the Christians. When smallpox ravaged the tribe, Cruz gave his life by nursing a chief who had been kind to them.

Martín was alone once more. At last, he escaped from the Indians. He rescued a white woman who had been beaten with the bowels of her own baby son. After weeks of weary travel, they returned to the plains, where Martín left the woman with a rancher and went on his way. He knew by then that even the evils of the government were better than life with savage Indians.

Martín, returning to his homeland, learned that he was no longer wanted by the government. The judge who had put him into the army was dead, and no one any longer cared about the black man and the gaucho he had killed in fair fights. In his new freedom, he went to a racing meet and there was reunited with two of his sons. From them, he learned that his wife was dead and that they had also been tortured and cheated by the government.

The older son sang his song first. He had been arrested and convicted for a killing that he did not do. Beaten, starved, abused, he spent a long time in the penitentiary. In his loneliness, he had had no friend to share his woes. He cautioned all who heard his tale to keep away from the law, for the law was not for the gaucho.

The second son sang his song. An aunt died and left him some property. The judge appointed a tutor who robbed the boy of his inheritance and beat him and starved him. Penniless, Martín's second son had roamed the land like a tramp until he was sent to the frontier with the army.

Father and sons sat singing and talking, when a stranger named Picardia appeared and sang his song. Like the others, he had been sent to serve in the army and endure the tortures of the wicked officials. At the end of his song, Picardia told Martín that he was the son of Cruz, Martín's old friend. The friends celebrated the meeting with wine and song. While they sang, a black man joined them. He and Martin held a singing match, a common thing among the gauchos. The African American sang that he was the brother of the black man Martín had killed long years before, and that he would avenge the death. Before they could fight, other gauchos stepped between them and sent Martín, his sons, and Picardia on their way.

They rode only a short distance together, then separated to seek new lives, each man alone. Before they departed, Martín Fierro gave the young men some advice out of his own experience. He told them to be true to their friends, to give every man his due, to obey the law, and never to cheat. If ever a woman should win their hearts, they must treat her well and be true. The four scattered, each one taking a new name from that day on. Martín, ending his song, commended his words to gauchos everywhere, for they came from the wisdom of an old man. Then he laid down his guitar, never to sing again.

Critical Evaluation:

Although it is not well known in the English-speaking world, the tale of Martín Fierro has had great popularity in the South American countries, particularly in Argentina. Fierro gave hope to a people long oppressed by the government and cheated by corrupt officials. He became a legend, and his tale was repeated over and over again. José Hernández himself was identified with his hero, and everywhere he went he was idolized as the spokesman for the gaucho. It is said that much of the romantic appeal of the poem is lost in translation; nevertheless, the English version is musical, vigorous, and exciting.

Martin Fierro is the poetic epic of the gauchos who settled the rich Argentine pampa. An ocean of land, pancake flat, the pampa has fertile brown soil and may be the only area on earth where one could yoke oxen to a plow and slice a furrow for six hundred miles without turning up a stone. Before the Spaniards arrived, it was peopled by warlike, nomadic Indians. Its deep grass supported birds and ostriches; its only tree was the rugged ombu, later sung about by Argentine poets, including Hernández. Cattle and horses introduced by the first Spaniards increased at an amazing rate around the port town of Buenos Aires, on the ocean's edge, and a cowboy type known as gaucho began to ride the plains near the town. Slowly, the first gauchos pushed inland, rolling back the Indians, thus starting what was to be their historic role of settling Argentina. Gauchos also settled the "purple land" of Uruguay and the extensive Brazilian pampa of Rio Grande do Sul, but in Argentina they built a nation.

Usually of Spanish or mestizo blood, the gaucho lived on horseback in his sea of grass. He ate only meat, sometimes killing a steer simply to eat its tongue or to have a seat. He was nervous, restless, and almost always in motion. His weapons were a huge knife and the bolas that he twirled to capture steers or ostriches. His games were rough and on horseback; he was tough and ignorant and despised city folk. He drank "Paraguay Tea," or *yerba maté*, and danced the tango. His literature was the so-called gaucho poetry, redolent of the pampa, that was sung around campfires at night by illiterate minstrels known as *payadores*. The *payador* was a medieval European minstrel of Spanish origin, transplanted to the New World, his songs comprising a new, regional literature describing the various types of gaucho, such as the outlaw, the tracker, the tamer of horses, the lover, or the storyteller. This literary genre was to tinge all Argentine literature centuries later, even the drama, and from it came *The Gaucho Martín Fierro*.

A dichotomized Argentina grew during three centuries of colonialism under Spain. White bread was eaten only in "the Port," Buenos Aires, where an urban class dressed in European style and had more contact with Europe than with the semicivilized gauchos of their own country's interior. After Argentina became independent, early in the nineteenth century, an army of gauchos, led by Juan Manuel de Rosas, captured Buenos Aires. To symbolize the capture of the city by the country, Rosas' gauchos tied their horses in front of the Pink House, Argentina's presidential palace. For twenty-three years, Rosas dominated Buenos Aires, persecuting the intellectual class and forcing everyone to wear red, his favorite color.

One young intellectual, Domingo Sarmiento, went into exile and wrote the book *Facundo* (1845). In *Facundo*, the gaucho was criticized as Argentina's barbaric drawback. The title referred to Facundo Quiroga, a gaucho tyrant who ruled La Rioja Province as head of a gaucho army flying a black death's-head flag of skull and crossbones. Sarmiento included a blueprint for a new Argentina, in which the gaucho would be tamed or replaced by European immigrants, the pampa fenced, railroads built, wheat planted, and higher-bred livestock introduced. Rosas finally fell in 1852, and Sarmiento and others lived to carry out his blueprint for a modernized Argentina.

José Hernández was born on an Argentine *estancia*, or large ranch, in Rosas' day. He grew up among gauchos and Indians, and loved their free way of life. He knew the gaucho thoroughly—his speech, folklore, psychology, heart, and soul. He also knew the pampa—its beauty, silence, climate, grass, sunrises, and sunsets. As the day of the gaucho began to wane, and Hernández realized that the antigaucho intellectuals were creating a new Argentina, he decided to tell the dying gaucho's story, to portray his manly virtues and his once-happy way of life.

The Gaucho Martín Fierro thus tells of the gaucho's passing. This took place after the 1850's, when the last wild Indian tribes were being pushed up against the setting sun and the Andes foothills. At the same time, the gaucho was being supplanted by progress in the form of barbed wire, railroads, immigrants, wheat, and the herds of purebred cattle and sheep and thoroughbred horses that have made Argentina famous. In telling the tragic story of Martín Fierro and his lost family and lost home, the poem includes many epic themes—the fight against injustice, against governmental power over individuals, the struggle against nature, the yearning for lost freedom and lost loved ones during bitter years of exile in a strange country. It also contains such themes as a temporary flight to the land of a hated enemy and the rescue of a maiden in distress. Drenched with the pampa's earthiness, *The Gaucho Martín Fierro* gives pictures of the land and sky, grass, birds, and creatures of the pampa, as well as of the gaucho himself, as symbolized by the redoubtable but bigoted Martín. The poem presents the life cycle of a group of people, and is as representative of Argentina as, say, the Mississippi is of the United States. The poetic style is brisk and clear, even though the language is replete with gaucho vocabulary and flavor of speech. Martín Fierro's character projects itself over the poem: The reader can empathize with him for the loss of his home and family; all the lonely bitterness of his cruel military years fighting the raiding Indians on the far frontier; and his sadness when he finally returns home to find his little cabin abandoned, his wife and children gone, and only one familiar figure, his old cat prowling unhappily around the well. *The Gaucho Martín Fierro* holds one's interest throughout most of its stanzas and stands at the summit of Argentine gaucho literature. It has attracted attention in Spanish America, Brazil, and Spain, where the noted Miguel de Unamuno often read it aloud to his classes at the Spanish Oxford, Salamanca University.

Gauchos no longer roam the unfenced pampas' grassy sea. They are often only peons on a mechanized *estancia*, but still have nostalgic yearnings for the past. At night, around campfires, they often produce old copies of *The Gaucho Martín Fierro*, bound in calfskin. Gauchos speak of Martín himself as if he still lives, and might, at any moment, flip open the cowhide door flap and walk in to sip *yerba maté* and sing his sorrows.

"Critical Evaluation" by William Freitas

Bibliography:
Carilla, Emilio. *La creación del "Martín Fierro."* Madrid: Editorial Gredos, 1973. In Spanish. A broad-based study of *The Gaucho Martín Fierro* that covers the author's life and the major themes of the poem.
Franco, Jean. *An Introduction to Spanish-American Literature.* Cambridge, England: Cambridge University Press, 1969. Pages 77-82 relate the poem's plot and demonstrate how Hernández's masterpiece transcends the regional dimensions of the pampas to become a universal myth.
Lindstrom, Naomi. "Argentina." In *Handbook of Latin American Literature*, edited by David William Foster. 2d ed. New York: Garland, 1992. Shows that, despite its harsh criticism of the contemporary Argentinian government's policy of waging war on the Indians in the pampas, this novel did not slow the campaign to convert the pampas to fenced private property.
Sommer, Doris. *Foundational Fictions: The National Romances of Latin America.* Berkeley: University of California Press, 1991. Compares the poem to José Mármol's novel *Amalia* (1851), and shows how the former projects an epic view of the Argentinian nation as rooted in the ruggedness of the gaucho way of life.
Vogeley, Nancy. "The Figure of the Black *Payador* in *Martín Fierro*." *College Language Association Journal* 26, no. 1 (September, 1982): 34-48. Compares the unfavorable depiction of the black singer in *The Gaucho Martín Fierro* with the favorable depiction of the gaucho.

A GENERAL INTRODUCTION TO PSYCHOANALYSIS

Type of work: Psychology
Author: Sigmund Freud (1856-1939)
First published: Vorlesungen zur Einführung in die Psychoanalyse, 1917 (English
translation, 1920)

A General Introduction to Psychoanalysis, which could more properly be entitled *Introductory Lectures in Psychoanalysis,* probably remains the most widely used and popular means of introducing Sigmund Freud's ideas of the psyche. Given during World War I, these lectures embody the results of Freud's analytical research between 1895 and 1910, when the basic groundwork was set forth for his revolutionary ideas about the role of the unconscious and the power of sexuality in the life of the mind. Freud undertook several other introductory surveys in later years, but these lectures remain the most concise and useful of the Freudian surveys. Although a veritable army of subsequent Freudian scholars and psychoanalysts have explicated the Viennese pioneer, none can replace Freud's own writings, for he is an excellent stylist and the power of his mind speaks in every paragraph, even in translation. Freud reproduces his own quest for meaning in these lectures and involves the reader in what is, among other things, one of the greatest detective stories ever written. Another device, which Freud employs here as elsewhere, is to have frequent recourse to dialogue between himself and an imaginary, quasi-hostile critic. With this rhetorical procedure, Freud succeeds in half convincing his readers even before he has begun to present his arguments in full.

In his first four lectures, Freud gives an analysis of the psychology of errors as a simple means of introducing what was at that time an extraordinary subject. The slip of the tongue or pen, misreading, forgetting, or mislaying things is often not due to chance but comes from something contrary to our rational intention that slips out and distorts speech or action. From the device of the errors that often are not what they appear, Freud turns in the next ten lectures to dreams. Freud is concerned to stress that his subject is not abnormal psychology, and that his analysis applies to all. It was because his patients spoke of dreams so often that Freud began this area of investigation. It was another radical idea, for the reading of dreams was tantamount to gypsy soothsaying. According to Freud, the dream must be interpreted, for the manifest dream content always condenses, displaces, or elaborates the latent content and replaces feelings with visual images. In interpretation, the analyst ignores surface confusion and waits for the central theme to emerge from the dreamer's retelling. In sleep people regress; the conscious mind idles at its customary control, and the mind returns to something like the womb. Moreover, dreamers know the meaning of their dreams, but they generally do not know that they know. Freud maintains that all the manifest or surface content of the dream comes from experience of the previous waking day. Because dreamers fear the censor or dread reality, their minds distort and condense. Thus all dream material is symbolic. To someone who knows the environment and circumstances in which a dreamer has dreamed, interpretation is simple. Whereas, however, it is unclear to Freud at this time why certain elements are symbolic and others are not, he is convinced that the overwhelming number of dream symbols are sexual. As Freud notes in his introduction, the greatest resistance to his work came because of his insistence on the importance of sexuality in the formation of character. In dreams, the male organ is represented by all pointed or elongated objects, fish and snakes, anything sharp, like a weapon. All hollows, apertures, and jewels represent the female organ. Birth is associated with water, and erection and intercourse with flying. Freud notes that all these associations can be found in folklore, legend, and jokes, and in daytime fantasies as well as in night dreams. So important is this material, he briefly suggests, that all conscious language, and thus rational thought, comes from the libido, or sexual hunger. In answer to his critics, Freud declares that these symbolic readings must not be applied mechanically; dreams require a sensitive and intelligent interpreter. Not all dreams are primarily sexual, though he insists that the oddest, most anxiety-ridden ones invariably are. The material in dreams is primitive in that it comes out of the childhood of the dreamer and perhaps the childhood of the race. Here Freud briefly suggests an idea that his quondam colleague, Carl G. Jung, was to make into a major tenet in his quite different analytical mode, in which he posited a racial unconsciousness within the psyche, as well as an individual one.

It is an untenable fallacy, Freud observes, to call children innocent, if we mean innocent of sexuality. The child has not yet focused upon sex as reproduction, a situation that adults often fail to observe. The child is "polymorphously perverse," in Freud's phrase. In dreams people regress to childhood, for the unconscious is the repository of infantile mental life. What adults call evil in dream and intent is merely childlike. What becomes apparent here is Freud's calm expectation that human beings can understand and consequently control everything. Known to popular culture as an exponent of free love and a demoniac prophet of uncontrollable sex, Freud actually was one of the greatest of the nineteenth century rationalists. His whole life went into extending understanding, so that control and utilization might follow. Rather than being a prophet of doom, he is a scientist with perhaps too much faith in human perfectibility.

In the last portion of the book, a series of twelve lectures, Freud outlines his general theory of sexuality and neurosis. The whole science of psychoanalysis came from the study of obsessional neurosis. In such a condition, the mind is taken over at times by seemingly useless and meaningless compulsions and forced to repeat trivial acts that nevertheless are endowed with unreasonable tension and anxiety. Through his work with Josef Breuer on hysteria—first through hypnosis and then through his own technique of free association—Freud found that patient after patient, in probing the past, came up with some event or situation over which the unconscious still brooded, causing neurosis in the present. Freud called this stumbling block a trauma, and he designed his analytical technique as a way of exploring and explaining this event to his patients, thus ridding them of the need to succumb to the trauma. Out of fear, patients will always resist such a probe, a situation that must be overcome by the analyst's seeking the patients' confidence and persuading them to participate in the quest themselves. Every neurosis contains such a trauma or fixation, Freud avers, though not every fixation need cause a neurosis. The mind could be described as two rooms: a large one crowded with unconscious feelings and memories, and a small preconscious room of control and censorship. (In later Freudian theory this metaphorical structure became the famous tripartite designation of id, ego, and superego.)

In the last lectures of this series, Freud describes the development of human sexuality as his analysis found it. Libido, or sex drive, is present in the child from the beginning, though unfocused. At first a child's libido is directed through sucking toward its mother's breast, which is the first object of sexual desire. Later the child is autoerotic, finding gratification for libido in exploring itself. Then the child becomes analytical, interested in objects and finding gratification in bowel movements, for example. From age seven on the child is latently mature, beginning to be concerned with adult or genital sex. The first object of love is the mother. Here Freud summarizes his famous analysis of the Oedipus myth, in which the hero is punished by society and the gods for killing his father and marrying his mother. This is the key myth in Western culture, Freud explains, because what society calls "maturity" consists of displacing the libidinal fixation from the mother and transferring it to another being of the opposite sex beyond the incest barrier. Those who cannot or will not do this revert to childlike sexuality, which in the adult is perversion.

In conclusion, Freud notes that psychoanalysis is only a superstructure, resting on some organic base (the electrochemistry of the brain) about which little is yet known. Psychoanalysis does not advocate free love or wild abandonment through destroying censorship. It seeks to free the libido from unhealthy repressions and re-educate the whole person for a responsible life in a world of adult maturity.

Bibliography:
Gay, Peter. *Freud: A Life for Our Time*. New York: W. W. Norton, 1988. Covers the whole of Freud's life. Devotes considerable attention to the history, techniques, implications, and applications of psychoanalysis. Includes some references to *A General Introduction to Psychoanalysis*.
Jones, Ernest. *The Life and Work of Sigmund Freud*. Edited by Lionel Trilling and Steven Marcus. 3 vols. New York: Basic Books, 1961. A superb reference for information on Freud. The discussion of *A General Introduction to Psychoanalysis* includes synopsis and information on its origin and creation.
Levin, Gerald. *Sigmund Freud*. Boston: Twayne, 1975. A concise yet efficient and thorough text of Freud. Includes biography, case histories, Freud's theory of literature, and discussions of several specific writings, including *A General Introduction to Psychoanalysis*.
McGlashan, Agnes M., and Christopher J. Reeve. *Sigmund Freud: Founder of Psychoanalysis*. New York: Praeger, 1970. A short account of the life of Freud through his work and theories. Biography as it is relevant to the advent of psychoanalysis. Illustrated.
Timms, Edward, and Naomi Segal, eds. *Freud in Exile: Psychoanalysis and Its Vicissitudes*. New Haven, Conn.: Yale University Press, 1988. Articles discuss the Jewish origins of psychoanalysis, Freud's library, and the impact of psychoanalysis on art criticism. Contains five writings on the problems of translating Freud and a final section on the future of psychoanalysis.

Plant City